TOOLS FOR ANALYSIS

Liquidity

Working capital	Current assets − Current liabilities	p. 59
Current ratio	$\dfrac{\text{Current assets}}{\text{Current liabilities}}$	p. 59
Current cash debt coverage ratio	$\dfrac{\text{Cash provided by operations}}{\text{Average current liabilities}}$	p. 607
Inventory turnover ratio	$\dfrac{\text{Cost of goods sold}}{\text{Average inventory}}$	p. 281
Days in inventory	$\dfrac{\text{365 days}}{\text{Inventory turnover ratio}}$	p. 281
Receivables turnover ratio	$\dfrac{\text{Net credit sales}}{\text{Average net receivables}}$	p. 388
Average collection period	$\dfrac{\text{365 days}}{\text{Receivables turnover ratio}}$	p. 388

Solvency

Debt to total assets ratio	$\dfrac{\text{Total liabilities}}{\text{Total assets}}$	p. 60
Cash debt coverage ratio	$\dfrac{\text{Cash provided by operations}}{\text{Average total liabilities}}$	p. 608
Times interest earned ratio	$\dfrac{\text{Net income + Interest expense + Tax expense}}{\text{Interest expense}}$	p. 493
Free cash flow	Cash provided by operations − Capital expenditures − Cash dividends	p. 63

Profitability

Earnings per share	$\dfrac{\text{Net income − Preferred stock dividends}}{\text{Average common shares outstanding}}$	p. 55
Price-earnings ratio	$\dfrac{\text{Stock price per share}}{\text{Earnings per share}}$	p. 662
Gross profit rate	$\dfrac{\text{Gross profit}}{\text{Net sales}}$	p. 234
Profit margin ratio	$\dfrac{\text{Net income}}{\text{Net sales}}$	p. 235
Return on assets ratio	$\dfrac{\text{Net income}}{\text{Average total assets}}$	p. 437
Asset turnover ratio	$\dfrac{\text{Net sales}}{\text{Average total assets}}$	p. 439
Payout ratio	$\dfrac{\text{Cash dividends declared on common stock}}{\text{Net income}}$	p. 556
Return on common stockholders' equity ratio	$\dfrac{\text{Net income − Preferred stock dividends}}{\text{Average common stockholders' equity}}$	p. 558

TO THE INSTRUCTOR

WileyPLUS is built around the activities you perform

Prepare & Present

Create outstanding class presentations using a wealth of resources, such as PowerPoint™ slides, image galleries, interactive simulations, and more. Plus you can easily upload any materials you have created into your course, and combine them with the resources Wiley provides you with.

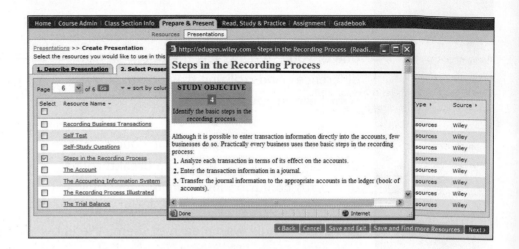

Create Assignments

Automate the assigning and grading of homework or quizzes by using the provided question banks, or by writing your own. Student results will be automatically graded and recorded in your gradebook. *WileyPLUS* also links homework problems to relevant sections of the online text, hints, or solutions—context-sensitive help where students need it most!

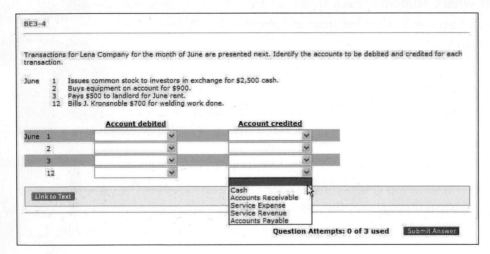

*Based on a spring 2005 survey of 972 student users of *WileyPLUS*

in your class each day. With Wiley**PLUS** you can:

Track Student Progress

Keep track of your students' progress via an instructor's gradebook, which allows you to analyze individual and overall class results. This gives you an accurate and realistic assessment of your students' progress and level of understanding.

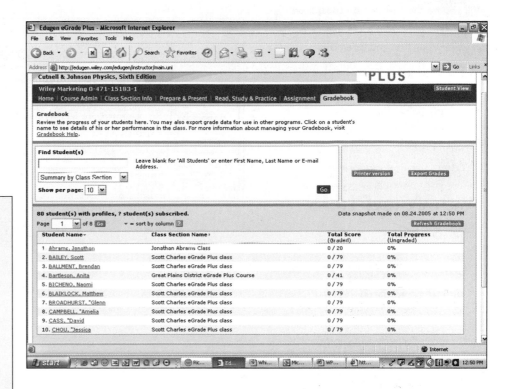

Now Available with WebCT and Blackboard!

Now you can seamlessly integrate all of the rich content and resources available with *WileyPLUS* with the power and convenience of your WebCT or BlackBoard course. You and your students get the best of both worlds with single sign-on, an integrated gradebook, list of assignments and roster, and more.
If your campus is using another course management system, contact your local Wiley Representative.

"I studied more for this class than I would have without *WileyPLUS*."

Melissa Lawler, *Western Washington Univ.*

For more information on what *WileyPLUS* can do to help your students reach their potential, please visit

www.wiley.com/college/wileyplus

76% of students surveyed said it made them better prepared for tests.

TO THE STUDENT

You have the potential to make a difference!

Will you be the first person to land on Mars? Will you invent a car that runs on water? But, first and foremost, will you get through this course?

WileyPLUS is a powerful online system packed with features to help you make the most of your potential, and get the best grade you can!

With Wiley**PLUS** you get:

A complete online version of your text and other study resources

Study more effectively and get instant feedback when you practice on your own. Resources like self-assessment quizzes, tutorials, and animations bring the subject matter to life, and help you master the material.

Problem-solving help, instant grading, and feedback on your homework and quizzes

You can keep all of your assigned work in one location, making it easy for you to stay on task. Plus, many homework problems contain direct links to the relevant portion of your text to help you deal with problem-solving obstacles at the moment they come up.

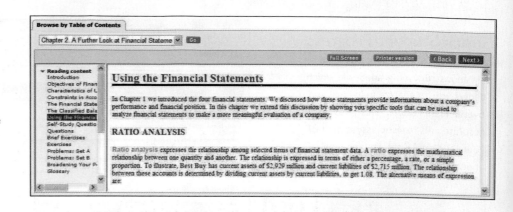

The ability to track your progress and grades throughout the term.

A personal gradebook allows you to monitor your results from past assignments at any time. You'll always know exactly where you stand.

If your instructor uses *WileyPLUS*, you will receive a URL for your class. If not, your instructor can get more information about *WileyPLUS* by visiting www.wiley.com/college/wileyplus

"It has been a great help, and I believe it has helped me to achieve a better grade."
Michael Morris, *Columbia Basin College*

69% of students surveyed said it helped them get a better grade.*

Financial Accounting

Tools for Business Decision Making
4th Edition

PAUL D. KIMMEL PHD, CPA
Associate Professor of Accounting
University of Wisconsin—Milwaukee

JERRY J. WEYGANDT PHD, CPA
Arthur Andersen Alumni Professor of Accounting
University of Wisconsin

DONALD E. KIESO PHD, CPA
KPMG Peat Marwick Emeritus Professor of Accountancy
Northern Illinois University

JOHN WILEY & SONS, INC.
WILEY

Dedicated to
our wives, Merlynn, Enid, and Donna
and to our children, Croix, Marais, and Kale;
Matt, Erin, and Lia; and Douglas and Debra

PUBLISHER	Susan Elbe
EXECUTIVE EDITOR	Christopher DeJohn
ASSISTANT EDITOR	Brian Kamins
DEVELOPMENT EDITOR	Ann Torbert
PRODUCTION SERVICES MANAGER	Jeanine Furino
MARKETING MANAGER	Amy Yarnevich
SENIOR DESIGNER	Kevin Murphy
SENIOR MEDIA EDITOR	Allie Morris
ASSOCIATE EDITOR	Ed Brislin
SENIOR ILLUSTRATION EDITOR	Anna Melhorn
SENIOR PHOTO EDITOR	Elle Wagner
EDITORIAL ASSISTANT	Alison Stanley
PRODUCTION SERVICES MANAGEMENT	Ingrao Associates
COVER PHOTO	SuperStock/AGE fotostock
COVER PHOTO	David Levy

This book was set in New Aster by Techbooks and printed and bound by Von Hoffmann. The cover was printed by Von Hoffmann.

This book is printed on acid free paper. ∞

To order books or for customer service, please call 1-800-CALL WILEY (225-5945).

ISBN-13 978-0-471-73051-4
ISBN-10 0-471-73051-3

Printed in the United States of America

10 9 8 7 6 5 4 3 2 1

Paul D. Kimmel, PhD, CPA, received his bachelor's degree from the University of Minnesota and his doctorate in accounting from the University of Wisconsin. He is an Associate Professor at the University of Wisconsin—Milwaukee, and has public accounting experience with Deloitte & Touche (Minneapolis). He was the recipient of the UWM School of Business Advisory Council Teaching Award, the Reggie Taite Excellence in Teaching Award, and a three-time winner of the Outstanding Teaching Assistant Award at the University of Wisconsin. He is also a recipient of the Elijah Watts Sells Award for Honorary Distinction for his results on the CPA exam.

He is a member of the American Accounting Association and the Institute of Management Accountants and has published articles in *Accounting Review, Accounting Horizons, Advances in Management Accounting, Managerial Finance, Issues in Accounting Education, Journal of Accounting Education,* as well as other journals. His research interests include accounting for financial instruments and innovation in accounting education. He has published papers and given numerous talks on incorporating critical thinking into accounting education, and helped prepare a catalog of critical thinking resources for the Federated Schools of Accountancy.

Jerry J. Weygandt, PhD, CPA, is Arthur Andersen Alumni Professor of Accounting at the University of Wisconsin—Madison. He holds a Ph.D. in accounting from the University of Illinois. Articles by Professor Weygandt have appeared in the *Accounting Review, Journal of Accounting Research, Accounting Horizons, Journal of Accountancy,* and other academic and professional journals. These articles have examined such financial reporting issues as accounting for price-level adjustments, pensions, convertible securities, stock option contracts, and interim reports. Professor Weygandt is author of other accounting and financial reporting books and is a member of the American Accounting Association, the American Institute of Certified Public Accountants, and the Wisconsin Society of Certified Public Accountants. He has served on numerous committees of the American Accounting Association and as a member of the editorial board of the *Accounting Review;* he also has served as President

and Secretary-Treasurer of the American Accounting Association. In addition, he has been actively involved with the American Institute of Certified Public Accountants and has been a member of the Accounting Standards Executive Committee (AcSEC) of that organization. He has served on the FASB task force that examined the reporting issues related to accounting for income taxes and is presently a trustee of the Financial Accounting Foundation. Professor Weygandt has received the Chancellor's Award for Excellence in Teaching and the Beta Gamma Sigma Dean's Teaching Award. He is on the board of directors of M & I Bank of Southern Wisconsin. He is the recipient of the Wisconsin Institute of CPA's Outstanding Educator's Award and the Lifetime Achievement Award. In 2001 he received the American Accounting Association's Outstanding Accounting Educator Award.

Donald E. Kieso, PhD, CPA, received his bachelor's degree from Aurora University and his doctorate in accounting from the University of Illinois. He has served as chairman of the Department of Accountancy and is currently the KPMG Emeritus Professor of Accountancy at Northern Illinois University. He has public accounting experience with Price Waterhouse & Co. (San Francisco and Chicago) and Arthur Andersen & Co. (Chicago) and research experience with the Research Division of the American Institute of Certified Public Accountants (New York). He has done postdoctorate work as a Visiting Scholar at the University of California at Berkeley and is a recipient of NIU's Teaching Excellence Award and four Golden Apple Teaching Awards. Professor Kieso is the author of other accounting and business books and is a member of the American Accounting Association, the American Institute of Certified Public Accountants, and the Illinois CPA Society. He has served as a member of the Board of Directors of the Illinois CPA

Society, the AACSB's Accounting Accreditation Committees, the State of Illinois Comptroller's Commission, as Secretary-Treasurer of the Federation of Schools of Accountancy, and as Secretary-Treasurer of the American Accounting Association. Professor Kieso is currently serving on the Board of Trustees and Executive Committee of Aurora University, as a member of the Board of Directors of Kishwaukee Community Hospital, and as Treasurer and Director of Valley West Community Hospital. From 1989 to 1993 he served as a charter member of the national Accounting Education Change Commission. He is the recipient of the Outstanding Accounting Educator Award from the Illinois CPA Society, the FSA's Joseph A. Silvoso Award of Merit, the NIU Foundation's Humanitarian Award for Service to Higher Education, a Distinguished Service Award from the Illinois CPA Society, and in 2003 an honorary doctorate from Aurora University.

The goal of this text is to introduce students to accounting in a way that demonstrates the importance of accounting to society and the relevance of accounting to their future careers. We strive to teach students those things that they really need to know and to do it in a way that maximizes their opportunities for successful completion of the course. To accomplish these goals, the foundation of this text relies on a few key beliefs.

"It really matters." The collapse of Enron, WorldCom, Arthur Andersen, and others had devastating consequences. A number of the book's features are designed to reveal accounting's critical role to society: Some of the *Feature Stories*, the *Business Insight—Ethics Perspective* boxes, and end-of-chapter *Ethics Cases* and *Research Cases* introduce students to the important effects of accounting on business and society. In short, it has never been more clear that accounting really matters.

"Less is more." Our instructional objective is to provide students with an understanding of those core concepts that are fundamental to the use of accounting. Most students will forget procedural details within a short period of time. On the other hand, students should remember well-taught concepts for a lifetime. Concepts are especially important in a world where the details are constantly changing.

Decision Checkpoints

"Don't just sit there – do something." The overriding pedagogical objective of this book is to provide students with continual opportunities for active learning. One of the best tools for active learning is strategically placed questions. Our discussions are framed by questions, often beginning with rhetorical questions and ending with review questions. Also, our analytical devices, called *Decision Toolkits*, use key questions to demonstrate the purpose of each.

"Get real." Students will be most willing to commit time and energy to a topic when they believe that it is relevant to their future careers. There is no better way to demonstrate relevance than to ground discussion in the real world. We do this in several ways: First, we use high-profile companies such as Nike, Microsoft, and Intel to frame our discussion of accounting issues. Second, the book employs a "macro" approach in its first two chapters teaching students how to understand and use the real financial statements of Tootsie Roll, Hershey, and Best Buy, before teaching how to record transactions. Many students determine their opinion of a course during the initial weeks, and this macro approach clearly demonstrates the relevance of accounting while students are forming their impression of the course. Finally, *Accounting across the Organization* boxes specifically connect accounting to business functions such as finance, marketing, and management and show uses of accounting for students with business majors other than accounting.

"Make a decision." All business people must make decisions. Decision making involves critical evaluation and analysis of the information at hand, and this takes practice. We have integrated important analytical tools throughout the book. After each new decision tool is presented, we summarize the key features of that tool in a *Decision Toolkit*. At the end of each chapter we provide a comprehensive demonstration of an analysis of a real company using the decision tools presented in the chapter. This sequence of decision tools culminates in a capstone analysis chapter at the end of the book.

"It's a small world." The Internet has made it possible for even small businesses to sell their products virtually anywhere in the world. Few business decisions can be made without consideration of international factors. To heighten student awareness of international issues, we have many references to international companies and issues, and many *Interpreting Financial Statements* problems have an international focus.

TOOLS FOR STUDENT SUCCESS

Financial Accounting, 4th Edition, provides many proven pedagogical tools to help students learn accounting concepts and apply them to decision making in the business world. This pedagogical framework emphasizes the *processes* students undergo as they learn. Turn to the **Student Owner's Manual** on page xx to see all the learning tools of the book in detail. Here are a few key features.

Learning How to Use the Text

- **The Student Owner's Manual**, p. xx, and notes in red in Chapter 1, explain to students how to take advantage of the text's learning tools to help achieve success in the course.

- A **Learning Styles Quiz**, p. xxix, includes tips on in-class and at-home learning strategies.

- **The Navigator** guides students through each chapter by pulling all the learning tools together into a learning system. Throughout the chapter, **The Navigator** prompts students to use the learning aids and to set priorities as they study.

Understanding the Context

- **Study Objectives**, listed at the beginning of each chapter, reappear in the margins and again in the **Summary of Study Objectives**.

- A **Feature Story** helps students picture how the chapter topic relates to the real world of accounting and business and serves as a recurrent example.

- A **Chapter Preview** links the Feature Story to the major topics of the chapter and provides a road map to the chapter.

PREVIEW OF CHAPTER 6

In the previous chapter, we discussed the accounting for merchandise inventory using a perpetual inventory system. In this chapter, we explain the methods used to calculate the cost of inventory on hand at the balance sheet date and the cost of goods sold. We conclude by illustrating methods for analyzing inventory. The content and organization of this chapter are as follows.

REPORTING AND ANALYZING INVENTORY

Classifying Inventory	Determining Inventory Quantities	Inventory Costing	Analysis of Inventory
• Finished goods • Work is process • Raw materials	• Taking a physical inventory • Determining ownership of goods	• Specific identification • Cost flow assumptions • Financial statement and tax effects • Consistent use • Lower of cost or market	• Inventory turnover ratio • LIFO reserve

TOOLS FOR STUDENT SUCCESS

Learning the Material

- The text emphasizes accounting experiences of **real companies and business situations throughout**.

- Three types of **Business Insight** boxes—highlighting ethics, investor, and international perspectives—give students glimpses into how real companies make decisions using accounting information. In addition, new **Accounting across the Organization** boxes give glimpses of how businesspeople in non-accounting functions use accounting information in their decision making.

- The **Business Insight** boxes and the new **Accounting across the Organization** boxes end with a question to test students' understanding of the real-world application in the box. Guideline answers for these questions appear at the end of the **Broadening Your Perspective** section, at the end of the chapter.

- **Color illustrations**, including **infographics**, create "visual anchors" that help students visualize and apply accounting concepts.

- **Before You Go On** sections provide learning checks (**Review It**) and mini demonstration problems (**Do It**). Questions marked with the **Tootsie Roll** send students to find information in Tootsie Roll's 2004 annual report printed in the book.

BEFORE YOU GO ON . . .

▶ **Review It**

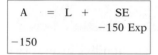

1. What are the phases of the product life cycle, and how do they affect the statement of cash flows?
2. Based on its statement of cash flows, in what stage of the product life cycle is Tootsie Roll Industries? The answer to this question appears on page 643.
3. What are the three major steps in preparing a statement of cash flows?

A	=	L	+	SE
				−150 Exp
−150				

Cash Flows
−150

- **Accounting Equation analyses** in the margin next to journal entries reinforce understanding of the impact of an accounting transaction on the financial statements. They report the **cash effect** of each transaction to reinforce understanding of the difference between cash effects and accrual accounting.

- **Helpful Hints, Alternative Terminology**, and blue-highlighted **key terms and concepts** help focus students on key concepts as they study the material.

- **International Notes** provide a convenient way to expose students to international issues.

- **Decision tools** useful for analyzing and solving business problems are presented and then summarized in **Decision Toolkits**. A **Using the Decision Toolkit** exercise asks students to use the decision tools presented in the chapter and takes them through the problem-solving steps.

Decision Toolkit

Decision Checkpoints	Info Needed for Decision	Tool to Use for Decision	How to Evaluate Results
Can the company meet its near-term obligations?	Current assets and current liabilities	$\text{Current ratio} = \dfrac{\text{Current assets}}{\text{Current liabilities}}$	Higher ratio suggests favorable liquidity.
Can the company meet its long-term obligations?	Total debt and total assets	$\text{Debt to total assets ratio} = \dfrac{\text{Total liabilities}}{\text{Total assets}}$	Lower value suggests favorable solvency.

TOOLS FOR STUDENT SUCCESS

Putting It Together

At the end of each chapter are several features useful for review and reference.

- A **Summary of Study Objectives** reviews the main points of the chapter.
- The **Decision Toolkit—A Summary** presents in one place the decision tools used throughout the chapter.
- A **Glossary** of key terms gives definitions with page references to the text.
- A **Demonstration Problem** with an **Action Plan** gives students another opportunity to refer to a detailed solution to a representative problem before they do homework assignments.

Demonstration Problem

Trillo Company's bank statement for May 2007 shows these data.

Balance May 1	$12,650	Balance May 31	$14,280
Debit memorandum:		Credit memorandum:	
NSF check	175	Collection of note receivable	505

The cash balance per books at May 31 is $13,319. Your review of the data reveals the following.

1. The NSF check was from Hup Co., a customer.
2. The note collected by the bank was a $500, 3-month, 12% note. The bank charged a $10 collection fee. No interest has been accrued.

Action Plan

- Follow the four steps used in reconciling items (p. 330).
- Work carefully to minimize mathematical errors in the reconciliation.
- Prepare entries based on reconciling items per books.

Developing Skills Through Practice

Each chapter is supported by a full complement of homework material. **Self-Study Questions, Questions, Brief Exercises, Exercises**, and three sets of **Problems** (one of which is at the book's website) are all keyed to the Study Objectives. In addition:

- Certain Questions, Exercises, and Problems use the decision tools presented in the chapter. These are marked with the icon ⊙▬▬𝒞. Also, certain Questions, Exercises, and Problems show applications of accounting issues for business functions across the organization. These are marked with the icon ➡.

- A new **Comprehensive Problem** (in Chapters 5-11) combines material of the current chapter with previous chapters so that students understand "how it all fits together." Each of these problems requires the recording of transactions and adjusting entries, and culminates in the preparation of financial statements.

- A new **Continuing Cookie Chronicle** problem in every chapter traces the growth of an entrepreneurial venture. Each week students apply their newly acquired accounting skills to solve the financial reporting issues faced by this small business.

Continuing Cookie Chronicle

(*Note:* This is a continuation of the Cookie Chronicle from Chapter 1.)

CCC2 After investigating the different forms of business organization, Natalie Koebel decides to operate her business as a corporation, Cookie Creations Inc., and she begins the process of getting her business running.

- Certain Exercises and Problems can be solved using the Excel supplement that is available to accompany the text and are identified by the following icon:

- Other Exercises and Problems can be solved with the **General Ledger Software** available with the text and are marked with the icon GLS.

TOOLS FOR STUDENT SUCCESS

Expanding and Applying Knowledge

Broadening Your Perspective at the end of each chapter offers a wealth of resources for those instructors who want to broaden the learning experience by bringing in more real-world decision making, analysis, and critical thinking activities.

BROADENING YOUR PERSPECTIVE

Financial Reporting and Analysis

FINANCIAL REPORTING PROBLEM: *Tootsie Roll Industries*

BYP3-1   The financial statements of Tootsie Roll in Appendix A at the back of this book contain the following selected accounts, all in thousands of dollars.

- A **Financial Reporting Problem** directs students to study various aspects of the financial statements of Tootsie Roll Industries, Inc., which are printed in Chapter 1 (in simplified form) and in Appendix A (in full)

- A **Comparative Analysis Problem** offers the opportunity to compare and contrast the financial reporting of Tootsie Roll Industries, Inc., with a competitor, Hershey Foods Corporation.

- A **Research Case** directs students to the *Wall Street Journal* and other business periodicals and references for further study and analysis of key topics.

- **Interpreting Financial Statements** problems offer minicases that ask students to read parts of financial statements of actual companies and use the decision tools of the chapter to interpret them. Some of these cases, indicated by a globe icon, focus on specific situations faced by actual international companies.

- **Financial Analysis on the Web** problems guide students to websites from which they can mine and analyze information related to the chapter topic.

- **Decision Making across the Organization** cases help promote group collaboration and build decision-making and business communication skills by requiring teams of students to consider business problems from various functional perspectives.

- **Communication Activities** provide practice in written communication, a skill much in demand among employers.

- **Ethics Cases** ask students to analyze situations, identify the ethical issues involved, and decide on an appropriate course of action.

The third edition was a tremendous success. In the spirit of continuous improvement, we have made many changes in this edition. These changes come in response to suggestions made by reviewers, focus group participants, and users. We sincerely appreciate your input.

Major Changes in the 4th Edition

- In this edition our "focus companies" are again Tootsie Roll Industries and Hershey Foods. We chose them because they have high name recognition with students, they operate primarily in a single industry, and they have relatively simple financial statements. This edition of the book uses their **2004 annual reports**. We have updated the **Review It** questions related to Tootsie Roll and the **Broadening Your Perspective** problems related to both companies to reflect the new data.

- In order to illustrate the importance of financial accounting knowledge to non-accounting majors, we have added 25 **Accounting across the Organization** boxes. These demonstrate the use of accounting to address issues in marketing, finance, management, and other business functions.

- To reflect recent events affecting financial reporting, we created nine new **Business Insight** boxes. All of the Business Insight boxes now end with a question to test student understanding. (Answers are provided at the end of the Broadening Your Perspective section, at the end of the chapter.) In addition, as suggested by users of the book, we actually reduced the total number of Business Insight boxes and instead inserted more of the "real-world references" directly into the text discussion.

- We added a new set of problems—**Problems: Set C**—to expand the homework options available to the instructor. The C Problems, which are available on the book's website, parallel the A and B problem sets.

- In addition, 52 new Exercises or Problems are included in this edition of the text.

- Over 500 **new questions** are included in this edition of the Test Bank. A new section of brief exercises is also included. Each problem is classified by study objective. New to this edition of the Test Bank is the classification by Bloom's taxonomy.

- New **Instructor's Manual** and **PowerPoint** presentations are available.

- To enhance students' conceptual understanding of the impact of transactions, accounting equation analyses in the margins next to each journal entry have been redesigned so that the effect on each account is more clearly associated with the accounting equation.

- We discuss the financial reporting implications of the Sarbanes–Oxley Act at numerous points throughout the text.

- We have added **Comprehensive Problems** to Chapters 5-11. These new problems require students to record transactions and adjusting entries and prepare financial statements. They are designed to reinforce the students' understanding of the accounting cycle throughout the course.

- We have added a **Continuing Cookie Chronicle** problem to every chapter. This problem illustrates the usefulness of accounting in a small-business setting throughout the various stages of a company's formation and growth, and it provides a comprehensive review of topics.

- We have entirely rewritten Chapter 12, on the Statement of Cash Flows, to provide a significantly shorter, more streamlined presentation of the basic concepts needed to prepare and understand that statement. In addition, we moved the presentation of the direct approach to an appendix.

Key Features of Each Chapter

Chapter 1, Introduction to Financial Statements

- Explains the purpose of each financial statement.
- Uses financial statements of a hypothetical company (to keep it simple), followed by those for a real company, Tootsie Roll Industries (to make it relevant).
- *Changes*: Added new Feature Story on open-book management; added new section, "Accounting and You"; revised ethics section with emphasis on Sarbanes-Oxley; moved section on assumptions and principles to Chapter 2.

Chapter 2, A Further Look at Financial Statements

- Discusses revenue, expenses, assets, and liabilities.
- Presents the classified balance sheet.
- Applies ratio analysis (current ratio, debt to total assets, earnings per share, and free cash flow) to real companies—Best Buy and Circuit City.
- *Changes*: Moved "The Financial Statements Revisited" section to beginning of chapter; moved some ratios (P-E, current cash debt coverage, and current cash coverage) and added free cash

flow; added section on assumptions and princi-ples (from Chapter 1).

Chapter 3, The Accounting Information System

- Covers transaction analysis—emphasizes funda-mentals while avoiding unnecessary detail.

Chapter 4, Accrual Accounting Concepts

- Emphasizes difference between cash and accrual accounting.
- Discusses how some companies manage earnings through accrual practices.
- Presents minimal discussion of closing and work sheets; provides additional detail on work sheets in an appendix.
- *Changes*: Added section on quality of earnings; simplified text presentation in several places.

Chapter 5, Merchandising Operations and the Multiple-Step Income Statement

- Introduces merchandising concepts using the perpetual inventory approach.
- Presents the multiple-step income statement.
- Applies ratio analysis (gross profit rate and profit margin ratio) to real companies—Target and Wal-Mart.

Chapter 6, Reporting and Analyzing Inventory

- Covers cost flow assumptions and their implica-tions for financial reporting, emphasizing the periodic approach (for simplicity).
- Applies ratio analysis (inventory turnover) to real companies—Target and Wal-Mart.
- Discusses implication of LIFO reserve for real company—Caterpillar Inc.
- Covers in an appendix cash flow assumptions under perpetual inventory systems.
- *Changes*: Slightly expanded discussion of lower of cost or market, including a numeric example.

Chapter 7, Internal Control and Cash

- Covers internal control concepts and implica-tions of control failures.
- Presents bank reconciliation as a control device.
- Discusses cash management, including operat-ing cycle and cash budgeting.
- *Changes*: Added new Feature Story; added new section on Sarbanes-Oxley.

Chapter 8, Reporting and Analyzing Receivables

- Presents the basics of accounts receivable and notes receivable, bad debt estimation, and inter-est calculations.
- Discusses receivables management, including determining to whom to extend credit, establish-ing the payment period, monitoring collections, evaluating the receivables balance, and acceler-ating receipts.

- Applies ratio analysis (receivables turnover) to a real company—McKesson.
- *Changes*: Added new financial statement disclo-sure for receivables.

Chapter 9, Reporting and Analyzing Long-Lived Assets

- Covers the basics of plant assets and intangible assets.
- Discusses the basics of the buy or lease decision.
- Covers the implications of depreciation method choice; shows details of accelerated methods in an appendix.
- Applies ratio analysis (asset turnover and return on assets) to real companies—Southwest Airlines and AirTran.
- Demonstrates implications of estimated useful life for amortization of intangibles.
- Discusses the statement of cash flows presenta-tion of fixed-asset transactions.
- *Changes*: Updated discussion and analysis of return on assets and updated section on intangible assets.

Chapter 10, Reporting and Analyzing Liabilities

- Covers current liabilities: notes payable, sales taxes, payroll, unearned revenues, and current maturities of long-term debt.
- Covers long-term liabilities, bond pricing, and various types of bonds.
- Presents straight-line amortization and the effective-interest method in a chapter-end appendix.
- Includes present value discussion in an appen-dix at the back of the book.
- Discusses the basics of contingent liabilities, lease obligations, and off-balance-sheet financing.
- Applies ratio analysis (current ratio, debt to total assets ratio, and times interest earned) to real companies—Ford and General Motors.
- Discusses the statement of cash flows presenta-tion of debt transactions.
- *Changes*: Moved into the text the key points from the appendix on contingent liabilities and leases, and eliminated the remainder of that appendix.

Chapter 11, Reporting and Analyzing Stockholders' Equity

- Presents pros and cons of the corporate form of organization.
- Covers issues related to common and preferred stock and the reasons that companies purchase treasury stock.
- Explains reasons for cash dividends, stock divi-dends, and stock splits, and implications for analysis.

- Discusses debt versus equity choice.
- Applies ratio analysis (return on common stockholders' equity and payout ratio) to real companies—Nike and Reebok.
- Discusses the statement of cash flows presentation of equity transactions.

Chapter 12, Statement of Cash Flows

- Explains the purpose and usefulness of the statement of cash flows.
- Presents the indirect method in the body of the chapter and the direct method in a chapter-end appendix.
- Applies ratio analysis (free cash flow, current cash debt coverage ratio, and cash debt coverage ratio) to real companies—Microsoft, Oracle, AMD, and Intel.
- *Changes*: Shortened coverage of preparing operating activities section, for both methods; condensed presentation from two years to one year; moved the direct method into an appendix.

Chapter 13, Financial Analysis: The Big Picture

- Capstone chapter—presents some new tools, and reinforces previous analytical tools and demonstrates their interrelationships.
- Demonstrates horizontal and vertical analysis of Kellogg.

- Discusses "sustainable income" and implications of discontinued operations, extraordinary items, accounting changes, nonrecurring charges, and comprehensive earnings.
- Discusses factors that affect the quality of earnings.
- In an appendix, applies comprehensive ratio analysis to real companies—Kellogg and General Mills.
- *Changes*: Added new section on the price-earning ratio; rewrote coverage of changes in accounting principle to reflect the new FASB standard.

Appendix A, Specimen Financial Statements: Tootsie Roll Industries, Inc.

Appendix B, Specimen Financial Statements: Hershey Food Corporation

Appendix C, Time Value of Money

- Provides coverage of present value and future value of single sums and annuities.

Appendix D, Reporting and Analyzing Investments

- Provides a comprehensive discussion of reporting and analyzing investments.
- Discusses statement of cash flows presentation of investments.

Active Teaching and Learning Supplementary Material

Financial Accounting, 4th Edition, features a full line of teaching and learning resources. Driven by the same basic beliefs as the textbook, these supplements provide a consistent and well-integrated learning system. This hands-on, real-world package guides *instructors* through the process of active learning and gives the tools to create an interactive learning environment. With its emphasis on activities, exercises, and the Internet, the package encourages *students* to take an active role in the course and prepares them for decision making in a real-world context.

 ## Wiley's Integrated Technology Solutions

Helping Teachers Teach and Students Learn

Book Companion Site
www.wiley.com/college/kimmel

The *Financial Accounting, 4th Edition*, companion website provides a seamless integration of text and media and keeps all of a book's online resources in one easily accessible location for instructors and students. Instructors will find electronic versions of the Solutions Manual, Computerized Test Bank, Set C Problems and solutions, and other resources. Students will benefit from the Self-Study and Self-Test Practice Quizzes, Excel templates, and PowerPoint presentations that reinforce chapter material from the textbook.

A collection of Wiley's premium resources and study tools, WileyPLUS offers even greater opportunity for instructors to teach more effectively and students to learn more productively.

For Instructors

Within WileyPLUS, instructors will find easy access to electronic versions of the Solutions Manual, Test Bank, Instructor's Manual, Computerized Test Bank, Set C Problems and solutions, and other resources.

In addition, instructors can create their own teaching and learning environment by organizing Wiley's materials in a way that best fits their course. Upon adoption of WileyPLUS, Wiley will create a unique course instance that instructors can begin to customize by employing the following helpful tools:

- **Class Section Information** helps instructors manage their course. Through this tool instructors can add and delete student names from class sections, import course documents, and customize their course home page.

- A **"Prepare and Present"** tool contains all of the Wiley-provided resources, such as PowerPoint slides, interactive Chapter Reviews, e-book resources, and Lecture Outlines, making your preparation time more efficient. You may easily adapt, customize, and add to Wiley content to meet the needs of your course.

- An **"Assignment"** area is one of the most powerful features of WileyPLUS. This area of the website allows professors to assign homework and quizzes comprised of text Exercises and Problems. Instructors save time as results are automatically graded and recorded in an instructor gradebook. Students benefit by the option to receive immediate feedback on their work, allowing them to determine right away how well they understand the course material.

- An **Instructor's Gradebook** will keep track of student progress and allow instructors to analyze individual and overall class results to determine their progress and level of understanding.

For Students

WileyPLUS provides a wealth of support materials that will help students develop their conceptual understanding of class material and increase their ability to solve problems. On the WileyPLUS website, students will find the following resources:

- **"Read, Study and Practice"** resources that can include select interactive, end-of-chapter problems linked directly to e-book content, allowing students to review the textbook while they study. Additional resources can include interactive Chapter Reviews and Activities, and other problem-solving resources.

- An **"Assignment"** area that helps students stay "on task" by containing all homework assignments in one location. Many homework problems contain a link to the relevant sections of the e-book, providing students with context-sensitive help that allows them to conquer problem-solving obstacles.

- A Personal **"Gradebook"** for each student will allow students to view their results from past assignments at any time.

Instructor's Active Teaching Aids

Instructor's Resource CD-ROM. The Instructor's Resource CD (IRCD) provides all instructor support material in an electronic format that is easy to navigate and use. The IRCD gives you the flexibility to access and prepare instructional material based on your individual needs.

Solutions Manual. The Solutions Manual contains detailed solutions to all Brief Exercises, Exercises, and Problems in the textbook and suggested answers to the questions and cases. Each chapter includes an *assignment classification table*, an *assignment characteristics table*, and a new *Bloom's taxonomy table*. Print is large and bold for easy readability in lecture settings. The Solutions Manual has been carefully verified by a team of independent accuracy checkers. (Also available at www.wiley.com/college/kimmel, on the IRCD, and via WileyPLUS.)

Solutions Transparencies. The solutions transparencies contain detailed solutions to Brief Exercises, Exercises, and Problems in the textbook. They feature large, bold type for better projection and easy readability in large classroom settings.

Teaching Transparencies. The teaching transparencies contain color illustrations found in the textbook.

Instructor's Manual. The new instructor's manual features a comprehensive chapter outline, and it also

discusses how to incorporate supplements and WileyPLUS assets into an active-learning classroom. Chapter review quizzes, activities, and sample syllabi are also provided. (Available at www.wiley.com/college/kimmel, on the IRCD, and via WileyPlus.)

PowerPoint Presentations. The new PowerPoint presentations contain a combination of key concepts, images, and problems from the textbook for use in the classroom. Designed to follow the organization of content in the textbook, they visually reinforce accounting principles. New "Let's Review" questions are included throughout to encourage classroom participation. (Available at www.wiley.com/college/kimmel, on the IRCD, and via WileyPlus.)

Test Bank. Revised and enhanced for this edition, the Test Bank is a comprehensive testing package that allows instructors to tailor examinations according to study objectives, learning skills, and content. The fourth edition Test Bank includes over 500 new questions. Each problem is classified by textbook study objective. Also new to this edition is the classification by Bloom's taxonomy. Examination questions focus on concepts, decision-making, and the real-world environment.

In addition to a *final exam*, the Test Bank provides an *achievement test for every two chapters* in the textbook and a *comprehensive exam for every four chapters* of the text. The tests, easy to photocopy and distribute to students, consist of problems and exercises as well as multiple-choice, matching, and true/false questions. (Available at www/wiley.com/college/kimmel and on the IRCD.)

Computerized Test Bank. The new Diploma computerized Test Bank allows instructors to create and print multiple versions of the same test by scrambling the order of all questions found in the print Test Bank. The computerized test bank also allows users to customize exams by altering or adding new problems. (Available at www/wiley.com/college/kimmel, on the IRCD, and via WileyPLUS.)

WebCT and Blackboard. WebCT™ and Blackboard™ offer an integrated set of course-management tools that enable instructors to easily design, develop, and manage web-based and web-enhanced courses.

The Wiley *Financial Accounting* WebCT™ and Blackboard™ courses contain the basic course management shell with all online resources for students. It allows the professor to present all or part of a course online and helps the student organize the course material, understand key concepts, and access additional tools. Your Wiley WebCT™ or Blackboard™ course can be customized to fit individual, professor needs. Contact your Wiley representative for more information.

Students' Active Learning Aids

 Take Action! CD-ROM. An exciting resource that can be made available with *Financial Accounting* is the interactive, **Take Action! CD-ROM.** Available as a supplement to accompany the main text, the Take Action! CD-ROM contains a Chapter Review Tutorial (one per chapter), Demonstration Problem (one per chapter), Glossary of Terms, Accounting Cycle Tutorial, Tootsie Roll Annual Report Walkthrough, Inventory Tutorial, Depreciation Tutorial, and Bad Debt Tutorial.

Student Workbook. The student workbook is a helpful tool for review and exam preparation. Each chapter contains a detailed review of all text study objectives. Multiple-choice, completion, and comprehensive problems are also provided with detailed solutions.

Working Papers. Working Papers are accounting templates for all end-of-chapter brief exercises, exercises, problems, and cases. A convenient resource for organizing and completing homework assignments, they demonstrate how to correctly set up solution formats and are directly tied to textbook assignments.

Excel Working Papers. An electronic version of the print working papers, these Excel-formatted templates help students properly format solutions to end-of-chapter exercises, problems, and cases. Available through premium WileyPLUS.

GLS **General Ledger Software.** The General Ledger Software program allows students to solve select end-of-chapter text problems or customized problems using a computerized accounting system. Easy to use, GLS demonstrates the immediate effects of each transaction and enables students to enter and post journal entries and to generate trial balances and income statements. The application is available on CD and through premium WileyPLUS.

Excel Workbook and Templates. This workbook and accompanying Excel templates allow students to complete select end-of-chapter exercises and problems identified by a spreadsheet icon in the margin of the main text. A useful introduction to computers, these electronic spreadsheets also enhance students' accounting skills. Spreadsheets and workbook are available only on the student companion site at www/wiley.com/college/kimmel.

Acknowledgments

The development of *Financial Accounting* has benefited greatly from the input of focus group participants, manuscript reviewers, those who have sent comments by letter or e-mail, ancillary authors, and proofers. We greatly appreciate the constructive suggestions and innovative ideas of reviewers and the creativity and accuracy of the ancillary authors and checkers.

Reviewers and Focus Group Participants for Prior Editions of *Financial Accounting*

Dawn Addington, *Albuquerque TVI Community College*; Solochidi Ahiarah, *Buffalo State College*; Sheila Ammons, *Austin Community College*; Thomas G. Amyot, *College of Santa Rose*; Victoria Beard, *University of North Dakota*; Angela H. Bell, *Jacksonville State University*; John A. Booker, *Tennessee Technological University*; Robert L. Braun, *Southeastern Louisiana University*; Sarah Ruth Brown, *University of North Alabama*; and James Byrne, *Oregon State University*.

Judy Cadle, *Tarleton State University*; David Carr, *Austin Community College*; Jack Cathey, *University of North Carolina–Charlotte*; Andy Chen, *Northeast Illinois University*; Jim Christianson, *Austin Community College*; Laura Claus, *Louisiana State University*; Leslie A. Cohen, *University of Arizona*; Teresa L. Conover, *University of North Texas*; Janet Courts, *San Bernadino Valley College*.

Helen Davis, *Johnson and Wales University*; Cheryl Dickerson, *Western Washington University*; George M. Dow, *Valencia Community College–West*; Kathy J. Dow, *Salem State College*; and Lola Dudley, *Eastern Illinois University*.

Mary Emery, *St. Olaf College*; Martin L. Epstein, *Albuquerque TVI Community College*; Larry R. Falcetto, *Emporia State University*; Scott Fargason, *Louisiana State University*; Sheila D. Foster, *The Citadel*; Jessica J. Frazier, *Eastern Kentucky University;* Norman H. Godwin, *Auburn University*; David Gotlob, *Indiana University-Purdue University–Fort Wayne*; and Emmett Griner, *Georgia State University*.

Leon J. Hanouille, *Syracuse University*; Kenneth M. Hiltebeitel, *Villanova University*; Judith A. Hora, *University of San Diego*; Carol Olson Houston, *San Diego State University*; Marianne L. James, *California State University–Los Angeles*; Christopher Jones, *George Washington University;* Jane Kaplan, *Drexel University*; John E. Karayan, *California State University–Pomona;* Susan Kattelus, *Eastern Michigan University*; Cindi Khanlarian, *University of North Carolina–Greensboro*; Robert J. Kirsch, *Southern Connecticut State University*; Frank Korman, *Mountain View College*; and Jerry G. Kreuze, *Western Michigan University*.

John Lacey, *California State University–Long Beach*; Doug Laufer, *Metropolitan State College of Denver*; Keith Leeseberg, *Manatee Community College*; Seth Levine, *DeVry University*; James Lukawitz, *University of Memphis*; Noel McKeon, *Florida Community College*; P. Merle Maddocks, *University of Alabama–Huntsville*; Janice Mardon, *Green River Community College*; John Marts, *University of North Carolina–Wilmington*; Alan Mayer-Sommer, *Georgetown University*; Elizabeth Minbiole, *Northwood University;* and Gale E. Newell, *Western Michigan University*.

Sarah N. Palmer, *University of North Carolina–Charlotte*; Patricia Parker, *Columbus State Community College;* Franklin J. Plewa, *Idaho State University*; John Purisky, *Salem State College*; Donald J. Raux, *Siena College*; Judith Resnick, *Borough of Manhattan Community College*; Mary Ann Reynolds, *Western Washington University*; Carla Rich, *Pensacola Junior College*; Ray Rigoli, *Ramapo College of New Jersey*; Jeff Ritter, *St. Norbert College;* Patricia A. Robinson, *Johnson and Wales University;* Marc A. Rubin, *Miami University*.

Alfredo Salas, *El Paso Community College;* Christine Schalow, *California State University–San Bernadino*; Michael Schoderbek, *Rutgers University*; Richard Schroeder, *University of North Carolina–Charlotte*; Cindy Seipel, *New Mexico State University*; Anne E. Selk,*University of Wisconsin–Green Bay*; William Seltz, *University of Massachusetts*; Suzanne Sevalstad, *University of Nevada*; Mary Alice Seville, *Oregon State University*; Aileen Smith, *Stephen F. Austin State University*; William E. Smith, *Xavier University*; Teresa A. Speck, *St. Mary's University of Minnesota*; Charles Stanley, *Baylor University*; Ron Stone, *California State University–Northridge*; Gary Stout, *California State University–Northridge*; and Ellen L. Sweatt, *Georgia Perimeter College*.

Pamadda Tantral, *Fairleigh Dickinson University*; Andrea B. Weickgenannt, *Northern Kentucky University*; David P. Weiner, *University of San Francisco*; Frederick Weis, *Claremont McKenna College*; T. Sterling Wetzel, *Oklahoma State University*; Allan Young, *DeVry University*; Michael F. van Breda, *Texas Christian University*; Linda G. Wade, *Tarleton State University*; Stuart K. Webster, *University of Wyoming*; V. Joyce Yearley, *New Mexico State University*.

Reviewers and Focus Group Participants for Financial Accounting, 4th Edition

Sheila Ammons, *Austin Community College*

Cheryl Bartlett, *Albuquerque TVI Community College*

Robert L. Braun, *Southeastern Louisiana University*

Daniel Brickner, *Eastern Michigan University*

Leslie A. Cohen, *University of Arizona*

Martin L. Epstein, *Albuquerque TVI Community College*

Janet Farler, *Pima Community College*

Harry Hooper, *Santa Fe Community College*

Norma Jacobs, *Austin Community College*

Marianne L. James, *California State University–Los Angeles*

Stanley Jenne, *University of Montana*

Dawn Kelly, *Texas Tech University*

Robert Kiddoo, *California State University–Northridge*

Glenda Levendowski, *Arizona State University*

Barbara Merino, *University of North Texas*

Jeanne Miller, *Cypress College*

Robert Miller, *California State University–Fullerton*

Marguerite Muise, *Santa Ana College*

James Neurath, *Central Michigan University*

Suzanne Ogilby, *Sacramento State University*

Charles Pier, *Appalachian State University*

Meg Pollard, *American River College*

Donald J. Raux, *Siena College*

Brandi Roberts, *Southeastern Louisiana University*
Nancy Rochman, *University of Arizona*
Jerry Searfoss, *University of Utah*

Donald Smillie, *Southwest Missouri State University*
Talitha Smith, *Auburn University*
Will Snyder, *San Diego State University*

Ancillary Authors, Contributers, and Proofers

Sheila Ammons, *Austin Community College* –
Test Bank author and Instructor's Manual author

Molly Brown, *James Madison University* – Test Bank
author

James M. Emig, *Villanova University* – Solutions Manual
and Test Bank proofer

Larry R. Falcetto, *Emporia Sate University* – Test Bank
and Checklist author, Solutions Manual proofer

Janet Farler, *Pima Community College* – Test Bank
author

Cecelia M. Fewox, *College of Charleston* – Student
Workbook author

Carol Hartley, *Providence College* – PowerPoint author

Wayne Higley, *Buena Vista University* – Text proofer

Laura McNally – WileyPlus author

Melanie Yon – WileyPlus reviewer

Rex Schildhouse, *San Diego Community College* – Excel
Workbook and Templates author

Alice Sineaath, *Forsyth Technical Community College* –
Test Bank proofer

Eileen Shifflett, *James Madison University* – Test Bank
author

Ellen L. Sweatt, *Georgia Perimeter College* – PowerPoint
author

Dick D. Wasson, *Southwestern College* – Working Papers
and Excel Working Papers author, Solutions Manual
proofer

Sheila Viel, *University of Wisconsin–Milwaukee* –
Solutions Manual Proofer

We appreciate the exemplary support and professional commitment given us by our publisher Susan Elbe, executive editor Christopher DeJohn, development editor Ann Torbert, project editors Brian Kamins and Ed Brislin, editorial assistant Alison Stanley, program assistant Kristin Babroski, senior media editor Allie Morris, vice-president of higher education production and manufacturing Ann Berlin, designer Kevin Murphy, illustration editor Anna Melhorne, photo editor Elle Wagner, production manager Jeanine Furino, project editor Suzanne Ingrao of Ingrao Associates, product manager Jane Shifflet at TECHBOOKS, director of marketing Frank Lyman, marketing manager Amy Yarnevich, and marketing assistant Vanessa Ahrens. Thanks, too, to Jay O'Callaghan for his energetic devotion to this project over the years.

We thank Tootsic Roll Industries and Hershey Foods Corporation for permitting us the use of their 2004 Annual Reports for our specimen financial statements and accompanying notes.

We appreciate and encourage suggestions and comments from users. Please feel free to email any one of us at *account@wiley.com*.

PAUL D. KIMMEL
Milwaukee, Wisconsin

JERRY J. WEYGANDT
Madison, Wisconsin

DONALD E. KIESO
DeKalb, Illinois

Study Objectives at the beginning of each chapter give you a framework for learning the specific concepts covered in the chapter. Each study objective reappears in the margin where the concept is discussed. You can review the concepts related to the study objectives in the **Summary** at the end of the chapter text.

The Navigator is a learning system designed to guide you through each chapter and help you succeed in learning the material. It consists of (1) a checklist at the beginning of the chapter, which outlines text features and study aids you will need, and (2) a series of check boxes that prompt you to use the learning aids in the chapter and set priorities as you study.

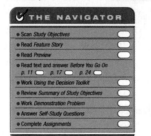

CHAPTER 1

Introduction to Financial Statements

STUDY OBJECTIVES

After studying this chapter, you should be able to:

1 Describe the primary forms of business organization.
2 Identify the users and uses of accounting information.
3 Explain the three principal types of business activity.
4 Describe the content and purpose of each of the financial statements.
5 Explain the meaning of assets, liabilities, and stockholders' equity, and state the basic accounting equation.
6 Describe the components that supplement the financial statements in an annual report.

THE NAVIGATOR

- Scan *Study Objectives*
- Read *Feature Story*
- Read *Preview*
- Read text and answer *Before You Go On*
  p. 11 ◯   p. 17 ◯   p. 24 ◯
- Work *Using the Decision Toolkit*
- Review *Summary of Study Objectives*
- Work *Demonstration Problem*
- Answer *Self-Study Questions*
- Complete *Assignments*

The Navigator is a learning system designed to prompt you to use the learning aids in and to set priorities as you study.

FEATURE STORY

Knowing the Numbers

Many students who take this course do not plan to be accountants. If you are in that group, you might be thinking, "If I'm not going to be an accountant, why do I need to know accounting?" In response, consider this quote from Harold Geneen, the former chairman of IT&T: "To be good at your business, you have to know the numbers—cold." Success in any business comes back to the numbers. You will rely on them to make decisions, and managers will use them to evaluate your performance. That is true whether your job involves marketing, production, management, or information systems.

In business, accounting and financial statements are the means for communicating the numbers. If you don't know how to read financial statements, you can't really know your business.

Many companies spend significant resources teaching their employees basic accounting so that they can read financial statements and understand how their actions affect the company's financial results. One such company is Springfield ReManufacturing Corporation (SRC). When Jack Stack and 11 other managers purchased SRC for 10 cents a share, it was a failing division of International Harvester. Jack had 119 employees who were counting on him for their livelihood, and he knew that the new company was on the verge of financial failure. He

The Feature Story helps you picture how the chapter topic relates to the real world of accounting and business. References in the chapter to the Feature Story will help you put new ideas in context, organize them, and remember them.

PREVIEW OF CHAPTER 1

How do you start a business? How do you make it grow into a widely recognized brand name like Tootsie Roll? How do you determine whether your business is making or losing money? When you need to expand your operations, where you get money to finance expansion—should you borrow, should you issue stock, should you use your own funds? How do you convince lenders to lend you money or investors to buy your stock? Success in business requires making countless decisions, and decisions require financial information.

The purpose of this chapter is to show you what role accounting plays in providing financial information. The content and organization of the chapter are as follows.

INTRODUCTION TO FINANCIAL STATEMENTS

Forms of Business Organization	Users and Uses of Financial Information	Business Activities	Communicating with Users	A Quick Look at Tootsie Roll's Financial Statements
• Sole proprietorship	• Internal users	• Financing	• Income statement	• Income statement
• Partnership	• External users	• Investing	• Retained earnings statement	• Retained earnings statement
• Corporation	• Ethics in financial reporting	• Operating	• Balance sheet	• Balance sheet
			• Statement of cash flows	• Statement of cash flows
			• Interrelationships of statements	• Other elements of an annual report

THE NAVIGATOR

The **Preview** links the Feature Story with the major topics of the chapter and describes the purpose of the chapter. It then outlines the topics that are discussed. This narrative and visual preview helps you organize the information you are learning.

Accounting across the Organization

Accounting can even serve as a useful recruiting tool for the human resources department. Rhino Foods, located in Burlington, VT, is a manufacturer of specialty ice cream novelties and ice cream ingredients. Its corporate website includes the following paragraphs:

> "Wouldn't it be great to work where you were part of a team? Where your input and hard work made a difference? Where you weren't kept in the dark about what management was thinking?
>
> Well—it's not a dream! It's the way we do business at Rhino Foods on Industrial Parkway in Burlington. Rhino Foods believes in family, honesty and open communication—we really care about and appreciate our employees—and it shows. Operating results are posted and monthly group meetings inform all employees about what's happening in the Company. Employees also share in the Company's profits, in addition to having an excellent comprehensive *benefits* package."

Source: www.rhinofoods.com/workforus/workforus.html.

? What are the benefits to the company and to the employees of making the financial statements available to all employees?

EXTERNAL USERS

There are several types of **external users** of accounting information. **Investors** (owners) use accounting information to make decisions to buy, hold, or sell stock. **Creditors** such as suppliers and bankers use accounting information to evaluate the risks of granting credit or lending money. Some questions that investors and creditors may ask about a company are shown in Illustration 1-3.

The information needs and questions of other external users vary considerably. **Taxing authorities**, such as the Internal Revenue Service, want to know whether the company complies with the tax laws. **Customers** are interested in whether a

Illustration 1-3

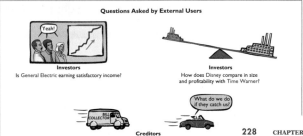

Questions Asked by External Users

Investors
Is General Electric earning satisfactory income?

Investors
How does Disney compare in size and profitability with Time Warner?

What do we do if they catch us!

Creditors
Will United Airlines be able to pay its debts as they come due?

Accounting across the Organization boxes demonstrate the use of accounting to address issues in marketing, finance, management, and other functional areas of business. If you are not an accounting major, these should be of particular interest. (A guideline answer to the question at the end of each box appears near the end of the chapter.)

Color illustrations, such as this **infographic,** help you visualize and apply information as you study. They reinforce important concepts and therefore often contain material that may appear on exams.

---

228   CHAPTER 5   Merchandising Operations and the Multiple-Step Income Statement

Junot Diaz Company

Sept.	5	Accounts Receivable	1,500	
		Sales		1,500
		(To record credit sale)		
	5	Cost of Goods Sold	800	
		Merchandise Inventory		800
		(To record cost of goods sold on account)		
Sept.	8	Sales Returns and Allowances	200	
		Accounts Receivable		200
		(To record credit granted for receipt of returned goods)		
	8	Merchandise Inventory	105	
		Cost of Goods Sold		105
		(To record cost of goods returned)		

THE NAVIGATOR

Income Statement Presentation

STUDY OBJECTIVE
4
Distinguish between a single-step and a multiple-step income statement.

Companies widely use two forms of the income statement. One is the **single-step income statement**. The statement is so named because only one step, subtracting total expenses from total revenues, is required in determining net income (or net loss).

In a single-step statement, all data are classified into two categories: (1) **revenues**, which include both operating revenues and nonoperating revenues and gains (for example, interest revenue and gain on sale of equipment); and (2) **expenses**, which include cost of goods sold, operating expenses, and nonoperating expenses and losses (for example, interest expense, loss on sale of equipment, or income tax expense). The single-step income statement is the form we have used thus far in the text. Illustration 5-5 shows a single-step statement for Wal-Mart.

Illustration 5-5
Single-step income statements

WAL★MART
ALWAYS LOW PRICES.
Always

WAL-MART STORES, INC.
Income Statements
(in millions)

	For the years ended January 31	
	2004	**2003**
Revenues		
Net sales	$256,329	$229,616
Other revenues, net	2,352	1,961
	258,681	231,577
Expenses		
Cost of goods sold	198,747	178,299
Selling, general, and administrative expenses	44,909	39,983
Interest expense	832	927
Other expense	21	56
Income taxes	5,118	4,357
	249,627	223,622
Net income	$ 9,054	$ 7,955

Study Objectives reappear in the margins where the related topic is discussed. End-of-chapter assignments are keyed to study objectives.

Financial statements appear regularly throughout the book. Those from actual companies are identified by a logo or photo. Often, numbers or categories are highlighted in red to draw your attention to key information.

Business Insight
Ethics Perspective

Allegations of abuse of the revenue recognition principle have become all too common in recent years. For example, it was alleged that Krispy Kreme sometimes doubled the number of doughnuts shipped to wholesale customers at the end of a quarter to boost quarterly results. The customers shipped the unsold doughnuts back after the beginning of the next quarter for a refund. Conversely, Computer Associates International was accused of backdating sales—that is, saying that a sale that occurred at the beginning of one quarter occurred at the end of the previous quarter in order to achieve the previous quarter's sales targets.

 What motivates sales executives and finance and accounting executives to participate in activities that result in inaccurate reporting of revenues?

BEFORE YOU GO ON . . .

▶**Review It**

1. What are the revenue recognition and matching principles?
2. What are the differences between the cash and accrual bases of accounting?

THE NAVIGATOR

The Basics of Adjusting Entries

In order for revenues to be recorded in the period in which they are earned, and for expenses to be recognized in the period in which they are incurred, companies make adjusting entries. Adjusting entries ensure that the revenue recognition and matching principles are followed.

Adjusting entries are necessary because the **trial balance**—the first pulling together of the transaction data—may not contain up-to-date and complete data. This is true for several reasons:

1. Some events are not recorded daily because it is not efficient to do so. Examples are the use of supplies and the earning of wages by employees.
2. Some costs are not recorded during the accounting period because these costs expire with the passage of time rather than as a result of recurring

STUDY OBJECTIVE

Explain why adjusting entries are needed, and identify the major types of adjusting entries.

Business Insight boxes give you more glimpses into how actual companies make decisions using accounting information. These high-interest boxes are classified by three different points of view—ethics, investor, and international. Each ends with a question to test your understanding. (Guideline answers appear near the end of the chapter.)

Key terms and concepts are printed in blue where they are first explained in the text. They are listed and defined again in the end-of-chapter **Glossary**.

---

224 CHAPTER 5 Merchandising Operations and the Multiple-Step Income Statement

When an invoice is paid within the discount period, the amount of the discount decreases Merchandise Inventory. Why? Because the merchandiser records inventory at its cost and, by paying within the discount period, it has reduced that cost. To illustrate, assume Sauk Stereo pays the balance due of $3,500 (gross invoice price of $3,800 less purchase returns and allowances of $300) on May 14, the last day of the discount period. The cash discount is $70 ($3,500 × 2%), and the amount of cash Sauk Stereo paid is $3,430 ($3,500 − $70). The entry Sauk makes to record its May 14 payment decreases Accounts Payable by the amount of the gross invoice price, reduces Merchandise Inventory by the $70 discount, and reduces Cash by the net amount owed.

A = L + SE
            −3,500
−3,430
−70

Cash Flows
−3,430

May 14	Accounts Payable	3,500	
	Cash		3,430
	Merchandise Inventory		70
	(To record payment within discount period)		

If Sauk Stereo failed to take the discount and instead made full payment of $3,500 on June 3, Sauk would debit Accounts Payable and credit Cash for $3,500 each.

A = L + SE
            −3,500
−3,500

Cash Flows
−3,500

June 3	Accounts Payable	3,500	
	Cash		3,500
	(To record payment with no discount taken)		

A merchandising company usually should take all available discounts. Passing up the discount may be viewed as **paying interest** for use of the money. For example, passing up the discount offered by PW Audio would be like Sauk Stereo paying an interest rate of 2% for the use of $3,500 for 20 days. This is the equivalent of an annual interest rate of approximately 36.5% (2% × 365/20). Obviously, it would be better for Sauk Stereo to borrow at prevailing bank interest rates of 6% to 10% than to lose the discount.

Accounting equation analyses appear in the margin next to key journal entries. They will help you understand the impact of an accounting transaction on the financial statements and on the company's cash flows.

---

of rising prices. For example, at Houston Electronics, income taxes are $7? der LIFO, compared to $990 under FIFO. The tax savings of $240 makes cash available for use in the business.

Decision Toolkit

Decision Checkpoints	Info Needed for Decision	Tool to Use for Decision	How to Evaluate Results
Which inventory costing method should be used?	Are prices increasing, or are they decreasing?	Income statement, balance sheet, and tax effects	Depends on objective. In a period of rising prices, income and inventory are higher and cash flow is lower under FIFO. LIFO provides opposite results. Average cost can moderate the impact of changing prices.

USING INVENTORY COST FLOW METHODS CONSISTENTLY

Whatever cost flow method a company chooses, it should use that method consistently from one accounting period to another. Consistent application enhances the comparability of financial statements over successive time periods. In contrast, using the FIFO method one year and the LIFO method the next year would make it difficult to compare the net incomes of the two years.

Although consistent application is preferred, it does not mean that a company may *never* change its method of inventory costing. When a company adopts a different method, it should disclose in the financial statements the change and its effects on net income. A typical disclosure is shown in Illustration 6-14, using information from recent financial statements of the Quaker Oats Company.

Helpful Hint As you learned in Chapter 2, consistency and comparability are important characteristics of accounting information.

Each chapter presents **decision tools** that help decision makers analyze and solve business problems. At the end of the text discussion, a **Decision Toolkit** summarizes the key features of a decision tool, and it reviews why and how you would use it.

Helpful Hints in the margins are like having an instructor with you as you read. They further clarify concepts being discussed.

The Classified Balance Sheet   **53**

STOCKHOLDERS' EQUITY

Stockholders' equity consists of two parts: common stock and retained earnings. Companies record as **common stock** the investments of assets into the business by the stockholders. They record as **retained earnings** the income retained for use in the business. These two parts, combined, make up **stockholders' equity** on the balance sheet. In Illustration 2-2 Franklin reported common stock of $14,000 and retained earnings of $20,050.

Alternative Terminology
Common stock is sometimes called *capital stock.*

BEFORE YOU GO ON . . .

▶**Review It**

1. What are the major sections in a classified balance sheet?
2. What is the primary determining factor to distinguish current assets from long-term assets?
3. What was Tootsie Roll's largest current asset at December 31, 2004? (The answer to this question appears on page 97.)
4. Where on the balance sheet do companies report accumulated depreciation?

▶**Do It**

Baxter Hoffman recently received the following information related to Hoffman Corporation's December 31, 2007, balance sheet.

Prepaid expenses	$ 2,300	Inventory	$3,400
Cash	800	Accumulated depreciation	2,700
Property, plant, and equipment	10,700	Accounts receivable	1,100

Prepare the assets section of Hoffman Corporation's balance sheet.

Action Plan

• Present current assets first. Current assets are cash and other resources that the company reasonably expects to consume in one year.
• Present current assets in the order in which the company expects to convert them into cash.
• Subtract accumulated depreciation from property, plant, and equipment to determine net property, plant, and equipment.

Solution

HOFFMAN CORPORATION
Balance Sheet (partial)
December 31, 2007

Assets

Current assets		
Cash	$ 800	
Accounts receivable	1,100	
Inventory	3,400	
Prepaid expenses	2,300	
Total current assets		$ 7,600
Property, plant, and equipment	10,700	
Less: Accumulated depreciation	2,700	8,000
Total assets		$15,600

THE NAVIGATOR

Alternative Terminology notes present synonymous terms that you may come across in practice.

Before You Go On sections follow each key topic. ***Review It*** questions prompt you to stop and review the key points you have just studied. If you cannot answer these questions, you should go back and read the section again. ***Review It*** questions marked with the Tootsie Roll icon direct you to find information in Tootsie Roll Industries' 2004 Annual Report, printed in Appendix A. Answers appear at the end of the chapter.

Brief ***Do It*** exercises ask you to put to work your newly acquired knowledge. They outline an **Action Plan** necessary to complete the exercise and show a **Solution**.

A **Using the Decision Toolkit** exercise follows the final set of ***Review It*** questions in the chapter. It asks you to use business information and the decision tools presented in the chapter. You should think through the questions related to the decision before you study the **Solution** provided.

Using the Decision Toolkit

Reebok remains one of Nike's fiercest competitors. In such a competitive and rapidly changing environment, one wrong step can spell financial disaster. After bottoming out at the end of 1999, Reebok's stock has rebounded sharply.

Instructions
The following facts are available for Reebok. Using this information, evaluate its (1) dividend record and (2) earnings performance, and contrast them with those for Nike for 2003 and 2004. Nike's earnings per share were $3.59 in 2004 and $2.80 in 2003.

(in thousands except per share data)	2004	2003	2002
Dividends declared	$ 17,839	$ 8,847	0
Net income	$ 192,425	$ 157,254	$126,458
Preferred stock dividends	0	0	0
Shares outstanding at end of year	101,827	101,081	99,235
Common stockholders' equity	$1,219,956	$1,033,710	$884,570

Solution

1. *Dividend record:* A measure to evaluate dividend record is the payout ratio. For Reebok, this measure in 2004 and 2003 is calculated as shown below.

	2004	2003
Payout ratio	$\dfrac{\$17,839}{\$192,425} = 9.3\%$	$\dfrac{\$8,847}{\$157,254} = 5.6\%$

Nike's payout ratio remained nearly constant at 21%. Reebok's payout ratio increased significantly from 2003 to 2004 but was still less than half Nike's ratio.

2. *Earnings performance:* There are many measures of earnings performance. Some of those presented thus far in the book were earnings per share (page 55) and the return on common stockholders' equity ratio (this chapter). These measures for Reebok in 2004 and 2003 are calculated as shown here.

	2004	2003
Earnings per share	$\dfrac{\$192,425 - 0}{(101,827 + 101,081)/2} = \$1.90$	$\dfrac{\$157,254 - 0}{(101,081 + 99,235)/2} = \$1.57$
Return on common stockholders' equity ratio	$\dfrac{\$192,425 - 0}{(\$1,219,956 + \$1,033,710)/2} = 17.1\%$	$\dfrac{\$157,254 - 0}{(\$1,033,710 + \$884,570)/2} = 16.4\%$

From 2003 to 2004, Reebok's net income improved 22% and its earnings per share increased 21%. During the same time period Nike's earnings per share increased 28%.

Reebok's return on common stockholders' equity increased from 16.4% to 17.1%. While this represents a healthy increase, it is still less than Nike's 21.6%.

THE NAVIGATOR

The **Summary of Study Objectives** reviews the main points related to the Study Objectives. It provides you with another opportunity to review what you have learned as well as to see how the key topics within the chapter fit together.

At the end of each chapter, the **Decision Toolkit— A Summary** reviews the techniques for decision making that were covered in the chapter.

The **Wiley Plus** icon at the chapter Summary and other places in the assignment materials indicates electronic book content that will enable you to review the text and complete homework online.

The **Glossary** defines all the **key terms** and **concepts** introduced in the chapter. Page references help you find any terms you need to study further.

A **Demonstration Problem** is the final step before you begin homework. These sample problems provide you with an **Action Plan** in the margin that lists the strategies needed to approach and solve the problem. The **Solution** demonstrates both the form and content of complete answers.

---

130 **CHAPTER 3** The Accounting Information System

Summary of Study Objectives

1 *Analyze the effect of business transactions on the basic accounting equation.* Each business transaction must have a dual effect on the accounting equation. For example, if an individual asset is increased, there must be a corresponding (a) decrease in another asset, or (b) increase in a specific liability, or (c) increase in stockholders' equity.

2 *Explain what an account is and how it helps in the recording process.* An account is an individual accounting record of increases and decreases in specific asset, liability, and stockholders' equity items.

3 *Define debits and credits and explain how they are used to record business transactions.* The terms *debit* and *credit* are synonymous with *left* and *right*. Assets, dividends, and expenses are increased by debits and decreased by credits. Liabilities, common stock, retained earnings, and revenues are increased by credits and decreased by debits.

4 *Identify the basic steps in the recording process.* The basic steps in the recording process are: (a) analyze each transaction in terms of its effect on the accounts, (b) enter the transaction information in a journal, and (c) transfer the journal information to the appropriate accounts in the ledger.

5 *Explain what a journal is and how it helps in the recording process.* The initial accounting record of a transaction is entered in a journal before the data are entered in the accounts. A journal (a) discloses in one place the complete effect of a transaction, (b) provides a chronological record of transactions, and (c) prevents or locates errors because the debit and credit amounts for each entry can be readily compared.

6 *Explain what a ledger is and how it helps in the recording process.* The entire group of accounts maintained by a company is referred to collectively as a ledger. The ledger keeps in one place all the information about changes in specific account balances.

7 *Explain what posting is and how it helps in the recording process.* Posting is the procedure of transferring journal entries to the ledger accounts. This phase of the recording process accumulates the effects of journalized transactions in the individual accounts.

8 *Explain the purposes of a trial balance.* A trial balance is a list of accounts and their balances at a given time. The primary purpose of the trial balance is to prove the mathematical equality of debits and credits after posting. A trial balance also uncovers errors in journalizing and posting and is useful in preparing financial statements.

THE NAVIGATOR

Decision Toolkit—A Summary

Decision Checkpoints	Info Needed for Decision	Tool to Use for Decision	How to Evaluate Results
Has an accounting transaction occurred?	Details of the event	Accounting equation	If the event affected assets, liabilities, or stockholders' equity, then record as a transaction.
How do you determine that debits equal credits?	All account balances	Trial balance	List the account titles and their balances; total the debit and credit columns; verify equality.

Glossary

Account An individual accounting record of increases and decreases in specific asset, liability, or stockholders' equity items. (p. 108)

Accounting information system The system of collecting and processing transaction data and communicating financial information to interested parties. (p. 100)

Accounting transactions Events that require recording in the financial statements because they affect assets, liabilities, or stockholders' equity. (p. 101)

Chart of accounts A list of a company's accounts. (p. 118)

Credit The right side of an account. (p. 109)

Debit The left side of an account. (p. 109)

Double-entry system A system that records the dual effect of each transaction in appropriate accounts. (p. 109)

General journal The most basic form of journal. (p. 114)

General ledger A ledger that contains all asset, liability, and stockholders' equity accounts. (p. 117)

Demonstration Problem

Rolman Corporation is authorized to issue 1,000,000 shares of $5 par value common stock. In its first year the company has the following stock transactions.

Jan. 10 Issued 400,000 shares of stock at $8 per share.
Sept. 1 Purchased 10,000 shares of common stock for the treasury at $9 per share.
Dec. 24 Declared a cash dividend of 10 cents per share on common stock outstanding.

Instructions
(a) Journalize the transactions.
(b) Prepare the stockholders' equity section of the balance sheet assuming the company had retained earnings of $150,600 at December 31.

Action Plan
- When common stock has a par value, credit Common Stock for par value and Paid-in Capital in Excess of Par Value for the amount above par value.
- Debit the Treasury Stock account at cost.

Solution to Demonstration Problem

(a) Jan. 10	Cash	3,200,000	
	Common Stock		2,000,000
	Paid-in Capital in Excess of Par Value		1,200,000
	(To record issuance of 400,000 shares of $5 par value stock)		
Sept. 1	Treasury Stock	90,000	
	Cash		90,000
	(To record purchase of 10,000 shares of treasury stock at cost)		
Dec. 24	Retained Earnings	39,000	
	Dividends Payable		39,000
	(To record declaration of 10 cents per share cash dividend)		

(b)

ROLMAN CORPORATION
Balance Sheet (partial)

Stockholders' equity	
Paid-in capital	
Capital stock	
Common stock, $5 par value, 1,000,000 shares authorized, 400,000 shares issued, 390,000 outstanding	$2,000,000
Additional paid-in capital in excess of par value	1,200,000
Total paid-in capital	3,200,000
Retained earnings	150,600
Total paid-in capital and retained earnings	3,350,600
Less: Treasury stock (10,000 shares)	90,000
Total stockholders' equity	$3,260,600

THE NAVIGATOR

Self-Study Questions provide a practice test, keyed to Study Objectives, that gives you an opportunity to check your knowledge of important topics. Answers appear at the end of the chapter. Additional opportunities for self-testing are available through WileyPlus.

Questions allow you to explain your understanding of concepts and relationships from the chapter. Use them to help prepare for class discussion and tests.

Self-Study Questions

Answers are at the end of the chapter.

(SO 1) **1.** Which is *not* one of the three forms of business organization?
(a) Sole proprietorship.   (c) Partnership.
(b) Creditorship.   (d) Corporation.

(SO 1) **2.** Which is an advantage of corporations relative to partnerships and sole proprietorships?
(a) Lower taxes.
(b) Harder to transfer ownership.
(c) Reduced legal liability for investors.
(d) Most common form of organization.

(SO 2) **3.** Which statement about users of accounting information is *incorrect*?
(a) Management is considered an internal user.
(b) Taxing authorities are considered external users.
(c) Present creditors are considered external users.
(d) Regulatory authorities are considered internal users.

(SO 3) **4.** Which is *not* one of the three primary business activities?
(a) Financing.   (c) Advertising.
(b) Operating.   (d) Investing.

(SO 3, 4) **5.** Net income will result during a time period when:
(a) assets exceed liabilities.

(c) The financing section.
(d) The cash flow statement does not give this information.

(SO 5) **7.** Which financial statement reports assets, liabilities, and stockholders' equity?
(a) Income statement.
(b) Retained earnings statement.
(c) Balance sheet.
(d) Statement of cash flows.

(SO 5) **8.** Stockholders' equity represents:
(a) claims of creditors.
(b) claims of employees.
(c) the difference between revenues and expenses.
(d) claims of owners.

(SO 5) **9.** As of December 31, 2007, Stoneland Corporation has assets of $3,500 and stockholders' equity of $2,000. What are the liabilities for Stoneland Corporation as of December 31, 2007?
(a) $1,500.   (c) $2,500.
(b) $1,000.   (d) $2,000.

(SO 6) **10.** The segment of a corporation's annual report that describes the corporation's accounting methods is the:
(a) notes to the financial statements.
(b) management discussion and analysis.
(c) auditor's report.
(d) income statement.

Go to the book's website, **www.wiley.com/college/kimmel**, to access additional Self-Study Questions.

THE NAVIGATOR

Questions

1. What are the three basic forms of business organizations?

2. What are the advantages to a business of being formed as a corporation? What are the disadvantages?

3. What are the advantages to a business of being formed as a partnership or sole proprietorship? What are the disadvantages?

4. "Accounting is ingrained in our society and is vital to our economic system." Do you agree? Explain.

5. Who are the internal users of accounting data? How does accounting provide relevant data to the internal users?

6. Who are the external users of accounting data? Give examples.

7. What are the three main types of business activity? Give examples of each activity.

8. Listed here are some items found in the financial statements of Ellyn Toth, Inc. Indicate in which financial statement(s) each item would appear.
(a) Service revenue.   (d) Accounts receivable.
(b) Equipment.   (e) Common stock.
(c) Advertising expense.   (f) Wages payable.

9. Why would a bank want to monitor the dividend payment practices of the corporations it lends money to?

This icon indicates review and homework material that relates to issues in marketing, finance, management, and other business areas other than accounting.

Brief Exercises help you focus on one Study Objective at a time and thus help you build confidence in your basic skills and knowledge.

Exercises, which are more difficult than Brief Exercises, help you continue to build confidence in your ability to use the material learned in the chapter.

The tool icon indicates review and homework material that asks you to use the **decision tools** presented in the chapter.

---

78   CHAPTER 2   A Further Look at Financial Statements

Brief Exercises

Classify accounts on balance sheet.
(SO 1)

BE2-1 The following are the major balance sheet classifications:

Current assets (CA)   Current liabilities (CL)
Long-term investments (LTI) Long-term liabilities (LTL)
Property, plant, and equipment (PPE)   Common stock (CS)
Intangible assets (IA)   Retained earnings (RE)

Match each of the following accounts to its proper balance sheet classification.

____ Accounts payable   ____ Income tax payable
____ Accounts receivable   ____ Investment in long-term bonds
____ Accumulated depreciation ____ Land
____ Building   ____ Merchandise inventory
____ Cash   ____ Patent
____ Goodwill   ____ Supplies

Identify placement of items on a multiple-step income statement.
(SO 4)

BE5-6 Explain where each of these items would appear on a multiple-step income statement: gain on sale of equipment, cost of goods sold, depreciation expense, and sales returns and allowances.

Compute net purchases and cost of goods purchased.
(SO 5)

BE5-7 Assume that Roshek Company uses a periodic inventory system and has these account balances: Purchases $424,000; Purchase Returns and Allowances $11,000; Purchase Discounts $7,000; and Freight-in $16,000. Determine net purchases and cost of goods purchased.

Certain Exercises and Problems, marked with a pencil icon help you practice **business writing skills,** which are much in demand among employers.

---

194   CHAPTER 4   Accrual Accounting Concepts

Exercises

PLUS

Identify point of revenue recognition.
(SO 1)

E4-1 The following independent situations require professional judgement for determining when to recognize revenue from the transactions.

(a) Southwest Airlines sells you an advance-purchase airline ticket in September for your flight home at Christmas.

(b) Ultimate Electronics sells you a home theatre on a "no money down, no interest, and no payments for one year" promotional deal.

(c) The Toronto Blue Jays sell season tickets online to games in the Skydome. Fans can purchase the tickets at any time, although the season doesn't officially begin until April. The major league baseball season runs from April through October.

(d) You borrow money in August from RBC Financial Group. The loan and the interest are repayable in full in November.

(e) In August, you order a sweater from Sears using its online catalog. The sweater arrives in September, and you charge it to your Sears credit card. You receive and pay the Sears bill in October.

Instructions
Identify when revenue should be recognized in each of the above situations.

Each **Problem** helps you pull together and apply several concepts from the chapter. Two sets of **Problems—A** and **B**—are keyed to the same Study Objectives and provide additional opportunities for practice.

Problems: Set A

P3-1A On April 1 Far and Wide Travel Agency Inc. was established. These transactions were completed during the month.

1. Stockholders invested $20,000 cash in the company in exchange for common stock.
2. Paid $900 cash for April office rent.
3. Purchased office equipment for $2,800 cash.
4. Purchased $200 of advertising in the *Chicago Tribune*, on account.
5. Paid $500 cash for office supplies.
6. Earned $9,000 for services provided: Cash of $1,000 is received from customers, and the balance of $8,000 is billed to customers on account.
7. Paid $400 cash dividends.
8. Paid *Chicago Tribune* amount due in transaction (4).
9. Paid employees' salaries $1,200.
10. Received $8,000 in cash from customers who have previously been billed in transaction (6).

Instructions
(a) Prepare a tabular analysis of the transactions using these column headings: Cash, Accounts Receivable, Supplies, Office Equipment, Accounts Payable, Common Stock, and Retained Earnings. Include margin explanations for any changes in Retained Earnings.
(b) From an analysis of the column Retained Earnings, compute the net income or net loss for April.

P3-2A Marie Blaesing started her own consulting firm, Blaesing Consulting Inc., on May 1, 2007. The following transactions occurred during the month of May.

Analyze transactions and compute net income.
(SO 1)
GLS

(a) Cash $23,000
Ret. earnings $ 6,300

Analyze transactions and prepare financial statements.
(SO 1)
GLS

Spreadsheet Exercises and **Problems**, identified by an icon, can be solved using the spreadsheet software *Solving Principles of Accounting Problems Using Excel.*

Problems: Set B

P5-1B Midwest Distributing Company completed these merchandising transactions in the month of April. At the beginning of April, the ledger of Midwest showed Cash of $9,000 and Common Stock of $9,000.

Apr. 2 Purchased merchandise on account from Kane Supply Co. $6,300, terms 2/10, n/30.
 4 Sold merchandise on account $5,000, terms 2/10, n/30. The cost of the merchandise sold was $3,700.
 5 Paid $200 freight on April 4 sale.
 6 Received credit from Kane Supply Co. for merchandise returned $300.
 11 Paid Kane Supply Co. in full, less discount.
 13 Received collections in full, less discounts, from customers billed on April 4.
 14 Purchased merchandise for cash $4,700.
 16 Received refund from supplier for returned merchandise on cash purchase of April 14, $500.
 18 Purchased merchandise from Great Plains Distributors $4,500, terms 2/10, n/30.
 20 Paid freight on April 18 purchase $100.
 23 Sold merchandise for cash $8,300. The cost of the merchandise sold was $5,820.
 26 Purchased merchandise for cash $2,300.
 27 Paid Great Plains Distributors in full, less discount.
 29 Made refunds to cash customers for returned merchandise $180. The returned merchandise had a cost of $120.
 30 Sold merchandise on account $3,980, terms n/30. The cost of the merchandise sold was $2,500.

Midwest Distributing Company's chart of accounts includes Cash, Accounts Receivable, Merchandise Inventory, Accounts Payable, Common Stock, Sales, Sales Returns and Allowances, Sales Discounts, Cost of Goods Sold, and Freight-out.

Journalize, post, prepare partial income statement, and calculate ratios.
(SO 2, 3, 4, 6)
GLS

General Ledger Problems, identified by an icon, are selected problems that can be solved using the *General Ledger Software* package.

Check figures in the margin provide key numbers to let you know you're on the right track as you do assignments.

A set of **C Problems** is available at the book's website.

Problems: Set C

Go to the book's website, **www.wiley.com/college/kimmel**, to access a set of C Problems.

Comprehensive Problem

CP10 Crow Corporation's balance sheet at December 31, 2006, is presented below.

CROW CORPORATION
Balance Sheet
December 31, 2006

Cash	$30,500	Accounts payable	$13,750
Inventory	25,750	Bond interest payable	3,000
Prepaid insurance	5,600	Bonds payable	50,000
Equipment	38,000	Common stock	20,000
	$99,850	Retained earnings	$13,100
			$99,850

During 2007, the following transactions occurred.
1. Crow paid $3,000 interest on the bonds on January 1, 2007.
2. Crow purchased $241,100 of inventory on account.
3. Crow sold for $400,000 cash inventory which cost $240,000. Crow also collected $24,000 sales taxes.
4. Crow paid $230,000 on accounts payable.
5. Crow paid $3,000 interest on the bonds on July 1, 2007.
6. The prepaid insurance ($5,600) expired on July 31.
7. On August 1, Crow paid $10,800 for insurance coverage from August 1, 2007, through July 31, 2008.
8. Crow paid $17,000 sales taxes to the state.
9. Paid other operating expenses, $91,000.
10. Retired the bonds on December 31, 2007, by paying $48,000 plus $3,000 interest.
11. Issued $70,000 of 8% bonds on December 31, 2007, at 104. The bonds pay interest every June 30 and December 31.

A **Comprehensive Problem** (in Chapters 5–11) combines material from the current and previous chapters, to show "how it all fits together."

Continuing Cookie Chronicle

(*Note:* This is a continuation of the Cookie Chronicle from Chapter 1.)

CCC2 After investigating the different forms of business organization, Natalie Koebel decides to operate her business as a corporation, Cookie Creations Inc., and she begins the process of getting her business running.

While at a trade show, Natalie is introduced to Gerry Richards, operations manager of "Biscuits," a national food retailer. After much discussion, Gerry asks Natalie to consider being Biscuits' major supplier of oatmeal chocolate chip cookies. He provides Natalie with the most recent copy of the financial statements of Biscuits. He expects that Natalie will need to supply Biscuits' Watertown warehouse with approximately 1,500 dozen cookies a week. Natalie is to send Biscuits a monthly invoice, and she will be paid approximately 30 days from the date the invoice is received in Biscuits' Chicago office.

Natalie is thrilled with the offer. However, she has recently read in the newspaper that Biscuits has a reputation for selling cookies and donuts with high amounts of sugar and fat, and as a result, consumer demand for the company's products has decreased.

Instructions
Natalie has several questions. Answer the following questions for Natalie.
(a) What type of information does each financial statement provide?
(b) How can Natalie evaluate whether Biscuits will be able to pay her invoices? What type of information can financial statements give that will reassure her that Biscuits will pay her invoices?
(c) Will Biscuits have enough cash to meet its current liabilities? Where can she find this information?
(d) Will Biscuits be able to survive over a long period of time? Where can she find this information?
(e) Is Biscuits profitable? Where can she find this information?
(f) Does Biscuits have any debt? Is Biscuits able to pay off both its debt and the interest on it? Where can she find this information?
(g) Does Biscuits pay any dividends? Where can she find this information?
(h) In deciding whether to go ahead with this opportunity, are there other areas of concern that she should be aware of?

The **Continuing Cookie Chronicle** in each chapter traces the growth of a small business and the financial reporting issues it encounters.

BROADENING YOUR PERSPECTIVE

FINANCIAL REPORTING PROBLEM: *Tootsie Roll Industries, Inc.*

BYP2-1   The financial statements of Tootsie Roll Industries, Inc., are presented in Appendix A at the end of this book.

Instructions
Answer the following questions using the Consolidated Balance Sheet and the Notes to Consolidated Financial Statements section.
(a) What were Tootsie Roll's total current assets at December 31, 2004, and December 31, 2003?
(b) Are the assets included in current assets listed in the proper order? Explain.
(c) How are Tootsie Roll's assets classified?
(d) What were Tootsie Roll's current liabilities at December 31, 2004, and December 31, 2003?

COMPARATIVE ANALYSIS PROBLEM: *Tootsie Roll vs. Hershey Foods*

BYP2-2   The financial statements of Hershey Foods are presented in Appendix B, following the financial statements for Tootsie Roll in Appendix A. Hershey's average number of shares outstanding was 253,881,000, and Tootsie Roll's was 52,366,000.

Instructions
(a) For each company calculate the following values for 2004.
    (1) Working capital.   (4) Free cash flow.
    (2) Current ratio.   (5) Earnings per share.
    (3) Debt to total assets ratio
       (*Hint:* When calculating free cash flow, consider business acquisitions to be part of capital expenditures.)
(b) Based on your findings above, discuss the relative liquidity, solvency, and profitability of the two companies.

RESEARCH CASE

BYP2-3   The March 2, 2004, issue of the *Wall Street Journal* includes an article by Mitchell Pacelle and Matthew Karnitschnig titled "Spiegel's European Owner Gets a Hard Lesson in U.S. Business."

Instructions
Read the article and answer the following.
(a) Mr. Otto controls 89 companies. What was unique about Spiegel, and how did this get him into trouble?
(b) Mr. Otto is German and is accustomed to the regulatory environment in Germany. How does the German regulatory environment differ from that of the U.S.? According to the article, how is the German regulatory environment changing?
(c) Briefly explain what is meant by the "going concern assumption."
(d) Explain why Spiegel's violation of its loan agreements caused its auditor to say that it would most likely issue an audit opinion that questioned the company's ability to continue as a going concern.
(e) How would the company's creditors react to the news that the auditor questioned the company's ability to continue as a going concern?
(f) Briefly explain the "full disclosure principle" and discuss whether Spiegel appears to have violated this principle

...by Gap, Inc. in its 2004 annual report.

	2002	2001	2000
	$10,283	$8,096	$7,387
	$2,972	$1,018	$(153)
	2.08:1	1.48:1	0.95:1
	.66:1	.64:1	.62:1
	$0.55	$(0.03)	$0.99

INTERPRETING FINANCIAL STATEMENTS

BYP5-4   Recently it was announced that two giant French retailers, Carrefour SA and Promodes SA, would merge. A headline in the *Wall Street Journal* blared, "French Retailers Create New Wal-Mart Rival." While Wal-Mart's total sales would still exceed those of the combined company, Wal-Mart's international sales are far less than those of the combined company. This is a serious concern for Wal-Mart, since its primary opportunity for future growth lies outside of the United States.
    Below are basic financial data for the combined corporation (in euros) and Wal-Mart (in U.S. dollars). Even though their results are presented in different currencies, by employing ratios we can make some basic comparisons.

	Carrefour (in millions)	Wal-Mart (in millions)
Sales	euros 70,486	$256,329
Cost of goods sold	54,630	198,747
Net income	1,738	9,054
Total assets	39,063	104,912
Current assets	14,521	34,421
Current liabilities	13,660	37,418
Total liabilities	29,434	61,289

FINANCIAL ANALYSIS ON THE WEB

BYP6-5   *Purpose:* Use SEC filings to learn about a company's inventory accounting practices.

Address: **http://biz.yahoo.com/p/_capgds-bldmch.html**
     (or go to **www.wiley.com/college/kimmel**)

Steps
1. Go to this site and click on the name of an equipment manufacturer other than those discussed in the chapter.
2. Click on **SEC filings**.
3. Under "Recent filings" choose **Form 10K** (annual report) and click on **Full Filing at Edgar Online**.
4. Choose option "3", **Online HTML Version**.
If the 10K is not listed among the recent filings then click on **View All Filings on EDGAR Online**.

Instructions
Review the 10K to answer the following questions.
(a) What is the name of the company?
(b) How has its inventory changed from the previous year?
(c) What is the amount of raw materials, work in process, and finished goods inventory?
(d) What inventory method does the company use?
(e) Calculate the inventory turnover ratio and days in inventory for the current year.
(f) If the company uses LIFO, what was the amount of its LIFO reserve?

The **Broadening Your Perspective** section helps you pull together concepts from the chapter and apply them to real-world business situations.

In the **Financial Reporting Problem** you study the financial statements of Tootsie Roll Industries, which are printed in Chapter 1 (in simplified form) and in Appendix A (in full).

A **Comparative Analysis Problem** compares and contrasts the financial reporting of Tootsie Roll with a competitor, Hershey Foods (whose financial statements appear in Appendix B).

Research Cases direct you to the *Wall Street Journal* and other business periodicals for further study and analysis of key topics.

Financial Analysis on the Web exercises guide you to websites where you can find and analyze information related to the chapter topic.

Interpreting Financial Statements are mini-cases that ask you to read parts of financial statements of actual companies and use the decision tools from the chapter to interpret this information. Those identified by a globe icon ask you to apply concepts to specific situations faced by actual foreign companies.

(d) What are the names of four companies in this industry?
(e) Choose one of the competitors. What is this competitor's name? What were its sales? What was its net income?

Critical Thinking

DECISION MAKING ACROSS THE ORGANIZATION

BYP1-6 Kim Perkins recently accepted a job in the production department at Tootsie Roll. Before she starts work, she decides to review the company's annual report to better understand its operations.

Instructions
Use the annual report provided in Appendix A to answer the following questions.
(a) What CPA firm performed the audit of Tootsie Roll's financial statements?
(b) What was the amount of Tootsie Roll's earnings per share in 2004?
(c) What are the company's net sales in foreign countries?
(d) What did management suggest as the cause of the increase in the sales in 2004?
(e) What were net sales in 2000?
(f) How many shares of Class B common stock have been authorized?
(g) How much cash was spent on capital expenditures in 2004?
(h) Over what life does the company depreciate its buildings?
(i) What was the value of raw material inventories in 2003?

COMMUNICATION ACTIVITY

BYP1-7 Carol Young is the bookkeeper for Evans Company, Inc. Carol has been trying to get the company's balance sheet to balance. She finally got it to balance, but she still isn't sure that it is correct.

EVANS COMPANY, INC.
Balance Sheet
For the Month Ended December 31, 2007

Assets		Liabilities and Stockholders' Equity	
Equipment	$20,500	Common stock	$11,000
Cash	10,500	Accounts receivable	(3,000)
Supplies	2,000	Dividends	(2,000)
Accounts payable	(5,000)	Notes payable	12,000
Total assets	$28,000	Retained earnings	10,000
		Total liabilities and	
		stockholders' equity	$28,000

Instructions
Explain to Carol Young in a memo (a) the purpose of a balance sheet, and (b) why this balance sheet is incorrect and what she should do to correct it.

ETHICS CASE

BYP1-8 Rules governing the investment practices of individual certified public accountants prohibit them from investing in the stock of a company that their firm audits. The Securities and Exchange Commission became concerned that some accountants were violating this rule. In response to an SEC investigation, PricewaterhouseCoopers fired 10 people and spent $25 million educating employees about the investment rules and installing an investment tracking system.

Instructions
~~Answer the following questions~~
~~...~~ auditors from investing in companies that
~~...~~ be allowed to invest in a company's stock
~~...~~ n working on the company's audit or con-

The **Decision Making across the Organization** cases help you build decision-making skills. They require you to consider the perspectives of various business functions. They also give practice in building communication skills.

Communication Activities help you build business communication skills by asking you to engage in real-world business situations using writing, speaking, or presentation skills.

Through the **Ethics Cases**, you will reflect on typical ethical dilemmas, analyze the issues involved, and decide on an appropriate course of action.

Answers to Business Insight and **Accounting across the Organization Questions** offer guideline answers for questions that appear in the chapter's boxed real-world examples.

Answers to Business Insight and Accounting across the Organization Questions

p. 60
Q. What can various company managers do to ensure that working capital is managed efficiently (so as to maximize net income)?
A. Marketing and sales managers must understand that by extending generous repayment terms they are expanding the company's receivables balance and slowing the company's cash flow. Production managers must strive to minimize the amount of excess inventory on hand. Managers must coordinate efforts to speed up the collection of receivables, while also ensuring that the company pays its payables on time, but never too early.

p. 61
Q. Discuss the difference in the debt to total assets ratio of Micro~~...~~
A. Microsoft has a very low debt to total assets ratio. The comp~~...~~ changing industry and thus should try to minimize th~~...~~risk ass~~...~~ debt. Also, because Microsoft generates significant ~~a~~mounts of ~~...~~ needs for large investments in plant assets, it d~~...~~es not need ~~...~~ General Motors needs to make huge investm~~...~~nts in plant ass~~...~~ large credit operation. Thus it has large ~~b~~orrowing needs.

p. 66
Q. What problems might Best Buy's y~~...~~ar-end create for analysts~~...~~
A. First, if Best Buy's competitors ~~...~~se a different year-end, then ~~...~~ their financial results, you a~~...~~e not comparing performance o~~...~~ time or financial position ~~...~~t the same point in time. Also, by no~~...~~ particular date, the n~~...~~mber of weeks in Best Buy's fiscal year will change. For example, fiscal years ~~...~~002, 2003, and 2004 had 52 weeks, but fisal year 2001 had 53 weeks.

Answer to Tootsie Roll Review It Question 3, p. 53
Tootsie Roll's largest current asset at December 31, 2004, was cash and cash equivalents, at $56,989,000.

Answers to Self-Study Questions
1. d   2. a   3. b   4. a   5. c   6. b   7. d   8. a   9. a   10. c   11. c
12. c

Answers to *Review It* questions based on the Tootsie Roll financial statements appear here.

Answers to Self-Study Questions provide feedback on your understanding of concepts in the Self-Study quiz.

After you complete your homework assignments, it's a good idea to go back to **The Navigator** checklist at the start of the chapter to see if you have used all the chapter's study aids.

This questionaire aims to find out something about your preferences for the way you work with information. You will have a preferred learning style and one part of that learning style is your preference for the intake and the output of ideas and information.

Circle the letter of the answer that best explains your preference. Circle more than one if a single answer does not match your perception. Leave blank any question that does not apply.

1. You are about to give directions to a person who is standing with you. She is staying in a hotel in town and wants to visit your house later. She has a rental car. Would you
   a. draw a map on paper?
   b. tell her the directions?
   c. write down the directions (without a map)?
   d. pick her up at the hotel in your car?

2. You are not sure whether a word should be spelled "dependent" or "dependant." Do you
   c. look it up in the dictionary?
   a. see the word in your mind and choose by the way it looks?
   b. sound it out in your mind?
   d. write both versions down on paper and choose one?

3. You have just received a copy of your itinerary for a world trip. This is of interest to a friend. Would you
   b. call her immediately and tell her about it?
   c. send her a copy of the printed itinerary?
   a. show her on a map of the world?
   d. share what you plan to do at each place you visit?

4. You are going to cook something as a special treat for your family. Do you
   d. cook something familiar without the need for instructions?
   a. thumb through the cookbook looking for ideas from the pictures?
   c. refer to a specific cookbook where there is a good recipe?

5. A group of tourists has been assigned to you to find out about wildlife reserves or parks. Would you
   d. drive them to a wildlife reserve or park?
   a. show them slides and photographs?
   c. give them pamphlets or a book on wildlife reserves or parks?
   b. give them a talk on wildlife reserves or parks?

6. You are about to purchase a new CD player. Other than price, what would most influence your decision?
   b. The salesperson telling you what you want to know.
   c. Reading the details about it.
   d. Playing with the controls and listening to it.
   a. Its fashionable and upscale appearance.

7. Recall a time in your life when you learned how to do something like playing a new board game. Try to avoid choosing a very physical skill, e.g. riding a bike. How did you learn best? By
   a. visual clues—pictures, diagrams, charts?
   c. written instructions?
   b. listening to somebody explaining it?
   d. doing it or trying it?

8. You have an eye problem. Would you prefer that the doctor
   b. tell you what is wrong?
   a. show you a diagram of what is wrong?
   d. use a model to show what is wrong?

9. You are about to learn to use a new program on a computer. Would you
   d. sit down at the keyboard and begin to experiment with the program's features?
   c. read the manual that comes with the program?
   b. call a friend and ask questions about it?

10. You are staying in a hotel and have a rental car. You would like to visit friends whose address/location you do not know. Would you like them to
   a. draw you a map on paper?
   b. tell you the directions?
   c. write down the directions (without a map)?
   d. pick you up at the hotel in their car?

11. Apart from price, what would most influence your decision to buy a particular book?
   d. You have used a copy before.
   b. A friend talking about it.
   c. Quickly reading parts of it.
   a. The appealing way it looks.

12. A new movie has arrived in town. What would most influence your decision to go (or not go)?
   b. You heard a radio review about it.
   c. You read a review about it.
   a. You saw a preview of it.

13. Do you prefer a lecturer or teacher who likes to use
   c. a textbook, handouts, readings?
   a. flow diagrams, charts, graphs?
   d. field trips, labs, practical sessions?
   b. discussion, guest speakers?

Count your choices:	a.	b.	c.	d.
	❑	❑	❑	❑
	V	A	R	K

Now match the letter or letters you have recorded most to the same letter or letters in the Learning Styles Chart. You may have more than one learning style preference—many people do. Next to each letter in the Chart are suggestions that will refer you to different learning aids throughout this text.

LEARNING STYLES CHART

VISUAL

INTAKE: TO TAKE IN THE INFORMATION	TO MAKE A STUDY PACKAGE	TEXT FEATURES THAT MAY HELP YOU THE MOST	OUTPUT: TO DO WELL ON EXAMS
• Pay close attention to charts, drawings, and handouts your instructor uses • Underline. • Use different colors. • Use symbols, flow charts, graphs, different arrangements on the page, white space.	Convert your lecture notes into "page pictures." To do this: • Use the "Intake" strategies. • Reconstruct images in different ways. • Redraw pages from memory. • Replace words with symbols and initials. • Look at your pages.	**The Navigator** **Preview** **Infographics/Illustrations/ Photos** **Accounting Equation/ Cash Flow Analysis** **Business Insight and Accounting across the Organization boxes** **Decision Toolkits** **Key Terms in blue** **Words in bold** **Using the Decision Toolkit** **Demonstration Problem** **Questions/Exercises/Problems** **Financial Analysis on the Web** **Exploring the Web**	• Recall your "page pictures." • Draw diagrams where appropriate. • Practice turning your visuals back into words.

AURAL

INTAKE: TO TAKE IN THE INFORMATION	TO MAKE A STUDY PACKAGE	TEXT FEATURES THAT MAY HELP YOU THE MOST	OUTPUT: TO DO WELL ON ON EXAMS
• Attend lectures and tutorials. • Discuss topics with students and instructors. • Explain new ideas to other people. • Use a tape recorder. • Leave spaces in your lecture notes for later recall. • Describe overheads, pictures, and visuals to somebody who was not in class.	You may take poor notes because you prefer to listen. Therefore: • Expand your notes by talking with others and with information from your textbook. • Tape record summarized notes and listen. • Read summarized notes out loud. • Explain your notes to another "aural" person.	**Feature Story** **Infographics/Illustrations** **Business Insights and Accounting across the Organization boxes** **Review It/Do It/Action Plan** **Using the Decision Toolkit** **Summary of Study Objectives** **Glossary** **Demonstration Problem** **Self-Study Questions** **Questions/Exercises/Problems** **Financial Analysis on the Web** **Decision Making across the Organization** **Communication Activity** **Ethics Case**	• Talk with the instructor. • Spend time in quiet places recalling the ideas. • Practice writing answers to old exam questions. • Say your answers out loud.

SOURCE: Adapted from VARK pack. Copyright Version 4.1 (2002) held by Neil D. Fleming, Christchurch, New Zealand and Charles C. Bonwell, Green Mountain Falls, Colorado 80819, U.S.A. The VARK website is at www.vark-learn.com.

READING/WRITING

INTAKE: TO TAKE IN THE INFORMATION	TO MAKE A STUDY PACKAGE	TEXT FEATURES THAT MAY HELP YOU THE MOST	OUTPUT: TO DO WELL ON EXAMS
• Use lists and headings. • Use dictionaries, glossaries, and definitions. • Read handouts, textbooks, and supplementary library readings. • Use lecture notes.	• Write out words again and again. • Reread notes silently. • Rewrite ideas and principles into other words. • Turn charts, diagrams, and other illustrations into statements.	**The Navigator** **Study Objectives** **Preview** **Review It/Do It/Action Plan** **Using the Decision Toolkit** **Summary of Study Objectives** **Glossary** **Self-Study Questions** **Questions/Exercises/Problems** **Writing Problems** **Research Case** **Interpreting Financial Statements** **Decision Making across the Organization** **Communication Activity** **Research and Ethics Cases**	• Write exam answers. • Practice with multiple-choice questions. • Write paragraphs, beginnings and endings. • Write your lists in outline form. • Arrange your words into hierarchies and points.

KINESTHETIC

INTAKE: TO TAKE IN THE INFORMATION	TO MAKE A STUDY PACKAGE	TEXT FEATURES THAT MAY HELP YOU THE MOST	OUTPUT: TO DO WELL ON EXAMS
• Use all your senses. • Go to labs, take field trips. • Listen to real-life examples. • Pay attention to applications. • Use hands-on approaches. • Use trial-and-error methods.	You may take poor notes because topics do not seem concrete or relevant. Therefore: • Put examples in your summaries. • Use case studies and applications to help with principles abstract concepts. • Talk about your notes with another "kinesthetic" person. • Use pictures and photographs that illustrate an idea.	**The Navigator** **Feature Story and Web links** **Preview** **Infographics/Illustrations/ Photos** **Accounting Equation/ Cash Flow Analysis** **Decision Toolkits** **Review It/Do It/Action Plan** **Using the Decision Toolkit** **Demonstration Problem** **Self-Study Questions** **Questions/Exercises/Problems** **Financial Reporting Problem** **Comparative Analysis Problem** **Research Case** **Decision Making across the Organization** **e-book content at WileyPLUS**	• Write practice answers. • Role-play the exam situation.

For all learning styles: Be sure to use WileyPLUS, the Take Action! CD, and the book companion site to enhance your understanding of the concepts and procedures of the text. In particular, use the **Interactive Self-Study** and **Self-Tests**, **Interactive Chapter Reviews**, and **Web-based Tutorials**.

BRIEF CONTENTS

CONTENTS

CHAPTER 4
Accrual Accounting Concepts 156

CHAPTER 5
Merchandising Operations and the Multiple-Step Income Statement 216

CHAPTER 6
Reporting and Analyzing Inventory 266

CHAPTER 7
Internal Control and Cash 314

CHAPTER 11

Reporting and Analyzing Stockholder's Equity *532*

CHAPTER 12

Statement of Cash Flows *564*

Introduction to Financial Statements

STUDY OBJECTIVES

After studying this chapter,
you should be able to:

1 Describe the primary forms of business organization.

2 Identify the users and uses of accounting information.

3 Explain the three principal types of business activity.

4 Describe the content and purpose of each of the financial statements.

5 Explain the meaning of assets, liabilities, and stock-holders' equity, and state the basic accounting equation.

6 Describe the components that supple-ment the financial statements in an annual report.

 THE NAVIGATOR

✓ THE NAVIGATOR

- Scan *Study Objectives* ⬭
- Read *Feature Story* ⬭
- Read *Preview* ⬭
- Read text and answer *Before You Go On*
  p. 11 ⬭   p. 17 ⬭   p. 24 ⬭
- Work *Using the Decision Toolkit* ⬭
- Review *Summary of Study Objectives* ⬭
- Work *Demonstration Problem* ⬭
- Answer *Self-Study Questions* ⬭
- Complete *Assignments* ⬭

The Navigator is a learning system designed to prompt you to use the learning aids in the chapter and to set priorities as you study.

FEATURE STORY

Knowing the Numbers

M any students who take this course do not plan to be accountants. If you are in that group, you might be thinking, "If I'm not going to be an accountant, why do I need to know accounting?" In response, consider this quote from Harold Geneen, the former chairman of IT&T: "To be good at your business, you have to know the numbers—cold." Success in any business comes back to the numbers. You will rely on them to make decisions, and managers will use them to evaluate your performance. That is true whether your job involves marketing, production, management, or information systems.

In business, accounting and financial statements are the means for communicating the numbers. If you don't know how to read financial statements, you can't really know your business.

Many companies spend significant resources teaching their employees basic accounting so that they can read financial statements and understand how their actions affect the company's financial results. One such company is Springfield ReManufacturing Corporation (SRC). When Jack Stack and 11 other managers purchased SRC for 10 cents a share, it was a failing division of International Harvester. Jack had 119 employees who were counting on him for their livelihood, and he knew that the new com-pany was on the verge of financial failure. He

decided that the only chance of survival was to encourage every employee to think like a businessperson and to act like an owner. To accomplish this, all employees at SRC took basic accounting courses and participated in weekly reviews of the company's financial statements. SRC survived, and eventually thrived. To this day, every employee (now numbering more than 1,000) undergoes this same training.

Many other companies have adopted this approach, which is called "open-book management." Even in companies that do not practice open-book management, employers generally assume that managers in all areas of the company are "financially literate."

Taking this course will go a long way to making you financially literate. In this book you will learn how to read and prepare financial statements, and how to use basic tools to evaluate financial results. In this first chapter we will introduce you to the financial statements of a real company whose products you are probably familiar with—Tootsie Roll. Tootsie Roll's presentation of its financial results is complete, yet also relatively easy to understand.

Tootsie Roll started off humbly in 1896 in a small New York City candy shop owned by an Austrian immigrant, Leo Hirshfield. The candy's name came from his five-year-old daughter's nickname—"Tootsie." Today the Chicago-based company produces more than 49 million Tootsie Rolls and 16 million Tootsie Pops *each day*. In fact, Tootsie Pops are at the center of one of science's most challenging questions: How many licks does it take to get to the Tootsie Roll center of a Tootsie Pop? The answer varies: Licking machines created at Purdue University and the University of Michigan report an average of 364 and 411 licks, respectively. In studies using human lickers, the answer ranges from 144 to 252. We recommend that you take a few minutes today away from your studies to determine your own results.

Source: Tootsie Roll information adapted from www.tootsie.com.

On the World Wide Web
Springfield ReManufacturing Corporation:
www.srcreman.com
Tootsie Roll Industries:
www.tootsie.com

3

PREVIEW OF CHAPTER 1

How do you start a business? How do you make it grow into a widely recognized brand name like Tootsie Roll? How do you determine whether your business is making or losing money? When you need to expand your operations, where do you get money to finance expansion—should you borrow, should you issue stock, should you use your own funds? How do you convince lenders to lend you money or investors to buy your stock? Success in business requires making countless decisions, and decisions require financial information.

The purpose of this chapter is to show you what role accounting plays in providing financial information. The content and organization of the chapter are as follows.

INTRODUCTION TO FINANCIAL STATEMENTS

Forms of Business Organization	Users and Uses of Financial Information	Business Activities	Communicating with Users	A Quick Look at Tootsie Roll's Financial Statements
• Sole proprietorship • Partnership • Corporation	• Internal users • External users • Ethics in financial reporting	• Financing • Investing • Operating	• Income statement • Retained earnings statement • Balance sheet • Statement of cash flows • Interrelationships of statements	• Income statement • Retained earnings statement • Balance sheet • Statement of cash flows • Other elements of an annual report

Forms of Business Organization

STUDY OBJECTIVE

1

Describe the primary forms of business organization.

Suppose you graduate with a marketing degree and open your own marketing agency. One of your initial decisions is what organizational form your business will have. You have three choices—sole proprietorship, partnership, or corporation. A business owned by one person is a **sole proprietorship**. A business owned by two or more persons associated as partners is a **partnership**. A business organized as a separate legal entity owned by stockholders is a **corporation**.

You will probably choose the sole proprietorship form for your marketing agency. It is **simple to set up** and **gives you control** over the business. Small owner-operated businesses such as barber shops, law offices, and auto repair shops are often sole proprietorships, as are farms and small retail stores.

Another possibility is for you to join forces with other individuals to form a partnership. Partnerships often are formed because one individual does not have **enough economic resources** to initiate or expand the business. Sometimes **partners bring unique skills or resources** to the partnership. You and your

*Terms that represent essential concepts are printed in blue. They are listed and defined again in the **glossary** at the end of the chapter.*

partners should formalize your duties and contributions in a written partnership agreement. Retail and service-type businesses, including professional practices (lawyers, doctors, architects, and certified public accountants), often organize as partnerships.

As a third alternative, you might organize as a corporation. As an investor in a corporation you receive shares of stock to indicate your ownership claim. Buying stock in a corporation is often more attractive than investing in a partnership because shares of stock are **easy to sell** (transfer ownership). Selling a proprietorship or partnership interest is much more involved. Also, individuals can become **stockholders** by investing relatively small amounts of money. Therefore, it is **easier for corporations to raise funds**. Successful corporations often have thousands of stockholders, and their stock is traded on organized stock exchanges like the New York Stock Exchange. Many businesses start as sole proprietorships or partnerships and eventually incorporate. For example, in 1896 Leo Hirshfield started Tootsie Roll as a sole proprietorship, and by 1919 the company had incorporated.

Other factors to consider in deciding which organizational form to choose are **taxes and legal liability**. If you choose a sole proprietorship or partnership, you generally receive more favorable tax treatment than a corporation. However, proprietors and partners are personally liable for all debts of the business; corporate stockholders are not. In other words, corporate stockholders generally pay higher taxes but have no personal liability. We will discuss these issues in more depth in a later chapter. Illustration 1-1 highlights the three types of organizations and the advantages of each.

Alternative Terminology notes present synonymous terms that you may come across in practice.

Alternative Terminology
Stockholders are sometimes called *shareholders*.

Illustrations like this one convey information in pictorial form to help you visualize and apply the ideas as you study.

Illustration 1-1 Forms of business organization

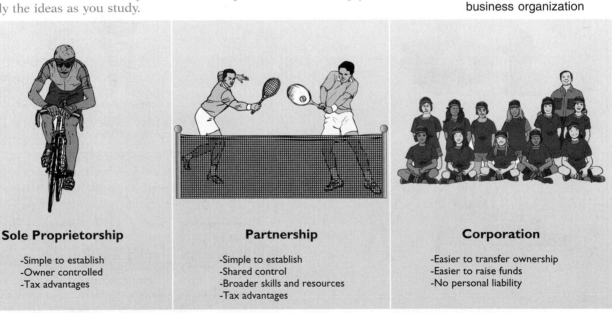

Sole Proprietorship

-Simple to establish
-Owner controlled
-Tax advantages

Partnership

-Simple to establish
-Shared control
-Broader skills and resources
-Tax advantages

Corporation

-Easier to transfer ownership
-Easier to raise funds
-No personal liability

The combined number of proprietorships and partnerships in the United States is more than five times the number of corporations. However, the revenue produced by corporations is eight times greater. Most of the largest enterprises in the United States—for example, Coca-Cola, ExxonMobil, General Motors, Citigroup, and Microsoft—are corporations. Because the majority of U.S. business is transacted by corporations, the emphasis in this book is on the corporate form of organization.

Users and Uses of Financial Information

The purpose of financial information is to provide inputs for decision making. **Accounting** is the information system that identifies, records, and communicates the economic events of an organization to interested users. Many people have an interest in knowing about the ongoing activities of the business. These people are **users** of accounting information. Users can be divided broadly into two groups: internal users and external users.

INTERNAL USERS

Internal users of accounting information are managers who plan, organize, and run a business. These include **marketing managers**, **production supervisors**, **finance directors**, **and company officers**. In running a business, managers must answer many important questions, as shown in Illustration 1-2.

Illustration 1-2

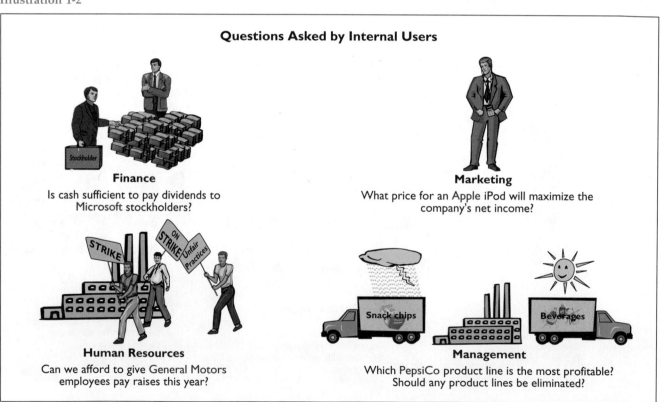

Questions Asked by Internal Users

Finance
Is cash sufficient to pay dividends to Microsoft stockholders?

Marketing
What price for an Apple iPod will maximize the company's net income?

Human Resources
Can we afford to give General Motors employees pay raises this year?

Management
Which PepsiCo product line is the most profitable? Should any product lines be eliminated?

To answer these and other questions, you need detailed information on a timely basis. For internal users, accounting provides internal reports, such as financial comparisons of operating alternatives, projections of income from new sales campaigns, and forecasts of cash needs for the next year. In addition, companies present summarized financial information in the form of financial statements.

Accounting across the Organization

Accounting can even serve as a useful recruiting tool for the human resources department. Rhino Foods, located in Burlington, VT, is a manufacturer of specialty ice cream novelties and ice cream ingredients. Its corporate website includes the following paragraphs:

> "Wouldn't it be great to work where you were part of a team? Where your input and hard work made a difference? Where you weren't kept in the dark about what management was thinking?
>
> Well—it's not a dream! It's the way we do business at Rhino Foods on Industrial Parkway in Burlington. Rhino Foods believes in family, honesty and open communication—we really care about and appreciate our employees—and it shows. Operating results are posted and monthly group meetings inform all employees about what's happening in the Company. Employees also share in the Company's profits, in addition to having an excellent comprehensive *benefits* package."

Source: www.rhinofoods.com/workforus/workforus.html.

 What are the benefits to the company and to the employees of making the financial statements available to all employees?

Accounting across the Organization stories demonstrate applications of accounting information in various business functions.

EXTERNAL USERS

There are several types of **external users** of accounting information. **Investors** (owners) use accounting information to make decisions to buy, hold, or sell stock. **Creditors** such as suppliers and bankers use accounting information to evaluate the risks of granting credit or lending money. Some questions that investors and creditors may ask about a company are shown in Illustration 1-3.

The information needs and questions of other external users vary considerably. **Taxing authorities**, such as the Internal Revenue Service, want to know whether the company complies with the tax laws. **Customers** are interested in whether a

Illustration 1-3

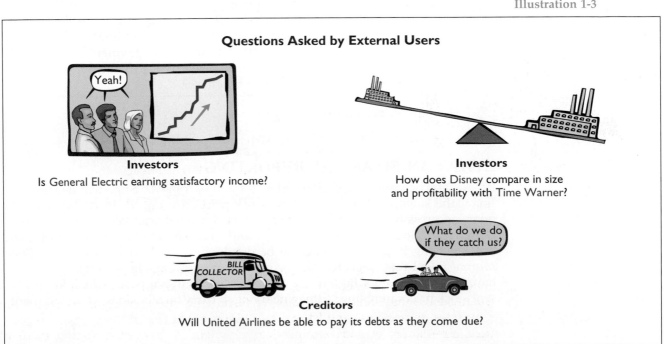

Questions Asked by External Users

Investors
Is General Electric earning satisfactory income?

Investors
How does Disney compare in size and profitability with Time Warner?

Creditors
Will United Airlines be able to pay its debts as they come due?

company like General Motors will continue to honor product warranties and otherwise support its product lines. **Labor unions** such as the Major League Baseball Players Association want to know whether the owners have the ability to pay increased wages and benefits. **Regulatory agencies**, such as the Securities and Exchange Commission or the Federal Trade Commission, want to know whether the company is operating within prescribed rules. For example, Enron, Dynegy, Duke Energy, and other big energy-trading companies reported record profits at the same time as California was paying extremely high prices for energy and suffering from blackouts. This disparity caused regulators to investigate the energy traders to make sure that the profits were earned by legitimate and fair practices.

Accounting across the Organization

One question that students of accounting frequently ask is, "How will the study of accounting help me?" It should help you a great deal, because a working knowledge of accounting is desirable for virtually every field of endeavor. Some examples of how accounting is used in other careers include:

General management: Imagine running Ford Motors, Massachusetts General Hospital, California State University–Fullerton, a McDonald's franchise, a Trek bike shop. All general managers need to understand accounting data in order to make wise business decisions.

Marketing: A marketing specialist at a company like Procter & Gamble develops strategies to help the sales force be successful. But making a sale is meaningless unless it is a profitable sale. Marketing people must be sensitive to costs and benefits, which accounting helps them quantify and understand.

Finance: Do you want to be a banker for Citicorp, an investment analyst for Goldman Sachs, a stock broker for Merrill Lynch? These fields rely heavily on accounting. In all of them you will regularly examine and analyze financial statements. In fact, it is difficult to get a good job in a finance function without two or three courses in accounting.

Real estate: Are you interested in being a real estate broker for Prudential Real Estate? Because a third party—the bank—is almost always involved in financing a real estate transaction, brokers must understand the numbers involved: Can the buyer afford to make the payments to the bank? Does the cash flow from an industrial property justify the purchase price? What are the tax benefits of the purchase?

 How might accounting help you?

ETHICS IN FINANCIAL REPORTING

People won't gamble in a casino if they think it is "rigged." Similarly, people won't "play" the stock market if they think stock prices are rigged. In recent years the financial press has been full of articles about financial scandals at Enron, World-Com, HealthSouth, and AIG. As more scandals came to light, a mistrust of financial reporting in general seemed to be developing. One article in the *Wall Street Journal* noted that "repeated disclosures about questionable accounting practices have bruised investors' faith in the reliability of earnings reports, which in turn has sent stock prices tumbling."[1] Imagine trying to carry on a business or invest money

---

[1]"U.S. Share Prices Slump," *Wall Street Journal* (February 21, 2002).

if you could not depend on the financial statements to be honestly prepared. Information would have no credibility. There is no doubt that a sound, well-functioning economy depends on accurate and dependable financial reporting.

United States regulators and lawmakers were very concerned that the economy would suffer if investors lost confidence in corporate accounting because of unethical financial reporting. In 2002 Congress passed the **Sarbanes-Oxley Act (SOX)** to try to reduce unethical corporate behavior and consequently decrease the likelihood of future corporate scandals. As a result of SOX, top management must now certify the accuracy of financial information. In addition, penalties for fraudulent financial activity by top management are now much more severe. Also, SOX calls for increased independence of the outside auditors who review the accuracy of corporate financial statements, and increased responsibility of boards of directors in their oversight role.

Effective financial reporting depends on sound ethical behavior. To sensitize you to ethical situations and to give you practice at solving ethical dilemmas, we address ethics in a number of ways in this book: (1) A number of the *Feature Stories* and other parts of the text discuss the central importance of ethical behavior to financial reporting. (2) *Business Insight boxes* with an ethics perspective highlight ethics situations and issues in actual business settings. (3) At the end of the chapter, an *Ethics Case* simulates a business situation and asks you to put yourself in the position of a decision maker in that case. (4) The *CD* that accompanies this book has video segments on critical accounting issues.

When analyzing these various ethics cases and your own ethical experiences, you should apply the three steps outlined in Illustration 1-4.

Illustration 1-4 Steps in analyzing ethics cases

Solving an Ethical Dilemma

1. Recognize an ethical situation and the ethical issues involved.	**2. Identify and analyze the principal elements in the situation.**	**3. Identify the alternatives, and weigh the impact of each alternative on various stakeholders.**
Use your personal ethics to identify ethical situations and issues. Some businesses and professional organizations provide written codes of ethics for guidance in some business situations.	Identify the *stakeholders*—persons or groups who may be harmed or benefited. Ask the question: What are the responsibilities and obligations of the parties involved?	Select the most ethical alternative, considering all the consequences. Sometimes there will be one right answer. Other situations involve more than one right solution; these situations require you to evaluate each alternative and select the best one.

Business Insight
International Perspective

Concern over the quality and integrity of financial reporting is not limited to the United States. Recently the Chinese Ministry of Finance reprimanded a large accounting firm for preparing fraudulent financial reports for a number of its publicly traded companies. Afterward, the state-run news agency noted that investors and analysts actually felt that the punishment of the firm was not adequate. In fact, a recent survey of investors in China found that less than 10 percent had full confidence in companies' annual reports. As a result of these concerns the Chinese Institute of Certified Public Accountants vowed to strengthen its policing of its members.

Business Insights provide examples of business situations from various perspectives—ethics, investor, and international.

 What has been done in the United States to improve the quality and integrity of financial reporting and to build investor confidence in financial reports?

Business Activities

STUDY OBJECTIVE

3

Explain the three principal types of business activity.

All businesses are involved in three types of activity—financing, investing, and operating. For example, Leo Hirshfield the founder of Tootsie Roll, needed financing to start and grow his business. Some of this **financing** came from personal savings, and some likely came from outside sources like banks. Hirshfield then **invested** the cash he had obtained by buying equipment necessary to run the business, such as mixing equipment and delivery vehicles. Once this equipment was in place, he could begin the **operating** activities of making and selling candy.

The **accounting information system** keeps track of the results of each of the various business activities—financing, investing, and operating. Let's look in more detail at each type of business activity.

FINANCING ACTIVITIES

Financing

It takes money to make money. The two primary sources of outside funds for corporations are borrowing money and issuing (selling) shares of stock in exchange for cash.

Tootsie Roll Industries may borrow money in a variety of ways. For example, it can take out a loan at a bank or borrow directly from investors by issuing debt securities called bonds. Persons or entities to whom Tootsie Roll owes money are its **creditors**. Amounts owed to creditors—in the form of debt and other obligations—are called liabilities. Specific names are given to different types of liabilities, depending on their source. Tootsie Roll may have a **note payable** to a bank for the money borrowed to purchase delivery trucks. Debt securities sold to investors that must be repaid at a particular date some years in the future are **bonds payable**.

A corporation may also obtain funds by selling shares of stock to investors. Common stock is the term used to describe the total amount paid in by stockholders for the shares they purchase.

The claims of creditors differ from those of stockholders. If you loan money to a company, you are one of its creditors. In lending money, you specify a payment schedule (e.g., payment at the end of three months). As a creditor, you have a legal right to be paid at the agreed time. In the event of nonpayment, you may legally force the company to sell property to pay its debts. In the case of financial difficulty, creditor claims must be paid before stockholders' claims.

Stockholders, on the other hand, have no claim to corporate resources until the claims of creditors are satisfied. If you buy a company's stock instead of loaning it money, you have no legal right to expect any payments until all of its creditors are paid. However, many corporations make payments to stockholders on a regular basis as long as there is sufficient cash to cover required payments to creditors. These payments to stockholders are called dividends.

INVESTING ACTIVITIES

Investing

Alternative Terminology
Property, plant, and equipment is sometimes called *fixed assets*.

Once the company has raised money through financing activities, it will then use that money in investing activities. Investing activities involve the purchase of those resources a company needs in order to operate. During the early stages of the company's life it must purchase many resources. For example, it obtains resources such as computers, delivery trucks, furniture, and buildings from investing activities. Resources owned by a business are called assets. Different types of assets are given different names. Tootsie Roll's mixing equipment is a type of asset referred to as **property**, **plant**, **and equipment**.

Cash is one of the more important assets owned by Tootsie Roll or any other business. If a company has excess cash that it does not need for a while, it might choose to invest it in debt or equity securities of other corporations. **Investments** are another example of an investing activity.

OPERATING ACTIVITIES

Operating

Once a business has the assets it needs to get started, it can begin its operations. Tootsie Roll is in the business of selling all things that taste, look, or smell like candy. It sells Tootsie Rolls, Tootsie Pops, Blow Pops, Caramel Apple Pops, Mason Dots, Mason Crows, Sugar Daddy, and Sugar Babies. In short, if it has anything to do with candy, Tootsie Roll sells it. We call amounts earned on the sale of these products *revenues*. Revenue is the increase in assets resulting from the sale of a product or service in the normal course of business. For example, Tootsie Roll records revenue when it sells a candy product.

Revenues arise from different sources and are identified by various names depending on the nature of the business. For instance, Tootsie Roll's primary source of revenue is the sale of candy products. However, it also generates interest revenue on debt securities held as investments. Sources of revenue common to many businesses are **sales revenue**, **service revenue**, and **interest revenue**.

The company purchases most of its longer-lived assets through investing activities as described earlier. Other assets with shorter lives, however, result from operating activities. For example, goods available for future sales to customers are assets called **inventory**. Also, if Tootsie Roll sells goods to a customer and does not receive cash immediately, then the company has a right to expect payment from that customer in the near future. This right to receive money in the future is called an **account receivable**.

Before Tootsie Roll can sell a single Tootsie Roll, Tootsie Pop, or Blow Pop, it must purchase sugar, corn syrup, and other ingredients, mix these ingredients, process the mix, and wrap and ship the finished product. It also incurs costs like salaries, rents, and utilities. All of these costs, referred to as *expenses*, are necessary to produce and sell the product. In accounting language, expenses are the cost of assets consumed or services used in the process of generating revenues.

Expenses take many forms and are identified by various names depending on the type of asset consumed or service used. For example, Tootsie Roll keeps track of these types of expenses: **cost of goods sold** (such as the cost of ingredients); **selling expenses** (such as the cost of salespersons' salaries); **marketing expenses** (such as the cost of advertising); **administrative expenses** (such as the salaries of administrative staff, and telephone and heat costs incurred at the corporate office); **interest expense** (amounts of interest paid on various debts); and **income taxes** (corporate taxes paid to government).

Tootsie Roll may also have liabilities arising from these expenses. For example, it may purchase goods on credit from suppliers; the obligations to pay for these goods are called **accounts payable**. Additionally, Tootsie Roll may have **interest payable** on the outstanding amounts owed to the bank. It may also have **wages payable** to its employees and **sales taxes payable**, **property taxes payable**, and **income taxes payable** to the government.

Tootsie Roll compares the revenues of a period with the expenses of that period to determine whether it earned a profit. When revenues exceed expenses, net income results. When expenses exceed revenues, a net loss results.

BEFORE YOU GO ON . . .

▶Review It

1. What are the three forms of business organization and the advantages of each?
2. What are the two primary categories of users of financial information? Give examples of each.
3. What are the three types of business activity?
4. What are assets, liabilities, common stock, revenues, expenses, and net income?

Before You Go On questions prompt you to stop and review the key points you have just studied.

▶Do It

Classify each item as an asset, liability, common stock, revenue, or expense.

Cost of renting property	Issuance of ownership shares
Truck purchased	Amount earned from providing service
Notes payable	Amounts owed to suppliers

Action Plan

• Classify each item based on its economic characteristics. Proper classification of items is critical if accounting is to provide useful information.

Solution

Cost of renting property is classified as expense.
Truck purchased is classified as an asset.
Notes payable are classified as liabilities.
Issuance of ownership shares is classified as common stock.
Amount earned from providing service is classified as revenue.
Amounts owed to suppliers are classified as liabilities.

Communicating with Users

STUDY OBJECTIVE
4
Describe the content and purpose of each of the financial statements.

Assets, liabilities, expenses, and revenues are of interest to users of accounting information. For business purposes, it is customary to arrange this information in the format of four different **financial statements**, which form the backbone of financial accounting:

• To present a picture at a point in time of what your business owns (its assets) and what it owes (its liabilities), you would present a **balance sheet**.

• To show how successfully your business performed during a period of time, you would report its revenues and expenses in an **income statement**.

• To indicate how much of previous income was distributed to you and the other owners of your business in the form of dividends, and how much was retained in the business to allow for future growth, you would present a **retained earnings statement**.

• To show from what sources your business obtained cash during a period of time and how that cash was used, you would present a **statement of cash flows**.

To introduce you to these statements, we have prepared the financial statements for a marketing agency, Sierra Corporation.

INCOME STATEMENT

The purpose of the income statement is to report the success or failure of the company's operations for a period of time. To indicate that its income statement reports the results of operations for a **period of time**, Sierra dates the income statement "For the Month Ended October 31, 2007." The income statement lists the company's revenues followed by its expenses. Finally, Sierra determines the net income (or net loss) by deducting expenses from revenues. Sierra Corporation's income statement is shown in Illustration 1-5.

Why are financial statement users interested in net income? Investors are interested in Sierra's past net income because it provides information about future net income. Investors buy and sell stock based on their beliefs about Sierra's future performance. If you believe that Sierra will be even more successful in the future and that this success will translate into a higher stock price, you should buy its stock. Creditors also use the income statement to predict the future. When

SIERRA CORPORATION Income Statement For the Month Ended October 31, 2007		
Revenues		
Service revenue		$10,600
Expenses		
Salaries expense	$5,200	
Supplies expense	1,500	
Rent expense	900	
Insurance expense	50	
Interest expense	50	
Depreciation expense	40	
Total expenses		7,740
Net income		$ 2,860

Illustration 1-5   Sierra Corporation's income statement

Helpful Hint The heading identifies the company, the type of statement, and the time period covered. Sometimes another line indicates the unit of measure—e.g., "in thousands" or "in millions."

a bank loans money to a company, it does so with the belief that it will be repaid in the future. If it didn't think it would be repaid, it wouldn't loan the money. Therefore, prior to making the loan the bank loan officer will use the income statement as a source of information to predict whether the company will be profitable enough to repay its loan.

Amounts received from issuing stock are not revenues, and amounts paid out as dividends are not expenses. As a result, they are not reported on the income statement. For example, Sierra Corporation did not treat as revenue the $10,000 of cash received from issuing new stock, nor did it regard as a business expense the $500 of dividends paid.

Decision Toolkit

Decision Toolkits summarize the financial decision-making process.

Decision Checkpoints	Info Needed for Decision	Tool to Use for Decision	How to Evaluate Results
Are the company's operations profitable?	Income statement	The income statement reports on the success or failure of the company's operations by reporting its revenues and expenses.	If the company's revenue exceeds its expenses, it will report net income; otherwise it will report a net loss.

RETAINED EARNINGS STATEMENT

If Sierra is profitable, at the end of each period it must decide what portion of profits to pay to shareholders in dividends. In theory it could pay all of its current-period profits, but few companies choose to do this. Why? Because they want to retain part of the profits to allow for further expansion. High-growth companies, such as Google and Cisco Systems, often choose to pay no dividends. **Retained earnings** is the net income retained in the corporation.

The **retained earnings statement** shows the amounts and causes of changes in retained earnings during the period. The time period is the same as that covered by the income statement. The beginning retained earnings amount appears on the first line of the statement. Then the company adds net income and deducts dividends to determine the retained earnings at the end of the period. If a company has a net loss, it deducts (rather than adds) that amount in the retained earnings statement. Illustration 1-6 presents Sierra Corporation's retained earnings statement.

Illustration 1-6 Sierra Corporation's retained earnings statement

SIERRA CORPORATION Retained Earnings Statement For the Month Ended October 31, 2007	
Retained earnings, October 1	$ 0
Add: Net income	2,860
	2,860
Less: Dividends	500
Retained earnings, October 31	$2,360

Helpful Hint The heading of this statement identifies the company, the type of statement, and the time period covered by the statement.

By monitoring the retained earnings statement, financial statement users can evaluate dividend payment practices. Some investors seek companies, such as Dow Chemical, that have a history of paying high dividends. Other investors seek companies, such as Amazon.com, that instead of paying dividends, reinvest earnings to increase the company's growth. Lenders monitor their corporate customers' dividend payments because any money paid in dividends reduces a company's ability to repay its debts.

Decision Toolkit

Decision Checkpoints	Info Needed for Decision	Tool to Use for Decision	How to Evaluate Results
What is the company's policy toward dividends and growth?	Retained earnings statement	How much of this year's income did the company pay out in dividends to shareholders?	A company striving for rapid growth will pay a low (or no) dividend.

BALANCE SHEET

STUDY OBJECTIVE
5
Explain the meaning of assets, liabilities, and stockholders' equity, and state the basic accounting equation.

The **balance sheet** reports assets and claims to those assets at a specific **point** in time. These claims are subdivided into two categories: claims of creditors and claims of owners. As noted earlier, claims of creditors are called **liabilities**. Claims of owners are called **stockholders' equity**.

The relationship among the categories on the balance sheet is shown in equation form in Illustration 1-7. This equation is referred to as the **basic accounting equation**.

Illustration 1-7 Basic accounting equation

$$\textbf{Assets = Liabilities + Stockholders' Equity}$$

This relationship is where the name "balance sheet" comes from. Assets must be in balance with the claims to the assets.

As you can see from looking at Sierra's balance sheet in Illustration 1-8, the balance sheet presents the company's financial position as of a specific date—in this case, October 31, 2007. It lists assets first, followed by liabilities and stockholders' equity. Stockholders' equity is comprised of two parts: (1) common stock and (2) retained earnings. As noted earlier, common stock results when the company sells new shares of stock; retained earnings is the net income retained in the corporation. Sierra has common stock of $10,000 and retained earnings of $2,360, for total stockholders' equity of $12,360.

SIERRA CORPORATION	
Balance Sheet	
October 31, 2007	
Assets	
Cash	$15,200
Accounts receivable	200
Advertising supplies	1,000
Prepaid insurance	550
Office equipment, net	4,960
Total assets	$21,910
Liabilities and Stockholders' Equity	
Liabilities	
Notes payable	$ 5,000
Accounts payable	2,500
Interest payable	50
Unearned revenue	800
Salaries payable	1,200
Total liabilities	$ 9,550
Stockholders' equity	
Common stock	10,000
Retained earnings	2,360
Total stockholders' equity	12,360
Total liabilities and stockholders' equity	$21,910

Illustration 1-8   Sierra Corporation's balance sheet

Helpful Hint The heading of a balance sheet must identify the company, the statement, and the date.

Creditors analyze a company's balance sheet to determine the likelihood that they will be repaid. They carefully evaluate the nature of the company's assets and liabilities. For example, does Sierra have assets that could be easily sold to repay its debts? Sierra's managers use the balance sheet to determine whether cash on hand is sufficient for immediate cash needs. They also look at the relationship between debt and stockholders' equity to determine whether the company has a satisfactory proportion of debt and common stock financing.

Decision Toolkit

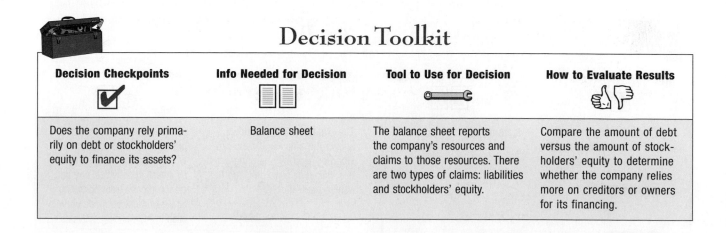

Decision Checkpoints	Info Needed for Decision	Tool to Use for Decision	How to Evaluate Results
Does the company rely primarily on debt or stockholders' equity to finance its assets?	Balance sheet	The balance sheet reports the company's resources and claims to those resources. There are two types of claims: liabilities and stockholders' equity.	Compare the amount of debt versus the amount of stockholders' equity to determine whether the company relies more on creditors or owners for its financing.

Business Insight
Ethics Perspective

What topic has performers such as Tom Waits, Clint Black, Sheryl Crow, and Madonna so concerned that they are pushing for new laws regarding its use? Accounting. Recording-company accounting to be more precise. Musicians receive royalty payments based on the accounting records kept by their recording companies. Many performers say that the recording companies—either intentionally or unintentionally—have very poor accounting systems, which, the performers say, has resulted in many inaccurate royalty payments. They would like to see laws created that would hit the recording companies with stiff fines for accounting errors.

 What is one way that some of these disputes might be resolved?

STATEMENT OF CASH FLOWS

The primary purpose of a statement of cash flows is to provide financial information about the cash receipts and cash payments of a business for a specific period of time. To help investors, creditors, and others in their analysis of a company's cash position, the statement of cash flows reports the cash effects of a company's **operating**, **investing**, and **financing** activities. In addition, the statement shows the net increase or decrease in cash during the period, and the amount of cash at the end of the period.

Users are interested in the statement of cash flows because they want to know what is happening to a company's most important resource. The statement of cash flows provides answers to these simple but important questions:

- Where did cash come from during the period?
- How was cash used during the period?
- What was the change in the cash balance during the period?

The statement of cash flows for Sierra, in Illustration 1-9, shows that cash increased $15,200 during the month. This increase resulted because operating activities (services to clients) increased cash $5,700, and financing activities increased cash $14,500. Investing activities used $5,000 of cash for the purchase of equipment.

Decision Toolkit

Decision Checkpoints	Info Needed for Decision	Tool to Use for Decision	How to Evaluate Results
Does the company generate sufficient cash from operations to fund its investing activities?	Statement of cash flows	The statement of cash flows shows the amount of cash provided or used by operating activities, investing activities, and financing activities.	Compare the amount of cash provided by operating activities with the amount of cash used by investing activities. Any deficiency in cash from operating activities must be made up with cash from financing activities.

SIERRA CORPORATION		
Statement of Cash Flows		
For the Month Ended October 31, 2007		
Cash flows from **operating** activities		
Cash receipts from operating activities	$11,200	
Cash payments for operating activities	(5,500)	
Net cash provided by operating activities		$ 5,700
Cash flows from **investing** activities		
Purchased office equipment	(5,000)	
Net cash used by investing activities		(5,000)
Cash flows from **financing** activities		
Issuance of common stock	10,000	
Issued note payable	5,000	
Payment of dividend	(500)	
Net cash provided by financing activities		14,500
Net increase in cash		15,200
Cash at beginning of period		0
Cash at end of period		$15,200

Illustration 1-9   Sierra Corporation's statement of cash flows

Helpful Hint The heading of this statement identifies the company, the type of statement, and the time period covered by the statement. Negative numbers are shown in parentheses.

INTERRELATIONSHIPS OF STATEMENTS

Because the results on some statements become inputs to other statements, the statements are interrelated. Illustration 1-10 (page 18) shows the interrelationships for Sierra's statements, which we describe below.

1. The retained earnings statement depends on the results of the income statement. Sierra reported net income of $2,860 for the period. It adds the net income amount to the beginning amount of retained earnings in order to determine ending retained earnings.

2. The balance sheet and retained earnings statement also are interrelated: Sierra reports the ending amount of $2,360 on the retained earnings statement as the retained earnings amount on the balance sheet.

3. Finally, the statement of cash flows relates to information on the balance sheet. The statement of cash flows shows how the cash account changed during the period. It shows the amount of cash at the beginning of the period, the sources and uses of cash during the period, and the $15,200 of cash at the end of the period. The ending amount of cash shown on the statement of cash flows must agree with the amount of cash on the balance sheet.

Study these interrelationships carefully. To prepare financial statements you must understand the sequence in which these amounts are determined, and how each statement impacts the next.

BEFORE YOU GO ON . . .

►Review It

1. What questions might each of the following decision makers ask that could be answered by financial information: marketing manager, production manager, bank loan officer, stock investor, labor union president, and federal bank regulator?

2. What are the content and purpose of each statement: income statement, balance sheet, retained earnings statement, and statement of cash flows?

3. The accounting equation is: Assets = Liabilities + Stockholders' Equity. Appendix A, at the end of this book, reproduces Tootsie Roll's financial statements. Replacing words in the equation with dollar amounts, what is

Review It questions marked with this **Tootsie Roll icon** require that you use Tootsie Roll's 2004 Annual Report in Appendix A at the back of the book.

Illustration 1-10 Sierra Corporation's financial statements

SIERRA CORPORATION
Income Statement
For the Month Ended October 31, 2007

Revenues		
Service revenue		$10,600
Expenses		
Salaries expense	$5,200	
Supplies expense	1,500	
Rent expense	900	
Insurance expense	50	
Interest expense	50	
Depreciation expense	40	
Total expenses		7,740
Net income		$ 2,860

SIERRA CORPORATION
Retained Earnings Statement
For the Month Ended October 31, 2007

Retained earnings, October 1	$ 0
Add: Net income	2,860
	2,860
Less: Dividends	500
Retained earnings, October 31	$ 2,360

SIERRA CORPORATION
Balance Sheet
October 31, 2007

Assets

Cash		$15,200
Accounts receivable		200
Advertising supplies		1,000
Prepaid insurance		550
Office equipment, net		4,960
Total assets		$21,910

Liabilities and Stockholders' Equity

Liabilities		
Notes payable	$5,000	
Accounts payable	2,500	
Interest payable	50	
Unearned revenue	800	
Salaries payable	1,200	
Total liabilities		$ 9,550
Stockholders' equity		
Common stock	10,000	
Retained earnings	2,360	
Total stockholders' equity		12,360
Total liabilities and stockholders' equity		$21,910

SIERRA CORPORATION
Statement of Cash Flows
For the Month Ended October 31, 2007

Cash flows from operating activities		
Cash receipts from operating activities	$11,200	
Cash payments for operating activities	(5,500)	
Net cash provided by operating activities		$ 5,700
Cash flows from investing activities		
Purchased office equipment	(5,000)	
Net cash used by investing activities		(5,000)
Cash flows from financing activities		
Issuance of common stock	10,000	
Issued note payable	5,000	
Payment of dividend	(500)	
Net cash provided by financing activities		14,500
Net increase in cash		15,200
Cash at beginning of period		0
Cash at end of period		$15,200

① ② ③

Tootsie Roll's accounting equation at December 31, 2004? (The answer to this question appears on page 45.)

▶Do It

CSU Corporation began operations on January 1, 2007. The following information is available for CSU Corporation on December 31, 2007: service revenue $17,000; accounts receivable $4,000; accounts payable $2,000; building rental expense $9,000; notes payable $5,000; common stock $10,000; retained earnings $?; equipment $16,000; insurance expense $1,000; supplies $1,800; supplies expense $200; cash $1,400; dividends $600.

Prepare an income statement, a retained earnings statement, and a balance sheet using this information.

Action Plan

- Report the revenues and expenses for a period of time in an income statement.
- Show the amounts and causes (net income and dividends) of changes in retained earnings during the period in the retained earnings statement.
- Present the assets and claims to those assets at a specific point in time in the balance sheet.

Solution

CSU CORPORATION
Income Statement
For the Year Ended December 31, 2007

Revenues		
Service revenue		$17,000
Expenses		
Rent expense	$9,000	
Insurance expense	1,000	
Supplies expense	200	
Total expenses		10,200
Net income		$ 6,800

CSU CORPORATION
Retained Earnings Statement
For the Year Ended December 31, 2007

Retained earnings, January 1	$ 0
Add: Net income	6,800
	6,800
Less: Dividends	600
Retained earnings, December 31	$6,200

CSU CORPORATION
Balance Sheet
December 31, 2007

Assets

Cash	$ 1,400
Accounts receivable	4,000
Supplies	1,800
Equipment	16,000
Total assets	$23,200

Liabilities and Stockholders' Equity

Liabilities		
Notes payable	$ 5,000	
Accounts payable	2,000	
Total liabilities		$ 7,000
Stockholders' equity		
Common stock	10,000	
Retained earnings	6,200	
Total stockholders' equity		16,200
Total liabilities and stockholders' equity		$23,200

A Quick Look at Tootsie Roll's Financial Statements

Tootsie Roll Annual Report Walkthrough

The same relationships that you observed among the financial statements of Sierra Corporation are evident in the 2004 financial statements of Tootsie Roll Industries, Inc., which are presented in Illustrations 1-11 through 1-14. We have simplified the financial statements to assist your learning—but they may look complicated to you anyway. Do not be alarmed by their seeming complexity. (If you could already read and understand them, there would be little reason to take this course, except possibly to add a high grade to your transcript—which we hope you'll do anyway.) By the end of the book, you'll have a great deal of experience in reading and understanding financial statements such as these. Tootsie Roll's **actual financial statements** are presented in **Appendix A** at the end of the book.

Before we dive in, we need to explain two points:

1. Note that numbers are reported in thousands on Tootsie Roll's financial statements—that is, the last three 000s are omitted. Thus, Tootsie Roll's net income in 2004 is $64,174,000, not $64,174.

2. Tootsie Roll, like most companies, presents its financial statements for more than one year. Financial statements that report information for more than one period are called **comparative statements**. Comparative statements allow users to compare the financial position of the business at the end of an accounting period with that of previous periods.

Helpful Hint The percentage change in any amount from one year to the next is calculated as follows:

$$\frac{\text{Change during period}}{\text{Previous value}}$$

Thus, the percentage change in income is:

$$\frac{\text{Change in income}}{\text{Previous year's income}}$$

INCOME STATEMENT

Tootsie Roll's income statement is presented in Illustration 1-11. It reports total revenues in 2004 of $424,894,000. It then subtracts three types of expenses—cost of goods sold; selling, marketing, and administrative expenses; and income tax expense—to arrive at net income of $64,174,000. This is a 1.3% decrease from income for the previous year.

Illustration 1-11
Tootsie Roll's income statement

TOOTSIE ROLL INDUSTRIES, INC.
Income Statements
For the Years Ended December 31, 2004, and December 31, 2003
(in thousands)

	2004	2003
Revenues		
Sales revenue	$420,110	$392,656
Other revenues	4,784	5,594
Total revenues	424,894	398,250
Expenses		
Cost of goods sold	244,501	222,547
Selling, marketing, and administrative expenses	85,705	77,756
Income tax expense	30,514	32,933
Total expenses	360,720	333,236
Net income	$ 64,174	$ 65,014

Illustration 1-12 Tootsie Roll's retained earnings statement

TOOTSIE ROLL INDUSTRIES, INC.
Retained Earnings Statements
For the Years Ended December 31, 2004, and December 31, 2003
(in thousands)

Retained earnings, December 31, 2002	$148,705
Add: Net income	65,014
	213,719
Less: Dividends	56,933
Retained earnings, December 31, 2003	156,786
Add: Net income	64,174
	220,960
Less: Dividends	71,905
Retained earnings, December 31, 2004	$149,055

RETAINED EARNINGS STATEMENT

Tootsie Roll presents information about its retained earnings in the retained earnings statement in Illustration 1-12. (Many companies present changes in retained earnings in a broader report called the Statement of Stockholders' Equity.) Find the line "Retained earnings, December 31, 2003." This number, $156,786,000, agrees with the retained earnings balance from the December 31, 2003, balance sheet.

As we proceed down the retained earnings statement, the next figure is net income of $64,174,000. Tootsie Roll distributed dividends of $71,905,000. The ending balance of retained earnings is $149,055,000 on December 31, 2004. Find this amount of retained earnings near the bottom of Tootsie Roll's balance sheet for December 31, 2004 (Illustration 1-13 on page 22).

BALANCE SHEET

As shown in its balance sheet in Illustration 1-13, Tootsie Roll's assets include the kinds previously mentioned in our discussion of Sierra Corporation. These are cash, inventories, and property, plant, and equipment, plus other types of assets that we will discuss in later chapters, such as prepaid expenses. Tootsie Roll's total assets increased from $665,297,000 on December 31, 2003, to $811,753,000 on December 31, 2004. Its liabilities include accounts payable as well as items not yet discussed, such as employee benefits payable.

You can see that Tootsie Roll relies far more on equity financing than on debt—it has more than twice as much stockholders' equity as it has liabilities. As you learn more about financial statements we will discuss how to interpret the relationships and changes in financial statement items.

STATEMENT OF CASH FLOWS

Tootsie Roll's cash decreased $27,095,000 during 2004. Tootsie Roll's balance sheet shows that cash was $84,084,000 at December 31, 2003, and $56,989,000 at December 31, 2004. The reasons for this decrease can be determined by examining the statement of cash flows in Illustration 1-14 (page 23). Tootsie Roll generated $76,228,000 from its operating activities during 2004. Its investing activities included capital expenditures (purchases of property, plant, and equipment) as well as purchases and sales of investment securities. The net effect of its investment activities was an outflow of cash of $164,039,000. Its financing activities involved the repurchase of its own common stock and the payment of

Illustration 1-13 Tootsie
Roll's balance sheet

TOOTSIE ROLL INDUSTRIES, INC.
Balance Sheets
December 31, 2004, and December 31, 2003
(in thousands)

Assets	2004	2003
Cash	$ 56,989	$ 84,084
Investments	32,369	86,961
Accounts receivable	37,457	21,207
Inventories	58,777	46,086
Prepaid expenses	7,101	5,367
Property, plant, and equipment, net	178,750	129,163
Other assets	440,310	292,429
Total assets	$811,753	$665,297

Liabilities and Stockholders' Equity	2004	2003
Liabilities		
Accounts payable	$ 19,315	$ 11,947
Dividends payable	3,659	3,589
Accrued liabilities	44,722	38,834
Income taxes payable	8,288	8,517
Bank loan	92,000	—
Employee benefits payable	10,075	9,302
Other liabilities	63,515	56,527
Total liabilities	241,574	128,716
Stockholders' equity		
Common stock	421,124	379,795
Retained earnings	149,055	156,786
Total stockholders' equity	570,179	536,581
Total liabilities and stockholders' equity	$811,753	$665,297

cash dividends. In all, the net effect of the cash generated from its operating and financing activities, less the cash used in its investing activities, was a decrease in cash of $27,095,000.

OTHER ELEMENTS OF AN ANNUAL REPORT

U.S. companies that are publicly traded must provide shareholders with an **annual report**. The annual report always includes the financial statements introduced in this chapter. The annual report also includes other important information such as a management discussion and analysis section, notes to the financial statements, and an independent auditor's report. No analysis of a company's financial situation and prospects is complete without a review of these items.

STUDY OBJECTIVE
6
Describe the components that supplement the financial statements in an annual report.

Management Discussion and Analysis

The **management discussion and analysis (MD&A)** section covers various financial aspects of a company, including **its ability to pay near-term obligations, its ability to fund operations and expansion, and its results of operations**. Management must highlight favorable or unfavorable trends and identify significant events and uncertainties that affect these three factors. This discussion obviously involves a number of subjective estimates and opinions.

TOOTSIE ROLL INDUSTRIES, INC.
Statements of Cash Flows
For the Years Ended December 31, 2004, and December 31, 2003
(in thousands)

	2004	2003
Cash flows from operating activities		
Cash receipts from operating activities	$420,783	$396,922
Cash payments for operating activities	(344,555)	(313,456)
Net cash provided by operating activities	76,228	83,466
Cash flows from investing activities		
Capital expenditures and acquisitions	(236,177)	(12,150)
Purchase of investment securities	(106,036)	(115,401)
Sales of investment securities	178,174	77,168
Net cash used in investing activities	(164,039)	(50,383)
Cash flows from financing activities		
Proceeds from bank loan	154,000	—
Repayment of bank loan	(62,000)	—
Repurchase of common stock	(16,407)	(40,096)
Dividends paid in cash	(14,877)	(14,410)
Net cash provided by financing activities	60,716	(54,506)
Net decrease in cash	(27,095)	(21,423)
Cash at beginning of year	84,084	105,507
Cash at end of year	$ 56,989	$ 84,084

Illustration 1-14 Tootsie Roll's statement of cash flows

TOOTSIE ROLL INDUSTRIES, INC.
Management's Discussion and Analysis of
Financial Condition and Results of Operations

The company has a simple financial structure, and aside from an immaterial amount of operating leases, the company has no "off-balance sheet" financing arrangements. We maintain a conservative financial posture and funds generated from operations plus maturities of short term investments are expected to be adequate to meet the company's financing needs over the coming year.

Illustration 1-15 Tootsie Roll's management discussion and analysis

A brief excerpt from the MD&A section of Tootsie Roll's annual report (above). is presented in Illustration 1-15.

Notes to the Financial Statements

Explanatory notes and supporting schedules accompany every set of financial statements and are an integral part of the statements. The **notes to the financial statements** clarify information presented in the financial statements, as well as expand upon it where additional detail is needed. Information in the notes does not have to be quantifiable (numeric). Examples of notes are descriptions of the significant accounting policies and methods used in preparing the statements, explanations of uncertainties and contingencies, and various statistics and details too voluminous to be included in the statements. The notes are essential to understanding a company's operating performance and financial position.

Illustration 1-16 is an excerpt from the notes to Tootsie Roll's financial statements. It describes the methods that Tootsie Roll uses to account for revenues.

Illustration 1-16 Notes to Tootsie Roll's financial statements

TOOTSIE ROLL INDUSTRIES, INC.
Notes to Financial Statements

Revenue recognition
Revenues are recognized when products are delivered to customers and collectibility is reasonably assured.

Auditor's Report

An **auditor's report** is a report prepared by an independent outside auditor. It states the auditor's opinion as to the fairness of the presentation of the financial position and results of operations and their conformance with generally accepted accounting standards.

An **auditor** is an accounting professional who conducts an independent examination of a company's financial statements. Only accountants who meet certain criteria and thereby attain the designation **Certified Public Accountant (CPA)** may perform audits. If the auditor is satisfied that the financial statements provide a fair representation of the company's financial position and results of operations in accordance with generally accepted accounting principles, then the auditor expresses an **unqualified opinion**. If the auditor expresses anything other than an unqualified opinion, then readers should only use the financial statements with caution. That is, without an unqualified opinion, we cannot have complete confidence that the financial statements give an accurate picture of the company's financial health.

Illustration 1-17 is an excerpt from the auditor's report from Tootsie Roll's 2004 annual report. Tootsie Roll received an unqualified opinion from its auditor, PricewaterhouseCoopers.

Illustration 1-17 Excerpt from auditor's report on Tootsie Roll's financial statements

TOOTSIE ROLL INDUSTRIES, INC.
Excerpt from Auditor's Report

To the Board of Directors and Shareholders of Tootsie Roll Industries, Inc.

In our opinion, the accompanying consolidated balance sheets and the related consolidated statements of earnings, comprehensive earnings, retained earnings, and cash flows present fairly, in all material respects, the financial position of Tootsie Roll Industries, Inc. and its subsidiaries at December 31, 2004 and 2003, and the results of their operations and their cash flows for each of the three years in the period ended December 31, 2004, in conformity with accounting principles generally accepted in the United States of America.

BEFORE YOU GO ON . . .

▶Review It

1. What is the intent of the management discussion and analysis section in the annual report?
2. Why are notes to the financial statements necessary? What kinds of items are included in these notes?
3. What is the purpose of the auditor's report?

Using the Decision Toolkit

Hershey Foods Corporation, located in Hershey, Pennsylvania, is the leading North American manufacturer of chocolate—for example, Hershey's Kisses, Reese's Peanut Butter Cups, Kit Kat, and Take 5 bars. Imagine that you are considering the purchase of shares of Hershey's common stock.

Using the Decision Toolkit exercises ask you to use information from financial statements to make financial decisions.

Instructions

Answer these questions related to your decision whether to invest.

(a) What financial statements should you request from the company?
(b) What should these financial statements tell you?
(c) Should you request audited financial statements? Explain.
(d) Illustrations 1-18 through 1-21 show simplified financial statements for Hershey Foods. What comparisons can you make between Tootsie Roll and Hershey in terms of their respective results from operations and financial position?

HERSHEY FOODS CORPORATION
Income Statements
For the Years Ended December 31, 2004, and
December 31, 2003 (in thousands)

	2004	2003
Revenues		
Sales revenue	$4,429,248	$4,172,551
Expenses		
Cost of goods sold	2,679,531	2,544,726
Selling, marketing, and administrative expenses	847,540	816,442
Other	—	22,395
Interest expense	66,533	63,529
Income tax expense	244,765	267,875
Total expenses	3,838,369	3,714,967
Net income	$ 590,879	$ 457,584

Illustration 1-18
Hershey Foods' income statement

HERSHEY FOODS CORPORATION
Retained Earnings Statements
For the Years Ended December 31, 2004, and
December 31, 2003 (in thousands)

Retained earnings December 31, 2002	$1,191,160
Add: Net income	457,584
	1,648,744
Less: Dividends	184,686
Other adjustments*	368,176
Retained earnings December 31, 2003	1,095,882
Add: Net income	590,879
	1,686,761
Less: Dividends	205,747
Other adjustments*	780,227
Retained earnings December 31, 2004	$ 700,787

Illustration 1-19
Hershey Foods' retained earnings statement

*Primarily the repurchase of common stock.

Illustration 1-20
Hershey Foods' balance
sheet

HERSHEY FOODS CORPORATION
Balance Sheets
December 31, 2004, and December 31, 2003
(in thousands)

Assets	2004	2003
Cash	$ 54,837	$ 114,793
Accounts receivable	408,930	407,612
Inventories	557,180	492,859
Prepaid expenses and other	161,494	116,305
Property, plant, and equipment, net	1,682,698	1,661,939
Other assets	932,392	789,032
Total assets	$3,797,531	$3,582,540
Liabilities and Stockholders' Equity		
Liabilities		
Accounts payable	$ 148,686	$ 132,222
Accrued liabilities	472,096	416,181
Income taxes payable	42,280	24,898
Short-term debt and other	622,320	12,509
Long-term debt and liabilities	1,093,958	1,339,275
Other liabilities	328,889	377,589
Total liabilities	2,708,229	2,302,674
Stockholders' equity		
Common stock	388,515	183,984
Retained earnings	700,787	1,095,882
Total stockholders' equity	1,089,302	1,279,866
Total liabilities and stockholders' equity	$3,797,531	$3,582,540

Illustration 1-21
Hershey Foods' statement
of cash flows

HERSHEY FOODS CORPORATION
Statements of Cash Flows
For the Years Ended December 31, 2004, and
December 31, 2003 (in thousands)

	2004	2003
Cash flows from operating activities		
Cash receipts from operating activities	$4,446,567	$4,135,915
Cash payments for operating activities	(3,649,117)	(3,542,972)
Net cash provided by operating activities	797,450	592,943
Cash flows from investing activities		
Capital expenditures	(362,745)	(237,054)
Proceeds from divestitures	—	20,049
Net cash used in investing activities	(362,745)	(217,005)
Cash flows from financing activities		
Issuance of debt	331,245	4,091
Repayment of long-term debt	(883)	(18,633)
Dividends paid in cash	(205,747)	(184,686)
Issuance of common stock	79,634	55,120
Repurchase of common stock	(616,977)	(329,433)
Other	(81,933)	(85,347)
Net cash used in financing activities	(494,661)	(558,888)
Net decrease in cash	(59,956)	(182,950)
Cash at beginning of year	114,793	297,743
Cash at end of year	$ 54,837	$ 114,793

Solution

(a) Before you invest, you should investigate the income statement, retained earnings statement, statement of cash flows, and balance sheet.

(b) You would probably be most interested in the income statement because it tells about past performance and thus gives an indication of future performance. The retained earnings statement provides a record of the company's dividend history. The statement of cash flows reveals where the company is getting and spending its cash. This is especially important for a company that wants to grow. Finally, the balance sheet reveals the relationship between assets and liabilities.

(c) You would want audited financial statements. These statements indicate that a CPA (certified public accountant) has examined and expressed an opinion that the statements present fairly the financial position and results of operations of the company. Investors and creditors should not make decisions without studying audited financial statements.

(d) Many interesting comparisons can be made between the two companies. Tootsie Roll is smaller, with total assets of $811,753,000 versus $3,797,531,000 for Hershey, and it has lower sales revenue—$420,110,000 versus $4,429,248,000 for Hershey. In addition, Tootsie Roll's cash provided by operating activities of $76,228,000 is less than Hershey's $797,450,000.

While useful, these basic measures are not enough to determine whether one company is a better investment than the other. In later chapters you will learn of tools that will allow you to compare the relative profitability and financial health of these and other companies.

Summary of Study Objectives

1 *Describe the primary forms of business organization.* A sole proprietorship is a business owned by one person. A partnership is a business owned by two or more people associated as partners. A corporation is a separate legal entity for which evidence of ownership is provided by shares of stock.

2 *Identify the users and uses of accounting information.* Internal users are managers who need accounting information to plan, organize, and run business operations. The primary external users are investors and creditors. Investors (stockholders) use accounting information to help them decide whether to buy, hold, or sell shares of a company's stock. Creditors (suppliers and bankers) use accounting information to assess the risk of granting credit or loaning money to a business. Other groups who have an indirect interest in a business are taxing authorities, customers, labor unions, and regulatory agencies.

3 *Explain the three principal types of business activity.* Financing activities involve collecting the necessary funds to support the business. Investing activities involve acquiring the resources necessary to run the business. Operating activities involve putting the resources of the business into action to generate a profit.

4 *Describe the content and purpose of each of the financial statements.* An income statement presents the revenues and expenses of a company for a specific period of time. A retained earnings statement summarizes the changes in retained earnings that have occurred for a specific period of time. A balance sheet reports the assets, liabilities, and stockholders' equity of a business at a specific date. A statement of cash flows summarizes information concerning the cash inflows (receipts) and outflows (payments) for a specific period of time.

5 *Explain the meaning of assets, liabilities, and stockholders' equity, and state the basic accounting equation.* Assets are resources owned by a business. Liabilities are the debts and obligations of the business. Liabilities represent claims of creditors on the assets of the business. Stockholders' equity represents the claims of owners on the assets of the business. Stockholders' equity is subdivided into two parts: common stock and retained earnings. The basic accounting equation is: Assets = Liabilities + Stockholders' Equity.

6 *Describe the components that supplement the financial statements in an annual report.* The management discussion and analysis provides management's interpretation of the company's results and financial position as well as a discussion of plans for the future. Notes to the financial statements provide additional explanation or detail to make the financial statements more informative. The auditor's report expresses an opinion as to whether the financial statements present fairly the company's results of operations and financial position.

Decision Toolkit—A Summary

Decision Checkpoints	Info Needed for Decision	Tool to Use for Decision	How to Evaluate Results
Are the company's operations profitable?	Income statement	The income statement reports on the success or failure of the company's operations by reporting its revenues and expenses.	If the company's revenue exceeds its expenses, it will report net income; otherwise it will report a net loss.
What is the company's policy toward dividends and growth?	Retained earnings statement	How much of this year's income did the company pay out in dividends to shareholders?	A company striving for rapid growth will pay a low (a no) dividend.
Does the company rely primarily on debt or stockholders' equity to finance its assets?	Balance sheet	The balance sheet reports the company's resources and claims to those resources. There are two types of claims: liabilities and stockholders' equity.	Compare the amount of debt versus the amount of stockholders' equity to determine whether the company relies more on creditors or owners for its financing.
Does the company generate sufficient cash from operations to fund its investing activities?	Statement of cash flows	The statement of cash flows shows the amount of cash provided or used by operating activities, investing activities, and financing activities.	Compare the amount of cash provided by operating activities with the amount of cash used by investing activities. Any deficiency in cash from operating activities must be made up with

Glossary

Accounting The information system that identifies, records, and communicates the economic events of an organization to interested users. (p. 6)

Annual report A report prepared by corporate management that presents financial information including financial statements, notes, a management discussion and analysis section, and an independent auditor's report. (p. 22)

Assets Resources owned by a business. (p. 10)

Auditor's report A report prepared by an independent outside auditor stating the auditor's opinion as to the fairness of the presentation of the financial position and results of operations and their conformance with generally accepted accounting standards. (p. 24)

Balance sheet A financial statement that reports the assets and claims to those assets at a specific point in time. (p. 14)

Basic accounting equation Assets = Liabilities + Stockholders' Equity. (p. 14)

Certified Public Accountant (CPA) An individual who has met certain criteria and is thus allowed to perform audits of corporations. (p. 24)

Common stock Term used to describe the total amount paid in by stockholders for the shares they purchase. (p. 10)

Comparative statements A presentation of the financial statements of a company for more than one year. (p. 20)

Corporation A business organized as a separate legal entity having ownership divided into transferable shares of stock. (p. 4)

Dividends Payments of cash from a corporation to its stockholders. (p. 10)

Expenses The cost of assets consumed or services used in the process of generating revenues. (p. 11)

Income statement A financial statement that presents the revenues and expenses and resulting net income or net loss of a company for a specific period of time. (p. 12)

Liabilities The debts and obligations of a business. Liabilities represent the amounts owed to creditors. (p. 10)

Management discussion and analysis (MD&A) A section of the annual report that presents management's views on the company's ability to pay near-term obligations, its ability to fund operations and expansion, and its results of operations. (p. 22)

Net income The amount by which revenues exceed expenses. (p. 11)

Net loss The amount by which expenses exceed revenues. (p. 11)

Notes to the financial statements Notes that clarify information presented in the financial statements, as well as expand upon it where additional detail is needed. (p. 23)

Partnership A business owned by two or more persons associated as partners. (p. 4)

Retained earnings The amount of net income retained in the corporation. (p. 13)

Retained earnings statement A financial statement that summarizes the amounts and causes of changes in retained earnings for a specific period of time. (p. 13)

Revenues The increase in assets that result from the sale of a product or service in the normal course of business. (p. 11)

Sarbanes-Oxley Act Regulations passed by Congress in 2002 to try to reduce unethical corporate behavior. (p. 9)

Sole proprietorship A business owned by one person. (p. 4)

Statement of cash flows A financial statement that provides financial information about the cash receipts and cash payments of a business for a specific period of time. (p. 16)

Stockholders' equity The stockholders' claim on total assets. (p. 14)

Demonstration Problem

Jeff Andringa, a former college hockey player, quit his job and started Ice Camp, a hockey camp for kids ages 8 to 18. Eventually he would like to open hockey camps nationwide. Jeff has asked you to help him prepare financial statements at the end of his first year of operations. He relates the following facts about his business activities.

In order to get the business off the ground, he decided to incorporate. He sold shares of common stock to a few close friends, as well as buying some of the shares himself. He initially raised $25,000 through the sale of these shares. In addition, the company took out a $10,000 loan at a local bank.

Ice Camp purchased, for $12,000 cash, a bus for transporting kids. The company also bought hockey goals and other miscellaneous equipment with $1,500 cash. The company earned camp tuition during the year of $100,000 but had collected only $80,000 of this amount. Thus, at the end of the year its customers still owed $20,000. The company rents time at a local rink for $50 per hour. Total rink rental costs during the year were $8,000, insurance was $10,000, salary expense was $20,000, and administrative expenses totaled $9,000, all of which were paid in cash. The company incurred $800 in interest expense on the bank loan, which it still owed at the end of the year.

The company paid dividends during the year of $5,000 cash. The balance in the corporate bank account at December 31, 2007, was $49,500.

Instructions

Using the format of the Sierra Corporation statements in this chapter, prepare an income statement, retained earnings statement, balance sheet, and statement of cash flows. (*Hint:* Prepare the statements in the order stated to take advantage of the flow of information from one statement to the next, as shown in Illustration 1-10 on page 18.)

Demonstration Problems are a final review before you begin homework. **Action Plans** that appear in the margins give you tips about how to approach the problem.

Solution to Demonstration Problem

ICE CAMP
Income Statement
For the Year Ended December 31, 2007

Revenues		
Camp tuition revenue		$100,000
Expenses		
Salaries expense	$20,000	
Insurance expense	10,000	
Administrative expense	9,000	
Rink rental expense	8,000	
Interest expense	800	
Total expenses		47,800
Net income		$ 52,200

Action Plan
- On the income statement: Show revenues and expenses for a period of time.
- On the retained earnings statement: Show the changes in retained earnings for a period of time.
- On the balance sheet: Report assets, liabilities, and stockholders' equity at a specific date.
- On the statement of cash flows: Report sources and uses of cash from operating, investing, and financing activities for a period of time.

ICE CAMP
Retained Earnings Statement
For the Year Ended December 31, 2007

Retained earnings, January 1, 2007		$ 0
Add: Net income		52,200
		52,200
Less: Dividends		5,000
Retained earnings, December 31, 2007		$47,200

ICE CAMP
Balance Sheet
December 31, 2007

Assets

Cash	$49,500
Accounts receivable	20,000
Bus	12,000
Equipment	1,500
Total assets	$83,000

Liabilities and Stockholders' Equity

Liabilities		
Bank loan payable	$10,000	
Interest payable	800	
Total liabilities		$10,800
Stockholders' equity		
Common stock	25,000	
Retained earnings	47,200	
Total stockholders' equity		72,200
Total liabilities and stockholders' equity		$83,000

ICE CAMP
Statement of Cash Flows
For the Year Ended December 31, 2007

Cash flows from operating activities		
Cash receipts from operating activities	$80,000	
Cash payments for operating activities	(47,000)	
Net cash provided by operating activities		$33,000
Cash flows from investing activities		
Purchase of bus	(12,000)	
Purchase of equipment	(1,500)	
Net cash used by investing activities		(13,500)
Cash flows from financing activities		
Issuance of bank loan payable	10,000	
Issuance of common stock	25,000	
Dividends paid	(5,000)	
Net cash provided by financing activities		30,000
Net increase in cash		49,500
Cash at beginning of period		0
Cash at end of period		$49,500

THE NAVIGATOR

This would be a good time to look at the **Student Owner's Manual** at the beginning of the book. Knowing the purpose of the different types of homework will help you understand what each contributes to your accounting skills and competencies.

The tool icon ⚒ indicates that an activity employs one of the decision tools presented in the chapter. The ➡ indicates that an activity relates to a business function beyond accounting. The pencil icon ✏➡ indicates that an activity requires written communication.

Self-Study Questions

Answers are at the end of the chapter.

(SO 1) **1.** Which is *not* one of the three forms of business organization?
(a) Sole proprietorship. (c) Partnership.
(b) Creditorship. (d) Corporation.

(SO 1) **2.** Which is an advantage of corporations relative to partnerships and sole proprietorships?
(a) Lower taxes.
(b) Harder to transfer ownership.
(c) Reduced legal liability for investors.
(d) Most common form of organization.

(SO 2) **3.** Which statement about users of accounting information is *incorrect*?
(a) Management is considered an internal user.
(b) Taxing authorities are considered external users.
(c) Present creditors are considered external users.
(d) Regulatory authorities are considered internal users.

(SO 3) **4.** Which is *not* one of the three primary business activities?
(a) Financing. (c) Advertising.
(b) Operating. (d) Investing.

(SO 3, 4) **5.** Net income will result during a time period when:
(a) assets exceed liabilities.
(b) assets exceed revenues.
(c) expenses exceed revenues.
(d) revenues exceed expenses.

(SO 4, 5) **6.** What section of a cash flow statement indicates the cash spent on new equipment during the past accounting period?
(a) The investing section.
(b) The operating section.

(c) The financing section.
(d) The cash flow statement does not give this information.

7. Which financial statement reports assets, liabilities, and stockholders' equity? (SO 5)
(a) Income statement.
(b) Retained earnings statement.
(c) Balance sheet.
(d) Statement of cash flows.

8. Stockholders' equity represents: (SO 5)
(a) claims of creditors.
(b) claims of employees.
(c) the difference between revenues and expenses.
(d) claims of owners.

9. As of December 31, 2007, Stoneland Corporation has assets of $3,500 and stockholders' equity of $2,000. What are the liabilities for Stoneland Corporation as of December 31, 2007? (SO 5)
(a) $1,500. (c) $2,500.
(b) $1,000. (d) $2,000.

10. The segment of a corporation's annual report that describes the corporation's accounting methods is the: (SO 6)
(a) notes to the financial statements.
(b) management discussion and analysis.
(c) auditor's report.
(d) income statement.

Go to the book's website, **www.wiley.com/college/kimmel**, to access additional Self-Study Questions.

Questions

1. What are the three basic forms of business organizations?

2. What are the advantages to a business of being formed as a corporation? What are the disadvantages?

3. What are the advantages to a business of being formed as a partnership or sole proprietorship? What are the disadvantages?

4. "Accounting is ingrained in our society and is vital to our economic system." Do you agree? Explain.

5. Who are the internal users of accounting data? How does accounting provide relevant data to the internal users?

6. Who are the external users of accounting data? Give examples.

7. What are the three main types of business activity? Give examples of each activity.

8. Listed here are some items found in the financial statements of Ellyn Toth, Inc. Indicate in which financial statement(s) each item would appear.
(a) Service revenue. (d) Accounts receivable.
(b) Equipment. (e) Common stock.
(c) Advertising expense. (f) Wages payable.

9. Why would a bank want to monitor the dividend payment practices of the corporations it lends money to?

10. "A company's net income appears directly on the income statement and the retained earnings statement, and it is included indirectly in the company's balance sheet." Do you agree? Explain.

11. What is the primary purpose of the statement of cash flows?

12. What are the three main categories of the statement of cash flows? Why do you think these categories were chosen?

13. What is retained earnings? What items increase the balance in retained earnings? What items decrease the balance in retained earnings?

14. What is the basic accounting equation?

15. (a) Define the terms *assets*, *liabilities*, and *stockholders' equity*.
    (b) What items affect stockholders' equity?

16. Which of these items are liabilities of White Glove Cleaning Service?
    (a) Cash. (f) Equipment.
    (b) Accounts payable. (g) Salaries payable.
    (c) Dividends. (h) Service revenue.
    (d) Accounts receivable. (i) Rent expense.
    (e) Supplies.

17. How are each of the following financial statements interrelated? (a) Retained earnings statement and income statement. (b) Retained earnings statement and balance sheet. (c) Balance sheet and statement of cash flows.

18. What is the purpose of the management discussion and analysis section (MD&A)?

19. Why is it important for financial statements to receive an unqualified auditor's opinion?

20. What types of information are presented in the notes to the financial statements?

Brief Exercises

Describe forms of business organization.
(SO 1)

BE1-1 Match each of the following forms of business organization with a set of characteristics: sole proprietorship (SP), partnership (P), corporation (C).
(a) ____ Shared control, tax advantages, increased skills and resources.
(b) ____ Simple to set up and maintains control with founder.
(c) ____ Easier to transfer ownership and raise funds, no personal liability.

Identify users of accounting information.
(SO 2)

BE1-2 Match each of the following types of evaluation with one of the listed users of accounting information.
1. Trying to determine whether the company complied with tax laws.
2. Trying to determine whether the company can pay its obligations.
3. Trying to determine whether a marketing proposal will be cost effective.
4. Trying to determine whether the company's net income will result in a stock price increase.
5. Trying to determine whether the company should employ debt or equity financing.
(a) ____ Investors in common stock. (d) ____ Chief Financial Officer.
(b) ____ Marketing managers. (e) ____ Internal Revenue Service.
(c) ____ Creditors.

Classify items by activity.
(SO 4, 5)

BE1-3 Indicate in which part of the statement of cash flows each item would appear: operating activities (O), investing activities (I), or financing activities (F).
(a) ____ Cash received from customers.
(b) ____ Cash paid to stockholders (dividends).
(c) ____ Cash received from issuing new common stock.
(d) ____ Cash paid to suppliers.
(e) ____ Cash paid to purchase a new office building.

Determine effect of transactions on stockholders' equity.
(SO 4)

BE1-4 Presented below are a number of transactions. Determine whether each transaction affects common stock (C), dividends (D), revenue (R), expense (E), or does not affect stockholders' equity (NSE). Provide titles for the revenues and expenses.
(a) Costs incurred for advertising.
(b) Assets received for services performed.
(c) Costs incurred for insurance.
(d) Amounts paid to employees.
(e) Cash distributed to stockholders.
(f) Assets received in exchange for allowing the use of the company's building.
(g) Costs incurred for utilities used.
(h) Paid cash to purchase equipment.
(i) Received cash from investors in exchange for common stock.

BE1-5 In alphabetical order below are balance sheet items for Gidget Company at December 31, 2007. Prepare a balance sheet following the format of Illustration 1-8.

Prepare a balance sheet. *(SO 4, 5)*

Accounts payable	$85,000
Accounts receivable	81,000
Cash	32,000
Common stock	28,000

BE1-6 **Eskimo Pie Corporation** markets a broad range of frozen treats, including its famous Eskimo Pie ice cream bars. The following items were taken from a recent income statement and balance sheet. In each case identify whether the item would appear on the balance sheet (BS) or income statement (IS).

Determine where items appear on financial statements. *(SO 4, 5)*

(a) ____ Income tax expense. *IS*
(b) ____ Inventories. *IS*
(c) ____ Accounts payable. *BS*
(d) ____ Retained earnings. *BS*
(e) ____ Property, plant, and equipment. *BS*

(f) ____ Net sales. *IS*
(g) ____ Cost of goods sold. *IS*
(h) ____ Common stock. *BS*
(i) ____ Receivables. *BS*
(j) ____ Interest expense. *IS*

BE1-7 Indicate which statement you would examine to find each of the following items: income statement (I), balance sheet (B), retained earnings statement (R), or statement of cash flows (C).
(a) Revenue during the period.
(b) Supplies on hand at the end of the year.
(c) Cash received from issuing new bonds during the period.
(d) Total debts outstanding at the end of the period.

Determine proper financial statement. *(SO 4)*

BE1-8 Use the basic accounting equation to answer these questions.
(a) The liabilities of Bergmann Company are $90,000 and the stockholders' equity is $230,000. What is the amount of Bergmann Company's total assets?
(b) The total assets of Buchanan Company are $170,000 and its stockholders' equity is $90,000. What is the amount of its total liabilities?
(c) The total assets of Lily Co. are $700,000 and its liabilities are equal to half of its total assets. What is the amount of Lily Co.'s stockholders' equity?

Use basic accounting equation. *(SO 5)*

BE1-9 At the beginning of the year, Megan Company had total assets of $900,000 and total liabilities of $500,000.
(a) If total assets increased $150,000 during the year and total liabilities decreased $80,000, what is the amount of stockholders' equity at the end of the year?
(b) During the year, total liabilities increased $100,000 and stockholders' equity decreased $70,000. What is the amount of total assets at the end of the year?
(c) If total assets decreased $90,000 and stockholders' equity increased $110,000 during the year, what is the amount of total liabilities at the end of the year?

Use basic accounting equation. *(SO 5)*

BE1-10 Indicate whether each of these items is an asset (A), a liability (L), or part of stockholders' equity (SE).
(a) Accounts receivable.
(b) Salaries payable.
(c) Equipment.
(d) Office supplies.
(e) Common stock.
(f) Notes payable.

Identify assets, liabilities, and stockholders' equity. *(SO 5)*

BE1-11 Which is *not* a required part of an annual report of a publicly traded company?
(a) Statement of cash flows.
(b) Notes to the financial statements.
(c) Management discussion and analysis.
(d) All of these are required.

Determine required parts of annual report. *(SO 6)*

Exercises

E1-1 Here is a list of words or phrases discussed in this chapter:
1. Corporation
2. Creditor
3. Accounts receivable
4. Partnership
5. Stockholder
6. Common stock
7. Accounts payable
8. Auditor's opinion

Match items with descriptions. *(SO 1, 2, 4, 6)*

Instructions

Match each word or phrase with the best description of it.

____ (a) An expression about whether financial statements are presented in a reasonable fashion.

____ (b) A business enterprise that raises money by issuing shares of stock.

____ (c) The portion of stockholders' equity that results from receiving cash from investors.

____ (d) Obligations to suppliers of goods.

____ (e) Amounts due from customers.

____ (f) A party to whom a business owes money.

____ (g) A party that invests in common stock.

____ (h) A business that is owned jointly by two or more individuals but that does not issue stock.

Identify business activities.
(SO 3)

E1-2   All business are involved in three types of activities—financing, investing, and operating. Listed below are the names and descriptions of companies in several different industries.

> Abitibi Consolidated Inc.—manufacturer and marketer of newsprint
> Cal State–Northridge Stdt Union—university student union
> Oracle Corporation—computer software developer and retailer
> Sportsco Investments—owner of the Vancouver Canucks hockey club
> Grant Thornton LLP—professional accounting and business advisory firm
> Southwest Airlines—discount airline

Instructions

(a) For each of the above companies, provide examples of (1) a financing activity, (2) an investing activity, and (3) an operating activity that the company likely engages in.

(b) Which of the activities that you identified in (a) are common to most businesses? Which activities are not?

Classify accounts.
(SO 3, 4)

E1-3 The Mill Run Golf & Country Club details the following accounts in its financial statements.

	(a)	(b)
Accounts payable and accrued liabilities	O	L
Accounts receivable (s/t)	O	A
Property, plant, and equipment (PPE)	I	A
Food and beverage operations revenue	O	R
Golf course operations revenue	O	R
Inventory (s/t)	O	A
Long-term debt	F	L
Office and general expense (s/t)	O	E
Professional fees expense	O	E
Wages and benefits expense	O	E
	F	SE

Instructions

(a) Classify each of the above accounts as an asset (A), liability (L), stockholders' equity (SE), revenue (R), or expense (E) item.

(b) Classify each of the above accounts as a financing activity (F), investing activity (I), or operating activity (O). If you believe a particular account doesn't fit in any of these activities, explain why.

Prepare income statement and retained earnings statement.
(SO 4)

E1-4   This information relates to Connor Co. for the year 2007.

Retained earnings, January 1, 2007	$64,000
Advertising expense	1,800
Dividends paid during 2007	6,000
Rent expense	10,400
Service revenue	58,000
Utilities expense	2,400
Salaries expense	30,000

Instructions

After analyzing the data, prepare an income statement and a retained earnings statement for the year ending December 31, 2007.

E1-5 The following information was taken from the 2004 financial statements of phar- maceutical giant Merck and Co. All dollar amounts are in millions.

Prepare income statement and retained earnings statement.
(SO 4)

Retained earnings, January 1, 2004	$34,142.0
Materials and production expense	4,959.8
Marketing and administrative expense	7,346.3
Dividends	3,329.1
Sales revenue	22,938.6
Research and development expense	4,010.2
Tax expense	2,161.1
Other revenue	1,352.2

Instructions
(a) After analyzing the data, prepare an income statement and a retained earnings state- ment for the year ending December 31, 2004.
(b) Suppose that Merck decided to reduce its research and development expense by 50%. What would be the short-term implications? What would be the long-term implica- tions? How do you think the stock market would react?

E1-6 Presented here is information for Anne Charlotte Inc. for 2007.

Prepare a retained earnings statement.
(SO 4)

Retained earnings, January 1	$130,000
Revenue from legal services	410,000
Total expenses	170,000
Dividends	82,000

Instructions
Prepare the 2007 retained earnings statement for Anne Charlotte Inc.

E1-7 Consider each of the following independent situations.
(a) The retained earnings statement of Motzek Corporation shows dividends of $68,000, while net income for the year was $75,000.
(b) The statement of cash flows for Cheung Corporation shows that cash provided by operating activities was $10,000, cash used in investing activities was $110,000, and cash provided by financing activities was $130,000.

Interpret financial facts.
(SO 4)

Instructions
For each company provide a brief discussion interpreting these financial facts. For exam- ple, you might discuss the company's financial health or its apparent growth philosophy.

E1-8 Here are incomplete financial statements for Brandon, Inc.

Calculate missing amounts.
(SO 4, 5)

BRANDON, INC.
Balance Sheet

Assets		**Liabilities and Stockholders' Equity**	
Cash	$ 5,000	Liabilities	
Inventory	10,000	Accounts payable	$ 5,000
Building	45,000	Stockholders' equity	
Total assets	$60,000	Common stock	(a)
		Retained earnings	(b)
		Total liabilities and	
		stockholders' equity	$60,000

Income Statement

Revenues	$80,000
Cost of goods sold	(c)
Administrative expenses	10,000
Net income	$ (d)

Retained Earnings Statement

Beginning retained earnings	$10,000
Net income	(e)
Dividends	5,000
Ending retained earnings	$29,000

Compute net income and prepare a balance sheet.
(SO 4, 5)

Instructions

Calculate the missing amounts.

E1-9   Sleep Cheap is a private camping ground near the Lathom Peak Recreation Area. It has compiled the following financial information as of December 31, 2007.

Revenues during 2007: camping fees	$137,000	Dividends	$ 9,000
Revenues during 2007: general store	25,000	Notes payable	50,000
Accounts payable	11,000	Expenses during 2007	129,000
Cash	8,500	Supplies	2,500
Equipment	119,000	Common stock	40,000
		Retained earnings (1/1/2007)	5,000

Instructions

(a) Determine net income from Sleep Cheap for 2007.
(b) Prepare a retained earnings statement and a balance sheet for Sleep Cheap as of December 31, 2007.
(c) Upon seeing this income statement, Terry Stevens, the campground manager immediately concluded, "The general store is more trouble than it is worth—let's get rid of it." The marketing director isn't so sure this is a good idea. What do you think?

Identify financial statement components and prepare an income statement.
(SO 4, 5)

E1-10   Kellogg Company is the world's leading producer of ready-to-eat cereal and a leading producer of grain-based convenience foods such as frozen waffles and cereal bars. The following items were taken from its 2004 income statement and balance sheet. All dollars are in millions.

SE	Retained earnings	$2,701.3	L	Long-term debt	$3,892.6
E	Cost of goods sold	5,298.7	A	Inventories	681.0
E	Selling and		K	Net sales	9,613.9
	administrative expenses	2,634.1	L	Accounts payable	767.2
A	Cash	417.4	SE	Common stock	103.8
L	Notes payable (loan)	709.7	E	Income tax expense	475.3
E	Interest expense	308.6	E	Other expense	6.6

Instructions

Perform each of the following.

(a) In each case identify whether the item is an asset (A), liability (L), stockholders' equity (SE), revenue (R), or expense (E).
(b) Prepare an income statement for Kellogg Company for the year ended December 31, 2004.

E1-11   This information is for Campo Corporation for the year ended December 31, 2007.

Prepare a statement of cash flows.
(SO 5)

Cash received from lenders	$20,000
Cash received from customers	65,000
Cash paid for new equipment	35,000
Cash dividends paid	6,000
Cash paid to suppliers	18,000
Cash balance 1/1/07	12,000

Instructions

(a) Prepare the 2007 statement of cash flows for Campo Corporation.
(b) Suppose you are one of Campo's creditors. Referring to the statement of cash flows, evaluate Campo's ability to repay its creditors.

Prepare a statement of cash flows.
(SO 5)

E1-12   The following data are derived from the 2004 financial statements of Southwest Airlines. All dollars are in millions. Southwest has a December 31 year-end.

Cash balance, January 1, 2004	$1,865
Cash paid for repayment of debt	207
Cash received from issuance of common stock	88
Cash received from issuance of long-term debt	512
Cash received from customers	6,455
Cash paid for property and equipment	1,850
Cash paid for dividends	14
Cash paid for repurchase of common stock	246
Cash paid for goods and services	5,298

Instructions

(a) After analyzing the data, prepare a statement of cash flows for Southwest Airlines for the year ended December 31, 2004.

(b) Discuss whether the company's cash from operations was sufficient to finance its investing activities. If it was not, how did the company finance its investing activities?

E1-13 John Paul is the bookkeeper for Gabelli Company. John has been trying to get the balance sheet of Gabelli Company to balance. It finally balanced, but now he's not sure it is correct.

Correct an incorrectly prepared balance sheet.
(SO 5)

GABELLI COMPANY
Balance Sheet
December 31, 2007

Assets		**Liabilities and Stockholders' Equity**	
Cash	$18,500	Accounts payable	$16,000
Supplies	9,500	Accounts receivable	(12,000)
Equipment	40,000	Common stock	40,000
Dividends	10,000	Retained earnings	34,000
Total assets	$78,000	Total liabilities and stockholders' equity	$78,000

Instructions

Prepare a correct balance sheet.

E1-14 The following items were taken from the balance sheet of Nike, Inc.

1. Cash	$ 828.0	7. Inventories	$1,633.6
2. Accounts receivable	2,120.2	8. Income taxes payable	118.2
3. Common stock	890.6	9. Property, plant, and equipment	1,586.9
4. Notes payable	146.0	10. Retained earnings	3,891.1
5. Other assets	1,722.9	11. Accounts payable	763.8
6. Other liabilities	2,081.9		

Classify items as assets, liabilities, and stockholders' equity and prepare accounting equation.
(SO 5)

Instructions

Perform each of the following.

(a) Classify each of these items as an asset, liability, or stockholders' equity. (All dollars are in millions.)

(b) Determine Nike's accounting equation by calculating the value of total assets, total liabilities, and total stockholders' equity.

(c) To what extent does Nike rely on debt versus equity financing?

E1-15 The summaries of data from the balance sheet, income statement, and retained earnings statement for two corporations, Bates Corporation and Wilson Enterprises, are presented below for 2007.

Use financial statement relationships to determine missing amounts.
(SO 5)

	Bates Corporation	**Wilson Enterprises**
Beginning of year		
Total assets	$110,000	$130,000
Total liabilities	80,000	(d)
Total stockholders' equity	(a)	90,000
End of year		
Total assets	(b)	180,000
Total liabilities	120,000	55,000
Total stockholders' equity	50,000	(e)
Changes during year in retained earnings		
Dividends	(c)	5,000
Total revenues	215,000	(f)
Total expenses	165,000	80,000

Instructions

Determine the missing amounts. Assume all changes in stockholders' equity are due to changes in retained earnings.

Classify various items in an annual report.
(SO 6)

E1-16 The annual report provides financial information in a variety of formats including the following.

> Management discussion and analysis (MD&A)
> Financial statements
> Notes to the financial statements
> Auditor's opinion

Instructions

For each of the following, state in what area of the annual report the item would be presented. If the item would probably not be found in an annual report, state "Not disclosed."

(a) The total cumulative amount received from stockholders in exchange for common stock.
(b) An independent assessment concerning whether the financial statements present a fair depiction of the company's results and financial position.
(c) The interest rate that the company is being charged on all outstanding debts.
(d) Total revenue from operating activities.
(e) Management's assessment of the company's results.
(f) The names and positions of all employees hired in the last year.

Problems: Set A

Determine forms of business organization.
(SO 1)

P1-1A Presented below are five independent situations.

(a) Three physics professors at MIT have formed a business to improve the speed of information transfer over the Internet for stock exchange transactions. Each has contributed an equal amount of cash and knowledge to the venture. Although their approach looks promising, they are concerned about the legal liabilities that their business might confront.
(b) Andrew Carpenter, a college student looking for summer employment, opened a bait shop in a small shed at a local marina.
(c) Dennis Lee and Paul Rowe each owned separate shoe manufacturing businesses. They have decided to combine their businesses. They expect that within the coming year they will need significant funds to expand their operations.
(d) Elaine, Jerry, and George recently graduated with marketing degrees. They have been friends since childhood. They have decided to start a consulting business focused on marketing sporting goods over the Internet.
(e) Liam O'Brien wants to rent CD players and CDs in airports across the country. His idea is that customers will be able to rent equipment and CDs at one airport, listen to the CDs on their flights, and return the equipment and CDs at their destination airport. Of course, this will require a substantial investment in equipment and CDs, as well as employees and locations in each airport. Liam has no savings or personal assets. He wants to maintain control over the business.

Instructions

In each case explain what form of organization the business is likely to take—sole proprietorship, partnership, or corporation. Give reasons for your choice.

Identify users and uses of financial statements.
(SO 2, 4, 5)

P1-2A Financial decisions often place heavier emphasis on one type of financial statement over the others. Consider each of the following hypothetical situations independently.

(a) The North Face, Inc. is considering extending credit to a new customer. The terms of the credit would require the customer to pay within 30 days of receipt of goods.
(b) An investor is considering purchasing common stock of Amazon.com. The investor plans to hold the investment for at least 5 years.
(c) Chase Manhattan is considering extending a loan to a small company. The company would be required to make interest payments at the end of each year for 5 years, and to repay the loan at the end of the fifth year.
(d) The president of Campbell Soup is trying to determine whether the company is generating enough cash to increase the amount of dividends paid to investors in this and future years, and still have enough cash to buy equipment as it is needed.

Instructions
In each situation, state whether the decision maker would be most likely to place primary emphasis on information provided by the income statement, balance sheet, or statement of cash flows. In each case provide a brief justification for your choice. Choose only one financial statement in each case.

P1-3A On June 1 Fix-It-Up Service Co. was started with an initial investment in the company of $26,200 cash. Here are the assets and liabilities of the company at June 30, and the revenues and expenses for the month of June, its first month of operations:

Prepare an income statement, retained earnings statement, and balance sheet, and discuss results.
(SO 4, 5)

Cash	$ 4,600	Notes payable	$14,000
Accounts receivable	4,000	Accounts payable	500
Revenue	8,000	Supplies expense	1,000
Supplies	2,400	Gas and oil expense	600
Advertising expense	400	Utilities expense	300
Equipment	32,000	Wage expense	1,400

In June, the company issued no additional stock, but paid dividends of $2,000.

Instructions
(a) Prepare an income statement and a retained earnings statement for the month of June and a balance sheet at June 30, 2007.
(b) Briefly discuss whether the company's first month of operations was a success.
(c) Discuss the company's decision to distribute a dividend.

P1-4A Presented below is selected financial information for Linus Corporation for December 31, 2007.

*Marginal **check figures** (in blue) provide a key number to let you know you're on the right track.*
(a) Net income $4,300
    Ret. earnings $2,300
    Tot. assets $43,000
Determine items included in a statement of cash flows, prepare the statement, and comment.
(SO 4, 5)

Inventory	$ 25,000	Cash paid to purchase equipment	$ 10,000
Cash paid to suppliers	108,000	Equipment	40,000
Building	200,000	Revenues	100,000
Common stock	50,000	Cash received from customers	137,000
Cash dividends paid	7,000	Cash received from issuing common stock	22,000

Instructions
(a) Determine which items should be included in a statement of cash flows and then prepare the statement for Linus Corporation.
(b) Comment on the adequacy of net cash provided by operating activities to fund the company's investing activities and dividend payments.

(a) Net increase $34,000

P1-5A Silberman Corporation was formed on January 1, 2007. At December 31, 2007, Scott Brantner, the president and sole stockholder, decided to prepare a balance sheet, which appeared as follows.

Comment on proper accounting treatment and prepare a corrected balance sheet.
(SO 4, 5)

SILBERMAN CORPORATION
Balance Sheet
December 31, 2007

Assets		**Liabilities and Stockholders' Equity**	
Cash	$20,000	Accounts payable	$40,000
Accounts receivable	55,000	Notes payable	15,000
Inventory	33,000	Boat loan	18,000
Boat	24,000	Stockholders' equity	55,000

Scott willingly admits that he is not an accountant by training. He is concerned that his balance sheet might not be correct. He has provided you with the following additional information.
1. The boat actually belongs to Brantner, not to Silberman Corporation. However, because he thinks he might take customers out on the boat occasionally, he decided to list it as an asset of the company. To be consistent he also listed as a liability of the corporation his personal loan that he took out at the bank to buy the boat.
2. The inventory was originally purchased for $21,000, but due to a surge in demand Scott now thinks he could sell it for $33,000. He thought it would be best to record it at $33,000.

3. Included in the accounts receivable balance is $12,000 that Scott loaned to his brother 5 years ago. Scott included this in the receivables of Silberman Corporation so he wouldn't forget that his brother owes him money.

Instructions

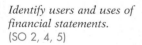

Tot.assets $84,000

(a) Comment on the proper accounting treatment of the three items above.
(b) Provide a corrected balance sheet for Silberman Corporation. (*Hint:* To get the balance sheet to balance, adjust stockholders' equity.)

Problems: Set B

Determine forms of business organization.
(SO 1)

P1-1B Presented below are five independent situations.
(a) Joyce Packee, a college student looking for summer employment, opened a vegetable stand along a busy local highway. Each morning she buys produce from local farmers, then sells it in the afternoon as people return home from work.
(b) Alex Rice and Peter Gould each owned separate swing-set manufacturing businesses. They have decided to combine their businesses and try to expand their reach beyond their local market. They expect that within the coming year they will need significant funds to expand their operations.
(c) Three chemistry professors at FIU have formed a business to employ bacteria to clean up toxic waste sites. Each has contributed an equal amount of cash and knowledge to the venture. The use of bacteria in this situation is experimental, and legal obligations could result.
(d) Emma Peale has run a successful, but small cooperative health food store for over 20 years. The increased sales of her store have made her believe that the time is right to open a national chain of health food stores across the country. Of course, this will require a substantial investment in stores, inventory, and employees in each store. Emma has no savings or personal assets. She wants to maintain control over the business.
(e) Tammy Laven and Ted Peterman recently graduated with masters degrees in economics. They have decided to start a consulting business focused on teaching the basics of international economics to small business owners interested in international trade.

Instructions

In each case explain what form of organization the business is likely to take—sole proprietorship, partnership, or corporation. Give reasons for your choice.

Identify users and uses of financial statements.
(SO 2, 4, 5)

P1-2B Financial decisions often place heavier emphasis on one type of financial statement over the others. Consider each of the following hypothetical situations independently.
(a) An investor is considering purchasing common stock of the Bally Total Fitness company. The investor plans to hold the investment for at least 3 years.
(b) Boeing is considering extending credit to a new customer. The terms of the credit would require the customer to pay within 60 days of receipt of goods.
(c) The president of Northwest Airlines is trying to determine whether the company is generating enough cash to increase the amount of dividends paid to investors in this and future years, and still have enough cash to buy new flight equipment as it is needed.
(d) Bank of America is considering extending a loan to a small company. The company would be required to make interest payments at the end of each year for 5 years, and to repay the loan at the end of the fifth year.

Instructions

In each of the situations above, state whether the decision maker would be most likely to place primary emphasis on information provided by the income statement, balance sheet, or statement of cash flows. In each case provide a brief justification for your choice. Choose only one financial statement in each case.

Prepare an income statement, retained earnings statement, and balance sheet, and discuss results.
(SO 4, 5)

P1-3B Special Delivery was started on May 1 with an investment of $45,000 cash. To "jump start" its sales, the company spent significant money on advertising. Following are the assets and liabilities of the company on May 31, 2007, and the revenues and expenses for the month of May, its first month of operations.

A Accounts receivable	$ 6,200	B Notes payable	$30,000
R Service revenue	10,800	E Wage expense	2,200
E Advertising expense	800	A Equipment	60,300
L Accounts payable	2,400	E Repair expense	500
C Cash	13,700	E Fuel expense	2,400
		E Insurance expense	400

(a) Net income $4,500
Ret. earnings $2,800
Tot. assets $80,200

No additional common stock was issued in May, but a dividend of $1,700 in cash was paid.

Instructions

(a) Prepare an income statement and a retained earnings statement for the month of May and a balance sheet at May 31, 2007.
(b) Briefly discuss whether the company's first month of operations was a success.
(c) Discuss the company's decision to distribute a dividend.

P1-4B Presented below are selected financial statement items for Daley Corporation for December 31, 2007.

Determine items included in a statement of cash flows, prepare the statement, and comment.
(SO 4, 5)

Inventory	$ 55,000	Cash paid to purchase equipment	$ 34,000
Cash paid to suppliers	154,000	Equipment	40,000
Building	400,000	Revenues	200,000
Common stock	20,000	Cash received from customers	173,000
Cash dividends paid	9,000	Cash received from issuing bonds payable	30,000

Instructions

(a) Determine which items should be included in a statement of cash flows, and then prepare the statement for Daley Corporation.
(b) Comment on the adequacy of net cash provided by operating activities to fund the company's investing activities and dividend payments.

(a) Net increase $6,000

P1-5B Wyoming Corporation was formed during 2006 by Sandra Lee. Sandra is the president and sole stockholder. At December 31, 2007, Sandra prepared an income statement for Wyoming Corporation. Sandra is not an accountant, but she thinks she did a reasonable job preparing the income statement by looking at the financial statements of other companies. She has asked you for advice. Sandra's income statement appears as follows.

Comment on proper accounting treatment and prepare a corrected income statement.
(SO 4, 5)

WYOMING CORPORATION
Income Statement
For the Year Ended December 31, 2007

Accounts receivable	$17,000
Revenue	60,000
Rent expense	12,000
Insurance expense	5,000
Vacation expense	2,000
Net income	58,000

Sandra has also provided you with these facts.

1. Included in the revenue account is $3,000 of revenue that the company earned and received payment for in 2006. She forgot to include it in the 2006 income statement, so she put it in this year's statement.
2. Sandra operates her business out of the basement of her parents' home. They do not charge her anything, but she thinks that if she paid rent it would cost her about $12,000 per year. She therefore included $12,000 of rent expense in the income statement.
3. To reward herself for a year of hard work, Sandra went to Greece. She did not use company funds to pay for the trip, but she reported it as an expense on the income statement since it was her job that made her need the vacation.

Instructions

(a) Comment on the proper accounting treatment of the three items above.
(b) Prepare a corrected income statement for Wyoming Corporation.

(a) Net income $52,000

Problems: Set C

Visit the book's website at **www.wiley.com/college/kimmel** and choose the Student Companion site to access Problem Set C.

Continuing Cookie Chronicle

CCC1 Natalie Koebel spent much of her childhood learning the art of cookie-making from her grandmother. They spent many happy hours mastering every type of cookie imaginable and later devised new recipes that were both healthy and delicious. Now at the start of her second year in college, Natalie is investigating possibilities for starting her own business as part of the entrepreneurship program in which she is enrolled.

A long-time friend insists that Natalie has to include cookies in her business plan. After a series of brainstorming sessions, Natalie settles on the idea of operating a cookie-making school. She will start on a part-time basis and offer her services in people's homes. Now that she has started thinking about it, the possibilities seem endless. During the fall, she will concentrate on holiday cookies. She will offer group sessions (which will probably be more entertainment than education) and individual lessons. Natalie also decides to include children in her target market. The first difficult decision is coming up with the perfect name for her business. She settles on "Cookie Creations," and then moves on to more important issues.

Instructions
(a) What form of business organization—proprietorship, partnership, or corporation—do you recommend that Natalie use for her business? Discuss the benefits and weaknesses of each form that Natalie might consider.
(b) Will Natalie need accounting information? If yes, what information will she need and why? How often will she need this information?
(c) Identify specific asset, liability, revenue, and expense accounts that Cookie Creations will likely use to record its business transactions.
(d) Should Natalie open a separate bank account for the business? Why or why not?
(e) Natalie expects she will have to use her car to drive to people's homes and to pick up supplies, but she also needs to use her car for personal reasons. She recalls from her first-year accounting course something about keeping business and personal assets separate. She wonders what she should do for accounting purposes. What do you recommend?

BROADENING YOUR PERSPECTIVE

Financial Reporting and Analysis

FINANCIAL REPORTING PROBLEM: *Tootsie Roll Industries, Inc.*

BYP1-1 Simplified 2004 financial statements of Tootsie Roll Industries, Inc. are given in Illustrations 1-11 through 1-14.

Instructions
Refer to Tootsie Roll's financial statements to answer the following questions.
(a) What were Tootsie Roll's total assets at December 31, 2004? At December 31, 2003?
(b) How much cash did Tootsie Roll have on December 31, 2004?
(c) What amount of accounts payable did Tootsie Roll report on December 31, 2004? On December 31, 2003?
(d) What were Tootsie Roll's sales revenue in 2004? In 2003?
(e) What is the amount of the change in Tootsie Roll's net income from 2003 to 2004?
(f) The accounting equation is: Assets = Liabilities + Stockholders' Equity. Replacing the words in that equation with dollar amounts, give Tootsie Roll's accounting equation at December 31, 2004.

COMPARATIVE ANALYSIS PROBLEM: *Tootsie Roll vs. Hershey Foods*

BYP1-2 Simplified financial statements of Hershey Foods Corporation are presented in Illustrations 1-18 through 1-21, and Tootsie Roll's simplified financial statements are presented in Illustrations 1-11 through 1-14.

Instructions
(a) Based on the information in these financial statements, determine the following for each company.
   (1) Total assets at December 31, 2004.
   (2) Accounts receivable at December 31, 2004.
   (3) Sales revenue for 2004.
   (4) Net income for 2004.

(b) What conclusions concerning the two companies can you draw from these data?

RESEARCH CASE

BYP1-3 The newsletter *Rural Roots*, published by The Rural School and Community Trust, includes an article titled "Student-Run Grocery Store Up and Running." The article is available at **www.ruraledu.org/roots/rr201d.htm**.

Instructions
Read the article and answer the following questions.
(a) List the various ways that accounting would be critical to the successful formation and operation of Wolf Den Market.
(b) Identify various accounts that would be used by Wolf Den Market. First list balance sheet accounts; then list income statement accounts.

INTERPRETING FINANCIAL STATEMENTS

BYP1-4 The year 2000 was not a particularly pleasant year for the managers of Xerox Corporation, or its shareholders. The company's stock price had already fallen in the previous year from $60 per share to $30. Just when it seemed things couldn't get worse, Xerox's stock fell to $4 per share. The data below were taken from the December 31, 2000, statement of cash flows of Xerox. All dollars are in millions.

Cash used in operating activities		$ (663)
Cash used in investing activities		(644)
Financing activities		
Dividends paid	$ (587)	
Net cash received from issuing debt	3,498	
Cash provided by financing activities		2,911

Instructions
Analyze the information above, and then answer the following questions.
(a) If you were a creditor of Xerox, what reaction might you have to the above information?
(b) If you were an investor in Xerox, what reaction might you have to the above information?
(c) If you were evaluating the company as either a creditor or a stockholder, what other information would you be interested in seeing?
(d) Xerox decided to pay a cash dividend in 2000. This dividend was approximately equal to the amount paid in 1999. Discuss the issues that were probably considered in making this decision.

FINANCIAL ANALYSIS ON THE WEB

BYP1-5 *Purpose:* Identify summary information about companies. This information includes basic descriptions of the company's location, activities, industry, financial health, and financial performance.

Address: **http://biz.yahoo.com/i** (or go to **www.wiley.com/college/kimmel**)

Steps
1. Type in a company name, or use the index to find company name.
2. Choose **Quote**, then choose **Profile**, then choose **Income Statement**. Perform instructions (a) and (b) below.
3. Choose **Industry** to identify others in this industry. Perform instructions (c)–(e) below.

Instructions
Answer the following questions.
(a) What was the company's net income? Over what period was this measured?
(b) What was the company's total sales? Over what period was this measured?
(c) What is the company's industry?

(d) What are the names of four companies in this industry?

(e) Choose one of the competitors. What is this competitor's name? What were its sales? What was its net income?

Critical Thinking

DECISION MAKING ACROSS THE ORGANIZATION

BYP1-6 Kim Perkins recently accepted a job in the production department at Tootsie Roll. Before she starts work, she decides to review the company's annual report to better understand its operations.

Instructions

Use the annual report provided in Appendix A to answer the following questions.

(a) What CPA firm performed the audit of Tootsie Roll's financial statements?

(b) What was the amount of Tootsie Roll's earnings per share in 2004?

(c) What are the company's net sales in foreign countries?

(d) What did management suggest as the cause of the increase in the sales in 2004?

(e) What were net sales in 2000?

(f) How many shares of Class B common stock have been authorized?

(g) How much cash was spent on capital expenditures in 2004?

(h) Over what life does the company depreciate its buildings?

(i) What was the value of raw material inventories in 2003?

COMMUNICATION ACTIVITY

BYP1-7 Carol Young is the bookkeeper for Evans Company, Inc. Carol has been trying to get the company's balance sheet to balance. She finally got it to balance, but she still isn't sure that it is correct.

EVANS COMPANY, INC.
Balance Sheet
For the Month Ended December 31, 2007

Assets		**Liabilities and Stockholders' Equity**	
Equipment	$20,500	Common stock	$11,000
Cash	10,500	Accounts receivable	(3,000)
Supplies	2,000	Dividends	(2,000)
Accounts payable	(5,000)	Notes payable	12,000
Total assets	$28,000	Retained earnings	10,000
		Total liabilities and stockholders' equity	$28,000

Instructions

Explain to Carol Young in a memo (a) the purpose of a balance sheet, and (b) why this balance sheet is incorrect and what she should do to correct it.

ETHICS CASE

BYP1-8 Rules governing the investment practices of individual certified public accountants prohibit them from investing in the stock of a company that their firm audits. The Securities and Exchange Commission became concerned that some accountants were violating this rule. In response to an SEC investigation, PricewaterhouseCoopers fired 10 people and spent $25 million educating employees about the investment rules and installing an investment tracking system.

Instructions

Answer the following questions.

(a) Why do you think rules exist that restrict auditors from investing in companies that are audited by their firms?

(b) Some accountants argue that they should be allowed to invest in a company's stock as long as they themselves aren't involved in working on the company's audit or consulting. What do you think of this idea?

(c) Today a very high percentage of publicly traded companies are audited by only four very large public accounting firms. These firms also do a high percentage of the consulting work that is done for publicly traded companies. How does this fact complicate the decision regarding whether CPAs should be allowed to invest in companies audited by their firm?

(d) Suppose you were a CPA and you had invested in IBM when IBM was not one of your firm's clients. Two years later, after IBM's stock price had fallen considerably, your firm won the IBM audit contract. You will not in any way be involved in working with the IBM audit, which will be done by one of your firm's other offices in a different state. You know that your firm's rules, as well as U.S. law, require that you sell your shares immediately. If you do sell immediately, you will sustain a large loss. Do you think this is fair? What would you do?

(e) Why do you think PricewaterhouseCoopers took such extreme steps in response to the SEC investigation?

Answers to Business Insight and Accounting across the Organization Questions

p. 7

Q: What are the benefits to the company and to the employees of making the financial statements available to all employees?

A: If employees can read and use financial reports, a company will benefit in the following ways. The *marketing department* will make better decisions about products to offer and prices to charge. The *finance department* will make better decisions about debt and equity financing and how much to distribute in dividends. The *production department* will make better decisions about when to buy new equipment and how much inventory to produce. The *human resources department* will be better able to determine whether employees can be given raises. Finally, *all employees* will be better informed about the basis on which they are evaluated, which will increase employee morale.

p. 8

Q: How might accounting help you?

A: You will need to understand financial reports in any enterprise with which you are associated. Whether you become a manager, a doctor, a lawyer, a social worker, a teacher, an engineer, an architect, or an entrepreneur, a working knowledge of accounting is relevant.

p. 9

Q: What has been done in the United States to improve the quality and integrity of financial reporting and to build investor confidence in financial reports?

A: Congress passed new laws to legislate fair business behavior and accounting and auditing practices. The *Sarbanes-Oxley Act* increases the resources for the government to combat fraud and to curb poor reporting practices. It introduces sweeping changes to the structure and practices of the accounting and auditing professions and increases the responsibility of corporate boards and officers.

p. 16

Q: What is one way that some of these disputes might be resolved?

A: Frequently, when contractual payments depend on accounting-based financial results, interested parties employ outside auditors to evaluate whether the financial information has been prepared fairly and accurately. The musicians would like auditors to have easy access to inventory and manufacturing information of the recording companies.

Answer to Tootsie Roll Review It Question 3, p. 17

Using dollar amounts, Tootsie Roll's accounting equation is:

Assets	=	Liabilities	+ Stockholders' Equity
$811,753,000	=	$241,574,000 +	$570,179,000

Answers to Self-Study Questions

1. b   2. c   3. d   4. c   5. d   6. a   7. c   8. d   9. a   10. a

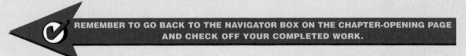

REMEMBER TO GO BACK TO THE NAVIGATOR BOX ON THE CHAPTER-OPENING PAGE AND CHECK OFF YOUR COMPLETED WORK.

A Further Look at Financial Statements

Just Fooling Around?

Few people could have predicted how dramatically the Internet would change the investment world. One of the most interesting results is how it has changed the way ordinary people invest their savings. More and more people are striking out on their own, making their own investment decisions.

Two early pioneers in providing investment information to the masses were Tom and David Gardner, brothers who created an online investor bulletin board called the Motley Fool. The name comes from Shakespeare's *As You Like It*. The fool in Shakespeare's plays was the only one who could speak unpleasant truths to kings and queens without being killed. Tom and David view themselves as 21st-century "fools," revealing the "truths" of Wall Street to the small investor, who they feel has been taken advantage of by Wall Street insiders. Their online bulletin board enables investors to exchange information and insights about companies.

Critics of these bulletin boards contend that they are high-tech rumor mills. They suggest that the fervor created by bulletin board chatter causes investors to bid up stock prices to unreasonable levels. Because bulletin board participants typically use aliases, there is little to stop people from putting misinformation on the board to influence a stock's price. For example, the stock of PairGain

Technologies jumped 32 percent in a single day as a result of a bogus takeover rumor on an investment bulletin board. Some observers are concerned that small investors—ironically, the very people the Gardner brothers are trying to help—will be hurt the most by misinformation and intentional scams.

To show how these bulletin boards work, suppose that in a recent year you had $10,000 to invest. You were considering Best Buy Company, the largest seller of electronics equipment in the United States. You scanned the Internet investment bulletin boards and found messages posted by two different investors. Here are excerpts from actual postings during the same recent year.

From: "TMPVenus": "Where are the prospects for positive movement for this company? Poor margins, poor management, astronomical P/E!"

From "broachman": "I believe that this is a LONG TERM winner, and presently at a good price."

One says sell, and one says buy. Whom should you believe? If you had taken "broachman's"

advice and purchased the stock, the $10,000 you invested would have been worth over $300,000 five years later. Best Buy was one of America's best-performing stocks during that period of time.

Deciding what information to rely on is becoming increasingly complex. For example, shortly before its share price completely collapsed, nearly every professional analyst who followed Enron was recommending its stock as a "buy."

Rather than getting swept away by rumors, investors must sort out the good information from the bad. One thing is certain—as information services such as the Motley Fool increase in number, gathering information will become even easier. Evaluating it will be the harder task.

On the World Wide Web
Motley Fool: www.fool.com.
Best Buy Company: www.bestbuy.com

If you are thinking of purchasing Best Buy stock, or any stock, how can you decide what the stock is worth? If you manage J. Crew's credit department, how should you determine whether to extend credit to a new customer? If you are a financial executive of IBM, how do you decide whether your company is generating adequate cash to expand operations without borrowing? Your decision in each of these situations will be influenced by a variety of considerations. One of them should be your careful analysis of a company's financial statements. The reason: Financial statements offer relevant and reliable information, which will help you in your decision making.

In this chapter we take a closer look at the balance sheet and introduce some useful ways for evaluating the information provided by the financial statements. We also examine the financial reporting concepts underlying the financial statements.

A FURTHER LOOK AT FINANCIAL STATEMENTS

The Financial Statements Revisited	Financial Reporting Concepts
• Classified balance sheet • Using the financial statements	• The standard-setting environment • Characteristics of useful information • Assumptions and principles • Constraints

THE NAVIGATOR

SECTION ONE
THE FINANCIAL STATEMENTS REVISITED

Tootsie Roll Annual Report Walkthrough

In Chapter 1 we introduced the four financial statements. In this section we review the financial statements and present tools that are useful for evaluating them. We begin by introducing the classified balance sheet.

The Classified Balance Sheet

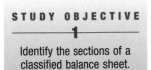

STUDY OBJECTIVE
1

Identify the sections of a classified balance sheet.

The balance sheet presents a snapshot of a company's financial position at a point in time. To improve users' understanding of a company's financial position, companies often group similar assets and similar liabilities together. This is useful because it tells you that items within a group have similar economic characteristics. A **classified balance sheet** generally contains the standard classifications listed in Illustration 2-1.

Illustration 2-1
Standard balance sheet classifications

Assets	Liabilities and Stockholders' Equity
Current assets Long-term investments Property, plant, and equipment Intangible assets	Current liabilities Long-term liabilities Stockholders' equity

These groupings help readers determine such things as (1) whether the company has enough assets to pay its debts as they come due, and (2) the claims of short- and long-term creditors on the company's total assets. Many of these groupings can be seen in the balance sheet of Franklin Corporation shown in Illustration 2-2. In the sections that follow, we explain each of these groupings.

CURRENT ASSETS

Current assets are assets that a company expects to convert to cash or use up within one year. In Illustration 2-2, Franklin Corporation had current assets of $22,100. For most businesses the cutoff for classification as current assets is one

Illustration 2-2   Classified balance sheet

FRANKLIN CORPORATION
Balance Sheet
October 31, 2007

Assets

Current assets			
Cash		$ 6,600	
Short-term investments		2,000	
Accounts receivable		7,000	
Notes receivable		1,000	
Inventories		3,000	
Supplies		2,100	
Prepaid insurance		400	
Total current assets			$22,100
Long-term investments			
Investment in stock of Walters Corp.		5,200	
Investment in real estate		2,000	7,200
Property, plant, and equipment			
Land		10,000	
Office equipment	$24,000		
Less: Accumulated depreciation	5,000	19,000	29,000
Intangible assets			
Patents			3,100
Total assets			$61,400

Liabilities and Stockholders' Equity

Current liabilities		
Notes payable	$11,000	
Accounts payable	2,100	
Salaries payable	1,600	
Unearned revenue	900	
Interest payable	450	
Total current liabilities		$16,050
Long-term liabilities		
Mortgage payable	10,000	
Notes payable	1,300	
Total long-term liabilities		11,300
Total liabilities		27,350
Stockholders' equity		
Common stock	14,000	
Retained earnings	20,050	
Total stockholders' equity		34,050
Total liabilities and stockholders' equity		$61,400

Helpful Hint Recall that the accounting equation is Assets = Liabilities + Stockholders' Equity.

year from the balance sheet date. For example, accounts receivable are current assets because the company will collect them and convert them to cash within one year. Supplies is a current asset because the company expects to use it up in operations within one year.

Some companies use a period longer than one year to classify assets and liabilities as current because they have an operating cycle longer than one year. The **operating cycle** of a company is the average time that it takes to purchase inventory, sell it on account, and then collect cash from customers. For most businesses this cycle takes less than a year, so they use a one-year cutoff. But, for some businesses, such as vineyards or airplane manufacturers, this period may be longer than a year. **Except where noted, we will assume that companies use one year to determine whether an asset or liability is current or long-term.**

Common types of current assets are (1) cash, (2) short-term investments (such as short-term U.S. government securities), (3) receivables (notes receivable, accounts receivable, and interest receivable), (4) inventories, and (5) prepaid expenses (insurance and supplies). **On the balance sheet, companies usually list these items in the order in which they expect to convert them into cash** (order of liquidity).

Illustration 2-3 presents the current assets of The Coca-Cola Company.

Illustration 2-3 Current assets section

THE COCA-COLA COMPANY Balance Sheet (partial) (in millions)	
Current assets	
Cash and cash equivalents	$ 6,707
Short-term investments	61
Trade accounts receivable	2,171
Inventories	1,420
Prepaid expenses and other assets	1,735
Total current assets	$12,094

As explained later in the chapter, a company's current assets are important in assessing its short-term debt-paying ability.

LONG-TERM INVESTMENTS

Long-term investments are generally investments in stocks and bonds of other corporations that are normally held for many years. This category also includes investments in long-term assets such as land or buildings that a company is not currently using in its operating activities. In Illustration 2-2 Franklin Corporation reported total long-term investments of $7,200 on its balance sheet.

Yahoo! Inc. reported long-term investments in its balance sheet as shown in Illustration 2-4.

Illustration 2-4 Long-term investments section

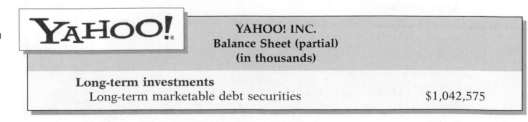

YAHOO! INC. Balance Sheet (partial) (in thousands)	
Long-term investments	
Long-term marketable debt securities	$1,042,575

PROPERTY, PLANT, AND EQUIPMENT

Property, plant, and equipment are assets with relatively long useful lives that a company is currently using in operating the business. This category includes land, buildings, machinery and equipment, delivery equipment, and furniture. In Illustration 2-2 Franklin Corporation reported property, plant, and equipment of $29,000.

Alternative Terminology
Property, plant, and equipment is sometimes called *fixed assets.*

Depreciation is the practice of allocating the cost of assets to a number of years. Companies do this by systematically assigning a portion of an asset's cost as an expense each year (rather than expensing the full purchase price in the year of purchase). The assets that the company depreciates are reported on the balance sheet at cost less accumulated depreciation. The **accumulated depreciation** account shows the total amount of depreciation that the company has expensed thus far in the asset's life. In Illustration 2-2 Franklin Corporation reported accumulated depreciation of $5,000.

Illustration 2-5 presents the property, plant, and equipment of ski and sporting goods manufacturer K2, Inc.

Illustration 2-5 Property, plant, and equipment section

K2, INC. Balance Sheet (partial) (in thousands)		
Property, plant, and equipment		
Land and land improvements	$ 6,794	
Buildings and leasehold improvements	55,900	
Machinery and equipment	204,651	
Construction in process	5,614	$272,959
Less: Accumulated depreciation		131,995
		$140,964

INTANGIBLE ASSETS

Many companies have assets that do not have physical substance yet often are very valuable. We call these assets **intangible assets**. They include patents, copyrights, and trademarks or trade names that give the company **exclusive right** of use for a specified period of time. Franklin Corporation reported intangible assets of $3,100.

Helpful Hint Sometimes intangible assets are reported under a broader heading called *"Other assets."*

Illustration 2-6 shows how media giant Time Warner, Inc. reported its intangible assets.

Illustration 2-6 Intangible assets section

TIME WARNER, INC. Balance Sheet (partial) (in millions)	
Intangible assets	
Film library	$ 3,361
Customer lists	868
Cable television franchises	29,751
Sports franchises	262
Brands, trademarks, and other intangible assets	9,643
	$43,885

CURRENT LIABILITIES

In the liabilities and stockholders' equity section of the balance sheet, the first grouping is current liabilities. **Current liabilities** are obligations that the company is to pay within the coming year. Common examples are accounts payable, wages payable, bank loans payable, interest payable, and taxes payable. Also included as current liabilities are current maturities of long-term obligations—payments to be made within the next year on long-term obligations. In Illustration 2-2 Franklin Corporation reported five different types of current liabilities, for a total of $16,050.

Within the current liabilities section, companies usually list notes payable first, followed by accounts payable. Other items then follow in the order of their magnitude. In your homework, you should present notes payable first, followed by accounts payable, and then other liabilities in order of magnitude.

Illustration 2-7 shows the current liabilities section adapted from the balance sheet of Marcus Corporation.

Illustration 2-7 Current liabilities section

MARCUS CORPORATION Balance Sheet (partial) (in thousands)	
Current liabilities	
Notes payable	$ 2,066
Accounts payable	17,516
Current maturities of long-term debt	26,321
Taxes payable	14,889
Other current liabilities	14,809
Accrued compensation payable	8,614
Total current liabilities	$84,215

LONG-TERM LIABILITIES

Long-term liabilities are obligations that a company expects to pay **after** one year. Liabilities in this category include bonds payable, mortgages payable, long-term notes payable, lease liabilities, and pension liabilities. Many companies report long-term debt maturing after one year as a single amount in the balance sheet and show the details of the debt in notes that accompany the financial statements. Others list the various types of long-term liabilities. In Illustration 2-2 Franklin Corporation reported long-term liabilities of $11,300. In your homework, list long-term liabilities in the order of their magnitude.

Illustration 2-8 shows the long-term liabilities that Northwest Airlines Corporation reported in its balance sheet.

Illustration 2-8 Long-term liabilities section

NORTHWEST AIRLINES CORPORATION Balance Sheet (partial) (in millions)	
Long-term liabilities	
Long-term debt	$ 7,715
Other liabilities	4,346
Long-term obligations under capital leases	308
Total long-term liabilities	$12,369

STOCKHOLDERS' EQUITY

Stockholders' equity consists of two parts: common stock and retained earnings. Companies record as **common stock** the investments of assets into the business by the stockholders. They record as **retained earnings** the income retained for use in the business. These two parts, combined, make up **stockholders' equity** on the balance sheet. In Illustration 2-2 Franklin reported common stock of $14,000 and retained earnings of $20,050.

Alternative Terminology
Common stock is sometimes called *capital stock.*

BEFORE YOU GO ON . . .

▶Review It

1. What are the major sections in a classified balance sheet?
2. What is the primary determining factor to distinguish current assets from long-term assets?
3. What was Tootsie Roll's largest current asset at December 31, 2004? (The answer to this question appears on page 97.)
4. Where on the balance sheet do companies report accumulated depreciation?

▶Do It

Baxter Hoffman recently received the following information related to Hoffman Corporation's December 31, 2007, balance sheet.

Prepaid expenses	$ 2,300	Inventory	$3,400
Cash	800	Accumulated depreciation	2,700
Property, plant, and equipment	10,700	Accounts receivable	1,100

Prepare the assets section of Hoffman Corporation's balance sheet.

Action Plan

• Present current assets first. Current assets are cash and other resources that the company reasonably expects to consume in one year.
• Present current assets in the order in which the company expects to convert them into cash.
• Subtract accumulated depreciation from property, plant, and equipment to determine net property, plant, and equipment.

Solution

HOFFMAN CORPORATION
Balance Sheet (partial)
December 31, 2007

Assets

Current assets		
Cash	$ 800	
Accounts receivable	1,100	
Inventory	3,400	
Prepaid expenses	2,300	
Total current assets		$ 7,600
Property, plant, and equipment	10,700	
Less: Accumulated depreciation	2,700	8,000
Total assets		$15,600

Using the Financial Statements

In Chapter 1 we introduced the four financial statements. We discussed how these statements provide information about a company's performance and financial position. In this chapter we extend this discussion by showing you specific tools that you can use to analyze financial statements in order to make a more meaningful evaluation of a company.

RATIO ANALYSIS

Ratio analysis expresses the relationship among selected items of financial statement data. A **ratio** expresses the mathematical relationship between one quantity and another. The relationship is expressed in terms of either a percentage, a rate, or a simple proportion.

To illustrate, Best Buy has current assets of $5,724 million and current liabilities of $4,501 million. We can determine a relationship between these accounts by dividing current assets by current liabilities, to get 1.27. The alternative means of expression are:

Percentage: Current assets are 127% of current liabilities.

Rate: Current assets are 1.27 times as great as current liabilities.

Proportion: The relationship of current assets to current liabilities is 1.27:1.

For analysis of the primary financial statements, we classify ratios as follows.

Illustration 2-9 Financial ratio classifications

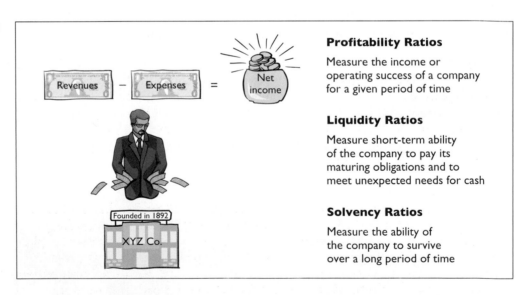

Profitability Ratios

Measure the income or operating success of a company for a given period of time

Liquidity Ratios

Measure short-term ability of the company to pay its maturing obligations and to meet unexpected needs for cash

Solvency Ratios

Measure the ability of the company to survive over a long period of time

Ratios can provide clues to underlying conditions that may not be apparent from examination of the individual items on the financial statements. However, a single ratio by itself is not very meaningful. Accordingly, in this and the following chapters we will use various comparisons to shed light on company performance:

1. **Intracompany comparisons** covering two years for the same company.
2. **Industry-average comparisons** based on average ratios for particular industries.
3. **Intercompany comparisons** based on comparisons with a competitor in the same industry.

USING THE INCOME STATEMENT

Best Buy Company generates profits for its shareholders by selling electronics goods. The income statement reports how successful it is at generating a profit from its sales. The income statement reports the amount earned during the period (revenues) and the costs incurred during the period (expenses). Illustration 2-10 shows a simplified income statement for Best Buy.

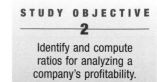

STUDY OBJECTIVE
2
Identify and compute ratios for analyzing a company's profitability.

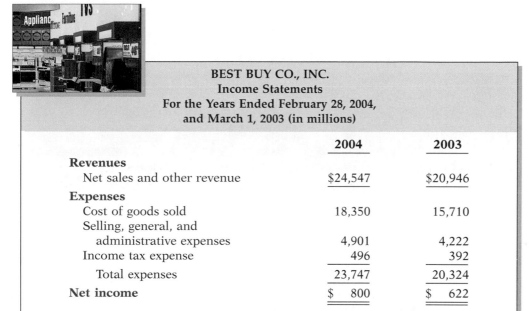

BEST BUY CO., INC.
Income Statements
For the Years Ended February 28, 2004,
and March 1, 2003 (in millions)

	2004	2003
Revenues		
Net sales and other revenue	$24,547	$20,946
Expenses		
Cost of goods sold	18,350	15,710
Selling, general, and administrative expenses	4,901	4,222
Income tax expense	496	392
Total expenses	23,747	20,324
Net income	$ 800	$ 622

Illustration 2-10   Best Buy's income statement

From this income statement we can see that Best Buy's sales and net income both increased during the year. Net income increased from $622,000,000 to $800,000,000. Best Buy's primary competitor is Circuit City. Circuit City reported a net loss of $787,000 for the year ended February 29, 2004.

To evaluate the profitability of Best Buy, we will use ratio analysis. Profitability ratios measure the operating success of a company for a given period of time.

EARNINGS PER SHARE.   Earnings per share (EPS) measures the net income earned on each share of common stock. We compute EPS by dividing **net income** by the **average number of common shares outstanding during the year**. Stockholders usually think in terms of the number of shares they own or plan to buy or sell, so stating net income earned as a per share amount provides a useful perspective for determining the investment return. Advanced accounting courses present more refined techniques for calculating earnings per share.

For now, a basic approach for calculating earnings per share is to divide earnings available to common stockholders by average common shares outstanding during the year. What is "earnings available to common stockholders"? It is an earnings amount calculated as net income less dividends paid on another type of stock, called preferred stock (Net income − Preferred stock dividends).

By comparing earnings per share of **a single company over time**, one can evaluate its relative earnings performance from the perspective of a shareholder—that is, on a per share basis. It is very important to note that comparisons of earnings per share across companies are **not meaningful** because of the wide variations in the numbers of shares of outstanding stock among companies.

Illustration 2-11 shows the earnings per share calculation for Best Buy in 2004 and 2003, based on the information presented below. (Note that to simplify our calculations, we assumed that any change in shares for Best Buy occurred in the middle of the year.)

(in millions)	2004	2003
Net income	$800	$622
Preferred stock dividends	–0–	–0–
Shares outstanding at beginning of year	322	319
Shares outstanding at end of year	325	322

Illustration 2-11 Best Buy earnings per share

$$\text{Earnings per Share} = \frac{\text{Net Income} - \text{Preferred Stock Dividends}}{\text{Average Common Shares Outstanding}}$$

($ and shares in millions)	2004	2003
Earnings per Share	$\frac{\$800 - \$0}{(325 + 322)/2} = \$2.47$	$\frac{\$622 - \$0}{(322 + 319)/2} = \$1.94$

Decision Toolkit

Decision Checkpoints	Info Needed for Decision	Tool to Use for Decision	How to Evaluate Results
How does the company's earnings performance compare with that of previous years?	Net income available to common shareholders and average common shares outstanding	$\text{Earnings per share} = \frac{\text{Net income} - \text{Preferred stock dividends}}{\text{Average common shares outstanding}}$	A higher measure suggests improved performance, although the number is subject to manipulation. Values should not be compared across companies.

USING THE STATEMENT OF STOCKHOLDERS' EQUITY

STUDY OBJECTIVE

3

Explain the relationship between a retained earnings statement and a statement of stockholders' equity.

As discussed in Chapter 1, the retained earnings statement describes the changes in retained earnings during the year. This statement adds net income and then subtracts dividends from the beginning retained earnings to arrive at ending retained earnings.

Recall, however, that stockholders' equity is comprised of two parts: retained earnings and common stock. Therefore, the stockholders' equity of most companies is affected by factors other than just changes in retained earnings. For example, the company may issue or retire shares of common stock. Most companies, therefore, use what is called a **statement of stockholders' equity**, rather than a retained earnings statement, so that they can report **all changes** in stockholders' equity accounts. Illustration 2-12 is a simplified statement of stockholders' equity for Best Buy.

BEST BUY CO., INC.
Statement of Stockholders' Equity
(in millions)

	Common Stock	Retained Earnings
Balances at March 3, 2001	$598	$1,224
Issuance of common stock	135	
Net income		564
Balances at March 2, 2002	733	1,788
Issuance of common stock	77	
Net income		622
Other adjustments		(490)
Balances at March 1, 2003	810	1,920
Issuance of common stock	58	
Net income		800
Dividends		(130)
Other adjustments		(36)
Balances at February 28, 2004	$868	$2,554

We can observe from this financial statement that Best Buy's common stock increased as the result of issuance of common stock in each of the three years. Another observation from this financial statement is that Best Buy paid no dividends until the most recent year. You might wonder why Best Buy paid no dividends during prior years when it was profitable. In fact, in a prior year, two Best Buy shareholders discussed this question about the company's dividend policy on an investor bulletin board. Here are excerpts:

From "Katwoman": "Best Buy has a nice price increase. Earnings are on the way up. But why no dividends?"

From "AngryCandy": "I guess they feel they can make better use of the money by investing back in the business. They still view Best Buy as a rapidly growing company and would prefer to invest in expanding the infrastructure (building new stores, advertising, etc.) than in paying out dividends. . . . If Best Buy gets to the stage of 'stable, big company' with little room for expansion, then I'm sure you'll see them elect to pay out a dividend."

AngryCandy's response is an excellent explanation of the thought process that management goes through in deciding whether to pay a dividend. Management must evaluate what its cash needs are. If it has uses for cash that will increase the value of the company (for example, building a new, centralized warehouse), then it should retain cash in the company. However, if it has more cash than it has valuable opportunities, it should distribute its excess cash as a dividend.

BEFORE YOU GO ON . . .

▶**Review It**

1. What are the three ways that ratios can be expressed?
2. What is the purpose of profitability ratios? Explain earnings per share.
3. What does a statement of stockholders' equity show?

USING A CLASSIFIED BALANCE SHEET

You can learn a lot about a company's financial health by also evaluating the relationship between its various assets and liabilities. Illustration 2-13 provides a simplified balance sheet for Best Buy.

Illustration 2-13 Best Buy's balance sheet

BEST BUY CO., INC.
Balance Sheets
(in millions)

Assets	February 28, 2004	March 1, 2003
Current assets		
Cash and cash equivalents	$2,600	$1,914
Receivables	343	312
Merchandise inventories	2,607	2,077
Other current assets	174	595
Total current assets	5,724	4,898
Property and equipment	3,574	3,089
Less: Accumulated depreciation	1,330	1,027
Net property and equipment	2,244	2,062
Other assets	684	734
Total assets	$8,652	$7,694
Liabilities and Stockholders' Equity		
Current liabilities		
Accounts payable	$2,535	$2,195
Accrued liabilities	949	760
Accrued income taxes	380	374
Other current liabilities	368	321
Accrued compensation payable	269	174
Total current liabilities	4,501	3,824
Long-term liabilities		
Long-term debt	482	828
Other long-term liabilities	247	312
Total long-term liabilities	729	1,140
Total liabilities	5,230	4,964
Stockholders' equity		
Common stock	868	810
Retained earnings	2,554	1,920
Total stockholders' equity	3,422	2,730
Total liabilities and stockholders' equity	$8,652	$7,694

Liquidity

Suppose you are a banker at CitiGroup considering lending money to Best Buy, or you are a sales manager at Hewlett-Packard interested in selling computers to Best Buy on credit. You would be concerned about Best Buy's liquidity—its ability to pay obligations expected to become due within the next year or operating cycle. You would look closely at the relationship of its current assets to current liabilities.

WORKING CAPITAL.   One measure of liquidity is working capital, which is the difference between the amounts of current assets and current liabilities:

Illustration 2-14   Working capital

$$\text{Working Capital} = \text{Current Assets} - \text{Current Liabilities}$$

When working capital is positive, current assets exceed current liabilities. When this occurs, there is greater likelihood that the company will pay its liabilities. When working capital is negative, a company might not be able to pay short-term creditors, and the company might ultimately be forced into bankruptcy. Best Buy had working capital in 2004 of $1,223,000,000 ($5,724,000,000 − $4,501,000,000).

CURRENT RATIO.   Liquidity ratios measure the short-term ability of the enterprise to pay its maturing obligations and to meet unexpected needs for cash. One liquidity ratio is the current ratio, computed as current assets divided by current liabilities.

The current ratio is a more dependable indicator of liquidity than working capital. Two companies with the same amount of working capital may have significantly different current ratios. Illustration 2-15 shows the 2004 and 2003 current ratios for Best Buy and for Circuit City, along with the 2004 industry average.

Illustration 2-15   Current ratio

$$\text{Current Ratio} = \frac{\text{Current Assets}}{\text{Current Liabilities}}$$

	2004	2003
Best Buy ($ in millions)	$\frac{\$5,724}{\$4,501} = 1.27:1$	$\frac{\$4,898}{\$3,824} = 1.28:1$
Circuit City	2.48:1	2.42:1
Industry average	1.40:1	

What does the ratio actually mean? Best Buy's 2004 current ratio of 1.27:1 means that for every dollar of current liabilities, Best Buy has $1.27 of current assets. Best Buy's current ratio decreased slightly in 2004. When compared to the industry average of 1.40:1, and Circuit City's 2.48:1 current ratio, Best Buy's liquidity needs further investigation.

The current ratio is only one measure of liquidity. It does not take into account the **composition** of the current assets. For example, a satisfactory current ratio does not disclose whether a portion of the current assets is tied up in slow-moving inventory. The composition of the assets matters because a dollar of cash is more readily available to pay the bills than is a dollar of inventory. For example, suppose a company's cash balance declined while its merchandise inventory increased substantially. If inventory increased because the company is having difficulty selling its products, then the current ratio might not fully reflect the reduction in the company's liquidity.

Accounting across the Organization

There actually is a point where a company can be too liquid—that is, it can have too much working capital. While it is important to be liquid enough to be able to pay short-term bills as they come due, a company does not want to tie up its cash in extra inventory or receivables that are not earning the company money.

By one estimate from the REL Consultancy Group, U.S. companies have on their books cumulative excess working capital of nearly $600 billion (K. Richardson, "Ignored Money Waiting to Be Spent," *Wall Street Journal*, August 30, 2004, p. C3). Based on this figure, companies could have reduced debt by 36 percent or increased net income by 9 percent. Given that managers throughout a company are interested in improving profitability, it is clear that they should have an eye toward managing working capital. They need to aim for a "Goldilocks solution"—not too much, not too little, but just right.

 What can various company managers do to ensure that working capital is managed efficiently (so as to maximize net income)?

Solvency

Now suppose that instead of being a short-term creditor, you are interested in either buying Best Buy's stock or extending the company a long-term loan. Long-term creditors and stockholders are interested in a company's long-run **solvency**—its ability to pay interest as it comes due and to repay the balance of a debt due at its maturity. **Solvency ratios** measure the ability of the enterprise to survive over a long period of time.

DEBT TO TOTAL ASSETS RATIO.   The **debt to total assets ratio** is one source of information about long-term debt-paying ability. It measures the percentage of assets financed by creditors rather than stockholders. Debt financing is more risky than equity financing because debt must be repaid at specific points in time, whether the company is performing well or not. Thus, the higher the percentage of debt financing, the riskier the company.

We compute the debt to total assets ratio as total debt (both current and long-term liabilities) divided by total assets. The higher the percentage of total liabilities (debt) to total assets, the greater the risk that the company may be unable to pay its debts as they come due. Illustration 2-16 (page 61) shows the debt to total assets ratios for Best Buy and Circuit City, along with the 2004 industry average.

The 2004 ratio of 60% means that Best Buy's creditors provided $0.60 of every dollar invested in assets by Best Buy. Best Buy's ratio exceeds the industry average of 15% and Circuit City's ratio of 39%. The higher the ratio, the lower the equity "buffer" available to creditors if the company becomes insolvent. Thus, from the creditors' point of view, a high ratio of debt to total assets is undesirable. Best Buy's solvency appears lower than that of Circuit City and lower than the average company in the industry.

Helpful Hint Some users evaluate solvency using a ratio of liabilities divided by stockholders' equity. The higher this "debt to equity" ratio, the lower is a company's solvency.

Illustration 2-16   Debt to total assets ratio

Debt to Total Assets Ratio = $\dfrac{\text{Total Liabilities}}{\text{Total Assets}}$		
	2004	**2003**
Best Buy ($ in millions)	$\dfrac{\$5,230}{\$8,652} = 60\%$	$\dfrac{\$4,964}{\$7,694} = 65\%$
Circuit City	39%	38%
Industry average	15%	

The adequacy of this ratio is often judged in the light of the company's earnings. Generally, companies with relatively stable earnings, such as public utilities, can support higher debt to total assets ratios than can cyclical companies with widely fluctuating earnings, such as many high-tech companies. In later chapters you will learn additional ways to evaluate solvency.

Business Insight
INVESTOR PERSPECTIVE

Debt financing differs greatly across industries and companies. Here are some debt to total assets ratios for selected companies:

	Debt to Total Assets Ratio
American Pharmaceutical Partners	19%
Callaway Golf Company	20%
Microsoft	21%
Sears Holdings Corporation	73%
Eastman Kodak Company	78%
General Motors Corporation	94%

 Discuss the difference in the debt to total assets ratio of Microsoft and General Motors.

Decision Toolkit

Decision Checkpoints	Info Needed for Decision	Tool to Use for Decision	How to Evaluate Results
Can the company meet its near-term obligations?	Current assets and current liabilities	Current ratio = $\dfrac{\text{Current assets}}{\text{Current liabilities}}$	Higher ratio suggests favorable liquidity.
Can the company meet its long-term obligations?	Total debt and total assets	Debt to total assets ratio = $\dfrac{\text{Total liabilities}}{\text{Total assets}}$	Lower value suggests favorable solvency.

BEFORE YOU GO ON . . .

▶Review It

1. What is liquidity? How can it be measured using a classified balance sheet?
2. What is solvency? How can it be measured using a classified balance sheet?

▶Do It

Selected financial data for Drummond Company at December 31, 2007, are as follows: cash $60,000; receivables (net) $80,000; inventory $70,000; total assets $540,000; current liabilities $140,000; and total liabilities $270,000. Compute the current ratio and debt to total assets ratio.

Action Plan

- Use the formula for the current ratio: Current assets ÷ Current liabilities.
- Use the formula for the debt to total assets ratio: Total liabilities ÷ Total assets.

Solution

The current ratio is 1.5 : 1 ($210,000 ÷ $140,000). The debt to total assets ratio is 50% ($270,000 ÷ $540,000).

THE NAVIGATOR

USING THE STATEMENT OF CASH FLOWS

STUDY OBJECTIVE
5
Use the statement of cash flows to evaluate solvency.

As you learned in Chapter 1, the statement of cash flows provides financial information about the sources and uses of a company's cash. Investors, creditors, and others want to know what is happening to a company's most liquid resource—its cash. In fact, people often say that "cash is king" because if a company cannot generate cash, it will not survive. To aid in the analysis of cash, the statement of cash flows reports the cash effects of (1) a company's **operating activities**, (2) its **investing activities**, and (3) its **financing activities**.

Sources of cash matter. For example, you would feel much better about a company's health if you knew that the company generates its cash from the operations of the business rather than borrows it. A cash flow statement provides this information. Similarly, net income does not tell you *how much* cash the company generated from operations. The statement of cash flows can tell you that. In summary, neither the income statement nor the balance sheet directly answers most of the important questions about cash, but the statement of cash flows does. Illustration 2-17 (page 63) shows a simplified statement of cash flows for Best Buy.

Different users have different reasons for being interested in the statement of cash flows. If you were a creditor of Best Buy (either short term or long term), you would be interested to know the source of its cash in recent years. This information would give you some indication of where it might get cash to pay you. If you have a long-term interest in Best Buy as a stockholder, you would look to the statement of cash flows for information regarding the company's ability to generate cash over the long run to meet its cash needs for growth.

Companies get cash from two sources: operating activities and financing activities. In the early years of a company's life it typically will not generate enough cash from operating activities to meet its investing needs, so it will have to issue stock or borrow money. An established company, however, will often be able to meet most of its cash needs with cash from operations. Best Buy's cash provided by operating activities during these two years was sufficient to meet its needs for acquisitions of property, plant, and equipment. For example, in 2004 cash provided by operating activities was $1,414,000,000, whereas cash spent on property, plant, and equipment was $545,000,000.

Illustration 2-17 Best Buy's statement of cash flows

BEST BUY CO., INC.
Statement of Cash Flows
(in millions)

	For fiscal year ending	
	February 28, 2004	March 1, 2003
Cash flows provided by operating activities		
Cash receipts from operating activities	$24,520	$20,857
Cash payments for operating activities	23,106	20,111
Net cash provided (used) by operations	1,414	746
Cash flows provided by investing activities		
(Increase) decrease in property and plant	(545)	(725)
Other cash inflow (outflow)	(50)	(13)
Net cash provided (used) by investing	(595)	(738)
Cash flows provided by financing activities		
Issue of equity securities	114	40
Increase (decrease) in borrowing	(17)	5
Dividends	(130)	0
Repurchase of common stock	(100)	0
Net cash provided (used) by financing	(133)	45
Net increase (decrease) in cash and equivalents	686	53
Cash and equivalents at start of year	1,914	1,861
Cash and equivalents at year-end	$ 2,600	$ 1,914

FREE CASH FLOW.   In the statement of cash flows, cash provided by operating activities is intended to indicate the cash-generating capability of the company. Analysts have noted, however, that **cash provided by operating activities fails to take into account that a company must invest in new property, plant, and equipment** (capital expenditures) just to maintain its current level of operations. Companies also must at least **maintain dividends at current levels** to satisfy investors. A measurement to provide additional insight regarding a company's cash-generating ability is free cash flow. Free cash flow describes the cash remaining from operations after adjusting for capital expenditures and dividends.

Consider the following example: Suppose that MPC produced and sold 10,000 personal computers this year. It reported $100,000 cash provided by operating activities. In order to maintain production at 10,000 computers, MPC invested $15,000 in equipment. It chose to pay $5,000 in dividends. Its free cash flow was $80,000 ($100,000 − $15,000 − $5,000). The company could use this $80,000 to purchase new assets to expand the business, to pay off debts, or to increase its dividend distribution. In practice, analysts often calculate free cash flow with the formula in Illustration 2-18. Alternative definitions also exist.

Illustration 2-18 Free cash flow

$$\text{Free Cash Flow} = \text{Cash Provided by Operations} - \text{Capital Expenditures} - \text{Cash Dividends}$$

Illustration 2-19 shows calculation of Best Buy's free cash flow.

Illustration 2-19
Calculation of Best Buy's
free cash flow ($ in
millions)

Cash provided by operating activities	$1,414
Less: Expenditures on property, plant, and equipment	545
Dividends paid	130
Free cash flow	$ 739

Best Buy generated free cash flow of $739 million which is available for the acquisition of new assets, the retirement of stock or debt, or the payment of additional dividends. Long-term creditors consider a high free cash flow amount an indication of solvency. Circuit City's free cash flow for 2004 is a negative $322 million. This lack of free cash flow calls into question Circuit City's ability to repay its long-term obligations as they come due.

Decision Toolkit

Decision Checkpoints	Info Needed for Decision	Tool to Use for Decision	How to Evaluate Results
How much cash did the company generate to expand operations, pay off debts, or distribute dividends?	Cash provided by operating activities, cash spent on fixed assets, and cash dividends	$$\text{Free cash flow} = \text{Cash provided by operations} - \text{Capital expenditures} - \text{Cash dividends}$$	Significant free cash flow indicates greater potential to finance new investment and pay additional dividends.

BEFORE YOU GO ON . . .

▶Review It

1. What information does the statement of cash flows provide that is not available in an income statement or a balance sheet?
2. What does free cash flow measure?

THE NAVIGATOR

SECTION TWO
FINANCIAL REPORTING CONCEPTS

In Chapter 1 you learned about the four financial statements, and in this chapter we introduced you to some basic ways to interpret those statements. In this last section we will discuss concepts that underly these financial statements. It would be unwise to make business decisions based on financial statements without understanding the implications of these concepts.

STUDY OBJECTIVE
6

Explain the meaning of
generally accepted
accounting principles.

The Standard-Setting Environment

How does a company like Best Buy decide on the amount and type of financial information to disclose? What format should it use? How should it measure assets, liabilities, revenues, and expenses? The answers to these questions are found in accounting guidelines referred to as **generally accepted accounting principles (GAAP)**. Various standard-setting bodies, in consultation with the accounting profession and the business community, determine these guidelines.

The **Securities and Exchange Commission (SEC)** is the agency of the U.S. government that oversees U.S. financial markets and accounting standard-setting bodies. The primary accounting standard-setting body in the United States is the **Financial Accounting Standards Board (FASB)**. Many countries outside of the United States have adopted the accounting standards issued by the **International Accounting Standards Board (IASB)**. In recent years the FASB and IASB have worked closely to try to minimize the differences in their standards.

CHARACTERISTICS OF USEFUL INFORMATION

In establishing guidelines for reporting financial information, the FASB believes that the overriding consideration should be the generation of financial information useful for making business decisions. To be useful, information should possess these characteristics: relevance, reliability, comparability, and consistency.

Relevance

Accounting information is **relevant** if it would make a difference in a business decision. For example, the information in Best Buy's financial statements is considered relevant because it provides a basis for forecasting Best Buy's future earnings. Accounting information is also relevant to business decisions because it confirms or corrects prior expectations. Financial statements provide relevant information that helps **predict** future events and **provide feedback** about prior expectations for the financial health of the company.

> **STUDY OBJECTIVE**
> **7**
> Discuss financial reporting concepts.

For accounting information to be relevant it must be **timely**. That is, it must be available to decision makers before it loses its capacity to influence decisions. The SEC requires that public companies provide their annual reports to investors within 60 days of their year-end.

Reliability

Reliability of information means that the information can be depended on. To be reliable, accounting information must be **verifiable**—we must be able to prove that it is free of error. Also, the information must be a **faithful representation** of what it purports to be—it must be factual. If Best Buy's income statement reports sales of $20 billion when it actually had sales of $10 billion, then the statement is not a faithful representation of Best Buy's financial performance. Finally, accounting information must be **neutral**—it cannot be selected, prepared, or presented to favor one set of interested users over another. As noted in Chapter 1, to ensure reliability, certified public accountants audit financial statements.

Comparability

In accounting, **comparability** results when different companies use the same accounting principles. U.S. accounting standards are relatively comparable because they are based on certain basic principles and assumptions. However, these principles and assumptions allow for some variation in methods. For example, there are a variety of ways to report inventory. Often these different methods result in different amounts of net income. To make comparison across companies easier, each company **must disclose** the accounting methods used.

Accounting across the Organization

Another issue related to comparability is the accounting time period. An accounting period that is one-year long is called a **fiscal year**. But a fiscal year need not match the calendar year. For example, a company could end its fiscal year on April 30, rather than December 31.

Why do companies choose the particular year-ends that they do? For example, why doesn't every company use December 31 as the accounting year-end? Many companies choose to end their accounting year when inventory or operations are at a low. This is advantageous because compiling accounting information requires much time and effort by managers, so they would rather do it when they aren't as busy operating the business. Also, inventory is easier and less costly to count when its volume is low.

Some companies whose year-ends differ from December 31 are Delta Air Lines, June 30; Walt Disney Productions, September 30; and Dunkin' Donuts, Inc., October 31. In the notes to its financial statements, Best Buy states that its accounting year-end is the Saturday nearest the end of February.

 What problems might Best Buy's year-end create for analysts?

Consistency

To compare Best Buy's net income over several years, you would need to know that it used the same accounting principles from year to year. **Consistency** means that a company uses the same accounting principles and methods from year to year. Thus, if a company selects one inventory accounting method in the first year of operations, it is expected to continue to use that same method in succeeding years.

A company *can* change to a new method of accounting if management can justify that the new method produces more useful financial information. In the year in which the change occurs, the change must be disclosed in the notes to the financial statements so that users of the statements are aware of the lack of consistency.

Illustration 2-20 summarizes the characteristics that make accounting information useful.

Illustration 2-20
Characteristics of useful information

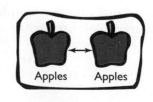

Relevance
1. Provides a basis for forecasts
2. Confirms or corrects prior expectations
3. Is timely

Reliability
1. Is verifiable
2. Is a faithful representation
3. Is neutral

Comparability
Different companies use similar accounting principles

Consistency
Company uses same accounting methods from year to year

ASSUMPTIONS AND PRINCIPLES IN FINANCIAL REPORTING

To develop accounting standards, the FASB relies on some key assumptions and principles.

Monetary Unit Assumption

The monetary unit assumption requires that only those things that can be expressed in money are included in the accounting records. Because the exchange of money is fundamental to business transactions, it makes sense that we measure a business in terms of money.

However, the monetary unit assumption also means that certain important information needed by investors, creditors, and managers is not reported in the financial statements. For example, customer satisfaction is important to every business, but it is not easily quantified in dollar terms; thus it is not reported in the financial statements.

Economic Entity Assumption

The economic entity assumption states that every economic entity can be separately identified and accounted for. For example, suppose you are a stockholder of Best Buy. The amount of cash you have in your personal bank account and the balance owed on your personal car loan are not reported in Best Buy's balance sheet. In order to accurately assess Best Buy's performance and financial position, it is important that we not blur it with your personal transactions, or the transactions of any other person (especially its managers) or company.

Time Period Assumption

Next, notice that the income statement, retained earnings statement, and statement of cash flows all cover periods of one year, and the balance sheet is prepared at the end of each year. The time period assumption states that the life of a business can be divided into artificial time periods and that useful reports covering those periods can be prepared for the business. All companies report financial results at least annually. Many also report every three months (quarterly) to stockholders, and many prepare monthly statements for internal purposes.

Going Concern Assumption

The going concern assumption states that the business will remain in operation for the foreseeable future. Of course many businesses do fail, but in general, it is reasonable to assume that the business will continue operating. If going concern is not assumed, then the company should state plant assets at their liquidation value (selling price less cost of disposal), rather than at their cost. Only when liquidation of the business appears likely is the going concern assumption inappropriate.

Illustration 2-21 (page 68) shows these four accounting assumptions graphically.

Cost Principle

The cost principle dictates that assets be recorded at their cost. This is true not only at the time the asset is purchased, but also over the time the asset is held. For example, if Best Buy were to purchase some land for $30,000, the company would initially report it on the balance sheet at $30,000. But what would Best Buy do if, by the end of the next year, the land had increased in value to $40,000?

Illustration 2-21
Accounting assumptions

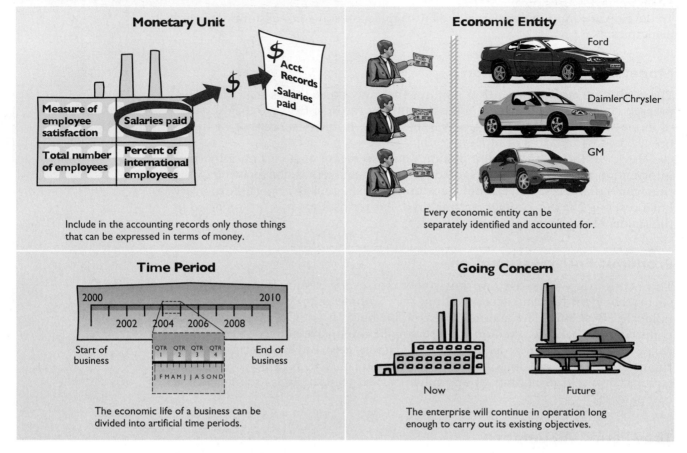

Under the cost principle the company would continue to report the land at $30,000.

The cost principle is often criticized as being irrelevant. Critics contend that market value would be more useful to financial decision makers. Proponents of the cost principle counter that cost is the best measure because it can be easily verified from transactions between two parties, whereas market value is often subjective. Recently, the FASB has changed some accounting rules requiring that certain investment securities be recorded at their market value. In choosing between cost and market value, the FASB weighed the reliability of cost figures versus the relevance of market value.

Full Disclosure Principle

The **full disclosure principle** requires that companies disclose all circumstances and events that would make a difference to financial statement users. Some important financial information is not easily reported on the face of the statements. For example, Best Buy has debt outstanding. Investors and creditors would like to know the terms of the debt; that is, when does it mature, what is its interest rate, and is it renewable? Or Best Buy might be sued by one of its customers. Investors and creditors might not know about this lawsuit. If an important item cannot reasonably be reported directly in one of the four types of financial statements, then it should be discussed in notes that accompany the statements. Some investors who lost money in Enron, WorldCom, and Global Crossing complained that the lack of full disclosure regarding some of the companies' transactions caused the financial statements to be misleading.

Illustration 2-22 depicts these two accounting principles.

Illustration 2-22
Accounting principles

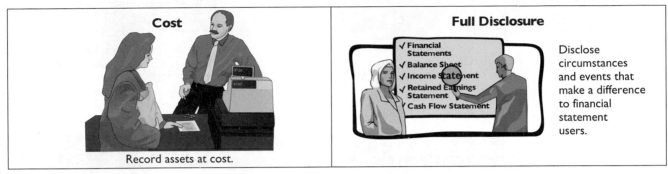

CONSTRAINTS IN ACCOUNTING

Taken to the extreme, efforts to provide useful financial information could be far too costly to a company. Therefore, the profession has agreed upon **constraints** to ensure that companies apply accounting rules in a reasonable fashion, from the perspectives of both the company and the user. The constraints are materiality and conservatism.

Materiality

Materiality relates to a financial statement item's impact on a company's overall financial condition and operations. An item is **material** when its **size** makes it likely to influence the decision of an investor or creditor. It is **immaterial** if it is too small to impact a decision maker. In short, if the item does not make a difference, the company does not have to follow GAAP in reporting it. To determine the materiality of an amount—that is, to determine its financial significance—the company compares the item with such items as total assets, sales revenue, and net income.

To illustrate, assume that Best Buy made a $100 error in recording revenue. Best Buy's total revenue is $24.5 billion; thus a $100 error is not material.

Conservatism

Conservatism in accounting means that when preparing financial statements, a company should choose the accounting method that will be least likely to overstate assets or income. It **does not mean, however, that a company should intentionally understate assets or income**.

A common application of the conservatism constraint is in valuing inventories. Companies normally record inventories at their cost. Conservatism, however, requires that companies write down inventories to market value if market value is below cost. Conservatism also requires that when the market value of inventory exceeds cost, the company should not increase the value of the inventory on the books, but instead keep it at cost. This practice results in lower net income on the income statement and a lower amount reported for inventory on the balance sheet.

Illustration 2-23 (page 70) graphically depicts the two constraints.

Illustration 2-23
Accounting constraints

Materiality	Conservatism

Companies do not have to follow GAAP for small amounts.	When in doubt, choose the solution that will be least likely to overstate assets and income.

BEFORE YOU GO ON . . .

▶Review It

1. What are generally accepted accounting principles?
2. What is the basic objective of financial information?
3. What qualitative characteristics make accounting information useful?
4. What are the materiality constraint and the conservatism constraint?

Using the Decision Toolkit

In this chapter we have evaluated a home electronics giant, Best Buy. Tweeter Home Entertainment sells consumer electronics products from 154 stores on the East Coast under various names. It specializes in products with high-end features. Illustrations 2-24 and 2-25 show a simplified balance sheet and income statement for Tweeter Home Entertainment. Additional information: Tweeter's cash provided by operating activities was $41,508,000 in 2004 and $10,307,000 in 2003. Its capital expenditures were $19,485,000 in 2004 and $24,188,000 in 2003. The company paid no dividends in either year. Assume that average shares outstanding during all of fiscal 2004 were 24.2 million and were 23.7 million during all of fiscal 2003. There was no preferred stock outstanding.

Instructions
Using these statements, answer the following questions.

1. Calculate the current ratio for Tweeter for 2004 and 2003 and discuss its liquidity position.
2. Calculate the debt to total assets ratio and free cash flow for Tweeter for 2004 and 2003 and discuss its solvency.
3. Calculate the earnings per share for Tweeter for 2004 and 2003, and discuss its change in profitability.
4. Best Buy's accounting year-end was February 28, 2004; Tweeter's was September 30, 2004. How does this difference affect your ability to compare their profitability?

Tweeter

TWEETER HOME ENTERTAINMENT GROUP
Balance Sheets
(in millions)

	September 30	
	2004	**2003**
Assets		
Current assets		
Cash and cash equivalents	$ 2.8	$ 1.9
Receivables	25.6	24.2
Inventories	106.6	117.6
Other current assets	17.0	26.9
Total current assets	152.0	170.6
Property, plant, and equipment, net	124.9	126.2
Other assets	24.3	11.6
Total assets	$301.2	$308.4
Liabilities and Stockholders' Equity		
Current liabilities		
Note payable	$ 3.2	$ 7.4
Accounts payable	70.0	55.2
Other current liabilities	22.5	21.4
Total current liabilities	95.7	84.0
Long-term debt	35.0	48.3
Other liabilities	14.1	11.1
Total liabilities	144.8	143.4
Stockholders' equity	156.4	165.0
Total liabilities and stockholders' equity	$301.2	$308.4

Illustration 2-24 Tweeter Home Entertainment's balance sheet

Tweeter

TWEETER HOME ENTERTAINMENT GROUP
Income Statements
(in millions)

	Years ended September 30	
	2004	**2003**
Sales	$778.2	$787.0
Cost of sales	476.2	516.9
Operating expenses	324.3	286.8
Interest expense	3.3	2.8
Other expense/(income)	(1.2)	(0.7)
Income tax expense (benefit)	(9.3)	(7.1)
Total expenses	793.3	798.7
Net loss	$ (15.1)	$ (11.7)

Illustration 2-25 Tweeter Home Entertainment's income statement

Solution

1. Current ratio:

$$2004\ (\$152.0/\$95.7) = 1.59 \qquad 2003\ (\$170.6/\$84.0) = 2.03$$

Tweeter's liquidity declined from 2003 to 2004. In 2003 there was $2.03 of current assets available for every dollar of current liabilities. In 2004 there was $1.59. Analysts probably would consider Tweeter's 2004 current ratio acceptable, but not strong. It is higher than that of Best Buy, but Tweeter is a much smaller company than Best Buy. Often, larger companies can get by with a lower current ratio.

2. Debt to total assets ratio:

$$2004\ (\$144.8/\$301.2) = 48\% \qquad 2003\ (\$143.4/\$308.4) = 46\%$$

Based on the change in its ratio of debt to total assets, Tweeter's reliance on debt financing increased slightly from 2003 to 2004. The increase in the value of this ratio suggests the company's solvency declined.

Free cash flow:

$$2004 \quad \$41,508,000 - \$19,485,000 - 0 = \$22,023,000$$

$$2003 \quad \$10,307,000 - \$24,188,000 - 0 = -\$13,881,000$$

Tweeter's free cash flow improved from a negative $13.9 million in 2003 to positive $22 million in 2004. Thus, although the debt to total assets ratio increased, the company's improved free cash flow suggests an improved ability to repay its long-term debt.

3. Loss per share:

$$2004\ (\$15.1/24.2) = \$0.62 \text{ per share} \qquad 2003\ (\$11.7/23.7) = \$0.49 \text{ per share}$$

Tweeter's loss per share increased from $0.49 to $0.62.

4. Tweeter's income statement covers seven months not covered by Best Buy's. Suppose that the economy changed dramatically during this seven-month period, either improving or declining. This change in the economy would be reflected in Tweeter's income statement but would not be reflected in Best Buy's income statement until the following March, thus reducing the usefulness of a comparison of the income statements of the two companies.

THE NAVIGATOR

Summary of Study Objectives

WILEY PLUS

1 *Identify the sections of a classified balance sheet.* In a classified balance sheet, companies classify assets as current assets; long-term investments; property, plant, and equipment; and intangibles. They classify liabilities as either current or long-term. A stockholders' equity section shows common stock and retained earnings.

2 *Identify and compute ratios for analyzing a company's profitability.* Profitability ratios, such as earnings per share (EPS), measure aspects of the operating success of a company for a given period of time.

3 *Explain the relationship between a retained earnings statement and a statement of stockholders' equity.* The retained earnings statement presents the factors that

changed the retained earnings balance during the period. A statement of stockholders' equity presents the factors that changed stockholders' equity during the period, including those that changed retained earnings. Thus, a statement of stockholders' equity is more inclusive.

4 *Identify and compute ratios for analyzing a company's liquidity and solvency using a balance sheet.* Liquidity ratios, such as the current ratio, measure the short-term ability of a company to pay its maturing obligations and to meet unexpected needs for cash. Solvency ratios, such as the debt to total assets ratio, measure the ability of an enterprise to survive over a long period.

5 *Use the statement of cash flows to evaluate solvency.* Free cash flow indicates a company's ability to generate cash from operations that is sufficient to pay debts, acquire assets, and distribute dividends.

6 *Explain the meaning of generally accepted accounting principles.* Generally accepted accounting principles are a set of rules and practices recognized as a general guide for financial reporting purposes. The basic objective of financial reporting is to provide information that is useful for decision making.

7 *Discuss financial reporting concepts.* To be judged useful, information should have relevance, reliability, comparability, and consistency.

The *monetary unit assumption* requires that companies include in the accounting records only transaction data that can be expressed in terms of money. The *economic entity assumption* states that economic events can be identified with a particular unit of accountability. The *time period assumption* states that the economic life of a business can be divided into artificial time periods and that meaningful accounting reports can be prepared for each period. The *going concern assumption* states that the enterprise will continue in operation long enough to carry out its existing objectives and commitments.

The *cost principle* states that companies should record assets at their cost. The *full disclosure principle* dictates that companies disclose circumstances and events that matter to financial statement users.

The major constraints are materiality and conservatism.

Decision Toolkit—A Summary

Decision Checkpoints ✔	Info Needed for Decision	Tool to Use for Decision	How to Evaluate Results
How does the company's earnings performance compare with that of previous years?	Net income available to common shareholders and average common shares outstanding	$\text{Earnings per share} = \dfrac{\text{Net income} - \text{Preferred stock dividends}}{\text{Average common shares outstanding}}$	A higher measure suggests improved performance, although the number is subject to manipulation. Values should not be compared across companies.
Can the company meet its near-term obligations?	Current assets and current liabilities	$\text{Current ratio} = \dfrac{\text{Current assets}}{\text{Current liabilities}}$	Higher ratio suggests favorable liquidity.
Can the company meet its long-term obligations?	Total debt and total assets	$\text{Debt to total assets ratio} = \dfrac{\text{Total liabilities}}{\text{Total assets}}$	Lower value suggests favorable solvency.
How much cash did the company generate to expand operations, pay off debts, or distribute dividends?	Cash provided by operating activities, cash spent on fixed assets, and cash dividends	$\text{Free cash flow} = \text{Cash provided by operations} - \text{Capital expenditures} - \text{Cash dividends}$	Significant free cash flow indicates greater potential to finance new investment and pay additional dividends.

Glossary

Classified balance sheet A balance sheet that contains a number of standard classifications or sections. (p. 48)

Comparability Ability to compare the accounting information of different companies because they use the same accounting principles. (p. 65)

Conservatism The approach of choosing an accounting method, when in doubt, that will least likely overstate assets and net income. (p. 69)

Consistency Use of the same accounting principles and methods from year to year within a company. (p. 66)

Cost principle An accounting principle that states that companies should record assets at their cost. (p. 67)

Current assets Cash and other resources that companies reasonably expect to convert to cash or use up within one year or the operating cycle, whichever is longer. (p. 49)

Current liabilities Obligations that companies reasonably expect to pay within the next year or operating cycle, whichever is longer. (p. 52)

Current ratio A measure used to evaluate a company's liquidity and short-term debt-paying ability; computed as current assets divided by current liabilities. (p. 59)

Debt to total assets ratio   Measures the percentage of total financing provided by creditors; computed as total debt divided by total assets. (p. 60)

Earnings per share (EPS)   A measure of the net income earned on each share of common stock; computed as net income minus preferred stock dividends divided by the average number of common shares outstanding during the year. (p. 55)

Economic entity assumption   An assumption that economic events can be identified with a particular unit of accountability. (p. 67).

Financial Accounting Standards Board (FASB)   The primary accounting standard-setting body in the United States. (p. 65)

Free cash flow   Cash provided by operating activities adjusted for capital expenditures and dividends paid. (p. 63)

Full disclosure principle   Accounting principle that dictates that companies disclose circumstances and events that make a difference to financial statements users. (p. 68)

Generally accepted accounting principles (GAAP)   A set of rules and practices, having substantial authoritative support, that the accounting profession recognizes as a general guide for financial reporting purposes. (p. 65)

Going concern assumption   The assumption that the enterprise will continue in operation for the foreseeable future. (p. 67).

Intangible assets   Assets that do not have physical substance. (p. 51)

International Accounting Standards Board (IASB)   An accounting standard-setting body that issues standards adopted by many countries outside of the United States. (p. 65)

Liquidity   The ability of a company to pay obligations that are expected to become due within the next year or operating cycle. (p. 59)

Liquidity ratios   Measures of the short-term ability of the company to pay its maturing obligations and to meet unexpected needs for cash. (p. 59)

Long-term investments   Generally, investments in stocks and bonds of other companies that companies normally hold for many years. Also includes long-term assets, such as land and buildings, not currently being used in the company's operations. (p. 50)

Long-term liabilities (Long-term debt)   Obligations that companies do not expect to pay within one year or the operating cycle. (p. 52)

Materiality   The constraint of determining whether an item is large enough to likely influence the decision of an investor or creditor. (p. 69)

Monetary unit assumption   An assumption that requires that only those things that can be expressed in money are included in the accounting records. (p. 67)

Operating cycle   The average time required to go from cash to cash in producing revenues. (p. 50)

Profitability ratios   Measures of the income or operating success of a company for a given period of time. (p. 55)

Property, plant, and equipment   Assets of a relatively permanent nature that companies use in the business and are not intended for resale. (p. 51)

Ratio   An expression of the mathematical relationship between one quantity and another; may be expressed as a percentage, a rate, or a proportion. (p. 54)

Ratio analysis   A technique for evaluating financial statements that expresses the relationship among selected financial statement data. (p. 54)

Relevance   The quality of information that indicates the information makes a difference in a decision. (p. 65)

Reliability   The quality of information that gives assurance that it is free of error and bias. (p. 65)

Securities and Exchange Commission (SEC)   The agency of the U.S. government that oversees U.S. financial markets and accounting standard-setting bodies. (p. 65)

Solvency   The ability of a company to pay interest as it comes due and to repay the face value of debt at maturity. (p. 60)

Solvency ratios   Measures of the ability of the company to survive over a long period of time. (p. 60)

Statement of stockholders' equity   A financial statement that presents the factors that caused stockholders' equity to change during the period, including those that caused retained earnings to change. (p. 56)

Time period assumption   An assumption that the life of a business can be divided into artificial time periods and that useful reports covering those periods can be prepared for the business. (p. 67)

Working capital   The difference between the amounts of current assets and current liabilities. (p. 59)

Demonstration Problem

Listed here are items taken from the income statement and balance sheet of Circuit City Stores, Inc. for the year ended February 29, 2004. Certain items have been combined for simplification. Amounts are given in millions.

Long-term debt, excluding current installments	$ 22.7
Cash and cash equivalents	783.5
Selling, general, and administrative expenses	2,259.5
Common stock	1,024.6

Accounts payable	$ 879.6
Prepaid expenses and other current assets	464.3
Property and equipment, net	585.9
Cost of goods sold	7,518.1
Current portion of long-term debt	1.1
Income taxes payable	161.4
Interest expense	1.8
Other long-term liabilities	209.6
Retained earnings	1,199.4
Merchandise inventory	1,517.3
Net sales and operating revenues	9,778.1
Accounts and notes receivable, net	154.0
Income tax (benefit)	(0.5)
Other assets	128.0
Accrued expenses and other current liabilities	134.6

Instructions

Prepare an income statement and a classified balance sheet using the items listed. Do not use any item more than once.

Solution

CIRCUIT CITY STORES, INC.
Income Statement
For the Year Ended February 29, 2004
(in millions)

Net sales and operating revenues		$9,778.1
Cost of goods sold	$7,518.1	
Selling, general, and administrative expenses	2,259.5	
Interest expense	1.8	
Income tax (benefit)	(0.5)	
Total expenses		9,778.9
Net loss		$ (0.8)

CIRCUIT CITY STORES, INC.
Balance Sheet
February 29, 2004
(in millions)

Assets

Current assets		
Cash and cash equivalents	$ 783.5	
Accounts and notes receivable, net	154.0	
Merchandise inventory	1,517.3	
Prepaid expenses and other current assets	464.3	
Total current assets		$2,919.1
Property and equipment, net		585.9
Other assets		128.0
Total assets		$3,633.0

Action Plan

- In preparing the income statement, list revenues, then expenses.
- In preparing a classified balance sheet, list current assets in order of liquidity.

CIRCUIT CITY STORES, INC.
Balance Sheet
February 29, 2004
(in millions)

Liabilities and Stockholders' Equity

Current liabilities		
Accounts payable	$ 879.6	
Income taxes payable	161.4	
Accrued expenses and other current liabilities	134.6	
Current portion of long-term debt	1.1	
Total current liabilities		$1,176.7
Long-term liabilities		
Long-term debt, excluding current installments	22.7	
Other long-term liabilities	209.6	232.3
Total liabilities		1,409.0
Stockholders' equity		
Common stock	1,024.6	
Retained earnings	1,199.4	
Total stockholders' equity		2,224.0
Total liabilities and stockholders' equity		$3,633.0

Self-Study Questions

Answers are at the end of the chapter.

(SO 1) **1.** In a classified balance sheet, assets are usually classified as:
(a) current assets; long-term assets; property, plant, and equipment; and intangible assets.
(b) current assets; long-term investments; property, plant, and equipment; and common stock.
(c) current assets; long-term investments; tangible assets; and intangible assets.
(d) current assets; long-term investments; property, plant, and equipment; and intangible assets.

(SO 1) **2.** Current assets are listed:
(a) by liquidity.
(b) by importance.
(c) by longevity.
(d) alphabetically.

(SO 2) **3.** Which is an indicator of profitability?
(a) Current ratio.
(b) Earnings per share.
(c) Debt to total assets ratio.
(d) Free cash flow.

(SO 2) **4.** For 2007 Stoneland Corporation reported net income $24,000; net sales $400,000; and average shares outstanding 6,000. There

were no preferred stock dividends. What was the 2007 earnings per share?
(a) $4.00   (c) $16.67
(b) $0.06   (d) $66.67

5. The balance in retained earnings is *not* affected by: (SO 3)
(a) net income.
(b) net loss.
(c) issuance of common stock.
(d) dividends.

6. Which of these measures is an evaluation of a company's ability to pay current liabilities? (SO 4)
(a) Earnings per share.
(b) Current ratio.
(c) Both (a) and (b).
(d) None of the above.

7. Companies can use free cash flow to: (SO 5)
(a) pay additional dividends.
(b) acquire property, plant, and equipment.
(c) pay off debts.
(d) All of the above.

8. Generally accepted accounting principles are: (SO 6)
(a) a set of standards and rules that are recognized as a general guide for financial reporting.

(b) usually established by the Internal Revenue Service.

(c) the guidelines used to resolve ethical dilemmas.

(d) fundamental truths that can be derived from the laws of nature.

(SO 6) **9.** What organization issues U.S. accounting standards?

(a) Financial Accounting Standards Board.

(b) International Accounting Standards Committee.

(c) International Auditing Standards Committee.

(d) None of the above.

(SO 7) **10.** What is the primary criterion by which accounting information can be judged?

(a) Consistency.

(b) Predictive value.

(c) Usefulness for decision making.

(d) Comparability.

11. Verifiability is an ingredient of: (SO 7)

	Reliability	Relevance
(a)	Yes	Yes
(b)	No	No
(c)	Yes	No
(d)	No	Yes

12. What accounting constraint refers to the tendency (SO 7) of accountants to resolve uncertainty in a way least likely to overstate assets and net income?

(a) Comparability. (c) Conservatism.

(b) Materiality. (d) Consistency.

Go to the book's website, **www.wilcy.com/college/kimmel**, to access additional Self-Study Questions.

Questions

1. What is meant by the term *operating cycle?*

2. Define current assets. What basis is used for ordering individual items within the current assets section?

3. Distinguish between long-term investments and property, plant, and equipment.

4. How do current liabilities differ from long-term liabilities?

5. Identify the two parts of stockholders' equity in a corporation and indicate the purpose of each.

6.

(a) Brenda Starr believes that the analysis of financial statements is directed at two characteristics of a company: liquidity and profitability. Is Brenda correct? Explain.

(b) Are short-term creditors, long-term creditors, and stockholders primarily interested in the same characteristics of a company? Explain.

7. Name ratios useful in assessing (a) liquidity, (b) solvency, and (c) profitability.

8. Dave Rose, the founder of Waterboots Inc., needs to raise $500,000 to expand his company's operations. He has been told that raising the money through debt will increase the riskiness of his company much more than issuing stock. He doesn't understand why this is true. Explain it to him.

9. What do these classes of ratios measure?

(a) Liquidity ratios.

(b) Profitability ratios.

(c) Solvency ratios.

10. Holding all other factors constant, indicate whether each of the following signals generally good or bad news about a company.

(a) Increase in earnings per share.

(b) Increase in the current ratio.

(c) Increase in the debt to total assets ratio.

(d) Decrease in free cash flow.

11. Which ratio or ratios from this chapter do you think should be of greatest interest to:

(a) a pension fund considering investing in a corporation's 20-year bonds?

(b) a bank contemplating a short-term loan?

(c) an investor in common stock?

12. (a) What are generally accepted accounting principles (GAAP)?

(b) What body provides authoritative support for GAAP?

13. (a) What is the basic objective of financial reporting?

(b) Identify the characteristics of useful accounting information.

14. Sue Leonard, the president of Leon Company, is pleased. Leon substantially increased its net income in 2007 while keeping its unit inventory relatively the same. Dan Noonan, chief accountant, cautions Sue, however. Noonan says that since Leon changed its method of inventory valuation, there is a consistency problem and it is difficult to determine whether Leon is better off. Is Noonan correct? Why or why not?

15. What is the distinction between comparability and consistency?

16. Describe the two constraints inherent in the presentation of accounting information.

17. Your roommate believes that international accounting standards are uniform throughout the world. Is your roommate correct? Explain.

18. What purpose does the going concern assumption serve?

19. Tamara Swan is president of Better Books. She has no accounting background. Swan cannot understand why market value is not used as the basis for accounting measurement and reporting. Explain what basis is used and why.

20. What is the economic entity assumption? Give an example of its violation.

Brief Exercises

Classify accounts on balance sheet.
(SO 1)

BE2-1 The following are the major balance sheet classifications:

Current assets (CA)   Current liabilities (CL)
Long-term investments (LTI)   Long-term liabilities (LTL)
Property, plant, and equipment (PPE)   Common stock (CS)
Intangible assets (IA)   Retained earnings (RE)

Match each of the following accounts to its proper balance sheet classification.

_____ Accounts payable   _____ Income tax payable
_____ Accounts receivable   _____ Investment in long-term bonds
_____ Accumulated depreciation   _____ Land
_____ Building   _____ Merchandise inventory
_____ Cash   _____ Patent
_____ Goodwill   _____ Supplies

Prepare the current assets section of a balance sheet.
(SO 1)

BE2-2 A list of financial statement items for Schweitz Company includes the following: accounts receivable $14,000; prepaid insurance $3,300; cash $12,400; supplies $3,800, and short-term investments $8,200. Prepare the current assets section of the balance sheet listing the items in the proper sequence.

Compute earnings per share.
(SO 2)

BE2-3 The following information (in millions of dollars) is available for The Limited for 2005: Sales revenue $9,408; net income $705; preferred stock dividend $0; average shares outstanding 470 million. Compute the earnings per share for The Limited for 2005.

Identify items affecting stockholders' equity.
(SO 3)

BE2-4 For each of the following events affecting the stockholders' equity of Haulmarke, indicate whether the event would: increase retained earnings (IRE), decrease retained earnings (DRE), increase common stock (ICS), or decrease common stock (DCS).

_____ (a) Issued new shares of common stock.
_____ (b) Paid a cash dividend.
_____ (c) Reported net income of $75,000.
_____ (d) Reported a net loss of $20,000.

Calculate liquidity ratios.
(SO 4)

BE2-5 These selected condensed data are taken from a recent balance sheet of Bob Evans Farms (in millions of dollars).

Cash	$ 4.0
Accounts receivable	22.3
Inventories	19.5
Other current assets	1.7
Total current assets	$ 47.5
Total current liabilities	$145.8

Compute working capital and the current ratio.

Calculate liquidity and solvency ratios.
(SO 4, 5)

BE2-6 Randy's Books & Music Inc. reported the following selected information at March 30.

	2007
Total current assets	$252,787
Total assets	439,832
Total current liabilities	293,625
Total liabilities	376,002
Cash provided by operating activities	55,472

Calculate (a) the current ratio, (b) the debt to total assets ratio, and (c) free cash flow for March 30, 2007. The company paid dividends of $11,000 and spent $24,787 on capital expenditures.

BE2-7 Indicate whether each statement is *true* or *false*.

Recognize generally accepted accounting principles.
(SO 6)

(a) GAAP is a set of rules and practices established by accounting standard-setting bodies to serve as a general guide for financial reporting purposes.

(b) Substantial authoritative support for GAAP usually comes from two standards-setting bodies: the FASB and the IRS.

BE2-8 The accompanying chart shows the qualitative characteristics of accounting information. Fill in the blanks.

Identify characteristics of useful information.
(SO 7)

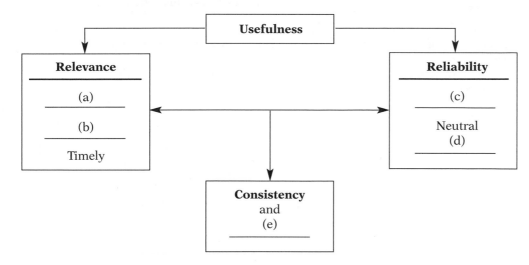

BE2-9 Given the *characteristics* of useful accounting information, complete each of the following statements.

Identify characteristics of useful information.
(SO 7)

(a) For information to be ____, it should have predictive or feedback value, and it must be presented on a timely basis.

(b) ____ is the quality of information that gives assurance that it is free of error and bias; it can be depended on.

(c) ____ means using the same accounting principles and methods from year to year within a company.

BE2-10 Here are some qualitative characteristics of accounting information:
1. Predictive value   3. Verifiable
2. Neutral   4. Timely

Identify characteristics of useful information.
(SO 7)

Match each qualitative characteristic to one of the following statements.

____ (a) Accounting information should help users make predictions about the outcome of past, present, and future events.

____ (b) Accounting information cannot be selected, prepared, or presented to favor one set of interested users over another.

____ (c) Accounting information must be proved to be free of error.

____ (d) Accounting information must be available to decision makers before it loses its capacity to influence their decisions.

BE2-11 The full disclosure principle dictates that:

Define full disclosure principle
(SO 7)

(a) financial statements should disclose all assets at their cost.

(b) financial statements should disclose only those events that can be measured in dollars.

(c) financial statements should disclose all events and circumstances that would matter to users of financial statements.

(d) financial statements should not be relied on unless an auditor has expressed an unqualified opinion on them.

BE2-12 Herbert Company uses these accounting practices:

Identify constraints that have been violated.
(SO 7)

(a) Inventory is reported at cost when market value is lower.

(b) Small tools are recorded as plant assets and depreciated.

(c) The income statement shows paper clips expense of $10.

Indicate the accounting constraint, if any, that each practice has violated.

Exercises

Classify accounts on balance sheet.
(SO 1)

E2-1   The following are the major balance sheet classifications.

Current assets (CA)	Current liabilities (CL)
Long-term investments (LTI)	Long-term liabilities (LTL)
Property, plant, and equipment (PPE)	Common stock (CS)
Intangible assets (IA)	Retained earnings (RE)

Instructions

Classify each of the following accounts taken from Hawthorne Corporation's balance sheet.

_____ Accounts payable and
accrued liabilities
_____ Accounts receivable
_____ Accumulated depreciation
_____ Buildings
_____ Cash and short-term investments
_____ Dividends payable
_____ Goodwill

_____ Income taxes payable
_____ Inventories
_____ Investments
_____ Land
_____ Long-term debt
_____ Materials and supplies
_____ Office equipment and furniture
_____ Prepaid expenses

Classify items as current or noncurrent, and prepare assets section of balance sheet.
(SO 1)

E2-2   The following items were taken from the December 31, 2004, assets section of the Boeing Company balance sheet. (All dollars are in millions.)

Inventories	$ 4,247	Other current assets	$ 2,061
Notes receivable—due after		Property, plant, and	
December 31, 2005	13,435	equipment	21,405
Notes receivable—due before		Cash and cash equivalents	3,204
December 31, 2005	616	Accounts receivable	4,653
Accumulated depreciation	12,962	Other noncurrent assets	14,082
Intangible assets	2,903	Short-term investments	319

Instructions

Prepare the assets section of a classified balance sheet, listing the current assets in order of their liquidity.

Prepare assets section of a classified balance sheet.
(SO 1)

E2-3   The following information (in thousands of dollars) is available for H.J. Heinz Company—famous for ketchup and other fine food products—for the year ended April 28, 2004.

Prepaid expenses	$ 165,177	Inventories	$1,156,932
Land	65,836	Buildings and equipment	3,661,388
Other current assets	15,493	Cash and cash equivalents	1,180,039
Intangible assets	2,753,735	Accounts receivable	1,093,155
Other noncurrent assets	1,455,372	Accumulated depreciation	1,669,938

Instructions

Prepare the assets section of a classified balance sheet, listing the items in proper sequence and including a statement heading.

Prepare a classified balance sheet.
(SO 1)

E2-4   These items are taken from the financial statements of Donovan Co. at December 31, 2007.

Building	$105,800
Accounts receivable	12,600
Prepaid insurance	4,680
Cash	16,840
Equipment	82,400
Land	61,200
Insurance expense	780
Depreciation expense	5,300
Interest expense	2,600
Common stock	62,000

Retained earnings (January 1, 2007)	40,000
Accumulated depreciation—building	45,600
Accounts payable	9,500
Mortgage payable	93,600
Accumulated depreciation—equipment	18,720
Interest payable	3,600
Bowling revenues	19,180

Instructions
Prepare a classified balance sheet. Assume that $13,600 of the mortgage payable will be paid in 2008.

E2-5 The following items were taken from the 2004 financial statements of Texas Instruments, Inc. (All dollars are in millions.)

Prepare a classified balance sheet.
(SO 1)

Long-term debt	$ 368	Cash	$ 2,668
Common stock	2,488	Accumulated depreciation	5,655
Prepaid expenses	326	Accounts payable	1,444
Property, plant, and equipment	9,573	Other noncurrent assets	1,927
Other current assets	554	Other noncurrent liabilities	943
Other current liabilities	470	Retained earnings	10,575
Long-term investments	264	Accounts receivable	1,696
Short-term investments	3,690	Inventories	1,256
Loans payable in 2005	11		

Instructions
Prepare a classified balance sheet in good form as of December 31, 2004.

E2-6 The following information is available for Callaway Golf Company for the years 2004 and 2003. (Dollars are in thousands, except share information.)

Compute and interpret profitability ratio.
(SO 2)

	2004	2003
Net sales	$934,564	$814,032
Net income (loss)	(10,103)	45,523
Total assets	735,737	748,566
Share information		
Shares outstanding at year-end	69,111,349	66,862,850
Preferred dividends	–0–	–0–

There were 65,676,326 shares outstanding at the end of 2002.

Instructions
(a) What was the company's earnings per share for each year?
(b) Based on your findings above, how did the company's profitability change from 2003 to 2004?

E2-7 These financial statement items are for Snyder Corporation at year-end, July 31, 2007.

Prepare financial statements.
(SO 1, 3, 4)

Salaries payable	$ 2,080
Salaries expense	51,700
Utilities expense	22,600
Equipment	18,500
Accounts payable	4,100
Commission revenue	61,100
Rent revenue	8,500
Long-term note payable	1,800
Common stock	16,000
Cash	24,200
Accounts receivable	9,780
Accumulated depreciation	6,000
Dividends	4,000
Depreciation expense	4,000
Retained earnings (beginning of the year)	35,200

what if [illegible] the [illegible] stock?

Instructions

(a) Prepare an income statement and a retained earnings statement for the year. Snyder Corporation did not issue any new stock during the year.

(b) Prepare a classified balance sheet at July 31.

(c) Compute the current ratio and debt to total assets ratio.

(d) Suppose that you are the president of Allied Equipment. Your sales manager has approached you with a proposal to sell $20,000 of equipment to Snyder. He would like to provide a loan to Snyder in the form of a 10%, 5-year note payable. Evaluate how this loan would change Snyder's current ratio and debt to total assets ratio, and discuss whether you would make the sale.

Compute liquidity ratios and compare results.
(SO 4)

E2-8 Nordstrom, Inc. operates department stores in numerous states. Selected financial statement data (in millions of dollars) for the year ended January 31, 2004, are as follows.

	End of Year	Beginning of Year
Cash and cash equivalents	$ 361	$ 340
Receivables (net)	646	667
Merchandise inventory	917	902
Other current assets	648	616
Total current assets	$2,572	$2,525
Total current liabilities	$1,341	$1,123

For the year, net sales were $7,131,000 and cost of goods sold was $4,559,000.

Instructions

(a) Compute working capital and the current ratio at the beginning of the year and at the end of the current year.

(b) Did Nordstrom's liquidity improve or worsen during the year?

(c) Using the data in the chapter, compare Nordstrom's liquidity with Best Buy's.

Compute liquidity measures and discuss findings.
(SO 4)

E2-9 The chief financial officer (CFO) of SuperClean Corporation requested that the accounting department prepare a preliminary balance sheet on December 30, 2007, so that the CFO could get an idea of how the company stood. He knows that certain debt agreements with its creditors require the company to maintain a current ratio of at least 2:1. The preliminary balance sheet is as follows.

SUPERCLEAN CORP.
Balance Sheet
December 30, 2007

Current assets			Current liabilities		
Cash	$30,000		Accounts payable	$ 25,000	
Accounts receivable	20,000		Salaries payable	15,000	$ 40,000
Prepaid insurance	10,000	$ 60,000	Long-term liabilities		
			Notes payable		80,000
			Total liabilities		120,000
Property, plant, and equipment (net)		200,000	Stockholders' equity		
Total assets		$260,000	Common stock	100,000	
			Retained earnings	40,000	140,000
			Total liabilities and stockholders equity		$260,000

Instructions

(a) Calculate the current ratio and working capital based on the preliminary balance sheet.

(b) Based on the results in (a), the CFO requested that $25,000 of cash be used to pay off the balance of the accounts payable account on December 31, 2007. Calculate the new current ratio and working capital after the company takes these actions.

(c) Discuss the pros and cons of the current ratio and working capital as measures of liquidity.

(d) Was it unethical for the CFO to take these steps?

E2-10 The following data were taken from the 2004 and 2003 financial statements of American Eagle Outfitters. (All dollars are in thousands.)

Compute and interpret solvency ratios.
(SO 4, 5)

	2004	**2003**
Current assets	$525,623	$427,878
Total assets	865,071	741,339
Current liabilities	189,035	141,586
Total liabilities	221,401	163,857
Total stockholders' equity	643,670	577,482
Cash provided by operating activities	189,469	104,548
Capital expenditures	64,173	61,407
Dividends paid	–0–	–0–

Instructions
Perform each of the following.
(a) Calculate the debt to total assets ratio for each year.
(b) Calculate the free cash flow for each year.
(c) Discuss American Eagle's solvency in 2004 versus 2003.
(d) Discuss American Eagle's ability to finance its investment activities with cash provided by operating activities, and how any deficiency would be met.

E2-11 Presented below are the assumptions and principles discussed in this chapter.

Identify accounting assumptions and principles.
(SO 7)

1. Full disclosure principle.
2. Going concern assumption.
3. Monetary unit assumption.
4. Time period assumption.
5. Cost principle.
6. Economic entity assumption.

Instructions
Identify by number the accounting assumption or principle that is described below. Do not use a number more than once.
(a) Is the rationale for why plant assets are not reported at liquidation value. (*Note:* Do not use the cost principle.)
(b) Indicates that personal and business record-keeping should be separately maintained.
(c) Assumes that the dollar is the "measuring stick" used to report on financial performance.
(d) Separates financial information into time periods for reporting purpose.
(e) Indicates that companies should not record in the accounts market value changes subsequent to purchase.
(f) Dictates that companies should disclose all circumstances and events that make a difference to financial statement users.

E2-12 Mere Co. had three major business transactions during 2007.
(a) Reported at its market value of $260,000 merchandise inventory with a cost of $208,000.
(b) The president of Mere Co., Issam Mere, purchased a truck for personal use and charged it to his expense account.
(c) Mere Co. wanted to make its 2007 income look better, so it added 2 more weeks to the year (a 54-week year). Previous years were 52 weeks.

Identify the assumption or principle that has been violated.
(SO 7)

Instructions
In each situation, identify the assumption or principle that has been violated, if any, and discuss what the company should have done.

Problems: Set A

Prepare a classified balance sheet.
(SO 1)

P2-1A The following items are taken from the 2004 balance sheet of **Yahoo!, Inc.** (All dollars are in thousands.)

Intangible assets	$3,031,623
Common stock	5,684,300
Property and equipment, net	531,696
Accounts payable	48,205
Other assets	481,832
Long-term investments	1,042,575
Accounts receivable	483,951
Prepaid expenses and other current assets	94,549
Short-term investments	2,688,252
Retained earnings	1,417,146
Cash and cash equivalents	823,723
Long-term debt	750,000
Accrued expenses and other current liabilities	853,115
Unearned revenue—current	279,387
Other long-term liabilities	146,048

Instructions

Tot. current assets $4,090,475
Tot. assets $9,178,201

Prepare a classified balance sheet for Yahoo! Inc. as of December 31, 2004.

Prepare financial statements.
(SO 1, 3)

P2-2A These items are taken from the financial statements of Drew Corporation for 2007.

Retained earnings (beginning of year)	$31,000
Utilities expense	2,000
Equipment	66,000
Accounts payable	13,300
Cash	17,900
Salaries payable	3,000
Common stock	13,000
Dividends	12,000
Service revenue	82,000
Prepaid insurance	3,500
Repair expense	1,800
Depreciation expense	3,300
Accounts receivable	14,200
Insurance expense	2,200
Salaries expense	37,000
Accumulated depreciation	17,600

Instructions

Net income $35,700
Tot. assets $84,000

Prepare an income statement, a retained earnings statement, and a classified balance sheet as of December 31, 2007.

Prepare financial statements.
(SO 1, 3)

P2-3A You are provided with the following information for Maxim Enterprises, effective as of its April 30, 2007, year-end.

Accounts. payable	$ 834
Accounts receivable	810
Building, net of accumulated depreciation	1,537
Cash	770
Common stock	900
Cost of goods sold	990
Current portion of long-term debt	450
Depreciation expense	335
Dividends paid during the year	325

Equipment, net of accumulated depreciation	1,220
Income tax expense	165
Income taxes payable	135
Interest expense	400
Inventories	967
Land	1,600
Long-term debt	3,500
Prepaid expenses	12
Retained earnings, beginning	1,600
Revenues	3,600
Selling expenses	210
Short-term investments	1,200
Wages expense	700
Wages payable	222

Instructions

(a) Prepare an income statement and a retained earnings statement for Maxim Enterprises for the year ended April 30, 2007.

(b) Prepare a classified balance sheet for Maxim Enterprises as of April 30, 2007.

Net income $800
Tot. current assets $3,759
Tot. assets $8,116

P2-4A Comparative financial statement data for Arthur Corporation and Lancelot Corporation, two competitors, appear below. All balance sheet data are as of December 31, 2007.

Compute ratios; comment on relative profitability, liquidity, and solvency.
(SO 2, 4, 5)

	Arthur Corporation	Lancelot Corporation
	2007	**2007**
Net sales	$1,950,000	$620,000
Cost of goods sold	1,175,000	340,000
Operating expenses	303,000	98,000
Interest expense	9,000	3,800
Income tax expense	85,000	36,000
Current assets	427,200	190,336
Plant assets (net)	532,000	139,728
Current liabilities	66,325	35,348
Long-term liabilities	108,500	29,620

Additional information:

Cash from operating activities	$148,000	$36,000
Capital expenditures	$90,000	$20,000
Dividends paid	$36,000	$15,000
Average number of shares outstanding	100,000	50,000

Instructions

(a) Comment on the relative profitability of the companies by computing the net income and earnings per share for each company for 2007.

(b) Comment on the relative liquidity of the companies by computing working capital and the current ratios for each company for 2007.

(c) Comment on the relative solvency of the companies by computing the debt to total assets ratio and the free cash flow for each company for 2007.

P2-5A Here and on page 86 are financial statements of Chiasson Company.

Compute and liquidity, solvency, and profitability ratios.
(SO 2, 4, 5)

CHIASSON COMPANY
Income Statement
For the Year Ended December 31

	2007
Net sales	$2,218,500
Cost of goods sold	1,012,400
Selling and administrative expenses	906,000
Interest expense	98,000
Income tax expense	69,000
Net income	$ 133,100

CHIASSON COMPANY
Balance Sheet
December 31

Assets	2007
Current assets	
Cash	$ 60,100
Short-term investments	54,000
Accounts receivable (net)	169,800
Inventory	125,000
Total current assets	408,900
Plant assets (net)	625,300
Total assets	$1,034,200

Liabilities and Stockholders' Equity	
Current liabilities	
Accounts payable	$ 180,000
Income taxes payable	35,500
Total current liabilities	215,500
Bonds payable	200,000
Total liabilities	415,500
Stockholders' equity	
Common stock	330,000
Retained earnings	288,700
Total stockholders' equity	618,700
Total liabilities and stockholders' equity	$1,034,200

Additional information: The cash provided by operating activities for 2007 was $190,800. The cash used for capital expenditures was $92,000. The cash used for dividends was $26,000. The average number of shares outstanding during the year was 50,000.

Instructions
Compute the following values and ratios for 2007.
(a) Working capital.
(b) Current ratio.
(c) Free cash flow.
(d) Debt to total assets ratio.
(e) Earnings per share.

Compute and interpret liquidity, solvency, and profitability ratios.
(SO 2, 4, 5)

P2-6A Condensed balance sheet and income statement data for Mere Corporation are presented here.

MERE CORPORATION
Balance Sheets
December 31

Assets	2007	2006
Cash	$ 25,000	$ 20,000
Receivables (net)	70,000	62,000
Other current assets	80,000	73,000
Long-term investments	75,000	60,000
Plant and equipment (net)	510,000	470,000
Total assets	$760,000	$685,000

Liabilities and Stockholders' Equity	2007	2006
Current liabilities	$ 85,000	$ 70,000
Long-term debt	80,000	90,000
Common stock	320,000	300,000
Retained earnings	275,000	225,000
Total liabilities and stockholders' equity	$760,000	$685,000

MERE CORPORATION
Income Statements
For the Years Ended December 31

	2007	2006
Sales	$750,000	$670,000
Cost of goods sold	440,000	400,000
Operating expenses (including income taxes)	240,000	220,000
Net income	$ 70,000	$ 50,000

Additional information:

Cash from operating activities	$87,000	$60,000
Cash used for capital expenditures	$45,000	$38,000
Dividends paid	$20,000	$15,000
Average number of shares outstanding	32,000	30,000

Instructions
Compute these values and ratios for 2006 and 2007.
(a) Earnings per share.
(b) Working capital.
(c) Current ratio.
(d) Debt to total assets ratio.
(e) Free cash flow.
(f) Based on the ratios calculated, discuss briefly the improvement or lack thereof in financial position and operating results from 2006 to 2007 of Mere Corporation.

P2-7A   Selected financial data of two competitors, Target and Wal-Mart, are presented here. (All dollars are in millions.)

Compute ratios and compare liquidity, solvency, and profitability for two companies.
(SO 2, 4, 5)

	Target (2/3/04)	Wal-Mart (1/31/04)
	Income Statement Data for Year	
Net sales	$46,781	$256,329
Cost of goods sold	31,790	198,747
Selling and administrative expenses	10,696	44,909
Interest expense	559	832
Other income (loss)	(776)	2,331
Income taxes	1,119	5,118
Net income	$ 1,841	$ 9,054

	Target	Wal-Mart
	Balance Sheet Data (End of Year)	
Current assets	$12,928	$ 34,421
Noncurrent assets	18,464	70,491
Total assets	$31,392	$104,912
Current liabilities	$ 8,314	$ 37,418
Long-term debt	12,013	23,871
Total stockholders' equity	11,065	43,623
Total liabilities and stockholders' equity	$31,392	$104,912
Cash from operating activities	$ 3,160	$ 15,996
Cash paid for capital expenditures	$ 3,004	$ 10,308
Dividends paid	$ 237	$ 1,569
Average shares outstanding	911	4,373

Instructions

For each company, compute these values and ratios.
(a) Working capital.
(b) Current ratio.
(c) Debt to total assets ratio.
(d) Free cash flow.
(e) Earnings per share.
(f) Compare the liquidity, solvency, and profitability of the two companies.

Comment on the objectives and qualitative characteristics of financial reporting.
(SO 6, 7)

P2-8A   A friend of yours, Diana Maher, recently completed an undergraduate degree in science and has just started working with a biotechnology company. Diana tells you that the owners of the business are trying to secure new sources of financing which are needed in order for the company to proceed with development of a new health care product. Diana said that her boss told her that the company must put together a report to present to potential investors.

Diana thought that the company should include in this package the detailed scientific findings related to the Phase I clinical trials for this product. She said, "I know that the biotech industry sometimes has only a 10% success rate with new products, but if we report all the scientific findings, everyone will see what a sure success this is going to be! The president was talking about the importance of following some set of accounting principles. Why do we need to look at some accounting rules? What they need to realize is that we have scientific results that are quite encouraging, some of the most talented employees around, and the start of some really great customer relationships. We haven't made any sales yet, but we will. We just need the funds to get through all the clinical testing and get government approval for our product. Then these investors will be quite happy that they bought in to our company early!"

Instructions

(a) What is financial reporting? Explain to Diana what is meant by generally accepted accounting principles.
(b) Comment on how Diana's suggestions for what should be reported to prospective investors conforms to the qualitative characteristics of accounting information. Do you think that the things that Diana wants to include in the information for investors will conform to financial reporting guidelines?

Problems: Set B

Prepare a classified balance sheet.
(SO 1)

P2-1B   The following items are from the 2004 balance sheet of Kellogg Company. (All dollars are in millions.)

Common stock	$ 103.8
Other assets	5,953.5
Notes payable—current	709.7
Other current assets	247.0
Current maturities of long-term debt	278.6
Cash and cash equivalents	417.4
Other long-term liabilities	1,794.6
Retained earnings	2,153.4
Accounts payable	767.2
Other current liabilities	1,090.5
Accounts receivable, net	776.4
Property, net	2,715.1
Inventories	681.0
Long-term debt	3,892.6

Instructions

Prepare a classified balance sheet for Kellogg Company as of December 31, 2004.

Tot. current assets $ 2,121.8
Tot. assets $10,790.4

P2-2B These items are taken from the financial statements of Stasik, Inc.

Prepare financial statements.
(SO 1, 3)

CL Prepaid insurance	$ 1,800
CA Equipment	34,000
E Salaries expense	36,000
E Utilities expense	2,100
CL Accumulated depreciation	8,600
CL Accounts payable	10,200
CA Cash	5,300
CA Accounts receivable	7,500
CL Salaries payable	2,000
SE Common stock	5,900
E Depreciation expense	4,300
SE Retained earnings (beginning)	14,000
SE Dividends	3,600
R Service revenue	58,000
E Repair expense	2,900
E Insurance expense	1,200

Instructions

Prepare an income statement, a retained earnings statement, and a classified balance sheet as of December 31, 2007.

Net income $11,500
Tot. assets $40,000

P2-3B You are provided with the following information for Kiltie Corporation, effective as of its April 30, 2007, year-end.

Prepare financial statements.
(SO 1, 3)

Accounts payable	$ 2,400
Accounts receivable	4,150
Accumulated depreciation	6,600
Depreciation expense	2,200
Cash	21,955
Common stock	20,000
Dividends	2,800
Equipment	23,050
Sales revenue	14,450
Income tax expense	1,100
Income taxes payable	300
Interest expense	350
Interest payable	175
Long-term notes payable	5,700
Prepaid rent	380
Rent expense	760
Retained earnings, beginning	13,960
Salaries expense	6,840

Instructions

(a) Prepare an income statement and a retained earnings statement for Kiltie Corporation for the year ended April 30, 2007.
(b) Prepare a classified balance sheet for Kiltie as of April 30, 2007.
(c) Explain how each financial statement interrelates with the others.

Net income $ 3,200
Tot. current assets $26,485
Tot. assets $42,935
Compute ratios; comment on relative profitability, liquidity, and solvency.
(SO 2, 4, 5)

P2-4B Comparative statement data for Oscar Company and Felix Company, two competitors, are presented on page 90. All balance sheet data are as of December 31, 2007.

	Oscar Company 2007	Felix Company 2007
Net sales	$450,000	$918,000
Cost of goods sold	260,000	620,000
Operating expenses	134,000	55,000
Interest expense	6,000	10,000
Income tax expense	10,000	65,000
Current assets	180,000	700,000
Plant assets (net)	600,000	800,000
Current liabilities	60,000	250,000
Long-term liabilities	190,000	200,000

Additional information:

Cash from operating activities	$ 26,000	$180,000
Capital expenditures	$ 20,000	$ 50,000
Dividends paid	$ 4,000	$ 15,000
Average number of shares outstanding	200,000	400,000

Instructions

(a) Comment on the relative profitability of the companies by computing the net income and earnings per share for each company for 2007.

(b) Comment on the relative liquidity of the companies by computing working capital and the current ratios for each company for 2007.

(c) Comment on the relative solvency of the companies by computing the debt to total assets ratio and the free cash flow for each company for 2007.

Compute and interpret liquidity, solvency, and profitability ratios.
(SO 2, 4, 5)

P2-5B   The financial statements of Jackson Company are presented here.

JACKSON COMPANY
Income Statement
For the Year Ended December 31

	2007
Net sales	$700,000
Cost of goods sold	400,000
Selling and administrative expenses	150,000
Interest expense	7,800
Income tax expense	43,000
Net income	$ 99,200

JACKSON COMPANY
Balance Sheet
December 31

Assets	2007
Current assets	
Cash	$ 23,100
Short-term investments	34,800
Accounts receivable (net)	106,200
Inventory	155,000
Total current assets	319,100
Plant assets (net)	465,300
Total assets	$784,400

Liabilities and Stockholders' Equity

Current liabilities
    Accounts payable $120,200
      Income taxes payable   24,000
        Total current liabilities   144,200
Bonds payable   130,000
    Total liabilities   274,200
Stockholders' equity
    Common stock   170,000
    Retained earnings   340,200
        Total stockholders' equity   510,200
Total liabilities and stockholders' equity $784,400

Cash from operating activities $ 71,300
Capital expenditures $ 42,000
Dividends paid $ 10,000
Average number of shares outstanding   70,000

Instructions

(a) Compute the following values and ratios for 2007. (We have provided the results from 2006 for comparative purposes.)
   (i) Current ratio. (2006: 2.4:1)
  (ii) Working capital. (2006: $178,000)
 (iii) Debt to total assets ratio. (2006: 31%)
 (iv) Free cash flow. (2006: $13,000)
  (v) Earnings per share. (2006: $1.35)

(b) Using your calculations from part (a), discuss changes from 2006 in liquidity, solvency, and profitability.

P2-6B   Condensed balance sheet and income statement data for Swann Corporation are presented below.

Compute and interpret liquidity, solvency, and profitability ratios.
(SO 2, 4, 5)

SWANN CORPORATION
Balance Sheets
December 31

Assets	2007	2006
Cash	$ 40,000	$ 24,000
Receivables (net)	90,000	55,000
Other current assets	74,000	73,000
Long-term investments	78,000	70,000
Plant and equipment (net)	525,000	427,000
Total assets	$807,000	$649,000

Liabilities and Stockholders' Equity	2007	2006
Current liabilities	$ 98,000	$ 75,000
Long-term debt	90,000	70,000
Common stock	370,000	340,000
Retained earnings	249,000	164,000
Total liabilities and stockholders' equity	$807,000	$649,000

SWANN CORPORATION
Income Statements
For the Years Ended December 31

	2007	2006
Sales	$760,000	$800,000
Cost of goods sold	420,000	400,000
Operating expenses (including income taxes)	200,000	237,000
Net income	$140,000	$163,000

Additional information:

Cash from operating activities	$165,000	$178,000
Capital expenditures	$ 85,000	$ 45,000
Dividends paid	$ 15,000	$ 13,000
Average number of shares outstanding	370,000	320,000

Instructions

Compute the following values and ratios for 2006 and 2007.

(a) Earnings per share.

(b) Working capital.

(c) Current ratio.

(d) Debt to total assets ratio.

(e) Free cash flow.

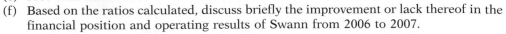 (f) Based on the ratios calculated, discuss briefly the improvement or lack thereof in the financial position and operating results of Swann from 2006 to 2007.

Compute ratios and compare liquidity, solvency, and profitability for two companies.
(SO 2, 4, 5)

P2-7B Selected financial data of two competitors, Blockbuster Inc. and Hollywood Entertainment Corp., in 2004 are presented here. (All dollars are in millions.)

	Blockbuster Inc.	Hollywood Entertainment Corp.
	Income Statement Data for Year	
Net sales	$ 6,053	$1,782
Cost of goods sold	2,441	717
Selling and administrative expenses	3,111	917
Interest expense	38	30
Other expense	1,749	2
Income tax expense (refund)	(37)	45
Net income	$(1,249)	$ 71

	Blockbuster Inc.	Hollywood Entertainment Corp.
	Balance Sheet Data (End of Year)	
Current assets	$1,218	$ 403
Property, plant, and equipment (net)	854	228
Intangible assets	1,630	69
Other assets	161	420
Total assets	$3,863	$1,120
Current liabilities	$1,424	$ 351
Long-term debt	1,376	395
Total stockholders' equity	1,063	374
Total liabilities and stockholders' equity	$3,863	$1,120
Average shares outstanding	180.9	60.5
Cash from operating activities	$1,215	$401
Cash used for capital expenditures	$289	$272
Dividends paid	$920	$–0–

Instructions

For each company, compute these values and ratios.

(a) Working capital.

(b) Current ratio. (Round to two decimal places.)

(c) Debt to total assets ratio.

(d) Free cash flow.

(e) Earnings per share.

(f) Compare the liquidity, profitability, and solvency of the two companies.

P2-8B Net Nanny Software International Inc., headquartered in Vancouver, specializes in Internet safety and computer security products for both the home and commercial markets. In a recent balance sheet, it reported a deficit (negative retained earnings) of US $5,678,288. It has reported only net losses since its inception. In spite of these losses, Net Nanny's common shares have traded anywhere from a high of $3.70 to a low of $0.32 on the Canadian Venture Exchange.

Comment on the objectives and qualitative characteristics of accounting information. (SO 6, 7)

Net Nanny's financial statements have historically been prepared in Canadian dollars. Recently, the company adopted the U.S. dollar as its reporting currency.

Instructions
(a) What is the objective of financial reporting? How does this objective meet or not meet Net Nanny's investor's needs?
(b) Why would investors want to buy Net Nanny's shares if the company has consistently reported losses over the last few years? Include in your answer an assessment of the relevance of the information reported on Net Nanny's financial statements.
(c) Comment on how the change in reporting information from Canadian dollars to U.S. dollars likely affected the readers of Net Nanny's financial statements. Include in your answer an assessment of the comparability of the information.

Problems: Set C

Visit the book's website at **www.wiley.com/college/kimmel** and choose the Student Companion site to access Problem Set C.

Continuing Cookie Chronicle

(*Note:* This is a continuation of the Cookie Chronicle from Chapter 1.)

CCC2 After investigating the different forms of business organization, Natalie Koebel decides to operate her business as a corporation, Cookie Creations Inc., and she begins the process of getting her business running.

While at a trade show, Natalie is introduced to Gerry Richards, operations manager of "Biscuits," a national food retailer. After much discussion, Gerry asks Natalie to consider being Biscuits' major supplier of oatmeal chocolate chip cookies. He provides Natalie with the most recent copy of the financial statements of Biscuits. He expects that Natalie will need to supply Biscuits' Watertown warehouse with approximately 1,500 dozen cookies a week. Natalie is to send Biscuits a monthly invoice, and she will be paid approximately 30 days from the date the invoice is received in Biscuits' Chicago office.

Natalie is thrilled with the offer. However, she has recently read in the newspaper that Biscuits has a reputation for selling cookies and donuts with high amounts of sugar and fat, and as a result, consumer demand for the company's products has decreased.

Instructions
Natalie has several questions. Answer the following questions for Natalie.
(a) What type of information does each financial statement provide?
(b) How can Natalie evaluate whether Biscuits will be able to pay her invoices? What type of information can financial statements give that will reassure her that Biscuits will pay her invoices?
(c) Will Biscuits have enough cash to meet its current liabilities? Where can she find this information?
(d) Will Biscuits be able to survive over a long period of time? Where can she find this information?
(e) Is Biscuits profitable? Where can she find this information?
(f) Does Biscuits have any debt? Is Biscuits able to pay off both its debt and the interest on it? Where can she find this information?
(g) Does Biscuits pay any dividends? Where can she find this information?
(h) In deciding whether to go ahead with this opportunity, are there other areas of concern that she should be aware of?

BROADENING YOUR PERSPECTIVE

FINANCIAL REPORTING PROBLEM: *Tootsie Roll Industries, Inc.*

BYP2-1 The financial statements of Tootsie Roll Industries, Inc., are presented in Appendix A at the end of this book.

Instructions

Answer the following questions using the Consolidated Balance Sheet and the Notes to Consolidated Financial Statements section.

(a) What were Tootsie Roll's total current assets at December 31, 2004, and December 31, 2003?

(b) Are the assets included in current assets listed in the proper order? Explain.

(c) How are Tootsie Roll's assets classified?

(d) What were Tootsie Roll's current liabilities at December 31, 2004, and December 31, 2003?

COMPARATIVE ANALYSIS PROBLEM: *Tootsie Roll vs. Hershey Foods*

BYP2-2 The financial statements of Hershey Foods are presented in Appendix B, following the financial statements for Tootsie Roll in Appendix A. Hershey's average number of shares outstanding was 253,881,000, and Tootsie Roll's was 52,366,000.

Instructions

(a) For each company calculate the following values for 2004.

   (1) Working capital.   (4) Free cash flow.

   (2) Current ratio.   (5) Earnings per share.

   (3) Debt to total assets ratio

   (*Hint:* When calculating free cash flow, consider business acquisitions to be part of capital expenditures.)

(b) Based on your findings above, discuss the relative liquidity, solvency, and profitability of the two companies.

RESEARCH CASE

BYP2-3 The March 2, 2004, issue of the *Wall Street Journal* includes an article by Mitchell Pacelle and Matthew Karnitschnig titled "Spiegel's European Owner Gets a Hard Lesson in U.S. Business."

Instructions

Read the article and answer the following.

(a) Mr. Otto controls 89 companies. What was unique about Spiegel, and how did this get him into trouble?

(b) Mr. Otto is German and is accustomed to the regulatory environment in Germany. How does the German regulatory environment differ from that of the U.S.? According to the article, how is the German regulatory environment changing?

(c) Briefly explain what is meant by the "going concern assumption."

(d) Explain why Spiegel's violation of its loan agreements caused its auditor to say that it would most likely issue an audit opinion that questioned the company's ability to continue as a going concern.

(e) How would the company's creditors react to the news that the auditor questioned the company's ability to continue as a going concern?

(f) Briefly explain the "full disclosure principle" and discuss whether Spiegel appears to have violated this principle.

INTERPRETING FINANCIAL STATEMENTS

BYP2-4 The following information was reported by Gap, Inc. in its 2004 annual report.

	2004	2003	2002	2001	2000
Total assets (millions)	$10,048	$10,713	$10,283	$8,096	$7,387
Working capital	$4,062	$4,156	$2,972	$1,018	$(153)
Current ratio	2.81:1	2.63:1	2.08:1	1.48:1	0.95:1
Debt to total assets ratio	.51:1	.57:1	.66:1	.64:1	.62:1
Earnings per share	$1.29	$1.15	$0.55	$(0.03)	$0.99

(a) Determine the overall percentage increase in Gap's total assets from 2000 to 2004. What was the average increase per year?
(b) Comment on the change in Gap's liquidity. Does working capital or the current ratio appear to provide a better indication of Gap's liquidity? What might explain the change in Gap's liquidity during this period?
(c) Comment on the change in Gap's solvency during this period.
(d) Comment on the change in Gap's profitability during this period. How might this affect your prediction about Gap's future profitability?

FINANCIAL ANALYSIS ON THE WEB

BYP2-5 *Purpose:* Identify summary liquidity, solvency, and profitability information about companies, and compare this information across companies in the same industry.

Address: **http://biz.yahoo.com/i** (or go to **www.wiley.com/college/kimmel**)

Steps
1. Type in a company name, or use the index to find a company name. Choose **Profile**. Choose **Key Statistics**. Perform instructions (a) and (b) below.
2. Go back to **Profile**. Click on the company's particular industry behind the heading "Industry." Perform instructions (c) and (d).

Instructions
Answer the following questions.
(a) What is the company's name? What was the company's current ratio and debt to equity ratio (a variation of the debt to total assets ratio)?
(b) What is the company's industry?
(c) What is the name of a competitor? What is the competitor's current ratio and its debt to equity ratio?
(d) Based on these measures: Which company is more liquid? Which company is more solvent?

BYP2-6 The opening story described the dramatic effect that investment bulletin boards are having on the investment world. This exercise will allow you to evaluate a bulletin board discussing a company of your choice.

Address: **http://biz.yahoo.com/i** (or go to **www.wiley.com/college/kimmel**)

Steps
1. Type in a company name, or use the index to find a company name.
2. Choose **Msgs** or **message Board.** (for messages).
3. Read the ten most recent messages.

Instructions
Answer the following questions.
(a) State the nature of each of these messages (e.g., offering advice, criticizing company, predicting future results, ridiculing other people who have posted messages).
(b) For those messages that expressed an opinion about the company, was evidence provided to support the opinion?
(c) What effect do you think it would have on bulletin board discussions if the participants provided their actual names? Do you think this would be a good policy?

Critical Thinking

DECISION MAKING ACROSS THE ORGANIZATION

BYP2-7 As a financial analyst in the planning department for Pre-Mold Industries, Inc., you have been requested to develop some key ratios from the comparative financial statements. This information is to be used to convince creditors that Pre-Mold Industries, Inc. is liquid, solvent, and profitable, and that it deserves their continued support. Lenders are particularly concerned about the company's ability to continue as a going concern.

Presented on page 96 are the data requested and the computations developed from the financial statements:

	2007	**2006**
Current ratio	3.1	2.1
Working capital	Up 22%	Down 7%
Free cash flow	Up 25%	Up 18%
Debt to total assets ratio	0.60	0.70
Net income	Up 32%	Down 8%
Earnings per share	$2.40	$1.15

Instructions

Pre-Mold Industries, Inc. asks you to prepare brief comments stating how each of these items supports the argument that its financial health is improving. The company wishes to use these comments to support presentation of data to its creditors. With the class divided into groups, prepare the comments as requested, giving the implications and the limitations of each item separately, and then the collective inference that may be drawn from them about Pre-Mold's financial well-being.

COMMUNICATION ACTIVITY

BYP2-8   P. J. Thews is the chief executive officer of Tomorrow's Products. Thews is an expert engineer but a novice in accounting.

Instructions

Write a letter to P. J. Thews that explains (a) the three main types of ratios; (b) examples of each, how they are calculated, and what they measure; and (c) the bases for comparison in analyzing Tomorrow's Products' financial statements.

ETHICS CASE

BYP2-9   A May 20, 2002, *Business Week* story by Stanley Holmes and Mike France entitled "Boeing's Secret" discusses issues surrounding the timing of the disclosure of information at the giant airplane manufacturer. To summarize, on December 11, 1996, Boeing closed a giant deal to acquire another manufacturer, McDonnell Douglas. Boeing paid for the acquisition by issuing shares of its own stock to the stockholders of McDonnell Douglas. In order for the deal not to be revoked, the value of Boeing's stock could not decline below a certain level for a number of months after the deal.

The article suggests that during the first half of 1997 Boeing suffered significant cost overruns because of severe inefficiencies in its production methods. Had these problems been disclosed in the quarterly financial statements during the first and second quarter of 1997, the company's stock most likely would have plummeted, and the deal would have been revoked. Company managers spent considerable time debating when the bad news should be disclosed. One public relations manager suggested that the company's problems be revealed on the date of either Princess Diana's or Mother Teresa's funeral, in the hope that it would be lost among those big stories that day. Instead, the company waited until October 22 of that year to announce a $2.6 billion write-off due to cost overruns. Within one week the company's stock price had fallen 20%, but by this time the McDonnell Douglas deal could not be reversed.

Instructions

Answer the following questions. Although it is not required in order to answer the questions, you may want to read the *Business Week* article.
(a) Who are the stakeholders in this situation?
(b) What are the ethical issues?
(c) What assumptions or principles of accounting are relevant to this case?
(d) Do you think it is ethical to try to "time" the release of a story so as to diminish its effect?
(e) What would you have done if you were the chief executive officer of Boeing?
(f) Boeing's top management maintains that it did not have an obligation to reveal its problems during the first half of 1997, and that it wouldn't do anything differently today. What implications does this have for investors and analysts who follow Boeing's stock?

Answers to Business Insight and Accounting across the Organization Questions

p. 60

Q. What can various company managers do to ensure that working capital is managed efficiently (so as to maximize net income)?

A. Marketing and sales managers must understand that by extending generous repayment terms they are expanding the company's receivables balance and slowing the company's cash flow. Production managers must strive to minimize the amount of excess inventory on hand. Managers must coordinate efforts to speed up the collection of receivables, while also ensuring that the company pays its payables on time, but never too early.

p. 61

Q. Discuss the difference in the debt to total assets ratio of Microsoft and General Motors.

A. Microsoft has a very low debt to total assets ratio. The company is in a rapidly changing industry and thus should try to minimize the risk associated with increased debt. Also, because Microsoft generates significant amounts of cash and has minimal needs for large investments in plant assets, it does not need to borrow a lot of cash. General Motors needs to make huge investments in plant assets, and it has a very large credit operation. Thus it has large borrowing needs.

p. 66

Q. What problems might Best Buy's year-end create for analysts?

A. First, if Best Buy's competitors use a different year-end, then when you compare their financial results, you are not comparing performance over the same period of time or financial position at the same point in time. Also, by not picking a particular date, the number of weeks in Best Buy's fiscal year will change. For example, fiscal years 2002, 2003, and 2004 had 52 weeks, but fisal year 2001 had 53 weeks.

Answer to Tootsie Roll Review It Question 3, p. 53

Tootsie Roll's largest current asset at December 31, 2004, was cash and cash equivalents, at $56,989,000.

Answers to Self-Study Questions

1. d   2. a   3. b   4. a   5. c   6. b   7. d   8. a   9. a   10. c   11. c
12. c

The Accounting Information System

STUDY OBJECTIVES

After studying this chapter,
you should be able to:

1 Analyze the effect of business transactions on the basic accounting equation.

2 Explain what an account is and how it helps in the recording process.

3 Define debits and credits and explain how they are used to record business transactions.

4 Identify the basic steps in the recording process.

5 Explain what a journal is and how it helps in the recording process.

6 Explain what a ledger is and how it helps in the recording process.

7 Explain what posting is and how it helps in the recording process.

8 Explain the purposes of a trial balance.

THE NAVIGATOR

- Scan *Study Objectives*
- Read *Feature Story*
- Read *Preview*
- Read text and answer *Before You Go On*
  p. 107 ◯ p. 113 ◯ p. 117 ◯ p. 126 ◯
  p. 128 ◯
- Work *Using the Decision Toolkit*
- Review *Summary of Study Objectives*
- Work *Demonstration Problem*
- Answer *Self-Study Questions*
- Complete *Assignments*

FEATURE STORY

Accidents Happen

How organized are you financially? Take a short quiz. Answer *yes* or *no* to each question:

• Does your wallet contain so many cash machine receipts that you've been declared a walking fire hazard?

• Is your wallet such a mess that it is often faster to fish for money in the crack of your car seat than to dig around in your wallet?

• Was Shaquille O'Neal playing high school basketball the last time you balanced your checkbook?

• Have you ever been tempted to burn down your house so you don't have to try to find all of the receipts and records that you need to fill out your tax returns?

If you think it is hard to keep track of the many transactions that make up *your* life, imagine what it is like for a major corporation like Fidelity Investments. Fidelity is one of the largest mutual fund management firms in the world. If you had your life savings invested at Fidelity Investments, you might be just slightly displeased if, when you called to find out your balance, the representative said, "You know, I kind of remember someone with a name like yours sending us some money—now what did we do with that?"

To ensure the accuracy of your balance and the security of your funds, Fidelity Investments, like all

other companies large and small, relies on a sophisticated accounting information system. That's not to say that Fidelity or any other company is error-free. In fact, if you've ever really messed up your checkbook register, you may take some comfort from one accountant's mistake at Fidelity Investments. The accountant failed to include a minus sign while doing a calculation, making what was actually a $1.3 billion loss look like a $1.3 billion gain—yes, *billion!* Fortunately, like most accounting errors, it was detected before any real harm was done.

No one expects that kind of mistake at a company like Fidelity, which has sophisticated computer systems and top investment managers.

In explaining the mistake to shareholders, a spokesperson wrote, "Some people have asked how, in this age of technology, such a mistake could be made. While many of our processes are computerized, accounting systems are complex and dictate that some steps must be handled manually by our managers and accountants, and people can make mistakes."

On the World Wide Web
Fidelity Investments: www.fidelity.com

PREVIEW OF CHAPTER 3

As indicated in the Feature Story, a reliable information system is a necessity for any company. The purpose of this chapter is to explain and illustrate the features of an accounting information system. The organization and content of the chapter are as follows.

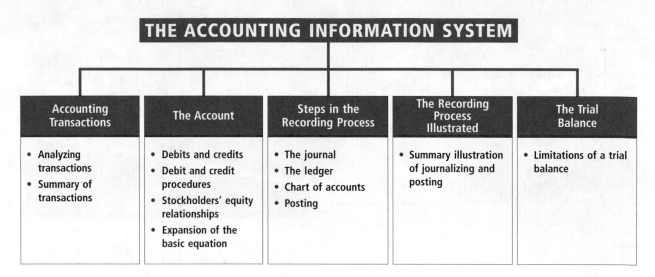

THE ACCOUNTING INFORMATION SYSTEM

Accounting Transactions	The Account	Steps in the Recording Process	The Recording Process Illustrated	The Trial Balance
• Analyzing transactions • Summary of transactions	• Debits and credits • Debit and credit procedures • Stockholders' equity relationships • Expansion of the basic equation	• The journal • The ledger • Chart of accounts • Posting	• Summary illustration of journalizing and posting	• Limitations of a trial balance

THE NAVIGATOR

The Accounting Information System

The system of collecting and processing transaction data and communicating financial information to decision makers is known as the **accounting information system**. Factors that shape these systems include: the nature of the company's business, the types of transactions, the size of the company, the volume of data, and the information demands of management and others.

Most businesses use computerized accounting systems—sometimes referred to as electronic data processing (EDP) systems. These systems handle all the steps involved in the recording process, from initial data entry to preparation of the financial statements. In order to remain competitive, companies continually improve their accounting systems to provide accurate and timely data for decision making. For example, in a recent annual report, Tootsie Roll states, "We also invested in additional processing and data storage hardware during the year. We view information technology as a key strategic tool, and are committed to deploying leading edge technology in this area." In addition, many companies have upgraded their accounting information systems in response to the requirements of Sarbanes-Oxley.

In this chapter we focus on a manual accounting system because the accounting concepts and principles do not change whether a system is computerized or manual, and manual systems are easier to illustrate. However, many of the problems in this and subsequent chapters can also be done using the computerized general ledger package that supplements this text.

Accounting Transactions

To use an accounting information system, you need to know which economic events to recognize (record). Not all events are recorded and reported in the financial statements. For example, suppose General Motors hired a new employee or purchased a new computer. Are these events entered in its accounting records? The first event would not be recorded, but the second event would. We call economic events that require recording in the financial statements **accounting transactions**.

An accounting transaction occurs when assets, liabilities, or stockholders' equity items change as a result of some economic event. The purchase of a computer by General Motors, the payment of rent by Microsoft, and the sale of advertising space by Sierra Corporation are examples of events that change a company's assets, liabilities, or stockholders' equity. Illustration 3-1 summarizes the decision process companies use to decide whether or not to record economic events.

Illustration 3-1
Transaction identification process

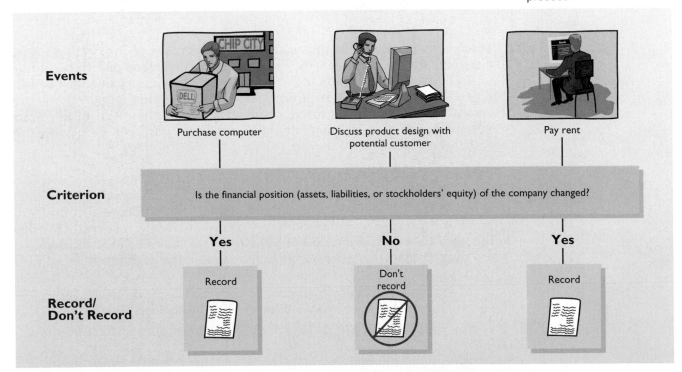

ANALYZING TRANSACTIONS

In Chapter 1 you learned the basic accounting equation:

STUDY OBJECTIVE

1

Analyze the effect of business transactions on the basic accounting equation.

Assets = Liabilities + Stockholders' Equity

In this chapter you will learn how to analyze transactions in terms of their effect on assets, liabilities, and stockholders' equity. **Transaction analysis** is the process of identifying the specific effects of economic events on the accounting equation.

The accounting equation must always balance. Each transaction has a dual (double-sided) effect on the equation. For example, if an individual asset is increased, there must be a corresponding:

Decrease in another asset, *or*
Increase in a specific liability, *or*
Increase in stockholders' equity.

Two or more items could be affected when an asset is increased. For example, if a company purchases a computer for $10,000 by paying $6,000 in cash and signing a note for $4,000, one asset (computer) increases $10,000, another asset (cash) decreases $6,000, and a liability (notes payable) increases $4,000. The result is that the accounting equation remains in balance—assets increased by a net $4,000 and liabilities increased by $4,000, as shown below.

Assets	=	Liabilities	+	Stockholders' Equity
+$10,000		+$4,000		
− 6,000				
$ 4,000	=	$4,000		

Chapter 1 presented the financial statements for Sierra Corporation for its first month. You should review those financial statements (on pp. 13–17) at this time. To illustrate how economic events affect the accounting equation, we will examine events affecting Sierra Corporation during its first month. If you are tempted to skip ahead after you've read a few of these, don't do it. Each has something unique to teach, something you'll need later. (We assure you that we've kept them to the minimum needed!)

EVENT (1). INVESTMENT OF CASH BY STOCKHOLDERS. On October 1 cash of $10,000 is invested in the business by investors in exchange for $10,000 of common stock. This event is an accounting transaction because it results in an increase in both assets and stockholders' equity. There is an increase of $10,000 in the asset Cash and an increase of $10,000 in Common Stock on the books of Sierra Corporation. The effect of this transaction on the basic equation is:

	Assets	=	Liabilities	+	Stockholders' Equity	
	Cash	=			Common Stock	
(1)	+$10,000	=			+$10,000	Issued stock

The equation is in balance. **The source of each change to stockholders' equity is noted to the right of the transaction.** In this case it was an issuance of common stock. Keeping track of the source of each change in stockholders' equity is essential for later accounting activities—in particular, for the calculation of net income.

EVENT (2). NOTE ISSUED IN EXCHANGE FOR CASH. On October 1 Sierra borrowed $5,000 on a 3-month, 12%, $5,000 note payable to Castle Bank. This transaction results in an equal increase in assets and liabilities: Cash (an asset) increases $5,000, and Notes Payable (a liability) increases $5,000. The specific effect of this transaction and the cumulative effect of the first two transactions are:

		Assets	=	Liabilities	+	Stockholders' Equity
		Cash	=	Notes Payable	+	Common Stock
Old Balance		$10,000				$10,000
(2)		+5,000		+$5,000		
New Balance		$15,000	=	$5,000	+	$10,000
			$15,000			

Total assets are now $15,000, and stockholders' equity plus the new liability also total $15,000.

EVENT (3). PURCHASE OF OFFICE EQUIPMENT FOR CASH.

On October 2 Sierra purchased office equipment by paying $5,000 cash to Superior Equipment Sales Co. This event is a transaction because an equal increase and decrease in Sierra's assets occur: Office Equipment (an asset) increases $5,000, and Cash (an asset) decreases $5,000.

		Assets			=	Liabilities	+	Stockholders' Equity
		Cash	+	Office Equipment	=	Notes Payable	+	Common Stock
Old Balance		$15,000				$5,000		$10,000
(3)		−5,000		+$5,000				
New Balance		$10,000	+	$5,000	=	$5,000	+	$10,000
			$15,000				$15,000	

The total assets are now $15,000, and stockholders' equity plus the liability also total $15,000.

EVENT (4). RECEIPT OF CASH IN ADVANCE FROM CUSTOMER.

On October 2 Sierra received a $1,200 cash advance from R. Knox, a client. This event is a transaction because Sierra received cash (an asset) for advertising services that are expected to be completed by Sierra in the future. Although Sierra received cash, **it does not record revenue until it has performed the work**. In some industries, such as the magazine and airline industries, customers are expected to prepay. These companies have a liability to the customer until they deliver the magazines or provide the flight. As soon as the company provides the product or service, it records the revenue.

Since Sierra received cash prior to performance of the service, Sierra has a liability for the work due. Cash increases by $1,200, and a liability, Unearned Service Revenue (abbreviated as Unearned Revenue), increases by an equal amount.

		Assets			=	Liabilities			+	Stockholders' Equity
		Cash	+	Office Equipment	=	Notes Payable	+	Unearned Revenue	+	Common Stock
Old Balance		$10,000		$5,000		$5,000				$10,000
(4)		+1,200						+$1,200		
New Balance		$11,200	+	$5,000	=	$5,000	+	$1,200	+	$10,000
			$16,200					$16,200		

EVENT (5). SERVICES PROVIDED FOR CASH. On October 3 Sierra received $10,000 in cash from Copa Company for advertising services performed. This event is a transaction because Sierra received an asset (cash) in exchange for services.

Advertising service is the principal revenue-producing activity of Sierra. **Revenue increases stockholders' equity.** This transaction, then, increases both assets and stockholders' equity. Cash is increased $10,000, and Retained Earnings is increased $10,000. The new balances in the equation are:

	Assets		=	Liabilities		+	Stockholders' Equity	
	Cash	+ Office Equipment	=	Notes Payable	+ Unearned Revenue	+	Common Stock	+ Retained Earnings
Old Balance	$11,200	$5,000		$5,000	$1,200		$10,000	
(5)	+10,000							+$10,000 Service Revenue
New Balance	$21,200 +	$5,000	=	$5,000 +	$1,200	+	$10,000 +	$10,000
	$26,200					$26,200		

Often companies provide services "on account." That is, they provide service for which they are paid at a later date. Revenue, however, is earned when services are performed. Therefore, stockholders' equity would increase when services are performed, even though cash has not been received. Instead of receiving cash, the company receives a different type of asset, an **account receivable**. Accounts receivable represent the right to receive payment at a later date. Suppose that Sierra had provided these services on account rather than for cash. This event would be reported using the accounting equation as:

Assets	=	Liabilities	+	Stockholders' Equity
Accounts Receivable	=			Retained Earnings
+$10,000				+$10,000 Service Revenue

Later, when Sierra collects the $10,000 from the customer, Accounts Receivable would decline by $10,000, and Cash would increase by $10,000.

Assets		=	Liabilities	+	Stockholders' Equity
Cash	Accounts Receivable	=			
+$10,000	−$10,000				

Note that in this case, stockholders' equity is not affected by the collection of cash. Instead we record an exchange of one asset (Accounts Receivable) for a different asset (Cash).

EVENT (6). PAYMENT OF RENT. On October 3 Sierra Corporation paid its office rent for the month of October in cash, $900. This rent payment is a transaction because it results in a decrease in an asset, cash.

Rent is an expense incurred by Sierra Corporation in its effort to generate revenues. **Expenses decrease stockholders' equity.** Sierra records the rent payment by decreasing cash and decreasing stockholders' equity (specifically, Retained Earnings) to maintain the balance of the accounting equation. To record this transaction, Sierra decreases Cash $900, and decreases Retained Earnings $900. The effect of these payments on the accounting equation is:

	Assets		=	Liabilities		+	Stockholders' Equity	
	Cash +	Office Equipment	=	Notes Payable +	Unearned Revenue	+	Common Stock +	Retained Earnings
Old Balance	$21,200	$5,000		$5,000	$1,200		$10,000	$10,000
(6)	−900							−900 **Rent Expense**
New Balance	$20,300 +	$5,000	=	$5,000 +	$1,200	+	$10,000 +	$ 9,100
	$25,300				$25,300			

EVENT (7). PURCHASE OF INSURANCE POLICY IN CASH.

On October 4 Sierra paid $600 for a one-year insurance policy that will expire next year on September 30. In this transaction the asset Cash is decreased $600. Payments of expenses that will benefit more than one accounting period are identified as assets called prepaid expenses or prepayments. Therefore the asset Prepaid Insurance is increased $600. The balance in total assets did not change; one asset account decreased by the same amount that another increased.

	Assets			=	Liabilities		+	Stockholders' Equity	
	Cash +	Prepaid Insurance +	Office Equipment	=	Notes Payable +	Unearned Revenue	+	Common Stock +	Retained Earnings
Old Balance	$20,300		$5,000		$5,000	$1,200		$10,000	$9,100
(7)	−600	+$600							
New Balance	$19,700 +	$ 600 +	$5,000	=	$5,000 +	$1,200	+	$10,000 +	$9,100
	$25,300					$25,300			

EVENT (8). PURCHASE OF SUPPLIES ON ACCOUNT.

On October 5 Sierra purchased a three-month supply of advertising materials on account from Aero Supply for $2,500. In this case, "on account" means that the company receives goods or services that it will pay for at a later date. Supplies, an asset, increases $2,500 by this transaction. Accounts Payable, a liability, increases $2,500, to indicate the amount due to Aero Supply. The effect on the equation is:

	Assets				=	Liabilities			+	Stockholders' Equity	
	Cash +	Supplies +	Prepaid Insurance +	Office Equipment	=	Notes Payable +	Accounts Payable +	Unearned Revenue	+	Common Stock +	Retained Earnings
Old Balance	$19,700		$600	$5,000		$5,000		$1,200		$10,000	$9,100
(8)		+$2,500					+$2,500				
New Balance	$19,700+	$ 2,500 +	$600 +	$5,000	=	$5,000 +	$ 2,500 +	$1,200	+	$10,000 +	$9,100
	$27,800						$27,800				

EVENT (9). HIRING OF NEW EMPLOYEES.

On October 9 Sierra hired four new employees to begin work on October 15. Each employee will receive a weekly salary of $500 for a five-day work week, payable every two weeks. Employees will receive their first paychecks on October 26. On the date Sierra hires the employees, there is no effect on the accounting equation because the assets, liabilities, and stockholders' equity of the company have not changed. **An accounting transaction has not occurred.** At this point there is only an agreement that the employees will begin work on October 15. [See Event (11) for the first payment.]

EVENT (10). PAYMENT OF DIVIDEND. On October 20 Sierra paid a $500 dividend. **Dividends** are a distribution of net income and not an expense. A dividend transaction affects assets and stockholders' equity: Cash and Retained Earnings are decreased $500.

		Cash	+ Supplies +	Prepaid Insurance	+	Office Equipment	=	Notes Payable	+	Accounts Payable	+	Unearned Revenue	+	Common Stock	+	Retained Earnings	
		Assets					**=**	**Liabilities**					**+**	**Stockholders' Equity**			
	Old Balance	$19,700	$2,500	$600		$5,000		$5,000		$2,500		$1,200		$10,000		$9,100	
(10)		−500														−500	Dividends
	New Balance	$19,200 +	$2,500 +	$600	+	$5,000	=	$5,000 +		$2,500 +		$1,200 +		$10,000 +		$8,600	
			$27,300								$27,300							

EVENT (11). PAYMENT OF CASH FOR EMPLOYEE SALARIES. Employees have worked two weeks, earning $4,000 in salaries, which were paid on October 26. Salaries are an expense which reduce stockholders' equity. This event is a transaction because assets and stockholders' equity are affected. Thus, Cash and Retained Earnings are each decreased $4,000.

		Cash	+ Supplies +	Prepaid Insurance	+	Office Equipment	=	Notes Payable	+	Accounts Payable	+	Unearned Revenue	+	Common Stock	+	Retained Earnings	
		Assets					**=**	**Liabilities**					**+**	**Stockholders' Equity**			
	Old Balance	$19,200	$2,500	$600		$5,000		$5,000		$2,500		$1,200		$10,000		$8,600	
(11)		−4,000														−4,000	Salaries
	New Balance	$15,200 +	$2,500 +	$600	+	$5,000	=	$5,000 +		$2,500 +		$1,200 +		$10,000 +		$4,600	Expense
			$23,300								$23,300							

Business Insight
Investor Perspective

While most companies record transactions very carefully, the reality is that mistakes still happen. For example, bank regulators fined Bank One Corporation (now Chase) $1.8 million because they felt that the unreliability of the bank's accounting system caused it to violate regulatory requirements.

Also, in recent years Fannie Mae, the government-chartered mortgage association, announced a series of large accounting errors. These announcements caused alarm among investors, regulators, and politicians because they fear that the errors may suggest larger, undetected problems. This is important because the home-mortgage market depends on Fannie Mae to buy hundreds of billions of dollars of mortgages each year from banks, thus enabling the banks to issue new mortgages.

Finally, before a major overhaul of its accounting system, the financial records of Waste Management Company were in such disarray that of the company's 57,000 employees, 10,000 were receiving pay slips that were in error.

The Sarbanes-Oxley Act of 2002 was created to minimize the occurrence of errors like these by increasing every employee's responsibility for accurate financial reporting.

 In order for these companies to prepare and issue financial statements, their accounting equations (debits and credits) must have been in balance at year-end. How could these errors or misstatements have occurred?

SUMMARY OF TRANSACTIONS

Illustration 3-2 summarizes the transactions of Sierra Corporation to show their cumulative effect on the basic accounting equation. It includes the transaction number in the first column on the left. The right-most column shows the specific effect of any transaction that affects stockholders' equity. Remember that Event (9) did not result in a transaction, so no entry is included for that event. The illustration demonstrates three important points:

1. Each transaction is analyzed in terms of its effect on assets, liabilities, and stockholders' equity.
2. The two sides of the equation must always be equal.
3. The cause of each change in stockholders' equity must be indicated.

Illustration 3-2
Summary of transactions

	Assets				=	Liabilities			+	Stockholders' Equity		
	Cash	+ Supplies +	Prepaid Insurance +	Office Equipment =		Notes Payable +	Accounts Payable +	Unearned Revenue +		Common Stock +	Retained Earnings	
(1)	+$10,000				=					+$10,000		Issued stock
(2)	+5,000					+$5,000						
(3)	−5,000			+$5,000								
(4)	+1,200							+$1,200				
(5)	+10,000										+$10,000	Service Revenue
(6)	−900										−900	Rent Expense
(7)	−600		+$600									
(8)		+$2,500					+$2,500					
(10)	−500										−500	Dividends
(11)	−4,000										−4,000	Salaries Expense
	$15,200 +	$2,500 +	$600 +	$5,000 =		$5,000 +	$2,500 +	$1,200 +		$10,000 +	$ 4,600	
		$23,300						$23,300				

Decision Toolkit

Decision Checkpoints	Info Needed for Decision	Tool to Use for Decision	How to Evaluate Results
✔			
Has an accounting transaction occurred?	Details of the event	Accounting equation	If the event affected assets, liabilities, or stockholders' equity, then record as a transaction.

BEFORE YOU GO ON . . .

▶Review It

1. What are the criteria that must be met for an event to be recorded in the financial statements? What is the name for events that require recording?
2. What is transaction analysis?
3. Why isn't the purchase of equipment treated as an expense at the time of purchase?
4. Why isn't an advance received from customers treated as revenue at the time of receipt?

▶Do It

A tabular analysis of the transactions made by Roberta Mendez & Co., a certified public accounting firm, for the month of August is shown below. Each increase and decrease in stockholders' equity is explained.

	Assets		=	Liabilities +		Stockholders' Equity		
	Cash	+ Office Equipment	=	Accounts Payable	+ Common Stock	+ Retained Earnings		
1.	+25,000				+25,000			Issued Stock
2.		+7,000		+7,000				
3.	+8,000					+8,000		Service Revenue
4.	−850					−850		Rent Expense

Describe each transaction that occurred for the month.

Action Plan

• Analyze the tabular analysis to determine the nature and effect of each transaction.
• Keep the accounting equation always in balance.
• Remember that a change in an asset will require a change in another asset, a liability, or in stockholders' equity.

Solution

1. The company issued shares of stock to stockholders for $25,000 cash.
2. The company purchased $7,000 of office equipment on account.
3. The company received $8,000 of cash in exchange for services performed.
4. The company paid $850 for this month's rent.

THE NAVIGATOR

The Account

STUDY OBJECTIVE
2
Explain what an account is and how it helps in the recording process.

Rather than using a tabular summary like the one in Illustration 3-2 for Sierra Corporation, an accounting information system uses accounts. An **account** is an individual accounting record of increases and decreases in a specific asset, liability, or stockholders' equity item. For example, Sierra Corporation has separate accounts for Cash, Accounts Receivable, Accounts Payable, Service Revenue, Salaries Expense, and so on. (Note that whenever we are referring to a specific account, we capitalize the name.)

In its simplest form, an account consists of three parts: (1) the title of the account, (2) a left or debit side, and (3) a right or credit side. Because the alignment of these parts of an account resembles the letter T, it is referred to as a **T account**. The basic form of an account is shown in Illustration 3-3.

Illustration 3-3 Basic form of account

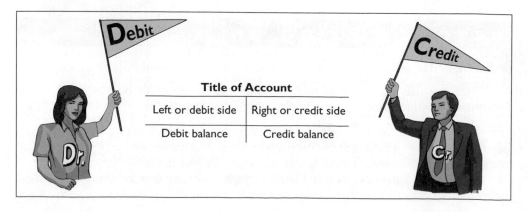

Title of Account	
Left or debit side	Right or credit side
Debit balance	Credit balance

We use this form of account often throughout this book to explain basic accounting relationships.

DEBITS AND CREDITS

The term debit indicates left, and credit indicates right. They are commonly abbreviated as **Dr.** for debit and **Cr.** for credit. They **do not** mean increase or decrease, as is commonly thought. We use the terms *debit* and *credit* repeatedly in the recording process to describe **where** entries are made in accounts. For example, the act of entering an amount on the left side of an account is called **debiting** the account. Making an entry on the right side is **crediting** the account.

When comparing the totals of the two sides, an account shows a **debit balance** if the total of the debit amounts exceeds the credits. An account shows a **credit balance** if the credit amounts exceed the debits. Note the position of the debit or credit balances in Illustration 3-3.

The procedure of recording debits and credits in an account is shown in Illustration 3-4 for the transactions affecting the Cash account of Sierra Corporation. The data are taken from the Cash column of the tabular summary in Illustration 3-2.

STUDY OBJECTIVE

3

Define debits and credits and explain how they are used to record business transactions.

Tabular Summary		Account Form			
Cash		**Cash**			
$10,000		(Debits)	10,000	(Credits)	5,000
5,000			5,000		900
−5,000			1,200		600
1,200			10,000		500
10,000					4,000
−900					
−600		Balance	15,200		
−500		(Debit)			
−4,000					
$15,200					

Illustration 3-4 Tabular summary and account form for Sierra Corporation's Cash account

Every positive item in the tabular summary represents a receipt of cash; every negative amount represents a payment of cash. **Notice that in the account form we record the increases in cash as debits, and the decreases in cash as credits.** For example, the $10,000 receipt of cash (in red) is debited to Cash, and the −$5,000 payment of cash (in blue) is credited to Cash.

Having increases on one side and decreases on the other reduces recording errors and helps in determining the totals of each side of the account as well as the balance in the account. The account balance, a debit of $15,200, indicates that Sierra Corporation had $15,200 more increases than decreases in cash. That is, since it started with a balance of zero, it has $15,200 in its Cash account.

DEBIT AND CREDIT PROCEDURES

Each transaction must affect two or more accounts to keep the basic accounting equation in balance. In other words, for each transaction, debits must equal credits. The equality of debits and credits provides the basis for the double-entry accounting system.

Under the **double-entry system**, the two-sided effect of each transaction is recorded in appropriate accounts. This system provides a logical method for recording transactions. The double-entry system also helps to ensure the accuracy of the recorded amounts and helps to detect errors such as those at Fidelity Investments as discussed in the Feature Story. If every transaction is recorded with equal debits and credits, then the sum of all the debits to the accounts must equal the sum of all the credits. The double-entry system for determining the equality of the accounting equation is much more efficient than the plus/minus procedure used earlier.

Dr./Cr. Procedures for Assets and Liabilities

In Illustration 3-4 for Sierra Corporation, increases in Cash—an asset—were entered on the left side, and decreases in Cash were entered on the right side. We know that both sides of the basic equation (Assets = Liabilities + Stockholders' Equity) must be equal. It therefore follows that increases and decreases in liabilities will have to be recorded *opposite from* increases and decreases in assets. Thus, increases in liabilities must be entered on the right or credit side, and decreases in liabilities must be entered on the left or debit side. The effects that debits and credits have on assets and liabilities are summarized in Illustration 3-5.

Illustration 3-5 Debit and credit effects—assets and liabilities

Debits	Credits
Increase assets	Decrease assets
Decrease liabilities	Increase liabilities

Asset accounts normally show debit balances. That is, debits to a specific asset account should exceed credits to that account. Likewise, **liability accounts normally show credit balances**. That is, credits to a liability account should exceed debits to that account. The **normal balances** may be diagrammed as in Illustration 3-6.

Illustration 3-6 Normal balances—assets and liabilities

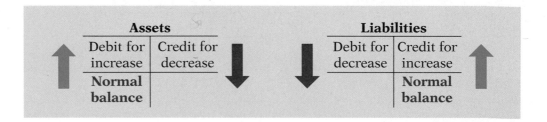

Knowing which is the normal balance in an account may help when you are trying to identify errors. For example, a credit balance in an asset account such as Land or a debit balance in a liability account such as Wages Payable usually indicates errors in recording. Occasionally, however, an abnormal balance may be correct. The Cash account, for example, will have a credit balance when a company has overdrawn its bank balance (written a check that "bounced"). In automated accounting systems, the computer is programmed to flag violations of the normal balance and to print out error or exception reports. In manual systems, careful visual inspection of the accounts is required to detect normal balance problems.

Dr./Cr. Procedures for Stockholders' Equity

In Chapter 1 we indicated that stockholders' equity is comprised of two parts: common stock and retained earnings. In the transaction events earlier in this chapter, you saw that revenues, expenses, and the payment of dividends affect retained earnings. We are now at the point where we can expand the subdivision of stockholders' equity. The subdivisions of stockholders' equity are: common stock, retained earnings, dividends, revenues, and expenses.

COMMON STOCK.   Common stock is issued to investors in exchange for the stockholders' investment. The Common Stock account is increased by credits and decreased by debits. For example, when cash is invested in the business, Cash is debited and Common Stock is credited. The effects of debits and credits on the Common Stock account are shown in Illustration 3-7.

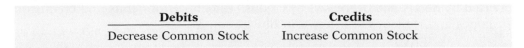

Debits	Credits
Decrease Common Stock	Increase Common Stock

Illustration 3-7 Debit and credit effects— Common Stock

The normal balance in the Common Stock account may be diagrammed as in Illustration 3-8.

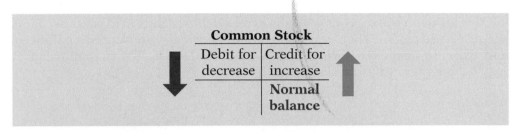

Illustration 3-8 Normal balance—Common Stock

RETAINED EARNINGS. Retained earnings is net income that is retained in the business. It represents the portion of stockholders' equity that has been accumulated through the profitable operation of the company. Retained Earnings is increased by credits (for example, by net income) and decreased by debits (for example, by a net loss), as shown in Illustration 3-9.

Debits	Credits
Decrease Retained Earnings	Increase Retained Earnings

Illustration 3-9 Debit and credit effects— Retained Earnings

The normal balance for Retained Earnings may be diagrammed as in Illustration 3-10.

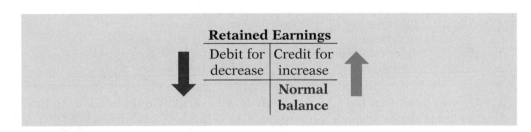

Illustration 3-10 Normal balance—Retained Earnings

DIVIDENDS. A dividend is a distribution by a corporation to its stockholders. The most common form of distribution is a cash dividend. Dividends result in a reduction of the stockholders' claims on retained earnings. Because dividends reduce stockholders' equity, increases in the Dividends account are recorded with debits. As shown in Illustration 3-11, the Dividends account normally has a debit balance.

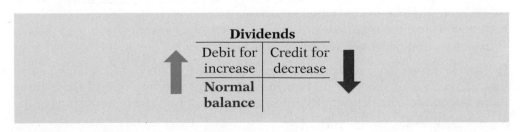

Illustration 3-11 Normal balance—Dividends

REVENUES AND EXPENSES. When a company earns revenues, stockholders' equity is increased. Revenue accounts are increased by credits and decreased by debits.

Expenses decrease stockholders' equity. Thus, expense accounts are increased by debits and decreased by credits. The effects of debits and credits on revenues and expenses are shown in Illustration 3-12.

Illustration 3-12 Debit and credit effects—revenues and expenses

Debits	Credits
Decrease revenues	Increase revenues
Increase expenses	Decrease expenses

Credits to revenue accounts should exceed debits; debits to expense accounts should exceed credits. Thus, **revenue accounts normally show credit balances, and expense accounts normally show debit balances.** The normal balances may be diagrammed as in Illustration 3-13.

Illustration 3-13 Normal balances—revenues and expenses

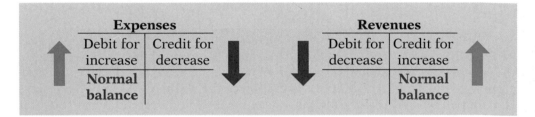

Expenses			Revenues	
Debit for increase	Credit for decrease		Debit for decrease	Credit for increase
Normal balance				**Normal balance**

Business Insight
Investor Perspective

The Chicago Cubs baseball team has these major revenue and expense accounts:

Revenues	Expenses
Admissions (ticket sales)	Players' salaries
Concessions	Administrative salaries
Television and radio	Travel
Advertising	Ballpark maintenance

 Do you think that the Chicago Bears football team would be likely to have the same major revenue and expense accounts as the Cubs?

STOCKHOLDERS' EQUITY RELATIONSHIPS

Companies report the subdivisions of stockholders' equity in various places in the financial statements:

- Common stock and retained earnings: in the stockholders' equity section of the balance sheet.
- Dividends: on the retained earnings statement.
- Revenues and expenses: on the income statement.

Dividends, revenues, and expenses are eventually transferred to retained earnings at the end of the period. As a result, a change in any one of these three items affects stockholders' equity. Illustration 3-14 shows the relationships of the accounts affecting stockholders' equity.

Illustration 3-14
Stockholders' equity
relationships

Balance Sheet

Assets

Liabilities

Stockholder's equity
   Common stock ← ──────── Investments by stockholders
   Retained earnings ← ──── Net income retained in the business

Income Statement

Revenues
Less: Expenses
Net income or net loss ──────

Retained Earnings Statement

Retained earnings, beginning
Add: Net income ←──────
Less: Dividends
Retained earnings, ending

EXPANSION OF THE BASIC EQUATION

You have already learned the basic accounting equation. Illustration 3-15 expands this equation to show the accounts that make up stockholders' equity. In addition, it illustrates the debit/credit rules and effects on each type of account. **Study this diagram carefully.** It will help you understand the fundamentals of the double-entry system. Like the basic equation, the expanded basic equation must be in balance: Total debits must equal total credits.

Illustration 3-15
Expansion of the basic
accounting equation

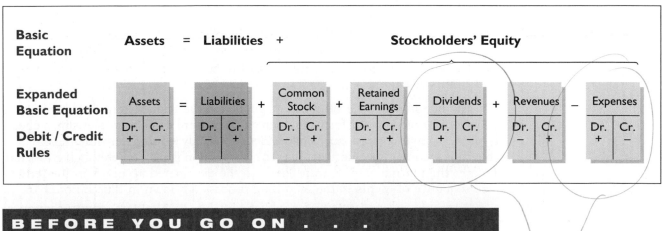

Basic Equation	Assets	=	Liabilities	+			Stockholders' Equity				

| Expanded Basic Equation | Assets | = | Liabilities | + | Common Stock | + | Retained Earnings | − | Dividends | + | Revenues | − | Expenses |
| Debit / Credit Rules | Dr. + / Cr. − | | Dr. − / Cr. + | | Dr. − / Cr. + | | Dr. − / Cr. + | | Dr. + / Cr. − | | Dr. − / Cr. + | | Dr. + / Cr. − |

B E F O R E   Y O U   G O   O N . . .

▶Review It

1. What do the terms *debit* and *credit* indicate?
2. What are the debit and credit effects on assets, liabilities, and stockholders' equity?
3. What are the debit and credit effects on revenues, expenses, and dividends?

4. What are the normal balances for the following accounts of Tootsie Roll Industries: Accounts Receivable; Income Taxes Payable; Sales; and Selling, Marketing, and Administrative Expense? (The answer to this question appears on page 155.)

▶Do It

Kate Browne, president of Hair It Is Inc., has just rented space in a shopping mall for the purpose of opening and operating a beauty salon. Long before opening day and before purchasing equipment, hiring assistants, and remodeling the space, Kate was strongly advised to set up a double-entry set of accounting records in which to record all of her business transactions.

Identify the balance sheet accounts that Hair It Is Inc. will likely need to record the transactions necessary to establish and open for business. Also, indicate whether the normal balance of each account is a debit or a credit.

Action Plan

• First identify asset accounts for each different type of asset invested in the business.

• Then identify liability accounts for debts incurred by the business.

• Remember that Hair It Is Inc. will need only one stockholders' equity account for common stock when it begins the business. The other stockholders' equity accounts will be needed only after the business is operating.

Solution

Hair It Is Inc. would likely need the following accounts in which to record the transactions necessary to establish and ready the beauty salon for opening day: Cash (debit balance); Equipment (debit balance); Supplies (debit balance); Accounts Payable (credit balance); Notes Payable (credit balance), if the business borrows money; and Common Stock (credit balance).

THE NAVIGATOR

Steps in the Recording Process

STUDY OBJECTIVE

4

Identify the basic steps in the recording process.

Although it is possible to enter transaction information directly into the accounts, few businesses do so. Practically every business uses these basic steps in the recording process:

1. Analyze each transaction in terms of its effect on the accounts.
2. Enter the transaction information in a journal.
3. Transfer the journal information to the appropriate accounts in the ledger (book of accounts).

The actual sequence of events begins with the transaction. Evidence of the transaction comes in the form of a **source document**, such as a sales slip, a check, a bill, or a cash register tape. This evidence is analyzed to determine the effect of the transaction on specific accounts. The transaction is then entered in the **journal**. Finally, the journal entry is transferred to the designated accounts in the **ledger**. The sequence of events in the recording process is shown in Illustration 3-16.

THE JOURNAL

STUDY OBJECTIVE

5

Explain what a journal is and how it helps in the recording process.

Transactions are initially recorded in chronological order in journals before they are transferred to the accounts. For each transaction the journal shows the debit and credit effects on specific accounts. (In a computerized system, journals are kept as files, and accounts are recorded in computer databases.)

Companies may use various kinds of journals, but every company has at least the most basic form of journal, a **general journal**. **The journal makes three significant contributions to the recording process:**

The Recording Process

Analyze each transaction

Enter transaction in a journal

Transfer journal information to ledger accounts

Illustration 3-16 The recording process

1. It discloses in one place the **complete effect of a transaction**.
2. It provides a **chronological record** of transactions.
3. It **helps to prevent or locate errors** because the debit and credit amounts for each entry can be readily compared.

Entering transaction data in the journal is known as journalizing. To illustrate the technique of journalizing, let's look at the first three transactions of Sierra Corporation in equation form.

On October 1, Sierra issued common stock in exchange for $10,000 cash:

Assets	**= Liabilities +**	**Stockholders' Equity**
Cash	=	Common Stock
+$10,000		+$10,000 Issued stock

On October 1, Sierra borrowed $5,000 by signing a note:

Assets	**= Liabilities +**	**Stockholders' Equity**
Cash	=	Notes Payable
+$5,000	+$5,000	

On October 2, Sierra purchased office equipment for $5,000:

Assets		**= Liabilities +**	**Stockholders' Equity**
Cash	Office Equipment		
−$5,000	+$5,000		

Sierra makes separate journal entries for each transaction. A complete entry consists of: (1) the date of the transaction, (2) the accounts and amounts to be debited and credited, and (3) a brief explanation of the transaction. These transactions are journalized in Illustration 3-17 (on page 116).

Note the following features of the journal entries.

1. The date of the transaction is entered in the Date column.
2. The account to be debited is entered first at the left. The account to be credited is then entered on the next line, indented under the line above. The indentation differentiates debits from credits and decreases the possibility of switching the debit and credit amounts.

Illustration 3-17
Recording transactions in
journal form

GENERAL JOURNAL			
Date	**Account Titles and Explanation**	**Debit**	**Credit**
2007			
Oct. 1	Cash	10,000	
	Common Stock		10,000
	(Issued stock for cash)		
1	Cash	5,000	
	Notes Payable		5,000
	(Issued 3-month, 12% note payable for cash)		
2	Office Equipment	5,000	
	Cash		5,000
	(Purchased office equipment for cash)		

3. The amounts for the debits are recorded in the Debit (left) column, and the amounts for the credits are recorded in the Credit (right) column.

4. A brief explanation of the transaction is given.

It is important to use correct and specific account titles in journalizing. Erroneous account titles lead to incorrect financial statements. Some flexibility exists initially in selecting account titles. The main criterion is that each title must appropriately describe the content of the account. For example, a company could use any of these account titles for recording the cost of delivery trucks: Delivery Equipment, Delivery Trucks, or Trucks. Once the company chooses the specific title to use, however, it should record under that account title all subsequent transactions involving the account.

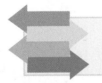

Accounting across the Organization

Bryan Lee is head of finance at Microsoft's Home and Entertainment Division. In recent years the division has lost over $4 billion, mostly due to losses on the original Xbox videogame player. With the new Xbox 360 videogame player, Mr. Lee hopes the division will become profitable. He has set strict goals for sales, revenue, and profit. "A manager seeking to spend more on a feature such as a disk drive has to find allies in the group to cut spending elsewhere, or identify new revenue to offset the increase," he explains.

For example, Microsoft originally designed the new Xbox to have 256 megabytes of memory. But the design department said that amount of memory wouldn't support the best special effects. The purchasing department said that adding more memory would cost $30—which is 10% of the estimated selling price of $300. But the marketing department "determined that adding the memory would let Microsoft reduce marketing costs and attract more game developers, boosting royalty revenue. It would also extend the life of the console, generating more sales." Microsoft doubled the memory to 512 megabytes.

Source: Robert A. Guth, "New Xbox Aim for Microsoft: Profitability," *Wall Street Journal*, May 24, 2005, p. C1.

 In what ways is this Microsoft division using accounting to assist in its effort to become more profitable?

BEFORE YOU GO ON . . .

▶Review It

1. What is the correct sequence of steps in the recording process?
2. What contribution does the journal make to the recording process?
3. What are the standard form and content of a journal entry made in the general journal?

▶Do It

The following events occurred during the first month of business of Hair It Is Inc., Kate Browne's beauty salon:

1. Issued common stock to shareholders in exchange for $20,000 cash.
2. Purchased $4,800 of equipment on account (to be paid in 30 days).
3. Interviewed three people for the position of beautician.

In what form (type of record) should the company record these three activities? Prepare the entries to record the transactions.

Action Plan

• Record the transactions in a journal, which is a chronological record of the transactions.
• Make sure to provide a complete and accurate representation of the transactions' effects on the assets, liabilities, and stockholders' equity of the business.

Solution

Each transaction that is recorded is entered in the general journal. The three activities are recorded as follows.

1. Cash	20,000	
Common Stock		20,000
(Issued stock for cash)		
2. Equipment	4,800	
Accounts Payable		4,800
(Purchased equipment on account)		
3. No entry because no transaction occurred.		

THE LEDGER

The entire group of accounts maintained by a company is referred to collectively as the **ledger**. The ledger keeps in one place all the information about changes in specific account balances.

Companies may use various kinds of ledgers, but every company has a general ledger. A **general ledger** contains all the assets, liabilities, and stockholders' equity accounts, as shown in Illustration 3-18 (page 118). Whenever we use the term *ledger* in this textbook without additional specification, it will mean the general ledger.

STUDY OBJECTIVE
6

Explain what a ledger is and how it helps in the recording process.

CHART OF ACCOUNTS

The number and type of accounts used differ for each company, depending on the size, complexity, and type of business. For example, the number of accounts depends on the amount of detail desired by management. The management of one company may want one single account for all types of utility expense. Another may keep separate expense accounts for each type of utility expenditure, such as gas, electricity, and water. A small corporation like Sierra Corporation will not have many accounts compared with a corporate giant like Ford Motor Company. Sierra may be able to manage and report its activities in 20 to 30 accounts, whereas Ford requires thousands of accounts to keep track of its worldwide activities.

Illustration 3-18 The general ledger

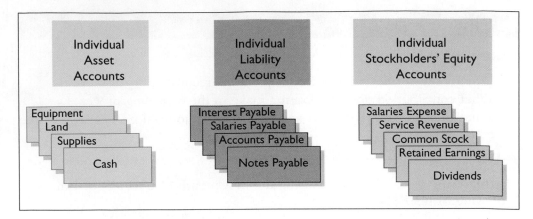

Most companies list the accounts in a **chart of accounts**. They may create new accounts as needed during the life of the business. Illustration 3-19 shows the chart of accounts for Sierra Corporation. **Accounts shown in red are used in this chapter**; accounts shown in black are explained in later chapters.

Illustration 3-19 Chart of accounts for Sierra Corporation

SIERRA CORPORATION—Chart of Accounts				
Assets	**Liabilities**	Stockholders' **Equity**	**Revenues**	**Expenses**
Cash	**Notes Payable**	**Common Stock**	**Service Revenue**	**Salaries Expense**
Accounts Receivable	**Accounts Payable**	**Retained Earnings**		Supplies Expense
Advertising Supplies	Interest Payable	**Dividends**		**Rent Expense**
Prepaid Insurance	**Unearned**	Income Summary		Insurance Expense
Office Equipment	**Service Revenue**			Interest Expense
Accumulated Depreciation—	Salaries Payable			Depreciation Expense
Office Equipment				

POSTING

The procedure of transferring journal entries to ledger accounts is called **posting**. **This phase of the recording process accumulates the effects of journalized transactions in the individual accounts.** Posting involves these steps:

1. In the ledger, enter in the appropriate columns of the debited account(s) the date and debit amount shown in the journal.
2. In the ledger, enter in the appropriate columns of the credited account(s) the date and credit amount shown in the journal.

The Recording Process Illustrated

Illustrations 3-20 through 3-30 on the following pages show the basic steps in the recording process using the October transactions of Sierra Corporation. Sierra's accounting period is a month. A basic analysis and a debit–credit analysis precede the journalizing and posting of each transaction. Study these transaction analyses carefully. **The purpose of transaction analysis is first to identify the type of account involved and then to determine whether a debit or a credit to the account is required.** You should always perform this type of analysis before preparing a journal entry. Doing so will help you understand the journal entries discussed in this chapter as well as more complex journal entries to be described in later chapters.

In addition, an Accounting Cycle Tutorial at the book's website, **www.wiley.com/ college/kimmel,** provides an interactive presentation of the steps in the accounting cycle, using the examples in the illustrations on the following pages. The illustration at the top of the next page is a shot of the tutorial's opening screen.

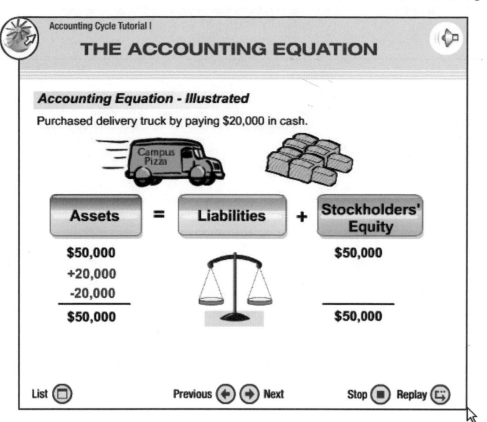

The Accounting Cycle Tutorial is available at **www.wiley.com/college/kimmel.**

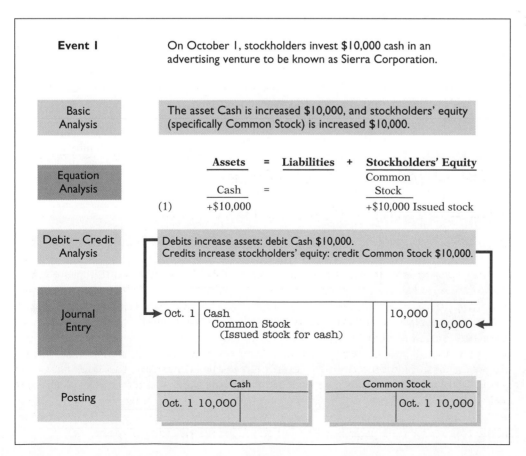

Illustration 3-20
Investment of cash by stockholders

Illustration 3-21 Issue of note payable

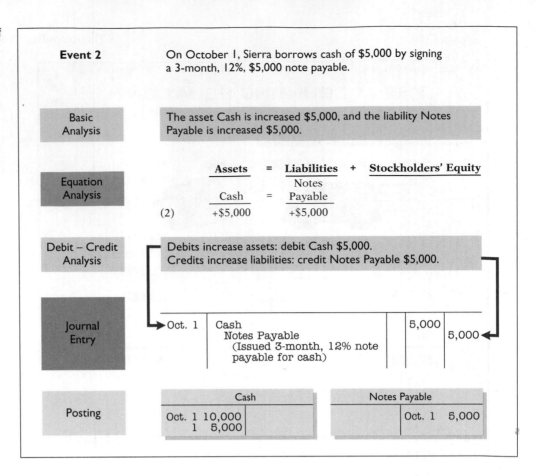

Illustration 3-22
Purchase of office equipment

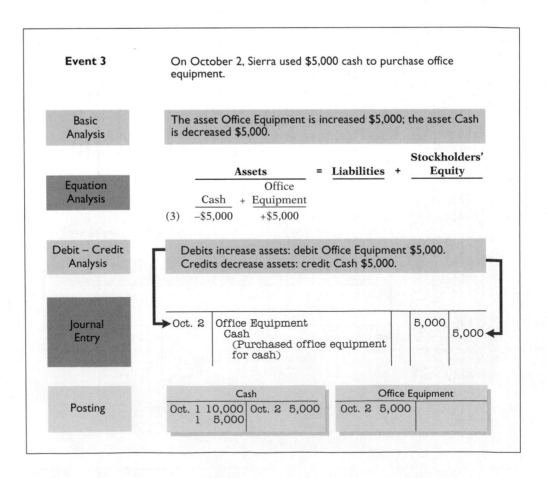

Illustration 3-23 Receipt of cash in advance from customer

Event 4

On October 2, Sierra received a $1,200 cash advance from R. Knox, a client, for advertising services that are expected to be completed by December 31.

Basic Analysis

The asset Cash is increased $1,200; the liability Unearned Service Revenue is increased $1,200 because the service has not been provided yet. That is, when an advance payment is received, an unearned revenue (a liability) should be recorded in order to recognize the obligation that exists.

Helpful Hint Many liabilities have the word "payable" in their title. But note that Unearned Service Revenue is considered a liability even though the word *payable* is not used.

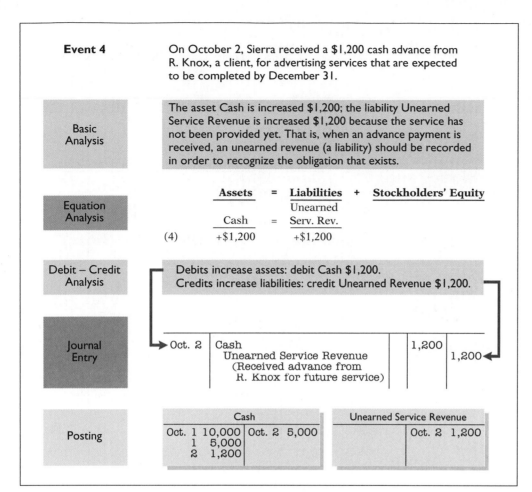

Equation Analysis

	Assets	=	Liabilities	+	Stockholders' Equity
	Cash	=	Unearned Serv. Rev.		
(4)	+$1,200		+$1,200		

Debit – Credit Analysis

Debits increase assets: debit Cash $1,200.
Credits increase liabilities: credit Unearned Revenue $1,200.

Journal Entry

Oct. 2	Cash	1,200	
	Unearned Service Revenue		1,200
	(Received advance from R. Knox for future service)		

Posting

Cash				Unearned Service Revenue	
Oct. 1	10,000	Oct. 2 5,000			Oct. 2 1,200
1	5,000				
2	1,200				

Illustration 3-24 Services provided for cash

Event 5

On October 3, Sierra received $10,000 in cash from Copa Company for advertising services provided in October.

Basic Analysis

The asset Cash is increased $10,000; the revenue Service Revenue is increased $10,000.

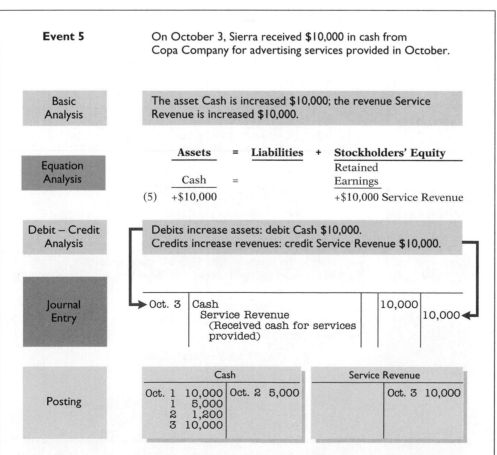

Equation Analysis

	Assets	=	Liabilities	+	Stockholders' Equity
	Cash	=			Retained Earnings
(5)	+$10,000				+$10,000 Service Revenue

Debit – Credit Analysis

Debits increase assets: debit Cash $10,000.
Credits increase revenues: credit Service Revenue $10,000.

Journal Entry

Oct. 3	Cash	10,000	
	Service Revenue		10,000
	(Received cash for services provided)		

Posting

Cash				Service Revenue	
Oct. 1	10,000	Oct. 2 5,000			Oct. 3 10,000
1	5,000				
2	1,200				
3	10,000				

Illustration 3-25
Payment of rent in cash

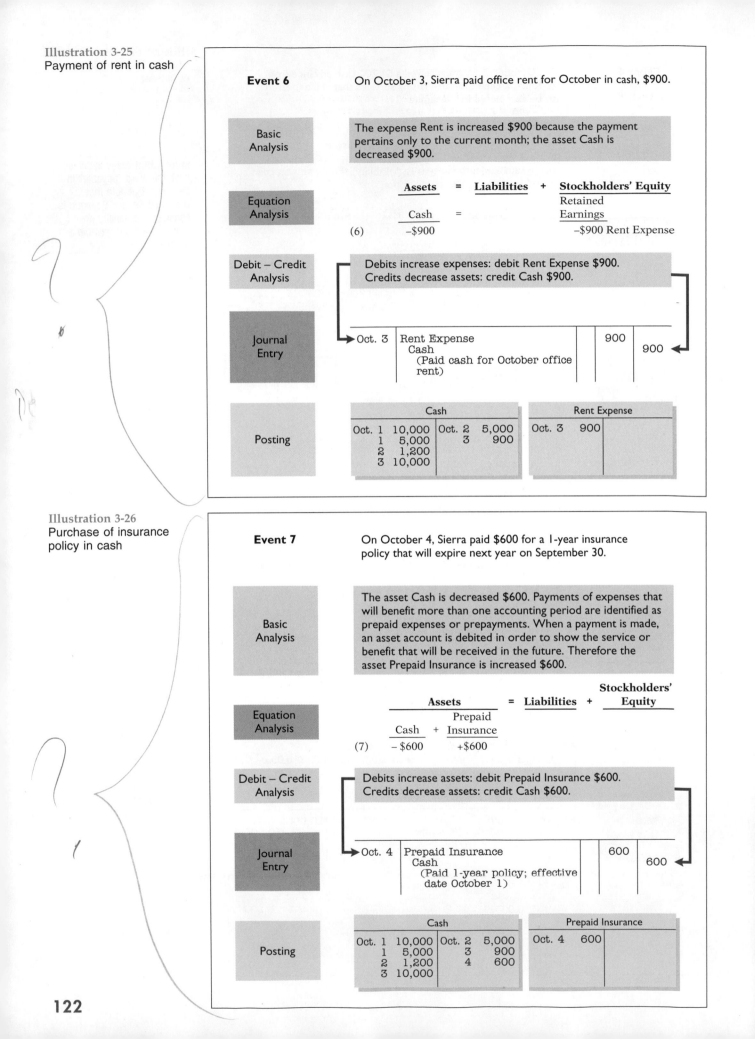

Event 6 On October 3, Sierra paid office rent for October in cash, $900.

Basic Analysis The expense Rent is increased $900 because the payment pertains only to the current month; the asset Cash is decreased $900.

Equation Analysis

	Assets	=	Liabilities	+	Stockholders' Equity
	Cash	=			Retained Earnings
(6)	−$900				−$900 Rent Expense

Debit – Credit Analysis Debits increase expenses: debit Rent Expense $900.
Credits decrease assets: credit Cash $900.

Journal Entry

Oct. 3	Rent Expense	900	
	Cash		900
	(Paid cash for October office rent)		

Posting

Cash				Rent Expense	
Oct. 1	10,000	Oct. 2	5,000	Oct. 3	900
1	5,000	3	900		
2	1,200				
3	10,000				

Illustration 3-26
Purchase of insurance policy in cash

Event 7 On October 4, Sierra paid $600 for a 1-year insurance policy that will expire next year on September 30.

Basic Analysis The asset Cash is decreased $600. Payments of expenses that will benefit more than one accounting period are identified as prepaid expenses or prepayments. When a payment is made, an asset account is debited in order to show the service or benefit that will be received in the future. Therefore the asset Prepaid Insurance is increased $600.

Equation Analysis

	Assets		=	Liabilities	+	Stockholders' Equity
	Cash	+	Prepaid Insurance	=		
(7)	− $600		+$600			

Debit – Credit Analysis Debits increase assets: debit Prepaid Insurance $600.
Credits decrease assets: credit Cash $600.

Journal Entry

Oct. 4	Prepaid Insurance	600	
	Cash		600
	(Paid 1-year policy; effective date October 1)		

Posting

Cash				Prepaid Insurance	
Oct. 1	10,000	Oct. 2	5,000	Oct. 4	600
1	5,000	3	900		
2	1,200	4	600		
3	10,000				

Illustration 3-27
Purchase of supplies on account

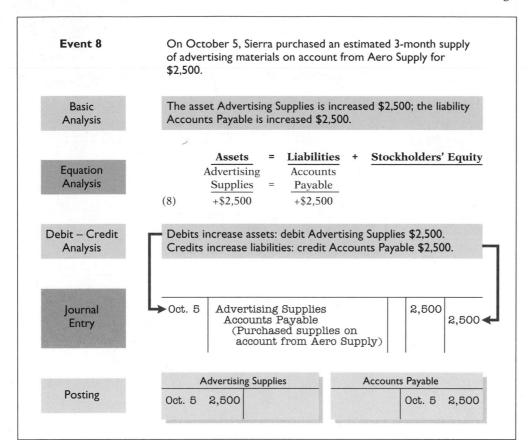

| | **Event 8** | On October 5, Sierra purchased an estimated 3-month supply of advertising materials on account from Aero Supply for $2,500. |

Basic Analysis

The asset Advertising Supplies is increased $2,500; the liability Accounts Payable is increased $2,500.

Equation Analysis

	Assets	=	**Liabilities**	+	**Stockholders' Equity**
	Advertising		Accounts		
	Supplies	=	Payable		
(8)	+$2,500		+$2,500		

Debit – Credit Analysis

Debits increase assets: debit Advertising Supplies $2,500.
Credits increase liabilities: credit Accounts Payable $2,500.

Journal Entry

Oct. 5	Advertising Supplies	2,500	
	Accounts Payable		2,500
	(Purchased supplies on account from Aero Supply)		

Posting

Advertising Supplies		Accounts Payable	
Oct. 5 2,500			Oct. 5 2,500

Illustration 3-28   Hiring of new employees

| | **Event 9** | On October 9, Sierra hired four employees to begin work on October 15. Each employee is to receive a weekly salary of $500 for a 5-day work week, payable every 2 weeks — first payment made on October 26. |

Basic Analysis

An accounting transaction has not occurred. There is only an agreement that the employees will begin work on October 15. Thus, a debit–credit analysis is not needed because there is no accounting entry. (See transaction of October 26 for first entry.)

Illustration 3-29
Payment of dividend

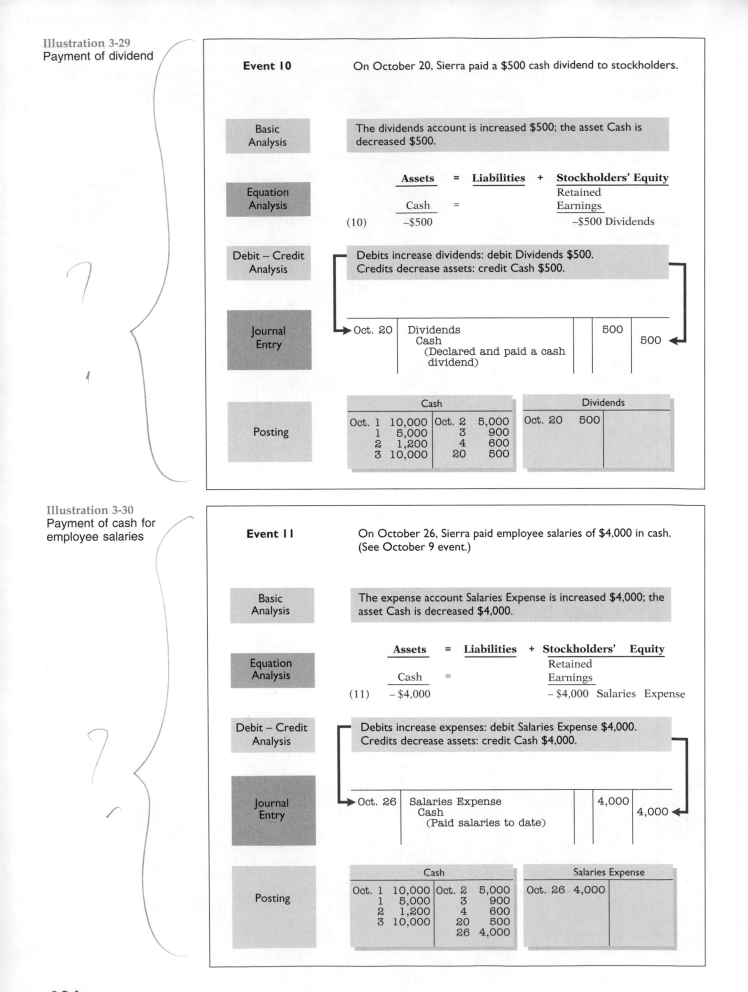

Event 10   On October 20, Sierra paid a $500 cash dividend to stockholders.

Basic Analysis   The dividends account is increased $500; the asset Cash is decreased $500.

Equation Analysis

	Assets	=	Liabilities	+	Stockholders' Equity
					Retained
	Cash	=			Earnings
(10)	–$500				–$500 Dividends

Debit – Credit Analysis   Debits increase dividends: debit Dividends $500.
Credits decrease assets: credit Cash $500.

Journal Entry

Oct. 20	Dividends	500	
	Cash		500
	(Declared and paid a cash		
	dividend)		

Posting

	Cash						Dividends	
Oct. 1	10,000	Oct. 2	5,000		Oct. 20	500	
1	5,000	3	900				
2	1,200	4	600				
3	10,000	20	500				

Illustration 3-30
Payment of cash for
employee salaries

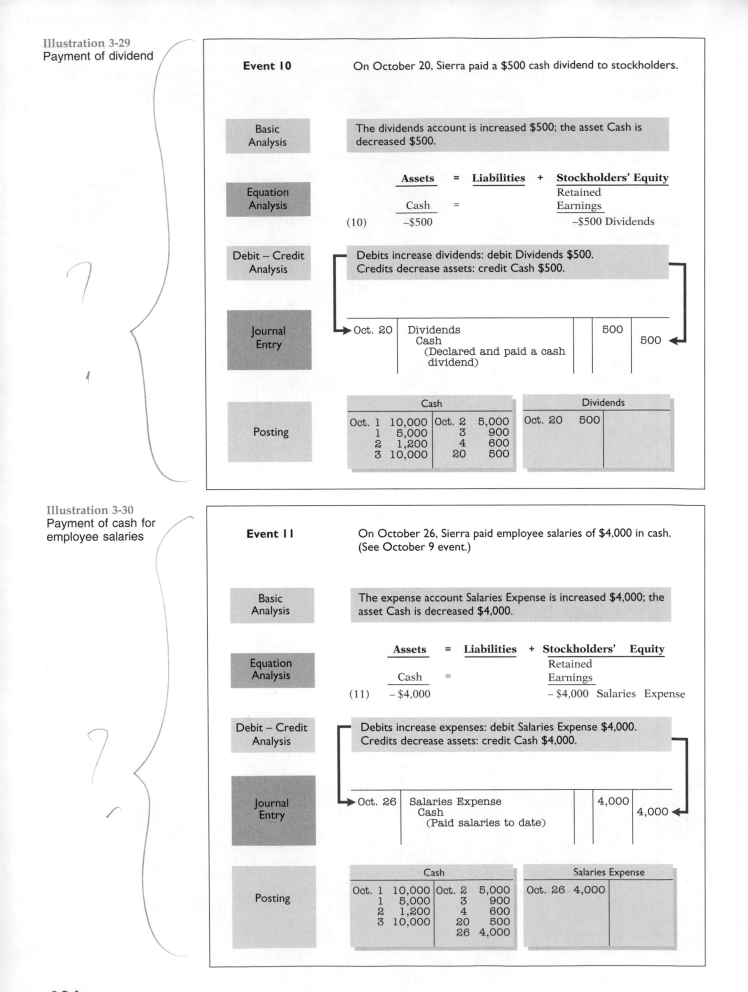

Event 11   On October 26, Sierra paid employee salaries of $4,000 in cash.
(See October 9 event.)

Basic Analysis   The expense account Salaries Expense is increased $4,000; the asset Cash is decreased $4,000.

Equation Analysis

	Assets	=	Liabilities	+	Stockholders' Equity
					Retained
	Cash	=			Earnings
(11)	–$4,000				–$4,000 Salaries Expense

Debit – Credit Analysis   Debits increase expenses: debit Salaries Expense $4,000.
Credits decrease assets: credit Cash $4,000.

Journal Entry

Oct. 26	Salaries Expense	4,000	
	Cash		4,000
	(Paid salaries to date)		

Posting

	Cash					Salaries Expense	
Oct. 1	10,000	Oct. 2	5,000		Oct. 26	4,000	
1	5,000	3	900				
2	1,200	4	600				
3	10,000	20	500				
		26	4,000				

SUMMARY ILLUSTRATION OF JOURNALIZING AND POSTING

The journal for Sierra Corporation for the month of October is summarized in Illustration 3-31. The ledger is shown in Illustration 3-32 with all balances highlighted in red.

Illustration 3-31 General journal for Sierra Corporation

GENERAL JOURNAL

Date	Account Titles and Explanation	Debit	Credit
2007 Oct. 1	Cash	10,000	
	Common Stock		10,000
	(Issued stock for cash)		
1	Cash	5,000	
	Notes Payable		5,000
	(Issued 3-month, 12% note payable for cash)		
2	Office Equipment	5,000	
	Cash		5,000
	(Purchased office equipment for cash)		
2	Cash	1,200	
	Unearned Service Revenue		1,200
	(Received advance from R. Knox for future service)		
3	Cash	10,000	
	Service Revenue		10,000
	(Received cash for services provided)		
3	Rent Expense	900	
	Cash		900
	(Paid cash for October office rent)		
4	Prepaid Insurance	600	
	Cash		600
	(Paid 1-year policy; effective date October 1)		
5	Advertising Supplies	2,500	
	Accounts Payable		2,500
	(Purchased supplies on account from Aero Supply)		
20	Dividends	500	
	Cash		500
	(Declared and paid a cash dividend)		
26	Salaries Expense	4,000	
	Cash		4,000
	(Paid salaries to date)		

Illustration 3-32 General ledger for Sierra Corporation

GENERAL LEDGER

Cash				Unearned Service Revenue	
Oct. 1	10,000	Oct. 2	5,000		Oct. 2	1,200
1	5,000	3	900		
2	1,200	4	600		Bal.	**1,200**
3	10,000	20	500		
		26	4,000		
Bal.	**15,200**				

Illustration 3-32
(continued) General
ledger for Sierra
Corporation

GENERAL LEDGER

Advertising Supplies				Common Stock		
Oct. 5	2,500				Oct. 1	10,000
Bal.	**2,500**				Bal.	**10,000**

Prepaid Insurance				Dividends		
Oct. 4	600			Oct. 20	500	
Bal.	**600**			Bal.	**500**	

Office Equipment				Service Revenue		
Oct. 2	5,000				Oct. 3	10,000
Bal.	**5,000**				Bal.	**10,000**

Notes Payable				Salaries Expense		
		Oct. 1	5,000	Oct. 26	4,000	
		Bal.	**5,000**	Bal.	**4,000**	

Accounts Payable				Rent Expense		
		Oct. 5	2,500	Oct. 3	900	
		Bal.	**2,500**	Bal.	**900**	

BEFORE YOU GO ON . . .

▶ Review It

1. How does journalizing differ from posting?
2. What is the purpose of (a) the ledger and (b) a chart of accounts?

▶ Do It

Selected transactions from the journal of Faital Inc. during its first month of operations are presented below. Post these transactions to T accounts.

Date		Account Titles	Debit	Credit
July	1	Cash	30,000	
		Common Stock		30,000
	9	Accounts Receivable	6,000	
		Service Revenue		6,000
	24	Cash	4,000	
		Accounts Receivable		4,000

Action Plan

• Journalize transactions to keep track of financial activities (receipts, payments, receivables, payables, etc.).
• To make entries useful, classify and summarize them by posting the entries to specific ledger accounts.

Solution

Cash				Accounts Receivable			
July 1	30,000			July 9	6,000	July 24	4,000
24	4,000						

Common Stock				Service Revenue			
		July 1	30,000			July 9	6,000

The Trial Balance

A trial balance lists accounts and their balances at a given time. A company usually prepares a trial balance at the end of an accounting period. The accounts are listed in the order in which they appear in the ledger. Debit balances are listed in the left column and credit balances in the right column. The totals of the two columns must be equal.

The trial balance proves the mathematical equality of debits and credits after posting. Under the double-entry system this equality occurs when the sum of the debit account balances equals the sum of the credit account balances. **A trial balance may also uncover errors in journalizing and posting.** For example, a trial balance may well have detected the error at Fidelity Investments discussed in the Feature Story. **In addition, a trial balance is useful in the preparation of financial statements.**

These are the procedures for preparing a trial balance:

1. List the account titles and their balances.
2. Total the debit column and total the credit column.
3. Verify the equality of the two columns.

Illustration 3-33 presents the trial balance prepared from the ledger of Sierra Corporation. Note that the total debits, $28,700, equal the total credits, $28,700.

> **STUDY OBJECTIVE**
> ——— **8** ———
> Explain the purposes of a trial balance.

SIERRA CORPORATION Trial Balance October 31, 2007		
	Debit	**Credit**
Cash	$15,200	
Advertising Supplies	2,500	
Prepaid Insurance	600	
Office Equipment	5,000	
Notes Payable		$ 5,000
Accounts Payable		2,500
Unearned Service Revenue		1,200
Common Stock		10,000
Dividends	500	
Service Revenue		10,000
Salaries Expense	4,000	
Rent Expense	900	
	$28,700	**$28,700**

Illustration 3-33 Sierra Corporation trial balance

LIMITATIONS OF A TRIAL BALANCE

A trial balance does not prove that all transactions have been recorded or that the ledger is correct. Numerous errors may exist even though the trial balance columns agree. For example, the trial balance may balance even when any of the following occurs: (1) a transaction is not journalized, (2) a correct journal entry is not posted, (3) a journal entry is posted twice, (4) incorrect accounts are used in journalizing or posting, or (5) offsetting errors are made in recording the amount of a transaction. In other words, as long as equal debits and credits are posted, even to the wrong account or in the wrong amount, the total debits will equal the total credits. Nevertheless, despite these limitations, the trial balance is a useful screen for finding errors and is frequently used in practice.

BEFORE YOU GO ON . . .

▶**Review It**

1. What is a trial balance, and how is it prepared?
2. What is the primary purpose of a trial balance?
3. What are the limitations of a trial balance?

THE NAVIGATOR

Decision Toolkit

Decision Checkpoints	Info Needed for Decision	Tool to Use for Decision	How to Evaluate Results
✔		⚋━━⚋	👍👎
How do you determine that debits equal credits?	All account balances	Trial balance	List the account titles and their balances; total the debit and credit columns; verify equality.

Using the Decision Toolkit

The Kansas Farmers' Vertically Integrated Cooperative, Inc. (K-VIC), was formed by over 200 northeast Kansas farmers in the late 1980s. Its purpose is to use raw materials, primarily grain and meat products grown by K-VIC's members, to process this material into end-user food products, and to distribute the products nationally. Profits not needed for expansion or investment are returned to the members annually, on a pro-rata basis, according to the market value of the grain and meat products received from each farmer.

Assume that the following information was prepared for K-VIC's trial balance.

KANSAS FARMERS' VERTICALLY INTEGRATED COOPERATIVE, INC.
Trial Balance
December 31, 2007
(in thousands)

	Debit	Credit
Accounts Receivable	$ 712,000	
Accounts Payable		$ 37,000
Advertising and Promotion Payable		141,000
Buildings	365,000	
Cash	32,000	
Cost of Goods Sold	2,384,000	
Current Maturity of Long-Term Debt		12,000
Inventories	1,291,000	
Land	110,000	
Long-Term Debt		873,000
Machinery and Equipment	63,000	
Notes Payable to Members		495,000
Retained Earnings		822,000
Sales Revenue		3,741,000
Salaries and Wages Payable		62,000
Selling and Administrative Expense	651,000	
Trucking Expense	500,000	
	$6,108,000	$6,183,000

Because the trial balance is not in balance, you have checked with various people responsible for entering accounting data and have discovered the following.

1. The purchase of 35 new trucks, costing $7 million and paid for with cash, was not recorded.
2. A data entry clerk accidentally deleted the account name for an account with a credit balance of $472 million, so the amount was added to the Long-Term Debt account in the trial balance.
3. December cash sales revenue of $75 million was credited to the Sales Revenue account, but the other half of the entry was not made.
4. $50 million of selling expenses were mistakenly charged to Trucking Expense.

Instructions
Answer these questions.
(a) Which mistake(s) have caused the trial balance to be out of balance?
(b) Should all of the items be corrected? Explain.
(c) What is the name of the account the data entry clerk deleted?
(d) Make the necessary corrections and balance the trial balance.
(e) On your trial balance, write BAL beside the accounts that go on the balance sheet and INC beside those that go on the income statement.

Solution

(a) Only mistake #3 has caused the trial balance to be out of balance.
(b) All of the items should be corrected. The misclassification error (mistake #4) on the selling expense would not affect bottom-line net income, but it does affect the amounts reported in the two expense accounts.
(c) There is no Common Stock account, so that must be the account that was deleted by the data entry clerk.
(d) and (e):

KANSAS FARMERS' VERTICALLY INTEGRATED COOPERATIVE, INC.
Trial Balance
December 31, 2007
(in thousands)

	Debit	Credit	
Accounts Receivable	$ 712,000		BAL
Accounts Payable		$ 37,000	BAL
Advertising and Promotion Payable		141,000	BAL
Buildings	365,000		BAL
Cash ($32,000 − $7,000 + $75,000)	100,000		BAL
Common Stock		472,000	BAL
Cost of Goods Sold	2,384,000		INC
Current Maturity of Long-Term Debt		12,000	BAL
Inventories	1,291,000		BAL
Land	110,000		BAL
Long-Term Debt		401,000	BAL
Machinery and Equipment	70,000		BAL
Notes Payable to Members		495,000	BAL
Retained Earnings		822,000	BAL
Sales Revenue		3,741,000	INC
Salaries and Wages Payable		62,000	BAL
Selling and Administrative Expense	701,000		INC
Trucking Expense	450,000		INC
	$6,183,000	$6,183,000	

Summary of Study Objectives

1 *Analyze the effect of business transactions on the basic accounting equation.* Each business transaction must have a dual effect on the accounting equation. For example, if an individual asset is increased, there must be a corresponding (a) decrease in another asset, or (b) increase in a specific liability, or (c) increase in stockholders' equity.

2 *Explain what an account is and how it helps in the recording process.* An account is an individual accounting record of increases and decreases in specific asset, liability, and stockholders' equity items.

3 *Define debits and credits and explain how they are used to record business transactions.* The terms *debit* and *credit* are synonymous with *left* and *right*. Assets, dividends, and expenses are increased by debits and decreased by credits. Liabilities, common stock, retained earnings, and revenues are increased by credits and decreased by debits.

4 *Identify the basic steps in the recording process.* The basic steps in the recording process are: (a) analyze each transaction in terms of its effect on the accounts, (b) enter the transaction information in a journal, and (c) transfer the journal information to the appropriate accounts in the ledger.

5 *Explain what a journal is and how it helps in the recording process.* The initial accounting record of a transaction is entered in a journal before the data are entered in the accounts. A journal (a) discloses in one place the complete effect of a transaction, (b) provides a chronological record of transactions, and (c) prevents or locates errors because the debit and credit amounts for each entry can be readily compared.

6 *Explain what a ledger is and how it helps in the recording process.* The entire group of accounts maintained by a company is referred to collectively as a ledger. The ledger keeps in one place all the information about changes in specific account balances.

7 *Explain what posting is and how it helps in the recording process.* Posting is the procedure of transferring journal entries to the ledger accounts. This phase of the recording process accumulates the effects of journalized transactions in the individual accounts.

8 *Explain the purposes of a trial balance.* A trial balance is a list of accounts and their balances at a given time. The primary purpose of the trial balance is to prove the mathematical equality of debits and credits after posting. A trial balance also uncovers errors in journalizing and posting and is useful in preparing financial statements.

THE NAVIGATOR

Decision Toolkit—A Summary

Decision Checkpoints	Info Needed for Decision	Tool to Use for Decision	How to Evaluate Results
Has an accounting transaction occurred?	Details of the event	Accounting equation	If the event affected assets, liabilities, or stockholders' equity, then record as a transaction.
How do you determine that debits equal credits?	All account balances	Trial balance	List the account titles and their balances; total the debit and credit colums; verify equality.

Glossary

Account An individual accounting record of increases and decreases in specific asset, liability, or stockholders' equity items. (p. 108)

Accounting information system The system of collecting and processing transaction data and communicating financial information to interested parties. (p. 100)

Accounting transactions Events that require recording in the financial statements because they affect assets, liabilities, or stockholders' equity. (p. 101)

Chart of accounts A list of a company's accounts. (p. 118)

Credit The right side of an account. (p. 109)

Debit The left side of an account. (p. 109)

Double-entry system A system that records the dual effect of each transaction in appropriate accounts. (p. 109)

General journal The most basic form of journal. (p. 114)

General ledger A ledger that contains all asset, liability, and stockholders' equity accounts. (p. 117)

Journal An accounting record in which transactions are initially recorded in chronological order. (p. 114)

Journalizing The procedure of entering transaction data in the journal. (p. 115)

Ledger The group of accounts maintained by a company. (p. 117)

Posting The procedure of transferring journal entries to the ledger accounts. (p. 118)

T account The basic form of an account. (p. 108)

Trial balance A list of accounts and their balances at a given time. (p. 127)

Demonstration Problem

Bob Sample and other student investors opened Campus Carpet Cleaning, Inc. on September 1, 2007. During the first month of operations the following transactions occurred.

Sept.	1	Stockholders invested $20,000 cash in the business.
	2	Paid $1,000 cash for store rent for the month of September.
	3	Purchased industrial carpet-cleaning equipment for $25,000, paying $10,000 in cash and signing a $15,000 6-month, 12% note payable.
	4	Paid $1,200 for 1-year accident insurance policy.
	10	Received bill from the *Daily News* for advertising the opening of the cleaning service, $200.
	15	Performed services on account for $6,200.
	20	Declared and paid a $700 cash dividend to stockholders.
	30	Received $5,000 from customers billed on September 15.

The chart of accounts for the company is the same as for Sierra Corporation except for the following additional accounts: Cleaning Equipment and Advertising Expense.

Instructions
(a) Journalize the September transactions.
(b) Open ledger accounts and post the September transactions.
(c) Prepare a trial balance at September 30, 2007.

Solution to Demonstration Problem

(a)

GENERAL JOURNAL

Date	Account Titles and Explanation	Debit	Credit
2007			
Sept. 1	Cash	20,000	
	Common Stock		20,000
	(Issued stock for cash)		
2	Rent Expense	1,000	
	Cash		1,000
	(Paid September rent)		
3	Cleaning Equipment	25,000	
	Cash		10,000
	Notes Payable		15,000
	(Purchased cleaning equipment for cash and 6-month, 12% note payable)		
4	Prepaid Insurance	1,200	
	Cash		1,200
	(Paid 1-year insurance policy)		
10	Advertising Expense	200	
	Accounts Payable		200
	(Received bill from *Daily News* for advertising)		
15	Accounts Receivable	6,200	
	Service Revenue		6,200
	(Services performed on account)		

Action Plan
- Proceed through the accounting cycle in the following sequence:

1. Make separate journal entries for each transaction.
2. Note that all debits precede all credit entries.
3. In journalizing, make sure debits equal credits.
4. In journalizing, use specific account titles taken from the chart of accounts.
5. Provide an appropriate explanation of each journal entry.
6. Arrange ledger in statement order, beginning with the balance sheet accounts.
7. Post in chronological order.
8. Prepare a trial balance, which lists accounts in the order in which they appear in the ledger.
9. List debit balances in the left column and credit balances in the right column.

20	Dividends		700	
	Cash			700
	(Declared and paid a cash dividend)			
30	Cash		5,000	
	Accounts Receivable			5,000
	(Collection of accounts receivable)			

(b) **GENERAL LEDGER**

Cash

Sept.	1	20,000	Sept.	2	1,000
	30	5,000		3	10,000
				4	1,200
				20	700
Bal.		**12,100**			

Accounts Receivable

Sept.	15	6,200	Sept.	30	5,000
Bal.		**1,200**			

Prepaid Insurance

Sept.	4	1,200		
Bal.		**1,200**		

Cleaning Equipment

Sept.	3	25,000		
Bal.		**25,000**		

Notes Payable

			Sept.	3	15,000
			Bal.		**15,000**

Accounts Payable

			Sept.	10	200
			Bal.		**200**

Common Stock

			Sept.	1	20,000
			Bal.		**20,000**

Dividends

Sept.	20	700		
Bal.		**700**		

Service Revenue

			Sept.	15	6,200
			Bal.		**6,200**

Advertising Expense

Sept.	10	200		
Bal.		**200**		

Rent Expense

Sept.	2	1,000		
Bal.		**1,000**		

(c)

CAMPUS CARPET CLEANING, INC.
Trial Balance
September 30, 2007

	Debit	Credit
Cash	$12,100	
Accounts Receivable	1,200	
Prepaid Insurance	1,200	
Cleaning Equipment	25,000	
Notes Payable		$15,000
Accounts Payable		200
Common Stock		20,000
Dividends	700	
Service Revenue		6,200
Advertising Expense	200	
Rent Expense	1,000	
	$41,400	$41,400

Self-Study Questions

Answers are at the end of the chapter.

(SO 1)   **1.** The effects on the basic accounting equation of performing services for cash are to:
(a) increase assets and decrease stockholders' equity.
(b) increase assets and increase stockholders' equity.
(c) increase assets and increase liabilities.
(d) increase liabilities and increase stockholders' equity.

(SO 1)   **2.** Genesis Company buys a $900 machine on credit. This transaction will affect the:
(a) income statement only.
(b) balance sheet only.
(c) income statement and retained earnings statement only.
(d) income statement, retained earnings statement, and balance sheet.

(SO 2)   **3.** Which statement about an account is *true*?
(a) In its simplest form, an account consists of two parts.
(b) An account is an individual accounting record of increases and decreases in specific asset, liability, and stockholders' equity items.
(c) There are separate accounts for specific assets and liabilities but only one account for stockholders' equity items.
(d) The left side of an account is the credit or decrease side.

(SO 3)   **4.** Debits:
(a) increase both assets and liabilities.
(b) decrease both assets and liabilities.
(c) increase assets and decrease liabilities.
(d) decrease assets and increase liabilities.

(SO 3)   **5.** A revenue account:
(a) is increased by debits.
(b) is decreased by credits.
(c) has a normal balance of a debit.
(d) is increased by credits.

(SO 3)   **6.** Which accounts normally have debit balances?
(a) Assets, expenses, and revenues.
(b) Assets, expenses, and retained earnings.
(c) Assets, liabilities, and dividends.
(d) Assets, dividends, and expenses.

(SO 4)   **7.** Which is *not* part of the recording process?
(a) Analyzing transactions.
(b) Preparing a trial balance.
(c) Entering transactions in a journal.
(d) Posting transactions.

(SO 5)   **8.** Which of these statements about a journal is *false*?
(a) It contains only revenue and expense accounts.
(b) It provides a chronological record of transactions.
(c) It helps to locate errors because the debit and credit amounts for each entry can be readily compared.
(d) It discloses in one place the complete effect of a transaction.

(SO 6)   **9.** A ledger:
(a) contains only asset and liability accounts.
(b) should show accounts in alphabetical order.
(c) is a collection of the entire group of accounts maintained by a company.
(d) provides a chronological record of transactions.

(SO 7)   **10.** Posting:
(a) normally occurs before journalizing.
(b) transfers ledger transaction data to the journal.
(c) is an optional step in the recording process.
(d) transfers journal entries to ledger accounts.

(SO 8)   **11.** A trial balance:
(a) is a list of accounts with their balances at a given time.
(b) proves the mathematical accuracy of journalized transactions.
(c) will not balance if a correct journal entry is posted twice.
(d) proves that all transactions have been recorded.

(SO 8)   **12.** A trial balance will *not* balance if:
(a) a correct journal entry is posted twice.
(b) the purchase of supplies on account is debited to Supplies and credited to Cash.
(c) a $100 cash dividend is debited to Dividends for $1,000 and credited to Cash for $100.
(d) a $450 payment on account is debited to Accounts Payable for $45 and credited to Cash for $45.

Go to the book's website, **www.wiley.com/college/kimmel**, to access additional Self-Study Questions.

✓ **THE NAVIGATOR**

Questions

1. Describe the accounting information system and the steps in the recording process.

2. Can a business enter into a transaction that affects only the left side of the basic accounting equation? If so, give an example.

3. Are the following events recorded in the accounting records? Explain your answer in each case.
   - *N* (a) A major stockholder of the company dies.
   - *Y* (b) Supplies are purchased on account.
   - *N* (c) An employee is fired.
   - *Y* (d) The company pays a cash dividend to its stockholders.

4. Indicate how each business transaction affects the basic accounting equation.
   - (a) Paid cash for janitorial services.
   - (b) Purchased equipment for cash.
   - (c) Issued common stock to investors in exchange for cash.
   - (d) Paid an account payable in full.

5. Why is an account referred to as a T account?

6. The terms *debit* and *credit* mean "increase" and "decrease," respectively. Do you agree? Explain.

7. Frank Fantazzi, a fellow student, contends that the double-entry system means each transaction must be recorded twice. Is Frank correct? Explain.

8. Emily Keshen, a beginning accounting student, believes debit balances are favorable and credit balances are unfavorable. Is Emily correct? Discuss.

9. State the rules of debit and credit as applied to (a) asset accounts, (b) liability accounts, and (c) the common stock account.

10. What is the normal balance for each of these accounts?
    - (a) Accounts Receivable.
    - (b) Cash.
    - (c) Dividends.
    - (d) Accounts Payable.
    - (e) Service Revenue.
    - (f) Salaries Expense.
    - (g) Common Stock.

11. Indicate whether each account is an asset, a liability, or a stockholders' equity account, and whether it would have a normal debit or credit balance.
    - (a) Accounts Receivable.
    - (b) Accounts Payable.
    - (c) Equipment.
    - (d) Dividends.
    - (e) Supplies.

12. For the following transactions, indicate the account debited and the account credited.
    - (a) Supplies are purchased on account.
    - (b) Cash is received on signing a note payable.
    - (c) Employees are paid salaries in cash.

13. For each account listed here, indicate whether it generally will have debit entries only, credit entries only, or both debit and credit entries.
    - (a) Cash.
    - (b) Accounts Receivable.
    - (c) Dividends.
    - (d) Accounts Payable.
    - (e) Salaries Expense.
    - (f) Service Revenue.

14. What are the basic steps in the recording process?

15. (a) When entering a transaction in the journal, should the debit or credit be written first?
    - (b) Which should be indented, the debit or the credit?

16. (a) Can accounting transaction debits and credits be recorded directly in the ledger accounts?
    - (b) What are the advantages of first recording transactions in the journal and then posting to the ledger?

17. Journalize these accounting transactions.
    - (a) Stockholders invested $12,000 in the business in exchange for common stock.
    - (b) Insurance of $800 is paid for the year.
    - (c) Supplies of $1,500 are purchased on account.
    - (d) Cash of $7,500 is received for services rendered.

18. (a) What is a ledger?
    - (b) Why is a chart of accounts important?

19. What is a trial balance and what are its purposes?

20. Russ Holub is confused about how accounting information flows through the accounting system. He believes information flows in this order:
    - (a) Debits and credits are posted to the ledger.
    - (b) Accounting transaction occurs.
    - (c) Information is entered in the journal.
    - (d) Financial statements are prepared.
    - (e) Trial balance is prepared.

    Indicate to Russ the proper flow of the information.

21. Two students are discussing the use of a trial balance. They wonder whether the following errors, each considered separately, would prevent the trial balance from balancing. What would you tell them?
    - (a) The bookkeeper debited Cash for $600 and credited Wages Expense for $600 for payment of wages.
    - (b) Cash collected on account was debited to Cash for $900, and Service Revenue was credited for $90.

Brief Exercises

Determine effect of transaction on basic accounting equation.
(SO 1)

BE3-1   Presented on page 135 are three economic events. On a sheet of paper, list the letters (a), (b), and (c) with columns for assets, liabilities, and stockholders' equity. In each column, indicate whether the event increased (+), decreased (−), or had no effect (NE) on assets, liabilities, and stockholders' equity.

(a) Purchased supplies on account.
(b) Received cash for providing a service.
(c) Expenses paid in cash.

BE3-2 During 2007, Walters Corp. entered into the following transactions.
1. Borrowed $80,000 by issuing bonds.
2. Paid $9,000 cash dividend to stockholders.
3. Received $17,000 cash from a customer who had previously been billed for services provided.
4. Purchased supplies on account for $3,100.

Determine effect of transactions on basic accounting equation.
(SO 1)

Using the following tabular analysis, show the effect of each transaction on the accounting equation. Put explanations for changes to Stockholders' Equity in the right-hand margin. Use Illustration 3-2 (page 107) as a model.

Assets			=	Liabilities		+	Stockholders' Equity	
Cash +	Accounts Receivable	+ Supplies =		Accounts Payable	+ Bonds Payable	+	Common Stock	+ Retained Earnings

BE3-3 During 2004, Starbucks entered into the following transactions.
1. Purchased property, plant, and equipment for $386,176,000 cash.
2. Issued common stock to investors for $137,590,000 cash.
3. Purchased inventory of $77,662,000 on account.

Determine effect of transactions on basic accounting equation.
(SO 1)

Using the following tabular analysis, show the effect of each transaction on the accounting equation. Put explanations for changes to Stockholders' Equity in the right-hand margin. Use Illustration 3-2 (page 107) as a model.

Assets			=	Liabilities +		Stockholders' Equity	
Cash +	Inventory +	Property, Plant, and Equipment	=	Accounts Payable	+	Common Stock	+ Retained Earnings

BE3-4 For each of the following accounts indicate the effect of a debit or a credit on the account and the normal balance.
(a) Accounts Payable.   (d) Accounts Receivable.
(b) Advertising Expense. (e) Retained Earnings.
(c) Service Revenue.   (f) Dividends.

Indicate debit and credit effects.
(SO 3)

BE3-5 Transactions for Alvarez Company for the month of June are presented next. Identify the accounts to be debited and credited for each transaction.

Identify accounts to be debited and credited.
(SO 3)

June 1 Issues common stock to investors in exchange for $2,500 cash.
        2 Buys equipment on account for $1,100.
        3 Pays $500 to landlord for June rent.
       12 Bills Chas. Thon $700 for welding work done.

BE3-6 Use the data in BE3-5 and journalize the transactions. (You may omit explanations.)

Journalize transactions.
(SO 5)

BE3-7 Jeremy Oslo, a fellow student, is unclear about the basic steps in the recording process. Identify and briefly explain the steps in the order in which they occur.

Identify steps in the recording process.
(SO 4)

BE3-8 Norris Corporation has the following transactions during August of the current year. Indicate (a) the basic analysis and (b) the debit–credit analysis illustrated on pages 119–124.

Indicate basic debit–credit analysis.
(SO 4)

Aug. 1 Issues shares of common stock to investors in exchange for $5,000.
        4 Pays insurance in advance for 3 months, $1,500.
       16 Receives $900 from clients for services rendered.
       27 Pays the secretary $500 salary.

BE3-9 Use the data in BE3-8 and journalize the transactions. (You may omit explanations.)

Journalize transactions.
(SO 5)

BE3-10 Selected transactions for Gonzales Company are presented in journal form (without explanations). Post the transactions to T accounts.

Post journal entries to T accounts.
(SO 7)

Date		Account Title	Debit	Credit
May	5	Accounts Receivable	2,800	
		Service Revenue		2,800
	12	Cash	1,900	
		Accounts Receivable		1,900
	15	Cash	2,000	
		Service Revenue		2,000

Prepare a trial balance.
(SO 8)

BE3-11   From the ledger balances below, prepare a trial balance for Shumway Company at June 30, 2007. All account balances are normal.

Accounts Payable	$ 3,000	Service Revenue	$6,600
Cash	3,400	Accounts Receivable	3,000
Common Stock	18,000	Salaries Expense	4,000
Dividends	1,200	Rent Expense	1,000
Equipment	15,000		

Prepare a corrected trial balance.
(SO 8)

BE3-12   An inexperienced bookkeeper prepared the following trial balance that does not balance. Prepare a correct trial balance, assuming all account balances are normal.

RICHARDSON COMPANY
Trial Balance
December 31, 2007

	Debit	Credit
Cash	$18,800	
Prepaid Insurance		$ 3,500
Accounts Payable		2,500
Unearned Revenue	1,800	
Common Stock		10,000
Retained Earnings		6,400
Dividends		5,000
Service Revenue		25,600
Salaries Expense	16,600	
Rent Expense		2,400
	$37,200	$55,400

Exercises

Analyze the effect of transactions.
(SO 1)

E3-1   Selected transactions for Sidhu Advertising Company, Inc., are listed here.
1. Issued common stock to investors in exchange for cash received from investors.
2. Paid monthly rent.
3. Received cash from customers when service was rendered.
4. Billed customers for services performed.
5. Paid dividend to stockholders.
6. Incurred advertising expense on account.
7. Received cash from customers billed in (4).
8. Purchased additional equipment for cash.
9. Purchased equipment on account.

Instructions
Describe the effect of each transaction on assets, liabilities, and stockholders' equity. For example, the first answer is: (1) Increase in assets and increase in stockholders' equity.

Analyze the effect of transactions on assets, liabilities, and stockholders' equity.
(SO 1)

E3-2   Downtown Company entered into these transactions during May 2007.
1. Purchased computers for office use for $35,000 from Dell on account.
2. Paid $4,000 cash for May rent on storage space.

3. Received $12,000 cash from customers for contracts billed in April.
4. Provided computer services to Brieske Construction Company for $5,000 cash.
5. Paid Southern States Power Co. $11,000 cash for energy usage in May.
6. Stockholders invested an additional $30,000 in the business in exchange for common stock of the company.
7. Paid Dell for the computers purchased in (1).
8. Incurred advertising expense for May of $1,000 on account.

Instructions
Using the following tabular analysis, show the effect of each transaction on the accounting equation. Put explanations for changes to Stockholders' Equity in the right-hand margin. Use Illustration 3-2 (page 107) as a model.

	Assets		= Liabilities +	Stockholders' Equity	
Cash +	Accounts Receivable +	Office Equipment =	Accounts Payable +	Common Stock +	Retained Earnings

E3-3 During 2007, its first year of operations as a delivery service, Cheng Corp. entered into the following transactions.

1. Issued shares of common stock to investors in exchange for $110,000 in cash.
2. Borrowed $45,000 by issuing bonds.
3. Purchased delivery trucks for $60,000 cash.
4. Received $16,000 from customers for services provided.
5. Purchased supplies for $4,200 on account.
6. Paid rent of $5,600.
7. Performed services on account for $8,000.
8. Paid salaries of $28,000.
9. Paid a dividend of $11,000 to shareholders.

Determine effect of transactions on basic accounting equation. (SO 1)

Instructions
Using the following tabular analysis, show the effect of each transaction on the accounting equation. Put explanations for changes to Stockholders' Equity in the right-hand margin. Use Illustration 3-2 (page 107) as a model.

	Assets			=	Liabilities	+	Stockholders' Equity	
Cash +	Accounts Receivable +	Supplies +	Property, Plant, and Equipment =		Accounts Payable +	Bonds Payable +	Common Stock +	Retained Earnings

E3-4 A tabular analysis of the transactions made during August 2007 by Verbos Company during its first month of operations is shown below. Each increase and decrease in stockholders' equity is explained.

Analyze transactions and compute net income. (SO 1)

	Assets				= Liabilities +	Stockholders' Equity	
Cash +	Accounts Receivable +	Supplies +	Office Equipment =	Accounts Payable +	Common Stock +	Retained Earnings	
1. +$15,000					+$15,000		Issued Common Stock
2. −1,000			+$5,000	+$4,000			
3. −750		+$750					
4. +4,400	+$3,400					+$7,800	Service Revenue
5. −1,500				−1,500			
6. −2,000						−2,000	Dividends
7. −800						−800	Rent Expense
8. +450	−450						
9. −3,000						−3,000	Salaries Expense
10.				+500		−500	Utilities Expense

Instructions
(a) Describe each transaction.
(b) Determine how much stockholders' equity increased for the month.
(c) Compute the net income for the month.

Prepare an income statement, retained earnings statement, and balance sheet.
(SO 1)

E3-5 The tabular analysis of transactions for Verbos Company is presented in E3-4.

Instructions
Prepare an income statement and a retained earnings statement for August and a classified balance sheet at August 31, 2007.

Identify debits, credits, and normal balances and journalize transactions.
(SO 3, 5)

E3-6 Selected transactions for Welcome Home, an interior decorator corporation, in its first month of business, are as follows.

1. Issued stock to investors for $12,000 in cash.
2. Purchased used car for $8,000 cash for use in business.
3. Purchased supplies on account for $300.
4. Billed customers $2,600 for services performed.
5. Paid $200 cash for advertising start of the business.
6. Received $1,100 cash from customers billed in transaction (4).
7. Paid creditor $300 cash on account.
8. Paid dividends of $400 cash to stockholders.

Instructions
(a) For each transaction indicate (a) the basic type of account debited and credited (asset, liability, stockholders' equity); (b) the specific account debited and credited (Cash, Rent Expense, Service Revenue, etc.); (c) whether the specific account is increased or decreased; and (d) the normal balance of the specific account. Use the following format, in which transaction 1 is given as an example.

	Account Debited				**Account Credited**			
	(a)	**(b)**	**(c)**	**(d)**	**(a)**	**(b)**	**(c)**	**(d)**
Trans-action	**Basic Type**	**Specific Account**	**Effect**	**Normal Balance**	**Basic Type**	**Specific Account**	**Effect**	**Normal Balance**
1	Asset	Cash	Increase	Debit	Stockholders' equity	Common Stock	Increase	Credit

(b) Journalize the transactions. Do not provide explanations.

Analyze transactions and determine their effect on accounts.
(SO 3)

E3-7 This information relates to Matthews Real Estate Agency Corporation.

Oct. 1 Stockholders invested $25,000 in exchange for common stock of the corporation.
   2 Hires an administrative assistant at an annual salary of $42,000.
   3 Buys office furniture for $3,600, on account.
   6 Sells a house and lot for M.E. Mills; commissions due from Mills, $10,800 (not paid by Mills at this time).
   10 Receives cash of $140 as commission for acting as rental agent renting an apartment.
   27 Pays $700 on account for the office furniture purchased on October 3.
   30 Pays the administrative assistant $3,500 in salary for October.

Instructions
Prepare the debit–credit analysis for each transaction as illustrated on pages 119–124.

Journalize transactions.
(SO 5)

E3-8 Transaction data for Matthews Real Estate Agency are presented in E3-7.

Instructions
Journalize the transactions. Do not provide explanations.

Post journal entries and prepare a trial balance.
(SO 7, 8)

E3-9 Transaction data and journal entries for Matthews Real Estate Agency are presented in E3-7 and E3-8.

Instructions
(a) Post the transactions to T accounts.
(b) Prepare a trial balance at October 31, 2007.

Analyze transactions, prepare journal entries, and post transactions to T accounts.
(SO 1, 5, 7)

E3-10 Selected transactions for P.F. Quick Corporation during its first month in business are presented below.

Sept. 1 Issued common stock in exchange for $15,000 cash received from investors.
    5 Purchased equipment for $12,000, paying $2,000 in cash and the balance on account.
  25 Paid $5,000 cash on balance owed for equipment.
  30 Paid $500 cash dividend.

P. F. Quick's chart of accounts shows: Cash, Equipment, Accounts Payable, Common Stock, and Dividends.

Instructions
(a) Prepare a tabular analysis of the September transactions. The column headings should be: Cash + Equipment = Accounts Payable + Stockholders' Equity. For transactions affecting stockholders' equity, provide explanations in the right margin, as shown on page 107.
(b) Journalize the transactions. Do not provide explanations.
(c) Post the transactions to T accounts.

Journalize transactions from T accounts and prepare a trial balance.
(SO 5, 8)

E3-11 These T accounts summarize the ledger of Hayley's Gardening Company Inc. at the end of the first month of operations.

Cash				Unearned Revenue	
Apr. 1	12,000	Apr. 15	900		Apr. 30	600
12	700	25	3,500		
29	800				
30	600				

Accounts Receivable				Common Stock	
Apr. 7	2,400	Apr. 29	800		Apr. 1	12,000

Supplies				Service Revenue	
Apr. 4	5,200				Apr. 7	2,400
					12	700

Accounts Payable				Salaries Expense	
Apr. 25	3,500	Apr. 4	5,200	Apr. 15	900	

Instructions
(a) Prepare in the order they occurred the journal entries (including explanations) that resulted in the amounts posted to the accounts.
(b) Prepare a trial balance at April 30, 2007. (*Hint:* Compute ending balances of T accounts first.)

Post journal entries and prepare a trial balance.
(SO 7, 8)

E3-12 Selected transactions from the journal of Dewitt Inc. during its first month of operations are presented here.

Date	Account Titles	Debit	Credit
Aug. 1	Cash	3,000	
	Common Stock		3,000
10	Cash	1,700	
	Service Revenue		1,700
12	Office Equipment	6,200	
	Cash		1,200
	Notes Payable		5,000
25	Accounts Receivable	3,100	
	Service Revenue		3,100
31	Cash	600	
	Accounts Receivable		600

Instructions

(a) Post the transactions to T accounts.

(b) Prepare a trial balance at August 31, 2007.

Journalize transactions from T accounts and prepare a trial balance.
(SO 5, 8)

E3-13 Here is the ledger for Arseneault Co.

Cash						Common Stock	
Oct. 1	4,800	Oct. 4	400			Oct. 1	4,800
10	750	12	1,500			25	2,000
10	8,000	15	250				
20	800	30	300				
25	2,000	31	500				

Accounts Receivable					Dividends		
Oct. 6	800	Oct. 20	800	Oct. 30	300		
20	920						

Supplies					Service Revenue		
Oct. 4	400	Oct. 31	180			Oct. 6	800
						10	750
						20	920

Furniture			Store Wages Expense	
Oct. 3	3,000		Oct. 31	500

Notes Payable			Supplies Expense	
	Oct. 10	8,000	Oct. 31	180

Accounts Payable			Rent Expense	
Oct. 12	1,500	Oct. 3	3,000	Oct. 15	250

Instructions

(a) Reproduce the journal entries for only the transactions that *occurred on October 1, 10, and 20*, and provide explanations for each.

(b) Prepare a trial balance at October 31, 2007. (*Hint:* Compute ending balances of T accounts first.)

Analyze errors and their effects on trial balance.
(SO 8)

E3-14 The bookkeeper for Beylea Corporation made these errors in journalizing and posting.

1. A credit posting of $400 to Accounts Receivable was omitted.

2. A debit posting of $750 for Prepaid Insurance was debited to Insurance Expense.

3. A collection on account of $100 was journalized and posted as a debit to Cash $100 and a credit to Accounts Payable $100.

4. A credit posting of $300 to Property Taxes Payable was made twice.

5. A cash purchase of supplies for $250 was journalized and posted as a debit to Supplies $25 and a credit to Cash $25.

6. A debit of $375 to Advertising Expense was posted as $357.

Instructions

For each error, indicate (a) whether the trial balance will balance; if the trial balance will not balance, indicate (b) the amount of the difference, and (c) the trial balance column that will have the larger total. Consider each error separately. Use the following form, in which error 1 is given as an example.

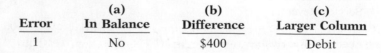

	(a)	(b)	(c)
Error	**In Balance**	**Difference**	**Larger Column**
1	No	$400	Debit

E3-15 The accounts in the ledger of Dependable Delivery Service contain the following balances on July 31, 2007.

Prepare a trial balance.
(SO 8)

Accounts Receivable	$13,400	Prepaid Insurance	$ 1,800
Accounts Payable	7,400	Repair Expense	1,200
Cash	?	Service Revenue	15,500
Delivery Equipment	59,360	Dividends	700
Gas and Oil Expense	758	Common Stock	40,000
Insurance Expense	600	Salaries Expense	4,428
Notes Payable, due 2010	28,450	Salaries Payable	900
		Retained Earnings	5,200
		(July 1, 2007)	

Instructions
(a) Prepare a trial balance with the accounts arranged as illustrated in the chapter, and fill in the missing amount for Cash.
(b) Prepare an income statement, a retained earnings statement, and a classified balance sheet for the month of July 2007.

E3-16 The following accounts, in alphabetical order, were selected from the 2004 financial statements of Krispy Kreme Doughnuts, Inc.

Identify normal account balance and corresponding financial statement.
(SO 3)

Accounts payable	Interest income
Accounts receivable	Inventories
Common stock	Prepaid expenses
Depreciation expense	Property and equipment
Interest expense	Revenues

Instructions
For each account, indicate (a) whether the normal balance is a debit or a credit, and (b) the financial statement—balance sheet or income statement—where the account should be presented.

Problems: Set A

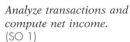

P3-1A On April 1 Far and Wide Travel Agency Inc. was established. These transactions were completed during the month.

Analyze transactions and compute net income.
(SO 1)

1. Stockholders invested $20,000 cash in the company in exchange for common stock.
2. Paid $900 cash for April office rent.
3. Purchased office equipment for $2,800 cash.
4. Purchased $200 of advertising in the *Chicago Tribune*, on account.
5. Paid $500 cash for office supplies.
6. Earned $9,000 for services provided: Cash of $1,000 is received from customers, and the balance of $8,000 is billed to customers on account.
7. Paid $400 cash dividends.
8. Paid *Chicago Tribune* amount due in transaction (4).
9. Paid employees' salaries $1,200.
10. Received $8,000 in cash from customers who have previously been billed in transaction (6).

Instructions
(a) Prepare a tabular analysis of the transactions using these column headings: Cash, Accounts Receivable, Supplies, Office Equipment, Accounts Payable, Common Stock, and Retained Earnings. Include margin explanations for any changes in Retained Earnings.
(b) From an analysis of the column Retained Earnings, compute the net income or net loss for April.

(a) Cash $23,000
    Ret. earnings $ 6,300

Analyze transactions and prepare financial statements.
(SO 1)

 P3-2A Marie Blaesing started her own consulting firm, Blaesing Consulting Inc., on May 1, 2007. The following transactions occurred during the month of May.

May   1   Stockholders invested $12,000 cash in the business in exchange for common stock.
2   Paid $700 for office rent for the month.
3   Purchased $500 of supplies on account.
5   Paid $150 to advertise in the *County News*.
9   Received $1,000 cash for services provided.
12   Paid $200 cash dividend.
15   Performed $3,200 of services on account.
17   Paid $2,500 for employee salaries.
20   Paid for the supplies purchased on account on May 3.
23   Received a cash payment of $1,500 for services provided on account on May 15.
26   Borrowed $5,000 from the bank on a note payable.
29   Purchased office equipment for $2,400 paying $200 in cash and the balance on account.
30   Paid $150 for utilities.

Instructions

(a) Cash $15,100
Ret. earnings $ 500

(a) Show the effects of the previous transactions on the accounting equation using the following format. Assume the note payable is to be repaid within the year.

			Assets			=	Liabilities			+	Stockholders' Equity	
Date	Cash	+	Accounts Receivable	+ Supplies +	Office Equipment	=	Notes Payable	+ Accounts Payable	+	Common Stock	+	Retained Earnings

Include margin explanations for any changes in Retained Earnings.

(b) Net income $700

(b) Prepare an income statement for the month of May.
(c) Prepare a classified balance sheet at May 31, 2007.

Analyze transactions and prepare an income statement, retained earnings statement, and balance sheet.
(SO 1)

 GLS

P3-3A   Mark Mader created a corporation providing legal services, Mark Mader Inc., on July 1, 2007. On July 31 the balance sheet showed: Cash $4,000; Accounts Receivable $2,500; Supplies $500; Office Equipment $5,000; Accounts Payable $4,200; Common Stock $6,200; and Retained Earnings $1,600. During August the following transactions occurred.

1. Collected $1,500 of accounts receivable due from customers.
2. Paid $2,700 cash for accounts payable due.
3. Earned revenue of $6,400, of which $3,000 is collected in cash and the balance is due in September.
4. Purchased additional office equipment for $2,000, paying $400 in cash and the balance on account.
5. Paid salaries $1,400, rent for August $900, and advertising expenses $350.
6. Declared and paid a cash dividend of $700.
7. Received $2,000 from Standard Federal Bank; the money was borrowed on a 4-month note payable.
8. Incurred utility expenses for the month on account $450.

(a) Cash $4,050
Ret. earnings $4,200

Instructions

(a) Prepare a tabular analysis of the August transactions beginning with July 31 balances. The column heading should be: Cash + Accounts Receivable + Supplies + Office Equipment = Notes Payable + Accounts Payable + Common Stock + Retained Earnings. Include margin explanations for any changes in Retained Earnings.

(b) Net income $3,300

(b) Prepare an income statement for August, a retained earnings statement for August, and a classified balance sheet at August 31.

Journalize a series of transactions.
(SO 3, 5)

GLS

P3-4A   Hometown Miniature Golf and Driving Range Inc. was opened on March 1 by Happy Gilmore. These selected events and transactions occurred during March.

Mar.   1   Stockholders invested $60,000 cash in the business in exchange for common stock of the corporation.
3   Purchased Arnie's Golf Land for $38,000 cash. The price consists of land $23,000, building $9,000, and equipment $6,000. (Record this in a single entry.)

5   Advertised the opening of the driving range and miniature golf course, paying advertising expenses of $1,600 cash.

6   Paid cash $2,400 for a 1-year insurance policy.

10 Purchased golf clubs and other equipment for $3,700 from Golden Bear Company, payable in 30 days.

18 Received golf fees of $1,200 in cash from customers for golf fees earned.

19 Sold 100 coupon books for $20 each in cash. Each book contains ten coupons that enable the holder to play one round of miniature golf or to hit one bucket of golf balls. (*Hint*: The revenue is not earned until the customers use the coupons.)

25 Declared and paid a $500 cash dividend.

30 Paid salaries of $700.

30 Paid Golden Bear Company in full for equipment purchased on March 10.

31 Received $800 of fees in cash from customers for golf fees earned.

The company uses these accounts: Cash, Prepaid Insurance, Land, Buildings, Equipment, Accounts Payable, Unearned Golf Revenue, Common Stock, Retained Earnings, Dividends, Golf Revenue, Advertising Expense, and Salaries Expense.

Instructions
Journalize the March transactions, including explanations.

P3-5A F.L. Wright Architects incorporated as licensed architects on April 1, 2007. During the first month of the operation of the business, these events and transactions occurred:

Journalize transactions, post, and prepare a trial balance.
(SO 3, 5, 6, 7, 8)

Apr. 1   Stockholders invested $14,000 cash in exchange for common stock of the corporation.

1   Hired a secretary-receptionist at a salary of $375 per week, payable monthly.

2   Paid office rent for the month $900.

3   Purchased architectural supplies on account from Spring Green Company $1,000.

10 Completed blueprints on a carport and billed client $1,100 for services.

11 Received $500 cash advance from J. Madison to design a new home.

20 Received $2,300 cash for services completed and delivered to M. Svetlana.

30 Paid secretary-receptionist for the month $1,500.

30 Paid $100 to Spring Green Company for accounts payable due.

The company uses these accounts: Cash, Accounts Receivable, Supplies, Accounts Payable, Unearned Revenue, Common Stock, Service Revenue, Salaries Expense, and Rent Expense.

Instructions
(a) Journalize the transactions, including explanations.
(b) Post to the ledger T accounts.
(c) Prepare a trial balance on April 30, 2007.

(c) Cash $14,300
Tot. trial
*   balance $18,800*

P3-6A This is the trial balance of Aladdin Company on September 30.

Journalize transactions, post, and prepare a trial balance.
(SO 3, 5, 6, 7, 8)

ALADDIN COMPANY
Trial Balance
September 30, 2007

	Debit	Credit
Cash	$ 8,300	
Accounts Receivable	2,600	
Supplies	2,100	
Equipment	8,000	
Accounts Payable		$ 5,100
Unearned Revenue		900
Common Stock		15,000
	$21,000	$21,000

The October transactions were as follows.

Oct. 5 Received $1,300 in cash from customers for accounts receivable due.
10 Billed customers for services performed $4,100.
15 Paid employee salaries $1,400.
17 Performed $600 of services for customers who paid in advance in August.
20 Paid $1,100 to creditors for accounts payable due.
29 Paid a $300 cash dividend.
31 Paid utilities $700.

Instructions

(a) Prepare a general ledger using T accounts. Enter the opening balances in the ledger accounts as of October 1. Provision should be made for these additional accounts: Dividends, Service Revenue, Salaries Expense, and Utilities Expense.

(d) Cash $ 6,100
    Tot. trial
      balance $24,000

(b) Journalize the transactions, including explanations.
(c) Post to the ledger accounts.
(d) Prepare a trial balance on October 31, 2007.

Prepare a correct trial balance.
(SO 8)

P3-7A This trial balance of Izo Co. does not balance.

IZO CO.
Trial Balance
June 30, 2007

	Debit	Credit
Cash		$ 2,180
Accounts Receivable	$ 3,370	
Supplies	800	
Equipment	3,000	
Accounts Payable		2,666
Unearned Revenue	1,200	
Common Stock		9,000
Dividends	800	
Service Revenue		3,480
Salaries Expense	3,600	
Office Expense	910	
	$13,680	$17,326

Each of the listed accounts has a normal balance per the general ledger. An examination of the ledger and journal reveals the following errors:

1. Cash received from a customer on account was debited for $690, and Accounts Receivable was credited for the same amount. The actual collection was for $960.
2. The purchase of a printer on account for $340 was recorded as a debit to Supplies for $340 and a credit to Accounts Payable for $340.
3. Services were performed on account for a client for $800. Accounts Receivable was debited for $80 and Service Revenue was credited for $800.
4. A debit posting to Salaries Expense of $500 was omitted.
5. A payment on account for $206 was credited to Cash for $206 and credited to Accounts Payable for $260.
6. Payment of a $600 cash dividend to Izo's stockholders was debited to Salaries Expense for $600 and credited to Cash for $600.

Tot. trial balance $15,880

Instructions

Prepare the correct trial balance. (*Hint:* All accounts have normal balances.)

Journalize transactions, post,
and prepare a trial balance.
(SO 3, 5, 6, 7, 8)

GLS

P3-8A The Three-Peat Theater Inc. was recently formed. It began operations in March 2007. The Three-Peat is unique in that it will show only triple features of sequential theme movies. On March 1, the ledger of The Three-Peat showed: Cash $16,000; Land $38,000; Buildings (concession stand, projection room, ticket booth, and screen) $22,000; Equipment $16,000; Accounts Payable $12,000; and Common Stock $80,000. During the month of March the following events and transactions occurred.

Mar. 2   Rented the three *Star Wars* movies (*Star Wars*®, *The Empire Strikes Back*, and *The Return of the Jedi*) to be shown for the first three weeks of March. The film rental was $12,000; $2,000 was paid in cash and $10,000 will be paid on March 10.

3   Ordered the first three *Star Trek* movies to be shown the last 10 days of March. It will cost $400 per night.

9   Received $9,200 cash from admissions.

10   Paid balance due on *Star Wars* movies rental and $2,600 on March 1 accounts payable.

11   Hired J. Bybee to operate the concession stand. Bybee agrees to pay The Three-Peat Theater 15% of gross receipts, payable monthly.

12   Paid advertising expenses $900.

20   Received $7,100 cash from customers for admissions.

20   Received the *Star Trek* movies and paid rental fee of $4,000.

31   Paid salaries of $3,800.

31   Received statement from J. Bybee showing gross receipts from concessions of $9,000 and the balance due to The Three-Peat of $1,350 for March. Bybee paid half the balance due and will remit the remainder on April 5.

31   Received $20,000 cash from customers for admissions.

In addition to the accounts identified above, the chart of accounts includes: Accounts Receivable, Admission Revenue, Concession Revenue, Advertising Expense, Film Rental Expense, and Salaries Expense.

Instructions
(a) Using T accounts, enter the beginning balances to the ledger.
(b) Journalize the March transactions, including explanations.
(c) Post the March journal entries to the ledger.
(d) Prepare a trial balance on March 31, 2007.

(d) Cash $ 29,675
Tot. trial
*   balance $127,050*

P3-9A   The bookkeeper for Shirley Temple's dance studio made the following errors in journalizing and posting.

Analyze errors and their effects on the trial balance.
(SO 8)

1. A credit to Supplies of $600 was omitted.
2. A debit posting of $300 to Accounts Payable was inadvertently debited to Accounts Receivable.
3. A purchase of supplies on account of $450 was debited to Supplies for $540 and credited to Accounts Payable for $540.
4. A credit posting of $250 to Wages Payable was posted twice.
5. A debit posting to Wages Payable for $250 and a credit posting to Cash for $250 were made twice.
6. A debit posting for $1,200 of Dividends was inadvertently posted to Travel Expense instead.
7. A credit to Service Revenue for $350 was inadvertently posted as a debit to Service Revenue.
8. A credit to Accounts Receivable of $250 was credited to Accounts Payable.

Instructions
For each error, indicate (a) whether the trial balance will balance; (b) the amount of the difference if the trial balance will not balance; and (c) the trial balance column that will have the larger total. Consider each error separately. Use the following form, in which error 1 is given as an example.

	(a)	(b)	(c)
Error	**In Balance**	**Difference**	**Larger Column**
1.	No	$600	Debit

Problems: Set B

Analyze transactions and compute net income.
(SO 1)

P3-1B   Blue Sky Window Washing Inc. was started on May 1. Here is a summary of the May transactions.

1. Stockholders invested $16,000 cash in the company in exchange for common stock.
2. Purchased equipment for $7,000 cash.
3. Paid $700 cash for May office rent.
4. Paid $400 cash for supplies.
5. Purchased $550 of advertising in the *Beacon News* on account.
6. Received $5,800 in cash from customers for service.
7. Declared and paid a $500 cash dividend.
8. Paid part-time employee salaries $1,700.
9. Paid utility bills $140.
10. Provided service on account to customers $500.
11. Collected cash of $240 for services billed in transaction (10).

Instructions

(a) Prepare a tabular analysis of the transactions using these column headings: Cash, Accounts Receivable, Supplies, Equipment, Accounts Payable, Common Stock, and Retained Earnings. Revenue is called Service Revenue. Include margin explanations for any changes in Retained Earnings.

(b) Net income $3,210

(b) From an analysis of the column Retained Earnings, compute the net income or net loss for May.

Analyze transactions and prepare financial statements.
(SO 1)

P3-2B   Patrick Coleman started his own delivery service, At Your Service Inc., on June 1, 2007. The following transactions occurred during the month of June.

June 1 Stockholders invested $16,000 cash in the business in exchange for common stock.
       2 Purchased a used van for deliveries for $10,000. Patrick paid $2,000 cash and signed a note payable for the remaining balance.
       3 Paid $500 for office rent for the month.
       5 Performed $1,900 of services on account.
       9 Paid $300 in cash dividends.
      12 Purchased supplies for $150 on account.
      15 Received a cash payment of $750 for services provided on June 5.
      17 Purchased gasoline for $200 on account.
      20 Received a cash payment of $1,500 for services provided.
      23 Made a cash payment of $800 on the note payable.
      26 Paid $250 for utilities.
      29 Paid for the supplies purchased on account on June 12.
      30 Paid $750 for employee salaries.

Instructions

(a) Cash $13,500

(a) Show the effects of the previous transactions on the accounting equation using the following format. Assume the note payable is to be repaid within the year.

		Assets			=	Liabilities		+	Stockholders' Equity	
Date	Cash +	Accounts Receivable +	Supplies +	Delivery Van	=	Notes Payable +	Accounts Payable +		Common Stock +	Retained Earnings

Include margin explanations for any changes in Retained Earnings.

(b) Net income $1,700

(b) Prepare an income statement for the month of June.
(c) Prepare a classified balance sheet at June 30, 2007.

Analyze transactions and prepare an income statement, retained earnings statement, and balance sheet.
(SO 1)

P3-3B   Janna Reed opened Reed Company, a veterinary business in Neosho, Wisconsin, on August 1, 2007. On August 31 the balance sheet showed: Cash $9,000; Accounts Receivable $1,700; Supplies $600; Office Equipment $5,000; Accounts Payable $3,600; Common Stock $12,000; and Retained Earnings $700. During September the following transactions occurred.

1. Paid $3,400 cash for accounts payable due.
2. Received $1,600 from customers in payment of accounts receivable.
3. Purchased additional office equipment for $4,100, paying $1,000 in cash and the balance on account.

4. Earned revenue of $8,500, of which $2,300 is paid in cash and the balance is due in October.
5. Declared and paid a $600 cash dividend.
6. Paid salaries $900, rent for September $800, and advertising expense $250.
7. Incurred utility expenses for the month on account $170.
8. Received $7,000 from Hilldale Bank; the money was borrowed on a 6-month note payable.

Instructions

(a) Prepare a tabular analysis of the September transactions beginning with August 31 balances. The column headings should be: Cash + Accounts Receivable + Supplies + Office Equipment = Notes Payable + Accounts Payable + Common Stock + Retained Earnings. Include margin explanations for any changes in Retained Earnings.

(b) Prepare an income statement for September, a retained earnings statement for September, and a classified balance sheet at September 30, 2007.

(a) Cash $12,950
*   Ret. earnings $ 6,480*

P3-4B   RV Haven was started on April 1 by Don Patter. These selected events and trans-actions occurred during April.

Journalize a series of transactions.
(SO 3, 5)

Apr.	1	Stockholders invested $75,000 cash in the business in exchange for common stock.
	4	Purchased land costing $50,000 for cash.
	8	Purchased advertising in local newspaper for $1,200 on account.
	11	Paid salaries to employees $1,700.
	12	Hired park manager at a salary of $3,000 per month, effective May 1.
	13	Paid $6,000 for a 1-year insurance policy.
	17	Paid $600 cash dividends.
	20	Received $5,000 in cash from customers for admission fees.
	25	Sold 100 coupon books for $70 each. Each book contains ten coupons that entitle the holder to one admission to the park. (*Hint*: The revenue is not earned until the coupons are used.)
	30	Received $7,900 in cash from customers for admission fees.
	30	Paid $500 of the balance owed for the advertising purchased on account on April 8.

The company uses the following accounts: Cash, Prepaid Insurance, Land, Accounts Payable, Unearned Admissions, Common Stock, Dividends, Admission Revenue, Advertising Expense, and Salaries Expense.

Instructions
Journalize the April transactions, including explanations.

P3-5B   Ricki Knapp incorporated Knapp Consulting, an accounting practice, on May 1, 2007. During the first month of operations, these events and transactions occurred.

Journalize transactions, post, and prepare a trial balance.
(SO 3, 5, 6, 7, 8)

May	1	Stockholders invested $52,000 cash in exchange for common stock of the corporation.
	2	Hired a secretary-receptionist at a salary of $2,000 per month.
	3	Purchased $800 of supplies on account from Keating Supply Company.
	7	Paid office rent of $1,100 for the month.
	11	Completed a tax assignment and billed client $1,500 for services provided.
	12	Received $4,200 advance on a management consulting engagement.
	17	Received cash of $3,600 for services completed for Goodman Co.
	31	Paid secretary-receptionist $2,000 salary for the month.
	31	Paid 40% of balance due Keating Supply Company.

The company uses the following chart of accounts: Cash, Accounts Receivable, Supplies, Accounts Payable, Unearned Revenue, Common Stock, Service Revenue, Salaries Expense, and Rent Expense.

Instructions
(a) Journalize the transactions, including explanations.
(b) Post to the ledger T accounts.
(c) Prepare a trial balance on May 31, 2007.

(c) Cash $56,380
*   Tot. trial*
*   balance $61,780*

Journalize transactions, post, and prepare a trial balance.
(SO 3, 5, 6, 7, 8)

P3-6B The trial balance of Artistic Dry Cleaners on June 30 is given here.

ARTISTIC DRY CLEANERS
Trial Balance
June 30, 2007

	Debit	Credit
Cash	$12,532	
Accounts Receivable	10,536	
Supplies	3,512	
Equipment	25,950	
Accounts Payable		$15,800
Unearned Revenue		1,730
Common Stock		35,000
	$52,530	$52,530

The July transactions were as follows.

July	8	Received $5,189 in cash on June 30 accounts receivable.
	9	Paid employee salaries $2,100.
	11	Received $5,100 in cash for services provided.
	14	Paid creditors $10,750 of accounts payable.
	17	Purchased supplies on account $520.
	22	Billed customers for services provided $4,700.
	30	Paid employee salaries $3,114, utilities $1,467, and repairs $492.
	31	Paid $400 cash dividend.

Instructions
(a) Prepare a general ledger using T accounts. Enter the opening balances in the ledger accounts as of July 1. Provision should be made for the following additional accounts: Dividends, Dry Cleaning Revenue, Repair Expense, Salaries Expense, and Utilities Expense.

(d) Cash $ 4,498
   Tot. trial
     balance $52,100

(b) Journalize the transactions, including explanations.
(c) Post to the ledger accounts.
(d) Prepare a trial balance on July 31, 2007.

Prepare a correct trial balance.
(SO 8)

P3-7B This trial balance of Rosenberger Company does not balance.

ROSENBERGER COMPANY
Trial Balance
May 31, 2007

	Debit	Credit
Cash	$ 5,340	
Accounts Receivable		$ 2,750
Prepaid Insurance	700	
Equipment	8,000	
Accounts Payable		4,100
Property Taxes Payable	750	
Common Stock		5,700
Retained Earnings		6,000
Service Revenue	6,690	
Salaries Expense	4,200	
Advertising Expense		1,100
Property Tax Expense	900	
	$26,580	$19,650

Your review of the ledger reveals that each account has a normal balance. You also discover the following errors.

1. The totals of the debit sides of Prepaid Insurance, Accounts Payable, and Property Tax Expense were each understated $100.
2. Transposition errors were made in Accounts Receivable and Service Revenue. Based on postings made, the correct balances were $2,570 and $6,960, respectively.
3. A debit posting to Salaries Expense of $400 was omitted.
4. An $800 cash dividend was debited to Common Stock for $800 and credited to Cash for $800.
5. A $350 purchase of supplies on account was debited to Equipment for $350 and credited to Cash for $350.
6. A cash payment of $250 for advertising was debited to Advertising Expense for $25 and credited to Cash for $25.
7. A collection from a customer for $240 was debited to Cash for $240 and credited to Accounts Payable for $240.

Instructions
Prepare the correct trial balance, assuming all accounts have normal balances. (*Note:* The chart of accounts also includes the following: Dividends and Supplies.)

Cash $ 5,465
Tot. trial balance $24,320

✗ **P3-8B**   Classic Theater Inc. was recently formed. All facilities were completed on March 31. On April 1, the ledger showed: Cash $6,300; Land $10,000; Buildings (concession stand, projection room, ticket booth, and screen) $8,000; Equipment $6,000; Accounts Payable $2,300; Mortgage Payable $8,000; and Common Stock $20,000. During April, the following events and transactions occurred.

Journalize transactions, post, and prepare a trial balance. (SO 3, 5, 6, 7, 8)

GLS

Apr. 2	Paid film rental fee of $800 on first movie.
𝐴𝑇 3	Ordered two additional films at $900 each.
9	Received $3,900 cash from admissions.
10	Paid $2,000 of mortgage payable and $1,000 of accounts payable.
11	Hired M. Norby to operate the concession stand. Norby agrees to pay Classic Theater 17% of gross receipts, payable monthly.
12	Paid advertising expenses $460.
20	Received one of the films ordered on April 3 and was billed $900. The film will be shown in April.
25	Received $3,000 cash from customers for admissions.
29	Paid salaries $1,900.
30	Received statement from M. Norby showing gross receipts of $1,000 and the balance due to Classic Theater of $170 for April. Norby paid half of the balance due and will remit the remainder on May 5.
30	Prepaid $1,000 rental fee on special film to be run in May.

Time Period

In addition to the accounts identified above, the chart of accounts shows: Accounts Receivable, Prepaid Rentals, Admission Revenue, Concession Revenue, Advertising Expense, Film Rental Expense, Salaries Expense.

Instructions
(a) Enter the beginning balances in the ledger T accounts as of April 1.
(b) Journalize the April transactions, including explanations.
(c) Post the April journal entries to the ledger T accounts.
(d) Prepare a trial balance on April 30, 2007.

(d) Cash $ 6,125
    Tot. trial
        balance $35,270

P3-9B   A first year co-op student working for UR Here.com recorded the transactions for the month. He wasn't exactly sure how to journalize and post, but he did the best he could. He had a few questions, however, about the following transactions.

Analyze errors and their effects on the trial balance. (SO 8)

1. Cash received from a customer on account was recorded as a debit to Cash of $560 and a credit to Accounts Receivable of $650, instead of $560.
2. A service provided for cash was posted as a debit to Cash of $2,000 and a credit to Service Revenue of $2,000.
3. A debit of $880 for services provided on account was neither recorded nor posted. The credit was recorded correctly.
4. The debit to record $1,000 of cash dividends was posted to the Salary Expense account.
5. The purchase, on account, of a computer that cost $2,500 was recorded as a debit to Supplies and a credit to Accounts Payable.
6. A cash payment of $495 for salaries was recorded as a debit to Dividends and a credit to Cash.

7. Payment of month's rent was debited to Rent Expense and credited to Cash, $850.
8. Issue of $7,000 of common shares was credited to the Common Stock account, but no debit was recorded.

Instructions
(a) Indicate which of the above transactions are correct, and which are incorrect.
(b) For each error identified in (a), indicate (1) whether the trial balance will balance; (2) the amount of the difference if the trial balance will not balance; and (3) the trial balance column that will have the larger total. Consider each error separately. Use the following form, in which transaction 1 is given as an example.

Error	(1) In Balance	(2) Difference	(3) Larger Column
1.	No	$90	Credit

Problems: Set C

Visit the book's website at **www.wiley.com/college/kimmel** and choose the Student Companion site to access Problem Set C.

Continuing Cookie Chronicle

(*Note*: This is a continuation of the Cookie Chronicle from Chapters 1 and 2.)

CCC3 In November 2006 after having incorporated Cookie Creations Inc., Natalie begins operations. She has decided to not pursue the offer to supply cookies to Biscuits. Instead she will focus on offering cooking classes. The following events occur.

Nov. 8 Natalie cashes in her U.S. Savings Bonds and receives $520, which she deposits in her personal bank account.
8 Natalie opens a bank account for Cookie Creations Inc.
8 Natalie purchases $500 of Cookie Creations' common stock.
11 Natalie designs a brochure and a poster to advertise the company and the services available.
11 The brochures and posters are printed, at a cost of $95. They will be distributed as the opportunity arises.
14 Cookie Creations purchases baking supplies, such as flour, sugar, butter, and chocolate chips, for $125.
15 Natalie starts to gather some baking equipment to take with her when teaching the cookie classes. She has an excellent top-of-the-line food processor and mixer that originally cost her $550. Natalie decides to start using it only in her new business. She estimates that the equipment is currently worth $300, and she transfers the equipment into the business in exchange for additional common stock.
16 The company needs more cash to sustain its operations. Natalie's grandmother lends the company $2,000 cash, in exchange for a two-year, 6% note payable. Interest and the principal are repayable at maturity.
17 Cookie Creations purchases more baking equipment for $900.
18 Natalie books her first class for November 29 for $100.
25 Natalie books a second class for December 5 for $125. She receives a $50 cash down payment, in advance.
29 Natalie teaches her first class, booked on November 18, and collects the $100 cash.
30 Natalie's brother develops a website for Cookie Creations Inc. that the company will use for advertising. He charges the company $600 for his work, payable at the end of December. (Because the website is expected to have a useful life of two years before upgrades are needed, it should be treated as an asset.)
30 Cookie Creations purchases a one-year insurance policy for $1,200.
30 Natalie teaches a group of elementary school students how to make Santa Claus cookies. At the end of the class, Natalie leaves an invoice for $250

with the school principal. The principal says that he will pass it along to the business office and it will be paid some time in December.

30   Natalie receives a $50 invoice for use of her cell phone. She uses the cell phone exclusively for Cookie Creations Inc. business. The invoice is for services provided in November, and payment is due on December 15.

Instructions

(a) Prepare journal entries to record the November transactions.

(b) Post the journal entries to the general ledger accounts.

(c) Prepare a trial balance at November 30, 2006.

(c) Trial balance total $3,850

BROADENING YOUR PERSPECTIVE

Financial Reporting and Analysis

FINANCIAL REPORTING PROBLEM: *Tootsie Roll Industries*

BYP3-1   The financial statements of Tootsie Roll in Appendix A at the back of this book contain the following selected accounts, all in thousands of dollars.

Common Stock	$24,139
Accounts Payable	19,315
Accounts Receivable	28,456
Selling, Marketing, and Administrative Expenses	85,705s
Prepaid Expenses	5,719
Property, Plant, and Equipment	321,054
Net Sales	420,110

Instructions

(a) What is the increase and decrease side for each account? What is the normal balance for each account?

(b) Identify the probable other account in the transaction and the effect on that account when:

  (1) Accounts Receivable is decreased.

  (2) Accounts Payable is decreased.

  (3) Prepaid Expenses is increased.

(c) Identify the other account(s) that ordinarily would be involved when:

  (1) Interest Expense is increased.

  (2) Property, Plant, and Equipment is increased.

COMPARATIVE ANALYSIS PROBLEM: *Tootsie Roll vs. Hershey Foods*

BYP3-2   The financial statements of Hershey Foods are presented in Appendix B, following the financial statements for Tootsie Roll in Appendix A.

Instructions

(a) Based on the information contained in these financial statements, determine the normal balance for:

Tootsie Roll Industries	**Hershey Foods**
(1) Accounts Receivable	(1) Inventories
(2) Property, Plant, and Equipment	(2) Provision for Income Taxes
(3) Accounts Payable	(3) Accrued Liabilities
(4) Retained Earnings	(4) Common Stock
(5) Net Sales	(5) Interest Expense

(b) Identify the other account ordinarily involved when:

  (1) Accounts Receivable is increased.

  (2) Notes Payable is decreased.

(3) Machinery is increased.

(4) Interest Income is increased.

RESEARCH CASE

BYP3-3 The October 13, 2003, issue of *Business Week* includes an article by Stephanie Anderson titled "Is This Any Way To Run a Bank?"

Instructions

Read the article and answer the following questions.

(a) Describe Sherry Colby's account of her experiences with the mortgage company Washington Mutual.

(b) What other types of complaints has Washington Mutual received?

(c) What might be contributing to Washington Mutual's accounting troubles?

(d) What are the potential implications of the company's apparent poor accounting practices for the success of its business?

INTERPRETING FINANCIAL STATEMENTS

BYP3-4 Chieftain International, Inc., is an oil and natural gas exploration and production company. A recent balance sheet reported $208 million in assets with only $4.6 million in liabilities, all of which were short-term accounts payable.

During the year, Chieftain expanded its holdings of oil and gas rights, drilled 37 new wells, and invested in expensive 3-D seismic technology. The company generated $19 million cash from operating activities and paid no dividends. It had a cash balance of $102 million at the end of the year.

Instructions

(a) Name at least two advantages to Chieftain from having no long-term debt. Can you think of disadvantages?

(b) What are some of the advantages to Chieftain from having this large a cash balance? What is a disadvantage?

(c) Why do you suppose Chieftain has the $4.6 million balance in accounts payable, since it appears that it could have made all its purchases for cash?

BYP3-5 Doman Industries Ltd., whose products are sold in 30 countries worldwide, is an integrated Canadian forest products company.

Doman sells the majority of its lumber products in the United States, and a significant amount of its pulp products in Asia. Doman also has loans from other countries. For example, the Company borrowed US$160 million at an annual interest rate of 12%. Doman must repay this loan, and interest, in U.S. dollars.

One of the challenges global companies face is to make themselves attractive to investors from other countries. This is difficult to do when different accounting rules in different countries blur the real impact of earnings. For example, in a recent year Doman reported a loss of $2.3 million, using Canadian accounting rules. Had it reported under U.S. accounting rules, its loss would have been $12.1 million.

Many companies that want to be more easily compared with U.S. and other global competitors have switched to U.S. accounting principles. Canadian National Railway, Corel, Cott, Inco, and Thomson Corporation are but a few examples of large Canadian companies whose financial statements are now presented in U.S. dollars, adhere to U.S. GAAP, or are reconciled to U.S. GAAP.

Instructions

(a) Identify advantages and disadvantages that companies should consider when switching to U.S. reporting standards.

(b) Suppose you compare Doman Industries to a U.S.-based competitor. Do you believe the use of country-specific accounting policies would hinder your ability to compare the companies? If so, explain how.

(c) Suppose you compare Doman Industries to a Canadian-based competitor. If the companies apply generally acceptable Canadian accounting policies differently, how could this affect your ability to compare their financial results?

(d) Do you see any significant distinction between comparing statements prepared using generally accepted accounting principles of different countries and comparing statements prepared using generally accepted accounting principles of the same country (e.g. U.S.) but that apply the principles differently?

FINANCIAL ANALYSIS ON THE WEB

BYP3-6 *Purpose:* This activity provides information about career opportunities for CPAs.

Address: **www.futurecpa.org** (or go to **www.wiley.com/college/kimmel**)

Steps
1. Go to the address shown above.
2. Click on CPA101.

Careers in Accounting

Instructions
Answer the following questions.
(a) What does CPA stand for? Where do CPAs work?
(b) What is meant by "public accounting"?
(c) What skills does a CPA need?
(d) What is the salary range for a CPA at a large firm during the first three years? What is the salary range for chief financial officers and treasurers at large corporations?

Critical Thinking

DECISION MAKING ACROSS THE ORGANIZATION

BYP3-7 Katie Kim operates Double K Riding Academy, Inc. The academy's primary sources of revenue are riding fees and lesson fees, which are provided on a cash basis. Katie also boards horses for owners, who are billed monthly for boarding fees. In a few cases, boarders pay in advance of expected use. For its revenue transactions, the academy maintains these accounts: Cash, Accounts Receivable, Unearned Revenue, Riding Revenue, Lesson Revenue, and Boarding Revenue.

The academy owns 10 horses, a stable, a riding corral, riding equipment, and office equipment. These assets are accounted for in the following accounts: Horses, Building, Riding Corral, Riding Equipment, and Office Equipment.

The academy employs stable helpers and an office employee, who receive weekly salaries. At the end of each month, the mail usually brings bills for advertising, utilities, and veterinary service. Other expenses include feed for the horses and insurance. For its expenses, the academy maintains the following accounts: Hay and Feed Supplies, Prepaid Insurance, Accounts Payable, Salaries Expense, Advertising Expense, Utilities Expense, Veterinary Expense, Hay and Feed Expense, and Insurance Expense.

Katie Kim's sole source of personal income is dividends from the academy. Thus, the corporation declares and pays periodic dividends. To record stockholders' equity in the business and dividends, two accounts are maintained: Common Stock and Dividends.

During the first month of operations an inexperienced bookkeeper was employed. Katie Kim asks you to review the following eight entries of the 50 entries made during the month. In each case, the explanation for the entry is correct.

May 1	Cash		15,000	
	Unearned Revenue			15,000
	(Issued common stock in exchange for $15,000 cash)			
5	Cash		250	
	Lesson Revenue			250
	(Received $250 cash for lesson fees)			
7	Cash		500	
	Boarding Revenue			500
	(Received $500 for boarding of horses beginning June 1)			
9	Hay and Feed Expense		1,700	
	Cash			1,700
	(Purchased estimated 5 months' supply of feed and hay for $1,700 on account)			

May 14	Riding Equipment	80	
	Cash		800
	(Purchased desk and other office equipment for $800 cash)		
15	Salaries Expense	400	
	Cash		400
	(Issued check to Katie Kim for personal use)		
20	Cash	145	
	Riding Revenue		154
	(Received $154 cash for riding fees)		
31	Veterinary Expense	75	
	Accounts Receivable		75
	(Received bill of $75 from veterinarian for services provided)		

Instructions

With the class divided into groups, answer the following.

(a) For each journal entry that is correct, so state. For each journal entry that is incorrect, prepare the entry that should have been made by the bookkeeper.

(b) Which of the incorrect entries would prevent the trial balance from balancing?

(c) What was the correct net income for May, assuming the bookkeeper originally reported net income of $4,500 after posting all 50 entries?

(d) What was the correct cash balance at May 31, assuming the bookkeeper reported a balance of $12,475 after posting all 50 entries?

COMMUNICATION ACTIVITY

BYP3-8 Clean Sweep Company offers home cleaning service. Two recurring transactions for the company are billing customers for services provided and paying employee salaries. For example, on March 15 bills totaling $6,000 were sent to customers, and $2,000 was paid in salaries to employees.

Instructions

Write a memorandum to your instructor that explains and illustrates the steps in the recording process for each of the March 15 transactions. Use the format illustrated in the text under the heading "The Recording Process Illustrated" (pp. 118–124).

ETHICS CASE

BYP3-9 Rachel McGaver is the assistant chief accountant at A2Z Company, a manufacturer of computer chips and cellular phones. The company presently has total sales of $20 million. It is the end of the first quarter and Rachel is hurriedly trying to prepare a general ledger trial balance so that quarterly financial statements can be prepared and released to management and the regulatory agencies. The total credits on the trial balance exceed the debits by $1,000.

In order to meet the 4 P.M. deadline, Rachel decides to force the debits and credits into balance by adding the amount of the difference to the Equipment account. She chose Equipment because it is one of the larger account balances; percentage-wise it will be the least misstated. Rachel plugs the difference! She believes that the difference is quite small and will not affect anyone's decisions. She wishes that she had another few days to find the error but realizes that the financial statements are already late.

Instructions

(a) Who are the stakeholders in this situation?

(b) What ethical issues are involved?

(c) What are Rachel's alternatives?

Answers to Business Insight and Accounting across the Organization Questions

p. 106

Q: In order for these companies to prepare and issue financial statements, their accounting equations (debit and credits) must have been in balance at year-end. How could these errors or misstatements have occurred?

A: A company's accounting equation (its books) can be in balance yet its financial statements have errors or misstatements because of the following: entire transactions were not recorded; transactions were recorded at wrong amounts; transactions were recorded in the wrong accounts; transactions were recorded in the wrong accounting period. Audits of financial statements uncover some, but obviously not all, errors or misstatements.

p. 112

Q: Do you think that the Chicago Bears football team would be likely to have the same major revenue and expense accounts as the Cubs?

A: Because their businesses are similar—professional sports—many of the revenue and expense accounts for the baseball and football teams might be similar.

p. 116

Q: In what ways is this Microsoft division using accounting to assist in its effort to become more profitable?

A: The division has used accounting to set very strict sales, revenue, and profit goals. In addition, the managers in this division use accounting to keep a tight reign on product costs. Also, accounting serves as the basis of communication so that the marketing managers and product designers can work with production managers, engineers, and accountants to achieve an exciting product within specified cost constraints.

Answer to Tootsie Roll Review It Question 4, p. 114

Normal balances for accounts in Tootsie Roll's financial statements: Accounts Receivable—debit; Income Taxes Payable—credit; Sales—credit; Selling, Marketing, and Administrative Expense—debit.

Answers to Self-Study Questions

1. b   2. b   3. b   4. c   5. d   6. d   7. b   8. a   9. c   10. d
11. a   12. c

CHAPTER 4

Accrual Accounting Concepts

STUDY OBJECTIVES

After studying this chapter, you should be able to:

1 Explain the revenue recognition principle and the matching principle.

2 Differentiate between the cash basis and the accrual basis of accounting.

3 Explain why adjusting entries are needed, and identify the major types of adjusting entries.

4 Prepare adjusting entries for prepayments.

5 Prepare adjusting entries for accruals.

6 Describe the nature and purpose of the adjusted trial balance.

7 Explain the purpose of closing entries.

8 Describe the required steps in the accounting cycle.

✔ THE NAVIGATOR

- Scan *Study Objectives*
- Read *Feature Story*
- Read *Preview*
- Read text and answer *Before You Go On*
  p. 161 ⬭ p. 169 ⬭ p. 174 ⬭ p. 183 ⬭
- Work *Using the Decision Toolkit*
- Review *Summary of Study Objectives*
- Work *Demonstration Problem*
- Answer *Self-Study Questions*
- Complete *Assignments*

FEATURE STORY

What Was Your Profit?

The accuracy of the financial reporting system depends on answers to a few fundamental questions. At what point has revenue been earned? At what point is the earnings process complete? When have expenses really been incurred?

During the 1990s' boom in the stock prices of dot-com companies, many dot-com companies earned most of their revenue from selling advertising space on their Web sites. To boost reported revenue, some dot-coms began swapping website ad space. Company A would put an ad for its website on company B's website, and company B would put an ad for its website on company A's website. No money ever changed hands, but each company recorded revenue (for the value of the space that it gave up on its site). This practice did little to boost net income and resulted in no additional cash flow—but it did boost *reported revenue*. Regulators eventually put an end to the practice.

Another type of transgression results from companies recording revenue or expenses in the wrong year. In fact, shifting revenues and expenses is one of the most common abuses of financial accounting. Xerox recently admitted reporting billions of dollars of lease revenue in periods earlier than it should have been reported. And WorldCom stunned the financial markets with its admission that it had boosted net income by billions of dollars

by delaying the recognition of expenses until later years.

Unfortunately, revelations such as these have become all too common in the corporate world. It is no wonder that recently the U.S. Trust Survey of affluent Americans reported that 85 percent of its respondents believed that there should be tighter regulation of financial disclosures, and 66 percent said they did not trust the management of publicly traded companies.

Why did so many companies violate basic financial reporting rules and sound ethics? Many speculate that as stock prices climbed, executives were under increasing pressure to meet higher and higher earnings expectations. If actual results weren't as good as hoped for, some gave in to temptation and "adjusted" their numbers to meet market expectations.

THE NAVIGATOR

On the World Wide Web
Xerox: www.xerox.com

PREVIEW OF CHAPTER 4

As indicated in the Feature Story, making adjustments is necessary to avoid misstatement of revenues and expenses such as those at Xerox and WorldCom. In this chapter we introduce you to the accrual accounting concepts that make such adjustments possible.

The organization and content of the chapter are as follows.

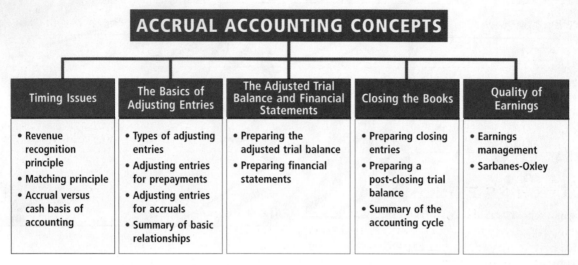

ACCRUAL ACCOUNTING CONCEPTS

Timing Issues	The Basics of Adjusting Entries	The Adjusted Trial Balance and Financial Statements	Closing the Books	Quality of Earnings
• Revenue recognition principle • Matching principle • Accrual versus cash basis of accounting	• Types of adjusting entries • Adjusting entries for prepayments • Adjusting entries for accruals • Summary of basic relationships	• Preparing the adjusted trial balance • Preparing financial statements	• Preparing closing entries • Preparing a post-closing trial balance • Summary of the accounting cycle	• Earnings management • Sarbanes-Oxley

THE NAVIGATOR

Helpful Hint An accounting time period that is one year long is called a **fiscal year**.

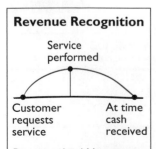

Revenue Recognition

Service performed

Customer requests service — At time cash received

Revenue should be recognized in the accounting period in which it is earned (generally when service is performed).

Timing Issues

Most businesses need immediate feedback about how well they are doing. For example, management usually wants monthly reports on financial results, most large corporations are required to present quarterly and annual financial statements to stockholders, and the Internal Revenue Service requires all businesses to file annual tax returns. **Accounting divides the economic life of a business into artificial time periods.** As indicated in Chapter 2, this is the time period assumption. **Accounting time periods are generally a month, a quarter, or a year.**

Many business transactions affect more than one of these arbitrary time periods. For example, a new building purchased by Citigroup or a new airplane purchased by Delta Air Lines will be used for many years. It doesn't make sense to expense the full cost of the building or the airplane at the time of purchase because each will be used for many subsequent periods. Instead, we determine the impact of each transaction on specific accounting periods.

Determining the amount of revenues and expenses to report in a given accounting period can be difficult. Proper reporting requires an understanding of the nature of the company's business. Two principles are used as guidelines: the revenue recognition principle and the matching principle.

THE REVENUE RECOGNITION PRINCIPLE

The **revenue recognition principle** requires that companies recognize revenue in the accounting period **in which it is earned**. In a service company, revenue is considered to be earned at the time the service is performed. To illustrate, assume Conrad Dry Cleaners cleans clothing on June 30, but customers do not claim and pay for their clothes until the first week of July. Under the revenue recognition principle, Conrad earns revenue in June when it performs the service, not in July when it receives the cash. At June 30 Conrad would report a receivable on its balance sheet and revenue in its income statement for the service performed.

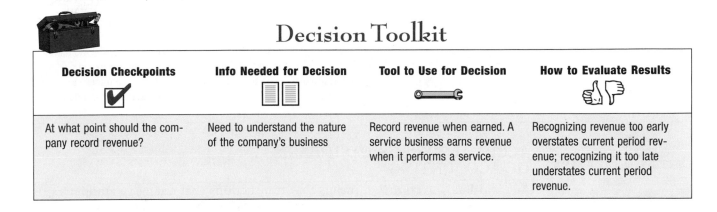

Decision Toolkit

Decision Checkpoints	Info Needed for Decision	Tool to Use for Decision	How to Evaluate Results
At what point should the company record revenue?	Need to understand the nature of the company's business	Record revenue when earned. A service business earns revenue when it performs a service.	Recognizing revenue too early overstates current period revenue; recognizing it too late understates current period revenue.

THE MATCHING PRINCIPLE

In recognizing expenses, a simple rule is followed: "Let the expenses follow the revenues." Thus, expense recognition is tied to revenue recognition. Applied to the preceding example, this means that the salary expense Conrad incurred in performing the cleaning service on June 30 should be reported in the same period in which it recognizes the service revenue. The critical issue in expense recognition is determining when the expense makes its contribution to revenue. This may or may not be the same period in which the expense is paid. If Conrad does not pay the salary incurred on June 30 until July, it would report salaries payable on its June 30 balance sheet.

The practice of expense recognition is referred to as the **matching principle** because it dictates that efforts (expenses) be matched with accomplishments (revenues). Illustration 4-1 shows these relationships.

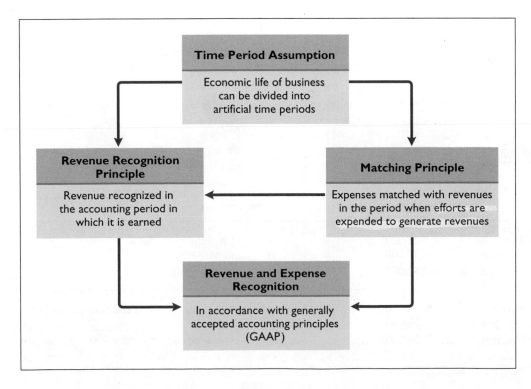

Illustration 4-1   **GAAP** relationships in revenue and expense recognition

Decision Toolkit

Decision Checkpoints	Info Needed for Decision	Tool to Use for Decision	How to Evaluate Results
At what point should the company record expenses?	Need to understand the nature of the company's business	Expenses should "follow" revenues—that is, match the effort (expense) with the result (revenue).	Recognizing expenses too early overstates current period expense; recognizing them too late understates current period expense.

ACCRUAL VERSUS CASH BASIS OF ACCOUNTING

Accrual-basis accounting means that transactions that change a company's financial statements are recorded **in the periods in which the events occur.** For example, using the accrual basis means that companies recognize revenues **when earned** (the revenue recognition principle) **rather than when they receive cash. Likewise, under the accrual basis, companies recognize expenses when incurred** (the matching principle) **rather than when paid.**

An alternative to the accrual basis is the cash basis. Under **cash-basis accounting, companies record revenue only when cash is received. They record expense only when cash is paid. The cash basis of accounting is prohibited under generally accepted accounting principles.** Why? Because it does not record revenue when earned, thus violating the revenue recognition principle. Similarly, it does not record expenses when incurred, which violates the matching principle.

Illustration 4-2 compares accrual-based numbers and cash-based numbers. Suppose that Fresh Colors paints a large building in 2006. In 2006 it incurs and pays total expenses (salaries and paint costs) of $50,000. It bills the customer $80,000, but does not receive payment until 2007. On an accrual basis, Fresh

 International Note

Although different accounting standards are often used by companies in other countries, the accrual basis of accounting is central to all of these standards.

Illustration 4-2   Accrual versus cash basis accounting

	2006	**2007**
Activity	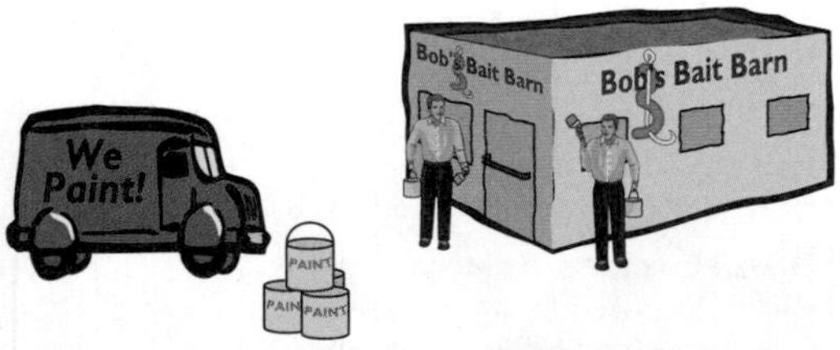 Purchased paint, painted building, paid employees	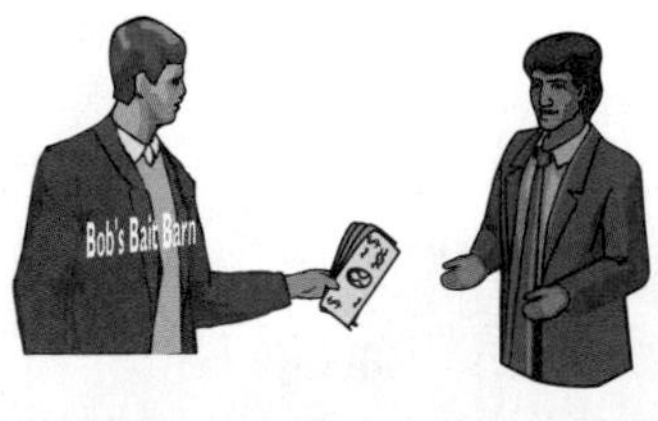 Received payment for work done in 2006
Accrual basis	Revenue $80,000 Expense 50,000 Net income $30,000	Revenue $ 0 Expense 0 Net income $ 0
Cash basis	Revenue $ 0 Expense 50,000 Net loss $(50,000)	Revenue $80,000 Expense 0 Net income $80,000

Colors reports $80,000 of revenue during 2006 because that is when it is earned. The company matches expenses of $50,000 to the $80,000 of revenue. Thus, 2006 net income is $30,000 ($80,000 − $50,000). The $30,000 of net income reported for 2006 indicates the profitability of Fresh Colors' efforts during that period.

If, instead, Fresh Paint were to use cash-basis accounting, it would report $50,000 of expenses in 2006 and $80,000 of revenues during 2007. As shown in Illustration 4-2, it would report a loss of $50,000 in 2006 and would report net income of $80,000 in 2007. Clearly, the cash-basis measures are misleading because the financial performance of the company would be misstated for both 2006 and 2007.

Business Insight
Ethics Perspective

Allegations of abuse of the revenue recognition principle have become all too common in recent years. For example, it was alleged that Krispy Kreme sometimes doubled the number of doughnuts shipped to wholesale customers at the end of a quarter to boost quarterly results. The customers shipped the unsold doughnuts back after the beginning of the next quarter for a refund. Conversely, Computer Associates International was accused of backdating sales—that is, saying that a sale that occurred at the beginning of one quarter occurred at the end of the previous quarter in order to achieve the previous quarter's sales targets.

 What motivates sales executives and finance and accounting executives to participate in activities that result in inaccurate reporting of revenues?

BEFORE YOU GO ON . . .

▶Review It

1. What are the revenue recognition and matching principles?
2. What are the differences between the cash and accrual bases of accounting?

☑ THE NAVIGATOR

The Basics of Adjusting Entries

In order for revenues to be recorded in the period in which they are earned, and for expenses to be recognized in the period in which they are incurred, companies make adjusting entries. Adjusting entries **ensure that the revenue recognition and matching principles are followed**.

Adjusting entries are necessary because the **trial balance**—the first pulling together of the transaction data—may not contain up-to-date and complete data. This is true for several reasons:

1. Some events are not recorded daily because it is not efficient to do so. Examples are the use of supplies and the earning of wages by employees.
2. Some costs are not recorded during the accounting period because these costs expire with the passage of time rather than as a result of recurring

STUDY OBJECTIVE
3

Explain why adjusting entries are needed, and identify the major types of adjusting entries.

daily transactions. Examples are charges related to the use of buildings and equipment, rent, and insurance.

3. Some items may be unrecorded. An example is a utility service bill that will not be received until the next accounting period.

Adjusting entries are required every time a company prepares financial statements. The company analyzes each account in the trial balance to determine whether it is complete and up to date for financial statement purposes.

TYPES OF ADJUSTING ENTRIES

Adjusting entries are classified as either prepayments or accruals. As Illustration 4-3 shows, each of these classes has two subcategories.

Illustration 4-3
Categories of adjusting entries

Prepayments:

1. **Prepaid expenses**: Expenses paid in cash and recorded as assets before they are used or consumed.
2. **Unearned revenues**: Cash received and recorded as liabilities before revenue is earned.

Accruals:

1. **Accrued revenues**: Revenues earned but not yet received in cash or recorded.
2. **Accrued expenses**: Expenses incurred but not yet paid in cash or recorded.

Subsequent sections give specific examples and explanations of each type of adjustment. Each example is based on the October 31 trial balance of Sierra Corporation, from Chapter 3, reproduced below in Illustration 4-4. Note that Retained Earnings, with a zero balance, has been added to this trial balance. We will explain its use later.

Illustration 4-4   Trial balance

SIERRA CORPORATION
Trial Balance
October 31, 2007

	Debit	Credit
Cash	$15,200	
Advertising Supplies	2,500	
Prepaid Insurance	600	
Office Equipment	5,000	
Notes Payable		$ 5,000
Accounts Payable		2,500
Unearned Service Revenue		1,200
Common Stock		10,000
Retained Earnings		0
Dividends	500	
Service Revenue		10,000
Salaries Expense	4,000	
Rent Expense	900	
	$28,700	$28,700

We assume that Sierra Corporation uses an accounting period of one month. Thus, monthly adjusting entries are made. The entries are dated October 31.

(handwritten margin notes: "prut exps / no return same yr", "got money / didn't earn yg")

ADJUSTING ENTRIES FOR PREPAYMENTS

Prepayments are either prepaid expenses or unearned revenues. Companies must make adjusting entries for prepayments at the statement date to record the portion of the prepayment that represents the expense incurred or the revenue earned in the current accounting period.

Prepaid Expenses

Companies record payments of expenses that will benefit more than one accounting period as assets called **prepaid expenses** or **prepayments**. When expenses are prepaid, an asset account is increased (debited) to show the service or benefit that the company will receive in the future. Examples of common prepayments are insurance, supplies, advertising, and rent. In addition, companies make prepayments when they purchase buildings and equipment.

Prepaid expenses are costs that expire either with the passage of time (e.g., rent and insurance) **or through use** (e.g., supplies). The expiration of these costs does not require daily entries, which would be impractical and unnecessary. Accordingly, companies postpone the recognition of such cost expirations until they prepare financial statements. At each statement date, they then make adjusting entries to record the expenses applicable to the current accounting period and to show the remaining amounts in the asset accounts.

Prior to adjustment, assets are overstated and expenses are understated. Therefore, as shown in Illustration 4-5, **an adjusting entry for prepaid expenses results in an increase (a debit) to an expense account and a decrease (a credit) to an asset account.**

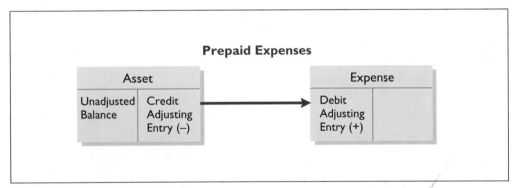

Illustration 4-5
Adjusting entries for prepaid expenses

Let's look in more detail at some specific types of prepaid expenses, beginning with supplies.

SUPPLIES. The purchase of supplies, such as paper and envelopes, results in an increase (a debit) to an asset account. During the accounting period, the company uses supplies. Rather than record supplies expense as the supplies are used, companies recognize supplies expense at the **end** of the accounting period. At the end of the accounting period the company must count the remaining supplies. The difference between the unadjusted balance in the Supplies (asset) account and the actual cost of supplies on hand represents the supplies used (an expense) for that period.

Recall from Chapter 3 that Sierra Corporation purchased advertising supplies costing $2,500 on October 5. Sierra recorded the payment by increasing (debiting) the asset Advertising Supplies. This account shows a balance of $2,500 in the October 31 trial balance. An inventory count at the close of business on October 31 reveals that $1,000 of supplies are still on hand. Thus, the cost of

Supplies

Oct.5

Supplies purchased; record asset

Oct.31
Supplies used; record supplies expense

supplies used is $1,500 ($2,500 − $1,000). This use of supplies decreases an asset, Advertising Supplies. It also decreases stockholders' equity by increasing an expense account, Advertising Supplies Expense. The use of supplies affects the accounting equation in the following way.

Assets	=	Liabilities	+	Stockholders' Equity
−$1,500				−$1,500

Thus, Sierra makes the following adjusting entry:

Oct. 31	Advertising Supplies Expense	1,500	
	Advertising Supplies		1,500
	(To record supplies used)		

After the adjusting entry is posted, the accounts, in T account form, appear as in Illustration 4-6.

Illustration 4-6 Supplies accounts after adjustment

Advertising Supplies				Advertising Supplies Expense	
Oct. 5	2,500	Oct.31 **Adj. 1,500**		Oct. 31 **Adj. 1,500**	
Oct. 31 Bal. 1,000				Oct. 31 Bal. 1,500	

The asset account Advertising Supplies now shows a balance of $1,000, which is equal to the cost of supplies on hand at the statement date. In addition, Advertising Supplies Expense shows a balance of $1,500, which equals the cost of supplies used in October. **If Sierra does not make the adjusting entry, October expenses will be understated and net income overstated by $1,500. Moreover, both assets and stockholders' equity will be overstated by $1,500 on the October 31 balance sheet.**

Accounting across the Organization

The method of accounting for advertising costs affects sales and marketing executives. In the past, companies sometimes recorded as assets the costs of media advertising for burgers, bleaches, athletic shoes, and such products and expensed those costs in subsequent periods as sales took place. The reasoning behind this treatment was that long ad campaigns provided benefits over multiple accounting periods. Today the accounting profession no longer allows this treatment because it was decided that the benefits were too difficult to measure.

Instead, companies now must expense advertising costs when the advertising takes place. The issue is important because the outlays for advertising can be substantial. Recent (2004) big spenders: Coca-Cola spent $2.2 billion, PepsiCo., Inc. $1.7 billion, Nike, Inc. $1,378 million, and Limited Brands $484 million.

 Why might the new accounting method cause companies sometimes to spend less on advertising?

INSURANCE.   Companies purchase insurance to protect themselves from losses due to fire, theft, and unforeseen events. Insurance must be paid in advance, often for more than one year. The cost of insurance (premiums) paid in advance is recorded as an increase (debit) in the asset account Prepaid Insurance. At the financial statement date companies increase (debit) Insurance Expense and decrease (credit) Prepaid Insurance for the cost of insurance that has expired during the period.

On October 4 Sierra Corporation paid $600 for a one-year fire insurance policy. Coverage began on October 1. Sierra recorded the payment by increasing (debiting) Prepaid Insurance. This account shows a balance of $600 in the October 31 trial balance. Insurance of $50 ($600 ÷ 12) expires each month. The expiration of Prepaid Insurance decreases an asset, Prepaid Insurance. It also decreases stockholders' equity by increasing an expense account, Insurance Expense. The expiration of Prepaid Insurance affects the accounting equation in October (and in each of the next 11 months) in the following way.

Assets	=	Liabilities	+	Stockholders' Equity
−$50				−$50

Thus, the following adjusting entry is made.

Oct. 31	Insurance Expense	50	
	Prepaid Insurance		50
	(To record insurance expired)		

After Sierra posts the adjusting entry, the accounts appear as in Illustration 4-7.

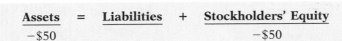

Prepaid Insurance			Insurance Expense	
Oct. 4 600	Oct. 31 **Adj. 50**		Oct. 31 **Adj. 50**	
Oct. 31 Bal. 550			Oct. 31 Bal. 50	

Illustration 4-7
Insurance accounts after adjustment

The asset Prepaid Insurance shows a balance of $550, which represents the unexpired cost for the remaining 11 months of coverage. At the same time the balance in Insurance Expense equals the insurance cost that expired in October. If Sierra does not make this adjustment, October expenses are understated by $50 and net income is overstated by $50. Moreover, as the accounting equation shows, both assets and stockholders' equity will be overstated by $50 on the October 31 balance sheet.

DEPRECIATION.   A company typically owns a variety of assets that have long lives, such as buildings, equipment, and motor vehicles. The period of service is referred to as the **useful life** of the asset. Because a building is expected to provide service for many years, it is recorded as an asset, rather than an expense, on the date it is acquired. As explained in Chapter 2, companies record such assets **at cost**, as required by the cost principle. According to the matching principle, companies then report a portion of this cost as an expense during each period of the asset's useful life. **Depreciation** is the process of allocating the cost of an asset to expense over its useful life.

Need for Adjustment.   The acquisition of long-lived assets is essentially a long-term prepayment for services. An adjusting entry for depreciation is

Insurance

Oct.4

Insurance purchased;
record asset

Insurance Policy			
Oct	Nov	Dec	Jan
$50	$50	$50	$50
Feb	March	April	May
$50	$50	$50	$50
June	July	Aug	Sept
$50	$50	$50	$50
I YEAR $600			

Oct.31
Insurance expired;
record insurance expense

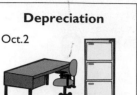

Depreciation

Oct.2

Office equipment purchased; record asset

Office Equipment			
Oct	Nov	Dec	Jan
$40	$40	$40	$40
Feb	March	April	May
$40	$40	$40	$40
June	July	Aug	Sept
$40	$40	$40	$40
Depreciation = $480/year			

Oct.31

Depreciation recognized; record depreciation expense

needed to recognize the cost that has been used (an expense) during the period and to report the unused cost (an asset) at the end of the period. One very important point to understand: **Depreciation is an allocation concept, not a valuation concept.** That is, depreciation **allocates an asset's cost to the periods in which it is used. Depreciation does not attempt to report the actual change in the value of the asset.**

For Sierra Corporation, assume that depreciation on the office equipment is $480 a year, or $40 per month. Depreciation decreases an asset (in this example, Office Equipment). It also decreases stockholders' equity by increasing an expense account, Depreciation Expense. Depreciation affects the accounting equation in the following way.

Assets	=	Liabilities	+	Stockholders' Equity
−$40				−$40

Sierra recognizes depreciation for October by this adjusting entry.

Oct. 31	Depreciation Expense	40	
	Accumulated Depreciation—Office		
	Equipment		40
	(To record monthly depreciation)		

After the company posts the adjusting entry, the accounts appear as in Illustration 4-8.

Illustration 4-8
Accounts after adjustment for depreciation

Office Equipment

Oct. 2	5,000	
Oct. 31	Bal. 5,000	

Accumulated Depreciation— Office Equipment

	Oct. 31	**Adj. 40**
	Oct. 31	Bal. 40

Depreciation Expense

Oct. 31	**Adj. 40**	
Oct. 31	Bal. 40	

The balance in the Accumulated Depreciation account will increase $40 each month, and the balance in Office Equipment remains $5,000.

Helpful Hint All contra accounts have increases, decreases, and normal balances **opposite to** the account to which they relate.

Statement Presentation. Accumulated Depreciation—Office Equipment is a contra asset account. That means that the account is offset against an asset account (Office Equipment) on the balance sheet. The normal balance of a contra asset account is a credit. A theoretical alternative to using a contra asset account would be to decrease (credit) the asset account by the amount of depreciation each period. But using the contra account is preferable for a simple reason: it discloses *both* the original cost of the equipment *and* the total cost that has expired to date. Thus, in the balance sheet, Sierra deducts Accumulated Depreciation—Office Equipment from the related asset account as shown in Illustration 4-9.

Illustration 4-9 Balance sheet presentation of accumulated depreciation

Office equipment	$ 5,000
Less: Accumulated depreciation—office equipment	40
	$4,960

Book value is the difference between the cost of any depreciable asset and its related accumulated depreciation. In Illustration 4-9, the book value of the equipment at the balance sheet date is $4,960. The book value and the market value of the asset are generally two different values. As noted earlier, **the purpose of depreciation is not valuation, but a means of cost allocation.**

Depreciation expense identifies the portion of an asset's cost that expired during the period (in this case, in October). The accounting equation shows that without this adjusting entry, total assets, total stockholders' equity, and net income are overstated by $40 and depreciation expense is understated by $40.

Alternative Terminology
Book value is also referred to as *carrying value.*

Unearned Revenues

Companies record cash received before revenue is earned by increasing (crediting) a liability account called **unearned revenues.** Items like rent, magazine subscriptions, and customer deposits for future service may result in unearned revenues. Airlines such as United, American, and Delta, for instance, treat receipts from the sale of tickets as unearned revenue until the flight service is provided.

Unearned revenues are the opposite of prepaid expenses. Indeed, unearned revenue on the books of one company is likely to be a prepayment on the books of the company that has made the advance payment. For example, if identical accounting periods are assumed, a landlord will have unearned rent revenue when a tenant has prepaid rent.

When a company receives payment for services to be provided in a future accounting period, it increases (credits) an unearned revenue (a liability) account to recognize the liability that exists. The company subsequently earns revenues by providing service. During the accounting period it is not practical to make daily entries as the company earns the revenue. Instead, we delay recognition of earned revenue until the adjustment process. Then the company makes an adjusting entry to record the revenue earned during the period and to show the liability that remains at the end of the accounting period. Typically, prior to adjustment, liabilities are overstated and revenues are understated. Therefore, as shown in Illustration 4-10, **the adjusting entry for unearned revenues results in a decrease (a debit) to a liability account and an increase (a credit) to a revenue account**.

Unearned Revenues

Oct.2 *Thank you in advance for your work*

I will finish by Dec. 31

~$1,200

Cash is received in advance; liability is recorded

Oct.31
Some service has been provided; some revenue is recorded

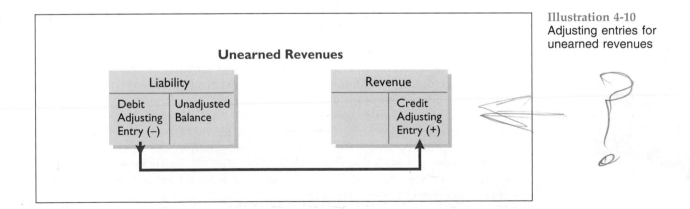

Unearned Revenues

Liability			Revenue	
Debit Adjusting Entry (−)	Unadjusted Balance			Credit Adjusting Entry (+)

Illustration 4-10
Adjusting entries for unearned revenues

Sierra Corporation received $1,200 on October 2 from R. Knox for advertising services expected to be completed by December 31. Sierra credited the payment to Unearned Service Revenue, and this liability account shows a balance of $1,200 in the October 31 trial balance. From an evaluation of the work Sierra performed for Knox during October, the company determines that it has earned $400 in October. The liability (Unearned Service Revenue) is therefore decreased, and stockholders' equity (Service Revenue) is increased. The accounting equation is affected in the following way.

Assets	=	Liabilities	+	Stockholders' Equity
		−$400		+$400

Thus, Sierra makes the following adjusting entry.

Oct. 31	Unearned Service Revenue	400	
	Service Revenue		400
	(To record revenue earned)		

After the company posts the adjusting entry, the accounts appear as in Illustration 4-11.

Illustration 4-11 Service revenue accounts after adjustment

Unearned Service Revenue				Service Revenue		
Oct. 31 **Adj. 400**	Oct. 2	1,200			Oct. 3	10,000
					31 **Adj.**	**400**
	Oct. 31	Bal. 800			Oct. 31 Bal.	10,400

The liability Unearned Service Revenue now shows a balance of $800. That amount represents the remaining advertising services expected to be performed in the future. At the same time, Service Revenue shows total revenue earned in October of $10,400. **Without this adjustment, revenues and net income are understated by $400 in the income statement. Moreover, liabilities are overstated and stockholders' equity is understated by $400 on the October 31 balance sheet.**

Accounting across the Organization

Those of you who are marketing majors (and even most of you who are not) know that gift cards are among the hottest marketing tools in merchandising today. Customers purchase gift cards and give them to someone for later use. In a recent year gift-card sales topped $95 billion.

Although these programs are popular with marketing executives, they create accounting questions. Should revenue be recorded at the time the gift card is sold, or when it is exercised? How should expired gift cards be accounted for? In its 2004 balance sheet Best Buy reported unearned revenue related to gift cards of $300 million.

Source: Robert Berner, "Gift Cards: No Gift to Investors," *Business Week* (March 14, 2005), p. 86.

 Suppose that Robert Jones purchases a $100 gift card at Best Buy on December 24, 2006, and gives it to his wife, Mary Jones, on December 25, 2006. On January 3, 2007, Mary uses the card to purchase $100 worth of CDs. When do you think Best Buy should recognize revenue and why?

BEFORE YOU GO ON . . .

▶Review It

1. What are the four types of adjusting entries?
2. What is the effect on assets, stockholders' equity, expenses, and net income if a prepaid expense adjusting entry is not made?
3. What is the effect on liabilities, stockholders' equity, revenues, and net income if an unearned revenue adjusting entry is not made?

▶ Do It

The ledger of Hammond, Inc., on March 31, 2007, includes these selected accounts before adjusting entries are prepared.

	Debit	Credit
Prepaid Insurance	$ 3,600	
Office Supplies	2,800	
Office Equipment	25,000	
Accumulated Depreciation—Office Equipment		$5,000
Unearned Service Revenue		9,200

An analysis of the accounts shows the following.

1. Insurance expires at the rate of $100 per month.
2. Supplies on hand total $800.
3. The office equipment depreciates $200 a month.
4. One-half of the unearned service revenue was earned in March.

Prepare the adjusting entries for the month of March.

Action Plan

- Make adjusting entries at the end of the period for revenues earned and expenses incurred in the period.
- Don't forget to make adjusting entries for prepayments. Failure to adjust for prepayments leads to overstatement of the asset or liability and understatement of the related expense or revenue.

Solution

		Debit	Credit
1. Insurance Expense		100	
Prepaid Insurance			100
(To record insurance expired)			
2. Office Supplies Expense		2,000	
Office Supplies			2,000
(To record supplies used)			
3. Depreciation Expense		200	
Accumulated Depreciation—Office Equipment			200
(To record monthly depreciation)			
4. Unearned Service Revenue		4,600	
Service Revenue			4,600
(To record revenue earned)			

ADJUSTING ENTRIES FOR ACCRUALS

The second category of adjusting entries is **accruals**. Prior to an accrual adjustment, the revenue account (and the related asset account) or the expense

STUDY OBJECTIVE
5
Prepare adjusting entries for accruals.

Accrued Revenues

Oct.31

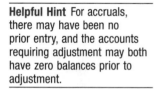

Revenue and receivable are recorded for unbilled services

Cash is received; receivable is reduced

account (and the related liability account) are understated. Thus, the adjusting entry for accruals will **increase both a balance sheet and an income statement account.**

Accrued Revenues

Revenues earned but not yet recorded at the statement date are accrued revenues. Accrued revenues may accumulate (accrue) with the passing of time, as in the case of interest revenue. These are unrecorded because the earning of interest does not involve daily transactions. Companies do not record interest revenue on a daily basis because it is often impractical to do so. Accrued revenues also may result from services that have been performed but not yet billed nor collected, as in the case of commissions and fees. These may be unrecorded because only a portion of the total service has been provided and the clients won't be billed until the service has been completed.

An adjusting entry records the receivable that exists at the balance sheet date and the revenue earned during the period. Prior to adjustment both assets and revenues are understated. As shown in Illustration 4-12, **an adjusting entry for accrued revenues results in an increase (a debit) to an asset account and an increase (a credit) to a revenue account.**

Illustration 4-12
Adjusting entries for accrued revenues

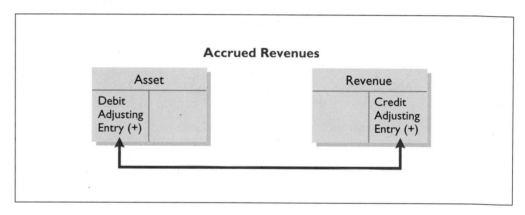

Helpful Hint For accruals, there may have been no prior entry, and the accounts requiring adjustment may both have zero balances prior to adjustment.

In October Sierra Corporation earned $200 for advertising services that were not billed to clients before October 31. Because these services are not billed, they are not recorded. The accrual of unrecorded service revenue increases an asset account, Accounts Receivable. It also increases stockholders' equity by increasing a revenue account, Service Revenue. The accrual of unrecorded service revenue affects the accounting equation in the following way.

Assets	=	Liabilities	+	Stockholders' Equity
+$200				+$200

Thus, Sierra makes the following adjusting entry.

Oct. 31	Accounts Receivable	200	
	Service Revenue		200
	(To record revenue earned)		

After the company posts the adjusting entry, the accounts appear as in Illustration 4-13.

Accounts Receivable		Service Revenue		
Oct. 31 **Adj. 200**		Oct. 3	10,000	
		31	400	
		31	**Adj. 200**	
Oct. 31 Bal. 200		Oct. 31 Bal. 10,600		

Illustration 4-13
Receivable and revenue
accounts after accrual
adjustments

The asset Accounts Receivable shows that clients owe Sierra $200 at the balance sheet date. The balance of $10,600 in Service Revenue represents the total revenue Sierra earned during the month ($10,000 + $400 + $200). **Without the adjusting entry, assets and stockholders' equity on the balance sheet and revenues and net income on the income statement are understated.**

On November 10, Sierra receives cash of $200 for the services performed in October and makes the following entry.

Equation analyses summarize the effects of transactions on the three elements of the accounting equation, as well as the effect on cash flows.

Nov. 10	Cash	200	
	Accounts Receivable		200
	(To record cash collected on account)		

A	=	L	+	SE
+200				
−200				

Cash Flows
+200

The company records the collection of the receivables by a debit (increase) to Cash and a credit (decrease) to Accounts Receivable.

Accrued Expenses

Expenses incurred but not yet paid or recorded at the statement date are called **accrued expenses**. Interest, taxes, and salaries are common examples of accrued expenses.

Companies make adjustments for accrued expenses to record the obligations that exist at the balance sheet date and to recognize the expenses that apply to the current accounting period. Prior to adjustment, both liabilities and expenses are understated. Therefore, **an adjusting entry for accrued expenses results in an increase (a debit) to an expense account and an increase (a credit) to a liability account.**

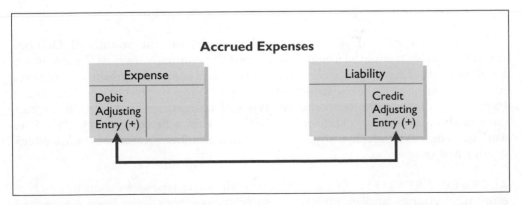

Illustration 4-14
Adjusting entries for
accrued expenses

Let's look in more detail at some specific types of accrued expenses, beginning with accrued interest.

ACCRUED INTEREST. Sierra Corporation signed a three-month note payable in the amount of $5,000 on October 1. The note requires Sierra to pay interest at an annual rate of 12%.

The amount of the interest recorded is determined by three factors: (1) the face value of the note, (2) the interest rate, which is always expressed as an annual rate, and (3) the length of time the note is outstanding. For Sierra, the total interest due on the $5,000 note at its maturity date three months in the future is $150 ($5,000 $\times$ 12% $\times \frac{3}{12}$), or $50 for one month. Illustration 4-15 shows the formula for computing interest and its application to Sierra Corporation for the month of October.

Illustration 4-15
Formula for computing interest

Face Value of Note	$\times$	Annual Interest Rate	$\times$	Time in Terms of One Year	=	Interest
$5,000	$\times$	12%	$\times$	$\frac{1}{12}$	=	**$50**

Helpful Hint In computing interest, we express the time period as a fraction of a year.

The accrual of interest at October 31 increases a liability account, Interest Payable. It also decreases stockholders' equity by increasing an expense account, Interest Expense. The accrual of interest at October 31 affects the accounting equation in the following way.

Assets	=	Liabilities	+	Stockholders' Equity
		+$50		−$50

Thus, Sierra makes an accrued expense adjusting entry at October 31 as follows.

Oct. 31	Interest Expense	50	
	Interest Payable		50
	(To record interest on notes payable)		

After the company posts this adjusting entry, the accounts appear as in Illustration 4-16.

Illustration 4-16 Interest accounts after adjustment

Interest Expense			Interest Payable	
Oct. 31 Adj. 50			Oct. 31	Adj. 50
Oct. 31 Bal. 50			Oct. 31	Bal. 50

Interest Expense shows the interest charges for the month of October. Interest Payable shows the amount of interest the company owes at the statement date. Sierra will not pay the interest until the note comes due at the end of three months. Companies use the Interest Payable account, instead of crediting Notes Payable, to disclose the two different types of obligations—interest and principal—in the accounts and statements. **Without this adjusting entry, liabilities and interest expense are understated, and net income and stockholders' equity are overstated.**

ACCRUED SALARIES. Companies pay for some types of expenses, such as employee salaries and commissions, after the services have been performed. Sierra Corporation last paid salaries on October 26; the next payment of salaries will not occur until November 9. As the calendar in Illustration 4-17 shows, three working days remain in October (October 29–31).

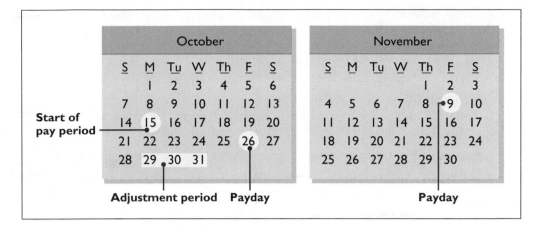

Illustration 4-17
Calendar showing Sierra
Corporation's pay periods

At October 31 the salaries for these three days represent an accrued expense and a related liability to Sierra. The employees receive total salaries of $2,000 for a five-day work week, or $400 per day. Thus, accrued salaries at October 31 are $1,200 ($400 × 3). This accrual increases a liability, Salaries Payable. It also decreases stockholders' equity by increasing an expense account, Salaries Expense. The accrual of salaries affects the accounting equation in the following way.

Assets	=	Liabilities	+	Stockholders' Equity
		+$1,200		−$1,200

Thus, Sierra makes the following adjusting entry:

Oct. 31	Salaries Expense	1,200	
	Salaries Payable		1,200
	(To record accrued salaries)		

After the company posts this adjusting entry, the accounts are as shown in Illustration 4-18.

Salaries Expense				Salaries Payable		
Oct. 26	4,000				Oct. 31	**Adj. 1,200**
31	**Adj. 1,200**					
Oct. 31	**Bal. 5,200**				Oct. 31	**Bal. 1,200**

Illustration 4-18 Salary accounts after adjustment

After this adjustment, the balance in Salaries Expense of $5,200 (13 days × $400) is the actual salary expense for October. The balance in Salaries Payable of $1,200 is the amount of the liability for salaries Sierra owes as of October 31. **Without the $1,200 adjustment for salaries, Sierra's expenses are understated $1,200 and its liabilities are understated $1,200.**

Sierra Corporation pays salaries every two weeks. Consequently, the next payday is November 9, when the company will again pay total salaries of $4,000. The payment consists of $1,200 of salaries payable at October 31 plus $2,800 of salaries expense for November (7 working days, as shown in the November calendar × $400). Therefore, Sierra makes the following entry on November 9.

Nov. 9	Salaries Payable	1,200	
	Salaries Expense	2,800	
	Cash		4,000
	(To record November 9 payroll)		

This entry eliminates the liability for Salaries Payable that Sierra recorded in the October 31 adjusting entry, and it records the proper amount of Salaries Expense for the period between November 1 and November 9.

BEFORE YOU GO ON . . .

▶Review It

1. What is the effect on assets, stockholders' equity, revenues, and net income if an accrued revenue adjusting entry is not made?
2. What is the effect on liabilities, stockholders' equity, expenses, and net income if an accrued expense adjusting entry is not made?
3. What was the amount of Tootsie Roll's 2004 depreciation expense? (*Hint:* Look in the notes to the financial statements.) The answer to this question appears on page 215.

▶ Do It

Micro Computer Services Inc. began operations on August 1, 2007. At the end of August 2007, management attempted to prepare monthly financial statements. The following information relates to August.

1. At August 31 the company owed its employees $800 in salaries that will be paid on September 1.
2. On August 1 the company borrowed $30,000 from a local bank on a 15-year mortgage. The annual interest rate is 10%.
3. Revenue earned but unrecorded for August totaled $1,100.

Prepare the adjusting entries needed at August 31, 2007.

Action Plan

• Make adjusting entries at the end of the period for revenues earned and expenses incurred in the period.
• Don't forget to make adjusting entries for accruals. Adjusting entries for accruals will increase both a balance sheet and an income statement account.

Solution

1. Salaries Expense	800	
	Salaries Payable		800
	(To record accrued salaries)		
2. Interest Expense	250	
	Interest Payable		250
	(To record accrued interest:		
	$30,000 \times 10\% \times \frac{1}{12} = \$250$)		
3. Accounts Receivable	1,100	
	Service Revenue		1,100
	(To record revenue earned)		

SUMMARY OF BASIC RELATIONSHIPS

Illustration 4-19 summarizes the four basic types of adjusting entries. Take some time to study and analyze the adjusting entries. Be sure to note that **each adjusting entry affects one balance sheet account and one income statement account**.

Type of Adjustment	Accounts Before Adjustment	Adjusting Entry
Prepaid expenses	Assets overstated Expenses understated	Dr. Expenses Cr. Assets
Unearned revenues	Liabilities overstated Revenues understated	Dr. Liabilities Cr. Revenues
Accrued revenues	Assets understated Revenues understated	Dr. Assets Cr. Revenues
Accrued expenses	Expenses understated Liabilities understated	Dr. Expenses Cr. Liabilities

Illustration 4-19
Summary of adjusting entries

Illustrations 4-20 and 4-21 (page 176) show the journalizing and posting of adjusting entries for Sierra Corporation on October 31. When reviewing the general ledger in Illustration 4-21, note that the adjustments are highlighted in color.

GENERAL JOURNAL

Date	Account Titles and Explanation	Debit	Credit
2007	Adjusting Entries		

Oct. 31	Advertising Supplies Expense
	    Advertising Supplies
	        (To record supplies used)
		1,500	1,500

31	Insurance Expense
	    Prepaid Insurance
	        (To record insurance expired)
		50	50

31	Depreciation Expense
	    Accumulated Depreciation—Office Equipment
	        (To record monthly depreciation)
		40	40

31	Unearned Service Revenue
	    Service Revenue
	        (To record revenue earned)
		400	400

31	Accounts Receivable
	    Service Revenue
	        (To record revenue earned)
		200	200

31	Interest Expense
	    Interest Payable
	        (To record interest on notes payable)
		50	50

31	Salaries Expense
	    Salaries Payable
	        (To record accrued salaries)
		1,200	1,200

Illustration 4-20 General journal showing adjusting entries

Illustration 4-21 General ledger after adjustments

GENERAL LEDGER

Cash

Oct.	1	10,000	Oct.	2	5,000
	1	5,000		3	900
	2	1,200		4	600
	3	10,000		20	500
				26	4,000

Oct. 31	Bal. 15,200	

Accounts Receivable

Oct. 31	**200**	

Oct. 31	Bal. 200	

Advertising Supplies

Oct.	5	2,500	Oct.	31	**1,500**

Oct. 31	Bal. 1,000	

Prepaid Insurance

Oct.	4	600	Oct.	31	**50**

Oct. 31	Bal. 550	

Office Equipment

Oct.	2	5,000	

Oct. 31	Bal. 5,000	

Accumulated Depreciation— Office Equipment

	Oct.	31	**40**

	Oct. 31	Bal. 40

Notes Payable

	Oct.	1	5,000

	Oct. 31	Bal. 5,000

Accounts Payable

	Oct.	5	2,500

	Oct. 31	Bal. 2,500

Interest Payable

	Oct.	31	**50**

	Oct. 31	Bal. 50

Unearned Service Revenue

Oct. 31	**400**	Oct.	2	1,200

	Oct. 31	Bal. 800

Salaries Payable

	Oct.	31	**1,200**

	Oct. 31	Bal. 1,200

Common Stock

	Oct.	1	10,000

	Oct. 31	Bal. 10,000

Retained Earnings

	Oct. 31	Bal. 0

Dividends

Oct. 20	500	

Oct. 31	Bal. 500	

Service Revenue

	Oct.	3	10,000
		31	**400**
		31	**200**

	Oct. 31	Bal. 10,600

Salaries Expense

Oct.	26	4,000	
	31	**1,200**	

Oct. 31	Bal. 5,200	

Advertising Supplies Expense

Oct. 31	**1,500**	

Oct. 31	Bal. 1,500	

Rent Expense

Oct.	3	900	

Oct. 31	Bal. 900	

Insurance Expense

Oct. 31	**50**	

Oct. 31	Bal. 50	

Interest Expense

Oct. 31	**50**	

Oct. 31	Bal. 50	

Depreciation Expense

Oct. 31	**40**	

Oct. 31	Bal. 40	

The Adjusted Trial Balance and Financial Statements

After a company has journalized and posted all adjusting entries, it prepares another trial balance from the ledger accounts. This trial balance is called an **adjusted trial balance**. It shows the balances of all accounts, including those adjusted, at the end of the accounting period. The purpose of an adjusted trial balance is to **prove the equality** of the total debit balances and the total credit balances in the ledger after all adjustments. Because the accounts contain all data needed for financial statements, the adjusted trial balance is the **primary basis for the preparation of financial statements**.

STUDY OBJECTIVE

6

Describe the nature and purpose of the adjusted trial balance.

PREPARING THE ADJUSTED TRIAL BALANCE

Illustration 4-22 presents the adjusted trial balance for Sierra Corporation prepared from the ledger accounts in Illustration 4-21. The amounts affected by the adjusting entries are highlighted in color.

Illustration 4-22
Adjusted trial balance

SIERRA CORPORATION Adjusted Trial Balance October 31, 2007		
	Dr.	**Cr.**
Cash	$15,200	
Accounts Receivable	200	
Advertising Supplies	1,000	
Prepaid Insurance	550	
Office Equipment	5,000	
Accumulated Depreciation—Office Equipment		$ 40
Notes Payable		5,000
Accounts Payable		2,500
Interest Payable		50
Unearned Service Revenue		800
Salaries Payable		1,200
Common Stock		10,000
Retained Earnings		0
Dividends	500	
Service Revenue		10,600
Salaries Expense	5,200	
Advertising Supplies Expense	1,500	
Rent Expense	900	
Insurance Expense	50	
Interest Expense	50	
Depreciation Expense	40	
	$30,190	$30,190

PREPARING FINANCIAL STATEMENTS

Companies can prepare financial statements directly from an adjusted trial balance. Illustrations 4-23 (page 178) and 4-24 (page 179) present the interrelationships of data in the adjusted trial balance of Sierra Corporation. As Illustration 4-23 shows, companies prepare the income statement from the revenue and expense accounts. Similarly, they derive the retained earnings statement from the retained earnings account, dividends account, and the net income (or net loss) shown in the income statement. As Illustration 4-24 shows, companies then prepare the balance sheet from the asset, liability, and stockholders' equity accounts. They obtain the amount reported for retained earnings on the balance sheet from the ending balance in the retained earnings statement.

Illustration 4-23
Preparation of the income statement and retained earnings statement from the adjusted trial balance

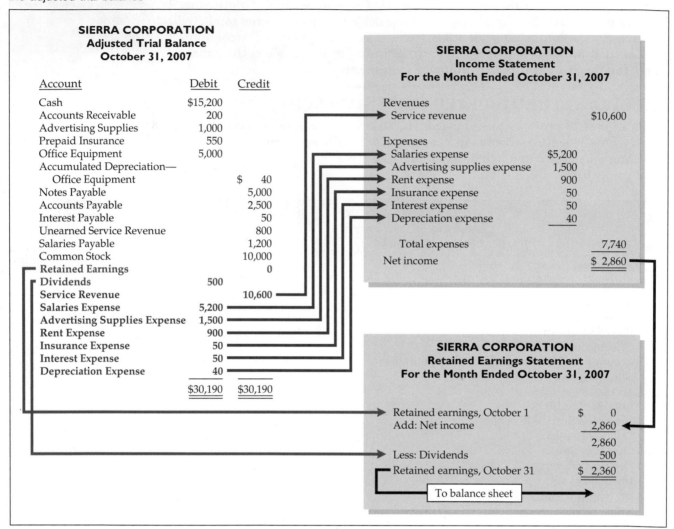

Closing the Books

Alternative Terminology
Temporary accounts are sometimes called *nominal accounts*, and permanent accounts are sometimes called *real accounts*.

In previous chapters you learned that revenue and expense accounts and the dividends account are subdivisions of retained earnings, which is reported in the stockholders' equity section of the balance sheet. Because revenues, expenses, and dividends relate to only a given accounting period, they are considered **temporary accounts**. In contrast, all balance sheet accounts are considered **permanent accounts** because their balances are carried forward into future accounting periods. Illustration 4-25 identifies the accounts in each category.

STUDY OBJECTIVE
7
Explain the purpose of closing entries.

PREPARING CLOSING ENTRIES

At the end of the accounting period, companies transfer the temporary account balances to the permanent stockholders' equity account—Retained Earnings—through the preparation of closing entries. **Closing entries** transfer net income (or net loss) and dividends to Retained Earnings, so the balance in Retained

Illustration 4-24
Preparation of the balance
sheet from the adjusted
trial balance

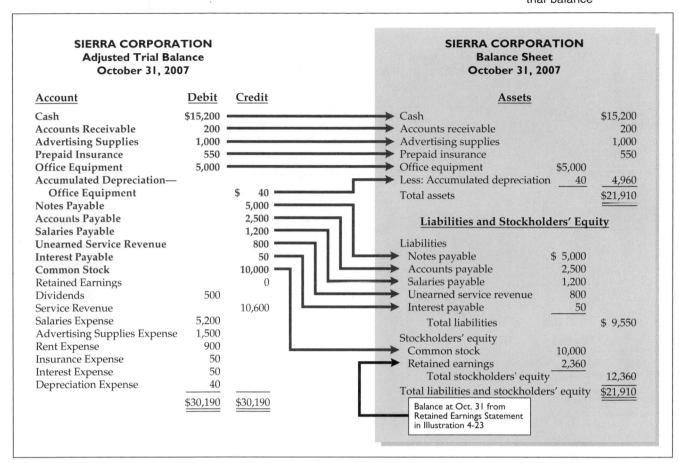

Illustration 4-25
Temporary versus
permanent accounts

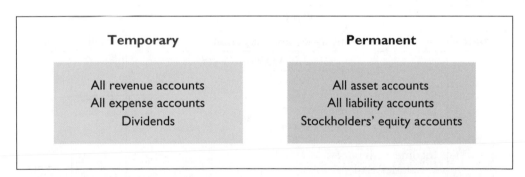

Earnings agrees with the retained earnings statement. For example, notice that in the adjusted trial balance in Illustration 4-24, Retained Earnings has a balance of zero. Prior to the closing entries, the balance in Retained Earnings will be its beginning-of-the-period balance. For Sierra this is zero because it is Sierra's first month of operations.

In addition to updating Retained Earnings to its correct ending balance, closing entries produce a **zero balance in each temporary account**. As a result, these accounts are ready to accumulate data about revenues, expenses, and dividends in the next accounting period separate from the data in the prior periods. **Permanent accounts are not closed.**

When companies prepare closing entries, they could close each income statement account directly to Retained Earnings. However, to do so would result in excessive detail in the retained earnings account. Accordingly, companies close the revenue and expense accounts to another temporary account, **Income Summary**, and they transfer only the resulting net income or net loss from this account to Retained Earnings. Illustration 4-26 depicts the closing process. While it still takes the average large company seven days to close, some companies such as Cisco employ technology that allows them to do a so-called "virtual close" almost instantaneously any time during the year. Besides dramatically reducing the cost of closing, the virtual close provides companies with accurate data for decision making whenever they desire it.

Illustration 4-26 The closing process

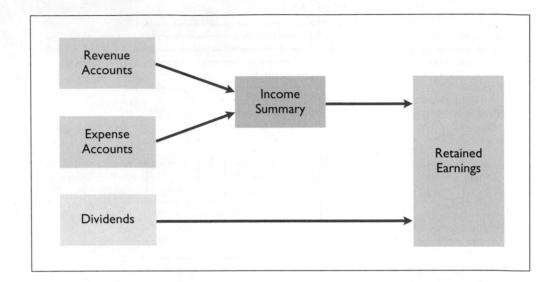

Illustration 4-27 shows the closing entries for Sierra Corporation. Illustration 4-28 (page 181) diagrams the posting process for Sierra Corporation's closing entries.

Illustration 4-27 Closing entries journalized

Helpful Hint Income Summary is a very descriptive title: Companies close total revenues to Income Summary and total expenses to Income Summary. The balance in the Income Summary is a net income or net loss.

GENERAL JOURNAL

Date		Account Titles and Explanation	Debit	Credit
		Closing Entries		
2007		(1)		
Oct.	31	Service Revenue	10,600	
		Income Summary		10,600
		(To close revenue account)		
		(2)		
	31	Income Summary	7,740	
		Salaries Expense		5,200
		Advertising Supplies Expense		1,500
		Rent Expense		900
		Insurance Expense		50
		Interest Expense		50
		Depreciation Expense		40
		(To close expense accounts)		
		(3)		
	31	Income Summary	2,860	
		Retained Earnings		2,860
		(To close net income to retained earnings)		
		(4)		
	31	Retained Earnings	500	
		Dividends		500
		(To close dividends to retained earnings)		

Illustration 4-28 Posting of closing entries

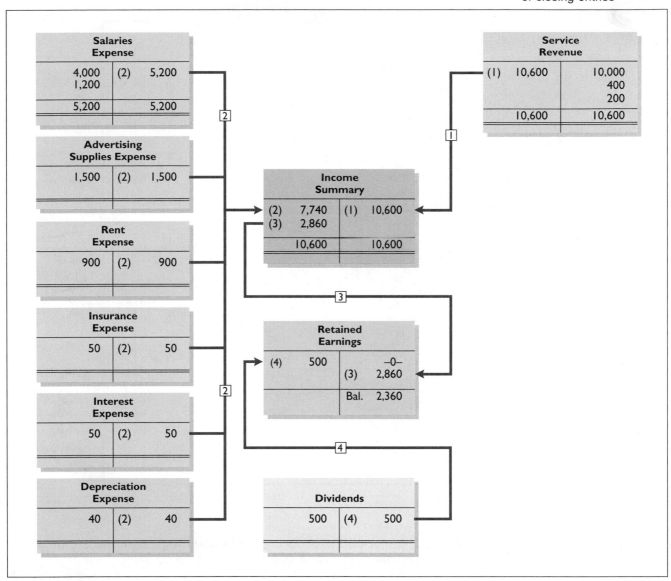

PREPARING A POST-CLOSING TRIAL BALANCE

After a company journalizes and posts all closing entries, it prepares another trial balance, called a **post-closing trial balance**, from the ledger. A post-closing trial balance is a list of all permanent accounts and their balances after closing entries are journalized and posted. **The purpose of this trial balance is to prove the equality of the permanent account balances that the company carries forward into the next accounting period.** Since all temporary accounts will have zero balances, **the post-closing trial balance will contain only permanent—balance sheet—accounts**.

SUMMARY OF THE ACCOUNTING CYCLE

Illustration 4-29 (page 182) shows the required steps in the accounting cycle. You can see that the cycle begins with the analysis of business transactions and ends with the preparation of a post-closing trial balance. Companies perform the steps in the cycle in sequence and repeat them in each accounting period.

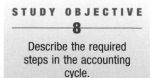

STUDY OBJECTIVE

8

Describe the required steps in the accounting cycle.

Illustration 4-29
Required steps in the accounting cycle

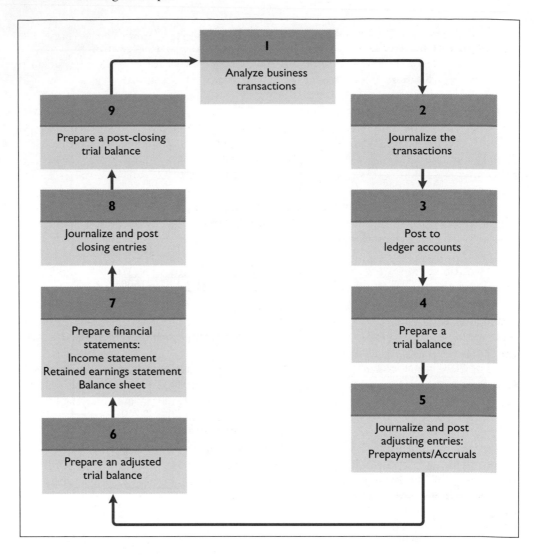

Steps 1–3 may occur daily during the accounting period, as explained in Chapter 3. Companies perform Steps 4–7 on a periodic basis, such as monthly, quarterly, or annually. Steps 8 and 9, closing entries and a post-closing trial balance, usually take place only at the end of a company's **annual** accounting period.

Quality of Earnings

"Did you make your numbers today?" is a question asked often in both large and small businesses. Companies and employees are continually under pressure to "make the numbers"—that is, to have earnings that are in line with expectations. As a consequence it is not surprising that many companies practice earnings management. **Earnings management** is the planned timing of revenues, expenses, gains, and losses to smooth out bumps in net income. The quality of earnings is greatly affected when a company manages earnings up or down to meet some targeted earnings number. A company that has a high **quality of earnings** provides full and transparent information that will not confuse or mislead users of the financial statements. A company with questionable quality of earnings may mislead investors and creditors, who believe they are relying on relevant and reliable information. As a consequence, investors and creditors lose confidence in financial reporting, and it becomes difficult for our capital markets to work efficiently.

Companies manage earnings in a variety of ways. One way is through the use of **one-time items** to prop up earnings numbers. For example, ConAgra Foods recorded a nonrecurring gain from the sale of Pilgrim's Pride stock for $186 million to help meet an earnings projection for the quarter.

Another way is to **inflate revenue** numbers in the short-run to the detriment of the long-run. For example, Bristol-Myers Squibb provided sales incentives to its wholesalers to encourage them to buy products at the end of the quarter. As a result Bristol-Myers was able to meet its sales projections. The problem was that the wholesalers could not sell that amount of merchandise and ended up returning it to Bristol-Myers. The result was that Bristol-Myers had to restate its income numbers.

Companies also manage earnings through **improper adjusting entries**. Regulators investigated Xerox for accusations that it was booking too much revenue up-front on multi-year contract sales. Financial executives at Office Max resigned amid accusations that the company was recognizing rebates from its vendors too early and therefore overstating revenue. Finally, WorldCom's abuse of adjusting entries to meet its net income targets is unsurpassed: It used adjusting entries to increase net income by reclassifying liabilities as revenue and reclassifying expenses as assets. Investigations of the company's books after it went bankrupt revealed adjusting entries of more than a billion dollars that had no supporting documentation.

The good news is that, as a result of investor pressure as well as the **Sarbanes-Oxley Act**, many companies are trying to improve the quality of their financial reporting. For example, hotel operator Marriott is now providing detailed information on the write-offs it has on loan guarantees it gives hotels. General Electric has decided to provide more detail on its revenues and operating profits for individual businesses it owns. IBM is attempting to provide a better breakdown of its earnings. At the same time, regulators are taking a tough stand on the issue of quality of earnings. For example, one regulator noted that companies may be required to restate their financials every single time that they account for any transaction that had no legitimate purpose but was done solely for an accounting purpose, such as to smooth net income.

BEFORE YOU GO ON . . .

▶ Review It

1. How do permanent accounts differ from temporary accounts?
2. What four different types of entries are required in closing the books?
3. What are the content and purpose of a post-closing trial balance?
4. What are the required steps in the accounting cycle?
5. Explain the term earnings management and describe the actions that companies take to manage earnings.

☑ THE NAVIGATOR

Using the Decision Toolkit

Humana Corporation provides managed health care services to approximately 7 million people. Headquartered in Louisville, Kentucky, it has over 13,700 employees in 15 states and Puerto Rico. A simplified version of Humana's December 31, 2004, adjusted trial balance is shown at the top of the next page.

Instructions

From the trial balance, prepare an income statement, retained earnings statement, and classified balance sheet. **Be sure to prepare them in that order, since each statement depends on information determined in the preceding statement.**

HUMANA.

HUMANA CORPORATION
Adjusted Trial Balance
December 31, 2004
(in millions)

Account	Dr.	Cr.
Cash	$ 580	
Short-Term Investments	2,146	
Receivables	580	
Other Current Assets	290	
Property and Equipment, Net	400	
Long-Term Investments	348	
Other Long-Term Assets	1,314	
Medical Costs Payable		$ 1,422
Accounts Payable		680
Other Current Liabilities		225
Long-Term Debt		1,241
Common Stock		1,046
Dividends	0	
Retained Earnings		764
Revenues		13,104
Medical Cost Expense	10,669	
Selling, General, and Administrative Expense	1,878	
Depreciation Expense	118	
Interest Expense	23	
Income Tax Expense	136	
	$18,482	$18,482

Solution

HUMANA.

HUMANA CORPORATION
Income Statement
For the Year Ended December 31, 2004
(in millions)

Revenues		$13,104
Medical cost expense	$10,669	
Selling, general, and administrative expense	1,878	
Depreciation expense	118	
Interest expense	23	
Income tax expense	136	12,824
Net income		$ 280

HUMANA.

HUMANA CORPORATION
Retained Earnings Statement
For the Year Ended December 31, 2004
(in millions)

Beginning retained earnings	$ 764
Add: Net income	280
Less: Dividends	0
Ending retained earnings	$1,044

HUMANA.

HUMANA CORPORATION
Balance Sheet
December 31, 2004
(in millions)

Assets

Current assets		
Cash	$ 580	
Short-term investments	2,146	
Receivables	580	
Other current assets	290	
Total current assets		$3,596
Long-term investments		348
Property and equipment, net		400
Other long-term assets		1,314
Total assets		$5,658

Liabilities and Stockholders' Equity

Liabilities		
Current liabilities		
Medical costs payable	$1,422	
Accounts payable	680	
Other current liabilities	225	
Total current liabilities		$2,327
Long-term debt		1,241
Total liabilities		3,568
Stockholders' equity		
Common stock	1,046	
Retained earnings	1,044	
Total stockholders' equity		2,090
Total liabilities and stockholders' equity		$5,658

Summary of Study Objectives

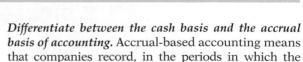

1 *Explain the revenue recognition principle and the matching principle.* The revenue recognition principle dictates that companies recognize revenue in the accounting period in which it is earned. The matching principle dictates that companies recognize expenses when expenses make their contribution to revenues.

2 *Differentiate between the cash basis and the accrual basis of accounting.* Accrual-based accounting means that companies record, in the periods in which the events occur, events that change a company's financial statements. Under the cash basis, companies record events only in the periods in which the company receives or pays cash.

3 *Explain why adjusting entries are needed, and identify the major types of adjusting entries.* Companies make adjusting entries at the end of an accounting period. These entries ensure that companies record revenues in the period in which they are earned and that companies recognize expenses in the period in which they are incurred. The major types of adjusting entries are prepaid expenses, unearned revenues, accrued revenues, and accrued expenses.

4 *Prepare adjusting entries for prepayments.* Prepayments are either prepaid expenses or unearned revenues. Companies make adjusting entries for prepayments at the statement date to record the portion of the prepayment that represents the expense incurred or the revenue earned in the current accounting period.

5 *Prepare adjusting entries for accruals.* Accruals are either accrued revenues or accrued expenses. Adjusting entries for accruals record revenues earned and expenses incurred in the current accounting period that have not been recognized through daily entries.

6 *Describe the nature and purpose of the adjusted trial balance.* An adjusted trial balance is a trial balance that shows the balances of all accounts, including those that have been adjusted, at the end of an accounting period. The purpose of an adjusted trial balance is to show the effects of all financial events that have occurred during the accounting period.

7 *Explain the purpose of closing entries.* One purpose of closing entries is to transfer the results of operations for the period to Retained Earnings. A second purpose is to "zero-out" all temporary accounts (revenue accounts, expense accounts, and dividends) so that they start each new period with a zero balance. To accomplish this, companies "close" all temporary accounts at the end of an accounting period. They make separate entries to close revenues and expenses to Income Summary, Income Summary to Retained Earnings, and Dividends to Retained Earnings. Only temporary accounts are closed.

8 *Describe the required steps in the accounting cycle.* The required steps in the accounting cycle are: (a) analyze business transactions, (b) journalize the transactions, (c) post to ledger accounts, (d) prepare a trial balance, (e) journalize and post adjusting entries, (f) prepare an adjusted trial balance, (g) prepare financial statements, (h) journalize and post closing entries, and (i) prepare a post-closing trial balance.

Decision Toolkit—A Summary

Decision Checkpoints	Info Needed for Decision	Tool to Use for Decision	How to Evaluate Results
At what point should the company record revenue?	Need to understand the nature of the company's business	Revenue should be recorded when earned. A service business earns revenue when it performs a service.	Recognizing revenue too early overstates current period revenue; recognizing it too late understates current period revenue.
At what point should the company record expenses?	Need to understand the nature of the company's business	Expenses should "follow" revenues—that is, match the effort (expense) with the result (revenue).	Recognizing expenses too early overstates current period expense; recognizing them too late understates current period expense.

APPENDIX
ADJUSTING ENTRIES IN AN AUTOMATED WORLD—USING A WORK SHEET

STUDY OBJECTIVE
9
Describe the purpose and the basic form of a work sheet.

In the previous discussion we used T accounts and trial balances to arrive at the amounts used to prepare financial statements. Accountants frequently use a device known as a work sheet to determine these amounts. A **work sheet** is a multiple-column form that may be used in the adjustment process and in preparing financial statements. Accountants can prepare work sheets manually, but today most use computer spreadsheets.

As its name suggests, the work sheet is a working tool for the accountant. **A work sheet is not a permanent accounting record**; it is neither a journal nor a part of the general ledger. The work sheet is merely a supplemental device used to make it easier to prepare adjusting entries and the financial statements. Small companies that have relatively few accounts and adjustments may not need a work sheet. In large companies with numerous accounts and many adjustments, a work sheet is almost indispensable.

Illustration 4A-1 shows the basic form of a work sheet. Note the headings: The work sheet starts with two columns for the Trial Balance. The next two columns record all Adjustments. Next is the Adjusted Trial Balance. The last two sets of columns correspond to the Income Statement and the Balance Sheet. All items listed in the Adjusted Trial Balance columns are included in either the Income Statement or the Balance Sheet columns.

Illustration 4A-1 Form and procedure for a work sheet

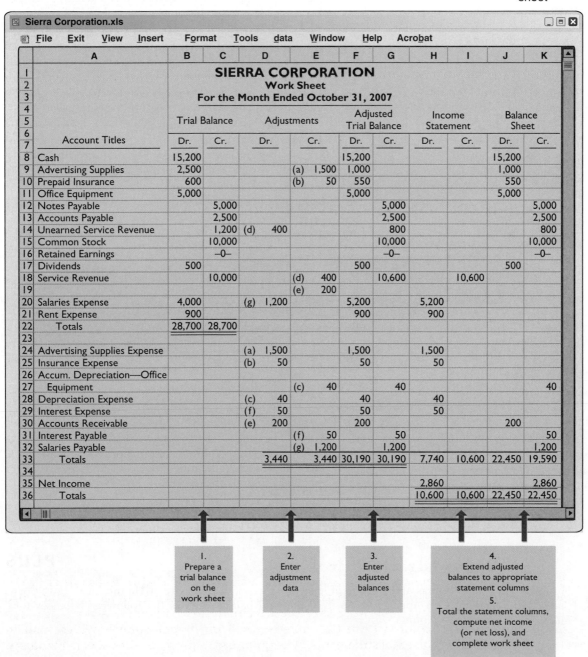

Summary of Study Objective for Appendix

9 *Describe the purpose and the basic form of a work sheet.* The work sheet is a device to make it easier to prepare adjusting entries and the financial statements. Companies often prepare a work sheet on a computer spreadsheet. The sets of columns of the work sheet are, from left to right, the unadjusted trial balance, adjustments, adjusted trial balance, income statement, and balance sheet.

Glossary

Accrual-basis accounting Accounting basis in which companies record, in the periods in which the events occur, transactions that change a company's financial statements, rather than in the periods in which the company receives or pays cash. (p. 160)

Accrued expenses Expenses incurred but not yet paid in cash or recorded. (p. 171)

Accrued revenues Revenues earned but not yet received in cash or recorded. (p. 170)

Adjusted trial balance A list of accounts and their balances after all adjustments have been made. (p. 177)

Adjusting entries Entries made at the end of an accounting period to ensure that the revenue recognition and matching principles are followed. (p. 161)

Book value The difference between the cost of a depreciable asset and its related accumulated depreciation. (p. 167)

Cash-basis accounting Accounting basis in which a company records revenue only when it receives cash, and an expense only when it pays out cash. (p. 160)

Closing entries Entries at the end of an accounting period to transfer the balances of temporary accounts to a permanent stockholders' equity account, Retained Earnings. (p. 178)

Contra asset account An account that is offset against an asset account on the balance sheet. (p. 166)

Depreciation The process of allocating the cost of an asset to expense over its useful life. (p. 165)

Earnings management The planned timing of revenues, expenses, gains, and losses to smooth out bumps in net income. (p. 182)

Fiscal year An accounting period that is one year long. (p. 158, in margin)

Income Summary A temporary account used in closing revenue and expense accounts. (p. 180)

Matching principle The principle that dictates that companies match efforts (expenses) with accomplishments (revenues). (p. 159)

Permanent accounts Balance sheet accounts whose balances are carried forward to the next accounting period. (p. 178)

Post-closing trial balance A list of permanent accounts and their balances after a company has journalized and posted closing entries. (p. 181)

Prepaid expenses (Prepayments) Expenses paid in cash and recorded as assets before they are used or consumed. (p. 163)

Quality of earnings Indicates the level of full and transparent information that a company provides to users of its financial statements. (p. 182)

Revenue recognition principle The principle that companies recognize revenue in the accounting period in which it is earned. (p. 158)

Reversing entry An entry made at the beginning of the next accounting period; the exact opposite of the adjusting entry made in the previous period. (p. 182, in margin)

Temporary accounts Revenue, expense, and dividend accounts whose balances a company transfers to Retained Earnings at the end of an accounting period. (p. 178)

Time period assumption An assumption that the economic life of a business can be divided into artificial time periods. (p. 158)

Unearned revenues Cash received before a company earns revenues and recorded as a liability until earned. (p. 167)

Useful life The length of service of a productive asset. (p. 165)

Work sheet A multiple-column form that companies may use in the adjustment process and in preparing financial statements. (p. 186)

Demonstration Problem

Terry Thomas and a group of investors incorporate the Green Thumb Lawn Care Corporation on April 1. At April 30 the trial balance shows the following balances for selected accounts.

Prepaid Insurance	$ 3,600
Equipment	28,000
Notes Payable	20,000
Unearned Service Revenue	4,200
Service Revenue	1,800

Analysis reveals the following additional data pertaining to these accounts.

1. Prepaid insurance is the cost of a 2-year insurance policy, effective April 1.
2. Depreciation on the equipment is $500 per month.
3. The note payable is dated April 1. It is a 6-month, 12% note.
4. Seven customers paid for the company's 6-month lawn service package of $600 beginning in April. These customers received the first month of services in April.
5. Lawn services performed for other customers but not billed at April 30 totaled $1,500.

Instructions
Prepare the adjusting entries for the month of April. Show computations.

Solution to Demonstration Problem				Action Plan

GENERAL JOURNAL

Date	Account Titles and Explanation	Debit	Credit
	Adjusting Entries		
Apr. 30	Insurance Expense	150	
	Prepaid Insurance		150
	(To record insurance expired:		
	$3,600 ÷ 24 = $150 per month)		
30	Depreciation Expense	500	
	Accumulated Depreciation—Equipment		500
	(To record monthly depreciation)		
30	Interest Expense	200	
	Interest Payable		200
	(To accrue interest on notes payable:		
	$20,000 × 12% × $\frac{1}{12}$ = $200)		
30	Unearned Service Revenue	700	
	Service Revenue		700
	(To record revenue earned: $600 ÷ 6 = $100;		
	$100 per month × 7 = $700)		
30	Accounts Receivable	1,500	
	Service Revenue		1,500
	(To accrue revenue earned but not billed		
	or collected)		

Action Plan
- Note that adjustments are being made for one month.
- Make computations carefully.
- Select account titles carefully.
- Make sure debits are made first and credits are indented.
- Check that debits equal credits for each entry.

Self-Study Questions

Answers are at the end of this chapter.

(SO 1) **1.** What is the time period assumption?
  (a) Companies should recognize revenue in the accounting period in which it is earned.
  (b) Companies should match expenses with revenues.

  (c) The economic life of a business can be divided into artificial time periods.
  (d) The fiscal year should correspond with the calendar year.

(SO 1)   **2.** Which principle dictates that efforts (expenses) be recorded with accomplishments (revenues)?
(a) Matching principle.
(b) Cost principle.
(c) Periodicity principle.
(d) Revenue recognition principle.

(SO 3)   **3.** Adjusting entries are made to ensure that:
(a) expenses are recognized in the period in which they are incurred.
(b) revenues are recorded in the period in which they are earned.
(c) balance sheet and income statement accounts have correct balances at the end of an accounting period.
(d) All of the above.

(SO 4, 5)   **4.** Each of the following is a major type (or category) of adjusting entry *except*:
(a) prepaid expenses.
(b) accrued revenues.
(c) accrued expenses.
(d) earned expenses.

(SO 4)   **5.** The trial balance shows Supplies $1,350 and Supplies Expense $0. If $600 of supplies are on hand at the end of the period, the adjusting entry is:

(a) Supplies	600	
Supplies Expense		600
(b) Supplies	750	
Supplies Expense		750
(c) Supplies Expense	750	
Supplies		750
(d) Supplies Expense	600	
Supplies		600

(SO 4)   **6.** Adjustments for unearned revenues:
(a) decrease liabilities and increase revenues.
(b) increase liabilities and increase revenues.
(c) increase assets and increase revenues.
(d) decrease revenues and decrease assets.

(SO 5)   **7.** Adjustments for accrued revenues:
(a) increase assets and increase liabilities.
(b) increase assets and increase revenues.
(c) decrease assets and decrease revenues.
(d) decrease liabilities and increase revenues.

(SO 5)   **8.** Colleen Mooney earned a salary of $400 for the last week of September. She will be paid on October 1. The adjusting entry for Colleen's employer at September 30 is:
(a) No entry is required.

(b) Salaries Expense	400	
Salaries Payable		400
(c) Salaries Expense	400	
Cash		400
(d) Salaries Payable	400	
Cash		400

(SO 6)   **9.** Which statement is *incorrect* concerning the adjusted trial balance?
(a) An adjusted trial balance proves the equality of the total debit balances and the total credit balances in the ledger after all adjustments are made.
(b) The adjusted trial balance provides the primary basis for the preparation of financial statements.
(c) The adjusted trial balance lists the account balances segregated by assets and liabilities.
(d) The company prepares the adjusted trial balance after it has journalized and posted the adjusting entries.

(SO 2)   **10.** Which one of these statements about the accrual basis of accounting is *false*?
(a) Companies record in the periods in which the events occur events that change a company's financial statements.
(b) Companies recognize revenue in the period in which it is earned.
(c) This basis is in accord with generally accepted accounting principles.
(d) Companies record revenue only when they receive cash, and record expense only when they pay out cash.

(SO 7)   **11.** Which account will have a zero balance after a company has journalized and posted closing entries?
(a) Service Revenue.
(b) Advertising Supplies.
(c) Prepaid Insurance.
(d) Accumulated Depreciation.

(SO 7)   **12.** Which types of accounts will appear in the post-closing trial balance?
(a) Permanent accounts.
(b) Temporary accounts.
(c) Accounts shown in the income statement columns of a work sheet.
(d) None of the above.

(SO 8)   **13.** All of the following are required steps in the accounting cycle *except*:
(a) journalizing and posting closing entries.
(b) preparing an adjusted trial balance.
(c) preparing a post-closing trial balance.
(d) preparing a work sheet.

Go to the book's website, **www.wiley.com/college/kimmel,** to access additional Self-Study Questions.

THE NAVIGATOR

Note: All asterisked Questions, Exercises, and Problems relate to material in the appendix to the chapter.

Questions

1. (a) How does the time period assumption affect an accountant's analysis of accounting transactions?
(b) Explain the term *fiscal year*.

2. Identify and state two generally accepted accounting principles that relate to adjusting the accounts.

3. Tony Galego, a lawyer, accepts a legal engagement in March, performs the work in April, and is paid in May. If Galego's law firm prepares monthly financial statements, when should it recognize revenue from this engagement? Why?

4. In completing the engagement in question 3, Galego pays no costs in March, $2,500 in April, and $2,500 in May (incurred in April). How much expense should the firm deduct from revenues in the month when it recognizes the revenue? Why?

5. "The cost principle of accounting requires adjusting entries." Do you agree? Explain.

6. Why may the financial information in a trial balance not be up-to-date and complete?

7. Distinguish between the two categories of adjusting entries, and identify the types of adjustments applicable to each category.

8. What accounts does a company debit and credit in a prepaid expense adjusting entry?

9. "Depreciation is a process of valuation that results in the reporting of the fair market value of the asset." Do you agree? Explain.

10. Explain the differences between depreciation expense and accumulated depreciation.

11. Genesis Company purchased equipment for $15,000. By the current balance sheet date, the company had depreciated $7,000. Indicate the balance sheet presentation of the data.

12. What accounts are debited and credited in an unearned revenue adjusting entry?

13. Computer Technologies provides maintenance service for computers and office equipment for companies throughout the Northeast. The sales managers is elated because she closed a $300,000 three-year maintenance contract on December 29, 2007, two days before the company's year-end. "Now we will hit this year's net income target for sure," she crowed. The customer is required to pay $100,000 on December 29 (the day the deal was closed). Two more payments of $100,000 each are also required on December 29, 2008 and 2009. Discuss the effect that this event will have on the company's financial statements.

14. SquareDeal, a large national retail chain, is nearing its fiscal year-end. It appears that the company is not going to hit its revenue and net income targets. The company's marketing manager, Randal Fox, suggests running a promotion selling $50 gift cards for $40.

He believes that this would be very popular and would enable the company to meet its targets for revenue and net income. What do you think of this idea?

15. A company fails to recognize revenue earned but not yet received. Which of the following accounts are involved in the adjusting entry: (a) asset, (b) liability, (c) revenue, or (d) expense? For the accounts selected, indicate whether they would be debited or credited in the entry.

16. A company fails to recognize an expense incurred but not paid. Indicate which of the following accounts is debited and which is credited in the adjusting entry: (a) asset, (b) liability, (c) revenue, or (d) expense.

17. A company makes an accrued revenue adjusting entry for $800 and an accrued expense adjusting entry for $300. How much was net income understated prior to these entries? Explain.

18. On January 9 a company pays $5,000 for salaries, of which $1,100 was reported as Salaries Payable on December 31. Give the entry to record the payment.

19. For each of the following items before adjustment, indicate the type of adjusting entry—prepaid expense, unearned revenue, accrued revenue, and accrued expense—that is needed to correct the misstatement. If an item could result in more than one type of adjusting entry, indicate each of the types.
(a) Assets are understated.
(b) Liabilities are overstated.
(c) Liabilities are understated.
(d) Expenses are understated.
(e) Assets are overstated.
(f) Revenue is understated

20. One-half of the adjusting entry is given below. Indicate the account title for the other half of the entry.
(a) Salaries Expense is debited.
(b) Depreciation Expense is debited.
(c) Interest Payable is credited.
(d) Supplies is credited.
(e) Accounts Receivable is debited.
(f) Unearned Service Revenue is debited.

21. "An adjusting entry may affect more than one balance sheet or income statement account." Do you agree? Why or why not?

22. Why is it possible to prepare financial statements directly from an adjusted trial balance?

23.
(a) What information do accrual basis financial statements provide that cash basis statements do not?
(b) What information do cash basis financial statements provide that accrual basis statements do not?

24. What is the relationship, if any, between the amount shown in the adjusted trial balance column for an account and that account's ledger balance?

25. Identify the account(s) debited and credited in each of the four closing entries, assuming the company has net income for the year.

26. Some companies employ technologies that allow them to do a so-called "virtual close." This enables them to close their books nearly instantaneously any time during the year. What advantages does a "virtual close" provide?

27. Describe the nature of the Income Summary account, and identify the types of summary data that may be posted to this account.

28. What items are disclosed on a post-closing trial balance, and what is its purpose?

29. Which of these accounts would not appear in the post-closing trial balance? Interest Payable, Equipment, Depreciation Expense, Dividends, Unearned Service Revenue, Accumulated Depreciation—Equipment, and Service Revenue.

30. Indicate, in the sequence in which they are made, the three required steps in the accounting cycle that involve journalizing.

31. Identify, in the sequence in which they are prepared, the three trial balances that are required in the accounting cycle.

32. Explain the terms earnings management and quality of earnings.

33. Give examples of how companies manage earnings.

* 34. What is the purpose of a work sheet?

* 35. What is the basic form of a work sheet?

Brief Exercises

WILEY PLUS

Identify impact of transactions on cash and net income.
(SO 2)

BE4-1 Transactions that affect earnings do not necessarily affect cash.

Instructions
Identify the effect, if any, that each of the following transactions would have upon cash and net income. The first transaction has been completed as an example.

	Cash	Net Income
(a) Purchased $100 of supplies for cash.	−$100	$ 0
(b) Recorded an adjusting entry to record use of $30 of the above supplies.		
(c) Made sales of $1,300, all on account.		
(d) Received $800 from customers in payment of their accounts.		
(e) Purchased capital asset for cash, $2,500.		
(f) Recorded depreciation of building for period used, $600.		

Indicate why adjusting entries are needed.
(SO 3)

BE4-2 The ledger of T. J. Bahr Company includes the following accounts. Explain why each account may require adjustment.
(a) Prepaid Insurance.
(b) Depreciation Expense.
(c) Unearned Service Revenue.
(d) Interest Payable.

Identify the major types of adjusting entries.
(SO 3)

BE4-3 Lena Company accumulates the following adjustment data at December 31. Indicate (1) the type of adjustment (prepaid expense, accrued revenue, and so on) and (2) the status of the accounts before adjustment (overstated or understated).
(a) Supplies of $400 are on hand. Supplies account shows $1,900 balance.
(b) Service Revenue earned but unbilled total $700.
(c) Interest of $300 has accumulated on a note payable.
(d) Rent collected in advance totaling $1,100 has been earned.

Prepare adjusting entry for supplies.
(SO 4)

BE4-4 Adler Advertising Company's trial balance at December 31 shows Advertising Supplies $8,800 and Advertising Supplies Expense $0. On December 31 there are $1,700 of supplies on hand. Prepare the adjusting entry at December 31 and, using T accounts, enter the balances in the accounts, post the adjusting entry, and indicate the adjusted balance in each account.

BE4-5 At the end of its first year, the trial balance of Riko Company shows Equipment $22,000 and zero balances in Accumulated Depreciation—Equipment and Depreciation Expense. Depreciation for the year is estimated to be $2,700. Prepare the adjusting entry for depreciation at December 31, post the adjustments to T accounts, and indicate the balance sheet presentation of the equipment at December 31.

Prepare adjusting entry for depreciation.
(SO 4)

BE4-6 On July 1, 2007, Lumas Co. pays $14,800 to Patel Insurance Co. for a 2-year insurance contract. Both companies have fiscal years ending December 31. For Lumas Co. journalize and post the entry on July 1 and the adjusting entry on December 31.   *Pre pard Insured*

Prepare adjusting entry for prepaid expense.
(SO 4)

BE4-7 Using the data in BE4-6, journalize and post the entry on July 1 and the adjusting entry on December 31 for Patel Insurance Co. Patel uses the accounts Unearned Insurance Revenue and Insurance Revenue.

Prepare adjusting entry for unearned revenue.
(SO 4)

BE4-8 The bookkeeper for Ahlet Company asks you to prepare the following accrual adjusting entries at December 31.
(a) Interest on notes payable of $400 is accrued.
(b) Service revenue earned but unbilled totals $1,400.
(c) Salaries of $780 earned by employees have not been recorded.
Use these account titles: Service Revenue, Accounts Receivable, Interest Expense, Interest Payable, Salaries Expense, and Salaries Payable.

Prepare adjusting entries for accruals.
(SO 5)

BE4-9 The trial balance of Cher Company includes the following balance sheet accounts. Identify the accounts that might require adjustment. For each account that requires adjustment, indicate (1) the type of adjusting entry (prepaid expenses, unearned revenues, accrued revenues, and accrued expenses) and (2) the related account in the adjusting entry.
(a) Accounts Receivable.
(b) Prepaid Insurance.
(c) Equipment.
(d) Accumulated Depreciation—Equipment.
(e) Notes Payable.
(f) Interest Payable.
(g) Unearned Service Revenue.

Analyze accounts in an adjusted trial balance.
(SO 6)

BE4-10 The adjusted trial balance of Sain Corporation at December 31, 2007, includes the following accounts: Retained Earnings $17,200; Dividends $6,000; Service Revenue $37,000; Salaries Expense $13,000; Insurance Expense $1,800; Rent Expense $3,500; Supplies Expense $1,200; and Depreciation Expense $1,000. Prepare an income statement for the year.

Prepare an income statement from an adjusted trial balance.
(SO 6)

BE4-11 Partial adjusted trial balance data for Sain Corporation are presented in BE4-10. The balance in Retained Earnings is the balance as of January 1. Prepare a retained earnings statement for the year assuming net income is $14,000.

Prepare a retained earnings statement from an adjusted trial balance.
(SO 6)

BE4-12 The following selected accounts appear in the adjusted trial balance for Shah Company. Indicate the financial statement on which each account would be reported.
(a) Accumulated Depreciation.
(b) Depreciation Expense.
(c) Retained Earnings.
(d) Dividends.
(e) Service Revenue.
(f) Supplies.
(g) Accounts Payable.

Identify financial statement for selected accounts.
(SO 6)

BE4-13 Using the data in BE4-12, identify the accounts that would be included in a post-closing trial balance.

Identify post-closing trial balance accounts.
(SO 7)

BE4-14 The required steps in the accounting cycle are listed in random order below. List the steps in proper sequence.
(a) Prepare a post-closing trial balance.
(b) Prepare an adjusted trial balance.
(c) Analyze business transactions.
(d) Prepare a trial balance.
(e) Journalize the transactions.
(f) Journalize and post closing entries.
(g) Prepare financial statements.
(h) Journalize and post adjusting entries.
(i) Post to ledger accounts.

List required steps in the accounting cycle sequence.
(SO 8)

Exercises

Identify point of revenue recognition.
(SO 1)

E4-1 The following independent situations require professional judgement for determining when to recognize revenue from the transactions.

(a) Southwest Airlines sells you an advance-purchase airline ticket in September for your flight home at Christmas.

(b) Ultimate Electronics sells you a home theatre on a "no money down, no interest, and no payments for one year" promotional deal.

(c) The Toronto Blue Jays sell season tickets online to games in the Skydome. Fans can purchase the tickets at any time, although the season doesn't officially begin until April. The major league baseball season runs from April through October.

(d) You borrow money in August from RBC Financial Group. The loan and the interest are repayable in full in November.

(e) In August, you order a sweater from Sears using its online catalog. The sweater arrives in September, and you charge it to your Sears credit card. You receive and pay the Sears bill in October.

Instructions

Identify accounting assumptions, principles, and constraints.
(SO 1)

Identify when revenue should be recognized in each of the above situations.

E4-2 These are the assumptions, principles, and constraints discussed in this and previous chapters.

1. Economic entity assumption.
2. Matching principle.
3. Monetary unit assumption.
4. Time period assumption.
5. Cost principle.
6. Materiality.
7. Full disclosure principle.
8. Going concern assumption.
9. Revenue recognition principle.
10. Conservatism.

Instructions

Identify by number the accounting assumption, principle, or constraint that describes each situation below. Do not use a number more than once.

_____ (a) Is the rationale for why plant assets are not reported at liquidation value. (Do not use the cost principle.)

_____ (b) Indicates that personal and business record-keeping should be separately maintained.

_____ (c) Ensures that all relevant financial information is reported.

_____ (d) Assumes that the dollar is the "measuring stick" used to report on financial performance.

_____ (e) Requires that accounting standards be followed for all *significant* items.

_____ (f) Separates financial information into time periods for reporting purposes.

_____ (g) Requires recognition of expenses in the same period as related revenues.

_____ (h) Indicates that market value changes subsequent to purchase are not recorded in the accounts.

Identify the violated assumption, principle, or constraint.
(SO 1)

E4-3 Here are some accounting reporting situations.

(a) Flanner Company recognizes revenue at the end of the production cycle but before sale. The price of the product, as well as the amount that can be sold, is not certain.

(b) Falk Company is in its fifth year of operation and has yet to issue financial statements. (Do not use the full disclosure principle.)

(c) Schleis, Inc. is carrying inventory at its original cost of $100,000. Inventory has a market value of $110,000.

reported as current assets and current liabilities, respectively. Liquidation of the company is unlikely.

(e) Judd Company has inventory on hand that cost $400,000. Judd reports inventory on its balance sheet at its current market value of $425,000.

(f) Kim Decker, president of Classic Music Company, bought a computer for her personal use. She paid for the computer by using company funds and debited the "Computers" account.

Instructions

For each situation, list the assumption, principle, or constraint that has been violated, if any. Some of these assumptions, principles, and constraints were presented in earlier chapters. List only one answer for each situation.

E4-4 Your examination of the records of a company that follows the cash basis of accounting tells you that the company's reported cash basis earnings in 2007 are $33,640. If this firm had followed accrual basis accounting practices, it would have reported the following year-end balances.

Convert earnings from cash to accrual basis.
(SO 2, 4, 5)

	2007	**2006**
Accounts receivable	$3,400	$2,300
Supplies on hand	1,300	1,160
Unpaid wages owed	1,500	2,400
Other unpaid amounts	1,400	1,600

Instructions

Determine the company's net earnings on an accrual basis for 2007. Show all your calculations in an orderly fashion.

E4-5 In its first year of operations Bere Company earned $28,000 in service revenue, $6,000 of which was on account and still outstanding at year-end. The remaining $22,000 was received in cash from customers.

Determine cash basis and accrual basis earnings.
(SO 2)

The company incurred operating expenses of $14,500. Of these expenses $13,000 were paid in cash; $1,500 was still owed on account at year-end. In addition, Bere prepaid $3,600 for insurance coverage that would not be used until the second year of operations.

Instructions

(a) Calculate the first year's net earnings under the cash basis of accounting, and calculate the first year's net earnings under the accrual basis of accounting.

(b) Which basis of accounting (cash or accrual) provides more useful information for decision makers?

E4-6 The Radical Edge, a ski tuning and repair shop, opened in November 2006. The company carefully kept track of all its cash receipts and cash payments. The following information is available at the end of the ski season, April 30, 2007.

Convert earnings from cash to accrual basis; prepare accrual-based financial statements.
(SO 2, 4, 5)

	Cash Receipts	**Cash Payments**
Issue of common shares	$20,000	
Payment for repair equipment		$ 9,200
Rent payments		1,225
Newspaper advertising payment		375
Utility bills payments		970
Part-time helper's wages payments		2,600
Income tax payment		10,000
Cash receipts from ski and snowboard repair services	32,150	
Subtotals	52,150	24,370
Cash balance		27,780
Totals	$52,150	$52,150

Deprec.   Rcle ?

You learn that the repair equipment has an estimated useful life of 5 years. The company rents space at a cost of $175 per month on a one-year lease. The lease contract requires payment of the first and last months' rent in advance, which was done. The part-timer helper is owed $220 at April 30, 2007, for unpaid wages. At April 30, 2007, customers owe The Radical Edge $650 for services they have received but have not yet paid for.

Instructions

(a) Prepare an accrual-basis income statement for the 6 months ended April 30, 2007.

(b) Prepare the April 30, 2007, classified balance sheet.

Identify differences between cash and accrual accounting.
(SO 2, 3)

E4-7 MaxPlay, a maker of electronic games for kids, has just completed its first year of operations. The company's sales growth was explosive. To encourage large national stores to carry its products MaxPlay offered 180-day financing—meaning its largest customers do not pay for nearly 6 months. Because MaxPlay is a new company, its components suppliers insist on being paid cash on delivery. Also, it had to pay up front for 2 years of insurance. At the end of the year MaxPlay owed employees for one full month of salaries, but due to a cash shortfall, it promised to pay them the first week of next year.

Instructions

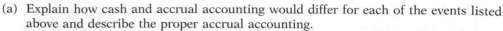

(a) Explain how cash and accrual accounting would differ for each of the events listed above and describe the proper accrual accounting.

(b) Assume that at the end of the year MaxPlay reported a favorable net income, yet the company's management is concerned because the company is very short of cash. Explain how MaxPlay could have positive net income and yet run out of cash.

Identify types of adjustments and accounts before adjustment.
(SO 3, 4, 5)

E4-8 Rollins Company accumulates the following adjustment data at December 31.

(a) Service Revenue earned but unbilled totals $600.

(b) Store supplies of $300 are on hand. Supplies account shows $1,900 balance.

(c) Utility expenses of $275 are unpaid.

(d) Service revenue of $490 collected in advance has been earned.

(e) Salaries of $800 are unpaid.

(f) Prepaid insurance totaling $400 has expired.

Instructions

For each item indicate (1) the type of adjustment (prepaid expense, unearned revenue, accrued revenue, or accrued expense) and (2) the status of the accounts before adjustment (overstated or understated).

Prepare adjusting entries from selected account data.
(SO 4, 5)

E4-9 The ledger of Reliable Rental Agency on March 31 of the current year includes these selected accounts before adjusting entries have been prepared.

	Debits	Credits
Prepaid Insurance	$ 3,600	
Supplies	3,000	
Equipment	25,000	
Accumulated Depreciation—Equipment		$ 8,400
Notes Payable		20,000
Unearned Rent Revenue		10,200
Rent Revenue		60,000
Interest Expense	0	
Wage Expense	14,000	

An analysis of the accounts shows the following.

1. The equipment depreciates $250 per month.

2. Half of the unearned rent revenue was earned during the quarter.

3. Interest of $440 is accrued on the notes payable.

4. Supplies on hand total $850.

5. Insurance expires at the rate of $300 per month.

Instructions

Prepare the adjusting entries at March 31, assuming that adjusting entries are made quarterly. Additional accounts are: Depreciation Expense, Insurance Expense, Interest Payable, and Supplies Expense.

Prepare adjusting entries.
(SO 4, 5)

E4-10 Gene Hoffman, D.D.S., opened an incorporated dental practice on January 1, 2007. During the first month of operations the following transactions occurred:

1. Performed services for patients who had dental plan insurance. At January 31, $680 of such services was earned but not yet billed to the insurance companies.

2. Utility expenses incurred but not paid prior to January 31 totaled $520.

3. Purchased dental equipment on January 1 for $80,000, paying $20,000 in cash and signing a $60,000, 3-year note payable (Interest is paid each December 31). The equipment depreciates $400 per month. Interest is $500 per month.

4. Purchased a 1-year malpractice insurance policy on January 1 for $18,000.

5. Purchased $1,750 of dental supplies. On January 31 determined that $350 of supplies were on hand.

Instructions

Prepare the adjusting entries on January 31. Account titles are: Accumulated Depreciation—Dental Equipment, Depreciation Expense, Service Revenue, Accounts Receivable, Insurance Expense, Interest Expense, Interest Payable, Prepaid Insurance, Supplies, Supplies Expense, Utilities Expense, and Utilities Payable.

E4-11 The unadjusted trial balance for Sierra Corp. is shown in Illustration 4-4 (page 162). In lieu of the adjusting entries shown in the text at October 31, assume the following adjustment data.

Prepare adjusting entries.
(SO 4, 5)

1. Advertising supplies on hand at October 31 total $700.

2. Expired insurance for the month is $100.

3. Depreciation for the month is $50.

4. As of October 31, $800 of the previously recorded unearned revenue had been earned.

5. Services provided but unbilled (and no receivable has been recorded) at October 31 are $300.

6. Interest expense accrued at October 31 is $70.

7. Accrued salaries at October 31 are $1,400.

Instructions

Prepare the adjusting entries for the items above.

E4-12 The income statement of Leno Co. for the month of July shows net income of $1,500 based on Service Revenue $5,500; Wages Expense $2,300; Supplies Expense $900, and Utilities Expense $800. In reviewing the statement, you discover the following:

Prepare a correct income statement.
(SO 1, 4, 5, 6)

1. Insurance expired during July of $350 was omitted.

2. Supplies expense includes $400 of supplies that are still on hand at July 31.

3. Depreciation on equipment of $150 was omitted.

4. Accrued but unpaid wages at July 31 of $300 were not included.

5. Revenue earned but unrecorded totaled $900.

Instructions

Prepare a correct income statement for July 2007.

E4-13 This is a partial adjusted trial balance of Marliss Company.

Analyze adjusted data.
(SO 1, 4, 5, 6)

MARLISS COMPANY
Adjusted Trial Balance
January 31, 2007

	Debit	Credit
Supplies	$ 700	
Prepaid Insurance	1,560	
Salaries Payable		$1,200
Unearned Service Revenue		750
Supplies Expense	950	
Insurance Expense	520	
Salaries Expense	1,800	
Service Revenue		2,000

Instructions

Answer these questions, assuming the year begins January 1.

(a) If the amount in Supplies Expense is the January 31 adjusting entry, and $850 of supplies was purchased in January, what was the balance in Supplies on January 1?

(b) If the amount in Insurance Expense is the January 31 adjusting entry, and the original insurance premium was for 1 year, what was the total premium and when was the policy purchased?

(c) If $2,500 of salaries was paid in January, what was the balance in Salaries Payable at December 31, 2006?

(d) If $1,600 was received in January for services performed in January, what was the balance in Unearned Service Revenue at December 31, 2006?

Journalize basic transactions and adjusting entries.
(SO 4, 5, 6)

E4-14   Selected accounts of Atlantis Company are shown here.

Supplies Expense				Salaries Payable		
July 31	850				July 31	1,200

Salaries Expense				Accounts Receivable		
July 15	1,200			July 31	500	
31	1,200					

Service Revenue				Unearned Service Revenue		
	July 14	4,100	July 31	900	July 1	Bal. 1,500
	31	900			20	700
	31	500				

Supplies			
July 1	Bal. 1,100	July 31	850
10	200		

Instructions

After analyzing the accounts, journalize (a) the July transactions and (b) the adjusting entries that were made on July 31. (*Hint:* July transactions were for cash.)

Prepare adjusting entries from analysis of trial balance.
(SO 4, 5, 6)

E4-15   The trial balances shown below are before and after adjustment for Hoi Company at the end of its fiscal year.

HOI COMPANY
Trial Balance
August 31, 2007

	Before Adjustment		After Adjustment	
	Dr.	Cr.	Dr.	Cr.
Cash	$10,900		$10,900	
Accounts Receivable	8,800		9,400	
Office Supplies	2,500		700	
Prepaid Insurance	4,000		2,500	
Office Equipment	16,000		16,000	
Accumulated Depreciation—Office Equipment		$ 3,600		$ 4,800
Accounts Payable		5,800		5,800
Salaries Payable		0		1,100
Unearned Rent Revenue		1,800		600
Common Stock		10,000		10,000
Retained Earnings		5,600		5,600
Dividends	2,800		2,800	
Service Revenue		34,000		34,600
Rent Revenue		13,200		14,400
Salaries Expense	17,000		18,100	
Office Supplies Expense	0		1,800	
Rent Expense	12,000		12,000	
Insurance Expense	0		1,500	
Depreciation Expense	0		1,200	
	$74,000	$74,000	$76,900	$76,900

Instructions
Prepare the adjusting entries that were made.

E4-16   The adjusted trial balance for Hoi Company is given in E4-15.

Instructions
Prepare the income and retained earnings statements for the year and the classified balance sheet at August 31.

E4-17   The adjusted trial balance for Hoi Company is given in E4-15.

Instructions
Prepare the closing entries for the temporary accounts at August 31.

Prepare financial statements from adjusted trial balance.
(SO 6)

Prepare closing entries.
(SO 7)

Problems: Set A

WILEY
PLUS

P4-1A   The following selected data are taken from the comparative financial statements of Alpine Curling Club. The Club prepares its financial statements using the accrual basis of accounting.

Record transactions on accrual basis; convert revenue to cash receipts.
(SO 2, 4)

September 30	2007	2006
Accounts receivable for member dues	$ 18,000	$ 11,000
Unearned ticket revenue	20,000	26,000
Dues revenue	148,000	135,000

Dues are billed to members based upon their use of the Club's facilities. Unearned ticket revenues arise from the sale of tickets to events such as the Skins Game.

Instructions
(*Hint:* You will find it helpful to use T accounts to analyze the following data. You must analyze these data sequentially, as missing information must first be deduced before moving on. Post your journal entries as you progress, rather than waiting until the end.)
(a) Prepare journal entries for each of the following events that took place during 2007.
   1. Dues receivable from members from 2006 were all collected during 2007.
   2. Unearned ticket revenue at the end of 2006 was all earned during 2007.
   3. Additional tickets were sold for $39,000 cash during 2007; a portion of these were used by the purchasers during the year. The entire balance remaining relates to the upcoming Skins Game in 2007.
   4. Dues for the 2006–2007 fiscal year were billed to members.
   5. Dues receivable for 2007 (i.e., those billed in item (4) above) were partially collected.
(b) Determine the amount of cash received by the Club from the above transactions during the year ended September 30, 2007.

(b) Cash received $180,000

P4-2A   Josh Stein started his own consulting firm, Astromech Consulting, on June 1, 2007. The trial balance at June 30 is as follows.

Prepare adjusting entries, post to ledger accounts, and prepare adjusted trial balance.
(SO 4, 5, 6)

ASTROMECH CONSULTING
Trial Balance
June 30, 2007

	Debit	Credit
Cash	$ 6,850	
Accounts Receivable	7,000	
Prepaid Insurance	2,640	
Supplies	2,000	
Office Equipment	15,000	
Accounts Payable		$ 4,540
Unearned Service Revenue		5,200
Common Stock		21,750
Service Revenue		8,000
Salaries Expense	4,000	
Rent Expense	2,000	
	$39,490	$39,490

In addition to those accounts listed on the trial balance, the chart of accounts for Astromech also contains the following accounts: Accumulated Depreciation—Office Equipment, Utilities Payable, Salaries Payable, Depreciation Expense, Insurance Expense, Utilities Expense, and Supplies Expense.

Other data:

1. Supplies on hand at June 30 total $980.
2. A utility bill for $180 has not been recorded and will not be paid until next month.
3. The insurance policy is for a year.
4. $2,900 of unearned service revenue has been earned at the end of the month.
5. Salaries of $1,250 are accrued at June 30.
6. The office equipment has a 5-year life with no salvage value and is being depreciated at $250 per month for 60 months.
7. Invoices representing $3,000 of services performed during the month have not been recorded as of June 30.

Instructions
(a) Prepare the adjusting entries for the month of June.

(b) Service rev. $13,900
(c) Tot. trial balance $44,170

(b) Post the adjusting entries to the ledger accounts. Enter the totals from the trial balance as beginning account balances. Use T accounts.
(c) Prepare an adjusted trial balance at June 30, 2007.

Prepare adjusting entries, adjusted trial balance, and financial statements.
(SO 4, 5, 6, 7)

 GLS

P4-3A The Julien Hotel opened for business on May 1, 2007. Here is its trial balance before adjustment on May 31.

JULIEN HOTEL
Trial Balance
May 31, 2007

	Debit	Credit
Cash	$ 2,500	
Prepaid Insurance	1,800	
Supplies	2,600	
Land	15,000	
Lodge	70,000	
Furniture	16,800	
Accounts Payable		$ 4,700
Unearned Rent Revenue		3,300
Mortgage Payable		36,000
Common Stock		60,000
Rent Revenue		9,000
Salaries Expense	3,000	
Utilities Expense	800	
Advertising Expense	500	
	$113,000	$113,000

Other data:

1. Insurance expires at the rate of $300 per month.
2. An inventory of supplies shows $1,350 of unused supplies on May 31.
3. Annual depreciation is $3,600 on the lodge and $3,000 on furniture.
4. The mortgage interest rate is 9%. (The mortgage was taken out on May 1.)
5. Unearned rent of $1,500 has been earned.
6. Salaries of $750 are accrued and unpaid at May 31.

Instructions
(a) Journalize the adjusting entries on May 31.

(c) Rent revenue $ 10,500
Tot. trial balance $114,570

(b) Prepare a ledger using T accounts. Enter the trial balance amounts and post the adjusting entries.
(c) Prepare an adjusted trial balance on May 31.

(d) Prepare an income statement and a retained earnings statement for the month of May and a classified balance sheet at May 31.

(e) Identify which accounts should be closed on May 31.

(d) Net income $ 3,080

P4-4A Highlands Golf Inc. was organized on July 1, 2007. Quarterly financial statements are prepared. The trial balance and adjusted trial balance on September 30 are shown here.

Prepare adjusting entries and financial statements; identify accounts to be closed.
(SO 4, 5, 6, 7)

GLS

HIGHLANDS GOLF INC.
Trial Balance
September 30, 2007

	Unadjusted		Adjusted	
	Dr.	**Cr.**	**Dr.**	**Cr.**
Cash	$ 6,700		$ 6,700	
Accounts Receivable	400		1,000	
Prepaid Rent	1,800		900	
Supplies	1,200		860	
Equipment	15,000		15,000	
Accumulated Depreciation—Equipment				$ 350
Notes Payable		$ 5,000		5,000
Accounts Payable		1,710		1,710
Salaries Payable				600
Interest Payable				50
Unearned Rent Revenue		1,000		600
Common Stock		14,000		14,000
Retained Earnings		0		0
Dividends	600		600	
Dues Revenue		13,800		14,400
Rent Revenue		400		800
Salaries Expense	8,800		9,400	
Rent Expense	900		1,800	
Depreciation Expense			350	
Supplies Expense			340	
Utilities Expense	510		510	
Interest Expense			50	
	$35,910	$35,910	$37,510	$37,510

Instructions

(a) Journalize the adjusting entries that were made.

(b) Prepare an income statement and a retained earnings statement for the 3 months ending September 30 and a classified balance sheet at September 30.

(c) Identify which accounts should be closed on September 30.

(d) If the note bears interest at 12%, how many months has it been outstanding?

(b) Net income $ 2,750
Tot. assets $24,110

P4-5A A review of the ledger of Kaffen Company at December 31, 2007, produces these data pertaining to the preparation of annual adjusting entries.

Prepare adjusting entries.
(SO 4, 5)

1. Prepaid Insurance $15,950. The company has separate insurance policies on its buildings and its motor vehicles. Policy B4564 on the building was purchased on July 1, 2006, for $10,500. The policy has a term of 3 years. Policy A2958 on the vehicles was purchased on January 1, 2007, for $7,200. This policy has a term of 2 years.

2. Unearned Subscription Revenue $29,400: The company began selling magazine subscriptions on October 1, 2007 on an annual basis. The selling price of a subscription is $30. A review of subscription contracts reveals the following.

Subscription Start Date	Number of Subscriptions
October 1	280
November 1	300
December 1	400
	980

3. Notes Payable, $40,000: This balance consists of a note for 6 months at an annual interest rate of 8%, dated October 1.

4. Salaries Payable $0: There are eight salaried employees. Salaries are paid every Friday for the current week. Five employees receive a salary of $600 each per week, and three employees earn $700 each per week. December 31 is a Wednesday. Employees do not work weekends. All employees worked the last 3 days of December.

Instructions

Prepare the adjusting entries at December 31, 2007.

Prepare adjusting entries and a corrected income statement.
(SO 4, 5)

P4-6A Happy Camper Travel Court was organized on July 1, 2006, by Brianna Brunn. Brianna is a good manager but a poor accountant. From the trial balance prepared by a part-time bookkeeper, Brianna prepared the following income statement for her fourth quarter, which ended June 30, 2007.

HAPPY CAMPER TRAVEL COURT
Income Statement
For the Quarter ended June 30, 2007

Revenues		
Travel court rental revenues		$216,000
Operating expenses		
Advertising	$ 3,800	
Wages	80,500	
Utilities	900	
Depreciation	2,700	
Repairs	4,000	
Total operating expenses		91,900
Net income		$124,100

Brianna suspected that something was wrong with the statement because net income had never exceeded $30,000 in any one quarter. Knowing that you are an experienced accountant, she asks you to review the income statement and other data.

You first look at the trial balance. In addition to the account balances reported above in the income statement, the ledger contains the following additional selected balances at June 30, 2007.

Supplies	$ 8,200
Prepaid Insurance	14,400
Note Payable	12,000

You then make inquiries and discover the following.

1. Travel court rental revenues include advanced rental payments received for summer occupancy, in the amount of $60,000.

2. There were $1,300 of supplies on hand at June 30.

3. Prepaid insurance resulted from the payment of a one-year policy on April 1, 2007.

4. The mail in July 2007 brought the following bills: advertising for the week of June 24, $110; repairs made June 18, $4,450; and utilities for the month of June, $215.

5. There are three employees who receive wages that total $250 per day. At June 30, two days' wages have been incurred but not paid.

6. The note payable is a 8% note dated May 1, 2007, and due on July 31, 2007.

7. Income tax of $13,400 for the quarter is due in July but has not yet been recorded.

Instructions

(a) Prepare any adjusting journal entries required as at June 30, 2007.

(b) Net income $34,765

(b) Prepare a correct income statement for the quarter ended June 30, 2007.

(c) Explain to Brianna the generally accepted accounting principles that she did not recognize in preparing her income statement and their effect on her results.

P4-7A On November 1, 2007, the following were the account balances of Coleman Equipment Repair.

Journalize transactions and follow through accounting cycle to preparation of financial statements.
(SO 4, 5, 6)

	Debits		Credits
Cash	$ 2,790	Accumulated Depreciation	$ 500
Accounts Receivable	2,910	Accounts Payable	2,300
Supplies	1,120	Unearned Service Revenue	400
Store Equipment	10,000	Salaries Payable	620
		Common Stock	10,000
		Retained Earnings	3,000
	$16,820		$16,820

During November the following summary transactions were completed.

Nov. 8 Paid $1,220 for salaries due employees, of which $600 is for November and $620 is for October salaries payable.
   10 Received $1,200 cash from customers in payment of account.
   12 Received $1,700 cash for services performed in November.
   15 Purchased store equipment on account $3,000.
   17 Purchased supplies on account $1,300.
   20 Paid creditors $2,500 of accounts payable due.
   22 Paid November rent $450.
   25 Paid salaries $1,000.
   27 Performed services on account and billed customers for services provided $900.
   29 Received $550 from customers for services to be provided in the future.

Adjustment data:

1. Supplies on hand are valued at $1,600.
2. Accrued salaries payable are $480.
3. Depreciation for the month is $250.
4. Unearned service revenue of $300 is earned.

Instructions
(a) Enter the November 1 balances in the ledger accounts. (Use T accounts.)
(b) Journalize the November transactions.
(c) Post to the ledger accounts. Use Service Revenue, Depreciation Expense, Supplies Expense, Salaries Expense, and Rent Expense.
(d) Prepare a trial balance at November 30.
(e) Journalize and post adjusting entries.
(f) Prepare an adjusted trial balance.
(g) Prepare an income statement and a retained earnings statement for November and a classified balance sheet at November 30.

(f) Cash $ 1,070
   Tot. trial balance $21,880
(g) Net loss $ 700

P4-8A Katie Gage opened New View Window Washing Inc. on July 1, 2007. During July the following transactions were completed.

Complete all steps in accounting cycle.
(SO 4, 5, 6, 7, 8)

July 1 Issued 11,000 shares of common stock for $11,000 cash.
    1 Purchased used truck for $9,000, paying $3,000 cash and the balance on account.
    3 Purchased cleaning supplies for $800 on account.
    5 Paid $1,440 cash on 1-year insurance policy effective July 1.
   12 Billed customers $3,200 for cleaning services.
   18 Paid $1,000 cash on amount owed on truck and $500 on amount owed on cleaning supplies.
   20 Paid $2,000 cash for employee salaries.
   21 Collected $1,400 cash from customers billed on July 12.
   25 Billed customers $2,000 for cleaning services.
   31 Paid $260 for gas and oil used in the truck during month.
   31 Declared and paid $600 cash dividend.

The chart of accounts for New View Window Washing contains the following accounts:
Cash, Accounts Receivable, Cleaning Supplies, Prepaid Insurance, Equipment, Accumulated

Depreciation—Equipment, Accounts Payable, Salaries Payable, Common Stock, Retained Earnings, Dividends, Income Summary, Service Revenue, Gas & Oil Expense, Cleaning Supplies Expense, Depreciation Expense, Insurance Expense, Salaries Expense.

Instructions
(a) Journalize the July transactions.
(b) Post to the ledger accounts. (Use T accounts.)
(c) Prepare a trial balance at July 31.
(d) Journalize the following adjustments.
  (1) Services provided but unbilled and uncollected at July 31 were $1,700.
  (2) Depreciation on equipment for the month was $250.
  (3) One-twelfth of the insurance expired.
  (4) An inventory count shows $360 of cleaning supplies on hand at July 31.
  (5) Accrued but unpaid employee salaries were $400.
(e) Post adjusting entries to the T accounts.

(f) Cash $ 3,600
(g) Tot. assets $19,530

(f) Prepare an adjusted trial balance.
(g) Prepare the income statement and a retained earnings statement for July and a classified balance sheet at July 31.
(h) Journalize and post closing entries and complete the closing process.
(i) Prepare a post-closing trial balance at July 31.

Problems: Set B

Record transactions on accrual basis; convert revenue to cash receipts.
(SO 2, 4)

P4-1B The following data are taken from the comparative balance sheets of EverGreen Club, which prepares its financial statements using the accrual basis of accounting.

December 31	2007	2006
Accounts receivable for member fees	$20,000	$ 6,000
Unearned fees revenue	17,000	18,000

Fees are billed to members based upon their use of the club's facilities. Unearned fees arise from the sale of gift certificates, which members can apply to their future use of club facilities. The 2007 income statement for the club showed that fee revenue of $157,000 was earned during the year.

Instructions
(*Hint:* You will find it helpful to use T accounts to analyze these data.)
(a) Prepare journal entries for each of the following events that took place during 2007.

1. Fees receivable from 2006 were all collected during 2007.

2. Gift certificates outstanding at the end of 2006 were all redeemed during 2007.

3. An additional $30,000 worth of gift certificates were sold during 2007; a portion of these were used by the recipients during the year; the remainder were still outstanding at the end of 2007.

(b) Cash received $142,000

Prepare adjusting entries, post to ledger accounts, and prepare an adjusted trial balance.
(SO 4, 5, 6)

4. Fees for 2007 were billed to members.

5. Fees receivable for 2007 (i.e., those billed in item (4) above) were partially collected.

(b) Determine the amount of cash received by the club with respect to fees during 2007.

P4-2B Jessica Naboo started her own consulting firm, Naboo Consulting, on May 1, 2007. The trial balance at May 31 is as shown on page 205.

NABOO CONSULTING
Trial Balance
May 31, 2007

	Debit	Credit
Cash	$ 7,500	
Accounts Receivable	3,000	
Prepaid Insurance	3,600	
Supplies	2,500	
Office Furniture	12,000	
Accounts Payable		$ 3,500
Unearned Service Revenue		4,000
Common Stock		19,100
Service Revenue		7,500
Salaries Expense	4,000	
Rent Expense	1,500	
	$34,100	$34,100

In addition to those accounts listed on the trial balance, the chart of accounts for Naboo Consulting also contains the following accounts: Accumulated Depreciation—Office Furniture, Travel Payable, Salaries Payable, Depreciation Expense, Insurance Expense, Travel Expense, and Supplies Expense.

Other data:

1. $500 of supplies have been used during the month.

2. Travel costs incurred but not paid are $260.

3. The insurance policy is for 2 years.

4. $1,000 of the balance in the Unearned Service Revenue account remains unearned at the end of the month.

5. May 31 is a Wednesday and employees are paid on Fridays. Naboo Consulting has two employees that are paid $600 each for a 5-day work week.

6. The office furniture has a 5-year life with no salvage value and is being depreciated at $200 per month for 60 months.

7. Invoices representing $1,400 of services performed during the month have not been recorded as of May 31.

Instructions
(a) Prepare the adjusting entries for the month of May.
(b) Post the adjusting entries to the ledger accounts. Enter the totals from the trial balance as beginning account balances. Use T accounts.
(c) Prepare an adjusted trial balance at May 31, 2007.

(c) Tot. trial
balance $36,680

P4-3B Happy Trails Resort opened for business on June 1 with eight air-conditioned units. Its trial balance before adjustment on August 31 is presented here.

Prepare adjusting entries,
adjusted trial balance, and
financial statements.
(SO 4, 5, 6, 7)

HAPPY TRAILS RESORT
Trial Balance
August 31, 2007

	Debit	Credit
Cash	$ 24,600	
Prepaid Insurance	5,400	
Supplies	4,300	
Land	40,000	
Cottages	132,000	
Furniture	36,000	
Accounts Payable		$ 6,500
Unearned Rent Revenue		6,800

	Debit	Credit
Mortgage Payable		120,000
Common Stock		100,000
Dividends	5,000	
Rent Revenue		80,000
Salaries Expense	53,000	
Utilities Expense	9,400	
Repair Expense	3,600	
	$313,300	$313,300

Other data:

1. Insurance expires at the rate of $450 per month.
2. An inventory count on August 31 shows $1,200 of supplies on hand.
3. Annual depreciation is $4,800 on cottages and $4,000 on furniture.
4. Unearned rent of $5,000 was earned prior to August 31.
5. Salaries of $600 were unpaid at August 31.
6. Rentals of $1,200 were due from tenants at August 31. (Use Accounts Receivable.)
7. The mortgage interest rate is 7% per year. (The mortgage was taken out August 1.)

Instructions

(a) Journalize the adjusting entries on August 31 for the 3-month period June 1–August 31.
(b) Prepare a ledger using T accounts. Enter the trial balance amounts and post the adjusting entries.

(c) Tot. trial balance $318,000
(d) Net income $12,250

(c) Prepare an adjusted trial balance on August 31.
(d) Prepare an income statement and a retained earnings statement for the 3 months ended August 31 and a classified balance sheet as of August 31.
(e) Identify which accounts should be closed on August 31.

Prepare adjusting entries and financial statements; identify accounts to be closed.
(SO 4, 5, 6, 7)

GLS

P4-4B   Khanna Advertising Agency was founded by Matt Khanna in January 2002. Presented here are both the adjusted and unadjusted trial balances as of December 31, 2007.

KHANNA ADVERTISING AGENCY
Trial Balance
December 31, 2007

	Unadjusted Dr.	Unadjusted Cr.	Adjusted Dr.	Adjusted Cr.
Cash	$ 11,000		$ 11,000	
Accounts Receivable	16,000		19,500	
Art Supplies	8,400		6,000	
Prepaid Insurance	3,350		1,790	
Printing Equipment	60,000		60,000	
Accumulated Depreciation		$ 25,000		$ 30,000
Accounts Payable		2,000		2,000
Interest Payable		0		320
Notes Payable		8,000		8,000
Unearned Advertising Revenue		4,000		3,600
Salaries Payable		0		1,300
Common Stock		20,000		20,000
Retained Earnings		5,500		5,500
Dividends	10,000		10,000	
Advertising Revenue		57,600		61,500
Salaries Expense	9,000		10,300	
Insurance Expense			1,560	
Interest Expense			320	

	Unadjusted		Adjusted	
	Dr.	**Cr.**	**Dr.**	**Cr.**
Depreciation Expense			5,000	
Art Supplies Expense			2,400	
Rent Expense	4,350		4,350	
	$122,100	$122,100	$132,220	$132,220

Instructions

(a) Journalize the annual adjusting entries that were made.

(b) Prepare an income statement and a retained earnings statement for the year ended December 31, and a classified balance sheet at December 31.

(c) Identify which accounts should be closed on December 31.

(d) If the note has been outstanding 6 months, what is the annual interest rate on that note?

(e) If the company paid $10,500 in salaries in 2007, what was the balance in Salaries Payable on December 31, 2006?

(b) Net income $37,570
Tot. assets $68,290

P4-5B A review of the ledger of Ordman Company at December 31, 2007, produces the following data pertaining to the preparation of annual adjusting entries.

Prepare adjusting entries.
(SO 4, 5)

1. Salaries Payable $0: There are eight salaried employees. Salaries are paid every Friday for the current week. Six employees receive a salary of $800 each per week, and two employees earn $600 each per week. December 31 is a Wednesday. Employees do not work weekends. All employees worked the last 3 days of December.

2. Unearned Rent Revenue $369,000: The company began subleasing office space in its new building on November 1. Each tenant is required to make a $5,000 security deposit that is not refundable until occupancy is terminated. At December 31 the company had the following rental contracts that are paid in full for the entire term of the lease.

Date	Term (in months)	Monthly Rent	Number of Leases
Nov. 1	6	$4,000	5
Dec. 1	6	8,500	4

3. Prepaid Advertising $13,200: This balance consists of payments on two advertising contracts. The contracts provide for monthly advertising in two trade magazines. The terms of the contracts are as follows.

Contract	Date	Amount	Number of Magazine Issues
A650	May 1	$6,000	12
B974	Sept. 1	7,200	18

The first advertisement runs in the month in which the contract is signed.

4. Notes Payable $80,000: This balance consists of a note for 1 year at an annual interest rate of 7%, dated October 1, 2007.

Instructions

Prepare the adjusting entries at December 31, 2007. Show all computations.

P4-6B The Fly Right Travel Agency was organized on January 1, 2005, by Sam Cheney. Sam is a good manager but a poor accountant. From the trial balance prepared by a part-time bookkeeper, Sam prepared the income statement on page 208 for the quarter that ended March 31, 2007.

Prepare adjusting entries and a corrected income statement.
(SO 4, 5)

FLY RIGHT TRAVEL AGENCY
Income Statement
For the Quarter Ended March 31, 2007

Revenues		
Travel service revenue		$50,000
Operating expenses		
Advertising	$2,600	
Depreciation	400	
Income tax	1,500	
Salaries	6,000	
Utilities	400	10,900
Net income		$39,100

Sam knew that something was wrong with the statement because net income had never exceeded $5,000 in any one quarter. Knowing that you are an experienced accountant, he asks you to review the income statement and other data.

You first look at the trial balance. In addition to the account balances reported above in the income statement, the trial balance contains the following additional selected balances at March 31, 2007.

Supplies	$ 2,900
Prepaid insurance	1,200
Note payable	10,000

You then make inquiries and discover the following:

1. Travel service revenue includes advance payments for cruises, $30,000.

2. There were $800 of supplies on hand at March 31.

3. Prepaid insurance resulted from the payment of a one-year policy on March 1, 2007.

4. The mail on April 1, 2007, brought the utility bill for the month of March's heat, light, and power, $210.

5. There are three employees who receive salaries of $75 each per day. At March 31, three days' salaries have been incurred but not paid.

6. The note payable is a 6-month, 8% note dated January 1, 2007.

Instructions
(a) Prepare any adjusting journal entries required as at March 31, 2007.

(b) Net income $5,815

(b) Prepare a correct income statement for the quarter ended March 31, 2007.

(c) Explain to Sam the generally accepted accounting principles that he did not recognize in preparing his income statement and their effect on his results.

Journalize transactions and follow through accounting cycle to preparation of financial statements.
(SO 4, 5, 6)

P4-7B   On September 1, 2007, the following were the account balances of Tech Know Equipment Repair.

	Debits		**Credits**
Cash	$ 4,880	Accumulated Depreciation	$ 1,600
Accounts Receivable	3,820	Accounts Payable	3,100
Supplies	800	Unearned Service Revenue	400
Store Equipment	15,000	Salaries Payable	700
	$24,500	Common Stock	10,000
		Retained Earnings	8,700
			$24,500

During September the following summary transactions were completed.

Sept. 8   Paid $1,100 for salaries due employees, of which $400 is for September and $700 is for August salaries payable.

10   Received $1,500 cash from customers in payment of account.

12   Received $3,400 cash for services performed in September.

15   Purchased store equipment on account $3,000.

Sept. 17   Purchased supplies on account $1,500.
    20   Paid creditors $4,500 of accounts payable due.
    22   Paid September rent $400.
    25   Paid salaries $1,200.
    27   Performed services on account and billed customers for services provided
          $850.
    29   Received $650 from customers for services to be provided in the future.

Adjustment data:

1. Supplies on hand $1,800.

2. Accrued salaries payable $400.

3. Depreciation $200 per month.

4. Unearned service revenue of $350 earned.

Instructions
(a) Enter the September 1 balances in the ledger T accounts.
(b) Journalize the September transactions.
(c) Post to the ledger T accounts. Use Service Revenue, Depreciation Expense, Supplies Expense, Salaries Expense, and Rent Expense.
(d) Prepare a trial balance at September 30.
(e) Journalize and post adjusting entries.
(f) Prepare an adjusted trial balance.
(g) Prepare an income statement and a retained earnings statement for September and a classified balance sheet at September 30.

(f) Tot. trial balance $29,300
(g) Tot. assets $24,400

P4-8B   Julie Molony opened Valet Cleaners on March 1, 2007. During March, the following transactions were completed.

Complete all steps in accounting cycle.
(SO 4, 5, 6, 7, 8)

Mar. 1   Issued 10,000 shares of common stock for $15,000 cash.
    1   Purchased used truck for $8,000, paying $5,000 cash and the balance on account.
    3   Purchased cleaning supplies for $1,200 on account.
    5   Paid $1,800 cash on 1-year insurance policy effective March 1.
    14   Billed customers $3,200 for cleaning services.
    18   Paid $1,500 cash on amount owed on truck and $500 on amount owed on cleaning supplies.
    20   Paid $1,750 cash for employee salaries.
    21   Collected $1,600 cash from customers billed on March 14.
    28   Billed customers $4,200 for cleaning services.
    31   Paid $350 for gas and oil used in truck during month.
    31   Declared and paid a $900 cash dividend.

The chart of accounts for Valet Cleaners contains the following accounts: Cash, Accounts Receivable, Cleaning Supplies, Prepaid Insurance, Equipment, Accumulated Depreciation—Equipment, Accounts Payable, Salaries Payable, Common Stock, Retained Earnings, Dividends, Income Summary, Service Revenue, Gas & Oil Expense, Cleaning Supplies Expense, Depreciation Expense, Insurance Expense, Salaries Expense.

Instructions
(a) Journalize the March transactions.
(b) Post to the ledger accounts. (Use T accounts.)
(c) Prepare a trial balance at March 31.
(d) Journalize the following adjustments.
    1. Earned but unbilled revenue at March 31 was $600.
    2. Depreciation on equipment for the month was $250.
    3. One-twelfth of the insurance expired.
    4. An inventory count shows $280 of cleaning supplies on hand at March 31.
    5. Accrued but unpaid employee salaries were $830.
(e) Post adjusting entries to the T accounts.
(f) Prepare an adjusted trial balance.
(g) Prepare the income statement and a retained earnings statement for March and a classified balance sheet at March 31.
(h) Journalize and post closing entries and complete the closing process.
(i) Prepare a post-closing trial balance at March 31.

(f) Tot. adj. trial
    balance $26,280
(g) Tot. assets $20,880

Problems: Set C

Visit the book's website at **www.wiley.com/college/kimmel** and choose the Student Companion site to access Problem Set C.

Continuing Cookie Chronicle

(*Note:* This is a continuation of the Cookie Chronicle from Chapters 1 through 3.)

CCC4   Cookie Creations is gearing up for the winter holiday season. During the month of December 2006, the following transactions occur.

Dec.   1   Natalie hires an assistant at an hourly wage of $8 to help with cookie making and some administrative duties.

5   Natalie teaches the class that was booked on November 25. The balance outstanding is received.

8   Cookie Creations receives a check for the amount due from the neighborhood school for the class given on November 30.

9   Cookie Creations receives $625 in advance from the local school board for five classes that the company will give during December and January.

15   Pays the cell phone invoice outstanding at November 30.

16   Issues a check to Natalie's brother for the amount owed for the design of the website.

19   Receives a deposit of $50 on a cookie class scheduled for early January.

23   Additional revenue earned during the month for cookie-making classes amounts to $3,500. (Natalie has not had time to account for each class individually.) $3,000 in cash has been collected and $500 is still outstanding. (This is in addition to the December 5 and December 9 transactions.)

23   Additional supplies purchased during the month for sugar, flour, and chocolate chips amount to $1,250 cash.

23   Issues a check to Natalie's assistant for $800. Her assistant worked approximately 100 hours from the time in which she was hired until December 23.

28   Pays a dividend of $500 to the common shareholder (Natalie).

As of December 31, Cookie Creations' year-end, the following adjusting entry data are provided.

1. A count reveals that $50 of brochures and posters remain at the end of December.
2. Depreciation is recorded on the baking equipment purchased in November. The baking equipment has a useful life of 5 years. Assume that 2 months' worth of depreciation is required.
3. Amortization (which is similar to depreciation) is recorded on the website. (Credit the Website account directly for the amount of the amortization.) The website is amortized over a useful life of 2 years and was available for use on December 1.
4. Interest on the note payable is accrued. (Assume that 1.5 months of interest accrued during November and December.)
5. One month's worth of insurance has expired.
6. Natalie is unexpectedly telephoned on December 28 to give a cookie class at the neighborhood community center. In early January Cookie Creations sends an invoice for $375 to the community center.
7. A count reveals that $1,025 of baking supplies were used.
8. A cell phone invoice is received for $75. The invoice is for services provided during the month of December and is due on January 15.
9. Because the cookie-making class occurred unexpectedly on December 28 and is for such a large group of children, Natalie's assistant helps out. Her assistant worked 7 hours at a rate of $8 per hour.
10. An analysis of the unearned revenue account reveals that two of the five classes paid for by the local school board on December 9 still have not been taught by the end of December. The $50 deposit received on December 19 for another class also remains unearned.

Instructions

Using the information that you have gathered and the general ledger accounts that you have prepared through Chapter 3, plus the new information on page 210, do the following.
(a) Journalize the above transactions.
(b) Post the December transactions. (Use the general ledger accounts prepared in Chapter 3.)
(c) Prepare a trial balance at December 31, 2006.
(d) Prepare and post adjusting journal entries for the month of December.
(e) Prepare an adjusted trial balance as of December 31, 2006.
(f) Prepare an income statement and a retained earnings statement for the 2-month period ending December 31, 2006, and a classified balance sheet as of December 31, 2006.
(g) Prepare and post closing entries as of December 31, 2006.
(h) Prepare a post-closing trial balance.

▶ **BROADENING YOUR PERSPECTIVE**

Financial Reporting and Analysis

FINANCIAL REPORTING PROBLEM: *Tootsie Roll Industries, Inc.*

BYP4-1 The financial statements of Tootsie Roll are presented in Appendix A at the end of this book.

Instructions
(a) Using the consolidated income statement and balance sheet, identify items that may result in adjusting entries for prepayments.
(b) Using the consolidated income statement, identify two items that may result in adjusting entries for accruals.
(c) What was the amount of depreciation expense for 2004 and 2003? (You will need to examine the notes to the financial statements or the statement of cash flows.) Where was accumulated depreciation reported?
(d) What was the cash paid for income taxes during 2004, reported at the bottom of the consolidated statement of cash flows? What was income tax expense (provision for income taxes) for 2004? Where is the remainder presumably reported in the balance sheet?

COMPARATIVE ANALYSIS PROBLEM: *Tootsie Roll vs. Hershey Foods*

BYP4-2 The financial statements of Hershey Foods are presented in Appendix B, following the financial statements for Tootsie Roll in Appendix A.

Instructions
(a) Identify two accounts on Hershey Foods' balance sheet that provide evidence that Hershey uses accrual accounting. In each case, identify the income statement account that would be affected by the adjustment process.
(b) Identify two accounts on Tootsie Roll's balance sheet that provide evidence that Tootsie Roll uses accrual accounting (different from the two you listed for Hershey). In each case, identify the income statement account that would be affected by the adjustment process.

RESEARCH CASE

BYP4-3 The July 2, 2004, issue of the *Wall Street Journal* includes an article by Gene Colter titled "Accrual Accounting Can Be Costly."

Instructions

Read the article and answer the following.

(a) How does the article define accrual accounting?

(b) What does the article say happens to companies in the "highest accrual category," and why does it happen?

(c) What high-accrual group companies does the article mention that experienced shareholder lawsuits?

(d) What was General Motors spokesperson's response to being included in the high-accrual group?

INTERPRETING FINANCIAL STATEMENTS

BYP4-4   Laser Recording Systems, founded in 1981, produces disks for use in the home market. The following is an excerpt from Laser Recording Systems' financial statements (all dollars in thousands).

LASER RECORDING SYSTEMS
Management Discussion

Accrued liabilities increased to $1,642 at January 31, from $138 at the end of the previous fiscal year. Compensation and related accruals increased $195 due primarily to increases in accruals for severance, vacation, commissions, and relocation expenses. Accrued professional services increased by $137 primarily as a result of legal expenses related to several outstanding contractual disputes. Other expenses increased $35, of which $18 was for interest payable.

Instructions

(a) Can you tell from the discussion whether Laser Recording Systems has prepaid its legal expenses and is now making an adjustment to the asset account Prepaid Legal Expenses, or whether the company is handling the legal expense via an accrued expense adjustment?

(b) Identify each of the adjustments Laser Recording Systems is discussing as one of the four types of possible adjustments discussed in the chapter. How is net income ultimately affected by each of the adjustments?

(c) What journal entry did Laser Recording make to record the accrued interest?

FINANCIAL ANALYSIS ON THE WEB

BYP4-5   *Purpose:* To learn about the functions of the Securities and Exchange Commission (SEC).

Address: **www.sec.gov/about/whatwedo.shtml** (or go to
www.wiley.com/college/kimmel)

Instructions

Use the information in this site to answer the following questions.

(a) What event spurred the creation of the SEC? Why was the SEC created?

(b) What are the four divisions of the SEC? Briefly describe the purpose of each.

(c) What are the responsibilities of the chief accountant?

Critical Thinking

DECISION MAKING ACROSS THE ORGANIZATION

BYP4-6   Swiss Valley Park was organized on April 1, 2006, by Erika Barnes. Erika is a good manager but a poor accountant. From the trial balance prepared by a part-time bookkeeper, Erika prepared the income statement shown at the top of page 213 for the quarter that ended March 31, 2007.

SWISS VALLEY PARK
Income Statement
For the Quarter Ended March 31, 2007

Revenues		
Rental revenues		$89,000
Operating expenses		
Advertising	$ 4,200	
Wages	27,600	
Utilities	900	
Depreciation	800	
Repairs	2,800	
Total operating expenses		36,300
Net income		$52,700

Erika knew that something was wrong with the statement because net income had never exceeded $20,000 in any one quarter. Knowing that you are an experienced accountant, she asks you to review the income statement and other data.

You first look at the trial balance. In addition to the account balances reported in the income statement, the ledger contains these selected balances at March 31, 2007.

Supplies	$ 5,200
Prepaid Insurance	7,200
Notes Payable	14,000

You then make inquiries and discover the following.

1. Rental revenues include advanced rentals for summer-month occupancy, $26,000.
2. There were $1,300 of supplies on hand at March 31.
3. Prepaid insurance resulted from the payment of a 1-year policy on January 1, 2007.
4. The mail on April 1, 2007, brought the following bills: advertising for week of March 24, $110; repairs made March 10, $380; and utilities $240.
5. There are four employees who receive wages totaling $290 per day. At March 31, 3 days' wages have been incurred but not paid.
6. The note payable is a 3-month, 8% note dated January 1, 2007.

Instructions
With the class divided into groups, answer the following.
(a) Prepare a correct income statement for the quarter ended March 31, 2007.
(b) Explain to Erika the generally accepted accounting principles that she did not follow in preparing her income statement and their effect on her results.

COMMUNICATION ACTIVITY

BYP4-7   On numerous occasions proposals have surfaced to put the federal government on the accrual basis of accounting. This is no small issue because if this basis were used, it would mean that billions in unrecorded liabilities would have to be booked and the federal deficit would increase substantially.

Instructions
(a) What is the difference between accrual basis accounting and cash basis accounting?
(b) Comment on why politicians prefer a cash basis accounting system over an accrual basis system.
(c) Write a letter to your senators explaining why you think the federal government should adopt the accrual basis of accounting.

ETHICS CASE

BYP4-8   Beegone Company is a pesticide manufacturer. Its sales declined greatly this year due to the passage of legislation outlawing the sale of several of Beegone's chemical pesticides. During the coming year, Beegone will have environmentally safe and competitive replacement chemicals to replace these discontinued products. Sales in the next year are expected to greatly exceed those of any prior year. Therefore, the decline in this year's sales and profits appears to be a one-year aberration.

Even so, the company president believes that a large dip in the current year's profits could cause a significant drop in the market price of Beegone's stock and make it a takeover target. To avoid this possibility, he urges Clare Bolton, controller, in making this period's year-end adjusting entries to accrue every possible revenue and to defer as many expenses as possible. The president says to Clare, "We need the revenues this year, and next year we can easily absorb expenses deferred from this year. We can't let our stock price be hammered down!" Clare didn't get around to recording the adjusting entries until January 17, but she dated the entries December 31 as if they were recorded then. Clare also made every effort to comply with the president's request.

Instructions
(a) Who are the stakeholders in this situation?
(b) What are the ethical considerations of the president's request and Clare's dating the adjusting entries December 31?
(c) Can Clare accrue revenues and defer expenses and still be ethical?

Answers to Business Insight and Accounting across the Organization Questions

p. 161

Q. What motivates sales executives and finance and accounting executives to participate in activities that result in inaccurate reporting of revenues?

A. Sales executives typically receive bonuses based on their ability to meet quarterly sales targets. In addition, they often face the possibility of losing their jobs if they miss those targets. Executives in accounting and finance are very aware of the earnings targets of Wall Street analysts and investors. If they fail to meet these targets, the company's stock price will fall. As a result of these pressures, executives sometimes knowingly engage in unethical efforts to misstate revenues. As a result of the Sarbanes-Oxley Act of 2002, the penalties for such behavior are now much more severe.

p. 164

Q. Why might the new accounting method cause companies sometimes to spend less on advertising?

A. Under the old approach companies could delay to future periods the expensing of advertising costs. Under that approach, money spent this period did not necessarily immediately reduce income. Under the new approach, a dollar spent on advertising immediately reduces this year's income. If the company is concerned that it might not hit this year's earnings target, it might decide to reduce its advertising spending.

p. 168

Q. Suppose that Robert Jones purchases a $100 gift card at Best Buy on December 24, 2006, and gives it to his wife Mary Jones on December 25, 2006. On January 3, 2007, Mary uses the card to purchase $100 worth of CDs. When do you think Best Buy should recognize revenue and why?

A. According to the revenue recognition principle, companies should recognize revenue when earned. In this case revenue is not earned until Best Buy provides the goods. Thus, when Best Buy receives cash in exchange for the gift card on December 24, 2006, it should recognize a liability, Unearned Revenue, for $100. On January 3, 2007, when Mary Jones exchanges the card for merchandise, Best Buy should recognize revenue and eliminate $100 from the balance in the Unearned Revenue account.

Answer to Tootsie Roll Review It Question 3, p. 174

Under the heading "Property, plant, and equipment" in Note 1, Tootsie Roll reports 2004 depreciation expense of $11,680,000.

Answers to Self-Study Questions

1. c   2. a   3. d   4. d   5. c   6. a   7. b   8. b   9. c
10. d   11. a   12. a   13. d

REMEMBER TO GO BACK TO THE NAVIGATOR BOX ON THE CHAPTER-OPENING PAGE AND CHECK OFF YOUR COMPLETED WORK.

CHAPTER 5

Merchandising Operations and the Multiple-Step Income Statement

STUDY OBJECTIVES

After studying this chapter,
you should be able to:

1 Identify the differences between a service enterprise and a merchandising company.

2 Explain the recording of purchases under a perpetual inventory system.

3 Explain the recording of sales revenues under a perpetual inventory system.

4 Distinguish between a single-step and a multiple-step income statement.

5 Determine cost of goods sold under a periodic system.

6 Explain the factors affecting profitability.

THE NAVIGATOR

THE NAVIGATOR

- Scan *Study Objectives*
- Read *Feature Story*
- Read *Preview*
- Read text and answer *Before You Go On*
  p. 224   p. 227   p. 232
  p. 233   p. 237
- Work *Using the Decision Toolkit*
- Review *Summary of Study Objectives*
- Work *Demonstration Problem*
- Answer *Self-Study Questions*
- Complete *Assignments*

FEATURE STORY

Who Doesn't Shop at Wal-Mart?

In his book *The End of Work,* Jeremy Rifkin notes that until the 20th century the word *consumption* evoked negative images; to be labeled a "consumer" was an insult. (In fact, one of the deadliest diseases in history, tuberculosis, was often referred to as "consumption.") Twentieth-century merchants realized, however, that in order to prosper, they had to convince people of the need for things not previously needed. For example, General Motors made annual changes in its cars so that people would be discontented with the cars they already owned. Thus began consumerism.

Today consumption describes the U.S. lifestyle in a nutshell. We consume twice as much today per person as we did at the end of World War II. The amount of U.S. retail space per person is vastly greater than that of any other country. It appears that we live to shop.

The first great retail giant was Sears, Roebuck. It started as a catalog company enabling people in rural areas to buy things by mail. For decades it was the uncontested merchandising leader.

Today Wal-Mart is the undisputed champion provider of basic (and perhaps not-so-basic) human needs. Wal-Mart opened its first store in 1962, and it now has more than 5,000 stores, serving more than 100 million customers every week. A key

cause of Wal-Mart's incredible growth is its amazing system of inventory control and distribution. Wal-Mart has a management information system that employs six satellite channels, from which company computers receive 8.4 million updates every minute on what items customers buy and the relationship among items sold to each person.

Measured by sales revenues, Wal-Mart is the largest company in the world. In six years it went from selling almost no groceries to being America's largest grocery retailer.

It would appear that things have never looked better at Wal-Mart. On the other hand, a *Wall Street Journal* article entitled "How to Sell More to Those Who Think It's Cool to Be Frugal" suggests that consumerism as a way of life might be dying. Don't bet your wide-screen TV on it, though.

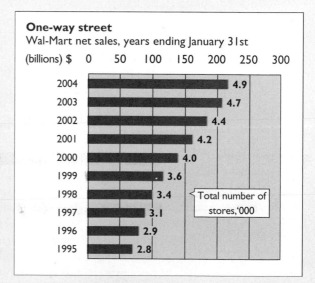

One-way street
Wal-Mart net sales, years ending January 31st

(billions) $	Net sales	Total number of stores, '000
2004		4.9
2003		4.7
2002		4.4
2001		4.2
2000		4.0
1999		3.6
1998		3.4
1997		3.1
1996		2.9
1995		2.8

Source: "How Big Can It Grow?" *The Economist* (April 17, 2004), pp. 67–69.

THE NAVIGATOR

On the World Wide Web
Wal-Mart: www.wal-mart.com

PREVIEW OF CHAPTER 5

Merchandising is one of the largest and most influential industries in the United States. It is likely that a number of you will work for a merchandiser. Therefore, understanding the financial statements of merchandising companies is important. In this chapter you will learn the basics about reporting merchandising transactions. In addition, you will learn how to prepare and analyze a commonly used form of the income statement—the multiple-step income statement. The content and organization of the chapter are as follows.

MERCHANDISING OPERATIONS

Merchandising Operations	Recording Purchases of Merchandise	Recording Sales of Merchandise	Income Statement Presentation	Evaluating Profitability
• Operating cycles • Inventory systems—perpetual and periodic	• Freight costs • Purchase returns and allowances • Purchase discounts • Summary of purchasing transactions	• Sales returns and allowances • Sales discounts	• Sales revenues • Gross profit • Operating expenses • Nonoperating activities • Determining cost of goods sold—periodic system	• Gross profit rate • Profit margin ratio

Merchandising Operations

STUDY OBJECTIVE

1

Identify the differences between a service enterprise and a merchandising company.

Wal-Mart, Kmart, and Target are called **merchandising companies** because they buy and sell merchandise rather than perform services as their primary source of revenue. Merchandising companies that purchase and sell directly to consumers are called **retailers**. Merchandising companies that sell to retailers are known as **wholesalers**. For example, retailer Walgreens might buy goods from wholesaler McKesson; retailer Office Depot might buy office supplies from wholesaler United Stationers. The primary source of revenues for merchandising companies is the sale of merchandise, often referred to simply as **sales revenue** or **sales**. A merchandising company has two categories of expenses: the cost of goods sold and operating expenses.

The **cost of goods sold** is the total cost of merchandise sold during the period. This expense is directly related to the revenue recognized from the sale of goods. Illustration 5-1 shows the income measurement process for a merchandising company. The items in the two blue boxes are unique to a merchandising company; they are not used by a service company.

OPERATING CYCLES

The **operating cycle** of a merchandising company ordinarily is longer than that of a service company. The purchase of merchandise inventory and its eventual

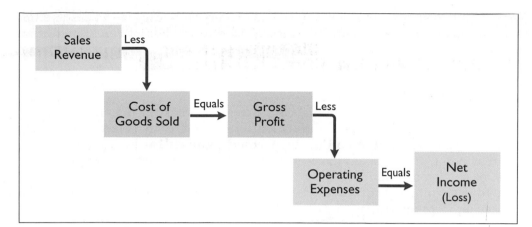

Illustration 5-1 Income measurement process for a merchandising company

sale lengthen the cycle. Illustration 5-2 contrasts the operating cycles of service and merchandising companies. Note that the added asset account for a merchandising company is the Merchandise Inventory account.

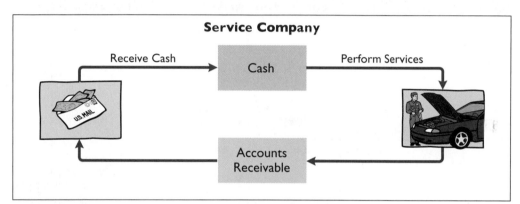

Illustration 5-2 Operating cycles for a service company and a merchandising company

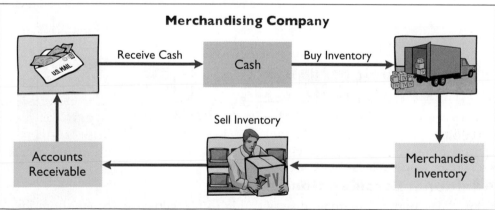

INVENTORY SYSTEMS

A merchandising company keeps track of its inventory to determine what is available for sale and what has been sold. Companies use one of two systems to account for inventory: a **perpetual inventory system** or a **periodic inventory system**.

Perpetual System

In a **perpetual inventory system**, companies maintain detailed records of the cost of each inventory purchase and sale. These records continuously—perpetually— show the inventory that should be on hand for every item. For example, a Ford dealership has separate inventory records for each automobile, truck, and van

Helpful Hint For control purposes companies take a physical inventory count under the perpetual system, even though it is not needed to determine cost of goods sold.

on its lot and showroom floor. Similarly, a grocery store uses bar codes and optical scanners to keep a daily running record of every box of cereal and every jar of jelly that it buys and sells. Under a perpetual inventory system, a company determines the cost of goods sold **each time a sale occurs**.

Periodic System

In a **periodic inventory system**, companies do not keep detailed inventory records of the goods on hand throughout the period. They determine the cost of goods sold **only at the end of the accounting period**—that is, periodically. At that point, the company takes a physical inventory count to determine the cost of goods on hand.

To determine the cost of goods sold under a periodic inventory system, the following steps are necessary:

1. Determine the cost of goods on hand at the beginning of the accounting period.
2. Add to it the cost of goods purchased.
3. Subtract the cost of goods on hand at the end of the accounting period.

Illustration 5-3 graphically compares the sequence of activities and the timing of the cost of goods sold computation under the two inventory systems.

Illustration 5-3
Comparing perpetual and periodic inventory systems

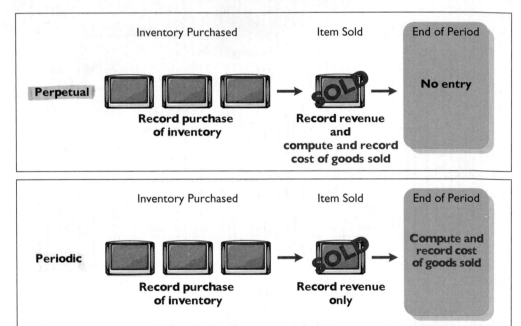

Additional Considerations

Companies that sell merchandise with high unit values, such as automobiles, furniture, and major home appliances, have traditionally used perpetual systems. The growing use of computers and electronic scanners has enabled many more companies to install perpetual inventory systems. The perpetual inventory system is so named because the accounting records continuously—perpetually—show the quantity and cost of the inventory that should be on hand at any time.

A perpetual inventory system provides better control over inventories than a periodic system. Since the inventory records show the quantities that should be on hand, the company can count the goods at any time to see whether the amount of goods actually on hand agrees with the inventory records. If shortages are uncovered, the company can investigate immediately. Although a perpetual inventory system requires additional clerical work and additional cost to maintain the subsidiary records, a computerized system can minimize this cost.

As noted in the Feature Story, much of Wal-Mart's success is attributed to its sophisticated inventory system.

Some businesses find it either unnecessary or uneconomical to invest in a computerized perpetual inventory system. Many small merchandising businesses, in particular, find that a perpetual inventory system costs more than it is worth. Managers of these businesses can control their merchandise and manage day-to-day operations using a periodic inventory system.

Because the perpetual inventory system is growing in popularity and use, we illustrate it in this chapter. An appendix to this chapter describes the journal entries for the periodic system.

Business Insight
Investor Perspective

Investors are often eager to invest in a company that has a hot new product. However, when snowboard maker Morrow Snowboards, Inc., issued shares of stock to the public for the first time, some investors expressed reluctance to invest in Morrow because of a number of accounting control problems. To reduce investor concerns, Morrow implemented a perpetual inventory system to improve its control over inventory. In addition, it stated that it would perform a physical inventory count every quarter until it felt that the perpetual inventory system was reliable.

 If a perpetual system keeps track of inventory on a daily basis, why do companies ever need to do a physical count?

Recording Purchases of Merchandise

Companies may purchase inventory for cash or on account (credit). They normally record purchases when they receive the goods from the seller. Every purchase should be supported by business documents that provide written evidence of the transaction. Each cash purchase should be supported by a canceled check or a cash register receipt indicating the items purchased and amounts paid. Companies record cash purchases by an increase in Merchandise Inventory and a decrease in Cash.

Each credit purchase should be supported by a **purchase invoice**, which indicates the total purchase price and other relevant information. However, the purchaser does not prepare a separate purchase invoice. Instead, the purchaser uses as a purchase invoice the copy of the sales invoice sent by the seller. In Illustration 5-4 (page 222), for example, Sauk Stereo (the buyer) uses as a purchase invoice the sales invoice prepared by PW Audio Supply, Inc. (the seller).

The associated entry for Sauk Stereo for the invoice from PW Audio Supply increases Merchandise Inventory and increases Accounts Payable.

STUDY OBJECTIVE
2

Explain the recording of purchases under a perpetual inventory system.

May 4	Merchandise Inventory	3,800	
	Accounts Payable		3,800
	(To record goods purchased on account from PW Audio Supply)		

A	=	L	+	SE
+3,800				
				+3,800

Cash Flows
no effect

Under the perpetual inventory system, companies record purchases of merchandise for sale in the Merchandise Inventory account. Thus, Wal-Mart would increase (debit) Merchandise Inventory for clothing, sporting goods, and anything else purchased for resale to customers. Not all purchases are debited to Merchandise Inventory, however. Companies record purchases of assets acquired

Illustration 5-4   Sales invoice used as purchase invoice by Sauk Stereo

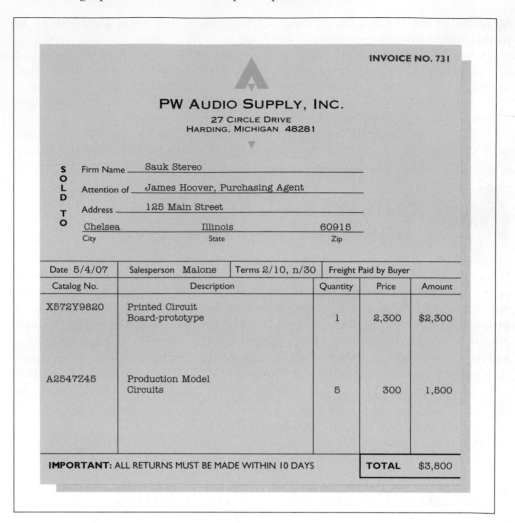

INVOICE NO. 731

PW AUDIO SUPPLY, INC.
27 CIRCLE DRIVE
HARDING, MICHIGAN 48281

S O L D T O

Firm Name _____ Sauk Stereo _____

Attention of _____ James Hoover, Purchasing Agent _____

Address _____ 125 Main Street _____

Chelsea   Illinois   60915
City   State   Zip

Date 5/4/07	Salesperson Malone	Terms 2/10, n/30	Freight Paid by Buyer		
Catalog No.	Description		Quantity	Price	Amount
X572Y9820	Printed Circuit Board-prototype		1	2,300	$2,300
A2547Z45	Production Model Circuits		5	300	1,500

IMPORTANT: ALL RETURNS MUST BE MADE WITHIN 10 DAYS	TOTAL	$3,800

Helpful Hint To better understand the contents of this invoice, identify these items:
1. Seller
2. Invoice date
3. Purchaser
4. Salesperson
5. Credit terms
6. Freight terms
7. Goods sold: catalog number, description, quantity, price per unit
8. Total invoice amount

for use and not for resale, such as supplies, equipment, and similar items, as increases to specific asset accounts rather than to Merchandise Inventory. For example, to record the purchase of materials used to make shelf signs or for cash register receipt paper, Wal-Mart would increase Supplies.

FREIGHT COSTS

Freight Costs Incurred by Buyer

The sales invoice indicates whether the seller or the buyer pays the cost of transporting the goods to the buyer's place of business. When the buyer pays the transportation costs, these costs are considered part of the cost of purchasing inventory. As a result, the account **Merchandise Inventory is increased**. For example, if Sauk Stereo (the buyer) pays Haul-It Freight Company $150 for freight charges on May 6, the entry on Sauk's books is:

A	=	L	+	SE
+150				
−150				

Cash Flows
−150

May	6	Merchandise Inventory	150	
		Cash		150
		(To record payment of freight on goods purchased)		

Freight Costs Incurred by Seller

In contrast, **freight costs incurred by the seller on outgoing merchandise are an operating expense to the seller**. These costs increase an expense account titled Freight-out or Delivery Expense. For example, if the freight terms on the invoice in Illustration 5-4 had required that PW Audio Supply (the seller) pay the $150 freight charges, the entry by PW Audio would be:

May 4	Freight-out	150	
	Cash		150
	(To record payment of freight on goods sold)		

A	=	L	+	SE
				−150 Exp
−150				

Cash Flows
−150

When the seller pays the freight charges, the seller will usually establish a higher invoice price for the goods, to cover the expense of shipping.

PURCHASE RETURNS AND ALLOWANCES

A purchaser may be dissatisfied with the merchandise received because the goods are damaged or defective, of inferior quality, or do not meet the purchaser's specifications. In such cases, the purchaser may return the goods to the seller for credit if the sale was made on credit, or for a cash refund if the purchase was for cash. This transaction is known as a **purchase return**. Alternatively, the purchaser may choose to keep the merchandise if the seller is willing to grant an allowance (deduction) from the purchase price. This transaction is known as a **purchase allowance**.

Assume that Sauk Stereo returned goods costing $300 to PW Audio Supply on May 8. The following entry by Sauk Stereo for the returned merchandise decreases Accounts Payable and decreases Merchandise Inventory.

May 8	Accounts Payable	300	
	Merchandise Inventory		300
	(To record return of goods purchased from PW Audio Supply)		

A	=	L	+	SE
		−300		
−300				

Cash Flows
no effect

Because Sauk Stereo increased Merchandise Inventory when the goods were received, Merchandise Inventory is decreased when Sauk returns the goods.

PURCHASE DISCOUNTS

The credit terms of a purchase on account may permit the buyer to claim a cash discount for prompt payment. The buyer calls this cash discount a **purchase discount**. This incentive offers advantages to both parties: The purchaser saves money, and the seller is able to shorten the operating cycle by converting the accounts receivable into cash earlier.

The **credit terms** specify the amount of the cash discount and time period during which it is offered. They also indicate the length of time in which the purchaser is expected to pay the full invoice price. In the sales invoice in Illustration 5-4, credit terms are 2/10, n/30, which is read "two-ten, net thirty." This means that a 2% cash discount may be taken on the invoice price less ("net of") any returns or allowances, if payment is made within 10 days of the invoice date (the **discount period**). Otherwise, the invoice price, less any returns or allowances, is due 30 days from the invoice date. Alternatively, the discount period may extend to a specified number of days following the month in which the sale occurs. For example, 1/10 EOM (end of month) means that a 1% discount is available if the invoice is paid within the first 10 days of the next month.

When the seller elects not to offer a cash discount for prompt payment, credit terms will specify only the maximum time period for paying the balance due. For example, the credit terms may state the time period as n/30, n/60, or n/10 EOM. This means, respectively, that the buyer must pay the net amount in 30 days, 60 days, or within the first 10 days of the next month.

Helpful Hint The term *net* in "net 30" means the remaining amount due after subtracting any sales returns and allowances and partial payments.

When an invoice is paid within the discount period, the amount of the discount decreases Merchandise Inventory. Why? Because the merchandiser records inventory at its cost and, by paying within the discount period, it has reduced that cost. To illustrate, assume Sauk Stereo pays the balance due of $3,500 (gross invoice price of $3,800 less purchase returns and allowances of $300) on May 14, the last day of the discount period. The cash discount is $70 ($3,500 × 2%), and the amount of cash Sauk Stereo paid is $3,430 ($3,500 − $70). The entry Sauk makes to record its May 14 payment decreases Accounts Payable by the amount of the gross invoice price, reduces Merchandise Inventory by the $70 discount, and reduces Cash by the net amount owed.

```
A  =  L  +  SE
     −3,500
−3,430
−70
```

Cash Flows
−3,430

May 14	Accounts Payable	3,500	
	Cash		3,430
	Merchandise Inventory		70
	(To record payment within discount period)		

If Sauk Stereo failed to take the discount and instead made full payment of $3,500 on June 3, Sauk would debit Accounts Payable and credit Cash for $3,500 each.

```
A  =  L  +  SE
     −3,500
−3,500
```
Cash Flows
−3,500

June 3	Accounts Payable	3,500	
	Cash		3,500
	(To record payment with no discount taken)		

A merchandising company usually should take all available discounts. Passing up the discount may be viewed as **paying interest** for use of the money. For example, passing up the discount offered by PW Audio would be like Sauk Stereo paying an interest rate of 2% for the use of $3,500 for 20 days. This is the equivalent of an annual interest rate of approximately 36.5% (2% × 365/20). Obviously, it would be better for Sauk Stereo to borrow at prevailing bank interest rates of 6% to 10% than to lose the discount.

SUMMARY OF PURCHASING TRANSACTIONS

The following T account (with transaction descriptions in blue) provides a summary of the effect of the previous transactions on Merchandise Inventory. Sauk originally purchased $3,800 worth of inventory for resale. It then returned $300 of goods. It paid $150 in freight charges, and finally, it received a $70 discount off the balance owed because it paid within the discount period. This results in a balance in Merchandise Inventory of $3,580.

Merchandise Inventory

Purchase	May 4	3,800	May 8	300	Purchase return
Freight-in	6	150	14	70	Purchase discount
Balance		3,580			

BEFORE YOU GO ON . . .

▶ **Review It**

1. How does a merchandising company measure net income differently from a service enterprise?

2. In what ways is a perpetual inventory system different from a periodic system?

3. Under the perpetual inventory system, what entries do companies make to record purchases, purchase returns and allowances, purchase discounts, and freight costs?

THE NAVIGATOR

Recording Sales of Merchandise

Companies record sales revenues, like service revenues, when earned, in compliance with the revenue recognition principle. Typically, companies earn sales revenues when the goods are transferred from the seller to the buyer. At this point the sales transaction is completed and the sales price is established.

Sales may be made on credit or for cash. Every sales transaction should be supported by a **business document** that provides written evidence of the sale. **Cash register tapes** provide evidence of cash sales. A sales invoice, like the one that was shown in Illustration 5-4 (page 222), provides support for a credit sale. The original copy of the invoice goes to the customer, and the seller keeps a copy for use in recording the sale. The invoice shows the date of sale, customer name, total sales price, and other relevant information.

The seller makes two entries for each sale: (1) It increases Accounts Receivable or Cash, as well as the Sales account. (2) It increases Cost of Goods Sold and decreases Merchandise Inventory. As a result, the Merchandise Inventory account will show at all times the amount of inventory that should be on hand.

To illustrate a credit sales transaction, PW Audio Supply records the sale of $3,800 on May 4 to Sauk Stereo (see Illustration 5-4) as follows (assume the merchandise cost PW Audio Supply $2,400).

May	4	Accounts Receivable	3,800	
		Sales		3,800
		(To record credit sale to Sauk Stereo per invoice #731)		
	4	Cost of Goods Sold	2,400	
		Merchandise Inventory		2,400
		(To record cost of merchandise sold on invoice #731 to Sauk Stereo)		

STUDY OBJECTIVE 3

Explain the recording of sales revenues under a perpetual inventory system.

A = L + SE
+3,800
+3,800 Rev

Cash Flows
no effect

A = L + SE
−2,400 Exp
−2,400

Cash Flows
no effect

Helpful Hint The merchandiser credits the Sales account only for sales of goods held for resale. Sales of assets not held for resale, such as equipment or land, are credited directly to the asset account.

For internal decision making purposes, merchandising companies may use more than one sales account. For example, PW Audio Supply may decide to keep separate sales accounts for its sales of TV sets, videocassette recorders, and microwave ovens. Wal-Mart might use separate accounts for sporting goods, children's clothing, and hardware—or it might have even more narrowly defined accounts. By using separate sales accounts for major product lines, rather than a single combined sales account, company management can monitor sales trends more closely and respond more strategically to changes in sales patterns. For example, if TV sales are increasing while microwave oven sales are decreasing, the company might reevaluate both its advertising and pricing policies on each of these items to ensure they are optimal.

On its income statement presented to outside investors a merchandising company would normally provide only a single sales figure—the sum of all of its individual sales accounts. This is done for two reasons. First, providing detail on all of its individual sales accounts would add considerable length to its income statement. Second, companies do not want their competitors to know the details of their operating results. However, Microsoft recently expanded its disclosure of revenue from three to five types. The reason: The additional categories will better enable financial statement users to evaluate the growth of the company's consumer and Internet businesses.

SALES RETURNS AND ALLOWANCES

We now look at the "flipside" of purchase returns and allowances, which the seller records as **sales returns and allowances**. PW Audio Supply's entries to record credit for returned goods involve (1) an increase in Sales Returns and Allowances and a decrease in Accounts Receivable at the $300 selling price, and (2) an increase in Merchandise Inventory (assume a $140 cost) and a decrease in Cost of Goods Sold as shown below. (We have assumed that the goods were not defective. If they were defective, PW Audio would make an adjustment to the inventory account to reflect their decline in value.)

A	=	L	+	SE
				−300 Rev
−300				

Cash Flows
no effect

A	=	L	+	SE
+140				
				+140 Exp

Cash Flows
no effect

May	8	Sales Returns and Allowances	300	
		Accounts Receivable		300
		(To record credit granted to Sauk Stereo for returned goods)		
	8	Merchandise Inventory	140	
		Cost of Goods Sold		140
		(To record cost of goods returned)		

Sales Returns and Allowances is a **contra revenue account** to Sales. The normal balance of Sales Returns and Allowances is a debit. Companies use a contra account, instead of debiting Sales, to disclose in the accounts and in the income statement the amount of sales returns and allowances. Disclosure of this information is important to management. Excessive returns and allowances suggest problems—inferior merchandise, inefficiencies in filling orders, errors in billing customers, or mistakes in delivery or shipment of goods. Moreover, a decrease (debit) recorded directly to Sales would obscure the relative importance of sales returns and allowances as a percentage of sales. It also could distort comparisons between total sales in different accounting periods.

Accounting across the Organization

In most industries sales returns are relatively minor. In the publishing industry, however, bookstores are allowed to return unsold hardcover books to the publisher. Marketing managers at the publishing companies argue that these generous return policies are necessary to encourage bookstores to buy a broader range of books, instead of focusing just on "sure things."

But with returns of hardcover books now exceeding 34% of sales, this generous return policy is taking its toll on net income. Production and inventory managers are quick to point out the many costs of excess returns. Publishers must pay to have the books shipped back to their warehouse, sorted, and then shipped to discounters. If the discounters don't sell them, the books are repackaged again, shipped back to the publisher, and destroyed. Some bookstores and publishers have proposed adopting a "no returns" policy, but no company wants to be the first one to implement it.

Source: Jeffrey A Trachtenberg, "Quest for Best Seller Creates a Pileup of Returned Books," *Wall Street Journal* (June 3, 2005), p. A1.

 If a company expects significant returns, what are the implications for revenue recognition?

SALES DISCOUNTS

As mentioned in our discussion of purchase transactions, the seller may offer the customer a cash discount—called by the seller a **sales discount**—for the prompt payment of the balance due. Like a purchase discount, a sales discount is based on the invoice price less returns and allowances, if any. The seller increases (debits) the Sales Discounts account for discounts that are taken. The entry by PW Audio Supply to record the cash receipt on May 14 from Sauk Stereo within the discount period is:

May 14	Cash	3,430	
	Sales Discounts	70	
	Accounts Receivable		3,500
	(To record collection within 2/10, n/30		
	discount period from Sauk Stereo)		

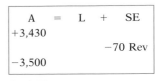

A	=	L	+	SE
+3,430				
				−70 Rev
−3,500				

Cash Flows
+3,430

Like Sales Returns and Allowances, Sales Discounts is a **contra revenue account** to Sales. Its normal balance is a debit. Sellers use this account, instead of debiting sales, to disclose the amount of cash discounts taken by customers. If the customer does not take the discount, PW Audio Supply increases Cash for $3,500 and decreases Accounts Receivable for the same amount at the date of collection.

BEFORE YOU GO ON . . .

▶ Review It

1. Under a perpetual inventory system, what are the two entries that a selling company must record at the time of each sale?
2. Why is it important to use the Sales Returns and Allowances account, rather than simply reducing the Sales account, when purchasers return goods?

▶ Do It

On September 5, De La Hoya Company buys merchandise on account from Junot Diaz Company. The selling price of the goods is $1,500, and the cost to Diaz Company was $800. On September 8, purchasers return goods with a selling price of $200 and a cost of $105. Record the transactions on the books of both companies.

Action Plan

• Purchaser records goods at cost.
• Seller records both the sale and the cost of goods sold at the time of the sale.
• When goods are returned, purchaser reduces Merchandise Inventory, but seller records the return in a contra account, Sales Returns and Allowances.

Solution

De La Hoya Company

Sept. 5	Merchandise Inventory	1,500	
	Accounts Payable		1,500
	(To record goods purchased on account)		
Sept. 8	Accounts Payable	200	
	Merchandise Inventory		200
	(To record return of defective goods)		

Junot Diaz Company

Sept.	5	Accounts Receivable	1,500	
		Sales		1,500
		(To record credit sale)		
	5	Cost of Goods Sold	800	
		Merchandise Inventory		800
		(To record cost of goods sold on account)		
Sept.	8	Sales Returns and Allowances	200	
		Accounts Receivable		200
		(To record credit granted for receipt of returned goods)		
	8	Merchandise Inventory	105	
		Cost of Goods Sold		105
		(To record cost of goods returned)		

THE NAVIGATOR

Income Statement Presentation

Companies widely use two forms of the income statement. One is the **single-step income statement**. The statement is so named because only one step, subtracting total expenses from total revenues, is required in determining net income (or net loss).

In a single-step statement, all data are classified into two categories: (1) **revenues**, which include both operating revenues and nonoperating revenues and gains (for example, interest revenue and gain on sale of equipment); and (2) **expenses**, which include cost of goods sold, operating expenses, and nonoperating expenses and losses (for example, interest expense, loss on sale of equipment, or income tax expense). The single-step income statement is the form we have used thus far in the text. Illustration 5-5 shows a single-step statement for Wal-Mart.

Illustration 5-5
Single-step income statements

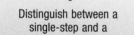

WAL-MART STORES, INC.
Income Statements
(in millions)

	For the years ended January 31	
	2004	**2003**
Revenues		
Net sales	$256,329	$229,616
Other revenues, net	2,352	1,961
	258,681	231,577
Expenses		
Cost of goods sold	198,747	178,299
Selling, general, and administrative expenses	44,909	39,983
Interest expense	832	927
Other expense	21	56
Income taxes	5,118	4,357
	249,627	223,622
Net income	$ 9,054	$ 7,955

There are two primary reasons for using the single-step form: (1) A company does not realize any type of profit or income until total revenues exceed total expenses, so it makes sense to divide the statement into these two categories. (2) The form is simple and easy to read.

A second form of the income statement is the **multiple-step income statement**. The multiple-step income statement is often considered more useful because it highlights the components of net income. The Wal-Mart income statement in Illustration 5-6 is an example.

WAL★MART
ALWAYS LOW PRICES.
Always

WAL-MART STORES, INC.
Income Statements
(in millions)

Illustration 5-6   Multiple-step income statements

	For the years ended January 31	
	2004	**2003**
Net sales	$256,329	$229,616
Cost of goods sold	198,747	178,299
Gross profit	57,582	51,317
Operating expenses		
Selling, general, and administrative expenses	44,909	39,983
Income from operations	12,673	11,334
Other revenues and gains		
Other revenues, net	2,352	1,961
Other expenses and losses		
Interest expense	832	927
Other expense	21	56
Income before income taxes	14,172	12,312
Income tax expense	5,118	4,357
Net income	$ 9,054	$ 7,955

The multiple-step income statement has three important line items: gross profit, income from operations, and net income. They are determined as follows.

1. Subtract cost of goods sold from sales to determine **gross profit**.
2. Deduct operating expenses from gross profit to determine **income from operations**.
3. Add or subtract the results of activities not related to operations to determine **net income**.

You should note that companies report income tax expense in a separate section of the income statement before net income. The following discussion provides additional information about the components of a multiple-step income statement.

SALES REVENUES

The income statement for a merchandising company typically presents gross sales revenues for the period. The company deducts sales returns and allowances and sales discounts (both contra accounts) from sales in the income statement to arrive at net sales. Illustration 5-7 (page 230) shows the sales revenues section of the income statement for PW Audio Supply.

Illustration 5-7
Statement presentation of
sales revenues section

PW AUDIO SUPPLY, INC.		
Income Statement (partial)		
Sales revenues		
Sales		$480,000
Less: Sales returns and allowances	$12,000	
Sales discounts	8,000	20,000
Net sales		**$460,000**

GROSS PROFIT

Alternative Terminology
Gross profit is sometimes
referred to as *gross margin*.

Companies deduct **cost of goods sold** from sales revenue to determine gross profit. As shown in Illustration 5-6, for example, Wal-Mart had a gross profit of $57.6 billion in fiscal year 2004. Sales revenue used for this computation is **net sales**, which takes into account sales returns and allowances and sales discounts.

On the basis of the PW Audio Supply sales data presented in Illustration 5-7 (net sales of $460,000) and the cost of goods sold (assume a balance of $316,000), PW Audio Supply's gross profit is $144,000, computed as follows.

GNet sales	$460,000
Cost of goods sold	316,000
Gross profit	**$144,000**

It is important to understand what gross profit is—and what it is not. Gross profit represents the **merchandising profit** of a company. Because operating expenses have not been deducted, it is *not* a measure of the overall profit of a company. Nevertheless, management and other interested parties closely watch the amount and trend of gross profit. Comparisons of current gross profit with past amounts and rates and with those in the industry indicate the effectiveness of a company's purchasing and pricing policies.

OPERATING EXPENSES

Operating expenses are the next component in measuring net income for a merchandising company. At Wal-Mart, for example, operating expenses were $44.9 billion in fiscal year 2004. These expenses are similar in merchandising and service enterprises.

At PW Audio Supply, operating expenses were $114,000. The firm determines its income from operations by subtracting operating expenses from gross profit. Thus, income from operations is $30,000, as shown below.

Gross profit	$144,000
Operating expenses	114,000
Income from operations	$ 30,000

NONOPERATING ACTIVITIES

Nonoperating activities consist of various revenues and expenses and gains and losses that are unrelated to the company's main line of operations. When nonoperating items are included, the label "**Income from operations**" (or "Operating income") precedes them. This label clearly identifies the results of the company's normal operations, an amount determined by subtracting cost of goods sold and operating expenses from net sales. The results of nonoperating activities are shown in the categories "**Other revenues and gains**" and "**Other expenses and losses**." Illustration 5-8 lists examples of each.

Illustration 5-8 Other items of nonoperating activities

Other Revenues and Gains
Interest revenue from notes receivable and marketable securities.
Dividend revenue from investments in capital stock.
Rent revenue from subleasing a portion of the store.
Gain from the sale of property, plant, and equipment.

Other Expenses and Losses
Interest expense on notes and loans payable.
Casualty losses from recurring causes, such as vandalism and accidents.
Loss from the sale or abandonment of property, plant, and equipment.
Loss from strikes by employees and suppliers.

The distinction between operating and nonoperating activities is crucial to many external users of financial data. These users view operating income as sustainable and many nonoperating activities as nonrecurring. Therefore, when forecasting next year's income, analysts put the most weight on this year's operating income, and less weight on this year's nonoperating activities.

Business Insight
Ethics Perspective

After Enron, increased investor criticism and regulator scrutiny forced many companies to improve the clarity of their financial disclosures. For example, IBM announced that it would begin providing more detail regarding its "Other gains and losses." It had previously included these items in its selling, general, and administrative expenses, with little disclosure.

Disclosing other gains and losses in a separate line item on the income statement will not have any effect on bottom-line income. However, analysts complained that burying these details in the selling, general, and administrative expense line reduced their ability to fully understand how well IBM was performing. For example, previously if IBM sold off one of its buildings at a gain, it would include this gain in the selling, general, and administrative expense line item, thus reducing that expense. This made it appear that the company had done a better job of controlling operating expenses than it actually had.

Other companies that also recently announced changes to increase the informativeness of their income statements included PepsiCo and General Electric.

 Why have investors and analysts demanded more accuracy in isolating "Other gains and losses" from operating items?

The nonoperating activities are reported in the income statement immediately after the operating activities. Included among these activities in Illustration 5-6 for Wal-Mart is net interest expense of $0.8 billion for fiscal year 2004. The amount remaining, after adding the operating and nonoperating sections together, is Wal-Mart's net income of $9.1 billion. Note that the net incomes in Illustrations 5-5 and 5-6 (pages 228 and 229) are the same. The difference in the two income statements is the amount of detail displayed and the order presented.

In Illustration 5-9 (on page 232) we have provided the multiple-step income statement of a hypothetical company. This statement provides more detail than that of Wal-Mart.

Illustration 5-9 Multiple-step income statement

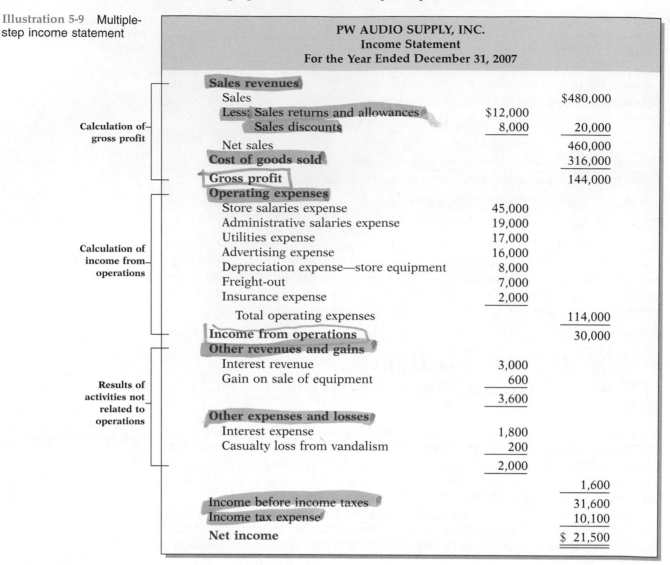

PW AUDIO SUPPLY, INC.
Income Statement
For the Year Ended December 31, 2007

Calculation of gross profit

Sales revenues		
Sales		$480,000
Less: Sales returns and allowances	$12,000	
Sales discounts	8,000	20,000
Net sales		460,000
Cost of goods sold		316,000
Gross profit		144,000

Calculation of income from operations

Operating expenses		
Store salaries expense	45,000	
Administrative salaries expense	19,000	
Utilities expense	17,000	
Advertising expense	16,000	
Depreciation expense—store equipment	8,000	
Freight-out	7,000	
Insurance expense	2,000	
Total operating expenses		114,000
Income from operations		30,000

Results of activities not related to operations

Other revenues and gains		
Interest revenue	3,000	
Gain on sale of equipment	600	
	3,600	
Other expenses and losses		
Interest expense	1,800	
Casualty loss from vandalism	200	
	2,000	
		1,600
Income before income taxes		31,600
Income tax expense		10,100
Net income		$ 21,500

For homework problems, use the multiple-step form of the income statement unless the requirements state otherwise.

BEFORE YOU GO ON . . .

▶ **Review It**

1. How are sales and contra revenue accounts reported in the income statement?
2. What is the significance of gross profit?
3. What title does Tootsie Roll use for gross profit? By what percentage did its gross profit change, and in what direction, in 2004? The answer to this question appears on p. 265.

THE NAVIGATOR

STUDY OBJECTIVE
5
Determine cost of goods sold under a periodic system.

DETERMINING COST OF GOODS SOLD UNDER A PERIODIC SYSTEM

Determining cost of goods sold is different under the periodic system than under the perpetual system. When a company uses a perpetual inventory system, it records all transactions affecting inventory (such as freight costs, returns, and discounts) directly to the Merchandise Inventory account. In addition, at the time of each sale the perpetual system requires a reduction in Merchandise Inventory and an increase in Cost of Goods Sold. But under a periodic system a company uses separate accounts to record freight costs, returns, and discounts. It does not maintain a running account of changes in inventory. Instead, it calculates the balance in ending inventory, as well as the cost of goods sold for the period, at the end of the period. Illustration 5-10 shows the determination of cost of goods sold for PW Audio Supply, using a periodic inventory system.

Illustration 5-10
Cost of goods sold for a merchandiser using a periodic inventory system

PW AUDIO SUPPLY, INC. Cost of Goods Sold For the Year Ended December 31, 2007			
Cost of goods sold			
Inventory, January 1			$ 36,000
Purchases		$325,000	
Less: Purchase returns and allowances	$10,400		
Purchase discounts	6,800	17,200	
Net purchases		307,800	
Add: Freight-in		12,200	
Cost of goods purchased			320,000
Cost of goods available for sale			356,000
Inventory, December 31			40,000
Cost of goods sold			$316,000

Helpful Hint The far right column identifies the primary items that make up cost of goods sold of $316,000. The middle column explains cost of goods purchased of $320,000. The left column reports contra purchase items of $17,200.

The use of the periodic inventory system does not affect the content of the balance sheet. As under the perpetual system, a company reports merchandise inventory at the same amount in the current assets section.

The appendix to this chapter provides further detail on the use of the periodic system.

BEFORE YOU GO ON . . .

▶ Review It

1. Discuss the steps used to determine cost of goods sold in a periodic inventory system.
2. What accounts do companies use in determining the cost of goods purchased?
3. In what ways is a perpetual inventory system different from a periodic inventory system?

▶ Do It

Aerosmith Company's accounting records show the following at the year-end December 31, 2007: Purchase Discounts $3,400; Freight-in $6,100; Purchases $162,500; Beginning Inventory $18,000; Ending Inventory $20,000; and Purchase Returns $5,200. Compute these amounts for Aerosmith Company using the periodic approach:
(a) Cost of goods purchased.
(b) Cost of goods sold.

Action Plan

• To determine cost of goods purchased, adjust purchases for returns, discounts, and freight-in.

• To determine cost of goods sold, add cost of goods purchased to beginning inventory, and subtract ending inventory.

Solution

(a) Cost of goods purchased:

Purchases − Purchase returns − Purchase discounts + Freight-in

$162,500 − $5,200 − $3,400 + $6,100 = $160,000

(b) Cost of goods sold:

Beginning inventory + Cost of goods purchased − Ending inventory

$18,000 + $160,000 − $20,000 = $158,000

Evaluating Profitability

GROSS PROFIT RATE

STUDY OBJECTIVE

6

Explain the factors affecting profitability.

A company's gross profit may be expressed as a **percentage** by dividing the amount of gross profit by net sales. This is referred to as the **gross profit rate**. For PW Audio Supply the gross profit rate is 31.3% ($144,000 ÷ $460,000).

Analysts generally consider the gross profit *rate* to be more informative than the gross profit *amount* because it expresses a more meaningful (qualitative) relationship between gross profit and net sales. For example, a gross profit amount of $1,000,000 may sound impressive. But if it was the result of sales of $100,000,000, the company's gross profit rate was only 1%. A 1% gross profit rate is acceptable in only a few industries. Illustration 5-11 presents gross profit rates of a variety of industries.

Illustration 5-11 Gross profit rate by industry

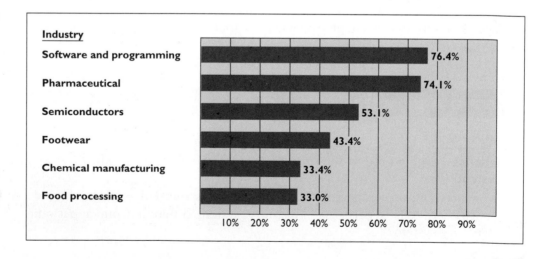

A decline in a company's gross profit rate might have several causes. The company may have begun to sell products with a lower "markup"—for example, budget blue jeans versus designer blue jeans. Increased competition may have resulted in a lower selling price. Or, the company may be forced to pay higher prices to its suppliers without being able to pass these costs on to its customers. The gross profit rates for Wal-Mart and Target, and the industry average, are presented in Illustration 5-12 on page 235.

Illustration 5-12 Gross profit rate

	Gross Profit Rate = $\dfrac{\text{Gross Profit}}{\text{Net Sales}}$	
	2004	**2003**
Wal-Mart ($ in millions)	$\dfrac{\$57,582}{\$256,329} = 22.5\%$	$\dfrac{\$51,317}{\$229,616} = 22.3\%$
Target	32.0%	31.5%
Industry average	26.9%	

Wal-Mart's gross profit rate increased from 22.3% in 2003 to 22.5% in 2004. In its Management Discussion and Analysis (MD&A), Wal-Mart explained, "This increase in gross margin occurred primarily due to a favorable shift in mix of products sold and our global sourcing efforts (which resulted in lower cost of merchandise sold), offset by increased apparel markdowns (price reductions) in the second half of the year."

At first glance it might be surprising that Wal-Mart has a lower gross profit rate than Target and the industry average. It is likely, however, that this can be explained by the fact that grocery products are becoming an increasingly large component of Wal-Mart's sales. In fact, in its MD&A, Wal-Mart says, "Because food items carry a lower gross margin than our other merchandise, increasing food sales tends to have an unfavorable impact on our total gross margin." Also, Wal-Mart has substantial warehouse-style sales in its Sam's Club stores, which are a low-margin, high-volume operation. In later chapters we will provide further discussion of the trade-off between sales volume and gross profit.

Decision Toolkit

Decision Checkpoints	Info Needed for Decision	Tool to Use for Decision	How to Evaluate Results
Is the price of goods keeping pace with changes in the cost of inventory?	Gross profit and net sales	$\text{Gross profit rate} = \dfrac{\text{Gross profit}}{\text{Net sales}}$	Higher ratio suggests the average margin between selling price and inventory cost is increasing. Too high a margin may result in lost sales.

PROFIT MARGIN RATIO

The **profit margin ratio** measures the percentage of each dollar of sales that results in net income. We compute this ratio by dividing net income by net sales (revenue) for the period.

How do the gross profit rate and profit margin ratio differ? The gross profit rate measures the margin by which selling price exceeds cost of goods sold. **The profit margin ratio measures the extent by which selling price covers all expenses** (including cost of goods sold). A company can improve its profit margin ratio by either increasing its gross profit rate and/or by controlling its operating expenses and other costs.

Profit margins vary across industries. Businesses with high turnover, such as grocery stores (Safeway and Kroger) and discount stores (Target and Wal-Mart), generally experience low profit margins. Low-turnover businesses, such as high-end jewelry stores (Tiffany and Co.) or major drug manufacturers (Merck), have high profit margins. Illustration 5-13 shows profit margin ratios from a variety of industries.

Illustration 5-13 Profit margin ratio by industry

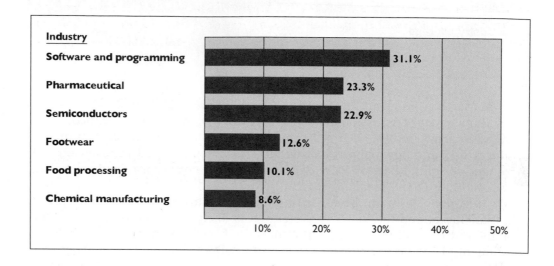

Profit margins for Wal-Mart and Target and the industry average are presented in Illustration 5-14.

Illustration 5-14 Profit margin ratio

Profit Margin Ratio = $\dfrac{\text{Net Income}}{\text{Net Sales}}$		
	2004	**2003**
Wal-Mart ($ in millions)	$\dfrac{\$9,054}{\$256,329} = 3.5\%$	$\dfrac{\$7,955}{\$229,616} = 3.5\%$
Target	3.9%	3.9%
Industry average	6.3%	

Wal-Mart's profit margin remained constant at 3.5% in 2003 and 2004. This means that the company generated 3.5 cents on each dollar of sales. How does Wal-Mart compare to its competitors? Its profit margin ratio was lower than Target's in both 2003 and 2004 and was less than the industry average. Thus, its profit margin ratio does not suggest exceptional profitability. However, we must again keep in mind that an increasing percentage of Wal-Mart's sales is from groceries. The average profit margin ratio for the grocery industry is only 3.1%.

Accounting across the Organization

In its death spiral toward bankruptcy, Kmart appeared to make two very costly strategic errors. First, in an effort to attract customers, it decided to reduce selling prices on over 30,000 items. The problem was that this reduced its gross profit rate—and didn't even have the intended effect of increasing sales because Wal-Mart quickly matched these price cuts. Since Wal-Mart operates much more efficiently than Kmart, Wal-Mart could afford to absorb these price cuts and still operate at a profit. Kmart could not. Its second error was to try to reduce operating costs by cutting its advertising expenditures. This resulted in a reduction in customers—and sales revenue.

 Explain how Wal-Mart's profitability gave it a strategic advantage over Kmart.

BEFORE YOU GO ON . . .

▶ **Review It**

1. How is the gross profit rate calculated? What might cause it to decline?
2. What effect does improved efficiency of operations have on the profit margin ratio?

 THE NAVIGATOR

Decision Toolkit

Decision Checkpoints	Info Needed for Decision	Tool to Use for Decision	How to Evaluate Results
Is the company maintaining an adequate margin between sales and expenses?	Net income and net sales	$\text{Profit margin ratio} = \dfrac{\text{Net income}}{\text{Net sales}}$	Higher value suggests favorable return on each dollar of sales.

Using the Decision Toolkit

After having once been as dominant as Wal-Mart, in recent years Sears has struggled to survive. It has enacted many changes trying to turn itself around. In the 1990s, it shocked and disappointed many loyal customers by closing its catalog business. It also closed 113 stores and eliminated 50,000 jobs. None of these changes was enough to make Sears truly competitive, so in March 2005 Sears merged with Kmart to form the third largest U.S. retailer. The following are pre-merger data for Sears.

	Year ended	
($ in millions)	01/03/04	12/28/02
Net income	$ 3,397	$ 1,376
Sales	36,372	35,698
Cost of goods sold	26,231	25,646

Instructions

Using the basic facts in the table, evaluate the following components of Sears's profitability for the years ended January 3, 2004 and December 28, 2002.

Profit margin ratio
Gross profit rate

How do Sears's profit margin ratio and gross profit rate compare to those of Wal-Mart and Target for 2004?

Solution

($ in millions)	Year ended	
	01/03/04	**12/28/02**
Profit margin ratio	$\dfrac{\$3,397}{\$36,372} = 9.3\%$	$\dfrac{\$1,376}{\$35,698} = 3.9\%$
Gross profit rate	$\dfrac{\$36,372 - \$26,231}{\$36,372} = 27.9\%$	$\dfrac{\$35,698 - \$25,646}{\$35,698} = 28.2\%$

Sears's profit margin ratio (income per dollar of sales) increased from 3.9% to 9.3%. This increase was due to the one-time sale of all of the assets and liabilities of its credit card and financial-products business, a nonoperating item. If we instead calculate the profit margin ratio using income from operations (see discussion on pages 235–236), Sears's profit margin ratio declined to 2.1%. This is well below both Wal-Mart's (3.5%) and Target's (3.9%). Thus, Sears is not as effective at turning its sales into net income as these two competitors.

Sears's gross profit rate declined from 28.2% to 27.9%. This suggests that its ability to maintain its mark-up above its cost of goods sold eroded during this period. Sears's gross profit rate of 27.9% is lower than Target's (32%) but higher than Wal-Mart's (22.5%). As discussed in the chapter, Wal-Mart's gross profit is depressed by the fact that it sells many grocery products, which are very low-margin. Target is superior to Sears both in its ability to maintain its mark-up above its costs of goods sold (its gross profit rate) and in its ability to control operating costs (its profit margin ratio).

Summary of Study Objectives

1 *Identify the differences between a service enterprise and a merchandising company.* Because of the presence of inventory, a merchandising company has sales revenue, cost of goods sold, and gross profit. To account for inventory, a merchandising company must choose between a perpetual inventory system and a periodic inventory system.

2 *Explain the recording of purchases under a perpetual inventory system.* The Merchandise Inventory account is debited for all purchases of merchandise and for freight costs, and it is credited for purchase discounts and purchase returns and allowances.

3 *Explain the recording of sales revenues under a perpetual inventory system.* When inventory is sold, Accounts Receivable (or Cash) is debited and Sales is credited for the selling price of the merchandise. At the same time, Cost of Goods Sold is debited and Merchandise Inventory is credited for the cost of inventory items sold. Subsequent entries are required for (a) sales returns and allowances and (b) sales discounts.

4 *Distinguish between a single-step and a multiple-step income statement.* In a single-step income statement, companies classify all data under two categories, revenues or expenses, and net income is determined in one step. A multiple-step income statement shows numerous steps in determining net income, including results of nonoperating activities.

5 *Determine cost of goods sold under a periodic system.* The periodic system uses multiple accounts to keep track of transactions that affect inventory. To determine cost of goods sold, first calculate cost of goods purchased by adjusting purchases for returns, allowances, discounts, and freight-in. Then calculate cost of goods sold by adding cost of goods purchased to beginning inventory and subtracting ending inventory.

6 *Explain the factors affecting profitability.* Profitability is affected by gross profit, as measured by the gross profit rate, and by management's ability to control costs, as measured by the profit margin ratio.

Decision Toolkit—A Summary

Decision Checkpoints	Info Needed for Decision	Tool to Use for Decision	How to Evaluate Results
Is the price of goods keeping pace with changes in the cost of inventory?	Gross profit and net sales	$\text{Gross profit rate} = \dfrac{\text{Gross profit}}{\text{Net sales}}$	Higher ratio suggests the average margin between selling price and inventory cost is increasing. Too high a margin may result in lost sales.
Is the company maintaining an adequate margin between sales and expenses?	Net income and net sales	$\text{Profit margin ratio} = \dfrac{\text{Net income}}{\text{Net sales}}$	Higher value suggests favorable return on each dollar of sales.

APPENDIX
PERIODIC INVENTORY SYSTEM

As described in this chapter, companies may use one of two basic systems of accounting for inventories: (1) the perpetual inventory system or (2) the periodic inventory system. In the chapter we focused on the characteristics of the perpetual inventory system. In this appendix we discuss and illustrate the **periodic inventory system.** One key difference between the two systems is the point at which the company computes cost of goods sold. For a visual reminder of this difference, you may want to refer back to Illustration 5-3 on page 220.

Recording Merchandise Transactions

In a **periodic inventory system,** companies record revenues from the sale of merchandise when sales are made, just as in a perpetual system. Unlike the perpetual system, however, companies **do not attempt on the date of sale to record the cost of the merchandise sold.** Instead, they take a physical inventory count at the **end of the period** to determine (1) the cost of the merchandise then on hand and (2) the cost of the goods sold during the period. And, **under a periodic system, companies record purchases of merchandise in the Purchases account rather than the Merchandise Inventory account.** Also, in a periodic system, purchase returns and allowances, purchase discounts, and freight costs on purchases are recorded in separate accounts.

To illustrate the recording of merchandise transactions under a periodic inventory system, we will use purchase/sale transactions between PW Audio Supply, Inc. and Sauk Stereo, as illustrated for the perpetual inventory system in this chapter.

> **STUDY OBJECTIVE**
> **7**
> Explain the recording of purchases and sales of inventory under a periodic inventory system.

Recording Purchases of Merchandise

On the basis of the sales invoice (Illustration 5-4, shown on page 222) and receipt of the merchandise ordered from PW Audio Supply, Sauk Stereo records the $3,800 purchase as follows.

May	4	Purchases	3,800	
		Accounts Payable		3,800
		(To record goods purchased on account		
		from PW Audio Supply)		

Purchases is a temporary account whose normal balance is a debit.

FREIGHT COSTS

When the purchaser directly incurs the freight costs, it debits the account Freight-in (or Transportation-in). For example, if Sauk pays Haul-It Freight Company $150 for freight charges on its purchase from PW Audio Supply on May 6, the entry on Sauk's books is:

May	6	Freight-in (Transportation-in)	150	
		Cash		150
		(To record payment of freight on goods		
		purchased)		

Like Purchases, Freight-in is a temporary account whose normal balance is a debit. **Freight-in is part of cost of goods purchased.** The reason is that cost of goods purchased should include any freight charges necessary to bring the goods to the purchaser. Freight costs are not subject to a purchase discount. Purchase discounts apply on the invoice cost of the merchandise.

PURCHASE RETURNS AND ALLOWANCES

Because $300 of merchandise received from PW Audio Supply is inoperable, Sauk Stereo returns the goods and prepares the following entry to recognize the return.

May	8	Accounts Payable	300	
		Purchase Returns and Allowances		300
		(To record return of goods		
		purchased from PW Audio Supply)		

Purchase Returns and Allowances is a temporary account whose normal balance is a credit.

PURCHASE DISCOUNTS

On May 14 Sauk Stereo pays the balance due on account to PW Audio Supply, taking the 2% cash discount allowed by PW Audio for payment within 10 days. Sauk Stereo records the payment and discount as follows.

May	14	Accounts Payable ($3,800 − $300)	3,500	
		Purchase Discounts ($3,500 × .02)		70
		Cash		3,430
		(To record payment within the		
		discount period)		

Purchase Discounts is a temporary account whose normal balance is a credit.

Recording Sales of Merchandise

The seller, PW Audio Supply, records the sale of $3,800 of merchandise to Sauk Stereo on May 4 (sales invoice No. 731, Illustration 5-4) as follows.

May	4	Accounts Receivable	3,800	
		Sales		3,800
		(To record credit sales per invoice #731 to Sauk Stereo)		

SALES RETURNS AND ALLOWANCES

To record the returned goods received from Sauk Stereo on May 8, PW Audio Supply records the $300 sales return as follows.

May	8	Sales Returns and Allowances	300	
		Accounts Receivable		300
		(To record credit granted to Sauk Stereo for returned goods)		

SALES DISCOUNTS

On May 14, PW Audio Supply receives payment of $3,430 on account from Sauk Stereo. PW Audio honors the 2% cash discount and records the payment of Sauk's account receivable in full as follows.

May	14	Cash	3,430	
		Sales Discounts ($3,500 × .02)	70	
		Accounts Receivable ($3,800 − $300)		3,500
		(To record collection within 2/10, n/30 discount period from Sauk Stereo)		

COMPARISON OF ENTRIES— PERPETUAL vs. PERIODIC

ENTRIES ON SAUK STEREO'S BOOKS

Transaction		Perpetual Inventory System			Periodic Inventory System		
May 4	Purchase of merchandise on credit.	Merchandise Inventory	3,800		Purchases	3,800	
		Accounts Payable		3,800	Accounts Payable		3,800
May 6	Freight costs on purchases.	Merchandise Inventory	150		Freight-in	150	
		Cash		150	Cash		150
May 8	Purchase returns and allowances.	Accounts Payable	300		Accounts Payable	300	
		Merchandise Inventory		300	Purchase Returns and Allowances		300
May 14	Payment on account with a discount.	Accounts Payable	3,500		Accounts Payable	3,500	
		Cash		3,430	Cash		3,430
		Merchandise Inventory		70	Purchase Discounts		70

ENTRIES ON PW AUDIO SUPPLY'S BOOKS

Transaction		Perpetual Inventory System			Periodic Inventory System		
May 4	Sale of merchandise on credit.	Accounts Receivable	3,800		Accounts Receivable	3,800	
		Sales Revenue		3,800	Sales Revenue		3,800
		Cost of Goods Sold	2,400		No entry for cost of goods sold		
		Merchandise Inventory		2,400			
May 8	Return of merchandise sold.	Sales Returns and Allowances	300		Sales Returns and Allowances	300	
		Accounts Receivable		300	Accounts Receivable		300
		Merchandise Inventory	140		No entry		
		Cost of Goods Sold		140			
May 14	Cash received on account with a discount.	Cash	3,430		Cash	3,430	
		Sales Discounts	70		Sales Discounts	70	
		Accounts Receivable		3,500	Accounts Receivable		3,500

Summary of Study Objective for Appendix

7 *Explain the recording of purchases and sales of inventory under a periodic inventory system.* To record purchases, entries are required for (a) cash and credit purchases, (b) purchase returns and allowances, (c) purchase discounts, and (d) freight costs. To record sales, entries are required for (a) cash and credit sales, (b) sales returns and allowances, and (c) sales discounts.

Glossary

Contra revenue account An account that is offset against a revenue account on the income statement. (p. 226)

Cost of goods sold The total cost of merchandise sold during the period. (p. 218)

Gross profit The excess of net sales over the cost of goods sold. (p. 230)

Gross profit rate Gross profit expressed as a percentage by dividing the amount of gross profit by net sales. (p. 234)

Net sales Sales less sales returns and allowances and sales discounts. (p. 229)

Periodic inventory system An inventory system in which a company does not maintain detailed records of goods on hand and determines the cost of goods sold only at the end of an accounting period. (p. 220)

Perpetual inventory system A detailed inventory system in which a company maintains the cost of each inventory item and the records continuously show the inventory that should be on hand. (p. 219)

Profit margin ratio Measures the percentage of each dollar of sales that results in net income, computed by dividing net income by net sales. (p. 235)

Purchase allowance A deduction made to the selling price of merchandise, granted by the seller so that the buyer will keep the merchandise. (p. 223)

Purchase discount A cash discount claimed by a buyer for prompt payment of a balance due. (p. 223)

Purchase invoice A document that supports each credit purchase. (p. 221)

Purchase return A return of goods from the buyer to the seller for cash or credit. (p. 223)

Sales discount A reduction given by a seller for prompt payment of a credit sale. (p. 227)

Sales invoice A document that provides support for credit sales. (p. 225)

Sales returns and allowances Purchase returns and allowances from the seller's perspective. See definitions for purchase returns and purchase allowances. (p. 226)

Sales revenue Primary source of revenue in a merchandising company. (p. 218)

Demonstration Problem

The adjusted trial balance for the year ended December 31, 2007, for Dykstra Company is shown below.

DYKSTRA COMPANY
Adjusted Trial Balance
For the Year Ended December 31, 2007

	Dr.	Cr.
Cash	$ 14,500	
Accounts Receivable	11,100	
Merchandise Inventory	29,000	
Prepaid Insurance	2,500	
Store Equipment	95,000	
Accumulated Depreciation		$ 18,000
Notes Payable		25,000
Accounts Payable		10,600
Common Stock		70,000
Retained Earnings		11,000
Dividends	12,000	

	Dr.	Cr.
Sales		536,800
Sales Returns and Allowances	6,700	
Sales Discounts	5,000	
Cost of Goods Sold	363,400	
Freight-out	7,600	
Advertising Expense	12,000	
Store Salaries Expense	56,000	
Utilities Expense	18,000	
Rent Expense	24,000	
Depreciation Expense	9,000	
Insurance Expense	4,500	
Interest Expense	3,600	
Interest Revenue		2,500
	$673,900	$673,900

Instructions

Prepare a multiple-step income statement for Dykstra Company.

Solution to Demonstration Problem

DYKSTRA COMPANY
Income Statement
For the Year Ended December 31, 2007

Sales revenues		
Sales		$536,800
Less: Sales returns and allowances	$ 6,700	
Sales discounts	5,000	11,700
Net sales		525,100
Cost of goods sold		363,400
Gross profit		161,700
Operating expenses		
Store salaries expense	56,000	
Rent expense	24,000	
Utilities expense	18,000	
Advertising expense	12,000	
Depreciation expense	9,000	
Freight-out	7,600	
Insurance expense	4,500	
Total operating expenses		131,100
Income from operations		30,600
Other revenues and gains		
Interest revenue	2,500	
Other expenses and losses		
Interest expense	3,600	1,100
Net income		$ 29,500

Action Plan

• In preparing the income statement, remember that the key components are net sales, cost of goods sold, gross profit, total operating expenses, and net income (loss). These components are reported in the right-hand column of the income statement.

• Present nonoperating items after income from operations.

Note: All Questions, Exercises, and Problems marked with an asterisk relate to material in the appendix to the chapter.

Self-Study Questions

Answers are at the end of the chapter.

(SO 1) **1.** Which of the following statements about a periodic inventory system is true?
  (a) Companies determine cost of goods sold only at the end of the accounting period.
  (b) Companies continuously maintain detailed records of the cost of each inventory purchase and sale.
  (c) The periodic system provides better control over inventories than a perpetual system.
  (d) The increased use of computerized systems has increased the use of the periodic system.

(SO 2) **2.** Which of the following items does *not* result in an adjustment in the merchandise inventory account under a perpetual system?
  (a) A purchase of merchandise.
  (b) A return of merchandise inventory to the supplier.
  (c) Payment of freight costs for goods shipped to a customer.
  (d) Payment of freight costs for goods received from a supplier.

(SO 3) **3.** Which sales accounts normally have a debit balance?
  (a) Sales discounts.
  (b) Sales returns and allowances.
  (c) Both (a) and (b).
  (d) Neither (a) nor (b).

(SO 3) **4.** A company makes a credit sale of $750 on June 13, terms 2/10, n/30, on which it grants a return of $50 on June 16. What amount is received as payment in full on June 23?
  (a) $700.   (c) $685.
  (b) $686.   (d) $650.

(SO 4) **5.** Gross profit will result if:
  (a) operating expenses are less than net income.
  (b) sales revenues are greater than operating expenses.
  (c) sales revenues are greater than cost of goods sold.
  (d) operating expenses are greater than cost of goods sold.

(SO 4) **6.** If sales revenues are $400,000, cost of goods sold is $310,000, and operating expenses are $60,000, what is the gross profit?
  (a) $30,000.   (c) $340,000.
  (b) $90,000.   (d) $400,000.

(SO 4) **7.** The income statement for a merchandising company shows each of these features *except:*
  (a) gross profit.
  (b) cost of goods sold.
  (c) a sales revenue section.
  (d) All of these are present.

(SO 5) **8.** If beginning inventory is $60,000, cost of goods purchased is $380,000, and ending inventory is $50,000, what is cost of goods sold under a periodic system?
  (a) $390,000.   (c) $330,000.
  (b) $370,000.   (d) $420,000.

(SO 6) **9.** Which of the following would affect the gross profit rate? (Assume sales remains constant.)
  (a) An increase in advertising expense.
  (b) A decrease in depreciation expense.
  (c) An increase in cost of goods sold.
  (d) A decrease in insurance expense.

(SO 6) **10.** The gross profit *rate* is equal to:
  (a) net income divided by sales.
  (b) cost of goods sold divided by sales.
  (c) net sales minus cost of goods sold, divided by net sales.
  (d) sales minus cost of goods sold, divided by cost of goods sold.

(SO 6) **11.** Which factor would *not* affect the gross profit rate?
  (a) An increase in the cost of heating the store.
  (b) An increase in the sale of luxury items.
  (c) An increase in the use of "discount pricing" to sell merchandise.
  (d) An increase in the price of inventory items.

(SO 7) ***12.** When goods are purchased for resale by a company using a periodic inventory system:
  (a) purchases on account are debited to Merchandise Inventory.
  (b) purchases on account are debited to Purchases.
  (c) purchase returns are debited to Purchase Returns and Allowances.
  (d) freight costs are debited to Purchases.

Go to the book's website, **www.wiley.com/college/kimmel**, to access additional Self-Study Questions.

Questions

1. (a) "The steps in the accounting cycle for a merchandising company differ from the steps in the accounting cycle for a service enterprise." Do you agree or disagree?
   (b) Is the measurement of net income in a merchandising company conceptually the same as in a service enterprise? Explain.

2. How do the components of revenues and expenses differ between a merchandising company and a service enterprise?

3. Jennifer Hopkins, CEO of Pay-A-Lot Discount Stores, is considering a recommendation made by both the company's purchasing manager and director of finance that the company should invest in a sophisticated new perpetual inventory system to replace its periodic system. Explain the primary difference between the two systems, and discuss the potential benefits of a perpetual inventory system.

4. (a) Explain the income measurement process in a merchandising company.
   (b) How does income measurement differ between a merchandising company and a service company?

5. Nick Bickler Co. has sales revenue of $100,000, cost of goods sold of $68,000, and operating expenses of $20,000. What is its gross profit?

6. Sheri Lynn believes revenues from credit sales may be earned before they are collected in cash. Do you agree? Explain.

7. (a) What is the primary source document for recording (1) cash sales and (2) credit sales?
   (b) Using XXs for amounts, give the journal entry for each of the transactions in part (a).

8. A credit sale is made on July 10 for $800, terms 2/10, n/30. On July 12, the purchaser returns $100 of goods for credit. Give the journal entry on July 19 to record the receipt of the balance due within the discount period.

9. As the end of Ray Company's fiscal year-end approached, it became clear that the company had considerable excess inventory. Alexander McBain, the head of marketing and sales, ordered salespeople to "add 20% more units to each order that you ship. The customers can always ship the extra back next period if they decide they don't want it. We've got to do it to meet this year's sales goal." Discuss the accounting implications of Alexander's action.

10. To encourage bookstores to buy a broader range of book titles, and to discourage price discounting, the publishing industry allows bookstores to return unsold books to the publisher. This results in very significant returns each year. To ensure proper recognition of revenues, how should publishing companies account for these returns?

11. Goods costing $1,600 are purchased on account on July 15 with credit terms of 2/10, n/30. On July 18 the purchaser receives a $200 credit memo from the supplier for damaged goods. Give the journal entry on July 24 to record payment of the balance due within the discount period.

12. Roscna Company reports net sales of $800,000, gross profit of $580,000, and net income of $260,000. What are its operating expenses?

13. DeGroot Company has always provided its customers with payment terms of 1/10, n/30. Members of its sale force have commented that competitors are offering customers 2/10, n/45. Explain what these terms mean, and discuss the implications to DeGroot of switching its payment terms to those of its competitors.

14. In its year-end earnings announcement press release, Optimistic Corp. announced that its earnings increased by $15 million relative to the previous year. This represented a 20% increase. Inspection of its income statement reveals that the company reported a $20 million gain under "Other revenues and gains" from the sale of one of its factories. Discuss the implications of this gain from the perspective of a potential investor.

15. Identify the distinguishing features of an income statement for a merchandising company.

16. Why is the normal operating cycle for a merchandising company likely to be longer than for a service company?

17. What merchandising account(s) will appear in the post-closing trial balance?

18. What types of businesses are most likely to use a perpetual inventory system?

19. Identify the accounts that are added to or deducted from purchases to determine the cost of goods purchased under a periodic system. For each account, indicate (a) whether it is added or deducted and (b) its normal balance.

20. In the following cases, use a periodic inventory system to identify the item(s) designated by the letters X and Y.
    (a) Purchases $- X - Y =$ Net purchases.
    (b) Cost of goods purchased $-$ Net purchases $= X$.
    (c) Beginning inventory $+ X =$ Cost of goods available for sale.
    (d) Cost of goods available for sale $-$ Cost of goods sold $= X$.

21. What two ratios measure factors that affect profitability?

22. What factors affect a company's gross profit rate—that is, what can cause the gross profit rate to increase and what can cause it to decrease?

23. Walter Lee, director of marketing, wants to reduce the selling price of his company's products by 15% to increase market share. He says, "I know this will reduce our gross profit rate, but the increased number of units sold will make up for the lost margin."

Before this action is taken, what other factors does the company need to consider?

*24. On July 15 a company purchases on account goods costing $1,600, with credit terms of 2/10, n/30. On July 18 the company receives a $200 credit memo from the supplier for damaged goods. Give the journal entry on July 24 to record payment of the balance due within the discount period assuming a periodic inventory system.

Brief Exercises

Compute missing amounts in determining net income.
(SO 1, 4)

BE5-1   Presented here are the components in Michelle Wilson Company's income statement. Determine the missing amounts.

Sales	Cost of Goods Sold	Gross Profit	Operating Expenses	Net Income
$ 71,200	(b)	$ 39,000	(d)	$10,800
$108,000	$65,000	(c)	(e)	$29,500
(a)	$71,900	$109,600	$46,200	(f)

Journalize perpetual inventory entries.
(SO 2, 3)

BE5-2   Clare Company buys merchandise on account from Muni Company. The selling price of the goods is $900 and the cost of the goods sold is $660. Both companies use perpetual inventory systems. Journalize the transactions on the books of both companies.

Journalize sales transactions.
(SO 3)

BE5-3   Prepare the journal entries to record the following transactions on Panther Company's books using a perpetual inventory system.
(a) On March 2 Panther Company sold $900,000 of merchandise to Eagle Company, terms 2/10, n/30. The cost of the merchandise sold was $540,000.
(b) On March 6 Eagle Company returned $110,000 of the merchandise purchased on March 2. The cost of the merchandise returned was $65,000.
(c) On March 12 Panther Company received the balance due from Eagle Company.

Journalize purchase transactions.
(SO 2)

BE5-4   From the information in BE5-3, prepare the journal entries to record these transactions on Eagle Company's books under a perpetual inventory system.

Prepare sales revenue section of income statement.
(SO 4)

BE5-5   Marquette Company provides this information for the month ended October 31, 2007: sales on credit $300,000; cash sales $130,000; sales discounts $5,000; and sales returns and allowances $22,000. Prepare the sales revenues section of the income statement based on this information.

Identify placement of items on a multiple-step income statement.
(SO 4)

BE5-6   Explain where each of these items would appear on a multiple-step income statement: gain on sale of equipment, cost of goods sold, depreciation expense, and sales returns and allowances.

Compute net purchases and cost of goods purchased.
(SO 5)

BE5-7   Assume that Roshek Company uses a periodic inventory system and has these account balances: Purchases $424,000; Purchase Returns and Allowances $11,000; Purchase Discounts $7,000; and Freight-in $16,000. Determine net purchases and cost of goods purchased.

Compute cost of goods sold and gross profit.
(SO 5)

BE5-8   Assume the same information as in BE5-7 and also that Roshek Company has beginning inventory of $60,000, ending inventory of $90,000, and net sales of $650,000. Determine the amounts to be reported for cost of goods sold and gross profit.

Calculate profitability ratios.
(SO 6)

BE5-9   Red Wall Corporation reported net sales of $250,000, cost of goods sold of $100,000, operating expenses of $50,000, net income of $87,500, beginning total assets of $500,000, and ending total assets of $600,000. Calculate each of the following values and explain what they mean.
(a) Profit margin ratio.   (b) Gross profit rate.

Calculate profitability ratios.
(SO 6)

BE5-10   Beardsley Corporation reported net sales $580,000; cost of goods sold $300,000; operating expenses $210,000; and net income $70,000. Calculate the following values and explain what they mean.
(a) Profit margin ratio.   (b) Gross profit rate.

*BE5-11 Prepare the journal entries to record these transactions on Powell Company's books using a periodic inventory system.

(a) On March 2, Powell Company purchased $900,000 of merchandise from Rice Company, terms 2/10, n/30.
(b) On March 6 Powell Company returned $110,000 of the merchandise purchased on March 2 because it was defective.
(c) On March 12 Powell Company paid the balance due to Rice Company.

Exercises

E5-1 The following transactions are for Kale Company.

1. On December 3 Kale Company sold $480,000 of merchandise to Thomson Co., terms 1/10, n/30. The cost of the merchandise sold was $320,000.
2. On December 8 Thomson Co. was granted an allowance of $28,000 for merchandise purchased on December 3.
3. On December 13 Kale Company received the balance due from Thomson Co.

Instructions
(a) Prepare the journal entries to record these transactions on the books of Kale Company. Kale uses a perpetual inventory system.
(b) Assume that Kale Company received the balance due from Thomson Co. on January 2 of the following year instead of December 13. Prepare the journal entry to record the receipt of payment on January 2.

E5-2 Assume that on September 1 Office Depot had an inventory that included a variety of calculators. The company uses a perpetual inventory system. During September these transactions occurred.

Sept.	6	Purchased calculators from Black Box Co. at a total cost of $1,620, terms n/30.
	9	Paid freight of $50 on calculators purchased from Black Box Co.
	10	Returned calculators to Black Box Co. for $38 credit because they did not meet specifications.
	12	Sold calculators costing $520 for $780 to University Book Store, terms n/30.
	14	Granted credit of $45 to University Book Store for the return of one calculator that was not ordered. The calculator cost $28.
	20	Sold calculators costing $570 for $900 to Campus Card Shop, terms n/30.

Instructions
Journalize the September transactions.

E5-3 This information relates to Sherper Co.

1. On April 5 purchased merchandise from Newport Company for $22,000, terms 2/10, n/30.
2. On April 6 paid freight costs of $900 on merchandise purchased from Newport.
3. On April 7 purchased equipment on account for $26,000.
4. On April 8 returned some of April 5 merchandise to Newport Company which cost $3,600.
5. On April 15 paid the amount due to Newport Company in full.

Instructions
(a) Prepare the journal entries to record the transactions listed above on the books of Sherper Co. Sherper Co. uses a perpetual inventory system.
(b) Assume that Sherper Co. paid the balance due to Newport Company on May 4 instead of April 15. Prepare the journal entry to record this payment.

E5-4 On June 10 Mawmey Company purchased $6,000 of merchandise from Lima Company, terms 3/10, n/30. Mawmey pays the freight costs of $400 on June 11. Damaged goods totaling $500 are returned to Lima for credit on June 12. On June 19 Mawmey Company pays Lima Company in full, less the purchase discount. Both companies use a perpetual inventory system.

Instructions
(a) Prepare separate entries for each transaction on the books of Mawmey Company.
(b) Prepare separate entries for each transaction for Lima Company. The merchandise purchased by Mawmey on June 10 cost Lima $3,000, and the goods returned cost Lima $240.

Prepare sales revenues section of income statement.
(SO 4)

E5-5 The adjusted trial balance of Brighton Company shows these data pertaining to sales at the end of its fiscal year, October 31, 2007: Sales $900,000; Freight-out $12,000; Sales Returns and Allowances $15,000; and Sales Discounts $13,500.

Instructions
Prepare the sales revenues section of the income statement.

Prepare an income statement and calculate profitability ratios.
(SO 4, 6)

E5-6 Presented below is information for Zales Co. for the month of January 2007.

Cost of goods sold	$212,000	Rent expense	$ 32,000
Freight-out	7,000	Sales discounts	8,000
Insurance expense	12,000	Sales returns and allowances	13,000
Salary expense	58,000	Sales	370,000

Instructions
(a) Prepare an income statement using the format presented on page 232.
(b) Calculate the profit margin ratio and the gross profit rate.

Compute missing amounts and calculate profitability ratios.
(SO 4, 6)

E5-7 Financial information is presented here for two companies.

	King Company	Queen Company
Sales	$90,000	?
Sales returns	?	$ 5,000
Net sales	81,000	100,000
Cost of goods sold	56,700	?
Gross profit	?	38,000
Operating expenses	14,580	?
Net income	?	18,000

Instructions
(a) Fill in the missing amounts. Show all computations.
(b) Calculate the profit margin ratio and the gross profit rate for each company.
(c) Discuss your findings in part (b).

Prepare multiple-step income statement and calculate profitability ratios.
(SO 4, 6)

E5-8 In its income statement for the year ended December 31, 2007, Knitz Company reported the following condensed data.

Administrative expenses	$435,000	Selling expenses	$ 690,000
Cost of goods sold	987,000	Loss on sale of equipment	83,500
Interest expense	68,000	Net sales	2,350,000
Interest revenue	45,000		

Instructions
(a) Prepare a multiple-step income statement.
(b) Calculate the profit margin ratio and gross profit rate.
(c) In 2006 Knitz had a profit margin ratio of 9%. Is the decline in 2007 a cause for concern?

E5-9 In its income statement for the year ended June 30, 2004, The Clorox Company reported the following condensed data (dollars in millions).

Prepare multiple-step income statement and calculate profitability ratios.
(SO 4, 6)

Selling and administrative expenses	$ 552	Research and development expense	$ 84
Net sales	4,324	Income tax expense	294
Interest expense	30	Other income	1
Advertising expense	429	Cost of goods sold	2,387

Instructions
(a) Prepare a multiple-step income statement.
(b) Calculate the gross profit rate and the profit margin ratio and explain what each means.
(c) Assume the marketing department has presented a plan to increase advertising expenses by $300 million. It expects this plan to result in an increase in both net sales and cost of goods sold of 25%. Redo parts (a) and (b) and discuss whether this plan has merit. (Assume a tax rate of 35%, and round all amounts to whole dollars.)

E5-10 The trial balance of Rachel Company at the end of its fiscal year, August 31, 2007, includes these accounts: Merchandise Inventory $19,200; Purchases $144,000; Sales $190,000; Freight-in $8,000; Sales Returns and Allowances $3,000; Freight-out $1,000; and Purchase Returns and Allowances $5,000. The ending merchandise inventory is $25,000.

Prepare cost of goods sold section.
(SO 5)

Instructions
Prepare a cost of goods sold section for the year ending August 31.

E5-11 Below is a series of cost of goods sold sections for companies X, F, L, and S.

Prepare cost of goods sold section.
(SO 5)

	X	F	L	S
Beginning inventory	$ 250	$ 120	$1,000	$ (j)
Purchases	1,500	1,080	(g)	43,590
Purchase returns and allowances	40	(d)	290	(k)
Net purchases	(a)	1,030	7,210	42,090
Freight-in	130	(e)	(h)	2,240
Cost of goods purchased	(b)	1,230	8,050	(l)
Cost of goods available for sale	1,840	1,350	(i)	49,530
Ending inventory	310	(f)	1,450	6,230
Cost of goods sold	(c)	1,230	7,600	43,300

Instructions
Fill in the lettered blanks to complete the cost of goods sold sections.

*E5-12 This information relates to Tandi Co.
1. On April 5 purchased merchandise from Buehler Company for $22,000, terms 2/10, net/30.
2. On April 6 paid freight costs of $900 on merchandise purchased from Buehler Company.
3. On April 7 purchased equipment on account for $26,000.
4. On April 8 returned some of the April 5 merchandise to Buehler Company which cost $3,600.
5. On April 15 paid the amount due to Buehler Company in full.

Journalize purchase transactions.
(SO 7)

Instructions
(a) Prepare the journal entries to record these transactions on the books of Tandi Co. using a periodic inventory system.
(b) Assume that Tandi Co. paid the balance due to Buehler Company on May 4 instead of April 15. Prepare the journal entry to record this payment.

Problems: Set A

Journalize, post, prepare partial income statement, and calculate ratios.
(SO 2, 3, 4, 6)

GLS

P5-1A Banff Hardware Store completed the following merchandising transactions in the month of May. At the beginning of May, Banff's ledger showed Cash of $5,000 and Common Stock of $5,000.

May	1	Purchased merchandise on account from Jasper Wholesale Supply for $6,000, terms 2/10, n/30.
	2	Sold merchandise on account for $5,200, terms 3/10, n/30. The cost of the merchandise sold was $3,300.
	5	Received credit from Jasper Wholesale Supply for merchandise returned $200.
	9	Received collections in full, less discounts, from customers billed on sales of $5,200 on May 2.
	10	Paid Jasper Wholesale Supply in full, less discount.
	11	Purchased supplies for cash $900.
	12	Purchased merchandise for cash $2,700.
	15	Received $230 refund for return of poor-quality merchandise from supplier on cash purchase.
	17	Purchased merchandise from Northern Distributors for $1,900, terms 2/10, n/30.
	19	Paid freight on May 17 purchase $250.
	24	Sold merchandise for cash $6,200. The cost of the merchandise sold was $4,020.
	25	Purchased merchandise from Toolware Inc. for $800, terms 3/10, n/30.
	27	Paid Northern Distributors in full, less discount.
	29	Made refunds to cash customers for returned merchandise $124. The returned merchandise had cost $90.
	31	Sold merchandise on account for $1,280, terms n/30. The cost of the merchandise sold was $830.

Banff Hardware's chart of accounts includes Cash, Accounts Receivable, Merchandise Inventory, Supplies, Accounts Payable, Common Stock, Sales, Sales Returns and Allowances, Sales Discounts, and Cost of Goods Sold.

Instructions
(a) Journalize the transactions using a perpetual inventory system.
(b) Post the transactions to T accounts. Be sure to enter the beginning cash and common stock balances.
(c) Gross profit $4,340
(c) Prepare an income statement through gross profit for the month of May 2007.
(d) Calculate the profit margin ratio and the gross profit rate. (Assume operating expenses were $2,400.)

Journalize purchase and sale transactions under a perpetual inventory system.
(SO 2, 3)

P5-2A Between the Lines Warehouse distributes hardback books to retail stores and extends credit terms of 2/10, n/30 to all of its customers. During the month of June the following merchandising transactions occurred.

June	1	Purchased 160 books on account for $5 each (including freight) from El Libro Publishers, terms 2/10, n/30.
	3	Sold 120 books on account to the Booked for Murder bookstore for $10 each.
	6	Received $50 credit for 10 books returned to El Libro Publishers.
	9	Paid El Libro Publishers in full.
	15	Received payment in full from the Booked for Murder bookstore.
	17	Sold 140 books on account to Curl Up N Read Bookstore for $10 each.
	20	Purchased 120 books on account for $5 each from Good Book Publishers, terms 1/15, n/30.
	24	Received payment in full from Curl Up N Read Bookstore.
	26	Paid Good Book Publishers in full.
	28	Sold 130 books on account to HomeTown Bookstore for $10 each.
	30	Granted HomeTown Bookstore $150 credit for 15 books returned costing $75.

Instructions

Journalize the transactions for the month of June for Between the Lines Warehouse, using a perpetual inventory system. Assume the cost of each book sold was $5.

P5-3A   At the beginning of the current season on April 1, the ledger of Fairway Pro Shop showed Cash $2,500; Merchandise Inventory $3,500; and Common Stock $6,000. The following transactions were completed during April 2007.

Journalize, post, and prepare trial balance and partial income statement.
(SO 2, 3, 4)

Apr.	5	Purchased golf bags, clubs, and balls on account from Kokott Co. $1,800, terms 3/10, n/60.
	7	Paid freight on Kokott purchase $80.
	9	Received credit from Kokott Co. for merchandise returned $200.
	10	Sold merchandise on account to members $910, terms n/30. The merchandise sold had a cost of $620.
	12	Purchased golf shoes, sweaters, and other accessories on account from Eagle Sportswear $730, terms 1/10, n/30.
	14	Paid Kokott Co. in full.
	17	Received credit from Eagle Sportswear for merchandise returned $30.
	20	Made sales on account to members $840, terms n/30. The cost of the merchandise sold was $550.
	21	Paid Eagle Sportswear in full.
	27	Granted an allowance to members for clothing that did not fit properly $60.
	30	Received payments on account from members $1,100.

The chart of accounts for the pro shop includes Cash, Accounts Receivable, Merchandise Inventory, Accounts Payable, Common Stock, Sales, Sales Returns and Allowances, and Cost of Goods Sold.

Instructions

(a) Journalize the April transactions using a perpetual inventory system.
(b) Using T accounts, enter the beginning balances in the ledger accounts and post the April transactions.
(c) Prepare a trial balance on April 30, 2007.
(d) Prepare an income statement through gross profit.

(c) Tot. trial
*   balance $7,750*
(d) Gross profit $ 520

P5-4A   Zwick Department Store is located in midtown Metropolis. During the past several years, net income has been declining because suburban shopping centers have been attracting business away from city areas. At the end of the company's fiscal year on November 30, 2007, these accounts appeared in its adjusted trial balance.

Prepare financial statements and calculate profitability ratios.
(SO 4, 6)

Accounts Payable	$ 18,300
Accounts Receivable	17,200
Accumulated Depreciation—Delivery Equipment	20,000
Accumulated Depreciation—Store Equipment	38,000
Cash	8,000
Common Stock	35,000
Cost of Goods Sold	633,300
Delivery Expense	6,200
Delivery Equipment	57,000
Depreciation Expense—Delivery Equipment	4,000
Depreciation Expense—Store Equipment	9,500
Dividends	12,000
Gain on sale of equipment	2,000
Insurance Expense	9,000
Interest Expense	5,000
Merchandise Inventory	36,200
Notes Payable	47,500
Prepaid Insurance	6,000
Property Tax Expense	3,500
Property Taxes Payable	3,500
Rent Expense	29,000
Retained Earnings	14,200
Salaries Expense	110,000

Sales	914,000
Sales Commissions Expense	17,000
Sales Commissions Payable	6,000
Sales Returns and Allowances	20,000
Store Equipment	105,000
Utilities Expense	10,600

Additional data: Notes payable are due in 2011.

Instructions

(a) Net income $ 58,900
Tot. assets $171,400

(a) Prepare a multiple-step income statement, a retained earnings statement, and a classified balance sheet.

(b) Calculate the profit margin ratio and the gross profit rate.

(c) The vice-president of marketing and the director of human resources have developed a proposal whereby the company would compensate the sales force on a strictly commission basis using 20% of net sales. Given the increased incentive, they expect net sales to increase by 15%. As a result, they estimate that gross profit will increase by $39,105 and operating expenses by $75,595. Compute the expected new net income. (*Hint:* You do not need to prepare an income statement). Then compute the revised profit margin ratio and gross profit rate. Comment on the effect that this plan would have on net income and on the ratios, and evaluate the merit of this proposal.

Prepare a correct multiple-step income statement.
(SO 4)

P5-5A An inexperienced accountant prepared this condensed income statement for Lahti Company, a retail firm that has been in business for a number of years.

LAHTI COMPANY
Income Statement
For the Year Ended December 31, 2007

Revenues		
Net sales	$850,000	
Other revenues	22,000	
	872,000	
Cost of goods sold	555,000	
Gross profit	317,000	
Operating expenses		
Selling expenses	104,000	
Administrative expenses	93,000	
	197,000	
Net earnings	$120,000	

As an experienced, knowledgeable accountant, you review the statement and determine the following facts.

1. Net sales consist of sales $906,000, less delivery expense on merchandise sold $26,000, and sales returns and allowances $30,000.

2. Other revenues consist of sales discounts $14,000 and rent revenue $8,000.

3. Selling expenses consist of salespersons' salaries $80,000; depreciation on accounting equipment $8,000; advertising $10,000; and sales commissions $6,000. The commissions represent commissions paid. At December 31, $3,000 of commissions have been earned by salespersons but have not been paid.

Net income $111,000

Journalize, post, and prepare adjusted trial balance and financial statements.
(SO 4)

4. Administrative expenses consist of office salaries $37,000; dividends $18,000; utilities $12,000; interest expense $2,000; and rent expense $24,000, which includes prepayments totaling $4,000 for the first quarter of 2008.

Instructions

Prepare a correct detailed multiple-step income statement.

P5-6A The trial balance of Save-More Wholesale Company contained the accounts shown at December 31, the end of the company's fiscal year.

SAVE-MORE WHOLESALE COMPANY
Trial Balance
December 31, 2007

	Debit	Credit
Cash	$ 33,400	
Accounts Receivable	37,600	
Merchandise Inventory	70,000	
Land	92,000	
Buildings	200,000	
Accumulated Depreciation—Buildings		$ 60,000 _+10,000_
Equipment	83,500	
Accumulated Depreciation—Equipment		40,500 _+9000_
Notes Payable		54,700
Accounts Payable		37,500
Common Stock		160,000
Retained Earnings		68,200
Dividends	10,000	
Sales		922,100
Sales Discounts	5,000	
Cost of Goods Sold	709,900	
Salaries Expense	71,300	
Utilities Expense	9,400	
Repair Expense	8,900	
Gas and Oil Expense	7,200	
Insurance Expense	4,800	
	$1,343,000	$1,343,000

Adjustment data:
1. Depreciation is $10,000 on buildings and $9,000 on equipment. (Both are operating expenses.)
2. Interest of $5,500 is due and unpaid on notes payable at December 31.

Other data: $15,000 of the notes payable are payable next year.

Instructions
(a) Journalize the adjusting entries.
(b) Create T accounts for all accounts used in part (a). Enter the trial balance amounts into the T accounts and post the adjusting entries.
(c) Prepare an adjusted trial balance.
(d) Prepare a multiple-step income statement and a retained earnings statement for the year, and a classified balance sheet at December 31, 2007.

(c) Tot. trial balance $1,367,500
(d) Net income $ 81,100
Tot. assets $ 397,000

P5-7A At the end of Jaxx Department Store's fiscal year on November 30, 2007, these accounts appeared in its adjusted trial balance.

Determine cost of goods sold and gross profit under periodic approach.
(SO 4, 5)

Freight-in	$ 5,060
Merchandise Inventory (beginning)	42,200
Purchases	636,000
Purchase Discounts	7,000
Purchase Returns and Allowances	6,760
Sales	914,000
Sales Returns and Allowances	20,000

Additional facts:
1. Merchandise inventory on November 30, 2007, is $36,200.
2. Note that Jaxx Department Store uses a periodic system.

Instructions
Prepare an income statement through gross profit for the year ended November 30, 2007.

P5-8A Yuan Li Inc. operates a retail operation that purchases and sells snowmobiles, amongst other outdoor products. The company purchases all merchandise inventory on

Gross profit $260,700
Calculate missing amounts and assess profitability.
(SO 4, 5, 6)

credit and uses a perpetual inventory system. The accounts payable account is used for recording inventory purchases only; all other current liabilities are accrued in separate accounts. You are provided with the following selected information for the fiscal years 2005 through 2008, inclusive.

	2005	2006	2007	2008
Income Statement Data				
Sales		$96,850	$ (e)	$82,220
Cost of goods sold		(a)	25,140	25,490
Gross profit		69,260	61,540	(i)
Operating expenses		63,640	(f)	52,870
Net income		$ (b)	$ 4,570	$ (j)
Balance Sheet Data				
Merchandise inventory	$13,000	$ (c)	$14,700	$ (k)
Accounts payable	5,800	6,500	4,600	(l)
Additional Information				
Purchases of merchandise inventory on account		$25,890	$ (g)	$24,050
Cash payments to suppliers		(d)	(h)	24,650

Instructions

(a) Calculate the missing amounts.

(b) The vice-presidents of sales, marketing, production, and finance are discussing the company's results with the CEO. They note that sales declined over the 3-year fiscal period, 2006–2008. Does that mean that profitability necessarily also declined? Explain, computing the gross profit rate and the profit margin ratio for each fiscal year to help support your answer.

Journalize, post, and prepare trial balance and partial income statement using periodic approach.
(SO 5, 7)

*P5-9A At the beginning of the current season on April 1, the ledger of Fairway Pro Shop showed Cash $2,500; Merchandise Inventory $3,500; and Common Stock $6,000. These transactions occured during April 2007.

Apr. 5 Purchased golf bags, clubs, and balls on account from Kokott Co. $1,800, terms 3/10, n/60.
7 Paid freight on Kokott Co. purchases $80.
9 Received credit from Kokott Co. for merchandise returned $200.
10 Sold merchandise on account to members $910, terms n/30.
12 Purchased golf shoes, sweaters, and other accessories on account from Eagle Sportswear $730, terms 1/10, n/30.
14 Paid Kokott Co. in full.
17 Received credit from Eagle Sportswear for merchandise returned $30.
20 Made sales on account to members $840, terms n/30.
21 Paid Eagle Sportswear in full.
27 Granted credit to members for clothing that did not fit properly $60.
30 Received payments on account from members $1,100.

The chart of accounts for the pro shop includes Cash, Accounts Receivable, Merchandise Inventory, Accounts Payable, Common Stock, Sales, Sales Returns and Allowances, Purchases, Purchase Returns and Allowances, Purchase Discounts, and Freight-in.

Instructions

(a) Journalize the April transactions using a periodic inventory system.

(b) Using T accounts, enter the beginning balances in the ledger accounts and post the April transactions.

(c) Prepare a trial balance on April 30, 2007.

(d) Prepare an income statement through Gross Profit, assuming merchandise inventory on hand at April 30 is $4,655.

(c) Tot. trial
balance $8,035
Gross profit $ 520

Problems: Set B

P5-1B   Midwest Distributing Company completed these merchandising transactions in the month of April. At the beginning of April, the ledger of Midwest showed Cash of $9,000 and Common Stock of $9,000.

Journalize, post, prepare partial income statement, and calculate ratios.
(SO 2, 3, 4, 6)

GLS

Apr. 2	Purchased merchandise on account from Kane Supply Co. $6,300, terms 2/10, n/30.
4	Sold merchandise on account $5,000, terms 2/10, n/30. The cost of the merchandise sold was $3,700.
5	Paid $200 freight on April 4 sale.
6	Received credit from Kane Supply Co. for merchandise returned $300.
11	Paid Kane Supply Co. in full, less discount.
13	Received collections in full, less discounts, from customers billed on April 4.
14	Purchased merchandise for cash $4,700.
16	Received refund from supplier for returned merchandise on cash purchase of April 14, $500.
18	Purchased merchandise from Great Plains Distributors $4,500, terms 2/10, n/30.
20	Paid freight on April 18 purchase $100.
23	Sold merchandise for cash $8,300. The cost of the merchandise sold was $5,820.
26	Purchased merchandise for cash $2,300.
27	Paid Great Plains Distributors in full, less discount.
29	Made refunds to cash customers for returned merchandise $180. The returned merchandise had a cost of $120.
30	Sold merchandise on account $3,980, terms n/30. The cost of the merchandise sold was $2,500.

Midwest Distributing Company's chart of accounts includes Cash, Accounts Receivable, Merchandise Inventory, Accounts Payable, Common Stock, Sales, Sales Returns and Allowances, Sales Discounts, Cost of Goods Sold, and Freight-out.

Instructions
(a) Journalize the transactions.
(b) Post the transactions to T accounts. Be sure to enter the beginning cash and common stock balances.
(c) Prepare the income statement through gross profit for the month of April 2007.
(d) Calculate the profit margin ratio and the gross profit rate. (Assume operating expenses were $2,050.)

(c) Gross profit $5,100

P5-2B   Good to Go Warehouse distributes suitcases to retail stores and extends credit terms of 1/10, n/30 to all of its customers. During the month of July the following merchandising transactions occurred.

Journalize purchase and sale transactions under a perpetual inventory system.
(SO 2, 3)

July 1	Purchased 70 suitcases on account for $30 each from Valise Manufacturers, terms 2/15, n/30.
3	Sold 40 suitcases on account to Globe Trotters for $50 each.
9	Paid Valise Manufacturers in full.
12	Received payment in full from Globe Trotters.
17	Sold 34 suitcases on account to Bon Voyage for $50 each.
18	Purchased 60 suitcases on account for $30 (including freight) each from Pak-N-Go Manufacturers, terms 1/10, n/30.
20	Received $300 credit for 10 suitcases returned to Pak-N-Go Manufacturers.
21	Received payment in full from Bon Voyage.
22	Sold 48 suitcases on account to Run Around for $52 each.
30	Paid Pak-N-Go Manufacturers in full.
31	Granted Run Around $260 credit for 5 suitcases returned costing $150.

Instructions
Journalize the transactions for the month of July for Good to Go Warehouse, using a perpetual inventory system. Assume the cost of each suitcase sold was $30.

Journalize, post, and prepare trial balance and partial income statement.
(SO 2, 3, 4)

P5-3B At the beginning of the current season, the ledger of Love All Tennis Shop showed Cash $2,500; Merchandise Inventory $1,700; and Common Stock $4,200. The following transactions were completed during April.

Apr.	4	Purchased racquets and balls from Connors Co. $880, terms 2/10, n/30.
	6	Paid freight on Connors Co. purchase $60.
	8	Sold merchandise to members $900, terms n/30. The merchandise sold cost $600.
	10	Received credit of $130 from Connors Co. for damaged racquets that were returned.
	11	Purchased tennis shoes from No Fault for cash $300.
	13	Paid Connors Co. in full.
	14	Purchased tennis shirts and shorts from Serena Sportswear $700, terms 3/10, n/60.
	15	Received cash refund of $50 from No Fault for damaged merchandise that was returned.
	17	Paid freight on Serena Sportswear purchase $30.
	18	Sold merchandise to members $860, terms n/30. The cost of the merchandise sold was $440.
	20	Received $500 in cash from members in settlement of their accounts.
	21	Paid Serena Sportswear in full.
	27	Granted an allowance of $30 to members for tennis clothing that did not fit properly.
	30	Received cash payments on account from members $350.

The chart of accounts for the tennis shop includes Cash, Accounts Receivable, Merchandise Inventory, Accounts Payable, Common Stock, Sales, Sales Returns and Allowances, and Cost of Goods Sold.

Instructions
(a) Journalize the April transactions.
(b) Using T accounts, enter the beginning balances in the ledger accounts and post the April transactions.

(c) Tot. trial
    balance $5,960
(d) Gross profit $ 690

(c) Prepare a trial balance on April 30, 2007.
(d) Prepare an income statement through gross profit.

Prepare financial statements and calculate profitability ratios.
(SO 4, 6)

P5-4B Danielle Department Store is located near the Crystal Shopping Mall. At the end of the company's fiscal year on December 31, 2007, the following accounts appeared in its adjusted trial balance.

Accounts Payable	$ 68,300
Accounts Receivable	50,300
Accumulated Depreciation—Building	52,500
Accumulated Depreciation—Equipment	42,600
Building	190,000
Cash	28,000
Common Stock	140,000
Cost of Goods Sold	418,000
Depreciation Expense—Building	10,400
Depreciation Expense—Equipment	13,000
Dividends	15,000
Equipment	100,000
Gain on sale of equipment	4,300
Insurance Expense	8,400
Interest Expense	7,000
Interest Payable	2,000
Merchandise Inventory	63,000
Mortgage Payable	80,000
Office Salaries Expense	32,000
Prepaid Insurance	2,400
Property Taxes Payable	4,800
Property Taxes Expense	6,200
Retained Earnings	19,200
Sales Salaries Expense	76,000

Sales	636,000
Sales Commissions Expense	14,500
Sales Commissions Payable	3,500
Sales Returns and Allowances	8,000
Utilities Expense	11,000

Additional data: $20,000 of the mortgage payable is due for payment next year.

Instructions
(a) Prepare a multiple-step income statement, a retained earnings statement, and a classified balance sheet.

(b) Calculate the profit margin ratio and the gross profit rate.

(c) The vice-president of marketing and the director of human resources have developed a proposal whereby the company would compensate the sales force on a strictly commission basis using 15% of net sales. Given the increased incentive, they expect net sales to increase by 25%. As a result, they estimate that gross profit will increase by $52,500 and operating expenses by $28,800. Compute the expected new net income. (*Hint*: You do not need to prepare an income statement.) Then compute the revised profit margin ratio and gross profit rate. Comment on the effect that this plan would have on net income and the ratios, and evaluate the merit of this proposal.

(a) Net income $ 35,800
Tot. assets $338,600

P5-5B A part-time bookkeeper prepared this income statement for Maquoketa Company for the year ending December 31, 2007.

Prepare a correct multiple-step income statement.
(SO 4)

MAQUOKETA COMPANY
Income Statement
December 31, 2007

Revenues		
Sales		$715,000
Less: Freight-out	$14,000	
Sales discounts	11,300	25,300
Net sales		689,700
Other revenues (net)		1,300
Total revenues		688,000
Expenses		
Cost of goods sold		450,000
Selling expenses		103,000
Administrative expenses		50,000
Dividends		12,000
Total expenses		615,000
Net income		$ 73,000

As an experienced, knowledgeable accountant, you review the statement and determine the following facts.
1. Sales include $16,000 of deposits from customers for future sales orders.
2. Other revenues contain two items: interest expense $4,000 and interest revenue $5,300.
3. Selling expenses consist of sales salaries $76,000, advertising $13,000, depreciation on store equipment $7,500, and sales commissions expense $6,500.
4. Administrative expenses consist of office salaries $19,000; utilities expense $9,500; rent expense $14,500; and insurance expense $7,000. Insurance expense includes $800 of insurance applicable to 2008.

Operating
expenses $166,200
Net income $ 72,800

Instructions
Prepare a correct detailed multiple-step income statement.

Journalize, post, and prepare adjusted trial balance and financial statements.
(SO 4)

P5-6B The trial balance of Stylynn Fashion Center contained the following accounts at November 30, the end of the company's fiscal year.

STYLYNN FASHION CENTER
Trial Balance
November 30, 2007

	Debit	Credit
Cash	$ 35,700	
Accounts Receivable	33,700	
Merchandise Inventory	43,000	
Store Supplies	8,800	
Store Equipment	105,000	
Accumulated Depreciation—Store Equipment		$ 35,000
Delivery Equipment	38,000	
Accumulated Depreciation—Delivery Equipment		6,000
Notes Payable		65,000
Accounts Payable		39,800
Common Stock		80,000
Retained Earnings		30,000
Dividends	12,000	
Sales		757,200
Sales Returns and Allowances	6,200	
Cost of Goods Sold	507,400	
Salaries Expense	130,000	
Advertising Expense	26,400	
Utilities Expense	14,000	
Repair Expense	12,100	
Delivery Expense	16,700	
Rent Expense	24,000	
	$1,013,000	$1,013,000

Adjustment data:
1. Store supplies on hand total $3,500.
2. Depreciation is $15,000 on the store equipment and $6,000 on the delivery equipment.
3. Interest of $8,000 is accrued on notes payable at November 30.

Other data: $30,000 of notes payable are due for payment next year.

Instructions
(a) Journalize the adjusting entries.
(b) Prepare T accounts for all accounts used in part (a). Enter the trial balance amounts into the T accounts and post the adjusting entries.

(c) Tot. trial
    balance $1,042,000
(d) Net loss $(13,900)
    Tot. assets $196,900

(c) Prepare an adjusted trial balance.
(d) Prepare a multiple-step income statement and a retained earnings statement for the year, and a classified balance sheet at November 30, 2007.

Determine cost of goods sold and gross profit under periodic approach.
(SO 4, 5)

P5-7B   At the end of Neiman Fields Department Store's fiscal year on December 31, 2007, these accounts appeared in its adjusted trial balance.

Freight-in	$ 5,600
Merchandise Inventory (beginning)	40,500
Purchases	446,000
Purchase Discounts	12,000
Purchase Returns and Allowances	6,400
Sales	727,000
Sales Returns and Allowances	8,000

Additional facts:
1. Merchandise inventory on December 31, 2007, is $71,000.
2. Note that Neiman Fields Department Store uses a periodic system.

Instructions
Gross profit $316,300
Calculate missing amounts and assess profitability.
(SO 4, 5, 6)

Prepare an income statement through gross profit for the year ended December 31, 2007.

P5-8B   Yelena Zhivago operates a clothing retail operation. She purchases all merchandise inventory on credit and uses a perpetual inventory system. The accounts payable account is used for recording inventory purchases only; all other current liabilities are accrued in separate accounts. You are provided with the following selected information for the fiscal years 2005, 2006, 2007, and 2008.

	2005	2006	2007	2008
Inventory (ending)	$13,000	$ 11,300	$ 16,400	$ 12,200
Accounts payable (ending)	17,000			
Sales		225,700	227,600	224,000
Purchases of merchandise inventory on account		141,000	150,700	136,000
Cash payments to suppliers		135,000	159,000	127,000

Instructions

(a) Calculate cost of goods sold for each of the 2006, 2007, and 2008 fiscal years.
(b) Calculate the gross profit for each of the 2006, 2007, and 2008 fiscal years.
(c) Calculate the ending balance of accounts payable for each of the 2006, 2007, and 2008 fiscal years.
(d) The vice-presidents of sales, marketing, production, and finance are discussing the company's results with the CEO. They note that sales declined in fiscal 2008. They wonder whether that means that profitability, as measured by the gross profit rate, necessarily also declined. Explain, calculating the gross profit rate for each fiscal year to help support your answer.

(a) 2007 $145,600
(c) 2007 $14,700

*P5-9B   At the beginning of the current season, the ledger of Love All Tennis Shop showed Cash $2,500; Merchandise Inventory $1,700; and Common Stock $4,200. The following transactions were completed during April.

Journalize, post, and prepare trial balance and partial income statement using periodic approach.
(SO 5, 7)

Apr. 4 Purchased racquets and balls from Connors Co. $880, terms 2/10, n/30.
6 Paid freight on Connors Co. purchase $60.
8 Sold merchandise to members $900, terms n/30.
10 Received credit of $130 from Connors Co. for damaged racquets that were returned.
11 Purchased tennis shoes from No Fault for cash $300.
13 Paid Connors Co. in full.
14 Purchased tennis shirts and shorts from Serena Sportswear $700, terms 3/10, n/60.
15 Received cash refund of $50 from No Fault for damaged merchandise that was returned.
17 Paid freight on Serena Sportswear purchase $30.
18 Sold merchandise to members $860, terms n/30.
20 Received $500 in cash from members in settlement of their accounts.
21 Paid Serena Sportswear in full.
27 Granted an allowance of $30 to members for tennis clothing that did not fit properly.
30 Received cash payments on account from members $350.

The chart of accounts for the tennis shop includes Cash, Accounts Receivable, Merchandise Inventory, Accounts Payable, Common Stock, Sales, Sales Returns and Allowances, Purchases, Purchase Returns and Allowances, Purchase Discounts, and Freight-in.

Instructions

(a) Journalize the April transactions using a periodic inventory system.
(b) Using T accounts, enter the beginning balances in the ledger accounts and post the April transactions.
(c) Prepare a trial balance on April 30, 2007.
(d) Prepare an income statement through Gross Profit, assuming merchandise inventory on hand at April 30 is $2,414.

(c) Tot. trial
*   balance $6,176*
(d) Gross profit $ 690

Problems: Set C

Visit the book's website at **www.wiley.com/college/kimmel** and choose the Student Companion site to access Problem Set C.

Comprehensive Problem

CP5   On December 1, 2007, Wheeler Distributing Company had the following account balances.

	Debits		Credits
Cash	$ 7,300	Accumulated Depreciation	$ 2,200
Accounts Receivable	5,600	Accounts Payable	4,600
Merchandise Inventory	12,000	Salaries Payable	1,000
Supplies	1,200	Common stock	15,000
Equipment	22,000	Retained Earnings	25,300
	$48,100		$48,100

During December the company completed the following summary transactions.

Dec. 6   Paid $1,600 for salaries due employees, of which $600 is for December and $1,000 is for November salaries payable.
   8   Received $1,800 cash from customers in payment of account (no discount allowed).
   10   Sold merchandise for cash $6,000. The cost of the merchandise sold was $4,000.
   13   Purchased merchandise on account from King Co. $8,000, terms 2/10, n/30.
   15   Purchased supplies for cash $2,000.
   18   Sold merchandise on account $9,000, terms 1/10, n/30. The cost of the merchandise sold was $6,000.
   20   Paid salaries $1,800.
   23   Paid King Co. in full, less discount.
   27   Received collections in full, less discounts, from customers billed on December 18.

Adjustment data:

1. Accrued salaries payable $600.
2. Depreciation $300 per month.
3. Supplies on hand $2,200.

Instructions

(a) Journalize the December transactions.
(b) Enter the December 1 balances in the ledger T accounts and post the December transactions. Use Cost of Goods Sold, Depreciation Expense, Salaries Expense, Sales, Sales Discounts, and Supplies Expense.
(c) Journalize and post adjusting entries.
(d) Prepare an adjusted trial balance.
(e) Prepare an income statement and a retained earnings statement for December and a classified balance sheet at December 31.

(d) Totals $63,000
(e) Net income $ 610

Continuing Cookie Chronicle

(*Note:* This is a continuation of the Cookie Chronicle from Chapters 1 through 4.)

CCC5   Because Natalie has had such a successful first few months, she is considering other opportunities to develop her business. One opportunity is the sale of fine European mixers. The owner of Mixer Deluxe has approached Natalie to become the exclusive distributor of these fine mixers. The current cost of a mixer is approximately $525, and Natalie would sell each one for $1,050. Natalie comes to you for advice on how to account for these mixers. Each appliance has a serial number and can be easily identified. Natalie asks you the following questions.

1. "Would you consider these mixers to be inventory? Or, should they be classified as supplies or equipment?"
2. "I've learned a little about keeping track of inventory using both the perpetual and the periodic systems of accounting for inventory. Which system do you think is better? Which one would you recommend for the type of inventory that I want to sell?"

3. "How often do I need to count inventory if I maintain it using the perpetual system? Do I need to count inventory at all?"

In the end, Natalie decides to use the perpetual method of accounting for inventory, and the following transactions happen during the month of January.

Jan.	4	She buys five deluxe mixers on account from Kzinski Supply Co. for $2,625, terms n/30.
	6	She pays $100 freight on the January 4 purchase.
	7	Natalie returns one of the mixers to Kzinski because it was damaged during shipping. Kzinski issues Cookie Creations credit for the cost of the mixer plus $20 for the cost of freight that was paid on January 6 for one mixer.
	8	She collects the amount due from the neighborhood community center that was accrued at the end of December 2006.
	12	She sells three deluxe mixers on account for $3,150, FOB destination, terms n/30.
	13	Natalie pays her cell phone bill previously accrued in the December adjusting journal entries.
	14	She pays $75 of delivery charges for the three mixers that were sold on January 12.
	14	She buys four deluxe mixers on account from Kzinski Supply Co. for $2,100, terms n/30.
	17	Natalie is concerned that there is not enough cash available to pay for all of the mixers purchased. She issues additional common stock for $1,000.
	18	She pays $80 freight on the January 14 purchase.
	20	She sells two deluxe mixers for $2,100 cash.
	28	Natalie issues a check to her assistant. Her assistant worked 20 hours in January and is also paid for amounts owing at December 31, 2006. Recall that Natalie's assistant earns $8 an hour.
	28	Natalie collects amounts due from customers in the January 12 transaction.
	31	She pays Kzinski all amounts due.
	31	Cash dividends of $750 are paid.

As of January 31, the following adjusting entry data are available.

1. A count of brochures and posters reveals that none were used in January.
2. A count of baking supplies reveals that none were used in January.
3. Another month's worth of depreciation needs to be recorded on the baking equipment bought in November. (Recall that the baking equipment has a useful life of 5 years or 60 months.)
4. One month's worth of amortization (write-off) needs to be recorded on the website. (Recall that the website has a useful life of 2 years or 24 months.)
5. An additional month's worth of interest on her grandmother's loan needs to be accrued. (The interest rate is 6%.)
6. One month's worth of insurance has expired.
7. Natalie receives her cell phone bill, $75. The bill is for services provided in January and is due February 15. (Recall that the cell phone is used only for business purposes.)
8. An analysis of the unearned revenue account reveals that Natalie has not had time to teach any of these lessons this month because she has been so busy selling mixers. As a result there is no change to the unearned revenue account. Natalie hopes to book the outstanding lessons in February.
9. An inventory count of mixers at the end of January reveals that Natalie has three mixers remaining.

Instructions

Using the information that you have gathered and the general ledger accounts that you have prepared through Chapter 4, plus the new information above, do the following.

(a) Answer Natalie's questions.
(b) Prepare and post the January 2007 transactions.
(c) Prepare a trial balance.   (c) Totals $11,399
(d) Prepare and post the adjusting journal entries required.
(e) Prepare an adjusted trial balance.
(f) Prepare a multiple-step income statement and retained earnings statement for the   (f) Net income $ 2,060
month ended January 31, 2007.
(g) Prepare a classified balance sheet as of January 31, 2007.   (g) Total assets $ 7,504

BROADENING YOUR PERSPECTIVE

Financial Reporting and Analysis

FINANCIAL REPORTING PROBLEM: *Tootsie Roll Industries, Inc.*

BYP5-1 The financial statements for Tootsie Roll Industries are presented in Appendix A at the end of this book.

Instructions
Answer these questions using the Consolidated Income Statement.
(a) What was the percentage change in sales and in net income from 2003 to 2004?
(b) What was the profit margin ratio in each of the 3 years? Comment on the trend.
(c) What was Tootsie Roll's gross profit rate in each of the 3 years? Comment on the trend.

COMPARATIVE ANALYSIS PROBLEM: *Tootsie Roll vs. Hershey Foods*

BYP5-2 The financial statements of Hershey Foods are presented in Appendix B, following the financial statements for Tootsie Roll in Appendix A.

Instructions
(a) Based on the information contained in these financial statements, determine the following values for each company.
(1) Profit margin ratio for 2004.
(2) Gross profit for 2004.
(3) Gross profit rate for 2004.
(4) Operating income for 2004.
(5) Percentage change in operating income from 2003 to 2004.
(b) What conclusions concerning the relative profitability of the two companies can be drawn from these data?

RESEARCH CASE

BYP5-3 The January 30, 2004, issue of the *Wall Street Journal* includes an article by Chad Terhune titled "Probe of Coke's Sales Leads to Japan."

Instructions
Read the article and answer the following questions.
(a) Describe the practice that Coke has been accused of.
(b) Explain why this practice is of concern to accountants and investors.
(c) What was suggested as the possible motivation for the alleged practice?

INTERPRETING FINANCIAL STATEMENTS

BYP5-4 Recently it was announced that two giant French retailers, Carrefour SA and Promodes SA, would merge. A headline in the *Wall Street Journal* blared, "French Retailers Create New Wal-Mart Rival." While Wal-Mart's total sales would still exceed those of the combined company, Wal-Mart's international sales are far less than those of the combined company. This is a serious concern for Wal-Mart, since its primary opportunity for future growth lies outside of the United States.

Below are basic financial data for the combined corporation (in euros) and Wal-Mart (in U.S. dollars). Even though their results are presented in different currencies, by employing ratios we can make some basic comparisons.

	Carrefour (in millions)	Wal-Mart (in millions)
Sales	euros 70,486	$256,329
Cost of goods sold	54,630	198,747
Net income	1,738	9,054
Total assets	39,063	104,912
Current assets	14,521	34,421
Current liabilities	13,660	37,418
Total liabilities	29,434	61,289

Instructions

Compare the two companies by answering the following.

(a) Calculate the gross profit rate for each of the companies, and discuss their relative abilities to control cost of goods sold.
(b) Calculate the profit margin ratio, and discuss the companies' relative profitability.
(c) Calculate the current ratio and debt to total assets ratios for the two companies, and discuss their relative liquidity and solvency.
(d) What concerns might you have in relying on this comparison?

FINANCIAL ANALYSIS ON THE WEB

BYP5-5   *Purpose:* No financial decision maker should ever rely solely on the financial information reported in the annual report to make decisions. It is important to keep abreast of financial news. This activity demonstrates how to search for financial news on the Web.

Address: **http://biz.yahoo.com/i** (or go to **www.wiley.com/college/kimmel**)

Steps

1. Type in either Wal-Mart, Target Corp., or Kmart.
2. Choose **News**.
3. Select an article that sounds interesting to you and that would be relevant to an investor in these companies.

Instructions

(a) What was the source of the article? (For example, Reuters, Businesswire, Prnewswire.)
(b) Assume that you are a personal financial planner and that one of your clients owns stock in the company. Write a brief memo to your client summarizing the article and explaining the implications of the article for their investment.

Critical Thinking

DECISION MAKING ACROSS THE ORGANIZATION

BYP5-6   Three years ago Zoe Biersack and her brother-in-law Tom Angsten opened Mallmart Department Store. For the first 2 years, business was good, but the following condensed income statement sresults for 2007 were disappointing.

MALLMART DEPARTMENT STORE
Income Statement
For the Year Ended December 31, 2007

Net sales		$700,000
Cost of goods sold		560,000
Gross profit		140,000
Operating expenses		
Selling expenses	$100,000	
Administrative expenses	15,000	
		115,000
Net income		$ 25,000

Zoe believes the problem lies in the relatively low gross profit rate of 20%. Tom believes the problem is that operating expenses are too high. Zoe thinks the gross profit rate can be improved by making two changes: (1) Increase average selling prices by 15%; this increase is expected to lower sales volume so that total sales dollars will increase only 5%. (2) Buy merchandise in larger quantities and take all purchase discounts; these changes are expected to increase the gross profit rate by 4%. Zoe does not anticipate that these changes will have any effect on operating expenses.

Tom thinks expenses can be cut by making these two changes: (1) Cut 2007 sales salaries of $60,000 in half and give sales personnel a commission of 2% of net sales. (2) Reduce store deliveries to one day per week rather than twice a week; this change will reduce 2007 delivery expenses of $30,000 by 40%. Tom feels that these changes will not have any effect on net sales.

Zoe and Tom come to you for help in deciding the best way to improve net income.

Instructions

With the class divided into groups, answer the following.

(a) Prepare a condensed income statement for 2008 assuming (1) Zoe's changes are implemented and (2) Tom's ideas are adopted.

(b) What is your recommendation to Zoe and Tom?

(c) Prepare a condensed income statement for 2008 assuming both sets of proposed changes are made.

(d) Discuss the impact that other factors might have. For example, would increasing the quantity of inventory increase costs? Would a salary cut affect employee morale? Would decreased morale affect sales? Would decreased store deliveries decrease customer satisfaction? What other suggestions might be considered?

COMMUNICATION ACTIVITY

BYP5-7 The following situation is presented in chronological order.
1. Dexter decides to buy a surfboard.
2. He calls Surfing USA Co. to inquire about their surfboards.
3. Two days later he requests Surfing USA Co. to make him a surfboard.
4. Three days later Surfing USA Co. sends him a purchase order to fill out.
5. He sends back the purchase order.
6. Surfing USA Co. receives the completed purchase order.
7. Surfing USA Co. completes the surfboard.
8. Dexter picks up the surfboard.
9. Surfing USA Co. bills Dexter.
10. Surfing USA Co. receives payment from Dexter.

Instructions

In a memo to the president of Surfing USA Co., answer the following questions.

(a) When should Surfing USA Co. record the sale?

(b) Suppose that with his purchase order, Dexter is required to make a down payment. Would that change your answer to part (a)?

ETHICS CASE

BYP5-8 Kalia Vang was just hired as the assistant treasurer of Yorkshire Stores, a specialty chain store company that has nine retail stores concentrated in one metropolitan area. Among other things, the payment of all invoices is centralized in one of the departments Kalia will manage. Her primary responsibility is to maintain the company's high credit rating by paying all bills when due and to take advantage of all cash discounts.

Dennis Hirt, the former assistant treasurer, who has been promoted to treasurer, is training Kalia in her new duties. He instructs Kalia that she is to continue the practice of preparing all checks "net of discount" and dating the checks the last day of the discount period. "But," Dennis Hirt continues, "we always hold the checks at least 4 days beyond the discount period before mailing them. That way we get another 4 days of interest on our money. Most of our creditors need our business and don't complain. And, if they scream about our missing the discount period, we blame it on the mail room or the post office. We've only lost one discount out of every hundred we take that way. I think everybody does it. By the way, welcome to our team!"

Instructions

(a) What are the ethical considerations in this case?

(b) What stakeholders are harmed or benefited?

(c) Should Kalia continue the practice started by Dennis? Does she have any choice?

Answers to Business Insight and Accounting across the Organization Questions

p. 221

Q: If a perpetual system keeps track of inventory on a daily basis, why do companies ever need to do a physical count?

A: A perpetual system keeps track of all sales and purchases on a continuous basic. This provides a constant record of the number of units in the inventory. However, if employees make errors in recording sales or purchases, the inventory value will not be correct. As a consequence, all companies do a physical count of inventory at least once a year.

p. 226

Q: If a company expects significant returns, what are the implications for revenue recognition?

A: If a company expects significant returns, it should make an adjusting entry at the end of the year reducing sales by the estimated amount of sales returns. This is necessary so as not to overstate the amount of revenue recognized in the period.

p. 231

Q: Why have investors and analysts demanded more accuracy in isolating "Other gains and losses" from operating items?

A: Greater accuracy in the classification of operating versus nonoperating ("Other gains and losses") items permit investors and analysts to judge the real operating margin, the results of continuing operations, and management's ability to control operating expenses.

p. 237

Q: Explain how Wal-Mart's profitability gave it a strategic advantage over Kmart.

A: If two competitors get into a "price war," the company with the higher profitability can reduce prices further (thus eroding its gross profit rate), but still operate at a profit. Thus, Wal-Mart's success at minimizing its operating costs has enabled it to drive many competitors out of business.

Answer to Tootsie Roll Review It Question 3, p. 232

Tootsie Roll's title for gross profit is "gross margin." Its gross profit (gross margin) increased 3.2% in 2004 ($175,609 − $170,109) ÷ $170,109.

Answers to Self-Study Questions

1. a   2. c   3. c   4. b   5. c   6. b   7. d   8. a   9. c
10. c   11. a   *12. b

CHAPTER 6

Reporting and Analyzing Inventory

STUDY OBJECTIVES

After studying this chapter,
you should be able to:

1 Describe the steps in determining inventory quantities.

2 Explain the basis of accounting for inventories and apply the inventory cost flow methods under a periodic inventory system.

3 Explain the financial statement and tax effects of each of the inventory cost flow assumptions.

4 Explain the lower of cost or market basis of accounting for inventories.

5 Compute and interpret the inventory turnover ratio.

6 Describe the LIFO reserve and explain its importance for comparing results of different companies.

 THE NAVIGATOR

✓ THE NAVIGATOR

- ● Scan *Study Objectives*
- ● Read *Feature Story*
- ● Read *Preview*
- ● Read text and answer *Before You Go On*
  p. 271 ◯   p. 280 ◯   p. 284 ◯
- ● Work *Using the Decision Toolkit*
- ● Review *Summary of Study Objectives*
- ● Work *Demonstration Problem*
- ● Answer *Self-Study Questions*
- ● Complete *Assignments*

FEATURE STORY

Where Is That Spare Bulldozer Blade?

Let's talk inventory—big, bulldozer-size inventory. Caterpillar Inc. is the world's largest manufacturer of construction and mining equipment, diesel and natural gas engines, and industrial gas turbines. It sells its products in over 200 countries, making it one of the most successful U.S. exporters. More than 70% of its productive assets are located domestically, and nearly 50% of its sales are foreign.

During the 1980s Caterpillar's profitability suffered, but today it is very successful. A big part of this turnaround can be attributed to effective management of its inventory. Imagine what a bulldozer costs. Now imagine what it costs Caterpillar to have too many bulldozers sitting around in inventory—a situation the company definitely wants to avoid. Conversely, Caterpillar must make sure it has enough inventory to meet demand.

During a recent 7-year period, Caterpillar's sales increased by 100%, while its inventory increased by only 50%. To achieve this dramatic reduction in the amount of resources tied up in inventory, while continuing to meet customers' needs, Caterpillar used a two-pronged approach. First, it completed a factory modernization program, which dramatically

increased its production efficiency. The program
reduced by 60% the amount of inventory the
company processed at any one time. It also
reduced by an incredible 75% the time it takes to
manufacture a part.

Second, Caterpillar dramatically improved
its parts distribution system. It ships more than
100,000 items daily from its 23 distribution centers
strategically located around the world (10 *million*
square feet of warehouse space—remember, we're
talking bulldozers). The company can virtually
guarantee that it can get any part to anywhere in
the world within 24 hours. Although this network
services 550,000 part numbers, Caterpillar is able to
ship 99.7% of its orders within hours. In fact,
Caterpillar's distribution system is so advanced that
it created a subsidiary, Caterpillar Logistics
Services, Inc., that warehouses and distributes other
companies' products. This subsidiary distributes
products as diverse as running shoes, computer
software, and auto parts all around the world.

In short, how Caterpillar manages and accounts
for its inventory goes a long way in explaining how
profitable it is.

On the World Wide Web
Caterpillar Inc.:
www.cat.com

267

In the previous chapter, we discussed the accounting for merchandise inventory using a perpetual inventory system. In this chapter, we explain the methods used to calculate the cost of inventory on hand at the balance sheet date and the cost of goods sold. We conclude by illustrating methods for analyzing inventory.

The content and organization of this chapter are as follows.

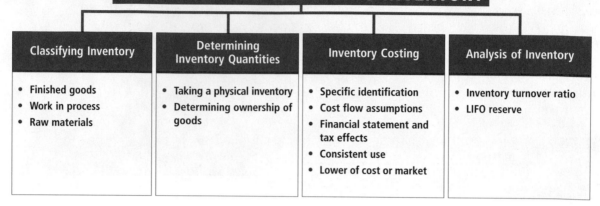

REPORTING AND ANALYZING INVENTORY

Classifying Inventory	Determining Inventory Quantities	Inventory Costing	Analysis of Inventory
• Finished goods • Work in process • Raw materials	• Taking a physical inventory • Determining ownership of goods	• Specific identification • Cost flow assumptions • Financial statement and tax effects • Consistent use • Lower of cost or market	• Inventory turnover ratio • LIFO reserve

THE NAVIGATOR

Classifying Inventory

How a company classifies its inventory depends on whether the firm is a merchandiser or a manufacturer. In a **merchandising** company, such as those described in Chapter 5, inventory consists of many different items. For example, in a grocery store, canned goods, dairy products, meats, and produce are just a few of the inventory items on hand. These items have two common characteristics: (1) They are owned by the company, and (2) they are in a form ready for sale to customers in the ordinary course of business. Thus, merchandisers need only one inventory classification, **merchandise inventory**, to describe the many different items that make up the total inventory.

In a **manufacturing** company, some inventory may not yet be ready for sale. As a result, manufacturers usually classify inventory into three categories: finished goods, work in process, and raw materials. **Finished goods inventory** is manufactured items that are completed and ready for sale. **Work in process** is that portion of manufactured inventory that has been placed into the production process but is not yet complete. **Raw materials** are the basic goods that will be used in production but have not yet been placed into production.

For example, Caterpillar classifies earth-moving tractors completed and ready for sale as **finished goods**. It classifies the tractors on the assembly line in various stages of production as **work in process**. The steel, glass, tires, and other components that are on hand waiting to be used in the production of tractors are identified as **raw materials**.

The accounting concepts discussed in this chapter apply to the inventory classifications of both merchandising and manufacturing companies. Our focus here is on merchandise inventory.

Helpful Hint Regardless of the classification, companies report all inventories under Current Assets on the balance sheet.

By observing the levels and changes in the levels of these three inventory types, financial statement users can gain insight into management's production plans. For example, low levels of raw materials and high levels of finished goods suggest that management believes it has enough inventory on hand, and production will be slowing down—perhaps in anticipation of a recession. On the other hand, high levels of raw materials and low levels of finished goods probably indicate that management is planning to step up production.

Many companies have significantly lowered inventory levels and costs using just-in-time (JIT) inventory methods. Under a just-in-time method, companies manufacture or purchase goods just in time for use. Dell is famous for having developed a system for making computers in response to individual customer requests. Even though it makes each computer to meet each customer's particular specifications, Dell is able to assemble the computer and put it on a truck in less than 48 hours. By integrating its information systems with those of its suppliers, Dell reduced its inventories to nearly zero. This is a huge advantage in an industry where products become obsolete nearly overnight.

Accounting across the Organization

Wal-Mart improved on its inventory control in 2004 with the introduction of electronic product codes (EPCs). Much like bar codes, which tell a retailer the number of boxes of a specific product it has, EPCs go a step farther, helping to distinguish one box of a specific product from another. EPCs use radio frequency identification (RFID) technology, the same technology behind keyless remotes used to unlock car doors.

Companies currently use EPCs to track shipments from supplier to distribution center to store. Other potential uses include help with monitoring product expiration dates and acting quickly on product recalls. Wal-Mart also anticipates faster returns and warranty processing using EPCs. This technology will further assist Wal-Mart managers in their efforts to ensure that their store has just the right type of inventory, in just the right amount, in just the right place.

 Why is inventory control important to managers such as those at Wal-Mart?

Determining Inventory Quantities

No matter whether they are using a periodic or perpetual inventory system, all companies need to determine inventory quantities at the end of the accounting period. If using a perpetual system, companies take a physical inventory for two purposes: The first purpose is to check the accuracy of their perpetual inventory records. The second is to determine the amount of inventory lost due to wasted raw materials, shoplifting, or employee theft.

Companies using a periodic inventory system must take a physical inventory for two *different* purposes: to determine the inventory on hand at the balance sheet date, and to determine the cost of goods sold for the period.

Determining inventory quantities involves two steps: (1) taking a physical inventory of goods on hand and (2) determining the ownership of goods.

STUDY OBJECTIVE

1

Describe the steps in determining inventory quantities.

TAKING A PHYSICAL INVENTORY

Taking a physical inventory involves actually counting, weighing, or measuring each kind of inventory on hand. In many companies, taking an inventory is a formidable task. Retailers such as Target, True Value Hardware, or Home Depot have thousands of different inventory items. An inventory count is generally more accurate when goods are not being sold or received during the counting. Consequently, companies often "take inventory" when the business is closed or when business is slow. Many retailers close early on a chosen day in January—after the holiday sales and returns, when inventories are at their lowest level—to count inventory. Recall from Chapter 5 that Wal-Mart had a year-end of January 31. Companies take the physical inventory at the end of the accounting period.

Business Insight
Ethics Perspective

Over the years inventory has played a role in many fraud cases. A classic case involved salad oil. Management of the salad-oil company filled storage tanks mostly with water. Since oil rises to the top, the auditors thought the tanks were full of oil. In addition, management said they had more tanks than they really did—they repainted numbers on the tanks to confuse auditors.

More recently, managers at women's apparel maker Leslie Fay were convicted of falsifying inventory records to boost net income—and consequently to boost management bonuses. In another case, executives at Craig Consumer Electronics were accused of defrauding lenders by manipulating inventory records. The indictment said the company classified "defective goods as new or refurbished" and claimed that it owned certain shipments "from overseas suppliers when, in fact, Craig either did not own the shipments or the shipments did not exist."

 What effect does an overstatement of inventory have on a company's financial statements?

DETERMINING OWNERSHIP OF GOODS

One challenge in determining inventory quantities is making sure a company owns the inventory. To determine ownership of goods, two questions must be answered: Do all of the goods included in the count belong to the company? Does the company own any goods that were not included in the count?

Goods in Transit

A complication in determining ownership is **goods in transit** (on board a truck, train, ship, or plane) at the end of the period. The company may have purchased goods that have not yet been received, or it may have sold goods that have not yet been delivered. To arrive at an accurate count, the company must determine ownership of these goods.

Goods in transit should be included in the inventory of the company that has legal title to the goods. Legal title is determined by the terms of the sale, as shown in Illustration 6-1 and described below.

1. When the terms are **FOB (free on board) shipping point**, ownership of the goods passes to the buyer when the public carrier accepts the goods from the seller.

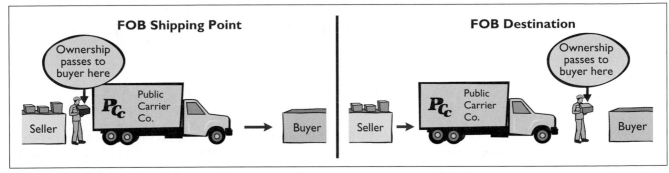

FOB Shipping Point

Ownership passes to buyer here

Seller

PCc Public Carrier Co.

Buyer

FOB Destination

Ownership passes to buyer here

Seller

PCc Public Carrier Co.

Buyer

Illustration 6-1
Terms of sale

2. When the terms are **FOB destination**, ownership of the goods remains with the seller until the goods reach the buyer.

Consigned Goods

In some lines of business, it is common to hold the goods of other parties and try to sell the goods for them for a fee, but without taking ownership of the goods. These are called **consigned goods**.

For example, you might have a used car that you would like to sell. If you take the item to a dealer, the dealer might be willing to put the car on its lot and charge you a commission if it is sold. Under this agreement the dealer **would not take ownership** of the car, which would still belong to you. Therefore, if an inventory count were taken, the car would not be included in the dealer's inventory.

Many car, boat, and antique dealers sell goods on consignment to keep their inventory costs down and to avoid the risk of purchasing an item that they won't be able to sell. Today even some manufacturers are making consignment agreements with their suppliers in order to keep their inventory levels low.

BEFORE YOU GO ON . . .

▶Review It

1. What are the three inventory categories a manufacturing company would be likely to use? Why should financial statement users be aware of these categories?
2. What steps are involved in determining inventory quantities?
3. How is ownership determined for goods in transit?
4. Who has title to consigned goods?

☑ THE NAVIGATOR

Inventory Costing

After a company has determined the quantity of units of inventory, it applies unit costs to the quantities to determine the total cost of the inventory and the cost of goods sold. This process can be complicated if a company has purchased inventory items at different times and at different prices.

For example, assume that Crivitz TV Company purchases three identical 46-inch TVs on different dates at costs of $700, $750, and $800. During the year Crivitz sold two sets at $1,200 each. These facts are summarized in Illustration 6-2.

STUDY OBJECTIVE

2

Explain the basis of accounting for inventories and apply the inventory cost flow methods under a periodic inventory system.

Illustration 6-2 Data for inventory costing example

Purchases			
February 3	1 TV	at	$700
March 5	1 TV	at	$750
May 22	1 TV	at	$800
Sales			
June 1	2 TVs	for	$2,400 ($1,200 × 2)

Cost of goods sold will differ depending on which two TVs the company sold. For example, it might be $1,450 ($700 + $750), or $1,500 ($700 + $800), or $1,550 ($750 + $800). In this section we discuss alternative costing methods available to Crivitz.

SPECIFIC IDENTIFICATION

If Crivitz sold the TVs it purchased on February 3 and May 22, then its cost of goods sold is $1,500 ($700 + $800), and its ending inventory is $750. If Crivitz can positively identify which particular units it sold and which are still in ending inventory, it can use the **specific identification method** of inventory costing (see Illustration 6-3). Using this method, companies can accurately determine ending inventory and cost of goods sold.

Illustration 6-3 Specific identification method

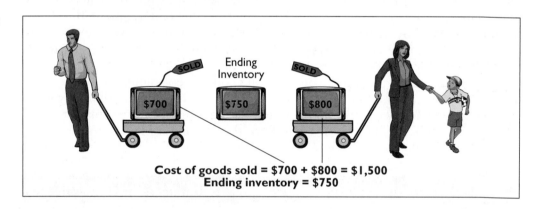

Cost of goods sold = $700 + $800 = $1,500
Ending inventory = $750

Ethics Note A major disadvantage of the specific identification method is that management may be able to manipulate net income. For example, it can boost net income by selling units purchased at a low cost, or reduce net income by selling units purchased at a high cost.

Specific identification requires that companies keep records of the original cost of each individual inventory item. Historically, specific identification was possible only when a company sold a limited variety of high-unit-cost items that could be identified clearly from the time of purchase through the time of sale. Examples of such products are cars, pianos, or expensive antiques.

Today, with bar coding, electronic product codes, and radio frequency identification, it is theoretically possible to do specific identification with nearly any type of product. The reality is, however, that this practice is still relatively rare. Instead, rather than keep track of the cost of each particular item sold, most companies make assumptions, called **cost flow assumptions**, about which units were sold.

COST FLOW ASSUMPTIONS

Because specific identification is often impractical, other cost flow methods are permitted. These differ from specific identification in that they **assume** flows of costs that may be unrelated to the physical flow of goods. There are three assumed cost flow methods:

1. First-in, first-out (FIFO)
2. Last-in, first-out (LIFO)
3. Average cost

There is no accounting requirement that the cost flow assumption be consistent with the physical movement of the goods. Company management selects the appropriate cost flow method.

To illustrate these three inventory cost flow methods, we will assume that Houston Electronics uses a periodic inventory system and has the information shown in Illustration 6-4 for its Astro condenser.[1] (An appendix to this chapter presents the use of these methods under a perpetual system.)

HOUSTON ELECTRONICS Astro Condensers				
Date	**Explanation**	**Units**	**Unit Cost**	**Total Cost**
Jan. 1	Beginning inventory	100	$10	$ 1,000
Apr. 15	Purchase	200	11	2,200
Aug. 24	Purchase	300	12	3,600
Nov. 27	Purchase	400	13	5,200
	Total	1,000		$12,000

Illustration 6-4   Cost of goods available for sale

The company had a total of 1,000 units available that it could have sold during the period. The total cost of these units was $12,000. A physical inventory at the end of the year determined that during the year Houston sold 550 units and had 450 units in inventory at December 31. The question then is how to determine what prices to use to value the goods sold and the ending inventory. The sum of the cost allocated to the units sold plus the cost of the units in inventory must add up to $12,000, the total cost of all goods available for sale.

First-In, First-Out (FIFO)

The **FIFO (first-in, first-out) method** assumes that the **earliest goods** purchased are the first to be sold. FIFO often parallels the actual physical flow of merchandise because it generally is good business practice to sell the oldest units first. Under the FIFO method, therefore, the **costs** of the earliest goods purchased are the first to be recognized in determining cost of goods sold. (Note that this does not necessarily mean that the oldest units *are* sold first, but that the costs of the oldest units are *recognized* first. In a bin of picture hangers at the hardware store, for example, no one really knows, nor would it matter, which hangers are sold first.) Illustration 6-5 (page 274) shows the allocation of the cost of goods available for sale at Houston Electronics under FIFO.

Under FIFO, since it is assumed that the first goods purchased were the first goods sold, ending inventory is based on the prices of the most recent units purchased. That is, **under FIFO, companies obtain the cost of the ending inventory by taking the unit cost of the most recent purchase and working backward until all units of inventory have been costed.** In this example, Houston Electronics prices the 450 units of ending inventory using the *most recent* prices. The last purchase was 400 units at $13 on November 27. The remaining 50 units are priced using the unit cost of the second most recent purchase, $12, on August 24. Next, Houston Electronics calculates cost of goods sold by subtracting the cost of the units **not sold** (ending inventory) from the cost of all goods available for sale.

---

[1]We have chosen to use the periodic approach for a number of reasons. First, many companies that use a perpetual inventory system use it to keep track of units on hand, but then determine cost of goods sold at the end of the period using one of the three cost flow approaches applied under essentially a periodic approach. In addition, because of the complexity, few companies use average cost on a perpetual basis. Also, most companies that use perpetual LIFO employ dollar-value LIFO, which is presented in more advanced texts. Furthermore, FIFO gives the same results under either perpetual or periodic. And finally, it is easier to demonstrate the cost flow assumptions under the periodic system, which makes it more pedagogically appropriate.

Illustration 6-5
Allocation of costs—FIFO
method

Helpful Hint Note the sequencing of the allocation: (1) Compute ending inventory, and (2) determine cost of goods sold.

Helpful Hint Another way of thinking about the calculation of FIFO **ending inventory** is the *LISH assumption*—last in still here.

COST OF GOODS AVAILABLE FOR SALE

Date	Explanation	Units	Unit Cost	Total Cost
Jan. 1	Beginning inventory	100	$10	$ 1,000
Apr. 15	Purchase	200	11	2,200
Aug. 24	Purchase	300	12	3,600
Nov. 27	Purchase	400	13	5,200
	Total	1,000		$12,000

STEP 1: ENDING INVENTORY   STEP 2: COST OF GOODS SOLD

Date	Units	Unit Cost	Total Cost		
Nov. 27	400	$13	$ 5,200	Cost of goods available for sale	$12,000
Aug. 24	50	12	600	Less: Ending inventory	5,800
Total	450		$5,800	Cost of goods sold	$ 6,200

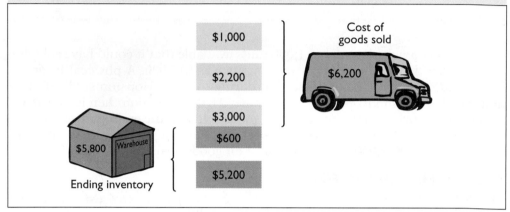

Illustration 6-6 demonstrates that companies also can calculate cost of goods sold by pricing the 550 units sold using the prices of the first 550 units acquired. Note that of the 300 units purchased on August 24, only 250 units are assumed sold. This agrees with our calculation of the cost of ending inventory, where 50 of these units were assumed unsold and thus included in ending inventory.

Illustration 6-6   Proof of
cost of goods sold

Date	Units	Unit Cost	Total Cost
Jan. 1	100	$10	$ 1,000
Apr. 15	200	11	2,200
Aug. 24	250	12	3,000
Total	550		$6,200

Last-In, First-Out (LIFO)

The **LIFO (last-in, first-out) method** assumes that the **latest goods** purchased are the first to be sold. LIFO seldom coincides with the actual physical flow of inventory. (Exceptions include goods stored in piles, such as coal or hay, where goods are removed from the top of the pile as they are sold.) Under the LIFO method, the **costs** of the latest goods purchased are the first to be recognized in determining cost of goods sold. Illustration 6-7 (page 275) shows the allocation of the cost of goods available for sale at Houston Electronics under LIFO.

Illustration 6-7
Allocation of costs—LIFO
method

COST OF GOODS AVAILABLE FOR SALE

Date	Explanation	Units	Unit Cost	Total Cost
Jan. 1	Beginning inventory	100	$10	$ 1,000
Apr. 15	Purchase	200	11	2,200
Aug. 24	Purchase	300	12	3,600
Nov. 27	Purchase	400	13	5,200
	Total	1,000		$12,000

STEP 1: ENDING INVENTORY   STEP 2: COST OF GOODS SOLD

Date	Units	Unit Cost	Total Cost		
Jan. 1	100	$10	$ 1,000	Cost of goods available for sale	$12,000
Apr. 15	200	11	2,200	Less: Ending inventory	5,000
Aug. 24	150	12	1,800	Cost of goods sold	$ 7,000
Total	450		$5,000		

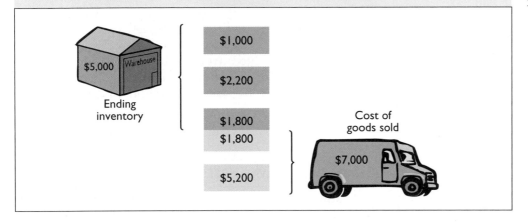

Helpful Hint Another way of thinking about the calculation of LIFO **ending inventory** is the *FISH assumption*—first in still here.

Under LIFO, since it is assumed that the first goods sold were those that were most recently purchased, ending inventory is based on the prices of the oldest units purchased. That is, **under LIFO, companies obtain the cost of the ending inventory by taking the unit cost of the earliest goods available for sale and working forward until all units of inventory have been costed**. In this example, Houston Electronics prices the 450 units of ending inventory using the *earliest* prices. The first purchase was 100 units at $10 in the January 1 beginning inventory. Then 200 units were purchased at $11. The remaining 150 units needed are priced at $12 per unit (August 24 purchase). Next, Houston Electronics calculates cost of goods sold by subtracting the cost of the units **not sold** (ending inventory) from the cost of all goods available for sale.

Illustration 6-8 demonstrates that companies also can calculate cost of goods sold by pricing the 550 units sold using the prices of the last 550 units acquired. Note that of the 300 units purchased on August 24, only 150 units are assumed sold. This agrees with our calculation of the cost of ending inventory, where 150 of these units were assumed unsold and thus included in ending inventory.

Illustration 6-8 Proof of cost of goods sold

Date	Units	Unit Cost	Total Cost
Nov. 27	400	$13	$ 5,200
Aug. 24	150	12	1,800
Total	550		$7,000

Under a periodic inventory system, which we are using here, **all goods purchased during the period are assumed to be available for the first sale, regardless of the date of purchase.**

Average Cost

The **average-cost method** allocates the cost of goods available for sale on the basis of the **weighted average unit cost** incurred. The average-cost method assumes that goods are similar in nature. Illustration 6-9 presents the formula and a sample computation of the weighted-average unit cost.

Illustration 6-9 Formula for weighted average unit cost

Cost of Goods Available for Sale	÷	Total Units Available for Sale	=	Weighted Average Unit Cost
$12,000	÷	1,000	=	$12.00

The company then applies the weighted average unit cost to the units on hand to determine the cost of the ending inventory. Illustration 6-10 shows the allocation of the cost of goods available for sale at Houston Electronics using average cost.

Illustration 6-10 Allocation of costs— average-cost method

COST OF GOODS AVAILABLE FOR SALE

Date	Explanation	Units	Unit Cost	Total Cost
Jan. 1	Beginning inventory	100	$10	$ 1,000
Apr. 15	Purchase	200	11	2,200
Aug. 24	Purchase	300	12	3,600
Nov. 27	Purchase	400	13	5,200
	Total	1,000		$12,000

STEP 1: ENDING INVENTORY

$12,000 ÷ 1,000 = $12.00

Units	Unit Cost	Total Cost
450	$12.00	$5,400

STEP 2: COST OF GOODS SOLD

Cost of goods available for sale	$12,000
Less: Ending inventory	5,400
Cost of goods sold	$ 6,600

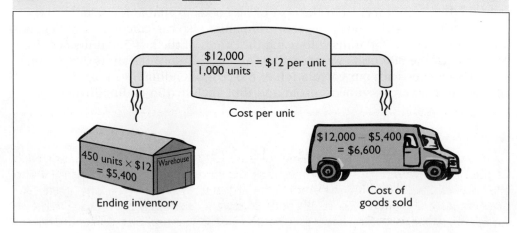

$$\frac{\$12,000}{1,000 \text{ units}} = \$12 \text{ per unit}$$

Cost per unit

450 units × $12 = $5,400 Warehouse

Ending inventory

$12,000 − $5,400 = $6,600

Cost of goods sold

We can verify the cost of goods sold under this method by multiplying the units sold times the weighted average unit cost (550 × $12 = $6,600). Note that this method does not use the average of the unit costs. That average is $11.50 ($10 + $11 + $12 + $13 = $46; $46 ÷ 4). The average cost method instead uses the average **weighted by** the quantities purchased at each unit cost.

FINANCIAL STATEMENT AND TAX EFFECTS OF COST FLOW METHODS

Each of the three assumed cost flow methods is acceptable for use. For example, Reebok International Ltd. and Wendy's International currently use the FIFO method of inventory costing. Campbell Soup Company, Krogers, and Walgreen Drugs use LIFO for part or all of their inventory. Bristol-Myers Squibb, Starbucks, and Motorola use the average cost method. In fact, a company may also use more than one cost flow method at the same time. Black & Decker Manufacturing Company, for example, uses LIFO for domestic inventories and FIFO for foreign inventories. Illustration 6-11 shows the use of the three cost flow methods in the 600 largest U.S. companies.

The reasons companies adopt different inventory cost flow methods are varied, but they usually involve one of three factors:

1. Income statement effects
2. Balance sheet effects
3. Tax effects

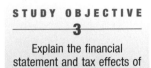

STUDY OBJECTIVE

3

Explain the financial statement and tax effects of each of the inventory cost flow assumptions.

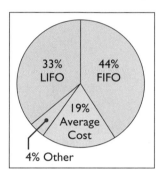

Illustration 6-11   Use of cost flow methods in major U.S. companies

Income Statement Effects

To understand why companies might choose a particular cost flow method, let's examine the effects of the different cost flow assumptions on the financial statements of Houston Electronics. The condensed income statements in Illustration 6-12 assume that Houston sold its 550 units for $11,500, had operating expenses of $2,000, and is subject to an income tax rate of 30%.

Illustration 6-12
Comparative effects of cost flow methods

HOUSTON ELECTRONICS Condensed Income Statements			
	FIFO	**LIFO**	**Average Cost**
Sales	$11,500	$11,500	$11,500
Beginning inventory	1,000	1,000	1,000
Purchases	11,000	11,000	11,000
Cost of goods available for sale	12,000	12,000	12,000
Ending inventory	**5,800**	**5,000**	**5,400**
Cost of goods sold	6,200	7,000	6,600
Gross profit	5,300	4,500	4,900
Operating expenses	2,000	2,000	2,000
Income before income taxes	3,300	2,500	2,900
Income tax expense (30%)	990	750	870
Net income	**$ 2,310**	**$ 1,750**	**$ 2,030**

Note the cost of goods available for sale ($12,000) is the same under each of the three inventory cost flow methods. However, the ending inventories and the costs of goods sold are different. This difference is due to the unit costs that the company allocated to cost of goods sold and to ending inventory. Each dollar of difference in ending inventory results in a corresponding dollar difference in income before income taxes. For Houston, an $800 difference exists between FIFO and LIFO cost of goods sold.

In periods of changing prices, the cost flow assumption can have a significant impact on income and on evaluations based on income. In most instances, prices are rising (inflation). In a period of inflation, FIFO produces a higher net income because the lower unit costs of the first units purchased are matched against revenues. In a period of rising prices (as is the case in the Houston example), FIFO reports the highest net income ($2,310) and LIFO the lowest ($1,750); average cost falls in the middle ($2,030). If prices are falling, the results from the use of FIFO and LIFO are reversed: FIFO will report the lowest net income and LIFO the highest.

To management, higher net income is an advantage: It causes external users to view the company more favorably. In addition, management bonuses, if based on net income, will be higher. Therefore, when prices are rising (which is usually the case), companies tend to prefer FIFO because it results in higher net income.

Some argue that the use of LIFO in a period of inflation enables the company to avoid reporting **paper** (or **phantom**) **profit** as economic gain. To illustrate, assume that Kralik Company buys 200 units of a product at $20 per unit on January 10 and 200 more on December 31 at $24 each. During the year, Kralik sells 200 units at $30 each. Illustration 6-13 shows the results under FIFO and LIFO.

Illustration 6-13 Income statement effects compared

	FIFO	**LIFO**
Sales (200 × $30)	$6,000	$6,000
Cost of goods sold	4,000 (200 × $20)	4,800 (200 × $24)
Gross profit	$2,000	$1,200

Under LIFO, Kralik Company has recovered the current replacement cost ($4,800) of the units sold. Thus, the gross profit in economic terms is real. However, under FIFO, the company has recovered only the January 10 cost ($4,000). To replace the units sold, it must reinvest $800 (200 × $4) of the gross profit. Thus, $800 of the gross profit is said to be phantom or illusory. As a result, reported net income is also overstated in real terms.

Balance Sheet Effects

A major advantage of the FIFO method is that in a period of inflation, the costs allocated to ending inventory will approximate their current cost. For example, for Houston Electronics, 400 of the 450 units in the ending inventory are costed under FIFO at the higher November 27 unit cost of $13.

Conversely, a major shortcoming of the LIFO method is that in a period of inflation, the costs allocated to ending inventory may be significantly understated in terms of current cost. The understatement becomes greater over prolonged periods of inflation if the inventory includes goods purchased in one or more prior accounting periods. For example, Caterpillar has used LIFO for 50 years. Its balance sheet shows ending inventory of $4,675 million. But the inventory's actual current cost if FIFO had been used is $6,799 million.

Tax Effects

Helpful Hint A tax rule, often referred to as the *LIFO conformity rule*, requires that if companies use LIFO for tax purposes they must also use it for financial reporting purposes. This means that if a company chooses the LIFO method to reduce its tax bills, it will also have to report lower net income in its financial statements.

We have seen that both inventory on the balance sheet and net income on the income statement are higher when companies use FIFO in a period of inflation. Yet, many companies have switched to LIFO. Why? The reason is that LIFO results in the lowest income taxes (because of lower net income) during times of rising prices. For example, at Houston Electronics, income taxes are $750 under LIFO, compared to $990 under FIFO. The tax savings of $240 makes more cash available for use in the business.

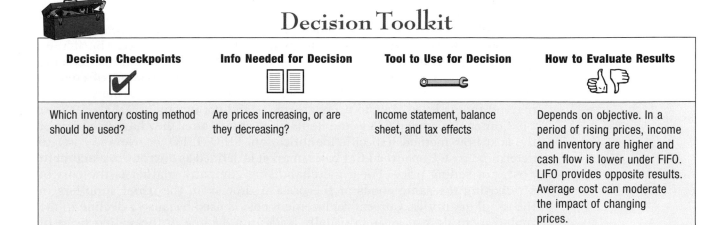

Decision Toolkit

Decision Checkpoints	Info Needed for Decision	Tool to Use for Decision	How to Evaluate Results
Which inventory costing method should be used?	Are prices increasing, or are they decreasing?	Income statement, balance sheet, and tax effects	Depends on objective. In a period of rising prices, income and inventory are higher and cash flow is lower under FIFO. LIFO provides opposite results. Average cost can moderate the impact of changing prices.

USING INVENTORY COST FLOW METHODS CONSISTENTLY

Whatever cost flow method a company chooses, it should use that method consistently from one accounting period to another. Consistent application enhances the comparability of financial statements over successive time periods. In contrast, using the FIFO method one year and the LIFO method the next year would make it difficult to compare the net incomes of the two years.

Although consistent application is preferred, it does not mean that a company may *never* change its method of inventory costing. When a company adopts a different method, it should disclose in the financial statements the change and its effects on net income. A typical disclosure is shown in Illustration 6-14, using information from recent financial statements of the Quaker Oats Company.

Helpful Hint As you learned in Chapter 2, consistency and comparability are important characteristics of accounting information.

Illustration 6-14
Disclosure of change in cost flow method

QUAKER OATS COMPANY
Notes to the Financial Statements

Note 1: Effective July 1, the Company adopted the LIFO cost flow assumption for valuing the majority of U.S. Grocery Products inventories. The Company believes that the use of the LIFO method better matches current costs with current revenues. The effect of this change on the current year was to decrease net income by $16.0 million.

LOWER OF COST OR MARKET

The value of inventory for companies selling high-technology or fashion goods can drop very quickly due to changes in technology or changes in fashions. These circumstances sometimes call for inventory valuation methods other than those presented so far. For example, in a recent year purchasing managers at Ford decided to make a large purchase of palladium, a precious metal used in vehicle emission devices. They made this large purchase because they

STUDY OBJECTIVE
4
Explain the lower of cost or market basis of accounting for inventories.

feared a future shortage. The shortage did not materialize, and by the end of the year the price of palladium had plummeted. Ford's inventory was then worth $1 billion less than its original cost. Do you think Ford's inventory should have been stated at cost, in accordance with the cost principle, or at its lower replacement cost?

As you probably reasoned, this situation requires a departure from the cost basis of accounting. When the value of inventory is lower than its cost, companies can write down the inventory to its market value. This is done by valuing the inventory at the **lower of cost or market (LCM)** in the period in which the price decline occurs. LCM is an example of the accounting **concept of conservatism**, which means that the best choice among accounting alternatives is the method that is least likely to overstate assets and net income.

Companies apply LCM to the items in inventory after they have used one of the cost flow methods (specific identification, FIFO, LIFO, or average cost) to determine cost. Under the LCM basis, market is defined as **current replacement cost**, not selling price. For a merchandising company, market is the cost of purchasing the same goods at the present time from the usual suppliers in the usual quantities. Current replacement cost is used because a decline in the replacement cost of an item usually leads to a decline in the selling price of the item.

To illustrate the application of LCM, assume that Ken Tuckie TV has the following lines of merchandise with costs and market values as indicated. LCM produces the results shown in Illustration 6-15. Note that the amounts shown in the final column are the lower of cost or market amounts for each item.

Illustration 6-15
Computation of lower of cost or market

	Cost	Market	Lower of Cost or Market
Console TVs	$ 60,000	$ 55,000	$ 55,000
Portable TVs	45,000	52,000	45,000
Video recorders	48,000	45,000	45,000
Movies	15,000	14,000	14,000
Total inventory	$168,000	$166,000	**$159,000**

BEFORE YOU GO ON . . .

►Review It

1. What factors should management consider in selecting an inventory cost flow method?

2. What inventory cost flow method does Tootsie Roll Industries use for U.S. inventories? What method does it use for foreign inventories? (*Hint:* You will need to examine the notes for Tootsie Roll's financial statements.) The answers to these questions appear on page 313.

3. Which inventory cost flow method produces the highest net income in a period of rising prices? Which results in the lowest income taxes?

4. When should inventory be reported at a value other than cost?

► Do It

The accounting records of Shumway Ag Implement show the following data.

Beginning inventory	4,000 units at $ 3
Purchases	6,000 units at $ 4
Sales	5,000 units at $12

Determine the cost of goods sold during the period under a periodic inventory system using (a) the FIFO method, (b) the LIFO method, and (c) the average-cost method.

Action Plan

- Understand the periodic inventory system.
- Allocate costs between goods sold and goods on hand (ending inventory) for each cost flow method,
- Compute cost of goods sold for each cost flow method.

Solution

(a) FIFO: (4,000 @ $3) + (1,000 @ $4) = $12,000 + $4,000 = $16,000
(b) LIFO: 5,000 @ $4 = $20,000
(c) Average-cost: [(4,000 @ $3) + (6,000 @ $4)] ÷ 10,000
$$= (\$12,000 + \$24,000) \div 10,000$$
$$= \$3.60 \text{ per unit}; 5,000 @ \$3.60 = \$18,000$$

Analysis of Inventory

For companies that sell goods, managing inventory levels can be one of the most critical tasks. Having too much inventory on hand costs the company money in storage costs, interest cost (on funds tied up in inventory), and costs associated with the obsolescence of technical goods (e.g., computer chips) or shifts in fashion (e.g., clothes). But having too little inventory on hand results in lost sales. In this section we discuss some issues related to evaluating inventory levels.

INVENTORY TURNOVER RATIO

The **inventory turnover ratio** is calculated as cost of goods sold divided by average inventory. It indicates how quickly a company sells its goods—how many times the inventory "turns over" (is sold) during the year. Inventory turnover can be divided into 365 days to compute **days in inventory**, which indicates the average age of the inventory.

High inventory turnover (low days in inventory) indicates the company is tying up little of its funds in inventory—that it has a minimal amount of inventory on hand at any one time. Although minimizing the funds tied up in inventory is efficient, too high an inventory turnover ratio may indicate that the company is losing sales opportunities because of inventory shortages. For example, investment analysts at one time suggested that Office Depot had gone too far in reducing its inventory—they said they were seeing too many empty shelves. Thus, management should closely monitor this ratio to achieve the best balance between too much and too little inventory.

In Chapter 5 we discussed the increasingly competitive environment of retailers like Wal-Mart and Target. Wal-Mart has implemented **just-in-time inventory procedures** as well as many technological innovations to improve the efficiency of its inventory management. The following data are available for Wal-Mart.

STUDY OBJECTIVE

5

Compute and interpret the inventory turnover ratio.

(in millions)	**2004**	**2003**	**2002**
Ending inventory	$ 26,612	$ 24,401	$22,053
Cost of goods sold	198,747	178,299	

Illustration 6-16 (page 282) presents the inventory turnover ratios and days in inventory for Wal-Mart and Target, using data from the financial statements of those corporations for 2004 and 2003.

The calculations in Illustration 6-16 show that Wal-Mart turns its inventory more frequently than Target (7.8 times for Wal-Mart versus 6.3 times for Target). Consequently, the average time an item spends on a Wal-Mart shelf is shorter (46.8 days for Wal-Mart versus 57.9 days for Target). This suggests that Wal-Mart is more efficient than Target in its inventory management.

Illustration 6-16
Inventory turnover ratio and days in inventory

$$\text{Inventory Turnover Ratio} = \frac{\text{Cost of Goods Sold}}{\text{Average Inventory}}$$

$$\text{Days in Inventory} = \frac{365}{\text{Inventory Turnover Ratio}}$$

		2004	2003
Wal-Mart ($ in millions)	Inventory turnover ratio	$\frac{\$198{,}747}{(\$26{,}612 + \$24{,}401)/2} = 7.8$ times	$\frac{\$178{,}299}{(\$24{,}401 + \$22{,}053)/2} = 7.7$ times
	Days in inventory	$\frac{365 \text{ days}}{7.8} = 46.8$ days	$\frac{365 \text{ days}}{7.7} = 47.4$ days
Target	Inventory turnover ratio	6.3 times	6.4 times
	Days in inventory	57.9 days	57.0 days

Note also that Wal-Mart's inventory turnover, which was already better than Target's in 2003, improved slightly in 2004. Wal-Mart's sophisticated inventory tracking and distribution system allows it to keep minimum amounts of inventory on hand, while still keeping the shelves full of what customers are looking for.

Accounting across the Organization

Demand for cell phones typically falls during the first quarter of each year. It is a widely held principle that a company should cut back its production and inventory levels when it anticipates that demand will decrease. Thus many industry observers were surprised when Samsung Electronics Co. chose to increase production during the first quarter of the year, for the third year in a row.

Why did Samsung do this? Its executives felt that this approach would enable it to stand out against competitors by putting "a slew of new cell phones on shelves next to graying models from its rivals." It is clear that even with just-in-time inventory techniques and highly efficient inventory systems, management still must make many critical strategic decisions regarding inventory.

Source: Evan Ramstad, "Samsung to Report Whether Counterintuitive Move Paid Off," *Wall Street Journal* (April 24, 2005), p. B3.

 If Samsung isn't successful in selling the units, what steps will it have to take, and how will this show up in its financial statements?

Decision Toolkit

Decision Checkpoints	Info Needed for Decision	Tool to Use for Decision	How to Evaluate Results
How long is an item in inventory?	Cost of goods sold; beginning and ending inventory	$$\text{Inventory turnover ratio} = \frac{\text{Cost of goods sold}}{\text{Average inventory}}$$ $$\text{Days in inventory} = \frac{365 \text{ days}}{\text{Inventory turnover ratio}}$$	A higher inventory turnover ratio or lower average days in inventory suggests that management is reducing the amount of inventory on hand, relative to sales.

ANALYSTS' ADJUSTMENTS FOR LIFO RESERVE

Earlier we noted that using LIFO rather than FIFO can result in significant differences in the results reported in the balance sheet and the income statement. With increasing prices, FIFO will result in higher income than LIFO. On the balance sheet, FIFO will result in higher reported inventory. The financial statement differences of using LIFO normally increase the longer a company uses LIFO.

Use of different inventory cost flow assumptions complicates analysts' attempts to compare companies' results. Fortunately, companies using LIFO are required to report the amount that inventory would increase (or occasionally decrease) if the company had instead been using FIFO. This amount is referred to as the **LIFO reserve**. Reporting the LIFO reserve enables analysts to make adjustments to compare companies that use different cost flow methods.

Illustration 6-17 presents an excerpt from the notes to Caterpillar's 2004 financial statements that discloses and discusses Caterpillar's LIFO reserve.

STUDY OBJECTIVE

6

Describe the LIFO reserve and explain its importance for comparing results of different companies.

CATERPILLAR INC.
Notes to the Financial Statements

Inventories: Inventories are stated at the lower of cost or market. Cost is principally determined using the last-in, first-out (LIFO) method. If the FIFO (first-in, first-out) method had been in use, inventories would have been $2,124, $1,863, and $1,977 million higher than reported at December 31, 2004, 2003, and 2002, respectively.

Illustration 6-17
Caterpillar LIFO reserve

Caterpillar has used LIFO for over 50 years. Thus, the cumulative difference between LIFO and FIFO reflected in the inventory account is very large. In fact, the 2004 LIFO reserve of $2,124 million is 45 percent of the 2004 LIFO inventory of $4,675 million. Such a huge difference would clearly distort any comparisons you might try to make with one of Caterpillar's competitors that used FIFO.

To adjust Caterpillar's inventory balance we add the LIFO reserve to reported inventory, as shown in Illustration 6-18. That is, if Caterpillar had used FIFO all along, its inventory would be $6,799 million, rather than $4,675 million.

	(in millions)
2004 inventory using LIFO	$ 4,675
2004 LIFO reserve	2,124
2004 inventory assuming FIFO	**$6,799**

Illustration 6-18
Conversion of inventory from LIFO to FIFO

The LIFO reserve can have a significant effect on ratios analysts commonly use. Using the LIFO reserve adjustment, Illustration 6-19 calculates the value of the current ratio (current assets ÷ current liabilities) for Caterpillar under both the LIFO and FIFO cost flow assumptions.

Illustration 6-19 Impact of LIFO reserve on ratios

($ in millions)	LIFO	FIFO
Current ratio	$\dfrac{\$20{,}856}{\$16{,}210} = 1.3:1$	$\dfrac{\$20{,}856 + \$2{,}124}{\$16{,}210} = 1.4:1$

As Illustration 6-19 shows, if Caterpillar used FIFO, its current ratio would be 1.4:1 rather than 1.3:1 under LIFO. Thus, Caterpillar's liquidity appears stronger if a FIFO assumption were used in valuing inventories. If a similar adjustment is made for the inventory turnover ratio, Caterpillar's inventory turnover actually would look worse under FIFO than under LIFO, dropping from 5.8 times for LIFO to 3.8 times for FIFO.[2] The reason: LIFO reports low inventory amounts, which cause inventory turnover to be overstated.

CNH Global, a competitor of Caterpillar, uses FIFO to account for its inventory. Comparing Caterpillar to CNH without converting Caterpillar's inventory to FIFO would lead to distortions and potentially erroneous decisions.

BEFORE YOU GO ON . . .

▶Review It

1. What is the purpose of the inventory turnover ratio? What is the relationship between the inventory turnover ratio and average days in inventory?
2. What is the LIFO reserve? What does it tell a financial statement user?

THE NAVIGATOR

Decision Toolkit

Decision Checkpoints	Info Needed for Decision	Tool to Use for Decision	How to Evaluate Results
What is the impact of LIFO on the company's reported inventory?	LIFO reserve, cost of goods sold, ending inventory, current assets, current liabilities	$\dfrac{\text{LIFO}}{\text{inventory}} + \dfrac{\text{LIFO}}{\text{reserve}} = \dfrac{\text{FIFO}}{\text{inventory}}$	If these adjustments are material, they can significantly affect such measures as the current ratio and the inventory turnover ratio.

[2]The LIFO reserve also affects cost of goods sold, although typically by a much less material amount. The cost of goods sold adjustment is discussed in more advanced financial statement analysis texts.

Using the Decision Toolkit

The Manitowoc Company is located in Manitowoc, Wisconsin. In recent years it has made a series of strategic acquisitions to grow and enhance its market-leading positions in each of its three business segments. These include: cranes and related products (crawler cranes, tower cranes, and boom trucks); food service equipment (commercial ice-cube machines, ice-beverage dispensers, and commercial refrigeration equipment); and marine operations (shipbuilding and ship-repair services). The company reported inventory of $287,036,000 for 2004 and of $232,877,000 for 2003. Here is the inventory note taken from the 2004 financial statements.

THE MANITOWOC COMPANY
Notes to the Financial Statements

Inventories: The components of inventories are summarized at December 31 as follows (in thousands).

	2004	2003
Components		
Raw materials	$111,400	$ 89,851
Work in process	87,825	81,378
Finished goods*	106,348	80,266
Net inventories at FIFO cost	305,573	251,495
Excess of FIFO cost over LIFO value	(18,537)	(18,618)
Inventories—net	$287,036	$232,877

*The finished goods inventories have been reduced to reflect the company's reserve for excess and obsolete inventory.

Manitowoc carries inventory at the lower of cost or market using the first-in, first-out (FIFO) method for 90% and 88% of total inventory for 2004 and 2003, respectively. The remainder of the inventory is costed using the last-in, first-out (LIFO) method.

Additional facts:

2004 Current liabilities	$ 652,680
2004 Current assets (as reported)	$ 845,961
2004 Cost of goods sold	$1,582,131

Instructions

Answer the following questions.

1. Why does the company report its inventory in three components?
2. Why might the company use two methods (LIFO and FIFO) to account for its inventory?
3. Perform each of the following.
   (a) Calculate the inventory turnover ratio and days in inventory using the LIFO inventory.
   (b) Show the conversion of the 2004 and 2003 LIFO inventory values to FIFO values.
   (c) Calculate the 2004 current ratio using LIFO and the current ratio using FIFO. Discuss the difference.

Solution

1. The Manitowoc Company is a manufacturer, so it purchases raw materials and makes them into finished products. At the end of each period, it has some goods that have been started but are not yet complete (work in process).

   By reporting all three components of inventory, a company reveals important information about its inventory position. For example, if amounts of raw materials have increased significantly compared to the previous year, we might assume the company is planning to step up production. On the other hand, if levels of finished goods have increased relative to last year and raw materials have declined, we might conclude that sales are slowing down—that the company has too much inventory on hand and is cutting back production.

2. Companies are free to choose different cost flow assumptions for different types of inventory. A company might choose to use FIFO for a product that is expected to decrease in price over time. One common reason for choosing a method other than LIFO is that many foreign countries do not allow LIFO; thus, the company cannot use LIFO for its foreign operations.

3. (a) $$\frac{\text{Inventory turnover}}{\text{ratio}} = \frac{\text{Cost of goods sold}}{\text{Average inventory}} = \frac{\$1,582,131}{(\$287,036 + \$232,877)/2} = 6.1$$

   $$\frac{\text{Days in}}{\text{inventory}} = \frac{365}{\text{Inventory turnover ratio}} = \frac{365}{6.1} = 59.8 \text{ days}$$

   (b) Conversion from LIFO to FIFO values

	2004	**2003**
LIFO inventory	$287,036	$ 232,877
LIFO reserve	18,537	18,618
FIFO inventory	$305,573	$251,495

   (c) Current ratio

	LIFO	**FIFO**
$\dfrac{\text{Current assets}}{\text{Current liabilities}}$	$\dfrac{\$845,961}{\$652,680} = 1.30:1$	$\dfrac{\$845,961 + \$18,537}{\$652,680} = 1.32:1$

   This represents a 1.5% increase in the current ratio $(1.32 - 1.30)/1.30$.

Summary of Study Objectives

1 *Describe the steps in determining inventory quantities.* The steps are (1) taking a physical inventory of goods on hand and (2) determining the ownership of goods in transit or on consignment.

2 *Explain the basis of accounting for inventories and apply the inventory cost flow methods under a periodic inventory system.* The primary basis of accounting for inventories is cost. Cost includes all expenditures necessary to acquire goods and place them in condition ready for sale. Cost of goods available for sale includes (a) cost of beginning inventory and (b) cost of goods purchased. The inventory cost flow methods are: specific identification and three assumed cost flow methods—FIFO, LIFO, and average cost.

3 *Explain the financial statement and tax effects of each of the inventory cost flow assumptions.* The cost of goods available for sale may be allocated to cost of goods sold and ending inventory by specific identification or by a method based on an assumed cost flow. When prices are rising, the first-in, first-out (FIFO) method results in lower cost of goods sold and higher net income than the average cost and the last-in, first-out (LIFO) methods. The reverse is true when prices are falling. In the balance sheet, FIFO results in an ending inventory that is closest to current value, whereas the inventory under LIFO is the farthest from current value. LIFO results in the lowest income taxes (because of lower taxable income).

4 *Explain the lower of cost or market basis of accounting for inventories.* Companies may use the lower of cost or market (LCM) basis when the current replacement cost (market) is less than cost. Under LCM, companies recognize the loss in the period in which the price decline occurs.

5 *Compute and interpret the inventory turnover ratio.* The inventory turnover ratio is calculated as cost of goods sold divided by average inventory. It can be converted to average days in inventory by dividing 365 days by the inventory turnover ratio. A higher turnover ratio or lower average days in inventory suggests that management is trying to keep inventory levels low relative to its sales level.

6 *Describe the LIFO reserve and explain its importance for comparing results of different companies.* The LIFO reserve represents the difference between ending inventory using LIFO and ending inventory if FIFO were employed instead. For some companies this difference can be significant, and ignoring it can lead to inappropriate conclusions when using the current ratio or inventory turnover ratio.

Decision Toolkit—A Summary

Decision Checkpoints	Info Needed for Decision	Tool to Use for Decision	How to Evaluate Results
Which inventory costing method should be used?	Are prices increasing, or are they decreasing?	Income statement, balance sheet, and tax effects	Depends on objective. In a period of rising prices, income and inventory are higher and cash flow is lower under FIFO. LIFO provides opposite results. Average cost can moderate the impact of changing prices.
How long is an item in inventory?	Cost of goods sold; beginning and ending inventory	$\text{Inventory turnover ratio} = \dfrac{\text{Cost of goods sold}}{\text{Average inventory}}$ $\text{Days in inventory} = \dfrac{365 \text{ days}}{\text{Inventory turnover ratio}}$	A higher inventory turnover ratio or lower average days in inventory suggests that management is reducing the amount of inventory on hand, relative to sales.
What is the impact of LIFO on the company's reported inventory?	LIFO reserve, cost of goods sold, ending inventory, current assets, current liabilities	$\text{LIFO inventory} + \text{LIFO reserve} = \text{FIFO inventory}$	If these adjustments are material, they can significantly affect such measures as the current ratio and the inventory turnover ratio.

APPENDIX 6A
INVENTORY COST FLOW METHODS IN PERPETUAL INVENTORY SYSTEMS

Each of the inventory cost flow methods described in the chapter for a periodic inventory system may be used in a perpetual inventory system. To illustrate the application of the three assumed cost flow methods (FIFO, LIFO, and average cost), we will use the data shown in Illustration 6A-1 (next page) and in this chapter for Houston Electronic's Astro Condenser.

STUDY OBJECTIVE

7

Apply the inventory cost flow methods to perpetual inventory records.

	HOUSTON ELECTRONICS Astro Condensers				
Date	**Explanation**	**Units**	**Unit Cost**	**Total Cost**	**Balance in Units**
1/1	Beginning inventory	100	$10	$ 1,000	100
4/15	Purchases	200	11	2,200	300
8/24	Purchases	300	12	3,600	600
9/10	Sale	550			50
11/27	Purchases	400	13	5,200	450
				$12,000	

First-In, First-Out (FIFO)

Under FIFO, the cost of the earliest goods on hand **prior to each sale** is charged to cost of goods sold. Therefore, the cost of goods sold on September 10 consists of the units on hand January 1 and the units purchased April 15 and August 24. Illustration 6A-2 shows the inventory under a FIFO method perpetual system.

Date	Purchases		Cost of Goods Sold	Balance	
January 1				(100 @ $10)	$ 1,000
April 15	(200 @ $11)	$2,200		(100 @ $10) (200 @ $11)	$ 3,200
August 24	(300 @ $12)	$3,600		(100 @ $10) (200 @ $11) (300 @ $12)	$ 6,800
September 10			(100 @ $10) (200 @ $11) (250 @ $12) **$6,200**	(50 @ $12)	$ 600
November 27	(400 @ $13)	$5,200		(50 @ $12) (400 @ $13)	**$5,800**

The ending inventory in this situation is $5,800, and the cost of goods sold is $6,200 [(100 @ $10) + (200 @ $11) + (250 @ $12)].

The results under FIFO in a perpetual system are the **same as in a periodic system**. (See Illustration 6-5 on page 274 where, similarly, the ending inventory is $5,800 and cost of goods sold is $6,200.) Regardless of the system, the first costs in are the costs assigned to cost of goods sold.

Last-In, First-Out (LIFO)

Under the LIFO method using a perpetual system, the cost of the most recent purchase prior to sale is allocated to the units sold. Therefore, the cost of the goods sold on September 10 consists of all the units from the August 24 and April 15 purchases plus 50 of the units in beginning inventory. The ending inventory under the LIFO method is computed in Illustration 6A-3.

The use of LIFO in a perpetual system will usually produce cost allocations that differ from use of LIFO in a periodic system. In a perpetual system, the latest units purchased *prior to each sale* are allocated to cost of goods sold. In contrast, in a periodic system, the latest units purchased *during the period* are allocated to cost of goods sold. Thus, when a purchase is made after the last sale, the LIFO periodic system will apply this purchase to the previous sale. See

Date	Purchases	Cost of Goods Sold	Balance	
January 1			(100 @ $10)	$ 1,000
April 15	(200 @ $11) $2,200		(100 @ $10)⎫ (200 @ $11)⎭	$ 3,200
August 24	(300 @ $12) $3,600		(100 @ $10)⎫ (200 @ $11)⎬ (300 @ $12)⎭	$ 6,800
September 10		(300 @ $12) (200 @ $11) (50 @ $10)	(50 @ $10)	$ 500
		$6,300		
November 27	(400 @ $13) $5,200		(50 @ $10)⎫ (400 @ $13)⎭	**$5,700**

Illustration 6-8 (on page 275) where the proof shows the 400 units at $13 purchased on November 27 applied to the sale of 550 units on September 10.

As shown above, under the LIFO perpetual system the 400 units at $13 purchased on November 27 are all applied to the ending inventory.

The ending inventory in this LIFO perpetual illustration is $5,700 and cost of goods sold is $6,300, as compared to the LIFO periodic illustration (on page 275) where the ending inventory is $5,000 and cost of goods sold is $7,000.

Average Cost

The average-cost method in a perpetual inventory system is called the **moving-average method**. Under this method the company computes a new average **after each purchase**. The average cost is computed by dividing the cost of goods available for sale by the units on hand. The average cost is then applied to: (1) the units sold, to determine the cost of goods sold, and (2) the remaining units on hand, to determine the ending inventory amount. Illustration 6A-4 shows the application of the average-cost method by Houston Electronics.

Date	Purchases	Cost of Goods Sold	Balance	
January 1			(100 @ $10)	$ 1,000
April 15	(200 @ $11) $2,200		(300 @ $10.667)	$ 3,200
August 24	(300 @ $12) $3,600		(600 @ $11.333)	$ 6,800
September 10		(550 @ $11.333)	(50 @ $11.333)	$ 567
		$6,233		
November 27	(400 @ $13) $5,200		(450 @ $12.816)	**$5,767**

As indicated above, the company computes **a new average each time it makes a purchase**. On April 15, after 200 units are purchased for $2,200, a total of 300 units costing $3,200 ($1,000 + $2,200) are on hand. The average unit cost is $10.667 ($3,200 ÷ 300). On August 24, after 300 units are purchased for $3,600, a total of 600 units costing $6,800 ($1,000 + $2,200 + $3,600) are on hand at an average cost per unit of $11.333 ($6,800 ÷ 600). Houston Electronics uses this unit cost of $11.333 in costing sales until another purchase is made, when the company computes a new unit cost. Accordingly, the unit cost of the 550 units sold on September 10 is $11.333, and the total cost of goods sold is $6,233. On November 27, following the purchase of 400 units for $5,200, there are 450 units on hand costing $5,767 ($567 + $5,200) with a new average cost of $12.816 ($5,767 ÷ 450).

Compare this moving-average cost under the perpetual inventory system to Illustration 6-10 (on page 276) showing the weighted-average method under a periodic inventory system.

Summary of Study Objective for Appendix 6A

7 *Apply the inventory cost flow methods to perpetual inventory records.* Under FIFO, the cost of the earliest goods on hand prior to each sale is charged to cost of goods sold. Under LIFO, the cost of the most re-cent purchase prior to sale is charged to cost of goods sold. Under the average-cost method, a new average cost is computed after each purchase.

APPENDIX 6B
INVENTORY ERRORS

STUDY OBJECTIVE
8
Indicate the effects of inventory errors on the financial statements.

Unfortunately, errors occasionally occur in accounting for inventory. In some cases, errors are caused by failure to count or price the inventory correctly. In other cases, errors occur because companies do not properly recognize the transfer of legal title to goods that are in transit. When errors occur, they affect both the income statement and the balance sheet.

Income Statement Effects

As you know, both the beginning and ending inventories appear in the income statement. The ending inventory of one period automatically becomes the beginning inventory of the next period. Thus, inventory errors affect the computation of cost of goods sold and net income in two periods.

The effects on cost of goods sold can be computed by entering incorrect data in the formula in Illustration 6B-1 and then substituting the correct data.

Illustration 6B-1
Formula for cost of goods sold

Beginning Inventory	+	Cost of Goods Purchased	−	Ending Inventory	=	Cost of Goods Sold

If *beginning* inventory is understated, cost of goods sold will be understated. If *ending* inventory is understated, cost of goods sold will be overstated. Illustration 6B-2 shows the effects of inventory errors on the current year's income statement.

Illustration 6B-2   Effects of inventory errors on current year's income statement

Inventory Error	Cost of Goods Sold	Net Income
Understate beginning inventory	Understated	Overstated
Overstate beginning inventory	Overstated	Understated
Understate ending inventory	Overstated	Understated
Overstate ending inventory	Understated	Overstated

An error in the ending inventory of the current period will have a **reverse effect on net income of the next accounting period**. This is shown in Illustration 6B-3. Note that the understatement of ending inventory in 2006 results in an understatement of beginning inventory in 2007 and an overstatement of net income in 2007.

Over the two years, total net income is correct because the errors offset each other. Notice that total income using incorrect data is $35,000 ($22,000 + $13,000), which is the same as the total income of $35,000 ($25,000 + $10,000) using correct data. Also note in this example that an error in the beginning inventory does not result in a corresponding error in the ending inventory for that period. The correctness of the ending inventory depends entirely on the accuracy of taking and costing the inventory at the balance sheet date under the periodic inventory system.

Illustration 6B-3   Effects of inventory errors on two years' income statements

SAMPLE COMPANY
Condensed Income Statements

	2006				2007			
	Incorrect		Correct		Incorrect		Correct	
Sales		$80,000		$80,000		$90,000		$90,000
Beginning inventory	$20,000		$20,000		**$12,000**		**$15,000**	
Cost of goods purchased	40,000		40,000		68,000		68,000	
Cost of goods available for sale	60,000		60,000		80,000		83,000	
Ending inventory	**12,000**		**15,000**		23,000		23,000	
Cost of goods sold		48,000		45,000		57,000		60,000
Gross profit		32,000		35,000		33,000		30,000
Operating expenses		10,000		10,000		20,000		20,000
Net income		$22,000		$25,000		$13,000		$10,000

$(3,000)
Net income
understated

$3,000
Net income
overstated

**The errors cancel. Thus the combined total
income for the 2-year period is correct.**

Business Insight
Investor Perspective

Inventory fraud increases during recessions. Such fraud includes pricing inventory at amounts in excess of its actual value, or claiming to have inventory when no inventory exists. Inventory fraud is usually done to overstate ending inventory, thereby understating cost of goods sold and creating higher income.

Balance Sheet Effects

The effect of ending inventory errors on the balance sheet can be determined by using the basic accounting equation: Assets = Liabilities + Stockholders' equity. Errors in the ending inventory have the effects shown in Illustration 6B-4.

Illustration 6B-4   Effects of ending inventory errors on balance sheet

Ending Inventory Error	Assets	Liabilities	Stockholders' Equity
Overstated	Overstated	No effect	Overstated
Understated	Understated	No effect	Understated

The effect of an error in ending inventory on the subsequent period was shown in Illustration 6B-3. Recall that if the error is not corrected, the combined total net income for the two periods would be correct. Thus, total stockholders' equity reported on the balance sheet at the end of 2007 will also be correct.

Summary of Study Objective for Appendix 6B

8 *Indicate the effects of inventory errors on the financial statements. In the income statement of the current year:* (a) An error in beginning inventory will have a reverse effect on net income (e.g., overstatement of inventory results in understatement of net income, and vice versa). (b) An error in ending inventory will have a similar effect on net income (e.g., overstatement of inventory results in overstatement of net in- come). If ending inventory errors are not corrected in the following period, their effect on net income for that period is reversed, and total net income for the two years will be correct.

In the balance sheet: Ending inventory errors will have the same effect on total assets and total stock- holders' equity and no effect on liabilities.

Glossary

Average-cost method An inventory costing method that uses the weighted average unit cost to allocate the cost of goods available for sale to ending inventory and cost of goods sold. (p. 276)

Consigned goods Goods held for sale by one party (the consignee) although ownership of the goods is retained by another party (the consignor). (p. 271)

Current replacement cost The current cost to replace an inventory item. (p. 280)

Days in inventory Measure of the average number of days inventory is held; calculated as 365 divided by in- ventory turnover ratio. (p. 281)

Finished goods inventory Manufactured items that are completed and ready for sale. (p. 268)

First-in, first-out (FIFO) method An inventory cost- ing method that assumes that the costs of the earliest goods purchased are the first to be recognized as cost of goods sold. (p. 273)

FOB destination Freight terms indicating that the goods are placed free on board at the buyer's place of business, and the seller pays the freight cost; goods be- long to the seller while in transit. (p. 271)

FOB shipping point Freight terms indicating that the goods are placed free on board the carrier by the seller, and the buyer pays the freight cost; goods belong to the buyer while in transit. (p. 270)

Inventory turnover ratio A ratio that measures the number of times on average the inventory sold during the period; computed by dividing cost of goods sold by the average inventory during the period. (p. 281)

Just-in-time (JIT) inventory Inventory system in which companies manufacture or purchase goods just in time for use. (p. 269)

Last-in, first-out (LIFO) method An inventory costing method that assumes that the costs of the latest units purchased are the first to be allocated to cost of goods sold. (p. 274)

LIFO reserve For a company using LIFO, the differ- ence between inventory reported using LIFO and inven- tory using FIFO. (p. 283)

Lower of cost or market (LCM) basis (inventories) A basis whereby inventory is stated at the lower of either its cost or its market cost as determined by current re- placement cost. (p. 280)

Raw materials Basic goods that will be used in produc- tion but have not yet been placed in production. (p. 268)

Specific identification method An actual physical flow costing method in which items still in inventory are specifically costed to arrive at the total cost of the end- ing inventory. (p. 272)

Weighted average unit cost Average cost that is weighted by the number of units purchased at each unit cost. (p. 276)

Work in process That portion of manufactured inven- tory that has begun the production process but is not yet complete. (p. 268)

Demonstration Problem

Englehart Company has the following inventory, purchases, and sales data for the month of March.

Inventory, March 1	200 units @ $4.00	$ 800
Purchases		
March 10	500 units @ $4.50	2,250
March 20	400 units @ $4.75	1,900
March 30	300 units @ $5.00	1,500
Sales		
March 15	500 units	
March 25	400 units	

The physical inventory count on March 31 shows 500 units on hand.

Instructions

Under a **periodic inventory system**, determine the cost of inventory on hand at March 31 and the cost of goods sold for March under (a) the first-in, first-out (FIFO) method; (b) the last-in, first-out (LIFO) method; and (c) the average-cost method. (For average cost, carry cost per unit to three decimal places.)

Solution to Demonstration Problem

The cost of goods available for sale is $6,450:

Inventory	200 units @ $4.00	$ 800
Purchases		
March 10	500 units @ $4.50	2,250
March 20	400 units @ $4.75	1,900
March 30	300 units @ $5.00	1,500
Total cost of goods available for sale		$6,450

(a)   **FIFO Method**

Ending inventory:

Date	Units	Unit Cost	Total Cost	
Mar. 30	300	$5.00	$1,500	
Mar. 20	200	4.75	950	$2,450

Cost of goods sold: $6,450 − $2,450 = $4,000

(b)   **LIFO Method**

Ending inventory:

Date	Units	Unit Cost	Total Cost	
Mar. 1	200	$4.00	$ 800	
Mar. 10	300	4.50	1,350	$2,150

Cost of goods sold: $6,450 − $2,150 = $4,300

(c)   **Weighted Average-Cost Method**

Weighted average unit cost: $6,450 ÷ 1,400 = $4.607
Ending inventory: 500 × $4.607 = $2,303.50

Cost of goods sold: $6,450 − $2,303.50 = $4,146.50

Action Plan

- For FIFO, allocate the latest costs to inventory.
- For LIFO, allocate the earliest costs to inventory.
- For average cost, use a weighted average.
- Remember, the costs allocated to cost of goods sold can be proved.
- Total purchases are the same under all three cost flow assumptions.

Note: All Questions, Exercises, and Problems marked with an asterisk relate to material in the appendixes to the chapter.

Self-Study Questions

Answers are at the end of the chapter.

(SO 1)   **1.** When is a physical inventory usually taken?
   (a) When the company has its greatest amount of inventory.
   (b) When goods are not being sold or received.
   (c) At the end of the company's fiscal year.
   (d) Both (b) and (c).

2. Which of the following should *not* be included   (SO 1)
in the physical inventory of a company?
   (a) Goods held on consignment from another company.
   (b) Goods shipped on consignment to another company.
   (c) Goods in transit from another company shipped FOB shipping point.
   (d) All of the above should be included.

(SO 2)

3. Kam Company has the following units and costs.

	Units	Unit Cost
Inventory, Jan. 1	8,000	$11
Purchase, June 19	13,000	12
Purchase, Nov. 8	5,000	13

If 9,000 units are on hand at December 31, what is the cost of the ending inventory under FIFO?
(a) $99,000.   (c) $113,000.
(b) $108,000.   (d) $117,000.

(SO 2)

4. From the data in question 3, what is the cost of the ending inventory under LIFO?
(a) $113,000.   (c) $99,000.
(b) $108,000.   (d) $100,000.

(SO 3)

5. In periods of rising prices, LIFO will produce:
(a) higher net income than FIFO.
(b) the same net income as FIFO.
(c) lower net income than FIFO.
(d) higher net income than average costing.

(SO 3)

6. Considerations that affect the selection of an inventory costing method do *not* include:
(a) tax effects.
(b) balance sheet effects.
(c) income statement effects.
(d) perpetual versus periodic inventory system.

(SO 4)

7. The lower of cost or market rule for inventory is an example of the application of:
(a) the conservatism constraint.
(b) the historical cost principle.
(c) the materiality constraint.
(d) the economic entity assumption.

(SO 5)

8. Which of these would cause the inventory turnover ratio to increase the most?
(a) Increasing the amount of inventory on hand.
(b) Keeping the amount of inventory on hand constant but increasing sales.

(c) Keeping the amount of inventory on hand constant but decreasing sales.
(d) Decreasing the amount of inventory on hand and increasing sales.

9. The LIFO reserve is: (SO 6)
(a) the difference between the value of the inventory under LIFO and the value under FIFO.
(b) an amount used to adjust inventory to the lower of cost or market.
(c) the difference between the value of the inventory under LIFO and the value under average cost.
(d) an amount used to adjust inventory to historical cost.

*10. In a perpetual inventory system,   (SO 7)
(a) LIFO cost of goods sold will be the same as in a periodic inventory system.
(b) average costs are based entirely on unit-cost simple averages.
(c) a new average is computed under the average cost method after each sale.
(d) FIFO cost of goods sold will be the same as in a periodic inventory system.

*11. Fran Company's ending inventory is understated by $4,000. The effects of this error on the current year's cost of goods sold and net income, respectively, are: (SO 8)
(a) understated and overstated.
(b) overstated and understated.
(c) overstated and overstated.
(d) understated and understated.

Go to the book's website, **www.wiley.com/college/kimmel**, to access additional Self-Study Questions.

Questions

1. "The key to successful business operations is effective inventory management." Do you agree? Explain.

2. An item must possess two characteristics to be classified as inventory. What are these two characteristics?

3. What is just-in-time inventory management? What are its potential advantages?

4. Your friend Carol Brandon has been hired to help take the physical inventory in Mozena's Hardware Store. Explain to Carol what this job will entail.

5. (a) Michelle Company ships merchandise to Matthew Corporation on December 30. The merchandise reaches the buyer on January 5. Indicate the terms of sale that will result in the goods being included in (1) Michelle's December 31 inventory and (2) Matthew's December 31 inventory.

(b) Under what circumstances should Michelle Company include consigned goods in its inventory?

6. Topp Hat Shop received a shipment of hats for which it paid the wholesaler $2,940. The price of the hats was $3,000, but Topp was given a $60 cash discount and required to pay freight charges of $95. In addition, Topp paid $100 to cover the travel expenses of an employee who negotiated the purchase of the hats. What amount should Topp include in inventory? Why?

7. What is the primary basis of accounting for inventories? What is the major objective in accounting for inventories?

8. Jon Compton believes that the allocation of cost of goods available for sale should be based on the actual physical flow of the goods. Explain to Jon why this may be both impractical and inappropriate.

9. What are the major advantage and major disadvantage of the specific identification method of inventory costing?

10. "The selection of an inventory cost flow method is a decision made by accountants." Do you agree? Explain. Once a method has been selected, what accounting requirement applies?

11. Which assumed inventory cost flow method:
    (a) usually parallels the actual physical flow of merchandise?
    (b) assumes that goods available for sale during an accounting period are similar in nature?
    (c) assumes that the latest units purchased are the first to be sold?

12. In a period of rising prices, the inventory reported in Alpha Company's balance sheet is close to the current cost of the inventory, whereas Omega Company's inventory is considerably below its current cost. Identify the inventory cost flow method used by each company. Which company probably has been reporting the higher gross profit?

13. Millott Corporation has been using the FIFO cost flow method during a prolonged period of inflation. During the same time period, Millott has been paying out all of its net income as dividends. What adverse effects may result from this policy?

14. Brian Birdsong, a mid-level product manager for Stella's Shoes, thinks his company should switch from LIFO to FIFO. He says, "My bonus is based on net income. If we switch it will increase net income and increase my bonus. The company would be better off and so would I." Is he correct? Explain.

15. Hayley Carter is studying for the next accounting midterm examination. What should Hayley know about (a) departing from the cost basis of accounting for inventories and (b) the meaning of "market" in the lower of cost or market method?

16. Moondog Music Center has five CD players on hand at the balance sheet date that cost $400 each. The current replacement cost is $320 per unit. Under the lower of cost or market basis of accounting for inventories, what value should Moondog report for the CD players on the balance sheet? Why?

17. What cost flow assumption may be used under the lower of cost or market basis of accounting for inventories?

18. Why is it inappropriate for a company to include freight-out expense in the Cost of Goods Sold account?

19. Dawn & Ken Company's balance sheet shows Inventories $162,800. What additional disclosures should be made?

20. Under what circumstances might the inventory turnover ratio be too high—that is, what possible negative consequences might occur?

21. What is the LIFO reserve? What are the consequences of ignoring a large LIFO reserve when analyzing a company?

*22. "When perpetual inventory records are kept, the results under the FIFO and LIFO methods are the same as they would be in a periodic inventory system." Do you agree? Explain.

*23. How does the average method of inventory costing differ between a perpetual inventory system and a periodic inventory system?

*24. Linx Company discovers in 2007 that its ending inventory at December 31, 2006, was $5,000 understated. What effect will this error have on (a) 2006 net income, (b) 2007 net income, and (c) the combined net income for the 2 years?

Brief Exercises

BE6-1 Mark Mader Company identifies the following items for possible inclusion in the physical inventory. Indicate whether each item should be included or excluded from the inventory taking.
(a) Goods shipped on consignment by Mader to another company.
(b) Goods in transit from a supplier shipped FOB destination.
(c) Goods sold but being held for customer pickup.
(d) Goods held on consignment from another company.

Identify items to be included in taking a physical inventory.
(SO 1)

BE6-2 In its first month of operations, Minh Lo Company made three purchases of merchandise in the following sequence: (1) 300 units at $6, (2) 400 units at $8, and (3) 500 units at $9. Assuming there are 400 units on hand, compute the cost of the ending inventory under (a) the FIFO method and (b) the LIFO method. Minh Lo uses a periodic inventory system.

Compute ending inventory using FIFO and LIFO.
(SO 2)

*Compute the ending
inventory using average
costs.*
(SO 2)

BE6-3   Data for Minh Lo Company are presented in BE6-2. Compute the cost of the ending inventory under the average cost method, assuming there are 400 units on hand. (Round the cost per unit to three decimal places.)

*Explain the financial
statement effect of inventory
cost flow assumptions.*
(SO 3)

BE6-4   The management of Laura Corp. is considering the effects of various inventory-costing methods on its financial statements and its income tax expense. Assuming that the price the company pays for inventory is increasing, which method will:
(a) provide the highest net income?
(b) provide the highest ending inventory?
(c) result in the lowest income tax expense?
(d) result in the most stable earnings over a number of years?

*Explain the financial
statement effect of inventory
cost flow assumptions.*
(SO 3)

BE6-5   In its first month of operation, Wier Company purchased 100 units of inventory for $6, then 200 units for $7, and finally 150 units for $8. At the end of the month, 160 units remained. Compute the amount of phantom profit that would result if the company used FIFO rather than LIFO. Explain why this amount is referred to as phantom profit. The company uses the periodic method.

*Determine the LCM
valuation.*
(SO 4)

BE6-6   Sunshine Video Center accumulates the following cost and market data at December 31.

Inventory Categories	Cost Data	Market Data
Cameras	$12,000	$13,400
Camcorders	9,000	9,500
DVDs	13,000	12,800

Compute the lower of cost or market valuation for Sunshine's inventory.

*Compute inventory turnover
ratio and days in inventory.*
(SO 5)

BE6-7   At December 31, 2004, the following information (in thousands) was available for sunglasses manufacturer Oakley, Inc.: ending inventory $115,061; beginning inventory $98,691; cost of goods sold $265,104; and sales revenue $585,468. Calculate the inventory turnover ratio and days in inventory for Oakley, Inc.

*Determine ending inventory
and cost of goods sold using
LIFO reserve.*
(SO 6)

BE6-8   Winnebago Industries, Inc. is a leading manufacturer of motor homes. Winnebago reported ending inventory at August 28, 2004, of $130,733,000 under the LIFO inventory method. In the notes to its financial statements, Winnebago reported a LIFO reserve of $27,192,000 at August 28, 2004. What would Winnebago Industries' ending inventory have been if it had used FIFO?

*Apply cost flow methods to
perpetual inventory records.*
(SO 7)

*BE6-9**   Bruno's Department Store uses a perpetual inventory system. Data for product E2-D2 include the following purchases.

Date	Number of Units	Unit Price
May 7	50	$12
July 28	30	15

On June 1 Bruno sold 35 units, and on August 27, 33 more units. Compute the cost of goods sold using (1) FIFO, (2) LIFO, and (3) average cost.

*Determine correct financial
statement amount.*
(SO 8)

*BE6-10**   Shaunna Company reports net income of $84,000 in 2007. However, ending inventory was understated by $7,000. What is the correct net income for 2007? What effect, if any, will this error have on total assets as reported in the balance sheet at December 31, 2007?

Exercises

E6-1 Springfield Bank and Trust is considering giving Homer Company a loan. Before doing so, they decide that further discussions with Homer's accountant may be desirable. One area of particular concern is the inventory account, which has a year-end balance of $295,000. Discussions with the accountant reveal the following.

Determine the correct inventory amount.
(SO 1)

1. Homer sold goods costing $55,000 to Moe Company FOB shipping point on December 28. The goods are not expected to reach Moe until January 12. The goods were not included in the physical inventory because they were not in the warehouse.
2. The physical count of the inventory did not include goods costing $95,000 that were shipped to Homer FOB destination on December 27 and were still in transit at year-end.
3. Homer received goods costing $25,000 on January 2. The goods were shipped FOB shipping point on December 26 by Lenny Co. The goods were not included in the physical count.
4. Homer sold goods costing $51,000 to Flanders of Canada FOB destination on December 30. The goods were received in Canada on January 8. They were not included in Homer's physical inventory.
5. Homer received goods costing $37,000 on January 2 that were shipped FOB destination on December 29. The shipment was a rush order that was supposed to arrive December 31. This purchase was included in the ending inventory of $295,000.

Instructions
Determine the correct inventory amount on December 31.

E6-2 Dennis Lee, an auditor with Knapp CPAs, is performing a review of Nathan Company's inventory account. Nathan did not have a good year, and top management is under pressure to boost reported income. According to its records, the inventory balance at year-end was $740,000. However, the following information was not considered when determining that amount.

Determine the correct inventory amount.
(SO 1)

1. Included in the company's count were goods with a cost of $250,000 that the company is holding on consignment. The goods belong to Anya Corporation.
2. The physical count did not include goods purchased by Nathan with a cost of $40,000 that were shipped FOB shipping point on December 28 and did not arrive at Nathan's warehouse until January 3.
3. Included in the inventory account was $17,000 of office supplies that were stored in the warehouse and were to be used by the company's supervisors and managers during the coming year.
4. The company received an order on December 29 that was boxed and was sitting on the loading dock awaiting pick-up on December 31. The shipper picked up the goods on January 1 and delivered them on January 6. The shipping terms were FOB shipping point. The goods had a selling price of $40,000 and a cost of $30,000. The goods were not included in the count because they were sitting on the dock.
5. On December 29 Nathan shipped goods with a selling price of $80,000 and a cost of $60,000 to Central Sales Corporation FOB shipping point. The goods arrived on January 3. Central Sales had only ordered goods with a selling price of $10,000 and a cost of $8,000. However, a sales manager at Nathan had authorized the shipment and said that if Central wanted to ship the goods back next week, it could.
6. Included in the count was $50,000 of goods that were parts for a machine that the company no longer made. Given the high-tech nature of Nathan's products, it was unlikely that these obsolete parts had any other use. However, management would prefer to keep them on the books at cost, "since that is what we paid for them, after all."

Instructions
Prepare a schedule to determine the correct inventory amount. Provide explanations for each item above, saying why you did or did not make an adjustment for each item.

E6-3 Shippers Inc. had the following inventory situations to consider at January 31, its year end.

Identify items in inventory.
(SO 1)

(a) Goods held on consignment for MailBoxes Corp. since December 12.
(b) Goods shipped on consignment to Rinehart Holdings Inc. on January 5.
(c) Goods shipped to a customer, FOB destination, on January 29 that are still in transit.

(d) Goods shipped to a customer, FOB shipping point, on January 29 that are still in transit.

(e) Goods purchased FOB destination from a supplier on January 25, that are still in transit.

(f) Goods purchased FOB shipping point from a supplier on January 25, that are still in transit.

(g) Office supplies on hand at January 31.

Instructions

Identify which of the preceding items should be included in inventory. If the item should not be included in inventory, state where it should be recorded.

Compute inventory and cost of goods sold using periodic FIFO and LIFO.
(SO 2)

E6-4   Boarders sells a snowboard, Xpert, that is popular with snowboard enthusiasts. Below is information relating to Boarders's purchases of Xpert snowboards during September. During the same month, 118 Xpert snowboards were sold. Boarders uses a periodic inventory system.

Date	Explanation	Units	Unit Cost	Total Cost
Sept. 1	Inventory	14	$ 97	$ 1,358
Sept. 12	Purchases	45	102	4,590
Sept. 19	Purchases	20	104	2,080
Sept. 26	Purchases	50	105	5,250
	Totals	129		$13,278

Instructions

(a) Compute the ending inventory at September 30 using the FIFO and LIFO methods. Prove the amount allocated to cost of goods sold under each method.

(b) For both FIFO and LIFO, calculate the sum of ending inventory and cost of goods sold. What do you notice about the answers you found for each method?

Calculate inventory and cost of goods sold using FIFO, average, and LIFO in a periodic inventory system.
(SO 2)

E6-5   Lois Inc. uses a periodic inventory system. Its records show the following for the month of May, in which 78 units were sold.

Date	Explanation	Units	Unit Cost	Total Cost
May 1	Inventory	30	$ 8	$240
15	Purchase	25	10	250
24	Purchase	40	11	440
	Total	95		$930

Instructions

Calculate the ending inventory at May 31 using the (a) FIFO, (b) average-cost, and (c) LIFO methods. (For average cost, round the average unit cost to three decimal places.) Prove the amount allocated to cost of goods sold under each method.

Calculate cost of goods sold using specific identification and FIFO periodic.
(SO 2, 3)

E6-6   On December 1, Bargain Electronics has three DVD players left in stock. All are identical, all are priced to sell at $85. One of the three DVD players left in stock, with serial #1012, was purchased on June 1 at a cost of $52. Another, with serial #1045, was purchased on November 1 for $45. The last player, serial #1056, was purchased on November 30 for $43.

Instructions

(a) Calculate the cost of goods sold using the FIFO periodic inventory method assuming that two of the three players were sold by the end of December, Bargain Electronic's year-end.

(b) If Bargain Electronics used the specific identification method instead of the FIFO method, how might it alter its earnings by "selectively choosing" which particular players to sell to the two customers? What would Bargain's cost of goods sold be if the company wished to minimize earnings? Maximize earnings?

(c) Which inventory method, FIFO or specific identification, do you recommend that Bargain use? Explain why.

E6-7 Plato Company reports the following for the month of June.

Instructions

Date	Explanation	Units	Unit Cost	Total Cost
June 1	Inventory	225	$5	$1,125
12	Purchase	375	6	2,250
23	Purchase	500	7	3,500
30	Inventory	180		

(a) Compute the cost of the ending inventory and the cost of goods sold under (1) FIFO, (2) LIFO, and (3) average cost.
(b) Which costing method gives the highest ending inventory? The highest cost of goods sold? Why?
(c) How do the average-cost values for ending inventory and cost of goods sold relate to ending inventory and cost of goods sold for FIFO and LIFO?
(d) Explain why the average cost is not $6.

Compute inventory and cost of goods sold using periodic FIFO, LIFO, and average cost.
(SO 2, 3)

E6-8 This information is available for PepsiCo, Inc. for 2002, 2003, and 2004.

(in millions)	2002	2003	2004
Beginning inventory	$ 1,310	$ 1,342	$ 1,412
Ending inventory	1,342	1,412	1,541
Cost of goods sold	11,497	12,379	13,406
Sales	25,112	26,971	29,261

Compute inventory turnover ratio, days in inventory, and gross profit rate.
(SO 5)

Instructions
Calculate the inventory turnover ratio, days in inventory, and gross profit rate for PepsiCo., Inc. for 2002, 2003, and 2004. Comment on any trends.

E6-9 Cody Camera Shop Inc. uses the lower of cost or market basis for its inventory. The following data are available at December 31.

Determine LCM valuation.
(SO 4)

	Units	Cost/Unit	Market Value/Unit
Cameras			
Minolta	5	$175	$160
Canon	7	150	152
Light Meters			
Vivitar	12	125	119
Kodak	10	115	135

Instructions
What amount should be reported on Cody Camera Shop's financial statements, assuming the lower of cost or market rule is applied?

E6-10 Deere & Company is a global manufacturer and distributor of agricultural, construction, and forestry equipment. It reported the following information in its 2004 annual report.

Determine the effect of the LIFO reserve on current ratio.
(SO 5, 6)

(in millions)	2004	2003
Inventories (LIFO)	$ 1,999	1,366
Current assets	21,844	
Current liabilities	7,889	
LIFO reserve	1,002	
Cost of goods sold	13,568	

Instructions
(a) Compute Deere's inventory turnover ratio and days in inventory for 2004.
(b) Compute Deere's current ratio using the 2004 data as presented, and then again after adjusting for the LIFO reserve.
(c) Comment on how ignoring the LIFO reserve might affect your evaluation of Deere's liquidity.

Calculate inventory and cost of goods sold using three cost flow methods in a perpetual inventory system.
(SO 7)

*E6-11 Inventory data for Plato Company are presented in E6-7.

Instructions
(a) Calculate the cost of the ending inventory and the cost of goods sold for each cost flow assumption, using a perpetual inventory system. Assume a sale of 430 units occurred on June 15 for a selling price of $8 and a sale of 490 units on June 27 for $9. (*Note:* For the average-cost method, round unit cost to three decimal places.)
(b) How do the results differ from E6-7?
(c) Why is the average unit cost not $6 [($5 + $6 + $7) ÷ 3 = $6]?

Apply cost flow methods to perpetual records.
(SO 7)

*E6-12 Information about Boarders is presented in E6-4. Additional data regarding the company's sales of Xpert snowboards are provided below. Assume that Boarders uses a perpetual inventory system.

Date		Units
Sept. 5	Sale	8
Sept. 16	Sale	48
Sept. 29	Sale	62
	Totals	118

Instructions
(a) Compute ending inventory at September 30 using FIFO, LIFO, and average cost. (*Note:* For average cost, round unit cost to three decimal places.)
(b) Compare ending inventory for FIFO and LIFO using a perpetual inventory system to ending inventory using a periodic inventory system (from E6-4).
(c) Which inventory cost flow method (FIFO, LIFO) gives the same ending inventory value under both periodic and perpetual? Which method gives different ending inventory values?

Determine effects of inventory errors.
(SO 8)

*E6-13 Disch Hardware reported cost of goods sold as follows.

	2008	2007
Beginning inventory	$ 30,000	$ 20,000
Cost of goods purchased	175,000	164,000
Cost of goods available for sale	205,000	184,000
Ending inventory	37,000	30,000
Cost of goods sold	$168,000	$154,000

Disch made two errors:
1. 2007 ending inventory was overstated by $4,000.
2. 2008 ending inventory was understated by $2,000.

Instructions
Compute the correct cost of goods sold for each year.

Prepare correct income statements.
(SO 8)

*E6-14 Miller Company reported these income statement data for a 2-year period.

	2008	2007
Sales	$250,000	$210,000
Beginning inventory	40,000	34,000
Cost of goods purchased	202,000	173,000
Cost of goods available for sale	242,000	207,000
Ending inventory	55,000	40,000
Cost of goods sold	187,000	167,000
Gross profit	$ 63,000	$ 43,000

Miller Company uses a periodic inventory system. The inventories at January 1, 2007, and December 31, 2008, are correct. However, the ending inventory at December 31, 2007, is overstated by $5,000.

Instructions
(a) Prepare correct income statement data for the 2 years.
(b) What is the cumulative effect of the inventory error on total gross profit for the 2 years?
(c) Explain in a letter to the president of Miller Company what has happened—that is, the nature of the error and its effect on the financial statements.

Problems: Set A

P6-1A   Schilling Limited is trying to determine the value of its ending inventory as of February 28, 2007, the company's year-end. The accountant counted everything that was in the warehouse, as of February 28, which resulted in an ending inventory valuation of $48,000. However, she didn't know how to treat the following transactions so she didn't record them.

Determine items and amounts to be recorded in inventory.
(SO 1)

(a) On February 26, Schilling shipped to a customer goods costing $800. The goods were shipped FOB shipping point, and the receiving report indicates that the customer received the goods on March 2.   *INCLUDE*
(b) On February 26, Seller Inc. shipped goods to Schilling FOB destination. The invoice price was $350 plus $25 for freight. The receiving report indicates that the goods were received by Schilling on March 2.   *Do not include*
(c) Schilling had $500 of inventory at a customer's warehouse "on approval." The customer was going to let Schilling know whether it wanted the merchandise by the end of the week, March 4.   *INCLUDE*
(d) Schilling also had $400 of inventory at a Balena craft shop, on consignment from Schilling.   *INCLUDE*
(e) On February 26, Schilling ordered goods costing $750. The goods were shipped FOB shipping point on February 27. Schilling received the goods on March 1.   *INCLUDE*
(f) On February 28, Schilling packaged goods and had them ready for shipping to a customer FOB destination. The invoice price was $350 plus $25 for freight; the cost of the items was $280. The receiving report indicates that the goods were received by the customer on March 2.   *No*
(g) Schilling had damaged goods set aside in the warehouse because they are no longer saleable. These goods originally cost $400 and, originally, Schilling expected to sell these items for $600.   *+400*

Instructions
For each of the above transactions, specify whether the item in question should be included in ending inventory, and if so, at what amount. For each item that is not included in ending inventory, indicate who owns it and what account, if any, it should have been recorded in.

15,500
17,000

P6-2A   Classic Distribution markets CDs of numerous performing artists. At the beginning of March, Classic had in beginning inventory 1,500 CDs with a unit cost of $7. During March Classic made the following purchases of CDs.

Determine cost of goods sold and ending inventory using FIFO, LIFO, and average cost, with analysis.
(SO 2, 3)

March 5	2,000 @ $8	March 21	6,000 @ $10
March 13	5,500 @ $9	March 26	2,000 @ $11

During March 13,000 units were sold. Classic uses a periodic inventory system.

Instructions
(a) Determine the cost of goods available for sale.
(b) Determine (1) the ending inventory and (2) the cost of goods sold under each of the assumed cost flow methods (FIFO, LIFO, and average cost). Prove the accuracy of the cost of goods sold under the FIFO and LIFO methods. (*Note:* For average cost, round cost per unit to three decimal places.)
(c) Which cost flow method results in (1) the highest inventory amount for the balance sheet and (2) the highest cost of goods sold for the income statement?

Cost of goods sold:
FIFO $116,000
LIFO $127,000
Average $120,824

Determine cost of goods sold and ending inventory using FIFO, LIFO, and average cost in a periodic inventory system, and assess financial statement effect.
(SO 2, 3)

Cost of goods sold:
FIFO $17,000
LIFO $18,200
Average $17,591

P6-3A McLean Company Inc. had a beginning inventory of 300 units of Product MLN at a cost of $8 per unit. During the year, purchases were:

Feb. 20	700 units at $ 9	Aug. 12	600 units at $11
May 5	500 units at $10	Dec. 8	100 units at $12

McLean Company uses a periodic inventory system. Sales totalled 1,800 units.

Instructions
(a) Determine the cost of goods available for sale.
(b) Determine the ending inventory and the cost of goods sold under each of the assumed cost flow methods (FIFO, LIFO, and average cost). Prove the accuracy of the cost of goods sold under the FIFO and LIFO methods. (Round average unit cost to three decimal places.)
(c) Which cost flow method results in the lowest inventory amount for the balance sheet? The lowest cost of goods sold for the income statement?

Compute ending inventory, prepare income statements, and answer questions using FIFO and LIFO.
(SO 2, 3)

P6-4A The management of Stampfer Inc. asks your help in determining the comparative effects of the FIFO and LIFO inventory cost flow methods. For 2007 the accounting

Inventory, January 1 (10,000 units)	$ 35,000
Cost of 120,000 units purchased	480,000
Šelling price of 100,000 units sold	730,000
Operating expenses	120,000

records show these data.
Units purchased consisted of 35,000 units at $3.70 on May 10; 60,000 units at $3.90 on August 15; and 25,000 units at $4.66 on November 20. Income taxes are 28%.

Instructions
(a) Prepare comparative condensed income statements for 2007 under FIFO and LIFO. (Show computations of ending inventory.)
(b) Answer the following questions for management in the form of a business letter.
   (1) Which inventory cost flow method produces the most meaningful inventory amount for the balance sheet? Why?
   (2) Which inventory cost flow method produces the most meaningful net income? Why?
   (3) Which inventory cost flow method is most likely to approximate the actual physical flow of the goods? Why?
   (4) How much more cash will be available under LIFO than under FIFO? Why?
   (5) How much of the gross profit under FIFO is illusionary in comparison with the gross profit under LIFO?

Gross profit:
FIFO $351,000
LIFO $324,000

Calculate ending inventory, cost of goods sold, gross profit, and gross profit rate under periodic method; compare results.
(SO 2, 3)

P6-5A You have the following information for Benton Inc. for the month ended October 31, 2007. Benton uses a periodic method for inventory.

Date	Description	Units	Unit Cost or Selling Price
October 1	Beginning inventory	60	$25
October 9	Purchase	120	27
October 11	Sale	100	35
October 17	Purchase	90	28
October 22	Sale	60	40
October 25	Purchase	80	29
October 29	Sale	120	40

Instructions
(a) Calculate (i) ending inventory, (ii) cost of goods sold, (iii) gross profit, and (iv) gross profit rate under each of the following methods.
   (1) LIFO.
   (2) FIFO.
   (3) Average cost. (Round cost per unit to three decimal places.)
(b) Compare results for the three cost flow assumptions.

Gross profit:
LIFO $2,890
FIFO $3,150
Average $3,036

P6-6A You have the following information for Rock Bottom Rocks. Rock Bottom uses the periodic method of accounting for its inventory transactions. Rock Bottom only carries one brand and size of diamonds—all are identical. Each batch of diamonds purchased is carefully coded and marked with its purchase cost.

Compare specific identification, FIFO, and LIFO under periodic method; use cost flow assumption to influence earnings.
(SO 2, 3)

March 1	Beginning inventory 200 diamonds at a cost of $300 per diamond.
March 3	Purchased 200 diamonds at a cost of $360 each.
March 5	Sold 180 diamonds for $600 each.
March 10	Purchased 330 diamonds at a cost of $375 each.
March 25	Sold 500 diamonds for $650 each.

Instructions
(a) Assume that Rock Bottom Rocks uses the specific identification cost flow method.
   (1) Demonstrate how Rock Bottom could maximize its gross profit for the month by specifically selecting which diamonds to sell on March 5 and March 25.
   (2) Demonstrate how Rock Bottom could minimize its gross profit for the month by selecting which diamonds to sell on March 5 and March 25.
(b) Assume that Rock Bottom uses the FIFO cost flow assumption. Calculate cost of goods sold. How much gross profit would Rock Bottom report under this cost flow assumption?
(c) Assume that Rock Bottom uses the LIFO cost flow assumption. Calculate cost of goods sold. How much gross profit would the company report under this cost flow assumption?
(d) Which cost flow method should Rock Bottom Rocks select? Explain.

Gross profit:
Maximum $196,000
Minimum $192,250

P6-7A This information is available for the Automotive and Other Operations Divisions of General Motors Corporation for 2004. General Motors uses the LIFO inventory method.

Compute inventory turnover ratio and days in inventory; compute current ratio based on LIFO and after adjusting for LIFO reserve.
(SO 5, 6)

(in millions)	**2004**
Beginning inventory	$ 10,960
Ending inventory	11,717
LIFO reserve	1,442
Current assets	55,515
Current liabilities	74,892
Cost of goods sold	150,053
Sales	161,545

Instructions
(a) Calculate the inventory turnover ratio and days in inventory.
(b) Calculate the current ratio based on inventory as reported using LIFO.
(c) Calculate the current ratio after adjusting for the LIFO reserve.
(d) Comment on any difference between parts (b) and (c).

*P6-8A Psang Inc. is a retailer operating in Edmonton, Alberta. Psang uses the perpetual inventory method. All sales returns from customers result in the goods being returned to inventory. (Assume that the inventory is not damaged.) Assume that there are no credit transactions; all amounts are settled in cash. You are provided with the following information for Psang Inc. for the month of January 2007.

Calculate cost of goods sold, ending inventory, and gross profit for LIFO, FIFO, and average cost under the perpetual system; compare results.
(SO 3, 7)

Date	Description	Quantity	Unit Cost or Selling Price
December 31	Ending inventory	160	$18
January 2	Purchase	100	20
January 6	Sale	180	40
January 9	Sale return	10	40
January 9	Purchase	75	24
January 10	Purchase return	15	24
January 10	Sale	50	45
January 23	Purchase	100	28
January 30	Sale	140	50

Gross profit:

LIFO	$8,010
FIFO	$8,610
Average	$8,396

Instructions

(a) For each of the following cost flow assumptions, calculate (i) cost of goods sold, (ii) ending inventory, and (iii) gross profit.

  (1) LIFO. (Assume sales returns had a cost of $18 and purchase returns had a cost of $24.)

  (2) FIFO. (Assume sales returns had a cost of $18 and purchase returns had a cost of $24.)

  (3) Moving-average. (Round cost per unit to three decimal places.)

(b) Compare results for the three cost flow assumptions.

Determine ending inventory under a perpetual inventory system.
(SO 3, 7)

*P6-9A Savings Center began operations on July 1. It uses a perpetual inventory system. During July the company had the following purchases and sales.

	Purchases		
Date	Units	Unit Cost	Sales Units
July 1	7	$ 93	
July 6			3
July 11	4	$ 99	
July 14			3
July 21	3	$106	
July 27			5

FIFO	$318
Average	$300
LIFO	$279

Instructions

(a) Determine the ending inventory under a perpetual inventory system using (1) FIFO, (2) average cost (round unit cost to three decimal places), and (3) LIFO.

(b) Which costing method produces the highest ending inventory valuation?

Problems: Set B

Determine items and amounts to be recorded in inventory.
(SO 1)

P6-1B Norby Limited is trying to determine the value of its ending inventory as of February 28, 2007, the company's year-end. The following transactions occurred, and the accountant asked your help in determining whether they should be recorded or not.

(a) On February 26, Norby shipped goods costing $800 to a customer and charged the customer $1,000. The goods were shipped with terms FOB destination and the receiving report indicates that the customer received the goods on March 2.

(b) On February 26, Seller Inc. shipped goods to Norby under terms FOB shipping point. The invoice price was $350 plus $25 for freight. The receiving report indicates that the goods were received by Norby on March 2.

(c) Norby had $500 of inventory isolated in the warehouse. The inventory is designated for a customer who has requested that the goods be shipped on March 10.

(d) Also included in Norby's warehouse is $400 of inventory that Meredith Producers shipped to Norby on consignment.

(e) On February 26, Norby issued a purchase order to acquire goods costing $750. The goods were shipped with terms FOB destination on February 27. Norby received the goods on March 2.

(f) On February 26, Norby shipped goods to a customer under terms FOB shipping point. The invoice price was $350 plus $25 for freight; the cost of the items was $280. The receiving report indicates that the goods were received by the customer on March 2.

Instructions

For each of the above transactions, specify whether the item in question should be included in ending inventory, and if so, at what amount.

Determine cost of goods sold and ending inventory using FIFO, LIFO, and average cost with analysis.
(SO 2, 3)

P6-2B Tween Distribution markets CDs of the performing artist Little Sister. At the beginning of October, Tween had in beginning inventory 1,000 Sister's CDs with a unit cost of $5. During October Tween made the following purchases of Sister's CDs.

Oct. 3	4,000 @ $6		Oct. 19	2,000 @ $8
Oct. 9	3,000 @ $7		Oct. 25	2,500 @ $9

During October 9,500 units were sold. Tween uses a periodic inventory system.

Instructions

(a) Determine the cost of goods available for sale.
(b) Determine (1) the ending inventory and (2) the cost of goods sold under each of the assumed cost flow methods (FIFO, LIFO, and average cost). Prove the accuracy of the cost of goods sold under the FIFO and LIFO methods.
(c) Which cost flow method results in (1) the highest inventory amount for the balance sheet and (2) the highest cost of goods sold for the income statement?

P6-3B   Prairie Company had a beginning inventory on January 1 of 100 units of Product SXL at a cost of $20 per unit. During the year, purchases were:

Mar. 15	300 units at $22	Sept. 4	350 units at $27
July 20	250 units at $25	Dec. 2	100 units at $30

Prairie Company sold 850 units, and it uses a periodic inventory system.

Instructions

(a) Determine the cost of goods available for sale.
(b) Determine the ending inventory and the cost of goods sold under each of the assumed cost flow methods (FIFO, LIFO, and average cost). Prove the accuracy of the cost of goods sold under each method. (Round cost per unit to three decimal places.)
(c) Which cost flow method results in the highest inventory amount for the balance sheet? The highest cost of goods sold for the income statement?

P6-4B   The management of Caradeo is reevaluating the appropriateness of using its present inventory cost flow method, which is average cost. The company requests your help in determining the results of operations for 2007 if either the FIFO or the LIFO method had been used. For 2007 the accounting records show these data:

Inventories		Purchases and Sales	
Beginning (10,000 units)	$22,800	Total net sales (222,000 units)	$862,000
Ending (18,000 units)		Total cost of goods purchased	
		(230,000 units)	571,000

Purchases were made quarterly as follows.

Quarter	Units	Unit Cost	Total Cost
1	60,000	$2.30	$138,000
2	50,000	2.40	120,000
3	50,000	2.55	127,500
4	70,000	2.65	185,500
	230,000		$571,000

Operating expenses were $147,000, and the company's income tax rate is 32%.

Instructions

(a) Prepare comparative condensed income statements for 2007 under FIFO and LIFO. (Show computations of ending inventory.)
(b) Answer the following questions for management in business-letter form.
   (1) Which cost flow method (FIFO or LIFO) produces the more meaningful inventory amount for the balance sheet? Why?
   (2) Which cost flow method (FIFO or LIFO) produces the more meaningful net income? Why?
   (3) Which cost flow method (FIFO or LIFO) is more likely to approximate the actual physical flow of goods? Why?
   (4) How much more cash will be available for management under LIFO than under FIFO? Why?
   (5) Will gross profit under the average cost method be higher or lower than FIFO? Than LIFO? (*Note:* It is not necessary to quantify your answer.)

Cost of goods sold:
  FIFO $62,000
  LIFO $71,500
  Average $67,260

Determine cost of goods sold and ending inventory using FIFO, LIFO, and average cost in a periodic inventory system and assess financial statement effects.
(SO 2, 3)

Cost of goods sold:
  FIFO $20,250
  LIFO $22,000
  Average $21,095

Compute ending inventory, prepare income statements, and answer questions using FIFO and LIFO.
(SO 2, 3)

Gross profit:
  FIFO $315,900
  LIFO $309,400

Calculate ending inventory, cost of goods sold, gross profit, and gross profit rate under periodic method; compare results.
(SO 2, 3)

P6-5B You have the following information for Venus Inc. for the month ended June 30, 2007. Venus uses the periodic method for inventory.

Date	Description	Quantity	Unit Cost or Selling Price
June 1	Beginning inventory	25	$60
June 4	Purchase	85	64
June 10	Sale	70	90
June 11	Sale return	5	90
June 18	Purchase	40	68
June 18	Purchase return	15	68
June 25	Sale	50	95
June 28	Purchase	20	75

Gross profit:
LIFO	$2,920
FIFO	$3,320
Average	$3,077

Instructions
(a) Calculate (i) ending inventory, (ii) cost of goods sold, (iii) gross profit, and (iv) gross profit rate under each of the following methods.
  (1) LIFO.
  (2) FIFO.
  (3) Average cost. (Round cost per unit to three decimal places.)
(b) Compare results for the three cost flow assumptions.

Compare specific identification, FIFO, and LIFO under periodic method; use cost flow assumption to justify price increase.
(SO 2, 3)

P6-6B You have the following information for Petrol Plus. Petrol Plus uses the periodic method of accounting for its inventory transactions.

March 1	Beginning inventory 1,200 litres at a cost of 40¢ per litre.
March 3	Purchased 2,000 litres at a cost of 45¢ per litre.
March 5	Sold 1,500 litres for 60¢ per litre.
March 10	Purchased 3,700 litres at a cost of 49¢ per litre.
March 20	Purchased 2,000 litres at a cost of 55¢ per litre.
March 30	Sold 5,000 litres for 70¢ per litre.

Gross profit:
Specific identification	$1,276
FIFO	$1,403
LIFO	$1,127

Instructions
(a) Prepare partial income statements through gross profit, and calculate the value of ending inventory that would be reported on the balance sheet, under each of the following cost flow assumptions.
  (1) Specific identification method assuming:
     (i) the March 5 sale consisted of 700 litres from the March 1 beginning inventory and 800 litres from the March 3 purchase; and
     (ii) the March 30 sale consisted of the following number of units sold from each purchase: 400 litres from March 1; 500 litres from March 3; 2,600 litres from March 10; 1,500 litres from March 20.
  (2) FIFO.
  (3) LIFO.
(b) How can companies use a cost flow method to justify price increases? Which cost flow method would best support an argument to increase prices?

Compute inventory turnover ratio, days in inventory, and current ratio based on LIFO and after adjusting for LIFO reserve.
(SO 5, 6)

P6-7B Gehl Company manufactures a full line of construction and agriculture equipment. The following information is available for Gehl for 2004. The company uses the LIFO inventory method.

(in thousands)	**2004**
Beginning inventory	$ 31,598
Ending inventory	38,925
LIFO reserve	27,810
Current assets	252,007
Current liabilities	89,159
Cost of goods sold	289,910
Sales	361,598

Instructions
(a) Calculate the inventory turnover ratio and days in inventory.
(b) Calculate the current ratio based on LIFO inventory.
(c) After adjusting for the LIFO reserve, calculate the current ratio.
(d) Comment on any difference between parts (b) and (c).

*P6-8B Skogmo Inc. is a retail company that uses the perpetual inventory method. All sales returns from customers result in the goods being returned to inventory. (Assume that the inventory is not damaged.) Assume that there are no credit transactions; all amounts are settled in cash. You have the following information for Skogmo Inc. for the month of January 2007.

Calculate cost of goods sold, ending inventory, and gross profit under LIFO, FIFO, and average cost under the perpetual system; compare results.
(SO 3, 7)

Date	Description	Quantity	Unit Cost or Selling Price
January 1	Beginning inventory	40	$12
January 5	Purchase	100	14
January 8	Sale	75	25
January 10	Sale return	10	25
January 15	Purchase	30	18
January 16	Purchase return	5	18
January 20	Sale	90	25
January 25	Purchase	20	20

Gross profit:
LIFO $1,665
FIFO $1,725
Average $1,691

Instructions
(a) For each of the following cost flow assumptions, calculate (i) cost of goods sold, (ii) ending inventory, and (iii) gross profit.
   (1) LIFO. (Assume sales returns had a cost of $14 and purchase returns had a cost of $18.)
   (2) FIFO. (Assume sales returns had a cost of $14 and purchase returns had a cost of $18.)
   (3) Moving-average cost. (Round cost per unit to three decimal places.)
(b) Compare results for the three cost flow assumptions.

*P6-9B Save-U-More Center began operations on July 1. It uses a perpetual inventory system. During July the company had the following purchases and sales.

Determine ending inventory under a perpetual inventory system.
(SO 3, 7)

	Purchases		
Date	Units	Unit Cost	Sales Units
July 1	6	$31	
July 6			4
July 11	5	$34	
July 14			3
July 21	3	$36	
July 27			2

Instructions
(a) Determine the ending inventory under a perpetual inventory system using (1) FIFO, (2) average cost, and (3) LIFO. (*Note:* For average cost, round cost per unit to three decimal places.)
(b) Which costing method produces the highest ending inventory valuation?

FIFO $176
Average $172
LIFO $166

Problems: Set C

Visit the book's website at **www.wiley.com/college/kimmel** and choose the Student Companion site to access Problem Set C.

Comprehensive Problem

CP6 On December 1, 2007, Rodriquez Company had the account balances shown on page 308.

Debits		Credits	
Cash	$ 4,800	Accumulated Depreciation—	$ 1,500
Accounts Receivable	3,900	Equipment	
Merchandise Inventory	1,800*	Accounts Payable	3,000
Equipment	21,000	Common Stock	10,000
	$31,500	Retained Earnings	17,000
			$31,500

*(3,000 × $0.60)

The following transactions occurred during December.

Dec. 3 Purchased 4,000 units on account at a cost of $0.70 per unit.
5 Sold 4,500 units on account for $0.90 per unit. (It sold 3,000 of the $0.60 units and 1,500 of the $0.70)
7 Granted the December 5 customer $180 credit for 200 units returned costing $140. These units were returned to inventory.
17 Purchased 2,400 units for cash at $0.75 each.
22 Sold 2,000 units on account for $0.95 per unit. (It sold 2,000 of the $0.70 units).

Adjustment data:

1. Accrued salaries payable $400.
2. Depreciation $200 per month.

Instructions

(a) Journalize the December transactions and adjusting entries assuming Rodriguez uses the perpetual inventory method.
(b) Enter the December 1 balances in the ledger T accounts and post the December transactions. In addition to the accounts mentioned above use the following additional accounts: Cost of Goods Sold, Depreciation Expense, Salaries Expense, Salaries Payable, Sales, and Sales Returns and Allowances.
(c) Prepare an adjusted trial balance as of December 31, 2007.
(d) Prepare an income statement for December 2007 and a classified balance sheet at December 31, 2007.
(e) Compute ending inventory and cost of goods sold under FIFO assuming Rodriquez Company uses the periodic inventory system.
(f) Compute ending inventory and cost of goods sold under LIFO assuming Rodriquez Company uses the periodic inventory system.

Continuing Cookie Chronicle

(*Note:* This is a continuation of the Cookie Chronicle from Chapters 1 through 5.)

CCC6 Natalie is busy establishing both divisions of her business (cookie classes and mixer sales) and completing her business degree. Her goals for the next 11 months are to sell one mixer per month and to give two to three classes per week.

The cost of the fine European mixers is expected to increase. Natalie has just negotiated new terms with Kzinski that include shipping costs in the negotiated purchase price (mixers will be shipped FOB destination), but the supplier cannot guarantee the invoice price. Natalie has decided to use a periodic inventory system and now must choose a cost flow assumption for her mixer inventory.

The following transactions occur in February to May 2007.

Feb. 2 Natalie buys two deluxe mixers on account from Kzinski Supply Co. for $1,100 ($550 each), FOB destination, terms n/30.
16 She sells one deluxe mixer for $1,050 cash.
25 She pays the amount owed to Kzinski.
Mar. 2 She buys one deluxe mixer on account from Kzinski Supply Co. for $567, FOB destination, terms n/30.
30 Natalie sells two deluxe mixers for a total of $2,100 cash.

31   She pays the amount owed to Kzinski.
Apr. 1   She buys two deluxe mixers on account from Kzinski Supply Co. for
        $1,122 ($561 each), FOB destination, terms n/30.
   13   She sells three deluxe mixers for a total of $3,150 cash.
   30   Natalie pays the amount owed to Kzinski.
May 4   She buys three deluxe mixers on account from Kzinski Supply Co. for
        $1,720 ($573.33 each), FOB destination, terms n/30.
   27   She sells one deluxe mixer for $1,050 cash.

Instructions
(a) Prepare journal entries for each of the transactions.
(b) Determine the cost of goods available for sale. Recall from Chapter 5 that at the end
     of January, Cookie Creations had three mixers on hand at a cost of $545 each.
(c) Calculate (i) ending inventory, (ii) cost of goods sold, (iii) gross profit, and (iv) gross
     profit rate under each of the following methods: LIFO, FIFO, and average cost.
     (Round average unit cost to three decimal places.)
(d) Natalie is thinking of getting a bank loan. If this is the only factor Natalie has to con-
     sider in choosing an inventory cost flow assumption, which cost flow assumption
     would you recommend that Natalie use? Why?

▶ BROADENING YOUR PERSPECTIVE

Financial Reporting and Analysis

FINANCIAL REPORTING PROBLEM: *Tootsie Roll Industries, Inc.*

BYP6-1   The notes that accompany a company's financial statements provide informative
details that would clutter the amounts and descriptions presented in the statements. Refer
to the financial statements of Tootsie Roll and the accompanying Notes to Consolidated
Financial Statements in Appendix A.

Instructions
Answer the following questions. (Give the amounts in thousands of dollars, as shown in
Tootsie Roll's annual report.)
(a) What did Tootsie Roll report for the amount of inventories in its Consolidated Balance
     Sheet at December 31, 2004? At December 31, 2003?
(b) Compute the dollar amount of change and the percentage change in inventories between
     2003 and 2004. Compute inventory as a percentage of current assets for 2004.
(c) What are the cost of goods sold reported by Tootsie Roll for 2004, 2003, and 2002?
     Compute the ratio of cost of goods sold to net sales in 2004.

COMPARATIVE ANALYSIS PROBLEM: *Tootsie Roll vs. Hershey Foods*

BYP6-2   The financial statements of Hershey Foods are presented in Appendix B, following the financial statements for Tootsie Roll in Appendix A.

Instructions
(a) Based on the information in the financial statements, compute these 2004 values for
     each company. (Do not adjust for the LIFO reserve.)
     (1) Inventory turnover ratio.
     (2) Days in inventory.
(b) What conclusions concerning the management of the inventory can you draw from
     these data?

RESEARCH CASE

BYP6-3 The April 16, 2005, issue of *The Washington Post* contains an article by David Brown titled, "Pediatric Vaccine Stockpile at Risk."

Instructions

Access the article on MSNBC.com at *www.msnbc.msn.com/id/7529480/print/1/display mode/1098/*. Then read the article and answer the following questions.

(a) What does the article suggest as the apparent cause of the decline of the vaccine stockpile?

(b) Describe the procedures that have been followed in the past in managing the stockpile, and how it was accounted for in the past.

(c) What was the motivation behind the SEC's decision to issue a new revenue recognition bulletin?

INTERPRETING FINANCIAL STATEMENTS

BYP6-4 The following information is from the 2005 annual report of American Greetings Corporation (all dollars in thousands).

	Feb. 28, 2005	Feb. 29, 2004
Inventories		
Finished goods	$228,088	$212,252
Work in process	19,719	30,047
Raw materials and supplies	50,957	69,526
	298,764	311,825
Less: LIFO reserve	75,890	73,213
Total (as reported)	$222,874	$238,612
Cost of goods sold	$905,201	$912,705
Current assets (as reported)	$1,281,639	$1,199,045
Current liabilities	$487,667	$424,579

The following information comes from the notes to the company's financial statements.

Finished products, work in process, and raw material inventories are carried at the lower-of-cost-or-market. The last-in, first-out (LIFO) cost method is used for approximately 65% of the domestic inventories in 2005 and approximately 50% in 2004. The foreign subsidiaries principally use the first-in, first-out method. Display material and factory supplies are carried at average cost.

Instructions

(a) Define each of the following: finished goods, work in process, and raw materials.

(b) The company experienced an increase in finished goods inventory and a decline in raw materials. Discuss the likely cause of this.

(c) What might be a possible explanation for why the company uses FIFO for its non-domestic inventories?

(d) Calculate the company's inventory turnover ratio and days in inventory for 2004 and 2005. (2003 inventory was $278,807.) Discuss the implications of any change in the ratios.

(e) What percentage of total inventory does the 2005 LIFO reserve represent? If the company used FIFO in 2005, what would be the value of its inventory? Do you consider this difference a "material" amount from the perspective of an analyst? Which value accurately represents the value of the company's inventory?

(f) Calculate the company's 2005 current ratio with the numbers as reported, then re-calculate after adjusting for the LIFO reserve.

FINANCIAL ANALYSIS ON THE WEB

BYP6-5 *Purpose:* Use SEC filings to learn about a company's inventory accounting practices.

Address: **http://biz.yahoo.com/p/_capgds-bldmch.html**

> (or go to **www.wiley.com/college/kimmel**)

Steps

1. Go to this site and click on the name of an equipment manufacturer other than those discussed in the chapter.
2. Click on **SEC filings**.
3. Under "Recent filings" choose **Form 10K** (annual report) and click on **Full Filing at Edgar Online**.
4. Choose option "3," **Online HTML Version**.

If the 10K is not listed among the recent filings then click on **View All Filingson EDGAR Online**.

Instructions

Review the 10K to answer the following questions.

(a) What is the name of the company?
(b) How has its inventory changed from the previous year?
(c) What is the amount of raw materials, work in process, and finished goods inventory?
(d) What inventory method does the company use?
(e) Calculate the inventory turnover ratio and days in inventory for the current year.
(f) If the company uses LIFO, what was the amount of its LIFO reserve?

Critical Thinking

DECISION MAKING ACROSS THE ORGANIZATION

BYP6-6   Hector Electronics has enjoyed tremendous sales growth during the last 10 years. However, even though sales have steadily increased, the company's CEO, Karen Stevens, is concerned about certain aspects of its performance. She has called a meeting with the corporate controller and the vice presidents of finance, operations, sales, and marketing to discuss the company's performance. Karen begins the meeting by making the following observations:

> "We have been forced to take significant write-downs on inventory during each of the last three years because of obsolescence. In addition, inventory storage costs have soared. We rent four additional warehouses to store our increasingly diverse inventory. Five years ago inventory represented only 20% of the value of our total assets. It now exceeds 35%. Yet, even with all of this inventory, "stock-outs" (measured by complaints by customers that the desired product is not available) have increased by 40% during the last three years. And worse yet, it seems that we constantly must discount merchandise that we have too much of."

Karen asks the group to review the following data and make suggestions as to how the company's performance might be improved.

(in millions)	2007	2006	2005	2004
Inventory				
Raw materials	$242	$198	$155	$128
Work in process	116	77	49	33
Finished goods	567	482	398	257
Total inventory	$925	$757	$602	$418
Current assets	$1,800	$1,623	$1,183	$841
Total assets	$2,643	$2,523	$2,408	$2,090
Current liabilities	$600	$590	$525	$420
Sales	$9,428	$8,974	$7,536	$6,840
Cost of goods sold	$6,128	$5,474	$4,145	$3,557
Net income	$754	$987	$979	$958

Instructions

Using the information provided, answer the following questions.

(a) Compute the current ratio, gross profit rate, profit margin ratio, inventory turnover ratio, and days in inventory for 2005, 2006, and 2007.

(b) Discuss the trends and potential causes of the changes in the ratios in part (a).

(c) Discuss potential remedies to any problems discussed in part (b).

(d) What concerns might be raised by some members of management with regard to your suggestions in part (c)?

COMMUNICATION ACTIVITIES

BYP6-7   In a discussion of dramatic increases in coffee bean prices, a *Wall Street Journal* article noted the following fact about Starbucks.

> Before this year's bean-price hike, Starbucks added several defenses that analysts say could help it maintain earnings and revenue. The company last year began accounting for its coffee-bean purchases by taking the average price of all beans in inventory.
>
> *Source:* Aaron Lucchetti, "Crowded Coffee Market May Keep a Lid on Starbucks After Price Rise Hurt Stock," *Wall Street Journal* (June 4, 1997), p. C1.

Prior to this change the company was using FIFO.

Instructions

Your client, the CEO of Hot Cup Coffee, Inc., read this article and sent you an e-mail message requesting that you explain why Starbucks might have taken this action. Your response should explain what impact this change in accounting method has on earnings, why the company might want to do this, and any possible disadvantages of such a change.

*BYP6-8   You are the controller of Blue Jays Inc. B. J. Dell, the president, recently mentioned to you that she found an error in the 2006 financial statements which she believes has corrected itself. She determined, in discussions with the purchasing department, that 2006 ending inventory was overstated by $1 million. B. J. says that the 2007 ending inventory is correct, and she assumes that 2007 income is correct. B. J. says to you, "What happened has happened—there's no point in worrying about it anymore."

Instructions

You conclude that B. J. is incorrect. Write a brief, tactful memo to her, clarifying the situation.

ETHICS CASE

BYP6-9   Becker Wholesale Corp. uses the LIFO cost flow method. In the current year, profit at Becker is running unusually high. The corporate tax rate is also high this year, but it is scheduled to decline significantly next year. In an effort to lower the current year's net income and to take advantage of the changing income tax rate, the president of Becker Wholesale instructs the plant accountant to recommend to the purchasing department a large purchase of inventory for delivery 3 days before the end of the year. The price of the inventory to be purchased has doubled during the year, and the purchase will represent a major portion of the ending inventory value.

Instructions

(a) What is the effect of this transaction on this year's and next year's income statement and income tax expense? Why?

(b) If Becker Wholesale had been using the FIFO method of inventory costing, would the president give the same directive?

(c) Should the plant accountant order the inventory purchase to lower income? What are the ethical implications of this order?

Answers to Business Insight and Accounting across the Organization Questions

p. 269

Q: Why is inventory control important to managers such as those at Wal-Mart?

A: In the very competitive environment of discount retailing, where Wal-Mart is the major player, small differences in price matter to the customer. Wal-Mart sells a high volume of inventory at a low gross profit rate. When operating in a high-volume, low-margin environment, small cost savings can mean the difference between being profitable or going out of business.

p. 270

Q: What effect does an overstatement of inventory have on a company's financial statements?

A: The balance sheet looks stronger because inventory and retained earnings are overstated. The income statement looks better because cost of goods sold is understated and income is overstated.

p. 282

Q. If Samsung isn't successful in selling the units, what steps will it have to take, and how will this show up in its financial statements?

A. If Samsung increases production, but then can't sell the units, its finished goods inventory will increase. Because cell phones are constantly changing, Samsung would want to take steps to sell off the inventory before it becomes obsolete. Thus, it would need to offer big discounts. Such a strategy would get its inventory down to desirable levels, but would severely depress the company's gross profit.

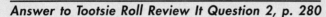

Answer to Tootsie Roll Review It Question 2, p. 280

Tootsie Roll uses LIFO for U.S. inventories and FIFO for foreign inventories.

Answers to Self-Study Questions

1. d   2. a   3. c   4. d   5. c   6. d   7. a   8. d   9. a
*10. d   *11. b

CHAPTER 7

Internal Control and Cash

STUDY OBJECTIVES

After studying this chapter, you should be able to:

1 Identify the principles of internal control.
2 Explain the applications of internal control to cash receipts.
3 Explain the applications of internal control to cash disbursements.
4 Prepare a bank reconciliation.
5 Explain the reporting of cash.
6 Discuss the basic principles of cash management.
7 Identify the primary elements of a cash budget.

THE NAVIGATOR

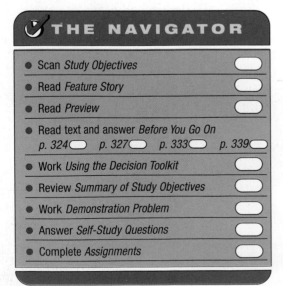

THE NAVIGATOR

- Scan *Study Objectives*
- Read *Feature Story*
- Read *Preview*
- Read text and answer *Before You Go On*
  p. 324◯   p. 327◯   p. 333◯   p. 339◯
- Work *Using the Decision Toolkit*
- Review *Summary of Study Objectives*
- Work *Demonstration Problem*
- Answer *Self-Study Questions*
- Complete *Assignments*

FEATURE STORY

Is There a Thief in the Next Cubicle?

According to some estimates, up to one-third of U.S. employees have stolen from their employers. Some of these thefts have a relatively minor impact on the business—such as high-school-age employees consuming cheese and sausage while making pizza at the local pizzeria. Other thefts, however, can be very serious. In the case of small businesses, employee theft can result in the failure of the business. About 90 percent of employee thefts involve cash. Consider the following examples.

A movie-theater manager printed out a ticket, but if he didn't think anyone was watching, he then allowed the customer to walk into the movie without giving the customer the ticket. The manager pocketed the cash. Later he sold the ticket to a different customer, so that the number of tickets issued matched the amount of cash in the register. Total take: $30,000.

A government employee stole taxpayer refund checks that the post office had returned due to incorrect addresses. The employee then forged the signatures and deposited the checks. Total take: $2,000,000.

A purchasing agent set up a vendor file using his wife's maiden name, and then made payments to her for consulting services that she never provided. Total take: $1,000,000.

Most disconcerting is that employee thieves often are people whom you would least expect. Kay Lemon, a grandmother, was a long-time employee of a small lighting store. She handled all aspects of the store's accounting and banking, including making bank deposits, signing checks, and reconciling the store's bank account. For more than a decade she didn't steal, even though the situation created many opportunities for theft. But once she started, she couldn't stop. Ultimately she stole $416,000. Here's how.

Lemon made out company checks to herself and deposited them in her own account. To cover the theft she wrote "void" on the check stub. Then, the next time she bought inventory she added the stolen amount to the check stub when she paid for the inventory. For example, if she stole $5,000 and was paying $10,000 for inventory, she would write $15,000 on the check stub for the inventory payment. This kept the cash account in balance. Then, when the check for the stolen amount was returned to the company with the bank statement, Lemon tore up the check.

How did she get caught? Actually she didn't. The pressure of all of those years of covering up the theft became too much for her to handle. She turned herself in. The company narrowly escaped financial ruin.

Companies design internal control systems to reduce the likelihood of thefts such as those listed above. In recent years a number of extremely large business failures resulting from employees acting in their own interest caused Congress to pass the Sarbanes-Oxley Act of 2002. The new law puts considerable emphasis on corporate internal control systems.

Source: Joseph T. Wells, "Enemies Within," *Journal of Accountancy* (December 2001), pp. 31–35.

315

Cash is the lifeblood of any company. Large and small companies alike must guard it carefully. Even companies that are in every other way successful can go bankrupt if they fail to manage cash. Managers must know both how to use cash efficiently and how to protect it. Due to its liquid nature, cash is the easiest asset to steal. As the Feature Story suggests, a particularly difficult problem arises when a company has a dishonest employee.

In this chapter you will learn ways to reduce the risk of theft of cash and other assets, how to report cash in the financial statements, and how to manage cash. The content and organization of the chapter are as follows.

INTERNAL CONTROL AND CASH

Internal Control	Cash Controls	Reporting Cash	Managing and Monitoring Cash
• Sarbanes-Oxley Act • Principles of internal control • Limitations of internal control	• Internal control over cash receipts • Internal control over cash disbursements • Use of a bank	• Cash equivalents • Restricted cash	• Basic principles • Cash budgeting

E.S.D.P.I.O,

Internal Control

A recent publication sponsored by the Association of Certified Fraud Examiners estimated that fraud costs U.S. organizations more than $600 billion annually. Findings such as these, as well as situations like those in the Feature Story, emphasize the need for a good system of internal control.

Internal control consists of all the related methods and measures adopted within a business to:

1. **Safeguard its assets** from employee theft, robbery, and unauthorized use; and

2. **Enhance the accuracy and reliability of its accounting records** by reducing the risk of errors (unintentional mistakes) and irregularities (intentional mistakes and misrepresentations) in the accounting process.

Under the Sarbanes-Oxley Act, all publicly traded U.S. corporations are required to maintain an adequate system of internal control. Companies that fail to comply are subject to fines, and company officers may be imprisoned.

THE SARBANES-OXLEY ACT

"Better get those controls under control" was a comment often made after the numerous corporate scandals of recent years. As a result, Congress passed the

Sarbanes-Oxley Act of 2002 (SOX). One of the most important laws to be passed in decades, SOX forces companies to pay more attention to internal controls.

SOX imposes more responsibilities on corporate executives and boards of directors to ensure that companies' internal controls are reliable and effective. Under one part of the law, companies must develop sound principles of control over financial reporting, and continually assess that these controls are working. In addition, independent outside auditors must attest to the level of internal control. SOX also created the Public Company Accounting Oversight Board (PCAOB), which now establishes auditing standards and regulates auditor activity.

One poll found that about 60% of investors believe that SOX will help safeguard their stock investments. Many say they would be unlikely to invest in a company that fails to follow SOX requirements. Although some corporate executives have criticized the time and expense involved in following the requirements of the law, SOX appears to be working well. For example, the chief accounting officer of Eli Lily noted that SOX triggered a comprehensive review of how the company documents its controls. This review uncovered redundancies and also pointed out controls that needed to be added. In short, it added up to time and money well spent. And the finance chief at General Electric noted, "We have seen value in SOX. It helps build investors' trust and gives them more confidence."[1]

PRINCIPLES OF INTERNAL CONTROL

To safeguard assets and enhance the accuracy and reliability of accounting records, companies follow internal control principles. The specific control measures used vary with the size and nature of the business and with management's control philosophy. The six principles listed in Illustration 7-1 apply to most enterprises. They are explained on the following pages.

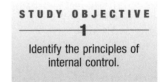

STUDY OBJECTIVE 1

Identify the principles of internal control.

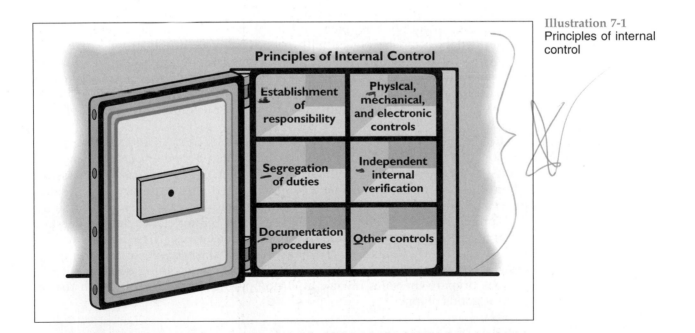

Illustration 7-1
Principles of internal control

Principles of Internal Control

Establishment of responsibility	Physical, mechanical, and electronic controls
Segregation of duties	Independent internal verification
Documentation procedures	Other controls

---

[1] "Corporate Regulation Must Be Working—There's a Backlash," *Wall Street Journal* (June 16, 2004), p. C1, and Judith Burns, "Is Sarbanes-Oxley Working?" *Wall Street Journal* (June 21, 2004), pp. R8–R9.

It's your shift now. I'm turning in my cash drawer and heading home.

Transfer of cash drawers

Establishment of Responsibility

An essential characteristic of internal control is the assignment of responsibility to specific individuals. **Control is most effective when only one person is responsible for a given task.**

To illustrate, assume that the cash on hand at the end of the day in a Safeway supermarket is $10 short of the cash rung up on the cash register. If only one person has operated the register, the shift manager can quickly assess responsibility for the shortage. If two or more individuals have worked the register, it may be impossible to determine who is responsible for the error unless each person has a separate cash drawer and register key.

Establishing responsibility includes the authorization and approval of transactions. The vice-president of sales should have the authority to establish policies for making credit sales. These policies ordinarily will require written credit department approval of credit sales.

Segregation of Duties

Segregation of duties is indispensable in a system of internal control. The rationale for segregation of duties is that **the work of one employee should, without a duplication of effort, provide a reliable basis for evaluating the work of another employee**. There are two common applications of this principle:

1. The responsibility for related activities should be assigned to different individuals.
2. The responsibility for record keeping for an asset should be separate from the physical custody of that asset.

RELATED ACTIVITIES. Companies should assign related activities to different individuals in both the purchasing and selling areas. **Making one individual responsible for all of the related activities**, as was the case in the Feature Story, **increases the potential for errors and irregularities**.

Related purchasing activities include ordering merchandise, receiving goods, and paying (or authorizing payment) for merchandise. In purchasing, for example, orders could be placed with friends or with suppliers who give kickbacks. In addition, a careless or dishonest employee might authorize payment without a careful review of the invoice, or, even worse, might approve fictitious invoices for payment. When a company assigns the responsibilities for ordering, receiving, and paying to different individuals, it minimizes the risk of such abuses.

Companies also should assign *related sales activities* to different individuals. Related sales activities include making a sale, shipping (or delivering) the goods to the customer, and billing the customer. Various frauds are possible when one person is responsible for these related sales transactions: A salesperson could make sales at unauthorized prices to increase sales commissions: A shipping clerk could ship goods to himself. A billing clerk could understate the amount billed for sales made to friends and relatives. These abuses are less likely to occur when salespersons make the sale, shipping department employees ship the goods on the basis of the sales order, and billing department employees prepare the sales invoice after comparing the sales order with the report of goods shipped.

RECORD KEEPING SEPARATE FROM PHYSICAL CUSTODY. If accounting is to provide a valid basis of accountability for an asset, the accountant, as record keeper, should have neither physical custody of the asset nor access to it.

Moreover, the custodian of the asset should not maintain or have access to the accounting records. **The custodian of the asset is not likely to convert the asset to personal use if one employee maintains the record of the asset that should be on hand and a different employee has physical custody of the asset.** The separation of accounting responsibility from the custody of assets is especially important for cash and inventories because these assets are very vulnerable to unauthorized use or misappropriation.

Illustration 7-2 shows the segregation of duties concept.

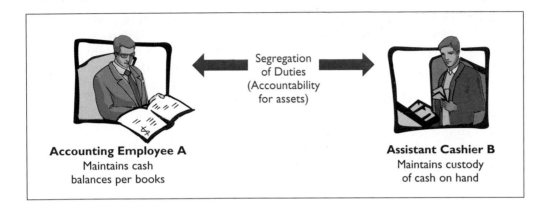

Illustration 7-2 The segregation of duties (accountability for assets) principle

Accounting across the Organization

Employee theft comes in a wide variety of flavors, affecting nearly every type of business. Consider the case of Simon WorldWide, which ran a number of promotional games for McDonald's. Customers searched newspapers and McDonald's products for winning pieces that in some cases were worth $1 million. The problem was that a Simon employee made sure that many of the winning pieces—more than $13 million worth of prizes—ended up in the hands of his friends. The friends then gave part of the winnings back to the employee.

 What controls would have reduced the likelihood of this type of theft?

Documentation Procedures

Documents provide evidence that transactions and events have occurred. For example, the shipping document indicates that the goods have been shipped, and the sales invoice indicates that the customer has been billed for the goods. By requiring signatures (or initials) on the documents, the company can identify the individual(s) responsible for the transaction or event.

Companies should establish procedures for documents. First, whenever possible, companies should use **prenumbered documents, and all documents should be accounted for**. Prenumbering helps to prevent an employee from recording a transaction more than once or, conversely, not recording the transactions at all. Second, **the control system should require that employees promptly forward source documents for accounting entries to the accounting department to help ensure timely recording of the transaction**

Helpful Hint An important corollary to prenumbering is keeping voided documents until all documents are accounted for.

and event. This control measure contributes directly to the accuracy and reliability of the accounting records.

Accounting across the Organization

The human resources (HR) department has always played an important role in internal control by carefully screening potential hires. The Sarbanes-Oxley Act has increased HR's role in a number of ways. Under SOX, a company needs to keep track of employees' degrees and certifications to ensure that employees continue to meet the specified requirements of a job. Also, to ensure proper employee supervision and proper separation of duties, companies must develop and monitor an organizational chart. When one corporation went through this exercise it found that out of 17,000 employees, there were "400 people who didn't report to anybody, and they had 35 people who reported to each other."

In addition, under SOX, if an employee complains of an unfair firing and mentions financial issues at the company, HR must refer the case to the company audit committee and possibly to its legal counsel.

 Why would unsupervised employees or employees who report to each other represent potential internal control threats?

Physical, Mechanical, and Electronic Controls

Use of physical, mechanical, and electronic controls is essential. Physical controls relate primarily to the safeguarding of assets. Mechanical and electronic controls safeguard assets and enhance the accuracy and reliability of the accounting records. Examples of these controls are shown in Illustration 7-3.

Illustration 7-3 Physical, mechanical, and electronic controls

Physical Controls

Safes, vaults, and safety deposit boxes for cash and business papers

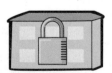

Locked warehouses and storage cabinets for inventories and records

Computer facilities with pass key access or fingerprint or eyeball scans

Mechanical and Electronic Controls

Alarms to prevent break-ins

Television monitors and garment sensors to deter theft

Time clocks for recording time worked

A crucial consideration in programming computerized systems is building in controls that limit unauthorized or unintentional tampering. Entire books and movies have used computer system tampering as a major theme. Most programmers would agree that tamper-proofing and debugging programs are the most difficult and time-consuming phases of their jobs.

Program controls built into the computer prevent intentional or unintentional errors or unauthorized access. To prevent unauthorized access, the computer system may require that users enter passwords or correctly answer random personal questions. Or, some systems authenticate users by means of fingerprint or retinal (eyeball) scans. Once access has been allowed, other program controls identify data having a value higher or lower than a predetermined amount (limit checks), validate computations (math checks), and detect improper processing order (sequence checks).

Independent Internal Verification

Most systems of internal control provide for **independent internal verification**. This principle involves the review, comparison, and reconciliation of data prepared by employees. Three measures are recommended to obtain maximum benefit from independent internal verification:

1. Companies should verify records periodically or on a surprise basis.
2. An employee who is independent of the personnel responsible for the information should make the verification.
3. Discrepancies and exceptions should be reported to a management level that can take appropriate corrective action.

Independent internal verification is especially useful in comparing recorded accountability with existing assets. The reconciliation of the cash register tape with the cash in the register is an example. Another common example is the reconciliation by an independent person of the cash balance per books with the cash balance per bank. Illustration 7-4 shows the relationship between this principle and the segregation of duties principle.

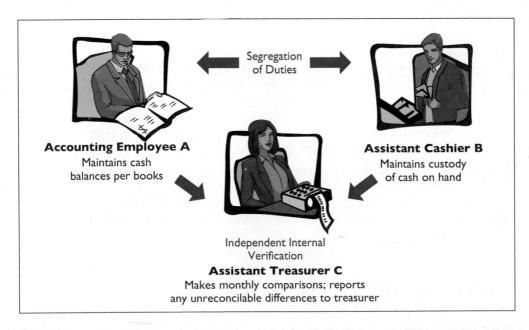

Illustration 7-4
Comparison of segregation of duties principle with independent internal verification principle

Accounting Employee A
Maintains cash balances per books

Segregation of Duties

Assistant Cashier B
Maintains custody of cash on hand

Independent Internal Verification
Assistant Treasurer C
Makes monthly comparisons; reports any unreconcilable differences to treasurer

Large companies often assign independent internal verification to internal auditors. **Internal auditors** are company employees who evaluate on a continuous basis the effectiveness of the company's system of internal control. They periodically review the activities of departments and individuals to determine whether prescribed internal controls are being followed.

Companies discover most fraud through internal mechanisms, such as internal controls and internal audits. That fact illustrates the importance of independent internal verification. The fraud at WorldCom involving billions of dollars, for example, was uncovered by an internal auditor.

Other Controls

Here are three other control measures:

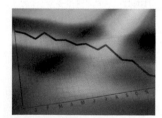

1. **Bond employees who handle cash.** Bonding involves obtaining insurance protection against misappropriation of assets by dishonest employees. This measure contributes to the safeguarding of cash in two ways: First, the insurance company carefully screens all individuals before adding them to the policy and may reject risky applicants. Second, bonded employees know that the insurance company will vigorously prosecute all offenders.

2. **Rotate employees' duties and require employees to take vacations.** These measures deter employees from attempting any thefts, since they will not be able to permanently conceal their improper actions. Many banks, for example, have discovered embezzlements when the perpetrator has been on vacation or assigned to a new position.

3. **Conduct thorough background checks.** Many believe that the most important and inexpensive measure any business can take to reduce employee theft and fraud is for the human resources department to conduct thorough background checks. Two tips: (1) Check to see whether job applicants actually graduated from the schools they list. (2) Never use the telephone numbers for previous employers given on the reference sheet; always look them up yourself.

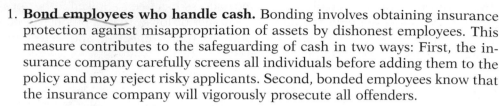

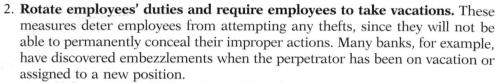

Poor internal controls can cost a company money even if no theft occurs. For example, Eastman Kodak Co., SunTrust Banks Inc., and Toys "R" Us Inc. all recently reported material weaknesses in internal controls. When a company announces that it has deficiencies in its internal controls, its stock price often falls.

Under the Sarbanes-Oxley Act companies must evaluate their internal controls systems and report on any deficiencies. Some analysts estimate that as many as 10% of all publicly traded companies will report weaknesses in their internal controls. The estimate for smaller companies is even higher.

Source: William M. Bulkeley and Robert Tomsho, "Kodak to Get Auditors Adverse View," *Wall Street Journal Online* (January 27, 2005).

 Why would a company's stock price fall if it reports deficiencies in its internal controls?

LIMITATIONS OF INTERNAL CONTROL

Companies generally design their systems of internal control to provide **reasonable assurance** of proper safeguarding of assets and reliability of accounting records. **The concept of reasonable assurance rests on the premise that the costs of establishing control procedures should not exceed their expected benefit.**

To illustrate, consider shoplifting losses in retail stores. Stores could completely eliminate such losses by having a security guard search customers as they leave the store. Store managers have concluded, however, that the negative effects of this procedure cannot be justified. Instead, stores have attempted to "control" shoplifting losses by less costly procedures: They post signs saying, "We reserve the right to inspect all packages" and "All shoplifters will be prosecuted." They also use hidden TV cameras and store detectives to monitor customer activity and put sensor equipment at exits.

The **human element** is an important factor in every system of internal control. A good system can become ineffective as a result of employee fatigue, carelessness, or indifference. For example, a receiving clerk may not bother to count goods received or may just "fudge" the counts. Occasionally, two or more individuals may work together to get around prescribed controls. Such **collusion** can significantly impair the effectiveness of a system because it eliminates the protection anticipated from segregation of duties. If a supervisor and a cashier collaborate to understate cash receipts, they may subvert the system of internal control (at least in the short run). No system of internal control is perfect.

The size of the business may impose limitations on internal control. A small company, for example, may find it difficult to apply the principles of segregation of duties and independent internal verification because it has few employees.

As indicated earlier, the Sarbanes-Oxley Act has a good system of checks and balances that will help enhance internal control. But SOX will not eliminate fraud. No matter how effective internal control is, ethical behavior cannot be imposed by law. Unfortunately some individuals will do illegal things. The "tone at the top" of a company is what counts. We need managers and executives with high moral standards to ensure that fraudulent and deceptive practices will not be tolerated.

 International Note

Other countries also have control problems. For example, a judge in France issued a 36-page book detailing many widespread scams, such as kickbacks in public-works contracts, the skimming of development aid money to Africa, and bribes on arms sales.

Business Insight
Ethics Perspective

A study by the Association of Certified Fraud Examiners indicates that businesses with fewer than 100 employees are most at risk for employee theft. Nearly 46% of frauds occurred at companies with fewer than 100 employees. The average loss at small companies was $98,000, which was only slightly less than the average fraud at companies with more than 10,000 employees. A $100,000 loss can threaten the very existence of a small company.

Source: 2004 Report to the Nation on Occupational Fraud and Abuse, Association of Certified Fraud Examiners, *http://www.cfenet.com/pdfs/2004RttN.pdf*, p. 6.

 Why are small companies more susceptible to employee theft?

Decision Toolkit

Decision Checkpoints	Info Needed for Decision	Tool to Use for Decision	How to Evaluate Results
Are the company's financial statements supported by adequate internal controls?	Auditor's report, management discussion and analysis, articles in financial press	The required measures of internal control are to (1) establish responsibility, (2) segregate duties, (3) document procedures, (4) employ physical or automated controls, and (5) use independent internal verification.	If any indication is given that these or other controls are lacking, use the financial statements with caution.

BEFORE YOU GO ON . . .

▶**Review It**

1. What are the two primary objectives of internal control?
2. Identify and describe the principles of internal control.
3. What are the limitations of internal control?

▶**Do It**

Li Song owns a small retail store. Li wants to establish good internal control procedures but is confused about the difference between segregation of duties and independent internal verification. Explain the differences to Li.

Action Plan

• Understand and explain the differences between (1) segregation of duties and (2) independent internal verification.

Solution

Segregation of duties relates to the assignment of responsibility so that (1) the work of one employee will check the work of another employee and (2) physical control of assets is separated from the records that keep track of the assets. Segregation of duties occurs daily in using assets and in executing and recording transactions.

In contrast, independent internal verification involves reviewing, comparing, and reconciling data prepared by one or several employees. Independent internal verification occurs after the fact, as in reconciling cash register totals at the end of the day with cash on hand.

THE NAVIGATOR

Cash Controls

Just as cash is the beginning of a company's operating cycle, it is usually the starting point for a company's system of internal control. Cash is the one asset that is readily convertible into any other type of asset; it is easily concealed and transported; and it is highly desired. Because of these characteristics, cash is the asset most susceptible to improper diversion and use. Moreover, because of the large volume of cash transactions, numerous errors may occur in executing and recording cash transactions. To safeguard cash and to ensure the accuracy of the accounting records for cash, effective internal control over cash is imperative.

Cash consists of coins, currency (paper money), checks, money orders, and money on hand or on deposit in a bank or similar depository. The general rule is that cash is whatever the bank will accept for deposit.

In the next sections we explain the application of internal control principles to cash receipts and cash disbursements.

INTERNAL CONTROL OVER CASH RECEIPTS

STUDY OBJECTIVE

2

Explain the applications of internal control to cash receipts.

Cash receipts result from a variety of sources: cash sales; collections on account from customers; the receipt of interest, rents, and dividends; investments by owners; bank loans; and proceeds from the sale of noncurrent assets. The internal control principles explained earlier apply to cash receipts transactions as shown in Illustration 7-5. As you might expect, companies vary considerably in how they apply these principles.

Illustration 7-5
Application of internal
control principles to cash
receipts

Internal Control over Cash Receipts

**Establishment of
Responsibility**

Only designated
personnel are
authorized to
handle cash receipts
(cashiers)

**Physical,
Mechanical, and
Electronic Controls**

Store cash in safes
and bank vaults;
limit access to
storage areas; use
cash registers

**Segregation
of Duties**

Different individuals
receive cash, record
cash receipts, and
hold the cash

**Independent
Internal
Verification**

Supervisors count
cash receipts daily;
treasurer compares
total receipts to
bank deposits daily

**Documentation
Procedures**

Use remittance
advice (mail
receipts), cash
register tapes, and
deposit slips

Other Controls

Bond personnel
who handle cash;
require employees
to take vacations;
deposit all cash
in bank daily

INTERNAL CONTROL OVER CASH DISBURSEMENTS

Companies disburse cash for a variety of reasons, such as to pay expenses and liabilities or to purchase assets. **Generally, internal control over cash disbursements is more effective when companies pay by check, rather than by cash, except for incidental amounts that are paid out of petty cash.** Companies generally issue checks only after following specified control procedures. In addition, the "paid" check provides proof of payment. The principles of internal control apply to cash disbursements as shown in Illustration 7-6 (page 326).

> **STUDY OBJECTIVE**
> **3**
> Explain the applications of internal control to cash disbursements.

Electronic Funds Transfer (EFT) System

Accounting for and controlling cash is an expensive and time-consuming process. The cost to process a check through a bank system is about $1 per check and is increasing. But it costs only 35¢ if the customer pays by credit card over the telephone and 1¢ if the customer pays via a computer.

Illustration 7-6
Application of internal
control principles to cash
disbursements

Internal Control over Cash Disbursements

Establishment of Responsibility

Only designated personnel are authorized to sign checks (treasurer)

Physical, Mechanical, and Electronic Controls

Store blank checks in safes, with limited access; print check amounts by machine in indelible ink

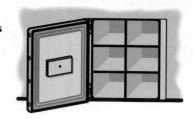

Segregation of Duties

Different individuals approve and make payments; check signers do not record disbursements

Independent Internal Verification

Compare checks to invoices; reconcile bank statement monthly

Documentation Procedures

Use prenumbered checks and account for them in sequence; each check must have approved invoice

Other Controls

Stamp invoices PAID

It is not surprising, therefore, that banking institutions have developed approaches to transfer funds among parties without the use of paper (deposit tickets, checks, etc.). Such procedures, called **electronic funds transfers (EFT)**, are disbursement systems that use wire, telephone, or computer to transfer cash from one location to another. Use of EFT is quite common. For example, many employees receive no formal payroll checks from their employers. Instead, the employers send magnetic tapes to the appropriate banks for deposit. In addition, individuals now frequently make regular payments such as those for house, car, or utilities by EFT.

Petty Cash Fund

As you learned earlier in the chapter, better internal control over cash disbursements is possible when companies make payments by check. However, using checks to pay such small amounts as those for postage due, employee working lunches, and taxi fares is both impractical and a nuisance. A common way of handling such payments, while maintaining satisfactory control, is to use a petty cash fund. A **petty cash fund** is a cash fund used to pay relatively small amounts. We explain the operation of a petty cash fund in the appendix at the end of this chapter.

Business Insight
Ethics Perspective

A recent study by the Association of Certified Fraud Examiners found that two-thirds of all employee thefts involved a fraudulent disbursement by an employee. The most common form (52% of cases) was fraudulent billing schemes. In these, the employee causes the company to issue a payment to the employee by submitting a bill for nonexistent goods or services, purchases of personal goods by the employee, or inflated invoices. The following graph shows the incidence of various types of fraudulent disbursements and the median loss from each.

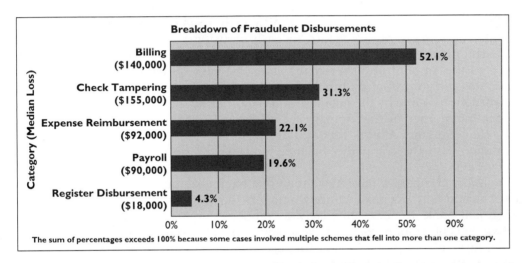

Breakdown of Fraudulent Disbursements

Category (Median Loss):
- Billing ($140,000) — 52.1%
- Check Tampering ($155,000) — 31.3%
- Expense Reimbursement ($92,000) — 22.1%
- Payroll ($90,000) — 19.6%
- Register Disbursement ($18,000) — 4.3%

The sum of percentages exceeds 100% because some cases involved multiple schemes that fell into more than one category.

Source: 2004 Report to the Nation on Occupational Fraud and Abuse, Association of Certified Fraud Examiners, *http://www.cfenet.com/pdfs/2004RttN.pdf,* p. 14.

 How can companies reduce the likelihood of fraudulent disbursements?

BEFORE YOU GO ON . . .

▶Review It

1. How do the principles of internal control apply to cash receipts?
2. How do the principles of internal control apply to cash disbursements?
3. What is the purpose of a petty cash fund?

▶Do It

L. R. Cortez is concerned about control over cash receipts in his fast-food restaurant, Big Cheese. The restaurant has two cash registers. At no time do more than two employees take customer orders and ring up sales. Work shifts for employees range from 4 to 8 hours. Cortez asks your help in installing a good system of internal control over cash receipts.

Action Plan

- Differentiate among the internal control principles of (1) establishing responsibility, (2) using electronic controls, and (3) independent internal verification.
- Design an effective system of internal control over cash receipts.

Solution

Cortez should assign a cash register to each employee at the start of each work shift, with register totals set at zero. Each employee should use only the assigned register and should ring up all sales. At the end of each work shift, Cortez or a supervisor/manager should total the register and make a cash count to see whether all cash is accounted for.

THE NAVIGATOR

USE OF A BANK

The use of a bank contributes significantly to good internal control over cash. A company can safeguard its cash by using a bank as a depository and clearinghouse for checks received and checks written. The use of a bank minimizes the amount of currency that must be kept on hand. In addition, it facilitates the control of cash because a double record is maintained of all bank transactions—one by the business and the other by the bank. The asset account Cash maintained by the company is the "flip-side" of the bank's liability account for that company. A **bank reconciliation** is the process of comparing the bank's balance with the company's balance, and explaining the differences to make them agree.

Many companies have more than one bank account. For efficiency of operations and better control, national retailers like Wal-Mart and Target often have regional bank accounts. Similarly, a company such as ExxonMobil with more than 100,000 employees may have a payroll bank account as well as one or more general bank accounts. In addition, a company may maintain several bank accounts in order to have more than one source for obtaining short-term loans when needed.

Bank Statements

Each month, the company receives from the bank a **bank statement** showing its bank transactions and balances.[2] For example, the statement for Laird Company in Illustration 7-7 (on page 329) shows the following: (1) checks paid and other debits that reduce the balance in the depositor's account, (2) deposits and other credits that increase the balance in the depositor's account, and (3) the account balance after each day's transactions.

Remember that bank statements are prepared from the *bank's* perspective. For example, every deposit the bank receives is an increase in the bank's liabilities (an account payable to the depositor). Therefore, in Illustration 7-7, National Bank and Trust *credits* to Laird Company every deposit it received from Laird. The reverse occurs when the bank "pays" a check issued by Laird Company on its checking account balance: Payment reduces the bank's liability and is therefore *debited* to Laird's account with the bank.

---

[2]Our presentation assumes that a company makes all adjustments at the end of the month. In practice, a company may also make journal entries during the month as it receives information from the bank regarding its account.

The bank statement lists in numerical sequence all paid checks along with the date the check was paid and its amount. Upon paying a check, the bank stamps the check "paid"; a paid check is sometimes referred to as a **canceled** check. In addition, the bank includes with the bank statement memoranda explaining other debits and credits it made to the depositor's account.

The bank uses a debit memorandum when a previously deposited customer's check "bounces" because of insufficient funds. In such a case, the customer's bank marks the check **NSF** (not sufficient funds) and returns it to the depositor's bank. The bank then debits (decreases) the depositor's account, as shown by the symbol NSF on the bank statement in Illustration 7-7, and sends the NSF check and debit memorandum to the depositor as notification of the charge. The NSF check creates an account receivable for the depositor and reduces cash in the bank account.

Helpful Hint Essentially, the bank statement is a copy of the bank's records sent to the customer for periodic review.

Illustration 7-7   Bank statement

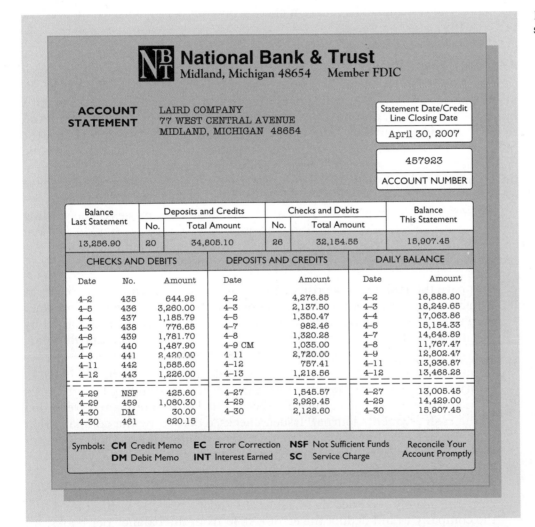

Reconciling the Bank Account

Because the bank and the company maintain independent records of the company's checking account, you might assume that the respective balances will always agree. In fact, the two balances are seldom the same at any given time. Therefore it is necessary to make the balance per books agree with the balance

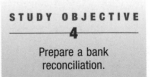

STUDY OBJECTIVE
4
Prepare a bank reconciliation.

per bank—a process called **reconciling the bank account**. The lack of agreement between the balances has two causes:

1. **Time lags** that prevent one of the parties from recording the transaction in the same period.
2. **Errors** by either party in recording transactions.

Time lags occur frequently. For example, several days may elapse between the time a company pays by check and the date the bank pays the check. Similarly, when a company uses the bank's night depository to make its deposits, there will be a difference of one day between the time the company records the receipts and the time the bank does so. A time lag also occurs whenever the bank mails a debit or credit memorandum to the company.

The incidence of errors depends on the effectiveness of the internal controls maintained by the company and the bank. Bank errors are infrequent. However, either party could accidentally record a $450 check as $45 or $540. In addition, the bank might mistakenly charge a check drawn by C. D. Berg to the account of C. D. Burg.

RECONCILIATION PROCEDURE.   In reconciling the bank account, it is customary to reconcile the balance per books and balance per bank to their adjusted (correct or true) cash balances. **To obtain maximum benefit from a bank reconciliation, an employee who has no other responsibilities related to cash should prepare the reconciliation**. When companies do not follow the internal control principle of independent internal verification in preparing the reconciliation, cash embezzlements may escape unnoticed. For example, in the Feature Story, a bank reconciliation by someone other than Kay Lemon might have exposed her embezzlement.

Illustration 7-8 (on page 331) shows the reconciliation process. The starting point in preparing the reconciliation is to enter the balance per bank statement and balance per books on a schedule. The following steps should reveal all the reconciling items that cause the difference between the two balances.

> **Helpful Hint** Deposits in transit and outstanding checks are reconciling items because of time lags.

1. Compare the individual deposits on the bank statement with the deposits in transit from the preceding bank reconciliation and with the deposits per company records or copies of duplicate deposit slips. Deposits recorded by the depositor that have not been recorded by the bank represent **deposits in transit**. Add these deposits to the balance per bank.
2. Compare the paid checks shown on the bank statement or the paid checks returned with the bank statement with (a) checks outstanding from the preceding bank reconciliation, and (b) checks issued by the company as recorded in the cash payments journal. Issued checks recorded by the company that have not been paid by the bank represent **outstanding checks**. Deduct outstanding checks from the balance per the bank.
3. Note any **errors** discovered in the foregoing steps and list them in the appropriate section of the reconciliation schedule. For example, if the company mistakenly recorded as $159 a paid check correctly written for $195, the company would deduct the error of $36 from the balance per books. All errors made by the depositor are reconciling items in determining the adjusted cash balance per books. In contrast, all errors made by the bank are reconciling items in determining the adjusted cash balance per the bank.
4. Trace **bank memoranda** to the depositor's records. The company lists in the appropriate section of the reconciliation schedule any unrecorded memoranda. For example, the company would deduct from the balance per books a $5 debit memorandum for bank service charges. Similarly, it would add to the balance per books a $32 credit memorandum for interest earned.

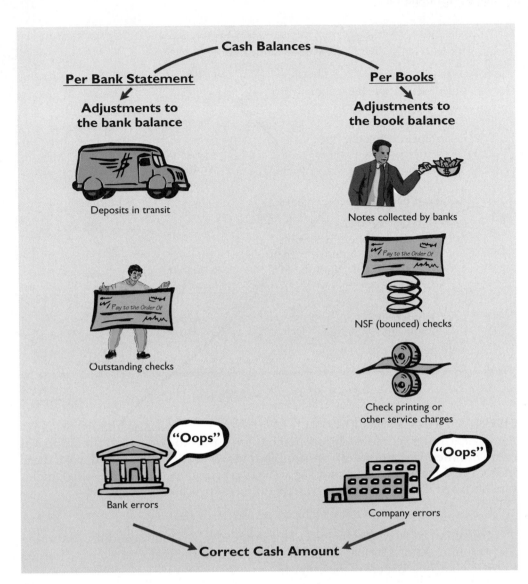

Cash Balances

Per Bank Statement — Per Books

Adjustments to the bank balance — Adjustments to the book balance

Deposits in transit — Notes collected by banks

Outstanding checks — NSF (bounced) checks

Check printing or other service charges

"Oops" — "Oops"

Bank errors — Company errors

Correct Cash Amount

BANK RECONCILIATION ILLUSTRATED. Illustration 7-7 presented the bank statement for Laird Company. It shows a balance per bank of $15,907.45 on April 30, 2007. On this date the balance of cash per books is $11,589.45. From the foregoing steps, Laird determines the following reconciling items.

1. **Deposits in transit:** April 30 deposit (received by bank on May 1). — $2,201.40

2. **Outstanding checks:** No. 453, $3,000.00; No. 457, $1,401.30; No. 460, $1,502.70. — 5,904.00

3. **Errors:** Check No. 443 was correctly written by Laird for $1,226.00 and was correctly paid by the bank. However, Laird recorded the check as $1,262.00. — 36.00

4. **Bank memoranda:**
   (a) Debit—NSF check from J. R. Baron for $425.60 — 425.60
   (b) Debit—Printing company checks charge, $30 — 30.00
   (c) Credit—Collection of note receivable for $1,000 plus interest earned $50, less bank collection fee $15 — 1,035.00

The bank reconciliation is shown in Illustration 7-9 (page 332).

Helpful Hint Note in the bank statement that the bank has paid checks No. 459 and 461, but check No. 460 is not listed. Thus, this check is outstanding. If a complete bank statement were provided, checks No. 453 and 457 also would not be listed. Laird obtains the amounts for these three checks from its cash payments records.

Illustration 7-9 Bank reconciliation

LAIRD COMPANY Bank Reconciliation April 30, 2007		
Cash balance per bank statement		$ 15,907.45
Add: Deposits in transit		2,201.40
		18,108.85
Less: Outstanding checks		
No. 453	$3,000.00	
No. 457	1,401.30	
No. 460	1,502.70	5,904.00
Adjusted cash balance per bank		**$12,204.85** ←
Cash balance per books		$ 11,589.45
Add: Collection of note receivable for $1,000 plus interest earned $50, less collection fee $15	$1,035.00	
Error in recording check No. 443	36.00	1,071.00
		12,660.45
Less: NSF check	425.60	
Bank service charge	30.00	455.60
Adjusted cash balance per books		**$12,204.85** ←

Helpful Hint These entries are adjusting entries. In prior chapters, we considered Cash an account that did not require adjustment because we had not yet explained a bank reconciliation.

ENTRIES FROM BANK RECONCILIATION. The depositor (that is, the company) next must record each reconciling item used to determine the **adjusted cash balance per books**. If the company does not journalize and post these items, the Cash account will not show the correct balance. The adjusting entries for the Laird Company bank reconciliation on April 30 are as follows.

Collection of Note Receivable. This entry involves four accounts. Assuming that the interest of $50 has not been recorded and the collection fee is charged to Miscellaneous Expense, the entry is:

```
A    =   L   +   SE
+1,035
                 -15 Exp
-1,000
                 +50 Rev
```
Cash Flows
+1,035

Apr.	30	Cash	1,035	
		Miscellaneous Expense	15	
		Notes Receivable		1,000
		Interest Revenue		50
		(To record collection of note receivable by bank)		

Book Error. An examination of the cash disbursements journal shows that check No. 443 was a payment on account to Andrea Company, a supplier. The correcting entry is:

```
A    =    L   +   SE
+36
          +36
```
Cash Flows
+36

Apr.	30	Cash	36	
		Accounts Payable—Andrea Company		36
		(To correct error in recording check No. 443)		

NSF Check. As indicated earlier, an NSF check becomes an accounts receivable to the depositor. The entry is:

Apr.	30	Accounts Receivable—J. R. Baron	425.60	
		Cash		425.60
		(To record NSF check)		

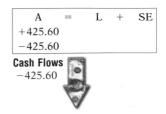

A	=	L	+	SE
+425.60				
−425.60				

Cash Flows
−425.60

Bank Service Charges. Companies typically debit to Miscellaneous Expense the check printing charges (DM) and other bank service charges (SC) because they are usually nominal in amount. Laird's entry is:

Apr.	30	Miscellaneous Expense	30	
		Cash		30
		(To record charge for printing company checks)		

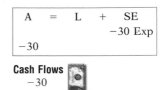

A	=	L	+	SE
				−30 Exp
−30				

Cash Flows
−30

The foregoing entries could also be combined into one compound entry.

After Laird posts the entries, the Cash account will appear as in Illustration 7-10. The adjusted cash balance in the ledger should agree with the adjusted cash balance per books in the bank reconciliation in Illustration 7-9.

Cash

Apr. 30	Bal.	11,589.45	Apr. 30	425.60
	30	1,035.00	30	30.00
	30	36.00		
Apr. 30	Bal.	**12,204.85**		

Illustration 7-10
Adjusted balance in cash account

What entries does the bank make? If the company discovers any bank errors in preparing the reconciliation, it should notify the bank so the bank can make the necessary corrections on its records. The bank does not make any entries for deposits in transit or outstanding checks. Only when these items reach the bank will the bank record these items.

BEFORE YOU GO ON . . .

▶ Review It

1. Why is it necessary to reconcile a bank account?
2. What steps are involved in the reconciliation procedure?
3. What information is included in a bank reconciliation?

▶ Do It

Sally Kist owns Linen Kist Fabrics. Sally asks you to explain how Linen Kist should treat the following items in reconciling the bank account at December 31: (1) a debit memorandum for an NSF check, (2) a credit memorandum for a note collected by the bank, (3) outstanding checks, and (4) a deposit in transit.

Action Plan

• Understand the purpose of a bank reconciliation.
• Identify time lags and explain how they cause reconciling items.

Solution

In reconciling the bank account, Linen Kist should treat the reconciling items as follows.

NSF check: Deduct from balance per books.
Collection of note: Add to balance per books.
Outstanding checks: Deduct from balance per bank.
Deposit in transit: Add to balance per bank.

Reporting Cash

STUDY OBJECTIVE
5
Explain the reporting of cash.

Companies report cash in two different statements: the balance sheet and the statement of cash flows. The balance sheet reports the amount of cash available at a given point in time. The statement of cash flows shows the sources and uses of cash during a period of time. The cash flow statement was introduced in Chapters 1 and 2 and will be discussed in much detail in Chapter 12. In this section we discuss some important points regarding the presentation of cash in the balance sheet.

When presented in a balance sheet, cash on hand, cash in banks, and petty cash are often combined and reported simply as **Cash**. Because it is the most liquid asset owned by the company, cash is listed first in the current assets section of the balance sheet.

CASH EQUIVALENTS

Many companies use the designation "Cash and cash equivalents" in reporting cash. (See Illustration 7-11 for an example.) **Cash equivalents** are short-term, highly liquid investments that are both:

1. Readily convertible to known amounts of cash, and
2. So near their maturity that their market value is relatively insensitive to changes in interest rates.

Examples of cash equivalents are Treasury bills, commercial paper (short-term corporate notes), and money market funds. All typically are purchased with cash that is in excess of immediate needs.

Illustration 7-11
Balance sheet
presentation of cash

▲ Delta

DELTA AIR LINES, INC.
Balance Sheet (partial)
December 31, 2004
(in millions)

Assets	
Current assets	
Cash and cash equivalents	**$1,463**
Short-term investments	336
Restricted cash	**348**
Accounts receivable, net	696
Parts inventories	203
Prepaid expenses and other	560
Total current assets	$3,606

Occasionally a company will have a net negative balance in its bank account. In this case, the company should report the negative balance among current liabilities. For example, farm equipment manufacturer Ag-Chem recently reported "Checks outstanding in excess of cash balances" of $2,145,000 among its current liabilities.

RESTRICTED CASH

A company may have cash that is not available for general use but, rather, is restricted for a special purpose. For example, landfill companies are often required to maintain a fund of restricted cash to ensure they will have adequate resources to cover closing and clean-up costs at the end of a landfill site's useful life.

Cash restricted in use should be reported separately on the balance sheet as **restricted cash**. If the company expects to use the restricted cash within the next year, it reports the amount as a current asset. When this is not the case, it reports the restricted funds as a noncurrent asset.

Illustration 7-11 shows restricted cash reported in the financial statements of **Delta Air Lines**. The company is required to maintain restricted cash as collateral to support insurance obligations related to workers' compensation claims. Delta does not have access to these funds for general use, and so it must report them separately, rather than as part of cash and cash equivalents.

Decision Toolkit

Decision Checkpoints	Info Needed for Decision	Tool to Use for Decision	How to Evaluate Results
Is all of the company's cash available for general use?	Balance sheet and notes to financial statements	Does the company report any cash as being restricted?	A restriction on the use of cash limits management's ability to use those resources for general obligations. This might be considered when assessing liquidity.

Managing and Monitoring Cash

Many companies struggle, not because they fail to generate sales, but because they can't manage their cash. A real-life example of this is a clothing manufacturing company owned by Sharon McCollick. McCollick gave up a stable, high-paying marketing job with Intel Corporation to start her own company. Soon she had more orders from stores such as JCPenney and Dayton Hudson (now Target) than she could fill. Yet she found herself on the brink of financial disaster, owing three mortgage payments on her house and $2,000 to the IRS. Her company could generate sales, but it was not collecting cash fast enough to support its operations. The bottom line is that a business must have cash.[3]

A merchandising company's operating cycle is generally shorter than that of a manufacturing company. Illustration 7-12 (page 336) shows the cash to cash operating cycle of a merchandising operation.

To understand cash management, consider the operating cycle of Sharon McCollick's clothing manufacturing company. First, it purchases cloth. Let's

---

[3]Adapted from T. Petzinger, Jr., "The Front Lines—Sharon McCollick Got Mad and Tore Down a Bank's Barriers," *Wall Street Journal* (May 19, 1995), p. B1.

Illustration 7-12
Operating cycle of a
merchandising company

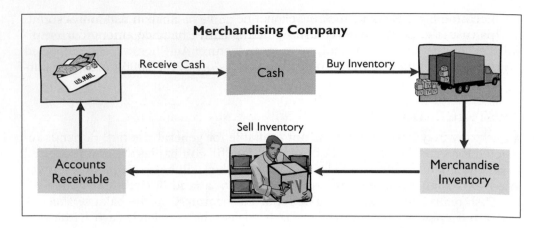

assume that it purchases the cloth on credit provided by the supplier, so the company owes its supplier money. Next, employees convert the cloth to clothing. Now the company also owes its employees money. Next, it sells the clothing to retailers, on credit. McCollick's company will have no money to repay suppliers or employees until its customers pay it. In a manufacturing operation there may be a significant lag between the original purchase of raw materials and the ultimate receipt of cash from customers.

Managing the often-precarious balance created by the ebb and flow of cash during the operating cycle is one of a company's greatest challenges. The objective is to ensure that a company has sufficient cash to meet payments as they come due, yet minimize the amount of non-revenue-generating cash on hand.

BASIC PRINCIPLES OF CASH MANAGEMENT

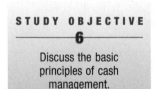

STUDY OBJECTIVE
6

Discuss the basic
principles of cash
management.

Management of cash is the responsibility of the company **treasurer**. Any company can improve its chances of having adequate cash by following five basic principles of cash management.

1. **Increase the speed of receivables collection.** Money owed Sharon McCollick by her customers is money that she can't use. The more quickly customers pay her, the more quickly she can use those funds. Thus, rather than have an average collection period of 30 days, she may want an average collection period of 15 days. However, she must carefully weigh any attempt to force her customers to pay earlier against the possibility that she may anger or alienate customers. Perhaps her competitors are willing to provide a 30-day grace period. As noted in Chapter 5, one common way to encourage customers to pay more quickly is to offer cash discounts for early payment under such terms as 2/10, n/30.

2. **Keep inventory levels low.** Maintaining a large inventory of cloth and finished clothing is costly. It ties up large amounts of cash, as well as warehouse space. Increasingly, companies are using techniques to reduce the inventory on hand, thus conserving their cash. Of course, if Sharon McCollick has inadequate inventory, she will lose sales. The proper level of inventory is an important decision.

3. **Delay payment of liabilities.** By keeping track of when her bills are due, Sharon McCollick's company can avoid paying bills too early. Let's say her supplier allows 30 days for payment. If she pays in 10 days, she has lost the use of that cash for 20 days. Therefore, she should use the full payment period. But she should not "stretch" payment past the point that could damage

her credit rating (and future borrowing ability). Sharon McCollick's company also should conserve cash by taking cash discounts offered by suppliers, when possible.

4. **Plan the timing of major expenditures.** To maintain operations or to grow, all companies must make major expenditures, which normally require some form of outside financing. In order to increase the likelihood of obtaining outside financing, McCollick should carefully consider the timing of major expenditures in light of her company's operating cycle. If at all possible, she should make any major expenditure when the company normally has excess cash—usually during the off-season.

5. **Invest idle cash.** Cash on hand earns nothing. An important part of the treasurer's job is to ensure that the company invests any excess cash, even if it is only overnight. Many businesses, such as Sharon McCollick's clothing company, are seasonal. During her slow season, when she has excess cash, she should invest it.

   To avoid a cash crisis, however, it is very important that investments of idle cash be highly liquid and risk-free. A *liquid investment* is one with a market in which someone is always willing to buy or sell the investment. A *risk-free investment* means there is no concern that the party will default on its promise to pay its principal and interest. For example, using excess cash to purchase stock in a small company because you heard that it was probably going to increase in value in the near term is totally inappropriate. First, the stock of small companies is often illiquid. Second, if the stock suddenly decreases in value, you might be forced to sell the stock at a loss in order to pay your bills as they come due. The most common form of liquid investments is interest-paying U.S. government securities.

⊕ **International Note**

International sales complicate cash management. For example, if Nike must repay a Japanese supplier 30 days from today in Japanese yen, Nike will be concerned about how the exchange rate of U.S. dollars for yen might change during those 30 days. Often corporate treasurers make investments known as *hedges* to lock in an exchange rate to reduce the company's exposure to exchange-rate fluctuation.

Illustration 7-13 summarizes these five principles of cash management.

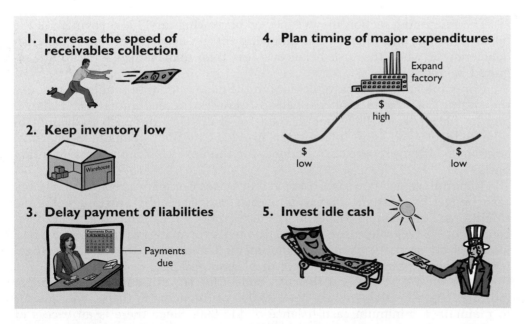

Illustration 7-13   Five principles of sound cash management

CASH BUDGETING

Because cash is so vital to a company, **planning the company's cash needs** is a key business activity. It enables the company to plan ahead to cover possible cash shortfalls and to make investments of idle funds. The **cash budget** shows anticipated cash flows, usually over a one- to two-year period. In this

STUDY OBJECTIVE

7

Identify the primary elements of a cash budget.

section we introduce the basics of cash budgeting. More advanced discussion of cash budgets and budgets in general is provided in managerial accounting texts.

As shown in Illustration 7-14, the cash budget contains three sections—cash receipts, cash disbursements, and financing—and the beginning and ending cash balances.

Illustration 7-14 Basic form of a cash budget

ANY COMPANY Cash Budget	
Beginning cash balance	$X,XXX
Add: **Cash receipts** (itemized)	X,XXX
Total available cash	X,XXX
Less: **Cash disbursements** (itemized)	X,XXX
Excess (deficiency) of available cash over cash disbursements	X,XXX
Financing needed	X,XXX
Ending cash balance	$X,XXX

The **Cash receipts** section includes expected receipts from the company's principal source(s) of cash, such as cash sales and collections from customers on credit sales. This section also shows anticipated receipts of interest and dividends, and proceeds from planned sales of investments, plant assets, and the company's capital stock.

The **Cash disbursements** section shows expected payments for direct materials, direct labor, manufacturing overhead, and selling and administrative expenses. This section also includes projected payments for income taxes, dividends, investments, and plant assets.

The **Financing** section shows expected borrowings and the repayment of the borrowed funds plus interest. The financing entry is needed when there is a cash deficiency or when the cash balance is less than management's minimum required balance.

Companies must prepare the data in the cash budget in sequence because the ending cash balance of one period becomes the beginning cash balance for the next period. They obtain data for preparing the cash budget from other budgets and from information provided by management. In practice, companies often prepare cash budgets for the next 12 months on a monthly basis.

To minimize detail, we will assume that Hayes Company prepares an annual cash budget by quarters. Preparing a cash budget requires making some assumptions. For example, Hayes makes assumptions regarding collection of accounts receivable, sales of securities, payments for materials and salaries, and purchases of property, plant, and equipment. The accuracy of the cash budget is very dependent on the accuracy of these assumptions.

Illustration 7–15 presents the cash budget for Hayes Company. The budget indicates that the company will need $3,000 of financing in the second quarter to maintain a minimum cash balance of $15,000. Since there is an excess of available cash over disbursements of $22,500 at the end of the third quarter, Hayes will repay the borrowing, plus $100 interest, in that quarter.

A cash budget contributes to more effective cash management. For example, it can show when a company will need additional financing, well before the actual need arises. Conversely, it can indicate when the company will have excess cash available for investments or other purposes.

Illustration 7-15   Cash budget

HAYES COMPANY Cash Budget For the Year Ending December 31, 2007				
	Quarter			
	1	**2**	**3**	**4**
Beginning cash balance	$ 38,000	$ 25,500	$ 15,000	$ 19,400
Add: **Cash receipts**				
Collections from customers	168,000	198,000	228,000	258,000
Sale of securities	2,000	0	0	0
Total receipts	170,000	198,000	228,000	258,000
Total available cash	208,000	223,500	243,000	277,400
Less: **Cash disbursements**				
Materials	23,200	27,200	31,200	35,200
Salaries	62,000	72,000	82,000	92,000
Selling and administrative expenses (excluding depreciation)	94,300	99,300	104,300	109,300
Purchase of truck	0	10,000	0	0
Income tax expense	3,000	3,000	3,000	3,000
Total disbursements	182,500	211,500	220,500	239,500
Excess (deficiency) of available cash over disbursements	25,500	12,000	22,500	37,900
Financing				
Borrowings	0	3,000	0	0
Repayments—plus $100 interest	0	0	3,100	0
Ending cash balance	$ 25,500	$ 15,000	$ 19,400	$ 37,900

Decision Toolkit

Decision Checkpoints	Info Needed for Decision	Tool to Use for Decision	How to Evaluate Results
Will the company be able to meet its projected cash needs?	Cash budget (typically available only to management)	The cash budget shows projected sources and uses of cash. If cash uses exceed internal cash sources, then the company must look for outside sources.	Two issues: (1) Are management's projections reasonable? (2) If outside sources are needed, are they available?

BEFORE YOU GO ON . . .

▶ Review It

1. What are the five principal elements of sound cash management?
2. What are the three sections of the cash budget?
3. What was Tootsie Roll's balance in cash and cash equivalents at December 31, 2004? Did it report any restricted cash? How did Tootsie Roll define cash equivalents? The answers to these questions appear on p. 369.

▶**Do It**

Martian Company's management wants to maintain a minimum monthly cash balance of $15,000. At the beginning of March the cash balance is $16,500; expected cash receipts for March are $210,000; and cash disbursements are expected to be $220,000. How much cash, if any, must Martian borrow to maintain the desired minimum monthly balance?

Action Plan

• Insert the dollar data into the basic form of the cash budget.

Solution

Beginning cash balance	$ 16,500
Add: Cash receipts for March	210,000
Total available cash	226,500
Less: Cash disbursements for March	220,000
Excess of available cash over cash disbursements	6,500
Financing	**8,500**
Ending cash balance	$ 15,000

To maintain the desired minimum cash balance of $15,000, Martian Company must borrow $8,500 of cash.

THE NAVIGATOR

Using the Decision Toolkit

Presented below is hypothetical financial information for Mattel Corporation. Included in this information is financial statement data from the year ended December 31, 2006, which should be used to evaluate Mattel's cash position.

Selected Financial Information
Year Ended December 31, 2006
(in millions)

Net cash provided by operations	$325
Capital expenditures	162
Dividends paid	80
Total expenses	680
Depreciation expense	40
Cash balance	206

Also provided are projected data which are management's best estimate of its sources and uses of cash during 2007. This information should be used to prepare a cash budget for 2007.

Projected Sources and Uses of Cash
(in millions)

Beginning cash balance	$206
Cash receipts from sales	355
Cash receipts from sale of short-term investments	20
Cash payments for inventory	357
Cash payments for selling and administrative expense	201
Cash payments for property, plant, and equipment	45
Cash payments for taxes	17

Mattel Corporation's management believes it should maintain a balance of $200 million cash.

Instructions

(a) Using the hypothetical projected sources and uses of cash information presented above, prepare a cash budget for 2007 for Mattel Corporation.

(b) Comment on the company's cash adequacy, and discuss steps that might be taken to improve its cash position.

Solution

(a)

MATTEL CORPORATION
Cash Budget
For the Year 2007
(in millions)

Beginning cash balance		$206
Add: Cash receipts		
From sales of product	$355	
From sale of short-term investments	20	375
Total available cash		581
Less: Cash disbursements		
Payments for inventory	357	
Payments for selling and administrative costs	201	
Payments for property, plant, and equipment	45	
Payments for taxes	17	
Total disbursements		620
Excess (deficiency) of available cash over disbursements		(39)
Financing needed		**239**
Ending cash balance		$200

(b) Using these hypothetical data, Mattel's cash position appears adequate. For 2007 Mattel is projecting a cash shortfall. This is not necessarily of concern, but it should be investigated. Given that its primary line of business is toys, and that most toys are sold during December, we would expect Mattel's cash position to vary significantly during the course of the year. After the holiday season it probably has a lot of excess cash. Earlier in the year, when it is making and selling its product but has not yet been paid, it may need to borrow to meet any temporary cash shortfalls.

    If Mattel's management is concerned with its cash position, it could take the following steps: (1) Offer its customers cash discounts for early payment, such as 2/10, n/30. (2) Implement inventory management techniques to reduce the need for large inventories of such things as the plastics used to make its toys. (3) Carefully time payments to suppliers by keeping track of when payments are due, so as not to pay too early. (4) If it has plans for major expenditures, time those expenditures to coincide with its seasonal period of excess cash.

Summary of Study Objectives

1 *Identify the principles of internal control.* The principles of internal control are establishment of responsibility; segregation of duties; documentation procedures; physical, mechanical, and electronic controls; independent internal verification; and other controls.

2 *Explain the applications of internal control to cash receipts.* Internal controls over cash receipts include: (a) designating only personnel such as cashiers to handle cash; (b) assigning the duties of receiving cash, recording cash, and having custody of cash to different individuals; (c) obtaining remittance advices for mail receipts, cash register tapes for over-the-counter receipts, and deposit slips for bank deposits; (d) using company safes and bank vaults to store cash with access limited to authorized personnel, and using cash registers in executing over-the-counter receipts; (e) making independent daily counts of register receipts and daily comparisons of total receipts with total deposits; and (f) bonding personnel who handle cash and requiring them to take vacations.

3 *Explain the applications of internal control to cash disbursements.* Internal controls over cash disbursements include: (a) having only specified individuals such as the treasurer authorized to sign checks; (b) assigning the duties of approving items for payment, paying the items, and recording the payment to different individuals; (c) using prenumbered checks and accounting for all checks, with each check supported by an approved invoice; (d) storing blank checks in a safe or vault with access restricted to authorized personnel, and using a machine with indelible ink to imprint amounts on checks; (e) comparing each check with the approved invoice before issuing the check, and making monthly reconciliations of bank and book balances; and (f) after payment, stamping each approved invoice "paid."

4 *Prepare a bank reconciliation.* In reconciling the bank account, it is customary to reconcile the balance per books and the balance per bank to their adjusted balance. The steps in determining the reconciling items are to ascertain deposits in transit, outstanding checks, errors by the depositor or the bank, and unrecorded bank memoranda.

5 *Explain the reporting of cash.* Cash is listed first in the current assets section of the balance sheet. In some cases, companies report cash together with cash equivalents. Cash restricted for a special purpose is reported separately as a current asset or as a noncurrent asset, depending on when the company expects to use the cash.

6 *Discuss the basic principles of cash management.* The basic principles of cash management include: (a) increase the speed of receivables collection, (b) keep inventory levels low, (c) delay payment of liabilities, (d) plan timing of major expenditures, and (e) invest idle cash.

7 *Identify the primary elements of a cash budget.* The three main elements of a cash budget are the cash receipts section, cash disbursements section, and financing section.

THE NAVIGATOR

Decision Toolkit—A Summary

Decision Checkpoints	Info Needed for Decision	Tool to Use for Decision	How to Evaluate Results
Are the company's financial statements supported by adequate internal controls?	Auditor's report, management discussion and analysis, articles in financial press	The required measures of internal control are to (1) establish responsibility, (2) segregate duties, (3) document procedures, (4) employ physical or automated controls, and (5) use independent internal verification.	If any indication is given that these or other controls are lacking, use the financial statements with caution.
Is all of the company's cash available for general use?	Balance sheet and notes to financial statements	Does the company report any cash as being restricted?	A restriction on the use of cash limits management's ability to use those resources for general obligations. This might be considered when assessing liquidity.
Will the company be able to meet its projected cash needs?	Cash budget (typically available only to management)	The cash budget shows projected sources and uses of cash. If cash uses exceed internal cash sources, then the company must look for outside sources.	Two issues: (1) Are management's projections reasonable? (2) If outside sources are needed, are they available?

APPENDIX
OPERATION OF THE PETTY CASH FUND

The operation of a petty cash fund involves (1) establishing the fund, (2) making payments from the fund, and (3) replenishing the fund.

Establishing the Petty Cash Fund

Two essential steps in establishing a petty cash fund are: (1) appointing a petty cash custodian who will be responsible for the fund, and (2) determining the size of the fund. Ordinarily, a company expects the amount in the fund to cover anticipated disbursements for a three- to four-week period.

When the company establishes the petty cash fund, it issues a check payable to the petty cash custodian for the stipulated amount. If Laird Company decides to establish a $100 fund on March 1, the entry in general journal form is:

Mar. 1	Petty Cash	100	
	Cash		100
	(To establish a petty cash fund)		

A	=	L	+	SE
+100				
−100				

Cash Flows
no effect

The fund custodian cashes the check and places the proceeds in a locked petty cash box or drawer. Most petty cash funds are established on a fixed-amount basis. Moreover, the company will make no additional entries to the Petty Cash account unless the stipulated amount of the fund is changed. For example, if Laird Company decides on July 1 to increase the size of the fund to $250, it would debit Petty Cash $150 and credit Cash $150.

Helpful Hint Petty cash funds are authorized and legitimate. In contrast, "slush" funds are unauthorized and hidden (under the table).

Making Payments from Petty Cash

The custodian of the petty cash fund has the authority to make payments from the fund that conform to prescribed management policies. Usually management limits the size of expenditures that come from petty cash and does not permit use of the fund for certain types of transactions (such as making short-term loans to employees).

Each payment from the fund must be documented on a prenumbered petty cash receipt (or petty cash voucher). The signatures of both the custodian and the individual receiving payment are required on the receipt. If other supporting documents such as a freight bill or invoice are available, they should be attached to the petty cash receipt.

Helpful Hint From the standpoint of internal control, the receipt satisfies two principles: (1) establishing responsibility (signature of custodian), and (2) documentation procedures.

The custodian keeps the receipts in the petty cash box until the fund is replenished. As a result, the sum of the petty cash receipts and money in the fund should equal the established total at all times. This means that management can make surprise counts at any time by an independent person, such as an internal auditor, to determine the correctness of the fund.

The company does not make an accounting entry to record a payment at the time it is taken from petty cash. It is considered both inexpedient and unnecessary to do so. Instead, the company recognizes the accounting effects of each payment when the fund is replenished.

Replenishing the Petty Cash Fund

When the money in the petty cash fund reaches a minimum level, the company replenishes the fund. The petty cash custodian initiates a request for reimbursement. This individual prepares a schedule (or summary) of the payments that have been made and sends the schedule, supported by petty cash receipts and other documentation, to the treasurer's office. The receipts and supporting documents are examined in the treasurer's office to verify that they were proper payments from the fund. The treasurer then approves the request, and a check is prepared to restore the fund to its established amount. At the same time, all supporting documentation is stamped "paid" so that it cannot be submitted again for payment.

To illustrate, assume that on March 15 the petty cash custodian requests a check for $87. The fund contains $13 cash and petty cash receipts for postage $44, supplies $38, and miscellaneous expenses $5. The entry, in general journal form, to record the check is:

```
A   =   L   +   SE
                -44 Exp
+38
                -5 Exp
-87
```

Cash Flows
−87

Mar. 15	Postage Expense	44	
	Supplies	38	
	Miscellaneous Expense	5	
	Cash		87
	(To replenish petty cash fund)		

Note that the reimbursement entry does not affect the Petty Cash account. Replenishment changes the composition of the fund by replacing the petty cash receipts with cash, but it does not change the balance in the fund.

Occasionally, in replenishing a petty cash fund the company may need to recognize a cash shortage or overage. To illustrate, assume in the preceding example that the custodian had only $12 in cash in the fund plus the receipts as listed. The request for reimbursement would therefore be for $88, and the following entry would be made.

```
A   =   L   +   SE
                -44 Exp
+38
                -5 Exp
                -1 Exp
-88
```

Cash Flows
−88

Mar. 15	Postage Expense	44	
	Supplies	38	
	Miscellaneous Expense	5	
	Cash Over and Short	1	
	Cash		88
	(To replenish petty cash fund)		

Conversely, if the custodian had $14 in cash, the reimbursement request would be for $86, and Cash Over and Short would be credited for $1. A debit balance in Cash Over and Short is reported in the income statement as miscellaneous expense; a credit balance is reported as miscellaneous revenue. The company closes Cash Over and Short to Income Summary at the end of the year.

Companies should replenish a petty cash fund **at the end of the accounting period, regardless of the cash in the fund**. Replenishment at this time is necessary in order to recognize the effects of the petty cash payments on the financial statements.

Internal control over a petty cash fund is strengthened by (1) having a supervisor make surprise counts of the fund to ascertain whether the paid vouchers and fund cash equal the designated amount, and (2) canceling or mutilating the paid vouchers so they cannot be resubmitted for reimbursement.

Summary of Study Objective for Appendix

8 *Explain the operation of a petty cash fund.* In operating a petty cash fund, a company establishes the fund by appointing a custodian and determining the size of the fund. The custodian makes payments from the fund for documented expenditures. The company replenishes the fund as needed, and at least at the end of each accounting period. Accounting entries to record payments are made at that time.

Glossary

Bank reconciliation The process of comparing the bank's account balance with the company's balance, and explaining the differences to make them agree. (p. 328)

Bank statement A statement received monthly from the bank that shows the depositor's bank transactions and balances. (p. 328)

Cash Resources that consist of coins, currency, checks, money orders, and money on hand or on deposit in a bank or similar depository. (p. 324)

Cash budget A projection of anticipated cash flows, usually over a one- to two-year period. (p. 337)

Cash equivalents Short-term, highly liquid investments that can be converted to a specific amount of cash. (p. 334)

Deposits in transit Deposits recorded by the depositor that have not been recorded by the bank. (p. 330)

Electronic funds transfer (EFT) A disbursement system that uses wire, telephone, telegraph, or computer to transfer cash from one location to another. (p. 326)

Internal auditors Company employees who evaluate on a continuous basis the effectiveness of the company's system of internal control. (p. 321)

Internal control The plan of organization and all the related methods and measures adopted within a business to safeguard its assets and enhance the accuracy and reliability of its accounting records. (p. 316)

NSF check A check that is not paid by a bank because of insufficient funds in a customer's bank account. (p. 329)

Outstanding checks Checks issued and recorded by a company that have not been paid by the bank. (p. 330)

Petty cash fund A cash fund used to pay relatively small amounts. (p. 327)

Restricted cash Cash that is not available for general use, but instead is restricted for a particular purpose. (p. 335)

Sarbanes-Oxley Act of 2002 (SOX) Law that forces companies to pay more attention to internal control. (p. 317)

Treasurer Employee responsible for the management of a company's cash. (p. 336)

Demonstration Problem

Trillo Company's bank statement for May 2007 shows these data.

Balance May 1	$12,650	Balance May 31		$14,280
Debit memorandum:		Credit memorandum:		
NSF check	175	Collection of note receivable		505

The cash balance per books at May 31 is $13,319. Your review of the data reveals the following.

1. The NSF check was from Hup Co., a customer.

2. The note collected by the bank was a $500, 3-month, 12% note. The bank charged a $10 collection fee. No interest has been accrued.

3. Outstanding checks at May 31 total $2,410.

4. Deposits in transit at May 31 total $1,752.

5. A Trillo Company check for $352 dated May 10 cleared the bank on May 25. This check, which was a payment on account, was journalized for $325.

Instructions
(a) Prepare a bank reconciliation at May 31.
(b) Journalize the entries required by the reconciliation.

Action Plan

- Follow the four steps used in reconciling items (p. 330).
- Work carefully to minimize mathematical errors in the reconciliation.
- Prepare entries based on reconciling items per books.
- Make sure the cash ledger balance after posting the reconciling entries agrees with the adjusted cash balance per books.

Solution to Demonstration Problem

(a)

Cash balance per bank statement	$14,280
Add: Deposits in transit	1,752
	16,032
Less: Outstanding checks	2,410
Adjusted cash balance per bank	$13,622
Cash balance per books	$13,319
Add: Collection of note receivable $500, plus $15 interest less collection fee $10	505
	13,824
Less: NSF check $175	
Error in recording check 27	202
Adjusted cash balance per books	$13,622

(b)

May 31	Cash	505	
	Miscellaneous Expense	10	
	Notes Receivable		500
	Interest Revenue		15
	(To record collection of note by bank)		
31	Accounts Receivable—Hup Co.	175	
	Cash		175
	(To record NSF check from Hup Co.)		
31	Accounts Payable	27	
	Cash		27
	(To correct error in recording check)		

Note: All Questions, Exercises, and Problems marked with an asterisk relate to material in the appendix to the chapter.

Self-Study Questions

Answers are at the end of the chapter.

(SO 1) **1.** Internal control is used in a business to enhance the accuracy and reliability of its accounting records and to:
(a) safeguard its assets.
(b) prevent fraud.
(c) produce correct financial statements.
(d) deter employee dishonesty.

(SO 1) **2.** The principles of internal control do *not* include:
(a) establishment of responsibility.
(b) documentation procedures.
(c) financial performance measures.
(d) independent internal verification.

(SO 1) **3.** Physical controls do *not* include:
(a) safes and vaults to store cash.
(b) independent bank reconciliations.
(c) locked warehouses for inventories.
(d) bank safety deposit boxes for important papers.

(SO 2) **4.** Permitting only designated personnel such as cashiers to handle cash receipts is an application of the principle of:
(a) documentation procedures.
(b) establishment of responsibility.
(c) independent internal verification.
(d) other controls.

(SO 3) **5.** The use of prenumbered checks in disbursing cash is an application of the principle of:
(a) establishment of responsibility.
(b) segregation of duties.
(c) physical, mechanical, and electronic controls.
(d) documentation procedures.

(SO 3) **6.** The control features of a bank account do *not* include:
(a) having bank auditors verify the correctness of the bank balance per books.
(b) minimizing the amount of cash that must be kept on hand.

(c) providing a double record of all bank transactions.

(d) safeguarding cash by using a bank as a depository.

(SO 4) **7.** In a bank reconciliation, deposits in transit are:
(a) deducted from the book balance.
(b) added to the book balance.
(c) added to the bank balance.
(d) deducted from the bank balance.

(SO 5) **8.** Which of the following items in a cash drawer at November 30 is *not* cash?
(a) Money orders.
(b) Coins and currency.
(c) A customer check dated December 1.
(d) A customer check dated November 28.

(SO 7) **9.** Which of the following is *not* one of the sections of a cash budget?
(a) Cash receipts section.
(b) Cash disbursements section.
(c) Financing section.
(d) Cash from operations section.

10. Which statement correctly describes   (SO 5)
the reporting of cash?
(a) Cash cannot be combined with cash equivalents.
(b) Restricted cash funds may be combined with Cash.
(c) Cash is listed first in the current assets section.
(d) Restricted cash funds cannot be reported as a current asset.

11. A check is written to replenish a $100 petty cash   (SO 8)
fund when the fund contains receipts of $94 and
$3 in cash. In recording the check:
(a) Cash Over and Short should be debited for $3.
(b) Petty Cash should be debited for $94.
(c) Cash should be credited for $94.
(d) Petty Cash should be credited for $3.

Go to the book's website,
www.wiley.com/college/kimmel, to access
additional Self-Study Questions.

Questions

1. "Internal control is concerned only with enhancing the accuracy of the accounting records." Do you agree? Explain.

2. Discuss how the Sarbanes-Oxley Act has increased the importance of internal control to all employees in a company.

3. What principles of internal control apply to most business enterprises?

4. In the corner grocery store, all sales clerks make change out of one cash register drawer. Is this a violation of internal control? Why?

5. Melody Wilson is reviewing the principle of segregation of duties. What are the two common applications of this principle?

6. How do documentation procedures contribute to good internal control?

7. What internal control objectives are met by physical, mechanical, and electronic controls?

8. (a) Explain the control principle of independent internal verification.
(b) What practices are important in applying this principle?

9. As the company accountant, explain the following ideas to the management of Jason Company.
(a) The concept of reasonable assurance in internal control.
(b) The importance of the human factor in internal control.

10. Discuss the human resources department's involvement in internal controls.

11. Fitzgerald Inc. owns the following assets at the balance sheet date.

Cash in bank—savings account	$ 5,000
Cash on hand	1,100
Cash refund due from the IRS	1,000
Checking account balance	12,000
Postdated checks	500

What amount should be reported as Cash in the balance sheet?

12. What principle(s) of internal control is (are) involved in making daily cash counts of over-the-counter receipts?

13. Assume that Kohl's Department Stores installed new electronic cash registers in its stores. How do cash registers improve internal control over cash receipts?

14. At Wells Wholesale Company two mail clerks open all mail receipts. How does this strengthen internal control?

15. "To have maximum effective internal control over cash disbursements, all payments should be made by check." Is this true? Explain.

16. Swendson Company's internal controls over cash disbursements provide for the treasurer to sign checks imprinted by a checkwriter after comparing the check with the approved invoice. Identify the internal control principles that are present in these controls.

17. How do these principles apply to cash disbursements:
(a) Physical, mechanical, and electronic controls?
(b) Other controls?

18. What is the essential feature of an electronic funds transfer (EFT) procedure?

19. "The use of a bank contributes significantly to good internal control over cash." Is this true? Why?

20. Raymond Bright is confused about the lack of agreement between the cash balance per books and the balance per bank. Explain the causes for the lack of agreement to Raymond, and give an example of each cause.

21. Describe the basic principles of cash management.

22. Kelly Mills asks your help concerning an NSF check. Explain to Kelly (a) what an NSF check is, (b) how it is treated in a bank reconciliation, and (c) whether it will require an adjusting entry on the company's books.

23.
    (a) "Cash equivalents are the same as cash." Do you agree? Explain.
    (b) How should restricted cash funds be reported on the balance sheet?

*24. (a) Identify the three activities that pertain to a petty cash fund, and indicate an internal control principle that is applicable to each activity.
    (b) When are journal entries required in the operation of a petty cash fund?

Brief Exercises

Explain the importance of internal control.
(SO 1)

BE7-1 Jo Duma is the new owner of JoJo Co. She has heard about internal control but is not clear about its importance for her business. Explain to Jo the two purposes of internal control, and give her one application of each purpose for JoJo Co.

Identify internal control principles.
(SO 1)

BE7-2 The internal control procedures in Barton Company make the following provisions. Identify the principles of internal control that are being followed in each case.
(a) Employees who have physical custody of assets do not have access to the accounting records.
(b) Each month the assets on hand are compared to the accounting records by an internal auditor.
(c) A prenumbered shipping document is prepared for each shipment of goods to customers.

Identify the internal control principles applicable to cash receipts.
(SO 2)

BE7-3 Allen Company has the following internal control procedures over cash receipts. Identify the internal control principle that is applicable to each procedure.
(a) All over-the-counter receipts are registered on cash registers.
(b) All cashiers are bonded.
(c) Daily cash counts are made by cashier department supervisors.
(d) The duties of receiving cash, recording cash, and having custody of cash are assigned to different individuals.
(e) Only cashiers may operate cash registers.

Identify the internal control principles applicable to cash disbursements.
(SO 3)

BE7-4 Pascal Company has the following internal control procedures over cash disbursements. Identify the internal control principle that is applicable to each procedure.
(a) Company checks are prenumbered.
(b) The bank statement is reconciled monthly by an internal auditor.
(c) Blank checks are stored in a safe in the treasurer's office.
(d) Only the treasurer or assistant treasurer may sign checks.
(e) Check signers are not allowed to record cash disbursement transactions.

Identify the control features of a bank account.
(SO 3)

BE7-5 Colton Amon is uncertain about the control features of a bank account. Explain the control benefits of (a) a check and (b) a bank statement.

Indicate location of reconciling items in a bank reconciliation.
(SO 4)

BE7-6 The following reconciling items are applicable to the bank reconciliation for Pileggi Co. Indicate how each item should be shown on a bank reconciliation.
(a) Outstanding checks.
(b) Bank debit memorandum for service charge.
(c) Bank credit memorandum for collecting a note for the depositor.
(d) Deposit in transit.

Identify reconciling items that require adjusting entries.
(SO 4)

BE7-7 Using the data in BE7-6, indicate (a) the items that will result in an adjustment to the depositor's records and (b) why the other items do not require adjustment.

BE7-8 At July 31 Ballah Company has this bank information: cash balance per bank $7,800; outstanding checks $762; deposits in transit $1,350; and a bank service charge $40. Determine the adjusted cash balance per bank at July 31.

Prepare partial bank reconciliation.
(SO 4)

BE7-9 In the month of November, Drajna Company Inc. wrote checks in the amount of $9,250. In December, checks in the amount of $11,880 were written. In November, $8,800 of these checks were presented to the bank for payment, and $10,889 in December. What is the amount of outstanding checks at the end of November? At the end of December?

Analyze outstanding checks.
(SO 4)

BE7-10 Elizondo Company has these cash balances: cash in bank $12,742; payroll bank account $6,000; and plant expansion fund cash $25,000. Explain how each balance should be reported on the balance sheet.

Explain the statement presentation of cash balances.
(SO 5)

BE7-11 The following information is available for Gurek Company for the month of January: expected cash receipts $60,000; expected cash disbursements $67,000; cash balance on January 1, $12,000. Management wishes to maintain a minimum cash balance of $8,000. Prepare a basic cash budget for the month of January.

Prepare a cash budget.
(SO 7)

*****BE7-12** On March 20 Slater's petty cash fund of $100 is replenished when the fund contains $21 in cash and receipts for postage $40, supplies $26, and travel expense $13. Prepare the journal entry to record the replenishment of the petty cash fund.

Prepare entry to replenish a petty cash fund.
(SO 8)

Exercises

E7-1 Bank employees use a system known as the "maker-checker" system. An employee will record an entry in the appropriate journal, and then a supervisor will verify and approve the entry. These days, as all of a bank's accounts are computerized, the employee first enters a batch of entries into the computer, and then the entries are posted automatically to the general ledger account after the supervisor approves them on the system.

Access to the computer system is password-protected and task-specific, which means that the computer system will not allow the employee to approve a transaction or the supervisor to record a transaction.

Identify the principles of internal control.
(SO 1)

Instructions
Identify the principles of internal control inherent in the "maker-checker" procedure used by banks.

E7-2 Culotti's Pizza operates strictly on a carryout basis. Customers pick up their orders at a counter where a clerk exchanges the pizza for cash. While at the counter, the customer can see other employees making the pizzas and the large ovens in which the pizzas are baked.

Identify the principles of internal control.
(SO 1)

Instructions
Identify the six principles of internal control and give an example of each principle that you might observe when picking up your pizza. (*Note:* It may not be possible to observe all the principles.)

E7-3 The following control procedures are used in Elke Company for over-the-counter cash receipts.

List internal control weaknesses over cash receipts and suggest improvements.
(SO 1, 2)

1. Cashiers are experienced; thus, they are not bonded.
2. All over-the-counter receipts are registered by three clerks who share a cash register with a single cash drawer.
3. To minimize the risk of robbery, cash in excess of $100 is stored in an unlocked attaché case in the stock room until it is deposited in the bank.
4. At the end of each day the total receipts are counted by the cashier on duty and reconciled to the cash register total.
5. The company accountant makes the bank deposit and then records the day's receipts.

Instructions
(a) For each procedure, explain the weakness in internal control and identify the control principle that is violated.

(b) For each weakness, suggest a change in the procedure that will result in good internal control.

*List internal control
weaknesses for cash
disbursements and suggest
improvements.*
(SO 1, 3)

E7-4   The following control procedures are used in Albina's Boutique Shoppe for cash disbursements.

1. Each week Albina leaves 100 company checks in an unmarked envelope on a shelf behind the cash register.

2. The store manager personally approves all payments before signing and issuing checks.

3. The company checks are unnumbered.

4. After payment, bills are "filed" in a paid invoice folder.

5. The company accountant prepares the bank reconciliation and reports any discrepancies to the owner.

Instructions

(a) For each procedure, explain the weakness in internal control and identify the internal control principle that is violated.

(b) For each weakness, suggest a change in the procedure that will result in good internal control.

*Identify internal control
weaknesses for cash
disbursements and suggest
improvements.*
(SO 1, 3)

E7-5   At Nystrom Company checks are not prenumbered because both the purchasing agent and the treasurer are authorized to issue checks. Each signer has access to unissued checks kept in an unlocked file cabinet. The purchasing agent pays all bills pertaining to goods purchased for resale. Prior to payment, the purchasing agent determines that the goods have been received and verifies the mathematical accuracy of the vendor's invoice. After payment, the invoice is filed by vendor and the purchasing agent records the payment in the cash disbursements journal. The treasurer pays all other bills following approval by authorized employees. After payment, the treasurer stamps all bills "paid," files them by payment date, and records the checks in the cash disbursements journal. Nystrom Company maintains one checking account that is reconciled by the treasurer.

Instructions

(a) List the weaknesses in internal control over cash disbursements.

(b) Identify improvements for correcting these weaknesses.

*Prepare bank reconciliation
and adjusting entries.*
(SO 4)

E7-6   Leng Xiong is unable to reconcile the bank balance at January 31. Leng's reconciliation is shown here.

Cash balance per bank	$3,660.20
Add: NSF check	370.00
Less: Bank service charge	25.00
Adjusted balance per bank	$4,005.20
Cash balance per books	$3,975.20
Less: Deposits in transit	590.00
Add: Outstanding checks	670.00
Adjusted balance per books	$4,055.20

Instructions

(a) What is the proper adjusted cash balance per bank?

(b) What is the proper adjusted cash balance per books?

(c) Prepare the adjusting journal entries necessary to determine the adjusted cash balance per books.

*Determine outstanding
checks.*
(SO 4)

E7-7   At April 30 the bank reconciliation of Engstrom Company shows three outstanding checks: No. 254 $650, No. 255 $800, and No. 257 $410. The May bank statement and the May cash payments journal are given here.

Bank Statement Checks Paid			Cash Payments Journal Checks Issued		
Date	Check No.	Amount	Date	Check No.	Amount
5-4	254	$650	5-2	258	$159
5-2	257	410	5-5	259	275
5-17	258	159	5-10	260	925
5-12	259	275	5-15	261	500
5-20	261	500	5-22	262	750
5-29	264	360	5-24	263	480
5-30	262	750	5-29	264	360

Instructions

Using step 2 in the reconciliation procedure (see page 330), list the outstanding checks at May 31.

Prepare bank reconciliation and adjusting entries.
(SO 4)

E7-8 The following information pertains to DeVries Company.

1. Cash balance per bank, July 31, $7,328.

2. July bank service charge not recorded by the depositor $40.

3. Cash balance per books, July 31, $7,280.

4. Deposits in transit, July 31, $1,700.

5. Note for $1,000 collected for DeVries in July by the bank, plus interest $36 less fee $20. The collection has not been recorded by Allied, and no interest has been accrued.

6. Outstanding checks, July 31, $772.

Instructions

(a) Prepare a bank reconciliation at July 31, 2007.
(b) Journalize the adjusting entries at July 31 on the books of DeVries Company.

E7-9 This information relates to the Cash account in the ledger of Espejel Company.

Prepare bank reconciliation and adjusting entries.
(SO 4)

Balance September 1—$16,400; Cash deposited—$64,000
Balance September 30—$17,600; Checks written—$62,800

The September bank statement shows a balance of $16,422 at September 30 and the following memoranda.

Credits		Debits	
Collection of $1,800 note plus interest $30	$1,830	NSF check: J. Hower	$360
Interest earned on checking account	45	Safety deposit box rent	50

At September 30 deposits in transit were $5,026 and outstanding checks totaled $2,383.

Instructions

(a) Prepare the bank reconciliation at September 30, 2007.
(b) Prepare the adjusting entries at September 30, assuming (1) the NSF check was from a customer on account, and (2) no interest had been accrued on the note.

E7-10 The cash records of Dana Company show the following.

For July:

Compute deposits in transit and outstanding checks for two bank reconciliations.
(SO 4)

1. The June 30 bank reconciliation indicated that deposits in transit total $750. During July the general ledger account Cash shows deposits of $16,200, but the bank statement indicates that only $15,600 in deposits were received during the month.

2. The June 30 bank reconciliation also reported outstanding checks of $990. During the month of July, Dana Company books show that $17,500 of checks were issued, yet the bank statement showed that $16,400 of checks cleared the bank in July.

For September:

3. In September deposits per bank statement totaled $25,900, deposits per books were $25,400, and deposits in transit at September 30 were $2,200.

4. In September cash disbursements per books were $23,700, checks clearing the bank were $24,000, and outstanding checks at September 30 were $2,100.

There were no bank debit or credit memoranda, and no errors were made by either the bank or Dana Company.

Instructions
Answer the following questions.
(a) In situation 1, what were the deposits in transit at July 31?
(b) In situation 2, what were the outstanding checks at July 31?
(c) In situation 3, what were the deposits in transit at August 31?
(d) In situation 4, what were the outstanding checks at August 31?

Prepare bank reconciliation and adjusting entries.
(SO 4)

E7-11   Mayo Inc.'s bank statement from Western Bank at August 31, 2007, gives the following information.

Balance, August 1	$16,400	Bank debit memorandum:	
August deposits	73,000	Safety deposit box fee	$ 25
Checks cleared in August	68,660	Service charge	50
Bank credit memorandum:		Balance, August 31	20,710
Interest earned	45		

A summary of the Cash account in the ledger for August shows the following: balance, August 1, $16,900; receipts $77,000; disbursements $73,570; and balance, August 31, $20,330. Analysis reveals that the only reconciling items on the July 31 bank reconciliation were a deposit in transit for $5,000 and outstanding checks of $4,500. In addition, you determine that there were two errors involving company checks drawn in August: (1) A check for $400 to a creditor on account that cleared the bank in August was journalized and posted for $40. (2) A salary check to an employee for $275 was recorded by the bank as $257.

Instructions
(a) Prepare a bank reconciliation at August 31.
(b) Journalize the adjusting entry(ies) to be made by Mayo Inc. at August 31.

Identify reporting of cash.
(SO 5)

E7-12   A new accountant at La Maison Inc. is trying to identify which of the following amounts should be reported as the current asset "Cash and cash equivalents" in the year-end balance sheet, as of April 30, 2007.

1. $60 of currency and coin in a locked box used for incidental cash transactions.
2. A $10,000 U.S. Treasury bill, due May 31, 2007.
3. $300 of April-dated checks that La Maison has received from customers but not yet deposited.
4. An $85 check received from a customer in payment of its April account, but postdated to May 1.
5. $2,500 in the company's checking account.
6. $4,000 in its savings account.
7. $75 of prepaid postage in its postage meter.
8. A $25 IOU from the company receptionist.

Instructions
(a) What balance should La Maison report as its "Cash and cash equivalents" balance at April 30, 2007?
(b) In what account(s) and in what financial statement(s) should the items not included in "Cash and cash equivalents" be reported?

Review cash management practices.
(SO 6)

E7-13   Adams, Hadzic, and Tene, three law students who have joined together to open a law practice, are struggling to manage their cash flow. They haven't yet built up sufficient clientele and revenues to support their legal practice's ongoing costs. Initial costs, such as advertising, renovations to their premises, and the like, all result in outgoing cash flow at a time when little is coming in. Adams, Hadzic, and Tene haven't had time to establish a billing system since most of their clients' cases haven't yet reached the courts, and the lawyers didn't think it would be right to bill them until "results were achieved."

Unfortunately, Adams, Hadzic, and Tene suppliers don't feel the same way. Their suppliers expect them to pay their accounts payable within a few days of receiving their bills.

So far, there hasn't even been enough money to pay the three lawyers, and they are not sure how long they can keep practicing law without getting some money into their pockets.

Instructions
Can you provide any suggestions for Adams, Hadzic, and Tene to improve their cash management practices?

E7-14 Schaefer Company expects to have a cash balance of $46,000 on January 1, 2007. These are the relevant monthly budget data for the first two months of 2007.

Prepare a cash budget for two months.
(SO 7)

1. Collections from customers: January $70,000, February $146,000

2. Payments to suppliers: January $40,000, February $75,000

3. Wages: January $30,000, February $40,000. Wages are paid in the month they are incurred.

4. Administrative expenses: January $21,000, February $28,000. These costs include depreciation of $1,000 per month. All other costs are paid as incurred.

5. Selling expenses: January $15,000, February $20,000. These costs are exclusive of depreciation. They are paid as incurred.

6. Sales of short-term investments in January are expected to realize $12,000 in cash. Schaefer has a line of credit at a local bank that enables it to borrow up to $25,000. The company wants to maintain a minimum monthly cash balance of $20,000.

Instructions
Prepare a cash budget for January and February.

*E7-15 During October, Guiding Light Company experiences the following transactions in establishing a petty cash fund.

Prepare journal entries for a petty cash fund.
(SO 8)

Oct. 1   A petty cash fund is established with a check for $100 issued to the petty cash custodian.

  31   A count of the petty cash fund disclosed the following items:

Currency	$5.00
Coins	0.40
Expenditure receipts (vouchers):	
Office supplies	$28.10
Telephone, Internet, and fax	16.40
Postage	42.00
Freight-out	6.80

  31   A check was written to reimburse the fund and increase the fund to $200.

Instructions
Journalize the entries in October that pertain to the petty cash fund.

*E7-16 Mora Company maintains a petty cash fund for small expenditures. These transactions occurred during the month of August.

Journalize and post petty cash fund transactions.
(SO 8)

Aug. 1   Established the petty cash fund by writing a check on Central Bank for $200.

  15   Replenished the petty cash fund by writing a check for $170. On this date, the fund consisted of $30 in cash and these petty cash receipts: freight-out $74.40, entertainment expense $36, postage expense $33.70 and miscellaneous expense $27.50.

  16   Increased the amount of the petty cash fund to $400 by writing a check for $200.

  31   Replenished the petty cash fund by writing a check for $283. On this date, the fund consisted of $117 in cash and these petty cash receipts: postage expense $145, entertainment expense $90.60, and freight-out $46.40.

Instructions
(a) Journalize the petty cash transactions.
(b) Post to the Petty Cash account.
(c) What internal control features exist in a petty cash fund?

Problems: Set A

Identify internal control weaknesses for cash receipts.
(SO 1, 2)

P7-1A Saratoga Theater is in the Federal Mall. A cashier's booth is located near the entrance to the theater. Two cashiers are employed. One works from 1:00 to 5:00 P.M., the other from 5:00 to 9:00 P.M. Each cashier is bonded. The cashiers receive cash from customers and operate a machine that ejects serially numbered tickets. The rolls of tickets are inserted and locked into the machine by the theater manager at the beginning of each cashier's shift.

After purchasing a ticket, the customer takes the ticket to a doorperson stationed at the entrance of the theater lobby some 60 feet from the cashier's booth. The doorperson tears the ticket in half, admits the customer, and returns the ticket stub to the customer. The other half of the ticket is dropped into a locked box by the doorperson.

At the end of each cashier's shift, the theater manager removes the ticket rolls from the machine and makes a cash count. The cash count sheet is initialed by the cashier. At the end of the day, the manager deposits the receipts in total in a bank night deposit vault located in the mall. In addition, the manager sends copies of the deposit slip and the initialed cash count sheets to the theater company treasurer for verification and to the company's accounting department. Receipts from the first shift are stored in a safe located in the manager's office.

Instructions
(a) Identify the internal control principles and their application to the cash receipts transactions of Saratoga Theater.
(b) If the doorperson and cashier decided to collaborate to misappropriate cash, what actions might they take?

Identify internal control weaknesses in cash receipts and cash disbursements.
(SO 1, 2, 3)

P7-2A Della Valle Middle School wants to raise money for a new sound system for its auditorium. The primary fund-raising event is a dance at which the famous disc jockey Jay Dee will play classic and not-so-classic dance tunes. Frank Cerra, the music and theater instructor, has been given the responsibility for coordinating the fund-raising efforts. This is Frank's first experience with fund-raising. He decides to put the eighth-grade choir in charge of the event; he will be a relatively passive observer.

Frank had 500 unnumbered tickets printed for the dance. He left the tickets in a box on his desk and told the choir students to take as many tickets as they thought they could sell for $5 each. In order to ensure that no extra tickets would be floating around, he told them to dispose of any unsold tickets. When the students received payment for the tickets, they were to bring the cash back to Frank, and he would put it in a locked box in his desk drawer.

Some of the students were responsible for decorating the gymnasium for the dance. Frank gave each of them a key to the money box and told them that if they took money out to purchase materials, they should put a note in the box saying how much they took and what it was used for. After two weeks the money box appeared to be getting full, so Frank asked Blair Norris to count the money, prepare a deposit slip, and deposit the money in a bank account Frank had opened.

The day of the dance, Frank wrote a check from the account to pay Jay Dee. The DJ said, however, that he accepted only cash and did not give receipts. So Frank took $200 out of the cash box and gave it to Jay. At the dance Frank had Sara Billings working at the entrance to the gymnasium, collecting tickets from students and selling tickets to those who had not pre-purchased them. Frank estimated that 400 students attended the dance.

The following day Frank closed out the bank account, which had $250 in it, and gave that amount plus the $180 in the cash box to Principal Skinner. Principal Skinner seemed surprised that, after generating roughly $2,000 in sales, the dance netted only $430 in cash. Frank did not know how to respond.

Instructions
Identify as many internal control weaknesses as you can in this scenario, and suggest how each could be addressed.

Prepare a bank reconciliation and adjusting entries.
(SO 4)

P7-3A On July 31, 2007, Hanlon Company had a cash balance per books of $6,140. The statement from Jackson State Bank on that date showed a balance of $7,695.80. A comparison of the bank statement with the cash account revealed the facts on page 355.

1. The bank service charge for July was $25.

2. The bank collected a note receivable of $1,800 for Hanlon Company on July 15, plus $30 of interest. The bank made a $10 charge for the collection. Hanlon has not accrued any interest on the note.

3. The July 31 receipts of $1,193.30 were not included in the bank deposits for July. These receipts were deposited by the company in a night deposit vault on July 31.

4. Company check No. 2480 issued to H. Coby, a creditor, for $384 that cleared the bank in July was incorrectly entered in the cash payments journal on July 10 for $348.

5. Checks outstanding on July 31 totaled $1,480.10.

6. On July 31 the bank statement showed an NSF charge of $490 for a check received by the company from P. Figura, a customer, on account.

Instructions
(a) Prepare the bank reconciliation as of July 31.
(b) Prepare the necessary adjusting entries at July 31.

(a) Cash bal. $7,409.00

P7-4A   The bank portion of the bank reconciliation for Kingston Company at October 31, 2007, is shown here.

Prepare a bank reconciliation and adjusting entries from detailed data.
(SO 4)

KINGSTON COMPANY
Bank Reconciliation
October 31, 2007

Cash balance per bank		$12,367.90
Add: Deposits in transit		1,530.20
		13,898.10
Less: Outstanding checks		

Check Number	Check Amount	
2451	$ 1,260.40	
2470	720.10	
2471	844.50	
2472	426.80	
2474	1,050.00	4,301.80
Adjusted cash balance per bank		$ 9,596.30

The adjusted cash balance per bank agreed with the cash balance per books at October 31. The November bank statement showed the following checks and deposits.

Bank Statement

	Checks			Deposits	
Date	Number	Amount	Date	Amount	
11-1	2470	$ 720.10	11-1	$ 1,530.20	
11-2	2471	844.50	11-4	1,211.60	
11-5	2474	1,050.00	11-8	990.10	
11-4	2475	1,640.70	11-13	2,575.00	
11-8	2476	2,830.00	11-18	1,472.70	
11-10	2477	600.00	11-21	2,945.00	
11-15	2479	1,750.00	11-25	2,567.30	
11-18	2480	1,330.00	11-28	1,650.00	
11-27	2481	695.40	11-30	1,186.00	
11-30	2483	575.50	Total	$16,127.90	
11-29	2487	398.00			
	Total	$12,434.20			

The cash records per books for November showed the following.

	Cash Payments Journal					Cash Receipts Journal	
Date	**Number**	**Amount**	**Date**	**Number**	**Amount**	**Date**	**Amount**
11-1	2475	$1,640.70	11-20	2483	$ 575.50	11-3	$ 1,211.60
11-2	2476	2,830.00	11-22	2484	829.50	11-7	990.10
11-2	2477	600.00	11-23	2485	974.80	11-12	2,575.00
11-4	2478	538.20	11-24	2486	900.00	11-17	1,472.70
11-8	2479	1,570.00	11-29	2487	398.00	11-20	2,954.00
11-10	2480	1,330.00	11-30	2488	800.00	11-24	2,567.30
11-15	2481	695.40	Total		$14,294.10	11-27	1,650.00
11-18	2482	612.00				11-29	1,186.00
						11-30	1,218.00
						Total	$15,824.70

The bank statement contained two bank memoranda:

1. A credit of $1,875 for the collection of an $1,800 note for Kingston Company plus interest of $90 and less a collection fee of $15. Kingston Company has not accrued any interest on the note.

2. A debit for the printing of additional company checks $85.

At November 30 the cash balance per books was $11,126.90 and the cash balance per bank statement was $17,851.60. The bank did not make any errors, but **two errors were made by Kingston Company**.

Instructions

(a) Cash bal. $12,727.90

(a) Using the four steps in the reconciliation procedure described on page 330, prepare a bank reconciliation at November 30, 2007.

(b) Prepare the adjusting entries based on the reconciliation. (*Note:* The correction of any errors pertaining to recording checks should be made to Accounts Payable. The correction of any errors relating to recording cash receipts should be made to Accounts Receivable.)

Prepare a bank reconciliation and adjusting entries.
(SO 4)

P7-5A Green Acres Company of Canton, Iowa, spreads herbicides and applies liquid fertilizer for local farmers. On May 31, 2007, the company's cash account per its general ledger showed a balance of $6,738.90.

The bank statement from Canton State Bank on that date showed the following balance.

CANTON STATE BANK

Checks and Debits	**Deposits and Credits**	**Daily Balance**
XXX	XXX	5-31 7,112.00

A comparison of the details on the bank statement with the details in the cash account revealed the following facts.

1. The statement included a debit memo of $40 for the printing of additional company checks.

2. Cash sales of $833.15 on May 12 were deposited in the bank. The cash receipts journal entry and the deposit slip were incorrectly made for $839.15. The bank credited Green Acres Company for the correct amount.

3. Outstanding checks at May 31 totaled $276.25, and deposits in transit were $1,180.15.

4. On May 18, the company issued check No. 1181 for $685 to R. Delzer, on account. The check, which cleared the bank in May, was incorrectly journalized and posted by Green Acres Company for $658.

5. A $2,200 note receivable was collected by the bank for Green Acres Company on May 31 plus $110 interest. The bank charged a collection fee of $20. No interest has been accrued on the note.

6. Included with the cancelled checks was a check issued by Green Day Company to P. Jonet for $360 that was incorrectly charged to Green Acres Company by the bank.

7. On May 31, the bank statement showed an NSF charge of $580 for a check issued by Natalie Fong, a customer, to Green Acres Company on account.

Instructions

(a) Prepare the bank reconciliation at May 31, 2007.

(b) Prepare the necessary adjusting entries for Green Acres Company at May 31, 2007.

(a) Cash bal. $8,375.90

P7-6A You are provided with the following information taken from Burlington Inc.'s March 31, 2007, balance sheet.

Prepare a cash budget.
(SO 7)

Cash	$ 8,000
Accounts receivable	20,000
Inventory	36,000
Property, plant, and equipment, net of depreciation	120,000
Accounts payable	22,400
Common stock	150,000
Retained earnings	11,600

Additional information concerning Burlington Inc. is as follows.

1. Gross profit is 25% of sales.

2. Actual and budgeted sales data:

March (actual)	$50,000
April (budgeted)	65,000

3. Sales are 60% for cash and 40% on credit. There are no sales discounts, and credit sales are collected in the month following the sale.

4. Half of a month's purchases are paid for in the month of purchase and half in the following month. Purchases of inventory totalled $44,800 for the month of March and are anticipated to total $52,200 for the month of April. Ending inventory is expected to be $39,450 at the end of April.

5. Cash operating costs are anticipated to be $12,700 for the month of April.

6. Equipment costing $2,500 will be purchased for cash in April.

7. The company wishes to maintain a minimum cash balance of $8,000. An open line of credit is available at the bank. All borrowing is done at the beginning of the month, and all repayments are made at the end of the month. The interest rate is 12% per year, and interest expense is accrued at the end of the month and paid in the following month.

Instructions

(a) Calculate cash collections in April for March and April sales.

(b) Calculate the cash disbursements in April related to March and April purchases.

(c) Prepare a cash budget for the month of April. Determine how much cash Burlington Inc. must borrow, or can repay, in April.

(a) Apr. customer collections $59,000
(c) Apr. borrowings $ 4,700

P7-7A BossaNova Corporation prepares monthly cash budgets. Here are relevant data from operating budgets for 2007.

Prepare a cash budget.
(SO 7)

	January	February
Sales	$350,000	$400,000
Purchases	110,000	130,000
Salaries	84,000	95,000
Administrative expenses	70,000	75,000
Selling expenses	79,000	88,000

All sales are on account. Collections are expected to be 60% in the month of sale, 30% in the first month following the sale, and 10% in the second month following the sale. Fifty percent (50%) of purchases are paid in cash in the month of purchase, and the balance due is paid in the month following the purchase. All other expenses are paid in the month incurred except for administrative expenses, which include $1,000 of depreciation per month.

Other data.

1. Credit sales — November 2006, $260,000; December 2006, $300,000
2. Purchases — December 2006, $100,000
3. Other receipts — January: collection of December 31, 2006, notes receivable $15,000; February: proceeds from sale of securities $6,000
4. Other disbursements—February: $12,000 cash dividend

The company's cash balance on January 1, 2007, is expected to be $52,000. The company wants to maintain a minimum cash balance of $50,000.

(a) Jan. customer
     collections $326,000
(b) Jan. 31
     cash bal. $ 56,000

Instructions

(a) Prepare schedules for (1) expected collections from customers and (2) expected payments for purchases for January and February.
(b) Prepare a cash budget for January and February.

Prepare a comprehensive bank reconciliation with theft and internal control deficiencies.
(SO 1, 2, 3, 4)

P7-8A Dusk 'til Dawn Company is a very profitable small business. It has not, however, given much consideration to internal control. For example, in an attempt to keep clerical and office expenses to a minimum, the company has combined the jobs of cashier and bookkeeper. As a result, Scott Dillon handles all cash receipts, keeps the accounting records, and prepares the monthly bank reconciliations.

The balance per the bank statement on October 31, 2007, was $18,415. Outstanding checks were: No. 62 for $126.75, No. 183 for $180, No. 284 for $253.25, No. 862 for $190.71, No. 863 for $226.80, and No. 864 for $165.28. Included with the statement was a credit memorandum of $265 indicating the collection of a note receivable for Dusk 'til Dawn Company by the bank on October 25. This memorandum has not been recorded by Dusk 'til Dawn.

The company's ledger showed one cash account with a balance of $21,992.72. The balance included undeposited cash on hand. Because of the lack of internal controls, Scott took for personal use all of the undeposited receipts in excess of $3,795.51. He then prepared the following bank reconciliation in an effort to conceal his theft of cash.

Cash balance per books, October 31		$21,992.72
Add: Outstanding checks		
No. 862	$190.71	
No. 863	226.80	
No. 864	165.28	482.79
		22,475.51
Less: Undeposited receipts		3,795.51
Unadjusted balance per bank, October 31		18,680.00
Less: Bank credit memorandum		265.00
Cash balance per bank statement, October 31		$18,415.00

Instructions

(a) Cash bal. $21,067.72

(a) Prepare a correct bank reconciliation. (*Hint:* Deduct the amount of the theft from the adjusted balance per books.)
(b) Indicate the three ways that Scott attempted to conceal the theft and the dollar amount involved in each method.
(c) What principles of internal control were violated in this case?

Problems: Set B

P7-1B Marais Company recently changed its system of internal control over cash disbursements. The system includes the following features.
1. Instead of being unnumbered and manually prepared, all checks must now be prenumbered and written by using the new checkwriter purchased by the company.
2. Before a check can be issued, each invoice must have the approval of Jane Bell, the purchasing agent, and Vorn Lor, the receiving department supervisor.
3. Checks must be signed by either Derek Madsen, the treasurer, or Sara Goss, the assistant treasurer. Before signing a check, the signer is expected to compare the amounts of the check with the amounts on the invoice.
4. After signing a check, the signer stamps the invoice "paid" and inserts within the stamp, the date, check number, and amount of the check. The "paid" invoice is then sent to the accounting department for recording.
5. Blank checks are stored in a safe in the treasurer's office. The combination to the safe is known by only the treasurer and assistant treasurer.
6. Each month the bank statement is reconciled with the bank balance per books by the assistant chief accountant.

Identify internal control principles for cash disbursements.
(SO 1, 3)

Instructions
Identify the internal control principles and their application to cash disbursements of Marais Company.

P7-2B The board of trustees of a local church is concerned about the internal accounting controls pertaining to the offering collections made at weekly services. They ask you to serve on a three-person audit team with the internal auditor of the university and a CPA who has just joined the church. At a meeting of the audit team and the board of trustees you learn the following.

Identify internal control weaknesses in cash receipts.
(SO 1, 2)

1. The church's board of trustees has delegated responsibility for the financial management and audit of the financial records to the finance committee. This group prepares the annual budget and approves major disbursements but is not involved in collections or recordkeeping. No audit has been made in recent years because the same trusted employee has kept church records and served as financial secretary for 15 years. The church does not carry any fidelity insurance.

2. The collection at the weekly service is taken by a team of ushers who volunteer to serve for 1 month. The ushers take the collection plates to a basement office at the rear of the church. They hand their plates to the head usher and return to the church service. After all plates have been turned in, the head usher counts the cash received. The head usher then places the cash in the church safe along with a notation of the amount counted. The head usher volunteers to serve for 3 months.

3. The next morning the financial secretary opens the safe and recounts the collection. The secretary withholds $150 – $200 in cash, depending on the cash expenditures expected for the week, and deposits the remainder of the collections in the bank. To facilitate the deposit, church members who contribute by check are asked to make their checks payable to "Cash."

4. Each month the financial secretary reconciles the bank statement and submits a copy of the reconciliation to the board of trustees. The reconciliations have rarely contained any bank errors and have never shown any errors per books.

Instructions
(a) Indicate the weaknesses in internal accounting control in the handling of collections.
(b) List the improvements in internal control procedures that you plan to make at the next meeting of the audit team for (1) the ushers, (2) the head usher, (3) the financial secretary, and (4) the finance committee.
(c) What church policies should be changed to improve internal control?

P7-3B On May 31, 2007, Galenti Company had a cash balance per books of $5,681.50. The bank statement from Community Bank on that date showed a balance of $7,964.60. A comparison of the statement with the cash account revealed the following facts.

Prepare a bank reconciliation and adjusting entries.
(SO 4)

1. The statement included a debit memo of $70 for the printing of additional company checks.

2. Cash sales of $786.15 on May 12 were deposited in the bank. The cash receipts journal entry and the deposit slip were incorrectly made for $796.15. The bank credited Galenti Company for the correct amount.

3. Outstanding checks at May 31 totaled $806.25, and deposits in transit were $836.15.

4. On May 18 the company issued check No. 1181 for $685 to N. Habben, on account. The check, which cleared the bank in May, was incorrectly journalized and posted by Galenti Company for $658.

5. A $3,000 note receivable was collected by the bank for Galenti Company on May 31 plus $80 interest. The bank charged a collection fee of $30. No interest has been accrued on the note.

6. Included with the cancelled checks was a check issued by Gallen Company to C. Young for $290 that was incorrectly charged to Galenti Company by the bank.

7. On May 31 the bank statement showed an NSF charge of $340 for a check issued by K. Uzong, a customer, to Galenti Company on account.

Instructions

(a) Cash bal. $8,284.50

(a) Prepare the bank reconciliation as of May 31, 2007.
(b) Prepare the necessary adjusting entries at May 31, 2007.

Prepare a bank reconciliation and adjusting entries from detailed data.
(SO 4)

P7-4B The bank portion of the bank reconciliation for Blue Diamond Company at November 30, 2007, is shown here.

BLUE DIAMOND COMPANY
Bank Reconciliation
November 30, 2007

Cash balance per bank		$14,367.90
Add: Deposits in transit		2,530.20
		16,898.10
Less: Outstanding checks		

Check Number	Check Amount	
3451	$2,260.40	
3470	1,100.10	
3471	844.50	
3472	1,426.80	
3474	1,050.00	6,681.80
Adjusted cash balance per bank		$10,216.30

The adjusted cash balance per bank agreed with the cash balance per books at November 30. The December bank statement showed the following checks and deposits.

			Bank Statement		
	Checks			**Deposits**	
Date	**Number**	**Amount**	**Date**		**Amount**
12-1	3451	$ 2,260.40	12-1		$ 2,530.20
12-2	3470	1,100.10	12-4		1,211.60
12-7	3472	1,426.80	12-8		2,365.10
12-4	3475	1,640.70	12-16		2,672.70
12-8	3476	1,300.00	12-21		2,945.00
12-10	3477	2,130.00	12-26		2,567.30
12-15	3479	3,080.00	12-29		2,836.00
12-27	3480	600.00	12-30		1,025.00
12-30	3482	475.50	Total		$18,152.90
12-29	3483	1,140.00			
12-31	3485	540.80			
	Total	$15,694.30			

The cash records per books for December showed the following.

	Cash Payments Journal					
Date	**Number**	**Amount**	**Date**	**Number**	**Amount**	
12-1	3475	$1,640.70	12-20	3482	$ 475.50	
12-2	3476	1,300.00	12-22	3483	1,140.00	
12-2	3477	2,130.00	12-23	3484	764.00	
12-4	3478	538.20	12-24	3485	450.80	
12-8	3479	3,080.00	12-30	3486	1,389.50	
12-10	3480	600.00	Total		$14,316.10	
12-17	3481	807.40				

Cash Receipts Journal	
Date	**Amount**
12-3	$ 1,211.60
12-7	2,365.10
12-15	2,672.70
12-20	2,954.00
12-25	2,567.30
12-28	2,836.00
12-30	1,025.00
12-31	1,190.40
Total	$16,822.10

The bank statement contained two memoranda.

1. A credit of $3,145 for the collection of a $3,000 note for Blue Diamond Company plus interest of $160 and less a collection fee of $15. Blue Diamond Company has not accrued any interest on the note.

2. A debit of $943.10 for an NSF check written by J. Waller, a customer. At December 31 the check had not been redeposited in the bank.

At December 31 the cash balance per books was $12,722.30, and the cash balance per bank statement was $19,028.40. The bank did not make any errors, **but two errors were made by Blue Diamond Company**.

Instructions
(a) Using the four steps in the reconciliation procedure described on page 330, prepare a bank reconciliation at December 31, 2007.
(b) Prepare the adjusting entries based on the reconciliation. [*Note:* The correction of any errors pertaining to recording checks should be made to Accounts Payable. The correction of any errors relating to recording cash receipts should be made to Accounts Receivable.]

(a) Cash bal. $14,825.20

P7-5B Fertile Crescent Company of Omaha, Nebraska, provides liquid fertilizer and herbicides to regional farmers. On July 31, 2007, the company's cash account per its general ledger showed a balance of $5,909.70.

Prepare a bank reconciliation and adjusting entries. (SO 4)

The bank statement from Tri-County Bank on that date showed the following balance.

TRI-COUNTY BANK

Checks and Debits	**Deposits and Credits**	**Daily Balance**
XXX	XXX	7-31 7,075.80

A comparison of the details on the bank statement with the details in the cash account revealed the following facts.

1. The bank service charge for July was $32.

2. The bank collected a note receivable of $1,200 for Fertile Crescent Company on July 15, plus $48 of interest. The bank made a $10 charge for the collection. Fertile Crescent has not accrued any interest on the note.

3. The July 31 receipts of $1,839 were not included in the bank deposits for July. These receipts were deposited by the company in a night deposit vault on July 31.

4. Company check No. 2480 issued to N. Teig, a creditor, for $492 that cleared the bank in July was incorrectly entered in the cash payments journal on July 10 for $429.

5. Checks outstanding on July 31 totaled $2,480.10.

6. On July 31, the bank statement showed an NSF charge of $618 for a check received by the company from N. O. Doe, a customer, on account.

Instructions

(a) Cash bal. $6,434.70

(a) Prepare the bank reconciliation as of July 31, 2007.
(b) Prepare the necessary adjusting entries at July 31, 2007.

Prepare a cash budget.
(SO 7)

P7-6B Tran Co. expects to have a cash balance of $26,000 on January 1, 2007. Relevant monthly budget data for the first two months of 2007 are as follows.

Collections from customers: January $70,000; February $160,000
Payments to suppliers: January $48,000; February $75,000

Salaries: January $35,000; February $40,000. Salaries are paid in the month they are incurred.
Selling and administrative expenses: January $27,000; February $39,000. These costs are exclusive of depreciation and are paid as incurred.
Sales of short-term investments in January are expected to realize $9,000 in cash.

Tran has a line of credit at a local bank that enables it to borrow up to $45,000. The company wants to maintain a minimum monthly cash balance of $25,000. Any excess cash above the $25,000 minimum is used to pay off the line of credit.

Instructions

(a) Jan. cash bal. $25,000

(a) Prepare a cash budget for January and February.
(b) Explain how a cash budget contributes to effective management.

Prepare a cash budget.
(SO 7)

P7-7B Zurich Inc. prepares monthly cash budgets. Here are relevant data from operating budgets for 2007.

	January	February
Sales	$340,000	$400,000
Purchases	100,000	130,000
Salaries	80,000	95,000
Selling and administrative expenses	135,000	160,000

All sales are on account. Collections are expected to be 50% in the month of sale, 30% in the first month following the sale, and 20% in the second month following the sale. Forty percent (40%) of purchases are paid in cash in the month of purchase, and the balance due is paid in the month following the purchase. All other items above are paid in the month incurred. Depreciation has been excluded from selling and administrative expenses.

Other data.

1. Credit sales — November 2006, $240,000; December 2006, $280,000

2. Purchases — December 2006, $90,000

3. Other receipts — January: collection of December 31, 2006, interest receivable $2,000; February: proceeds from sale of short-term investments $8,000

4. Other disbursements—February: payment of $20,000 for land

The company's cash balance on January 1, 2007, is expected to be $60,000. The company wants to maintain a minimum cash balance of $50,000.

Instructions

(a) Jan. customer
    collections $302,000
(b) Jan. 31 cash bal. $ 55,000

(a) Prepare schedules for (1) expected collections from customers and (2) expected payments for purchases for January and February.
(b) Prepare a cash budget for January and February.

Prepare a comprehensive bank reconciliation with theft and internal control deficiencies.
(SO 1, 2, 3, 4)

P7-8B Emporia Company is a very profitable small business. It has not, however, given much consideration to internal control. For example, in an attempt to keep clerical and office expenses to a minimum, the company has combined the jobs of cashier and bookkeeper. As a result, M. Kohnert handles all cash receipts, keeps the accounting records, and prepares the monthly bank reconciliations.

The balance per the bank statement on October 31, 2007, was $12,800. Outstanding checks were: No. 62 for $126.75, No. 183 for $180, No. 284 for $253.25, No. 862 for $190.71, No. 863 for $226.80, and No. 864 for $165.28. Included with the statement was a credit memorandum of $790 indicating the collection of a note receivable for Emporia Company by the bank on October 25. This memorandum has not been recorded by Emporia Company.

The company's ledger showed one cash account with a balance of $15,847.21. The balance included undeposited cash on hand. Because of the lack of internal controls, Kohnert took for personal use all of the undeposited receipts in excess of $2,740. He then prepared the following bank reconciliation in an effort to conceal his theft of cash.

Cash balance per books, October 31		$15,847.21
Add: Outstanding checks		
No. 862	$190.71	
No. 863	226.80	
No. 864	165.28	482.79
		16,330.00
Less: Undeposited receipts		2,740.00
Unadjusted balance per bank, October 31		13,590.00
Less: Bank credit memorandum		790.00
Cash balance per bank statement, October 31		$12,800.00

Instructions
(a) Prepare a correct bank reconciliation. (*Hint:* Deduct the amount of the theft from the adjusted balance per books.)

(a) Cash bal. $14,397.21

(b) Indicate the three ways that Kohnert attempted to conceal the theft and the dollar amount pertaining to each method.
(c) What principles of internal control were violated in this case?

Problems: Set C

Visit the book's website at **www.wiley.com/college/kimmel** and choose the Student Companion site to access Problem Set C.

Comprehensive Problem

CP7 On December 1, 2007, Stephens Company had the following account balances.

	Debits		Credits
Cash	$18,000	Accumulated Depreciation	$ 3,000
Notes Receivable	2,700	Accounts Payable	6,100
Accounts Receivable	7,500	Common Stock	20,000
Merchandise Inventory	16,000	Retained Earnings	44,700
Prepaid Insurance	1,600		$73,800
Equipment	28,000		
	$73,800		

During December the company completed the following transactions.

Dec. 7 Received $3,200 cash from customers in payment of account (no discount allowed).
12 Purchased merchandise on account from King Co. $10,000, terms 2/10, n/30.
17 Sold merchandise on account $12,000, terms 1/10, n/30. The cost of the merchandise sold was $8,000.
19 Paid salaries $2,500.
22 Paid King Co. in full, less discount.
26 Received collections in full, less discounts, from customers billed on December 17.

Adjustment data:
1. Depreciation $200 per month.
2. Insurance expired $400.

Instructions
(a) Journalize the December transactions.
(b) Enter the December 1 balances in the ledger T accounts and post the December trans-
    actions. Use Cost of Goods Sold, Depreciation Expense, Insurance Expense, Salaries
    Expense, Sales, and Sales Discounts.
(c) The statement from Lyon County Bank on December 31 showed a balance of $22,164.
    A comparison of the bank statement with the cash account revealed the following
    facts.
    1. The bank collected a note receivable of $2,700 for Stephens Company on Decem-
       ber 15.
    2. The December 31 receipts of $2,736 were not included in the bank deposits for
       December. The company deposited these receipts in a night deposit vault on
       December 31.
    3. Checks outstanding on December 31 totaled $2,220.
    4. On December 31 the bank statement showed a NSF charge of $800 for a check
       received by the company from C. Park, a customer, on account.

    Prepare a bank reconciliation as of December 31 based on the available information.
    (*Hint:* The cash balance per books is $20,780. This can be proven by finding the bal-
    ance in the Cash account from parts (a) and (b).)
(d) Journalize the adjusting entries resulting from the bank reconciliation and adjust-
    ment data.
(e) Post the adjusting entries to the ledger T accounts.
(f) Prepare an adjusted trial balance.
(g) Prepare an income statement for December and a classified balance sheet at
    December 31.

(f) Totals $76,000
(g) Net income $ 780
    Total assets $61,580

Continuing Cookie Chronicle

(Note: This is a continuation of the Cookie Chronicle from Chapters 1 through 6.)

CCC7   Part 1   Natalie is struggling to keep up with the recording of her accounting
transactions. She is spending a lot of time marketing and selling mixers and giving her
cookie classes. Her friend John is an accounting student who runs his own accounting
service. He has asked Natalie if she would like to have him do her accounting.

John and Natalie meet and discuss her business. John suggests that he do the following for Natalie.

1. Hold onto cash until there is enough to be deposited. (He would keep the cash locked
   up in his vehicle). He would also take all of the deposits to the bank at least twice a
   month.
2. Write and sign all of the checks.
3. Record all of the deposits in the accounting records.
4. Record all of the checks in the accounting records.
5. Prepare the monthly bank reconciliation.
6. Transfer all of Natalie's manual accounting records to his computer accounting program. John maintains all of the accounting information that he keeps for his clients
   on his laptop computer.
7. Prepare monthly financial statements for Natalie to review.
8. Write himself a check every month for the work he has done for Natalie.

Instructions
Identify the weaknesses in internal control that you see in the system that John is recommending. (Consider the principles of internal control identified in the chapter.) Can
you suggest any improvements if John is hired to do Natalie's accounting?

Part 2 Natalie decides that she cannot afford to hire John to do her accounting. One way that she can ensure that her cash account does not have any errors and is accurate and up-to-date is to prepare a bank reconciliation at the end of each month.

Natalie would like you to help her. She asks you to prepare a bank reconciliation for June 2007 using the following information.

GENERAL LEDGER—COOKIE CREATIONS

Cash

Date	Explanation	Ref.	Debit	Credit	Balance
2007					
June 1	Balance				2,657
1			750		3,407
3	Check #600			625	2,782
3	Check #601			95	2,687
8	Check #602			56	2,631
9			1,050		3,681
13	Check #603			425	3,256
20			155		3,411
28	Check #604			247	3,164
28			110		3,274

PREMIER BANK
Statement of Account—Cookie Creations
June 30, 2007

Date	Explanation	Checks and Other Debits	Deposits	Balance
May 31	Balance			3,256
June 1	Deposit		750	4,006
6	Check #600	625		3,381
6	Check #601	95		3,286
8	Check #602	56		3,230
9	Deposit		1,050	4,280
10	NSF check	100		4,180
10	NSF–fee	35		4,145
14	Check #603	452		3,693
20	Deposit		125	3,818
23	EFT–Telus	85		3,733
28	Check #599	361		3,372
30	Bank charges	13		3,359

Additional information:

1. On May 31, there were two outstanding checks: #595 for $238 and #599 for $361.
2. Premier Bank made a posting error to the bank statement: check #603 was issued for $425, not $452.
3. The deposit made on June 20 was for $125 that Natalie received for teaching a class. Natalie made an error in recording this transaction.
4. The electronic funds transfer (EFT) was for Natalie's cell phone use. Remember that she uses this phone only for business.
5. The NSF check was from Ron Black. Natalie received this check for teaching a class to Ron's children. Natalie contacted Ron and he assured her that she will receive a check in the mail for the outstanding amount of the invoice and the NSF bank charge.

Instructions
(a) Prepare Cookie Creations' bank reconciliation for June 2007.
(b) Prepare any necessary general journal entries.
(c) If a balance sheet is prepared for Cookie Creations at June 30, 2007, what balance will be reported as cash in the current assets section?

Financial Reporting and Analysis

FINANCIAL REPORTING PROBLEM: *Tootsie Roll Industries, Inc.*

BYP7-1 The financial statements of Tootsie Roll are presented in Appendix A of this book, together with an auditor's report—Report of Independent Auditors.

Instructions
Using the financial statements and reports, answer these questions about Tootsie Roll's internal controls and cash.
(a) What comments, if any, are made about cash in the report of the independent auditors?
(b) What data about cash and cash equivalents are shown in the consolidated balance sheet (statement of financial condition)?
(c) What activities are identified in the consolidated statement of cash flows as being responsible for the changes in cash during 2004?
(d) How are cash equivalents defined in the Notes to Consolidated Financial Statements?
(e) Read the section of the report titled "Management's Report on Internal Control Over Financial Reporting." Summarize the statements made in that section of the report.

COMPARATIVE ANALYSIS PROBLEM: *Tootsie Roll vs. Hershey Foods*

BYP7-2 The financial statements of Hershey Foods are presented in Appendix B, following the financial statements for Tootsie Roll in Appendix A.

Instructions
Answer the following questions for each company.
(a) What is the balance in cash and cash equivalents at December 31, 2004?
(b) What percentage of total assets does cash represent for each company over the last two years? Has it changed significantly for either company?
(c) How much cash was provided by operating activities during 2004?
(d) Comment on your findings in parts (a) through (c).

RESEARCH CASE

BYP7-3 The January 27, 2005, issue of the *Wall Street Journal* contains an article by William M. Bulkeley and Robert Tomsho titled "Kodak to Get Auditors' Adverse View."

Instructions
Read the article and answer the following questions.
(a) How does the article define a "material weakness" in internal financial controls? Does the existence of a material weakness mean that a misstatement of the company's results has occurred?
(b) What other well-known companies received similar opinions from their auditors, and what percentage of U.S. companies are expected to report problems in their internal controls?
(c) What type of company is expected to be particularly affected by this problem?

INTERPRETING FINANCIAL STATEMENTS

BYP7-4 The international accounting firm Ernst and Young recently performed a global survey. The results of that survey are summarized in a report titled "Fraud: The Unmanaged Risk."

You can find this report at **www.ey.com/global/download.nsf/Belgium_E/8th_Global_Fraud_Survey/$file/EY_8th_Global_Fraud_Survey.pdf** (or go to **www. wiley.com/college/kimmel**).

Instructions
Read the Key Findings section, and then skim the remainder of the report to answer the following questions.
(a) Examining the graphs presented under the heading "General Fraud Experience," what percentage of respondents experienced a significant fraud during the year? Do the findings differ by geographic region?

(b) What percentage of frauds does the report estimate are actually both detected and made public by companies?

(c) How did respondents rank various factors in terms of their ability to detect fraud and prevent fraud?

(d) What percentage of employees committing fraud are part of management? Are new managers more or less likely to commit fraud?

FINANCIAL ANALYSIS ON THE WEB

BYP7-5 The Financial Accounting Standards Board (FASB) is a private organization established to improve accounting standards and financial reporting. The FASB conducts extensive research before issuing a "Statement of Financial Accounting Standards," which represents an authoritative expression of generally accepted accounting principles.

Address: **www.fasb.org**
  (or go to **www.wiley.com/college/kimmel**)

Steps:

Choose **Facts about FASB**.

Instructions
Answer the following questions.
(a) What is the mission of the FASB?
(b) How are topics added to the FASB technical agenda?
(c) What characteristics make the FASB's procedures an "open" decision-making process?

BYP7-6 The Public Company Accounting Oversight Board (PCAOB) was created as a result of the Sarbanes-Oxley Act. It has oversight and enforcement responsibilities over accounting firms in the U.S.

Address: **http://www.pcaobus.org/**
  (or go to **www.wiley.com/college/kimmel**)

Instructions
Answer the following questions.
(a) What is the mission of the PCAOB?
(b) Briefly summarize its responsibilities related to inspections.
(c) Briefly summarize its responsibilities related to enforcement.

Critical Thinking

DECISION MAKING ACROSS THE ORGANIZATION

BYP7-7 Alternative Distributor Corp., a distributor of groceries and related products, is headquartered in Medford, Massachusetts.

During a recent audit, Alternative Distributor Corp. was advised that existing internal controls necessary for the company to develop reliable financial statements were inadequate. The audit report stated that the current system of accounting for sales, receivables, and cash receipts constituted a material weakness. Among other items, the report focused on nontimely deposit of cash receipts, exposing Alternative Distributor to potential loss or misappropriation, excessive past due accounts receivable due to lack of collection efforts, disregard of advantages offered by vendors for prompt payment of invoices, absence of appropriate segregation of duties by personnel consistent with appropriate control objectives, inadequate procedures for applying accounting principles, lack of qualified management personnel, lack of supervision by an outside board of directors, and overall poor recordkeeping.

Instructions
(a) Identify the principles of internal control violated by Alternative Distributor Corporation.
(b) Explain why managers of various functional areas in the company should be concerned about internal controls.

COMMUNICATION ACTIVITY

BYP7-8 As a new auditor for the CPA firm of Ticke and Tie, you have been assigned to review the internal controls over mail cash receipts of Rangel Company. Your review reveals that checks are promptly endorsed "For Deposit Only," but no list of the checks is prepared by the person opening the mail. The mail is opened either by the cashier or by the employee who maintains the accounts receivable records. Mail receipts are deposited in the bank weekly by the cashier.

Instructions

Write a letter to S.A. Forness, owner of the Rangel Company, explaining the weaknesses in internal control and your recommendations for improving the system.

ETHICS CASE

BYP7-9 As noted in the chapter, banks charge fees of up to $30 for "bounced" checks—that is, checks that exceed the balance in the account. It has been estimated that processing bounced checks costs a bank roughly $1.50 per check. Thus, the profit margin on bounced checks is very high. Recognizing this, some banks have started to process checks from largest to smallest. By doing this, they maximize the number of checks that bounce if a customer overdraws an account. For example, NationsBank (now Bank of America) projected a $14 million increase in fee revenue as a result of processing largest checks first. In response to criticism, banks have responded that their customers prefer to have large checks processed first, because those tend to be the most important. At the other extreme, some banks will cover their customers' bounced checks, effectively extending them an interest-free loan while their account is overdrawn.

Instructions

Answer each of the following questions.
(a) Antonio Freeman had a balance of $1,500 in his checking account at First National Bank on a day when the bank received the following five checks for processing against his account.

Check Number	Amount	Check Number	Amount
3150	$ 35	3165	$ 550
3162	400	3166	1,510
		3169	180

Assuming a $30 fee assessed by the bank for each bounced check, how much fee revenue would the bank generate if it processed checks (1) from largest to smallest, (2) from smallest to largest, and (3) in order of check number?
(b) Do you think that processing checks from largest to smallest is an ethical business practice?
(c) In addition to ethical issues, what other issues must a bank consider in deciding whether to process checks from largest to smallest?
(d) If you were managing a bank, what policy would you adopt on bounced checks?

BYP7-10 Fraud Bureau is a free service, established to alert consumers and investors about prior complaints relating to online vendors, including sellers at online auctions, and to provide consumers, investors, and users with information and news. One of the services it provides is a collection of online educational articles related to fraud.

Address: **www.fraudbureau.com/articles/** (or go to **www.wiley.com/college/kimmel**)

Instructions

Go to this site and choose an article of interest to you. Write a short summary of your findings.

Answers to Business Insight and Accounting across the Organization Questions

p. 319

Q: What controls would have reduced the likelihood of this type of theft?

A: One step would have been segregation of duties. The same employee who determined the winning number should not also have had physical control of that ticket.

p. 320

Q: Why would unsupervised employees or employees who report to each other represent potential internal control threats?

A. An unsupervised employee may have a fraudulent job (or may even be a fictitious person)—e.g., a person drawing a paycheck without working. Or, if two employees supervise each other, there is no real separation of duties, and they can conspire to defraud the company.

p. 322

Q. Why would a company's stock price fall if it reports deficiencies in its internal controls?

A. Internal controls protect against employee theft, but they also provide protection against manipulation of accounting numbers. If a company has poor internal controls, investors will have less confidence that its financial statements are accurate. As a consequence, its stock price will suffer.

p. 323

Q. Why are small companies more susceptible to employee theft?

A. The high degree of trust often found in small companies makes them more vulnerable. Also, small companies tend to have less sophisticated systems of internal control, and they usually lack internal auditors. In addition, it is very hard to achieve some internal control features, such as segregation of duties, when you have very few employees.

p. 327

Q. How can companies reduce the likelihood of fraudulent disbursements?

A. To reduce the occurrence of fraudulent disbursements a company should follow the procedures discussed in this chapter. These include having only designated personnel sign checks; having different personnel approve payments and make payments; ensuring that check signers do not record disbursements; using prenumbered checks and matching each check to an approved invoice; storing blank checks securely; reconciling the bank statement; and stamping invoices PAID.

Answer to Tootsie Roll Review It Question 3, p. 339

At December 31, 2004, Tootsie Roll reported cash and cash equivalents of $56,989,000. It reported no restricted cash. In Note 1 to its financial statements it defines cash equivalents as "temporary cash investments with an original maturity of three months or less."

Answers to Self-Study Questions

1. a   2. c   3. b   4. b   5. d   6. a   7. c   8. c   9. d   10. c
*11. a

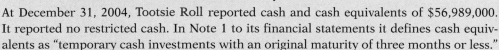

REMEMBER TO GO BACK TO THE NAVIGATOR BOX ON THE CHAPTER-OPENING PAGE AND CHECK OFF YOUR COMPLETED WORK.

CHAPTER 8

Reporting and Analyzing Receivables

STUDY OBJECTIVES

After studying this chapter,
you should be able to:

1 Identify the different types of receivables.

2 Explain how accounts receivable are recognized in the accounts.

3 Describe the methods used to account for bad debts.

4 Compute the interest on notes receivable.

5 Describe the entries to record the disposition of notes receivable.

6 Explain the statement presentation of receivables.

7 Describe the principles of sound accounts receivable management.

8 Identify ratios to analyze a company's receivables.

9 Describe methods to accelerate the receipt of cash from receivables.

THE NAVIGATOR

- Scan *Study Objectives* ⬭
- Read *Feature Story* ⬭
- Read *Preview* ⬭
- Read text and answer *Before You Go On*
  p. 379⬭   p. 384⬭   p. 385⬭   p. 393⬭
- Work *Using the Decision Toolkit* ⬭
- Review *Summary of Study Objectives* ⬭
- Work *Demonstration Problem* ⬭
- Answer *Self-Study Questions* ⬭
- Complete *Assignments* ⬭

FEATURE STORY

A Dose of Careful Management Keeps Receivables Healthy

"Sometimes you have to know when to be very tough, and sometimes you can give them a bit of a break," says Vivi Su. She's not talking about her children, but about the customers of a subsidiary of pharmaceutical company Whitehall-Robins, where she works as supervisor of credit and collections.

For example, while the company's regular terms are 1/15, n/30 (1% discount if paid within 15 days), a customer might ask for and receive a few days of grace and still get the discount. Or a customer might place orders above its credit limit, in which case, depending on its payment history and the circumstances, Ms. Su might authorize shipment of the goods anyway.

"It's not about drawing a line in the sand, and that's all," she explains. "You want a good relationship with your customers—but you also need to bring in the money."

"The money," in Whitehall-Robins's case amounts to some $170 million in sales a year. Nearly all of it comes in through the credit accounts Ms. Su manages. The process starts with the decision to grant a customer an account in the first place, Ms. Su explains. The sales rep gives the customer a

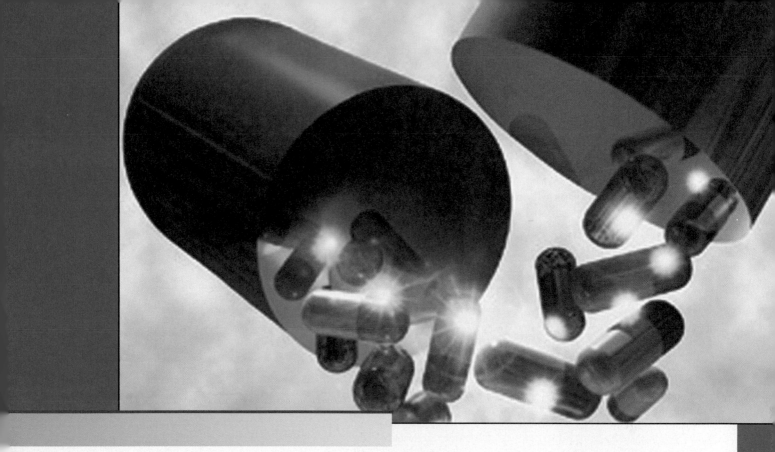

credit application. "My department reviews this application very carefully; a customer needs to supply three good references, and we also run a check with a credit firm like Equifax. If we accept them, then based on their size and history, we assign a credit limit."

Once accounts are established, the company supervises them very carefully. "I get an aging report every single day," says Ms. Su.

"The rule of thumb is that we should always have at least 85% of receivables current—meaning they were billed less than 30 days ago," she continues. "But we try to do even better than that—I like to see 90%." Similarly, her guideline is never to have more than 5% of receivables at over 90 days. But long before that figure is reached, "we jump on it," she says firmly.

At 15 days overdue, Whitehall-Robins phones the client. Often there's a reasonable explanation for the delay—an invoice may have gone astray, or the payables clerk is away. "But if a customer keeps on delaying, and tells us several times that it'll only be a few more days, we know there's a problem," says Ms. Su. After 45 days, "I send a letter. Then a second notice is sent in writing.

After the third and final notice, the client has 10 days to pay, and then I hand it over to a collection agency, and it's out of my hands."

Ms. Su's boss, Terry Norton, records an estimate for bad debts every year, based on a percentage of receivables. What percentage depends on the current aging history. He also calculates and monitors the company's receivables turnover ratio, which the company reports in its financial statements. "I think of it in terms of collection period of DSO—days of sales outstanding," he explains.

Ms. Su knows that she and Mr. Norton are crucial to the profitability of Whitehall-Robins. "Receivables are generally the second-largest asset of any company (after its capital assets)," she points out. "So it's no wonder we keep a very close eye on them."

On the World Wide Web
Whitehall-Robins Healthcare, Inc.
www.whitehall-robins.com

In this chapter we discuss some of the decisions related to reporting and analyzing receivables. As indicated in the Feature Story, receivables are a significant asset on the books of pharmaceutical company Whitehall-Robins. Receivables are significant to companies in other industries as well, because a significant portion of sales are made on credit in the United States. As a consequence, companies must pay close attention to their receivables balances and manage them carefully.

The organization and content of the chapter are as follows.

REPORTING AND ANALYZING RECEIVABLES

Types of Receivables	Accounts Receivable	Notes Receivable	Statement Presentation of Receivables	Managing Receivables
• Accounts receivable • Notes receivable • Other receivables	• Recognizing accounts receivable • Valuing accounts receivable	• Computing interest • Recognizing notes receivable • Valuing notes receivable • Disposing of notes receivable	• Balance sheet or notes • Income statement	• Extending credit • Establishing a payment period • Monitoring collections • Evaluating liquidity of receivables • Accelerating cash receipts

THE NAVIGATOR

Types of Receivables

STUDY OBJECTIVE
1
Identify the different types of receivables.

The term **receivables** refers to amounts due from individuals and companies. Receivables are claims that are expected to be collected in cash. The management of receivables is a very important activity for any company that sells goods or services on credit.

Receivables are important because they represent one of a company's most liquid assets. For many companies, receivables are also one of the largest assets. For example, receivables represented 11% of the current assets of pharmacy giant Rite Aid in 2004. Illustration 8-1 lists receivables as a percentage of total assets for five other well-known companies in a recent year.

Illustration 8-1
Receivables as a percentage of assets

Company	Receivables as a Percentage of Total Assets
General Electric	44%
Ford Motor Company	40%
Minnesota Mining and Manufacturing Company (3M)	13%
Krispy Kreme	11%
Intel Corporation	6%

The relative significance of a company's receivables as a percentage of its assets depends on various factors: its industry, the time of year, whether it extends long-term financing, and its credit policies. To reflect important differences among receivables, they are frequently classified as (1) accounts receivable, (2) notes receivable, and (3) other receivables.

Accounts receivable are amounts customers owe on account. They result from the sale of goods and services. Companies generally expect to collect accounts receivable within 30 to 60 days. They are usually the most significant type of claim held by a company.

Notes receivable represent claims for which formal instruments of credit are issued as evidence of the debt. The credit instrument normally requires the debtor to pay interest and extends for time periods of 60–90 days or longer. Notes and accounts receivable that result from sales transactions are often called **trade receivables**.

Other receivables include non-trade receivables such as interest receivable, loans to company officers, advances to employees, and income taxes refundable. These do not generally result from the operations of the business. Therefore, they are generally classified and reported as separate items in the balance sheet.

Accounts Receivable

Two accounting problems associated with accounts receivable are:

1. Recognizing accounts receivable.
2. Valuing accounts receivable.

A third issue, accelerating cash receipts from receivables, is discussed later in the chapter.

RECOGNIZING ACCOUNTS RECEIVABLE

Initial recognition of accounts receivable is relatively straightforward. A service organization records a receivable when it provides service on account. A merchandiser records accounts receivable at the point of sale of merchandise on account. When a merchandiser sells goods, it increases both the Accounts Receivable and Sales accounts.

Sales discounts reduce receivables. The seller may offer terms that encourage early payment by providing a discount. For example, terms of 2/10, n/30 provide the buyer with a 2% discount if it pays within 10 days. If the buyer chooses to pay within the discount period, the seller reduces its accounts receivable.

Sales returns also reduce receivables. The buyer might find some of the goods unacceptable and choose to return the unwanted goods. For example, if the buyer returns merchandise with a selling price of $100, the seller reduces Accounts Receivable by $100 upon receipt of the returned merchandise.

STUDY OBJECTIVE
2
Explain how accounts receivable are recognized in the accounts.

VALUING ACCOUNTS RECEIVABLE

Once companies record receivables in the accounts, the next question is: How should they report receivables in the financial statements? Companies report accounts receivable on the balance sheet as an asset. Determining the **amount** to report is sometimes difficult because some receivables will become uncollectible.

Although each customer must satisfy the credit requirements of the seller before the credit sale is approved, inevitably some accounts receivable become uncollectible. For example, a corporate customer may not be able to pay because it experienced a sales decline due to an economic downturn. Similarly, individuals may be laid off from their jobs or be faced with unexpected hospital bills. The seller debits such credit losses to **Bad Debts Expense** (or Uncollectible Accounts Expense). Such losses are a normal and necessary risk of doing business on a credit basis.

STUDY OBJECTIVE
3
Describe the methods used to account for bad debts.

The accounting profession uses two methods for uncollectible accounts: (1) the direct write-off method, and (2) the allowance method. We explain each of these methods in the following sections.

Direct Write-off Method for Uncollectible Accounts

Under the **direct write-off method**, when a company determines a particular account to be uncollectible, it charges the loss to Bad Debts Expense. Assume, for example, that Warden Co. writes off M. E. Doran's $200 balance as uncollectible on December 12. Warden's entry is:

```
A  =  L  +  SE
            -200 Exp
-200
```
Cash Flows
no effect

Dec.	12	Bad Debts Expense	200	
		Accounts Receivable—M. E. Doran		200
		(To record write-off of M. E. Doran		
		account)		

Under this method, bad debts expense will show only **actual losses** from uncollectibles. The company will report accounts receivable at its gross amount.

Use of the direct write-off method can reduce the usefulness of both the income statement and balance sheet. Consider the following example. In 2007, Quick Buck Computer Company decided it could increase its revenues by offering computers to college students without requiring any money down, and with no credit-approval process. It went on campuses across the country and sold one million computers at a selling price of $800 each. This promotion increased Quick Buck's revenues and receivables by $800,000,000. It was a huge success: The 2007 balance sheet and income statement looked wonderful. Unfortunately, during 2008, nearly 40% of the college student customers defaulted on their loans. The 2008 income statement and balance sheet looked terrible. Illustration 8-2 shows the effect of these events on the financial statements using the direct write-off method.

Illustration 8-2 Effects of direct write-off method

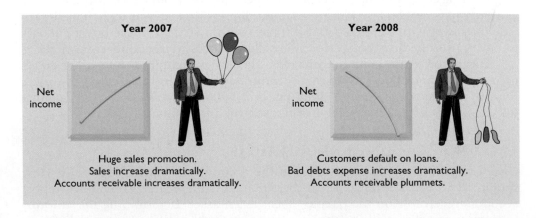

Year 2007
Net income
Huge sales promotion.
Sales increase dramatically.
Accounts receivable increases dramatically.

Year 2008
Net income
Customers default on loans.
Bad debts expense increases dramatically.
Accounts receivable plummets.

Under the direct write-off method, companies often record bad debts expense in a period different from the period in which they recorded the revenue. Thus, no attempt is made to match bad debts expense to sales revenues in the income statement. Nor does the company try to show accounts receivable in the balance sheet at the amount actually expected to be received. **Consequently, unless a company expects bad debts losses to be insignificant, the direct write-off method is not acceptable for financial reporting purposes.**

Allowance Method for Uncollectible Accounts

The **allowance method** of accounting for bad debts involves estimating uncollectible accounts at the end of each period. This provides better matching of expenses with revenues on the income statement. It also ensures that receivables are stated at their cash (net) realizable value on the balance sheet. **Cash (net) realizable value** is the net amount a company expects to receive in cash. It excludes amounts that the company estimates it will not collect. Estimated uncollectible receivables therefore reduce receivables on the balance sheet through use of the allowance method.

Companies must use the allowance method for financial reporting purposes when bad debts are material in amount. It has three essential features:

1. Companies **estimate** uncollectible accounts receivable and **match them against revenues** in the same accounting period in which the revenues are recorded.

2. Companies record estimated uncollectibles as an increase (a debit) to Bad Debts Expense and an increase (a credit) to Allowance for Doubtful Accounts (a contra asset account) through an adjusting entry at the end of each period.

3. Companies debit actual uncollectibles to Allowance for Doubtful Accounts and credit them to Accounts Receivable at the time the specific account is written off as uncollectible.

Helpful Hint In this context, *material* means significant or important to financial statement users.

RECORDING ESTIMATED UNCOLLECTIBLES. To illustrate the allowance method, assume that Hampson Furniture has credit sales of $1,200,000 in 2007, of which $200,000 remains uncollected at December 31. The credit manager estimates that $12,000 of these sales will prove uncollectible. The adjusting entry to record the estimated uncollectibles is:

Dec. 31	Bad Debts Expense	12,000	
	Allowance for Doubtful Accounts		12,000
	(To record estimate of uncollectible		
	accounts)		

A	=	L	+	SE
				−12,000 Exp
−12,000				

Cash Flows
no effect

Companies report Bad Debts Expense in the income statement as an operating expense (usually as a selling expense). Thus, Hampson matches the estimated uncollectibles with sales in 2007 because the expense is recorded in the same year the company makes the sales.

Allowance for Doubtful Accounts shows the estimated amount of claims on customers that companies expect will become uncollectible in the future. Companies use a contra account instead of a direct credit to Accounts Receivable because they do not know *which* customers will not pay. The credit balance in the allowance account will absorb the specific write-offs when they occur. The company deducts the allowance account from Accounts Receivable in the current assets section of the balance sheet as shown in Illustration 8-3.

HAMPSON FURNITURE Balance Sheet (partial)		
Current assets		
Cash		$ 14,800
Accounts receivable	**$200,000**	
Less: Allowance for doubtful accounts	**12,000**	**188,000**
Merchandise inventory		310,000
Prepaid expense		25,000
Total current assets		$ 537,800

Illustration 8-3
Presentation of allowance for doubtful accounts

The amount of $188,000 in Illustration 8-3 represents the expected **cash realizable value** of the accounts receivable at the statement date. **Companies do not close Allowance for Doubtful Accounts at the end of the fiscal year.**

RECORDING THE WRITE-OFF OF AN UNCOLLECTIBLE ACCOUNT.
Companies use various methods of collecting past-due accounts, as discussed in the Feature Story. When a company has exhausted all means of collecting a past-due account and collection appears unlikely, the company should write off the account. In the credit card industry it is standard practice to write off accounts that are 210 days past due. To prevent premature or unauthorized write-offs, authorized management personnel should formally approve each write-off. To maintain good internal control, companies should not authorize someone to write off accounts who also has daily responsibilities related to cash or receivables.

To illustrate a receivables write-off, assume that the vice-president of finance of Hampson Furniture on March 1, 2008, authorizes a write-off of the $500 balance owed by R. A. Ware. The entry to record the write-off is:

A	=	L	+	SE
+500				
−500				

Cash Flows
no effect

Mar. 1	Allowance for Doubtful Accounts		500	
	Accounts Receivable—R. A. Ware			500
	(Write-off of R. A. Ware account)			

The company does not increase Bad Debts Expense when the write-off occurs. **Under the allowance method, a company debits every bad debt write-off to the allowance account and not to Bad Debts Expense.** A debit to Bad Debts Expense would be incorrect because the company has already recognized the expense, when it made the adjusting entry for estimated bad debts. Instead, the entry to record the write-off of an uncollectible account reduces both Accounts Receivable and the Allowance for Doubtful Accounts. After posting, the general ledger accounts will appear as in Illustration 8-4.

Illustration 8-4 General ledger balances after write-off

Accounts Receivable		Allowance for Doubtful Accounts	
Jan. 1 Bal. 200,000	Mar. 1 **500**	Mar. 1 **500**	Jan. 1 Bal. 12,000
Mar. 1 Bal. 199,500			Mar. 1 Bal. 11,500

A write-off affects only balance sheet accounts. Cash realizable value in the balance sheet, therefore, remains the same, as shown in Illustration 8-5.

Illustration 8-5 Cash realizable value comparison

	Before Write-off	After Write-off
Accounts receivable	$ 200,000	$ 199,500
Allowance for doubtful accounts	12,000	11,500
Cash realizable value	**$188,000**	**$188,000**

RECOVERY OF AN UNCOLLECTIBLE ACCOUNT.
Occasionally, a company collects from a customer after the account has been written off as uncollectible. The company must make two entries to record the recovery of a bad debt: (1) It reverses the entry made in writing off the account. This reinstates the customer's account. (2) It journalizes the collection in the usual manner.

To illustrate, assume that on July 1, R. A. Ware pays the $500 amount that Hampson Furniture had written off on March 1. Hampson makes these entries:

	(1)				A	=	L	+	SE
July 1	Accounts Receivable—R. A. Ware	500			+500				
	Allowance for Doubtful Accounts		500		−500				
	(To reverse write-off of R. A. Ware account)								

Cash Flows no effect

	(2)				A	=	L	+	SE
1	Cash	500			+500				
	Accounts Receivable—R. A. Ware		500		−500				
	(To record collection from R. A. Ware)								

Cash Flows +500

Note that the recovery of a bad debt, like the write-off of a bad debt, affects only balance sheet accounts. The net effect of the two entries is an increase in Cash and an increase in Allowance for Doubtful Accounts for $500. Accounts Receivable and the Allowance for Doubtful Accounts both increase in entry (1) for two reasons: First, the company made an error in judgment when it wrote off the account receivable. Second, R. A. Ware did pay, and therefore the Accounts Receivable account should show this collection for possible future credit purposes.

Helpful Hint Like the write-off, a recovery does not involve the income statement.

ESTIMATING THE ALLOWANCE. For Hampson Furniture in Illustration 8-3, the amount of the expected uncollectibles was given. However, in "real life," companies must estimate the amount of expected uncollectible accounts if they use the allowance method. Frequently they estimate the allowance as a percentage of the outstanding receivables.

Under the **percentage of receivables basis**, management establishes a percentage relationship between the amount of receivables and expected losses from uncollectible accounts. The company prepares a schedule in which it classifies customer balances by the length of time they have been unpaid. Because of its emphasis on time, this schedule is often called an **aging schedule**, and the analysis of it is often called aging the accounts receivable.

After the company arranges the accounts by age, it determines the expected bad debt losses by applying percentages, based on past experience, to the totals of each category. The longer a receivable is past due, the less likely it is to be collected. As a result, the estimated percentage of uncollectible debts increases as the number of days past due increases. Illustration 8-6 shows an aging schedule for Dart Company. Note the increasing uncollectible percentages from 2% to 40%.

Illustration 8-6 Aging schedule

Customer	Total	Not Yet Due	Number of Days Past Due			
			1–30	31–60	61–90	Over 90
T. E. Adert	$ 600		$ 300		$ 200	$ 100
R. C. Bortz	300	$ 300				
B. A. Carl	450		200	$ 250		
O. L. Diker	700	500			200	
T. O. Ebbet	600			300		300
Others	36,950	26,200	5,200	2,450	1,600	1,500
	$39,600	$27,000	$5,700	$3,000	$2,000	$1,900
Estimated percentage uncollectible		2%	4%	10%	20%	40%
Total estimated uncollectible accounts	$ 2,228	$ 540	$ 228	$ 300	$ 400	$ 760

Total estimated uncollectible accounts for Dart Company ($2,228) represent the existing customer claims expected to become uncollectible in the future. Thus, this amount represents the **required balance** in Allowance for Doubtful Accounts at the balance sheet date. Accordingly, **the amount of the bad debts expense adjusting entry is the difference between the required balance and the existing balance in the allowance account**.

For example, if the trial balance shows Allowance for Doubtful Accounts with a credit balance of $528, then an adjusting entry for $1,700 ($2,228 − $528) is necessary:

A = L + SE		
		−1,700 Exp
−1,700		

Cash Flows
no effect

Dec. 31	Bad Debts Expense	1,700	
	Allowance for Doubtful Accounts		1,700
	(To adjust allowance account to total estimated uncollectibles)		

After Dart posts the adjusting entry, its accounts will appear as in Illustration 8-7.

Illustration 8-7 Bad debts accounts after posting

Bad Debts Expense		Allowance for Doubtful Accounts	
Dec. 31 Adj. **1,700**			Jan. 1 Bal. 528
			Dec. 31 Adj. **1,700**
			Dec. 31 Bal. 2,228

An important aspect of accounts receivable management is simply maintaining a close watch on the accounts. Studies have shown that accounts more than 60 days past due lose approximately 50% of their value if no payment activity occurs within the next 30 days. For each additional 30 days that pass, the collectible value halves once again. As noted in our Feature Story, Vivi Su of Whitehall-Robins monitors accounts receivable closely, using an aging schedule to set the percentage of bad debts and computing the company's receivables turnover.

Occasionally the allowance account will have a **debit balance** prior to adjustment because write-offs during the year have **exceeded** previous estimates for bad debts. In such a case, the company **adds the debit balance to the required balance** when it makes the adjusting entry. Thus, if there had been a $500 debit balance in the allowance account before adjustment, the adjusting entry would have been for $2,728 ($2,228 + $500) in order to arrive at a credit balance of $2,228.

The percentage of receivables basis provides an estimate of the cash realizable value of the receivables. It also provides a reasonable matching of expense to revenue.

Decision Toolkit

Decision Checkpoints	Info Needed for Decision	Tool to Use for Decision	How to Evaluate Results
☑			
Is the amount of past due accounts increasing? Which accounts require management's attention?	List of outstanding receivables and their due dates	Prepare an aging schedule showing the receivables in various stages: outstanding 0–30 days, 31–60 days, 61–90 days, and over 90 days.	Accounts in the older categories require follow-up: letters, phone calls, and possible renegotiation of terms.

The following note regarding accounts receivable comes from the annual report of healthcare company McKesson Corp.

McKESSON CORP. Notes to the Financial Statements		
Receivables, net		
	March 31,	
(In millions)	**2004**	**2003**
Customer accounts	$4,986.1	$4,305.9
Other	609.5	574.2
Total	5,595.6	4,880.1
Allowances	(176.8)	(285.4)
Net	$5,418.8	$4,594.7

The allowances are for uncollectible accounts, discounts, returns, refunds, customer settlements and other adjustments. Allowances declined in 2004 primarily due to a $66.4 million reversal of accrued customer settlements into operating expenses and a $44.1 million write-off of a previously reserved note receivable.

Illustration 8-8 Note disclosure of accounts receivable

Business Insight
Investor Perspective

Recently Nortel Networks announced that half of its previous year's earnings were "fake." Should investors have seen this coming? Well, there were issues in its annual report that should have caused investors to ask questions. The company had cut its allowance for doubtful accounts on all receivables from $1,253 million to $544 million, even though its total balance of receivables remained relatively unchanged.

This reduction in bad debt expense was responsible for a very large part of the company's earnings that year. At the time it was unclear whether Nortel might have set the reserves too high originally and needed to reduce them, or whether it slashed the allowance to artificially boost earnings. But one thing is certain—when a company makes an accounting change of this magnitude, investors need to ask questions.

Source: Jonathan Weil, "Outside Audit: At Nortel, Warning Signs Existed Months Ago," *Wall Street Journal* (May, 18, 2004), p. C3.

? When would it be appropriate for a company to lower its allowance for doubtful accounts as a percentage of its receivables?

BEFORE YOU GO ON . . .

 Review It

1. What types of receivables does Tootsie Roll report on its balance sheet? Does it use the allowance method or the direct write-off method to account for uncollectibles? The answer to these questions appears on page 417.

2. To maintain adequate internal controls over receivables, who should authorize receivables write-offs?
3. What are the essential features of the allowance method?
4. What is the primary criticism of the direct write-off method?

▶ Do It

Brule Corporation has been in business for 5 years. The ledger at the end of the current year shows: Accounts Receivable $30,000; Sales $180,000; and Allowance for Doubtful Accounts with a debit balance of $2,000. Brule estimates bad debts to be 10% of accounts receivable. Prepare the entry necessary to adjust the Allowance for Doubtful Accounts.

Action Plan

- Report receivables at their cash (net) realizable value—that is, the amount the company expects to collect in cash.
- Estimate the amount the company does not expect to collect.
- Consider the existing balance in the allowance account when using the percentage of receivables basis.

Solution

Brule should make the following entry to bring the balance in the Allowance for Doubtful Accounts up to a balance of $3,000 (.1 × $30,000):

Bad Debts Expense	5,000	
Allowance for Doubtful Accounts		5,000
(To record estimate of		
uncollectible accounts)		

Helpful Hint The debit to Bad Debts Expense is calculated as follows:

Allowance for Doubtful Accounts

2,000	5,000
	3,000

THE NAVIGATOR

Notes Receivable

Companies also may grant credit in exchange for a formal credit instrument known as a promissory note. A **promissory note** is a written promise to pay a specified amount of money on demand or at a definite time. Promissory notes may be used (1) when individuals and companies lend or borrow money, (2) when the amount of the transaction and the credit period exceed normal limits, and (3) in settlement of accounts receivable.

In a promissory note, the party making the promise to pay is called the **maker**. The party to whom payment is to be made is called the **payee**. The promissory note may specifically identify the payee by name or may designate the payee simply as the bearer of the note.

In the note shown in Illustration 8-9 (page 381), Brent Company is the maker, and Wilma Company is the payee. To Wilma Company, the promissory note is a note receivable; to Brent Company, the note is a note payable.

Notes receivable give the holder a stronger legal claim to assets than do accounts receivable. Like accounts receivable, notes receivable can be readily sold to another party. Promissory notes are negotiable instruments (as are checks), which means that, when sold, the seller can transfer them to another party by endorsement.

Companies frequently accept notes receivable from customers who need to extend the payment of an outstanding account receivable, and they often require them from high-risk customers. In some industries (e.g., the pleasure and sport boat industry) all credit sales are supported by notes. The majority of notes, however, originate from lending transactions.

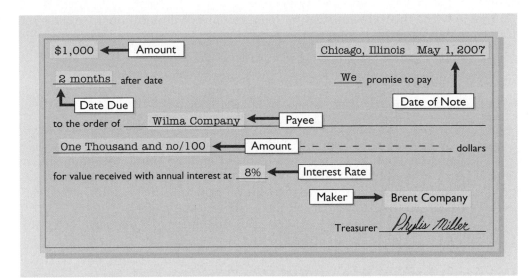

Illustration 8-9
Promissory note

Helpful Hint Who are the two key parties to a note? What entry does each party make when the note is issued?
Answer:
1. The maker, Brent Company, credits Notes Payable.
2. The payee, Wilma Company, debits Notes Receivable.

There are three basic issues in accounting for notes receivable:

1. **Recognizing** notes receivable.
2. **Valuing** notes receivable.
3. **Disposing** of notes receivable.

We will look at each of these issues, but first we need to consider an issue that did not apply to accounts receivable: computing interest.

COMPUTING INTEREST

STUDY OBJECTIVE
4
Compute the interest on notes receivable.

Illustration 8-10 gives the basic formula for computing interest on an interest-bearing note.

Illustration 8-10 Formula for computing interest

$$\begin{array}{c} \text{Face Value} \\ \text{of Note} \end{array} \times \begin{array}{c} \text{Annual} \\ \text{Interest} \\ \text{Rate} \end{array} \times \begin{array}{c} \text{Time} \\ \text{in Terms of} \\ \text{One Year} \end{array} = \text{Interest}$$

The interest rate specified on the note is an **annual** rate of interest. The time factor in the computation expresses the fraction of a year that the note is outstanding. When the maturity date is stated in days, the time factor is frequently the number of days divided by 360. When the due date is stated in months, the time factor is the number of months divided by 12. Illustration 8-11 shows computation of interest for various time periods.

Helpful Hint The maturity date of a 60-day note dated July 17 is determined as follows:

Term of note	60 days
July (31 − 17)	14
August	31 45
September (Maturity date)	**15**

Illustration 8-11
Computation of interest

Terms of Note	Interest Computation				
	Face	× Rate	× Time	=	Interest
$ 730, 12%, 120 days	$ 730 ×	12% ×	120/360	=	$ 29.20
$1,000, 9%, 6 months	$1,000 ×	9% ×	6/12	=	$ 45.00
$2,000, 6%, 1 year	$2,000 ×	6% ×	1/1	=	$120.00

There are different ways to calculate interest. For example, the computation in Illustration 8-11 assumed 360 days for the year. Most financial institutions use 365 days to compute interest. (*For homework problems, assume 360 days to simplify computations.*)

RECOGNIZING NOTES RECEIVABLE

To illustrate the basic entry for notes receivable, we will use Brent Company's $1,000, two-month, 8% promissory note dated May 1. Assuming that Brent

Company wrote the note to settle an open account, Wilma Company makes the following entry for the receipt of the note.

A	=	L	+	SE
+1,000				
−1,000				

Cash Flows
no effect

May	1	Notes Receivable	1,000	
		Accounts Receivable—Brent Company		1,000
		(To record acceptance of Brent Company note)		

The company records the note receivable at its **face value**, the value shown on the face of the note. No interest revenue is reported when the company accepts the note because the revenue recognition principle does not recognize revenue until earned. Interest is earned (accrued) as time passes.

If a company exchanges a note for cash, the entry is a debit to Notes Receivable and a credit to Cash in the amount of the loan.

VALUING NOTES RECEIVABLE

Like accounts receivable, companies report short-term notes receivable at their **cash (net) realizable value**. The notes receivable allowance account is Allowance for Doubtful Accounts. Valuing short-term notes receivable is the same as valuing accounts receivable. The computations and estimations involved in determining cash realizable value and in recording the proper amount of bad debts expense and related allowance are similar.

Long-term notes receivable, however, pose additional estimation problems. As an example, we need only look at the problems large U.S. banks sometimes have in collecting their receivables. Loans to less-developed countries are particularly worrisome. Developing countries need loans for development but often

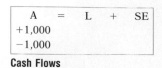

Accounting across the Organization

Management must decide to whom it will grant credit. This is one of the hardest, and most critical, decisions that it makes. Consider the case of Mitsubishi Motors. It had been floundering, reporting large losses for a number of years in a row. Then management came up with what appeared to be a great plan. It began a marketing campaign aimed at giving Mitsubishi a hip image (think flashy ads with loud music), thus making its vehicles attractive to single people in their early twenties. The company combined this campaign with easy credit-terms—so called "zero-zero-zero" deals. This meant no down-payment, no payments for the first six months, and 0% financing.

The plan worked great—sort of. Sales took off. But then the twenty-somethings started defaulting on their loans. Soon Mitsubishi's losses were even bigger than before. It has since refocused its ads and credit terms. It now focuses on people who are "young at heart" (as opposed to just young)—and "economically safer."

Source: Todd Zaun, "Bad Loans Bump Mitsubishi Motors Off Road to Recovery," *Wall Street Journal Online* (November 12, 2003).

 How would reported net income likely differ during the first year of this promotion if Mitsubishi used the direct write-off method versus the allowance method?

find repayment difficult. U.S. loans (notes) to less-developed countries at one time totaled approximately $135 billion. In Brazil alone, Citigroup at one time had loans equivalent to 80% of its stockholders' equity. In some cases, developed nations have intervened to provide financial assistance to the financially troubled borrowers so as to minimize the political and economic turmoil to the borrower and to ensure the survival of the lender.

DISPOSING OF NOTES RECEIVABLE

Notes may be held to their maturity date, at which time the face value plus accrued interest is due. In some situations, the maker of the note defaults, and the payee must make appropriate adjustment. In other situations, similar to accounts receivable, the holder of the note speeds up the conversion to cash by selling the receivables.

Honor of Notes Receivable

A note is **honored** when its maker pays in full at its maturity date. For each interest-bearing note, the **amount due at maturity** is the face value of the note plus interest for the length of time specified on the note.

To illustrate, assume that Wolder Co. lends Higley Inc. $10,000 on June 1, accepting a five-month, 9% interest note. In this situation, interest is $375 ($10,000 × 9% × $\frac{5}{12}$). The amount due, the maturity value, is $10,375 ($10,000 + $375). To obtain payment, Wolder (the payee) must present the note either to Higley Inc. (the maker) or to the maker's agent, such as a bank. If Wolder presents the note to Higley Inc. on November 1, the maturity date, Wolder's entry to record the collection is:

Helpful Hint How many days of interest should be accrued at September 30 for a 90-day note issued on August 16? *Answer:* 45 days (15 days in August plus 30 days in September).

Nov. 1	Cash	10,375	
	Notes Receivable		10,000
	Interest Revenue ($10,000 × 9% × $\frac{5}{12}$)		375
	(To record collection of Higley Inc. note and interest)		

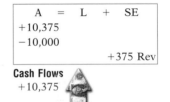

Accrual of Interest Receivable

If Wolder Co. prepares financial statements as of September 30, it must accrue interest. In this case, the adjusting entry by Wolder is for four months, or $300, as shown below.

Sept. 30	Interest Receivable ($10,000 × 9% × $\frac{4}{12}$)	300	
	Interest Revenue		300
	(To accrue 4 months' interest on Higley note)		

When interest has been accrued, the company must credit Interest Receivable at maturity. Also, since an additional month has passed, the company records one month of interest revenue. Wolder's entry to record the honoring of the Higley note on November 1 is:

Nov. 1	Cash	10,375	
	Notes Receivable		10,000
	Interest Receivable		300
	Interest Revenue ($10,000 × 9% × $\frac{1}{12}$)		75
	(To record collection of Higley Inc. note and interest)		

In this case, Wolder credits Interest Receivable because the receivable was established in the adjusting entry on September 30.

Dishonor of Notes Receivable

A **dishonored note** is a note that is not paid in full at maturity. A dishonored note receivable is no longer negotiable; however, the payee still has a claim against the maker of the note for both the note and the interest. If the lender expects that it eventually will be able to collect, the Notes Receivable account is transferred to an Account Receivable for both the face value of the note and the interest due. Sometimes the two parties negotiate new terms to make it easier for the borrower to repay the debt. If there is no hope of collection, the payee should write off the face value of the note.

BEFORE YOU GO ON . . .

▶ Review It

1. What is the basic formula for computing interest?
2. At what value do companies report notes receivable on the balance sheet?
3. Explain the difference between honoring and dishonoring a note receivable.

▶ Do It

Gambit Stores accepts from Leonard Co. a $3,400, 90-day, 6% note dated May 10 in settlement of Leonard's overdue open account. The note matures on August 8. What entry does Gambit make at the maturity date, assuming Leonard pays the note and interest in full at that time?

Action Plan

• Determine whether interest was accrued.
• Compute the accrued interest.
• Prepare the entry for payment of the note and the interest. The entry to record interest at maturity in this solution assumes that no interest has been previously accrued on this note.

Solution

The interest payable at maturity date is $51, computed as follows.

$$\text{Face} \times \text{Rate} \times \text{Time} = \text{Interest}$$

$$\$3,400 \times 6\% \times \frac{90}{360} = \$51$$

Gambit Stores records this entry at the maturity date:

Cash	3,451	
Notes Receivable		3,400
Interest Revenue		51
(To record collection of Leonard note and interest)		

THE NAVIGATOR

Financial Statement Presentation of Receivables

Companies should identify in the balance sheet or in the notes to the financial statements each of the major types of receivables. Short-term receivables are reported in the current assets section of the balance sheet, below short-term investments. Short-term investments appear before short-term receivables because these investments are nearer to cash. Companies report both the gross amount of receivables and the allowance for doubtful accounts.

Illustration 8-12 shows a presentation of receivables for Deere & Company from its 2004 balance sheet and notes.

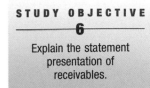

STUDY OBJECTIVE
6
Explain the statement presentation of receivables.

DEERE & COMPANY
Balance Sheet (partial)
(in millions)

Receivables	
Receivables from unconsolidated subsidiaries	$ 17.6
Trade accounts and notes receivable	3,262.9
Financing receivables	11,377.6
Other receivables	663.0
Total receivables	15,321.1
Less: Allowance for doubtful trade receivables	201.0
Net receivables	$15,120.1

Illustration 8-12 Balance sheet presentation of receivables

In the income statement, companies report bad debts expense under "Selling expenses" in the operating expenses section. They show interest revenue under "Other revenues and gains" in the nonoperating section of the income statement.

If a company has significant risk of uncollectible accounts or other problems with its receivables, it is required to discuss this possibility in the notes to the financial statements.

BEFORE YOU GO ON . . .

► Review It

1. Explain where companies report receivables on the balance sheet and in what order.
2. Where do companies report bad debts expense and interest revenue on the income statement?

THE NAVIGATOR

Managing Receivables

Managing accounts receivable involves five steps:

1. Determine to whom to extend credit.
2. Establish a payment period.
3. Monitor collections.
4. Evaluate the liquidity of receivables.
5. Accelerate cash receipts from receivables when necessary.

STUDY OBJECTIVE
7
Describe the principles of sound accounts receivable management.

EXTENDING CREDIT

A critical part of managing receivables is determining who should be extended credit and who should not. Many companies increase sales by being generous with their credit policy, but, like Mitsubishi in the *Accounting across the Organization* story, they may end up extending credit to risky customers who do not pay. If the credit policy is too tight, you will lose sales. If it is too loose, you may sell to "deadbeats" who will pay either very late or not at all. One CEO noted that prior to getting his credit and collection department in order, his salespeople had 300 square feet of office space **per person**, while the people in credit and collections had six people crammed into a single 300-square-foot space. Although this arrangement boosted sales, it had very expensive consequences in bad debts expense.

Companies can take certain steps to help minimize losses as they relax credit standards. They might require risky customers to provide letters of credit or bank guarantees. Then if the customer does not pay, the bank that provided the guarantee will do so. Particularly risky customers might be required to pay cash on delivery.

In addition, companies should ask potential customers for references from banks and suppliers, to determine their payment history. It is important to check these references on potential new customers as well as periodically to check the financial health of continuing customers. Many resources are available for investigating customers. For example, *The Dun & Bradstreet Reference Book of American Business* (*www.dnb.com*) lists millions of companies and provides credit ratings for many of them.

Accounting across the Organization

In the weeks prior to Kmart's decision to file for Chapter 11 bankruptcy protection, many of its suppliers were taking concrete steps to protect themselves. For example, the garden supply company The Scotts Company, which in the previous year sold Kmart $175 million in goods, decided to quit shipping to Kmart until its survival plans were more clear. This was a big decision for Scotts, since Kmart represented 10% of its sales in the previous year.

One consultant said that in an informal survey of Kmart suppliers, one-third weren't shipping to Kmart, one-third were holding back shipments until they learned more, and one-third were doing business as usual. The result: Kmart had a lot of empty shelves, at a time when it was hard pressed for cash.

Source: Amy Merrick, "Kmart Suppliers Limit Risk in Case of Chapter 11 Filing," *Wall Street Journal Online* (January 21, 2002).

 Rather than refusing to ship to Kmart, what could suppliers have done to protect their interests?

ESTABLISHING A PAYMENT PERIOD

Companies that extend credit should determine a required payment period and communicate that policy to their customers. It is important to make sure that your company's payment period is consistent with that of your competitors. For example, if you decide to require payment within 15 days, but your competitors require payment within 45 days, you may lose sales to your competitors. However, to match competitors' terms yet still encourage prompt payment of accounts, you might allow up to 45 days to pay but offer a sales discount for people paying within 15 days.

MONITORING COLLECTIONS

We discussed preparation of the accounts receivable aging schedule earlier in the chapter (page 377). Companies should prepare an accounts receivable aging schedule at least monthly. In addition to estimating the allowance for doubtful accounts, the aging schedule has other uses: It helps managers estimate the timing of future cash inflows, which is very important to the treasurer's efforts to prepare a cash budget. It provides information about the overall collection experience of the company and identifies problem accounts. For example, management would compute and compare the percentage of receivables that are over 90 days past due.

The aging schedule identifies problem accounts that the company needs to pursue with phone calls, letters, and occasionally legal action. Sometimes special arrangements must be made with problem accounts. For example, it was reported that Intel Corporation (a major manufacturer of computer chips) required that Packard Bell (at one time one of the largest U.S. sellers of personal computers) give Intel an interest-bearing note receivable in exchange for a past-due account receivable. This caused concern within the investment community, first because it suggested that Packard Bell was in trouble, and second because of the impact on Intel's accounts receivable, since Packard Bell was one of its largest customers.

Decision Toolkit

Decision Checkpoints	Info Needed for Decision	Tool to Use for Decision	How to Evaluate Results
Is the company's credit risk increasing?	Customer account balances and due dates	Accounts receivable aging schedule	Compute and compare the percentage of receivables over 90 days old.

If a company has significant concentrations of credit risk, it must discuss this risk in the notes to its financial statements. A **concentration of credit risk** is a threat of nonpayment from a single customer or class of customers that could adversely affect the financial health of the company. Illustration 8-13 shows an excerpt from the credit risk note from the 2004 annual report of McKesson Corp. McKesson reports that its ten largest customers account for 50% of its total revenues and receivables.

McKESSON CORP.
Notes to the Financial Statements

Concentrations of Credit Risk: Trade receivables subject us to a concentration of credit risk with customers primarily in our Pharmaceutical Solutions segment. A significant proportion of our revenue growth has been with a limited number of large customers and as a result, our credit concentration has increased. Accordingly, any defaults in payment by or a reduction in purchases from these large customers could have a significant negative impact on our financial condition, results of operations and liquidity. At March 31, 2004, revenues and accounts receivable from our ten largest customers accounted for approximately 50% of total consolidated revenues and accounts receivable. Fiscal 2004 revenues and March 31, 2004 receivables from our largest customer, Rite Aid Corporation, represented approximately 11% of total consolidated revenues and 8% of accounts receivable. We have also provided financing arrangements to certain of our customers within our Pharmaceutical Solutions segment, some of which are on a revolving basis. At March 31, 2004, these arrangements totaled $196.1 million and we have a security interest in the customers' assets.

Illustration 8-13
Excerpt from note on concentration of credit risk

This note to McKesson Corp.'s financial statements indicates it has a high level of credit concentration. A default by any of these large customers could have a significant negative impact on its financial performance.

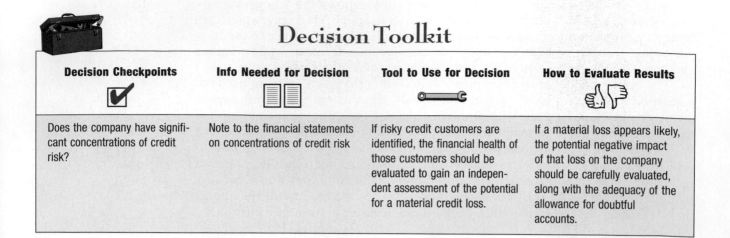

Decision Toolkit

Decision Checkpoints	Info Needed for Decision	Tool to Use for Decision	How to Evaluate Results
Does the company have significant concentrations of credit risk?	Note to the financial statements on concentrations of credit risk	If risky credit customers are identified, the financial health of those customers should be evaluated to gain an independent assessment of the potential for a material credit loss.	If a material loss appears likely, the potential negative impact of that loss on the company should be carefully evaluated, along with the adequacy of the allowance for doubtful accounts.

STUDY OBJECTIVE
8

Identify ratios to analyze a company's receivables.

EVALUATING LIQUIDITY OF RECEIVABLES

Investors and managers keep a watchful eye on the relationship among sales, accounts receivable, and cash collections. If sales increase, then accounts receivable are also expected to increase. But a disproportionate increase in accounts receivable might signal trouble. Perhaps the company increased its sales by loosening its credit policy, and these receivables may be difficult or impossible to collect. Such receivables are considered less liquid. Recall that liquidity is measured by how quickly certain assets can be converted to cash.

The ratio analysts use to assess the liquidity of the receivables is the **receivables turnover ratio**. This ratio measures the number of times, on average, a company collects receivables during the period. The receivables turnover ratio is computed by dividing net credit sales (net sales less cash sales) by the average net accounts receivable during the year. Unless seasonal factors are significant, **average** accounts receivable outstanding can be computed from the beginning and ending balances of the net receivables.[1]

A popular variant of the receivables turnover ratio is to convert it into an **average collection period** in terms of days. This is done by dividing the receivables turnover ratio into 365 days. Companies frequently use the average collection period to assess the effectiveness of a company's credit and collection policies. The general rule is that the average collection period should not greatly exceed the credit term period (i.e., the time allowed for payment).

The following data (in millions) are available for McKesson Corp.

	For the year ended March 31,	
	2004	**2003**
Sales	$69,506.1	$57,120.8
Accounts receivable (net)	$ 5,418.8	$ 4,594.7

---

[1]If seasonal factors are significant, the company might determine the average accounts receivable balance by using monthly amounts.

Illustration 8-14 shows the receivables turnover ratio and average collection period for McKesson Corp., along with comparative industry data. These calculations assume that all sales were credit sales.

Illustration 8-14
Receivables turnover and average collection period

$$\text{Receivables Turnover Ratio} = \frac{\text{Net Credit Sales}}{\text{Average Net Receivables}}$$

$$\text{Average Collection Period} = \frac{365}{\text{Receivables Turnover Ratio}}$$

($ in millions)		2004	2003
McKesson	Receivables turnover	$\frac{\$69,506.1}{(\$5,418.8 + \$4,594.7)/2} = 13.9$ times	$\frac{\$57,120.8}{(\$4,594.7 + \$3,998.1)/2*} = 13.3$ times
	Average collection period	$\frac{365}{13.9} = 26.3$ days	$\frac{365}{13.3} = 27.4$ days
Industry average	Receivables turnover	10.4 times	
	Average collection period	35.1 days	

*The receivables balance at March 31, 2002, was $3,998.1 million.

McKesson's receivables turnover was 13.9 times in 2004, with a corresponding average collection period of 26.3 days. This was slightly better than its 2003 collection period of 27.4 days. It compares favorably with the industry average collection period of 35.1 days. What this means is that McKesson is able to turn its receivables into cash more quickly than most of its competitors. Therefore, it has a better likelihood of paying its current obligations than a company with a slower receivables turnover.

Decision Toolkit

Decision Checkpoints	Info Needed for Decision	Tool to Use for Decision	How to Evaluate Results
Are collections being made in a timely fashion?	Net credit sales and average receivables balance	$\text{Receivables turnover ratio} = \frac{\text{Net credit sales}}{\text{Average net receivables}}$ $\text{Average collection period} = \frac{365 \text{ days}}{\text{Receivables turnover ratio}}$	Average collection period should be consistent with corporate credit policy. An increase may suggest a decline in financial health of customers.

In some cases, receivables turnover may be misleading. Some companies, especially large retail chains, encourage credit and revolving charge sales, and they slow collections in order to earn a healthy return on the outstanding receivables in the form of interest at rates of 18% to 22%. On the other hand, companies that sell their receivables on a consistent basis will have a faster turnover than those that do not. Thus, to interpret receivables turnover, you must know how a company manages its receivables. In general, the faster the turnover, the greater the reliability of the current ratio for assessing liquidity.

ACCELERATING CASH RECEIPTS

In the normal course of events, companies collect accounts receivable in cash and remove them from the books. However, as credit sales and receivables have grown in size and significance, the "normal course of events" has changed. Two common expressions apply to the collection of receivables: (1) "Time is money"—that is, waiting for the normal collection process costs money. (2) "A bird in the hand is worth two in the bush"—that is, getting the cash now is better than getting it later or not at all. Therefore, in order to accelerate the receipt of cash from receivables, companies frequently sell their receivables to another company for cash, thereby shortening the cash-to-cash operating cycle.

There are three reasons for the sale of receivables. The first is their **size**. In recent years, for competitive reasons, sellers (retailers, wholesalers, and manufacturers) often have provided financing to purchasers of their goods. For example, many major companies in the automobile, truck, industrial and farm equipment, computer, and appliance industries have created companies that accept responsibility for accounts receivable financing. General Motors has General Motors Acceptance Corp. (GMAC), General Electric has GE Capital, and Ford has Ford Motor Credit Corp. (FMCC). These companies are referred to as **captive finance companies** because they are wholly owned by the company selling the product. The purpose of captive finance companies is to encourage the sale of the company's products by assuring financing to buyers. However, the parent companies involved do not necessarily want to hold large amounts of receivables, so they may sell them.

Second, **companies may sell receivables because they may be the only reasonable source of cash**. When credit is tight, companies may not be able to borrow money in the usual credit markets. Even if credit is available, the cost of borrowing may be prohibitive.

A final reason for selling receivables is that **billing and collection are often time-consuming and costly**. As a result, it is often easier for a retailer to sell the receivables to another party that has expertise in billing and collection matters. Credit card companies such as MasterCard, Visa, American Express, and Discover specialize in billing and collecting accounts receivable.

National Credit Card Sales

Approximately one billion credit cards were in use recently—more than three credit cards for every man, woman, and child in this country. A common type of credit card is a national credit card such as Visa and MasterCard. Three parties are involved when national credit cards are used in making retail sales: (1) the credit card issuer, who is independent of the retailer, (2) the retailer, and (3) the customer. **A retailer's acceptance of a national credit card is another form of selling—factoring—the receivable by the retailer.**

The use of national credit cards translates to more sales and zero bad debts for the retailer. Both are powerful reasons for a retailer to accept such cards. Illustration 8-15 shows the major advantages of national credit cards to the

Illustration 8-15
Advantages of credit
cards to the retailer

Issuer does credit investigation of customer

Credit card issuer — Customer — Retailer

Issuer maintains customer accounts

Issuer undertakes collection process and absorbs any losses

Retailer receives cash more quickly from credit card issuer

retailer. In exchange for these advantages, the retailer pays the credit card issuer a fee of 2% to 4% of the invoice price for its services.

The retailer considers sales resulting from the use of Visa and MasterCard as **cash sales**. Upon notification of a credit card charge from a retailer, the bank that issued the card immediately adds the amount to the seller's bank balance. Companies therefore record these credit card charges in the same manner as checks deposited from a cash sale. The banks that issue national credit cards generally charge retailers a fee of 2% to 4% of the credit card sales slips for this service.

To illustrate, Morgan Marie purchases $1,000 of compact discs for her restaurant from Sondgeroth Music Co., and she charges this amount on her Visa First Bank Card. The service fee that First Bank charges Sondgeroth Music is 3%. Sondgeroth Music's entry to record this transaction is:

Cash	970	
Service Charge Expense	30	
Sales		1,000
(To record Visa credit card sales)		

A	=	L	+	SE
+970				
				−30 Exp
				+1,000 Rev

Cash Flows
+970

Sale of Receivables to a Factor

A common way to accelerate receivables collection is a sale to a factor. A **factor** is a finance company or bank that buys receivables from businesses for a fee and then collects the payments directly from the customers.

Factoring was traditionally associated with the textiles, apparel, footwear, furniture, and home furnishing industries. It has now spread to other types of businesses and is a multibillion dollar industry. For example, Sears, Roebuck & Co. (now Sears Holdings) once sold $14.8 billion of customer accounts receivable.

McKesson has a pre-arranged agreement allowing it to sell up to $850 million of its receivables. McKesson's sale of receivables may explain why its receivables turnover ratio exceeds the industry average.

Factoring arrangements vary widely, but typically the factor charges a commission. It ranges from 1% to 3% of the amount of receivables purchased. To illustrate, assume that Hendredon Furniture factors $600,000 of receivables to Federal Factors, Inc. Federal Factors assesses a service charge of 2% of the amount of receivables sold. The following journal entry records Hendredon's sale of receivables.

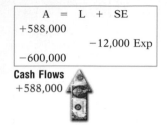

A = L + SE
+588,000
                    −12,000 Exp
−600,000

Cash Flows
+588,000

Cash	588,000	
Service Charge Expense (2% × $600,000)	12,000	
Accounts Receivable		600,000
(To record the sale of accounts receivable)		

If the company usually sells its receivables, it records the service charge expense as a selling expense. If the company sells receivables infrequently, it may report this amount under "Other expenses and losses" in the income statement.

Accounting across the Organization

In the past, smaller companies primarily factored receivables. Today, businesses of all sizes and types factor their receivables. For example, Wal-Mart's suppliers, many of them large companies, need their cash more quickly than Wal-Mart wants to pay, so many of them factor their receivables. Also, some businesses have found it economical to outsource their whole billing and collection function to factors. One factor, CDS Capital, will provide all billing and collecting, as well as a record of clients' daily cash position, cash received, bills paid, and receivables still outstanding.

Source: Martin Mayer, "Taking the Fear Out of Factoring," *Inc. Magazine* (December 2003), pp. 90–97.

 What factors should management consider in deciding whether to factor its receivables?

Illustration 8-16 summarizes the basic principles of managing accounts receivable.

Illustration 8-16
Managing receivables

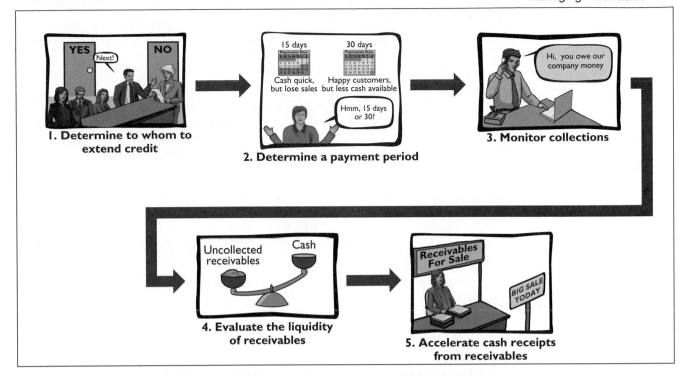

1. Determine to whom to extend credit
2. Determine a payment period
3. Monitor collections
4. Evaluate the liquidity of receivables
5. Accelerate cash receipts from receivables

BEFORE YOU GO ON . . .

▶ Review It

1. What is meant by a concentration of credit risk?
2. What is the interpretation of the receivables turnover ratio and the average collection period?
3. For whom is the service charge on a credit card sale an expense?
4. Why do companies sell their receivables?

▶ Do It

Peter M. Kell Wholesalers Co. needs to raise $120,000 in cash to safely cover next Friday's employee payroll. Kell has reached its debt ceiling. Kell's present balance of outstanding receivables totals $750,000. What might Kell do to alleviate this cash crunch? Record the entry that Kell would make when it raises the needed cash. (Assume a 1% service charge.)

Action Plan

• Consider sale of receivables to a factor.
• Weigh cost of factoring against benefit of having cash in hand.

Solution

If Kell Co. factors $125,000 of its accounts receivable at a 1% service charge, it would make this entry:

Cash	123,750	
Service Charge Expense	1,250	
Accounts Receivable		125,000
(To record sale of receivables to factor)		

THE
NAVIGATOR

Using the Decision Toolkit

The information below was taken from the December 31, 2004, financial statements of Amerisource Bergen Corp., Inc. Similar to McKesson Corp., Amerisource Bergen distributes drugs and related services to pharmaceutical manufacturers and health-care providers in the United States and Puerto Rico.

Instructions

Comment on Amerisource Bergen's accounts receivable management and liquidity relative to that of McKesson, using (1) the current ratio and (2) the receivables turnover ratio and average collection period. McKesson's current ratio was 1.38:1. The other ratio values for McKesson were calculated earlier in the chapter.

AMERISOURCE BERGEN CORP., INC.
Selected Financial Information
(in millions)

	2004		2003	
Sales		$53,179		$49,657
Current assets				
Cash and cash equivalents		$ 871		$ 800
Accounts receivable	$2,725		$2,488	
Allowance for doubtful accounts	464		192	
Net accounts receivable		2,261		2,296
Inventories		5,136		5,734
Other current assets		27		29
Total current assets		$ 8,295		$ 8,859
Total current liabilities		$ 6,104		$ 6,256

Solution

1. Here is the current ratio (Current assets ÷ Current liabilities) for each company.

McKesson	**Amerisource Bergen**
1.38:1	$\dfrac{\$8,295}{\$6,104} = 1.36:1$

This suggests that McKesson and Amerisource Bergen have similar liquidity.

2. The receivables turnover ratio and average collection period for each company are:

	McKesson	**Amerisource Bergen**
Receivables turnover ratio	13.9 times	$\dfrac{\$53,179}{(\$2,261 + \$2,296)/2} = 23.3$ times
Average collection period	26.3 days	$\dfrac{365}{23.3} = 15.7$ days

Amerisource Bergen's receivables turnover ratio of 23.3 compared to McKesson's 13.9, and its average collection days of 15.7 days versus McKesson's 26.3 days, suggest that Amerisource Bergen is able to collect from its customers much more rapidly.

THE NAVIGATOR

Summary of Study Objectives

1 *Identify the different types of receivables.* Receivables are frequently classified as accounts, notes, and other. Accounts receivable are amounts customers owe on account. Notes receivable represent claims that are evidenced by formal instruments of credit. Other receivables include nontrade receivables such as interest receivable, loans to company officers, advances to employees, and income taxes refundable.

2 *Explain how accounts receivable are recognized in the accounts.* Accounts receivable are recorded at invoice price. They are reduced by sales returns and allowances. Cash discounts reduce the amount received on accounts receivable.

3 *Describe the methods used to account for bad debts.* The two methods of accounting for uncollectible accounts are the allowance method and the direct write-off method. Under the allowance method, companies estimate uncollectible accounts as a percentage of receivables. It emphasizes the cash realizable value of the accounts receivable. An aging schedule is frequently used with this approach.

4 *Compute the interest on notes receivable.* The formula for computing interest is: Face value × Interest rate × Time.

5 *Describe the entries to record the disposition of notes receivable.* Notes can be held to maturity, at which time the borrower (maker) pays the face value plus accrued interest and the payee removes the note from the accounts. In many cases, however, similar to accounts receivable, the holder of the note speeds up the conversion by selling the receivable to another party. In some situations, the maker of the note dishonors the note (defaults), and the note is written off.

6 *Explain the statement presentation of receivables.* Companies should identify each major type of receivable in the balance sheet or in the notes to the financial statements. Short-term receivables are considered current assets. Companies report the gross amount of receivables and allowance for doubtful accounts. They report bad debts and service charge expenses in the income statement as operating (selling) expenses, and interest revenue as other revenues and gains in the nonoperating section of the statement.

Decision Toolkit—A Summary

Decision Checkpoints	Info Needed for Decision	Tool to Use for Decision	How to Evaluate Results
Is the amount of past due accounts increasing? Which accounts require management's attention?	List of outstanding receivables and their due dates	Prepare an aging schedule showing the receivables in various stages: outstanding 0–30 days, 31–60 days, 61–90 days, and over 90 days.	Accounts in the older categories require follow-up: letters, phone calls, and possible renegotiation of terms.
Is the company's credit risk increasing?	Customer account balances and due dates	Accounts receivable aging schedule	Compute and compare the percentage of receivables over 90 days old.
Does the company have significant concentrations of credit risk?	Note to the financial statements on concentrations of credit risk	If risky credit customers are identified, the financial health of those customers should be evaluated to gain an independent assessment of the potential for a material credit loss.	If a material loss appears likely, the potential negative impact of that loss on the company should be carefully evaluated, along with the adequacy of the allowance for doubtful accounts.
Are collections being made in a timely fashion?	Net credit sales and average receivables balance	$$\text{Receivables turnover ratio} = \frac{\text{Net credit sales}}{\text{Average net receivables}}$$ $$\text{Average collection period} = \frac{365 \text{ days}}{\text{Receivables turnover ratio}}$$	Average collection period should be consistent with corporate credit policy. An increase may suggest a decline in financial health of customers.

Describe the principles of sound accounts receivable management. To properly manage receivables, management must (a) determine to whom to extend credit, (b) establish a payment period, (c) monitor collections, (d) evaluate the liquidity of receivables, and (e) accelerate cash receipts from receivables when necessary.

8 *Identify ratios to analyze a company's receivables.* The receivables turnover ratio and the average collection period both are useful in analyzing management's

effectiveness in managing receivables. The accounts receivable aging schedule also provides useful information.

9 *Describe methods to accelerate the receipt of cash from receivables.* If the company needs additional cash, management can accelerate the collection of cash from receivables by selling (factoring) its receivables or by allowing customers to pay with bank credit cards.

Glossary

Accounts receivable   Amounts customers owe on account. (p. 373)

Aging the accounts receivable   The analysis of customer balances by the length of time they have been unpaid. (p. 377)

Allowance method   A method of accounting for bad debts that involves estimating uncollectible accounts at the end of each period. (p. 375)

Average collection period   The average amount of time that a receivable is outstanding, calculated by dividing 365 days by the receivables turnover ratio. (p. 388)

Bad debts expense   An expense account to record credit losses. (p. 373)

Cash (net) realizable value   The net amount a company expects to receive in cash. (p. 375)

Concentration of credit risk   The threat of nonpayment from a single customer or class of customers that could adversely affect the financial health of the company. (p. 387)

Direct write-off method   A method of accounting for bad debts that involves expensing accounts at the time they are determined to be uncollectible. (p. 374)

Dishonored note   A note that is not paid in full at maturity. (p. 384)

Factor   A finance company or bank that buys receivables from businesses for a fee and then collects the payments directly from the customers. (p. 391)

Maker   The party in a promissory note who is making the promise to pay. (p. 380)

Notes receivable   Claims for which formal instruments of credit are issued as evidence of the debt. (p. 373)

Payee   The party to whom payment of a promissory note is to be made. (p. 380)

Percentage of receivables basis   Management establishes a percentage relationship between the amount of receivables and the expected losses from uncollectible accounts. (p. 377)

Promissory note   A written promise to pay a specified amount of money on demand or at a definite time. (p. 380)

Receivables   Amounts due from individuals and companies that are expected to be collected in cash. (p. 372)

Receivables turnover ratio   A measure of the liquidity of receivables, computed by dividing net credit sales by average net receivables. (p. 388)

Trade receivables   Notes and accounts receivable that result from sales transactions. (p. 373)

Demonstration Problem

Presented here are selected transactions related to B. Dylan Corp.

Mar.	1	Sold $20,000 of merchandise to Potter Company, terms 2/10, n/30.
	11	Received payment in full from Potter Company for balance due.
	12	Accepted Juno Company's $20,000, 6-month, 12% note for balance due on outstanding account receivable.
	13	Made B. Dylan Corp. credit card sales for $13,200.
	15	Made Visa credit sales totaling $6,700. A 5% service fee is charged by Visa.
Apr.	11	Sold accounts receivable of $8,000 to Harcot Factor. Harcot Factor assesses a service charge of 2% of the amount of receivables sold.
	13	Received collections of $8,200 on B. Dylan Corp. credit card sales.
May	10	Wrote off as uncollectible $16,000 of accounts receivable. (B. Dylan Corp. uses the percentage of receivables basis to estimate bad debts.)
June	30	The balance in accounts receivable at the end of the first 6 months is $200,000 and the bad debt percentage is 10%. At June 30 the credit balance in the allowance account prior to adjustment is $3,500. Recorded bad debt expense.

July   16   One of the accounts receivable written off in May pays the amount due,
$4,000, in full.

Instructions

Prepare the journal entries for the transactions.

Solution to Demonstration Problem

Mar.	1	Accounts Receivable—Potter Company
		    Sales
		       (To record sales on account)
			20,000	20,000

	11	Cash
		Sales Discounts (2% × $20,000)
		    Accounts Receivable—Potter Company
		       (To record collection of accounts
		       receivable)
			19,600
			400
				20,000

	12	Notes Receivable
		    Accounts Receivable—Juno Company
		       (To record acceptance of Juno
		       Company note)
			20,000	20,000

	13	Accounts Receivable
		    Sales
		       (To record company credit card sales)
			13,200	13,200

	15	Cash
		Service Charge Expense (5% × $6,700)
		    Sales
		       (To record credit card sales)
			6,365
			335
				6,700

Apr.	11	Cash
		Service Charge Expense (2% × $8,000)
		    Accounts Receivable
		       (To record sale of receivables to factor)
			7,840
			160
				8,000

	13	Cash
		    Accounts Receivable
		       (To record collection of accounts
		       receivable)
			8,200	8,200

May	10	Allowance for Doubtful Accounts
		    Accounts Receivable
		       (To record write-off of accounts
		       receivable)
			16,000	16,000

June	30	Bad Debts Expense
		    Allowance for Doubtful Accounts
		       [($200,000 × 10%) − $3,500]
		       (To record estimate of uncollectible
		       accounts)
			16,500	16,500

July	16	Accounts Receivable
		    Allowance for Doubtful Accounts
		       (To reverse write-off of accounts
		       receivable)
			4,000	4,000

		Cash
		    Accounts Receivable
		       (To record collection of accounts
		       receivable)
			4,000	4,000

Action Plan

• Generally, record accounts receivable at invoice price.

• Recognize that sales returns and allowances and cash discounts reduce the amount received on accounts receivable.

• Record a service charge expense on the seller's books when accounts receivable are sold.

• Prepare an adjusting entry for bad debts expense.

• Recognize the balance in the allowance account under the percentage of receivables basis.

• Record write-offs of accounts receivable only in balance sheet accounts.

THE NAVIGATOR

Self-Study Questions

Answers are at the end of the chapter.

(SO 2) **1.** Kersee Company on June 15 sells merchandise on account to Soo Eng Co. for $1,000, terms 2/10, n/30. On June 20 Eng Co. returns merchandise worth $300 to Kersee Company. On June 24 payment is received from Eng Co. for the balance due. What is the amount of cash received?
  (a) $700. (c) $686.
  (b) $680. (d) None of the above.

(SO 3) **2.** Net credit sales for the month are $800,000. The accounts receivable balance is $160,000. The allowance is calculated as 7.5% of the receivables balance using the percentage of receivables basis. If the Allowance for Doubtful Accounts has a credit balance of $5,000 before adjustment, what is the balance after adjustment?
  (a) $12,000. (c) $17,000.
  (b) $7,000. (d) $31,000.

(SO 3) **3.** In 2007 Patterson Wholesale Company had net credit sales of $750,000. On January 1, 2007, Allowance for Doubtful Accounts had a credit balance of $18,000. During 2007, $30,000 of uncollectible accounts receivable were written off. Past experience indicates that the allowance should be 10% of the balance in receivables (percentage of receivables basis). If the accounts receivable balance at December 31 was $200,000, what is the required adjustment to the Allowance for Doubtful Accounts at December 31, 2007?
  (a) $20,000. (c) $32,000.
  (b) $75,000. (d) $30,000.

(SO 3) **4.** An analysis and aging of the accounts receivable of Raja Company at December 31 reveal these data:

Accounts receivable	$800,000
Allowance for doubtful accounts per books before adjustment (credit)	50,000
Amounts expected to become uncollectible	65,000

What is the cash realizable value of the accounts receivable at December 31, after adjustment?
  (a) $685,000. (c) $800,000.
  (b) $750,000. (d) $735,000.

(SO 4) **5.** Which of these statements about promissory notes is *incorrect*?
  (a) The party making the promise to pay is called the maker.
  (b) The party to whom payment is to be made is called the payee.
  (c) A promissory note is not a negotiable instrument.
  (d) A promissory note is more liquid than an account receivable.

(SO 4) **6.** Michael Co. accepts a $1,000, 3-month, 12% promissory note in settlement of an account with Tani Co. The entry to record this transaction is:

(a) Notes Receivable	1,030	
Accounts Receivable		1,030
(b) Notes Receivable	1,000	
Accounts Receivable		1,000
(c) Notes Receivable	1,000	
Sales		1,000
(d) Notes Receivable	1,020	
Accounts Receivable		1,020

(SO 5) **7.** Schleis Co. holds Murphy Inc.'s $10,000, 120-day, 9% note. The entry made by Schleis Co. when the note is collected, assuming no interest has previously been accrued, is:

(a) Cash	10,300	
Notes Receivable		10,300
(b) Cash	10,000	
Notes Receivable		10,000
(c) Accounts Receivable	10,300	
Notes Receivable		10,000
Interest Revenue		300
(d) Cash	10,300	
Notes Receivable		10,000
Interest Revenue		300

(SO 8) **8.** Eddy Corporation had net credit sales during the year of $800,000 and cost of goods sold of $500,000. The balance in receivables at the beginning of the year was $100,000 and at the end of the year was $150,000. What was the receivables turnover ratio?
  (a) 6.4 (b) 8.0 (c) 5.3 (d) 4.0

(SO 8) **9.** Prall Corporation sells its goods on terms of 2/10, n/30. It has a receivables turnover ratio of 7. What is its average collection period (days)?
  (a) 2,555 (b) 30 (c) 52 (d) 210

(SO 9) **10.** Which of these statements about **Visa** credit card sales is *incorrect*?
  (a) The credit card issuer conducts the credit investigation of the customer.
  (b) The retailer is not involved in the collection process.
  (c) The retailer must wait to receive payment from the issuer.
  (d) The retailer receives cash more quickly than it would from individual customers.

(SO 9) **11.** Good Stuff Retailers accepted $50,000 of Citibank Visa credit card charges for merchandise sold on July 1. Citibank charges 4% for its credit card use. The entry to record this transaction by Good Stuff Retailers will include a credit to Sales of $50,000 and a debit(s) to:

(a) Cash $48,000 and Service Charge Expense $2,000.

(b) Accounts Receivable $48,000 and Service Charge Expense $2,000.

(c) Cash $50,000.

(d) Accounts Receivable $50,000.

Go to the book's website, **www.wiley.com/college/kimmel**, to access additional Self-Study Questions.

Questions

1. What is the difference between an account receivable and a note receivable?

2. What are some common types of receivables other than accounts receivable or notes receivable?

3. What are the essential features of the allowance method of accounting for bad debts?

4. Lauren Anderson cannot understand why the cash realizable value does not decrease when an uncollectible account is written off under the allowance method. Clarify this point for Lauren.

5. Essex Company has a credit balance of $3,200 in Allowance for Doubtful Accounts before adjustment. The estimated uncollectibles under the percentage of receivables basis is $5,800. Prepare the adjusting entry.

6. How are bad debts accounted for under the direct write-off method? What are the disadvantages of this method?

7. ➡ Susan Lowe, the vice president of sales for Holiday Pools and Spas, wants the company's credit department to be less restrictive in granting credit. "How can we sell anything when you guys won't approve anybody?" she asks. Discuss the pros and cons of "easy credit." What are the accounting implications?

8. Your roommate is uncertain about the advantages of a promissory note. Compare the advantages of a note receivable with those of an account receivable.

9. How may the maturity date of a promissory note be stated?

10. Compute the missing amounts for each of the following notes.

Principal	Annual Interest Rate	Time	Total Interest
(a)	9%	60 days	$ 270
$30,000	8%	3 years	(d)
$60,000	(b)	5 months	$2,500
$50,000	11%	(c)	$1,375

11. Searcy Company dishonors a note at maturity. What are the options available to the lender?

12. General Motors Company has accounts receivable and notes receivable. How should the receivables be reported on the balance sheet?

13. ➡ ⚙ What are the steps to good receivables management?

14. ⚙ How might a company monitor the risk related to its accounts receivable?

15. ⚙ What is meant by a concentration of credit risk?

16. ⚙ The President of Hutley Inc. proudly announces her company's improved liquidity since its current ratio has increased substantially from one year to the next. Does an increase in the current ratio always indicate improved liquidity? What other ratio or ratios might you review to determine whether or not the increase in the current ratio is an improvement in financial health?

17. ➡ Since hiring a new sales director, Steps Inc. has enjoyed a 50% increase in sales. The CEO has also noticed, however, that the company's average collection period has increased from 17 days to 38 days. What might be the cause of this increase? What are the implications to management of this increase?

18. ⚙ The Coca-Cola Company's receivables turnover ratio was 10.31 in 2004, and its average amount of net receivables during the period was $2,131 million. What is the amount of its net credit sales for the period? What is the average collection period in days?

19. ➡ ⚙ JCPenney Company accepts both its own credit cards and national credit cards. What are the advantages of accepting both types of cards?

20. ➡ ⚙ An article in the *Wall Street Journal* indicated that companies are selling their receivables at a record rate. Why do companies sell their receivables?

21. Calico Corners decides to sell $630,000 of its accounts receivable to First Central Factors Inc. First Central Factors assesses a service charge of 3% of the amount of receivables sold. Prepare the journal entry that Calico Corners makes to record this sale.

Brief Exercises

BE8-1   Presented on page 400 are three receivables transactions. Indicate whether these receivables are reported as accounts receivable, notes receivable, or other receivables on a balance sheet.

Identify different types of receivables.

(SO 1)

(a) Advanced $10,000 to an employee.
(b) Received a promissory note of $34,000 for services performed.
(c) Sold merchandise on account for $60,000 to a customer.

Record basic accounts receivable transactions.
(SO 2)

BE8-2 Record the following transactions on the books of Massey Co.
(a) On July 1 Massey Co. sold merchandise on account to Opal Inc. for $17,000, terms 2/10, n/30.
(b) On July 8 Opal Inc. returned merchandise worth $2,400 to Massey Co.
(c) On July 11 Opal Inc. paid for the merchandise.

Prepare entry for write-off, and determine cash realizable value.
(SO 3)

BE8-3 At the end of 2007, Wendy Co. has accounts receivable of $700,000 and an allowance for doubtful accounts of $28,000. On January 24, 2008, it is learned that the company's receivable from Mayfield Inc. is not collectible and therefore management authorizes a write-off of $3,000.
(a) Prepare the journal entry to record the write-off.
(b) What is the cash realizable value of the accounts receivable (1) before the write-off and (2) after the write-off?

Prepare entries for collection of bad debt write-off.
(SO 3)

BE8-4 Assume the same information as BE8-3 and that on March 4, 2008, Wendy Co. receives payment of $3,000 in full from Mayfield Inc. Prepare the journal entries to record this transaction.

Prepare entry using percentage of receivables method.
(SO 3)

BE8-5 Jaya Co. uses the percentage of receivables basis to record bad debts expense and concludes that 2% of accounts receivable will become uncollectible. Accounts receivable are $500,000 at the end of the year, and the allowance for doubtful accounts has a credit balance of $1,500.
(a) Prepare the adjusting journal entry to record bad debts expense for the year.
(b) If the allowance for doubtful accounts had a debit balance of $600 instead of a credit balance of $1,500, prepare the adjusting journal entry for bad debts expense.

Compute interest rate and interest on note.
(SO 4)

BE8-6 Presented below are three promissory notes. Determine the missing amounts.

Date of Note	Terms	Principal	Annual Interest Rate	Total Interest
April 1	2 years	$900,000	8%	(a)
July 2	30 days	79,000	(b)	$592.50
March 7	6 months	56,000	11%	(c)

Prepare entry for note receivable exchanged for accounts receivable.
(SO 4)

BE8-7 On January 10, 2007, Santiago Co. sold merchandise on account to Croix for $8,000, terms n/30. On February 9 Croix gave Santiago Co. a 7% promissory note in settlement of this account. Prepare the journal entry to record the sale and the settlement of the accounts receivable.

Prepare entry for estimated uncollectibles and classifications, and compute ratios.
(SO 3, 6, 7, 8)

BE8-8 During its first year of operations, Salizar Company had credit sales of $3,000,000, of which $600,000 remained uncollected at year-end. The credit manager estimates that $24,000 of these receivables will become uncollectible.
(a) Prepare the journal entry to record the estimated uncollectibles. (Assume an unadjusted balance of zero.)
(b) Prepare the current assets section of the balance sheet for Salizar Company, assuming that in addition to the receivables it has cash of $90,000, merchandise inventory of $180,000, and prepaid expenses of $13,000.
(c) Calculate the receivables turnover ratio and average collection period. Assume that average net receivables were $300,000. Explain what these measures tell us.

Analyze accounts receivable.
(SO 8)

BE8-9 The 2004 financial statements of 3M Company report net sales of $20.0 billion. Accounts receivable (net) are $2.7 billion at the beginning of the year and $2.8 billion at the end of the year. Compute 3M's receivables turnover ratio. Compute 3M's average collection period for accounts receivable in days.

Prepare entries for credit card sale and sale of accounts receivable.
(SO 9)

BE8-10 Consider these transactions:
(a) Albanese Restaurant accepted a Visa card in payment of a $100 lunch bill. The bank charges a 3% fee. What entry should Albanese make?
(b) Beverly Company sold its accounts receivable of $68,000. What entry should Beverly make, given a service charge of 3% on the amount of receivables sold?

Exercises

E8-1 On January 6 Trisha Co. sells merchandise on account to Alma Inc. for $6,000, terms 1/10, n/30. On January 16 Alma pays the amount due.

Prepare entries for recognizing accounts receivable.
(SO 2)

Instructions
Prepare the entries on Trisha Co.'s books to record the sale and related collection.

E8-2 On January 10 Alana Davis uses her Idaho Co. credit card to purchase merchandise from Idaho Co. for $1,400. On February 10 Davis is billed for the amount due of $1,400. On February 12 Davis pays $1,000 on the balance due. On March 10 Davis is billed for the amount due, including interest at 1% per month on the unpaid balance as of February 12.

Prepare entries for recognizing accounts receivable.
(SO 2)

Instructions
Prepare the entries on Idaho Co.'s books related to the transactions that occurred on January 10, February 12, and March 10.

E8-3 At the beginning of the current period, Huang Corp. had balances in Accounts Receivable of $200,000 and in Allowance for Doubtful Accounts of $9,000 (credit). During the period, it had net credit sales of $800,000 and collections of $743,000. It wrote off as uncollectible accounts receivable of $7,000. However, a $4,000 account previously written off as uncollectible was recovered before the end of the current period. Uncollectible accounts are estimated to total $25,000 at the end of the period.

Journalize receivables transactions.
(SO 2, 3)

Instructions
(a) Prepare the entries to record sales and collections during the period.
(b) Prepare the entry to record the write-off of uncollectible accounts during the period.
(c) Prepare the entries to record the recovery of the uncollectible account during the period.
(d) Prepare the entry to record bad debts expense for the period.
(e) Determine the ending balances in Accounts Receivable and Allowance for Doubtful Accounts.
(f) What is the net realizable value of the receivables at the end of the period?

E8-4 The ledger of Garcia Company at the end of the current year shows Accounts Receivable $96,000; Credit Sales $780,000; and Sales Returns and Allowances $40,000.

Prepare entries to record allowance for doubtful accounts.
(SO 3)

Instructions
(a) If Garcia uses the direct write-off method to account for uncollectible accounts, journalize the adjusting entry at December 31, assuming Garcia determines that Allied's $900 balance is uncollectible.
(b) If Allowance for Doubtful Accounts has a credit balance of $1,100 in the trial balance, journalize the adjusting entry at December 31, assuming bad debts are expected to be 10% of accounts receivable.
(c) If Allowance for Doubtful Accounts has a debit balance of $500 in the trial balance, journalize the adjusting entry at December 31, assuming bad debts are expected to be 8% of accounts receivable.

E8-5 Hachey Company has accounts receivable of $95,100 at March 31, 2007. An analysis of the accounts shows these amounts.

Determine bad debt expense, and prepare the adjusting entry.
(SO 3)

	Balance, March 31	
Month of Sale	**2007**	**2006**
March	$65,000	$75,000
February	12,600	8,000
December and January	10,100	2,400
November and October	7,400	1,100
	$95,100	$86,500

Credit terms are 2/10, n/30. At March 31, 2007, there is a $2,200 credit balance in Allowance for Doubtful Accounts prior to adjustment. The company uses the percentage of receivables basis for estimating uncollectible accounts. The company's estimates of bad debts are as shown on page 402.

Age of Accounts	Estimated Percentage Uncollectible
Current	2%
1–30 days past due	7
31–90 days past due	30
Over 90 days	50

Instructions

(a) Determine the total estimated uncollectibles.

(b) Prepare the adjusting entry at March 31, 2007, to record bad debts expense.

(c) Discuss the implications of the changes in the aging schedule from 2006 to 2007.

Prepare entry for estimated uncollectibles, write-off, and recovery.
(SO 3)

E8-6   On December 31, 2007, when its Allowance for Doubtful Accounts had a debit balance of $1,000, North Star Co. estimates that 9% of its accounts receivable balance of $70,000 will become uncollectible and records the necessary adjustment to the Allowance for Doubtful Accounts. On May 11, 2008, North Star Co. determined that J. Tory's account was uncollectible and wrote off $1,200. On June 12, 2008, Tory paid the amount previously written off.

Instructions

Prepare the journal entries on December 31, 2007, May 11, 2008, and June 12, 2008.

Prepare entries for notes receivable transactions.
(SO 4, 5)

E8-7   Great Plains Supply Co. has the following transactions related to notes receivable during the last 2 months of the year.

Nov.	1	Loaned $30,000 cash to B. Wedunn on a 1-year, 8% note.
Dec.	11	Sold goods to R. P. Meier, Inc., receiving a $3,600, 90-day, 7% note.
	16	Received an $8,000, 6-month, 9% note to settle an open account from M. Fong.
	31	Accrued interest revenue on all notes receivable.

Instructions

Journalize the transactions for Great Plains Supply Co.

Journalize notes receivable transactions.
(SO 4, 5)

E8-8   These transactions took place for Pautsch Co.

2006

May	1	Received a $4,000, 1-year, 9% note in exchange for an outstanding account receivable from S. Bajwa.
Dec.	31	Accrued interest revenue on the S. Bajwa note.

2007

May	1	Received principal plus interest on the S. Bajwa note. (No interest has been accrued since December 31, 2006.)

Instructions

Record the transactions in the general journal.

Prepare a balance sheet presentation of receivables.
(SO 6)

E8-9   Milne Corp. had the following balances in receivable accounts at October 31, 2007 (in thousands): Allowance for Doubtful Accounts $56; Accounts Receivable $2,870; Other Receivables $189; Notes Receivable $853.

Instructions

Prepare the balance sheet presentation of Milne Corp.'s receivables in good form.

Identify the principles of receivables management.
(SO 7)

E8-10   The following is a list of activities that companies perform in relation to their receivables.

1. Selling receivables to a factor.
2. Reviewing company ratings in *The Dun and Bradstreet Reference Book of American Business*.
3. Collecting information on competitors' payment period policies.
4. Preparing monthly accounts receivable aging schedule and investigating problem accounts.
5. Calculating the receivables turnover ratio and average collection period.

Instructions
Match each of the activities listed above with a purpose of the activity listed below.
(a) Determine to whom to extend credit.
(b) Establish a payment period.
(c) Monitor collections.
(d) Evaluate the liquidity of receivables.
(e) Accelerate cash receipts from receivables when necessary.

E8-11 The following information was taken from the 2004 financial statements of FedEx Corporation, a major global transportation/delivery company.

Compute ratios to evaluate a company's receivables balance.
(SO 7, 8)

(in millions)	2004	2003
Accounts receivable (gross)	$ 3,178	$ 2,776
Accounts receivable (net)	$ 3,027	$ 2,627
Allowance for doubtful accounts	151	149
Sales	24,710	22,487
Total current assets	4,970	3,941

Instructions
Answer each of the following questions.
(a) Calculate the receivables turnover ratio and the average collection period for 2004 for FedEx.
(b) Is accounts receivable a material component of the company's total current assets?
(c) Evaluate the balance in FedEx's allowance for uncollectible accounts.

E8-12 The following ratios are available for Tianjin Inc.

Evaluate liquidity.
(SO 7, 8, 9)

	2004	2003
Current ratio	1.3:1	1.5:1
Receivables turnover	12 times	10 times
Inventory turnover	11 times	9 times

Instructions
(a) Is Tianjin's short-term liquidity improving or deteriorating in 2004? Be specific in your answer, referring to relevant ratios.
(b) Do changes in turnover ratios affect profitability? Explain.
(c) Identify any steps Tianjin might have taken, or might wish to take, to improve its management of its receivables and inventory turnover.

E8-13 On March 3 Metro Appliances sells $760,000 of its receivables to Universal Factors Inc. Universal Factors Inc. assesses a finance charge of 5% of the amount of receivables sold.

Prepare entry for sale of accounts receivable.
(SO 9)

Instructions
Prepare the entry on Metro Appliances' books to record the sale of the receivables.

E8-14 In a recent annual report, Office Depot, Inc. notes that the company entered into an agreement to sell all of its credit card program receivables to financial service companies.

Identify reason for sale of receivables.
(SO 9)

Instructions
Explain why Office Depot, a financially stable company with positive cash flow, would choose to sell its receivables.

E8-15 On May 10 Oman Company sold merchandise for $4,000 and accepted the customer's First Business Bank MasterCard. At the end of the day, the First Business Bank MasterCard receipts were deposited in the company's bank account. First Business Bank charges a 3.5% service charge for credit card sales.

Prepare entry for credit card sale.
(SO 9)

Instructions
Prepare the entry on Oman Company's books to record the sale of merchandise.

*Prepare entry for credit card
sale.*
(SO 9)

E8-16 On July 4 Alice's Restaurant accepts a Visa card for a $300 dinner bill. Visa charges a 3% service fee.

Instructions

Prepare the entry on Alice's books related to the transaction.

Problems: Set A

*Journalize transactions
related to bad debts.*
(SO 2, 3)

P8-1A Donedeal.com uses the allowance method to estimate uncollectible accounts receivable. The company produced the following aging of the accounts receivable at year end.

| | Total | **Number of Days Outstanding** | | | | |
		0–30	**31–60**	**61–90**	**91–120**	**Over 120**
Accounts receivable	$378,000	$222,000	$90,000	$38,000	$10,000	$18,000
% uncollectible		1%	4%	5%	6%	10%
Estimated bad debts		$ 2,200	$ 3,600	$ 1,900	$ 600	$ 1,800	→10,120

Est. Bad debts

Instructions

(a) Tot. est.
   bad debts $10,120

(a) Calculate the total estimated bad debts based on the above information.

(b) Prepare the year-end adjusting journal entry to record the bad debts using the aged uncollectible accounts receivable determined in (a). Assume the unadjusted balance in Allowance for Doubtful Accounts is a $4,000 debit. *Allowance*

(c) Of the above accounts, $5,000 is determined to be specifically uncollectible. Prepare the journal entry to write off the uncollectible account.

(d) The company collects $5,000 subsequently on a specific account that had previously been determined to be uncollectible in (c). Prepare the journal entry(ies) necessary to restore the account and record the cash collection.

(e) Comment on how your answers to (a)–(d) would change if Donedeal.com used 3% of *total* accounts receivable, rather than aging the accounts receivable. What are the advantages to the company of aging the accounts receivable rather than applying a percentage to total accounts receivable?

*Prepare journal entries
related to bad debt expense,
and compute ratios.*
(SO 2, 3, 8)

P8-2A At December 31, 2007, Curtis Imports reported this information on its balance sheet.

Accounts receivable	$600,000
Less: Allowance for doubtful accounts	40,000

During 2008 the company had the following transactions related to receivables.

1. Sales on account	$2,600,000
2. Sales returns and allowances	40,000
3. Collections of accounts receivable	2,200,000
4. Write-offs of accounts receivable deemed uncollectible	45,000
5. Recovery of bad debts previously written off as uncollectible	18,000

Instructions

(a) Prepare the journal entries to record each of these five transactions. Assume that no cash discounts were taken on the collections of accounts receivable.

(b) A/R bal. $915,000

(b) Enter the January 1, 2008, balances in Accounts Receivable and Allowance for Doubtful Accounts, post the entries to the two accounts (use T accounts), and determine the balances.

(c) Prepare the journal entry to record bad debts expense for 2008, assuming that aging the accounts receivable indicates that estimated bad debts are $46,000.

(d) Compute the receivables turnover ratio and average collection period.

P8-3A Presented below is an aging schedule for Joplin Company.

Journalize transactions related to bad debts.
(SO 2, 3)

Customer	Total	Not Yet Due	Number of Days Past Due				
			1–30	31–60	61–90	Over 90	
Adisy	$ 20,000		$ 9,000	$11,000			
Bloom	30,000	$ 30,000					
Cai	50,000	5,000	5,000		$40,000		
Dahl	38,000					$38,000	
Others	120,000	72,000	35,000	13,000			
	$258,000	$107,000	$49,000	$24,000	$40,000	$38,000	
Estimated percentage uncollectible		3%	5%	12%	24%	50%	
Total estimated bad debts	$ 37,140	$ 3,210	$ 2,450	$ 2,880	$ 9,600	$19,000	

At December 31, 2007, the unadjusted balance in Allowance for Doubtful Accounts is a credit of $8,000.

Instructions
(a) Journalize and post the adjusting entry for bad debts at December 31, 2007. (Use T accounts.)
(b) Journalize and post to the allowance account these 2008 events and transactions:
   1. March 1, a $600 customer balance originating in 2007 is judged uncollectible.
   2. May 1, a check for $600 is received from the customer whose account was written off as uncollectible on March 1.
(c) Journalize the adjusting entry for bad debts at December 31, 2008, assuming that the unadjusted balance in Allowance for Doubtful Accounts is a debit of $1,100 and the aging schedule indicates that total estimated bad debts will be $32,700.

P8-4A Here is information related to Kettle Moraine Company for 2007.

Compute bad debt amounts.
(SO 3)

Total credit sales	$1,500,000
Accounts receivable at December 31	440,000
Bad debts written off	31,000 ~~3000~~

Instructions
(a) What amount of bad debts expense will Kettle Moraine Company report if it uses the direct write-off method of accounting for bad debts?
(b) Assume that Kettle Moraine Company decides to estimate its bad debts expense based on 3% of accounts receivable. What amount of bad debts expense will the company record if Allowance for Doubtful Accounts has a credit balance of $3,000?
(c) Assume the same facts as in part (b), except that there is a $1,000 debit balance in Allowance for Doubtful Accounts. What amount of bad debts expense will Kettle Moraine record?
(d) ▭▭▭▷ What is a weakness of the direct write-off method of reporting bad debts expense?

P8-5A At December 31, 2007, the trial balance of Nora Company contained the following amounts before adjustment.

Journalize entries to record transactions related to bad debts.
(SO 2, 3)

	Debits	Credits
Accounts Receivable	$250,000	
Allowance for Doubtful Accounts		$ 1,500
Sales		875,000

Instructions
(a) Prepare the adjusting entry at December 31, 2007, to record bad debts expense assuming that the aging schedule indicates that $11,800 of accounts receivable will be uncollectible.

(b) Repeat part (a) assuming that instead of a credit balance there is a $1,500 debit balance in the Allowance for Doubtful Accounts.

(c) During the next month, January 2008, a $2,200 account receivable is written off as uncollectible. Prepare the journal entry to record the write-off.

(d) Repeat part (c) assuming that Nora Company uses the direct write-off method instead of the allowance method in accounting for uncollectible accounts receivable.

(e) What are the advantages of using an aging schedule and the allowance method in accounting for uncollectible accounts as compared to the direct write-off method?

Journalize various receivables transactions.
(SO 1, 2, 4, 5)

P8-6A On January 1, 2007, Paris Company had Accounts Receivable of $54,200 and Allowance for Doubtful Accounts of $3,700. Paris Company prepares financial statements annually and uses a perpetual inventory system. During the year the following selected transactions occurred.

Jan.	5	Sold $6,000 of merchandise to London Company, terms n/30. Cost of the merchandise sold was $4,000.
Feb.	2	Accepted a $6,000, 4-month, 9% promissory note from London Company for balance due.
	12	Sold $8,100 of merchandise costing $5,000 to Dublin Company and accepted Dublin's $8,100, 2-month, 10% note for the balance due.
	26	Sold $5,200 of merchandise costing $3,300 to Florence Co., terms n/10.
Apr.	5	Accepted a $5,200, 3-month, 8% note from Florence Co. for balance due.
	12	Collected Dublin Company note in full.
June	2	Collected London Company note in full.
	15	Sold $2,000 of merchandise costing $1,500 to Madrid Inc. and accepted a $2,000, 6-month, 12% note for the amount due.

Instructions
Journalize the transactions.

Explain the impact of transactions on ratios.
(SO 8)

P8-7A The president of Starz Enterprises asks if you could indicate the impact certain transactions have on the following ratios.

Transaction	Current Ratio (2:1)	Receivables Turnover (10X)	Average Collection Period (36.5 days)
1. Recorded $2,500 sales on account. The cost of the goods sold was $1,500.			
2. Recorded bad debts expense of $500 using allowance method.			
3. Wrote off a $100 account receivable as uncollectible.			
4. Received $3,000 on cash sale. The cost of the goods sold was $1,800.			

Instructions
Complete the table, indicating whether each transaction will increase (I), decrease (D), or have no effect (NE) on the specific ratios provided for Starz Enterprises.

Prepare entries for various credit card and notes receivable transactions.
(SO 2, 4, 5, 6, 9)

GLS

P8-8A NewBay Company closes its books on July 31. On June 30 the Notes Receivable account balance is $23,800. Notes Receivable include the following.

Date	Maker	Face Value	Term	Maturity Date	Interest Rate
May 21	Emery Inc.	$ 9,000	60 days	July 20	8%
May 25	Tulane Co.	4,800	60 days	July 24	10%
June 30	LSU Corp.	10,000	6 months	December 31	9%

During July the following transactions were completed.

July 5   Made sales of $7,100 on NewBay credit cards.
     14   Made sales of $600 on Visa credit cards. The credit card service charge is 3%.
     20   Received payment in full from Emery Inc. on the amount due.
     25   Received payment in full from Tulane Co. on the amount due.

Instructions
(a) Journalize the July transactions and the July 31 adjusting entry for accrued interest receivable. (Interest is computed using 360 days.)
(b) Enter the balances at July 1 in the receivable accounts and post the entries to all of the receivable accounts. (Use T accounts.)
(c) Show the balance sheet presentation of the receivable accounts at July 31.

(b) A/R bal. $ 7,100
(c) Tot.
*   receivables $17,175*

P8-9A   Presented here is basic financial information (in millions) from the 2004 annual reports of Nike and Reebok.

Calculate and interpret various ratios.
(SO 7, 8)

	Nike	Reebok
Sales	$12,253.1	$3,785.3
Allowance for doubtful accounts, Jan. 1	81.9	70.8
Allowance for doubtful accounts, Dec. 31	95.3	81.3
Accounts receivable balance (gross), Jan. 1	2,165.8	532.3
Accounts receivable balance (gross), Dec. 31	2,215.5	660.6

Instructions
Calculate the receivables turnover ratio and average collection period for both companies. Comment on the difference in their collection experiences.

Problems: Set B

P8-1B   The following represents selected information taken from a company's aging schedule to estimate uncollectible accounts receivable at year end.

Journalize transactions related to bad debts.
(SO 2, 3)

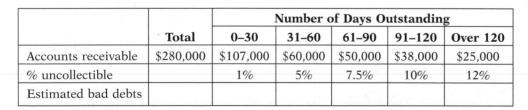

	Total	Number of Days Outstanding				
		0–30	**31–60**	**61–90**	**91–120**	**Over 120**
Accounts receivable	$280,000	$107,000	$60,000	$50,000	$38,000	$25,000
% uncollectible		1%	5%	7.5%	10%	12%
Estimated bad debts						

Instructions
(a) Calculate the total estimated bad debts based on the above information.
(b) Prepare the year-end adjusting journal entry to record the bad debts using the allowance method and the aged uncollectible accounts receivable determined in (a). Assume the unadjusted balance in the Allowance for Doubtful Accounts account is a $10,000 credit.
(c) Of the above accounts, $2,600 is determined to be specifically uncollectible. Prepare the journal entry to write off the uncollectible accounts.
(d) The company subsequently collects $1,000 on a specific account that had previously been determined to be uncollectible in (c). Prepare the journal entry(ies) necessary to restore the account and record the cash collection.
(e) Explain how establishing an allowance account satisfies the matching principle.

(a) Tot. est.
*   bad debts $14,620*

Prepare journal entries related to bad debt expense, and compute ratios.
(SO 2, 3, 8)

P8-2B At December 31, 2007, Guardian Company reported this information on its balance sheet.

Accounts receivable	$960,000
Less: Allowance for doubtful accounts	84,000

During 2008 the company had the following transactions related to receivables.

1. Sales on account	$3,800,000
2. Sales returns and allowances	50,000
3. Collections of accounts receivable	3,000,000
4. Write-offs of accounts receivable deemed uncollectible	92,000
5. Recovery of bad debts previously written off as uncollectible	40,000

Instructions
(a) Prepare the journal entries to record each of these five transactions. Assume that no cash discounts were taken on the collections of accounts receivable.

(b) A/R bal. $1,618,000

(b) Enter the January 1, 2008, balances in Accounts Receivable and Allowance for Doubtful Accounts, post the entries to the two accounts (use T accounts), and determine the balances.
(c) Prepare the journal entry to record bad debts expense for 2008, assuming that aging the accounts receivable indicates that expected bad debts are $113,000.
(d) Compute the receivables turnover ratio and average collection period.

Journalize transactions related to bad debts.
(SO 2, 3)

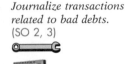

P8-3B Presented here is an aging schedule for West Beach Company.

Customer	Total	Not Yet Due	Number of Days Past Due			
			1–30	31–60	61–90	Over 90
Aaron	$ 22,000		$12,000	$10,000		
Brett	40,000	$ 40,000				
Cara	60,000	16,000	6,000		$38,000	
Dustin	28,000					$28,000
Others	126,000	96,000	16,000	14,000		
	$276,000	$152,000	$34,000	$24,000	$38,000	$28,000
Estimated percentage uncollectible		4%	9%	15%	25%	50%
Total estimated bad debts	$ 36,240	$ 6,080	$ 3,060	$ 3,600	$ 9,500	$14,000

At December 31, 2007, the unadjusted balance in Allowance for Doubtful Accounts is a credit of $11,700.

Instructions
(a) Journalize and post the adjusting entry for bad debts at December 31, 2007. (Use T accounts.)
(b) Journalize and post to the allowance account these 2008 events and transactions:
   1. March 31, a $500 customer balance originating in 2007 is judged uncollectible.
   2. May 31, a check for $500 is received from the customer whose account was written off as uncollectible on March 31.
(c) Journalize the adjusting entry for bad debts on December 31, 2008, assuming that the unadjusted balance in Allowance for Doubtful Accounts is a debit of $800 and the aging schedule indicates that total estimated bad debts will be $33,300.

Compute bad debt amounts.
(SO 3)

P8-4B Here is information related to Virtual Company for 2007.

Total credit sales	$2,000,000
Accounts receivable at December 31	500,000
Bad debts written off	19,000

Instructions
(a) What amount of bad debts expense will Virtual Company report if it uses the direct write-off method of accounting for bad debts?
(b) Assume that Virtual Company decides to estimate its bad debts expense based on 4% of accounts receivable. What amount of bad debts expense will the company record if it has an Allowance for Doubtful Accounts credit balance of $4,000?
(c) Assume the same facts as in part (b), except that there is a $2,000 debit balance in Allowance for Doubtful Accounts. What amount of bad debts expense will Virtual record?
(d) What is the weakness of the direct write-off method of reporting bad debts expense?

P8-5B   At December 31, 2007, the trial balance of Thews Company contained the following amounts before adjustment.

Journalize entries to record transactions related to bad debts.
(SO 2, 3)

	Debits	Credits
Accounts Receivable	$400,000	
Allowance for Doubtful Accounts		$ 4,800
Sales		2,200,000

Instructions
(a) Based on the information given, which method of accounting for bad debts is Thews Company using—the direct write-off method or the allowance method? How can you tell?
(b) Prepare the adjusting entry at December 31, 2007, for bad debts expense assuming that the aging schedule indicates that $17,500 of accounts receivable will be uncollectible.
(c) Repeat part (b) assuming that instead of a credit balance there is a $4,800 debit balance in the Allowance for Doubtful Accounts.
(d) During the next month, January 2008, a $5,000 account receivable is written off as uncollectible. Prepare the journal entry to record the write-off.
(e) Repeat part (d) assuming that Thews uses the direct write-off method instead of the allowance method in accounting for uncollectible accounts receivable.
(f) ▮▮▭▭▭▷ What type of account is the allowance for doubtful accounts? How does it affect how accounts receivable is reported on the balance sheet at the end of the accounting period?

P8-6B   On January 1, 2007, Kenyan Company had Accounts Receivable $154,000; Notes Receivable of $11,000; and Allowance for Doubtful Accounts of $13,200. The note receivable is from Brennan Company. It is a 4-month, 9% note dated December 31, 2006. Kenyan Company prepares financial statements annually. During the year the following selected transactions occurred. (Kenyan Company uses a periodic inventory system.)

Journalize various receivables transactions.
(SO 1, 2, 4, 5)

Jan.	5	Sold $12,000 of merchandise to Dorfner Company, terms n/15.
	20	Accepted Dorfner Company's $12,000, 3-month, 9% note for balance due.
Feb.	18	Sold $5,000 of merchandise to Cheng Company and accepted Cheng's $5,000, 6-month, 10% note for the amount due.
Apr.	20	Collected Dorfner Company note in full.
	30	Received payment in full from Brennan Company on the amount due.
May	25	Accepted Ardan Inc.'s $9,000, 6-month, 8% note in settlement of a past-due balance on account.
Aug.	18	Received payment in full from Cheng Company on note due.
Sept.	1	Sold $8,000 of merchandise to Charles Company and accepted an $8,000, 6-month, 10% note for the amount due.

Instructions
Journalize the transactions.

*Explain the impact of
transactions on ratios:
discuss acceleration of
receipt of cash from
receivables.*
(SO 8, 9)

P8-7B The president of Castle Enterprises Ltd., Nicole Castle, is considering the impact that certain transactions have on its receivables turnover and average collection period ratios. Prior to the following transactions, Castle's receivables turnover was 6 times, and its average collection period was 61 days.

Transaction	Receivables Turnover (6×)	Average Collection Period (61 days)
1. Recorded sales on account $100,000.		
2. Collected $25,000 owing from customers.		
3. Recorded bad debts expense for the year $7,500, using the allowance method.		
4. Recorded sales returns of $1,500 and credited the customers' accounts.		
5. Wrote off a $2,500 account from a customer as uncollectible.		

Instructions
(a) Complete the table, indicating whether each transaction will increase (I), decrease (D), or have no effect (NE) on the ratios.
(b) Nicole was reading through the financial statements for some publicly traded companies and noticed that they had recorded a loss on sale of receivables. She would like you to explain why companies sell their receivables.

*Prepare entries for various
credit card and notes
receivable transactions.*
(SO 2, 4, 5, 6, 9)

GLS

P8-8B Haley Company closes its books on October 31. On September 30 the Notes Receivable account balance is $24,700. Notes Receivable include the following.

Date	Maker	Face Value	Term	Maturity Date	Interest Rate
Aug. 16	Vinje Inc.	$ 8,500	60 days	Oct. 15	9%
Aug. 25	Rath Co.	6,000	2 months	Oct. 25	7%
Sept. 30	Flagg Corp.	10,200	6 months	Mar. 30	8%

Interest is computed using a 360-day year. During October the following transactions were completed.

Oct. 7 Made sales of $5,600 on Haley credit cards.
12 Made sales of $600 on Visa credit cards. The credit card service charge is 3%.
15 Received payment in full from Vinje Inc. on the amount due.
25 Received payment in full from Rath Co. on amount due.

Instructions
(a) Journalize the October transactions and the October 31 adjusting entry for accrued interest receivable.
(b) Enter the balances at October 1 in the receivable accounts and post the entries to all of the receivable accounts. (Use T accounts.)
(c) Show the balance sheet presentation of the receivable accounts at October 31.

(b) A/R bal.　$ 5,600
(c) Tot.
　　receivables $15,868

*Calculate and interpret
various ratios.*
(SO 7, 8)

P8-9B Presented here is basic financial information from the 2004 annual reports of Intel and Advanced Micro Devices (AMD), the two primary manufacturers of silicon chips for personal computers.

(in millions)	Intel	AMD
Sales	$34,209	$3,924.3
Allowance for doubtful accounts, Jan. 1	55	20.7
Allowance for doubtful accounts, Dec. 31	43	17.8
Accounts receivable balance (gross), Jan. 1	3,015	585.5
Accounts receivable balance (gross), Dec. 31	3,042	737.4

Instructions

Calculate the receivables turnover ratio and average collection period for both companies. Comment on the difference in their collection experiences.

Problems: Set C

Visit the book's website at **www.wiley.com/college/kimmel** and choose the Student Companion site to access Problem Set C.

Comprehensive Problem

CP8 Mulder Corporation's balance sheet at December 31, 2006, is presented below.

MULDER CORPORATION
Balance Sheet
December 31, 2006

Cash	$13,100	Accounts payable	$ 8,750
Accounts receivable	19,780	Common stock	20,000
Allowance for doubtful accounts	(1,000)	Retained earnings	12,530
Merchandise inventory	9,400		$41,280
	$41,280		

During January 2007, the following transactions occurred. Mulder uses the perpetual inventory method.

Jan. 1   Mulder accepted a 4-month, 12% note from Alien Company in payment of Alien's $1,000 account.
  3   Mulder wrote off as uncollectible the accounts of Ex Corporation ($450) and Files Company ($230).
  8   Mulder purchased $17,200 of inventory on account.
  11   Mulder sold for $25,000 on account inventory that cost $15,000.
  15   Mulder sold inventory that cost $600 to Ben Borke for $1,000. Borke charged this amount on his Visa First Bank card. The service fee charged Mulder by First Bank is 3%.
  17   Mulder collected $21,900 from customers on account.
  21   Mulder paid $16,300 on accounts payable.
  24   Mulder received payment in full ($230) from Files Company on the account written off on January 3.
  27   Mulder purchased advertising supplies for $1,400 cash.
  31   Mulder paid other operating expenses, $4,218.

Adjustment data:

1. Interest is recorded for the month on the note from January 1.
2. Bad debts are expected to be 6% of the January 31, 2007, accounts receivable.
3. A count of advertising supplies on January 31, 2007, reveals that $560 remains unused.
4. The income tax rate is 30%. (*Hint:* Prepare the income statement up to "Income before taxes" and multiply by 30% to compute the amount.)

Instructions

(You may want to set up T accounts to determine ending balances.)
(a) Prepare journal entries for the transactions listed above and adjusting entries.

(b) Prepare an adjusted trial balance at January 31, 2007.
(c) Prepare an income statement and a retained earnings statement for the month ending January 31, 2007, and a classified balance sheet as of January 31, 2007.

Continuing Cookie Chronicle

(*Note:* This is a Continuation of the Cookie Chronicle from Chapters 1 through 7.)

CCC8 One of Natalie's friends, Curtis Lesperance, runs a coffee shop where he sells specialty coffees and prepares and sells muffins and cookies. He is eager to buy one of Natalie's fine European mixers, which would enable him to make larger batches of muffins and cookies. However, Curtis cannot afford to pay for the mixer for at least 30 days. He asks Natalie if she would be willing to sell him the mixer on credit.

Natalie comes to you for advice and asks the following questions.

1. "Curtis has provided me with a set of his most recent financial statements. What calculations should I do with the data from these statements, and what questions should I ask him after I have analyzed the statements? How will this information help me decide if I should extend credit to Curtis?"
2. "Is there an alternative other than extending credit to Curtis for 30 days?"
3. "I am thinking seriously about permitting my customers to use credit cards. What are some of the advantages and disadvantages of letting my customers pay by credit card?"

The following transactions occurred in June through August.

June 1	After much thought, Natalie sells a mixer to Curtis on credit, terms n/30, for $1,025 (cost of mixer $566).
2	Natalie meets with the bank manager and arranges to get access to a credit card account. The terms of credit card transactions are 3% of the sales transactions and a monthly equipment rental charge of $75.
30	Natalie teaches 12 classes in June. Seven classes were paid for in cash, $875; the other five classes were paid for by credit card, $750.
30	Natalie receives and reconciles her bank statement. She makes sure that the bank has correctly processed the monthly $75 charge for the rental of the credit card equipment and the 3% fee on the credit card transactions.
30	Curtis calls Natalie. He is unable to pay the amount outstanding for another month, so he signs a one-month, 8.25% note receivable.
July 15	Natalie sells a mixer to a friend of Curtis's. The friend pays $1,025 for the mixer by credit card (cost of mixer $566).
30	Natalie teaches 15 classes in July. Eight classes are paid for in cash, $1,000; seven classes are paid for by credit card, $1,050.
31	Natalie reconciles her bank statement and makes sure the bank has recorded the correct amounts for the rental of the credit card equipment and the credit card sales.
31	Curtis calls Natalie. He cannot pay today but hopes to have a check for her at the end of the week. Natalie prepares the appropriate journal entry.
Aug. 10	Curtis calls again and promises to pay at the end of August, including interest for 2 months.
31	Natalie receives a check from Curtis in payment of his balance plus interest outstanding.

Instructions
(a) Answer Natalie's questions.
(b) Prepare journal entries for the transactions that occurred in June, July, and August.

Financial Reporting and Analysis

FINANCIAL REPORTING PROBLEM: *Tootsie Roll Industries*

BYP8-1   Refer to the financial statements of Tootsie Roll Industries and the accompanying notes to its financial statements in Appendix A.

Instructions

(a) Calculate the receivables turnover ratio and average collection period for 2004.
(b) Did Tootsie Roll have any potentially significant credit risks in 2004? (*Hint:* Review Note 9 to the financial statements.)
(c) What conclusions can you draw from the information in parts (a) and (b)?

COMPARATIVE ANALYSIS PROBLEM: *Tootsie Roll vs. Hershey Foods*

BYP8-2   The financial statements of Hershey Foods are presented in Appendix B, following the financial statements for Tootsie Roll in Appendix A.

Instructions

(a) Based on the information contained in these financial statements, compute the following 2004 values for each company.
   (1) Receivables turnover ratio. (Assume all sales were credit sales.)
   (2) Average collection period for receivables.
(b) What conclusions concerning the management of accounts receivable can be drawn from these data?

RESEARCH CASE

BYP8-3   The February 21, 2005, issue of *Business Week* includes an article by Amey Stone titled "How Banks Pretty up the Profit Picture."

Instructions

Read the article and answer the following questions.
(a) According to the article, what was one way that banks increased their net income in 2004? Why does the author think that this is a problem?
(b) What evidence did banks provide to justify their actions?
(c) According to the author, what problems do the banks' actions pose for investors?

INTERPRETING FINANCIAL STATEMENTS

BYP8-4   The information below and the notes on page 414 are from the 2004 financial statements and accompanying notes of The Scotts Company, a major manufacturer of lawn-care products.

(in millions)	2004	2003
Accounts receivable	$ 321.4	$ 319.5
Allowance for uncollectible accounts	29.0	29.0
Sales	2,037.9	1,887.7
Total current assets	830.3	812.6

Instructions

Answer each of the following questions.
(a) Calculate the receivables turnover ratio and average collection period for 2004 for the company.
(b) Is accounts receivable a material component of the company's total current assets?
(c) Scotts sells seasonal products. How might this affect the accuracy of your answer to part (a)?

THE SCOTTS COMPANY
Notes to the Financial Statements

Note 17. Concentrations of Credit Risk

Financial instruments which potentially subject the Company to concentration of credit risk consist principally of trade accounts receivable. The Company sells its consumer products to a wide variety of retailers, including mass merchandisers, home centers, independent hardware stores, nurseries, garden outlets, warehouse clubs and local and regional chains. Professional products are sold to commercial nurseries, greenhouses, landscape services, and growers of specialty agriculture crops.

At September 30, 2004, 71% of the Company's accounts receivable was due in North America, with 6% related to on-going litigation documented in Note 16 to the Consolidated Financial Statements. Approximately 84% of the North American accounts receivable was generated from the Company's consumer business. The most significant concentration of receivables within the North American consumer business was from our top 3 customers, which accounted for 68% of the total.

The remaining 16% of North American accounts receivable was generated from customers of Scotts LawnService and North American Professional businesses. Nearly all of the accounts receivable for the North America Professional business at September 30, 2004 were due from distributors.

The 29% of accounts receivable generated outside of North America was due from retailers, distributors, nurseries and growers. No concentrations of customers or individual customers within this group account for more than 10% of the Company's accounts receivable balance at September 30, 2004.

At September 30, 2004, the Company's concentrations of credit risk were similar to those existing at September 30, 2003.

The Company's two largest customers accounted for the following percentage of net sales in each respective period:

	Largest Customer	2nd Largest Customer
2004	25.9%	13.3%
2003	24.8%	13.9%
2002	25.8%	13.2%

Sales to the Company's two largest customers are reported within Scotts' North America segment. No other customers accounted for more that 10% of fiscal 2004, 2003 or 2002 net sales.

(d) Evaluate the credit risk of Scotts' concentrated receivables.
(e) Comment on the informational value of Scotts' Note 17 on concentrations of credit risk.

BYP8-5 Art World Industries, Inc., was incorporated in 1986 in Delaware, although it is located in Los Angeles. The company prints, publishes, and sells limited-edition graphics and reproductive prints in the wholesale market.

The company's balance sheet at the end of a recent year showed an allowance for doubtful accounts of $175,477. The allowance was set up against certain Japanese accounts receivable that average more than one year in age. The Japanese acknowledge the amount due, but with the slow economy in Japan, they lack the resources to pay at this time.

Instructions
(a) Which method of accounting for uncollectible accounts does Art World Industries use?
(b) Explain the difference between the direct write-off and percentage of receivables methods. Based on Art World's disclosure above, what important factor would you have

to consider in arriving at appropriate percentages to apply for the percentage of receivables method?

(c) What are the implications for a company's receivables management of selling its products internationally?

FINANCIAL ANALYSIS ON THE WEB

BYP8-6 *Purpose:* To learn more about factoring from a website that provides factoring services.

Address: **www.invoicefinancial.com** (or go to **www.wiley.com/college/kimmel**)

Instructions
Go to the website and answer the following questions.
(a) What are some of the benefits of factoring?
(b) What amount of accounts receivable are factored each year?
(c) What is the range of the percentages of the typical discount rate?
(d) If a company factors its receivables, what percentage of the value of the receivables can it expect to receive from the factor in the form of cash, and how quickly will it receive the cash?

Critical Thinking

DECISION MAKING ACROSS THE ORGANIZATION

BYP8-7 Rae and Rob Tillman own Glad Rags. From its inception Glad Rags has sold merchandise on either a cash or credit basis, but no credit cards have been accepted. During the past several months, the Tillmans have begun to question their credit-sales policies. First, they have lost some sales because of their refusal to accept credit cards. Second, representatives of two metropolitan banks have convinced them to accept their national credit cards. One bank, City National Bank, has stated that (1) its credit card fee is 4% and (2) it pays the retailer 96 cents on each $1 of sales within 3 days of receiving the credit card billings.

The Tillmans decide that they should determine the cost of carrying their own credit sales. From the accounting records of the past 3 years they accumulate these data:

	2007	2006	2005
Net credit sales	$520,000	$580,000	$430,000
Collection agency fees for slow-paying customers	2,900	2,600	1,600
Salary of part-time accounts receivable clerk	4,400	4,400	4,400

Credit and collection expenses as a percentage of net credit sales are as follows: uncollectible accounts 1.6%, billing and mailing costs .5%, and credit investigation fee on new customers .2%.

Rae and Rob also determine that the average accounts receivable balance outstanding during the year is 5% of net credit sales. The Tillmans estimate that they could earn an average of 10% annually on cash invested in other business opportunities.

Instructions
With the class divided into groups, answer the following.
(a) Prepare a tabulation for each year showing total credit and collection expenses in dollars and as a percentage of net credit sales.
(b) Determine the net credit and collection expenses in dollars and as a percentage of sales after considering the revenue not earned from other investment opportunities. (*Note:* The income lost on the cash held by the bank for 3 days is considered to be immaterial.)
(c) Discuss both the financial and nonfinancial factors that are relevant to the decision.

COMMUNICATION ACTIVITY

BYP8-8 Home Fibers Corporation is a recently formed business selling the "World's Best Doormat." The corporation is selling doormats faster than Home Fibers can make them. It has been selling the product on a credit basis, telling customers to "pay when they can." Oddly, even though sales are tremendous, the company is having trouble paying its bills.

Instructions

Write a memo to the president of Home Fibers Corporation discussing these questions:
(a) What steps should be taken to improve the company's ability to pay its bills?
(b) What accounting steps should be taken to measure its success in improving collections and in recording its collection success?
(c) If the corporation is still unable to pay its bills, what additional steps can be taken with its receivables to ease its liquidity problems?

ETHICS CASE

BYP8-9 The controller of Rojas Corporation believes that the company's yearly allowance for doubtful accounts should be 2% of net credit sales. The president of Rojas Corporation, nervous that the stockholders might expect the company to sustain its 10% growth rate, suggests that the controller increase the allowance for doubtful accounts to 4%. The president thinks that the lower net income, which reflects a 6% growth rate, will be a more sustainable rate for Rojas Corporation.

Instructions

(a) Who are the stakeholders in this case?
(b) Does the president's request pose an ethical dilemma for the controller?
(c) Should the controller be concerned with Rojas Corporation's growth rate in estimating the allowance? Explain your answer.

Answers to Business Insight and Accounting across the Organization Questions

p. 379

Q: When would it be appropriate for a company to lower its allowance for doubtful accounts as a percentage of its receivables?

A: It would be appropriate for a company to lower its allowance for doubtful accounts as a percentage of receivables if the company's collection experience had improved, or was expected to improve, and therefore the company expected lower defaults as a percentage of receivables.

p. 382

Q: How would reported net income likely differ during the first year of this promotion if Mitsubishi used the direct write-off method versus the allowance method?

A: Under the direct write-off method, Mitsubishi would not record bad debt expense until a customer actually defaulted on a loan. Under the allowance method, Mitsubishi would estimate how many of its loans would default rather than waiting until they actually default. For Mitsubishi, the direct write-off method would have resulted in higher net income during the first year of the promotion.

p. 386

Q: Rather than refusing to ship to Kmart, what could suppliers have done to protect their interests?

A: Suppliers could have demanded cash payment upon delivery, no longer offering Kmart the option of purchasing on credit.

p. 392

Q: What factors should management consider in deciding whether to factor its receivables?

A: Management must prepare a cash budget and evaluate its projected cash needs. If it projects a cash deficiency, it should first pursue more traditional bank financing, since it tends to be less expensive than factoring. If traditional bank financing is not available, management could pursue factoring. If carefully structured, a factoring arrangement can be quite cost-effective since it can enable the company to outsource much of its billing and collection activities.

Answer to Tootsie Roll Review It Question 1, p. 379

Tootsie Roll reports two types of receivables on its balance sheet: Accounts receivable trade, and Other receivables. Since Tootsie Roll's balance sheet reports allowance amounts for receivables, we know that Tootsie Roll uses the allowance method rather than the direct write-off method.

Answers to Self-Study Questions

1. c   2. a   3. c   4. d   5. c   6. b   7. d   8. a   9. c
10. c   11. a

REMEMBER TO GO BACK TO THE NAVIGATOR BOX ON THE CHAPTER-OPENING PAGE AND CHECK OFF YOUR COMPLETED WORK.

CHAPTER 9

Reporting and Analyzing Long-Lived Assets

STUDY OBJECTIVES

After studying this chapter,
you should be able to:

1 Describe how the cost principle applies to plant assets.

2 Explain the concept of depreciation.

3 Compute periodic depreciation using the straight-line method, and contrast its expense pattern with those of other methods.

4 Describe the procedure for revising periodic depreciation.

5 Explain how to account for the disposal of plant assets.

6 Describe methods for evaluating the use of plant assets.

7 Identify the basic issues related to reporting intangible assets.

8 Indicate how long-lived assets are reported on the balance sheet.

THE NAVIGATOR

THE NAVIGATOR

- Scan *Study Objectives* ⬭
- Read *Feature Story* ⬭
- Read *Preview* ⬭
- Read text and answer *Before You Go On*
  p. 425 ⬭   p. 428 ⬭   p. 433 ⬭
  p. 436 ⬭   p. 440 ⬭   p. 446 ⬭
- Work *Using the Decision Toolkit* ⬭
- Review *Summary of Study Objectives* ⬭
- Work *Demonstration Problems* ⬭
- Answer *Self-Study Questions* ⬭
- Complete *Assignments* ⬭

FEATURE STORY

A Tale of Two Airlines

So, you're interested in starting a new business. Have you thought about the airline industry? Your only experience with airlines is as a passenger? Don't let that stop you. Today the most profitable airlines in the industry are not well-known majors like American Airlines and United. In fact, most giant, old airlines are either bankrupt or on the verge of bankruptcy. During 2004, five major airlines representing 24% of total U.S. capacity were operating under bankruptcy protection.

Not all airlines are hurting. The growth and profitability in the airline industry today is found at relative newcomers like Southwest Airlines and JetBlue. These and other new airlines compete primarily on ticket prices. During the most recent five years the low-fare airline market share has increased by 47%; the low-fare airlines now have over 22% of U.S. airline capacity.

Southwest was the first upstart to make it big. It did so by taking a different approach. It bought small, new, fuel-efficient planes. Also, instead of the "hub-and-spoke" approach used by the majors, it opted for direct, short hop, no frills flights. It was all about controlling costs—getting the most out of its efficient new planes.

Other upstarts, such as Valujet, chose a different approach. They bought planes that were 20 to 30

years old (known in the industry as *zombies*). By buying used planes Valujet was able to add one or two planes a month to its fleet—an unheard of expansion. Valujet started with a $3.4 million investment and grew to be worth $630 million in its first three years.

But a terrible crash of a Valujet aircraft focused the spotlight on its strategy of using old planes. Although the cause of the crash appears to have been unrelated to the age of its planes, in the aftermath of the crash Valujet struggled to survive under the weight of government scrutiny and lack of customer confidence. In the face of continuing financial problems and customer skepticism, Valujet merged with AirWays Corp. and took the name of its airline, AirTran Airways. Today AirTran is one of the most profitable airlines in the industry.

But with fuel costs at record high levels, AirTran is no longer in the market for old planes. Nobody is. In fact, the old Boeing 727, which until very recently was a mainstay of nearly every airline, is no longer used for passenger flights because it couldn't be operated efficiently. Today success in the airline business comes from owning the newest and most efficient equipment, and knowing how to get the most out of it.

On the World Wide Web
Southwest Airlines:
www.southwest.com
AirTran Airways: www.airtran.com
JetBlue Airways: www.jetblue.com

PREVIEW OF CHAPTER 9

Was Valujet's approach to buying equipment really the "right formula," or was it a recipe for disaster? For airlines and many other companies, making the right decisions regarding long-lived assets is critical because these assets represent huge investments. Management must make many ongoing decisions about long-lived assets—what assets to acquire and when, how to finance them, how to account for them, and when to dispose of them.

In this chapter we address these and other issues surrounding long-lived assets. The discussion is in two parts: plant assets and intangible assets. *Plant assets* are the property, plant, and equipment (physical assets) that commonly come to mind when we think of what a company owns. Companies also have many important *intangible assets*. These assets, such as copyrights and patents, lack physical substance but can be extremely valuable and vital to a company's success.

The content and organization of this chapter are as follows.

REPORTING AND ANALYZING LONG-LIVED ASSETS

Plant Assets

- Determining the cost of plant assets
- Accounting for plant assets
- Analyzing plant assets

Intangible Assets

- Accounting for intangible assets
- Types of intangible assets
- Financial statement presentation of long-lived assets

THE NAVIGATOR

SECTION ONE
PLANT ASSETS

Plant assets are resources that have physical substance (a definite size and shape), are used in the operations of a business, and are not intended for sale to customers. They are called various names—*property, plant, and equipment; plant and equipment;* and *fixed assets.* By whatever name, these assets are expected to provide services to the company for a number of years. Except for land, plant assets decline in service potential (value) over their useful lives.

Plant assets are critical to a company's success because they determine the company's capacity and therefore its ability to satisfy customers. With too few planes, for example, AirTran and Southwest Airlines would lose customers to their competitors. But with too many planes, they would be flying with empty seats. Management must constantly monitor its needs and acquire assets accordingly. Failure to do so results in lost business opportunities or inefficient use of existing assets and is likely to show up eventually in poor financial results.

It is important for a company to (1) keep assets in good operating condition, (2) replace worn-out or outdated assets, and (3) expand its productive assets as needed. The decline of rail travel in the United States can be traced in part to the failure of railroad companies to maintain and update their assets. Conversely, the growth of air travel in this country can be attributed in part to the general willingness of airline companies to follow these essential guidelines.

For many companies, investments in plant assets are substantial. Illustration 9-1 shows the percentages of plant assets in relation to total assets in various companies.

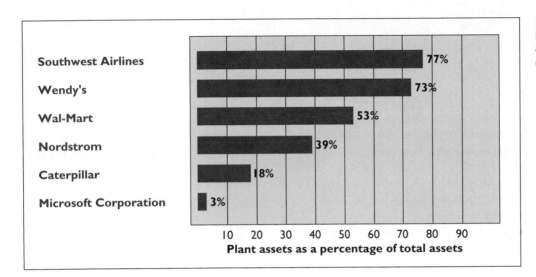

Illustration 9-1
Percentages of plant assets in relation to total assets

Determining the Cost of Plant Assets

The **cost principle** requires that companies record plant assets at cost. Thus, AirTran and Southwest Airlines record their planes at cost. **Cost consists of all expenditures necessary to acquire an asset and make it ready for its intended use.** For example, the purchase price, freight costs paid by the purchaser, and installation costs are all part of the cost of factory machinery.

Determining which costs to include in a plant asset account and which costs not to include is very important. If a cost is not included in a plant asset account, then it must be expensed immediately. Such costs are referred to as revenue expenditures. On the other hand, costs that are not expensed immediately but are instead included in a plant asset account are referred to as capital expenditures.

This distinction is important; it has immediate, and often material, implications for the income statement. Some companies, in order to boost current income, have improperly capitalized expenditures that they should have expensed. For example, suppose that a company improperly capitalizes to a building account $1,000 of maintenance costs incurred at the end of the year. (That is, the costs are included in the asset account Buildings rather than being expensed immediately.) If the company is allocating the cost of the building as an expense (depreciating it) over a 40-year life, then the maintenance cost of $1,000 will be incorrectly spread across 40 years instead of being expensed in the current year. As a result, the company will understate current-year expenses by $1,000, and will overstate current-year income by $1,000. Thus, determining which costs to capitalize and which to expense is very important.

STUDY OBJECTIVE
1
Describe how the cost principle applies to plant assets.

 **International Note**

The United Kingdom is flexible regarding asset valuation. Companies revalue to fair value when they believe this information is more relevant. Switzerland and the Netherlands also permit revaluations.

Cost is measured by the cash paid in a cash transaction or by the **cash equivalent price** paid when companies use noncash assets in payment. **The cash equivalent price is equal to the fair market value of the asset given up or the fair market value of the asset received, whichever is more clearly determinable.** Once cost is established, it becomes the basis of accounting for the plant asset over its useful life. Current market value is not used to increase the recorded cost after acquisition. We explain the application of the cost principle to each of the major classes of plant assets in the following sections.

Business Insight
Ethics Perspective

In what has been one of the largest accounting frauds in history, WorldCom announced the discovery of $7 billion in expenses improperly booked as capital expenditures, a gimmick that boosted profit over a five-quarter period. If these expenses had been booked properly, WorldCom, at one time one of the biggest stock market stars, would have reported losses. Instead, WorldCom reported billions of dollars of profit. As a result of these problems, WorldCom declared bankruptcy, to the dismay of its investors and creditors.

   How did the capitalization of expenses increase WorldCom's income?

LAND

Companies often use land as a building site for a manufacturing plant or office site. The cost of land includes (1) the cash purchase price, (2) closing costs such as title and attorney's fees, (3) real estate brokers' commissions, and (4) accrued property taxes and other liens on the land assumed by the purchaser. For example, if the cash price is $50,000 and the purchaser agrees to pay accrued taxes of $5,000, the cost of the land is $55,000.

All necessary costs incurred in making land **ready for its intended use** increase (debit) the Land account. When a company acquires vacant land, its cost includes expenditures for clearing, draining, filling, and grading. If the land has a building on it that must be removed to make the site suitable for construction of a new building, the company includes all demolition and removal costs, less any proceeds from salvaged materials, in the Land account.

To illustrate, assume that Hayes Manufacturing Company acquires real estate at a cash cost of $100,000. The property contains an old warehouse that is razed at a net cost of $6,000 ($7,500 in costs less $1,500 proceeds from salvaged materials). Additional expenditures are for the attorney's fee $1,000 and the real estate broker's commission $8,000. Given these factors, the cost of the land is $115,000, computed as shown in Illustration 9-2.

Illustration 9-2
Computation of cost of land

Land	
Cash price of property	$ 100,000
Net removal cost of warehouse	6,000
Attorney's fee	1,000
Real estate broker's commission	8,000
Cost of land	**$115,000**

When Hayes records the acquisition, it debits Land for $115,000 and credits Cash for $115,000.

LAND IMPROVEMENTS

Land improvements are structural additions made to land, such as driveways, parking lots, fences, landscaping, and underground sprinklers. The cost of land improvements includes all expenditures necessary to make the improvements ready for their intended use. For example, the cost of a new company parking lot includes the amount paid for paving, fencing, and lighting. Thus the company would debit the total of all of these costs to Land Improvements.

Land improvements have limited useful lives, and their maintenance and replacement are the responsibility of the company. Because of their limited useful life, companies expense (depreciate) the cost of land improvements over their useful lives.

BUILDINGS

Buildings are facilities used in operations, such as stores, offices, factories, warehouses, and airplane hangers. Companies charge to the Buildings account all necessary expenditures relating to the purchase or construction of a building. When a building is **purchased**, such costs include the purchase price, closing costs (attorney's fees, title insurance, etc.), and real estate broker's commission. Costs to make the building ready for its intended use consist of expenditures for remodeling rooms and offices and replacing or repairing the roof, floors, electrical wiring, and plumbing. When a new building is **constructed**, its cost consists of the contract price plus payments made by the owner for architects' fees, building permits, and excavation costs.

In addition, companies charge certain interest costs to the cost of a building: Interest costs incurred to finance a construction project are included in the cost of the asset when a significant period of time is required to get the asset ready for use. In these circumstances, interest costs are considered as necessary as materials and labor. However, the inclusion of interest costs in the cost of a constructed building is **limited to interest costs incurred during the construction period**. When construction has been completed, subsequent interest payments on funds borrowed to finance the construction are recorded as increases (debits) to Interest Expense.

EQUIPMENT

Equipment includes assets used in operations, such as store check-out counters, office furniture, factory machinery, delivery trucks, and airplanes. The cost of equipment consists of the cash purchase price, sales taxes, freight charges, and insurance during transit paid by the purchaser. It also includes expenditures required in assembling, installing, and testing the unit. However, companies treat as expenses the costs of motor vehicle licenses and accident insurance on company trucks and cars. Such items are annual recurring expenditures and do not benefit future periods. Two criteria apply in determining the cost of equipment: (1) the frequency of the cost—one time or recurring, and (2) the benefit period—the life of the asset or one year.

To illustrate, assume that Lenard Company purchases a delivery truck at a cash price of $22,000. Related expenditures are sales taxes $1,320, painting and lettering $500, motor vehicle license $80, and a three-year accident insurance policy $1,600. The cost of the delivery truck is $23,820, computed as shown in Illustration 9-3 on the next page.

Illustration 9-3
Computation of cost of
delivery truck

Delivery Truck	
Cash price	$ 22,000
Sales taxes	1,320
Painting and lettering	500
Cost of delivery truck	**$23,820**

Lenard treats the cost of a motor vehicle license as an expense and the cost of an insurance policy as a prepaid asset. Thus, the company records the purchase of the truck and related expenditures as follows.

A = L + SE	
+23,820	
	−80 Exp
+1,600	
−25,500	

Cash Flows
−25,500

Delivery Truck	23,820	
License Expense	80	
Prepaid Insurance	1,600	
Cash		25,500
(To record purchase of delivery truck and related expenditures)		

For another example, assume Merten Company purchases factory machinery at a cash price of $50,000. Related expenditures are sales taxes $3,000, insurance during shipping $500, and installation and testing $1,000. The cost of the factory machinery is $54,500, computed as in Illustration 9-4.

Illustration 9-4
Computation of cost of
factory machinery

Factory Machinery	
Cash price	$ 50,000
Sales taxes	3,000
Insurance during shipping	500
Installation and testing	1,000
Cost of factory machinery	**$54,500**

Thus, Merten records the purchase and related expenditures as follows.

A = L + SE	
+54,500	
−54,500	

Cash Flows
−54,500

Factory Machinery	54,500	
Cash		54,500
(To record purchase of factory machinery and related expenditures)		

TO BUY OR LEASE?

In this chapter we focus on purchased assets, but we want to expose you briefly to an alternative—leasing. In a lease, a party that owns an asset (the **lessor**) agrees to allow another party (the **lessee**) to use the asset for an agreed period of time at an agreed price. In many industries leasing is quite common. For example, one-third of heavy-duty commercial trucks are leased.

Some advantages of leasing an asset versus purchasing it are:

1. **Reduced risk of obsolescence.** Frequently, lease terms allow the party using the asset (the lessee) to exchange the asset for a more modern one if it becomes outdated. This is much easier than trying to sell an obsolete asset.

2. **Little or no down payment.**   To purchase an asset, most companies must borrow money, which usually requires a down payment of at least 20%. Leasing an asset requires little or no down payment.

3. **Shared tax advantages.**   Startup companies typically do not make much money in their early years, and so they have little need for the tax deductions available from owning an asset. In a lease, the lessor gets the tax advantage because it owns the asset. It often will pass these tax savings on to the lessee in the form of lower lease payments.

4. **Assets and liabilities not reported.**   Many companies prefer to keep assets and especially liabilities off their books. Certain types of leases, called operating leases, allow the lessee to account for the transaction as a rental, with neither an asset nor a liability recorded.

Airlines often choose to lease many of their airplanes in long-term lease agreements. In its 2004 financial statements, Southwest Airlines stated that it leased 88 of its 417 planes under operating leases. Because operating leases are accounted for as a rental, these 88 planes did not show up on its balance sheet.

Under another type of lease, a capital lease, companies show both the asset and the liability on the balance sheet. The lessee under a capital lease, accounts for long-term lease agreements in a way that is very similar to purchases: The lessee shows the leased item as an asset on its balance sheet, and the obligation owed to the lessor as a liability. The lessee depreciates the leased asset in a manner similar to purchased assets. Southwest Airlines' balance sheet accounts for about 0.5% of the company's property, plant, and equipment as capital leases. We discuss leasing further in Chapter 10 on liabilities.

Accounting across the Organization

Leasing is big business for U.S. companies. For example, business investment in equipment in 2004 totaled $709 billion. Leasing accounted for about 31% of all business investment ($218 billion).

Who does the most leasing? Interestingly major banks, such as Continental Bank, J.P. Morgan Leasing, and US Bancorp Equipment Finance, are the major lessors. Also, many companies have established separate leasing companies, such as Boeing Capital Corporation, Dell Financial Services, and John Deere Capital Corporation. And, as an excellent example of the magnitude of leasing, leased planes account for nearly 40% of the U.S. fleet of commercial airlines. In addition, leasing is becoming increasingly common in the hotel industry. Marriott, Hilton, and InterContinental are increasingly choosing to lease hotels that are owned by someone else.

 Why might airline managers choose to lease rather than purchase their planes?

BEFORE YOU GO ON . . .

▶ **Review It**

1. What are plant assets? What are the major classes of plant assets? At what value should companies record plant assets?

2. What are revenue expenditures? What are capital expenditures?

3. What are the primary advantages of leasing?

▶ **Do It**

Assume that a company purchases a delivery truck for $15,000 cash plus sales taxes of $900 and delivery costs of $500. The buyer also pays $200 for painting and lettering, $600 for an annual insurance policy, and $80 for a motor vehicle license. Explain how the company should account for each of these costs.

Action Plan

• Identify expenditures made in order to get delivery equipment ready for its intended use.

• Expense operating costs incurred during the useful life of the equipment.

Solution

The first four payments ($15,000, $900, $500, and $200) are expenditures necessary to make the truck ready for its intended use. Thus, the cost of the truck is $16,600. The payments for insurance and the license are operating expenses incurred during the useful life of the asset.

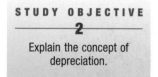

Accounting for Plant Assets

DEPRECIATION

STUDY OBJECTIVE

2

Explain the concept of depreciation.

As explained in Chapter 4, **depreciation is the process of allocating to expense the cost of a plant asset over its useful (service) life in a rational and systematic manner**. Such cost allocation is designed to properly match expenses with revenues. (See Illustration 9-5.)

Illustration 9-5
Depreciation as an allocation concept

Depreciation Tutorial

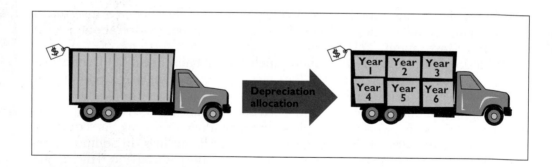

Depreciation affects the balance sheet through accumulated depreciation, which companies report as a deduction from plant assets. It affects the income statement through depreciation expense.

It is important to understand that **depreciation is a cost allocation process, not an asset valuation process**. No attempt is made to measure the change in an asset's market value during ownership. Thus, the **book value**—cost less accumulated depreciation—of a plant asset may differ significantly from its **market value**. In fact, if an asset is fully depreciated, it can have zero book value but still have a significant market value.

Helpful Hint Remember that depreciation is the process of *allocating cost* over the useful life of an asset. It is not a measure of value.

Depreciation applies to **three classes of plant assets**: land improvements, buildings, and equipment. Each of these classes is considered to be a **depreciable asset** because the usefulness to the company and the revenue-producing ability of each class decline over the asset's useful life. Depreciation **does not**

apply to land because its usefulness and revenue-producing ability generally remain intact as long as the land is owned. In fact, in many cases, the usefulness of land increases over time because of the scarcity of good sites. Thus, **land is not a depreciable asset**.

During a depreciable asset's useful life its revenue-producing ability declines because of wear and tear. A delivery truck that has been driven 100,000 miles will be less useful to a company than one driven only 800 miles.

A decline in revenue-producing ability may also occur because of obsolescence. **Obsolescence** is the process by which an asset becomes out of date before it physically wears out. The rerouting of major airlines from Chicago's Midway Airport to Chicago-O'Hare International Airport because Midway's runways were too short for giant jets is an example. Similarly, many companies replace their computers long before they originally planned to do so because improvements in new computers make their old computers obsolete.

Recognizing depreciation for an asset does not result in the accumulation of cash for replacement of the asset. The balance in Accumulated Depreciation represents the total amount of the asset's cost that the company has charged to expense to date; **it is not a cash fund**.

Helpful Hint Land does not depreciate because it does not wear out.

Factors in Computing Depreciation

Three factors affect the computation of depreciation, as shown in Illustration 9-6.

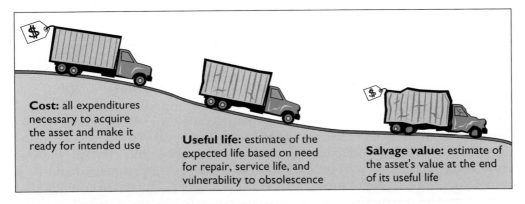

Illustration 9-6 Three factors in computing depreciation

Cost: all expenditures necessary to acquire the asset and make it ready for intended use

Useful life: estimate of the expected life based on need for repair, service life, and vulnerability to obsolescence

Salvage value: estimate of the asset's value at the end of its useful life

1. **Cost.** Earlier in the chapter we explained the considerations that affect the cost of a depreciable asset. Remember that companies record plant assets at cost, in accordance with the cost principle.

2. **Useful life.** Useful life is an estimate of the expected productive life, also called *service life*, of the asset for its owner. Useful life may be expressed in terms of time, units of activity (such as machine hours), or units of output. Useful life is an estimate. In making the estimate, management considers such factors as the intended use of the asset, repair and maintenance policies, and vulnerability of the asset to obsolescence. The company's past experience with similar assets is often helpful in deciding on expected useful life.

3. **Salvage value.** Salvage value is an estimate of the asset's value at the end of its useful life for its owner. Companies may base the value on the asset's worth as scrap or on its expected trade-in value. Like useful life, salvage value is an estimate. In making the estimate, management considers how it plans to dispose of the asset and its experience with similar assets.

BEFORE YOU GO ON . . .

▶ **Review It**

1. What is the relationship, if any, of depreciation to (a) cost allocation, (b) asset valuation, and (c) cash accumulation?
2. Explain the factors that affect the computation of depreciation.
3. What does Tootsie Roll use as the estimated useful life on its buildings? On its machinery and equipment? The answer to this question appears on page 471.

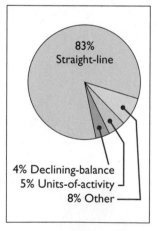

STUDY OBJECTIVE

3

Compute periodic depreciation using the straight-line method, and contrast its expense pattern with those of other methods.

Illustration 9-7 Use of depreciation methods in major U.S. companies

83% Straight-line

4% Declining-balance
5% Units-of-activity
8% Other

Depreciation Methods

Although a number of methods exist, depreciation is generally computed using one of three methods:

1. Straight-line
2. Declining-balance
3. Units-of-activity

Like the alternative inventory methods discussed in Chapter 6, each of these depreciation methods is acceptable under generally accepted accounting principles. Management selects the method it believes best measures an asset's contribution to revenue over its useful life. Once a company chooses a method, it should apply that method consistently over the useful life of the asset. Consistency enhances the comparability of financial statements.

Illustration 9-7 shows the distribution of the *primary* depreciation methods in 600 of the largest U.S. companies. Clearly, straight-line depreciation is the most widely used approach. In fact, because some companies use more than one method, **straight-line depreciation is used for some or all of the depreciation taken by more than 95% of U.S. companies.** For this reason, we illustrate procedures for straight-line depreciation and discuss the alternative depreciation approaches only at a conceptual level. This coverage introduces you to the basic idea of depreciation as an allocation concept without entangling you in too much procedural detail. (Also, note that many hand-held calculators are preprogrammed to perform the basic depreciation methods.) Details on the alternative approaches are presented in the appendix to this chapter (pages 449–451).

Our illustration of depreciation methods, both here and in the appendix, is based on the following data relating to a small delivery truck purchased by Bill's Pizzas on January 1, 2007.

Cost	$13,000
Expected salvage value	$1,000
Estimated useful life (in years)	5
Estimated useful life (in miles)	100,000

STRAIGHT-LINE. Under the straight-line method, companies expense an equal amount of depreciation each year of the asset's useful life. Management must choose the useful life of an asset based on its own expectations and experience.

To compute the annual depreciation expense, we divide depreciable cost by the estimated useful life. Depreciable cost represents the total amount subject to depreciation; it is calculated as the cost of the asset less its salvage value. Illustration 9-8 shows the computation of depreciation expense in the first year for Bill's Pizzas' delivery truck.

Illustration 9-8   Formula for straight-line method

Cost	−	Salvage Value	=	Depreciable Cost
$13,000	−	$1,000	=	$12,000

Depreciable Cost	÷	Useful Life (in years)	=	Depreciation Expense
$12,000	÷	5	=	**$2,400**

Alternatively, we can compute an annual *rate* at which the company depreciates the delivery truck. In this case, the rate is 20% (100% ÷ 5 years). When an annual rate is used under the straight-line method, the company applies the percentage rate to the depreciable cost of the asset, as shown in the **depreciation schedule** in Illustration 9-9.

Illustration 9-9
Straight-line depreciation schedule

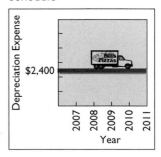

BILL'S PIZZAS

	Computation			Annual	End of Year	
Year	Depreciable Cost	×	Depreciation Rate	=	Depreciation Expense	Accumulated Depreciation	Book Value
2007	$12,000		20%		$ 2,400	$ 2,400	$10,600*
2008	12,000		20		2,400	4,800	8,200
2009	12,000		20		2,400	7,200	5,800
2010	12,000		20		2,400	9,600	3,400
2011	12,000		20		2,400	12,000	**1,000**
				Total	$12,000		

*$13,000 − $2,400

Note that the depreciation expense of $2,400 is the same each year. The book value at the end of the useful life is equal to the estimated $1,000 salvage value.

What happens when an asset is purchased **during** the year, rather than on January 1 as in our example? In that case, it is necessary to **prorate the annual depreciation** for the portion of a year used. If Bill's Pizzas had purchased the delivery truck on April 1, 2007, the company would use the truck for 9 months in 2007. The depreciation for 2007 would be $1,800 ($12,000 × 20% × $\frac{9}{12}$ of a year).

As indicated earlier, the straight-line method predominates in practice. For example, such large companies as Campbell Soup, Marriott, and General Mills use the straight-line method. It is simple to apply, and it matches expenses with revenues appropriately when the use of the asset is reasonably uniform throughout the service life. The types of assets that give equal benefits over useful life generally are those for which daily use does not affect productivity. Examples are office furniture and fixtures, buildings, warehouses, and garages for motor vehicles.

DECLINING-BALANCE.   The **declining-balance method** computes periodic depreciation using a declining book value. This method is called an **accelerated-depreciation method** because it results in more depreciation in the early years of an asset's life than does the straight-line approach. However, because the total amount of depreciation (the depreciable cost) taken over an asset's life is the same **no matter what approach** is used, the declining-balance method produces a decreasing annual depreciation expense over the asset's useful life. In early years declining-balance depreciation expense will exceed straight-line, but in later years it will be less than straight-line. Managers might choose an accelerated approach if they think that an asset's utility will decline quickly.

Companies can apply the declining-balance approach at different rates, which result in varying speeds of depreciation. A common declining-balance rate is double the straight-line rate. Using that rate, the method is referred to as the **double-declining-balance method**.

If we apply the double-declining-balance method to Bill's Pizzas' delivery truck, assuming a five-year life, we get the pattern of depreciation shown in Illustration 9-10. **The chapter's appendix, page 449, presents the computations behind these numbers.** Again, note that total depreciation over the life of the truck is $12,000, the depreciable cost.

Illustration 9-10
Declining-balance depreciation schedule

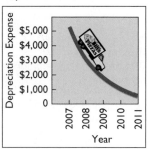

			End of Year	
		Annual		
		Depreciation	**Accumulated**	**Book**
Year		**Expense**	**Depreciation**	**Value**
2007		**$ 5,200**	$ 5,200	$ 7,800
2008		**3,120**	8,320	4,680
2009		**1,872**	10,192	2,808
2010		**1,123**	11,315	1,685
2011		**685**	12,000	**1,000**
	Total	$12,000		

BILL'S PIZZAS

UNITS-OF-ACTIVITY. As indicated earlier, useful life can be expressed in ways other than a time period. Under the **units-of-activity method**, useful life is expressed in terms of the total units of production or the use expected from the asset. The units-of-activity method is ideally suited to factory machinery: Companies can measure production in terms of units of output or in terms of machine hours used in operating the machinery. It is also possible to use the method for such items as delivery equipment (miles driven) and airplanes (hours in use). The units-of-activity method is generally not suitable for such assets as buildings or furniture because activity levels are difficult to measure for these assets.

Applying the units-of-activity method to the delivery truck owned by Bill's Pizzas, we first must know some basic information. Bill's expects to be able to drive the truck a total of 100,000 miles. Illustration 9-11 shows depreciation over the five-year life based on an assumed mileage pattern. **The chapter's appendix, pages 450–451, presents the computations used to arrive at these results.**

Illustration 9-11
Units-of-activity depreciation schedule

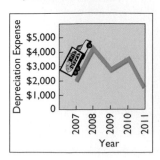

BILL'S PIZZAS

	Units of	**Annual**	End of Year	
	Activity	**Depreciation**	**Accumulated**	**Book**
Year	**(miles)**	**Expense**	**Depreciation**	**Value**
2007	15,000	**$ 1,800**	$ 1,800	$11,200
2008	30,000	**3,600**	5,400	7,600
2009	20,000	**2,400**	7,800	5,200
2010	25,000	**3,000**	10,800	2,200
2011	10,000	**1,200**	12,000	**1,000**
Total	100,000	$12,000		

As the name implies, under units-of-activity depreciation, the amount of depreciation is proportional to the activity that took place during that period. For example, the delivery truck was driven twice as many miles in 2008 as in 2007, and depreciation was exactly twice as much in 2008 as it was in 2007.

Management's Choice: Comparison of Methods

Illustration 9-12 compares annual and total depreciation expense for Bill's Pizzas under the three methods.

Year	Straight-Line	Declining-Balance	Units-of-Activity
2007	$ 2,400	$ 5,200	$ 1,800
2008	2,400	3,120	3,600
2009	2,400	1,872	2,400
2010	2,400	1,123	3,000
2011	2,400	685	1,200
	$12,000	$12,000	$12,000

Illustration 9-12
Comparison of depreciation methods

Periodic depreciation varies considerably among the methods, but **total depreciation is the same for the five-year period**. Each method is acceptable in accounting because each recognizes the decline in service potential of the asset in a rational and systematic manner. Illustration 9-13 graphs the depreciation expense pattern under each method.

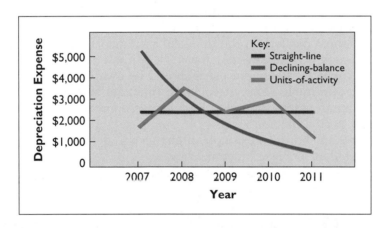

Illustration 9-13
Patterns of depreciation

Depreciation and Income Taxes

The Internal Revenue Service (IRS) allows corporate taxpayers to deduct depreciation expense when computing taxable income. However, the tax regulations of the IRS do not require the taxpayer to use the same depreciation method on the tax return that it uses in preparing financial statements.

Consequently, many large corporations use straight-line depreciation in their financial statements in order to maximize net income; at the same time they use a special accelerated-depreciation method on their tax returns in order to minimize their income taxes. For tax purposes, taxpayers must use on their tax returns either the straight-line method or a special accelerated-depreciation method called the **Modified Accelerated Cost Recovery System** (MACRS).

Helpful Hint Depreciation per GAAP is usually different from depreciation per IRS rules.

Depreciation Disclosure in the Notes

Companies must disclose the choice of depreciation method in their financial statements or in related notes that accompany the statements. Illustration 9-14 shows the "Property and equipment" notes from the financial statements of Southwest Airlines.

Illustration 9-14
Disclosure of depreciation policies

SOUTHWEST AIRLINES
Notes to the Financial Statements

Property and equipment Depreciation is provided by the straight-line method to estimated residual values over periods ranging from 20 to 25 years for flight equipment and 5 to 30 years for ground property and equipment once the asset is placed in service. Amortization of property under capital leases is on a straight-line basis over the lease term and is included in depreciation expense.

From this note we learn that Southwest Airlines uses the straight-line method to depreciate its planes over periods of 20 to 25 years.

Revising Periodic Depreciation

STUDY OBJECTIVE
4

Describe the procedure for revising periodic depreciation.

Management should periodically review annual depreciation expense. If wear and tear or obsolescence indicates that annual depreciation is either inadequate or excessive, the company should change the depreciation expense amount.

When a change in an estimate is required, the company makes the change in **current and future years but not to prior periods**. Thus, when making the change, the company (1) does not correct previously recorded depreciation expense, but (2) revises depreciation expense for current and future years. The rationale for this treatment is that continual restatement of prior periods would adversely affect users' confidence in financial statements.

Companies must disclose in the financial statements significant changes in estimates. Although a company may have a legitimate reason for changing an estimated life, financial statement users should be aware that some companies might change an estimate simply to achieve financial statement goals. For example, extending an asset's estimated life reduces depreciation expense and increases current period income.

Illustration 9-15 shows an example of changes in depreciation estimates for AirTran Airways that increased income.

Illustration 9-15
Disclosure of changes in depreciation estimates

AIR TRAN AIRWAYS
Notes to the Financial Statements

Note 1. Property and equipment Property and equipment is stated on the basis of cost. Flight equipment is depreciated to its salvage values using the straight-line method.

The estimated salvage values and depreciable lives are periodically reviewed for reasonableness, and revised if necessary. The Boeing 717 (B717) fleet has a salvage value of 10 percent. At July 1, 2001, we revised the useful lives on our B717 fleet, as outlined below, in order to more accurately reflect the estimated useful life of the aircraft:

	2001 Useful Life	2000 Useful Life
Airframes	30 years	25 years
Engines	30 years	25 years
Aircraft parts	30 years	5 years

The effect of this change for the year ended December 31, 2001, was to decrease our net loss by approximately $0.6 million, or $0.01 per share.

AirTran was operating at a loss at the time of these changes. Whether these changes are reasonable depends on the accuracy of the assumptions regarding these planes. Our Feature Story suggests that although many planes last a long time, safety concerns might ground many older planes.

BEFORE YOU GO ON . . .

▶ **Review It**

1. Why is depreciation an allocation concept rather than a valuation concept?
2. What is the formula for computing annual depreciation under the straight-line method?
3. How do the depreciation methods differ in their effects on annual depreciation over the useful life of an asset?
4. Are revisions of periodic depreciation made to prior periods? Explain.

▶ **Do It**

On January 1, 2007, Iron Mountain Ski Corporation purchased a new snow grooming machine for $50,000. The machine is estimated to have a 10-year life with a $2,000 salvage value. What journal entry would Iron Mountain Ski Corporation make at December 31, 2007, if it uses the straight-line method of depreciation?

Action Plan

• Calculate depreciable cost (Cost − Salvage value).
• Divide the depreciable cost by the asset's estimated useful life.

Solution

$$\text{Depreciation expense} = \frac{\text{Cost} - \text{Salvage value}}{} = \frac{\$50,000 - \$2,000}{} = \$4,800$$

Iron Mountain would record the first year's depreciation as follows:

Dec. 31	Depreciation Expense	4,800	
	Accumulated Depreciation—Machinery		4,800
	(To record annual depreciation on snow grooming machine)		

EXPENDITURES DURING USEFUL LIFE

During the useful life of a plant asset, a company may incur costs for ordinary repairs, additions, and improvements. Ordinary repairs are expenditures to maintain the operating efficiency and expected productive life of the unit. They usually are fairly small amounts that occur frequently throughout the service life. Examples are motor tune-ups and oil changes, the painting of buildings, and the replacing of worn-out gears on factory machinery. Ordinary repairs are debited to Repair (or Maintenance) Expense as incurred. Because they are immediately charged against revenues as an expense, these costs are **revenue expenditures**.

Additions and improvements are costs incurred to **increase** the operating efficiency, productive capacity, or expected useful life of the plant asset. These expenditures are usually material in amount and occur infrequently during the period of ownership. Expenditures for additions and improvements increase the company's investment in productive facilities and are generally debited to the plant asset affected. Thus, they are **capital expenditures**. The accounting for capital expenditures varies depending on the nature of the expenditure.

Northwest Airlines at one time spent $120 million to spruce up 40 DC9-30 jets. The improvements were designed to extend the lives of the planes, meet stricter government noise limits, and save money. The capital expenditure was expected to extend the life of the jets by 10 to 15 years and save about $560 million compared to the cost of buying new planes. The DC9 jets were, on average, 24 years old.

IMPAIRMENTS

As noted earlier, the book value of plant assets is rarely the same as the market value. In instances where the value of a plant asset declines substantially, its market value might fall materially below book value. This may happen because a machine has become obsolete, or the market for the product made by the machine has dried up or has become very competitive. A **permanent decline** in the market value of an asset is referred to as an impairment. So as not to overstate the asset on the books, the company writes the asset down to its new market value during the year in which the decline in value occurs. For example, AirTran recently announced a $28 million impairment loss on its DC9s and a $10.8 million impairment loss on its B737s. AirTran used appraisals and considered recent transactions and market trends involving similar aircraft in determining the fair market values.

In the past, some companies delayed recording losses on impairments until a year when it was "convenient" to do so—when the impact on the company's reported results was minimized. For example, if a company has record profits in one year, it can then afford to write down some of its bad assets without hurting its reported results too much. As discussed in Chapter 4, the practice of timing the recognition of gains and losses to achieve certain income results is known as **earnings management**. Earnings management reduces earnings quality. Immediate recognition of these write-downs is now required.

Write-downs can create problems for users of financial statements. Critics of write-downs note that after a company writes down assets, its depreciation expense will be lower in all subsequent periods. Some companies intentionally write down assets in bad years, when they are going to report poor results anyway. Then in subsequent years, when the company recovers, its results will look even better because of lower depreciation expense.

PLANT ASSET DISPOSALS

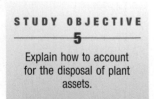

STUDY OBJECTIVE
5

Explain how to account for the disposal of plant assets.

Companies dispose of plant assets that are no longer useful to them. Illustration 9-16 shows the three ways in which companies make plant asset disposals.

Whatever the disposal method, the company must determine the book value of the plant asset at the time of disposal in order to determine the gain or loss. Recall that the book value is the difference between the cost of the plant asset

| **Sale** | **Retirement** | **Exchange** |
| Equipment is sold to another party. | Equipment is scrapped or discarded. | Existing equipment is traded for new equipment. |

Illustration 9-16
Methods of plant asset disposal

and the accumulated depreciation to date. If the disposal occurs at any time during the year, the company must record depreciation for the fraction of the year to the date of disposal. The company then eliminates the book value by reducing (debiting) Accumulated Depreciation for the total depreciation associated with that asset to the date of disposal and reducing (crediting) the asset account for the cost of the asset.

Sale of Plant Assets

In a disposal by sale, the company compares the book value of the asset with the proceeds received from the sale. If the proceeds from the sale **exceed** the book value of the plant asset, a **gain on disposal** occurs. If the proceeds from the sale **are less than** the book value of the plant asset sold, a **loss on disposal** occurs.

Only by coincidence will the book value and the fair market value of the asset be the same at the time the asset is sold. Gains and losses on sales of plant assets are therefore quite common. As an example, Delta Air Lines reported a $94,343,000 gain on the sale of five Boeing B-727-200 aircraft and five Lockheed L-1011-1 aircraft.

GAIN ON SALE. To illustrate a gain on sale of plant assets, assume that on July 1, 2007, Wright Company sells office furniture for $16,000 cash. The office furniture originally cost $60,000 and as of January 1, 2007, had accumulated depreciation of $41,000. Depreciation for the first six months of 2007 is $8,000. Wright records depreciation expense and updates accumulated depreciation to July 1 as follows.

July 1	Depreciation Expense	8,000	
	Accumulated Depreciation—Office Furniture		8,000
	(To record depreciation expense for the first 6 months of 2007)		

A	=	L	+	SE
				−8,000 Exp
−8,000				

Cash Flows
no effect

After the accumulated depreciation balance is updated, the company computes the gain or loss as the difference between the proceeds from sale and the book value at the date of disposal. Wright Company has a gain on disposal of $5,000, as computed in Illustration 9-17.

Cost of office furniture	$60,000
Less: Accumulated depreciation ($41,000 + $8,000)	49,000
Book value at date of disposal	11,000
Proceeds from sale	16,000
Gain on disposal of plant asset	**$ 5,000**

Illustration 9-17
Computation of gain on disposal

Wright records the sale and the gain on sale of the plant asset as follows.

July 1	Cash	16,000	
	Accumulated Depreciation—Office Furniture	49,000	
	Office Furniture		60,000
	Gain on Disposal		5,000
	(To record sale of office furniture at a gain)		

A	=	L	+	SE
+16,000				
+49,000				
−60,000				
				+5,000 Rev

Cash Flows
+16,000

Companies report a gain on disposal of the plant asset in the "Other revenues and gains" section of the income statement.

LOSS ON SALE. Assume that instead of selling the office furniture for $16,000, Wright sells it for $9,000. In this case, Wright experiences a loss of $2,000, as computed in Illustration 9-18.

Illustration 9-18
Computation of loss on disposal

Cost of office furniture	$60,000
Less: Accumulated depreciation	49,000
Book value at date of disposal	11,000
Proceeds from sale	9,000
Loss on disposal of plant asset	**$ 2,000**

Wright records the sale and the loss on sale of the plant asset as follows.

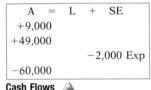

A	=	L	+	SE
+9,000				
+49,000				
				−2,000 Exp
−60,000				

Cash Flows
+9,000

July 1	Cash		9,000	
	Accumulated Depreciation—Office Furniture		49,000	
	Loss on Disposal		2,000	
	Office Furniture			60,000
	(To record sale of office furniture at a loss)			

Companies report a loss on disposal of the plant asset in the "Other expenses and losses" section of the income statement.

Retirement of Plant Assets

Companies simply retire, rather than sell, some assets at the end of their useful life. For example, some productive assets used in manufacturing may have very specific uses, and they consequently have no ready market when the company no longer needs them. In such a case the asset is simply retired.

Companies record retirement of an asset as a special case of a disposal where no cash is received. They decrease (debit) Accumulated Depreciation for the full amount of depreciation taken over the life of the asset and decrease (credit) the asset account for the original cost of the asset. The loss (a gain is not possible on a retirement) is equal to the asset's book value on the date of retirement.[1]

BEFORE YOU GO ON . . .

▶Review It

1. What is the difference between an ordinary repair and an addition or improvement? Why is this distinction important to financial reporting?
2. What is an impairment? In what way do critics suggest that companies manage their earnings through the write-downs associated with impairments?
3. What is the proper accounting for sales and retirements of plant assets?

▶Do It

Overland Trucking has an old truck that cost $30,000 and has accumulated depreciation of $16,000. Assume two different situations:

1. The company sells the old truck for $17,000 cash.
2. The truck is worthless, so the company simply retires it.

What entry should Overland use to record each scenario?

---

[1]More advanced courses discuss the accounting for exchanges, the third method of plant asset disposal.

Action Plan

• Compare the asset's book value and its fair value to determine whether a gain or loss has occurred.
• Make sure that both the Truck account and Accumulated Depreciation—Truck are reduced upon disposal.

Solution

1. Sale of truck for cash:

Cash	17,000	
Accumulated Depreciation—Truck	16,000	
Truck		30,000
Gain on Disposal [$17,000 − ($30,000 − $16,000)]		3,000
(To record sale of truck at a gain)		

2. Retirement of truck:

Accumulated Depreciation—Truck	16,000	
Loss on Disposal	14,000	
Truck		30,000
(To record retirement of truck at a loss)		

THE NAVIGATOR

Analyzing Plant Assets

The presentation of financial statement information about plant assets enables decision makers to analyze the company's use of its plant assets. We will use two measures to analyze plant assets: return on assets ratio, and asset turnover ratio.

STUDY OBJECTIVE 6

Describe methods for evaluating the use of plant assets.

RETURN ON ASSETS RATIO

An overall measure of profitability is the **return on assets ratio**. This ratio is computed by dividing net income by average assets. (Average assets are commonly calculated by adding the beginning and ending values of assets and dividing by 2.) The return on assets ratio indicates the amount of net income generated by each dollar invested in assets. Thus, the higher the return on assets, the more profitable the company.

Information is provided below related to AirTran and Southwest Airlines.

	AirTran (in millions)	Southwest Airlines (in millions)
Net income, 2004	$ 12	$ 313
Net income,* 2003	63	171
Total assets, 12/31/04	906	11,337
Total assets, 12/31/03	808	9,878
Total assets, 12/31/02	473	8,954
Net sales, 2004	1,041	6,530
Net sales, 2003	918	5,937

*In 2003, AirTran received $38 million and Southwest received $271 million in federal grants resulting from the Emergency Wartime Supplemental Appropriations Act. We have excluded these "one-time" sources of income from the net income reported here, to make the amounts more comparable to 2004's reported net income.

Illustration 9-19 (page 438) presents the 2004 and 2003 return on assets of AirTran, Southwest Airlines, and industry averages.

Illustration 9-19 Return on assets ratio

Return on Assets Ratio =	$\dfrac{\text{Net Income}}{\text{Average Total Assets}}$	
	2004	**2003**
AirTran **($ in millions)**	$\dfrac{\$12}{(\$906 + \$808)/2^*} = 1.4\%$	$\dfrac{\$63}{(\$808 + \$473)/2} = 9.8\%$
Southwest Airlines **($ in millions)**	$\dfrac{\$313}{(\$11{,}337 + \$9{,}878)/2} = 3.0\%$	$\dfrac{\$171}{(\$9{,}878 + \$8{,}954)/2} = 1.8\%$
Industry average	0.65%	

*Amounts in the ratio calculations have been rounded.

Southwest Airline's 2004 return on assets was better than that of AirTran and the airline industry, but its 2003 return was less than AirTran's. The airline industry has experienced financial difficulties in recent years as it attempted to cover high labor, fuel, and security costs while offering fares low enough to attract customers. Such difficulties are reflected in the very low industry average for return on assets and in the volatility of this ratio between years for a single airline.

Accounting across the Organization

Marketing executives now are using the basic finance concept underlying return on assets to determine "marketing return on investment (ROI)." They calculate *marketing ROI* as the profit generated by a marketing initiative divided by the investment in that initiative.

It can be tricky to determine what to include in the "investment" amount and how to attribute profit to a particular marketing initiative. However, many firms feel that measuring marketing ROI is worth the effort because it allows managers to evaluate the relative effectiveness of various programs. In addition, it helps quantify the benefits that marketing provides to the organization. In periods of tight budgets, the marketing ROI number can provide particularly valuable evidence to help a marketing manager avoid budget cuts.

Source: James O. Mitchel, "Marketing ROI," *LIMRA's MarketFacts Quarterly* (Summer 2004), p. 15.

 How does measuring marketing ROI support the overall efforts of the organization?

Decision Toolkit

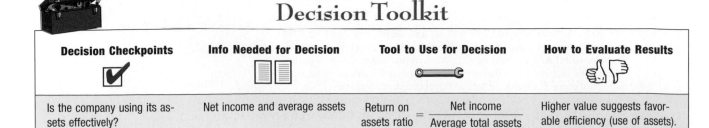

Decision Checkpoints	Info Needed for Decision	Tool to Use for Decision	How to Evaluate Results
Is the company using its assets effectively?	Net income and average assets	$\text{Return on assets ratio} = \dfrac{\text{Net income}}{\text{Average total assets}}$	Higher value suggests favorable efficiency (use of assets).

ASSET TURNOVER RATIO

The **asset turnover ratio** indicates how efficiently a company uses its assets—that is, how many dollars of sales a company generates for each dollar invested in assets. It is calculated by dividing net sales by average total assets. When we compare two companies in the same industry, the one with the higher asset turnover ratio is operating more *efficiently:* It is generating more sales per dollar invested in assets.

Illustration 9-20 presents the asset turnover ratios for AirTran and Southwest Airlines for 2004.

Illustration 9-20   Asset turnover ratio for 2004

$$\text{Asset Turnover Ratio} = \frac{\text{Net Sales}}{\text{Average Total Assets}}$$

AirTran ($ in millions)	Southwest Airlines ($ in millions)
$\dfrac{\$1,041}{(\$906 + \$808)/2} = 1.21 \text{ times}$	$\dfrac{\$6,530}{(\$11,337 + \$9,878)/2} = .62 \text{ times}$

These asset turnover ratios tell us that for each dollar invested in assets, AirTran generates sales of $1.21 and Southwest $0.62. AirTran is more successful in generating sales per dollar invested in assets, perhaps due in part to its decision to purchase older planes. The average asset turnover ratio for the airline industry is .75 times, more in line with Southwest's asset turnover.

Asset turnover ratios vary considerably across industries. The average asset turnover for electric utility companies is .34; the grocery industry has an average asset turnover of 2.89. Asset turnover ratios, therefore, are only comparable within—not between—industries.

PROFIT MARGIN RATIO REVISTED

In Chapter 5 you learned about the profit margin ratio. The profit margin ratio is calculated by dividing net income by net sales. It tells how effective a company is in turning its sales into income—that is, how much income each dollar of sales provides. Illustration 9-21 shows that the return on assets ratio can be computed from the profit margin ratio and the asset turnover ratio.

Illustration 9-21 Composition of return on assets ratio

Profit Margin	×	Asset Turnover	=	Return on Assets
$\dfrac{\text{Net Income}}{\text{Net Sales}}$	×	$\dfrac{\text{Net Sales}}{\text{Average Total Assets}}$	=	$\dfrac{\text{Net Income}}{\text{Average Total Assets}}$

This relationship has very important strategic implications for management. From Illustration 9-21 we can see that if a company wants to increase its return on assets, it can do so in two ways: (1) by increasing the margin it generates from each dollar of goods that it sells (the profit margin ratio), or (2) by increasing the volume of goods that it sells (the asset turnover). For example, most grocery stores have very low profit margins, often in the range of 1 or 2 cents for every dollar of goods sold. Grocery stores, therefore, focus on asset turnover: They rely on high turnover to increase their return on assets. Alternatively, a store selling luxury goods, such as expensive jewelry, doesn't generally have a high turnover. Consequently, a seller of luxury goods focuses on having a high profit margin. Recently Apple decided to offer a less expensive version of its popular iPod. This new product would provide a lower margin, but higher volume, than Apple's more expensive version.

Let's evaluate the return on assets ratio of Southwest Airlines for 2004 by evaluating its components—the profit margin ratio and the asset turnover ratio. See Illustration 9-22.

Illustration 9-22
Components of Southwest Airlines' rate of return

	Profit Margin	×	Asset Turnover	=	Return on Assets
Southwest Airlines	4.8%	×	.62 times	=	3.0%

Southwest Airlines has a profit margin ratio of 4.8% ($313 ÷ $6,530). Compared to the industry average of 1.72%, this suggests that Southwest has better control of its costs than most in the industry. As noted previously, Southwest's asset turnover is about equal to the industry average. Therefore, it would appear that if Southwest can increase its asset turnover by increasing the amount of sales it generates per dollar invested in planes, it will increase its reputation even further as one of the most profitable companies in the industry.

Decision Toolkit

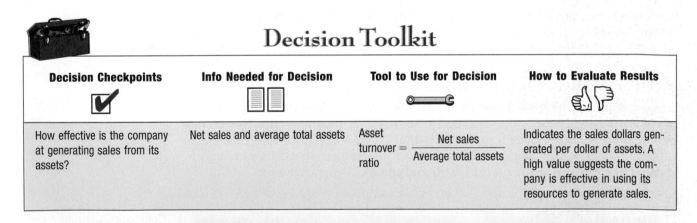

Decision Checkpoints	Info Needed for Decision	Tool to Use for Decision	How to Evaluate Results
How effective is the company at generating sales from its assets?	Net sales and average total assets	$\text{Asset turnover ratio} = \dfrac{\text{Net sales}}{\text{Average total assets}}$	Indicates the sales dollars generated per dollar of assets. A high value suggests the company is effective in using its resources to generate sales.

BEFORE YOU GO ON . . .

▶**Review It**

1. What is the purpose of the return on assets ratio? How is it calculated?
2. What is the purpose of the asset turnover ratio? How is it computed?
3. What are the two key components that explain the return on assets ratio?

THE NAVIGATOR

SECTION TWO
INTANGIBLE ASSETS

Intangible assets are rights, privileges, and competitive advantages that result from ownership of long-lived assets that do not possess physical substance. Many companies' most valuable assets are intangible. Some widely known intangibles are Microsoft's patents, McDonald's franchises, the trade name iPod, and Nike's trademark "swoosh."

Analysts estimated that in the early 1980s the market value of intangible assets to total assets was close to 40%. By 2000, the percentage was over 80%— quite a difference. What has happened is that research and development (e.g., hi-tech and bio-tech) has grown substantially. At the same time, many companies (e.g., Nike and Gatorade) have developed brand power which enables them to maintain their market position.

As you will learn in this section, financial statements do report numerous intangibles. Yet, many other financially significant intangibles are not reported. To give an example, according to its 2004 financial statements, Microsoft had a net book value of $64.9 billion. But its *market* value—the total market price of all its shares on that same date—was roughly $306 billion. Thus, its actual market value was about $241 billion greater than what its balance sheet said the company was worth. It is not uncommon for a company's reported book value to differ from its market value, because balance sheets are reported at historical cost. But such an extreme difference seriously diminishes the usefulness of the balance sheet to decision makers. In the case of Microsoft, the difference is due to unrecorded intangibles. For many high-tech or so-called intellectual-property companies, most of their value is from intangibles, many of which are not reported under current accounting rules.

Intangibles may be evidenced by contracts, licenses, and other documents. Intangibles may arise from the following sources:

1. Government grants such as patents, copyrights, franchises, trademarks, and trade names.
2. Acquisition of another business in which the purchase price includes a payment for goodwill.
3. Private monopolistic arrangements arising from contractual agreements, such as franchises and leases.

Accounting for Intangible Assets

Companies record intangible assets at cost. Intangibles are categorized as having either a limited life or an indefinite life. If an intangible has a **limited life**, the company allocates its cost over the asset's useful life using a process similar to depreciation. The process of allocating the cost of intangibles is referred to as **amortization**. The cost of intangible assets with **indefinite lives should not be amortized**.

To record amortization of an intangible asset, a company increases (debits) Amortization Expense, and decreases (credits) the specific intangible asset. (Unlike depreciation, no contra account, such as Accumulated Amortization, is usually used.)

Intangible assets are typically amortized on a straight-line basis. For example, the legal life of a patent is 20 years. Companies **amortize the cost of a patent over its 20-year life or its useful life, whichever is shorter.** To illustrate the computation of patent amortization, assume that National Labs purchases a

STUDY OBJECTIVE

7

Identify the basic issues related to reporting intangible assets.

patent at a cost of $60,000. If National estimates the useful life of the patent to be eight years, the annual amortization expense is $7,500 ($60,000 ÷ 8). National records the annual amortization as follows.

A	=	L	+	SE	
				−7,500 Exp	
−7,500					

Cash Flows
no effect

Dec. 31	Amortization Expense—Patent	7,500	
	Patent		7,500
	(To record patent amortization)		

When a company has significant intangibles, analysts should evaluate the reasonableness of the useful life estimates. In determining useful life, the company should consider obsolescence, inadequacy, and other factors. These may cause a patent or other intangible to become economically ineffective before the end of its legal life.

For example, suppose Intel obtained a patent on a new computer chip it had developed. The legal life of the patent is 20 years. From experience, however, we know that the useful life of a computer chip patent is rarely more than five years. Because new superior chips are developed so rapidly, existing chips become obsolete. Consequently, we would question the amortization expense of Intel if it amortized its patent on a computer chip for a life significantly longer than a five-year period. Amortizing an intangible over a period that is too long will understate amortization expense, overstate Intel's net income, and overstate its assets.

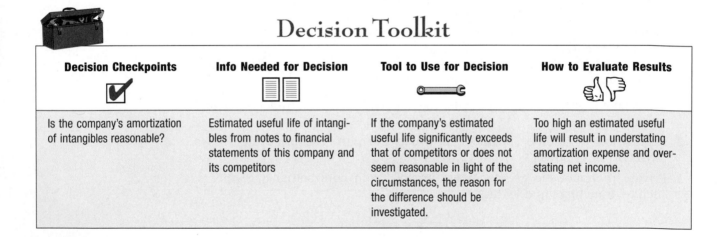

Decision Toolkit

Decision Checkpoints	Info Needed for Decision	Tool to Use for Decision	How to Evaluate Results
Is the company's amortization of intangibles reasonable?	Estimated useful life of intangibles from notes to financial statements of this company and its competitors	If the company's estimated useful life significantly exceeds that of competitors or does not seem reasonable in light of the circumstances, the reason for the difference should be investigated.	Too high an estimated useful life will result in understating amortization expense and overstating net income.

Types of Intangible Assets

PATENTS

A **patent** is an exclusive right issued by the United States Patent Office that enables the recipient to manufacture, sell, or otherwise control an invention for a period of 20 years from the date of the grant. **The initial cost of a patent is the cash or cash equivalent price paid to acquire the patent.**

The saying "A patent is only as good as the money you're prepared to spend defending it" is very true. Most patents are subject to some type of litigation by competitors. A well-known example is the patent infringement suit brought by Amazon.com against Barnes & Noble.com regarding its online shopping software. If the owner incurs legal costs in successfully defending the patent in an infringement suit, such costs are considered necessary to establish the validity of the patent. Thus, **the owner adds those costs to the Patent account and amortizes them over the remaining life of the patent**.

RESEARCH AND DEVELOPMENT COSTS

Research and development costs are expenditures that may lead to patents, copyrights, new processes, and new products. Many companies spend considerable sums of money on research and development (R&D) in an ongoing effort to develop new products or processes. For example, in a recent year IBM spent over $5.1 billion on research and development. There are uncertainties in identifying the extent and timing of the future benefits of these expenditures. As a result, companies usually record research and development costs **as an expense when incurred**, whether the R&D is successful or not.

To illustrate, assume that Laser Scanner Company spent $3 million on research and development that resulted in two highly successful patents. It spent $20,000 on legal fees for the patents. It can include the legal fees in the cost of the patents, but cannot include the R&D costs in the cost of the patents. Instead, Laser Scanner records the R&D costs as an expense when incurred.

Many disagree with this accounting approach. They argue that to expense these costs leads to understated assets and net income. Others argue that capitalizing these costs would lead to highly speculative assets on the balance sheet. Who is right is difficult to determine.

COPYRIGHTS

The federal government grants copyrights, which give the owner the exclusive right to reproduce and sell an artistic or published work. Copyrights last for the life of the creator plus 70 years. The cost of the copyright consists of the **cost of acquiring and defending it**. The cost may be only the $10 fee paid to the U.S. Copyright Office, or it may amount to a great deal more if a copyright infringement suit is involved. The useful life of a copyright generally is significantly shorter than its legal life.

TRADEMARKS AND TRADE NAMES

A trademark or trade name is a word, phrase, jingle, or symbol that distinguishes or identifies a particular enterprise or product. Trade names like Wheaties, Monopoly, Sunkist, Kleenex, Coca-Cola, Big Mac, and Jeep create immediate product identification and generally enhance the sale of the product. The creator or original user may obtain the exclusive legal right to the trademark or trade name by registering it with the U.S. Patent Office. Such registration provides 20 years' protection and may be renewed indefinitely as long as the trademark or trade name is in use.

If a company purchases the trademark or trade name, the cost is the purchase price. If the company develops the trademark or trade name itself, the cost includes attorney's fees, registration fees, design costs, successful legal defense costs, and other expenditures directly related to securing it. Because trademarks and trade names have indefinite lives, they are not amortized.

FRANCHISES AND LICENSES

When you drive down the street in your RAV4 purchased from a Toyota dealer, fill up your tank at the corner Shell station, eat lunch at Wendy's, or make plans to vacation at a Marriott resort, you are dealing with franchises. A franchise is a contractual arrangement under which the franchisor grants the franchisee the right to sell certain products, to provide specific services, or to use certain trademarks or trade names, usually within a designated geographic area.

Another type of franchise, granted by a governmental body, permits the enterprise to use public property in performing its services. Examples are the use of city streets for a bus line or taxi service; the use of public land for telephone, electric, and cable television lines; and the use of airwaves for radio or TV broadcasting. Such operating rights are referred to as **licenses**.

Franchises and licenses may be granted for a definite period of time, an indefinite period, or perpetual. **When a company can identify costs with the acquisition of the franchise or license, it should recognize an intangible asset.** Companies record as **operating expenses** annual payments made under a franchise agreement in the period in which they are incurred. In the case of a limited life, a company amortizes the cost of a franchise (or license) as operating expense over the useful life. If the life is indefinite or perpetual, the cost is not amortized.

Accounting across the Organization

What is a well-known franchise worth? Recently ESPN outbid its rivals for the right to broadcast Monday Night Football. At a price of $1.1 billion per year—nearly twice what rival ABC paid in previous years—it isn't clear who won and who lost.

When bidding for a unique franchise like Monday Night Football, management must consider many factors to determine a price. As part of the deal, ESPN also got wireless rights and Spanish-language telecasts. By its estimation, ESPN will generate a profit of $200 million per year from Monday Night Football. ABC was losing $150 million per year.

Another factor in the decision was ESPN management's concern that if ESPN didn't win the bid, a buyer would emerge that would use Monday Night Football as a launching pad for a new sports network. ESPN doesn't want any more competitors than it already has. It is hard to put a price tag on the value of keeping the competition to a minimum.

Source: Ronald Grover and Tom Lowry, "A Ball ESPN Couldn't Afford to Drop," *BusinessWeek* (May 2, 2005), p. 42.

 How should ESPN account for the $1.1 billion per year franchise fee?

GOODWILL

Usually the largest intangible asset that appears on a company's balance sheet is goodwill. **Goodwill** represents the value of all favorable attributes that relate to a business enterprise. These include exceptional management, desirable location, good customer relations, skilled employees, high-quality products, fair pricing policies, and harmonious relations with labor unions. Goodwill is unique because unlike other assets such as investments, plant assets, and even other intangibles, which can be sold *individually* in the marketplace, goodwill can be identified only with the business *as a whole*.

If goodwill can be identified only with the business as a whole, how can it be determined? Certainly, many business enterprises have many of the factors cited above (exceptional management, desirable location, and so on). However, to determine the amount of goodwill in these situations would be difficult and very subjective. In other words, to recognize goodwill without an exchange transaction that puts a value on the goodwill would lead to subjective valuations that do not contribute to the reliability of financial statements. **Therefore, companies record goodwill only when there is an exchange transaction that involves the purchase of an entire business. When an entire business is purchased, goodwill is the excess of cost over the fair market value of the net assets (assets less liabilities) acquired.**

In recording the purchase of a business, a company debits the net assets at their fair market values, credits cash for the purchase price, and records the difference as the cost of goodwill. Goodwill is not amortized because it is considered to have an indefinite life. However, it must be written down if a company determines the value of goodwill has been permanently impaired.

Financial Statement Presentation of Long-Lived Assets

BALANCE SHEET PRESENTATION

Usually companies show plant assets in the financial statements under "Property, plant, and equipment," and they show intangibles separately under "Intangible assets." Illustration 9-23 shows a typical balance sheet presentation of long-lived assets, adapted from The Coca-Cola Company's 2004 balance sheet.

Intangibles do not usually use a contra asset account like the contra asset account Accumulated Depreciation used for plant assets. Instead, companies record amortization of intangibles as a direct decrease (credit) to the asset account.

> **STUDY OBJECTIVE**
> **8**
> Indicate how long-lived assets are reported on the balance sheet.

The Coca-Cola Company

THE COCA-COLA COMPANY Balance Sheet (partial) (in millions)	
Property, plant, and equipment	
Land	$ 479
Buildings and improvements	2,853
Machinery and equipment	6,337
Containers	480
	10,149
Less: Accumulated depreciation	4,058
	6,091
Trademarks and other intangible assets	3,836
Total	$ 9,927

Illustration 9-23
Presentation of property, plant, and equipment and intangible assets

Either within the balance sheet or in the notes, companies should disclose the balances of the major classes of assets, such as land, buildings, and equipment, and of accumulated depreciation by major classes or in total. In addition, they should describe the depreciation and amortization methods used and disclose the amount of depreciation and amortization expense for the period.

STATEMENT OF CASH FLOWS PRESENTATION

It is also interesting to examine the statement of cash flows to determine the amount of property, plant, and equipment a company purchased and the cash it received from property, plant, and equipment sold in a given year. For example, the investing activities section of Coca-Cola reports the following.

Illustration 9-24
Purchases and dispositions of property, plant, and equipment

The Coca-Cola Company

THE COCA-COLA COMPANY Statement of Cash Flows (partial) (in millions)	
Cash flow from investing activities	
Purchases of property, plant, and equipment	$(755)
Proceeds from disposals of property, plant, and equipment	341

As indicated, Coca-Cola made significant investments in property, plant, and equipment which should be viewed positively given the company's overall profitability. The level of investment suggests that Coca-Cola believes that it can earn a reasonable rate of return on these assets.

BEFORE YOU GO ON . . .

►Review It

1. Identify the major types of intangible assets and the proper accounting for them.
2. Explain the accounting for research and development costs.
3. How are intangible assets presented on the balance sheet?

 THE NAVIGATOR

Using the Decision Toolkit

JetBlue Airways Corporation is a low-cost airline operating primarily out of New York. It operates 280 flights to 30 destinations daily. Although it has operated for only five years, it is now the tenth largest U.S. airline based on total passenger miles. It currently operates 70 planes, and expects to add more than 350 planes over the next 11 years. While the major airlines suffer, JetBlue appears to have found a formula for success.

Instructions

Review the excerpts from the company's 2004 annual report that follow and then answer the following questions.

1. What method does the company use to depreciate its aircraft? Over what period is the company depreciating these aircraft?
2. What type of intangible assets does the company have, and how are they being accounted for?
3. Compute the company's return on assets ratio, asset turnover ratio, and profit margin ratio for 2003 and 2004. Comment on your results.

(in thousands)	**2004**	**2003**
Net income	$47	$104
Net sales	$1,266	$998
Beginning total assets	$2,186	$1,379
Ending total assets	$2,799	$2,186

JETBLUE AIRWAYS CORPORATION
Notes to the Financial Statements

Property and Equipment: We record our property and equipment at cost and depreciate these assets on a straight-line basis to their estimated residual values over their estimated useful lives. Additions, modifications that enhance the operating performance of our assets, and interest related to predelivery deposits to acquire new aircraft and for the construction of facilities are capitalized.

Estimated useful lives and residual values for our property and equipment are as follows:

	Estimated Useful Life	Residual Value
Aircraft	25 years	20%
In-flight entertainment systems	12 years	0%
Aircraft parts	Fleet life	10%
Flight equipment leasehold improvements	Lease term	0%
Ground property and equipment	3–10 years	0%
Leasehold improvements	15 years or lease term	0%

We record impairment losses on long-lived assets used in operations when events and circumstances indicate that the assets may be impaired and the undiscounted future cash flows estimated to be generated by these assets are less than the assets' net book value. If impairment occurs, the loss is measured by comparing the fair value of the asset to its carrying amount.

Note 5—LiveTV Purchased technology, which is an intangible asset related to our September 2002 acquisition of the membership interests of LiveTV, is being amortized over six years based on the average number of aircraft expected to be in service as of the date of acquisition. Projected amortization expense is $10.9 million in 2005, $13.1 million in 2006, $15.5 million in 2007 and $14.7 million in 2008.

Solution

1. The company depreciates property and equipment using the straight-line approach. It depreciates aircraft over a 25-year life.
2. The company has an intangible asset called "purchased technology" related to its purchase of membership interests in "LiveTV." It amortizes this intangible asset based on the company's estimate of the average number of aircraft expected to be in service over a six-year period from 2003 through 2008.
3.

	2004	2003
Return on assets	$\dfrac{\$47}{(\$2{,}799 + \$2{,}186)/2} = 1.9\%$	$\dfrac{\$104}{(\$2{,}186 + \$1{,}379)/2} = 5.8\%$
Asset turnover	$\dfrac{\$1{,}266}{(\$2{,}799 + \$2{,}186)/2} = .51 \text{ times}$	$\dfrac{\$998}{(\$2{,}186 + \$1{,}379)/2} = .56 \text{ times}$
Profit margin	$\dfrac{\$47}{\$1{,}266} = 3.7\%$	$\dfrac{\$104}{\$998} = 10.4\%$

JetBlue's return on assets ratio declined from 5.8% in 2003 to 1.9% in 2004. This means that the company was earning less net income per dollar of assets in 2004 than it did in 2003. This decline was the result of two factors. First, as shown by the asset turnover ratio, the company was not generating as many sales per dollar of assets. Its asset turnover ratio declined from .56 times to .51 times. Second, the company's ability to generate net income from its sales declined, as evidenced by its profit margin decline from 10.4% to 3.7%.

THE NAVIGATOR

Summary of Study Objectives

1 *Describe how the cost principle applies to plant assets.* The cost of plant assets includes all expenditures necessary to acquire the asset and make it ready for its intended use. Cost is measured by the cash or cash equivalent price paid.

2 *Explain the concept of depreciation.* Depreciation is the process of allocating to expense the cost of a plant asset over its useful (service) life in a rational and systematic manner. Depreciation is not a process of valuation, and it is not a process that results in an accumulation of cash. Depreciation reflects an asset's decreasing usefulness and revenue-producing ability, resulting from wear and tear and from obsolescence.

3 *Compute periodic depreciation using the straight-line method, and contrast its expense pattern with those of other methods.* The formula for straight-line depreciation is:

$$\frac{\text{Cost} - \text{Salvage value}}{\text{Useful life (in years)}}$$

The expense patterns of the three depreciation methods are as follows.

Method	Annual Depreciation Pattern
Straight-line	Constant amount
Declining-balance	Decreasing amount
Units-of-activity	Varying amount

4 *Describe the procedure for revising periodic depreciation.* Companies make revisions of periodic depreciation in present and future periods, not retroactively.

5 *Explain how to account for the disposal of plant assets.* The procedure for accounting for the disposal of a plant asset through sale or retirement is: (a) Eliminate the book value of the plant asset at the date of disposal. (b) Record cash proceeds, if any. (c) Account for the difference between the book value and the cash proceeds as a gain or a loss on disposal.

6 *Describe methods for evaluating the use of plant assets.* Plant assets may be analyzed using the return on assets ratio and the asset turnover ratio. The return on assets ratio consists of two components: the asset turnover ratio and the profit margin ratio.

7 *Identify the basic issues related to reporting intangible assets.* Companies report intangible assets at their cost less any amounts amortized. If an intangible asset has a limited life, its cost should be allocated over its useful life. Intangible assets with indefinite lives should not be amortized.

8 *Indicate how long-lived assets are reported on the balance sheet.* Companies usually show plant assets under "Property, plant, and equipment"; they show intangibles separately under "Intangible assets." Either within the balance sheet or in the notes, companies disclose the balances of the major classes of assets, such as land, buildings, and equipment, and accumulated depreciation by major classes or in total. They describe the depreciation and amortization methods used, and disclose the amount of depreciation and amortization expense for the period.

Decision Toolkit—A Summary

Decision Checkpoints	Info Needed for Decision	Tool to Use for Decision	How to Evaluate Results
Is the company using its assets effectively?	Net income and average assets	$\text{Return on assets ratio} = \dfrac{\text{Net income}}{\text{Average total assets}}$	Higher value suggests favorable efficiency (use of assets).
How effective is the company at generating sales from its assets?	Net sales and average total assets	$\text{Asset turnover ratio} = \dfrac{\text{Net sales}}{\text{Average total assets}}$	Indicates the sales dollars generated per dollar of assets. A high value suggests the company is effective in using its resources to generate sales.
Is the company's amortization of intangibles reasonable?	Estimated useful life of intangibles from notes to financial statements of this company and its competitors	If the company's estimated useful life significantly exceeds that of competitors or does not seem reasonable in light of the circumstances, the reason for the difference should be investigated.	Too high an estimated useful life will result in understating amortization expense and overstating net income.

APPENDIX
CALCULATION OF DEPRECIATION USING OTHER METHODS

In this appendix we show the calculations of the depreciation expense amounts that we used in the chapter for the declining-balance and units-of-activity methods.

Declining-Balance

The **declining-balance method** produces a decreasing annual depreciation expense over the useful life of the asset. The method is so named because the computation of periodic depreciation is based on a **declining book value** (cost less accumulated depreciation) of the asset. Annual depreciation expense is computed by multiplying the book value at the beginning of the year by the declining-balance depreciation rate. **The depreciation rate remains constant from year to year, but the book value to which the rate is applied declines each year.**

Book value for the first year is the cost of the asset because the balance in accumulated depreciation at the beginning of the asset's useful life is zero. In subsequent years, book value is the difference between cost and accumulated depreciation at the beginning of the year. **Unlike other depreciation methods, the declining-balance method ignores salvage value in determining the amount to which the declining-balance rate is applied.** Salvage value, however, does limit the total depreciation that can be taken. Depreciation stops when the asset's book value equals its expected salvage value.

As noted in the chapter, a common declining-balance rate is double the straight-line rate—the **double-declining-balance method**. If Bill's Pizzas uses the double-declining-balance method, the depreciation rate is 40% (2 × the straight-line rate of 20%). Illustration 9A-1 presents the formula and computation of depreciation for the first year on the delivery truck.

> **STUDY OBJECTIVE**
> **9**
> Compute periodic depreciation using the declining-balance method and the units-of-activity method.

Helpful Hint The straight-line rate is approximated as 1 ÷ Estimated life. In this case it is 1 ÷ 5 = 20%.

Book Value at Beginning of Year	×	Declining-Balance Rate	=	Depreciation Expense
$13,000	×	40%	=	**$5,200**

Illustration 9A-1 Formula for declining-balance method

Illustration 9A-2 presents the depreciation schedule under this method.

BILL'S PIZZAS

Year	Computation — Book Value Beginning of Year	× Depreciation Rate =	Annual Depreciation Expense	End of Year — Accumulated Depreciation	Book Value
2007	$13,000	40%	**$5,200**	$ 5,200	$ 7,800*
2008	7,800	40	**3,120**	8,320	4,680
2009	4,680	40	**1,872**	10,192	2,808
2010	2,808	40	**1,123**	11,315	1,685
2011	1,685	40	**685****	12,000	**1,000**

*$13,000 − $5,200
**Computation of $674 ($1,685 × 40%) is adjusted to $685 in order for book value to equal salvage value.

Illustration 9A-2 Double-declining-balance depreciation schedule

Helpful Hint Depreciation stops when the asset's book value equals its expected salvage value.

The delivery equipment is 69% depreciated ($8,320 ÷ $12,000) at the end of the second year. Under the straight-line method it would be depreciated 40% ($4,800 ÷ $12,000) at that time. Because the declining-balance method produces higher depreciation expense in the early years than in the later years, it is considered an **accelerated-depreciation method**.

The declining-balance method is compatible with the matching principle. It matches the higher depreciation expense in early years with the higher benefits received in these years. Conversely, it recognizes lower depreciation expense in later years when the asset's contribution to revenue is less. Also, some assets lose their usefulness rapidly because of obsolescence. In these cases, the declining-balance method provides a more appropriate depreciation amount.

When an asset is purchased during the year, it is necessary to prorate the declining-balance depreciation in the first year on a time basis. For example, if Bill's Pizzas had purchased the delivery equipment on April 1, 2007, depreciation for 2007 would be $3,900 ($13,000 × 40% × $\frac{9}{12}$). The book value for computing depreciation in 2008 then becomes $9,100 ($13,000 − $3,900), and the 2008 depreciation is $3,640 ($9,100 × 40%).

Units-of-Activity

Alternative Terminology
Another term often used is the *units-of-production method.*

Under the **units-of-activity method**, useful life is expressed in terms of the total units of production or use expected from the asset. The units-of-activity method is ideally suited to equipment whose activity can be measured in units of output, miles driven, or hours in use. The units-of-activity method is generally not suitable for assets for which depreciation is a function more of time than of use.

To use this method, a company estimates the total units of activity for the entire useful life and divides that amount into the depreciable cost to determine the depreciation cost per unit. It then multiplies the depreciation cost per unit by the units of activity during the year to find the annual depreciation for that year.

To illustrate, assume that Bill's Pizzas estimates it will drive its new delivery truck 15,000 miles in the first year. Illustration 9A-3 presents the formula and computation of depreciation expense in the first year.

Illustration 9A-3
Formula for units-of-activity method

$$\frac{\text{Depreciable}}{\text{Cost}} \div \frac{\text{Total Units}}{\text{of Activity}} = \frac{\text{Depreciation}}{\text{Cost per Unit}}$$

$$\$12,000 \div 100,000 \text{ miles} = \$0.12$$

$$\frac{\text{Depreciation}}{\text{Cost per Unit}} \times \frac{\text{Units of}}{\text{Activity during the Year}} = \frac{\text{Depreciation}}{\text{Expense}}$$

$$\$0.12 \times 15,000 \text{ miles} = \$1,800$$

Illustration 9A-4 shows the depreciation schedule, using assumed mileage data.

BILL'S PIZZAS					
	Computation		Annual	End of Year	
Year	Units of Activity	× Depreciation Cost/Unit	= Depreciation Expense	Accumulated Depreciation	Book Value
2007	15,000	$0.12	$1,800	$ 1,800	$11,200*
2008	30,000	0.12	3,600	5,400	7,600
2009	20,000	0.12	2,400	7,800	5,200
2010	25,000	0.12	3,000	10,800	2,200
2011	10,000	0.12	1,200	12,000	1,000

*$13,000 − $1,800

Illustration 9A-4
Units-of-activity
depreciation schedule

Helpful Hint Depreciation stops when the asset's book value equals its expected salvage value.

The units-of-activity method is not nearly as popular as the straight-line method, primarily because it is often difficult to make a reasonable estimate of total activity. However, this method is used by some very large companies, such as Standard Oil Company of California and Boise Cascade Corporation. When the productivity of the asset varies significantly from one period to another, the units-of-activity method results in the best matching of expenses with revenues.

This method is easy to apply when assets are purchased during the year. In such a case, companies use the productivity of the asset for the partial year in computing the depreciation.

Summary of Study Objective for Appendix

9 *Compute periodic depreciation using the declining-balance method and the units-of-activity method.* The depreciation expense calculation for each of these methods is:

Declining-balance:

$$\begin{array}{c}\text{Book value at} \\ \text{beginning of year}\end{array} \times \begin{array}{c}\text{Declining-balance} \\ \text{rate}\end{array} = \begin{array}{c}\text{Depreciation} \\ \text{expense}\end{array}$$

Units-of-activity:

$$\begin{array}{c}\text{Depreciable} \\ \text{cost}\end{array} \div \begin{array}{c}\text{Total units} \\ \text{of activity}\end{array} = \begin{array}{c}\text{Depreciation} \\ \text{cost per unit}\end{array}$$

$$\begin{array}{c}\text{Depreciation cost} \\ \text{per unit}\end{array} \times \begin{array}{c}\text{Units of activity} \\ \text{during year}\end{array} = \begin{array}{c}\text{Depreciation} \\ \text{expense}\end{array}$$

Glossary

Accelerated-depreciation method A depreciation method that produces higher depreciation expense in the early years than the straight-line approach. (p. 429)

Additions and improvements Costs incurred to increase the operating efficiency, productive capacity, or expected useful life of a plant asset. (p. 433)

Amortization The process of allocating to expense the cost of an intangible asset. (p. 441)

Asset turnover ratio Indicates how efficiently a company uses its assets; calculated as net sales divided by average total assets. (p. 439)

Capital expenditures Expenditures that increase the company's investment in plant assets. (p. 421)

Capital lease A long-term agreement allowing one party (the lessee) to use another party's asset (the lessor); accounted for like a purchase. (p. 425)

Cash equivalent price An amount equal to the fair market value of the asset given up or the fair market value of the asset received, whichever is more clearly determinable. (p. 422)

Copyright An exclusive right granted by the federal government allowing the owner to reproduce and sell an artistic or published work. (p. 443)

Declining-balance method A depreciation method that applies a constant rate to the declining book value of the asset and produces a decreasing annual depreciation expense over the useful life of the asset. (pp. 429, 449)

Depreciable cost The cost of a plant asset less its salvage value. (p. 428)

Depreciation The process of allocating to expense the cost of a plant asset over its useful life in a rational and systematic manner. (p. 426)

Franchise A contractual arrangement under which the franchisor grants the franchisee the right to sell certain products, to render specific services, or to use certain trademarks or trade names, usually within a designated geographic area. (p. 443)

Goodwill The value of all favorable attributes that relate to a business enterprise. (p. 444)

Impairment A permanent decline in the market value of an asset. (p. 434)

Intangible assets Rights, privileges, and competitive advantages that result from the ownership of long-lived assets that do not possess physical substance. (p. 441)

Lessee A party that has made contractual arrangements to use another party's asset without purchasing it. (p. 424)

Lessor A party that has agreed contractually to let another party use its asset. (p. 424)

Licenses Operating rights to use public property, granted by a governmental agency to a business enterprise. (p. 444)

Operating lease An arrangement allowing one party (the lessee) to use the asset of another party (the lessor); accounted for as a rental. (p. 425)

Ordinary repairs Expenditures to maintain the operating efficiency and expected productive life of the asset. (p. 433)

Patent An exclusive right issued by the U.S. Patent Office that enables the recipient to manufacture, sell, or otherwise control an invention for a period of 20 years from the date of the grant. (p. 442)

Plant assets Tangible resources that have physical substance, are used in the operations of the business, and are not intended for sale to customers. (p. 420)

Research and development costs Expenditures that may lead to patents, copyrights, new processes, and new products. (p. 443)

Return on assets ratio A profitability measure that indicates the amount of net income generated by each dollar invested in assets; computed as net income divided by average assets. (p. 437)

Revenue expenditures Expenditures that are immediately charged against revenues as an expense. (p. 421)

Straight-line method A method in which periodic depreciation is the same for each year of the asset's useful life. (p. 428)

Trademark (trade name) A word, phrase, jingle, or symbol that distinguishes or identifies a particular enterprise or product. (p. 443)

Units-of-activity method A depreciation method in which useful life is expressed in terms of the total units of production or use expected from the asset. (pp. 430, 450)

Demonstration Problem 1

DuPage Company purchased a factory machine at a cost of $18,000 on January 1, 2007. DuPage expected the machine to have a salvage value of $2,000 at the end of its 4-year useful life.

Instructions
Prepare a depreciation schedule using the straight-line method.

Action Plan
• Under the straight-line method, apply the depreciation rate to depreciable cost.

Solution to Demonstration Problem

DUPAGE COMPANY
Depreciation Schedule—Straight-Line Method

| | Computation | | Annual | End of Year | |
| | Depreciable | Depreciation | Depreciation | Accumulated | Book |
Year	Cost (a) ×	Rate (b) =	Expense	Depreciation	Value (c)
2007	$16,000	25%	$4,000	$ 4,000	$14,000
2008	16,000	25	4,000	8,000	10,000
2009	16,000	25	4,000	12,000	6,000
2010	16,000	25	4,000	16,000	2,000

(a) $18,000 − $2,000   (b) $\frac{1}{4}$ = 25%   (c) Cost less accumulated depreciation.

Demonstration Problem 2

On January 1, 2004, Skyline Limousine Co. purchased a limousine at an acquisition cost of $28,000. Skyline depreciated the vehicle by the straight-line method using a 4-year service life and a $4,000 salvage value. The company's fiscal year ends on December 31.

Instructions
Prepare the journal entry or entries to record the disposal of the limousine assuming that it was:
(a) Retired and scrapped with no salvage value on January 1, 2008.
(b) Sold for $5,000 on July 1, 2007.

Solution to Demonstration Problem			
(a) Jan. 1, 2008	Accumulated Depreciation—Limousine	24,000	
	Loss on Disposal	4,000	
	Limousine		28,000
	(To record retirement of limousine)		
(b) July 1, 2007	Depreciation Expense	3,000	
	Accumulated Depreciation—Limousine		3,000
	(To record depreciation to date of disposal)		
	Cash	5,000	
	Accumulated Depreciation—Limousine	21,000	
	Loss on Disposal	2,000	
	Limousine		28,000
	(To record sale of limousine)		

Action Plan
• Calculate accumulated depreciation (depreciation expense per year × years in use).
• At the time of disposal, determine the book value of the asset.
• Recognize any gain or loss from disposal of the asset.

Note: All Questions, Exercises, and Problems marked with an asterisk relate to material in the appendix to the chapter.

Self-Study Questions

Answers are at the end of the chapter.

(SO 1) **1.** Corrieten Company purchased equipment and incurred these costs:

Cash price	$24,000
Sales taxes	1,200
Insurance during transit	200
Installation and testing	400
Total costs	$25,800

What amount should be recorded as the cost of the equipment?
(a) $24,000.   (c) $25,400.
(b) $25,200.   (d) $25,800.

(SO 1) **2.** Harrington Corporation recently leased a number of trucks from Andre Corporation. In inspecting the books of Harrington Corporation, you notice that the trucks have not been recorded as assets on its balance sheet. From this you can conclude that Harrington is accounting for this transaction as a/an:
(a) operating lease.   (c) purchase.
(b) capital lease.   (d) None of the above.

3. Depreciation is a process of: (SO 2)
(a) valuation.   (c) cash accumulation.
(b) cost allocation.   (d) appraisal.

4. Cuso Company purchased equipment on January   (SO 3)
1, 2006, at a total invoice cost of $400,000. The equipment has an estimated salvage value of $10,000 and an estimated useful life of 5 years. What is the amount of accumulated depreciation at December 31, 2007, if the straight-line method of depreciation is used?
(a) $80,000.   (c) $78,000.
(b) $160,000.   (d) $156,000.

5. A company would minimize its de-   (SO 3)
preciation expense in the first year of owning an asset if it used:
(a) a high estimated life, a high salvage value, and declining-balance depreciation.
(b) a low estimated life, a high salvage value, and straight-line depreciation.
(c) a high estimated life, a high salvage value, and straight-line depreciation.
(d) a low estimated life, a low salvage value, and declining-balance depreciation.

(SO 4)   **6.** When there is a change in estimated depreciation:
   (a) previous depreciation should be corrected.
   (b) current and future years' depreciation should be revised.
   (c) only future years' depreciation should be revised.
   (d) None of the above.

(SO 5)   **7.** Additions to plant assets:
   (a) are revenue expenditures.
   (b) increase a Repair Expense account.
   (c) increase a Purchases account.
   (d) are capital expenditures.

(SO 6)   **8.** Which of the following measures provides an indication of how efficient a company is in employing its assets?
   (a) Current ratio.
   (b) Profit margin ratio.
   (c) Debt to total assets ratio.
   (d) Asset turnover ratio.

(SO 7)   **9.** Pierce Company incurred $150,000 of research and development costs in its laboratory to develop a new product. It spent $20,000 in legal fees for a patent granted on January 2, 2007. On July 31, 2007, Pierce paid $15,000 for legal fees in a successful defense of the patent. What is the total amount that should be debited to Patents through July 31, 2007?
   (a) $150,000.   (c) $185,000.
   (b) $35,000.   (d) Some other amount.

(SO 7, 8)   **10.** Indicate which one of these statements is *true*.
   (a) Since intangible assets lack physical substance, they need to be disclosed only in the notes to the financial statements.
   (b) Goodwill should be reported as a contra account in the stockholders' equity section.
   (c) Totals of major classes of assets can be shown in the balance sheet, with asset details disclosed in the notes to the financial statements.
   (d) Intangible assets are typically combined with plant assets and natural resources and then shown in the property, plant, and equipment section.

11. If a company reports goodwill as an intangible   (SO 7)
asset on its books, what is the one thing you know with certainty?
   (a) The company is a valuable company worth investing in.
   (b) The company has a well-established brand name.
   (c) The company purchased another company.
   (d) The goodwill will generate a lot of positive business for the company for many years to come.

*****12.** Kant Enterprises purchased a truck for $11,000   (SO 9)
on January 1, 2006. The truck will have an estimated salvage value of $1,000 at the end of 5 years. If you use the units-of-activity method, the balance in accumulated depreciation at December 31, 2007, can be computed by the following formula:
   (a) ($11,000 ÷ Total estimated activity) × Units of activity for 2007.
   (b) ($10,000 ÷ Total estimated activity) × Units of activity for 2007.
   (c) ($11,000 ÷ Total estimated activity) × Units of activity for 2006 and 2007.
   (d) ($10,000 ÷ Total estimated activity) × Units of activity for 2006 and 2007.

Go to the book's website, **www.wiley.com/college/kimmel**, to access additional Self-Study Questions.

Questions

1. Mrs. Whistler is uncertain about how the cost principle applies to plant assets. Explain the principle to Mrs. Whistler.

2. How is the cost for a plant asset measured in a cash transaction? In a noncash transaction?

3. What are the primary advantages of leasing?

4. HaiFat Company acquires the land and building owned by Benz Company. What types of costs may be incurred to make the asset ready for its intended use if HaiFat Company wants to use only the land? If it wants to use both the land and the building?

5. ➡ Stellar Inc. needs to upgrade its diagnostic equipment. At the time of purchase, Stellar had expected the equipment to last 8 years. Unfortunately, it was obsolete after only 4 years. Randy Waters, CFO of Stellar Inc., is considering leasing new equipment rather than buying it. What are the potential benefits of leasing?

6. In a recent newspaper release, the president of Heller Company asserted that something has to be done about depreciation. The president said, "Depreciation does not come close to accumulating the cash needed to replace the asset at the end of its useful life." What is your response to the president?

7. Daria is studying for the next accounting examination. She asks your help on two questions: (a) What is salvage value? (b) How is salvage value used in determining depreciable cost under the straight-line method? Answer Daria's questions.

8. ◖━━━◗ Contrast the straight-line method and the units-of-activity method in relation to (a) useful life and (b) the pattern of periodic depreciation over useful life.

9. ◖━━━◗ Contrast the effects of the three depreciation methods on annual depreciation expense.

10. In the fourth year of an asset's 5-year useful life, the company decides that the asset will have a 6-year service life. How should the revision of depreciation be recorded? Why?

11. Distinguish between revenue expenditures and capital expenditures during an asset's useful life.

12. How is a gain or a loss on the sale of a plant asset computed?

13. LaBelle Corporation owns a machine that is fully depreciated but is still being used. How should LaBelle account for this asset and report it in the financial statements?

14. What are the similarities and differences between depreciation and amortization?

15. ➡ During a recent management meeting, Roger Bees, director of marketing, proposed that the company should begin capitalizing its marketing expenditures as goodwill. In his words, "Marketing expenditures create goodwill for the company which benefits the company for multiple periods. Therefore it doesn't make good sense to have to expense it as it is incurred. Besides, if we capitalize it as goodwill we won't have to amortize it, and this will boost reported income." Discuss the merits of Roger's proposal.

16. Omega Company hires an accounting intern who says that intangible assets should always be amortized over their legal lives. Is the intern correct? Explain.

17. Goodwill has been defined as the value of all favorable attributes that relate to a business enterprise. What types of attributes could result in goodwill?

18. Susan Day, a business major, is working on a case problem for one of her classes. In this case problem, the company needs to raise cash to market a new product it developed. Anthony Capp, an engineering major, takes one look at the company's balance sheet and says, "This company has an awful lot of goodwill. Why don't you recommend that they sell some of it to raise cash?" How should Susan respond to Anthony?

19. Under what conditions is goodwill recorded? What is the proper accounting treatment for amortizing goodwill?

20. Often research and development costs provide companies with benefits that last a number of years. (For example, these costs can lead to the development of a patent that will increase the company's income for many years.) However, generally accepted accounting principles require that such costs be recorded as an expense when incurred. Why?

21. ◖━━━◗ In 2004 Campbell Soup Company reported average total assets of $6,440 million, net sales of $7,109 million, and net income of $647 million. What was Campbell Soup's return on assets ratio?

22. ➡ Stacy Simmons, a marketing executive for Fresh Views Inc., has proposed expanding its product line of framed graphic art by producing a line of lower-quality products. These would require less processing by the company and would provide a lower profit margin. Terry Concord, the company's CFO, is concerned that this new product line would reduce the company's return on assets. Discuss the potential effect on return on assets that this product might have.

23. ➡ ◖━━━◗ Give an example of an industry that would be characterized by (a) a high asset turnover ratio and a low profit margin ratio, and (b) a low asset turnover ratio and a high profit margin ratio.

24. ◖━━━◗ Caitlin Corporation and Samantha Corporation both operate in the same industry. Caitlin uses the straight-line method to account for depreciation, whereas Samantha uses an accelerated method. Explain what complications might arise in trying to compare the results of these two companies.

25. ➡ ◖━━━◗ Rocky Corporation uses straight-line depreciation for financial reporting purposes but an accelerated method for tax purposes. Is it acceptable to use different methods for the two purposes? What is Rocky Corporation's motivation for doing this?

26. ◖━━━◗ You are comparing two companies in the same industry. You have determined that Leno Corp. depreciates its plant assets over a 40-year life, whereas Letterman Corp. depreciates its plant assets over a 20-year life. Discuss the implications this has for comparing the results of the two companies.

Brief Exercises

BE9-1 These expenditures were incurred by Gerald Ford Company in purchasing land: cash price $50,000; accrued taxes $5,000; attorney's fees $2,100; real estate broker's commission $2,800; and clearing and grading $3,500. What is the cost of the land?

Determine the cost of land.
(SO 1)

BE9-2 HeFlin Company incurs these expenditures in purchasing a truck: cash price $18,000; accident insurance (during use) $2,000; sales taxes $1,080; motor vehicle license $300; and painting and lettering $1,200. What is the cost of the truck?

Determine the cost of a truck.
(SO 1)

Compute straight-line depreciation.
(SO 3)

BE9-3 Apex Chemicals Company acquires a delivery truck at a cost of $26,000 on January 1, 2007. The truck is expected to have a salvage value of $4,000 at the end of its 5-year useful life. Compute annual depreciation for the first and second years using the straight-line method.

Compute revised depreciation.
(SO 4)

BE9-4 On January 1, 2007, the Ewing Company ledger shows Equipment $32,000 and Accumulated Depreciation $14,000. The depreciation resulted from using the straight-line method with a useful life of 10 years and a salvage value of $2,000. On this date the company concludes that the equipment has a remaining useful life of only 2 years with the same salvage value. Compute the revised annual depreciation.

Journalize entries for disposal of plant assets.
(SO 5)

BE9-5 Prepare journal entries to record these transactions: (a) Blaska Company retires its delivery equipment, which cost $41,000. Accumulated depreciation is also $41,000 on this delivery equipment. No salvage value is received. (b) Assume the same information as in part (a), except that accumulated depreciation for Blaska Company is $36,800 instead of $41,000.

Journalize entries for sale of plant assets.
(SO 5)

BE9-6 Carlton Company sells office equipment on September 30, 2007, for $21,000 cash. The office equipment originally cost $72,000 and as of January 1, 2007, had accumulated depreciation of $42,000. Depreciation for the first 9 months of 2007 is $7,500. Prepare the journal entries to (a) update depreciation to September 30, 2007, and (b) record the sale of the equipment.

Account for intangibles— patents.
(SO 7)

BE9-7 Jazz Company purchases a patent for $180,000 on January 2, 2007. Its estimated useful life is 5 years.
  (a) Prepare the journal entry to record amortization expense for the first year.
  (b) Show how this patent is reported on the balance sheet at the end of the first year.

Compute return on assets ratio and asset turnover ratio.
(SO 6)

BE9-8 In its 2004 annual report, McDonald's Corporation reports beginning total assets of $25.5 billion; ending total assets of $27.8 billion; net sales of $19.1 billion, and net income of $2.3 billion.
  (a) Compute McDonald's return on assets ratio.
  (b) Compute McDonald's asset turnover ratio.

Classification of long-lived assets on balance sheet.
(SO 8)

BE9-9 Nike, Inc. reported the following plant assets and intangible assets for the year ended May 31, 2004 (in millions): other plant assets $530.6; land $179.5; patents and trademarks (at cost) $400.5; machinery and equipment $1,608.6; buildings $813.6; goodwill (at cost) $135.4; accumulated amortization $34.2; accumulated depreciation $1,545.4. Prepare a partial balance sheet for Nike for these items.

Compute declining-balance depreciation.
(SO 9)

*BE9-10 Depreciation information for Apex Chemicals Company is given in BE9-3. Assuming the declining-balance depreciation rate is double the straight-line rate, compute annual depreciation for the first and second years under the declining-balance method.

Compute depreciation using units-of-activity method.
(SO 9)

*BE9-11 Pack in Taxi Service uses the units-of-activity method in computing depreciation on its taxicabs. Each cab is expected to be driven 150,000 miles. Taxi 10 cost $24,500 and is expected to have a salvage value of $500. Taxi 10 was driven 28,000 miles in 2006 and 30,000 miles in 2007. Compute the depreciation for each year.

Exercises

Determine cost of plant acquisitions.
(SO 1)

E9-1 The following expenditures relating to plant assets were made by Bel Air Company during the first 2 months of 2007.
1. Paid $7,000 of accrued taxes at the time the plant site was acquired.
2. Paid $200 insurance to cover a possible accident loss on new factory machinery while the machinery was in transit.
3. Paid $850 sales taxes on a new delivery truck.
4. Paid $21,000 for parking lots and driveways on the new plant site.
5. Paid $250 to have the company name and slogan painted on the new delivery truck.
6. Paid $8,000 for installation of new factory machinery.
7. Paid $900 for a 1-year accident insurance policy on the new delivery truck.
8. Paid $75 motor vehicle license fee on the new truck.

Instructions
(a) Explain the application of the cost principle in determining the acquisition cost of plant assets.
(b) List the numbers of the transactions, and opposite each indicate the account title to which each expenditure should be debited.

E9-2 On March 1, 2007, Geoffrey Company acquired real estate, on which it planned to construct a small office building, by paying $90,000 in cash. An old warehouse on the property was demolished at a cost of $8,200; the salvaged materials were sold for $1,700. Additional expenditures before construction began included $1,500 attorney's fee for work concerning the land purchase, $5,000 real estate broker's fee, $9,100 architect's fee, and $14,000 to put in driveways and a parking lot.

Determine acquisition costs of land.
(SO 1)

Instructions
(a) Determine the amount to be reported as the cost of the land.
(b) For each cost not used in part (a), indicate the account to be debited.

E9-3 Hillary Company purchased a new machine on September 1, 2007, at a cost of $96,000. The company estimated that the machine has a salvage value of $6,000. The machine is expected to be used for 70,000 working hours during its 8-year life.

Determine straight-line depreciation for partial period.
(SO 3)

Instructions
Compute the depreciation expense under the straight-line method for 2007 and 2008, assuming a December 31 year-end.

E9-4 Will Smith, the new controller of Fresh Prince Company, has reviewed the expected useful lives and salvage values of selected depreciable assets at the beginning of 2007. Here are his findings:

Compute revised annual depreciation.
(SO 3,4)

Type of Asset	Date Acquired	Cost	Accumulated Depreciation, Jan. 1, 2007	Useful Life (in years) Old	Useful Life (in years) Proposed	Salvage Value Old	Salvage Value Proposed
Building	Jan. 1, 1999	$900,000	$172,000	40	50	$40,000	$47,600
Warehouse	Jan. 1, 2001	120,000	27,600	25	20	5,000	3,600

All assets are depreciated by the straight-line method. Fresh Prince Company uses a calendar year in preparing annual financial statements. After discussion, management has agreed to accept Will's proposed changes. (The "Proposed" useful life is total life, not remaining life.)

Instructions
(a) Compute the revised annual depreciation on each asset in 2007. (Show computations.)
(b) Prepare the entry (or entries) to record depreciation on the building in 2007.

E9-5 Phill Co. has delivery equipment that cost $54,000 and has been depreciated $20,000.

Journalize transactions related to disposals of plant assets.
(SO 5)

Instructions
Record entries for the disposal under the following assumptions.
(a) It was scrapped as having no value.
(b) It was sold for $37,000.
(c) It was sold for $18,000.

E9-6 Here are selected 2007 transactions of Beck Corporation.

Record disposal of equipment.
(SO 5)

Jan. 1   Retired a piece of machinery that was purchased on January 1, 1997. The machine cost $62,000 and had a useful life of 10 years with no salvage value.

June 30   Sold a computer that was purchased on January 1, 2005. The computer cost $33,000 and had a useful life of 3 years with no salvage value. The computer was sold for $5,000 cash.

Dec. 31   Sold a delivery truck for $9,000 cash. The truck cost $27,000 when it was purchased on January 1, 2004, and was depreciated based on a 5-year useful life with a $3,000 salvage value.

Instructions

Journalize all entries required on the above dates, including entries to update depreciation on assets disposed of, where applicable. Beck Corporation uses straight-line depreciation.

Apply accounting concepts.
(SO 1, 6, 7)

E9-7   The following situations are independent of one another:

1. An accounting student can't understand why the company is only depreciating its buildings and equipment, but not its land. The student prepared journal entries to depreciate all the company's property, plant, and equipment for the current year-end.
2. The same student also thinks the company's amortization policy on its intangible assets is wrong. The company is currently amortizing its patents but not its goodwill. The student fixed that for the current year-end by adding goodwill to her adjusting entry for amortization. She told a fellow student that she felt she had improved the consistency of the company's accounting policies by making these changes.
3. The same company has a building still in use that has a zero book value but a substantial market value. The student felt that this practice didn't benefit the company's users—especially the bank—and wrote the building up to its market value. After all, she reasoned, you can write down assets if market values are lower. Writing them up if market value is higher is yet another example of the improved consistency that her employment has brought to the company's accounting practices.

Instructions

Explain whether or not the accounting treatment in each of the above situations is in accordance with generally accepted accounting principles. Explain what accounting principle or assumption, if any, has been violated and what the appropriate accounting treatment should be.

Calculate asset turnover ratio and return on assets ratio.
(SO 6)

E9-8   During 2004 Federal Express reported the following information (in millions): net sales of $24,710 and net income of $838. Its balance sheet also showed total assets at the beginning of the year of $15,385 and total assets at the end of the year of $19,134.

Instructions

Calculate the (a) asset turnover ratio and (b) return on assets ratio.

Calculate and interpret ratios.
(SO 6)

E9-9   Optix International is considering a significant expansion to its product line. The sales force is excited about the opportunities that the new products will bring. The new products are a significant step up in quality above the company's current offerings, but offer a complementary fit to its existing product line. Frank Renolds, senior production department manager, is very excited about the high-tech new equipment that will have to be acquired to produce the new products. Carol Fischer, the company's CFO, has provided the following projections based on results with and without the new products.

	Without New Products	**With New Products**
Sales	$10,000,000	$18,000,000
Net income	$800,000	$1,800,000
Average total assets	$5,000,000	$15,000,000

Instructions

(a) Compute the company's return on assets ratio, profit margin ratio, and asset turnover ratio, both with and without the new product line.
(b) Discuss the implications that your findings in part (a) have for the company's decision.

Calculate and interpret ratios.
(SO 6)

E9-10   Empire Company reports the following information (in millions) during a recent year: net sales, $9,926.5; net earnings, $195.9; total assets, ending, $4,312.6; and total assets, beginning, $4,254.3.

Instructions

(a) Calculate the (1) return on assets, (2) asset turnover, and (3) profit margin ratios.
(b) Prove mathematically how the profit margin and asset turnover ratios work together to explain return on assets, by showing the appropriate calculation.
(c) Empire Company owns Sobeys (grocery), Empire Theaters, Lawton Drugstores, and Wajax (heavy equipment), and manages commercial real estate, among other activities. Does this diversity of activities affect your ability to interpret the ratios you calculated in (a)? Explain.

E9-11 These are selected 2007 transactions for Neuman Corporation:

Prepare adjusting entries for amortization.
(SO 7)

Jan. 1   Purchased a copyright for $140,000. The copyright has a useful life of 8
years and a remaining legal life of 30 years.

May 1   Purchased a patent with an estimated useful life of 4 years and a legal
life of 20 years for $36,000.

Instructions
Prepare all adjusting entries at December 31 to record amortization required by the events.

E9-12 Keshan Company, organized in 2007, has these transactions related to intangible assets in that year:

Prepare entries to set up appropriate accounts for different intangibles; calculate amortization.
(SO 7)

Jan. 2   Purchased a patent (5-year life) $330,000.
Apr. 1   Goodwill purchased (indefinite life) $360,000.
July 1   Acquired a 9-year franchise; expiration date July 1, 2016, $450,000.
Sept. 1   Research and development costs $185,000.

Instructions
(a) Prepare the necessary entries to record these intangibles. All costs incurred were for cash.
(b) Make the entries as of December 31, 2007, recording any necessary amortization.
(c) Indicate what the balances should be on December 31, 2007.

E9-13 Alliance Atlantis Communications Inc. changed its accounting policy to amortize broadcast rights over the contracted exhibition period, which is based on the estimated useful life of the program. Previously, the company amortized broadcast rights
over the lesser of 2 years or the contracted exhibition period.

Discuss implications of amortization period.
(SO 7)

Instructions
 Write a short memo to your client explaining the implications this has for the
analysis of Alliance Atlantis's results. Also, discuss whether this change in amortization
period appears reasonable.

E9-14 The questions listed below are independent of one another.

Answer questions on depreciation and intangibles.
(SO 2, 7)

Instructions
Provide a brief answer to each question.
(a) Why should a company depreciate its buildings?
(b) How can a company have a building that has a zero reported book value but substantial market value?
(c) What are some examples of intangibles that you might find on your college campus?
(d) Give some examples of company or product trademarks or trade names. Are trade
names and trademarks reported on a company's balance sheet?

*E9-15 Blue Highway Bus Lines uses the units-of-activity method in depreciating its buses.
One bus was purchased on January 1, 2007, at a cost of $120,000. Over its 4 year useful
life, the bus is expected to be driven 160,000 miles. Salvage value is expected to be $8,000.

Compute depreciation under units of activity method.
(SO 9)

Instructions
(a) Compute the depreciation cost per unit.
(b) Prepare a depreciation schedule assuming actual mileage was: 2007, 40,000; 2008,
52,000; 2009, 41,000; and 2010, 27,000.

*E9-16 Basic information relating to a new machine purchased by Hillary Company is
presented in E9-3.

Compute declining-balance and units-of-activity depreciation.
(SO 9)

Instructions
Using the facts presented in E9-3, compute depreciation using the following methods in
the year indicated.
(a) Declining-balance using double the straight-line rate for 2007 and 2008.
(b) Units-of-activity for 2007, assuming machine usage was 2,900 hours. (Round
depreciation per unit to the nearest cent.)

Problems: Set A

P9-1A Basler Company was organized on January 1. During the first year of operations,
the following plant asset expenditures and receipts were recorded in random order.

Determine acquisition costs of land and building.
(SO 1)

Debits

1. Cost of real estate purchased as a plant site (land $255,000 and building $25,000)	$280,000
2. Installation cost of fences around property	6,800
3. Cost of demolishing building to make land suitable for construction of new building	19,000
4. Excavation costs for new building	23,000
5. Accrued real estate taxes paid at time of purchase of real estate	2,179
6. Cost of parking lots and driveways	29,000
7. Architect's fees on building plans	38,000
8. Real estate taxes paid for the current year on land	5,800
9. Full payment to building contractor	640,000
	$1,043,779

Credits

10. Proceeds from salvage of demolished building	$8,000

Instructions

Analyze the transactions using the following table column headings. Enter the number of each transaction in the Item column, and enter the amounts in the appropriate columns. For amounts in the Other Accounts column, also indicate the account title.

Land $293,179

Item	Land	Building	Other Accounts

Journalize equipment transactions related to purchase, sale, retirement, and depreciation.
(SO 5, 8)

P9-2A At December 31, 2007, Ruiz Corporation reported the following plant assets.

Land		$ 3,000,000
Buildings	$26,500,000	
Less: Accumulated depreciation—buildings	12,100,000	14,400,000
Equipment	40,000,000	
Less: Accumulated depreciation—equipment	5,000,000	35,000,000
Total plant assets		$52,400,000

During 2008, the following selected cash transactions occurred.

Apr. 1 Purchased land for $2,200,000.
May 1 Sold equipment that cost $660,000 when purchased on January 1, 2001. The equipment was sold for $200,000.
June 1 Sold land for $1,800,000. The land cost $700,000.
July 1 Purchased equipment for $1,300,000.
Dec. 31 Retired equipment that cost $500,000 when purchased on December 31, 1998. No salvage value was received.

Instructions

(a) Journalize the transactions. (*Hint:* You may wish to set up T accounts, post beginning balances, and then post 2008 transactions.) Ruiz uses straight-line depreciation for buildings and equipment. The buildings are estimated to have a 40-year useful life and no salvage value; the equipment is estimated to have a 10-year useful life and no salvage value. Update depreciation on assets disposed of at the time of sale or retirement.

(c) Tot. plant assets
$50,340,500

(b) Record adjusting entries for depreciation for 2008.
(c) Prepare the plant assets section of Ruiz's balance sheet at December 31, 2008.

Journalize entries for disposal of plant assets.
(SO 5)

P9-3A Presented here are selected transactions for Riley Company for 2007.

Jan. 1 Retired a piece of machinery that was purchased on January 1, 1997. The machine cost $71,000 on that date and had a useful life of 10 years with no salvage value.

June 30   Sold a computer that was purchased on January 1, 2004. The computer cost $32,000 and had a useful life of 5 years with no salvage value. The computer was sold for $10,000.

Dec. 31   Discarded a delivery truck that was purchased on January 1, 2002. The truck cost $27,000 and was depreciated based on an 8-year useful life with a $3,000 salvage value.

Instructions
Journalize all entries required on the above dates, including entries to update depreciation, where applicable, on assets disposed of. Riley Company uses straight-line depreciation. (Assume depreciation is up to date as of December 31, 2006.)

P9-4A   The intangible assets section of El-Gazzar Corporation's balance sheet at December 31, 2007, is presented here.

Prepare entries to record transactions related to acquisition and amortization of intangibles; prepare the intangible assets section and note.
(SO 7, 8)

Patents ($60,000 cost less $6,000 amortization)	$54,000
Copyrights ($36,000 cost less $25,200 amortization)	10,800
Total	$64,800

The patent was acquired in January 2007 and has a useful life of 10 years. The copyright was acquired in January 2001 and also has a useful life of 10 years. The following cash transactions may have affected intangible assets during 2008.

Jan.   2   Paid $36,000 legal costs to successfully defend the patent against infringement by another company.

Jan.–June   Developed a new product, incurring $210,000 in research and development costs. A patent was granted for the product on July 1, and its useful life is equal to its legal life. Legal and other costs for the patent were $9,000.

Sept.   1   Paid $40,000 to a quarterback to appear in commercials advertising the company's products. The commercials will air in September and October.

Oct.   1   Acquired a copyright for $180,000. The copyright has a useful life and legal life of 50 years.

Instructions
(a) Prepare journal entries to record the transactions.
(b) Prepare journal entries to record the 2008 amortization expense for intangible assets.
(c) Prepare the intangible assets section of the balance sheet at December 31, 2008.
(d) Prepare the note to the financial statements on El-Gazzar Corporation's intangible assets as of December 31, 2008.

(c) Tot. intangibles $275,075

P9-5A   Due to rapid employee turnover in the accounting department, the following transactions involving intangible assets were improperly recorded by Dische Corporation in 2007.

1. Dische developed a new manufacturing process, incurring research and development costs of $150,000. The company also purchased a patent for $37,400. In early January Dische capitalized $187,400 as the cost of the patents. Patent amortization expense of $9,370 was recorded based on a 20-year useful life.

2. On July 1, 2007, Dische purchased a small company and as a result acquired goodwill of $60,000. Dische recorded a half-year's amortization in 2007, based on a 40-year life ($750 amortization). The goodwill has an indefinite life.

Prepare entries to correct errors in recording and amortizing intangible assets.
(SO 7)

Instructions
Prepare all journal entries necessary to correct any errors made during 2007. Assume the books have not yet been closed for 2007.

P9-6A   Roger Corporation and Sean Corporation, two companies of roughly the same size, are both involved in the manufacture of shoe-tracing devices. Each company depreciates its plant assets using the straight-line approach. An investigation of their financial statements reveals the information shown on page 462.

Calculate and comment on return on assets, profit margin, and asset turnover ratio.
(SO 6)

	Roger Corp.	Sean Corp.
Net income	$ 400,000	$ 500,000
Sales	1,300,000	1,200,000
Total assets (average)	3,300,000	2,900,000
Plant assets (average)	2,400,000	1,800,000
Intangible assets (goodwill)	300,000	0

Instructions

(a) For each company, calculate these values:
   (1) Return on assets ratio.
   (2) Profit margin.
   (3) Asset turnover ratio.

(b) Based on your calculations in part (a), comment on the relative effectiveness of the two companies in using their assets to generate sales. What factors complicate your ability to compare the two companies?

Compute depreciation under different methods.
(SO 3, 9)

*P9-7A   In recent years Ping Company has purchased three machines. Because of frequent employee turnover in the accounting department, a different accountant was in charge of selecting the depreciation method for each machine, and various methods have been used. Information concerning the machines is summarized in the table below.

Machine	Acquired	Cost	Salvage Value	Useful Life (in years)	Depreciation Method
1	Jan. 1, 2004	$96,000	$ 6,000	6	Straight-line
2	July 1, 2005	80,000	10,000	5	Declining-balance
3	Nov. 1, 2005	78,000	6,000	6	Units-of-activity

For the declining-balance method, Ping Company uses the double-declining rate. For the units-of-activity method, total machine hours are expected to be 24,000. Actual hours of use in the first 3 years were: 2005, 400; 2006, 4,500; and 2007, 5,000.

Instructions

(a) Machine 2 $56,960

(a) Compute the amount of accumulated depreciation on each machine at December 31, 2007.

(b) If machine 2 was purchased on October 1 instead of July 1, what would be the depreciation expense for this machine in 2005? In 2006?

Compute depreciation under different methods.
(SO 3, 9)

*P9-8A   Tabesh Corporation purchased machinery on January 1, 2007, at a cost of $210,000. The estimated useful life of the machinery is 4 years, with an estimated residual value at the end of that period of $10,000. The company is considering different depreciation methods that could be used for financial reporting purposes.

Instructions

(a) Double-declining-balance expense 2009
$26,250

(a) Prepare separate depreciation schedules for the machinery using the straight-line method, and the declining-balance method using double the straight-line rate. Round to the nearest dollar.

(b) Which method would result in the higher reported 2007 income? In the highest total reported income over the 4-year period?

(c) Which method would result in the lower reported 2007 income? In the lowest total reported income over the 4-year period?

Determine acquisition costs of land and building.
(SO 1)

Problems: Set B

P9-1B   Cairo Company was organized on January 1. During the first year of operations, the following plant asset expenditures and receipts were recorded in random order.

Debits

1. Cost of real estate purchased as a plant site (land $180,000 and
   building $70,000) $ 250,000
2. Accrued real estate taxes paid at time of purchase of real estate   6,000
3. Cost of demolishing building to make land suitable for
   construction of new building   27,000
4. Cost of filling and grading the land   7,100
5. Excavation costs for new building   21,900
6. Architect's fees on building plans   45,000
7. Full payment to building contractor   629,500
8. Cost of parking lots and driveways   36,000
9. Real estate taxes paid for the current year on land   7,300
                                                                      $1,029,800

Credits

10. Proceeds for salvage of demolished building $ 12,700

Instructions

Analyze the transactions using the table column headings provided here. Enter the number of each transaction in the Item column, and enter the amounts in the appropriate columns. For amounts in the Other Accounts column, also indicate the account titles.

Item	Land	Building	Other Accounts

Land $277,400

P9-2B At December 31, 2007, Harrington Corporation reported these plant assets.

Journalize equipment transactions related to purchase, sale, retirement, and depreciation.
(SO 5, 8)

Land		$ 4,000,000
Buildings	$28,500,000	
Less: Accumulated depreciation—buildings	12,100,000	16,400,000
Equipment	48,000,000	
Less: Accumulated depreciation—equipment	5,000,000	43,000,000
Total plant assets		$63,400,000

During 2008, the following selected cash transactions occurred.

Apr.   1   Purchased land for $2,630,000.
May   1   Sold equipment that cost $600,000 when purchased on January 1, 2003.
          The equipment was sold for $350,000.
June 1   Sold land purchased on June 1, 1995, for $1,800,000. The land cost
          $500,000.
July   1   Purchased equipment for $800,000.
Dec. 31   Retired fully depreciated equipment that cost $470,000 when purchased
          on December 31, 1998. No salvage value was received.

Instructions

(a) Journalize the transactions. *(Hint:* You may wish to set up T accounts, post beginning balances, and then post 2008 transactions.) Harrington uses straight-line depreciation for buildings and equipment. The buildings are estimated to have a 40-year life and no salvage value; the equipment is estimated to have a 10-year useful life and no salvage value. Update depreciation on assets disposed of at the time of sale or retirement.

(b) Record adjusting entries for depreciation for 2008. *(Note:* The only assets that are fully depreciated are those that were retired on December 31.)

(c) Prepare the plant assets section of Harrington's balance sheet at December 31, 2008.

(c) Tot. plant assets
$60,537,500

P9-3B Here are selected transactions for Andre Corporation for 2007.

Journalize entries for disposal of plant assets.
(SO 5)

Jan.   1   Retired a piece of machinery that was purchased on January 1, 1997.
          The machine cost $52,000 and had a useful life of 10 years with no
          salvage value.

June 30   Sold a computer that was purchased on January 1, 2004. The computer cost $35,000 and had a useful life of 7 years with no salvage value. The computer was sold for $23,000.

Dec. 31   Discarded a delivery truck that was purchased on January 1, 2003. The truck cost $30,000 and was depreciated based on a 6-year useful life with a $3,000 salvage value.

Instructions

Journalize all entries required on the above dates, including entries to update depreciation on assets disposed of, where applicable. Andre Corporation uses straight-line depreciation.

Prepare entries to record transactions related to acquisition and amortization of intangibles; prepare the intangible assets section and notes.
(SO 7, 8)

P9-4B   The intangible assets section of the balance sheet for Cuso Company at December 31, 2007, is presented here.

Patents ($70,000 cost less $7,000 amortization)	$63,000
Copyrights ($48,000 cost less $18,000 amortization)	30,000
Total	$93,000

The patent was acquired in January 2007 and has a useful life of 10 years. The copyright was acquired in January 2005 and also has a useful life of 8 years. The following cash transactions may have affected intangible assets during 2008.

Jan. 2   Paid $22,500 legal costs to successfully defend the patent against infringement by another company.

Jan.–June   Developed a new product, incurring $220,000 in research and development costs. A patent was granted for the product on July 1, and its useful life is equal to its legal life. Legal and other costs for the patent were $14,000.

Sept. 1   Paid $110,000 to an extremely large defensive lineman to appear in commercials advertising the company's products. The commercials will air in September and October.

Oct. 1   Acquired a copyright for $150,000. The copyright has a useful life and legal life of 50 years.

Instructions

(a) Prepare journal entries to record the transactions.

(b) Prepare journal entries to record the 2008 amortization expense.

(c) Tot. intangibles $262,900   (c) Prepare the intangible assets section of the balance sheet at December 31, 2008.

(d) Prepare the notes to the financial statements on Cuso Company's intangible assets as of December 31, 2008.

Prepare entries to correct errors in recording and amortizing intangible assets.
(SO 7)

P9-5B   Due to rapid employee turnover in the accounting department, the following transactions involving intangible assets were improperly recorded by the Mooney Company in 2007.

1. Mooney developed a new manufacturing process, incurring research and development costs of $120,000. The company also purchased a patent for $72,000. In early January Mooney capitalized $192,000 as the cost of the patents. Patent amortization expense of $16,000 was recorded based on a 12-year useful life.

2. On July 1, 2007, Mooney purchased a small company and as a result acquired goodwill of $80,000. Mooney recorded a half-year's amortization in 2007 based on a 40-year life ($1,000 amortization). The goodwill has an indefinite life.

Instructions

Calculate and comment on return on assets, profit margin, and asset turnover ratio.
(SO 6)

Prepare all journal entries necessary to correct any errors made during 2007. Assume the books have not yet been closed for 2007.

P9-6B   Montreal Corporation and Quebec Corporation, two corporations of roughly the same size, are both involved in the manufacture of umbrellas. Each company depreciates its plant assets using the straight-line approach. An investigation of their financial statements reveals the following information.

	Montreal Corp.	Quebec Corp.
Net income	$ 800,000	$ 900,000
Sales	1,400,000	1,500,000
Total assets (average)	2,000,000	1,800,000
Plant assets (average)	1,400,000	1,200,000
Intangible assets (goodwill)	400,000	0

Instructions
(a) For each company, calculate these values:
    (1) Return on assets ratio.
    (2) Profit margin.
    (3) Asset turnover ratio.
(b) ▭▭▭▶ Based on your calculations in part (a), comment on the relative effectiveness of the two companies in using their assets to generate sales. What factors complicate your ability to compare the two companies?

P9-7B   In recent years Brian Transportation purchased three used buses. Because of frequent employee turnover in the accounting department, a different accountant selected the depreciation method for each bus, and various methods have been used. Information concerning the buses is summarized in the table below.

Compute depreciation under different methods.
(SO 3, 9)

Bus	Acquired	Cost	Salvage Value	Useful Life (in years)	Depreciation Method
1	Jan. 1, 2005	$ 86,000	$ 6,000	4	Straight-line
2	Jan. 1, 2005	150,000	10,000	4	Declining-balance
③	Jan. 1, 2005	100,000	9,000	5	Units-of-activity

For the declining-balance method, Brian Transportation uses the double-declining rate. For the units-of-activity method, total miles are expected to be 130,000. Actual miles of use in the first 3 years were: 2005, 26,000; 2006, 34,000; and 2007, 30,000.

Instructions
(a) Compute the amount of accumulated depreciation on each bus at December 31, 2007.
(b) If Bus 2 was purchased on March 1 instead of January 1, what would be the depreciation expense for this bus in 2005? In 2006?

(a) Bus 1 $60,000

P9-8B   Shumway Corporation purchased machinery on January 1, 2007, at a cost of $290,000. The estimated useful life of the machinery is 5 years, with an estimated salvage value at the end of that period of $30,000. The company is considering different depreciation methods that could be used for financial reporting purposes.

Compute depreciation under different methods.
(SO 3, 9)

Instructions
(a) Prepare separate depreciation schedules for the machinery using the straight-line method, and the declining-balance method using double the straight-line rate.
(b) Which method would result in the higher reported 2007 income? In the higher total reported income over the 5-year period?
(c) Which method would result in the lower reported 2007 income? In the lower total reported income over the 5-year period?

(a) Double-declining-balance exp. 2008 $69,600

Problems: Set C

Visit the book's website at **www.wiley.com/college/kimmel** and choose the Student Companion site to access Problem Set C.

Comprehensive Problem

CP9   Squarepants Corporation's trial balance at December 31, 2007, is presented on page 466. All 2007 transactions have been recorded except for the items described after the trial balance.

	Debit	Credit
Cash	$ 28,000	
Accounts Receivable	36,800	
Notes Receivable	10,000	
Interest Receivable	–0–	
Merchandise Inventory	36,200	
Prepaid Insurance	3,600	
Land	20,000	
Building	150,000	
Equipment	60,000	
Patent	9,000	
Allowance for Doubtful Accounts		$ 500
Accumulated Depreciation—Building		50,000
Accumulated Depreciation—Equipment		24,000
Accounts Payable		27,300
Salaries Payable		–0–
Unearned Rent		6,000
Notes Payable (short-term)		11,000
Interest Payable		–0–
Notes Payable (long-term)		35,000
Common Stock		50,000
Retained Earnings		63,600
Dividends	12,000	
Sales		900,000
Interest Revenue		–0–
Rent Revenue		–0–
Gain on Disposal		–0–
Bad Debts Expense	–0–	
Cost of Goods Sold	630,000	
Depreciation Expense—Buildings	–0–	
Depreciation Expense—Equipment	–0–	
Insurance Expense	–0–	
Interest Expense	–0–	
Other Operating Expenses	61,800	
Amortization Expense—Patents	–0–	
Salaries Expense	110,000	
Total	$1,167,400	$1,167,400

Unrecorded transactions

1. On May 1, 2007, Squarepants purchased equipment for $12,000 plus sales taxes of $600 (all paid in cash).
2. On July 1, 2007, Squarepants sold for $3,500 equipment which originally cost $5,000. Accumulated depreciation on this equipment at January 1, 2007, was $1,800; 2007 depreciation prior to the sale of equipment was $450.
3. On December 31, 2007, Squarepants sold for $3,000 on account inventory that cost $2,100.
4. Squarepants estimates that uncollectible accounts receivable at year-end are $4,000.
5. The note receivable is a one-year, 12% note dated April 1, 2007. No interest has been recorded.
6. The balance in prepaid insurance represents payment of a $3,600, 6-month premium on September 1, 2007.
7. The building is being depreciated using the straight-line method over 30 years. The salvage value is $30,000.
8. The equipment owned prior to this year is being depreciated using the straight-line method over 5 years. The salvage value is 10% of cost.
9. The equipment purchased on May 1, 2007, is being depreciated using the straight-line method over 5 years, with a salvage value of $1,800.
10. The patent was acquired on January 1, 2007, and has a useful life of 10 years from that date.
11. Unpaid salaries at December 31, 2007, total $2,200.
12. The unearned rent of $6,000 was received on December 1, 2007, for 3 months rent.
13. Both the short-term and long-term notes payable are dated January 1, 2007, and carry a 12% interest rate. All interest is payable in the next 12 months.

Instructions
(a) Prepare journal entries for the transactions listed above.
(b) Prepare an updated December 31, 2007, trial balance.
(c) Prepare a 2007 income statement and a 2007 retained earnings statement.
(d) Prepare a December 31, 2007, balance sheet.

(b) Totals $1,19
(c) Net income $72,440
(d) Total assets $259,060

Continuing Cookie Chronicle

(Note: This is a continuation of the Cookie Chronicle from Chapters 1 through 8.)

CCC9

Part 1   Now that she is selling mixers and her customers can use credit cards to pay for them, Natalie is thinking of upgrading her website to include the online sale of mixers and payment by credit card. This would enable her to sell these mixers to a wider range of customers using the Internet.

Natalie contacts her brother who originally prepared the website for her. He agrees to upgrade the site so it can handle credit card security issues as well as direct order entry. The cost of the upgrade is $1,800. This cost would be incurred and paid for during the month of August 2007, and the upgrade would be operational September 1, 2007. Recall that Natalie's website had an original cost of $600 and is being amortized using the straight-line method over 24 months, starting December 1, 2006, with zero residual value. Additional costs for website maintenance and insurance are estimated to be $1,200 per year.

If Natalie decides to upgrade the website, its useful life will not change and there will be no change in residual value.

Instructions
(a) Prepare the journal entry to record the upgrade.
(b) Calculate the monthly amortization expense before the upgrade and the accumulated amortization and book value on August 31, 2007.
(c) Calculate the revised monthly amortization expense as of September 1, 2007.
(d) Calculate the accumulated amortization and book value on December 31, 2007.
(e) Explain to Natalie the difference in accounting for the website upgrade costs and accounting for the costs incurred for website maintenance and insurance. In your explanation, comment on the generally accepted accounting principles that affect the accounting for these transactions.

Part 2   Natalie is also thinking of buying a van that will be used only for business. The cost of the van is estimated at $32,500. Natalie would spend an additional $2,500 to have the van painted. In addition, she wants the back seat of the van removed so that she will have lots of room to transport her mixer inventory as well as her baking supplies. The cost of taking out the back seat and installing shelving units is estimated at $1,500. She expects the van to last her about 5 years, and she expects to drive it for 100,000 miles. The annual cost of vehicle insurance will be $2,400. Natalie estimates that at the end of the 5-year useful life the van will sell for $6,500. Assume that she will buy the van on August 15, 2007, and it will be ready for use on September 1, 2007.

Natalie is concerned about the impact of the van's cost on her income statement and balance sheet. She has come to you for advice on calculating the van's depreciation.

Instructions
(a) Determine the cost of the van.
(b) Prepare a depreciation table for straight-line depreciation (similar to the one in Illustration 9-9). Recall that Cookie Creations has a December 31 fiscal year-end.
(c) What method should Natalie use for tax purposes? Provide a justification for your choice. Is she required to use the same approach for financial reporting and tax reporting?

BROADENING YOUR PERSPECTIVE

Financial Reporting and Analysis

FINANCIAL REPORTING PROBLEM: *Tootsie Roll Industries, Inc.*

BYP9-1   Refer to the financial statements and the Notes to Consolidated Financial Statements of Tootsie Roll Industries in Appendix A.

Instructions
Answer the following questions.
(a) What were the total cost and book value of property, plant, and equipment at December 31, 2004?
(b) What method or methods of depreciation are used by Tootsie Roll for financial reporting purposes?
(c) What was the amount of depreciation and amortization expense for each of the 3 years 2002–2004? (*Hint:* Use statement of cash flows.)
(d) Using the statement of cash flows, what are the amounts of property, plant, and equipment purchased (capital expenditures) in 2004 and 2003?
(e) Explain how Tootsie Roll accounted for its intangible assets in 2004.
(f) Read Tootsie Roll's note 8 on commitments. Does the company primarily engage in capital leases or operating leases? What are the implications for analysis of its financial statements?

COMPARATIVE ANALYSIS PROBLEM: *Tootsie Roll vs. Hershey Foods*

BYP9-2 The financial statements of Hershey Foods are presented in Appendix B, following the financial statements for Tootsie Roll Industries in Appendix A.

Instructions
(a) Based on the information in these financial statements and the accompanying notes and schedules, compute the following values for each company in 2004.
(1) Return on assets ratio.
(2) Profit margin.
(3) Asset turnover ratio.
(b) What conclusions concerning the management of plant assets can be drawn from these data?

RESEARCH CASE

BYP9-3 The May 16, 2005, issue of the *Wall Street Journal* includes an article by Pui-Wing Tam titled "Will H-P's Hurd Wipe the Slate Clean?"

Instructions
Read the article and answer the following questions.
(a) What are some of the reasons given for expecting that Hewlett-Packard will make a significant write-down against its goodwill? What would this charge relate to?
(b) According to accounting standards, how is goodwill to be accounted for?
(c) What is one possible reason given for why Mr. Hurd's predecessor CEO at Hewlett-Packard did not take a large write-off on goodwill?
(d) What other examples of large goodwill write-offs are given in the article?

INTERPRETING FINANCIAL STATEMENTS

BYP9-4 Bob Evans Farms, Inc. operates 568 restaurants in 22 states and produces fresh and fully cooked sausage products, fresh salads, and related products distributed to grocery stores in the Midwest, Southwest, and Southeast. For a recent 3-year period Bob Evans Farms reported the following selected income statement data (in millions of dollars).

	2004	2003	2002
Sales	$1,198.0	$1,091.3	$1,061.8
Cost of goods sold	340.8	287.0	298.3
Net income	72.0	75.1	67.7
Total assets	868.2	784.6	722.0

In his letters to stockholders, the chief executive officer (CEO) explained the decline in earnings. An excerpt from that letter is shown on page 469.

BOB EVANS FARMS, INC.
Letter to Stockholders (partial)

During fiscal 2004, we continued building long-term value for Bob Evans stockholders by pursuing our time-tested strategies for steady, complementary growth of our family-casual restaurants and food products. However, financial results for the year were affected primarily by increased commodity costs, which resulted in a slight decline in earnings per share from fiscal 2003's record level.

Instructions
(a) Compute the percentage change in sales and in net income from 2002 to 2004.
(b) What contribution, if any, did the company's gross profit rate make to the decline in earnings?
(c) What was Bob Evans's profit margin ratio in each of the 3 years? Comment on any trend in this percentage.
(d) The CEO's letter also stated that the company continued to invest prudently in restaurants, opening 37 new restaurants in 2004, compared to 29 openings in 2003. What effect would you expect this change to have on return on assets? Calculate the company's return on assets for 2003 and 2004 to see if it reflects the increase in number of stores.
(e) Based on the trends in these ratios, does the CEO's explanation seem appropriate?

BYP9-5   The accounting for goodwill differs in countries around the world. The discussion of a change in goodwill accounting practices shown below was taken from the notes to the financial statements of J Sainsbury Plc, one of the world's leading retailers. Headquartered in the United Kingdom, it serves 11 million customers a week.

J SAINSBURY PLC
Notes to the Financial Statements

Accounting Policies   Goodwill arising in connection with the acquisition of shares in subsidiaries and associated undertakings is calculated as the excess of the purchase price over the fair value of the net tangible assets acquired. In prior years goodwill has been deducted from reserves in the period of acquisition. FRS 10 is applicable in the current financial year, and in accordance with the standard acquired goodwill is now shown as an asset on the Group's Balance Sheet. As permitted by FRS 10, goodwill written off to reserves in prior periods has not been restated as an asset.

Goodwill is treated as having an indefinite economic life where it is considered that the acquired business has strong customer loyalty built up over a long period of time, based on advantageous store locations and a commitment to maintain the marketing advantage of the retail brand. The carrying value of the goodwill will be reviewed annually for impairment and adjusted to its recoverable amount if required. Where goodwill is considered to have a finite life, amortisation will be applied over that period.

For amounts stated as goodwill which are considered to have indefinite life, no amortisation is charged to the Profit and Loss Account.

Instructions
Answer the following questions.
(a) How does the initial determination and recording of goodwill compare with that in the United States? That is, is goodwill initially recorded in the same circumstances, and is the calculation of the amount the same in both the United Kingdom and the United States?
(b) Prior to adoption of the new accounting standard (*FRS 10*), how did the company account for goodwill? What were the implications for the income statement?
(c) Under the new accounting standard, how does the company account for its goodwill? Is it possible, under the new standard, for a company to avoid charging goodwill amortization to net income?
(d) In what ways is the new standard similar to U.S. standards, and in what ways is it different?

FINANCIAL ANALYSIS ON THE WEB

BYP9-6   *Purpose:* Use an annual report to identify a company's plant assets and the depreciation method used.

Address: **www.reportgallery.com** (or go to **www.wiley.com/college/kimmel**)

Steps
1. From Report Gallery Homepage, choose **View the Library of Annual Reports**.
2. Select a particular company.
3. Choose **Annual Report**.
4. Follow instructions below.

Instructions
Answer the following questions.
(a) What is the name of the company?
(b) What is the Internet address of the annual report?
(c) At fiscal year-end, what is the net amount of its plant assets?
(d) What is the accumulated depreciation?
(e) Which method of depreciation does the company use?

Critical Thinking

DECISION MAKING ACROSS THE ORGANIZATION

BYP9-7   Kreugers Furniture Corp. is nationally recognized for making high-quality products. Management is concerned that it is not fully exploiting its brand power. Kreugers' production managers are also concerned because their plants are not operating at anywhere near full capacity. Management is currently considering a proposal to offer a new line of affordable furniture.

Those in favor of the proposal (including the vice president of production) believe that, by offering these new products, the company could attract a clientele that it is not currently servicing. Also, it could operate its plants at full capacity, thus taking better advantage of its assets.

The vice president of marketing, however, believes that the lower-priced (and lower-margin) product would have a negative impact on the sales of existing products. The vice president believes that $10,000,000 of the sales of the new product will be from customers that would have purchased the more expensive product, but switched to the lower-margin product because it was available. (This is often referred to as *cannibalization* of existing sales). Top management feels, however, that even with cannibalization, the company's sales will increase and the company will be better off.

The following data are available.

(in thousands)	Current results	Proposed results without cannibalization	Proposed results with cannibalization
Sales	$40,000	$60,000	$50,000
Net income	$10,000	$12,500	$10,000
Average total assets	$100,000	$100,000	$100,000

Instructions
(a) Compute Kreugers' return on assets ratio, profit margin ratio, and asset turnover ratio, both with and without the new product line.
(b) Discuss the implications that your findings in part (a) have for Kreugers' decision.
(c) Are there any other options that Kreugers should consider? What impact would each of these have on the above ratios?

COMMUNICATION ACTIVITY

BYP9-8   The chapter presented some concerns regarding the current accounting standards for research and development expenditures.

Instructions
Assume that you are either (a) the president of a company that is very dependent on ongoing research and development, writing a memo to the FASB complaining about the current accounting standards regarding research and development, or (b) the FASB member defending the current standards regarding research and development. Your memo should address the questions shown on page 471.

1. By requiring expensing of R&D, do you think companies will spend less on R&D? Why or why not? What are the possible implications for the competitiveness of U.S. companies?
2. If a company makes a commitment to spend money for R&D, it must believe it has future benefits. Shouldn't these costs therefore be capitalized just like the purchase of any long-lived asset that you believe will have future benefits?

ETHICS CASE

BYP9-9 Green Line Anti-Pollution Company is suffering declining sales of its principal product, nonbiodegradable plastic cartons. The president, Peter Wall, instructs his controller, Chuck Meitz, to lengthen asset lives to reduce depreciation expense. A processing line of automated plastic extruding equipment, purchased for $2.5 million in January 2006, was originally estimated to have a useful life of 8 years and a salvage value of $400,000. Depreciation has been recorded for 2 years on that basis. Peter wants the estimated life changed to 12 years total and the straight-line method continued. Chuck is hesitant to make the change, believing it is unethical to increase net income in this manner. Peter says, "Hey, the life is only an estimate, and I've heard that our competition uses a 12-year life on their production equipment."

Instructions
(a) Who are the stakeholders in this situation?
(b) Is the proposed change in asset life unethical, or is it simply a good business practice by an astute president?
(c) What is the effect of Peter's proposed change on income before taxes in the year of change?

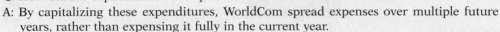

Answers to Business Insight and Accounting across the Organization Questions

p. 422
Q: How did the capitalization of expenses increase WorldCom's income?
A: By capitalizing these expenditures, WorldCom spread expenses over multiple future years, rather than expensing it fully in the current year.

p. 425
Q: Why might airline managers choose to lease rather than purchase their planes?
A: The reasons for leasing include favorable tax treatment, better financing options, increased flexibility, reduced risk of obsolescence, and low airline income.

p. 438
Q: How does measuring marketing ROI support the overall efforts of the organization?
A: Top management is ultimately concerned about maximizing the company's return on assets. Holding marketing managers accountable for the marketing ROI will contribute to the company's overall goal of maximizing return on assets.

p. 444
Q: How should ESPN account for the $1.1 billion per year franchise fee?
A: Since this is an annual franchise fee, ESPN should expense it each year, rather than capitalizing and amortizing it.

Answer to Tootsie Roll Review It Question 3, p. 428

Tootsie Roll depreciates its buildings over 20 to 35 years and its machinery and equipment over 5 to 20 years.

Answers to Self-Study Questions

1. d   2. a   3. b   4. d   5. c   6. b   7. d   8. d   9. b   10. c
11. c   *12. d

REMEMBER TO GO BACK TO THE NAVIGATOR BOX ON THE CHAPTER-OPENING PAGE AND CHECK OFF YOUR COMPLETED WORK.

Reporting and Analyzing Liabilities

FEATURE STORY

And Then There Were Two

Debt can help a company acquire the things it needs to grow, but it is often the very thing that kills a company. A brief history of Maxwell Car Company illustrates the role of debt in the U.S. auto industry. In 1920 Maxwell Car Company was on the brink of financial ruin. Because it was axle-deep in debt and unable to pay its bills, its creditors stepped in and took over. They hired a former General Motors executive named Walter Chrysler to reorganize the company. By 1925 he had taken over the company and renamed it Chrysler. By 1933 Chrysler was booming, with sales surpassing even those of Ford.

But the next few decades saw Chrysler make a series of blunders. During the 1940s, while its competitors were making yearly design changes to boost customer interest, Chrysler made no changes. During the 1960s, when customers wanted large cars, Chrysler produced small cars. During the 1970s, when customers wanted small cars, Chrysler offered big "boats." By 1980, with its creditors pounding at the gates, Chrysler was again on the brink of financial ruin.

At that point Chrysler brought in a former Ford executive named Lee Iacocca to save the company. Iacocca, considered by many as good a politician as a businessman, argued that the United States could not afford to let Chrysler fail because of the loss of jobs.

He convinced the federal government to grant loan guarantees—promises that if Chrysler failed to pay its creditors, the government would pay them. Iacocca then streamlined operations and brought out some profitable products. Chrysler repaid all of its government-guaranteed loans by 1983, seven years ahead of the scheduled final payment.

What has happened since? In the 1990s Chrysler knew both feast and famine: In 1991 it operated in the red, with Iacocca leaving the company under pressure in 1992. By 1995 Chrysler was the most profitable U.S.-based car manufacturer and the envy of the entire industry.

But to compete in today's global vehicle market, you must be big—really big. So in 1998 Chrysler merged with German automaker Daimler-Benz, to form DaimlerChrysler. This left just two U.S.-based auto manufacturers—General Motors and Ford.

These companies are giants. General Motors and Ford typically rank among the top five U.S. firms in total assets. But General Motors and Ford have accumulated a truckload of debt on their way to getting this big. Combined, they have approximately $600 billion in total outstanding liabilities. Although debt has made it possible to get so big, the Chrysler story makes it clear that debt can also threaten a company's survival.

On the World Wide Web
DaimlerChrysler:
    www.daimlerchrysler.com
Ford: www.ford.com
General Motors: www.gm.com

PREVIEW OF CHAPTER 10

The Feature Story suggests that General Motors and Ford have tremendous amounts of debt. It is unlikely that they could have grown so large without this debt, but at times the debt threatens their very existence. Given this risk, why do companies borrow money? Why do they sometimes borrow short-term and other times long-term? Besides bank borrowings, what other kinds of debts do companies incur? In this chapter we address these issues.

The content and organization of the chapter are as follows.

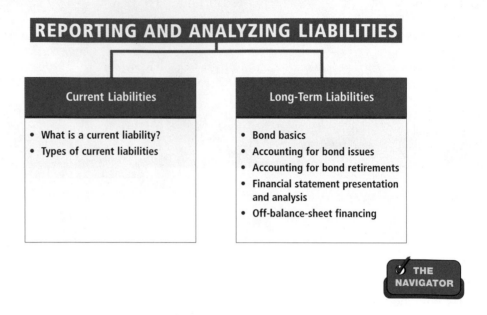

REPORTING AND ANALYZING LIABILITIES

Current Liabilities

- What is a current liability?
- Types of current liabilities

Long-Term Liabilities

- Bond basics
- Accounting for bond issues
- Accounting for bond retirements
- Financial statement presentation and analysis
- Off-balance-sheet financing

THE NAVIGATOR

SECTION ONE
CURRENT LIABILITIES

What Is a Current Liability?

STUDY OBJECTIVE

1

Explain a current liability and identify the major types of current liabilities.

You have learned that liabilities are defined as "creditors' claims on total assets" and as "existing debts and obligations." Companies must settle or pay these claims, debts, and obligations at some time in the future by transferring assets or services. The future date on which they are due or payable (the maturity date) is a significant feature of liabilities.

As explained in Chapter 2, a **current liability** is a debt that a company reasonably expects to pay (1) from existing current assets or through the creation of other current liabilities, and (2) within one year or the operating cycle, whichever is longer. Debts that do not meet both criteria are **long-term liabilities**.

Financial statement users want to know whether a company's obligations are current or long-term. A company that has more current liabilities than current assets often lacks liquidity, or short-term debt-paying ability. In addition, users want to know the types of liabilities a company has. If a company declares bankruptcy, a specific, predetermined order of payment to creditors exists. Thus, the amount and type of liabilities are of critical importance.

Types of Current Liabilities

The different types of current liabilities include notes payable, accounts payable, unearned revenues, and accrued liabilities such as taxes, salaries and wages, and interest. In this section we discuss a few of the common and more important types of current liabilities.

NOTES PAYABLE

Companies record obligations in the form of written notes as **notes payable**. They often use notes payable instead of accounts payable because notes payable give the lender written documentation of the obligation in case legal remedies are needed to collect the debt. Companies frequently issue notes payable to meet short-term financing needs. Notes payable usually require the borrower to pay interest.

STUDY OBJECTIVE

2

Describe the accounting for notes payable.

Notes are issued for varying periods of time. **Those due for payment within one year of the balance sheet date are usually classified as current liabilities.** Most notes are interest-bearing.

To illustrate the accounting for notes payable, assume that First National Bank agrees to lend $100,000 on September 1, 2007, if Cole Williams Co. signs a $100,000, 12%, four-month note maturing on January 1. When a company issues an interest-bearing note, the amount of assets it receives generally equals the note's face value. Cole Williams Co. therefore will receive $100,000 cash and will make the following journal entry.

Sept. 1	Cash	100,000	
	Notes Payable		100,000
	(To record issuance of 12%, 4-month		
	note to First National Bank)		

A	=	L	+	SE
+100,000				+100,000

Cash Flows
+100,000
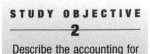

Interest accrues over the life of the note, and the issuer must periodically record that accrual. If Cole Williams Co. prepares financial statements annually, it makes an adjusting entry at December 31 to recognize interest expense and interest payable of $4,000 ($100,000 \times 12\% \times \frac{4}{12}$):

Dec. 31	Interest Expense	4,000	
	Interest Payable		4,000
	(To accrue interest for 4 months on First		
	National Bank note)		

A	=	L	+	SE
				−4,000 Exp
		+4,000		

Cash Flows
no effect

In the December 31 financial statements, the current liabilities section of the balance sheet will show notes payable $100,000 and interest payable $4,000. In addition, the company will report interest expense of $4,000 under "Other expenses and losses" in the income statement.

At maturity (January 1), Cole Williams Co. must pay the face value of the note ($100,000) plus $4,000 interest ($100,000 \times 12\% \times \frac{4}{12}$). It records payment of the note and accrued interest as follows.

Jan. 1	Notes Payable	100,000	
	Interest Payable	4,000	
	Cash		104,000
	(To record payment of First National		
	Bank interest-bearing note and		
	accrued interest at maturity)		

A	=	L	+	SE
		−100,000		
		−4,000		
−104,000				

Cash Flows
−104,000
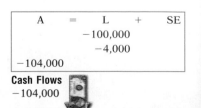

Appendix 10C at the end of this chapter discusses the accounting for long-term installment notes payable.

SALES TAXES PAYABLE

Many of the products we purchase at retail stores are subject to sales taxes. Many states are now implementing sales taxes on purchases made on the Internet as well. Sales taxes are expressed as a percentage of the sales price. The retailer (or selling company) collects the tax from the customer when the sale occurs and periodically (usually monthly) remits the collections to the state's department of revenue.

Helpful Hint Watch how sales are rung up at local retailers to see whether the sales tax is computed separately.

Under most state laws, the selling company must ring up separately on the cash register the amount of the sale and the amount of the sales tax collected. (Gasoline sales are a major exception.) The company then uses the cash register readings to credit Sales and Sales Taxes Payable. For example, if the March 25 cash register readings for Cooley Grocery show sales of $10,000 and sales taxes of $600 (sales tax rate of 6%), the journal entry is:

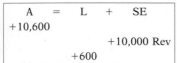

A = L + SE
+10,600
                    +10,000 Rev
        +600

Cash Flows
+10,600

Mar. 25	Cash	10,600	
	Sales		10,000
	Sales Taxes Payable		600
	(To record daily sales and sales taxes)		

When the company remits the taxes to the taxing agency, it decreases (debits) Sales Taxes Payable and decreases (credits) Cash. The company does not report sales taxes as an expense; it simply forwards to the government the amount paid by the customer. Thus, Cooley Grocery serves only as a **collection agent** for the taxing authority.

Sometimes companies do not ring up sales taxes separately on the cash register. To determine the amount of sales in such cases, divide total receipts by 100% plus the sales tax percentage. For example, assume that Cooley Grocery rings up total receipts of $10,600. Because the amount received from the sale is equal to the sales price 100% plus 6% of sales, or 1.06 times the sales total, we can compute sales as follows: $10,600 ÷ 1.06 = $10,000. Thus, we can find the sales tax amount of $600 by either (1) subtracting sales from total receipts ($10,600 − $10,000) or (2) multiplying sales by the sales tax rate ($10,000 × 6%).

PAYROLL AND PAYROLL TAXES PAYABLE

Assume that Susan Alena works 40 hours this week for Pepitone Inc., earning a wage of $10 per hour. Will Susan receive a $400 check at the end of the week? Not likely. The reason: Pepitone is required to withhold amounts from her wages to pay various governmental authorities. For example, Pepitone will withhold amounts for Social Security taxes and for federal and state income taxes. If these withholdings total $100, Susan will receive a check for only $300. Illustration 10-1 summarizes the types of payroll deductions that normally occur for most companies.

As a result of these deductions, companies withhold from employee paychecks amounts that must be paid to other parties. Pepitone therefore has incurred a liability to pay these third parties, and must report this liability in its balance sheet.

As a second illustration, assume that Cargo Corporation records its payroll for the week of March 7 with the journal entry shown on page 477.

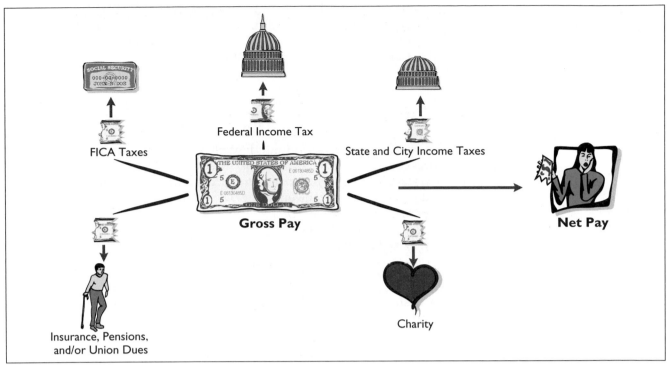

Illustration 10-1
Payroll deductions

			A	=	L	+	SE
							−100,000 Exp
Mar. 7	Salaries and Wages Expense	100,000					
	FICA Taxes Payable[1]		7,650		+7,650		
	Federal Income Taxes Payable		21,864		+21,864		
	State Income Taxes Payable		2,922		+2,922		
	Salaries and Wages Payable		67,564		+67,564		
	(To record payroll and withholding taxes for the week ending March 7)						

Cash Flows
no effect

Cargo then records payment of this payroll on March 7 as follows.

			A	=	L	+	SE
					−67,564		
Mar. 7	Salaries and Wages Payable	67,564	−67,564				
	Cash		67,564				
	(To record payment of the March 7 payroll)						

Cash Flows
−67,564

In this case Cargo reports $100,000 in wages and salaries expense. In addition, it reports liabilities for the wages payable as well as liabilities to governmental agencies. Rather than pay the employees $100,000, Cargo instead must withhold the taxes and make the tax payments directly. In summary, Cargo is essentially serving as a tax collector.

In addition to the liabilities incurred as a result of withholdings, employers also incur a second type of payroll-related liability. With every payroll, the employer incurs liabilities to pay various **payroll taxes** levied upon the employer. These payroll taxes include the *employer's share* of Social Security (FICA) taxes and state and federal unemployment taxes. Based on Cargo Corp.'s $100,000 payroll, the company would record the employer's expense and liability for these payroll taxes as follows.

---

[1]Social Security taxes are commonly called FICA taxes. In 1937 Congress enacted the Federal Insurance Contribution Act (FICA). As can be seen in this journal entry and the payroll tax journal entry, the employee and employer must make equal contributions to Social Security. The Social Security rate in 2005 was 7.65% for each.

A	=	L	+	SE	
				−13,850 Exp	
+7,650					
+800					
+5,400					

Cash Flows
no effect

Mar. 7	Payroll Tax Expense	13,850	
	FICA Taxes Payable		7,650
	Federal Unemployment Taxes Payable		800
	State Unemployment Taxes Payable		5,400
	(To record employer's payroll taxes on March 7 payroll)		

Companies classify the payroll and payroll tax liability accounts as current liabilities because they must be paid to employees or remitted to taxing authorities periodically and in the near term. Taxing authorities impose substantial fines and penalties on employers if the withholding and payroll taxes are not computed correctly and paid on time.

UNEARNED REVENUES

A magazine publisher such as Sports Illustrated may receive a customer's check when magazines are ordered. An airline company such as American Airlines often receives cash when it sells tickets for future flights. Season tickets for concerts, sporting events, and theatre programs are also paid for in advance. How do companies account for unearned revenues that are received before goods are delivered or services are provided?

1. When the company receives an advance, it increases (debits) Cash and also increases (credits) a current liability account identifying the source of the unearned revenue.
2. When the company earns the revenue, it decreases (debits) the unearned revenue account and increases (credits) an earned revenue account.

To illustrate, assume that Superior University sells 10,000 season football tickets at $50 each for its five-game home schedule. The entry for the sales of season tickets is:

A	=	L	+	SE
+500,000				
		+500,000		

Cash Flows
+500,000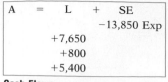

Aug. 6	Cash	500,000	
	Unearned Football Ticket Revenue		500,000
	(To record sale of 10,000 season tickets)		

As each game is completed, Superior records the earning of revenue with the following entry.

A	=	L	+	SE
		−100,000		
				+100,000 Rev

Cash Flows
no effect

Sept. 7	Unearned Football Ticket Revenue	100,000	
	Football Ticket Revenue		100,000
	(To record football ticket revenues earned)		

The account Unearned Football Ticket Revenue represents unearned revenue, and the university would report it as a current liability. As the school earns the revenue, it reclassifies the amount from unearned revenue to earned revenue. Unearned revenue is material for some companies: In the airline industry, tickets sold for future flights represent almost 50% of total current liabilities. At United Airlines, unearned ticket revenue recently was the largest current liability, amounting to more than $1 billion.

Illustration 10-2 shows specific unearned and earned revenue accounts used in selected types of businesses.

Type of Business	Account Title	
	Unearned Revenue	**Earned Revenue**
Airline	Unearned Passenger Ticket Revenue	Passenger Ticket Revenue
Magazine publisher	Unearned Subscription Revenue	Subscription Revenue
Hotel	Unearned Rental Revenue	Rental Revenue

Illustration 10-2
Unearned and earned
revenue accounts

CURRENT MATURITIES OF LONG-TERM DEBT

Companies often have a portion of long-term debt that comes due in the current year. As an example, assume that Wendy Construction issues a five-year, interest-bearing $25,000 note on January 1, 2006. This note specifies that each January 1, starting January 1, 2007, Wendy should pay $5,000 of the note. When the company prepares financial statements on December 31, 2006, it should report $5,000 as a current liability and $20,000 as a long-term liability. Companies often identify current maturities of long-term debt on the balance sheet as **long-term debt due within one year**. At December 31, 2003, the Automotive Division of General Motors had $1,090 million of such debt.

It is not necessary to prepare an adjusting entry to recognize the current maturity of long-term debt. At the balance sheet date, all obligations due within one year are classified as current, and all other obligations are classified as long-term.

Accounting across the Organization

A decision that all companies must make is to what extent to rely on short-term versus long-term financing. The critical nature of this decision was highlighted in the fall of 2001, after the World Trade Center disaster. Prior to September 11, short-term interest rates had been extremely low relative to long-term rates. In order to minimize interest costs, many companies were relying very heavily on short-term financing to purchase things they normally would have used long-term debt for. The problem with short-term financing is that it requires companies to continually find new financing as each loan comes due. This makes them vulnerable to sudden changes in the economy.

After September 11, lenders and short-term investors became very reluctant to loan money. This put the squeeze on many companies: as short-term loans came due, they were unable to refinance. Some were able to get other financing, but at extremely high rates (for example, 12% as compared to 3%). Others were unable to get loans and instead had to sell assets to generate cash for their immediate needs.

Source: Henny Sender, "Firms Feel Consequences of Short-Term Borrowing," *Wall Street Journal Online* (October 12, 2001).

 Based on this story, what is a good general rule to use in choosing between short-term and long-term financing?

BEFORE YOU GO ON . . .

▶ Review It

1. What are the two criteria for classifying a debt as a current liability?
2. What are some examples of current liabilities?
3. What are three items generally withheld from employees' wages or salaries?

4. List three examples of unearned revenues.

5. Identify the liabilities classified as current by Tootsie Roll. The answer to this question appears on page 531.

▶ **Do It**

During the month of September, Lake Corporation's employees earned wages of $60,000. Withholdings related to these wages were $3,500 for Social Security (FICA), $6,500 for federal income tax, and $2,000 for state income tax. Costs incurred for unemployment taxes were $90 for federal and $150 for state.

Prepare the September 30 journal entries for (a) wages expense and wages payable assuming that all September wages will be paid in October and (b) the company's payroll tax expense.

Action Plan

• Remember that wages earned are an expense to the company, but withholdings reduce the amount due to be paid to the employee.
• Payroll taxes are taxes the company incurs related to its employees.

Solution

(a) To determine wages payable, reduce wages expense by the withholdings for FICA, federal income tax, and state income tax.

Sept. 30	Wages Expense	60,000	
	FICA Taxes Payable		3,500
	Federal Income Taxes Payable		6,500
	State Income Taxes Payable		2,000
	Wages Payable		48,000

(b) Payroll taxes would be for the company's share of FICA, as well as for federal and state unemployment tax.

Sept. 30	Payroll Tax Expense	3,740	
	FICA Taxes Payable		3,500
	Federal Unemployment Taxes Payable		90
	State Unemployment Taxes Payable		150

SECTION TWO
LONG-TERM LIABILITIES

Long-term liabilities are obligations that a company expects to pay after one year. In this section we explain the accounting for the principal types of obligations reported in the long-term liabilities section of the balance sheet. These obligations often are in the form of bonds or long-term notes.

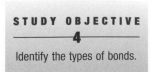

Bond Basics

Bonds are a form of interest-bearing note payable issued by corporations, universities, and governmental agencies. Bonds, like common stock, are sold in small denominations (usually $1,000 or multiples of $1,000). As a result, bonds attract many investors.

TYPES OF BONDS

Bonds may have different features. In the following sections we describe some commonly issued types of bonds.

Secured and Unsecured Bonds

Secured bonds have specific assets of the issuer pledged as collateral for the bonds. **Unsecured bonds** are issued against the general credit of the borrower. Large corporations with good credit ratings use unsecured bonds extensively. For example, in a recent annual report, Dupont reported more than $2 billion of unsecured bonds outstanding.

Convertible and Callable Bonds

Bonds that can be converted into common stock at the bondholder's option are **convertible bonds**. Bonds that the issuing company can retire at a stated dollar amount prior to maturity are **callable bonds**. Convertible bonds have features that are attractive both to bondholders and to the issuer. The conversion often gives bondholders an opportunity to benefit if the market price of the common stock increases substantially. Furthermore, until conversion, the bondholder receives interest on the bond. For the issuer, the bonds sell at a higher price and pay a lower rate of interest than comparable debt securities that do not have a conversion option. Many corporations, such as USAir, United States Steel Corp., and General Motors Corporation, have convertible bonds outstanding.

Convertible Bonds

Callable Bonds

Accounting across the Organization

During the boom times of the late 1990s, many rapidly growing companies issued large quantities of convertible bonds. Investors found the convertible bonds attractive because they paid regular interest but also had the upside potential of being converted to stock if the stock price increased. At the time, stock prices were increasing rapidly, so many investors viewed convertible bonds as a cheap and safe way to buy stock.

As a consequence, companies were able to pay much lower interest rates on convertible bonds than on standard bonds. When the bonds were issued, company managers assumed that the bonds would be converted. Thus the company would never have to repay the debt with cash. It seemed too good to be true—and it was.

When stock prices plummeted in the early 2000s, investors no longer had an incentive to convert, since the market price was below the conversion price. Now many of these massive bonds are coming due, and companies are being forced either to pay them off or to issue new debt at much higher rates.

 The drop in stock prices did not change the debt to total assets ratios of these companies. Discuss how the perception of a high debt to total assets ratio changed before and after the fall in stock prices.

ISSUING PROCEDURES

A **bond certificate** is issued to the investor to provide evidence of the investor's claim against the company. As Illustration 10-3 (page 482) shows, the bond certificate provides information such as the name of the company that issued the bonds, the face value of the bonds, the maturity date of the bonds, and the contractual interest rate. The **face value** is the amount due at the maturity date. The **maturity date** is the date that the final payment is due to the investor from the issuing company. The **contractual interest rate** is the rate used to determine the amount of cash interest the borrower pays and the investor receives. Usually the contractual rate is stated as an annual rate, and interest is generally paid semiannually.

Alternative Terminology
The contractual rate is often referred to as the *stated rate*.

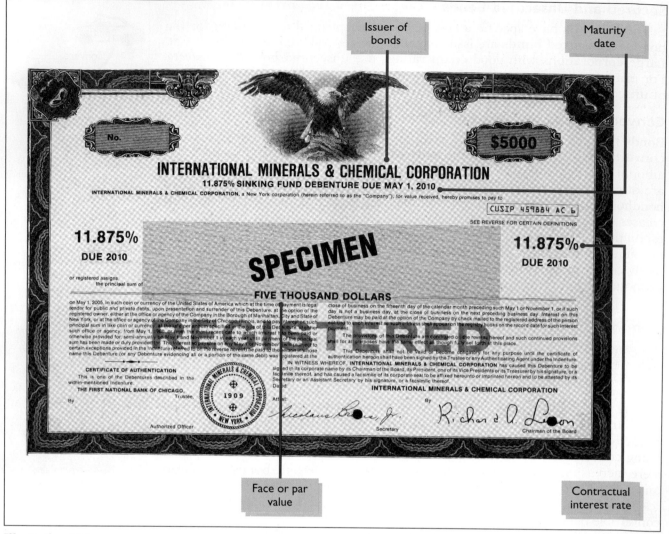

Illustration 10-3
Bond certificate

DETERMINING THE MARKET VALUE OF BONDS

If you were an investor wanting to purchase a bond, how would you determine how much to pay? To be more specific, assume that Coronet, Inc. issues a zero-interest (pays no interest) bond with a face value of $1,000,000 due in 20 years. For this bond, the only cash you receive is $1 million at the end of 20 years. Would you pay $1 million for this bond?

We hope not, because $1 million received 20 years from now is not the same as $1 million received today. The term **time value of money** is used to indicate the relationship between time and money—that a dollar received today is worth more than a dollar promised at some time in the future. If you had $1 million today, you would invest it and earn interest so that at the end of 20 years, your investment would be worth much more than $1 million. Thus, if someone is going to pay you $1 million 20 years from now, you would want to find its equivalent today, or its **present value**. In other words, you would want to determine how much must be invested today at current interest rates to have $1 million in 20 years.

The current market value (present value) of a bond is therefore a function of three factors: (1) the dollar amounts to be received, (2) the length of time until the amounts are received, and (3) the market interest rate. The **market interest**

Same dollars at different times are not equal.

rate is the rate investors demand for loaning funds. The process of finding the present value is referred to as **discounting** the future amounts.

To illustrate, assume that Acropolis Company on January 1, 2007, issues $100,000 of 9% bonds, due in five years, with interest payable annually at year-end. The purchaser of the bonds would receive the following two types of cash payments: (1) **principal** of $100,000 to be paid at maturity, and (2) five $9,000 **interest payments** ($100,000 × 9%) over the term of the bonds. Illustration 10-4 shows a time diagram depicting both cash flows.

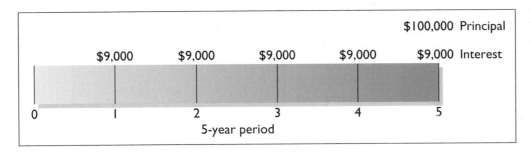

Illustration 10-4
Time diagram depicting cash flows

The current market value of a bond is equal to the present value of all the future cash payments promised by the bond. Illustration 10-5 lists and totals the present values of these amounts, assuming the market rate of interest is 9%.

Present value of $100,000 received in 5 years	$ 64,993
Present value of $9,000 received annually for 5 years	35,007
Market price of bonds	**$100,000**

Illustration 10-5
Computing the market price of bonds

Tables are available to provide the present value numbers to be used, or these values can be determined mathematically.[2] Appendix C, near the end of the book, provides further discussion of the concepts and the mechanics of the time value of money computations.

BEFORE YOU GO ON . . .

▶ Review It

1. What are bonds?
2. What are secured versus unsecured bonds and callable versus convertible bonds?
3. Explain the terms *face value* and *contractual interest rate*.
4. Explain why you would prefer to receive $1 million today rather than five years from now.

✔ THE NAVIGATOR

Accounting for Bond Issues

A corporation records bond transactions when it issues or retires (buys back) bonds and when bondholders convert bonds into common stock. If bondholders sell their bond investments to other investors, the issuing firm receives no

---

[2]For those knowledgable in the use of present value tables, the computations in this example are:
$100,000 × .64993 = $64,993 and $9,000 × 3.88965 = $35,007 (rounded).

further money on the transaction, **nor does the issuing corporation journalize the transaction** (although it does keep records of the names of bondholders in some cases).

Bonds may be issued at face value, below face value (discount), or above face value (premium). Bond prices for both new issues and existing bonds are quoted as **a percentage of the face value of the bond. Face value is usually $1,000.** Thus, a $1,000 bond with a quoted price of 97 means that the selling price of the bond is 97% of face value, or $970.

ISSUING BONDS AT FACE VALUE

To illustrate the accounting for bonds issued at face value, assume that Devor Corporation issues 100, five-year, 10%, $1,000 bonds dated January 1, 2007, at 100 (100% of face value). The entry to record the sale is:

A	=	L	+	SE
+100,000				
		+100,000		

Cash Flows
+100,000

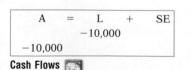

Jan. 1	Cash	100,000	
	Bonds Payable		100,000
	(To record sale of bonds at face value)		

Devor reports bonds payable in the long-term liabilities section of the balance sheet because the maturity date is January 1, 2012 (more than one year away).

Over the term (life) of the bonds, companies make entries to record bond interest. Interest on bonds payable is computed in the same manner as interest on notes payable, as explained earlier. If we assume that interest is payable annually on January 1 on the bonds described above, Devor accrues interest of $10,000 ($100,000 $\times$ 10% $\times$ $\frac{12}{12}$) on December 31.

At December 31 Devor recognizes the $10,000 of interest expense incurred with the following adjusting entry.

Helpful Hint Interest Expense = Principal $\times$ Rate $\times$ Time

A	=	L	+	SE
				−10,000 Exp
		+10,000		

Cash Flows
no effect

Dec. 31	Bond Interest Expense	10,000	
	Bond Interest Payable		10,000
	(To accrue bond interest)		

The company classifies **bond interest payable as a current liability** because it is scheduled for payment within the next year. When Devor pays the interest on January 1, 2008, it decreases (debits) Bond Interest Payable and decreases (credits) Cash for $10,000.

Devor records the payment on January 1 as follows.

A	=	L	+	SE
		−10,000		
−10,000				

Cash Flows
−10,000

Jan. 1	Bond Interest Payable	10,000	
	Cash		10,000
	(To record payment of bond interest)		

DISCOUNT OR PREMIUM ON BONDS

The previous illustrations assumed that the contractual (stated) interest rate and the market (effective) interest rate paid on bonds were the same. Recall that the **contractual interest rate** is the rate applied to the face (par) value to arrive at the interest paid in a year. The **market interest rate** is the rate investors demand for loaning funds to the corporation. When the contractual interest rate and the market interest rate are the same, **bonds sell at face value**.

However, market interest rates change daily. The type of bond issued, the state of the economy, current industry conditions, and the company's individual performance all affect market interest rates. As a result, the contractual and market interest rates often differ. To make bonds salable when the two rates differ, bonds sell below or above face value.

To illustrate, suppose that a company issues 10% bonds at a time when other bonds of similar risk are paying 12%. Investors will not be interested in buying the 10% bonds, so their value will fall below their face value. In this case, we say the 10% bonds are **selling at a** discount. As a result of the decline in the bonds' selling price, the actual interest rate incurred by the company increases to the level of the current market interest rate.

Conversely, if the market rate of interest is **lower than** the contractual interest rate, investors will have to pay more than face value for the bonds. That is, if the market rate of interest is 8% but the contractual interest rate on the bonds is 10%, the issuer will require more funds from the investor. In these cases, **bonds sell at a** premium. Illustration 10-6 shows these relationships graphically.

> **Helpful Hint** Bond prices *vary inversely* with changes in the market interest rate: As market interest rates decline, bond prices will increase. When a bond is issued, if the market interest rate is below the contractual rate, the price will be higher than the face value.

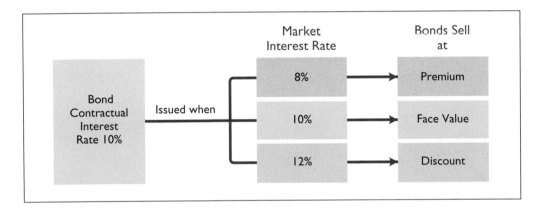

Illustration 10-6 Interest rates and bond prices

Issuance of bonds at an amount different from face value is quite common. By the time a company prints the bond certificates and markets the bonds, it will be a coincidence if the market rate and the contractual rate are the same. Thus, the issuance of bonds at a discount does not mean that the financial strength of the issuer is suspect. Conversely, the sale of bonds at a premium does not indicate that the financial strength of the issuer is exceptional.

> **Helpful Hint** Some bonds are sold at a discount by design. "Zero-coupon" bonds, which pay no interest, sell at a deep discount to face value.

ISSUING BONDS AT A DISCOUNT

To illustrate the issuance of bonds at a discount, assume that on January 1, 2007, Candlestick Inc. sells $100,000, five-year, 10% bonds at 98 (98% of face value) with interest payable on January 1. The entry to record the issuance is:

Jan. 1	Cash	98,000	
	Discount on Bonds Payable	2,000	
	Bonds Payable		100,000
	(To record sale of bonds at a discount)		

A	=	L	+	SE
+98,000				
				−2,000
				+100,000

Cash Flows
+98,000

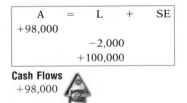

Although Discount on Bonds Payable has a debit balance, **it is not an asset.** Rather it is a **contra account**, which is **deducted from bonds payable** on the balance sheet as shown in Illustration 10-7 (page 486).

Illustration 10-7
Statement presentation of discount on bonds payable

CANDLESTICK INC. Balance Sheet (partial)		
Long-term liabilities		
Bonds payable	$100,000	
Less: Discount on bonds payable	2,000	$98,000

Helpful Hint The carrying value (book value) of bonds issued at a discount is determined by subtracting the balance of the discount account from the balance of the Bonds Payable account.

The $98,000 represents the **carrying (or book) value** of the bonds. On the date of issue this amount equals the market price of the bonds.

The issuance of bonds below face value causes the total cost of borrowing to differ from the bond interest paid. That is, the issuing corporation not only must pay the contractual interest rate over the term of the bonds but also must pay the face value (rather than the issuance price) at maturity. Therefore, the difference between the issuance price and the face value of the bonds—the discount—is an **additional cost of borrowing**. The company records this cost as **bond interest expense** over the life of the bonds. The total cost of borrowing $98,000 for Candlestick Inc. is $52,000, computed as shown in Illustration 10-8.

Illustration 10-8
Computation of total cost of borrowing—bonds issued at discount

Bonds Issued at a Discount	
Annual interest payments	
($100,000 × 10% = $10,000; $10,000 × 5)	$ 50,000
Add: Bond discount ($100,000 − $98,000)	2,000
Total cost of borrowing	**$52,000**

Alternatively, we can compute the total cost of borrowing as shown in Illustration 10-9.

Illustration 10-9
Alternative computation of total cost of borrowing—bonds issued at discount

Bonds Issued at a Discount	
Principal at maturity	$100,000
Annual interest payments ($10,000 × 5)	50,000
Cash to be paid to bondholders	150,000
Cash received from bondholders	98,000
Total cost of borrowing	**$ 52,000**

To follow the matching principle, companies allocate bond discount to expense in each period in which the bonds are outstanding. This is referred to as **amortizing the discount**. Amortization of the discount **increases** the amount of interest expense reported each period. That is, after the company amortizes the discount, the amount of interest expense it reports in a period will exceed the contractual amount. As shown in Illustration 10-8, for the bonds issued by Candlestick Inc., total interest expense will exceed the contractual interest by $2,000 over the life of the bonds.

As the discount is amortized, its balance declines. As a consequence, the carrying value of the bonds will increase, until at maturity the carrying value of the bonds equals their face amount. This is shown in Illustration 10-10. Appendix 10A and Appendix 10B at the end of this chapter discuss procedures for amortizing bond discount.

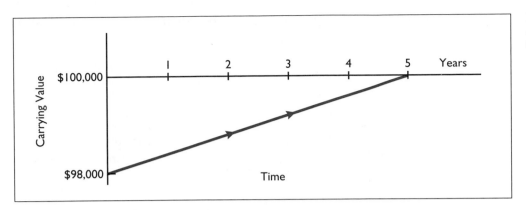

Illustration 10-10
Amortization of bond
discount

ISSUING BONDS AT A PREMIUM

We can illustrate the issuance of bonds at a premium by now assuming the Candlestick Inc. bonds described above sell at 102 (102% of face value) rather than at 98. The entry to record the sale is:

Helpful Hint Both a discount and a premium account are valuation accounts. A *valuation account* is one that is needed to value properly the item to which it relates.

Jan. 1	Cash	102,000	
	Bonds Payable		100,000
	Premium on Bonds Payable		2,000
	(To record sale of bonds at a premium)		

A	=	L	+	SE
+102,000				
		+100,000		
		+2,000		

Cash Flows
+102,000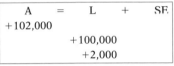

Candlestick adds the premium on bonds payable **to the bonds payable** amount on the balance sheet, as shown in Illustration 10-11.

CANDLESTICK INC. Balance Sheet (partial)		
Long-term liabilities		
Bonds payable	$100,000	
Add: Premium on bonds payable	**2,000**	$102,000

Illustration 10-11
Statement presentation of bond premium

The sale of bonds above face value causes the total cost of borrowing to be **less than the bond interest paid** because the borrower is not required to pay the bond premium at the maturity date of the bonds. Thus, the premium is considered to be **a reduction in the cost of borrowing** that reduces bond interest expense over the life of the bonds. The total cost of borrowing $102,000 for Candlestick Inc. is $48,000, computed as in Illustration 10-12.

Bonds Issued at a Premium	
Annual interest payments	
($100,000 × 10% = $10,000; $10,000 × 5)	$ 50,000
Less: Bond premium ($102,000 − $100,000)	2,000
Total cost of borrowing	**$48,000**

Illustration 10-12
Computation of total cost of borrowing—bonds issued at a premium

Alternatively, we can compute the cost of borrowing as shown in Illustration 10-13.

Illustration 10-13
Alternative computation of total cost of borrowing—bonds issued at a premium

Bonds Issued at a Premium	
Principal at maturity	$100,000
Annual interest payments ($10,000 × 5)	50,000
Cash to be paid to bondholders	150,000
Cash received from bondholders	102,000
Total cost of borrowing	**$ 48,000**

Similar to bond discount, companies allocate bond premium to expense in each period in which the bonds are outstanding. This is referred to as **amortizing the premium**. Amortization of the premium **decreases** the amount of interest expense reported each period. That is, after the company amortizes the premium, the amount of interest expense it reports in a period will be less than the contractual amount. As shown in Illustration 10-12, for the bonds issued by Candlestick Inc., contractual interest will exceed the interest expense by $2,000 over the life of the bonds.

As the premium is amortized, its balance declines. As a consequence, the carrying value of the bonds will decrease, until at maturity the carrying value of the bonds equals their face amount. This is shown in Illustration 10-14. Appendix 10A and Appendix 10B at the end of this chapter discuss procedures for amortizing bond premium.

Illustration 10-14
Amortization of bond premium

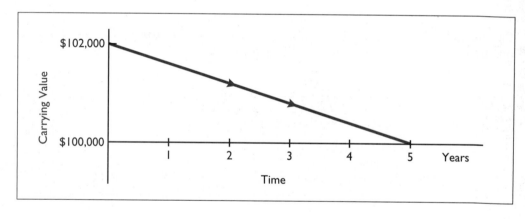

Accounting for Bond Retirements

Bonds are retired when the issuing corporation purchases (redeems) them. The appropriate entries for these transactions are explained next.

STUDY OBJECTIVE
6

Describe the entries when bonds are redeemed.

REDEEMING BONDS AT MATURITY

Regardless of the issue price of bonds, the book value of the bonds at maturity will equal their face value. Assuming that the company pays and records separately the interest for the last interest period, Candlestick records the redemption of its bonds at maturity as:

A	=	L	+	SE
		−100,000		
−100,000				

Cash Flows
−100,000

Bonds Payable	100,000	
Cash		100,000
(To record redemption of bonds at maturity)		

REDEEMING BONDS BEFORE MATURITY

Bonds may be redeemed before maturity. A company may decide to retire bonds before maturity in order to reduce interest cost and remove debt from its balance sheet. A company should retire debt early only if it has sufficient cash resources.

When bonds are retired before maturity, it is necessary to: (1) eliminate the carrying value of the bonds at the redemption date, (2) record the cash paid, and (3) recognize the gain or loss on redemption. The **carrying value** of the bonds is the face value of the bonds less unamortized bond discount or plus unamortized bond premium at the redemption date.

To illustrate, assume at the end of the fourth period, Candlestick Inc., having sold its bonds at a premium, retires the bonds at 103 after paying the annual interest. Assume that the carrying value of the bonds at the redemption date is $100,400. Candlestick records the redemption at the end of the fourth interest period (January 1, 2011) as:

Jan. 1	Bonds Payable	100,000	
	Premium on Bonds Payable	400	
	Loss on Bond Redemption	2,600	
	Cash		103,000
	(To record redemption of bonds at 103)		

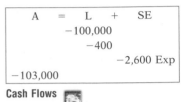

```
A  =   L   +   SE
     -100,000
       -400
            -2,600 Exp
-103,000
```

Cash Flows
−103,000

Note that the loss of $2,600 is the difference between the $103,000 cash paid and the $100,400 carrying value of the bonds.

BEFORE YOU GO ON . . .

▶ Review It

1. What entry is made to record the issuance of bonds payable of $1 million at 100? At 96? At 102?
2. Why do bonds sell at a discount? At a premium? At face value?
3. Explain the accounting for redemption of bonds at maturity and before maturity by payment in cash.

▶ Do It

Assume a company issued bonds with the following characteristics: (a) interest to be paid $50,000, (b) interest expense to be recorded $52,000, and (c) amortization $2,000. Answer these questions: (1) Were the bonds sold at a premium or a discount? (2) After recording the interest expense, will the bond carrying value increase or decrease?

Action Plan

• Know the effects that the amortization of bond discount and bond premium have on bond interest expense and on the carrying value of the bonds.
• Remember bond discount amortization increases both bond interest expense and the carrying value of the bonds. Bond premium amortization has the reverse effects.

Solution

(1) Interest expense is $2,000 greater than the interest paid. This difference is equal to the amortization amount. Thus, the bonds were sold at a discount. (2) The interest entry will decrease Discount on Bonds Payable and increase the carrying value of the bonds.

✓ THE NAVIGATOR

STUDY OBJECTIVE
7
Identify the requirements
for the financial statement
presentation and analysis of
liabilities.

Financial Statement Presentation and Analysis

BALANCE SHEET PRESENTATION

Current liabilities are the first category under Liabilities on the balance sheet. Companies list each of the principal types of current liabilities separately within the category.

Within the current liabilities section, companies usually list notes payable first, followed by accounts payable. Other items sometimes are listed in the order of their magnitude. *In your homework, you should present notes payable first, followed by accounts payable, and then other liabilities in order of magnitude.*

Companies report long-term liabilities in a separate section of the balance sheet immediately following "Current liabilities." An example is shown in Illustration 10-15.

Illustration 10-15
Balance sheet
presentation of liabilities

MARAIS COMPANY Balance Sheet (partial)		
Liabilities		
Current liabilities		
Notes payable	$ 250,000	
Accounts payable	125,000	
Current maturities of long-term debt	300,000	
Accrued liabilities	75,000	
Total current liabilities		$ 750,000
Long-term liabilities		
Bonds payable	1,000,000	
Less: Discount on bonds payable	80,000	920,000
Notes payable, secured by plant assets		540,000
Lease liability		500,000
Total long-term liabilities		1,960,000
Total liabilities		$2,710,000

Disclosure of debt is very important. Failures at Enron, WorldCom, and Global Crossing, have made investors very concerned about companies' debt obligations. Summary data regarding debts may be presented in the balance sheet with detailed data (such as interest rates, maturity dates, conversion privileges, and assets pledged as collateral) shown in a supporting schedule in the notes. Companies should report current maturities of long-term debt as a current liability.

STATEMENT OF CASH FLOWS PRESENTATION

The balance sheet presents the balances of a company's debts at a point in time. The statement of cash flows also presents information about a company's debts. Information regarding cash inflows and outflows during the year that resulted from the principal portion of debt transactions appears in the "Financing activities" section of the statement of cash flows. Interest expense is reported in the "Operating activities" section, even though it resulted from debt transactions.

Illustration 10-16 presents the cash flows from financing activities from the statement of cash flows for the Automotive Division of General Motors. From this we learn that the division issued new long-term debt of $758 million and repaid long-term debt of $79 million.

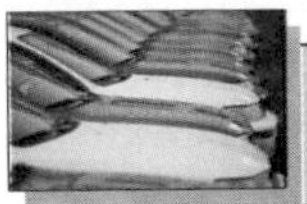

Illustration 10-16
Financing activities
section of statement of
cash flows

**GENERAL MOTORS CORPORATION—
AUTOMOTIVE DIVISION
Statement of Cash Flows (partial)
2004
(in millions)**

Cash flows from financing activities	
Net increase (decrease) in loans payable	$ (803)
Long-term debt—borrowings	**758**
Long-term debt—repayments	**(79)**
Cash dividends paid to stockholders	(1,129)
Net cash (used in) provided by financing activities	$ (1,253)

ANALYSIS

Careful examination of debt obligations helps you assess a company's ability to pay its current and long-term obligations. It also helps you determine whether a company can obtain debt financing in order to grow. We will use the following information from the financial statements of General Motors to illustrate the analysis of a company's liquidity and solvency.

Illustration 10-17
Simplified balance sheets
for General Motors
Corporation

**GENERAL MOTORS CORPORATION—
AUTOMOTIVE DIVISION
Balance Sheets
December 31, 2004 and 2003
(in millions)**

Assets	2004	2003
Total current assets	$ 55,515	$ 57,855
Noncurrent assets	103,788	103,930
Total assets	$159,303	$161,785
Liabilities and Stockholders' Equity		
Total current liabilities	$ 74,892	$ 71,264
Noncurrent liabilities	78,894	85,397
Total liabilities	153,786	156,661
Total stockholders' equity	5,517	5,124
Total liabilities and stockholders' equity	$159,303	$161,785

Liquidity

Liquidity ratios measure the short-term ability of a company to pay its maturing obligations and to meet unexpected needs for cash. A commonly used measure of liquidity is the current ratio (presented in Chapter 2). The current ratio is calculated as current assets divided by current liabilities. Illustration 10-18 presents the current ratio for General Motors along with the industry average.

Illustration 10-18
Current ratio

($ in millions)	General Motors		Industry Average
	2004	**2003**	**2004**
Current Ratio	$\frac{\$55,515}{\$74,892} = .74{:}1$	$\frac{\$57,855}{\$71,264} = .81{:}1$	1.59:1

General Motors' current assets are less than its current liabilities. Therefore its current ratio is less than 1 in both 2003 and 2004. The industry average current ratio for manufacturers of autos and trucks is 1.59:1.[3] Thus, General Motors appears to lack liquidity.

Many companies today minimize their liquid assets (such as cash, accounts receivable, and inventory) in order to improve profitability measures, such as return on assets. This is particularly true of large companies such as GM. Companies that keep fewer liquid assets on hand must rely on other sources of liquidity. One such source is a **bank line of credit**. A line of credit is a prearranged agreement between a company and a lender that permits the company, should it be necessary, to borrow up to an agreed-upon amount. The disclosure regarding debt in General Motors' financial statements states that it has $8.3 billion of unused lines of credit. This represents a substantial amount of available cash. In addition, the Management Discussion and Analysis section of GM's annual report provides an extensive discussion of the company's liquidity. In it, GM notes that even though its credit rating was downgraded during the year, its "access to the capital markets remained sufficient to meet the Corporation's capital needs." Thus, even though General Motors has a low current ratio, its available lines of credit as well as other sources of financing appear adequate to meet any short-term cash deficiency it might experience.

Decision Toolkit

Decision Checkpoints	Info Needed for Decision	Tool to Use for Decision	How to Evaluate Results
Can the company obtain short-term financing when necessary?	Available lines of credit, from notes to the financial statements.	Compare available lines of credit to current liabilities. Also, evaluate liquidity ratios.	If liquidity ratios are low, then lines of credit should be high to compensate.

Solvency

Solvency ratios measure the ability of a company to survive over a long period of time. The Feature Story in this chapter mentioned that although there once were many U.S. automobile manufacturers, only two U.S.-based companies remain today. Many of the others went bankrupt. This highlights the fact that when making a long-term loan or purchasing a company's stock, you must give consideration to a company's solvency.

To reduce the risks associated with having a large amount of debt during an economic downturn, U.S. automobile manufacturers have taken two precautionary steps. First, they have built up large balances of cash and cash equivalents to avoid a cash crisis. Second, recently they have been reluctant to build new plants or hire new workers to meet their production needs. Instead, they have asked existing workers to put in overtime, or they "outsource" work to other companies. In this way, if an economic downturn occurs, they avoid having to make debt payments on idle production plants, and they minimize layoffs.

In Chapter 2 you learned that one measure of a company's solvency is the debt to total assets ratio. This is calculated as total liabilities divided by total assets. This ratio indicates the extent to which a company's assets are financed with debt.

---

[3]Market Guide based this and subsequent industry ratios used in this chapter on a group of 29 companies that manufacture cars and trucks (see *multex.com*).

Other measures can also be useful in assessing solvency. One such measure is the **times interest earned ratio**, which provides an indication of a company's ability to meet interest payments as they come due. It is computed by dividing income before interest expense and income taxes by interest expense. It uses income before interest expense and taxes because this number best represents the amount available to pay interest.

We can use the balance sheet information presented on page 491 and the additional information below to calculate solvency ratios for the Automotive Division of General Motors.

($ in millions)	2004	2003
Net income (loss)	$(89)	$995
Interest expense	2,480	1,780
Tax expense (refund)	(2,325)	(869)

The debt to total assets ratios and times interest earned ratios for General Motors and averages for the industry are shown in Illustration 10-19.

Illustration 10-19
Solvency ratios

$$\text{Debt to Total Assets Ratio} = \frac{\text{Total Liabilities}}{\text{Total Assets}}$$

$$\text{Times Interest Earned Ratio} = \frac{\text{Net Income + Interest Expense + Tax Expense}}{\text{Interest Expense}}$$

	General Motors		Industry Average
($ in millions)	2004	2003	2004
Debt to Total Assets Ratio	$\frac{\$153,786}{\$159,303} = 97\%$	$\frac{\$156,661}{\$161,785} = 97\%$	84.6%
Times Interest Earned Ratio	$\frac{\$(89) + \$2,480 - \$2,325}{\$2,480}$ $= .03$ times	$\frac{\$995 + \$1,780 - \$869}{\$1,780}$ $= 1.07$ times	6.38 times

General Motors' debt to total assets ratio remained constant at 97%. The industry average for manufacturers of autos and trucks is 84.6%. Thus, General Motors' ratio is very high, especially considering that we are looking only at the automotive division and have excluded the financing division of the company, which traditionally has a very high debt to total assets ratio.

General Motors' times interest earned ratio declined from 1.07 times in 2003 to .03 in 2004. The industry average for manufacturers of autos and trucks is much higher at 6.38 times. In 2004, General Motors' income before interest expense and taxes—that is, income after adding back interest expense and in this case, deducting a tax refund—was only $66 million. The company's high debt to total assets ratio, combined with its interest coverage ratio of .03, should be of obvious concern to the company's creditors and investors. This concern was reflected in a downgrade to GM's credit rating by debt-rating services.

Business Insight
Investor Perspective

The Williams Companies recently faced the prospect of a credit-rating downgrade by Moody's Investors Service Inc. Lenders are heavily influenced by these ratings, so a downgrade would make it harder for the company to borrow funds, as well as make borrowing more expensive. The company quickly announced plans to improve its liquidity and solvency. It said it would sell assets of $1.5 to $3.0 billion, issue common stock of $1 to $1.5 billion, and cut annual costs by $100 million. It also said it would continue to evaluate the size of its dividend payment on common stock. It said it would use the funds generated by these actions to pay down existing debt and to increase its liquidity.

Source: "Williams Unveils Measures to Bolster its Balance Sheet," *Wall Street Journal Online* (May 28, 2002).

 Explain how the sale of plant assets could improve the company's solvency.

Decision Toolkit

Decision Checkpoints	Info Needed for Decision	Tool to Use for Decision	How to Evaluate Results
Can the company meet its obligations in the long term?	Interest expense and net income before interest and taxes	Times interest earned ratio = $\frac{\text{Net income} + \text{Interest expense} + \text{Tax expense}}{\text{Interest expense}}$	High ratio indicates ability to meet interest payments as scheduled.

Off-Balance-Sheet Financing

A concern for analysts when they evaluate a company's liquidity and solvency is whether that company has properly recorded all of its obligations. The bankruptcy of Enron Corporation, one of the largest bankruptcies in U.S. history, demonstrated how much damage can result when a company does not properly record or disclose all of its debts. Many would say Enron was practicing off-balance-sheet financing. **Off-balance-sheet financing** is an attempt to borrow funds in such a way that the obligations are not recorded. Two common types of off-balance-sheet financing result from contingencies and lease transactions.

CONTINGENCIES

One reason a company's balance sheet might not fully reflect its potential obligations is due to contingencies. **Contingencies** are events with uncertain outcomes. A common type of contingency is lawsuits. Suppose, for example, that you were analyzing the financial statements of a cigarette manufacturer and did not consider the possible negative implications of existing unsettled lawsuits. Your analysis of the company's financial position would certainly be misleading. Other common types of contingencies are product warranties and environmental clean-up obligations. For example, in 2004 Novartis AG began offering a money-back guarantee on its blood-pressure medications The creation of this guarantee will necessitate an accrual for the estimated claims that will result from returns.

Accounting rules require that companies disclose contingencies in the notes; in some cases they must accrue them as liabilities. For example, suppose that Waterbury Inc. is sued by a customer for $1 million due to an injury sustained by a defective product. If at the company's year-end, the lawsuit had not yet been resolved, how should Waterbury account for this event? If the company can determine **a reasonable estimate** of the expected loss and if it is **probable** it will lose the suit, then the company should accrue for the loss. It records the loss by increasing (debiting) a loss account and increasing (crediting) a liability such as Lawsuit Liability. If *both* of these conditions are not met, then the company discloses the basic facts regarding this suit in the notes to its financial statements.

LEASING

One common type of off-balance-sheet financing results from leasing. Most lessees do not like to report leases on their balance sheets because the lease increases the company's total liabilities. Recall from Chapter 9 that operating leases are treated like rentals—no asset or liabilities show on the books. Capital leases are treated like a purchase—increasing both assets and liabilities. **As a result, many companies structure their lease agreements to avoid meeting the criteria of a capital lease.**

Recall from Chapter 9 that many U.S. airlines lease a large portion of their planes without showing any debt related to them on their balance sheets. For example, the total increase in assets and liabilities that would result if Southwest Airlines recorded on the balance sheet its off-balance-sheet **"operating"** leases would be approximately $2.7 billion. Illustration 10-20 presents Southwest Airlines' debt to total assets ratio using the numbers presented in its balance sheet and also shows the ratio after adjusting for the off-balance-sheet leases. After those adjustments, Southwest has a ratio of 61% versus 51% before. This means that of every dollar of assets, 61 cents was funded by debt. This would be of interest to analysts evaluating Southwest's solvency.

	Using numbers as presented on balance sheet	**Adjusted for off-balance-sheet leases**
Debt to total assets ratio	$\dfrac{\$5,813}{\$11,337} = 51\%$	$\dfrac{\$5,813 + \$2,677}{\$11,337 + \$2,677} = 61\%$

Illustration 10-20
Debt to total assets ratio adjusted for leases

Critics of off-balance-sheet financing contend that many leases represent unavoidable obligations that meet the definition of a liability, and therefore companies should report them as liabilities on the balance sheet. To reduce these concerns, companies are required to report in a note their operating lease obligations for subsequent years. This allows analysts and other financial statement users to adjust a company's financial statements by adding leased assets and lease liabilities if they feel that this treatment is more appropriate.

Decision Toolkit

Decision Checkpoints	Info Needed for Decision	Tool to Use for Decision	How to Evaluate Results
Does the company have any contingent liabilities?	Knowledge of events with uncertain negative outcomes	Notes to financial statements and financial statements	If negative outcomes are possible, determine the probability, the amount of loss, and the potential impact on financial statements.
Does the company have significant off-balance-sheet financing, such as unrecorded lease obligations?	Information on unrecorded obligations, such as a schedule of minimum lease payments from the lease note	Compare liquidity and solvency ratios with and without unrecorded obligations included.	If ratios differ significantly after including unrecorded obligations, these obligations should not be ignored in analysis.

BEFORE YOU GO ON . . .

▶ Review It

1. What is meant by solvency?
2. What information does the times interest earned ratio provide, and how is the ratio calculated?
3. What is meant by "off-balance-sheet financing"? What is a common example of off-balance-sheet financing?
4. What are contingent liabilities?

Using the Decision Toolkit

Ford Motor Company has enjoyed some tremendous successes, including its popular Taurus and Explorer vehicles. Yet observers are looking for the next big hit. Development of a new vehicle costs billions. A flop is financially devastating, and the financial effect is magnified if the company has large amounts of outstanding debt.

The balance sheets below provide financial information for the Automotive Division of Ford Motor Company as of December 31, 2004 and 2003. We have chosen to analyze only the Automotive Division rather than the total corporation, which includes Ford's giant financing division. In an actual analysis you would want to analyze the major divisions individually as well as the combined corporation as a whole.

Instructions

1. Evaluate Ford's liquidity using appropriate ratios, and compare to those of General Motors and to industry averages.

2. Evaluate Ford's solvency using appropriate ratios, and compare to those of General Motors and to industry averages.

3. Comment on Ford's available lines of credit.

FORD MOTOR COMPANY—AUTOMOTIVE DIVISION
Balance Sheets
December 31, 2004 and 2003
(in millions)

Assets	2004	2003
Current assets	$ 44,703	$ 43,742
Noncurrent assets	71,719	71,702
Total assets	$116,422	$115,444
Liabilities and Shareholders' Equity		
Current liabilities	$ 55,027	$ 52,292
Noncurrent liabilities	57,612	64,612
Total liabilities	112,639	116,904
Total shareholders' equity	3,783	(1,460)
Total liabilities and shareholders' equity	$116,422	$115,444
Other Information		
Net income (loss)	$ (155)	$ (1,908)
Tax expense (refund)	(30)	(175)
Interest expense	1,221	1,323
Available lines of credit (Automotive Division)	7,100	

Solution

1. Ford's liquidity can be measured using the current ratio:

	2004	**2003**
Current ratio	$\dfrac{\$44,703}{\$55,027} = .81:1$	$\dfrac{\$43,742}{\$52,292} = .84:1$

Like that of General Motors, Ford's current ratio is well below the industry average of 1.59:1 and below 1—indicating that its current assets are less than its current liabilities. These are increasingly common levels for large companies that have reduced the amount of cash, inventory, and receivables they hold. As noted earlier, these low current ratios are not necessarily cause for concern, but they do require more careful monitoring. Ford must also make sure to have other short-term financing options available, such as lines of credit.

2. Ford's solvency can be measured with the debt to total assets ratio and the times interest earned ratio:

	2004	**2003**
Debt to total assets ratio	$\dfrac{\$112,639}{\$116,422} = 97\%$	$\dfrac{\$116,904}{\$115,444} = 101\%$
Times interest earned ratio	$\dfrac{\$(155) + \$1,221 - \$30}{\$1,221}$	$\dfrac{\$(1,908) + \$1,323 - \$175}{\$1,323}$
	$= .85$ times	$= 0$ times

The debt to total assets ratio suggests that Ford, like General Motors, relies very heavily on debt financing. The ratio decreased from 2003 to 2004, indicating that the company's solvency improved slightly. In 2003 its ratio exceeds 1. This is possible because we have calculated the ratio for the Automotive Division only, rather than the whole company. The debt to total assets ratio for the entire company is 94.5%. This is extremely high.

   The times interest earned ratio increased from a zero in 2003 to .85 in 2004. The 2003 ratio is zero because, even after adding back interest and taxes, the company's income was negative. This is well below the industry average of 6.38 times. It is likely that the company's solvency was a concern to investors and creditors and would be closely monitored.

3. Ford has available lines of credit of $7.1 billion. These financing sources significantly improve its liquidity.

Summary of Study Objectives

1 *Explain a current liability and identify the major types of current liabilities.* A current liability is a debt that a company can reasonably expect to pay (a) from existing current assets or through the creation of other current liabilities, and (b) within one year or the operating cycle, whichever is longer. The major types of current liabilities are notes payable, accounts payable, sales taxes payable, unearned revenues, and accrued liabilities such as taxes, salaries and wages, and interest payable.

2 *Describe the accounting for notes payable.* When a promissory note is interest-bearing, the amount of assets received upon the issuance of the note is

generally equal to the face value of the note, and interest expense is accrued over the life of the note. At maturity, the amount paid is equal to the face value of the note plus accrued interest.

3 *Explain the accounting for other current liabilities.* Companies record sales taxes payable at the time the related sales occur. The company serves as a collection agent for the taxing authority. Sales taxes are not an expense to the company. Companies hold employee withholding taxes, and credit them to appropriate liability accounts, until they remit these taxes to the governmental taxing authorities. Unearned revenues are initially recorded in an unearned revenue account.

As the company earns the revenue, a transfer from unearned revenue to earned revenue occurs. Companies should report the current maturities of long-term debt as a current liability in the balance sheet.

4 *Identify the types of bonds.* The following different types of bonds may be issued: secured and unsecured bonds, and convertible and callable bonds.

5 *Prepare the entries for the issuance of bonds and interest expense.* When companies issue bonds, they debit Cash for the cash proceeds and credit Bonds Payable for the face value of the bonds. In addition, they use the accounts Premium on Bonds Payable and Discount on Bonds Payable to show the bond premium and bond discount, respectively. Bond discount and bond premium are amortized over the life of the bond.

6 *Describe the entries when bonds are redeemed.* When companies redeem bonds at maturity, they credit Cash and debit Bonds Payable for the face value of the bonds. When companies redeem bonds before maturity, they (a) eliminate the carrying value of the bonds at the redemption date, (b) record the cash paid, and (c) recognize the gain or loss on redemption.

7 *Identify the requirements for the financial statement presentation and analysis of liabilities.* Current liabilities appear first on the balance sheet, followed by long-term liabilities. Companies should report the nature and amount of each liability in the balance sheet or in schedules in the notes accompanying the statements. They report inflows and outflows of cash related to the principal portion of long-term debt in the financing section of the statement of cash flows.

The liquidity of a company may be analyzed by computing the current ratio. The long-run solvency of a company may be analyzed by computing the debt to total assets ratio and the times interest earned ratio. Other factors to consider are contingent liabilities and lease obligations.

Decision Toolkit—A Summary

Decision Checkpoints	Info Needed for Decision	Tool to Use for Decision	How to Evaluate Results
Can the company obtain short-term financing when necessary?	Available lines of credit, from notes to the financial statements	Compare available lines of credit to current liabilities. Also, evaluate liquidity ratios.	If liquidity ratios are low, then lines of credit should be high to compensate.
Can the company meet its obligations in the long term?	Interest expense and net income before interest and taxes	$\text{Times interest earned ratio} = \dfrac{\text{Net income} + \text{Interest expense} + \text{Tax expense}}{\text{Interest expense}}$	High ratio indicates ability to meet interest payments as scheduled.
Does the company have any contingent liabilities?	Knowledge of events with uncertain negative outcomes	Notes to financial statements and financial statements	If negative outcomes are possible, determine the probability, the amount of loss, and the potential impact on financial statements.
Does the company have significant off-balance-sheet financing, such as unrecorded lease obligations?	Information on unrecorded obligations, such as a schedule of minimum lease payments from the lease note	Compare liquidity and solvency ratios with and without unrecorded obligations included.	If ratios differ significantly after including unrecorded obligations, these obligations should not be ignored in analysis.

APPENDIX 10A
STRAIGHT-LINE AMORTIZATION

STUDY OBJECTIVE

8

Apply the straight-line method of amortizing bond discount and bond premium.

Amortizing Bond Discount

To follow the matching principle, companies allocate bond discount to expense in each period in which the bonds are outstanding. The **straight-line method of amortization** allocates the same amount to interest expense in each interest period. The calculation is presented in Illustration 10A-1.

Bond Discount	÷	Number of Interest Periods	=	Bond Discount Amortization

In the Candlestick Inc. example (page 485), the company sold $100,000, five-year, 10% bonds on January 1, 2007, for $98,000. This resulted in a $2,000 bond discount ($100,000 − $98,000). The bond discount amortization is $400 ($2,000 ÷ 5) for each of the five amortization periods. Candlestick records the first accrual of bond interest and the amortization of bond discount on December 31 as follows.

Dec. 31	Bond Interest Expense	10,400	
	Discount on Bonds Payable		400
	Bond Interest Payable		10,000
	(To record accrued bond interest and amortization of bond discount)		

A	=	L	+	SE
				−10,400 Exp
		+400		
		+10,000		

Cash Flows
no effect

Over the term of the bonds, the balance in Discount on Bonds Payable will decrease annually by the same amount until it has a zero balance at the maturity date of the bonds. Thus, the carrying value of the bonds at maturity will be equal to the face value of the bonds.

Preparing a bond discount amortization schedule, as shown in Illustration 10A-2, is useful to determine interest expense, discount amortization, and the carrying value of the bond. As indicated, the interest expense recorded each period is $10,400. Also note that the carrying value of the bond increases $400 each period until it reaches its face value of $100,000 at the end of period 5.

BOND DISCOUNT AMORTIZATION SCHEDULE
Straight-Line Method—Annual Interest Payments
$100,000 of 10%, 5-Year Bonds

Interest Periods	(A) Interest To Be Paid (10% × $100,000)	(B) Interest Expense To Be Recorded (A) + (C)	(C) Discount Amortization ($2,000 ÷ 5)	(D) Unamortized Discount (D) − (C)	(E) Bond Carrying Value ($100,000 − D)
Issue date				$2,000	$ 98,000
1	$10,000	$10,400	$ 400	1,600	98,400
2	10,000	10,400	400	1,200	98,800
3	10,000	10,400	400	800	99,200
4	10,000	10,400	400	400	99,600
5	10,000	10,400	400	0	100,000
	$50,000	$52,000	$2,000		

Column (A) remains constant because the face value of the bonds ($100,000) is multiplied by the annual contractual interest rate (10%) each period.
Column (B) is computed as the interest paid (Column A) plus the discount amortization (Column C).
Column (C) indicates the discount amortization each period.
Column (D) decreases each period by the same amount until it reaches zero at maturity.
Column (E) increases each period by the amount of discount amortization until it equals the face value at maturity.

Amortizing Bond Premium

The amortization of bond premium parallels that of bond discount. Illustration 10A-3 presents the formula for determining bond premium amortization under the straight-line method.

Illustration 10A-3
Formula for straight-line
method of bond premium
amortization

Bond Premium	÷	Number of Interest Periods	=	Bond Premium Amortization

Continuing our example, assume Candlestick Inc., sells the bonds described above for $102,000, rather than $98,000. This results in a bond premium of $2,000 ($102,000 − $100,000). The premium amortization for each interest period is $400 ($2,000 ÷ 5). Candlestick records the first accrual of interest on December 31 as follows.

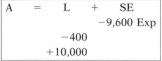

Cash Flows
no effect

Dec. 31	Bond Interest Expense	9,600	
	Premium on Bonds Payable	400	
	Bond Interest Payable		10,000
	(To record accrued bond interest and amortization of bond premium)		

Over the term of the bonds, the balance in Premium on Bonds Payable will decrease annually by the same amount until it has a zero balance at maturity.

A bond premium amortization schedule, as shown in Illustration 10A-4, is useful to determine interest expense, premium amortization, and the carrying value of the bond. As indicated, the interest expense Candlestick records each period is $9,600. Note that the carrying value of the bond decreases $400 each period until it reaches its face value of $100,000 at the end of period 5.

Illustration 10A-4 Bond premium amortization schedule

BOND PREMIUM AMORTIZATION SCHEDULE Straight-Line Method—Annual Interest Payments $100,000 of 10%, 5-Year Bonds				
Interest Periods	(A) Interest To Be Paid (10% × $100,000)	(B) Interest Expense To Be Recorded (A) − (C)	(C) Premium Amortization ($2,000 ÷ 5)	(D) Unamortized Premium (D) − (C)	(E) Bond Carrying Value ($100,000 + D)
Issue date				$2,000	$102,000
1	$10,000	$ 9,600	$ 400	1,600	101,600
2	10,000	9,600	400	1,200	101,200
3	10,000	9,600	400	800	100,800
4	10,000	9,600	400	400	100,400
5	10,000	9,600	400	0	100,000
	$50,000	$48,000	$2,000		

Column **(A)** remains constant because the face value of the bonds ($100,000) is multiplied by the annual contractual interest rate (10%) each period.
Column **(B)** is computed as the interest paid (Column A) less the premium amortization (Column C).
Column **(C)** indicates the premium amortization each period.
Column **(D)** decreases each period by the same amount until it reaches zero at maturity.
Column **(E)** decreases each period by the amount of premium amortization until it equals the face value at maturity.

Summary of Study Objective for Appendix 10A

8 *Apply the straight-line method of amortizing bond discount and bond premium.* The straight-line method of amortization results in a constant amount of amortization and interest expense per period.

APPENDIX 10B
EFFECTIVE-INTEREST AMORTIZATION

To follow the matching principle, companies allocate bond discount to expense in each period in which the bonds are outstanding. However, to completely comply with the matching principle, interest expense as a percentage of carrying value should not change over the life of the bonds. This percentage, referred to as the **effective-interest rate**, is established when the bonds are issued and remains constant in each interest period. Unlike the straight-line method, the effective-interest method of amortization accomplishes this result.

> **STUDY OBJECTIVE**
> **9**
> Apply the effective-interest method of amortizing bond discount and bond premium.

Under the **effective-interest method**, the amortization of bond discount or bond premium results in periodic interest expense equal to a constant percentage of the carrying value of the bonds. The effective-interest method results in **varying amounts** of amortization and interest expense per period but a **constant percentage rate.** In contrast, the straight-line method results in constant amounts of amortization and interest expense per period but a varying percentage rate.

Companies follow three steps under the effective-interest method:

1. Compute the **bond interest expense** by multiplying the carrying value of the bonds at the beginning of the interest period by the effective-interest rate.
2. Compute the **bond interest paid** (or accrued) by multiplying the face value of the bonds by the contractual interest rate.
3. Compute the **amortization amount** by determining the difference between the amounts computed in steps (1) and (2).

Illustration 10B-1 depicts these steps.

(1) **Bond Interest Expense**		**(2)** **Bond Interest Paid**		**(3)**
Carrying Value of Bonds at Beginning of Period	× Effective Interest Rate	− Face Amount of Bonds	× Contractual Interest Rate	= **Amortization Amount**

Illustration 10B-1
Computation of amortization using effective-interest method

Both the straight-line and effective-interest methods of amortization result in the same total amount of interest expense over the term of the bonds. Furthermore, interest expense each interest period is generally comparable in amount. However, **when the amounts are materially different, generally accepted accounting principles (GAAP) require use of the effective-interest method.**

Amortizing Bond Discount

To illustrate the effective-interest method of bond discount amortization, assume that Wrightway Corporation issues $100,000 of 10%, five-year bonds on January 1, 2007, with interest payable each January 1. The bonds sell for $92,790 (92.79% of face value), which results in bond discount of $7,210 ($100,000 − $92,790) and an effective-interest rate of 12%. (Note that the $92,790 can be proven as shown in Appendix C at the end of this book.)

Preparing a bond discount amortization schedule as shown in Illustration 10B-2 facilitates the recording of interest expense and the discount amortization. Note that interest expense as a percentage of carrying value remains constant at 12%.

Illustration 10B-2
Bond discount amortization schedule

WRIGHTWAY CORPORATION
Bond Discount Amortization
Effective-Interest Method—Annual Interest Payments
10% Bonds Issued at 12%

Interest Periods	(A) Interest to Be Paid (10% × $100,000)	(B) Interest Expense to Be Recorded (12% × Preceding Bond Carrying Value)		(C) Discount Amortization (B) − (A)	(D) Unamortized Discount (D) − (C)	(E) Bond Carrying Value ($100,000 − D)
Issue date					$7,210	$ 92,790
1	$10,000	$11,135	(12% × $92,790)	$1,135	6,075	93,925
2	10,000	11,271	(12% × $ 93,925)	1,271	4,804	95,196
3	10,000	11,424	(12% × $ 95,196)	1,424	3,380	96,620
4	10,000	11,594	(12% × $ 96,620)	1,594	1,786	98,214
5	10,000	11,786	(12% × $ 98,214)	1,786	–0–	100,000
	$ 50,000	$ 57,210		$ 7,210		

Column **(A)** remains constant because the face value of the bonds ($100,000) is multiplied by the annual contractual interest rate (10%) each period.
Column **(B)** is computed as the preceding bond carrying value times the annual effective-interest rate (12%).
Column **(C)** indicates the discount amortization each period.
Column **(D)** decreases each period until it reaches zero at maturity.
Column **(E)** increases each period until it equals face value at maturity.

For the first interest period, the computations of bond interest expense and the bond discount amortization are as follows.

Illustration 10B-3
Computation of bond discount amortization

Bond interest expense ($92,790 × 12%)	$11,135
Bond interest paid ($100,000 × 10%)	10,000
Bond discount amortization	**$ 1,135**

As a result, Wrightway Corporation records the accrual of interest and amortization of bond discount on December 31, as follows.

A	=	L	+	SE
				−11,135 Exp
		+1,135		
		+10,000		

Cash Flows
no effect

Dec. 31	Bond Interest Expense	11,135	
	Discount on Bonds Payable		1,135
	Bond Interest Payable		10,000
	(To record accrued interest and		
	amortization of bond discount)		

For the second interest period, bond interest expense will be $11,271 ($93,925 × 12%), and the discount amortization will be $1,271. At December 31, Wrightway makes the following adjusting entry.

Dec. 31	Bond Interest Expense	11,271	
	Discount on Bonds Payable		1,271
	Bond Interest Payable		10,000
	(To record accrued interest and		
	amortization of bond discount)		

A	=	L	+	SE
				−11,271 Exp
		+1,271		
		+10,000		

Cash Flows
no effect

Amortizing Bond Premium

The amortization of bond premium by the effective-interest method is similar to the procedures described for bond discount. As an example, assume that Wrightway Corporation issues $100,000, 10%, five-year bonds on January 1, with interest payable on January 1. In this case, the bonds sell for $107,985, which results in bond premium of $7,985 and an effective-interest rate of 8%. Illustration 10B-4 shows the bond premium amortization schedule.

Helpful Hint When a bond sells for $107,985 it is quoted at 107.985% of face value. Note that $107,985 can be proven as shown in Appendix C.

Illustration 10B-4
Bond premium amortization schedule

		(B) Interest Expense to Be Recorded	(C)	(D)	(E)
	(A)		Premium	Unamortized	Bond
Interest Periods	**Interest to Be Paid (10% × $100,000)**	**(8% × Preceding Bond Carrying Value)**	**Amortization (A) − (B)**	**Premium (D) − (C)**	**Carrying Value ($100,000 + D)**
Issue date				$7,985	$107,985
1	$10,000	$ 8,639 (8% × $107,985)	$1,361	6,624	106,624
2	10,000	8,530 (8% × $ 106,624)	1,470	5,154	105,154
3	10,000	8,412 (8% × $ 105,154)	1,588	3,566	103,566
4	10,000	8,285 (8% × $ 103,566)	1,715	1,851	101,851
5	10,000	8,149* (8% × $ 101,851)	1,851	–0–	100,000
	$50,000	$ 42,015	$7,985		

WRIGHTWAY CORPORATION
Bond Premium Amortization
Effective-Interest Method—Annual Interest Payments
10% Bonds Issued at 8%

Column **(A)** remains constant because the face value of the bonds ($100,000) is multiplied by the contractual interest rate (10%) each period.
Column **(B)** is computed as the carrying value of the bonds times the annual effective-interest rate (8%).
Column **(C)** indicates the premium amortization each period.
Column **(D)** decreases each period until it reaches zero at maturity.
Column **(E)** decreases each period until it equals face value at maturity.

*$1 difference due to rounding.

For the first interest period, the computations of bond interest expense and the bond premium amortization are:

Bond interest paid ($100,000 × 10%)	$10,000
Bond interest expense ($107,985 × 8%)	8,639
Bond premium amortization	**$ 1,361**

Illustration 10B-5
Computation of bond premium amortization

The entry Wrightway makes on December 31 is:

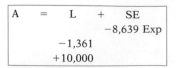

Cash Flows
no effect

Dec. 31	Bond Interest Expense	8,639	
	Premium on Bonds Payable	1,361	
	Bond Interest Payable		10,000
	(To record accrued interest and		
	amortization of bond premium)		

For the second interest period, interest expense will be $8,530, and the premium amortization will be $1,470. Note that the amount of periodic interest expense decreases over the life of the bond when companies apply the effective-interest method to bonds issued at a premium. The reason is that a constant percentage is applied to a decreasing bond carrying value to compute interest expense. The carrying value is decreasing because of the amortization of the premium.

Summary of Study Objective for Appendix 10B

9 *Apply the effective-interest method of amortizing bond discount and bond premium.* The effective-interest method results in varying amounts of amortization and interest expense per period but a constant percentage rate of interest. When the difference between the straight-line and effective-interest method is material, GAAP requires use of the effective-interest method.

APPENDIX 10C
ACCOUNTING FOR
LONG-TERM NOTES PAYABLE

STUDY OBJECTIVE
10

Describe the accounting for long-term notes payable.

The use of notes payable in long-term debt financing is quite common. Long-term notes payable are similar to short-term interest-bearing notes payable except that the terms of the notes exceed one year. In periods of unstable interest rates, lenders may tie the interest rate on long-term notes to changes in the market rate for comparable loans. Examples are the 8.03% adjustable rate notes issued by General Motors and the floating-rate notes issued by American Express Company.

A long-term note may be secured by a document called a **mortgage** that pledges title to specific assets as security for a loan. Individuals widely use mortgage notes payable to purchase homes, as do many small and some large companies to acquire plant assets. For example, at one time approximately 18% of McDonalds' long-term debt related to mortgage notes on land, buildings, and improvements.

Like other long-term notes payable, the mortgage loan terms may stipulate either a fixed or an adjustable interest rate. Typically, the terms require the borrower to make equal installment payments over the term of the loan. Each payment consists of (1) interest on the unpaid balance of the loan and (2) a reduction of loan principal. The interest decreases each period, while the portion applied to the loan principal increases.

Companies initially record mortgage notes payable at face value, and subsequently make entries for each installment payment. To illustrate, assume that Porter Technology Inc. issues a $500,000, 12%, 20-year mortgage note on December 31, 2007, to obtain needed financing for the construction of a new research laboratory.

Helpful Hint Electronic spreadsheet programs can create a schedule of installment loan payments. This allows you to put in the data for your own mortgage loan and get an illustration that really hits home.

The terms provide for semiannual installment payments of $33,231 (not including real estate taxes and insurance). The installment payment schedule for the first two years is as follows.

Illustration 10C-1
Mortgage installment payment schedule

Semiannual Interest Period	(A) Cash Payment	(B) Interest Expense (D) × 6%	(C) Reduction of Principal (A) − (B)	(D) Principal Balance (D) − (C)
Issue date				$500,000
1	$33,231	$30,000	$3,231	496,769
2	33,231	29,806	3,425	493,344
3	33,231	29,601	3,630	489,714
4	33,231	29,383	3,848	485,866

Porter Technology records the mortgage loan and first installment payment as follows.

Dec. 31	Cash	500,000	
	Mortgage Notes Payable		500,000
	(To record mortgage loan)		

June 30	Interest Expense	30,000	
	Mortgage Notes Payable	3,231	
	Cash		33,231
	(To record semiannual payment on mortgage)		

In the balance sheet, the company reports the reduction in principal for the next year as a current liability, and classifies the remaining unpaid principal balance as a long-term liability. At December 31, 2008, the total liability is $493,344, of which $7,478 ($3,630 + $3,848) is current and $485,866 ($493,344 − $7,478) is long-term.

Summary of Study Objective for Appendix 10C

10 *Describe the accounting for long-term notes payable.* Each payment consists of (1) interest on the unpaid balance of the loan, and (2) a reduction of loan principal. The interest decreases each period, while the portion applied to the loan principal increases each period.

Glossary

Bond certificate A legal document that indicates the name of the issuer, the face value of the bonds, and such other data as the contractual interest rate and the maturity date of the bonds. (p. 481)

Bonds A form of interest-bearing notes payable issued by corporations, universities, and governmental entities. (p. 480)

Callable bonds Bonds that are the issuing company can retire at a stated dollar amount prior to maturity. (p. 481)

Capital lease A type of lease whose characteristics make it similar to a debt-financed purchase and that is consequently accounted for in that fashion. (p. 495)

Contingencies   Events with uncertain outcomes, such as a potential liability that may become an actual liability sometime in the future. (p. 494)

Contractual (stated) interest rate   Rate used to determine the amount of interest the borrower pays and the investor receives. (p. 481)

Convertible bonds   Bonds that permit bondholders to convert them into common stock at their option. (p. 481)

Current liability   A debt that a company reasonably expects to pay (1) from existing current assets or through the creation of other current liabilities, and (2) within one year or the operating cycle, whichever is longer. (p. 474)

Discount (on a bond)   The difference between the face value of a bond and its selling price, when a bond is sold for less than its face value. (p. 485)

Effective-interest method of amortization   A method of amortizing bond discount or bond premium that results in periodic interest expense equal to a constant percentage of the carrying value of the bonds. (p. 501)

Effective-interest rate   Rate established when bonds are issued that remains constant in each interest period. (p. 501)

Face value   Amount of principal due at the maturity date of the bond. (p. 481)

Long-term liabilities   Obligations that a company expects to pay more than one year in the future. (p. 480)

Market interest rate   The rate investors demand for loaning funds to the corporation. (p. 482)

Maturity date   The date on which the final payment on a bond is due from the bond issuer to the investor. (p. 481)

Mortgage note payable   A long-term note secured by a mortgage that pledges title to specific units of property as security for the loan. (p. 504)

Notes payable   An obligation in the form of a written promissory note. (p. 475)

Off-balance-sheet financing   The intentional effort by a company to structure its financing arrangements so as to avoid showing liabilities on its books. (p. 494)

Operating lease   A contractual arrangement giving the lessee temporary use of the property with continued ownership of the property by the lessor. Accounted for as a rental. (p. 495)

Premium (on a bond)   The difference between the selling price and the face value of a bond when a bond is sold for more than its face value. (p. 485)

Present value   The value today of an amount to be received at some date in the future after taking into account current interest rates. (p. 482)

Secured bonds   Bonds that have specific assets of the issuer pledged as collateral. (p. 481)

Straight-line method of amortization   A method of amortizing bond discount or bond premium that allocates the same amount to interest expense in each interest period. (p. 498)

Time value of money   The relationship between time and money. A dollar received today is worth more than a dollar promised at some time in the future. (p. 482)

Times interest earned ratio   A measure of a company's solvency, calculated by dividing income before interest expense and taxes by interest expense. (p. 493)

Unsecured bonds   Bonds issued against the general credit of the borrower. (p. 481)

Demonstration Problem

Snyder Software Inc. successfully developed a new spreadsheet program. However, to produce and market the program, the company needed $2.0 million of additional financing. On January 1, 2007, Snyder borrowed money as follows.

1. Snyder issued $500,000, 11%, 10-year bonds. The bonds sold at face value and pay interest on January 1.
2. Snyder issued $1.0 million, 10%, 10-year bonds for $886,996. Interest is payable on January 1. Snyder uses the straight-line method of amortization.

Instructions

(a) For the 11% bonds, prepare journal entries for the following items.
    (1) The issuance of the bonds on January 1, 2007.
    (2) Accrue interest expense on December 31, 2007.
    (3) The payment of interest on January 1, 2008.

(b) For the 10-year, 10% bonds:
    (1) Journalize the issuance of the bonds on January 1, 2007.
    (2) Prepare the entry for the redemption of the bonds at 101 on January 1, 2010, after paying the interest due on this date. The carrying value of the bonds at the redemption date was $920,897.

Solution to Demonstration Problem

(a) (1) 2007

Jan. 1	Cash	500,000	
	Bonds Payable		500,000
	(To record issue of 11%, 10-year bonds at face value)		

(2) 2007

Dec. 31	Bond Interest Expense	55,000	
	Bond Interest Payable		55,000
	(To record accrual of bond interest)		

(3) 2008

Jan. 1	Bond Interest Payable	55,000	
	Cash		55,000
	(To record payment of accrued interest)		

(b) (1) 2007

Jan. 1	Cash	886,996	
	Discount on Bonds Payable	113,004	
	Bonds Payable		1,000,000
	(To record issuance of bonds at a discount)		

(2) 2008

Jan. 1	Bonds Payable	1,000,000	
	Loss on Bond Redemption	89,103*	
	Discount on Bonds Payable		79,103
	Cash		1,010,000
	(To record redemption of bonds at 101)		
	*($1,010,000 − $920,897)		

Action Plan

- Record the discount on bonds issued as a contra liability account.

- Compute the loss on bond redemption as the excess of the cash paid over the carrying value of the redeemed bonds.

THE NAVIGATOR

Note: All Questions, Exercises, and Problems marked with an asterisk relate to material in the appendixes to the chapter.

Self-Study Questions

WILEY PLUS

Answers are at the end of the chapter.

(SO 1) **1.** The time period for classifying a liability as current is one year or the operating cycle, whichever is:
(a) longer.   (c) probable.
(b) shorter.   (d) possible.

(SO 1) **2.** To be classified as a current liability, a debt must be expected to be paid:
(a) out of existing current assets.
(b) by creating other current liabilities.
(c) within 2 years.
(d) Either (a) or (b)

(SO 2) **3.** Corricten Company borrows $88,500 on September 1, 2007, from Harrington State Bank by signing an $88,500, 12%, one-year note. What is the accrued interest at December 31, 2007?

(a) $2,655.   (c) $4,425.
(b) $3,540.   (d) $10,620.

(SO 3) **4.** Andre Company has total proceeds from sales of $4,515. If the proceeds include sales taxes of 5%, what is the amount to be credited to Sales?
(a) $4,000.
(b) $4,300.
(c) $4,289.25.
(d) The correct answer is not given.

(SO 7) **5.** Which of the following is *not* a measure of liquidity?
(a) Debt to total assets ratio.
(b) Working capital.
(c) Current ratio.
(d) Current cash debt coverage.

(SO 4)

6. What term is used for bonds that have specific assets pledged as collateral?
(a) Callable bonds.
(b) Convertible bonds.
(c) Secured bonds.
(d) Discount bonds.

(SO 5)

7. Cuso Inc. issues 10-year bonds with a maturity value of $200,000. If the bonds are issued at a premium, this indicates that:
(a) the contractual interest rate exceeds the market interest rate.
(b) the market interest rate exceeds the contractual interest rate.
(c) the contractual interest rate and the market interest rate are the same.
(d) no relationship exists between the two rates.

(SO 5)

8. On January 1, 2007, Scissors Corp. issues $200,000, 5-year, 7% bonds at face value. The entry to record the issuance of the bonds would include a:
(a) debit to cash for $14,000.
(b) debit to bonds payable for $200,000.
(c) credit to bonds payable for $200,000.
(d) credit to bond interest expense of $14,000.

(SO 6)

9. Kant Corporation retires its $100,000 face value bonds at 105 on January 1, following the payment of interest. The carrying value of the bonds at the redemption date is $103,745. The entry to record the redemption will include a:
(a) credit of $3,745 to Loss on Bond Redemption.
(b) debit of $3,745 to Premium on Bonds Payable.
(c) credit of $1,255 to Gain on Bond Redemption.
(d) debit of $5,000 to Premium on Bonds Payable.

(SO 7)

10. ⚙ In a recent year Day Corporation had net income of $150,000, interest expense of $30,000, and tax expense of $20,000. What was Day Corporation's times interest earned ratio for the year?
(a) 5.00.   (c) 6.67.
(b) 4.00.   (d) 7.50.

*11. On January 1 Pierce Corporation issues (SO 8) $500,000, 5-year, 12% bonds at 96 with interest payable on January 1. The entry on December 31 to record accrued bond interest and the amortization of bond discount using the straight-line method will include a:
(a) debit to Interest Expense, $57,600.
(b) debit to Interest Expense, $60,000.
(c) credit to Discount on Bonds Payable, $4,000.
(d) credit to Discount on Bonds Payable, $2,000.

*12. For the bonds issued in question 11, what is the (SO 8) carrying value of the bonds at the end of the third interest period?
(a) $492,000.   (c) $472,000.
(b) $488,000.   (d) $464,000.

*13. On January 1, Daisey Duke Inc. issued (SO 9) $1,000,000, 9% bonds for $939,000. The market rate of interest for these bonds is 10%. Interest is payable annually on December 31. Daisey Duke uses the effective-interest method of amortizing bond discount. At the end of the first year, Daisey Duke should report unamortized bond discount of:
(a) $54,900.   (c) $51,610.
(b) $57,100.   (d) $51,000.

*14. On January 1, Anthony Corporation issued (SO 9) $1,000,000, 14%, 5-year bonds with interest payable on December 31. The bonds sold for $1,072,096. The market rate of interest for these bonds was 12%. On the first interest date, using the effective-interest method, the debit entry to Bond Interest Expense is for:
(a) $120,000.
(b) $125,581.
(c) $128,652.
(d) $140,000.

Go to the book's website, **www.wiley.com/college/kimmel**, to access additional Self-Study Questions.

Questions

1. Georgia Lazenby believes a current liability is a debt that can be expected to be paid in one year. Is Georgia correct? Explain.

2. Travelyan Company obtains $25,000 in cash by signing a 9%, 6-month, $25,000 note payable to First Bank on July 1. Travelyan's fiscal year ends on Sep-

tember 30. What information should be reported for the note payable in the annual financial statements?

3. (a) Your roommate says, "Sales taxes are reported as an expense in the income statement." Do you agree? Explain.

(b) Hard Wok Cafe has cash proceeds from sales of $10,550. This amount includes $550 of sales taxes. Give the entry to record the proceeds.

4. Holt University sold 8,000 season football tickets at $90 each for its five-game home schedule. What entries should be made (a) when the tickets are sold and (b) after each game?

5. Identify three taxes commonly withheld by the employer from an employee's gross pay.

6. (a) Identify three taxes commonly paid by employers on employees' salaries and wages.
   (b) Where in the financial statements does the employer report taxes withheld from employees' pay?

7. (a) What are long-term liabilities? Give two examples.
   (b) What is a bond?

8. Contrast these types of bonds:
   (a) Secured and unsecured.
   (b) Convertible and callable.

9. Explain each of these important terms in issuing bonds:
   (a) Face value.
   (b) Contractual interest rate.
   (c) Bond certificate.

10. (a) What is a convertible bond?
    (b) Discuss the advantages of a convertible bond from the standpoint of the bondholders and of the issuing corporation.

11. Describe the two major obligations incurred by a company when bonds are issued.

12. Assume that Mimi Inc. sold bonds with a face value of $100,000 for $104,000. Was the market interest rate equal to, less than, or greater than the bonds' contractual interest rate? Explain.

13. Magda and Helga are discussing how the market price of a bond is determined. Magda believes that the market price of a bond is solely a function of the amount of the principal payment at the end of the term of a bond. Is she right? Discuss.

14. If a 6%, 10-year, $600,000 bond is issued at face and interest is paid annually, what is the amount of the interest payment at the end of the first period?

15. If the Bonds Payable account has a balance of $900,000 and the Discount on Bonds Payable account has a balance of $36,000, what is the carrying value of the bonds?

16. Which accounts are debited and which are credited if a bond issue originally sold at a premium is redeemed before maturity at 97 immediately following the payment of interest?

17. Stephanie Wolcott, the chief financial officer of Hangers Inc., is considering the options available to her for financing the company's new plant. Short-term interest rates right now are 6%, and long-term rates are 8%. The company's current ratio is 2.2:1. If she finances the new plant with short-term debt, the current ratio will fall to 1.5:1. Briefly discuss the issues that Stephanie should consider.

18. (a) In general, what are the requirements for the financial statement presentation of long-term liabilities?
    (b) What ratios may be computed to evaluate a company's liquidity and solvency?

19. Valentin Zukovsky says that liquidity and solvency are the same thing. Is he correct? If not, how do they differ?

20. The management of Ultra Vehicle Corporation is concerned because survey data suggest that many potential customers do not buy vehicles due to quality concerns. It is considering taking the bold step of increasing the length of its warranty from the industry standard of 3 years up to an unprecedented 10 years in an effort to increase confidence in its quality. Discuss the business as well as accounting implications of this move.

21. Hector Gonzales needs a few new trucks for his business. He is considering buying the trucks but is concerned that the additional debt he will need to borrow will make his liquidity and solvency ratios look bad. What options does he have other than purchasing the trucks, and how will these options affect his financial statements?

22. Empire Corporation has a current ratio of 1.1. Tom has always been told that a corporation's current ratio should exceed 2.0. Empire argues that its ratio is low because it has a minimal amount of inventory on hand so as to reduce operating costs. Empire also points out that it has significant available lines of credit. Is Tom still correct? What do some companies do to compensate for having fewer liquid assets?

23. What are the implications for analysis if a company has significant operating leases?

24. What criteria must be met before a contingency must be recorded as a liability? How should the contingency be disclosed if the criteria are not met?

*25. Explain the straight-line method of amortizing discount and premium on bonds payable.

*26. Osato Corporation issues $200,000 of 6%, 5-year bonds on January 1, 2007, at 104. Assuming that the straight-line method is used to amortize the premium, what is the total amount of interest expense for 2007?

*27. Maria Lopez is discussing the advantages of the effective-interest method of bond amortization with her accounting staff. What do you think Maria is saying?

*28. Snooper Corporation issues $400,000 of 9%, 5-year bonds on January 1, 2007, at 104. If Snooper uses the effective-interest method in amortizing the premium, will the annual interest expense increase or decrease over the life of the bonds? Explain.

Brief Exercises

Identify whether obligations are current liabilities.
(SO 1)

BE10-1   Kananga Company has these obligations at December 31: (a) a note payable for $100,000 due in 2 years, (b) a 10-year mortgage payable of $200,000 payable in ten $20,000 annual payments, (c) interest payable of $15,000 on the mortgage, and (d) accounts payable of $60,000. For each obligation, indicate whether it should be classified as a current liability.

Prepare entries for an interest-bearing note payable.
(SO 2)

BE10-2   Popp Company borrows $70,000 on July 1 from the bank by signing a $70,000, 8%, 1-year note payable. Prepare the journal entries to record (a) the proceeds of the note and (b) accrued interest at December 31, assuming adjusting entries are made only at the end of the year.

Compute and record sales taxes payable.
(SO 3)

BE10-3   Gold Supply does not segregate sales and sales taxes at the time of sale. The register total for March 16 is $10,388. All sales are subject to a 6% sales tax. Compute sales taxes payable and make the entry to record sales taxes payable and sales.

Prepare entries for unearned revenues.
(SO 3)

BE10-4   Denton University sells 3,800 season basketball tickets at $60 each for its 10-game home schedule. Give the entry to record (a) the sale of the season tickets and (b) the revenue earned by playing the first home game.

Compare bond financing to stock financing.
(SO 4)

BE10-5   Domino Inc. is considering these two alternatives to finance its construction of a new $2 million plant:
  (a) Issuance of 200,000 shares of common stock at the market price of $10 per share.
  (b) Issuance of $2 million, 6% bonds at face value.

Complete the table and indicate which alternative is preferable.

	Issue Stock	Issue Bond
Income before interest and taxes	$1,000,000	$1,000,000
Interest expense from bonds	_____	_____
Income before income taxes		
Income tax expense (30%)	_____	_____
Net income	$ _____	$ _____
Outstanding shares	_____	700,000
Earnings per share	$ _____	$ _____

Prepare journal entries for bonds issued at face value.
(SO 5)

BE10-6   Lazar Corporation issued 1,000 7%, 5-year, $1,000 bonds dated January 1, 2007, at face value. Interest is paid each January 1.
  (a) Prepare the journal entry to record the sale of these bonds on January 1, 2007.
  (b) Prepare the adjusting journal entry on December 31, 2007, to record interest expense.
  (c) Prepare the journal entry on January 1, 2008, to record interest paid.

Prepare journal entry for redemption of bonds.
(SO 6)

BE10-7   The balance sheet for Tiffany Company reports the following information on July 1, 2007.

TIFFANY COMPANY
Balance Sheet (partial)

Long-term liabilities		
Bonds payable	$1,000,000	
Less: Discount on bonds payable	30,000	$970,000

Tiffany decides to redeem these bonds at 102 after paying annual interest. Prepare the journal entry to record the redemption on July 1, 2007.

Prepare statement presentation of long-term liabilities.
(SO 7)

BE10-8   Presented here are long-term liability items for Carlton Inc. at December 31, 2007. Prepare the long-term liabilities section of the balance sheet for Carlton Inc.

Bonds payable, due 2011	$900,000
Notes payable, due 2009	80,000
Discount on bonds payable	21,000

BE10-9 Presented here are liability items for Warner Inc. at December 31, 2007. Prepare the liabilities section of Warner's balance sheet.

Prepare liabilities section of balance sheet.
(SO 7)

Accounts payable	$135,000	Employee benefits payable	$ 7,800
Bank note payable			
(due May 1, 2008)	20,000	Interest payable	40,000
Bonds payable, due 2011	900,000	Notes payable, due 2009	80,000
Current portion of			
long-term debt	240,000	Property tax payable	3,500
Discount on bonds payable	45,000	Sales taxes payable	1,400

BE10-10 The 2004 Reebok financial statements contain the following selected data (in millions).

Analyze solvency.
(SO 7)

Current assets	$1,858	Interest expense	$ 26
Total assets	2,441	Income taxes	68
Current liabilities	806	Net income	192
Total liabilities	1,221		
Cash	565		

Compute the following values and provide a brief interpretation of each.
(a) Working capital.   (c) Debt to total assets ratio.
(b) Current ratio.   (d) Times interest earned ratio.

BE10-11 The Canadian National Railway Company's (CN) total assets in a recent year were $18,924 million and its total liabilities were $12,297 million. That year, CN reported operating lease commitments for its locomotives, freight cars, and equipment totalling $1,154 million. If these assets had been recorded as capital leases, assume that assets and liabilities would have risen by approximately $1,154 million.

Analyze solvency.
(SO 7)

(a) Calculate CN's debt to total assets ratio, first using the figures reported, and then after increasing assets and liabilities for the unrecorded operating leases.
(b) Discuss the potential effect of these operating leases on your assessment of CN's solvency.

*BE10-12 Vijay Company issues $2 million, 10-year, 6% bonds at 99, with interest payable on December 31. The straight-line method is used to amortize bond discount.

Prepare journal entries for bonds issued at a discount.
(SO 8)

(a) Prepare the journal entry to record the sale of these bonds on January 1, 2007.
(b) Prepare the journal entry to record interest expense and bond discount amortization on December 31, 2007, assuming no previous accrual of interest.

*BE10-13 Sydor Inc. issues $5 million, 5-year, 8% bonds at 103, with interest payable on January 1. The straight-line method is used to amortize bond premium.

Prepare journal entries for bonds issued at a premium.
(SO 8)

(a) Prepare the journal entry to record the sale of these bonds on January 1, 2007.
(b) Prepare the journal entry to record interest expense and bond premium amortization on December 31, 2007, assuming no previous accrual of interest.

*BE10-14 Presented below is the partial bond discount amortization schedule for Nuong Tu Corp., which uses the effective-interest method of amortization.

Use effective-interest method of bond amortization.
(SO 9)

Interest Periods	Interest to Be Paid	Interest Expense to Be Recorded	Discount Amortization	Unamortized Discount	Bond Carrying Value
Issue date				$62,311	$937,689
1	$45,000	$46,884	$1,884	60,427	939,573
2	45,000	46,979	1,979	58,448	941,552

Instructions
(a) Prepare the journal entry to record the payment of interest and the discount amortization at the end of period 1.
(b) Explain why interest expense is greater than interest paid.
(c) Explain why interest expense will increase each period.

Exercises

Prepare entries for interest-bearing notes.
(SO 2)

E10-1 Rebecca Fleming and Carrie Platt borrowed $12,000 on a 7-month, 9% note from Gopher State Bank to open their business, RC's Coffee House. The money was borrowed on June 1, 2007, and the note matures January 1, 2008.

Instructions
(a) Prepare the entry to record the receipt of the funds from the loan.
(b) Prepare the entry to accrue the interest on June 30.
(c) Assuming adjusting entries are made at the end of each month, determine the balance in the interest payable account at December 31, 2007.
(d) Prepare the entry required on January 1, 2008, when the loan is paid back.

Prepare entries for interest-bearing notes.
(SO 2)

E10-2 On May 15, Kiwi's Outback Clothiers borrowed some money on a 4-month note to provide cash during the slow season of the year. The interest rate on the note was 8%. At the time the note was due, the amount of interest owed was $320.

Instructions
(a) Determine the amount borrowed by Kiwi's.
(b) Assume the amount borrowed was $18,500. What was the interest rate if the amount of interest owed was $740?
(c) Prepare the entry for the initial borrowing and the repayment for the facts in part (a).

Prepare entries for interest-bearing notes.
(SO 2)

E10-3 On June 1, Avery Company Ltd. borrows $50,000 from First Bank on a 6-month, $50,000, 9% note. The note matures on December 1.

Instructions
(a) Prepare the entry on June 1.
(b) Prepare the adjusting entry on June 30.
(c) Prepare the entry at maturity (December 1), assuming monthly adjusting entries have been made through November 30.
(d) What was the total financing cost (interest expense)?

Journalize sales and related taxes.
(SO 3)

E10-4 In providing accounting services to small businesses, you encounter the following situations pertaining to cash sales.
1. Mariella Company rings up sales and sales taxes separately on its cash register. On April 10 the register totals are sales $25,000 and sales taxes $1,250.
2. Brent Company does not segregate sales and sales taxes. Its register total for April 15 is $11,660, which includes a 6% sales tax.

Instructions
Prepare the entries to record the sales transactions and related taxes for (a) Mariella Company and (b) Brent Company.

Journalize payroll entries.
(SO 3)

E10-5 During the month of March, Pouncer Company's employees earned wages of $70,000. Withholdings related to these wages were $5,355 for Social Security (FICA), $7,500 for federal income tax, $3,100 for state income tax, and $400 for union dues. The company incurred no cost related to these earnings for federal unemployment tax, but incurred $700 for state unemployment tax.

Instructions
(a) Prepare the necessary March 31 journal entry to record wages expense and wages payable. Assume that wages earned during March will be paid during April.
(b) Prepare the entry to record the company's payroll tax expense.

Journalize unearned revenue transactions.
(SO 3)

E10-6 Season tickets for the Lame Ducks are priced at $230 and include 20 games. Revenue is recognized after each game is played. When the season began, the amount credited to Unearned Season Ticket Revenue was $1,104,000. By the end of October, $772,800 of the Unearned Season Ticket Revenue had been recorded as earned.

Instructions
(a) How many season tickets did the Lame Ducks sell?
(b) How many home games had the Lame Ducks played by the end of October?

(c) Prepare the entry for the initial recording of the Unearned Season Ticket Revenue.
(d) Prepare the entry to recognize the revenue after the first home game had been played.

E10-7 Walter Company Ltd. publishes a monthly sports magazine, *Fishing Preview*. Subscriptions to the magazine cost $22 per year. During November 2007, Walter sells 6,000 subscriptions for cash, beginning with the December issue. Walter prepares financial statements quarterly and recognizes subscription revenue earned at the end of the quarter. The company uses the accounts Unearned Subscription Revenue and Subscription Revenue. The company has a December 31 year-end.

Journalize unearned subscription revenue.
(SO 3)

Instructions
(a) Prepare the entry in November for the receipt of the subscriptions.
(b) Prepare the adjusting entry at December 31, 2007, to record subscription revenue earned in December 2007.
(c) Prepare the adjusting entry at March 31, 2008, to record subscription revenue earned in the first quarter of 2008.

E10-8 On September 1, 2007, Chardin Corporation issued $300,000, 8%, 10-year bonds at face value. Interest is payable annually on September 1. Chardin's year-end is December 31.

Prepare journal entries for issuance of bonds and payment of accrual of interest.
(SO 5)

Instructions
Prepare journal entries to record the following events.
(a) The issuance of the bonds.
(b) The accrual of interest on December 31, 2007.
(c) The payment of interest on September 1, 2008.

E10-9 On January 1 Stanhope Company issued $100,000, 7%, 10-year bonds at face value. Interest is payable annually on January 1.

Prepare journal entries for issuance of bonds and payment and accrual of interest.
(SO 5)

Instructions
Prepare journal entries to record the following events.
(a) The issuance of the bonds.
(b) The accrual of interest on December 31.
(c) The payment of interest on January 1.

E10-10 Assume that the following are independent situations recently reported in the *Wall Street Journal*.
1. General Electric (GE) 7% bonds, maturing January 28, 2010, were issued at 111.12.
2. Boeing 7% bonds, maturing September 24, 2027, were issued at 99.08.

Prepare entries for issue of bonds.
(SO 5)

Instructions
(a) Were GE and Boeing bonds issued at a premium or a discount?
(b) Explain how bonds, both paying the same contractual interest rate, could be issued at different prices.
(c) Prepare the journal entry to record the issue of each of these two bonds, assuming each company issued $500,000 of bonds in total.

E10-11 Boone Company issued $240,000 of 8%, 20-year bonds on January 1, 2007, at face value. Interest is payable annually on January 1.

Prepare journal entries to record issuance of bonds, payment of interest, and redemption at maturity.
(SO 5, 6)

Instructions
Prepare the journal entries to record the following events.
(a) The issuance of the bonds
(b) The accrual of interest on December 31, 2007.
(c) The payment of interest on January 1, 2008.
(d) The redemption of the bonds at maturity, assuming interest for the last interest period has been paid and recorded.

E10-12 The situations presented here are independent of each other.

Prepare journal entries for redemption of bonds.
(SO 6)

Instructions
For each situation prepare the appropriate journal entry for the redemption of the bonds.
(a) Thunder Corporation retired $130,000 face value, 12% bonds on June 30, 2007, at 102. The carrying value of the bonds at the redemption date was $122,500. The bonds

pay annual interest, and the interest payment due on June 30, 2007, has been made and recorded.

(b) Lightning, Inc., retired $180,000 face value, 12.5% bonds on June 30, 2007, at 98. The carrying value of the bonds at the redemption date was $184,000. The bonds pay annual interest, and the interest payment due on June 30, 2007, has been made and recorded.

Prepare liabilities section of balance sheet.
(SO 7)

E10-13 Cyclone, Inc. reports the following liabilities (in thousands) on its January 31, 2007, balance sheet and notes to the financial statements.

Accounts payable	$3,263.9	Notes payable—long-term	$5,746.7
Accrued pension liability	1,215.2	Operating leases	1,641.7
Accrued liabilities	1,258.1	Loans payable—long-term	335.6
Bonds payable	1,961.2	Payroll-related liabilities	558.1
Current portion of		Short-term borrowings	2,563.6
long-term debt	1,992.2	Unused operating line of credit	3,337.6
Income taxes payable	235.2	Warranty liability—current	1,417.3

Instructions
(a) Identify which of the above liabilities are likely current and which are likely long-term. Say if an item fits in neither category. Explain the reasoning for your selection.
(b) Prepare the liabilities section of Cyclone's balance sheet as at January 31, 2007.

Calculate liquidity and solvency ratios; discuss impact of unrecorded obligations on liquidity and solvency.
(SO 7)

E10-14 McDonald's 2004 financial statements contain the following selected data (in millions).

Current assets	$ 2,857.8	Interest expense	$ 358.4
Total assets	27,837.5	Income taxes	923.9
Current liabilities	3,520.5	Net income	2,278.5
Total liabilities	13,636		

Instructions
(a) Compute the following values and provide a brief interpretation of each.
 (1) Working capital.   (3) Debt to total assets ratio.
 (2) Current ratio.   (4) Times interest earned ratio.
(b) The notes to McDonald's financial statements show that subsequent to 2004 the company will have future minimum lease payments under operating leases of $11,442.6 million. If these assets had been purchased with debt, assets and liabilities would rise by approximately $10,500 million. Recompute the debt to total assets ratio after adjusting for this. Discuss your result.

Calculate current ratio before and after paying accounts payable.
(SO 7)

E10-15   3M Company reported the following financial data for 2004 and 2003 ($ in millions).

3M COMPANY
Balance Sheet (partial)

	2004	**2003**
Current assets		
Cash and cash equivalents	$2,757	$1,836
Accounts receivable, net	2,792	2,714
Inventories	1,897	1,816
Other current assets	1,274	1,354
Total current assets	$8,720	$7,720
Current liabilities	$6,071	$5,082

Instructions
(a) Calculate the current ratio for 3M for 2004 and 2003.
(b) Suppose that at the end of 2004 3M management used $300 million cash to pay off $300 million of accounts payable. How would its current ratio change?

E10-16   Unique Boutique reported the following financial data for 2007 and 2006.

Calculate current ratio before and after paying accounts payable.
(SO 7)

UNIQUE BOUTIQUE
Balance Sheet (partial)
September 30 (in thousands)

	2007	2006
Current assets		
Cash and short-term deposits	$2,574	$1,021
Accounts receivable	2,347	1,575
Inventories	1,201	1,010
Other current assets	322	192
Total current assets	$6,444	$3,798
Current liabilities	$5,303	$4,008

Instructions

(a) Calculate the current ratio for Unique Boutique for 2007 and 2006.

(b) Suppose that at the end of 2007, the Unique Boutique used $1.5 million cash to pay off $1.5 million of accounts payable. How would its current ratio change?

(c) At September 30, the Unique Boutique has an undrawn operating line of credit of $12.5 million. Would this affect any assessment that you might make of the Unique Boutique's short-term liquidity? Explain.

E10-17   Wal-Mart was sued nearly 5,000 times in a recent year—about once every two hours every day of the year. Wal-Mart has been sued for everything imaginable—ranging from falls on icy parking lots to injuries sustained in shoppers' stampedes to a murder with a rifle purchased at Wal-Mart.

Discuss contingent liabilities.
(SO 7)

Wal-Mart does not adhere to the legal strategy many businesses use of "Settle quickly and cut your losses." Instead, Wal-Mart aggressively fights lawsuits, even when it would be cheaper to settle. The company reported the following in the notes to its financial statements:

> The Company and its subsidiaries are involved from time to time in claims, proceedings, and litigation arising from the operation of its business. The Company does not believe that any such claim, proceeding, or litigation, either alone or in the aggregate, will have a material adverse effect on the Company's financial position or results of its operations.

Instructions

(a) Explain why Wal-Mart does not have to record these contingent liabilities.

(b) Comment on any implications for analysis of the financial statements.

*E10-18   Columbo Company issued $300,000, 7%, 20-year bonds on January 1, 2007, at 103. Interest is payable annually on January 1. Columbo uses straight-line amortization for bond premium or discount.

Prepare journal entries to record issuance of bonds, payment of interest, amortization of premium using straight-line, and redemption at maturity.
(SO 5, 6, 8)

Instructions

Prepare the journal entries to record the following events.

(a) The issuance of the bonds.

(b) The accrual of interest and the premium amortization on December 31, 2007.

(c) The payment of interest on January 1, 2008.

(d) The redemption of the bonds at maturity, assuming interest for the last interest period has been paid and recorded.

*E10-19   Pierce Company issued $220,000, 8%, 10-year bonds on December 31, 2006, for $215,000. Interest is payable annually on December 31. Pierce uses the straight-line method to amortize bond premium or discount.

Prepare journal entries to record issuance of bonds, payment of interest, amortization of discount using straight-line, and redemption at maturity.
(SO 5, 6, 8)

Instructions

Prepare the journal entries to record the following events.

(a) The issuance of the bonds.

(b) The payment of interest and the discount amortization on December 31, 2007.

(c) The redemption of the bonds at maturity, assuming interest for the last interest period has been paid and recorded.

Prepare journal entries for issuance of bonds, payment of interest, and amortization of discount using effective-interest method.
(SO 5, 9)

*E10-20   Midas Corporation issued $260,000, 7%, 10-year bonds on January 1, 2007, for $242,554. This price resulted in an effective interest rate of 8% on the bonds. Interest is payable annually on January 1. Midas uses the effective-interest method to amortize bond premium or discount.

Instructions
Prepare the journal entries to record (round to the nearest dollar):
(a) The issuance of the bonds.
(b) The accrual of interest and the discount amortization on December 31, 2007.
(c) The payment of interest on January 1, 2008.

Prepare journal entries for issuance of bonds, payment of interest, and amortization of premium using effective-interest method.
(SO 5, 9)

*E10-21   Melina Company issued $180,000, 7%, 10-year bonds on January 1, 2007, for $193,248. This price resulted in an effective interest rate of 6% on the bonds. Interest is payable annually on January 1. Melina uses the effective-interest method to amortize bond premium or discount.

Instructions
Prepare the journal entries (rounded to the nearest dollar) to record:
(a) The issuance of the bonds.
(b) The accrual of interest and the premium amortization on December 31, 2007.
(c) The payment of interest on January 1, 2008.

Prepare journal entries to record mortgage note and installment payments.
(SO 10)

*E10-22   Moore Co. receives $110,000 when it issues a $110,000, 8%, mortgage note payable to finance the construction of a building at December 31, 2007. The terms provide for semiannual installment payments of $7,041 on June 30 and December 31.

Instructions
Prepare the journal entries to record the mortgage loan and the first two installment payments.

Problems: Set A

Prepare current liability entries, adjusting entries, and current liabilities section.
(SO 1, 2, 3, 7)

`GLS`

P10-1A   On January 1, 2007, the ledger of Daniels Company contained these liability accounts.

Accounts Payable	$42,500
Sales Taxes Payable	6,600
Unearned Service Revenue	19,000

During January the following selected transactions occurred.

Jan.   1   Borrowed $12,000 in cash from Midland Bank on a 4-month, 8%, $12,000 note.

      5   Sold merchandise for cash totaling $6,510, which includes 5% sales taxes.

    12   Provided services for customers who had made advance payments of $10,000. (Credit Service Revenue.)

    14   Paid state treasurer's department for sales taxes collected in December 2006, $6,600.

    20   Sold 500 units of a new product on credit at $48 per unit, plus 5% sales tax.

During January the company's employees earned wages of $60,000. Withholdings related to these wages were $4,590 for Social Security (FICA), $5,000 for federal income tax, and $1,500 for state income tax. The company owed no money related to these earnings for federal or state unemployment tax. Assume that wages earned during January will be paid during February. No entry had been recorded for wages or payroll tax expense as of January 31.

Instructions
(a) Journalize the January transactions.
(b) Journalize the adjusting entries at January 31 for the outstanding note payable and for wages expense and payroll tax expense.
(c) Prepare the current liabilities section of the balance sheet at January 31, 2007. Assume no change in Accounts Payable.

(c) Tot. current liabilities $129,680

P10-2A On the Edge Corporation sells rock-climbing products and also operates an indoor climbing facility for climbing enthusiasts. During the last part of 2007, On the Edge had the following transactions related to notes payable.

Journalize and post note transactions; show balance sheet presentation.
(SO 2, 7)

Sept. 1 Issued a $9,000 note to Gibraltar to purchase inventory. The 3-month note payable bears interest of 8% and is due December 1.

Sept. 30 Recorded accrued interest for the Gibraltar note.

Oct. 1 Issued a $18,000, 9%, 4-month note to Apex Bank to finance the purchase of a new climbing wall for advanced climbers. The note is due February 1.

Oct. 31 Recorded accrued interest for the Gibraltar note and the Apex Bank note.

Nov. 1 Issued a $20,000 note and paid $8,000 cash to purchase a vehicle to transport clients to nearby climbing sites as part of a new series of climbing classes. This note bears interest of 6% and matures in 12 months.

Nov. 30 Recorded accrued interest for the Gibraltar note, the Apex Bank note, and the vehicle note.

Dec. 1 Paid principal and interest on thc Gibraltar note.

Dec. 31 Recorded accrued interest for the Apex Bank note and the vehicle note.

Instructions
(a) Prepare journal entries for the transactions noted above.
(b) Post the above entries to the Notes Payable, Interest Payable, and Interest Expense accounts. (Use T accounts.)
(c) Show the balance sheet presentation of notes payable and interest payable at December 31.
(d) How much interest expense relating to notes payable did On the Edge incur during the year?

*(b) Interest
Payable $605*

P10-3A The following section is taken from Majestic's balance sheet at December 31, 2006.

Prepare journal entries to record interest payments and redemption of bonds.
(SO 5, 6)

Current liabilities	
Bond interest payable	$ 24,000
Long-term liabilities	
Bonds payable, 8%, due January 1, 2013	300,000

Interest is payable annually on January 1. The bonds are callable on any annual interest date.

Instructions
(a) Journalize the payment of the bond interest on January 1, 2007.
(b) Assume that on January 1, 2007, after paying interest, Majestic calls bonds having a face value of $50,000. The call price is 104. Record the redemption of the bonds.
(c) Prepare the adjusting entry on December 31, 2007, to accrue the interest on the remaining bonds.

P10-4A On October 1, 2006, Ferdinand Corp. issued $500,000, 7%, 10-year bonds at face value. The bonds were dated October 1, 2006, and pay interest annually on October 1. Financial statements are prepared annually on December 31.

Prepare journal entries to record issuance of bonds, interest, balance sheet presentation, and bond redemption.
(SO 5, 6, 7)

Instructions
(a) Prepare the journal entry to record the issuance of the bonds.
(b) Prepare the adjusting entry to record the accrual of interest on December 31, 2006.
(c) Show the balance sheet presentation of bonds payable and bond interest payable on December 31, 2006.
(d) Prepare the journal entry to record the payment of interest on October 1, 2007.
(e) Prepare the adjusting entry to record the accrual of interest on December 31, 2007.
(f) Assume that on January 1, 2008, Ferdinand pays the accrued bond interest and calls the bonds. The call price is 102. Record the payment of interest and redemption of the bonds.

(f) Loss $10,000

Prepare journal entries to record issuance of bonds, show balance sheet presentation, and record bond redemption.
(SO 5, 6, 7)

P10-5A Margaret Rose Company sold $4,000,000, 8%, 20-year bonds on January 1, 2007. The bonds were dated January 1, 2007, and pay interest on December 31. The bonds were sold at 98.

Instructions

(a) Prepare the journal entry to record the issuance of the bonds on January 1, 2007.

(b) At December 31, 2007, $4,000 of the bond discount had been amortized. Show the balance sheet presentation of the bond liability at December 31, 2007. (Assume that interest has been paid.)

(c) Loss $152,000

(c) At December 31, 2008, when the carrying value of the bonds was $3,928,000, the company redeemed the bonds at 102. Record the redemption of the bonds assuming that interest for the year had already been paid.

Calculate and comment on ratios.
(SO 7)

P10-6A You have been presented with the following selected information taken from the financial statements of Southwest Airlines Co.

SOUTHWEST AIRLINES CO.
Balance Sheet (partial)
December 31
(in millions)

	2004	2003
Total current assets	$2,172	$2,313
Noncurrent assets	9,165	7,565
Total assets	$11,337	$9,878
Current liabilities	$2,142	$1,723
Long-term liabilities	3,671	3,103
Total liabilities	5,813	4,826
Shareholders' equity	5,524	5,052
Total liabilities and shareholders' equity	$11,337	$9,878

Other information:

	2004	2003
Net income (loss)	$ 313	$ 442
Income tax expense	176	266
Interest expense	88	91
Cash provided by operations	1,157	1,336
Capital expenditures	1,775	1,238
Cash dividends	14	14

Note 8. Leases

The majority of the Company's terminal operations space, as well as 88 aircraft, were under operating leases at December 31, 2004. Future minimum lease payments under noncancelable operating leases are as follows: 2005, $343,000; 2006, $279,000; 2007, $256,000; 2008, $226,000; 2009, $204,000; after 2009, $1,369,000.

Instructions

(a) Calculate each of the following ratios for 2004 and 2003.

   (1) Current ratio.
   (2) Free cash flow.
   (3) Debt to total assets.
   (4) Times interest earned ratio.

(b) Comment on the trend in ratios.

(c) Read the company's note on leases. If the operating leases had instead been accounted for like a purchase, assets and liabilities would increase by approximately $1,500 million. Recalculate the debt to total assets ratio for 2004 in light of this information, and discuss the implictions for analysis.

Prepare journal entries to record interest payments, straight-line discount amortization, and redemption of bonds.
(SO 5, 6, 8)

*P10-7A The information on page 519 is taken from Simon Corp.'s balance sheet at December 31, 2007.

Current liabilities		
Bond interest payable		$ 192,000
Long-term liabilities		
Bonds payable, 8%, due January 1, 2018	$2,400,000	
Less: Discount on bonds payable	42,000	2,358,000

Interest is payable annually on January 1. The bonds are callable on any annual interest date. Simon uses straight-line amortization for any bond premium or discount. From December 31, 2007, the bonds will be outstanding for an additional 10 years (120 months).

Instructions
(Round all computations to the nearest dollar.)
(a) Journalize the payment of bond interest on January 1, 2008.
(b) Prepare the entry to amortize bond discount and to accrue the interest on December 31, 2008.
(c) Assume on January 1, 2009, after paying interest, that Simon Corp. calls bonds having a face value of $300,000. The call price is 103. Record the redemption of the bonds.
(d) Prepare the adjusting entry at December 31, 2009, to amortize bond discount and to accrue interest on the remaining bonds.

(c) Loss $13,725

*P10-8A   Peru Corporation sold $1,500,000, 6%, 10-year bonds on January 1, 2007. The bonds were dated January 1, 2007, and pay interest on January 1. Peru Corporation uses the straight-line method to amortize bond premium or discount.

Prepare journal entries to record issuance of bonds, interest, and straight-line amortization, and balance sheet presentation.
(SO 5, 7, 8)

Instructions
(a) Prepare all the necessary journal entries to record the issuance of the bonds and bond interest expense for 2007, assuming that the bonds sold at 103.
(b) Prepare journal entries as in part (a) assuming that the bonds sold at 98.
(c) Show the balance sheet presentation for the bond issue at December 31, 2007, using (1) the 103 selling price, and then (2) the 98 selling price.

*P10-9A   McGraw Co. sold $4,000,000, 9%, 5-year bonds on January 1, 2007. The bonds were dated January 1, 2007, and pay interest on January 1. The company uses straight-line amortization on bond premiums and discounts. Financial statements are prepared annually.

Prepare journal entries to record issuance of bonds, interest, and straight-line amortization, and balance sheet presentation.
(SO 5, 6, 8)

Instructions
(a) Prepare the journal entries to record the issuance of the bonds assuming they sold at:
    (1) 101.
    (2) 97.
(b) Prepare amortization tables for both assumed sales for the first three interest payments.
(c) Prepare the journal entries to record interest expense for 2007 under both assumed sales.
(d) Show the balance sheet presentation for both assumed sales at December 31, 2007.

*P10-10A   On January 1, 2007, Lucy Corporation issued $1,200,000 face value, 7%, 10-year bonds at $1,119,479. This price resulted in an effective-interest rate of 8% on the bonds. Lucy uses the effective-interest method to amortize bond premium or discount. The bonds pay annual interest January 1.

Prepare journal entries to record issuance of bonds, payment of interest, and amortization of bond discount using effective-interest method.
(SO 9)

Instructions
(Round all computations to the nearest dollar.)
(a) Prepare the journal entry to record the issuance of the bonds on January 1, 2007.
(b) Prepare an amortization table through December 31, 2009 (three interest periods) for this bond issue.
(c) Prepare the journal entry to record the accrual of interest and the amortization of the discount on December 31, 2007.
(d) Prepare the journal entry to record the payment of interest on January 1, 2008.
(e) Prepare the journal entry to record the accrual of interest and the amortization of the discount on December 31, 2008.

(c) Interest
Expense $89,558

Prepare journal entries to record issuance of bonds, payment of interest, and effective-interest amortization, and balance sheet presentation.
(SO 5, 7, 9)
(a) (4) Interest
      Expense $136,324

*P10-11A On January 1, 2007, HiLo Company issued $2,000,000 face value, 8%, 10-year bonds at $2,294,403. This price resulted in a 6% effective-interest rate on the bonds. HiLo uses the effective-interest method to amortize bond premium or discount. The bonds pay annual interest on each January 1.

Instructions
(a) Prepare the journal entries to record the following transactions.
   (1) The issuance of the bonds on January 1, 2007.
   (2) Accrual of interest and amortization of the premium on December 31, 2007.
   (3) The payment of interest on January 1, 2008.
   (4) Accrual of interest and amortization of the premium on December 31, 2008.
(b) Show the proper balance sheet presentation for the liability for bonds payable on the December 31, 2008, balance sheet.
(c) Provide the answers to the following questions in narrative form.
   (1) What amount of interest expense is reported for 2008?
   (2) Would the bond interest expense reported in 2008 be the same as, greater than, or less than the amount that would be reported if the straight-line method of amortization were used?

Prepare installment payments schedule, journal entries, and balance sheet presentation for a mortgage note payable.
(SO 7, 10)

*P10-12A Fowler purchased a new piece of equipment to be used in its new facility. The $550,000 piece of equipment was purchased with a $50,000 down payment and with cash received through the issuance of a $500,000, 8%, 4-year mortgage note payable issued on October 1, 2007. The terms provide for quarterly installment payments of $36,825 on December 31, March 31, June 30, and September 30.

Instructions
(Round all computations to the nearest dollar.)
(a) Prepare an installment payments schedule for the first five payments of the notes payable.
(b) Prepare all journal entries related to the notes payable for December 31, 2007.

(c) Current portion $112,773

(c) Show the balance sheet presentation for this obligation for December 31, 2007. (*Hint:* Be sure to distinguish between the current and long-term portions of the note.)

Prepare journal entries to record payments for long-term note payable, and balance sheet presentation.
(SO 7, 10)

*P10-13A Cindy Davito has just approached a venture capitalist for financing for her new business venture, the development of a local ski hill. On July 1, 2007, Cindy was loaned $100,000 at an annual interest rate of 7%. The loan is repayable over 5 years in annual installments of $24,389, principal and interest, due each June 30. The first payment is due June 30, 2008. Cindy uses the effective-interest method for amortizing debt. Her ski hill company's year-end will be June 30.

Instructions
(a) Prepare an amortization schedule for the 5 years, 2007–2012. Round all calculations to the nearest dollar.

(b) 6/30/08 Interest
      Expense $7,000

(b) Prepare all journal entries for Cindy Davito for the first 2 fiscal years ended June 30, 2008, and June 30, 2009. Round all calculations to the nearest dollar.
(c) Show the balance sheet presentation of the note payable as of June 30, 2009. (*Hint:* Be sure to distinguish between the current and long-term portions of the note.)

Problems: Set B

Prepare current liability entries, adjusting entries, and current liabilities section.
(SO 1, 2, 3, 7)

GLS

P10-1B On January 1, 2007, the ledger of Cramer Company contained the following liability accounts.

Accounts Payable	$52,000
Sales Taxes Payable	8,500
Unearned Service Revenue	11,000

During January the following selected transactions occurred.

Jan. 1 Borrowed $18,000 from TriCounty Bank on a 3-month, 6%, $18,000 note.
      5 Sold merchandise for cash totaling $17,172, which includes 6% sales taxes.
   12 Provided services for customers who had made advance payments of $8,000. (Credit Service Revenue.)

14   Paid state revenue department for sales taxes collected in December 2006 ($8,500).

20   Sold 500 units of a new product on credit at $50 per unit, plus 6% sales tax.

During January the company's employees earned wages of $40,000. Withholdings related to these wages were $3,060 for Social Security (FICA), $3,800 for federal income tax, and $1,100 for state income tax. The company owed no money related to these earnings for federal or state unemployment tax. Assume that wages earned during January will be paid during February. No entry had been recorded for wages or payroll tax expense as of January 31.

Instructions
(a) Journalize the January transactions.
(b) Journalize the adjusting entries at January 31 for the outstanding notes payable and for wages expense and payroll tax expense.
(c) Prepare the current liabilities section of the balance sheet at January 31, 2007. Assume no change in accounts payable.

(c) Tot. current liabilities $118,622

P10-2B   Cougar Mountain Bikes markets mountain-bike tours to clients vacationing in various locations in the mountains of Colorado. In preparation for the upcoming summer biking season, Cougar entered into the following transactions related to notes payable.

Journalize and post note transactions; show balance sheet presentation.
(SO 2, 7)

Mar. 1   Purchased Puma bikes for use as rentals by issuing an $8,000, 3-month, 6% note payable that is due June 1.

Mar. 31   Recorded accrued interest for the Puma note.

Apr. 1   Issued a $24,000 9-month note for the purchase of mountain property on which to build bike trails. The note bears 8% interest and is due January 1.

Apr. 30   Recorded accrued interest for the Puma note and the land note.

May 1   Issued a 4-month note to Rocky National Bank for $20,000 at 6%. The funds will be used for working capital for the beginning of the season; the note is due September 1.

May 31   Recorded accrued interest for all three notes.

June 1   Paid principal and interest on the Puma note.

June 30   Recorded accrued interest for the land note and the Rocky Bank note.

Instructions
(a) Prepare journal entries for the transactions noted above.
(b) Post the above entries to the Notes Payable, Interest Payable, and Interest Expense accounts. (Use T accounts.)
(c) Assuming that Cougar's year-end is June 30, show the balance sheet presentation of notes payable and interest payable at that date.
(d) How much interest expense relating to notes payable did Cougar incur during the year?

(b) Interest Payable $680

P10-3B   The following section is taken from Barnaby Corp.'s balance sheet at December 31, 2006.

Prepare journal entries to record interest payments and redemption of bonds.
(SO 5, 6)

Current liabilities	
Bond interest payable	$ 128,000
Long-term liabilities	
Bonds payable, 8%, due January 1, 2011	1,600,000

Interest is payable annually on January 1. The bonds are callable on any annual interest date.

Instructions
(a) Journalize the payment of the bond interest on January 1, 2007.
(b) Assume that on January 1, 2007, after paying interest, Barnaby Corp. calls bonds having a face value of $400,000. The call price is 105. Record the redemption of the bonds.
(c) Prepare the adjusting entry on December 31, 2007, to accrue the interest on the remaining bonds.

(b) Loss $20,000

Prepare journal entries to record issuance of bonds, interest, balance sheet presentation, and bond redemption.
(SO 5, 6, 7)

(f) Loss   16,000

P10-4B On April 1, 2006, ERV Corp. issued $800,000, 7%, 5-year bonds at face value. The bonds were dated April 1, 2006, and pay interest annually on April 1. Financial statements are prepared annually on December 31.

Instructions
(a) Prepare the journal entry to record the issuance of the bonds.
(b) Prepare the adjusting entry to record the accrual of interest on December 31, 2006.
(c) Show the balance sheet presentation of bonds payable and bond interest payable on December 31, 2006.
(d) Prepare the journal entry to record the payment of interest on April 1, 2007.
(e) Prepare the adjusting entry to record the accrual of interest on December 31, 2007.
(f) Assume that on January 1, 2008, ERV pays the accrued bond interest and calls the bonds. The call price is 102. Record the payment of interest and redemption of the bonds.

Prepare journal entries to record issuance of bonds, show balance sheet presentation, and record bond redemption.
(SO 5, 6, 7)

(c) Loss $39,000

P10-5B Buzz Electric sold $3,000,000, 9%, 20-year bonds on January 1, 2007. The bonds were dated January 1 and pay interest on January 1. The bonds were sold at 103.

Instructions
(a) Prepare the journal entry to record the issuance of the bonds on January 1, 2007.
(b) At December 31, 2007, $4,500 of the bond premium had been amortized. Show the balance sheet presentation of the bond liability at December 31, 2007. (Assume that interest has been paid.)
(c) At December 31, 2008, when the carrying value of the bonds was $3,081,000, the company redeemed the bonds at 104. Record the redemption of the bonds assuming that interest for the year had already been paid.

Calculate and comment on ratios.
(SO 7)

P10-6B The following selected information was taken from the financial statements of Krispy Kreme Doughnuts, Inc.

KRISPY KREME DOUGHNUTS, INC.
Balance Sheet (partial)

(in thousands)

	Feb. 1, 2004	Feb. 2, 2003
Total current assets	$138,644	$141,128
Capital assets and other long-term assets	522,020	269,359
	$660,664	$410,487
Current liabilities	$ 53,493	$ 59,687
Long-term liabilities	154,964	77,448
Total liabilities	208,457	137,135
Shareholders' equity	452,207	273,352
Total liabilities and shareholders' equity	$660,664	$410,487

Other information:

	2004	2003
Interest expense	$ 4,409	$ 1,781
Tax expense	37,590	21,295
Net income	33,478	57,087
Cash provided by operations	95,553	51,036
Capital expenditures	79,649	83,196
Cash dividends	-0-	-0-

Note 8. Lease Commitments
The Company conducts some of its operations from leased facilities and, additionally, leases certain equipment under operating leases. Generally, these have initial terms of 3 to 20 years and contain provisions for renewal options of 5 to 10 years.

At February 1, 2004, future minimum annual rental commitments, gross, under non-cancelable operating leases, including lease commitments on consolidated joint ventures, are as follows:

Fiscal Year Ending in	Amount (in thousands)
2005	$ 21,119
2006	18,560
2007	15,657
2008	13,099
2009	11,692
Thereafter	75,599
	$155,726

Rental expense, net of rental income, totaled $10,576,000 in fiscal 2002, $13,169,000 in fiscal 2003 and $19,574,000 in fiscal 2004.

Instructions
(a) Calculate each of the following ratios for 2004 and 2003.
    (1) Current ratio.
    (2) Free cash flow.
    (3) Debt to total assets ratio.
    (4) Times interest earned ratio.
(b) Comment on Krispy Kreme's liquidity and solvency.
(c) Read the company's note on leases (Note 8). If the operating leases had instead been accounted for like a purchase, assets and liabilities would have increased by approximately $110,000,000. Recalculate the debt to total assets ratio for 2004 and discuss the implications for analysis.

*P10-7B The following section is taken from Clampette Oil Company's balance sheet at December 31, 2007.

Prepare journal entries to record interest payments, straight-line premium amortization, and redemption of bonds
(SO 5, 6, 8)

Current liabilities		
Bond interest payable		$ 342,000
Long-term liabilities		
Bonds payable, 9% due January 1, 2018	$3,800,000	
Add: Premium on bonds payable	200,000	4,000,000

Interest is payable annually on January 1. The bonds are callable on any annual interest date. Clampette uses straight-line amortization for any bond premium or discount. From December 31, 2007, the bonds will be outstanding for an additional 10 years (120 months).

Instructions
(Round all computations to the nearest dollar.)
(a) Journalize the payment of bond interest on January 1, 2008.
(b) Prepare the entry to amortize bond premium and to accrue interest due on December 31, 2008.
(c) Assume on January 1, 2009, after paying interest, that Clampette Company calls bonds having a face value of $1,900,000. The call price is 102. Record the redemption of the bonds.
(d) Prepare the adjusting entry at December 31, 2009, to amortize bond premium and to accrue interest on the remaining bonds.

(c) Gain $52,000

Prepare journal entries to record issuance of bonds, interest, and straight-line amortization, and balance sheet presentation.
(SO 5, 7, 8)

*P10-8B Smudge Company sold $1,500,000, 10%, 10-year bonds on January 1, 2007. The bonds were dated January 1, 2007, and pay interest on January 1. Smudge Company uses the straight-line method to amortize bond premium or discount.

Instructions
(a) Prepare all the necessary journal entries to record the issuance of the bonds and bond interest expense for 2007, assuming that the bonds sold at 102.
(b) Prepare journal entries as in part (a) assuming that the bonds sold at 96.
(c) Show the balance sheet presentation for the bond issue at December 31, 2007, using (1) the 102 selling price, and then (2) the 96 selling price.

Prepare journal entries to record issuance of bonds, interest, and straight-line amortization, and balance sheet presentation.
(SO 5, 7, 8)

*P10-9B Zorin Corporation sold $3,500,000, 7%, 20-year bonds on December 31, 2006. The bonds were dated December 31, 2006, and pay interest on December 31. The company uses straight-line amortization for premiums and discounts. Financial statements are prepared annually.

Instructions
(a) Prepare the journal entry to record the issuance of the bonds assuming they sold at:
   (1) 97½.
   (2) 104.
(b) Prepare amortization tables for both of the assumed sales for the first three interest payments.

(c) (2) 12/31/07 Interest Expense $238,000

(c) Prepare the journal entries to record interest expense for the first two interest payments under both assumed sales.
(d) Show the balance sheet presentation for both assumed sales at December 31, 2007.

Prepare journal entries to record issuance of bonds, payment of interest, and amortization of bond premium using effective-interest method.
(SO 5, 9)

*P10-10B On January 1, 2007, Stavlund Corporation issued $1,400,000 face value, 12%, 10-year bonds at $1,572,048. This price resulted in an effective-interest rate of 10% on the bonds. Stavlund uses the effective-interest method to amortize bond premium or discount. The bonds pay annual interest January 1.

Instructions
(Round all computations to the nearest dollar.)
(a) Prepare the journal entry to record the issuance of the bonds on January 1, 2007.
(b) Prepare an amortization table through December 31, 2009 (three interest periods) for this bond issue.

(c) Interest Expense $157,205

(c) Prepare the journal entry to record the accrual of interest and the amortization of the premium on December 31, 2007.
(d) Prepare the journal entry to record the payment of interest on January 1, 2008.
(e) Prepare the journal entry to record the accrual of interest and the amortization of the premium on December 31, 2008.

Prepare journal entries to record issuance of bonds, payment of interest, and effective-interest amortization, and balance sheet presentation.
(SO 5, 7, 9)

*P10-11B On January 1, 2007, Gelber Company issued $2,200,000 face value, 10%, 15-year bonds at $1,900,322. This price resulted in an effective interest rate of 12% on the bonds. Gelber uses the effective-interest method to amortize bond premium or discount. The bonds pay annual interest January 1.

Instructions
(a) Prepare the journal entries to record the following transactions.
   (1) The issuance of the bonds on January 1, 2007.
   (2) The accrual of interest and the amortization of the discount on December 31, 2007.
   (3) The payment of interest on January 1, 2008.
   (4) The accrual of interest and the amortization of the discount on December 31, 2008.
(b) Show the proper balance sheet presentation for the liability for bonds payable on the December 31, 2008, balance sheet.

(c) (1) $229,003

(c) Provide the answers to the following questions in narrative form.
   (1) What amount of interest expense is reported for 2008?
   (2) Would the bond interest expense reported in 2008 be the same as, greater than, or less than the amount that would be reported if the straight-line method of amortization were used?
   (3) Determine the total cost of borrowing over the life of the bond.
   (4) Would the total bond interest expense be greater than, the same as, or less than the total interest expense that would be reported if the straight-line method of amortization were used?

Prepare installment payments schedule, journal entries for a mortgage note payable, and balance sheet presentation.
(SO 7, 10)

*P10-12B Angela Corporation purchased a new piece of equipment to be used in its new facility. The $750,000 piece of equipment was purchased with a $50,000 down payment and with cash received through the issuance of a $700,000, 8%, 4-year mortgage note payable issued on October 1, 2007. The terms provide for quarterly installment payments of $51,555 on December 31, March 31, June 30, and September 30.

Instructions
(Round all computations to the nearest dollar.)
(a) Prepare an installment payments schedule for the first five payments of the notes payable.
(b) Prepare all necessary journal entries related to the notes payable for December 31, 2007.
(c) Show the balance sheet presentation for these obligations for December 31, 2007. (*Hint:* Be sure to distinguish between the current and long-term portions of the note.)

(b) Interest Expense $14,000

P10-13B James Clark has just approached a venture capitalist for financing for his sailing school. The venture capitalist is willing to loan James $70,000 at a high-risk annual interest rate of 24%. The loan is payable over 3 years in monthly installments of $2,746. Each payment includes principal and interest, calculated using the effective-interest method for amortizing debt. James receives the loan on May 1, 2007, which is the first day of his fiscal year. James makes the first payment on May 31, 2007.

Prepare journal entries to record payments for long-term note payable.
(SO 10)

Instructions
(a) Prepare an amortization schedule for the period from May 1, 2007, to August 31, 2007. Round all calculations to the nearest dollar.
(b) Prepare all journal entries for James Clark for the period beginning May 1, 2007, and ending July 31, 2007. Round all calculations to the nearest dollar.

(b) 6/30 Interest
    Expense $1,373

Problems: Set C

Visit the book's website at **www.wiley.com/college/kimmel** and choose the Student Companion site to access Problem Set C.

Comprehensive Problem

CP10 Crow Corporation's balance sheet at December 31, 2006, is presented below.

<table>
<tr><td colspan="4" align="center">**CROW CORPORATION**
Balance Sheet
December 31, 2006</td></tr>
<tr><td>Cash</td><td>$30,500</td><td>Accounts payable</td><td>$13,750</td></tr>
<tr><td>Inventory</td><td>25,750</td><td>Bond interest payable</td><td>3,000</td></tr>
<tr><td>Prepaid insurance</td><td>5,600</td><td>Bonds payable</td><td>50,000</td></tr>
<tr><td>Equipment</td><td>38,000</td><td>Common stock</td><td>20,000</td></tr>
<tr><td></td><td>$99,850</td><td>Retained earnings</td><td>$13,100</td></tr>
<tr><td></td><td></td><td></td><td>$99,850</td></tr>
</table>

During 2007, the following transactions occurred.
1. Crow paid $3,000 interest on the bonds on January 1, 2007.
2. Crow purchased $241,100 of inventory on account.
3. Crow sold for $400,000 cash inventory which cost $240,000. Crow also collected $24,000 sales taxes.
4. Crow paid $230,000 on accounts payable.
5. Crow paid $3,000 interest on the bonds on July 1, 2007.
6. The prepaid insurance ($5,600) expired on July 31.
7. On August 1, Crow paid $10,800 for insurance coverage from August 1, 2007, through July 31, 2008.
8. Crow paid $17,000 sales taxes to the state.
9. Paid other operating expenses, $91,000.
10. Retired the bonds on December 31, 2007, by paying $48,000 plus $3,000 interest.
11. Issued $70,000 of 8% bonds on December 31, 2007, at 104. The bonds pay interest every June 30 and December 31.

Adjustment data:
1. Recorded the insurance expired from item 7.
2. The equipment was acquired on December 31, 2006, and will be depreciated on a straight-line basis over 5 years with a $3,000 salvage value.
3. The income tax rate is 30%. (*Hint*: Prepare the income statement up to income before taxes and multiply by 30% to compute the amount.)

Instructions
(You may want to set up T accounts to determine ending balances.)
(a) Prepare journal entries for the transactions listed above and adjusting entries.
(b) Prepare an adjusted trial balance at December 31, 2007.
(c) Prepare an income statement and a retained earnings statement for the year ending December 31, 2007, and a classified balance sheet as of December 31, 2007.

Continuing Cookie Chronicle

(*Note:* This is a continuation of the Cookie Chronicle from Chapters 1 through 9.)

CCC10 Natalie is thinking of repaying all amounts outstanding to her grandmother. Recall that Cookie Creations borrowed $2,000 on November 16, 2006, from Natalie's grandmother. Interest on the note is 6% per year, and the note plus interest was to be repaid in 24 months. Recall that a monthly adjusting journal entry was prepared for the months of November 2006 (1/2 month), December 2006, and January 2007.

Instructions
(a) Calculate the interest payable that was accrued and recorded to January 31, 2007.
(b) Calculate the total interest expense and interest payable to August 31, 2007. Prepare the journal entry at August 31, 2007, to bring the accounting records up to date.
(c) Natalie repays her grandmother on September 15, 2007—10 months after her grandmother extended the loan to Cookie Creations. Prepare the journal entry for the loan repayment.

BROADENING YOUR PERSPECTIVE

Financial Reporting and Analysis

FINANCIAL REPORTING PROBLEM: *Tootsie Roll Industries*

BYP10-1 Refer to the financial statements of Tootsie Roll Industries and the Notes to Consolidated Financial Statements in Appendix A.

Instructions
Answer the following questions.
(a) What were Tootsie Roll's total current liabilities at December 31, 2004? What was the increase/decrease in Tootsie Roll's total current liabilities from the prior year?
(b) How much were the accounts payable at December 31, 2004?
(c) What were the components of total current liabilities on December 31, 2004 (other than accounts payable already discussed above)?

COMPARATIVE ANALYSIS PROBLEM: *Tootsie Roll vs. Hershey Foods*

BYP10-2 The financial statements of Hershey Foods are presented in Appendix B, following the financial statements for Tootsie Roll Industries in Appendix A.

Instructions
(a) Based on the information contained in these financial statements, compute the current ratio for 2004 for each company.

What conclusions concerning the companies' liquidity can be drawn from these ratios?

(b) Based on the information contained in these financial statements, compute the following 2004 ratios for each company.

    (1) Debt to total assets.

    (2) Times interest earned. (Hershey's total interest expense for 2004 was $67,919,000.)

What conclusions about the companies' long-run solvency can be drawn from the ratios?

RESEARCH CASE

BYP10-3 The July 2, 2004, edition of the *Wall Street Journal* contains an article by Ken Brown and Mark Heinzl titled "Nortel Board Finds Accounting Tricks Behind '03 Profits."

Instructions

Read the article and answer the following questions.

(a) Describe the process of "cookie jar" accounting. Include the example used in the article.

(b) What motivation did Nortel's executives have to engage in the practice of "cookie jar" accounting?

(c) What actions did Nortel's board of directors take once the improper accounting was revealed?

INTERPRETING FINANCIAL STATEMENTS

BYP10-4 Hechinger Co. and Home Depot are two home improvement retailers. Compared to Hechinger, founded in the early 1900s, Home Depot is a relative newcomer. But, in recent years, while Home Depot was reporting large increases in net income, Hechinger was reporting increasingly large net losses. Finally, largely due to competition from Home Depot, Hechinger was forced to file for bankruptcy. Here are financial data for both companies (in millions).

	Hechinger	Home Depot
Cash	$ 21	$ 62
Receivables	0	469
Total current assets	1,153	4,933
Beginning total assets	1,668	11,229
Ending total assets	1,577	13,465
Beginning current liabilities	935	2,456
Ending current liabilities	938	2,857
Beginning total liabilities	1,392	4,015
Ending total liabilities	1,339	4,716
Interest expense	67	37
Income tax expense	3	1,040
Cash provided (used) by operations	(257)	1,917
Net income	(93)	1,614
Net sales	3,444	30,219

Instructions

Using the data, perform the following analysis.

(a) Calculate working capital and the current ratio for each company. Discuss their relative liquidity.

(b) Calculate the debt to total assets ratio and times interest earned for each company. Discuss their relative solvency.

(c) Calculate the return on assets ratio and profit margin ratio for each company. Comment on their relative profitability.

(d) The notes to Home Depot's financial statements indicate that it leases many of its facilities using operating leases. If these assets had instead been purchased with debt, assets and liabilities would have increased by approximately $2,347 million. Calculate the company's debt to total assets ratio employing this adjustment. Discuss the implications.

BYP10-5 Many multinational companies find it beneficial to have their shares listed on stock exchanges in foreign countries. In order to do this, they must comply with the securities laws of those countries. Some of these laws relate to the form of financial disclosure the company must provide, including disclosures related to contingent liabilities. This exercise investigates the Tokyo Stock Exchange, the largest stock exchange in Japan.

Address: **www.tse.or.jp/english/index.shtml** (or go to **www.wiley.com/college/kimmel**)

Steps

1. Choose **About TSE**.
2. Choose **History**. Answer questions (a) and (b).
3. Choose **Listed Companies**.
4. Choose **Disclosure**. Answer questions (c) and (d).

Instructions
Answer the following questions.
(a) When was the first stock exchange opened in Japan? How many exchanges does Japan have today?
(b) What event caused trading to stop for a period of time in Japan?
(c) What are four examples of decisions by corporations that must be disclosed at the time of their occurrence?
(d) What are four examples of "occurrence of material fact" that must be disclosed at the time of their occurrence?

FINANCIAL ANALYSIS ON THE WEB

BYP10-6 *Purpose:* Bond or debt securities pay a stated rate of interest. This rate of interest is dependent on the risk associated with the investment. Moody's Investment Service provides ratings for companies that issue debt securities.

Address: **www.moodys.com/** (or go to **www.wiley.com/college/kimmel**)

Steps: From Moody's homepage, choose **About Moody's**.

Instructions
Answer the following questions.
(a) In what year did Moody's introduce the first bond rating? (See **Moody's History**.)
(b) What is the total amount of debt securities that Moody's analysts "track"? (See **An Introduction**.)
(c) What characteristics must debt ratings have in order to be useful to the capital markets? (See **Understand Risk: The Truth About Credit Ratings**.)

BYP10-7 *Purpose:* To illustrate the usefulness of financial calculators on the Web.

Address: **www.centura.com/tools** (or go to **www.wiley.com/college/kimmel**)

Steps: Go to the site shown above.

Instructions
Choose one of the many financial decisions listed at the site. Fill in inputs based on two different sets of assumptions. Print out your results, and then write up a short description of the decision model for your instructor. Describe the inputs and assumptions the model uses. Also try to identify the strengths and weaknesses of the site.

Critical Thinking

DECISION MAKING ACROSS THE ORGANIZATION

BYP10-8   On January 1, 2005, Troy Corporation issued $1,200,000 of 5-year, 8% bonds at 97. The bonds pay interest annually on January 1. By January 1, 2007, the market rate of interest for bonds of risk similar to those of Troy Corporation had risen. As a result the market value of these bonds was $1,000,000 on January 1, 2007—below their carrying value of $1,178,400.

Troy Athens, president of the company, suggests repurchasing all of these bonds in the open market at the $1,000,000 price. But to do so the company will have to issue $1,000,000 (face value) of new 10-year, 12% bonds at par. The president asks you, as controller, "What is the feasibility of my proposed repurchase plan?"

Instructions
With the class divided into groups, answer the following.
(a) Prepare the journal entry to retire the 5-year bonds on January 1, 2007. Prepare the journal entry to issue the new 10-year bonds.
(b) Prepare a short memo to the president in response to his request for advice. List the economic factors that you believe should be considered for his repurchase proposal.

COMMUNICATION ACTIVITY

BYP10-9   Adam Merritt, president of Good to Go, is considering the issuance of bonds to finance an expansion of his business. He has asked you to do the following: (1) discuss the advantages of bonds over common stock financing, (2) indicate the types of bonds he might issue, and (3) explain the issuing procedures used in bond transactions.

Instructions
Write a memorandum to the president, answering his request.

ETHICS CASE

BYP10-10   The July 1998 issue of *Inc.* magazine includes an article by Jeffrey L. Seglin entitled "Would You Lie to Save Your Company?" It recounts the following true situation:

"A Chief Executive Officer (CEO) of a $20-million company that repairs aircraft engines received notice from a number of its customers that engines that it had recently repaired had failed, and that the company's parts were to blame. The CEO had not yet determined whether his company's parts were, in fact, the cause of the problem. The Federal Aviation Administration (FAA) had been notified and was investigating the matter.

What complicated the situation was that the company was in the midst of its year-end audit. As part of the audit, the CEO was required to sign a letter saying that he was not aware of any significant outstanding circumstances that could negatively impact the company—in accounting terms, of any contingent liabilities. The auditor was not aware of the customer complaints or the FAA investigation.

The company relied heavily on short-term loans from eight banks. The CEO feared that if these lenders learned of the situation, they would pull their loans. The loss of these loans would force the company into bankruptcy, leaving hundreds of people without jobs. Prior to this problem, the company had a stellar performance record."

Instructions
Answer the following questions.
(a) Who are the stakeholders in this situation?
(b) What are the CEO's possible courses of action? What are the potential results of each course of action? (Take into account the two alternative outcomes: the FAA determines the company (1) was not at fault, and (2) was at fault.)
(c) What would you do, and why?

(d) Suppose the CEO decides to conceal the situation, and that during the next year the company is found to be at fault and is forced into bankruptcy. What losses are incurred by the stakeholders in this situation? Do you think the CEO should suffer legal consequences if he decides to conceal the situation?

BYP10-11 During the summer of 2002 the financial press reported that Citigroup was being investigated for allegations that it had arranged transactions for Enron so as to intentionally misrepresent the nature of the transactions and consequently achieve favorable balance sheet treatment. Essentially, the deals were structured to make it appear that money was coming into Enron from trading activities, rather than from loans.

A July 23, 2002, *New York Times* article by Richard Oppel and Kurt Eichenwald entitled "Citigroup Said to Mold Deal to Help Enron Skirt Rules" suggested that Citigroup intentionally kept certain parts of a secret oral agreement out of the written record for fear that it would change the accounting treatment. Critics contend that this had the effect of significantly understating Enron's liabilities, thus misleading investors and creditors. Citigroup maintains that, as a lender, it has no obligation to ensure that its clients account for transactions properly. The proper accounting, Citigroup insists, is the responsibility of the client and its auditor.

Instructions
Answer the following questions.
  (a) Who are the stakeholders in this situation?
  (b) Do you think that a lender, in general, in arranging so called "structured financing" has a responsibility to ensure that its clients account for the financing in an appropriate fashion, or is this the responsibility of the client and its auditor?
  (c) What effect did the fact that the written record did not disclose all characteristics of the transaction probably have on the auditor's ability to evaluate the accounting treatment of this transaction?
  (d) The *New York Times* article noted that in one presentation made to sell this kind of deal to Enron and other energy companies, Citigroup stated that using such an arrangement "eliminates the need for capital markets disclosure, keeping structure mechanics private." Why might a company wish to conceal the terms of a financing arrangement from the capital markets (investors and creditors)? Is this appropriate? Do you think it is ethical for a lender to market deals in this way?
  (e) Why was this deal more potentially harmful to shareholders than other off-balance-sheet transactions (for example, lease financing)?

Answers to Business Insight and Accounting across the Organization Questions

p. 479
Q: Based on this story, what is a good general rule to use in choosing between short-term and long-term financing?
A: In general, it is best to finance short-term assets with short-term liabilities and long-term assets with long-term liabilities in order to reduce the likelihood of a liquidity crunch such as this.

p. 481
Q: The drop in stock prices did not change the debt to total assets ratios of these companies. Discuss how the perception of a high debt to total assets ratio changed before and after the fall in stock prices.
A: When stock prices fell, the debt to total assets of these companies was unchanged: The debt was outstanding before the fall, and it was outstanding after the fall. However, before the fall, many investors did not worry if a company had a high debt to total assets ratio; they assumed that the debt would be converted to stock and so would never have to be repaid with cash. After the fall it became clear that the debt would not be converted to stock; suddenly, a high debt to total assets ratio was a real concern.

p. 494

Q: Explain how the sale of plant assets could improve the company's solvency.

A: A common measure of solvency is the debt to total assets ratio. By selling some of its fixed assets and using the cash to pay off debt, the company would reduce its reliance on debt financing and improve its debt to assets ratio.

Answer to Tootsie Roll Review It Question 5, p. 480

The liabilities that Tootsie Roll has identified as current are: Bank loan, Accounts payable, Dividends payable, Accrued liabilities, and Income taxes payable.

Answers to Self-Study Questions

1. a   2. d   3. b   4. b   5. a   6. c   7. a   8. c   9. b   10. c
11. c   12. a   13. b   14. c

REMEMBER TO GO BACK TO THE NAVIGATOR BOX ON THE CHAPTER-OPENING PAGE AND CHECK OFF YOUR COMPLETED WORK.

CHAPTER 11

Reporting and Analyzing Stockholders' Equity

STUDY OBJECTIVES

After studying this chapter,
you should be able to:

1 Identify and discuss the major characteristics of a corporation.

2 Record the issuance of common stock.

3 Explain the accounting for the purchase of treasury stock.

4 Differentiate preferred stock from common stock.

5 Prepare the entries for cash dividends and understand the effect of stock dividends and stock splits.

6 Identify the items that affect retained earnings.

7 Prepare a comprehensive stockholders' equity section.

8 Evaluate a corporation's dividend and earnings performance from a stock-holder's perspective.

THE NAVIGATOR

✓ THE NAVIGATOR

- Scan *Study Objectives* ⬭
- Read *Feature Story* ⬭
- Read *Preview* ⬭
- Read text and answer *Before You Go On* ⬭
  - p. 539 ⬭ p. 543 ⬭ p. 545 ⬭
  - p. 552 ⬭ p. 556 ⬭ p. 560 ⬭
- Work *Using the Decision Toolkit* ⬭
- Review *Summary of Study Objectives* ⬭
- Work *Demonstration Problem* ⬭
- Answer *Self-Study Questions* ⬭
- Complete *Assignments* ⬭

FEATURE STORY

What's Cooking?

What major U.S. corporation got its start 35 years ago with a waffle iron? Hint: It doesn't sell food. Another hint: Swoosh. Another hint: "Just do it." That's right, Nike. In 1971 Nike co-founder Bill Bowerman put a piece of rubber into a kitchen waffle iron, and the trademark waffle sole was born. It seems fair to say that at Nike, "They don't make 'em like they used to."

Nike was co-founded by Bowerman and Phil Knight, a member of Bowerman's University of Oregon track team. Each began in the shoe business independently during the early 1960s. Bowerman got his start by making hand-crafted running shoes for his University of Oregon track team. Knight, after completing graduate school, started a small business importing low-cost, high-quality shoes from Japan. In 1964 the two joined forces, each contributing $500, and formed Blue Ribbon Sports, a partnership, marketing Japanese shoes.

It wasn't until 1971 that the company began manufacturing its own line of shoes. With the new shoes came a new corporate name—Nike—the Greek goddess of victory. It is hard to imagine that the company that now boasts a stable full of world-class athletes as promoters at one time had part-time employees selling shoes out of car trunks at track meets. Nike has achieved its success through

relentless innovation combined with unbridled promotion.

By 1980 Nike was sufficiently established that it was able to issue its first stock to the public. In that same year it also created a stock ownership program for its employees, allowing them to share in the company's success. Since then Nike has enjoyed phenomenal growth, with 2004 sales reaching $12.3 billion and total dividends paid of $179 million.

Nike is not alone in its quest for the top of the sport shoe world. Competitor Reebok pushes Nike every step of the way. However, Nike's recent success has resulted in sales that are three times those of Reebok.

Is the race over? Probably not. The shoe market is fickle, with new styles becoming popular almost daily and vast international markets still lying untapped. Whether one of these two giants does eventually take control of the planet remains to be seen. Meanwhile the shareholders sit anxiously in the stands as this Olympic-size drama unfolds.

On the World Wide Web
Nike: www.nike.com
Reebok: www.reebok.com

Corporations like Nike and Reebok have substantial resources at their disposal. In fact, the corporation is the dominant form of business organization in the United States in terms of sales, earnings, and number of employees. All of the 500 largest U.S. companies are corporations. In this chapter we look at the essential features of a corporation and explain the accounting for a corporation's capital stock transactions.

The content and organization of the chapter are as follows.

REPORTING AND ANALYZING STOCKHOLDERS' EQUITY

The Corporate Form of Organization	Stock Issue Considerations	Accounting for Treasury Stock	Preferred Stock	Dividends and Retained Earnings	Financial Statement Presentation and Corporate Performance
• Characteristics • Formation • Stockholder rights	• Authorized stock • Issuance • Par and no-par value • Accounting for common stock issues	• Purchase of treasury stock	• Dividend preferences • Liquidation preference	• Cash dividends • Stock dividends • Stock splits • Retained earnings restrictions	• Balance sheet • Statement of cash flows • Dividend record • Earnings performance • Debt vs. equity decision

THE NAVIGATOR

The Corporate Form of Organization

A corporation is created by law. As a legal entity, a corporation has most of the rights and privileges of a person. The major exceptions relate to privileges that can be exercised only by a living person, such as the right to vote or to hold public office. Similarly, a corporation is subject to the same duties and responsibilities as a person. For example, it must abide by the law and it must pay taxes.

We can classify corporations in a variety of ways. Two common classifications are **by purpose** and **by ownership**. A corporation may be organized for the purpose of making a profit (such as Nike or General Motors), or it may be a nonprofit charitable, medical, or educational corporation (such as Salvation Army or the American Cancer Society).

Classification by ownership differentiates publicly held and privately held corporations. A publicly held corporation may have thousands of stockholders, and its stock is regularly traded on a national securities market such as the New York Stock Exchange. Examples are IBM, Caterpillar, and General Electric. In contrast, a privately held corporation, often referred to as a closely held corporation, usually has only a few stockholders and does not offer its stock for sale to the general public. Privately held companies are generally much smaller than publicly held companies, although some notable exceptions exist. Cargill Inc., a private corporation that trades in grain and other commodities, is one of the largest companies in the United States. This chapter deals primarily with issues related to publicly held companies.

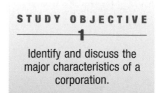

STUDY OBJECTIVE

1

Identify and discuss the major characteristics of a corporation.

CHARACTERISTICS OF A CORPORATION

In 1964, when Nike's founders, Knight and Bowerman, were just getting started in the running shoe business, they formed their original organization as a partnership. In 1968 they reorganized the company as a corporation. A number of characteristics distinguish a corporation from sole proprietorships and partnerships. The most important of these characteristics are explained below.

Separate Legal Existence

As an entity separate and distinct from its owners, the corporation acts under its own name rather than in the name of its stockholders. Nike, for example, may buy, own, and sell property, borrow money, and enter into legally binding contracts in its own name. It may also sue or be sued. It pays taxes as a separate entity.

In contrast to a partnership, in which the acts of the owners (partners) bind the partnership, the acts of the owners (stockholders) do not bind the corporation unless such owners are agents of the corporation. For example, if you owned shares of Nike stock, you would not have the right to purchase inventory for the company unless you were designated as an agent of the corporation.

Stockholders

Legal existence separate from owners

Limited Liability of Stockholders

Since a corporation is a separate legal entity, creditors ordinarily have recourse only to corporate assets to satisfy their claims. The liability of stockholders is normally limited to their investment in the corporation. Creditors have no legal claim on the personal assets of the stockholders unless fraud has occurred. Thus, even in the event of bankruptcy of the corporation, stockholders' losses are generally limited to the amount of capital they have invested in the corporation.

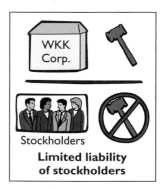

Stockholders

Limited liability of stockholders

Transferable Ownership Rights

Ownership of a corporation is held in shares of capital stock, which are transferable units. Stockholders may dispose of part or all of their interest in a corporation simply by selling their stock. The transfer of an ownership interest in a partnership requires the consent of each partner. In contrast, the transfer of stock is entirely at the discretion of the stockholder. It does not require the approval of either the corporation or other stockholders.

The transfer of ownership rights among stockholders normally has no effect on the operating activities of the corporation. Nor does it affect the corporation's assets, liabilities, and total stockholders' equity. The transfer of ownership rights is a transaction between individual owners. The company does not participate in the transfer of these ownership rights after the original sale of the capital stock.

Transferable ownership rights

Ability to Acquire Capital

It is relatively easy for a corporation to obtain capital through the issuance of stock. Buying stock in a corporation is often attractive to an investor because a stockholder has limited liability and shares of stock are readily transferable. Also, numerous individuals can become stockholders by investing small amounts of money.

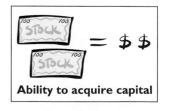

Ability to acquire capital

Continuous Life

The life of a corporation is stated in its charter. The life may be perpetual or it may be limited to a specific number of years. If it is limited, the company can extend the period of existence through renewal of the charter. Since a corporation is a separate legal entity, its continuance as a going concern is not affected by

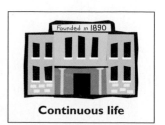

Continuous life

the withdrawal, death, or incapacity of a stockholder, employee, or officer. As a result, a successful corporation can have a continuous and perpetual life.

Corporation Management

Although stockholders legally own the corporation, they manage it indirectly through a board of directors they elect. Philip Knight is the chairman of Nike's board of directors. The board, in turn, formulates the operating policies for the company. The board also selects officers, such as a president and one or more vice-presidents, to execute policy and to perform daily management functions. As a result of the Sarbanes-Oxley Act, the board is now required to monitor management's actions more closely. Many feel that the failures at Enron and WorldCom could have been avoided by more diligent boards.

Illustration 11-1 depicts a typical organization chart showing the delegation of responsibility.

Illustration 11-1
Corporation organization chart

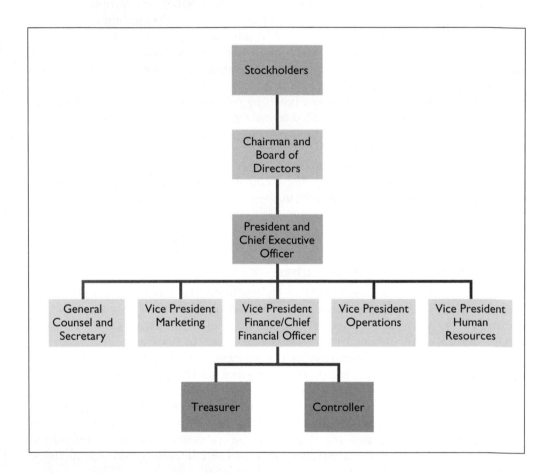

The chief executive officer (CEO) has overall responsibility for managing the business. As the organization chart shows, the CEO delegates responsibility to other officers. The chief accounting officer is the **controller**. The controller's responsibilities are to (1) maintain the accounting records, (2) maintain an adequate system of internal control and (3) prepare financial statements, tax returns, and internal reports. The **treasurer** has custody of the corporation's funds and is responsible for maintaining the company's cash position.

The organizational structure of a corporation enables a company to hire professional managers to run the business. On the other hand, the separation of ownership and management often reduces an owner's ability to actively manage the company.

Government Regulations

A corporation is subject to numerous state and federal regulations. For example, state laws usually prescribe the requirements for issuing stock, the distributions of earnings permitted to stockholders, and acceptable methods for retiring stock. Federal securities laws govern the sale of capital stock to the general public. Also, most publicly held corporations are required to make extensive disclosure of their financial affairs to the Securities and Exchange Commission (SEC) through quarterly and annual reports. The Sarbanes-Oxley Act increased the company's responsibility for the accuracy of these reports. In addition, when a corporate stock is listed and traded on organized securities exchanges, the corporation must comply with the reporting requirements of these exchanges.

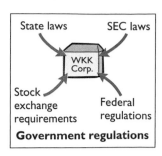

Government regulations

Accounting across the Organization

During the hot stock market of the late 1990s, the dream of nearly every entrepreneur was to "take the company public." But times have changed, and now top managers at small- to medium-sized companies are reevaluating the costs versus the benefits of being a publicly traded company.

In 2004 and 2005 a record number of publicly traded companies repurchased all of their shares and took their companies private. Most cited the increased regulatory costs associated with Sarbanes-Oxley as the reason for going private. Estimates of these costs were about $2.3 million per year—roughly ten times what they were a few years earlier. In about two-thirds of the deals it was the managers themselves who bought the company's shares.

Source: Emily Thorton, "A Little Privacy Please," *Business Week* (May 24, 2004), pp. 74–75.

 In addition to regulatory cost, what is another reason why some owners choose not to take their companies public?

Additional Taxes

Owners of proprietorships and partnerships report their share of earnings on their personal income tax returns. The individual owner then pays taxes on this amount. Corporations, on the other hand, must pay federal and state income taxes as a separate legal entity. These taxes are substantial: They can amount to as much as 40% of taxable income.

In addition, stockholders are required to pay taxes on cash dividends. Thus, many argue that corporate income is **taxed twice (double taxation)**—once at the corporate level and again at the individual level.

Illustration 11-2 shows the advantages and disadvantages of a corporation compared to a sole proprietorship and partnership.

Additional taxes

Advantages	Disadvantages
• Separate legal existence	• Corporation management—separation of ownership and management
• Limited liability of stockholders	• Government regulations
• Transferable ownership rights	• Additional taxes
• Ability to acquire capital	
• Continuous life	
• Corporation management—professional managers	

Illustration 11-2
Advantages and disadvantages of a corporation

Other Forms of Business Organization

A variety of "hybrid" organizational forms—forms that combine different attributes of partnerships and corporations—now exist. For example, one type of corporate form, called an **S corporation**, allows for legal treatment as a corporation but tax treatment as a partnership—that is, no double taxation. Because of changes to the S corporation's rules, more small- and medium-sized businesses now may choose S corporation treatment. One of the primary criteria is that the company cannot have more than 75 shareholders. Other forms of organization include limited partnerships, limited liability partnerships (LLPs), and limited liability corporations (LLCs).

Decision Toolkit

Decision Checkpoints	Info Needed for Decision	Tool to Use for Decision	How to Evaluate Results
Should the company incorporate?	Capital needs, growth expectations, type of business, tax status	Corporations have limited liability, easier capital raising ability, and professional managers; but they suffer from additional taxes, government regulations, and separation of ownership from management.	Must carefully weigh the costs and benefits in light of the particular circumstances.

FORMING A CORPORATION

A corporation is formed by grant of a state **charter**. Regardless of the number of states in which a corporation has operating divisions, it is incorporated in only one state. It is to the company's advantage to incorporate in a state whose laws are favorable to the corporate form of business organization. For example, although General Motors has its headquarters in Michigan, it is incorporated in New Jersey. In fact, more and more corporations have been incorporating in states with rules that favor existing management. For example, Gulf Oil changed its state of incorporation to Delaware to thwart possible unfriendly takeovers. There, certain defensive tactics against takeovers can be approved by the board of directors alone, without a vote by shareholders.

Upon receipt of its charter from the state of incorporation, the corporation establishes **by-laws**. The by-laws establish the internal rules and procedures for conducting the affairs of the corporation. Corporations engaged in interstate commerce must also obtain a **license** from each state in which they do business. The license subjects the corporation's operating activities to the general corporation laws of the state.

STOCKHOLDER RIGHTS

When chartered, the corporation may begin selling shares of stock. When a corporation has only one class of stock, it is identified as **common stock**. Each share of common stock gives the stockholder the ownership rights pictured in Illustration 11-3 (page 539). The articles of incorporation or the by-laws state the ownership rights of a share of stock.

Illustration 11-3
Ownership rights of
stockholders

Stockholders have the right to:

1. Vote in election of board of directors at annual meeting and vote on actions that require stockholder approval.

2. Share the corporate earnings through receipt of dividends.

dividends

Before   **After**

New shares issued

3. Keep the same percentage ownership when new shares of stock are issued (**preemptive right**[1]).

14%   14%

4. Share in assets upon liquidation in proportion to their holdings. This is called a **residual claim** because owners are paid with assets that remain after all claims have been paid.

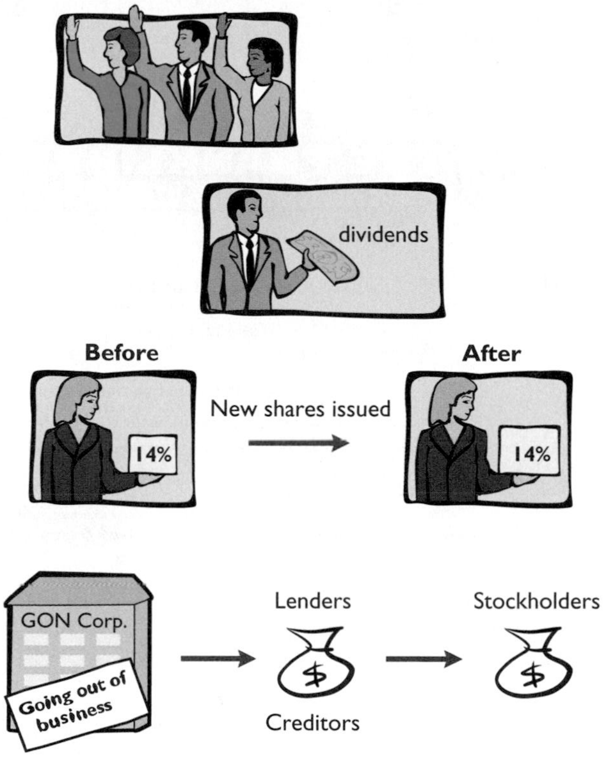

GON Corp. Going out of business   Lenders / Creditors   Stockholders

Proof of stock ownership is evidenced by a printed or engraved form known as a **stock certificate**. As shown in Illustration 11-4 (page 540), the face of the certificate shows the name of the corporation, the stockholder's name, the class and special features of the stock, the number of shares owned, and the signatures of authorized corporate officials. Certificates are prenumbered to ensure proper control over their use; they may be issued for any quantity of shares.

BEFORE YOU GO ON . . .

▶ **Review It**

1. What are the advantages and disadvantages of a corporation compared to a proprietorship and a partnership?
2. Identify the principal steps in forming a corporation.
3. What are the ownership rights of owning a share of stock in a corporation?

THE NAVIGATOR

[1] A number of companies have eliminated the preemptive right because they believe it places an unnecessary and cumbersome demand on management. For example, IBM, by stockholder approval, has dropped its preemptive right for stockholders.

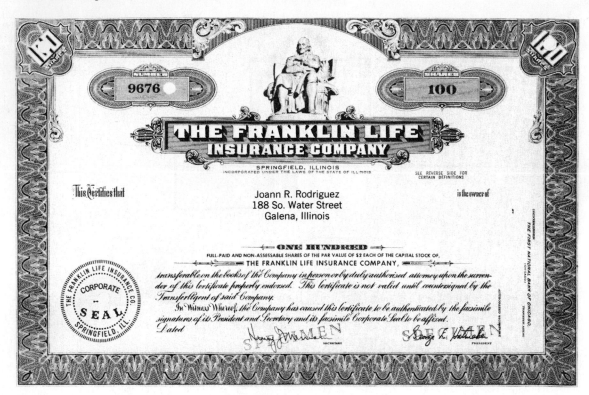

Illustration 11-4
A stock certificate

Stock Issue Considerations

Although Nike incorporated in 1968, it did not sell stock to the public until 1980. At that time Nike evidently decided it would benefit from the infusion of cash that a public sale of its shares would bring. When a corporation decides to issue stock, it must resolve a number of basic questions: How many shares should it authorize for sale? How should it issue the stock? What value should it assign to the stock? We address these questions in the following sections.

AUTHORIZED STOCK

The amount of stock that a corporation is authorized to sell is indicated in its charter. If the corporation has sold all of its **authorized stock**, then it must obtain consent of the state to amend its charter before it can issue additional shares.

The authorization of common stock does not result in a formal accounting entry. The reason is that the event has no immediate effect on either corporate assets or stockholders' equity. However, the corporation must disclose in the stockholders' equity section of the balance sheet the number of shares authorized.

ISSUANCE OF STOCK

A corporation can issue common stock **directly** to investors. Alternatively, it can issue common stock **indirectly** through an investment banking firm that specializes in bringing securities to the attention of prospective investors. Direct issue is typical in closely held companies. Indirect issue is customary for a publicly held corporation.

New issues of stock may be offered for sale to the public through various organized U.S. securities exchanges: the New York Stock Exchange, the American Stock Exchange, and 13 regional exchanges. Stock may also be traded on the NASDAQ national market.

⊕ **International Note**

U.S. and U.K. corporations raise most of their capital through millions of outside shareholders and bondholders. In contrast, companies in Germany, France, and Japan acquire financing mostly from large banks or other financial institutions. Consequently, in the latter environment, shareholders are less important, and external reporting and auditing receive less emphasis.

PAR AND NO-PAR VALUE STOCKS

Par value stock is capital stock that has been assigned a value per share in the corporate charter. Years ago, par value was used to determine the **legal capital** per share that must be retained in the business for the protection of corporate creditors. That amount is not available for withdrawal by stockholders. Thus, in the past, most states required the corporation to sell its shares at par or above.

However, the usefulness of par value as a protective device to creditors was questionable because par value was often immaterial relative to the value of the company's stock in the securities markets—even at the time of issue. For example, Reebok's par value is $0.01 per share, yet a new issue in 2004 would have sold at a **market value** in the $38 per share range. Thus, par has no relationship with market value and in the vast majority of cases is an immaterial amount. As a consequence, today many states do not require a par value. Instead, they use other means to determine legal capital to protect creditors.

No-par value stock is capital stock that has not been assigned a value in the corporate charter. No-par value stock is quite common today. For example, Nike, Procter & Gamble, and North American Van Lines all have no-par stock. In many states the board of directors assigns a **stated value** to the no-par shares.

ACCOUNTING FOR COMMON STOCK ISSUES

The stockholders' equity section of a corporation's balance sheet includes: (1) **paid-in (contributed) capital** and (2) **retained earnings (earned capital)**. The distinction between paid-in capital and retained earnings is important from both a legal and an economic point of view. **Paid-in capital** is the amount stockholders paid to the corporation in exchange for shares of ownership. **Retained earnings** is earned capital held for future use in the business. In this section we discuss the accounting for paid-in capital. In a later section we discuss retained earnings.

Let's now look at how to account for new issues of common stock. The primary objectives in accounting for the issuance of common stock are: (1) to identify the specific sources of paid-in capital and (2) to maintain the distinction between paid-in capital and retained earnings. As shown below, **the issuance of common stock affects only paid-in capital accounts**.

As discussed earlier, par value does not indicate a stock's market value. The cash proceeds from issuing par value stock may be equal to, greater than, or less than par value. When a company records the issuance of common stock for cash, it credits the par value of the shares to Common Stock, and records in a separate paid-in capital account the portion of the proceeds that is above or below par value.

To illustrate, assume that Hydro-Slide, Inc. issues 1,000 shares of $1 par value common stock at par for cash. The entry to record this transaction is:

Helpful Hint Stock is sometimes issued in exchange for services (payment to attorneys or consultants, for example) or other noncash assets (land or buildings). The value recorded for the shares issued is determined by either the market value of the shares, or the value of the good or service received depending upon which value the company can more readily determine.

Cash	1,000	
Common Stock		1,000
(To record issuance of 1,000 shares of $1 par		
common stock at par)		

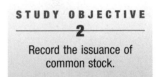

A = L + SE
+1,000
          +1,000 CS

Cash Flows
 +1,000

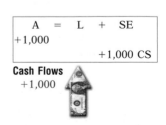

If Hydro-Slide, Inc. issues an additional 1,000 shares of the $1 par value common stock for cash at $5 per share, the entry is:

Cash	5,000	
Common Stock		1,000
Paid-in Capital in Excess of Par Value		4,000
(To record issuance of 1,000 shares of common		
stock in excess of par)		

A = L + SE
+5,000
          +1,000 CS
          +4,000 CS

Cash Flows
 +5,000

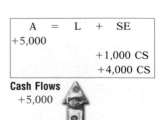

The total paid-in capital from these two transactions is $6,000. If Hydro-Slide, Inc. has retained earnings of $27,000, the stockholders' equity section of the balance sheet is as shown in Illustration 11-5.

Illustration 11-5
Stockholders' equity—
paid-in capital in excess
of par value

HYDRO-SLIDE, INC.	
Balance Sheet (partial)	
Stockholders' equity	
Paid-in capital	
Common stock	$ 2,000
Paid-in capital in excess of par value	**4,000**
Total paid-in capital	6,000
Retained earnings	27,000
Total stockholders' equity	$33,000

Some companies issue no-par stock with a stated value. For accounting purposes, companies treat the stated value in the same way as the par value. For example, if in our Hydro-Slide example the stock was no-par stock with a stated value of $1, the entries would be the same as those presented for the par stock except the term "Par Value" would be replaced with "Stated Value." If a company issues no-par stock that does not have a stated value, then it credits to the Common Stock account the full amount received. In such a case, there is no need for the Paid-in Capital in Excess of Stated Value account.

Business Insight
Investor Perspective

Organized exchanges trade the stock of publicly held companies at dollar prices per share established by the interaction between buyers and sellers. For each listed security the financial press reports the high and low prices of the stock during the year, the total volume of stock traded on a given day, the high and low prices for the day, and the closing market price, with the net change for the day. Nike is listed on the New York Stock Exchange. Here is a recent listing for Nike:

	52 Weeks						
Stock	**High**	**Low**	**Volume**	**High**	**Low**	**Close**	**Net Change**
Nike	92.43	68.61	263,000	87.49	86.80	87.03	+.09

These numbers indicate the following: The high and low market prices for the last 52 weeks have been $92.43 and $68.61. The trading volume for the previous day was 263,000 shares. The high, low, and closing prices for that date were $87.49, $86.80, and $87.03, respectively. The net change for the day was an increase of $0.09 per share.

 For stocks traded on organized exchanges, how are the dollar prices per share established? What factors might influence the price of shares in the marketplace?

BEFORE YOU GO ON . . .

▶ **Review It**

1. Of what significance to a corporation is the amount of authorized stock?
2. What alternative approaches may a corporation use to sell new shares to investors?
3. Distinguish between par value and market value.
4. Explain the accounting for par and no-par common stock issued for cash.

▶ **Do It**

Cayman Corporation begins operations on March 1 by issuing 100,000 shares of $10 par value common stock for cash at $12 per share. Journalize the issuance of the shares.

Action Plan

• In issuing shares for cash, credit Common Stock for par value per share.
• Credit any additional proceeds in excess of par value to a separate paid-in capital account.

Solution

Mar. 1	Cash	1,200,000	
	Common Stock		1,000,000
	Paid-in Capital in Excess of Par Value		200,000
	(To record issuance of 100,000 shares at $12 per share)		

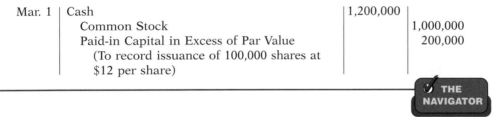

Accounting for Treasury Stock

Treasury stock is a corporation's own stock that has been issued, fully paid for, and reacquired by the corporation and is being held in its treasury for future use. A corporation may acquire treasury stock for various reasons:

STUDY OBJECTIVE
3
Explain the accounting for the purchase of treasury stock.

1. To reissue the shares to officers and employees under bonus and stock compensation plans.
2. To increase trading of the company's stock in the securities market. Companies expect that buying their own stock will signal that management believes the stock is underpriced, which they hope will enhance its market value.
3. To have additional shares available for use in acquiring other companies.
4. To reduce the number of shares outstanding and thereby increase earnings per share.

Another infrequent reason for purchasing treasury shares is that management may want to eliminate hostile shareholders by buying them out.

Many corporations have treasury stock. For example, in the United States approximately 68% of companies have treasury stock.[2] Specifically, in 2004 Nike purchased 6.4 million treasury shares, IBM, 78.6 million, and Limited Brands, 125 million shares. Stock repurchases have been so substantial that a recent study by two Federal Reserve economists suggested that a sharp reduction in

---

[2]*Accounting Trends & Techniques—2004* (New York: American Institute of Certified Public Accountants).

corporate purchases of treasury shares might result in a sharp drop in the value of the U.S. stock market.

PURCHASE OF TREASURY STOCK

The purchase of treasury stock is generally accounted for by the **cost method**. This method derives its name from the fact that the Treasury Stock account is maintained at the cost of shares purchased. Under the cost method, **companies increase (debit) Treasury Stock by the price paid to reacquire the shares. Treasury Stock decreases by the same amount when the company later sells the shares.**

To illustrate, assume that on January 1, 2007, the stockholders' equity section for Mead, Inc. has 100,000 shares of $5 par value common stock outstanding (all issued at par value) and Retained Earnings of $200,000. Illustration 11-6 shows the stockholders' equity section of the balance sheet before purchase of treasury stock.

Illustration 11-6
Stockholders' equity with no treasury stock

MEAD, INC. Balance Sheet (partial)	
Stockholders' equity	
Paid-in capital	
Common stock, $5 par value, 100,000 shares	
issued and outstanding	$500,000
Retained earnings	200,000
Total stockholders' equity	$700,000

On February 1, 2007, Mead acquires 4,000 shares of its stock at $8 per share. The entry is:

```
A   =   L   +   SE
                -32,000 TS
-32,000
Cash Flows
-32,000
```

Feb. 1	Treasury Stock	32,000	
	Cash		32,000
	(To record purchase of 4,000 shares of treasury stock at $8 per share)		

The Treasury Stock account would increase by the cost of the shares purchased ($32,000). The original paid-in capital account, Common Stock, would not be affected because **the number of issued shares does not change**.

Companies show treasury stock as a deduction from total paid-in capital and retained earnings in the stockholders' equity section of the balance sheet. Illustration 11-7 shows this presentation for Mead, Inc. Thus, the acquisition of treasury stock reduces stockholders' equity.

Helpful Hint Treasury Stock is a contra stockholders' equity account.

Illustration 11-7
Stockholders' equity with treasury stock

MEAD, INC. Balance Sheet (partial)	
Stockholders' equity	
Paid-in capital	
Common stock, $5 par value, 100,000 shares	
issued and 96,000 shares outstanding	$500,000
Retained earnings	200,000
Total paid-in capital and retained earnings	700,000
Less: Treasury stock (4,000 shares)	**32,000**
Total stockholders' equity	$668,000

Companies disclose in the balance sheet both the number of shares issued (100,000) and the number in the treasury (4,000). The difference is the number of shares of stock outstanding (96,000). The term **outstanding stock** means the number of shares of issued stock that are being held by stockholders.

Accounting across the Organization

In a bold (and some would say risky) move, Reebok at one time bought back nearly a *third* of its shares. This repurchase of shares dramatically reduced Reebok's available cash. In fact, the company borrowed significant funds to accomplish the repurchase. In a press release, management stated that it was repurchasing the shares because it believed that the stock was severely underpriced. The repurchase of so many shares was meant to signal management's belief in good future earnings.

Skeptics, however, suggested that Reebok's management was repurchasing shares to make it less likely that the company would be acquired by another company (in which case Reebok's top managers would likely lose their jobs). Acquiring companies like to purchase companies with large cash reserves so they can pay off debt used in the acquisition. By depleting its cash, Reebok became a less likely acquisition target.

 What signal might a large stock repurchase send to investors regarding management's belief about the company's growth opportunities?

BEFORE YOU GO ON . . .

▶ Review It

1. What is treasury stock, and why do companies acquire it?
2. How do companies record treasury stock?
3. Where in the financial statements do companies report treasury stock?

▶ Do It

Santa Anita Inc. purchases 3,000 shares of its $50 par value common stock for $180,000 cash on July 1. It expects to hold the shares in the treasury until resold. Journalize the treasury stock transaction.

Action Plan

- Record the purchase of treasury stock at cost.
- Report treasury stock as a deduction from stockholders' equity (contra account) at the bottom of the stockholders' equity section.

Solution

July 1	Treasury Stock	180,000	
	Cash		180,000
	(To record the purchase of 3,000 shares at $60 per share)		

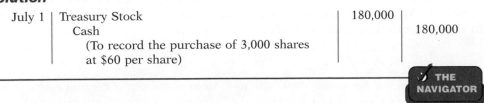

THE NAVIGATOR

Preferred Stock

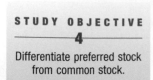

STUDY OBJECTIVE

4

Differentiate preferred stock from common stock.

To appeal to a larger segment of potential investors, a corporation may issue an additional class of stock, called preferred stock. **Preferred stock** has contractual provisions that give it preference or priority over common stock in certain areas. Typically, preferred stockholders have a priority in relation to (1) dividends and (2) assets in the event of liquidation. However, they sometimes do not have voting rights. Reebok has no outstanding preferred stock, whereas Nike has a very minor amount outstanding. Approximately 15% of U.S. companies have one or more classes of preferred stock.[3]

Like common stock, companies may issue preferred stock for cash or for noncash consideration. The entries for these transactions are similar to the entries for common stock. When a corporation has more than one class of stock, each paid-in capital account title should identify the stock to which it relates (e.g., Preferred Stock, Common Stock, Paid-in Capital in Excess of Par Value—Preferred Stock, and Paid-in Capital in Excess of Par Value—Common Stock).

Assume that Stine Corporation issues 10,000 shares of $10 par value preferred stock for $12 cash per share. The entry to record the issuance is:

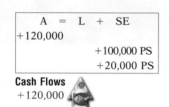

		A	=	L	+	SE
+120,000						
					+100,000 PS	
					+20,000 PS	

Cash Flows
+120,000

	Debit	Credit
Cash	120,000	
Preferred Stock		100,000
Paid-in Capital in Excess of Par Value—Preferred Stock		20,000
(To record the issuance of 10,000 shares of $10 par value preferred stock)		

Preferred stock may have either a par value or no-par value. In the stockholders' equity section of the balance sheet, companies show preferred stock first because of its dividend and liquidation preferences over common stock.

DIVIDEND PREFERENCES

As indicated above, **preferred stockholders have the right to share in the distribution of corporate income before common stockholders**. For example, if the dividend rate on preferred stock is $5 per share, common shareholders will not receive any dividends in the current year until preferred stockholders have received $5 per share. The first claim to dividends does not, however, **guarantee** dividends. Dividends depend on many factors, such as adequate retained earnings and availability of cash.

For preferred stock, companies state the per share dividend amount as a percentage of the par value of the stock or as a specified amount. For example, EarthLink specifies a 3% dividend, whereas Nike pays 10 cents per share on its $1 par preferred stock.

Cumulative Dividend

Preferred stock contracts often contain a **cumulative dividend** feature. This right means that preferred stockholders must be paid both current-year dividends and any unpaid prior-year dividends before common stockholders receive dividends. When preferred stock is cumulative, preferred dividends not declared in a given period are called **dividends in arrears**.

---

[3]*Accounting Trends & Techniques—2004* (New York: American Institute of Certified Public Accountants).

To illustrate, assume that Scientific Leasing has 5,000 shares of 7%, $100 par value cumulative preferred stock outstanding. Each $100 share pays a $7 dividend (.07 × $100). The annual dividend is $35,000 (5,000 × $7 per share). If dividends are two years in arrears, preferred stockholders are entitled to receive in the current year the dividends as shown in Illustration 11-8.

Dividends in arrears ($35,000 × 2)	$	70,000
Current-year dividends		35,000
Total preferred dividends		**$105,000**

Illustration 11-8
Computation of total dividends to preferred stock

No distribution can be made to common stockholders until Scientific Leasing pays this entire preferred dividend. In other words, companies cannot pay dividends to common stockholders while any preferred stock dividend is in arrears.

Dividends in arrears are not considered a liability. No obligation exists until the board of directors formally "declares" that the corporation will pay a dividend. However, companies should disclose in the notes to the financial statements the amount of dividends in arrears. Doing so enables investors to assess the potential impact of this commitment on the corporation's financial position.

The investment community does not look favorably upon companies that are unable to meet their dividend obligations. As a financial officer noted in discussing one company's failure to pay its cumulative preferred dividend for a period of time, "Not meeting your obligations on something like that is a major black mark on your record."

LIQUIDATION PREFERENCE

Most preferred stocks have a preference on corporate assets if the corporation fails. This feature provides security for the preferred stockholder. The preference to assets may be for the par value of the shares or for a specified liquidating value. For example, Commonwealth Edison issued preferred stock that entitles the holders to receive $31.80 per share, plus accrued and unpaid dividends, in the event of involuntary liquidation. The liquidation preference is used in litigation pertaining to bankruptcy lawsuits involving the respective claims of creditors and preferred stockholders.

Dividends

As noted earlier, a **dividend is a distribution by a corporation to its stockholders on a pro rata basis.** *Pro rata* means that if you own, say, 10% of the common shares, you will receive 10% of the dividend. Dividends can take four forms: cash, property, script (promissory note to pay cash), or stock. Cash dividends, which predominate in practice, and stock dividends, which are declared with some frequency, are the focus of our discussion.

Investors are very interested in a company's dividend practices. In the financial press, **dividends are generally reported quarterly as a dollar amount per share**. (Sometimes they are reported on an annual basis.) For example, Nike's **quarterly** dividend rate in the fourth quarter of 2004 was 20 cents per share; the dividend rate for that quarter for Target was 7 cents, and for PepsiCo it was 23 cents.

CASH DIVIDENDS

A **cash dividend** is a pro rata distribution of cash to stockholders. For a corporation to pay a cash dividend, it must have the following.

1. **Retained earnings.** Many states prohibit payment of dividends from legal capital. However, payment of dividends from paid-in capital in excess of par is legal in some states. **Payment of dividends from retained earnings is legal in all states.** In addition, loan agreements frequently constrain companies to pay dividends only from retained earnings.

2. **Adequate cash.** Recently Nike had a balance in retained earnings of $3,983 million but a cash balance of only $828 million. If it had wanted to pay a dividend equal to its retained earnings, Nike would have had to raise $3,155 million more in cash. It would have been unlikely to do this because it would not be able to pay this much in dividends in future years. In addition, such a dividend would completely deplete Nike's balance in retained earnings, so it would not be able to pay a dividend in the next year unless it had positive net income.

3. **Declared dividends.** The board of directors has full authority to determine the amount of income to distribute in the form of dividends and the amount to retain in the business. Dividends do not accrue like interest on a note payable, and they are not a liability until they are declared.

In order to remain in business, companies must honor their interest payments to creditors, bankers, and bondholders. But the payment of dividends to stockholders is another matter. Many companies can survive, and even thrive, without such payouts. "Why give money to those strangers?" was the response of one company president.

The amount and timing of a dividend are important issues for management to consider. The payment of a large cash dividend could lead to liquidity problems for the company. Conversely, a small dividend or a missed dividend may cause unhappiness among stockholders who expect to receive a reasonable cash payment from the company on a periodic basis. Many companies declare and pay cash dividends quarterly. On the other hand, a number of high-growth companies pay no dividends, preferring to retain earnings and use them to finance capital expenditures.

Investors must keep an eye on the company's dividend policy and understand what it may mean. For most companies, for example, regular dividend boosts in the face of irregular earnings can be a warning signal. Companies with high dividends and rising debt may be borrowing money to pay shareholders. On the other hand, low dividends may not be a negative sign because they may mean the company is reinvesting in itself, which may result in high returns through increases in the stock price. Presumably, investors for whom regular dividends are important tend to buy stock in companies that pay periodic dividends, and those for whom growth in the stock price (capital gains) is more important tend to buy stock in companies that retain their earnings.

Entries for Cash Dividends

Three dates are important in connection with dividends: (1) the declaration date, (2) the record date, and (3) the payment date. Companies make accounting entries on the declaration date and the payment date.

On the **declaration date**, the board of directors formally authorizes the cash dividend and announces it to stockholders. The declaration of a cash dividend **commits the corporation to a binding legal obligation**. Thus, the company must make an entry to recognize the decrease in retained earnings and the increase in the liability Dividends Payable.

To illustrate, assume that on December 1, 2007, the directors of Media General declare a $0.50 per share cash dividend on 100,000 shares of $10 par value common stock. The dividend is $50,000 (100,000 × $0.50). The entry to record the declaration is:

Declaration Date

Dec. 1	Retained Earnings (or Cash Dividends)	50,000	
	Dividends Payable		50,000
	(To record declaration of cash dividend)		

A = L + SE
  −50,000 Div
+50,000

Cash Flows
no effect

Dividends Payable is a current liability: It will normally be paid within the next several months.

You may recall that in Chapter 3, instead of decreasing Retained Earnings, we used the account Dividends. The Dividends account provides additional information in the ledger. For example, a company may have separate dividend accounts for each class of stock or each type of dividend. When a company uses a separate dividend account, it transfers the account's balance to Retained Earnings at the end of the year by a closing entry. Whichever account is used for the dividend declaration, the effect is the same: The company decreases retained earnings and increases a current liability. To avoid additional detail in the textbook, we have chosen to use the Retained Earnings account. *For homework problems, you should use the Retained Earnings account for recording dividend declarations.*

At the **record date**, the company determines ownership of the outstanding shares for dividend purposes. The stockholders' records maintained by the corporation supply this information.

For Media General, the record date is December 22. No entry is required on the record date.

Helpful Hint The record date is important in determining the dividend to be paid to each stockholder but not the total dividend.

Record Date

Dec. 22	No entry necessary		

On the **payment date**, the company mails dividend checks to the stockholders on record as of December 22, and it also records the payment of the dividend. If January 20 is the payment date for Media General, the entry on that date is:

Payment Date

Jan. 20	Dividends Payable	50,000	
	Cash		50,000
	(To record payment of cash dividend)		

A = L + SE
  −50,000
−50,000

Cash Flows
−50,000

Note that payment of the dividend reduces both current assets and current liabilities, but it has no effect on stockholders' equity. The cumulative effect of the **declaration and payment** of a cash dividend on a company's financial statements is to **decrease both stockholders' equity and total assets**.

Accounting across the Organization

The decision whether to pay a cash dividend, and how much, is a very important management decision. During 2004 cash dividend payments were a record $181 billion—not including a one-time $32.6 billion dividend by Microsoft. The $181 billion does include a 44% dividend increase by Wal-Mart and a doubling of the dividend payment by Intel.

One explanation for the increase is that Congress lowered, from 39% to 15%, the tax rate paid by investors on dividends received, making dividends more attractive to investors. Another driving force for the dividend increases was that companies were sitting on record amounts of cash. Because they did not see a lot of good expansion opportunities, companies decided to return the cash to shareholders.

Bigger dividends are still possible in the future. Large companies paid out 34% of their earnings as dividends in 2004—well below the historical average payout of 54% of earnings.

Source: Alan Levinsohn, "Divine Dividends," *Strategic Finance* (May 2005), pp. 59–60.

 What factors must management consider in deciding how large a dividend to pay?

STOCK DIVIDENDS

A **stock dividend** is a pro rata distribution of the corporation's own stock to stockholders. Whereas a cash dividend is paid in cash, a stock dividend is paid in stock. **A stock dividend results in a decrease in retained earnings and an increase in paid-in capital.** Unlike a cash dividend, a stock dividend does not decrease total stockholders' equity or total assets.

Because a stock dividend does not result in a distribution of assets, many view it as nothing more than a publicity gesture. Stock dividends are often issued by companies that do not have adequate cash to issue a cash dividend. These companies may not want to announce that they are not going to be issuing a cash dividend at their normal time to do so. By issuing a stock dividend they "save face" by giving the appearance of distributing a dividend. Note that since a stock dividend neither increases nor decreases the assets in the company, investors are not receiving anything they didn't already own. In a sense it is like asking for two pieces of pie and having your host take one piece of pie and cut it into two smaller pieces. You are not better off, but you got your two pieces of pie.

To illustrate a stock dividend, assume that you have a 2% ownership interest in Cetus Inc.; you own 20 of its 1,000 shares of common stock. If Cetus declares a 10% stock dividend, it would issue 100 shares (1,000 × 10%) of stock. You would receive two shares (2% × 100), but your ownership interest would remain at 2% (22 ÷ 1,100). **You now own more shares of stock, but your ownership interest has not changed.** Moreover, the company disburses no cash, and assumes no liabilities.

What, then, are the purposes and benefits of a stock dividend? Corporations generally issue stock dividends for one of the following reasons.

Helpful Hint Because of its effects, a stock dividend is also referred to as *capitalizing retained earnings.*

1. To satisfy stockholders' dividend expectations without spending cash.
2. To increase the marketability of the stock by increasing the number of shares outstanding and thereby decreasing the market price per share. Decreasing

the market price of the stock makes it easier for smaller investors to purchase the shares.

3. To emphasize that the company has permanently reinvested in the business a portion of stockholders' equity, which therefore is unavailable for cash dividends.

When the dividend is declared, the board of directors determines the size of the stock dividend and the value to be assigned to each dividend share. In order to meet legal requirements, the per share amount must be at least equal to the par or stated value.

The accounting profession distinguishes between a **small stock dividend** (less than 20%–25% of the corporation's issued stock) and a **large stock dividend** (greater than 20%–25%). It recommends that the directors assign the **fair market value per share** for small stock dividends. The recommendation is based on the assumption that a small stock dividend will have little effect on the market price of the shares previously outstanding. Thus, many stockholders consider small stock dividends to be distributions of earnings equal to the fair market value of the shares distributed. The accounting profession does not specify the amount to be assigned for a large stock dividend. However, companies normally assign **par or stated value per share**. Small stock dividends predominate in practice. In the appendix at the end of the chapter, we illustrate the journal entries for small stock dividends.

Effects of Stock Dividends

How do stock dividends affect stockholders' equity? They **change the composition of stockholders' equity** because they result in a transfer of a portion of retained earnings to paid-in capital. However, **total stockholders' equity remains the same**. Stock dividends also have no effect on the par or stated value per share, but the number of shares outstanding increases.

To illustrate, assume that Medland Corp. declares a 10% stock dividend on its $10 par common stock when 50,000 shares were outstanding. The market price was $15 per share.

	Before Dividend	After Dividend
Stockholders' equity		
Paid-in capital		
Common stock, $10 par	$ 500,000	$ 550,000
Paid-in capital in excess of par value	—	25,000
Total paid-in capital	500,000	575,000
Retained earnings	300,000	225,000
Total stockholders' equity	$800,000	$800,000
Outstanding shares	50,000	55,000

Illustration 11-9
Stock dividend effects

In this example, total paid-in capital increased by $75,000 (50,000 shares × 10% × $15), and retained earnings is decreased by the same amount. Note also that total stockholders' equity remains unchanged at $800,000.

STOCK SPLITS

A **stock split**, like a stock dividend, involves the issuance of additional shares of stock to stockholders according to their percentage ownership. However, **a stock split results in a reduction in the par or stated value per share**. The purpose of a stock split is to increase the marketability of the stock by lowering

Helpful Hint A stock split changes the par value per share but does not affect any balances in stockholders' equity.

its market value per share. This, in turn, makes it easier for the corporation to issue additional stock.

The effect of a split on market value is generally **inversely proportional** to the size of the split. For example, after a recent 2-for-1 stock split, the market value of Nike's stock fell from $111 to approximately $55.

In a stock split, the company increases the number of shares in the same proportion that it decreases the par or stated value per share. For example, in a 2-for-1 split, the company exchanges one share of $10 par value stock for two shares of $5 par value stock. **A stock split does not have any effect on paid-in capital, retained earnings, and total stockholders' equity.** However, the number of shares outstanding increases. These effects are shown in Illustration 11-10, assuming that instead of issuing a 10% stock dividend, Medland splits its 50,000 shares of common stock on a 2-for-1 basis.

Illustration 11-10 Stock split effects

Stockholders' equity	Before Stock Split	After Stock Split
Paid-in capital		
Common stock (Before: 50,000 $10 par shares; after: 100,000 $5 par shares)	$ 500,000	$ 500,000
Paid-in capital in excess of par value	0	0
Total paid-in capital	500,000	500,000
Retained earnings	300,000	300,000
Total stockholders' equity	$800,000	$800,000
Outstanding shares	50,000	100,000

Because a stock split does not affect the balances in any stockholders' equity accounts, a company **does not need to journalize a stock split**. However, a memorandum entry explaining the effect of the split is typically made.

The differences between the effects of stock dividends and stock splits are shown in Illustration 11-11.

Illustration 11-11 Effects of stock splits and stock dividends differentiated

Item	Stock Dividend	Stock Split
Total paid-in capital	Increase	No change
Total retained earnings	Decrease	No change
Total par value (common stock)	Increase	No change
Par value per share	No change	Decrease

BEFORE YOU GO ON . . .

▶ Review It

1. What factors affect the size of a company's cash dividend?
2. Why do companies issue stock dividends? Why do companies declare stock splits?
3. Distinguish between a small and a large stock dividend and indicate the basis for valuing each kind of dividend.
4. Contrast the effects of a small stock dividend and a 2-for-1 stock split on (a) stockholders' equity and (b) outstanding shares.

▶ Do It

Due to five years of record earnings at Sing CD Corporation, the market price of its 500,000 shares of $2 par value common stock tripled from $15 per share to $45. During this period, paid-in capital remained the same at $2,000,000. Retained earnings increased from $1,500,000 to $10,000,000. President Joan Elbert is considering either a 10% stock dividend or a 2-for-1 stock split. She asks you to show the before and after effects of each option on retained earnings.

Action Plan

- Calculate the stock dividend's effect on retained earnings by multiplying the number of new shares times the market price of the stock (or par value for a large stock dividend).
- Recall that a stock dividend increases the number of shares without affecting total equity.
- Recall that a stock split only increases the number of shares outstanding and decreases the par value per share without affecting total equity.

Solution

The stock dividend amount is $2,250,000 [(500,000 × 10%) × $45]. The new balance in retained earnings is $7,750,000 ($10,000,000 − $2,250,000). The retained earnings balance after the stock split is the same as it was before the split: $10,000,000. The effects on the stockholders' equity accounts are as follows.

	Original Balances	After Dividend	After Split
Paid-in capital	$ 2,000,000	$ 4,250,000	$ 2,000,000
Retained earnings	10,000,000	7,750,000	10,000,000
Total stockholders' equity	$12,000,000	$12,000,000	$12,000,000
Shares outstanding	500,000	550,000	1,000,000

✔ THE NAVIGATOR

Retained Earnings

Retained earnings is net income that a company retains in the business. The balance in retained earnings is part of the stockholders' claim on the total assets of the corporation. It does not, however, represent a claim on any specific asset. Nor can the amount of retained earnings be associated with the balance of any asset account. For example, a $100,000 balance in retained earnings does not mean that there should be $100,000 in cash. The reason is that the company may have used the cash resulting from the excess of revenues over expenses to purchase buildings, equipment, and other assets. Illustration 11-12 shows recent amounts of retained earnings and cash in selected companies.

STUDY OBJECTIVE
6
Identify the items that affect retained earnings.

	(in millions)	
Company	**Retained Earnings**	**Cash**
Circuit City Stores, Inc.	$1,199	$783
Nike, Inc.	3,983	828
Starbucks Coffee Company	1,449	299
Amazon.com	(2,386)	1,303

Illustration 11-12
Retained earnings and cash balances

When expenses exceed revenues, a **net loss** results. In contrast to net income, a net loss decreases retained earnings. In closing entries a company debits a net loss to the Retained Earnings account. **It does not debit net losses to**

paid-in capital accounts. To do so would destroy the distinction between paid-in and earned capital. If cumulative losses exceed cumulative income over a company's life, a debit balance in Retained Earnings results. A debit balance in retained earnings, such as that of Amazon.com in 2004, is a deficit. A company reports a deficit as a deduction in the stockholders' equity section of the balance sheet, as shown in Illustration 11-13.

Illustration 11-13
Stockholders' equity with deficit

AMAZON.COM Balance Sheet (partial) December 31, 2004 (in thousands)		
Stockholders' equity		
Paid-in capital		
Common stock	$	4,097
Paid-in capital in excess of par value		2,154,669
Total paid-in capital		2,158,766
Accumulated deficit		**(2,385,977)**
Total stockholders' equity (deficit)	$	(227,211)

RETAINED EARNINGS RESTRICTIONS

The balance in retained earnings is generally available for dividend declarations. Some companies state this fact. In some cases, however, there may be **retained earnings restrictions**. These make a portion of the balance currently unavailable for dividends. Restrictions result from one or more of these causes: legal, contractual, or voluntary.

Companies generally disclose retained earnings restrictions in the notes to the financial statements. For example, Tektronix Inc., a manufacturer of electronic measurement devices, recently had total retained earnings of $774 million, but the unrestricted portion was only $223.8 million.

Illustration 11-14
Disclosure of unrestricted retained earnings

TEKTRONIX INC. Notes to the Financial Statements
Certain of the Company's debt agreements require compliance with debt covenants. Management believes that the Company is in compliance with such requirements for the fiscal year ended May 26, 2001. The Company had unrestricted retained earnings of $223.8 million after meeting those requirements.

Financial Statement Presentation of Stockholders' Equity

BALANCE SHEET PRESENTATION

STUDY OBJECTIVE
7
Prepare a comprehensive stockholders' equity section.

In the stockholders' equity section of the balance sheet, companies report paid-in capital and retained earnings and identify the specific sources of paid-in capital. Within paid-in capital, two classifications are recognized:

1. **Capital stock**, which consists of preferred and common stock. Companies show preferred stock before common stock because of its preferential rights. They report information about the par value, shares authorized, shares issued, and shares outstanding for each class of stock.

2. **Additional paid-in capital**, which includes the excess of amounts paid in over par or stated value.

Illustration 11-15 presents the stockholders' equity section of the balance sheet of Graber Inc. The company discloses a retained earnings restriction in the notes.

GRABER INC. Balance Sheet (partial)		
Stockholders' equity		
Paid-in capital		
Capital stock		
9% preferred stock, $100 par value, cumulative, 10,000 shares authorized, 6,000 shares issued and outstanding		$ 600,000
Common stock, no par, $5 stated value, 500,000 shares authorized, 400,000 shares issued, and 390,000 outstanding		2,000,000
Total capital stock		2,600,000
Additional paid-in capital		
In excess of par value—preferred stock	$ 30,000	
In excess of stated value—common stock	1,050,000	
Total additional paid-in capital		1,080,000
Total paid-in capital		3,680,000
Retained earnings **(see Note R)**		1,160,000
Total paid-in capital and retained earnings		4,840,000
Less: Treasury stock—common (10,000 shares)		(80,000)
Total stockholders' equity		$4,760,000

Note R: Retained earnings is restricted for the cost of treasury stock, $80,000.

Illustration 11-15
Comprehensive stockholders' equity section

⊕ **International Note**

In Switzerland, there are no specific disclosure requirements for stockholders' equity. However, companies typically disclose separate categories of capital on the balance sheet.

The stockholders' equity section for Graber Inc. includes most of the accounts discussed in this chapter. The disclosures pertaining to Graber's common stock indicate that 400,000 shares are issued; 100,000 shares are unissued (500,000 authorized less 400,000 issued); and 390,000 shares are outstanding (400,000 issued less 10,000 shares in treasury).

In published annual reports, companies seldom present subclassifications within the stockholders' equity section. Moreover, they often combine and report as a single amount the individual sources of additional paid-in capital. Notes often provide additional detail. Illustration 11-16 is an excerpt from Columbia Sportswear Company's 2004 balance sheet.

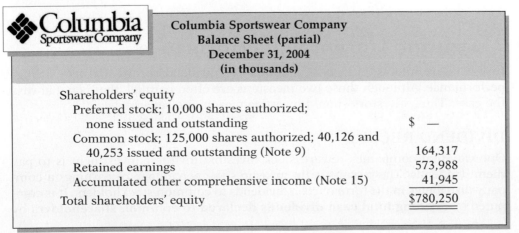

Columbia Sportswear Company Balance Sheet (partial) December 31, 2004 (in thousands)	
Shareholders' equity	
Preferred stock; 10,000 shares authorized; none issued and outstanding	$ —
Common stock; 125,000 shares authorized; 40,126 and 40,253 issued and outstanding (Note 9)	164,317
Retained earnings	573,988
Accumulated other comprehensive income (Note 15)	41,945
Total shareholders' equity	$780,250

Illustration 11-16
Stockholders' equity section

STATEMENT OF CASH FLOWS PRESENTATION

The balance sheet presents the balances of a company's stockholders' equity accounts at a point in time. Companies report in the "Financing Activities" section of the statement of cash flows information regarding cash inflows and outflows during the year that resulted from equity transactions. Illustration 11-17 presents the cash flows from financing activities from the statement of cash flows of Sara Lee Corporation. From this information we learn that the company's purchases of treasury stock during the period far exceeded its issuances of new common stock, and its financing activities resulted in a net reduction in its cash balance.

Illustration 11-17
Financing activities of statement of cash flows

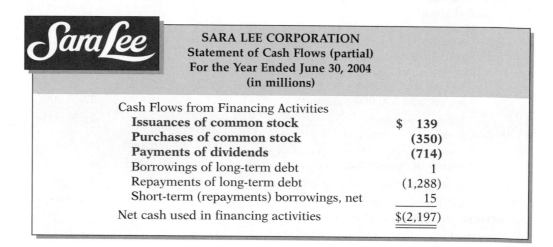

SARA LEE CORPORATION
Statement of Cash Flows (partial)
For the Year Ended June 30, 2004
(in millions)

Cash Flows from Financing Activities	
Issuances of common stock	$ 139
Purchases of common stock	(350)
Payments of dividends	(714)
Borrowings of long-term debt	1
Repayments of long-term debt	(1,288)
Short-term (repayments) borrowings, net	15
Net cash used in financing activities	$(2,197)

BEFORE YOU GO ON . . .

▶ Review It

1. Identify the classifications within the paid-in capital section and the totals that are stated in the stockholders' equity section of a balance sheet.
2. What is a retained earnings restriction?
3. What was the total cost of Tootsie Roll's treasury stock in 2004? What was the total value of the 2004 cash dividend? What was the total charge to retained earnings of the 2004 stock dividend? The answer to these questions appears on p. 583.

THE NAVIGATOR

Measuring Corporate Performance

Investors are interested in both a company's dividend record and its earnings performance. Although those two measures are often parallel, that is not always the case. Thus, investors should investigate each one separately.

STUDY OBJECTIVE

8

Evaluate a corporation's dividend and earnings performance from a stockholder's perspective.

DIVIDEND RECORD

One way that companies reward stock investors for their investment is to pay them dividends. The **payout ratio** measures the percentage of earnings a company distributes in the form of cash dividends to common stockholders. It is computed by **dividing total cash dividends declared to common shareholders by**

net income. Using the information shown below, the payout ratio for Nike in 2004 and 2003 is calculated in Illustration 11-18.

	2004	**2003**
Dividends (in millions)	$194.9	$142.7
Net income (in millions)	945.6	740.1*

Illustration 11-18 Nike's payout ratio

Payout Ratio	=	Cash Dividends Declared on Common Stock / Net Income

($ in millions)	2004	2003
Payout Ratio	$\dfrac{\$194.9}{\$945.6} = 21\%$	$\dfrac{\$142.7}{\$740.1^*} = 19\%$

*Nike's reported net income for 2003 included a one-time charge of $266.1 due to an accounting change. Net income of $740.1 was used to make 2003 more comparable to 2004. Using reported net income of $474.0 produces a payout ratio of 30%.

Companies that have high growth rates are characterized by low payout ratios because they reinvest most of their net income in the business. Thus, a low payout ratio is not necessarily bad news. Companies that believe they have many good opportunities for growth, such as Nike and Reebok, will reinvest those funds in the company rather than pay high dividends. In fact, dividend payout ratios for the 500 largest U.S. companies currently are very low relative to historical rates. However, low dividend payments, or a cut in dividend payments, might signal that a company has liquidity or solvency problems and is trying to free up cash by not paying dividends. Thus, investors and analysts should investigate the reason for low dividend payments.

Illustration 11-19 lists recent payout ratios of four well-known companies.

Company	Payout Ratio
Microsoft	312.7%
Kellogg	45.0%
Johnson & Johnson	37.9%
Sears Holdings Corp.	0%

Illustration 11-19
Variability of payout ratios among companies

Decision Toolkit

Decision Checkpoints	Info Needed for Decision	Tool to Use for Decision	How to Evaluate Results
What portion of its earnings does the company pay out in dividends?	Net income and total cash dividends on common stock	$\text{Payout ratio} = \dfrac{\text{Cash dividends declared on common stock}}{\text{Net income}}$	A low ratio may suggest that the company is retaining its earnings for investment in future growth.

EARNINGS PERFORMANCE

Another way to measure corporate performance is through profitability. A widely used ratio that measures profitability from the common stockholders' viewpoint is **return on common stockholders' equity**. This ratio shows how many dollars of net income a company earned for each dollar invested by common stockholders. It is computed by dividing net income available to common stockholders (Net income − Preferred stock dividends) by average common stockholders' equity.

Using the additional information presented below, Illustration 11-20 shows Nike's return on common stockholders' equity ratios, calculated for 2004 and 2003.

(in thousands)	2004	2003	2002
Net income	$ 945,600	$ 740,100	$ 668,300
Preferred stock dividends	30	30	30
Common stockholders' equity	4,781,400	3,990,400	3,838,700

Illustration 11-20 Nike's return on common stockholders' equity

$$\text{Return on Common Stockholders' Equity Ratio} = \frac{\text{Net Income} - \text{Preferred Stock Dividends}}{\text{Average Common Stockholders' Equity}}$$

($ in thousands)	2004	2003
Return on Common Stockholders' Equity Ratio	$\frac{\$945,600 - \$30}{(\$4,781,400 + \$3,990,400)/2} = 21.6\%$	$\frac{\$740,100 - \$30}{(\$3,990,400 + \$3,838,700)/2} = 18.9\%$

From 2003 to 2004, Nike's return on common shareholders' equity increased more than 14%. As a company grows larger, it becomes increasingly hard to sustain a high return. In Nike's case, since many believe the U.S. market for expensive sports shoes is saturated, it will need to grow either along new product lines, such as hiking shoes and golf equipment, or in new markets, such as Europe and Asia.

DEBT VERSUS EQUITY DECISION

To obtain large amounts of long-term capital, corporate managers must decide whether to issue bonds or to sell common stock. Bonds have three primary advantages relative to common stock, as shown in Illustration 11-21.

Illustration 11-21 Advantages of bond financing over common stock

Bond Financing	Advantages
	1. **Stockholder control is not affected.** Bondholders do not have voting rights, so current owners (stockholders) retain full control of the company.
	2. **Tax savings result.** Bond interest is deductible for tax purposes; dividends on stock are not.
	3. **Return on common stockholders' equity may be higher.** Although bond interest expense reduces net income, return on common stockholders' equity often is higher under bond financing because no additional shares of common stock are issued.

How does the debt versus equity decision affect the return on common stockholders' equity ratio? Illustration 11-22 shows that the return on common stockholders' equity is affected by the return on assets ratio and the amount of leverage a company uses—that is, by the company's reliance on debt (often measured by the debt to total assets ratio). If a company wants to increase its return on common stockholders' equity, it can either increase its return on assets or increase its reliance on debt financing.

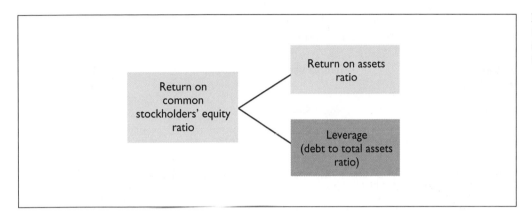

Illustration 11-22
Components of the return on common stockholders' equity

To illustrate the potential effect of debt financing on the return on common stockholders' equity, assume that Microsystems Inc. is considering two plans for financing the construction of a new $5 million plant: Plan A involves issuing 200,000 shares of common stock at the current market price of $25 per share. Plan B involves issuing $5 million of 12% bonds at face value. Income before interest and taxes on the new plant will be $1.5 million; income taxes are expected to be 30%. Microsystems currently has 100,000 shares of common stock outstanding issued at $25 per share. The alternative effects on the return on common stockholders' equity are shown in Illustration 11-23.

	Plan A: Issue stock	Plan B: Issue bonds
Income before interest and taxes	$1,500,000	$1,500,000
Interest (12% × $5,000,000)	—	600,000
Income before income taxes	1,500,000	900,000
Income tax expense (30%)	450,000	270,000
Net income	$1,050,000	$ 630,000
Common stockholders' equity	$7,500,000	$2,500,000
Return on common stockholders' equity	14%	25.2%

Illustration 11-23
Effects on return on common stockholders' equity of issuing debt

Note that with long-term debt financing (bonds), net income is $420,000 ($1,050,000 − $630,000) less. However, the return on common stockholders' equity increases from 14% to 25.2% with the use of debt financing because there is less common stockholders' equity to spread the income across. **In general, as long as the return on assets rate exceeds the rate paid on debt, a company will increase the return on common stockholders' equity by the use of debt.**

After seeing this illustration, one might ask, why don't companies rely almost exclusively on debt financing, rather than equity? Debt has one major disadvantage: **The company locks in fixed payments that it must make in good times and bad. The company must pay interest on a periodic basis,**

and must pay the principal (face value) of the bonds at maturity. A company with fluctuating earnings and a relatively weak cash position may experience great difficulty in meeting interest requirements in periods of low earnings. In the extreme, this can result in bankruptcy. With common stock financing, on the other hand, the company can decide to pay low (or no) dividends if earnings are low.

Decision Toolkit

Decision Checkpoints	Info Needed for Decision	Tool to Use for Decision	How to Evaluate Results
What is the company's return on common stockholders' investment?	Earnings available to common stockholders and average common stockholders' equity	Return on common stockholders' equity ratio $= \dfrac{\text{Net income} - \text{Preferred stock dividends}}{\text{Average common stockholders' equity}}$	A high measure suggests strong earnings performance from common stockholders' perspective.

BEFORE YOU GO ON . . .

▶ **Review It**

1. What measure can be used to evaluate a company's dividend record, and how is it calculated?
2. What factors affect the return on common stockholders' equity ratio?
3. What are the advantages and disadvantages of debt and equity financing?

THE NAVIGATOR

Using the Decision Toolkit

Reebok remains one of Nike's fiercest competitors. In such a competitive and rapidly changing environment, one wrong step can spell financial disaster. After bottoming out at the end of 1999, Reebok's stock has rebounded.

Instructions

The following facts are available for Reebok. Using this information, evaluate its (1) dividend record and (2) earnings performance, and contrast them with those for Nike for 2003 and 2004. Nike's earnings per share were $3.59 in 2004 and $2.80 in 2003.

(in thousands except per share data)	2004	2003	2002
Dividends declared	$ 17,839	$ 8,847	0
Net income	$ 192,425	$ 157,254	$126,458
Preferred stock dividends	0	0	0
Shares outstanding at end of year	101,827	101,081	99,235
Common stockholders' equity	$1,219,956	$1,033,710	$884,570

Solution

1. *Dividend record:* A measure to evaluate dividend record is the payout ratio. For Reebok, this measure in 2004 and 2003 is calculated as shown below.

	2004	**2003**
Payout ratio	$\dfrac{\$17,839}{\$192,425} = 9.3\%$	$\dfrac{\$8,847}{\$157,254} = 5.6\%$

Nike's payout ratio remained nearly constant at 21%. Reebok's payout ratio increased significantly from 2003 to 2004 but was still less than half Nike's ratio.

2. *Earnings performance:* There are many measures of earnings performance. Some of those presented thus far in the book were earnings per share (page 55) and the return on common stockholders' equity ratio (this chapter). These measures for Reebok in 2004 and 2003 are calculated as shown here.

	2004	**2003**
Earnings per share	$\dfrac{\$192,425 - 0}{(101,827 + 101,081)/2} = \$1.90$	$\dfrac{\$157,254 - 0}{(101,081 + 99,235)/2} = \$1.57$
Return on common stockholders' equity ratio	$\dfrac{\$192,425 - 0}{(\$1,219,956 + \$1,033,710)/2} = 17.1\%$	$\dfrac{\$157,254 - 0}{(\$1,033,710 + \$884,570)/2} = 16.4\%$

From 2003 to 2004, Reebok's net income improved 22% and its earnings per share increased 21%. During the same time period Nike's earnings per share increased 28%.

Reebok's return on common stockholders' equity increased from 16.4% to 17.1%. While this represents a healthy increase, it is still less than Nike's 21.6%.

Summary of Study Objectives

1 *Identify and discuss the major characteristics of a corporation.* The major characteristics of a corporation are separate legal existence, limited liability of stockholders, transferable ownership rights, ability to acquire capital, continuous life, corporation management, government regulations, and additional taxes.

2 *Record the issuance of common stock.* When a company records issuance of common stock for cash, it credits the par value of the shares to Common Stock; it records in a separate paid-in capital account the portion of the proceeds that is above par value. When no-par common stock has a stated value, the entries are similar to those for par value stock. When no-par common stock does not have a stated value, the entire proceeds from the issue are credited to Common Stock.

3 *Explain the accounting for the purchase of treasury stock.* Companies generally use the cost method in accounting for treasury stock. Under this approach, a company debits Treasury Stock at the price paid to reacquire the shares.

4 *Differentiate preferred stock from common stock.* Preferred stock has contractual provisions that give it priority over common stock in certain areas. Typically, preferred stockholders have a preference as to (1) dividends and (2) assets in the event of liquidation. However, they often do not have voting rights.

5 *Prepare the entries for cash dividends and understand the effect of stock dividends and stock splits.* Companies make entries for dividends at the declaration date and the payment date. At the declaration date the entries for a cash dividend are: debit Retained Earnings and credit Dividends Payable. The effects of stock dividends and splits: Small *stock dividends* transfer an amount equal to the fair market value of the shares issued from retained earnings to the paid-in capital accounts. *Stock splits* reduce the par value per share of the common stock while increasing the number of shares so that total par value remains the same.

6 *Identify the items that affect retained earnings.* Additions to retained earnings consist of net income. Deductions consist of net loss and cash and stock dividends. In some instances, portions of retained earnings are restricted, making that portion un-available for the payment of dividends.

7 *Prepare a comprehensive stockholders' equity section.* In the stockholders' equity section of the balance sheet, companies report paid-in capital and retained earnings and identify specific sources of paid-in capital. Within paid-in capital, companies show two classifications: capital stock and additional paid-in capital. If a corporation has treasury stock, it deducts the cost of treasury stock from total paid-in capital and retained earnings to determine total stockholders' equity.

8 *Evaluate a corporation's dividend and earnings performance from a stockholder's perspective.* A company's dividend record can be evaluated by looking at what percentage of net income it chooses to pay out in dividends, as measured by the dividend payout ratio (dividends divided by net income). Earnings performance is measured with the return on common stockholders' equity ratio (income available to common shareholders divided by average common shareholders' equity).

THE NAVIGATOR

Decision Toolkit—A Summary

Decision Checkpoints	Info Needed for Decision	Tool to Use for Decision	How to Evaluate Results
Should the company incorporate?	Capital needs, growth expectations, type of business, tax status	Corporations have limited liability, easier capital raising ability, and professional managers; but they suffer from additional taxes, government regulations, and separation of ownership from management.	Must carefully weigh the costs and benefits in light of the particular circumstances.
What portion of its earnings does the company pay out in dividends?	Net income and total cash dividends on common stock	$$\text{Payout ratio} = \frac{\text{Cash dividends declared on common stock}}{\text{Net income}}$$	A low ratio may suggest that the company is retaining its earnings for investment in future growth.
What is the company's return on common stockholders' investment?	Earnings available to common stockholders and average common stockholders' equity	$$\text{Return on common stockholders' equity ratio} = \frac{\text{Net income} - \text{Preferred stock dividends}}{\text{Average common stockholders' equity}}$$	A high measure suggests strong earnings performance from common stockholders' perspective.

APPENDIX
ENTRIES FOR STOCK DIVIDENDS

STUDY OBJECTIVE
9
Prepare entries for stock dividends.

To illustrate the accounting for stock dividends, assume that Medland Corporation has a balance of $300,000 in retained earnings and declares a 10% stock dividend on its 50,000 shares of $10 par value common stock. The current fair market value of its stock is $15 per share. The number of shares to be issued is 5,000 (10% × 50,000), and the total amount to be debited to Retained Earnings is $75,000 (5,000 × $15). The entry to record this transaction at the declaration date is:

A	=	L	+	SE
				−75,000 Div
				+50,000 CS
				+25,000 CS

Cash Flows
no effect

Retained Earnings (or Stock Dividends)	75,000	
Common Stock Dividends Distributable		50,000
Paid-in Capital in Excess of Par Value		25,000
(To record declaration of 10% stock dividend)		

At the declaration date Medland decreases (debits) Retained Earnings for the fair market value of the stock issued; increases (credits) Common Stock Dividends Distributable for the par value of the dividend shares (5,000 × $10); and credits the excess over par (5,000 × $5) to an additional paid-in capital account.

Common Stock Dividends Distributable is a stockholders' equity account; it is not a liability because assets will not be used to pay the dividend. If Medland prepares a balance sheet before it issues the dividend shares, it reports the distributable account in paid-in capital as an addition to common stock issued, as shown in Illustration 11A-1.

MEDLAND CORPORATION Balance Sheet (partial)		
Paid-in capital		
Common stock	$500,000	
Common stock dividends distributable	**50,000**	**$550,000**

Illustration 11A-1
Statement presentation of common stock dividends distributable

When Medland issues the dividend shares, it decreases Common Stock Dividends Distributable and increases Common Stock as follows.

Helpful Hint Note that the dividend account title is *distributable*, not *payable*.

Common Stock Dividends Distributable	50,000	
Common Stock		50,000
(To record issuance of 5,000 shares in a stock dividend)		

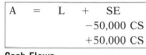

A	=	L	+	SE
				−50,000 CS
				+50,000 CS

Cash Flows
no effect

Summary of Study Objective for Appendix

9 *Prepare entries for stock dividends.* To record the declaration of a small stock dividend (less than 20%), reduce Retained Earnings for an amount equal to the fair value of the shares issued. Record a credit to a temporary stockholders' equity account—Common Stock Dividends Distributable—for the par value of the shares, and credit the balance to Paid-in Capital in Excess of Par Value. When the shares are issued, debit Common Stock Dividends Distributable and credit Common Stock.

Glossary

Authorized stock The amount of stock that a corporation is authorized to sell as indicated in its charter. (p. 540)

Cash dividend A pro rata distribution of cash to stockholders. (p. 548)

Corporation A company organized as a separate legal entity, with most of the rights and privileges of a person. (p. 534)

Cumulative dividend A feature of preferred stock entitling the stockholder to receive current and unpaid prior-year dividends before common stockholders receive any dividends. (p. 546)

Declaration date The date the board of directors formally authorizes the dividend and announces it to stockholders. (p. 548)

Deficit A debit balance in retained earnings. (p. 554)

Dividend A distribution by a corporation to its stockholders on a pro rata (proportional) basis. (p. 547)

Dividends in arrears Preferred dividends that were supposed to be declared but were not declared during a given period. (p. 546)

Legal capital The amount per share of stock that must be retained in the business for the protection of corporate creditors. (p. 541)

No-par value stock Capital stock that has not been assigned a value in the corporate charter. (p. 541)

Outstanding stock Capital stock that has been issued and is being held by stockholders. (p. 545)

Paid-in capital The amount stockholders paid in to the corporation in exchange for shares of ownership. (p. 541)

Par value stock Capital stock that has been assigned a value per share in the corporate charter. (p. 541)

Payment date The date dividend checks are mailed to stockholders. (p. 549)

Payout ratio A measure of the percentage of earnings a company distributes in the form of cash dividends to common stockholders. (p. 556)

Preferred stock Capital stock that has contractual preferences over common stock in certain areas. (p. 546)

Privately held corporation A corporation that has only a few stockholders and whose stock is not available for sale to the general public. (p. 534)

Publicly held corporation   A corporation that may have thousands of stockholders and whose stock is regularly traded on a national securities market. (p. 534)

Record date   The date when the company determines ownership of outstanding shares for dividend purposes. (p. 549)

Retained earnings   Net income that a company retains in the business. (p. 553)

Retained earnings restrictions   Circumstances that make a portion of retained earnings currently unavailable for dividends. (p. 554)

Return on common stockholders' equity ratio   A measure of profitability from the stockholders' point of view; computed by dividing net income minus preferred stock dividends by average common stockholders' equity. (p. 558)

Stated value   The amount per share assigned by the board of directors to no-par stock. (p. 541)

Stock dividend   A pro rata distribution of the corporation's own stock to stockholders. (p. 550)

Stock split   The issuance of additional shares of stock to stockholders accompanied by a reduction in the par or stated value per share. (p. 551)

Treasury stock   A corporation's own stock that has been issued, fully paid for, and reacquired by the corporation and is being held in the treasury for future use. (p. 543)

Demonstration Problem

Rolman Corporation is authorized to issue 1,000,000 shares of $5 par value common stock. In its first year the company has the following stock transactions.

Jan. 10   Issued 400,000 shares of stock at $8 per share.
Sept. 1   Purchased 10,000 shares of common stock for the treasury at $9 per share.
Dec. 24   Declared a cash dividend of 10 cents per share on common stock outstanding.

Instructions
(a) Journalize the transactions.
(b) Prepare the stockholders' equity section of the balance sheet assuming the company had retained earnings of $150,600 at December 31.

Action Plan
- When common stock has a par value, credit Common Stock for par value and Paid-in Capital in Excess of Par Value for the amount above par value.
- Debit the Treasury Stock account at cost.

Solution to Demonstration Problem

(a)

Jan. 10	Cash		3,200,000	
	Common Stock			2,000,000
	Paid-in Capital in Excess of Par Value			1,200,000
	(To record issuance of 400,000 shares of $5 par value stock)			
Sept. 1	Treasury Stock		90,000	
	Cash			90,000
	(To record purchase of 10,000 shares of treasury stock at cost)			
Dec. 24	Retained Earnings		39,000	
	Dividends Payable			39,000
	(To record declaration of 10 cents per share cash dividend)			

(b)

ROLMAN CORPORATION
Balance Sheet (partial)

Stockholders' equity	
Paid-in capital	
Capital stock	
Common stock, $5 par value, 1,000,000 shares authorized, 400,000 shares issued, 390,000 outstanding	$2,000,000
Additional paid-in capital	
In excess of par value—common stock	1,200,000
Total paid-in capital	3,200,000
Retained earnings	150,600
Total paid-in capital and retained earnings	3,350,600
Less: Treasury stock (10,000 shares)	90,000
Total stockholders' equity	$3,260,600

THE NAVIGATOR

Note: All Questions, Exercises, and Problems marked with an asterisk relate to material in the appendix to the chapter.

Self-Study Questions

Answers are at the end of the chapter.

(SO 1) **1.** Which of these is *not* a major advantage of a corporation?
    (a) Separate legal existence.
    (b) Continuous life.
    (c) Government regulations.
    (d) Transferable ownership rights.

(SO 1) **2.** A major disadvantage of a corporation is:
    (a) limited liability of stockholders.
    (b) additional taxes.
    (c) transferable ownership rights.
    (d) None of the above.

(SO 1) **3.** Which of these statements is *false?*
    (a) Ownership of common stock gives the owner a voting right.
    (b) The stockholders' equity section begins with paid-in capital.
    (c) The authorization of capital stock does not result in a formal accounting entry.
    (d) Legal capital is intended to protect stockholders.

(SO 2) **4.** ABC Corp. issues 1,000 shares of $10 par value common stock at $12 per share. When the transaction is recorded, credits are made to:
    (a) Common Stock $10,000 and Paid-in Capital in Excess of Stated Value $2,000.
    (b) Common Stock $12,000.
    (c) Common Stock $10,000 and Paid-in Capital in Excess of Par Value $2,000.
    (d) Common Stock $10,000 and Retained Earnings $2,000.

(SO 4) **5.** Preferred stock may have which of the following features?
    (a) dividend preference.
    (b) preference to assets in the event of liquidation.
    (c) cumulative dividends.
    (d) all of the above.

(SO 5) **6.** Entries for cash dividends are required on the:
    (a) declaration date and the record date.
    (b) record date and the payment date.

    (c) declaration date, record date, and payment date.
    (d) declaration date and the payment date.

7. Which of these statements about stock divi- (SO 5)
dends is *true?*
    (a) Stock dividends reduce a company's cash balance.
    (b) A stock dividend has no effect on total stockholders' equity.
    (c) A stock dividend decreases total stockholders' equity.
    (d) A stock dividend ordinarily will increase total stockholders' equity.

8. In the stockholders' equity section, the cost of (SO 7)
treasury stock is deducted from:
    (a) total paid-in capital and retained earnings.
    (b) retained earnings.
    (c) total stockholders' equity.
    (d) common stock in paid-in capital.

9. The return on stockholders' equity (SO 8)
is increased by all of the following, *except:*
    (a) an increase in the return on assets ratio.
    (b) an increase in the use of debt financing.
    (c) an increase in the company's stock price.
    (d) an increase in the company's net income.

10. Roger is nearing retirement and (SO 8)
would like to invest in a stock that will provide a good steady income supply. Roger should choose a stock with a:
    (a) high current ratio.
    (b) high dividend payout.
    (c) high earnings per share.
    (d) high price-earnings ratio.

Go to the book's website, **www.wiley.com/college/kimmel**, to access additional Self-Study Questions.

Questions

1. Warren, a student, asks your help in understanding some characteristics of a corporation. Explain each of these to Warren.
    (a) Separate legal existence.
    (b) Limited liability of stockholders.
    (c) Transferable ownership rights.

2. (a) Your friend R. L. Duran cannot understand how the characteristic of corporate management is both an advantage and a disadvantage. Clarify this problem for R. L.

    (b) Identify and explain two other disadvantages of a corporation.

3. Ann Adler believes a corporation must be incorporated in the state in which its headquarters office is located. Is Ann correct? Explain.

4. What are the basic ownership rights of common stockholders in the absence of restrictive provisions?

5. A corporation has been defined as an entity separate and distinct from its owners. In what ways is a corporation a separate legal entity?

6. What are the two principal components of stockholders' equity?

7. The corporate charter of Clio Corporation allows the issuance of a maximum of 100,000 shares of common stock. During its first 2 years of operation, Clio sold 60,000 shares to shareholders and reacquired 4,000 of these shares. After these transactions, how many shares are authorized, issued, and outstanding?

8. Which is the better investment—common stock with a par value of $5 per share or common stock with a par value of $20 per share?

9. For what reasons might a company like **IBM** repurchase some of its stock (treasury stock)?

10. Malon, Inc. purchases 1,000 shares of its own previously issued $5 par common stock for $11,000. Assuming the shares are held in the treasury, what effect does this transaction have on (a) net income, (b) total assets, (c) total paid-in capital, and (d) total stockholders' equity?

11. (a) What are the principal differences between common stock and preferred stock?
(b) Preferred stock may be cumulative. Discuss this feature.
(c) How are dividends in arrears presented in the financial statements?

12. Identify the events that result in credits and debits to retained earnings.

13. Indicate how each of these accounts should be classified in the stockholders' equity section of the balance sheet.
(a) Common Stock.
(b) Paid-in Capital in Excess of Par Value.
(c) Retained Earnings.
(d) Treasury Stock.
(e) Paid-in Capital in Excess of Stated Value.
(f) Preferred Stock.

14. What three conditions must be met before a cash dividend is paid?

15. Three dates associated with Mega Company's cash dividend are May 1, May 15, and May 31. Discuss the significance of each date and give the entry at each date.

16. Contrast the effects of a cash dividend and a stock dividend on a corporation's balance sheet.

17. Wendy Naylor asks, "Since stock dividends don't change anything, why declare them?" What is your answer to Wendy?

18. Flynn Corporation has 10,000 shares of $15 par value common stock outstanding when it announces a 2-for-1 split. Before the split, the stock had a market price of $120 per share. After the split, how many shares of stock will be outstanding, and what will be the approximate market price per share?

19. The board of directors is considering a stock split or a stock dividend. They understand that total stockholders' equity will remain the same under either action. However, they are not sure of the different effects of the two actions on other aspects of stockholders' equity. Explain the differences to the directors.

20. (a) What is the purpose of a retained earnings restriction?
(b) Identify the possible causes of retained earnings restrictions.

21. Reo Inc.'s common stock has a par value of $1 and a current market value of $15. Explain why these amounts are different.

22. What is the formula for the payout ratio? What does it indicate?

23. Explain the circumstances under which debt financing will increase the return on stockholders' equity ratio.

24. Under what circumstances will the return on assets ratio and the return on common stockholders' equity ratio be equal?

25. Kirk Corp. has a return on assets ratio of 12%. It plans to issue bonds at 8% and use the cash to retire debt. What effect will this have on its debt to total assets ratio and on its return on common stockholders' equity?

Brief Exercises

Cite advantages and disadvantages of a corporation.
(SO 1)

BE11-1   Jeni Phelps is planning to start a business. Identify for Jeni the advantages and disadvantages of the corporate form of business organization.

Journalize issuance of par value common stock.
(SO 2)

BE11-2   On May 10 McLain Corporation issues 1,000 shares of $5 par value common stock for cash at $13 per share. Journalize the issuance of the stock.

Journalize issuance of no-par common stock.
(SO 2)

BE11-3   On June 1 Harmon Inc. issues 2,000 shares of no-par common stock at a cash price of $6 per share. Journalize the issuance of the shares.

Journalize issuance of preferred stock.
(SO 4)

BE11-4   Duggen Inc. issues 5,000 shares of $100 par value preferred stock for cash at $108 per share. Journalize the issuance of the preferred stock.

Prepare entries for a cash dividend.
(SO 5)

BE11-5   Michelle Corporation has 7,000 shares of common stock outstanding. It declares a $1 per share cash dividend on November 1 to stockholders of record on December

1. The dividend is paid on December 31. Prepare the entries on the appropriate dates to record the declaration and payment of the cash dividend.

BE11-6   The stockholders' equity section of Saber Corporation's balance sheet consists of common stock ($10 par) $1,000,000 and retained earnings $400,000. A 10% stock dividend (10,000 shares) is declared when the market value per share is $19. Show the before and after effects of the dividend on (a) the components of stockholders' equity and (b) the shares outstanding.

Show before and after effects of a stock dividend.
(SO 5)

BE11-7   Indicate whether each of the following transactions would increase (+), decrease (−), or not affect (N/A) total assets, total liabilities, and total stockholders' equity.

Compare impact of cash dividend, stock dividend, and stock split.
(SO 5)

Transaction	Assets	Liabilities	Stockholders' Equity
(a) Declared cash dividend.			
(b) Paid cash dividend declared in (a).			
(c) Declared stock dividend.			
(d) Distributed stock dividend declared in (c).			
(e) Split stock 3-for-1.			

BE11-8   Duffy Corporation has these accounts at December 31: Common Stock, $10 par, 5,000 shares issued, $50,000; Paid-in Capital in Excess of Par Value $18,000; Retained Earnings $32,000; and Treasury Stock—Common, 500 shares, $12,000. Prepare the stockholders' equity section of the balance sheet.

Prepare a stockholders' equity section.
(SO 7)

BE11-9   Nick Gross, president of Gross Corporation, believes that it is a good practice for a company to maintain a constant payout of dividends relative to its earnings. Last year net income was $600,000, and the corporation paid $150,000 in dividends. This year, due to some unusual circumstances, the corporation had income of $1,500,000. Nick expects next year's net income to be about $700,000. What was Gross Corporation's payout ratio last year? If it is to maintain the same payout ratio, what amount of dividends would it pay this year? Is this necessarily a good idea—that is, what are the pros and cons of maintaining a constant payout ratio in this scenario?

Evaluate a company's dividend record.
(SO 8)

BE11-10   SUPERVALU, one of the largest grocery retailers in the United States, is headquartered in Minneapolis. The following financial information (in millions) was taken from the company's 2005 annual report. Net sales $19,543.2; net income $385.8; beginning stockholders' equity $2,209.6; ending stockholders' equity $2,510.6. Compute the return on stockholders' equity ratio. Provide a brief interpretation of your findings.

Calculate the return on stockholders' equity.
(SO 8)

BE11-11   Howell Corporation has 100,000 shares of $10 par value common stock outstanding. It declares a 10% stock dividend on December 1 when the market value per share is $17. The dividend shares are issued on December 31. Prepare the entries for the declaration and distribution of the stock dividend.

Prepare entries for a stock dividend.
(SO 9)

Exercises

E11-1   During its first year of operations, Ritter Corporation had these transactions pertaining to its common stock.

Journalize issuance of common stock.
(SO 2)

        Jan. 10   Issued 90,000 shares for cash at $5 per share.
        July 1   Issued 50,000 shares for cash at $7 per share.

Instructions
(a) Journalize the transactions, assuming that the common stock has a par value of $5 per share.
(b) Journalize the transactions, assuming that the common stock is no-par with a stated value of $1 per share.

E11-2   Somer Co. had these transactions during the current period.

Journalize issuance of common stock and preferred stock and purchase of treasury stock.
(SO 2, 3, 4)

June 12   Issued 60,000 shares of $1 par value common stock for cash of $300,000.
July 11   Issued 1,000 shares of $100 par value preferred stock for cash at $104 per share.
Nov. 28   Purchased 2,000 shares of treasury stock for $11,000.

Instructions
Prepare the journal entries for the transactions shown on page 567.

Journalize preferred stock transactions and indicate statement presentation.
(SO 4, 7)

E11-3 Oritz Corporation is authorized to issue both preferred and common stock. The par value of the preferred is $50. During the first year of operations, the company had the following events and transactions pertaining to its preferred stock.

Feb. 1 Issued 40,000 shares for cash at $51 per share.
July 1 Issued 20,000 shares for cash at $56 per share.

Instructions
(a) Journalize the transactions.
(b) Post to the stockholders' equity accounts. (Use T accounts.)
(c) Discuss the statement presentation of the accounts.

Answer questions about stockholders' equity section.
(SO 2, 3, 4, 7)

E11-4 The stockholders' equity section of MaiStyle Corporation's balance sheet at December 31 is presented here.

MAISTYLE CORPORATION
Balance Sheet (partial)

Stockholders' equity	
Paid-in capital	
Preferred stock, cumulative, 10,000 shares authorized,	
6,000 shares issued and outstanding	$ 900,000
Common stock, no par, 750,000 shares authorized,	
600,000 shares issued	1,800,000
Total paid-in capital	2,700,000
Retained earnings	1,158,000
Total paid-in capital and retained earnings	3,858,000
Less: Treasury stock (8,000 common shares)	(32,000)
Total stockholders' equity	$3,826,000

Instructions
From a review of the stockholders' equity section, answer the following questions.
(a) How many shares of common stock are outstanding?
(b) Assuming there is a stated value, what is the stated value of the common stock?
(c) What is the par value of the preferred stock?
(d) If the annual dividend on preferred stock is $36,000, what is the dividend rate on preferred stock?
(e) If dividends of $72,000 were in arrears on preferred stock, what would be the balance reported for retained earnings?

Prepare correct entries for capital stock transactions.
(SO 2, 3, 4)

E11-5 Yanik Corporation recently hired a new accountant with extensive experience in accounting for partnerships. Because of the pressure of the new job, the accountant was unable to review what he had learned earlier about corporation accounting. During the first month, he made the following entries for the corporation's capital stock.

May 2	Cash		120,000	
		Capital Stock		120,000
		(Issued 10,000 shares of $5 par value common stock at $12 per share)		
	10	Cash	530,000	
		Capital Stock		530,000
		(Issued 10,000 shares of $50 par value preferred stock at $53 per share)		
	15	Capital Stock	7,200	
		Cash		7,200
		(Purchased 600 shares of common stock for the treasury at $12 per share)		

Instructions
On the basis of the explanation for each entry, prepare the entries that should have been made for the capital stock transactions.

E11-6 On January 1 Weiss Corporation had 75,000 shares of no-par common stock issued and outstanding. The stock has a stated value of $5 per share. During the year, the following transactions occurred.

Journalize cash dividends and indicate statement presentation.
(SO 5)

Apr.	1	Issued 8,000 additional shares of common stock for $11 per share.
June	15	Declared a cash dividend of $1.50 per share to stockholders of record on June 30.
July	10	Paid the $1.50 cash dividend.
Dec.	1	Issued 4,000 additional shares of common stock for $12 per share.
	15	Declared a cash dividend on outstanding shares of $1.70 per share to stockholders of record on December 31.

Instructions
(a) Prepare the entries, if any, on each of the three dates that involved dividends.
(b) How are dividends and dividends payable reported in the financial statements prepared at December 31?

E11-7 On October 31 the stockholders' equity section of Davis Company's balance sheet consists of common stock $648,000 and retained earnings $400,000. Davis is considering the following two courses of action: (1) declaring a 5% stock dividend on the 54,000 $12 par value shares outstanding or (2) effecting a 3-for-1 stock split that will reduce par value to $4 per share. The current market price is $15 per share.

Compare effects of a stock dividend and a stock split.
(SO 5)

Instructions
Prepare a tabular summary of the effects of the alternative actions on the company's stockholders' equity and outstanding shares. Use these column headings: **Before Action**, **After Stock Dividend**, and **After Stock Split**.

E11-8 Wells Fargo & Company, headquartered in San Francisco, is one of the nation's largest financial institutions. It reported the following selected accounts (in millions) as of December 31, 2004.

Prepare a stockholders' equity section.
(SO 7)

Retained earnings	$27,143
Preferred stock	270
Common stock—$1⅔ par value, authorized 6,000,000,000 shares;	
issued 1,736,381,025 shares	2,894
Treasury stock—41,789,388 shares	(2,247)
Additional paid-in capital—common stock	9,806

Instructions
Prepare the stockholders' equity section of the balance sheet for Wells Fargo as of December 31, 2004.

E11-9 The following stockholders' equity accounts, arranged alphabetically, are in the ledger of Marvel Corporation at December 31, 2007.

Prepare a stockholders' equity section.
(SO 7)

Common Stock ($5 stated value)	$1,500,000
Paid-in Capital in Excess of Par Value—Preferred Stock	45,000
Paid-in Capital in Excess of Stated Value—Common Stock	1,050,000
Preferred Stock (8%, $100 par, noncumulative)	500,000
Retained Earnings	1,134,000
Treasury Stock—Common (8,000 shares)	78,000

Instructions
Prepare the stockholders' equity section of the balance sheet at December 31, 2007.

E11-10 The following accounts appear in the ledger of Sycamore Inc. after the books are closed at December 31, 2007.

Prepare a stockholders' equity section.
(SO 7)

Common Stock (no-par, $1 stated value, 400,000 shares authorized,	
200,000 shares issued)	$ 200,000
Paid-in Capital in Excess of Stated Value—Common Stock	1,200,000
Preferred Stock ($50 par value, 8%, 40,000 shares authorized, 12,000	
shares issued)	600,000
Retained Earnings	900,000
Treasury Stock (10,000 common shares)	64,000
Paid-in Capital in Excess of Par Value—Preferred Stock	24,000

Instructions

Prepare the stockholders' equity section at December 31, assuming $100,000 of retained earnings is restricted for plant expansion. (Use Note R.)

Calculate ratios to evaluate dividend and earnings performance.
(SO 8)

E11-11   The following financial information is available for Sara Lee Corporation.

(in millions)	2004	2003
Average common stockholders' equity	$2,500	$1,897
Dividends declared for common stockholders	594	497
Dividends declared for preferred stockholders	0	10
Net income	1,272	1,221

Instructions

Calculate the payout ratio and return on common stockholders' equity ratio for 2004 and 2003. Comment on your findings.

Calculate ratios to evaluate dividend and earnings performance.
(SO 8)

E11-12   The following financial information is available for Walgreen Company.

(in millions)	2004	2003
Average common stockholders' equity	$7,628.8	$6,640.4
Dividends declared for common stockholders	186.4	159.6
Dividends declared for preferred stockholders	0	0
Net income	1,349.8	1,165.1

Instructions

Calculate the payout ratio and return on common stockholders' equity ratio for 2004 and 2003. Comment on your findings.

Calculate ratios to evaluate profitability and solvency.
(SO 8)

E11-13   Mann Corporation decided to issue common stock and used the $400,000 proceeds to retire all of its outstanding bonds on January 1, 2007. The following information is available for the company for 2006 and 2007.

	2007	2006
Net income	$ 182,000	$ 150,000
Average stockholders' equity	1,100,000	700,000
Total assets	1,200,000	1,200,000
Current liabilities	100,000	100,000
Total liabilities	100,000	500,000

Instructions

(a) Compute the return on stockholder's equity ratio for both years.
(b) Explain how it is possible that net income increased, but the return on common stockholders' equity decreased.
(c) Compute the debt to total assets ratio for both years, and comment on the implications of this change in the company's solvency.

Journalize stock dividends.
(SO 5, 9)

*E11-14   On January 1, 2007, Kern Corporation had $1,500,000 of common stock outstanding that was issued at par and retained earnings of $750,000. The company issued 30,000 shares of common stock at par on July 1 and earned net income of $400,000 for the year.

Instructions

Journalize the declaration of a 15% stock dividend on December 10, 2007, for the following two independent assumptions.

(a) Par value is $10 and market value is $12.
(b) Par value is $5 and market value is $9.

Problems: Set A

P11-1A   Norris Corporation was organized on January 1, 2007. It is authorized to issue 20,000 shares of 6%, $50 par value preferred stock and 500,000 shares of no-par common stock with a stated value of $1 per share. The following stock transactions were completed during the first year.

Jan. 10   Issued 60,000 shares of common stock for cash at $4 per share.
Mar. 1   Issued 12,000 shares of preferred stock for cash at $54 per share.
May 1   Issued 100,000 shares of common stock for cash at $5 per share.
Sept. 1   Issued 5,000 shares of common stock for cash at $6 per share.
Nov. 1   Issued 2,000 shares of preferred stock for cash at $56 per share.

Instructions
(a) Journalize the transactions.
(b) Post to the stockholders' equity accounts. (Use T accounts.)
(c) Prepare the paid-in capital portion of the stockholders' equity section at December 31, 2007.

Journalize stock transactions, post, and prepare paid-in capital section.
(SO 2, 4, 7)

GLS

(c) Tot. paid-in capital
$1,530,000

P11-2A   The stockholders' equity accounts of Alpha Corporation on January 1, 2007, were as follows.

Preferred Stock (8%, $100 par noncumulative, 5,000 shares authorized)	$ 400,000
Common Stock ($5 stated value, 300,000 shares authorized)	1,000,000
Paid-in Capital in Excess of Par Value—Preferred Stock	15,000
Paid-in Capital in Excess of Stated Value—Common Stock	480,000
Retained Earnings	688,000
Treasury Stock—Common (5,000 shares)	40,000

Journalize transactions, post, and prepare a stockholders' equity section; calculate ratios.
(SO 2, 3, 5, 7, 8)

GLS

During 2007 the corporation had the following transactions and events pertaining to its stockholders' equity.

Feb. 1   Issued 3,000 shares of common stock for $18,600.
Mar. 20   Purchased 1,000 additional shares of common treasury stock at $7 per share.
Oct. 1   Declared an 8% cash dividend on preferred stock, payable November 1.
Nov. 1   Paid the dividend declared on October 1.
Dec. 1   Declared a $0.50 per share cash dividend to common stockholders of record on December 15, payable December 31, 2007.
31   Determined that net income for the year was $280,000. Paid the dividend declared on December 1.

Instructions
(a) Journalize the transactions. (Include entries to close net income to Retained Earnings.)
(b) Enter the beginning balances in the accounts and post the journal entries to the stockholders' equity accounts. (Use T accounts.)
(c) Prepare the stockholders' equity section of the balance sheet at December 31, 2007.
(d) Calculate the payout ratio, earnings per share, and return on common stockholders' equity ratio. (*Note:* Use the common shares outstanding on January 1 and December 31 to determine the average shares outstanding.)

(c) Tot. paid-in capital
$1,913,600

P11-3A   On December 31, 2006, Pepp Company had 1,300,000 shares of $5 par common stock issued and outstanding. The stockholders' equity accounts at December 31, 2006, had the balances listed here.

Prepare a stockholders' equity section.
(SO 7)

Common Stock	$6,500,000
Additional Paid-in Capital	1,800,000
Retained Earnings	1,200,000

Transactions during 2007 and other information related to stockholders' equity accounts were as follows.

1. On January 10, 2007, issued at $109 per share 100,000 shares of $100 par value, 8% cumulative preferred stock.

2. On February 8, 2007, reacquired 15,000 shares of its common stock for $11 per share.
3. On June 8, 2007, declared a cash dividend of $1.20 per share on the common stock outstanding, payable on July 10, 2007, to stockholders of record on July 1, 2007.
4. On December 9, 2007, declared the yearly cash dividend on preferred stock, payable January 10, 2008, to stockholders of record on December 15, 2007.
5. Net income for the year was $3,600,000.

Tot. stockholders' equity
$21,493,000

Instructions

Prepare the stockholders' equity section of Pepp's balance sheet at December 31, 2007.

Reproduce retained earnings account, and prepare a stockholders' equity section.
(SO 5, 6, 7)

P11-4A The ledger of Omega Corporation at December 31, 2007, after the books have been closed, contains the following stockholders' equity accounts.

Preferred Stock (10,000 shares issued)	$1,000,000
Common Stock (450,000 shares issued)	2,250,000
Paid-in Capital in Excess of Par Value—Preferred Stock	200,000
Paid-in Capital in Excess of Stated Value—Common Stock	1,600,000
Retained Earnings	3,060,000

A review of the accounting records reveals this information:

1. Preferred stock is 7%, $100 par value, noncumulative. Since January 1, 2006, 10,000 shares have been outstanding; 20,000 shares are authorized.
2. Common stock is no-par with a stated value of $5 per share; 600,000 shares are authorized.
3. The January 1, 2007, balance in Retained Earnings was $2,580,000.
4. On October 1, 60,000 shares of common stock were sold for cash at $8 per share.
5. A cash dividend of $400,000 was declared and properly allocated to preferred and common stock on November 1. No dividends were paid to preferred stockholders in 2006.
6. Net income for the year was $880,000.
7. On December 31, 2007, the directors authorized disclosure of a $130,000 restriction of retained earnings for plant expansion. (Use Note A.)

Instructions

(b) Tot. paid-in capital
$5,050,000

(a) Reproduce the retained earnings account (T account) for the year.
(b) Prepare the stockholders' equity section of the balance sheet at December 31.

Prepare entries for stock transactions, and prepare a stockholders' equity section.
(SO 2, 3, 4, 7)

P11-5A Milner Corporation has been authorized to issue 20,000 shares of $100 par value, 10%, noncumulative preferred stock and 1,000,000 shares of no-par common stock. The corporation assigned a $5 stated value to the common stock. At December 31, 2007, the ledger contained the following balances pertaining to stockholders' equity.

Preferred Stock	$ 130,000
Paid-in Capital in Excess of Par Value—Preferred Stock	20,000
Common Stock	2,000,000
Paid-in Capital in Excess of Stated Value—Common Stock	1,850,000
Treasury Stock—Common (5,000 shares)	55,000
Retained Earnings	82,000

The preferred stock was issued for $150,000 cash. All common stock issued was for cash. In November 5,000 shares of common stock were purchased for the treasury at a per share cost of $11. No dividends were declared in 2007.

Instructions

(a) Prepare the journal entries for the following.

    (1) Issuance of preferred stock for cash.
    (2) Issuance of common stock for cash.
    (3) Purchase of common treasury stock for cash.

(b) Tot. stockholders' equity
$4,027,000

(b) Prepare the stockholders' equity section of the balance sheet at December 31, 2007.

Prepare a stockholders' equity section.
(SO 7)

P11-6A On January 1, 2007, Rothchild Inc. had these stockholders' equity balances.

Common Stock, $1 par (2,000,000 shares authorized, 800,000 shares issued and outstanding)	$800,000
Paid-in Capital in Excess of Par Value	1,500,000
Retained Earnings	600,000

During 2007, the following transactions and events occurred.

1. Issued 50,000 shares of $1 par value common stock for $3 per share.
2. Issued 40,000 shares of common stock for cash at $4 per share.
3. Purchased 15,000 shares of common stock for the treasury at $3.50 per share.
4. Declared and paid a cash dividend of $115,000.
5. Earned net income of $300,000.

Instructions
Prepare the stockholders' equity section of the balance sheet at December 31, 2007.

Tot. stockholders' equity
$3,342,500

P11-7A Stuffitt Company manufactures backpacks. During 2007 Stuffitt issued bonds at 10% interest and used the cash proceeds to purchase treasury stock. The following financial information is available for Stuffitt Company for the years 2007 and 2006.

Evaluate a company's profitability and solvency.
(SO 8)

	2007	2006
Sales	$ 9,000,000	$ 9,000,000
Net income	2,340,000	2,700,000
Interest expense	500,000	140,000
Tax cxpense	670,000	780,000
Dividends paid	890,000	1,026,000
Total assets (year-end)	14,500,000	16,875,000
Average total assets	14,937,500	17,647,000
Total liabilities (year-end)	6,000,000	3,000,000
Average total stockholders' equity	9,400,000	14,100,000

Instructions
(a) Use the information above to calculate the following ratios for both years: (i) return on assets ratio, (ii) return on common stockholders' equity ratio, (iii) payout ratio, (iv) debt to total assets ratio, (v) times interest earned ratio.
(b) Referring to your findings in part (a), discuss the changes in the company's profitability from 2006 to 2007.
(c) Referring to your findings in part (a), discuss the changes in the company's solvency from 2006 to 2007.
(d) Based on your findings in (b), was the decision to issue debt to purchase common stock a wise one?

*P11-8A On January 1, 2007, Aglar Corporation had these stockholders' equity accounts.

Prepare dividend entries, prepare a stockholders' equity section, and calculate ratios.
(SO 5, 7, 8, 9)

Common Stock ($10 par value, 60,000 shares issued and outstanding)	$600,000
Paid-in Capital in Excess of Par Value	500,000
Retained Earnings	620,000

GLS

During the year, the following transactions occurred.

Jan. 15	Declared a $0.50 cash dividend per share to stockholders of record on January 31, payable February 15.
Feb. 15	Paid the dividend declared in January.
Apr. 15	Declared a 10% stock dividend to stockholders of record on April 30, distributable May 15. On April 15 the market price of the stock was $14 per share.
May 15	Issued the shares for the stock dividend.
Dec. 1	Declared a $0.55 per share cash dividend to stockholders of record on December 15, payable January 10, 2006.
31	Determined that net income for the year was $370,000.

Instructions
(a) Journalize the transactions. (Include entries to close net income to Retained Earnings.)
(b) Enter the beginning balances and post the entries to the stockholders' equity T accounts. (*Note:* Open additional stockholders' equity accounts as needed.)
(c) Prepare the stockholders' equity section of the balance sheet at December 31.
(d) Calculate the payout ratio and return on common stockholders' equity ratio.

(c) Tot. stockholders' equity
$2,023,700

Problems: Set B

Journalize stock transactions, post, and prepare paid-in capital section.
(SO 2, 4, 7)

P11-1B Hawes Corporation was organized on January 1, 2007. It is authorized to issue 10,000 shares of 8%, $100 par value preferred stock and 500,000 shares of no-par common stock with a stated value of $2 per share. The following stock transactions were completed during the first year.

Jan. 10	Issued 80,000 shares of common stock for cash at $3.50 per share.	
Mar. 1	Issued 5,000 shares of preferred stock for cash at $102 per share.	
May 1	Issued 60,000 shares of common stock for cash at $4 per share.	
Sept. 1	Issued 10,000 shares of common stock for cash at $5 per share.	
Nov. 1	Issued 2,000 shares of preferred stock for cash at $104 per share.	

Instructions

(c) Tot. paid-in capital
    $1,288,000

(a) Journalize the transactions.
(b) Post to the stockholders' equity accounts. (Use T accounts.)
(c) Prepare the paid-in capital section of stockholders' equity at December 31, 2007.

Journalize transactions, post, and prepare a stockholders' equity section; calculate ratios.
(SO 2, 3, 5, 7, 8)

P11-2B The stockholders' equity accounts of Sosa Corporation on January 1, 2007, were as follows.

Preferred Stock (7%, $50 par cumulative, 10,000 shares authorized)	$ 400,000
Common Stock ($1 stated value, 2,000,000 shares authorized)	1,000,000
Paid-in Capital in Excess of Par Value—Preferred Stock	80,000
Paid-in Capital in Excess of Stated Value—Common Stock	1,400,000
Retained Earnings	1,716,000
Treasury Stock—Common (10,000 shares)	30,000

During 2007 the corporation had these transactions and events pertaining to its stockholders' equity.

Feb. 1	Issued 15,000 shares of common stock for $60,000.	
Nov. 10	Purchased 4,000 shares of common stock for the treasury at a cost of $18,000.	
Nov. 15	Declared a 7% cash dividend on preferred stock, payable December 15.	
Dec. 1	Declared a $0.30 per share cash dividend to stockholders of record on December 15, payable December 31, 2007.	
15	Paid the dividend declared on November 15.	
31	Determined that net income for the year was $408,000. The market price of the common stock on this date was $5 per share. Paid the dividend declared on December 1.	

Instructions

(c) Tot. paid-in capital
    $2,940,000

(a) Journalize the transactions. (Include entries to close net income to Retained Earnings.)
(b) Enter the beginning balances in the accounts, and post the journal entries to the stockholders' equity accounts. (Use T accounts.)
(c) Prepare the stockholders' equity section of the balance sheet at December 31, 2007.
(d) Calculate the payout ratio, earnings per share, and return on common stockholders' equity ratio. (*Hint:* Use the common shares outstanding on January 1 and December 31 to determine average shares outstanding.)

Prepare a stockholders' equity section.
(SO 7)

P11-3B On December 31, 2006, Klein Company had 1,000,000 shares of $1 par common stock issued and outstanding. The stockholders' equity accounts at December 31, 2006, had the balances listed here.

Common Stock	$1,000,000
Additional Paid-in Capital	100,000
Retained Earnings	800,000

Transactions during 2007 and other information related to stockholders' equity accounts were as follows.

1. On January 9, 2007, issued at $8 per share 100,000 shares of $5 par value, 9% cumulative preferred stock.

2. On February 8, 2007, reacquired 12,000 shares of its common stock for $9 per share.
3. On June 10, 2007, declared a cash dividend of $1 per share on the common stock outstanding, payable on July 10, 2007, to stockholders of record on July 1, 2007.
4. On December 15, 2007, declared the yearly cash dividend on preferred stock, payable December 28, 2007, to stockholders of record on December 15, 2007.
5. Net income for the year is $2,400,000. At December 31, 2007, the market price of the common stock was $12 per share.

Instructions
Prepare the stockholders' equity section of Klein Company's balance sheet at December 31, 2007.

Tot. stockholders' equity
$3,959,000

P11-4B   The post-closing trial balance of Mantelle Corporation at December 31, 2007, contains these stockholders' equity accounts.

Preferred Stock (8,000 shares issued)	$ 400,000
Common Stock (250,000 shares issued)	2,500,000
Paid-in Capital in Excess of Par Value—Preferred Stock	250,000
Paid-in Capital in Excess of Par Value—Common Stock	700,000
Retained Earnings	1,215,000

Reproduce retained earnings account, and prepare a stockholders' equity section.
(SO 5, 6, 7)

A review of the accounting records reveals this information:

1. Preferred stock is $50 par, 10%, and cumulative; 8,000 shares have been outstanding since January 1, 2006.
2. Authorized stock is 20,000 shares of preferred and 500,000 shares of common with a $10 par value.
3. The January 1, 2007, balance in Retained Earnings was $960,000.
4. On July 1, 20,000 shares of common stock were sold for cash at $16 per share.
5. A cash dividend of $220,000 was declared and properly allocated to preferred and common stock on October 1. No dividends were paid to preferred stockholders in 2006.
6. Net income for the year was $475,000.
7. On December 31, 2007, the directors authorized disclosure of a $150,000 restriction of retained earnings for plant expansion. (Use Note X.)

Instructions
(a) Reproduce the retained earnings account for the year.
(b) Prepare the stockholders' equity section of the balance sheet at December 31.

(b) Tot. paid-in capital
$3,850,000

P11-5B   The following stockholders' equity accounts, arranged alphabetically, are in the ledger of Aaron Corporation at December 31, 2007.

Prepare a stockholders' equity section.
(SO 7)

Common Stock ($5 stated value, 800,000 shares authorized)	$2,600,000
Paid-in Capital in Excess of Par Value—Preferred Stock	108,000
Paid-in Capital in Excess of Stated Value—Common Stock	1,500,000
Preferred Stock (8%, $50 par, noncumulative, 50,000 shares	
authorized)	900,000
Retained Earnings	1,958,000
Treasury Stock—Common (20,000 shares)	150,000

Instructions
Prepare the stockholders' equity section of the balance sheet at December 31, 2007.

Tot. stockholders' equity
$6,916,000

P11-6B   On January 1, 2007, Willow Inc. had these stockholder equity balances.

Prepare a stockholders' equity section.
(SO 7)

Common Stock, $1 par (1,000,000 shares authorized;	
500,000 shares issued and outstanding)	$ 500,000
Paid-in Capital in Excess of Par Value	1,000,000
Retained Earnings	600,000

During 2007, the following transactions and events occurred.

1. Issued 50,000 shares of $1 par common stock for $125,000.
2. Issued 30,000 common shares for cash at $4 per share.
3. Purchased 10,000 shares of common stock for the treasury at $4 per share.
4. Declared and paid a cash dividend of $160,000.
5. Reported net income of $400,000.

Tot. stockholders' equity
            $2,545,000

*Evaluate a company's
profitability and solvency.*
(SO 8)

Instructions

Prepare the stockholders' equity section of the balance sheet at December 31, 2007.

P11-7B   Gene Kelly Company manufactures raingear. During 2007 Gene Kelly Company decided to issue bonds at 8% interest and then used the cash to purchase a significant amount of treasury stock. The following information is available for Gene Kelly Company.

	2007	2006
Sales	$3,000,000	$3,000,000
Net income	830,000	900,000
Interest expense	120,000	50,000
Tax expense	166,000	200,000
Total assets	5,000,000	5,625,000
Average total assets	5,312,500	6,250,000
Total liabilities	2,000,000	1,000,000
Average total stockholders' equity	3,312,500	5,250,000
Dividends	270,000	300,000

Instructions

(a) Use the information above to calculate the following ratios for both years: (i) return on assets ratio, (ii) return on common stockholders' equity ratio, (iii) payout ratio, (iv) debt to total assets ratio, (v) times interest earned ratio.

(b) Referring to your findings in part (a), discuss the changes in the company's profitability from 2006 to 2007.

(c) Referring to your findings in part (a), discuss the changes in the company's solvency from 2006 to 2007.

(d) Based on your findings in (b), was the decision to issue debt to purchase common stock a wise one?

*Prepare dividend entries,
prepare a stockholders' equity
section, and calculate ratios.*
(SO 5, 7, 8, 9)

GLS

*P11-8B   On January 1, 2007, Frenz Corporation had these stockholders' equity accounts.

Common Stock ($20 par value, 60,000 shares issued and outstanding)	$1,200,000
Paid-in Capital in Excess of Par Value	240,000
Retained Earnings	750,000

During the year, the following transactions occurred.

Feb.	1	Declared a $0.50 cash dividend per share to stockholders of record on February 15, payable March 1.
Mar.	1	Paid the dividend declared in February.
July	1	Declared a 10% stock dividend to stockholders of record on July 15, distributable July 31. On July 1 the market price of the stock was $26 per share.
	31	Issued the shares for the stock dividend.
Dec.	1	Declared a $1 per share dividend to stockholders of record on December 15, payable January 5, 2008.
	31	Determined that net income for the year was $440,000. The market price of the common stock on this date was $32.

Instructions

(a) Journalize the transactions. (Include entries to close net income to Retained Earnings.)

(b) Enter the beginning balances and post the entries to the stockholders' equity T accounts. (*Note:* Open additional stockholders' equity accounts as needed.)

(c) Tot. stockholders' equity
            $2,534,000

(c) Prepare the stockholders' equity section of the balance sheet at December 31.

(d) Calculate the payout ratio and return on common stockholders' equity ratio.

Problems: Set C

Visit the book's website at **www.wiley.com/college/kimmel** and choose the Student Companion site to access Problem Set C.

Comprehensive Problem

CP11   Servo Corporation's balance sheet at December 31, 2006, is presented below.

SERVO CORPORATION
Balance Sheet
December 31, 2006

Cash	$ 24,600	Accounts payable	$ 25,600
Accounts receivable	45,500	Common stock ($10 par)	80,000
Allowance for doubtful		Retained earnings	127,400
accounts	(1,500)		$233,000
Supplies	4,400		
Land	40,000		
Building	142,000		
Accumulated depreciation-			
building	(22,000)		
	$233,000		

During 2007, the following transactions occurred.

1. On January 1, 2007, Servo issued 1,500 shares of $20 par, 7% preferred stock for $33,000.
2. On January 1, 2007, Servo also issued 600 shares of the $10 par value common stock for $21,000.
3. Servo performed services for $280,000 on account.
4. On April 1, 2007, Servo collected fees of $48,000 in advance for services to be performed from April 1, 2007, to March 31, 2008.
5. Servo collected $267,000 from customers on account.
6. Servo bought $30,100 of supplies on account.
7. Servo paid $32,200 on accounts payable.
8. Servo reacquired 400 shares of its common stock on June 1, 2007, for $38 per share.
9. Paid other operating expenses of $188,200.
10. On December 31, 2007, Servo declared the annual preferred stock dividend and a $1.20 per share dividend on the outstanding common stock, all payable on January 15, 2008.
11. An account receivable of $1,300 which originated in 2006 is written off as uncollectible.

Adjustment data:

1. A count of supplies indicates that $5,900 of supplies remain unused at year-end.
2. Recorded revenue earned from item 4 above.
3. The allowance for doubtful accounts should have a balance of $3,500 at year end.
4. Depreciation is recorded on the building on a straight-line basis based on a 30-year life and a salvage value of $10,000.
5. The income tax rate is 30%. (*Hint:* Prepare the income statement up to income before taxes and multiply by 30% to compute the amount.)

Instructions
(You may want to set up T accounts to determine ending balances.)

(a) **Prepare** journal entries for the transactions listed above and adjusting entries.
(b) **Prepare** an adjusted trial balance at December 31, 2007.
(c) **Prepare** an income statement and a retained earnings statement for the year ending December 31, 2007, and a classified balance sheet as of December 31, 2007.

(b) Totals $670,250
(c) Net income $64,050
Tot. assets $373,200

Continuing Cookie Chronicle

(*Note:* This is a continuation of the Cookie Chronicle from Chapters 1 through 10.)

CCC11

Part 1   Because Natalie has been so successful with Cookie Creations and Curtis has been just as successful with his coffee shop, they both conclude that they could benefit from each other's business expertise. Curtis and Natalie next evaluate the different types of business organization, and because of the advantage of limited personal liability, decide to form a new corporation.

Curtis has operated his coffee shop for 2 years. He buys coffee, muffins, and cookies from a local supplier. Natalie's business consists of giving cookie-making classes and selling fine European mixers. The plan is for Natalie to use the premises Curtis currently rents as a location for her cookie-making classes and demonstrations of the mixers that she sells. Natalie will also hire, train, and supervise staff hired to bake cookies and muffins sold in the coffee shop. By offering her classes on the premises, Natalie will save on travel, and the coffee shop will provide one central location for selling the mixers. Combining forces will also allow Natalie and Curtis to pool their resources and buy a few more assets to run their new business venture.

The current market values of the assets of both businesses are as follows.

Description	Curtis' Coffee	Cookie Creations
Cash	$ 7,500	$10,000
Accounts receivable	100	500
Merchandise inventory	450	1,130
Equipment	2,500	1,000
	$10,550	$12,630

Curtis and Natalie meet with a lawyer and form their corporation, called Cookie & Coffee Creations Inc., on November 1, 2007. The new corporation is authorized to issue 50,000 shares of $1 par common stock and 10,000 shares of no par, $6 cumulative preferred stock.

The assets held by each business will be transferred into the corporation at current market value of $1 per share. Curtis will receive 10,550 common shares, and Natalie will receive 12,630 common shares in the corporation.

Natalie and Curtis are very excited about this new business venture. They come to you with the following questions.

1. Curtis' Dad and Natalie's grandmother are interested in investing $5,000 each in the new business venture. Curtis and Natalie are considering issuing them preferred shares. What would be the advantage of issuing them preferred stock instead of common?
2. What would be the advantages and disadvantages of issuing cumulative preferred?
3. "Our lawyer sent us a bill for $750. When we talked the bill over with her, she said she would be willing to receive common stock in our corporation instead of cash. We would be happy to issue her stock, but we're worried about accounting for this transaction. Can we do this? If so, how do we determine how many shares to give her?"

Instructions

(a) Answer Natalie and Curtis' questions.
(b) Prepare the journal entries required on November 1, 2007, the date when Natalie and Curtis transfer the assets of their respective businesses into Cookie & Coffee Creations Inc.
(c) Assume that Cookie & Coffee Creations Inc. issues 1,000 $6 cumulative preferred shares to Curtis' Dad and the same number to Natalie's grandmother, in both cases for $5,000. Also assume that Cookie & Coffee Creations Inc. issues 750 common shares to its lawyer. Prepare the journal entries required for each of these transactions that also occurred on November 1.
(d) Prepare the opening balance sheet for Cookie & Coffee Creations Inc. as of November 1, 2007, including the journal entries in (b) and (c) above.

Part 2 After establishing their company's fiscal year-end to be October 31, Natalie and Curtis began operating Cookie & Coffee Creations Inc. on November 1, 2007. The company had the following selected transactions during its first year of operations, 2008.

Jan. 1 Issued an additional 500 preferred shares to Natalie's brother for $2,500 cash.

June 30 Repurchased 750 shares issued to the lawyer, for $500 cash. The lawyer had decided to retire and wanted to liquidate all of her assets.

Oct. 15 The company had a very successful first year of operations and as a result declared dividends of $25,000, payable November 15, 2008. (Indicate the amounts payable to the preferred stockholders and to the common stockholders.)

Oct. 31 The company earned revenues of $462,500 and incurred expenses of $406,500 (including the $750 legal expense from November 1 but excluding income tax). Record income tax expense, assuming the company has a 20% income tax rate.

Instructions
(a) Prepare the journal entries to record each of the above transactions.
(b) Prepare all of the closing entries required on October 31, 2008.
(c) Prepare the retained earnings statement for the year ended October 31, 2008.
(d) Prepare the stockholders' equity section of the balance sheet as of October 31, 2008.   (d) Tot. stockholders' equity
$55,730

 BROADENING YOUR PERSPECTIVE

Financial Reporting and Analysis

FINANCIAL REPORTING PROBLEM: *Tootsie Roll Industries, Inc.*

BYP11-1 The stockholders' equity section of Tootsie Roll Industries' balance sheet is shown in the Consolidated Statement of Financial Position in Appendix A. You will also find data relative to this problem on other pages of Appendix A. (Note that Tootsie Roll has two classes of common stock. To answer the following questions, add the two classes of stock together.)

Instructions
Answer the following questions.
(a) What is the par or stated value per share of Tootsie Roll's common stock?
(b) What percentage of Tootsie Roll's authorized common stock was issued at December 31, 2004? (Round to the nearest full percent.)
(c) How many shares of common stock were outstanding at December 31, 2003, and at December 31, 2004?
(d) Calculate the payout ratio, earnings per share, and return on common stockholders' equity ratio for 2004.

COMPARATIVE ANALYSIS PROBLEM: *Tootsie Roll vs. Hershey Foods*

BYP11-2 The financial statements of Hershey Foods are presented in Appendix B, following the financial statements for Tootsie Roll in Appendix A.

Instructions
(a) Based on the information in these financial statements, compute the 2004 return on common stockholders' equity, debt to total assets ratio, and return on assets ratio for each company.
(b) What conclusions concerning the companies' profitability can be drawn from these ratios? Which company relies more on debt to boost its return to common shareholders?
(c) Compute the payout ratio for each company. Which pays out a higher percentage of its earnings?

RESEARCH CASE

BYP11-3   The May 2003 edition of *Strategic Finance* has an article by Alan Levinsohn titled "Does it Make Sense to Pay Dividends?"

Instructions

Read the article and answer the following questions.
(a) According to the author of the article, what are some potential benefits of paying dividends?
(b) What are some potential disadvantages of paying dividends?
(c) If a company has excess cash that it would like to distribute, what alternative exists to paying a dividend? Why might this alternative be preferred by some investors?
(d) What is meant by "double taxation of dividends," and what implications does this have for the choice that companies make between debt and equity financing?

INTERPRETING FINANCIAL STATEMENTS

BYP11-4   Marriott Corporation split into two companies: Host Marriott Corporation and Marriott International. Host Marriott retained ownership of the corporation's vast hotel and other properties, while Marriott International, rather than owning hotels, managed them. The purpose of this split was to free Marriott International from the "baggage" associated with Host Marriott, thus allowing it to be more aggressive in its pursuit of growth. The following information (in millions) is provided for each corporation for their first full year operating as independent companies.

	Host Marriott	**Marriott International**
Sales	$1,501	$8,415
Net income	(25)	200
Total assets	3,822	3,207
Total liabilities	3,112	2,440
Stockholders' equity	710	767

Instructions

(a) The two companies were split by the issuance of shares of Marriott International to all shareholders of the previous combined company. Discuss the nature of this transaction.
(b) Calculate the debt to total assets ratio for each company.
(c) Calculate the return on assets and return on common stockholders' equity ratios for each company.
(d) The company's debtholders were fiercely opposed to the original plan to split the two companies because the original plan had Host Marriott absorbing the majority of the company's debt. They relented only when Marriott International agreed to absorb a larger share of the debt. Discuss the possible reasons the debtholders were opposed to the plan to split the company.

BYP11-5   The January 25, 2005, edition of the *Wall Street Journal* has an article by Mary Kissel (on p. C1) titled "Known for Growth, Asian Firms Answer Call of the Dividend."

Instructions

Read the article and answer the following questions.
(a) What is the "dividend yield"? How does the dividend yield of Asian companies compare to that of companies in other regions?
(b) What has happened to Asian company debt levels in recent years? What implications has this had for return on equity? Explain why this would be the case.
(c) What measure is used to determine whether a company is paying out a high percentage of its earnings in the form of dividends? What percentage of their earnings are Asian firms paying out? According to the article, how have the stock prices of dividend-paying companies performed relative to non-dividend-paying companies? What explanations are given for this?

FINANCIAL ANALYSIS ON THE WEB

BYP11-6   *Purpose:* Use the stockholders' equity section of an annual report and identify the major components.

Address: **www.reportgallery.com** (or go to **www.wiley.com/college/kimmel**)

Steps
1. From Report Gallery Homepage, choose **Viewing Library**.
2. Select a particular company.
3. Choose **Annual Report**.
4. Follow instructions below.

Instructions
Answer the following questions.
(a) What is the company's name?
(b) What classes of capital stock has the company issued?
(c) For each class of stock:
   (1) How many shares are authorized, issued, and/or outstanding?
   (2) What is the par value?
(d) What are the company's retained earnings?
(e) Has the company acquired treasury stock? How many shares?

Critical Thinking

DECISION MAKING ACROSS THE ORGANIZATION

BYP11-7   In recent years the fast-food chain Wendy's International has purchased many treasury shares. From January 3, 1999, to December 30, 2001, the number of shares outstanding has fallen from 124 million to 105 million. The following information was drawn from the company's financial statements (in millions).

	Year ended	
	Dec. 30, 2001	**Jan. 3, 1999**
Net income	$ 193.6	$ 123.4
Total assets	2,076.0	1,837.9
Average total assets	2,016.9	1,889.8
Total common stockholders' equity	1,029.8	1,068.1
Average common stockholders' equity	1,078.0	1,126.2
Total liabilities	1,046.3	769.9
Average total liabilities	939.0	763.7
Interest expense	30.2	19.8
Income taxes	113.7	84.3
Cash provided by operations	305.2	233.8
Cash dividends paid on common stock	26.8	31.0
Preferred stock dividends	0	0
Average number of common shares outstanding	109.7	119.9

Instructions
Use the information provided to answer the following questions.
(a) Compute earnings per share, return on common stockholders' equity, and return on assets for both years. Discuss the change in the company's profitability over this period.
(b) Compute the dividend payout ratio. Also compute the average cash dividend paid per share of common stock (dividends paid divided by the average number of common shares outstanding). Discuss any change in these ratios during this period and the implications for the company's dividend policy.
(c) Compute the debt to total assets ratio and interest coverage ratio. Discuss the change in the company's solvency.
(d) Based on your findings in (a) and (c), discuss to what extent any change in the return on common stockholders' equity was the result of increased reliance on debt.
(e) Do the purchase of treasury stock and the shift toward more reliance on debt appear to have been wise strategic moves?

COMMUNICATION ACTIVITY

BYP11-8 Scott Kreiter, your uncle, is an inventor who has decided to incorporate. Uncle Scott knows that you are an accounting major at U.N.O. In a recent letter to you, he ends with the question, "I'm filling out a state incorporation application. Can you tell me the difference among the following terms: (1) authorized stock, (2) issued stock, (3) outstanding stock, and (4) preferred stock?"

Instructions

In a brief note, differentiate for Uncle Scott the four different stock terms. Write the letter to be friendly, yet professional.

ETHICS CASES

BYP11-9 The R&D division of Renew Corp. has just developed a chemical for sterilizing the vicious Brazilian "killer bees" which are invading Mexico and the southern United States. The president of Renew is anxious to get the chemical on the market because Renew profits need a boost—and his job is in jeopardy because of decreasing sales and profits. Renew has an opportunity to sell this chemical in Central American countries, where the laws are much more relaxed than in the United States.

The director of Renew's R&D division strongly recommends further research in the laboratory to test the side effects of this chemical on other insects, birds, animals, plants, and even humans. He cautions the president, "We could be sued from all sides if the chemical has tragic side effects that we didn't even test for in the lab." The president answers, "We can't wait an additional year for your lab tests. We can avoid losses from such lawsuits by establishing a separate wholly owned corporation to shield Renew Corp. from such lawsuits. We can't lose any more than our investment in the new corporation, and we'll invest just the patent covering this chemical. We'll reap the benefits if the chemical works and is safe, and avoid the losses from lawsuits if it's a disaster." The following week Renew creates a new wholly owned corporation called Offspring Inc., sells the chemical patent to it for $10, and watches the spraying begin.

Instructions

(a) Who are the stakeholders in this situation?
(b) Are the president's motives and actions ethical?
(c) Can Renew shield itself against losses of Offspring Inc.?

BYP11-10 Greenwood Corporation has paid 60 consecutive quarterly cash dividends (15 years). The last 6 months have been a real cash drain on the company, however, as profit margins have been greatly narrowed by increasing competition. With a cash balance sufficient to meet only day-to-day operating needs, the president, Gil Mailor, has decided that a stock dividend instead of a cash dividend should be declared. He tells Greenwood's financial vice-president, Vicki Lemke, to issue a press release stating that the company is extending its consecutive dividend record with the issuance of a 5% stock dividend. "Write the press release convincing the stockholders that the stock dividend is just as good as a cash dividend," he orders. "Just watch our stock rise when we announce the stock dividend; it must be a good thing if that happens."

Instructions

(a) Who are the stakeholders in this situation?
(b) Is there anything unethical about president Mailor's intentions or actions?
(c) What is the effect of a stock dividend on a corporation's stockholders' equity accounts? Which would you rather receive as a stockholder—a cash dividend or a stock dividend? Why?

Answers to Business Insight and Accounting across the Organization Questions

p. 537

Q: In addition to regulatory cost, what is another reason why some owners choose not to take their companies public?

A: One reason for being a private company is that managers then have more control over the company's future. For example, they can make decisions that they feel might be best for the company over the long-term, and not have to worry about the short-term stock price implications.

p. 542

Q: For stocks traded on organized stock exchanges, how are the dollar prices per share established? What factors might influence the price of shares in the marketplace?

A: The dollar prices per share are established by the interaction between buyers and sellers of the shares. The prices of shares are influenced by a company's earnings and dividends as well as by factors beyond a company's control, such as changes in interest rates, labor strikes, scarcity of supplies or resources, and politics. The number of willing buyers and sellers (demand and supply) also plays a part in the price of shares.

p. 545

Q: What signal might a large stock repurchase send to investors regarding management's belief about the company's growth opportunities?

A: When a company has many growth opportunities it will normally conserve its cash in order to be better able to fund expansion. A large use of cash to buy back stock (and essentially shrink the company) would suggest that management was not optimistic about its growth opportunities.

p. 550

Q: What factors must management consider in deciding how large a dividend to pay?

A: Management must consider the size of its retained earnings balance, the amount of available cash, its expected near-term cash needs, its growth opportunities, and what level of dividend it will be able to sustain based upon its expected future earnings.

Answer to Tootsie Roll Review It Question 3, p. 556

The cost of Tootsie Roll's treasury stock in 2004 was $1,992,000. It declared cash dividends of $14,547,000. The stock dividend reduced retained earnings by $57,358,000.

Answers to Self-Study Questions

1. c   2. b   3. d   4. c   5. d   6. d   7. b   8. a   9. c   10. b

CHAPTER 12

Statement of Cash Flows

STUDY OBJECTIVES

After studying this chapter,
you should be able to:

1 Indicate the usefulness of the statement of cash flows.

2 Distinguish among operating, investing, and financing activities.

3 Explain the impact of the product life cycle on a company's cash flows.

4 Prepare a statement of cash flows using the indirect method.

5 Use the statement of cash flows to evaluate a company.

THE NAVIGATOR

FEATURE STORY

Got Cash?

In today's environment, companies must be ready to respond to changes quickly in order to survive and thrive. They need to produce new products and expand into new markets continually. To do this takes cash—lots and lots of cash. Keeping lots of cash available is a real challenge for a young company. It requires careful cash management and attention to cash flow.

One company that managed cash successfully in its early years was Microsoft. During those years the company paid much of its payroll with stock options (rights to purchase company stock in the future at a given price) instead of cash. This strategy conserved cash, and turned more than a thousand of its employees into millionaires during the company's first 20 years of business.

In recent years Microsoft has had a different kind of cash problem. Now that it has reached a more "mature" stage in life, it generates so much cash—roughly $1 billion per month—that it cannot always figure out what to do with it. By 2004 Microsoft had accumulated $60 billion.

The company said it was accumulating cash to invest in new opportunities, buy other companies, and pay off pending lawsuits. But for years, the federal government has blocked attempts by Microsoft to buy anything other than small firms

THE NAVIGATOR

- Scan *Study Objectives*
- Read *Feature Story*
- Read *Preview*
- Read text and answer *Before You Go On*
  p. 590   p. 594   p. 602
  p. 609
- Work *Using the Decision Toolkit*
- Review *Summary of Study Objectives*
- Work *Demonstration Problem*
- Answer *Self-Study Questions*
- Complete *Assignments*

because it feared that purchase of a large firm would only increase Microsoft's monopolistic position. In addition, even the largest estimates of Microsoft's legal obligations related to pending lawsuits would use up only about $6 billion in cash.

Microsoft's stockholders have complained for years that holding all this cash was putting a drag on the company's profitability. Why? Because Microsoft had the cash invested in very low-yielding government securities. Stockholders felt that the company either should find new investment projects that would bring higher returns, or return some of the cash to stockholders.

Finally, in July 2004 Microsoft announced a plan to return cash to stockholders, by paying a special one-time $32 billion dividend in December 2004. This special dividend was so large that, according to the U.S. Commerce Department, it caused total personal income in the United States to rise by 3.7% in one month—the largest increase ever recorded by the agency. (It also made the holiday season brighter, especially for retailers in the Seattle area.) Microsoft also doubled its regular annual dividend to $3.50 per share. Further, it announced that it would spend another

$30 billion over the next four years buying treasury stock. These actions will help to deplete some of its massive cash horde, but as you will see in this chapter, for a cash-generating machine like Microsoft, the company will be anything but cash-starved.

Source: "Business: An End to Growth? Microsoft's Cash Bonanza," *The Economist* (July 23, 2005), p. 61.

On the World Wide Web
Microsoft: www.microsoft.com

PREVIEW OF CHAPTER 12

The balance sheet, income statement, and retained earnings statement do not always show the whole picture of the financial condition of a company or institution. In fact, looking at the financial statements of some well-known companies, a thoughtful investor might ask questions like these: How did Eastman Kodak finance cash dividends of $649 million in a year in which it earned only $17 million? How could United Airlines purchase new planes that cost $1.9 billion in a year in which it reported a net loss of over $2 billion? How did the companies that spent a combined fantastic $3.4 trillion on mergers and acquisitions in a recent year finance those deals? Answers to these and similar questions can be found in this chapter, which presents the statement of cash flows.

The content and organization of this chapter are as follows.

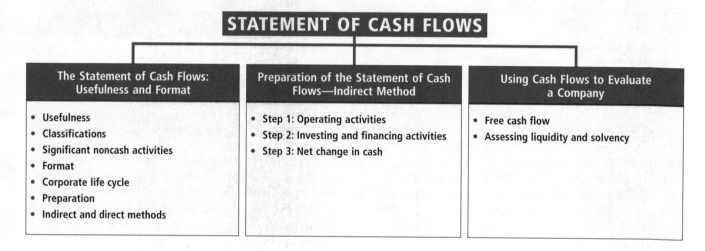

STATEMENT OF CASH FLOWS

The Statement of Cash Flows: Usefulness and Format	Preparation of the Statement of Cash Flows—Indirect Method	Using Cash Flows to Evaluate a Company
• Usefulness • Classifications • Significant noncash activities • Format • Corporate life cycle • Preparation • Indirect and direct methods	• Step 1: Operating activities • Step 2: Investing and financing activities • Step 3: Net change in cash	• Free cash flow • Assessing liquidity and solvency

The Statement of Cash Flows: Usefulness and Format

The balance sheet, income statement, and retained earnings statement provide only limited information about a company's cash flows (cash receipts and cash payments). For example, comparative balance sheets show the increase in property, plant, and equipment during the year. But they do not show how the additions were financed or paid for. The income statement shows net income. But it does not indicate the amount of cash generated by operating activities. The retained earnings statement shows cash dividends declared but not the cash dividends paid during the year. None of these statements presents a detailed summary of where cash came from and how it was used.

USEFULNESS OF THE STATEMENT OF CASH FLOWS

The **statement of cash flows** reports the cash receipts, cash payments, and net change in cash resulting from operating, investing, and financing activities during a period. The information in a statement of cash flows should help investors, creditors, and others assess:

1. **The entity's ability to generate future cash flows.** By examining relationships between items in the statement of cash flows, investors can make predictions of the amounts, timing, and uncertainty of future cash flows better than they can from accrual basis data.

2. **The entity's ability to pay dividends and meet obligations.** If a company does not have adequate cash, it cannot pay employees, settle debts, or pay dividends. Employees, creditors, and stockholders should be particularly interested in this statement, because it alone shows the flows of cash in a business.

3. **The reasons for the difference between net income and net cash provided (used) by operating activities.** Net income provides information on the success or failure of a business enterprise. However, some financial statement users are critical of accrual-basis net income because it requires many estimates. As a result, users often challenge the reliability of the number. Such is not the case with cash. Many readers of the statement of cash flows want to know the reasons for the difference between net income and net cash provided by operating activities. Then they can assess for themselves the reliability of the income number.

4. **The cash investing and financing transactions during the period.** By examining a company's investing and financing transactions, a financial statement reader can better understand why assets and liabilities changed during the period.

> **STUDY OBJECTIVE**
> **1**
> Indicate the usefulness of the statement of cash flows.

> *E*THICS NOTE
> Though we would discourage reliance on cash flows to the exclusion of accrual accounting, comparing cash from operations to net income can reveal important information about the "quality" of reported net income. Such a comparison can reveal the extent to which net income provides a good measure of actual performance.

CLASSIFICATION OF CASH FLOWS

The statement of cash flows classifies cash receipts and cash payments as operating, investing, and financing activities. Transactions and other events characteristic of each kind of activity are as follows.

1. **Operating activities** include the cash effects of transactions that create revenues and expenses. They thus enter into the determination of net income.

2. **Investing activities** include (a) acquiring and disposing of investments and property, plant, and equipment, and (b) lending money and collecting the loans.

3. **Financing activities** include (a) obtaining cash from issuing debt and repaying the amounts borrowed, and (b) obtaining cash from stockholders, repurchasing shares, and paying dividends.

> **STUDY OBJECTIVE**
> **2**
> Distinguish among operating, investing, and financing activities.

The operating activities category is the most important. It shows the cash provided by company operations. This source of cash is generally considered to be the best measure of a company's ability to generate sufficient cash to continue as a going concern.

Illustration 12-1 (next page) lists typical cash receipts and cash payments within each of the three classifications. **Study the list carefully.** It will prove very useful in solving homework exercises and problems.

Illustration 12-1
Typical receipt and
payment classifications

Types of Cash Inflows and Outflows

Operating activities—Income statement items

Cash inflows:

From sale of goods or services.

From interest received and dividends received.

Cash outflows:

To suppliers for inventory.

To employees for services.

To government for taxes.

To lenders for interest.

To others for expenses.

**Operating
activities**

Investing activities—Changes in investments and long-term assets

Cash inflows:

From sale of property, plant, and equipment.

From sale of investments in debt or equity securities of other entities.

From collection of principal on loans to other entities.

Cash outflows:

To purchase property, plant, and equipment.

To purchase investments in debt or equity securities of other entities.

To make loans to other entities.

Investing activities

**Financing activities—Changes in long-term liabilities and stockholders'
equity**

Cash inflows:

From sale of common stock.

From issuance of debt (bonds and notes).

Cash outflows:

To stockholders as dividends.

To redeem long-term debt or reacquire capital stock (treasury stock).

**Financing
activities**

Note the following general guidelines:

1. Operating activities involve income statement items.

2. Investing activities involve cash flows resulting from changes in investments
   and long-term asset items.

3. Financing activities involve cash flows resulting from changes in long-term
   liability and stockholders' equity items.

Companies classify as operating activities some cash flows related to investing
or financing activities. For example, receipts of investment revenue (interest and dividends) are classified as operating activities. So are payments of interest to lenders.
Why are these considered operating activities? **Because companies report these
items in the income statement, where results of operations are shown.**

SIGNIFICANT NONCASH ACTIVITIES

Not all of a company's significant activities involve cash. Examples of significant
noncash activities are:

1. Direct issuance of common stock to purchase assets.

2. Conversion of bonds into common stock.

3. Direct issuance of debt to purchase assets.

4. Exchanges of plant assets.

**Companies do not report in the body of the statement of cash flows
significant financing and investing activities that do not affect cash.** Instead,
they report these activities in either a **separate schedule** at the bottom of the

statement of cash flows or in a **separate note or supplementary schedule** to the financial statements. The reporting of these noncash activities in a separate schedule satisfies the **full disclosure principle**.

In solving homework assignments you should present significant noncash investing and financing activities in a separate schedule at the bottom of the statement of cash flows. (See the last entry in Illustration 12-2, at the bottom of this page, for an example.)

Accounting across the Organization

Net income is not the same as net cash provided by operations. The differences are illustrated by the following results from annual reports for 2004 ($ in millions). Note the wide disparity among these companies that all engaged in retail merchandising.

Company	Net Income	Net Cash Provided by Operations
Kohl's Corporation	$ 730	$ 948
Wal-Mart Stores, Inc.	10,267	15,044
JCPenney Company, Inc.	524	61
Costco Wholesale Corp.	882	2,099
Target Corporation	3,198	3,195

In general, why do differences exist between net income and net cash provided by operating activities?

FORMAT OF THE STATEMENT OF CASH FLOWS

The general format of the statement of cash flows presents the results of the three activities discussed previously—operating, investing, and financing— plus the significant noncash investing and financing activities. Illustration 12–2 shows a widely used form of the statement of cash flows.

COMPANY NAME Statement of Cash Flows Period Covered		
Cash flows from operating activities		
(List of individual items)	XX	
Net cash provided (used) by operating activities		XXX
Cash flows from investing activities		
(List of individual inflows and outflows)	XX	
Net cash provided (used) by investing activities		XXX
Cash flows from financing activities		
(List of individual inflows and outflows)	XX	
Net cash provided (used) by financing activities		XXX
Net increase (decrease) in cash		XXX
Cash at beginning of period		XXX
Cash at end of period		XXX
Noncash investing and financing activities		
(List of individual noncash transactions)		XXX

Illustration 12-2
Format of statement of cash flows

The cash flows from operating activities section always appears first, followed by the investing activities section and then the financing activities section.

BEFORE YOU GO ON . . .

▶ Review It

1. Why is the statement of cash flows useful?
2. What are the major classifications of cash flows on the statement of cash flows?
3. What are some examples of significant noncash activities?
4. What is the general format of the statement of cash flows? In what sequence are the three types of business activities presented?

▶ Do It

During its first week, Duffy & Stevenson Company had these transactions.

1. Issued 100,000 shares of $5 par value common stock for $800,000 cash.
2. Borrowed $200,000 from Castle Bank, signing a 5-year note bearing 8% interest.
3. Purchased two semi-trailer trucks for $170,000 cash.
4. Paid employees $12,000 for salaries and wages.
5. Collected $20,000 cash for services provided.

Classify each of these transactions by type of cash flow activity.

Action Plan

• Identify the three types of activities used to report all cash inflows and outflows.
• Report as operating activities the cash effects of transactions that create revenues and expenses and enter into the determination of net income.
• Report as investing activities transactions that (a) acquire and dispose of investments and productive long-lived assets and (b) lend money and collect loans.
• Report as financing activities transactions that (a) obtain cash from issuing debt and repay the amounts borrowed and (b) obtain cash from stockholders and pay them dividends.

Solution

1. Financing activity
2. Financing activity
3. Investing activity
4. Operating activity
5. Operating activity

THE CORPORATE LIFE CYCLE

All products go through a series of phases called the **product life cycle**. The phases (in order of their occurrence) are: **introductory phase**, **growth phase**, **maturity phase**, and **decline phase**. The introductory phase occurs at the beginning of a company's life, when it is purchasing fixed assets and beginning to produce and sell products. During the growth phase, the company is striving to expand its production and sales. In the maturity phase, sales and production level off. During the decline phase, sales of the product fall due to a weakening in consumer demand.

If a company had only one product and that product was nearing the end of its salable life, we could easily say that the company was in the decline phase. Companies generally have more than one product, however, and not all of a company's products are in the same phase of the product life cycle at the same time. Still, we can characterize a company as being in one of the four phases, because the majority of its products are in a particular phase.

Illustration 12-3 shows that the phase a company is in affects its cash flows. In the **introductory phase**, we expect that the company will not be generating positive cash from operations. That is, cash used in operations will exceed cash generated by operations in the introductory phase. Also, the company will be spending considerable amounts to purchase productive assets such as buildings and equipment. To support its asset purchases the company will have to issue stock or debt. Thus, during the introductory phase we expect cash from operations to be negative, cash from investing to be negative, and cash from financing to be positive.

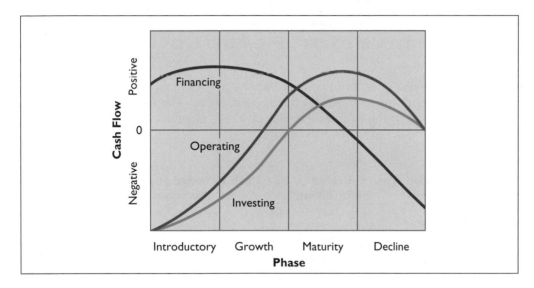

Illustration 12-3
Impact of product life
cycle on cash flows

During the **growth phase**, we expect to see the company start to generate small amounts of cash from operations. During this phase, cash from operations on the statement of cash flows will be less than net income on the income statement. One reason income will exceed cash flow from operations during this period is explained by the difference between the cash paid for inventory and the amount expensed as cost of goods sold. Since the company projects increasing sales, the size of inventory purchases must increase. Thus, in the growth phase the company will expense less inventory on an accrual basis than it purchases on a cash basis. Also, collections on accounts receivable will lag behind sales, and accrual sales during a period will exceed cash collections during that period. Cash needed for asset acquisitions will continue to exceed cash provided by operations, requiring that the company make up the deficiency by issuing new stock or debt. Thus, in the growth phase, the company continues to show negative cash from investing and positive cash from financing.

During the **maturity phase**, cash from operations and net income are approximately the same. Cash generated from operations exceeds investing needs. Thus, in the maturity phase the company can actually start to pay dividends, retire debt, or buy back stock.

Finally, during the **decline phase**, cash from operations decreases. Cash from investing might actually become positive as the company sells off excess assets. Cash from financing may be negative as the company buys back stock and retires debt.

Consider Microsoft: During its early years it had significant product development costs and little revenue. Microsoft was lucky in that its agreement with IBM to provide the operating system for IBM PCs gave it an early steady source of cash to support growth. As noted in the Feature Story, one way Microsoft conserved cash was to pay employees with stock options rather than cash. Today Microsoft could best be characterized as being in the maturity phase. It continues to spend considerable amounts on research and development and investment in new assets. For the last three years, though its cash from operations has exceeded its net income. Also, cash from operations over this period exceeded cash used for investing, and common stock repurchased exceeded common stock issued. For Microsoft, as for any large company, the challenge is to maintain its growth. In the software industry, where products become obsolete very quickly, the challenge is particularly great.

Business Insight
Investor Perspective

Listed here are recent amounts of net income and cash from operations, investing, and financing for some well-known companies. The final column suggests their likely phase in the life cycle based on these figures.

Company ($ in millions)	Net Income	Cash Provided by Operations	Cash Provided (Used) by Investing	Cash Provided (Used) by Financing	Likely Phase in Life Cycle
Amazon.com	$ 588	$ 567	$ (318)	$ (97)	Growth
Real Networks Inc.	(21)	(9)	(22)	107	Introductory
United States Steel	1,091	1,400	(484)	(203)	Early decline
Kellogg	891	1,229	(270)	(716)	Early decline
Southwest Airlines	313	1,157	(1,850)	133	Early maturity
Starbucks	391	820	(659)	(67)	Late growth

 Why do companies have negative cash from operations during the introductory phase?

PREPARING THE STATEMENT OF CASH FLOWS

Companies prepare the statement of cash flows differently from the three other basic financial statements. First, it is not prepared from an adjusted trial balance. It requires detailed information concerning the changes in account balances that occurred between two points in time. An adjusted trial balance will not provide the necessary data. Second, the statement of cash flows deals with cash receipts and payments. As a result, the company **must adjust** the effects of the use of accrual accounting **to determine cash flows**.

The information to prepare this statement usually comes from three sources:

- **Comparative balance sheets.** Information in the comparative balance sheets indicates the amount of the changes in assets, liabilities, and stockholders' equities from the beginning to the end of the period.
- **Current income statement.** Information in this statement helps determine the amount of cash provided or used by operations during the period.

- **Additional information.** Such information includes transaction data that are needed to determine how cash was provided or used during the period.

Preparing the statement of cash flows from these data sources involves three major steps, explained in Illustration 12-4 below.

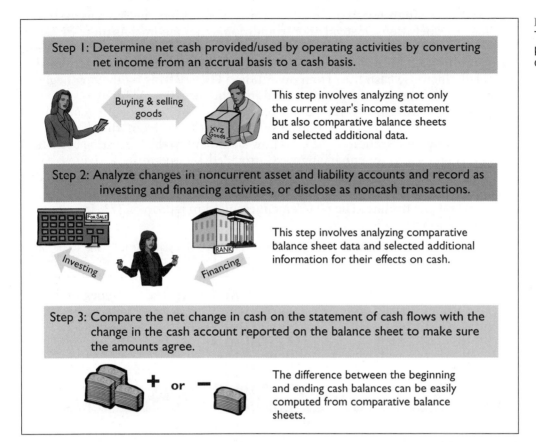

Step 1: Determine net cash provided/used by operating activities by converting net income from an accrual basis to a cash basis.

Buying & selling goods

This step involves analyzing not only the current year's income statement but also comparative balance sheets and selected additional data.

Step 2: Analyze changes in noncurrent asset and liability accounts and record as investing and financing activities, or disclose as noncash transactions.

Investing   Financing

This step involves analyzing comparative balance sheet data and selected additional information for their effects on cash.

Step 3: Compare the net change in cash on the statement of cash flows with the change in the cash account reported on the balance sheet to make sure the amounts agree.

+ or −

The difference between the beginning and ending cash balances can be easily computed from comparative balance sheets.

Illustration 12-4
Three major steps in preparing the statement of cash flows

INDIRECT AND DIRECT METHODS

In order to perform step 1, a company **must convert net income from an accrual basis to a cash basis**. This conversion may be done by either of two methods: (1) the indirect method or (2) the direct method. **Both methods arrive at the same total amount** for "Net cash provided by operating activities." They differ in **how** they arrive at the amount.

The indirect method adjusts net income for items that do not affect cash. A great majority of companies (98.8%) use this method, as shown in the nearby chart.[1] Companies favor the indirect method for two reasons: (1) It is easier and less costly to prepare, and (2) it focuses on the differences between net income and net cash flow from operating activities.

The direct method shows operating cash receipts and payments, making it more consistent with the objective of a statement of cash flows. The FASB has expressed a preference for the direct method, but allows the use of either method.

The next section illustrates the more popular indirect method. The appendix to this chapter illustrates the direct method.

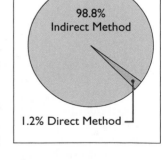

Usage of Methods

98.8% Indirect Method

1.2% Direct Method

[1]*Accounting Trends and Techniques—2004* (New York: American Institute of Certified Public Accountants, 2004).

Business Insight
Investor Perspective

Analysts increasingly use cash-flow-based measures of income, such as cash flow provided by operations, instead of or in addition to net income. As more investors focus on cash flow from operations, and as some compensation contracts now have bonuses tied to cash-flow numbers, some managers have taken actions that artificially increase cash flow from operations. They do this by moving negative amounts out of the operating section and into the investing or financing section. For example, WorldCom, Inc. disclosed that it had improperly capitalized expenses: It had moved $3.8 billion of cash outflows from the "Cash from operating activities" section of the cash flow statement to the "Investing activities" section, thereby greatly enhancing cash provided by operating activities. Similarly, Dynegy, Inc. restated its cash flow statement because it had improperly included in operating activities, instead of in financing activities, $300 million from natural gas trading. The restatement resulted in a drop of 37% in cash flow from operations.

Source: Henny Sender, "Sadly, These Days Even Cash Flow Isn't Always What It Seems To Be," *Wall Street Journal Online* (May 8, 2002).

 For what reasons might managers at WorldCom and at Dynegy take the actions noted above?

BEFORE YOU GO ON . . .

▶ Review It

1. What are the phases of the product life cycle, and how do they affect the statement of cash flows?
2. Based on its statement of cash flows, in what stage of the product life cycle is Tootsie Roll Industries? The answer to this question appears on page 643.
3. What are the three major steps in preparing a statement of cash flows?
4. What is the primary difference between the indirect and direct approaches to the statement of cash flows? Which method is more commonly used in practice?

STUDY OBJECTIVE
4

Prepare a statement of cash flows using the indirect method.

Preparation of the Statement of Cash Flows—Indirect Method

To explain how to prepare a statement of cash flows using the indirect method, we use financial information from Computer Services Company. Illustration 12-5 (page 595) presents Computer Services' current and previous-year balance sheets, its current-year income statement, and related financial information.

COMPUTER SERVICES COMPANY
Comparative Balance Sheets
December 31

Assets	2007	2006	Change in Account Balance Increase/Decrease
Current assets			
Cash	$ 55,000	$ 33,000	$ 22,000 Increase
Accounts receivable	20,000	30,000	10,000 Decrease
Merchandise inventory	15,000	10,000	5,000 Increase
Prepaid expenses	5,000	1,000	4,000 Increase
Property, plant, and equipment			
Land	130,000	20,000	110,000 Increase
Building	160,000	40,000	120,000 Increase
Accumulated depreciation—building	(11,000)	(5,000)	6,000 Increase
Equipment	27,000	10,000	17,000 Increase
Accumulated depreciation—equipment	(3,000)	(1,000)	2,000 Increase
Total assets	$398,000	$138,000	
Liabilities and Stockholders' Equity			
Current liabilities			
Accounts payable	$ 28,000	$ 12,000	$ 16,000 Increase
Income tax payable	6,000	8,000	2,000 Decrease
Long-term liabilities			
Bonds payable	130,000	20,000	110,000 Increase
Stockholders' equity			
Common stock	70,000	50,000	20,000 Increase
Retained earnings	164,000	48,000	116,000 Increase
Total liabilities and stockholders' equity	$398,000	$138,000	

Illustration 12-5
Comparative balance sheets, income statement, and additional information for Computer Services Company

COMPUTER SERVICES COMPANY
Income Statement
For the Year Ended December 31, 2007

Revenues		$507,000
Cost of goods sold	$150,000	
Operating expenses (excluding depreciation)	111,000	
Depreciation expense	9,000	
Loss on sale of equipment	3,000	
Interest expense	42,000	315,000
Income before income tax		192,000
Income tax expense		47,000
Net income		$145,000

Additional information for 2007:
1. The company declared and paid a $29,000 cash dividend.
2. Issued $110,000 of long-term bonds in direct exchange for land.
3. A building costing $120,000 was purchased for cash. Equipment costing $25,000 was also purchased for cash.
4. The company sold equipment with a book value of $7,000 (cost $8,000, less accumulated depreciation $1,000) for $4,000 cash.
5. Issued common stock for $20,000 cash.
6. Depreciation expense was comprised of $6,000 for building and $3,000 for equipment.

We will now apply the three steps to the information provided for Computer Services Company.

STEP 1: OPERATING ACTIVITIES

DETERMINE NET CASH PROVIDED/USED BY OPERATING ACTIVITIES BY CONVERTING NET INCOME FROM AN ACCRUAL BASIS TO A CASH BASIS

To determine net cash provided by operating activities under the indirect method, companies **adjust net income in numerous ways**. A useful starting point is to understand **why** net income must be converted to net cash provided by operating activities.

Under generally accepted accounting principles, most companies use the accrual basis of accounting. As you have learned, this basis requires that companies record revenue when earned and record expenses when incurred. Earned revenues may include credit sales for which the company has not yet collected cash. Expenses incurred may include some items that it has not yet paid in cash. Thus, under the accrual basis of accounting, net income is not the same as net cash provided by operating activities.

Therefore, under the **indirect method**, companies must adjust net income to convert certain items to the cash basis. The indirect method (or reconciliation method) starts with net income and converts it to net cash provided by operating activities. Illustration 12-6 lists the three types of adjustments.

Illustration 12-6
Three types of adjustments to convert net income to net cash provided by operating activities

Net Income +/−	Adjustments	=	Net Cash Provided/ Used by Operating Activities
	• **Add back noncash expenses**, such as depreciation expense, amortization, or depletion. • **Deduct gains and add losses** that resulted from investing and financing activities. • **Analyze changes** to noncash current asset and current liability accounts.		

We explain the three types of adjustments in the next three sections.

Depreciation Expense

Helpful Hint Depreciation is similar to any other expense in that it reduces net income. It differs in that it does not involve a current cash outflow; that is why it must be *added back* to net income to arrive at cash provided by operations.

Computer Services' income statement reports depreciation expense of $9,000. Although depreciation expense reduces net income, it does not reduce cash. In other words, depreciation expense is a noncash charge. The company must add it back to net income to arrive at net cash provided by operating activities. Computer Services reports depreciation expense as follows in the statement of cash flows.

Illustration 12-7
Adjustment for depreciation

Cash flows from operating activities	
Net income	$145,000
Adjustments to reconcile net income to net cash provided by operating activities:	
Depreciation expense	**9,000**
Net cash provided by operating activities	$154,000

As the first adjustment to net income in the statement of cash flows, companies frequently list depreciation and similar noncash charges such as amortization of intangible assets, depletion expense, and bad debt expense.

Loss on Sale of Equipment

Illustration 12-1 states that the investing activities section should report cash received from the sale of plant assets. Because of this, **companies must eliminate from net income all gains and losses, to arrive at cash provided by operating activities**.

In our example, Computer Services' income statement reports a $3,000 loss on the sale of equipment (book value $7,000, less cash received from sale of equipment $4,000). The company's loss of $3,000 should not be included in the operating activities section of the statement of cash flows. Illustration 12-8 shows that the $3,000 loss is eliminated by adding $3,000 back to net income to arrive at net cash provided by operating activities.

Cash flows from operating activities			
Net income			$145,000
Adjustments to reconcile net income to net cash provided by operating activities:			
Depreciation expense		$9,000	
Loss on sale of equipment		3,000	12,000
Net cash provided by operating activities			$157,000

Illustration 12-8
Adjustment for loss on sale of equipment

If a gain on sale occurs, the company deducts the gain from its net income in order to determine net cash provided by operating activities. **In the case of either a gain or a loss, companies report as a source of cash in the investing activities section of the statement of cash flows the actual amount of cash received from the sale.**

Changes to Noncash Current Asset and Current Liability Accounts

A final adjustment in reconciling net income to net cash provided by operating activities involves examining all changes in current asset and current liability accounts. The accrual accounting process records revenues in the period earned and expenses in the period incurred. For example, companies use Accounts Receivable to record amounts owed to the company for sales that have been made but for which cash collections have not yet been received. They use the Prepaid Insurance account to reflect insurance that has been paid for, but which has not yet expired, and therefore has not been expensed. Similarly, the Salaries Payable account reflects salaries expense that has been incurred by the company but has not been paid.

As a result, we need to adjust net income for these accruals and prepayments to determine net cash provided by operating activities. Thus we must analyze the change in each current asset and current liability account to determine its impact on net income and cash.

CHANGES IN NONCASH CURRENT ASSETS.   The adjustments required for changes in noncash current asset accounts are as follows: **Deduct from net income increases in current asset accounts, and add to net income decreases in current asset accounts, to arrive at net cash provided by operating activities.** We can observe these relationships by analyzing the accounts of Computer Services Company.

DECREASE IN ACCOUNTS RECEIVABLE. Computer Services Company's accounts receivable decreased by $10,000 (from $30,000 to $20,000) during the period. For Computer Services this means that cash receipts were $10,000 higher than revenues. The Accounts Receivable account in Illustration 12-9 shows that Computer Services Company had $507,000 in revenues (as reported on the income statement), but it collected $517,000 in cash. As shown in Illustration 12-10, to adjust net income to net cash provided by operating activities, the company adds to net income the decrease of $10,000 in accounts receivable.

Illustration 12-9
Analysis of accounts receivable

Accounts Receivable

1/1/07	Balance	30,000	**Receipts from customers**	**517,000**
	Revenues	**507,000**		
12/31/07	Balance	20,000		

When the Accounts Receivable balance increases, cash receipts are lower than revenue earned under the accrual basis. Therefore, the company deducts from net income the amount of the increase in accounts receivable, to arrive at net cash provided by operating activities.

INCREASE IN MERCHANDISE INVENTORY. Computer Services' Company's Merchandise Inventory balance increased $5,000 (from $10,000 to $15,000) during the period. The change in the Merchandise Inventory account reflects the difference between the amount of inventory purchased and the amount sold. For Computer Services this means that the cost of merchandise purchased exceeded the cost of goods sold by $5,000. As a result, cost of goods sold does not reflect $5,000 of cash payments made for merchandise. The company deducts from net income this inventory increase of $5,000 during the period, to arrive at net cash provided by operating activities (see Illustration 12-10). If inventory decreases, the company adds to net income the amount of the change, to arrive at net cash provided by operating activities.

INCREASE IN PREPAID EXPENSES. Computer Services' prepaid expenses increased during the period by $4,000. This means that cash paid for expenses is higher than expenses reported on an accrual basis. In other words, the company has made cash payments in the current period, but will not charge expenses to income until future periods (as charges to the income statement). To adjust net income to net cash provided by operating activities, the company deducts from net income the $4,000 increase in prepaid expenses (see Illustration 12-10).

Illustration 12-10
Adjustments for changes in current asset accounts

Cash flows from operating activities		
Net income		$145,000
Adjustments to reconcile net income to net cash provided by operating activities:		
Depreciation expense	$ 9,000	
Loss on sale of equipment	3,000	
Decrease in accounts receivable	**10,000**	
Increase in merchandise inventory	**(5,000)**	
Increase in prepaid expenses	**(4,000)**	13,000
Net cash provided by operating activities		$158,000

If prepaid expenses decrease, reported expenses are higher than the expenses paid. Therefore, the company adds to net income the decrease in prepaid expense, to arrive at net cash provided by operating activities.

CHANGES IN CURRENT LIABILITIES.   The adjustments required for changes in current liability accounts are as follows: **Add to net income increases in current liability accounts, and deduct from net income decreases in current liability accounts, to arrive at net cash provided by operating activities.**

INCREASE IN ACCOUNTS PAYABLE.   For Computer Services Company, Accounts Payable increased by $16,000 (from $12,000 to $28,000) during the period. That means the company received $16,000 more in goods than it actually paid for. As shown in Illustration 12-11 (below), to adjust net income to determine net cash provided by operating activities, the company adds to net income the $16,000 increase in Accounts Payable.

DECREASE IN INCOME TAXES PAYABLE.   When a company incurs income tax expense but has not yet paid its taxes, it records income tax payable. A change in the Income Tax Payable account reflects the difference between income tax expense incurred and income tax actually paid. Computer Services' Income Tax Payable account decreased by $2,000. That means the $47,000 of income tax expense reported on the income statement was $2,000 less than the amount of taxes paid during the period of $49,000. As shown in Illustration 12-11, to adjust net income to a cash basis, the company must reduce net income by $2,000.

Cash flows from operating activities			
Net income			$145,000
Adjustments to reconcile net income to net cash			
provided by operating activities:			
Depreciation expense		$ 9,000	
Loss on sale of equipment		3,000	
Decrease in accounts receivable		10,000	
Increase in merchandise inventory		(5,000)	
Increase in prepaid expenses		(4,000)	
Increase in accounts payable		**16,000**	
Decrease in income tax payable		**(2,000)**	27,000
Net cash provided by operating activities			$172,000

Illustration 12-11
Adjustments for changes
in current liability accounts

Illustration 12-11 shows that, after starting with net income of $145,000, the sum of all of the adjustments to net income was $27,000. This resulted in net cash provided by operating activities of $172,000.

SUMMARY OF CONVERSION TO NET CASH PROVIDED BY OPERATING ACTIVITIES—INDIRECT METHOD

As shown in the previous illustrations, the statement of cash flows prepared by the indirect method starts with net income. It then adds or deducts items to arrive at net cash provided by operating activities. The required adjustments are of three types:

1. Noncash charges such as depreciation, amortization, and depletion.
2. Gains and losses on the sale of plant assets.
3. Changes in noncash current asset and current liability accounts.

Illustration 12-12 (page 600) provides a summary of these changes.

Illustration 12-12
Adjustments required to convert net income to net cash provided by operating activities

		Adjustment Required to Convert Net Income to Net Cash Provided by Operating Activities
Noncash charges	Depreciation expense	Add
	Patent amortization expense	Add
	Depletion expense	Add
Gains and losses	Loss on sale of plant asset	Add
	Gain on sale of plant asset	Deduct
Changes in current assets and current liabilities	Increase in current asset account	Deduct
	Decrease in current asset account	Add
	Increase in current liability account	Add
	Decrease in current liability account	Deduct

Accounting across the Organization

Market share matters—and it shows up in the accounting numbers. Just ask General Motors (GM). In recent years GM has seen its market share erode until, at 25.6% of the market, the company reached the point where it actually consumes more cash than it generates. It isn't time to panic yet—GM has about $20 billion in cash on hand—but it is time to come up with a plan.

To address immediate cash needs, GM management may be forced to quit paying its $1.1 billion annual dividend, and it may sell off some assets and businesses. But in the long term, GM must either increase its market share or shrink its operations to fit its sales figures. The following table shows net income and cash provided by operating activities at various market-share levels.

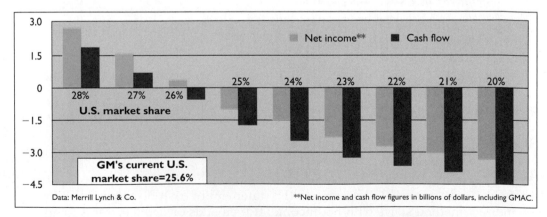

* Assumes overall North American car sales hold steady at a 16.9 million vehicle annual rate.

Source: David Welch and Dan Beucke, "Why GM's Plan Won't Work," *Business Week* (May 9, 2005), pp. 85–93.

 Why does GM's cash provided by operating activities drop so precipitously when the company's sales figures decline?

STEP 2: INVESTING AND FINANCING ACTIVITIES

ANALYZE CHANGES IN NONCURRENT ASSET AND LIABILITY ACCOUNTS AND RECORD AS INVESTING AND FINANCING ACTIVITIES, OR AS NONCASH INVESTING AND FINANCING ACTIVITIES

INCREASE IN LAND. As indicated from the change in the Land account and the additional information, the company purchased land of $110,000 through the issuance of long-term bonds. The issuance of bonds payable for land has no effect on cash. But it is a significant noncash investing and financing activity that merits disclosure in a separate schedule. (See Illustration 12–14 on next page.)

INCREASE IN BUILDING. As the additional data indicate, Computer Services Company acquired an office building for $120,000 cash. This is a cash outflow reported in the investing section. (See Illustration 12–14 on next page.)

INCREASE IN EQUIPMENT. The Equipment account increased $17,000. The additional information explains that this was a net increase that resulted from two transactions: (1) a purchase of equipment of $25,000, and (2) the sale for $4,000 of equipment costing $8,000. These transactions are investing activities. The company should report each transaction separately. Thus it reports the purchase of equipment as an outflow of cash for $25,000. It reports the sale as an inflow of cash for $4,000. The T account below shows the reasons for the change in this account during the year.

> **Helpful Hint** The investing and financing activities are measured and reported the same under both the direct and indirect methods.

Equipment			
1/1/07 Balance	10,000	Cost of equipment sold	8,000
Purchase of equipment	**25,000**		
12/31/07 Balance	27,000		

Illustration 12-13
Analysis of equipment

The following entry shows the details of the equipment sale transaction.

Cash	4,000	
Accumulated Depreciation	1,000	
Loss on Sale of Equipment	3,000	
Equipment		8,000

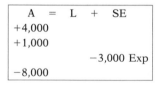

Cash Flows
+4,000

A	=	L	+	SE
+4,000				
+1,000				
				−3,000 Exp
−8,000				

INCREASE IN BONDS PAYABLE. The Bonds Payable account increased $110,000. As indicated in the additional information, the company acquired land from the issuance of these bonds. It reports this noncash transaction in a separate schedule at the bottom of the statement.

INCREASE IN COMMON STOCK. The balance sheet reports an increase in Common Stock of $20,000. The additional information section notes that this increase resulted from the issuance of new shares of stock. This is a cash inflow reported in the financing section.

> **Helpful Hint** When companies issue stocks or bonds for cash, the actual proceeds will appear in the statement of cash flows as a financing inflow (rather than the par value of the stocks or face value of bonds).

INCREASE IN RETAINED EARNINGS. Retained earnings increased $116,000 during the year. This increase can be explained by two factors: (1) Net income of $145,000 increased retained earnings. (2) Dividends of $29,000 decreased retained earnings. The company adjusts net income to net cash provided by operating activities in the operating activities section. Payment of the dividends (not the declaration) is a **cash outflow that the company reports as a financing activity**.

Statement of Cash Flows—2007

Using the previous information, we can now prepare a statement of cash flows for 2007 for Computer Services Company as shown in Illustration 12-14.

Illustration 12-14
Statement of cash flows, 2007—indirect method

Helpful Hint Note that in the investing and financing activities sections, positive numbers indicate cash inflows (receipts), and negative numbers indicate cash outflows (payments).

COMPUTER SERVICES COMPANY		
Statement of Cash Flows—Indirect Method		
For the Year Ended December 31, 2007		
Cash flows from operating activities		
Net income		$ 145,000
Adjustments to reconcile net income to net cash		
provided by operating activities:		
Depreciation expense	$ 9,000	
Loss on sale of equipment	3,000	
Decrease in accounts receivable	10,000	
Increase in merchandise inventory	(5,000)	
Increase in prepaid expenses	(4,000)	
Increase in accounts payable	16,000	
Decrease in income tax payable	(2,000)	27,000
Net cash provided by operating activities		172,000
Cash flows from investing activities		
Purchase of building	(120,000)	
Purchase of equipment	(25,000)	
Sale of equipment	4,000	
Net cash used by investing activities		(141,000)
Cash flows from financing activities		
Issuance of common stock	20,000	
Payment of cash dividends	(29,000)	
Net cash used by financing activities		(9,000)
Net increase in cash		22,000
Cash at beginning of period		33,000
Cash at end of period		$ 55,000
Noncash investing and financing activities		
Issuance of bonds payable to purchase land		$ 110,000

STEP 3: NET CHANGE IN CASH

COMPARE THE NET CHANGE IN CASH ON THE STATEMENT OF CASH FLOWS WITH THE CHANGE IN THE CASH ACCOUNT REPORTED ON THE BALANCE SHEET TO MAKE SURE THE AMOUNTS AGREE

Illustration 12-14 indicates that the net change in cash during the period was an increase of $22,000. This agrees with the change in Cash account reported on the balance sheet in Illustration 12-5 (page 595).

BEFORE YOU GO ON . . .

▶ **Review It**

1. What is the format of the operating activities section of the statement of cash flows using the indirect method?
2. Where is depreciation expense shown on a statement of cash flows using the indirect method?
3. Where are significant noncash investing and financing activities shown in a statement of cash flows? Give some examples.

▶ **Do It**

Presented below is information related to Reynolds Company. Use it to prepare a statement of cash flows using the indirect method.

REYNOLDS COMPANY
Comparative Balance Sheets
December 31

Assets	2007	2006	Change Increase/Decrease
Cash	$ 54,000	$ 37,000	$ 17,000 Increase
Accounts receivable	68,000	26,000	42,000 Increase
Inventories	54,000	–0–	54,000 Increase
Prepaid expenses	4,000	6,000	2,000 Decrease
Land	45,000	70,000	25,000 Decrease
Buildings	200,000	200,000	–0–
Accumulated depreciation—buildings	(21,000)	(11,000)	10,000 Increase
Equipment	193,000	68,000	125,000 Increase
Accumulated depreciation—equipment	(28,000)	(10,000)	18,000 Increase
Totals	$569,000	$386,000	

Liabilities and Stockholders' Equity			
Accounts payable	$ 23,000	$ 40,000	$ 17,000 Decrease
Accrued expenses payable	10,000	–0–	10,000 Increase
Bonds payable	110,000	150,000	40,000 Decrease
Common stock ($1 par)	220,000	60,000	160,000 Increase
Retained earnings	206,000	136,000	70,000 Increase
Totals	$569,000	$386,000	

REYNOLDS COMPANY
Income Statement
For the Year Ended December 31, 2007

Revenues		$890,000
Cost of goods sold	$465,000	
Operating expenses	221,000	
Interest expense	12,000	
Loss on sale of equipment	2,000	700,000
Income before income taxes		190,000
Income tax expense		65,000
Net income		$125,000

Additional information:
1. Operating expenses include depreciation expense of $33,000 and charges from prepaid expenses of $2,000.
2. Land was sold at its book value for cash.
3. Cash dividends of $55,000 were declared and paid in 2007.
4. Interest expense of $12,000 was paid in cash.
5. Equipment with a cost of $166,000 was purchased for cash. Equipment with a cost of $41,000 and a book value of $36,000 was sold for $34,000 cash.
6. Bonds of $10,000 were redeemed at their book value for cash. Bonds of $30,000 were converted into common stock.
7. Common stock ($1 par) of $130,000 was issued for cash.
8. Accounts payable pertain to merchandise suppliers.

Action Plan

- Determine net cash provided/used by operating activities by adjusting net income for items that did not affect cash.
- Determine net cash provided/used by investing activities and financing activities.
- Determine the net increase/decrease in cash.

Solution

REYNOLDS COMPANY Statement of Cash Flows—Indirect Method For the Year Ended December 31, 2007		
Cash flows from operating activities		
Net income		$ 125,000
Adjustments to reconcile net income to net cash provided by operating activities:		
Depreciation expense	$ 33,000	
Loss on sale of equipment	2,000	
Increase in accounts receivable	(42,000)	
Increase in inventories	(54,000)	
Decrease in prepaid expenses	2,000	
Decrease in accounts payable	(17,000)	
Increase in accrued expenses payable	10,000	(66,000)
Net cash provided by operating activities		59,000
Cash flows from investing activities		
Sale of land	25,000	
Sale of equipment	34,000	
Purchase of equipment	(166,000)	
Net cash used by investing activities		(107,000)
Cash flows from financing activities		
Redemption of bonds	(10,000)	
Sale of common stock	130,000	
Payment of dividends	(55,000)	
Net cash provided by financing activities		65,000
Net increase in cash		17,000
Cash at beginning of period		37,000
Cash at end of period		$ 54,000
Noncash investing and financing activities		
Conversion of bonds into common stock		$ 30,000

Using Cash Flows to Evaluate a Company

Traditionally, investors and creditors have most commonly used ratios based on accrual accounting. These days, cash-based ratios are gaining increased acceptance among analysts. In this section we review free cash flow and introduce two new measures.

FREE CASH FLOW

In the statement of cash flows, cash provided by operating activities is intended to indicate the cash-generating capability of the company. Analysts have noted, however, that **cash provided by operating activities fails to take into account that a company must invest in new fixed assets** just to maintain its current level of operations. Companies also must at least **maintain dividends at current**

levels to satisfy investors. As we discussed in Chapter 2, the measurement of free cash flow provides additional insight regarding a company's cash-generating ability. **Free cash flow** describes the cash remaining from operations after adjustment for capital expenditures and dividends.

Consider the following example: Suppose that MPC produced and sold 10,000 personal computers this year. It reported $100,000 cash provided by operating activities. In order to maintain production at 10,000 computers, MPC invested $15,000 in equipment. It chose to pay $5,000 in dividends. Its free cash flow was $80,000 ($100,000 − $15,000 − $5,000). The company could use this $80,000 either to purchase new assets to expand the business or to pay an $80,000 dividend and continue to produce 10,000 computers. In practice, free cash flow is often calculated with the formula in Illustration 12-15. Alternative definitions also exist.

Free Cash Flow	=	Cash Provided by Operations	−	Capital Expenditures	−	Cash Dividends

Illustration 12-15 Free cash flow

Illustration 12-16 provides basic information excerpted from the 2004 statement of cash flows of Microsoft Corporation.

MICROSOFT CORPORATION Statement of Cash Flows (partial) 2004		
Cash provided by operations		$14,626
Cash flows from investing activities		
Additions to property and equipment	$ (1,109)	
Purchases of investments	(92,495)	
Sales of investments	85,302	
Acquisitions of companies	(4)	
Maturities of investments	5,561	
Cash used by investing activities		(2,745)
Cash paid for dividends		(1,729)

Illustration 12-16 Microsoft cash flow information ($ in millions)

Microsoft's free cash flow is calculated as shown in Illustration 12-17.

Cash provided by operating activities	$14,626
Less: Expenditures on property, plant, and equipment	1,109
Dividends paid	1,729
Free cash flow	$11,788

Illustration 12-17 Calculation of Microsoft's free cash flow ($ in millions)

This is a tremendous amount of cash generated in a single year. It is available for the acquisition of new assets, the retirement of stock or debt, or the payment of dividends. Also note that this amount far exceeds Microsoft's 2004 net income of $8,168 million. This lends additional credibility to Microsoft's income number as an indicator of potential future performance. If anything, Microsoft's net income might understate its actual performance.

Oracle Corporation is one of the world's largest sellers of database software and information management services. Like Microsoft, its success depends on continuing to improve its existing products while developing new products to keep pace with rapid changes in technology. Oracle's free cash flow for 2004 was $2,988 million. This is impressive, but significantly less than Microsoft's amazing ability to generate cash.

Decision Toolkit

Decision Checkpoints	Info Needed for Decision	Tool to Use for Decision	How to Evaluate Results
How much cash did the company generate to either expand operations or pay dividends?	Cash provided by operating activities, cash spent on fixed assets, and cash dividends	Free cash flow = Cash provided by operations − Capital expenditures − Cash dividends	Significant free cash flow indicates greater potential to finance new investment and pay additional dividends.

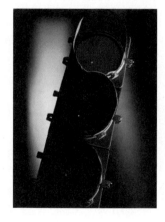

Business Insight
Investor Perspective

Investors and analysts are placing increasing emphasis on the statement of cash flows. As one person put it, "If you really want to put the quality of a company's earnings to the test, you need to examine the cash flow statement, too."

Here are some tips from the pros. David Zion, a Bear Stearns accounting analyst, says that you should compare net income with net cash flow from operating activities: "Generally, the closer a ratio of these numbers is to one, the higher-quality the earnings." Howard Schilit, of the Center for Financial Research and Analysis, says to compare the growth rate of net income with the growth rate of cash from operating activities. He says that if the two normally increase at similar rates, but now cash suddenly lags, "it's a terrific early warning sign."

Source: Anne Tergesen, "The Ins and Outs of Cash Flow," *Business Week* (January 22, 2001), pp. 102–103.

 If the ratio of net income to cash from operations differs significantly from 1, does that always mean that a company has poor-quality earnings?

ASSESSING LIQUIDITY AND SOLVENCY USING CASH FLOWS

Previous chapters have presented ratios used to analyze a company's liquidity and solvency. Many of those ratios used accrual-based numbers from the income statement and balance sheet. In this section we focus on ratios that are *cash-based* rather than accrual-based. That is, instead of using numbers from the income statement, these ratios use numbers from the statement of cash flows.

As discussed earlier, many analysts are critical of accrual-based numbers because they feel that the adjustment process allows too much management discretion. These analysts like to supplement accrual-based analysis with measures that use the cash flow statement. One disadvantage of these cash-based measures is that, unlike the more commonly employed accrual-based measures, there are no readily available industry averages for comparison. In the following discussion we use cash flow-based ratios to analyze Microsoft. In addition to the cash flow information provided in Illustration 12-16, we need the following information related to Microsoft.

($ in millions)	2004	2003
Current liabilities	$14,969	$13,974
Total liabilities	17,564	16,820

Liquidity

Liquidity is the ability of a business to meet its immediate obligations. You learned (in Chapter 2) that one measure of liquidity is the *current ratio*: current assets divided by current liabilities. A disadvantage of the current ratio is that it uses year-end balances of current asset and current liability accounts. These year-end balances may not be representative of the company's position during most of the year.

A ratio that partially corrects this problem is the **current cash debt coverage ratio**. It is computed as cash provided by operating activities divided by average current liabilities. Because cash provided by operating activities involves the entire year rather than a balance at one point in time, this ratio is often considered a better representation of liquidity on the average day. In general, a value below .40 times is cause for additional investigation of a company's liquidity.

Illustration 12-18 shows the current cash debt coverage ratio for Microsoft, with comparative numbers for Oracle. For comparative purposes, we have also provided each company's current ratio.

Illustration 12-18 Current cash debt coverage ratio

$$\text{Current Cash Debt Coverage Ratio} = \frac{\text{Cash Provided by Operations}}{\text{Average Current Liabilities}}$$

	Current cash debt coverage ratio	Current ratio
Microsoft ($ in millions)	$\dfrac{\$14,626}{(\$14,969 + \$13,974)/2} = 1.01$ times	4.71:1
Oracle	.75 times	2.65:1

Microsoft's net cash provided by operating activities is approximately equal to its average current liabilities. Oracle's ratio of .75 times, though not a cause for concern, is 26% lower than that of Microsoft. Keep in mind that Microsoft's cash position is extraordinary. For example, many large companies now have current ratios in the range of 1.0. By this standard, Oracle's current ratio of 2.65:1 and Microsoft's current ratio of 4.71:1 are both very strong.

Decision Toolkit

Decision Checkpoints	Info Needed for Decision	Tool to Use for Decision	How to Evaluate Results
✔		⚒	👍👎
Is the company generating sufficient cash provided by operating activities to meet its current obligations?	Cash provided by operating activities and average current liabilities	$\text{Current cash debt coverage ratio} = \dfrac{\text{Cash provided by operations}}{\text{Average current liabilities}}$	A high value suggests good liquidity. Since the numerator contains a "flow" measure, it provides a good supplement to the current ratio.

Solvency

Solvency is the ability of a company to survive over the long term. A measure of solvency that uses cash figures is the **cash debt coverage ratio**. It is computed as the ratio of cash provided by operating activities to total debt as represented by average total liabilities. This ratio indicates a company's ability to repay its liabilities from cash generated from operations—that is, without having to liquidate productive assets such as property, plant, and equipment. A general rule of thumb is that a cash debt coverage ratio below .20 times is cause for additional investigation.

Illustration 12-19 shows the cash debt coverage ratios for Microsoft and Oracle for 2004. For comparative purposes, we have also provided the debt to total assets ratios for each company.

Illustration 12-19 Cash debt coverage ratio

$$\text{Cash Debt Coverage Ratio} = \frac{\text{Cash Provided by Operations}}{\text{Average Total Liabilities}}$$

	Cash debt coverage ratio	Debt to total assets ratio
Microsoft ($ in millions)	$\dfrac{\$14,626}{(\$17,564 + \$16,820)/2} = .85$ times	19%
Oracle	.66 times	38%

Microsoft has few long-term obligations. Thus, its cash debt coverage ratio is similar to its current cash debt coverage ratio. Obviously, Microsoft is very solvent. Oracle has some long-term debt with a debt to total assets ratio of 38%. Its cash debt coverage ratio of .66 times is three-fourths as strong as Microsoft's. Neither the cash nor accrual measures suggest any cause for concern for either company.

Decision Toolkit

Decision Checkpoints	Info Needed for Decision	Tool to Use for Decision	How to Evaluate Results
Is the company generating sufficient cash provided by operating activities to meet its long-term obligations?	Cash provided by operating activities and average total liabilities	Cash debt coverage ratio $= \dfrac{\text{Cash provided by operations}}{\text{Average total liabilities}}$	A high value suggests the company is solvent; that is, it will meet its obligations in the long term.

BEFORE YOU GO ON . . .

▶ **Review It**

1. What is the difference between cash from operations and free cash flow?
2. What does it mean if a company has negative free cash flow?
3. Why might an analyst want to supplement accrual-based ratios with cash-based ratios? What are some cash-based ratios?

✓ THE NAVIGATOR

Using the Decision Toolkit

Intel Corporation is the leading producer of computer chips for personal computers. It makes the hugely successful Pentium chip. Its primary competitor is AMD (formerly Advanced Micro Devices). The two are vicious competitors, with frequent lawsuits filed between them. Financial statement data for Intel are provided below.

Instructions
Calculate the following cash-based measures for Intel, and compare them with the data for AMD provided on page 610.

1. Free cash flow.
2. Current cash debt coverage ratio.
3. Cash debt coverage ratio.

INTEL CORPORATION Balance Sheets December 31, 2004 and 2003 (in millions)		
Assets	**2004**	**2003**
Current assets	$24,058	$22,882
Noncurrent assets	24,085	24,261
Total assets	$48,143	$47,143
Liabilities and Stockholders' Equity		
Current liabilities	$ 8,006	$ 6,879
Long-term liabilities	1,558	2,418
Total liabilities	9,564	9,297
Stockholders' equity	38,579	37,846
Total liabilities and stockholders' equity	$48,143	$47,143

INTEL CORPORATION Income Statements For the Years Ended December 31, 2004 and 2003 (in millions)		
	2004	**2003**
Net revenues	$34,209	$ 30,141
Expenses	26,693	24,500
Net income	$ 7,516	$ 5,641

INTEL CORPORATION Statements of Cash Flows For the Years Ended December 31, 2004 and 2003 (in millions)		
	2004	**2003**
Net cash provided by operating activities	$ 13,119	$ 11,515
Net cash used for investing activities	(5,032)	(7,090)
Net cash used for financing activities	(7,651)	(3,858)
Net increase (decrease) in cash and cash equivalents	$ 436	$ 567

Note.   Cash spent on property, plant, and equipment in 2004 was $3,843. Cash paid for dividends was $1,022.

Comparative data for AMD:

1. Free cash flow   −$354 million
2. Current cash debt coverage ratio   .67 times
3. Cash debt coverage ratio   .23 times

Solution

1. Intel's free cash flow is $8,254 million ($13,119 − $3,843 − $1,022). AMD's is actually a negative $354 million. This gives Intel a huge advantage in the ability to move quickly to invest in new projects.
2. The current cash debt coverage ratio for Intel is calculated as follows.

$$\frac{\$13,119}{(\$8,006 + \$6,879)/2} = 1.76 \text{ times}$$

Compared to AMD's value of .67 times, Intel appears to be significantly more liquid.
3. The cash debt coverage ratio for Intel is calculated as follows.

$$\frac{\$13,119}{(\$9,564 + \$9,297)/2} = 1.39 \text{ times}$$

Compared to AMD's value of .23 times, Intel appears to be significantly more solvent.

THE NAVIGATOR

WILEY PLUS

Summary of Study Objectives

1   *Indicate the usefulness of the statement of cash flows.* The statement of cash flows provides information about the cash receipts, cash payments, and net change in cash resulting from the operating, investing, and financing activities of a company during the period.

2 *Distinguish among operating, investing, and financing activities.* Operating activities include the cash effects of transactions that enter into the determination of net income. Investing activities involve cash flows resulting from changes in investments and long-term asset items. Financing activities involve cash flows resulting from changes in long-term liability and stockholders' equity items.

3 *Explain the impact of the product life cycle on a company's cash flows.* During the introductory stage, cash provided by operating activities and cash from investing are negative, and cash from financing is positive. During the growth stage, cash provided by operating activities becomes positive. During the maturity stage, cash provided by operating activities exceeds investing needs, so the company begins to retire debt. During the decline stage, cash provided by operating activities is reduced, cash from investing becomes positive, and cash from financing becomes more negative.

4 *Prepare a statement of cash flows using the indirect method.* The preparation of a statement of cash flows involves three major steps: (1) Determine net cash provided/used by operating activities by converting net income from an accrual basis to a cash basis. (2) Analyze changes in noncurrent asset and liability accounts and record as investing and financing activities, or disclose as noncash transactions. (3) Compare the net change in cash on the statement of cash flows with the change in the cash account reported on the balance sheet to make sure the amounts agree.

5 *Use the statement of cash flows to evaluate a company.* A number of measures can be derived by using information from the statement of cash flows as well as the other required financial statements. Free cash flow indicates the amount of cash a company generated during the current year that is available for the payment of dividends or for expansion. Liquidity can be measured with the current cash debt coverage ratio (cash provided by operating activities divided by average current liabilities). Solvency can be measured by the cash debt coverage ratio (cash provided by operating activities divided by average total liabilities).

THE NAVIGATOR

Decision Toolkit—A Summary

Decision Checkpoints	Info Needed for Decision	Tool to Use for Decision	How to Evaluate Results
How much cash did the company generate to either expand operations or pay dividends?	Cash provided by operating activities, cash spent on fixed assets, and cash dividends	$$\text{Free cash flow} = \text{Cash provided by operations} - \text{Capital expenditures} - \text{Cash dividends}$$	Significant free cash flow indicates greater potential to finance new investment and pay additional dividends.
Is the company generating sufficient cash provided by operating activities to meet its current obligations?	Cash provided by operating activities and average current liabilities	$$\text{Current cash debt coverage ratio} = \frac{\text{Cash provided by operations}}{\text{Average current liabilities}}$$	A high value suggests good liquidity. Since the numerator contains a "flow" measure, it provides a good supplement to the current ratio.
Is the company generating sufficient cash provided by operating activities to meet its long-term obligations?	Cash provided by operating activities and average total liabilities	$$\text{Cash debt coverage ratio} = \frac{\text{Cash provided by operations}}{\text{Average total liabilities}}$$	A high value suggests the company is solvent; that is, it will meet its obligations in the long term.

APPENDIX
STATEMENT OF CASH FLOWS—DIRECT METHOD

STUDY OBJECTIVE

6

Prepare a statement of cash flows using the direct method.

To explain and illustrate the direct method, we will use the transactions of Juarez Company for 2007, to prepare a statement of cash flows. Illustration 12A-1 (page 612) presents information related to 2007 for Juarez Company.

Illustration 12A-1
Comparative balance
sheets, income statement,
and additional information
for Juarez Company

JUAREZ COMPANY
Comparative Balance Sheets
December 31

Assets	2007	2006	Change Increase/Decrease
Cash	$191,000	$159,000	$ 32,000 Increase
Accounts receivable	12,000	15,000	3,000 Decrease
Inventory	170,000	160,000	10,000 Increase
Prepaid expenses	6,000	8,000	2,000 Decrease
Land	140,000	80,000	60,000 Increase
Equipment	160,000	–0–	160,000 Increase
Accumulated depreciation—equipment	(16,000)	–0–	16,000 Increase
Total	$663,000	$422,000	

Liabilities and Stockholders' Equity			
Accounts payable	$ 52,000	$ 60,000	$ 8,000 Decrease
Accrued expenses payable	15,000	20,000	5,000 Decrease
Income taxes payable	12,000	–0–	12,000 Increase
Bonds payable	130,000	–0–	130,000 Increase
Common stock	360,000	300,000	60,000 Increase
Retained earnings	94,000	42,000	52,000 Increase
Total	$663,000	$422,000	

JUAREZ COMPANY
Income Statement
For the Year Ended December 31, 2007

Revenues		$975,000
Cost of goods sold	$660,000	
Operating expenses (excluding depreciation)	176,000	
Depreciation expense	18,000	
Loss on sale of store equipment	1,000	855,000
Income before income taxes		120,000
Income tax expense		36,000
Net income		$ 84,000

Additional information:
1. In 2007, the company declared and paid a $32,000 cash dividend.
2. Bonds were issued at face value for $130,000 in cash.
3. Equipment costing $180,000 was purchased for cash.
4. Equipment costing $20,000 was sold for $17,000 cash when the book value of the equipment was $18,000.
5. Common stock of $60,000 was issued to acquire land.

Preparation of the Statement of Cash Flows—Direct Method

To prepare a statement of cash flows under the direct approach, we will apply the three steps outlined in Illustration 12-4 (page 593).

STEP 1: OPERATING ACTIVITIES

DETERMINE NET CASH PROVIDED/USED BY OPERATING ACTIVITIES BY CONVERTING NET INCOME FROM AN ACCRUAL BASIS TO A CASH BASIS

Under the **direct method**, companies compute net cash provided by operating activities by **adjusting each item in the income statement** from the accrual basis to the cash basis. To simplify and condense the operating activities section, companies **report only major classes of operating cash receipts and cash payments**. For these major classes, the difference between cash receipts and cash payments is the net cash provided by operating activities. These relationships are as shown in Illustration 12A-2.

Illustration 12A-2 Major classes of cash receipts and payments

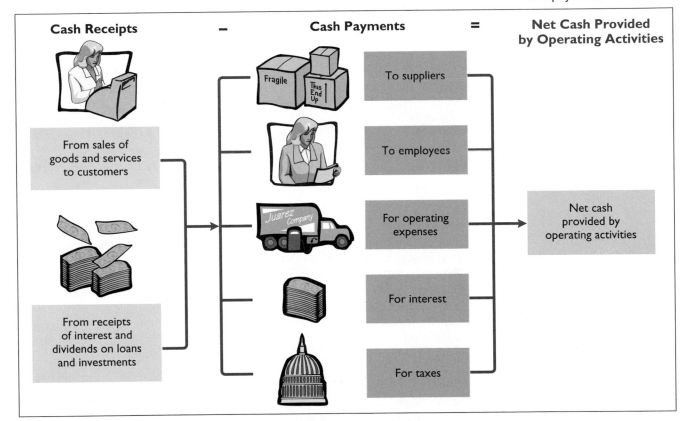

An efficient way to apply the direct method is to analyze the items reported in the income statement in the order in which they are listed. We then determine cash receipts and cash payments related to these revenues and expenses. The following pages present the adjustments required to prepare a statement of cash flows for Juarez Company using the direct approach.

CASH RECEIPTS FROM CUSTOMERS. The income statement for Juarez Company reported revenues from customers of $975,000. How much of that was cash receipts? To answer that, companies need to consider the change in accounts receivable during the year. When accounts receivable increase during the year, revenues on an accrual basis are higher than cash receipts from customers. Operations led to revenues, but not all of these revenues resulted in cash receipts.

To determine the amount of cash receipts, the company deducts from sales revenues the increase in accounts receivable. On the other hand, there may be a decrease in accounts receivable. That would occur if cash receipts from customers exceeded sales revenues. In that case, the company adds to sales revenues the decrease in accounts receivable.

For Juarez Company, accounts receivable decreased $3,000. Thus, cash receipts from customers were $978,000, computed as shown in Illustration 12A-3 (page 614).

Illustration 12A-3
Computation of cash
receipts from customers

Revenues from sales	$ 975,000
Add: Decrease in accounts receivable	3,000
Cash receipts from customers	**$ 978,000**

Juarez can also determine cash receipts from customers from an analysis of the Accounts Receivable account, as shown in Illustration 12A-4.

Illustration 12A-4
Analysis of accounts
receivable

Accounts Receivable

1/1/07	Balance	15,000	**Receipts from customers**	**978,000**	
	Revenues from sales	975,000			
12/31/07	Balance	12,000			

Helpful Hint The T account shows that revenue plus decrease in receivables equals cash receipts.

Illustration 12A-5 shows the relationships among cash receipts from customers, revenues from sales, and changes in accounts receivable.

Illustration 12A-5
Formula to compute cash
receipts from customers—
direct method

Cash Receipts from Customers	**=**	**Revenues from Sales**	{ **+ Decrease in Accounts Receivable** **or** **− Increase in Accounts Receivable**

CASH PAYMENTS TO SUPPLIERS. Juarez Company reported cost of goods sold of $660,000 on its income statement. How much of that was cash payments to suppliers? To answer that, it is first necessary to find purchases for the year. To find purchases, companies adjust cost of goods sold for the change in inventory. When inventory increases during the year, purchases for the year have exceeded cost of goods sold. As a result, to determine the amount of purchases, the company adds to cost of goods sold the increase in inventory.

In 2007, Juarez Company's inventory increased $10,000. It computes purchases as follows.

Illustration 12A-6
Computation of purchases

Cost of goods sold	$ 660,000
Add: Increase in inventory	10,000
Purchases	**$670,000**

After computing purchases, a company can determine cash payments to suppliers. This is done by adjusting purchases for the change in accounts payable. When accounts payable increase during the year, purchases on an accrual basis are higher than they are on a cash basis. As a result, to determine cash payments to suppliers, a company deducts from purchases the increase in accounts payable. On the other hand, if cash payments to suppliers exceed purchases, there may be a decrease in accounts payable. In that case, a company adds to purchases the decrease in accounts payable.

For Juarez Company, cash payments to suppliers were $678,000, computed as follows.

Illustration 12A-7
Computation of cash
payments to suppliers

Purchases	$ 670,000
Add: Decrease in accounts payable	8,000
Cash payments to suppliers	**$678,000**

Juarez also can determine cash payments to suppliers from an analysis of the Accounts Payable account, as shown in Illustration 12A-8.

Accounts Payable

Payments to suppliers	678,000	1/1/07	Balance	60,000
			Purchases	670,000
		12/31/07	Balance	52,000

Illustration 12A-9 shows the relationships among cash payments to suppliers, cost of goods sold, changes in inventory, and changes in accounts payable.

Illustration 12A-9
Formula to compute cash
payments to suppliers—
direct method

$$
\begin{array}{l}
\text{Cash} \\
\text{Payments} \\
\text{to} \\
\text{Suppliers}
\end{array}
=
\begin{array}{l}
\text{Cost} \\
\text{of} \\
\text{Goods} \\
\text{Sold}
\end{array}
\left\{
\begin{array}{l}
\text{+ Increase in Inventory} \\
\text{or} \\
\text{– Decrease in Inventory}
\end{array}
\right.
\left\{
\begin{array}{l}
\text{+ Decrease in} \\
\text{Accounts Payable} \\
\text{or} \\
\text{– Increase in} \\
\text{Accounts Payable}
\end{array}
\right.
$$

CASH PAYMENTS FOR OPERATING EXPENSES. Juarez reported on its income statement operating expenses of $176,000. How much of that amount was cash paid for operating expenses? To answer that, we need to adjust this amount for any changes in prepaid expenses and accrued expenses payable. For example, if prepaid expenses increased during the year, cash paid for operating expenses is higher than operating expenses reported on the income statement. To convert operating expenses to cash payments for operating expenses, a company adds the increase to operating expenses. On the other hand, if prepaid expenses decrease during the year, it deducts the decrease from operating expenses.

Companies must also adjust operating expenses for changes in accrued expenses payable. When accrued expenses payable increase during the year, operating expenses on an accrual basis are higher than they are in a cash basis. As a result, to determine cash payments for operating expenses, a company deducts from operating expenses an increase in accrued expenses payable. On the other hand, a company adds to operating expenses a decrease in accrued expenses payable because cash payments exceed operating expenses.

Juarez Company's cash payments for operating expenses were $179,000, computed as follows.

Illustration 12A-10
Computation of cash
payments for operating
expenses

Operating expenses	$ 176,000
Deduct: Decrease in prepaid expenses	(2,000)
Add: Decrease in accrued expenses payable	5,000
Cash payments for operating expenses	**$ 179,000**

Illustration 12A-11 shows the relationships among cash payments for operating expenses, changes in prepaid expenses, and changes in accrued expenses payable.

Illustration 12A-11
Formula to compute cash
payments for operating
expenses—direct method

$$
\begin{array}{l}
\text{Cash} \\
\text{Payments} \\
\text{for} \\
\text{Operating} \\
\text{Expenses}
\end{array}
=
\begin{array}{l}
\text{Operating} \\
\text{Expenses}
\end{array}
\left\{
\begin{array}{l}
\text{+ Increase in} \\
\text{Prepaid Expense} \\
\text{or} \\
\text{– Decrease in} \\
\text{Prepaid Expense}
\end{array}
\right.
\left\{
\begin{array}{l}
\text{+ Decrease in Accrued} \\
\text{Expenses Payable} \\
\text{or} \\
\text{– Increase in Accrued} \\
\text{Expenses Payable}
\end{array}
\right.
$$

DEPRECIATION EXPENSE AND LOSS ON SALE OF EQUIPMENT. Companies show operating expenses exclusive of depreciation. Juarez's depreciation expense in 2007 was

$18,000. Depreciation expense is not shown on a statement of cash flows because it is a noncash charge. If the amount for operating expenses includes depreciation expense, the company must reduce operating expenses by the amount of depreciation to determine cash payments for operating expenses.

The loss on sale of equipment of $1,000 is also a noncash charge. The loss on sale of equipment reduces net income, but it does not reduce cash. Thus, companies do not report on a statement of cash flows the loss on sale of equipment.

Other charges to expense that do not require the use of cash, such as the amortization of intangible assets, depletion expense, and bad debt expense, are treated in the same manner as depreciation.

CASH PAYMENTS FOR INCOME TAXES. Juarez reported income tax expense of $36,000 on the income statement. Income taxes payable, however, increased $12,000. This increase means that the company has not yet paid $12,000 of the income taxes. As a result, income taxes paid were less than income taxes reported in the income statement. Cash payments for income taxes were, therefore, $24,000 as shown below.

Illustration 12A-12
Computation of cash payments for income taxes

Income tax expense	$ 36,000
Deduct: Increase in income taxes payable	12,000
Cash payments for income taxes	**$ 24,000**

Illustration 12A-13 shows the relationships among cash payments for income taxes, income tax expense, and changes in income taxes payable.

Illustration 12A-13
Formula to compute cash payments for income taxes—direct method

$$\begin{array}{l} \textbf{Cash} \\ \textbf{Payments for} = \begin{array}{c} \textbf{Income Tax} \\ \textbf{Expense} \end{array} \left\{ \begin{array}{l} \textbf{+ Decrease in Income Taxes Payable} \\ \textbf{or} \\ \textbf{- Increase in Income Taxes Payable} \end{array} \right. \\ \textbf{Income Taxes} \end{array}$$

The operating activities section of the statement of cash flows of Juarez Company is shown in Illustration 12A-14.

Illustration 12A-14
Operating activities section of the statement of cash flows

Cash flows from operating activities		
Cash receipts from customers		$978,000
Less: Cash payments:		
To suppliers	$678,000	
For operating expenses	179,000	
For income taxes	24,000	881,000
Net cash provided by operating activities		$ 97,000

When a company uses the direct method, it must also provide in a **separate schedule** (not shown here) the net cash flows from operating activities as computed under the indirect method.

STEP 2: INVESTING AND FINANCING ACTIVITIES

ANALYZE CHANGES IN NONCURRENT ASSET AND LIABILITY ACCOUNTS AND RECORD AS INVESTING AND FINANCING ACTIVITIES, OR AS SIGNIFICANT NONCASH TRANSACTIONS

INCREASE IN LAND. Juarez's land increased $60,000. The additional information section indicates that the company issued common stock to purchase the land.

The issuance of common stock for land has no effect on cash. But it is a **significant noncash investing and financing transaction**. This transaction requires disclosure in a separate schedule at the bottom of the statement of cash flows.

INCREASE IN EQUIPMENT. The comparative balance sheets show that equipment increased $160,000 in 2007. The additional information in Illustration 12A-1 indicates that the increase resulted from two investing transactions: (1) Juarez purchased for cash equipment costing $180,000. And (2) it sold for $17,000 cash equipment costing $20,000, whose book value was $18,000. The relevant data for the statement of cash flows is the cash paid for the purchase and the cash proceeds from the sale. For Juarez Company, the investing activities section will show the following: The $180,000 purchase of equipment as an outflow of cash, and the $17,000 sale of equipment also as an inflow of cash. The company **should not net** the two amounts. **Both individual outflows and inflows of cash should be shown.**

The analysis of the changes in equipment should include the related Accumulated Depreciation account. These two accounts for Juarez Company are shown in Illustration 12A-15.

Illustration 12A-15
Analysis of equipment and related accumulated depreciation

Equipment

1/1/07	Balance	–0–	Cost of equipment sold	20,000
	Cash purchase	180,000		
12/31/07	Balance	160,000		

Accumulated Depreciation—Equipment

Sale of equipment	2,000	1/1/07	Balance	–0–
			Depreciation expense	18,000
		12/31/07	Balance	16,000

INCREASE IN BONDS PAYABLE. Bonds Payable increased $130,000. The additional information in Illustration 12A-1 (page 612) indicated that Juarez issued, for $130,000 cash, bonds with a face value of $130,000. The issuance of bonds is a financing activity. For Juarez Company, there is an inflow of cash of $130,000 from the issuance of bonds.

INCREASE IN COMMON STOCK. The Common Stock account increased $60,000. The additional information indicated that Juarez acquired land from the issuance of common stock. This transaction is a **significant noncash investing and financing transaction** which the company should report separately at the bottom of the statement.

INCREASE IN RETAINED EARNINGS. The $52,000 net increase in Retained Earnings resulted from net income of $84,000 and the declaration and payment of a cash dividend of $32,000. Companies **do not report net income in the statement of cash flows under the direct method**. Cash dividends paid of $32,000 are reported in the financing activities section as an outflow of cash.

Statement of Cash Flows—2007

Illustration 12A-16 (page 618) shows the statement of cash flows for Juarez.

JUAREZ COMPANY
Statement of Cash Flows—Direct Method
For the Year Ended December 31, 2007

Cash flows from operating activities		
Cash receipts from customers		$ 978,000
Less: Cash payments:		
To suppliers	$ 678,000	
For operating expenses	179,000	
For income taxes	24,000	881,000
Net cash provided by operating activities		97,000
Cash flows from investing activities		
Purchase of equipment	(180,000)	
Sale of equipment	17,000	
Net cash used by investing activities		(163,000)
Cash flows from financing activities		
Issuance of bonds payable	130,000	
Payment of cash dividends	(32,000)	
Net cash provided by financing activities		98,000
Net increase in cash		32,000
Cash at beginning of period		159,000
Cash at end of period		$ 191,000
Noncash investing and financing activities		
Issuance of common stock to purchase land		$ 60,000

STEP 3: NET CHANGE IN CASH

COMPARE THE NET CHANGE IN CASH ON THE STATEMENT OF CASH FLOWS WITH THE CHANGE IN THE CASH ACCOUNT REPORTED ON THE BALANCE SHEET TO MAKE SURE THE AMOUNTS AGREE

Illustration 12A-16 indicates that the net change in cash during the period was an increase of $32,000. This agrees with the change in balances in the cash account reported on the balance sheets in Illustration 12A-1 (page 612).

Summary of Study Objective for Appendix

6 *Prepare a statement of cash flows using the direct method.* The preparation of the statement of cash flows involves three major steps: (1) Determine net cash provided/used by operating activities by converting net income from an accrual basis to a cash basis. (2) Analyze changes in noncurrent asset and liability accounts and record as investing and financing activities, or disclose as noncash transactions. (3) Compare the net change in cash on the statement of cash flows with the change in the cash account reported on the balance sheet to make sure the amounts agree. The direct method reports cash receipts less cash payments to arrive at net cash provided by operating activities.

Glossary

Cash debt coverage ratio A cash-basis ratio used to evaluate solvency, calculated as cash provided by operating activities divided by average total liabilities. (p. 608)

Current cash debt coverage ratio A cash-basis ratio used to evaluate liquidity, calculated as cash provided by operations divided by average current liabilities. (p. 607)

Direct method A method of determining net cash provided by operating activities by adjusting each item in the income statement from the accrual basis to the cash basis. (pp. 593, 613)

Financing activities Cash flow activities that include (a) obtaining cash from issuing debt and repaying the amounts borrowed and (b) obtaining cash from stockholders, repurchasing shares, and paying dividends. (p. 587)

Free cash flow Cash provided by operating activities adjusted for capital expenditures and dividends paid. (p. 605)

Indirect method A method of preparing a statement of cash flows in which net income is adjusted for items that do not affect cash, to determine net cash provided by operating activities. (pp. 593, 596)

Investing activities Cash flow activities that include (a) purchasing and disposing of investments and property, plant, and equipment using cash and (b) lending money and collecting the loans. (p. 587)

Operating activities Cash flow activities that include the cash effects of transactions that create revenues and expenses and thus enter into the determination of net income. (p. 587)

Product life cycle A series of phases in a product's sales and cash flows over time; these phases, in order of occurrence, are introductory, growth, maturity, and decline. (p. 590)

Statement of cash flows A basic financial statement that provides information about the cash receipts and cash payments of an entity during a period, classified as operating, investing, and financing activities, in a format that reconciles the beginning and ending cash balances. (p. 587)

Demonstration Problem

The income statement for Kosinski Manufacturing Company contains the following condensed information.

KOSINSKI MANUFACTURING COMPANY
Income Statement
For the Year Ended December 31, 2007

Revenues		$6,583,000
Operating expenses, excluding depreciation	$4,920,000	
Depreciation expense	880,000	5,800,000
Income before income taxes		783,000
Income tax expense		353,000
Net income		$ 430,000

Included in operating expenses is a $24,000 loss resulting from the sale of machinery for $270,000 cash. Machinery was purchased at a cost of $750,000. The following balances are reported on Kosinski's comparative balance sheet at December 31.

	2007	2006
Cash	$672,000	$130,000
Accounts receivable	775,000	610,000
Inventories	834,000	867,000
Accounts payable	521,000	501,000

Income tax expense of $353,000 represents the amount paid in 2007. Dividends declared and paid in 2007 totaled $200,000.

Instructions

(a) Prepare the statement of cash flows using the indirect method.
*(b) Prepare the statement of cash flows using the direct method.

Solution to Demonstration Problem

(a)
KOSINSKI MANUFACTURING COMPANY
Statement of Cash Flows—Indirect Method
For the Year Ended December 31, 2007

Cash flows from operating activities		
Net income		$ 430,000
Adjustments to reconcile net income to net cash provided by operating activities:		
Depreciation expense	$ 880,000	
Loss on sale of machinery	24,000	
Increase in accounts receivable	(165,000)	
Decrease in inventories	33,000	
Increase in accounts payable	20,000	792,000
Net cash provided by operating activities		1,222,000

Action Plan

- Apply the same data to the preparation of a statement of cash flows under both the indirect and direct methods.

- Note the similarities of the two methods: Both methods report the same information in the investing and financing sections.

- Note the differences between the two methods: The cash flows from operating activities sections report different information, but the amount of net cash provided by operating activities is the same for both methods.

Cash flows from investing activities		
Sale of machinery	270,000	
Purchase of machinery	(750,000)	
Net cash used by investing activities		(480,000)
Cash flows from financing activities		
Payment of cash dividends	(200,000)	
Net cash used by financing activities		(200,000)
Net increase in cash		542,000
Cash at beginning of period		130,000
Cash at end of period		$ 672,000

*(b)

KOSINSKI MANUFACTURING COMPANY
Statement of Cash Flows—Direct Method
For the Year Ended December 31, 2007

Cash flows from operating activities		
Cash collections from customers		$6,418,000*
Cash payments:		
For operating expenses	$4,843,000**	
For income taxes	353,000	5,196,000
Net cash provided by operating activities		1,222,000
Cash flows from investing activities		
Sale of machinery	270,000	
Purchase of machinery	(750,000)	
Net cash used by investing activities		(480,000)
Cash flows from financing activities		
Payment of cash dividends	(200,000)	
Net cash used by financing activities		(200,000)
Net increase in cash		542,000
Cash at beginning of period		130,000
Cash at end of period		$ 672,000

Direct-Method Computations:

*Computation of cash collections from customers:	
Revenues per the income statement	$6,583,000
Deduct: Increase in accounts receivable	(165,000)
Cash collections from customers	$6,418,000
**Computation of cash payments for operating expenses:	
Operating expenses per the income statement	$4,920,000
Deduct: Loss from sale of machinery	(24,000)
Deduct: Decrease in inventories	(33,000)
Deduct: Increase in accounts payable	(20,000)
Cash payments for operating expenses	$4,843,000

Note: All Questions, Exercises, and Problems marked with an asterisk relate to material in the appendix to the chapter.

Self-Study Questions

(SO 1)   **1.** Which of the following is *incorrect* about the statement of cash flows?
(a) It is a fourth basic financial statement.
(b) It provides information about cash receipts and cash payments of an entity during a period.
(c) It reconciles the ending cash account balance to the balance per the bank statement.

(d) It provides information about the operating, investing, and financing activities of the business.

(SO 2) **2.** The statement of cash flows classifies cash receipts and cash payments by these activities:
(a) operating and nonoperating.
(b) investing, financing, and operating.
(c) financing, operating, and nonoperating.
(d) investing, financing, and nonoperating.

(SO 2) **3.** Which is an example of a cash flow from an operating activity?
(a) Payment of cash to lenders for interest.
(b) Receipt of cash from the sale of capital stock.
(c) Payment of cash dividends to the company's stockholders.
(d) None of the above.

(SO 2) **4.** Which is an example of a cash flow from an investing activity?
(a) Receipt of cash from the issuance of bonds payable.
(b) Payment of cash to repurchase outstanding capital stock.
(c) Receipt of cash from the sale of equipment.
(d) Payment of cash to suppliers for inventory.

(SO 2) **5.** Cash dividends paid to stockholders are classified on the statement of cash flows as:
(a) operating activities.
(b) investing activities.
(c) a combination of (a) and (b).
(d) financing activities.

(SO 2) **6.** Which is an example of a cash flow from a financing activity?
(a) Receipt of cash from sale of land.
(b) Issuance of debt for cash.
(c) Purchase of equipment for cash.
(d) None of the above

(SO 2) **7.** Which of the following is *incorrect* about the statement of cash flows?
(a) The direct method may be used to report cash provided by operations.
(b) The statement shows the cash provided (used) for three categories of activity.
(c) The operating section is the last section of the statement.
(d) The indirect method may be used to report cash provided by operations.

(SO 3) **8.** During the introductory phase of a company's life cycle, one would normally expect to see:
(a) negative cash from operations, negative cash from investing, and positive cash from financing.
(b) negative cash from operations, positive cash from investing, and positive cash from financing.
(c) positive cash from operations, negative cash from investing, and negative cash from financing.

(d) positive cash from operations, negative cash from investing, and positive cash from financing.

Questions 9 and 10 apply only to the indirect method.

(SO 4) **9.** Net income is $132,000, accounts payable increased $10,000 during the year, inventory decreased $6,000 during the year, and accounts receivable increased $12,000 during the year. Under the indirect method, what is net cash provided by operations?
(a) $102,000.   (c) $124,000.
(b) $112,000.   (d) $136,000.

(SO 4) **10.** Items that are added back to net income in determining cash provided by operations under the indirect method do *not* include:
(a) depreciation expense.
(b) an increase in inventory.
(c) amortization expense.
(d) loss on sale of equipment.

(SO 5) **11.** The statement of cash flows should *not* be used to evaluate an entity's ability to:
(a) earn net income.
(b) generate future cash flows.
(c) pay dividends.
(d) meet obligations.

(SO 5) **12.** Free cash flow provides an indication of a company's ability to:
(a) generate net income.
(b) generate cash to pay dividends.
(c) generate cash to invest in new capital expenditures.
(d) both (b) and (c).

Questions 13 and 14 apply only to the direct method.

(SO 6) ***13.** The beginning balance in accounts receivable is $44,000, the ending balance is $42,000, and sales during the period are $129,000. What are cash receipts from customers?
(a) $127,000.   (c) $131,000.
(b) $129,000.   (d) $141,000.

(SO 6) ***14.** Which of the following items is reported on a cash flow statement prepared by the direct method?
(a) Loss on sale of building.
(b) Increase in accounts receivable.
(c) Depreciation expense.
(d) Cash payments to suppliers.

Go to the book's website, **www.wiley.com/college/kimmel**, to access additional Self-Study Questions.

Questions

1. (a) What is a statement of cash flows?
   (b) John Norris maintains that the statement of cash flows is an optional financial statement. Do you agree? Explain.

2. What questions about cash are answered by the statement of cash flows?

3. Distinguish among the three activities reported in the statement of cash flows.

4. (a) What are the major sources (inflows) of cash in a statement of cash flows?
   (b) What are the major uses (outflows) of cash?

5. Why is it important to disclose certain noncash transactions? How should they be disclosed?

6. Wilma Flintstone and Barny Rublestone were discussing the format of the statement of cash flows of Hart Candy Co. At the bottom of Hart Candy's statement of cash flows was a separate section entitled "Noncash investing and financing activities." Give three examples of significant noncash transactions that would be reported in this section.

7. Why is it necessary to use comparative balance sheets, a current income statement, and certain transaction data in preparing a statement of cash flows?

8. (a) What are the phases of the corporate life cycle?
   (b) What effect does each phase have on the numbers reported in a statement of cash flows?

9. Contrast the advantages and disadvantages of the direct and indirect methods of preparing the statement of cash flows. Are both methods acceptable? Which method is preferred by the FASB? Which method is more popular?

10. When the total cash inflows exceed the total cash outflows in the statement of cash flows, how and where is this excess identified?

11. Describe the indirect method for determining net cash provided (used) by operating activities.

12. Why is it necessary to convert accrual-based net income to cash-basis income when preparing a statement of cash flows?

13. The president of Ferneti Company is puzzled. During the last year, the company experienced a net loss of $800,000, yet its cash increased $300,000 during the same period of time. Explain to the president how this could occur.

14. Identify five items that are adjustments to convert net income to net cash provided by operating activities under the indirect method.

15. Why and how is depreciation expense reported in a statement prepared using the indirect method?

16. Why is the statement of cash flows useful?

17. During 2007 Doubleday Company converted $1,700,000 of its total $2,000,000 of bonds payable into common stock. Indicate how the transaction would be reported on a statement of cash flows, if at all.

18. Give examples of accrual-based and cash-based ratios to measure each of these characteristics of a company:
    (a) Liquidity.
    (b) Solvency.

*19. Describe the direct method for determining net cash provided by operating activities.

*20. Give the formulas under the direct method for computing (a) cash receipts from customers and (b) cash payments to suppliers.

*21. Garcia Inc. reported sales of $2 million for 2007. Accounts receivable decreased $200,000 and accounts payable increased $300,000. Compute cash receipts from customers, assuming that the receivable and payable transactions related to operations.

*22. In the direct method, why is depreciation expense not reported in the cash flows from operating activities section?

Brief Exercises

Indicate statement presentation of selected transactions.
(SO 2)

BE12-1 Each of these items must be considered in preparing a statement of cash flows for Kiner Co. for the year ended December 31, 2007. For each item, state how it should be shown in the statement of cash flows for 2007.
(a) Issued bonds for $200,000 cash.
(b) Purchased equipment for $150,000 cash.
(c) Sold land costing $20,000 for $20,000 cash.
(d) Declared and paid a $50,000 cash dividend.

Classify items by activities.
(SO 2)

BE12-2 Classify each item as an operating, investing, or financing activity. Assume all items involve cash unless there is information to the contrary.
(a) Purchase of equipment.   (d) Depreciation.
(b) Sale of building.   (e) Payment of dividends.
(c) Redemption of bonds.   (f) Issuance of capital stock.

BE12-3 The following T account is a summary of the cash account of Edmonds Company.

Identify financing activity transactions.
(SO 2)

Cash (Summary Form)

Balance, Jan. 1	8,000		
Receipts from customers	364,000	Payments for goods	200,000
Dividends on stock investments	6,000	Payments for operating expenses	140,000
Proceeds from sale of equipment	36,000	Interest paid	10,000
Proceeds from issuance of		Taxes paid	8,000
bonds payable	300,000	Dividends paid	50,000
Balance, Dec. 31	306,000		

What amount of net cash provided (used) by financing activities should be reported in the statement of cash flows?

BE12-4
(a) Why is cash from operations likely to be lower than reported net income during the growth phase?
(b) Why is cash from investing often positive during the late maturity phase and during the decline phase?

Answer questions related to the phases of product life cycle.
(SO 3)

BE12-5 Martinez, Inc. reported net income of $2.5 million in 2007. Depreciation for the year was $160,000, accounts receivable decreased $350,000, and accounts payable decreased $280,000. Compute net cash provided by operating activities using the indirect approach.

Compute cash provided by operating activities—indirect method.
(SO 4)

BE12-6 The net income for Adcock Co. for 2007 was $280,000. For 2007 depreciation on plant assets was $70,000, and the company incurred a loss on sale of plant assets of $12,000. Compute net cash provided by operating activities under the indirect method.

Compute cash provided by operating activities—indirect method.
(SO 4)

BE12-7 The comparative balance sheets for Goltra Company show these changes in noncash current asset accounts: accounts receivable decrease $80,000, prepaid expenses increase $28,000, and inventories increase $30,000. Compute net cash provided by operating activities using the indirect method assuming that net income is $200,000.

Compute net cash provided by operating activities—indirect method.
(SO 4)

BE12-8 The T accounts for Equipment and the related Accumulated Depreciation for Pettengill Company at the end of 2007 are shown here.

Determine cash received from sale of equipment.
(SO 4)

Equipment

Beg. bal.	80,000	Disposals	22,000
Acquisitions	41,600		
End. bal.	99,600		

Accumulated Depreciation

Disposals	5,500	Beg. bal.	44,500
		Depr. exp.	12,000
		End. bal.	51,000

In addition, Pettengill Company's income statement reported a loss on the sale of equipment of $5,500. What amount was reported on the statement of cash flows as "cash flow from sale of equipment"?

BE12-9 During 2004 Cypress Semiconductor Corporation reported cash provided by operations of $155,793,000 cash used in investing of $207,826,000, and cash used in financing of $33,372,000. In addition, cash spent for fixed assets during the period was $132,280,000. Average current liabilities were $226,238,500, and average total liabilities were $959,567,000. No dividends were paid. Calculate these values:
(a) Free cash flow.
(b) Current cash debt coverage ratio.
(c) Cash debt coverage ratio.

Calculate cash-based ratios.
(SO 5)

BE12-10 Lott Corporation reported cash provided by operating activities of $360,000, cash used by investing activities of $250,000, and cash provided by financing activities of $70,000. In addition, cash spent for capital assets during the period was $200,000.

Calculate cash-based ratios.
(SO 5)

Average current liabilities were $150,000, and average total liabilities were $225,000. No dividends were paid. Calculate these values:
(a) Free cash flow.
(b) Current cash debt coverage ratio.
(c) Cash debt coverage ratio.

Calculate cash-based ratios.
(SO 5)

BE12-11   Alliance Atlantis Communications Inc. reported a $35.8 million increase in operating cash flow for its first quarter of 2005. Alliance reported cash provided by operating activities of $45,600,000 and revenues of $264,800,000. Cash spent on plant asset additions during the quarter was $1,600,000. Calculate free cash flow.

Calculate and analyze free cash flow.
(SO 5)

BE12-12   The management of Radar Inc. is trying to decide whether it can increase its dividend. During the current year it reported net income of $875,000. It had cash provided by operating activities of $734,000, paid cash dividends of $70,000, and had capital expenditures of $280,000. Compute the company's free cash flow, and discuss whether an increase in the dividend appears warranted. What other factors should be considered?

Compute receipts from customers—direct method.
(SO 6)

*BE12-13   Columbia Sportswear Company had accounts receivable of $206,024,000 at January 1, 2004, and $267,653,000 at December 31, 2004. Sales revenues were $1,095,307,000 for the year 2004. What is the amount of cash receipts from customers in 2004?

Compute cash payments for income taxes—direct method.
(SO 6)

*BE12-14   Young Corporation reported income taxes of $340,000,000 on its 2007 income statement and income taxes payable of $277,000,000 at December 31, 2006, and $522,000,000 at December 31, 2006. What amount of cash payments were made for income taxes during 2006?

Compute cash payments for operating expenses—direct method.
(SO 6)

*BE12-15   Flynn Corporation reports operating expenses of $80,000 excluding depreciation expense of $15,000 for 2007. During the year prepaid expenses decreased $6,600 and accrued expenses payable increased $4,400. Compute the cash payments for operating expenses in 2007.

Exercises

Classify transactions by type of activity.
(SO 2)

E12-1   Pioneer Corporation had these transactions during 2007.
(a) Issued $50,000 par value common stock for cash.
(b) Purchased a machine for $30,000, giving a long-term note in exchange.
(c) Issued $200,000 par value common stock upon conversion of bonds having a face value of $200,000.
(d) Declared and paid a cash dividend of $18,000.
(e) Sold a long-term investment with a cost of $15,000 for $15,000 cash.
(f) Collected $16,000 of accounts receivable.
(g) Paid $18,000 on accounts payable.

Instructions
Analyze the transactions and indicate whether each transaction resulted in a cash flow from operating activities, investing activities, financing activities, or noncash investing and financing activities.

Classify transactions by type of activity.
(SO 2)

E12-2   An analysis of comparative balance sheets, the current year's income statement, and the general ledger accounts of Gagliano Corp. uncovered the following items. Assume all items involve cash unless there is information to the contrary.

(a) Payment of interest on notes payable.
(b) Exchange of land for patent.
(c) Sale of building at book value.
(d) Payment of dividends.
(e) Depreciation.
(f) Receipt of dividends on investment in stock.
(g) Receipt of interest on notes receivable.
(h) Issuance of capital stock.
(i) Amortization of patent.
(j) Issuance of bonds for land.
(k) Purchase of land.
(l) Conversion of bonds into common stock.
(m) Loss on sale of land.
(n) Retirement of bonds.

Instructions
Indicate how each item should be classified in the statement of cash flows using these four major classifications: operating activity (indirect method), investing activity, financing activity, and significant noncash investing and financing activity.

E12-3   The information in the table is from the statement of cash flows for a company at four different points in time (A, B, C, and D). Negative values are presented in parentheses.

Identify phases of product life cycle.
(SO 3)

	Point in Time			
	A	**B**	**C**	**D**
Cash provided by operations	$ (60,000)	$ 30,000	$120,000	$(10,000)
Cash provided by investing	(100,000)	25,000	30,000	(40,000)
Cash provided by financing	70,000	(110,000)	(50,000)	120,000
Net income	(40,000)	10,000	100,000	(5,000)

Instructions
For each point in time, state whether the company is most likely in the introductory phase, growth phase, maturity phase, or decline phase. In each case explain your choice.

E12-4   Villa Company reported net income of $195,000 for 2007. Villa also reported depreciation expense of $45,000 and a loss of $5,000 on the sale of equipment. The comparative balance sheet shows a decrease in accounts receivable of $15,000 for the year, a $17,000 increase in accounts payable, and a $4,000 decrease in prepaid expenses.

Prepare the operating activities section—indirect method.
(SO 4)

Instructions
Prepare the operating activities section of the statement of cash flows for 2007. Use the indirect method.

E12-5   The current sections of Bellinham Inc.'s balance sheets at December 31, 2006 and 2007, are presented here.
Bellinham's net income for 2007 was $153,000. Depreciation expense was $24,000.

Prepare the operating activities section—indirect method.
(SO 4)

	2007	**2006**
Current assets		
Cash	$105,000	$ 99,000
Accounts receivable	110,000	89,000
Inventory	158,000	172,000
Prepaid expenses	27,000	22,000
Total current assets	$400,000	$382,000
Current liabilities		
Accrued expenses payable	$ 15,000	$ 5,000
Accounts payable	85,000	92,000
Total current liabilities	$100,000	$ 97,000

Instructions
Prepare the net cash provided by operating activities section of the company's statement of cash flows for the year ended December 31, 2007, using the indirect method.

E12-6   The three accounts shown below and on page 626 appear in the general ledger of Cesar Corp. during 2007.

Prepare partial statement of cash flows—indirect method.
(SO 4)

Equipment

Date		Debit	Credit	Balance
Jan. 1	Balance			160,000
July 31	Purchase of equipment	70,000		230,000
Sept. 2	Cost of equipment constructed	53,000		283,000
Nov. 10	Cost of equipment sold		49,000	234,000

Accumulated Depreciation—Equipment

Date		Debit	Credit	Balance
Jan. 1	Balance			71,000
Nov. 10	Accumulated depreciation on equipment sold	30,000		41,000
Dec. 31	Depreciation for year		28,000	69,000

Retained Earnings

Date		Debit	Credit	Balance
Jan. 1	Balance			105,000
Aug. 23	Dividends (cash)	14,000		91,000
Dec. 31	Net income		67,000	158,000

Instructions

From the postings in the accounts, indicate how the information is reported on a statement of cash flows using the indirect method. The loss on sale of equipment was $5,000. (*Hint:* Cost of equipment constructed is reported in the investing activities section as a decrease in cash of $53,000.)

Prepare a statement of cash flows—indirect method, and compute cash-based ratios. (SO 4, 5)

E12-7 Here are comparative balance sheets for Taguchi Company.

TAGUCHI COMPANY
Comparative Balance Sheets
December 31

Assets	2007	2006
Cash	$ 73,000	$ 22,000
Accounts receivable	85,000	76,000
Inventories	170,000	189,000
Land	75,000	100,000
Equipment	260,000	200,000
Accumulated depreciation	(66,000)	(32,000)
Total	$597,000	$555,000

Liabilities and Stockholders' Equity	2007	2006
Accounts payable	$ 39,000	$ 47,000
Bonds payable	150,000	200,000
Common stock ($1 par)	216,000	174,000
Retained earnings	192,000	134,000
Total	$597,000	$555,000

Additional information:
1. Net income for 2007 was $103,000.
2. Cash dividends of $45,000 were declared and paid.
3. Bonds payable amounting to $50,000 were redeemed for cash $50,000.
4. Common stock was issued for $42,000 cash.
5. No equipment was sold during 2007.

Instructions
(a) Prepare a statement of cash flows for 2007 using the indirect method.
(b) Compute these cash-basis ratios:

    (1) Current cash debt coverage.
    (2) Cash debt coverage.

Compare two companies by using cash-based ratios. (SO 5)

E12-8 Presented on page 627 is 2004 information for PepsiCo, Inc. and The Coca-Cola Company.

($ in millions)	PepsiCo	Coca-Cola
Cash provided by operations	$ 5,054	$ 5,968
Average current liabilities	6,584	9,429
Average total liabilities	13,959	14,322
Net income	4,212	4,847
Sales	29,261	21,962
Capital expenditures	1,387	755
Dividends paid	1,329	2,429

Instructions

Using the cash-based measures presented in this chapter, compare the (a) liquidity and (b) solvency of the two companies.

E12-9   Information for two companies in the same industry, Linn Corporation and Nye Corporation, is presented here.

Compare two companies by using cash-based ratios.
(SO 5)

	Linn Corporation	Nye Corporation
Cash provided by operating activities	$150,000	$150,000
Average current liabilities	50,000	100,000
Average total liabilities	200,000	250,000
Net earnings	200,000	200,000
Capital expenditures	40,000	70,000
Dividends paid	5,000	10,000

Instructions

Using the cash-based measures presented in this chapter, compare the (a) liquidity and (b) solvency of the two companies.

*E12-10   Hairston Company completed its first year of operations on December 31, 2007. Its initial income statement showed that Hairston had revenues of $192,000 and operating expenses of $78,000. Accounts receivable and accounts payable at year-end were $60,000 and $23,000, respectively. Assume that accounts payable related to operating expenses. Ignore income taxes.

Compute cash provided by operating activities—direct method.
(SO 6)

Instructions

Compute net cash provided by operating activities using the direct method.

*E12-11   The 2004 income statement for McDonald's Corporation shows cost of goods sold $4,852.7 million and operating expenses (including depreciation expense of $1,201 million) $10,671.5 million. The comparative balance sheet for the year shows that inventory increased $18.1 million, prepaid expenses increased $56.3 million, accounts payable (merchandise suppliers) increased $136.9 million, and accrued expenses payable increased $160.9 million.

Compute cash payments—direct method.
(SO 6)

Instructions

Using the direct method, compute (a) cash payments to suppliers and (b) cash payments for operating expenses.

*E12-12   The 2007 accounting records of Verlander Transport reveal these transactions and events.

Compute cash flow from operating activities—direct method.
(SO 6)

Payment of interest	$ 10,000	Collection of accounts receivable	$182,000
Cash sales	48,000	Payment of salaries and wages	53,000
Receipt of dividend revenue	18,000	Depreciation expense	16,000
Payment of income taxes	12,000	Proceeds from sale of vehicles	812,000
Net income	38,000	Purchase of equipment for cash	22,000
Payment of accounts payable		Loss on sale of vehicles	3,000
for merchandise	115,000	Payment of dividends	14,000
Payment for land	74,000	Payment of operating expenses	28,000

Instructions

Prepare the cash flows from operating activities section using the direct method. (Not all of the items will be used.)

Calculate cash flows—direct method.
(SO 6)

*E12-13 The following information is taken from the 2007 general ledger of Pierzynski Company.

Rent	Rent expense	$ 40,000
	Prepaid rent, January 1	5,900
	Prepaid rent, December 31	9,000
Salaries	Salaries expense	$ 54,000
	Salaries payable, January 1	10,000
	Salaries payable, December 31	8,000
Sales	Revenue from sales	$170,000
	Accounts receivable, January 1	16,000
	Accounts receivable, December 31	7,000

Instructions

In each case, compute the amount that should be reported in the operating activities section of the statement of cash flows under the direct method.

Problems: Set A

Distinguish among operating, investing, and financing activities.
(SO 6)

P12-1A You are provided with the following transactions that took place during a recent fiscal year.

Transaction	Where Reported on Statement	Cash Inflow, Outflow, or No Effect?
(a) Recorded depreciation expense on the plant assets.		
(b) Recorded and paid interest expense.		
(c) Recorded cash proceeds from a sale of plant assets.		
(d) Acquired land by issuing common stock.		
(e) Paid a cash dividend to preferred stockholders.		
(f) Distributed a stock dividend to common stockholders.		
(g) Recorded cash sales.		
(h) Recorded sales on account.		
(i) Purchased inventory for cash.		
(j) Purchased inventory on account.		

Instructions

Complete the table indicating whether each item (1) should be reported as an operating (O) activity, investing (I) activity, financing (F) activity, or as a noncash (NC) transaction reported in a separate schedule, and (2) represents a cash inflow or cash outflow or has no cash flow effect. Assume use of the indirect approach.

Determine cash flow effects of changes in equity accounts.
(SO 4)

P12-2A The following account balances relate to the stockholders' equity accounts of Gore Corp. at year-end.

	2007	2006
Common stock, 10,500 and 10,000 shares, respectively, for 2007 and 2006	$160,000	$140,000
Preferred stock, 5,000 shares	125,000	125,000
Retained earnings	300,000	260,000

A small stock dividend was declared and issued in 2007. The market value of the shares was $10,500. Cash dividends were $15,000 in both 2007 and 2006. The common stock has no par or stated value.

Instructions
(a) What was the amount of net income reported by Gore Corp. in 2007?
(b) Determine the amounts of any cash inflows or outflows related to the common stock and dividend accounts in 2007.
(c) Indicate where each of the cash inflows or outflows identified in (b) would be classified on the statement of cash flows.

(a) Net income $65,500

P12-3A The income statement of Elbert Company is presented here.

Prepare the operating activities section—indirect method.
(SO 4)

ELBERT COMPANY
Income Statement
For the Year Ended November 30, 2007

Sales		$7,700,000
Cost of goods sold		
Beginning inventory	$1,900,000	
Purchases	4,400,000	
Goods available for sale	6,300,000	
Ending inventory	1,400,000	
Total cost of goods sold		4,900,000
Gross profit		2,800,000
Operating expenses		
Selling expenses	450,000	
Administrative expenses	700,000	1,150,000
Net income		$1,650,000

Additional information:
1. Accounts receivable increased $250,000 during the year, and inventory decreased $500,000.
2. Prepaid expenses increased $150,000 during the year.
3. Accounts payable to suppliers of merchandise decreased $340,000 during the year.
4. Accrued expenses payable decreased $100,000 during the year.
5. Administrative expenses include depreciation expense of $90,000.

Instructions
Prepare the operating activities section of the statement of cash flows for the year ended November 30, 2007, for Elbert Company, using the indirect method.

Cash from operations
$1,400,000

*P12-4A Data for Elbert Company are presented in P12-3A.

Instructions
Prepare the operating activities section of the statement of cash flows using the direct method.

Prepare the operating activities section—direct method.
(SO 6)
Cash from operations
$1,400,000

P12-5A Grania Company's income statement contained the condensed information below.

Prepare the operating activities section—indirect method.
(SO 4)

GRANIA COMPANY
Income Statement
For the Year Ended December 31, 2007

Revenues		$970,000
Operating expenses, excluding depreciation	$624,000	
Depreciation expense	60,000	
Loss on sale of equipment	16,000	700,000
Income before income taxes		270,000
Income tax expense		40,000
Net income		$230,000

Grania's balance sheet contained the comparative data at December 31, shown on page 630.

	2007	2006
Accounts receivable	$75,000	$60,000
Accounts payable	41,000	28,000
Income taxes payable	11,000	7,000

Accounts payable pertain to operating expenses.

Cash from operations
$308,000

Instructions
Prepare the operating activities section of the statement of cash flows using the indirect method.

Prepare the operating activities section—direct method.
(SO 6)   Cash from
operations
$308,000

*P12-6A   Data for Grania Company are presented in P12-5A.

Instructions
Prepare the operating activities section of the statement of cash flows using the direct method.

Prepare a statement of cash flows—indirect method, and compute cash-based ratios.
(SO 4, 5)

P12-7A   Presented below are the financial statements of Weller Company.

WELLER COMPANY
Comparative Balance Sheets
December 31

Assets	2007	2006
Cash	$ 35,000	$ 20,000
Accounts receivable	33,000	14,000
Merchandise inventory	27,000	20,000
Property, plant, and equipment	60,000	78,000
Accumulated depreciation	(29,000)	(24,000)
Total	$126,000	$108,000

Liabilities and Stockholders' Equity		
Accounts payable	$ 29,000	$ 15,000
Income taxes payable	7,000	8,000
Bonds payable	27,000	33,000
Common stock	18,000	14,000
Retained earnings	45,000	38,000
Total	$126,000	$108,000

WELLER COMPANY
Income Statement
For the Year Ended December 31, 2007

Sales		$242,000
Cost of goods sold		175,000
Gross profit		67,000
Selling expenses	$18,000	
Administrative expenses	6,000	24,000
Income from operations		43,000
Interest expense		3,000
Income before income taxes		40,000
Income tax expense		8,000
Net income		$ 32,000

Additional data:
1. Dividends declared and paid were $25,000.
2. During the year equipment was sold for $8,500 cash. This equipment cost $18,000 originally and had a book value of $8,500 at the time of sale.

3. All depreciation expense is in the selling expense category.
4. All sales and purchases are on account.

Instructions
(a) Prepare a statement of cash flows using the indirect method.
(b) Compute these cash-basis measures:
    (1) Current cash debt coverage ratio.
    (2) Cash debt coverage ratio.
    (3) Free cash flow.

(a) Cash from operations
$33,500

*P12-8A Data for Weller Company are presented in P12-7A. Further analysis reveals the following.

1. Accounts payable pertain to merchandise suppliers.
2. All operating expenses except for depreciation were paid in cash.

Prepare a statement of cash flows—direct method, and compute cash-based ratios. (SO 5, 6)

Instructions
(a) Prepare a statement of cash flows for Weller Company using the direct method.
(b) Compute these cash-basis measures:
    (1) Current cash debt coverage ratio.
    (2) Cash debt coverage ratio.
    (3) Free cash flow.

(a) Cash from operations
$33,500

P12-9A Condensed financial data of Arma Inc. follow.

Prepare a statement of cash flows—indirect method. (SO 4)

ARMA INC.
Comparative Balance Sheets
December 31

Assets	2007	2006
Cash	$ 90,800	$ 48,400
Accounts receivable	92,800	33,000
Inventories	112,500	102,850
Prepaid expenses	28,400	26,000
Investments	138,000	114,000
Plant assets	270,000	242,500
Accumulated depreciation	(50,000)	(52,000)
Total	$682,500	$514,750

Liabilities and Stockholders' Equity		
Accounts payable	$112,000	$ 67,300
Accrued expenses payable	16,500	17,000
Bonds payable	110,000	150,000
Common stock	220,000	175,000
Retained earnings	224,000	105,450
Total	$682,500	$514,750

ARMA INC.
Income Statement Data
For the Year Ended December 31, 2007

Sales		$392,780
Less:		
Cost of goods sold	$135,460	
Operating expenses, excluding depreciation	12,410	
Depreciation expense	46,500	
Income taxes	27,280	
Interest expense	4,730	
Loss on sale of plant assets	7,500	233,880
Net income		$158,900

Additional information:

1. New plant assets costing $85,000 were purchased for cash during the year.
2. Old plant assets having an original cost of $57,500 were sold for $1,500 cash.
3. Bonds matured and were paid off at face value for cash.
4. A cash dividend of $40,350 was declared and paid during the year.

Cash from operations
$185,250

Instructions

Prepare a statement of cash flows using the indirect method.

Prepare a statement of cash
flows—direct method.
(SO 6)
Cash from operations
$185,250

*P12-10A   Data for Arma Inc. are presented in P12-9A. Further analysis reveals that accounts payable pertain to merchandise creditors.

Instructions

Prepare a statement of cash flows for Arma Inc. using the direct method.

Prepare a statement of cash
flows—indirect method.
(SO 4)

P12-11A   The comparative balance sheets for Ramirez Company as of December 31 are presented below.

RAMIREZ COMPANY
Comparative Balance Sheets
December 31

Assets	2007	2006
Cash	$ 71,000	$ 45,000
Accounts receivable	44,000	62,000
Inventory	151,450	142,000
Prepaid expenses	15,280	21,000
Land	105,000	130,000
Equipment	228,000	155,000
Accumulated depreciation—equipment	(45,000)	(35,000)
Building	200,000	200,000
Accumulated depreciation—building	(60,000)	(40,000)
Total	$709,730	$680,000

Liabilities and Stockholders' Equity		
Accounts payable	$ 47,730	$ 40,000
Bonds payable	260,000	300,000
Common stock, $1 par	200,000	160,000
Retained earnings	202,000	180,000
Total	$709,730	$680,000

Additional information:

1. Operating expenses include depreciation expense of $42,000 and charges from prepaid expenses of $5,720.
2. Land was sold for cash at book value.
3. Cash dividends of $15,000 were paid.
4. Net income for 2007 was $37,000.
5. Equipment was purchased for $95,000 cash. In addition, equipment costing $22,000 with a book value of $10,000 was sold for $6,000 cash.
6. Bonds were converted at face value by issuing 40,000 shares of $1 par value common stock.

Instructions

Cash from operations
$105,000

Prepare a statement of cash flows for the year ended December 31, 2007, using the indirect method.

P12-12A   You are provided with the following transactions that took place during the year.

Identify the impact of transactions on ratios.
(SO 5)

Transactions	Free Cash Flow ($125,000)	Current Cash Debt Coverage Ratio (0.5 times)	Cash Debt Coverage Ratio (0.3 times)
(a) Recorded credit sales $2,500.			
(b) Collected $1,500 owing from customers.			
(c) Paid amount owing to suppliers $2,750.			
(d) Recorded sales returns of $500 and credited the customer's account.			
(e) Purchased new equipment $5,000; signed a long-term note payable for the cost of the equipment.			
(f) Purchased a patent and paid $15,000 cash for the asset.			

Instructions

For each transaction listed above, indicate whether it will increase (I), decrease (D), or have no effect (NE) on the ratios.

Problems: Set B

P12-1B   You are provided with the following transactions that took place during a recent fiscal year.

Distinguish among operating, investing, and financing activities.
(SO 2)

Transaction	Where Reported on Statement	Cash Inflow, Outflow, or No Effect?
(a) Recorded depreciation expense on the plant assets.		
(b) Incurred a loss on disposal of plant assets.		
(c) Acquired a building by paying cash.		
(d) Made principal repayments on a mortgage.		
(e) Issued common stock.		
(f) Purchased shares of another company to be held as a long-term equity investment.		
(g) Paid dividends to common stockholders.		
(h) Sold inventory on credit. The company uses a perpetual inventory system.		
(i) Purchased inventory on credit.		
(j) Paid wages to employees.		

Instructions

Complete the table indicating whether each item (1) should be reported as an operating (O) activity, investing (I) activity, financing (F) activity, or as a noncash (NC) transaction reported in a separate schedule, and (2) represents a cash inflow or cash outflow or has no cash flow effect. Assume use of the indirect approach.

Determine cash flow effects of changes in plant asset accounts.
(SO 4)

P12-2B The following selected account balances relate to the plant asset accounts of Zambia Inc. at year-end.

	2007	2006
Accumulated depreciation—buildings	$337,500	$300,000
Accumulated depreciation—equipment	144,000	96,000
Buildings	750,000	750,000
Depreciation expense	101,500	85,500
Equipment	300,000	240,000
Land	100,000	70,000
Loss on sale of equipment	3,000	0

Additional information:

1. Zambia purchased $85,000 of equipment and $30,000 of land for cash in 2007.
2. Zambia also sold equipment in 2007.
3. Depreciation expense in 2007 was $37,500 on building and $64,000 on equipment.

Instructions

(a) Cash proceeds $6,000

(a) Determine the amounts of any cash inflows or outflows related to the plant asset accounts in 2007.
(b) Indicate where each of the cash inflows or outflows identified in (a) would be classified on the statement of cash flows.

Prepare the operating activities section—indirect method.
(SO 4)

P12-3B The income statement of Marquette Company is presented below.

Additional information:

1. Accounts receivable decreased $520,000 during the year, and inventory increased $140,000.
2. Prepaid expenses increased $175,000 during the year.
3. Accounts payable to merchandise suppliers increased $50,000 during the year.
4. Accrued expenses payable increased $165,000 during the year.

MARQUETTE COMPANY
Income Statement
For the Year Ended December 31, 2007

Sales		$5,400,000
Cost of goods sold		
Beginning inventory	$1,780,000	
Purchases	3,430,000	
Goods available for sale	5,210,000	
Ending inventory	1,920,000	
Total cost of goods sold		3,290,000
Gross profit		2,110,000
Operating expenses		
Selling expenses	420,000	
Administrative expense	525,000	
Depreciation expense	105,000	
Amortization expense	20,000	1,070,000
Net income		$1,040,000

Cash from operations
$1,585,000

Instructions
Prepare the operating activities section of the statement of cash flows for the year ended December 31, 2007, for Marquette Company, using the indirect method.

Prepare the operating activities section—direct method.
(SO 6)
Cash from operations
$1,585,000

P12-4B Data for Marquette Company are presented in P12-3B.

Instructions
Prepare the operating activities section of the statement of cash flows using the direct method.

P12-5B The income statement of Shapiro Inc. reported the following condensed information.

Prepare the operating activities section—indirect method.
(SO 4)

SHAPIRO INC.
Income Statement
For the Year Ended December 31, 2007

Revenues	$545,000
Operating expenses	400,000
Income from operations	145,000
Income tax expense	47,000
Net income	$ 98,000

Shapiro's balance sheet contained these comparative data at December 31.

	2007	2006
Accounts receivable	$50,000	$75,000
Accounts payable	30,000	51,000
Income taxes payable	10,000	4,000

Shapiro has no depreciable assets. Accounts payable pertain to operating expenses.

Instructions
Prepare the operating activities section of the statement of cash flows using the indirect method.

Cash from operations
$108,000

P12-6B Data for Shapiro Inc. are presented in P12-5B.

Prepare the operating activities section—direct method.
(SO 6)

Instructions
Prepare the operating activities section of the statement of cash flows using the direct method.

Cash from operations
$108,000

P12-7B Here and on page 636 are the financial statements of Molina Company.

Prepare a statement of cash flows—indirect method, and compute cash-based ratios.
(SO 4, 5)

MOLINA COMPANY
Comparative Balance Sheets
December 31

Assets		2007		2006
Cash		$ 28,000		$ 33,000
Accounts receivable		23,000		14,000
Merchandise inventory		41,000		25,000
Property, plant, and equipment	$ 70,000		$ 78,000	
Less: Accumulated depreciation	(27,000)	43,000	(24,000)	54,000
Total		$135,000		$126,000

Liabilities and Stockholders' Equity	2007	2006
Accounts payable	$ 31,000	$ 43,000
Income taxes payable	26,000	20,000
Bonds payable	20,000	10,000
Common stock	25,000	25,000
Retained earnings	33,000	28,000
Total	$135,000	$126,000

MOLINA COMPANY
Income Statement
For the Year Ended December 31, 2007

Sales		$286,000
Cost of goods sold		194,000
Gross profit		92,000
Selling expenses	$28,000	
Administrative expenses	9,000	37,000
Income from operations		55,000
Interest expense		7,000
Income before income taxes		48,000
Income tax expense		10,000
Net income		$ 38,000

Additional data:

1. Dividends of $33,000 were declared and paid.
2. During the year equipment was sold for $10,000 cash. This equipment cost $13,000 originally and had a book value of $10,000 at the time of sale.
3. All depreciation expense, $6,000, is in the selling expense category.
4. All sales and purchases are on account.
5. Additional equipment was purchased for $5,000 cash.

Instructions

(a) Cash from operations
$13,000

(a) Prepare a statement of cash flows using the indirect method.
(b) Compute these cash-basis measures:
    (1) Current cash debt coverage ratio.
    (2) Cash debt coverage ratio.
    (3) Free cash flow.

Prepare a statement of cash flows—direct method, and compute cash-based ratios.
(SO 5, 6)

*P12-8B   Data for Molina Company are presented in P12-7B. Further analysis reveals the following.

1. Accounts payable pertains to merchandise creditors.
2. All operating expenses except for depreciation are paid in cash.

Instructions

(a) Cash from operations
$13,000

(a) Prepare a statement of cash flows using the direct method.
(b) Compute these cash-basis measures:
    (1) Current cash debt coverage ratio.
    (2) Cash debt coverage ratio.
    (3) Free cash flow.

Prepare a statement of cash flows—indirect method.
(SO 4)

P12-9B   Condensed financial data of Yaeger Company are shown below and on page 637.

YAEGER COMPANY
Comparative Balance Sheets
December 31

Assets	2007	2006
Cash	$ 97,700	$ 33,400
Accounts receivable	70,800	37,000
Inventories	121,900	102,650
Investments	89,500	107,000
Plant assets	310,000	205,000
Accumulated depreciation	(49,500)	(40,000)
Total	$640,400	$445,050

Liabilities and Stockholders' Equity

Accounts payable	$ 62,700	$ 48,280
Accrued expenses payable	15,100	18,830
Bonds payable	140,000	70,000
Common stock	250,000	200,000
Retained earnings	172,600	107,940
Total	$640,400	$445,050

YAEGER COMPANY
Income Statement Data
For the Year Ended December 31, 2007

Sales		$297,500
Gain on sale of plant assets		5,000
		302,500
Less:		
Cost of goods sold	$99,460	
Operating expenses, excluding depreciation expense	14,670	
Depreciation expense	35,500	
Income taxes	27,270	
Interest expense	2,940	179,840
Net income		$122,660

Additional information:

1. New plant assets costing $141,000 were purchased for cash during the year.
2. Investments were sold at cost.
3. Plant assets costing $36,000 were sold for $15,000, resulting in a gain of $5,000.
4. A cash dividend of $58,000 was declared and paid during the year.

Instructions
Prepare a statement of cash flows using the indirect method.

Cash from operations
$110,800

*P12-10B   Data for Yaeger Company are presented in P12-9B. Further analysis reveals that accounts payable pertain to merchandise creditors.

Prepare a statement of cash flows—direct method.
(SO 6)

Instructions
Prepare a statement of cash flows for Yaeger Company using the direct method.

Cash from operations
$110,800

P12-11B   Presented below and on the next page are the comparative balance sheets for Lewis Company at December 31.

Prepare a statement of cash flows—indirect method.
(SO 4)

LEWIS COMPANY
Comparative Balance Sheets
December 31

Assets	2007	2006
Cash	$ 31,000	$ 57,000
Accounts receivable	77,000	64,000
Inventory	192,000	140,000
Prepaid expenses	12,140	16,540
Land	100,000	150,000
Equipment	215,000	175,000
Accumulated depreciation—equipment	(70,000)	(42,000)
Building	250,000	250,000
Accumulated depreciation—building	(70,000)	(50,000)
Total	$737,140	$760,540

Liabilities and Stockholders' Equity		
Accounts payable	$ 58,000	$ 45,000
Bonds payable	235,000	265,000
Common stock, $1 par	280,000	250,000
Retained earnings	164,140	200,540
Total	$737,140	$760,540

Additional information:

1. Operating expenses include depreciation expense $65,000 and charges from prepaid expenses of $4,400.
2. Land was sold for cash at cost.
3. Cash dividends of $69,290 were paid.
4. Net income for 2007 was $32,890.
5. Equipment was purchased for $80,000 cash. In addition, equipment costing $40,000 with a book value of $23,000 was sold for $25,000 cash.
6. Bonds were converted at face value by issuing 30,000 shares of $1 par value common stock.

Instructions

Cash from operations
$48,290

Prepare a statement of cash flows for 2007 using the indirect method.

Problems: Set C

Visit the book's website at **www.wiley.com/college/kimmel** and choose the Student Companion site to access Problem Set C.

Continuing Cookie Chronicle

(*Note:* This is a continuation of the Cookie Chronicle from Chapters 1 through 11.)

CCC12 Natalie is preparing the balance sheet and income statement of Cookie & Coffee Creations Inc. and would like you to prepare the cash flow statement. The comparative balance sheet of Cookie & Coffee Creations Inc. at October 31, 2009 for the years 2009 and 2008 and the income statement for the year ended October 31, 2009, are presented on page 639.

Additional information:

1. All of the computer equipment was disposed of at the beginning of the year for $500 cash. New computer equipment was then bought for $4,000 cash.
2. Additional kitchen equipment was bought for $14,000 on November 1, 2008. A $9,000 note payable was signed. The terms provide for equal semi-annual installment payments of $1,500 on May 1 and November 1 of each year, plus interest of 5% on the outstanding principal balance.
3. Additional furniture was bought for $7,500 cash.
4. Dividends were declared on the preferred and common stock on October 15, 2009, to be paid on November 15, 2009.
5. Accounts payable relate only to merchandise creditors.
6. Prepaid expenses relate only to other operating expenses.

Instructions

(a) Prepare a statement of cash flows for Cookie & Coffee Creations Inc. for the year ended October 31, 2009, using the indirect method.
*(b) Prepare a statement of cash flows for Cookie & Coffee Creations Inc. for the year ended October 31, 2009, using the direct method.

COOKIE & COFFEE CREATIONS INC.
Balance Sheet
October 31, 2009

Assets	2009	2008
Cash	$ 34,324	$13,050
Accounts receivable	3,250	2,710
Inventory	7,897	7,450
Prepaid expenses	6,300	6,050
Furniture and fixtures	12,500	5,000
Accumulated depreciation—furniture and fixtures	(2,000)	(1,000)
Computer equipment	4,000	4,500
Accumulated depreciation—computer equipment	(600)	(1,500)
Kitchen equipment	80,000	66,000
Accumulated depreciation—kitchen equipment	(22,600)	(6,600)
Total assets	$123,071	$95,660

Liabilities and Stockholders' Equity		
Accounts payable	$ 3,650	$ 2,450
Income taxes payable	10,251	11,200
Dividends payable	28,000	25,000
Salaries payable	2,250	1,280
Interest payable	188	0
Note payable	7,500	0
Preferred stock, no par, $6 cumulative, 3,000 and 2,500 shares issued, respectively	15,000	12,500
Common stock, $1 par—23,180 shares issued and outstanding	23,180	23,180
Additional paid-in capital—Treasury stock	250	250
Retained earnings	32,802	19,800
Total liabilities and stockholders' equity	$123,071	$95,660

COOKIE & COFFEE CREATIONS INC.
Income Statement
Year Ended October 31, 2009

Sales		$485,625
Cost of goods sold		222,694
Gross profit		262,931
Operating expenses		
Depreciation expense	$ 17,600	
Salaries and wages expense	147,979	
Other operating expenses	43,186	208,765
Income from operations		54,166
Other expenses		
Interest expense	$ 413	
Loss on sale of computer equipment	2,500	2,913
Income before income tax		51,253
Income tax expense		10,251
Net income		$ 41,002

Financial Reporting and Analysis

FINANCIAL REPORTING PROBLEM: *Tootsie Roll Industries, Inc.*

BYP12-1 The financial statements of Tootsie Roll Industries are presented in Appendix A.

Instructions
Answer the following questions.
(a) What was the amount of net cash provided by operating activities for 2004? For 2003? What were some causes of any significant changes in cash from operations between 2003 and 2004?
(b) What was the amount of increase or decrease in cash and cash equivalents for the year ended December 31, 2004?
(c) Which method of computing net cash provided by operating activities does Tootsie Roll use?
(d) From your analysis of the 2004 statement of cash flows, was the change in accounts receivable a decrease or an increase? Was the change in inventories a decrease or an increase? Was the change in accounts payable a decrease or an increase?
(e) What was the net cash used by investing activities for 2004?
(f) What was the amount of interest paid in 2004? What was the amount of income taxes paid in 2004?

COMPARATIVE ANALYSIS PROBLEM: *Tootsie Roll vs. Hershey Foods*

BYP12-2 The financial statements of Hershey Foods are presented in Appendix B, following the financial statements for Tootsie Roll Industries in Appendix A.

Instructions
(a) Based on the information in these financial statements, compute these 2004 ratios for each company:
  (1) Current cash debt coverage.
  (2) Cash debt coverage.
(b) What conclusions about the management of cash can you draw from these data?

RESEARCH CASE

BYP12-3 The April 16, 2004, edition of the *Wall Street Journal* contains an article by Jonathan Weil titled, "Outside Audit: 'Cash Flow Never Lies'—Or Does It?"

Instructions
Read the article and answer the following questions.
(a) According to the article, why do investors pay close attention to the statement of cash flows?
(b) In what section of the statement of cash flows are customer-related cash flows usually reported? In what section of the statement of cash flows are loans to other entities usually reported?
(c) In what section of the statement of cash flows does Ford Motor Co. report loans to customers? In what section of the statement of cash flows does Navistar report loans to customers? What implication does this have for cash flows from operations?

INTERPRETING FINANCIAL STATEMENTS

BYP12-4 The incredible growth of Amazon.com has put fear into the hearts of traditional retailers. Its stock price has soared to amazing levels. However, in 2001 many investors were very concerned about whether Amazon would survive since it had never earned a profit, and it was burning through cash. Some investors sold, but others decided to hold on to their investment in the company's stock. The following information is taken from the 2001 and 2004 financial statements of Amazon.com.

($ in millions)	2001	2004
Current assets	$1,207.9	$2,539.4
Total assets	1,637.5	3,248.5
Current liabilities	921.4	1,620.4
Total liabilities	3,077.5	5,096.1
Cash provided by operations	(119.8)	566.6
Capital expenditures	50.3	89.1
Dividends paid	0	0
Net income (loss)	(567.3)	588.5
Average current liabilities	948.2	1,436.6
Average total liabilities	3,090.0	4,773.4

Instructions

(a) Calculate the current ratio and current cash debt coverage ratio for Amazon.com for 2001 and 2004, and discuss its comparative liquidity.

(b) Calculate the cash debt coverage ratio and the debt to total assets ratio for Amazon.com for 2001 and 2004, and discuss its comparative solvency.

(c) Amazon.com has avoided purchasing large warehouses. Instead, it has used those of others. In order to increase customer satisfaction Amazon may have to build its own warehouses. Calculate free cash flow for Amazon.com for 2001 and 2004, and discuss its ability to purchase warehouses and to finance expansion from internally generated cash.

(d) Based on your findings in parts (a) through (d), can you conclude whether or not Amazon.com's amazing stock price is justified?

FINANCIAL ANALYSIS ON THE WEB

BYP12-5   *Purpose:* Use the Internet to view SEC filings.

Address: **biz.yahoo.com/i** (or go to **www.wiley.com/college/kimmel**)

Steps

1. Enter a company's name.
2. Choose **Quote**. Answer questions (a) and (b).
3. Choose **Profile;** then choose **SEC**. Answer questions (c) and (d).

Instructions

Answer the following questions.

(a) What company did you select?

(b) What is its stock symbol? What is its selling price?

(c) What recent SEC filings are available for your viewing?

(d) Which filing is the most recent? What is the date?

Critical Thinking

DECISION MAKING ACROSS THE ORGANIZATION

BYP12-6   Ron Nord and Lisa Smith are examining the following statement of cash flows for Carpino Company for the year ended January 31, 2007.

CARPINO COMPANY
Statement of Cash Flows
For the Year Ended January 31, 2007

Sources of cash	
From sales of merchandise	$380,000
From sale of capital stock	420,000
From sale of investment (purchased below)	80,000
From depreciation	55,000
From issuance of note for truck	20,000
From interest on investments	6,000
Total sources of cash	961,000

(continues on next page)

Uses of cash	
For purchase of fixtures and equipment	330,000
For merchandise purchased for resale	258,000
For operating expenses (including depreciation)	160,000
For purchase of investment	75,000
For purchase of truck by issuance of note	20,000
For purchase of treasury stock	10,000
For interest on note payable	3,000
Total uses of cash	856,000
Net increase in cash	$ 105,000

Ron claims that Carpino's statement of cash flows is an excellent portrayal of a superb first year with cash increasing $105,000. Lisa replies that it was not a superb first year. Rather, she says, the year was an operating failure, that the statement is presented incorrectly, and that $105,000 is not the actual increase in cash. The cash balance at the beginning of the year was $140,000.

Instructions
With the class divided into groups, answer the following.
(a) Using the data provided, prepare a statement of cash flows in proper form using the indirect method. The only noncash items in the income statement are depreciation and the gain from the sale of the investment.
(b) With whom do you agree, Ron or Lisa? Explain your position.

COMMUNICATION ACTIVITY

BYP12-7   Kyle Benson, the owner-president of Iris Co., is unfamiliar with the statement of cash flows that you, as his accountant, prepared. He asks for further explanation.

Instructions
Write him a brief memo explaining the form and content of the statement of cash flows as shown in Illustration 12-14 (page 602).

ETHICS CASE

BYP12-8   On The Road Again Corp. is a medium-sized wholesaler of automotive parts. It has 10 stockholders who have been paid a total of $1 million in cash dividends for 8 consecutive years. The board's policy requires that, for this dividend to be declared, net cash provided by operating activities as reported in On The Road Again's current year's statement of cash flows must exceed $1 million. President and CEO Willie Morton's job is secure so long as he produces annual operating cash flows to support the usual dividend.

At the end of the current year, controller Robert Jennings presents president Willie Morton with some disappointing news: The net cash provided by operating activities is calculated by the indirect method to be only $970,000. The president says to Robert, "We must get that amount above $1 million. Isn't there some way to increase operating cash flow by another $30,000?" Robert answers, "These figures were prepared by my assistant. I'll go back to my office and see what I can do." The president replies, "I know you won't let me down, Robert."

Upon close scrutiny of the statement of cash flows, Robert concludes that he can get the operating cash flows above $1 million by reclassifying a $60,000, 2-year note payable listed in the financing activities section as "Proceeds from bank loan—$60,000." He will report the note instead as "Increase in payables—$60,000" and treat it as an adjustment of net income in the operating activities section. He returns to the president, saying, "You can tell the board to declare their usual dividend. Our net cash flow provided by operating activities is $1,030,000." "Good man, Robert! I knew I could count on you," exults the president.

Instructions
(a) Who are the stakeholders in this situation?
(b) Was there anything unethical about the president's actions? Was there anything unethical about the controller's actions?
(c) Are the board members or anyone else likely to discover the misclassification?

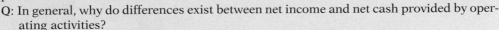

Answers to Business Insight and Accounting across the Organization Questions

p. 589

Q: In general, why do differences exist between net income and net cash provided by operating activities?

A: The differences are explained by differences in the timing of the reporting of revenues and expenses under accrual accounting versus cash. Under accrual accounting, companies report revenues when earned, even if cash hasn't been received, and they report expenses when incurred, even if cash hasn't been paid.

p. 592

Q: Why do companies have negative cash from operations during the introductory phase?

A: During the introductory phase companies usually spend more on inventory than the amount expensed for cost of goods sold because they are building up inventory, and their cash collections frequently lag the amount reported for sales. Therefore, even if they are reporting positive net income, they frequently report negative cash from operations.

p. 594

Q: For what reasons might managers at WorldCom and at Dynegy take the actions noted above?

A: Analysts increasingly use cash-flow-based measures of income, such as cash flow provided by operations, in addition to net income. More investors now focus on cash flow from operations, and some compensation contracts now have bonuses tied to cash-flow numbers. Thus, some managers have taken actions that artificially increase cash flow from operations.

p. 600

Q: Why does GM's cash provided by operating activities drop so precipitously when the company's sales figures decline?

A: GM's cash inflow is directly related to how many cars it sells. But many of its cash outflows are not tied to sales—they are "fixed." For example, many of its employee payroll costs are very rigid due to labor contracts. Therefore, even though sales (and therefore cash inflows) fall, these cash outflows don't decline.

p. 606

Q: If the ratio of net income to cash from operations differs significantly from 1, does that always mean that a company has poor-quality earnings?

A: When the ratio of net income to cash from operations differs significantly from 1, it means that an investor should closely examine the reasons why net income and cash from operations differ. However, as discussed in this chapter, at various stages in a company's life cycle, there can be legitimate reasons why net income and cash flow differ.

Answer to Tootsie Roll Review It Question 2, p. 594

Tootsie Roll has positive cash from operations that exceeds its net income. Its cash from operations exceeded its dividends paid and its capital expenditures. Tootsie Roll appears to be in the middle to late maturity phase.

Answers to Self-Study Questions

1. c   2. b   3. a   4. c   5. d   6. b   7. c   8. a   9. d   10. b
11. a   12. d   *13. c   *14. d

13

Financial Analysis: The Big Picture

STUDY OBJECTIVES

After studying this chapter,
you should be able to:

1 Understand the concept of sustainable income.

2 Indicate how irregular items are presented.

3 Explain the concept of comprehensive income.

4 Describe and apply horizontal analysis.

5 Describe and apply vertical analysis.

6 Identify and compute ratios used in analyzing a company's liquidity, solvency, and profitability.

7 Understand the concept of quality of earnings.

THE NAVIGATOR

THE NAVIGATOR

- Scan *Study Objectives*
- Read *Feature Story*
- Read *Preview*
- Read text and answer *Before You Go On*
  p. 653   p. 661   p. 663
- Work *Using the Decision Toolkit*
- Review *Summary of Study Objectives*
- Work *Demonstration Problem*
- Answer *Self-Study Questions*
- Complete *Assignments*

FEATURE STORY

Making the Numbers

There it is again, perched near the top of *Fortune*'s "Most Admired Companies" list. But when the people who run General Electric go out in public these days, they don't exactly get to bask in adulation. Instead, they have to explain how their company is *not* like Enron, or Global Crossing, or Tyco.

At one level, that's a pretty easy argument to make. GE is not about to collapse or to break up. It has tons of cash, and its businesses generate upwards of a billion dollars every month. It is one of only a handful of companies with a triple-A credit rating. It makes real things like turbines and refrigerators that people spend real money to buy.

GE also has an enviable record of pleasing Wall Street. Quarter after quarter, year after year, GE's earnings come gushing in, usually at least 10% higher than the year before, and almost invariably in line with analysts' estimates.

This used to be seen as a good thing. "Making the numbers" became the most watched measure of corporate performance. By missing only once during a 10-year period (by a penny, in the fourth quarter of 1997), GE ensured itself a hallowed place in the corporate hall of fame.

But as one analyst noted, "Smoking used to be chic and fashionable and cool; now it's not. The

companies that reliably deliver 15% earnings growth year after year are the new smokers." All of which means that GE's chief executive, Jeffrey Immelt, now finds himself having to tell interviewer after interviewer that no, he's not an earnings cheat.

"Would a miss be more honest?" Immelt asks, with exasperation in his voice. "I think that's terrible. That's where the world has gotten totally turned on its head, where somewhere I'd walk up to a podium and get a Nobel Peace Prize for saying 'I missed my numbers—aren't you proud of me?' "

Source: Adapted from Justin Fox, "What's So Great About GE?" *Fortune* (March 4, 2002), pp. 65–66.

☑ THE NAVIGATOR

On the World Wide Web
General Electric: www.ge.com

As indicated in our Feature Story, even the most admired companies in the United States are under attack for their earnings and disclosure practices. A climate of skepticism has caused many companies to lose billions of dollars in market value if there is even the slightest hint that the company is involved in some form of creative accounting. The purpose of this chapter is to explain the importance of **performance measurement** and to highlight the difficulties of developing **high-quality earnings numbers**, given the complexities of modern business transactions.

The content and organization of this chapter are as follows.

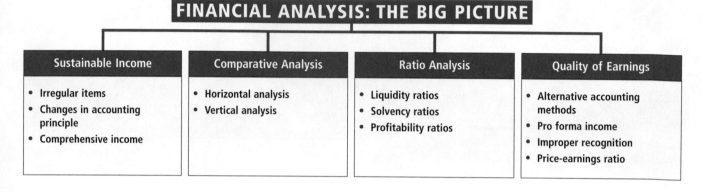

FINANCIAL ANALYSIS: THE BIG PICTURE

Sustainable Income	Comparative Analysis	Ratio Analysis	Quality of Earnings
• Irregular items • Changes in accounting principle • Comprehensive income	• Horizontal analysis • Vertical analysis	• Liquidity ratios • Solvency ratios • Profitability ratios	• Alternative accounting methods • Pro forma income • Improper recognition • Price-earnings ratio

THE NAVIGATOR

Sustainable Income

STUDY OBJECTIVE

1

Understand the concept of sustainable income.

Ultimately, the value of a company is a function of its future cash flows. When analysts use this year's net income to estimate future cash flows, they must make sure that this year's net income does not include irregular (i.e., out of the ordinary) revenues, expenses, gains, or losses. Net income adjusted for irregular items is referred to as sustainable income. **Sustainable income is the most likely level of income to be obtained in the future.** Sustainable income differs from actual net income by the amount of irregular revenues, expenses, gains, and losses included in this year's net income.

Users are interested in sustainable income because it helps them derive an estimate of future earnings without the "noise" of irregular items. For example, suppose Rye Corporation reports that this year's net income is $500,000 but included in that amount is a once-in-a-lifetime gain of $400,000. In estimating next year's net income for Rye Corporation, we would likely ignore this $400,000 gain and estimate that next year's net income will be in the neighborhood of $100,000. That is, based on this year's results, the company's sustainable income is roughly $100,000. Therefore, identifying irregular items is important if you are going to use reported earnings to estimate a company's value.

In earlier chapters you learned how to prepare and use a basic multiple-step income statement. In this chapter we will explain additional components of the income statement as well as a broader measure of performance called *comprehensive income*. Illustration 13-1 (page 647) presents the components of the income statement and comprehensive income; new items are presented in red. When estimating future cash flows, analysts must consider the implications that each of these components has for future cash flows.

Illustration 13-1
Components of the
income statement

Income Statement	
Sales	$XX
Cost of goods sold	XX
Gross profit	XX
Operating expenses	XX
Income from operations	XX
Other revenues (expenses) and gains (losses)	XX
Income before income taxes	XX
Income tax expense	XX
Income before irregular items	XX
Irregular items (net of tax)	XX
Net income	XX
Other comprehensive income items (net of tax)	XX
Comprehensive income	$XX

IRREGULAR ITEMS

As an aid in determining sustainable income, we identify irregular items by type on the income statement. There, companies report two types of irregular items:

1. Discontinued operations
2. Extraordinary items

Irregular items are reported net of income taxes. That is, a company first calculates income tax expense for the income before irregular items. Then it calculates income tax expense for each individual irregular item. The general concept is, "Let the tax follow the income or loss."

STUDY OBJECTIVE

2

Indicate how irregular items
are presented.

Discontinued Operations

To downsize its operations, General Dynamics Corp. sold its missile business to Hughes Aircraft Co. for $450 million. In its income statement, General Dynamics reported the sale in a separate section entitled "Discontinued operations." **Discontinued operations** refers to the disposal of a significant component of a business, such as the elimination of a major class of customers or an entire activity. When the disposal of a significant component occurs, the income statement should report the gain (or loss) from discontinued operations, net of tax.

To illustrate, assume that Rozek Inc. has revenues of $2.5 million and expenses of $1.7 million from continuing operations in 2007. The company therefore has income before income taxes of $800,000. During 2007 the company discontinued and sold its unprofitable chemical division. The loss on disposal of the chemical division (net of $90,000 taxes) was $210,000. Illustration 13-2 shows the income statement presentation, assuming a 30% tax rate on income before income taxes.

Illustration 13-2
Statement presentation of
discontinued operations

ROZEK INC. Income Statement (partial) For the Year Ended December 31, 2007	
Income before income taxes	$ 800,000
Income tax expense	240,000
Income before irregular items	560,000
Discontinued operations	
Loss from disposal of chemical division, net of $90,000 income tax savings	(210,000)
Net income	$ 350,000

This presentation clearly indicates the separate effects of continuing operations and discontinued operations on net income.

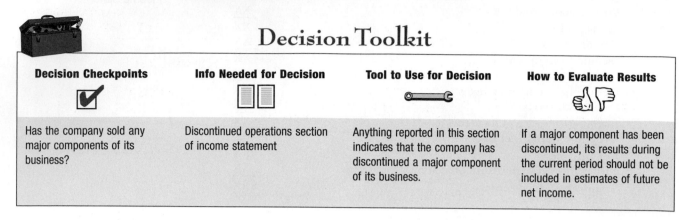

Decision Toolkit

Decision Checkpoints	Info Needed for Decision	Tool to Use for Decision	How to Evaluate Results
Has the company sold any major components of its business?	Discontinued operations section of income statement	Anything reported in this section indicates that the company has discontinued a major component of its business.	If a major component has been discontinued, its results during the current period should not be included in estimates of future net income.

Extraordinary Items

Extraordinary items are events and transactions that meet two conditions: They are **unusual in nature** and **infrequent in occurrence**. To be considered *unusual*, the item should be abnormal and only incidentally related to the customary activities of the entity. To be regarded as *infrequent*, the event or transaction should not be reasonably expected to recur in the foreseeable future.

A company must evaluate both criteria in terms of the environment in which it operates. Thus, Weyerhaeuser Co. reported the $36 million in damages to its timberland caused by the eruption of Mount St. Helens as an extraordinary item because the event was both unusual and infrequent. In contrast, Florida Citrus Company does not report frost damage to its citrus crop as an extraordinary item because frost damage is not viewed as infrequent.

Companies report extraordinary items net of taxes in a separate section of the income statement, immediately below discontinued operations. To illustrate, assume that in 2007 a revolutionary foreign government expropriated property held as an investment by Rozek Inc. If the loss is $70,000 before applicable income taxes of $21,000, the income statement presentation will show a deduction of $49,000, as in Illustration 13-3.

Helpful Hint Ordinary gains and losses are reported at pretax amounts in arriving at income before income taxes.

Illustration 13-3
Statement presentation of extraordinary items

ROZEK INC. Income Statement (partial) For the Year Ended December 31, 2007	
Income before income taxes	$ 800,000
Income tax expense	240,000
Income before irregular items	560,000
Discontinued operations: Loss from disposal of	
chemical division, net of $90,000 income tax savings	(210,000)
Extraordinary item: Expropriation of investment,	
net of $21,000 income tax savings	(49,000)
Net income	$ 301,000

If a transaction or event meets one but not both of the criteria for an extraordinary item, a company should report it in a separate line item in the upper half of the income statement, rather than in the bottom half as an extraordinary item. Usually companies report these items under either "Other revenues and gains" or "Other expenses and losses" at their gross amount (not net of tax). This is true, for example, of gains (losses) resulting from the sale of property, plant, and equipment, as explained in Chapter 9. Illustration 13-4 shows the appropriate classification of extraordinary and ordinary items.

Illustration 13-4
Classification of extraordinary and ordinary items

Extraordinary items

1. Effects of major natural casualties, if rare in the area.

2. Expropriation (takeover) of property by a foreign government.

3. Effects of a newly enacted law or regulation, such as a condemnation action.

Ordinary items

1. Effects of major natural casualties, not uncommon in the area.

2. Write-down of inventories or write-off of receivables.

3. Losses attributable to labor strikes.

4. Gains or losses from sales of property, plant, or equipment.

In summary, in evaluating a company, it generally makes sense to eliminate all irregular items in estimating future sustainable income.

Business Insight
Investor Perspective

Many companies these days are incurring restructuring charges as a result of attempting to reduce costs. Are these costs ordinary or extraordinary? Some companies report "one-time" restructuring charges over and over. Case in point: Toothpaste and diapers giant Procter & Gamble Co. reported a restructuring charge in 12 consecutive quarters, and Motorola had "special" charges 14 quarters in a row. On the other hand, some companies take a restructuring charge only once in five years. The one-size-fits-all classification therefore will not work. There appears to be no substitute for a careful analysis of the numbers that comprise net income.

 If a company takes a large restructuring charge, what is the effect on the company's current income statements versus future ones?

Decision Toolkit

Decision Checkpoints	Info Needed for Decision	Tool to Use for Decision	How to Evaluate Results
Has the company experienced any extraordinary events or transactions?	Extraordinary item section of income statement	Anything reported in this section indicates that the company experienced an event that was both unusual and infrequent.	These items should usually be ignored in estimating future net income.

CHANGES IN ACCOUNTING PRINCIPLE

For ease of comparison, users of financial statements expect companies to prepare such statements on a basis **consistent** with the preceding period. A **change in accounting principle** occurs when the principle used in the current year is different from the one used in the preceding year. Accounting rules permit a change when management can show that the new principle is preferable to the old principle. An example is a change in inventory costing methods (such as FIFO to average cost).

Companies report most changes in accounting principle retroactively.[1] That is, they report both the current period and previous periods using the new principle. As a result the same principle applies in all periods. This treatment improves the ability to compare results across years.

Decision Toolkit

Decision Checkpoints	Info Needed for Decision	Tool to Use for Decision	How to Evaluate Results
Has the company changed any of its accounting principles?	Effect of change in accounting principle on current and prior periods.	Management indicates that the new principle is preferable to the old principle.	Examine current and prior years reported, using new-principle basis to assess trends for estimating future income.

COMPREHENSIVE INCOME

STUDY OBJECTIVE

3

Explain the concept of comprehensive income.

Most revenues, expenses, gains, and losses are included in net income. However, certain gains and losses bypass net income. Instead, companies record these items as direct adjustments to stockholders' equity. Many analysts have expressed concern about this practice because they believe it reduces the usefulness of the income statement. To address this concern, the FASB requires companies to report not only net income, but also comprehensive income. **Comprehensive income** includes all changes in stockholders' equity during a period except those

---

[1]An exception to the general rule is a change in depreciation methods. The effects of this change are reported in current and future periods. Discussion of this approach in left for more advanced courses.

changes resulting from investments by stockholders and distributions (dividends) to stockholders.

Illustration of Comprehensive Income

Accounting standards require that companies adjust most investments in stocks and bonds up or down to their market value at the end of each accounting period. For example, assume that during 2007 Stassi Company purchased IBM stock for $10,000 as an investment. At the end of 2007 Stassi was still holding the investment, but the stock's market value was now $8,000. In this case, Stassi is required to reduce the recorded value of its IBM investment by $2,000. The $2,000 difference is an unrealized loss.

Should Stassi include this $2,000 unrealized loss in net income? It depends on whether Stassi classifies the IBM stock as a trading security or an available-for-sale security. A trading security is bought and held primarily for sale in the near term to generate income on short-term price differences. Companies report unrealized losses on trading securities in the "Other expenses and losses" section of the income statement. The rationale: It is likely that the company will realize the unrealized loss (or an unrealized gain), so the company should report the loss (gain) as part of net income.

If Stassi did not purchase the investment for trading purposes, it is classified as available-for-sale. Available-for-sale securities are held with the intent of selling them sometime in the future. Companies do not include unrealized gains or losses on available-for-sale securities in net income. Instead, they report them as part of "Other comprehensive income." For example, if Stassi does not intend to sell its IBM stock in the near term, it may not ever have to realize the loss. By the time Stassi sells the IBM stock, its value may have recovered, and Stassi may actually end up with a gain.

Format

One format for reporting comprehensive income is to report a combined statement of income and comprehensive income.[2] For example, assuming that Stassi Company has a net income of $300,000, the unrealized loss would adjust net income as follows.

STASSI CORPORATION Combined Statement of Income and Comprehensive Income (partial)	
Net income	$300,000
Unrealized loss on available-for-sale securities	2,000
Comprehensive income	$298,000

Illustration 13-5 Lower portion of combined statement of income and comprehensive income

Companies also report the unrealized loss on available-for-sale securities as a separate component of stockholders' equity. To illustrate, assume Stassi Corporation has common stock of $3,000,000, retained earnings of $1,500,000, and an unrealized loss on available-for-sale securities of $2,000. Illustration 13-6 (page 652) shows the balance sheet presentation of the unrealized loss.

---

[2]Computation of comprehensive income is sometimes shown in a separate statement of comprehensive income or as a section in the stockholders' equity statement.

Illustration 13-6
Unrealized loss in stockholders' equity section

STASSI CORPORATION Balance Sheet (partial)		
Stockholders' equity		
Common stock		$3,000,000
Retained earnings		1,500,000
Total paid-in capital and retained earnings		4,500,000
Less: **Unrealized loss on available-for-sale securities**		(2,000)
Total stockholders' equity		$4,498,000

Note that the presentation of the loss is similar to the presentation of the cost of treasury stock in the stockholders' equity section. (An unrealized gain would be added in this section of the balance sheet.) Reporting the unrealized gain or loss in the stockholders' equity section serves two important purposes: (1) It reduces the volatility of net income due to fluctuations in fair value, and (2) it informs the financial statement user of the gain or loss that would occur if the company sold the securities at fair value.

Complete Income Statement

The income statement for Pace Corporation in Illustration 13-7 presents the types of items found on this statement, such as net sales, cost of goods sold, operating expenses, and income taxes. In addition, it shows how companies report irregular items and comprehensive income (highlighted in red).

Illustration 13-7
Complete income statement

PACE CORPORATION Income Statement and Statement of Comprehensive Income For the Year Ended December 31, 2007		
Net sales		$440,000
Cost of goods sold		260,000
Gross profit		180,000
Operating expenses		110,000
Income from operations		70,000
Other revenues and gains	$ 5,600	
Other expenses and losses	(9,600)	(4,000)
Income before income taxes		66,000
Income tax expense ($66,000 × 30%)		19,800
Income before irregular items		46,200
Discontinued operations: Gain on disposal of Plastics Division, net of $15,000 income taxes ($50,000 × 30%)		35,000
Extraordinary item: Tornado loss, net of income tax savings $18,000 ($60,000 × 30%)		(42,000)
Net income		39,200
Add: Unrealized gain on available-for-sale securities		10,000
Comprehensive income		$ 49,200

CONCLUDING REMARKS

We have shown that the computation of the correct net income number can be elusive. In assessing the future prospects of a company, some investors focus on income from operations and therefore ignore all irregular and other items.

Others use measures such as net income, comprehensive income, or some modified version of one of these amounts.

BEFORE YOU GO ON . . .

▶ Review It

1. What is sustainable income?
2. What are irregular items, and what effect might they have on the estimation of future earnings and future cash flows?
3. What amount did Tootsie Roll Industries report as "Other comprehensive earnings" in 2004? By what percentage did Tootsie Roll's "Comprehensive earnings" differ from its "Net earnings"? The answer to this question appears on page 703.

Comparative Analysis

As indicated, in assessing the financial performance of a company, investors are interested in the core or sustainable earnings of a company. In addition, investors are interested in making comparisons from period to period. Throughout this book, we have relied on three types of comparisons to improve the decision usefulness of financial information.

1. **Intracompany basis.** Comparisons within a company are often useful to detect changes in financial relationships and significant trends. For example, a comparison of Kellogg's current year's cash amount with the prior year's cash amount shows either an increase or a decrease. Likewise, a comparison of Kellogg's year-end cash amount with the amount of its total assets at year-end shows the proportion of total assets in the form of cash.
2. **Intercompany basis.** Comparisons with other companies provide insight into a company's competitive position. For example, investors can compare Kellogg's total sales for the year with the total sales of its competitors in the breakfast cereal area, such as Quaker Oats and General Mills.
3. **Industry averages.** Comparisons with industry averages provide information about a company's relative position within the industry. For example, financial statement readers can compare Kellogg's financial data with the averages for its industry compiled by financial ratings organizations such as Dun & Bradstreet, Moody's, and Standard & Poor's, or with information provided on the Internet by organizations such as Yahoo! on its financial site.

We use three basic tools in financial statement analysis to highlight the significance of financial statement data:

1. Horizontal analysis
2. Vertical analysis
3. Ratio analysis

In previous chapters we relied primarily on ratio analysis, supplemented with some basic horizontal and vertical analysis. In the remainder of this section, we introduce more formal forms of horizontal and vertical analysis. In the next section we review ratio analysis in some detail.

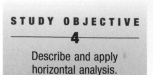

HORIZONTAL ANALYSIS

Horizontal analysis, also known as trend analysis, is a technique for evaluating a series of financial statement data over a period of time. Its purpose is to determine the increase or decrease that has taken place, expressed as either an amount or a percentage. For example, here are recent net sales figures (in millions) of Kellogg Company:

2004	2003	2002	2001	2000
$9,613.9	$8,811.5	$8,304.1	$7,548.4	$6,086.7

Alternative Terminology
Horizontal analysis is also often referred to as *trend analysis.*

If we assume that 2000 is the base year, we can measure all percentage increases or decreases relative to this base-period amount with the formula shown in Illustration 13-8.

Illustration 13-8
Horizontal analysis—
Computation of changes since base period

$$\text{Change Since Base Period} = \frac{\text{Current-Year Amount} - \text{Base-Year Amount}}{\text{Base-Year Amount}}$$

For example, we can determine that net sales for Kellogg Company increased approximately 24.0% [($7,548.4 − $6,086.7) ÷ $6,086.7] from 2000 to 2001. Similarly, we can also determine that net sales increased by 57.9% [($9,613.9 − $6,086.7) ÷ $6,086.7] from 2000 to 2004.

Alternatively, we can express current-year sales as a percentage of the base period. To do so, we would divide the current-year amount by the base-year amount, as shown in Illustration 13-9.

Illustration 13-9
Horizontal analysis—
Computation of current year in relation to base year

$$\text{Current Results in Relation to Base Period} = \frac{\text{Current-Year Amount}}{\text{Base-Year Amount}}$$

Current-period sales expressed as a percentage of the base period for each of the five years, using 2000 as the base period, are shown in Illustration 13-10.

Illustration 13-10
Horizontal analysis of net sales

KELLOGG COMPANY				
Net Sales (in millions)				
Base Period 2000				
2004	**2003**	**2002**	**2001**	**2000**
$9,613.9	$8,811.5	$8,304.1	$7,548.4	$6,086.7
157.95%	144.77%	136.43%	124.01%	100%

The large increase in net sales during 2001 would raise questions regarding possible reasons for such a significant change. Kellogg's 2001 notes to the financial statements explain that "the Company completed its acquisition of Keebler Foods Company" during 2001. This major acquisition would help explain the increase in sales highlighted by horizontal analysis.

To further illustrate horizontal analysis, we use the financial statements of Kellogg Company. Its two-year condensed balance sheets for 2004 and 2003, showing dollar and percentage changes, are presented in Illustration 13-11.

KELLOGG COMPANY, INC.
Condensed Balance Sheets
December 31
(in millions)

Illustration 13-11
Horizontal analysis of a
balance sheet

Assets	2004	2003	Increase (Decrease) during 2004 Amount	Percent
Current assets	$ 2,121.8	$ 1,787.9	$333.9	18.7
Property assets (net)	2,715.1	2,780.2	(65.1)	(2.3)
Other assets	5,953.5	5,574.6	378.9	6.8
Total assets	$10,790.4	$10,142.7	$647.7	6.4
Liabilities and Stockholders' Equity				
Current liabilities	$ 2,846.0	$ 2,766.0	$ 80.0	2.9
Long-term liabilities	5,687.2	5,933.5	(246.3)	(4.2)
Total liabilities	8,533.2	8,699.5	(166.3)	(1.9)
Stockholders' equity				
Common stock	103.8	128.3	(24.5)	(19.1)
Retained earnings	2,261.4	1,518.5	742.9	48.9
Treasury stock (cost)	(108.0)	(203.6)	(95.6)	(47.0)
Total stockholders' equity	2,257.2	1,443.2	814.0	56.4
Total liabilities and stockholders' equity	$10,790.4	$10,142.7	$647.7	6.4

The comparative balance sheet shows that a number of changes occurred in Kellogg's financial position from 2003 to 2004. In the assets section, current assets increased $333.9 million, or 18.7% ($333.9 ÷ $1,787.9), and property assets (net) decreased $65.1 million, or 2.3%. Other assets increased $378.9, or 6.8%. In the liabilities section, current liabilities increased $80.0 million, or 2.9%, while long-term liabilities decreased $246.3 million, or 4.2%. In the stockholders' equity section, we find that retained earnings increased $742.9 million, or 48.9%.

Illustration 13-12 presents a two-year comparative income statement of Kellogg Company for 2004 and 2003, showing dollar and percentage changes.

Helpful Hint When using horizontal analysis, be sure to examine both dollar amount changes and percentage changes. It is not necessarily bad if a company's earnings are growing at a declining rate. The **amount** of increase may be the same as or more than the base year, but the **percentage** change may be less because the base is greater each year.

KELLOGG COMPANY, INC.
Condensed Income Statements
For the Years Ended December 31
(in millions)

Illustration 13-12
Horizontal analysis of
an income statement

	2004	2003	Increase (Decrease) during 2004 Amount	Percent
Net sales	$9,613.9	$8,811.5	$802.4	9.1
Cost of goods sold	5,298.7	4,898.9	399.8	8.2
Gross profit	4,315.2	3,912.6	402.6	10.3
Selling and administrative expenses	2,634.1	2,368.5	265.6	11.2
Income from operations	1,681.1	1,544.1	137.0	8.9
Interest expense	308.6	371.4	(62.8)	(16.9)
Other income (expense), net	(6.6)	(3.2)	3.4	106.3
Income before income taxes	1,365.9	1,169.5	196.4	16.8
Income tax expense	475.3	382.4	92.9	24.3
Net income	$ 890.6	$ 787.1	$103.5	13.1

Helpful Hint Note that, in a horizontal analysis, while the amount column is additive (the total is $103.5 million), the percentage column is not additive (13.1% is **not a total**).

Horizontal analysis of the income statements shows the following changes: Net sales increased $802.4 million, or 9.1% ($802.4 ÷ $8,811.5). Cost of goods sold increased $399.8 million, or 8.2% ($399.8 ÷ $4,898.9). Selling and administrative expenses increased $265.6 million, or 11.2% ($265.6 ÷ $2,368.5). Overall, gross profit increased 10.3% and net income increased 13.1%. The increase in net income can be attributed to the increase in net sales and a decrease in interest expense.

The measurement of changes from period to period in percentages is relatively straightforward and quite useful. However, complications can result in making the computations. If an item has no value in a base year or preceding year and a value in the next year, no percentage change can be computed. Likewise, no percentage change can be computed if a negative amount appears in the base or preceding period and a positive amount exists the following year.

Decision Toolkit

Decision Checkpoints	Info Needed for Decision	Tool to Use for Decision	How to Evaluate Results
How do the company's financial position and operating results compare with those of the previous period?	Income statement and balance sheet	Comparative financial statements should be prepared over at least two years, with the first year reported being the base year. Changes in each line item relative to the base year should be presented both by amount and by percentage. This is called horizontal analysis.	Significant changes should be investigated to determine the reason for the change.

VERTICAL ANALYSIS

STUDY OBJECTIVE
5
Describe and apply vertical analysis.

Alternative Terminology
Vertical analysis is sometimes referred to as *common-size analysis.*

Vertical analysis, also called common-size analysis, is a technique for evaluating financial statement data that expresses each item in a financial statement as a **percent of a base amount**. For example, on a balance sheet we might say that current assets are 22% of total assets (total assets being the base amount). Or on an income statement we might say that selling expenses are 16% of net sales (net sales being the base amount).

Presented in Illustration 13-13 (page 657) is the comparative balance sheet of Kellogg for 2004 and 2003, analyzed vertically. The base for the asset items is **total assets**, and the base for the liability and stockholders' equity items is **total liabilities and stockholders' equity**.

In addition to showing the relative size of each category on the balance sheet, vertical analysis may show the percentage change in the individual asset, liability, and stockholders' equity items. In this case, current assets increased $333.9 million from 2003 to 2004, and they increased from 17.6% to 19.7% of total assets. Property assets (net) decreased from 27.4% to 25.1% of total assets. Other assets increased from 55% to 55.2% of total assets. Also, retained earnings increased by $742.9 million from 2003 to 2004, and total stockholders' equity increased from 14.2% to 20.9% of total liabilities and stockholders' equity. This switch to a higher percentage of equity financing has two causes: First, total liabilities decreased by $166.3 million, going from 85.8% to 79.1% of total liabilities and stockholders' equity. Second, retained earnings increased by $742.9 million, going from 15.0% to 20.9% of total liabilities and stockholders' equity. Thus, the

Kellogg's

KELLOGG COMPANY, INC.
Condensed Balance Sheets
December 31
(in millions)

Illustration 13-13
Vertical analysis of a
balance sheet

	2004		2003	
Assets	**Amount**	**Percent***	**Amount**	**Percent***
Current assets	$ 2,121.8	19.7	$ 1,787.9	17.6
Property assets (net)	2,715.1	25.1	2,780.2	27.4
Other assets	5,953.5	55.2	5,574.6	55.0
Total assets	$10,790.4	100.0	$10,142.7	100.0
Liabilities and Stockholders' Equity				
Current liabilities	$ 2,846.0	26.4	$ 2,766.0	27.3
Long-term liabilities	5,687.2	52.7	5,933.5	58.5
Total liabilities	8,533.2	79.1	8,699.5	85.8
Stockholders' equity				
Common stock	103.8	1.0	128.3	1.2
Retained earnings	2,261.4	20.9	1,518.5	15.0
Treasury stock (cost)	(108.0)	(1.0)	(203.6)	(2.0)
Total stockholders' equity	2,257.2	20.9	1,443.2	14.2
Total liabilities and stockholders' equity	$10,790.4	100.0	$10,142.7	100.0

*Numbers have been rounded to total 100%.

company shifted toward a heavier reliance on equity financing both by using less long-term debt and by increasing the amount of retained earnings.

Vertical analysis of the comparative income statements of Kellogg, shown in Illustration 13-14, reveals that cost of goods sold **as a percentage of net sales** decreased from 55.6% to 55.1%, and selling and administrative expenses increased from 26.9% to 27.4%. Net income as a percent of net sales increased from 8.9% to 9.3%. Kellogg's increase in net income as a percentage of sales is due primarily to the decrease in interest expense as a percent of sales.

Kellogg's

KELLOGG COMPANY, INC.
Condensed Income Statements
For the Years Ended December 31
(in millions)

Illustration 13-14
Vertical analysis of an
income statement

	2004		2003	
	Amount	**Percent***	**Amount**	**Percent***
Net sales	$9,613.9	100.0	$8,811.5	100.0
Cost of goods sold	5,298.7	55.1	4,898.9	55.6
Gross profit	4,315.2	44.9	3,912.6	44.4
Selling and administrative expenses	2,634.1	27.4	2,368.5	26.9
Income from operations	1,681.1	17.5	1,544.1	17.5
Interest expense	308.6	3.2	371.4	4.2
Other income (expense), net	(6.6)	.1	(3.2)	.1
Income before income taxes	1,365.9	14.2	1,169.5	13.2
Income tax expense	475.3	4.9	382.4	4.3
Net income	$ 890.6	9.3	$ 787.1	8.9

*Numbers have been rounded to total 100%.

Vertical analysis also enables you to compare companies of different sizes. For example, one of Kellogg's main competitors is General Mills. Using vertical analysis, we can more meaningfully compare the condensed income statements of Kellogg and General Mills, as shown in Illustration 13-15.

Illustration 13-15
Intercompany comparison by vertical analysis

	CONDENSED INCOME STATEMENTS For the Year Ended December 31, 2004 (in millions)			
	Kellogg Company, Inc.		**General Mills, Inc.**	
	Amount	**Percent***	**Amount**	**Percent***
Net sales	$9,613.9	100.0	$11,070.0	100.0
Cost of goods sold	5,298.7	55.1	6,584.0	59.5
Gross profit	4,315.2	44.9	4,486.0	40.5
Selling and administrative expenses	2,634.1	27.4	2,443.0	22.1
Nonrecurring charges	0.0	—	26.0	.2
Income from operations	1,681.1	17.5	2,017.0	18.2
Other expenses and revenues (including income taxes)	790.5	8.2	962.0	8.7
Net income	$ 890.6	9.3	$ 1,055.0	9.5

*Numbers have been rounded to total 100%.

Although Kellogg's net sales are 13% less than those of General Mills, vertical analysis eliminates the impact of this size difference for our analysis. Kellogg has a higher gross profit, 44.9%, compared to 40.5% for General Mills, but Kellogg's selling and administrative expenses are 27.4% of net sales, while those of General Mills are 22.1% of net sales. Looking at net income, we see that the companies report similar percentages: Kellogg's net income as a percentage of net sales is 9.3%, compared to 9.5% for General Mills.

Decision Toolkit

Decision Checkpoints	Info Needed for Decision	Tool to Use for Decision	How to Evaluate Results
How do the relationships between items in this year's financial statements compare with those of last year or those of competitors?	Income statement and balance sheet	Each line item on the income statement should be presented as a percentage of net sales, and each line item on the balance sheet should be presented as a percentage of total assets or total liabilities and stockholders' equity. These percentages should be investigated for differences either across years in the same company or in the same year across different companies. This is called vertical analysis.	Any differences either across years or between companies should be investigated to determine the cause.

Ratio Analysis

In previous chapters we presented many ratios used for evaluating the financial health and performance of a company. Here we provide a summary listing of those ratios. (Page references to prior discussions are provided if you feel you need to review any individual ratios.) The appendix to this chapter provides an example of a comprehensive financial analysis employing these ratios.

STUDY OBJECTIVE

6

Identify and compute ratios used in analyzing a company's liquidity, solvency, and profitability.

LIQUIDITY RATIOS

Liquidity ratios (Illustration 13-16) measure the short-term ability of the enterprise to pay its maturing obligations and to meet unexpected needs for cash. Short-term creditors such as bankers and suppliers are particularly interested in assessing liquidity.

Illustration 13-16
Summary of liquidity ratios

Liquidity Ratios		
Working capital	Current assets $-$ Current liabilities	p. 59
Current ratio	$\dfrac{\text{Current assets}}{\text{Current liabilities}}$	p. 59
Current cash debt coverage ratio	$\dfrac{\text{Cash provided by operations}}{\text{Average current liabilities}}$	p. 607
Inventory turnover ratio	$\dfrac{\text{Cost of goods sold}}{\text{Average inventory}}$	p. 281
Days in inventory	$\dfrac{\text{365 days}}{\text{Inventory turnover ratio}}$	p. 281
Receivables turnover ratio	$\dfrac{\text{Net credit sales}}{\text{Average net receivables}}$	p. 388
Average collection period	$\dfrac{\text{365 days}}{\text{Receivables turnover ratio}}$	p. 388

SOLVENCY RATIOS

Solvency ratios (Illustration 13-17) measure the ability of the enterprise to survive over a long period of time. Long-term creditors and stockholders are interested in a company's long-run solvency, particularly its ability to pay interest as it comes due and to repay the face value of debt at maturity.

Illustration 13-17
Summary of solvency ratios

Solvency Ratios		
Debt to total assets ratio	$\dfrac{\text{Total liabilities}}{\text{Total assets}}$	p. 60
Cash debt coverage ratio	$\dfrac{\text{Cash provided by operations}}{\text{Average total liabilities}}$	p. 608
Times interest earned ratio	$\dfrac{\text{Net income} + \text{Interest expense} + \text{Tax expense}}{\text{Interest expense}}$	p. 493
Free cash flow	Cash provided by operations $-$ Capital expenditures $-$ Cash dividends	p. 63

PROFITABILITY RATIOS

Profitability ratios (Illustration 13-18) measure the income or operating success of an enterprise for a given period of time. A company's income, or lack of it, affects its ability to obtain debt and equity financing, its liquidity position, and its ability to grow. As a consequence, creditors and investors alike are interested in evaluating profitability. Profitability is frequently used as the ultimate test of management's operating effectiveness.

Illustration 13-18
Summary of profitability ratios

Profitability Ratios		
Earnings per share	$\dfrac{\text{Net income} - \text{Preferred stock dividends}}{\text{Average common shares outstanding}}$	p. 55
Price-earnings ratio	$\dfrac{\text{Stock price per share}}{\text{Earnings per share}}$	p. 662
Gross profit rate	$\dfrac{\text{Gross profit}}{\text{Net sales}}$	p. 234
Profit margin ratio	$\dfrac{\text{Net income}}{\text{Net sales}}$	p. 235
Return on assets ratio	$\dfrac{\text{Net income}}{\text{Average total assets}}$	p. 437
Asset turnover ratio	$\dfrac{\text{Net sales}}{\text{Average total assets}}$	p. 439
Payout ratio	$\dfrac{\text{Cash dividends declared on common stock}}{\text{Net income}}$	p. 556
Return on common stockholders' equity ratio	$\dfrac{\text{Net income} - \text{Preferred stock dividends}}{\text{Average common stockholders' equity}}$	p. 558

Business Insight
Investor Perspective

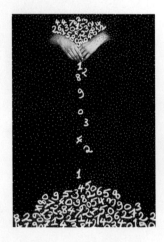

The apparent simplicity of the current ratio can have real-world limitations because adding equal amounts to both the numerator and the denominator causes the ratio to decrease.

Assume, for example, that a company has $2,000,000 of current assets and $1,000,000 of current liabilities; its current ratio is 2:1. If it purchases $1,000,000 of inventory on account, it will have $3,000,000 of current assets and $2,000,000 of current liabilities; its current ratio decreases to 1.5:1. If, instead, the company pays off $500,000 of its current liabilities, it will have $1,500,000 of current assets and $500,000 of current liabilities; its current ratio increases to 3:1. Thus, any trend analysis should be done with care because the ratio is susceptible to quick changes and is easily influenced by management.

 How might management influence a company's current ratio?

BEFORE YOU GO ON . . .

▶ **Review It**

1. What different bases can be used to compare financial information?
2. What is horizontal analysis?
3. What is vertical analysis?
4. Describe ratios that measure liquidity, solvency, and profitability.

Quality of Earnings

In evaluating the financial performance of a company, the quality of a company's earnings is of extreme importance to analysts. A company that has a high **quality of earnings** provides full and transparent information that will not confuse or mislead users of the financial statements.

The issue of quality of earnings has taken on increasing importance because recent accounting scandals suggest that some companies are spending too much time managing their income and not enough time managing their business. Here are some of the factors affecting quality of earnings.

STUDY OBJECTIVE

7

Understand the concept of quality of earnings.

ALTERNATIVE ACCOUNTING METHODS

Variations among companies in the application of generally accepted accounting principles may hamper comparability and reduce quality of earnings. For example, one company may use the FIFO method of inventory costing, while another company in the same industry may use LIFO. If inventory is a significant asset to both companies, it is unlikely that their current ratios are comparable. For example, if General Motors Corporation had used FIFO instead of LIFO for inventory valuation, its inventories in a recent year would have been 26% higher, which significantly affects the current ratio (and other ratios as well).

In addition to differences in inventory costing methods, differences also exist in reporting such items as depreciation, depletion, and amortization. Although these differences in accounting methods might be detectable from reading the notes to the financial statements, adjusting the financial data to compensate for the different methods is often difficult, if not impossible.

PRO FORMA INCOME

Companies whose stock is publicly traded are required to present their income statement following generally accepted accounting principles (GAAP). In recent years, many companies have been also reporting a second measure of income, called pro forma income. **Pro forma income** usually excludes items that the company thinks are unusual or nonrecurring. For example, in a recent year, Cisco Systems (a high-tech company) reported a quarterly net loss under GAAP of $2.7 billion. Cisco reported pro forma income for the same quarter as a profit of $230 million. This large difference in profits between GAAP income numbers and pro forma income is not unusual these days. For example, during one recent 9-month period the 100 largest firms on the Nasdaq stock exchange reported a total pro forma income of $19.1 billion, but a total loss as measured by GAAP of $82.3 billion—a difference of about $100 billion!

To compute pro forma income, companies generally can exclude any items they deem inappropriate for measuring their performance. Many analysts and investors are critical of the practice of using pro forma income because these numbers often make companies look better than they really are. As the financial press noted, pro forma numbers might be called EBS, which stands for "earnings before bad stuff." Companies, on the other hand, argue that pro forma numbers more clearly indicate sustainable income because they exclude unusual and non-recurring expenses. "Cisco's technique gives readers of financial statements a clear picture of Cisco's normal business activities," the company said in a statement issued in response to questions about its pro forma income accounting.

Recently, the SEC provided some guidance on how companies should present pro forma information. Stay tuned: Everyone seems to agree that pro forma numbers can be useful if they provide insights into determining a company's sustainable income. However, many companies have abused the flexibility that pro forma numbers allow and have used the measure as a way to put their companies in a good light.

IMPROPER RECOGNITION

Because some managers have felt pressure from Wall Street to continually increase earnings, they have manipulated the earnings numbers to meet these expectations. The most common abuse is the improper recognition of revenue. One practice that companies are using is *channel stuffing*: Offering deep discounts on their products to customers, companies encourage their customers to buy early (stuff the channel) rather than later. This lets the company report good earnings in the current period, but it often leads to a disaster in subsequent periods because customers have no need for additional goods. To illustrate, Bristol-Myers Squibb recently indicated that it used sales incentives to encourage wholesalers to buy more drugs than needed to meet patients' demands. As a result, the company had to issue revised financial statements showing corrected revenues and income.

Another practice is the improper capitalization of operating expenses. The classic case is WorldCom. It capitalized over $7 billion dollars of operating expenses so that it would report positive net income. In other situations, companies fail to report all their liabilities. Enron had promised to make payments on certain contracts if financial difficulty developed, but these guarantees were not reported as liabilities. In addition, disclosure was so lacking in transparency that it was impossible to understand what was happening at the company.

PRICE-EARNINGS RATIO

Earnings per share is net income available to common stockholders divided by the average number of common shares outstanding. The market value of a company's stock changes based on investors' expectations about a company's future earnings per share. In order to make a meaningful comparison of market values and earnings across firms, investors calculate the **price-earnings (P-E) ratio**. The P-E ratio divides the market price of a share of common stock by earnings per share.

Illustration 13-19
Formula for price-earnings (P-E) ratio

$$\text{Price-Earnings (P-E) Ratio} = \frac{\text{Stock Price per Share}}{\text{Earnings per Share}}$$

The P-E ratio reflects investors' assessment of a company's future earnings. The ratio of price to earnings will be higher if investors think that earnings will increase substantially in the future and therefore are willing to pay more per share of stock. A low price-earnings ratio often signifies that investors think the company's future earnings will not be strong. In addition, sometimes a low P-E ratio reflects the market's belief that a company has poor-quality earnings.

To illustrate, assume that two identical firms each have earnings per share of $5, but that one of the companies manipulated its accounting numbers to achieve the $5 figure. If investors perceive that one firm has lower-quality earnings, this perception will be reflected in a lower stock price, and consequently, a lower P-E.

Illustration 13-20 shows earnings per share and P-E ratios for five companies for 2004. Note the extreme difference in the P-E ratio of United States Steel versus Google Inc.

Company	Earnings Per Share	Price-Earnings Ratio
Kellogg Company	$ 2.22	20.5
Google Inc.	3.41	86.6
United States Steel	11.40	3.9
eBay Inc.	0.68	62.4
Nike	19.50	4.3

Illustration 13-20
Earnings per share and P-E ratios of various companies

Accounting across the Organization

Many company managers preparing their annual reports are piling on the paper in order to ease Enron-type worries on the part of investors. Natural-gas producer Williams Companies, Inc. turned out an eye-glazing annual report 1,234 pages in length. Nortel Networks Corporation added an extra two dozen pages to its annual report. Other companies have followed suit.

The trend to fuller disclosure has been a long time coming, observers say. But they caution that more paper does not necessarily mean more information that the average investor will understand. In addition, it is important to remember that annual reports are just one piece of the puzzle as to how companies present information to decision-makers.

Source: Elizabeth Church, "No Item Too Small as Firms Cave to Enron Disclosure Craze," *The (Toronto) Globe and Mail* (April 1, 2002), p. B1.

 Why might adding extra pages to the annual report not be beneficial to investors and analysts? What should be management's overriding objective in financial reporting?

BEFORE YOU GO ON . . .

▶ Review It

1. Explain what is meant by pro forma income.
2. Describe factors that reduce the quality of earnings.
3. Give an example of improper recognition.
4. What is the purpose of the P-E ratio?

✓ THE NAVIGATOR

Using the Decision Toolkit

In analyzing a company, you should always investigate an extended period of time in order to determine whether the condition and performance of the company are changing. The condensed financial statements of Kellogg Company for 2002 and 2001 are presented here. (The appendix to this chapter provides a complete analysis of Kellogg's 2004 and 2003 financial statements.)

Kellogg's
KELLOGG COMPANY, INC.
Balance Sheets
December 31
(in millions)

Assets	2002	2001
Current assets		
Cash and short-term investments	$ 100.6	$ 231.8
Accounts receivable (net)	741.0	762.3
Inventories	603.2	574.5
Prepaid expenses and other current assets	318.6	333.4
Total current assets	1,763.4	1,902.0
Property assets (net)	2,840.2	2,952.8
Intangibles and other assets	5,615.7	5,513.8
Total assets	$10,219.3	$10,368.6
Liabilities and Stockholders' Equity		
Current liabilities	$ 3,014.9	$ 2,207.6
Long-term liabilities	6,309.3	7,289.5
Stockholders' equity—common	895.1	871.5
Total liabilities and stockholders' equity	$10,219.3	$10,368.6

Kellogg's
KELLOGG COMPANY, INC.
Condensed Income Statements
For the Years Ended December 31
(in millions)

	2002	2001
Net sales	$8,304.1	$7,548.4
Cost of goods sold	4,569.0	4,211.4
Gross profit	3,735.1	3,337.0
Selling and administrative expenses	2,227.0	2,135.8
Nonrecurring charges	0	33.3
Income from operations	1,508.1	1,167.9
Interest expense	391.2	351.5
Other income (expense), net	27.4	(24.9)
Income before income taxes	1,144.3	791.5
Income tax expense	423.4	317.9
Net income	$ 720.9	$ 473.6

Instructions

Compute the following ratios for Kellogg for 2002 and 2001 and discuss your findings.

1. Liquidity:
  (a) Current ratio.
  (b) Inventory turnover ratio. (Inventory on December 31, 2000, was $443.8 million.)

2. Solvency:
   (a) Debt to total assets ratio.
   (b) Times interest earned ratio.

3. Profitability:
   (a) Return on common stockholders' equity ratio. (Stockholders' equity on December 31, 2000, was $897.5 million.)
   (b) Return on assets ratio. (Assets on December 31, 2000, were $4,886 million.)
   (c) Profit margin ratio.

Solution

1. Liquidity
   (a) Current ratio:

   $$2002: \quad \frac{\$1,763.4}{\$3,014.9} = .58:1$$

   $$2001: \quad \frac{\$1,902.0}{\$2,207.6} = .86:1$$

   (b) Inventory turnover ratio:

   $$2002: \quad \frac{\$4,569.0}{(\$603.2 + \$574.5)/2} = 7.8 \text{ times}$$

   $$2001: \quad \frac{\$4,211.4}{(\$574.5 + \$443.8)/2} = 8.3 \text{ times}$$

   We see that between 2001 and 2002 the current ratio decreased. The inventory turnover ratio also decreased. Both measures indicate that the company was less liquid in 2002.

2. Solvency
   (a) Debt to total assets ratio:

   $$2002: \quad \frac{\$9,324.2}{\$10,219.3} = 91\%$$

   $$2001: \quad \frac{\$9,497.1}{\$10,368.6} = 92\%$$

   (b) Times interest earned ratio:

   $$2002: \quad \frac{\$720.9 + \$423.4 + \$391.2}{\$391.2} = 3.9 \text{ times}$$

   $$2001: \quad \frac{\$473.6 + \$317.9 + \$351.5}{\$351.5} = 3.3 \text{ times}$$

   Kellogg's solvency as measured by the debt to total assets ratio improved slightly in 2002. We also can see that the times interest earned ratio increased.

3. Profitability
   (a) Return on common stockholders' equity ratio:

   $$2002: \quad \frac{\$720.9}{(\$895.1 + \$871.5)/2} = 82\%$$

   $$2001: \quad \frac{\$473.6}{(\$871.5 + \$897.5)/2} = 54\%$$

   (b) Return on assets ratio:

   $$2002: \quad \frac{\$720.9}{(\$10,219.3 + \$10,368.6)/2} = 7\%$$

   $$2001: \quad \frac{\$473.6}{(\$10,368.6 + \$4,886.0)/2} = 6\%$$

(c) Profit margin ratio:

$$2002: \quad \frac{\$720.9}{\$8,304.1} = 9\%$$

$$2001: \quad \frac{\$473.6}{\$7,548.4} = 6\%$$

Kellogg's return on common stockholders' equity ratio increased sharply. This increase was the result of increases in both its return on assets and its profit margin ratios.

Summary of Study Objectives

1 *Understand the concept of sustainable income.* Sustainable income refers to a company's ability to sustain its profits from operations.

2 *Indicate how irregular items are presented.* Irregular items—discontinued operations and extraordinary items—are presented on the income statement net of tax below "Income before irregular items" to highlight their unusual nature. Changes in accounting principle are reported retroactively.

3 *Explain the concept of comprehensive income.* Comprehensive income includes all changes in stockholders' equity during a period except those resulting from investments by stockholders and distributions to stockholders. "Other comprehensive income" is added to net income to arrive at comprehensive income.

4 *Describe and apply horizontal analysis.* Horizontal analysis is a technique for evaluating a series of data over a period of time to determine the increase or decrease that has taken place, expressed as either an amount or a percentage.

5 *Describe and apply vertical analysis.* Vertical analysis is a technique that expresses each item in a financial statement as a percentage of a relevant total or a base amount.

6 *Identify and compute ratios used in analyzing a company's liquidity, solvency, and profitability.* Financial ratios are provided in Illustration 13-16 (liquidity), Illustration 13-17 (solvency), and Illustration 13-18 (profitability).

7 *Understand the concept of quality of earnings.* A high quality of earnings provides full and transparent information that will not confuse or mislead users of the financial statements. Issues related to quality of earnings are (1) alternative accounting methods, (2) pro forma income, and (3) improper recognition. The price-earnings (P-E) ratio reflects investors' assessment of a company's future earnings potential.

Decision Toolkit—A Summary

Decision Checkpoints	Info Needed for Decision	Tool to Use for Decision	How to Evaluate Results
Has the company sold any major components of its business?	Discontinued operations section of income statement	Anything reported in this section indicates that the company has discontinued a major component of its business.	If a major component has been discontinued, its results during the current period should not be included in estimates of future net income.
Has the company experienced any extraordinary events or transactions?	Extraordinary item section of income statement	Anything reported in this section indicates that the company experienced an event that was both unusual and infrequent.	These items should usually be ignored in estimating future net income.
Has the company changed any of its accounting principles?	Effect of change in accounting principle on current and prior periods.	Management indicates that the new principle is preferable to the old principle.	Examine current and prior years reported, using new-principle basis to assess trends for estimating future income.
How do the company's financial position and operating results compare with those of the previous period?	Income statement and balance sheet	Comparative financial statements should be prepared over at least two years, with the first year reported being the base year. Changes in each line item relative to the base year should be presented both by amount and by percentage. This is called horizontal analysis.	Significant changes should be investigated to determine the reason for the change.
How do the relationships between items in this year's financial statements compare with those of last year or those of competitors?	Income statement and balance sheet	Each line item on the income statement should be presented as a percentage of net sales, and each line item on the balance sheet should be presented as a percentage of total assets or total liabilities and stockholders' equity. These percentages should be investigated for differences either across years in the same company or in the same year across different companies. This is called vertical analysis.	Any differences either across years or between companies should be investigated to determine the cause.

APPENDIX
COMPREHENSIVE ILLUSTRATION
OF RATIO ANALYSIS

In previous chapters we presented many ratios used for evaluating the financial health and performance of a company. In this appendix we provide a comprehensive review of those ratios and discuss some important relationships among them. Since earlier chapters demonstrated the calculation of each of these ratios, in this chapter we instead focus on their interpretation. Page references to prior discussions point you to any individual ratios you feel you need to review.

We used the financial information in Illustrations 13A-1 through 13A-4 to calculate Kellogg's 2004 ratios. You can use these data to review the computations.

Illustration 13A-1
Kellogg Company's
balance sheet

KELLOGG COMPANY, INC.
Balance Sheets
December 31
(in millions)

Assets	2004	2003
Current assets		
Cash and short-term investments	$ 417.4	$ 141.2
Accounts receivable	776.4	754.8
Inventories	681.0	649.8
Prepaid expenses and other current assets	247.0	242.1
Total current assets	2,121.8	1,787.9
Property assets (net)	2,715.1	2,780.2
Intangibles and other assets	5,953.5	5,574.6
Total assets	$10,790.4	$10,142.7
Liabilities and Stockholders' Equity		
Current liabilities	$ 2,846.0	$ 2,766.0
Long-term liabilities	5,687.2	5,933.5
Stockholders' equity—common	2,257.2	1,443.2
Total liabilities and stockholders' equity	$10,790.4	$10,142.7

As indicated in the chapter, we can classify ratios into three types for analysis of the primary financial statements.

1. **Liquidity ratios:** Measures of the short-term ability of the enterprise to pay its maturing obligations and to meet unexpected needs for cash.
2. **Solvency ratios:** Measures of the ability of the enterprise to survive over a long period of time.
3. **Profitability ratios:** Measures of the income or operating success of an enterprise for a given period of time.

As a tool of analysis, ratios can provide clues to underlying conditions that may not be apparent from an inspection of the individual components of a particular ratio. But a single ratio by itself is not very meaningful. Accordingly, in this discussion we use the three comparisons listed on the top of page 670.

KELLOGG COMPANY, INC.
Condensed Income Statements
For the Years Ended December 31
(in millions)

	2004	2003
Net sales	$9,613.9	$8,811.5
Cost of goods sold	5,298.7	4,898.9
Gross profit	4,315.2	3,912.6
Selling and administrative expenses	2,634.1	2,368.5
Income from operations	1,681.1	1,544.1
Interest expense	308.6	371.4
Other income (expense), net	(6.6)	(3.2)
Income before income taxes	1,365.9	1,169.5
Income tax expense	475.3	382.4
Net income	$ 890.6	$ 787.1

Illustration 13A-2 Kellogg Company's income statement

KELLOGG COMPANY, INC.
Condensed Statements of Cash Flows
For the Years Ended December 31
(in millions)

	2004	2003
Cash flows from operating activities		
Cash receipts from operating activities	$ 9,592.3	$8,797.7
Cash payments for operating activities	8,363.3	7,626.7
Net cash provided by operating activities	1,229.0	1,171.0
Cash flows from investing activities		
Purchases of property, plant, and equipment	(278.6)	(247.2)
Other investing activities	8.2	28.2
Net cash used in investing activities	(270.4)	(219.0)
Cash flows from financing activities		
Issuance of common stock	291.8	121.6
Issuance of debt	537.6	773.6
Reductions of debt	(823.9)	(1,331.6)
Payment of dividends	(417.6)	(412.4)
Repurchase of common stock and other items	(304.2)	(90.6)
Net cash provided by (used in) financing activities	(716.3)	(939.4)
Other	33.9	28.0
Increase (decrease) in cash and cash equivalents	276.2	40.6
Cash and cash equivalents at beginning of year	141.2	100.6
Cash and cash equivalents at end of year	$ 417.4	$ 141.2

Illustration 13A-3 Kellogg Company's statement of cash flows

Additional information	2004	2003
Average number of shares (millions)	412	407.9
Stock price at year-end	$44.66	$38.80

Illustration 13A-4
Additional information for Kellogg Company

1. **Intracompany comparisons** covering two years for Kellogg Company (using comparative financial information from Illustrations 13A-1, 13A-2, and 13A-3).
2. **Intercompany comparisons** using General Mills as one of Kellogg's principal competitors.
3. **Industry average comparisons** based on Reuters.com's median ratios for manufacturers of flour and other grain mill products and comparisons with other sources. For some of the ratios that we use, industry comparisons are not available. (These are denoted "na.")

Liquidity Ratios

Liquidity ratios measure the short-term ability of the enterprise to pay its maturing obligations and to meet unexpected needs for cash. Short-term creditors such as bankers and suppliers are particularly interested in assessing liquidity. The measures used to determine the enterprise's short-term debt-paying ability are the current ratio, the current cash debt coverage ratio, the receivables turnover ratio, the average collection period, the inventory turnover ratio, and average days in inventory.

1. **Current ratio.** The current ratio expresses the relationship of current assets to current liabilities, computed by dividing current assets by current liabilities. It is widely used for evaluating a company's liquidity and short-term debt-paying ability. The 2004 and 2003 current ratios for Kellogg and comparative data are shown in Illustration 13A-5.

Illustration 13A-5
Current ratio

| | | | Kellogg | | General Mills | Industry | Page in |
Ratio	Formula	Indicates:	2004	2003	2004	2004	book
Current ratio	Current assets / Current liabilities	Short-term debt-paying ability	.75	.65	1.17	1.41	59

What do the measures tell us? Kellogg's 2004 current ratio of .75 means that for every dollar of current liabilities, Kellogg has $0.75 of current assets. We sometimes state such ratios as .75:1 to reinforce this interpretation. Kellogg's current ratio—and therefore its liquidity—increased significantly in 2004. It is well below the industry average and that of General Mills.

2. **Current cash debt coverage ratio.** A disadvantage of the current ratio is that it uses year-end balances of current asset and current liability accounts. These year-end balances may not represent the company's current position during most of the year. The current cash debt coverage ratio partially corrects for this problem. It is the ratio of cash provided by operating activities to average current liabilities. Because it uses cash provided by operating activities rather than a balance at one point in time, it may provide a better representation of liquidity. Kellogg's current cash debt coverage ratio is shown in Illustration 13A-6.

Illustration 13A-6
Current cash debt coverage ratio

| | | | Kellogg | | General Mills | Industry | Page in |
Ratio	Formula	Indicates:	2004	2003	2004	2004	book
Current cash debt coverage ratio	Cash provided by operations / Average current liabilities	Short-term debt-paying ability (cash basis)	.44	.41	.47	na	607

Like the current ratio, this ratio increased in 2004 for Kellogg. Is the coverage adequate? Probably so. Kellogg's operating cash flow coverage of average current liabilities is similar to that of General Mills, and it exceeds a commonly accepted threshold of .40. No industry comparison is available.

3. **Receivables turnover ratio.**   Analysts can measure liquidity by how quickly a company converts certain assets to cash. Low values of the previous ratios can sometimes be compensated for if some of the company's current assets are highly liquid.

How liquid, for example, are the receivables? The ratio used to assess the liquidity of the receivables is the receivables turnover ratio, which measures the number of times, on average, a company collects receivables during the period. The receivables turnover ratio is computed by dividing net credit sales (net sales less cash sales) by average net receivables during the year. The receivables turnover ratio for Kellogg is shown in Illustration 13A-7.

Illustration 13A-7
Receivables turnover ratio

Ratio	Formula	Indicates:	Kellogg 2004	Kellogg 2003	General Mills 2004	Industry 2004	Page in book
Reccivables turnover ratio	Net credit sales / Average net receivables	Liquidity of receivables	12.6	11.8	11.1	11.5	388

We have assumed that all Kellogg's sales are credit sales. The receivables turnover ratio for Kellogg rose in 2004. The turnover of 12.6 times compares favorably with the industry median of 11.5 times, and is much higher than General Mills's turnover of 11.1 times.

4. **Average collection period.**   A popular variant of the receivables turnover ratio converts it into an average collection period in days. This is done by dividing the receivables turnover ratio into 365 days. The average collection period for Kellogg is shown in Illustration 13A-8.

Illustration 13A-8
Average collection period

Ratio	Formula	Indicates:	Kellogg 2004	Kellogg 2003	General Mills 2004	Industry 2004	Page in book
Average collection period	365 days / Receivables turnover ratio	Liquidity of receivables and collection success	29.0	30.9	32.9	31.7	388

Kellogg's 2004 receivables turnover of 12.6 times is divided into 365 days to obtain approximately 29 days. This means that the average collection period for receivables is about 29 days.

Analysts frequently use the average collection period to assess the effectiveness of a company's credit and collection policies. The general rule is that the collection period should not greatly exceed the credit term period (i.e., the time allowed for payment). Kellogg's average collection period is similar to those of General Mills and the industry.

5. **Inventory turnover ratio.**   The inventory turnover ratio measures the number of times on average a company sells the inventory during the period. Its purpose is to measure the liquidity of the inventory. The inventory turnover ratio is computed by dividing the cost of goods sold by the average inventory during the period. Unless seasonal factors are significant, average inventory can be computed from the beginning and ending inventory balances. Kellogg's inventory turnover ratio is shown in Illustration 13A-9.

Ratio	Formula	Indicates:	Kellogg 2004	Kellogg 2003	General Mills 2004	Industry 2004	Page in book
Inventory turnover ratio	Cost of goods sold / Average inventory	Liquidity of inventory	8.0	7.8	6.1	6.6	281

Illustration 13A-9
Inventory turnover ratio

Kellogg's inventory turnover ratio increased slightly in 2004. The turnover ratio of 8 times is higher than the industry average of 6.6 times and significantly better than General Mills's 6.1 times. Generally, the faster the inventory turnover, the less cash is tied up in inventory and the less the chance of inventory becoming obsolete. Of course, a downside of high inventory turnover is that the company can run out of inventory when it is needed.

6. **Days in inventory.** A variant of the inventory turnover ratio is the **days in inventory**, which measures the average number of days it takes to sell the inventory. The days in inventory for Kellogg is shown in Illustration 13A-10.

Illustration 13A-10
Days in inventory

Ratio	Formula	Indicates:	Kellogg 2004	Kellogg 2003	General Mills 2004	Industry 2004	Page in book
Days in inventory	365 days / Inventory turnover ratio	Liquidity of inventory and inventory management	45.6	46.8	59.8	55.3	281

Kellogg's 2004 inventory turnover ratio of 8 divided into 365 is approximately 45.6 days. An average selling time of 45 days is faster than the industry average and significantly faster than that of General Mills. Some of this difference might be explained by differences in product lines across the two companies, although in many ways the types of products of these two companies are quite similar.

Inventory turnover ratios vary considerably among industries. For example, grocery store chains have a turnover of 10 times and an average selling period of 37 days. In contrast, jewelry stores have an average turnover of 1.3 times and an average selling period of 281 days. Within a company there may even be significant differences in inventory turnover among different types of products. Thus, in a grocery store the turnover of perishable items such as produce, meats, and dairy products is faster than the turnover of soaps and detergents.

To conclude, nearly all of these liquidity measures suggest that Kellogg's liquidity increased slightly during 2004. Its liquidity appears acceptable when compared to the industry as a whole and better than that of General Mills.

Solvency Ratios

Solvency ratios measure the ability of the enterprise to survive over a long period of time. Long-term creditors and stockholders are interested in a company's long-run solvency, particularly its ability to pay interest as it comes due and to repay the face value of debt at maturity. The debt to total assets ratio, the times interest earned ratio, and the cash debt coverage ratio provide information about debt-paying ability. In addition, free cash flow provides information about the company's solvency and its ability to pay additional dividends or invest in new projects.

7. **Debt to total assets ratio.** The debt to total assets ratio measures the percentage of the total assets provided by creditors. It is computed by dividing total liabilities (both current and long-term) by total assets. This ratio indicates the degree of financial leveraging. It also provides some indication of the company's ability to withstand losses without impairing the interests of its creditors. The higher the percentage of debt to total assets, the greater the risk that the company may be unable to meet its maturing obligations. The lower the ratio, the more equity "buffer" is available to creditors if the company becomes insolvent. Thus, from the creditors' point of view, a low ratio of debt to total assets is desirable. Kellogg's debt to total assets ratio is shown in Illustration 13A-11.

Illustration 13A-11
Debt to total assets ratio

Ratio	Formula	Indicates:	Kellogg 2004	Kellogg 2003	General Mills 2004	Industry 2004	Page in book
Debt to total assets ratio	Total liabilities / Total assets	Percentage of total assets provided by creditors	79%	86%	72%	48%	60

Kellogg's 2004 ratio of 79% means that creditors have provided financing sufficient to cover 79% of the company's total assets. Alternatively, it says that Kellogg would have to liquidate 79% of its assets at their book value in order to pay off all of its debts. Kellogg's 79% is above the industry average of 48% as well as the 72% ratio of General Mills. Kellogg's solvency improved during the year. In that time, Kellogg's use of debt financing changed in two ways: First, Kellogg decreased its use of long-term debt slightly, and second, increased its equity by 56%. Both of these factors improved its solvency.

The adequacy of this ratio is often judged in light of the company's earnings. Generally, companies with relatively stable earnings, such as public utilities, have higher debt to total assets ratios than cyclical companies with widely fluctuating earnings, such as many high-tech companies.

Another ratio with a similar meaning is the **debt to equity ratio**. It shows the relative use of borrowed funds (total liabilities) compared with resources invested by the owners. Because this ratio can be computed in several ways, be careful when making comparisons with it. Debt may be defined to include only the noncurrent portion of liabilities, and intangible assets may be excluded from stockholders' equity (which would equal tangible net worth). If debt and assets are defined as above (all liabilities and all assets), then when the debt to total assets ratio equals 50%, the debt to equity ratio is 1:1.

8. **Times interest earned ratio.** The times interest earned ratio (also called interest coverage) indicates the company's ability to meet interest payments as they come due. It is computed by dividing income before interest expense and income taxes by interest expense. Note that this ratio uses income before interest expense and income taxes because this amount represents what is available to cover interest. Kellogg's times interest earned ratio is shown in Illustration 13A-12.

Illustration 13A-12
Times interest earned ratio

Ratio	Formula	Indicates:	Kellogg 2004	Kellogg 2003	General Mills 2004	Industry 2004	Page in book
Times interest earned ratio	(Net Income + Interest expense + Tax expense) / Interest expense	Ability to meet interest payments as they come due	5.4	4.1	4.1	5.9	493

For Kellogg the 2004 interest coverage was 5.4, which indicates that income before interest and taxes was 5.4 times the amount needed for interest expense. This exceeds the rate for General Mills, but it is less than the average rate for the industry. The debt to total assets ratio decreased for Kellogg during 2004, and its times interest earned ratio increased. These ratios indicate that Kellogg is better able to service its debt.

9. **Cash debt coverage ratio.** The ratio of cash provided by operating activities to average total liabilities, called the **cash debt coverage ratio**, is a cash-basis measure of solvency. This ratio indicates a company's ability to repay its liabilities from cash generated from operating activities without having to liquidate the assets used in its operations. Illustration 13A-13 shows Kellogg's cash debt coverage ratio.

Illustration 13A-13
Cash debt coverage ratio

Ratio	Formula	Indicates:	Kellogg 2004	Kellogg 2003	General Mills 2004	Industry 2004	Page in book
Cash debt coverage ratio	$\dfrac{\text{Cash provided by operations}}{\text{Average total liabilities}}$	Long-term debt-paying ability (cash basis)	.14	.13	.11	na	608

An industry average for this measure is not available. Kellogg's .14 is higher than General Mills's .11, and it increased from .13 in 2003. One way of interpreting this ratio is to say that net cash generated from one year of operations would be sufficient to pay off 14% of Kellogg's total liabilities. If 14% of this year's liabilities were retired each year, it would take approximately seven years to retire all of its debt. It would take General Mills approximately nine years to do so. A general rule of thumb is that a measure above .20 is acceptable.

10. **Free cash flow.** One indication of a company's solvency, as well as of its ability to pay dividends or expand operations, is the amount of excess cash it generated after investing to maintain its current productive capacity and paying dividends. This amount is referred to as **free cash flow**. For example, if you generate $100,000 of cash from operations but you spend $30,000 to maintain and replace your productive facilities at their current levels and pay $10,000 in dividends, you have $60,000 ($100,000 − $30,000 − $10,000) to use either to expand operations or to pay additional dividends. Kellogg's free cash flow is shown in Illustration 13A-14.

Illustration 13A-14
Free cash flow

Ratio	Formula	Indicates:	Kellogg 2004	Kellogg 2003	General Mills 2004	Industry 2004	Page in book
Free cash flow	Cash provided by operations − Capital expenditures − Cash dividends	Cash available for paying dividends or expanding operations	$532.8 (in millions)	$511.4	$421.0 (in millions)	na	63

Kellogg's free cash flow increased slightly from 2003 to 2004. During both years, the cash provided by operations was more than enough to allow Kellogg to acquire additional productive assets and maintain dividend payments. Kellogg could have used the remaining cash to reduce debt if necessary.

Profitability Ratios

Profitability ratios measure the income or operating success of an enterprise for a given period of time. A company's income, or the lack of it, affects its ability to obtain debt and equity financing, its liquidity position, and its ability to grow. As a consequence, creditors and investors alike are interested in evaluating profitability. Analysts frequently use profitability as the ultimate test of management's operating effectiveness.

Throughout this book we have introduced numerous measures of profitability. The relationships among measures of profitability are very important. Understanding them can help management determine where to focus its efforts to improve profitability. Illustration 13A-15 diagrams these relationships. Our discussion of Kellogg's profitability is structured around this diagram.

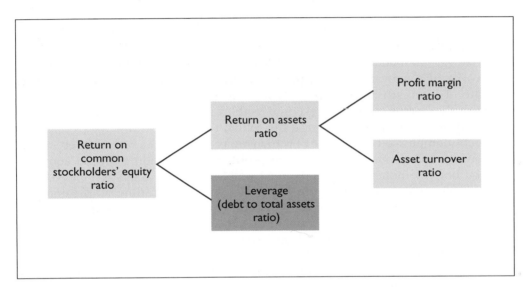

Illustration 13A-15
Relationships among profitability measures

11. **Return on common stockholders' equity ratio.** A widely used measure of profitability from the common stockholder's viewpoint is the **return on common stockholders' equity ratio**. This ratio shows how many dollars of net income the company earned for each dollar invested by the owners. It is computed by dividing net income minus any preferred stock dividends—that is, income available to common stockholders—by average common stockholders' equity. The return on common stockholders' equity for Kellogg is shown in Illustration 13A-16.

Illustration 13A-16
Return on common stockholders' equity ratio

| | | | Kellogg | | General Mills | Industry | Page in |
| | | | 2004 | 2003 | 2004 | 2004 | |
Ratio	Formula	Indicates:					book
Return on common stockholders' equity ratio	$\dfrac{\text{Net income} - \text{Preferred stock dividends}}{\text{Average common stockholders' equity}}$	Profitability of common stockholders' investment	48%	67%	22%	23%	558

Kellogg's 2004 rate of return on common stockholders' equity is unusually high at 48%, considering an industry average of 23% and General Mills's return of 22%. In the subsequent sections we investigate the causes of this high return.

12. **Return on assets ratio.** The return on common stockholders' equity ratio is affected by two factors: the **return on assets ratio** and the degree of leverage. The return on assets ratio measures the overall profitability of assets in terms of the income earned on each dollar invested in assets. It is computed by dividing net income by average total assets. Kellogg's return on assets ratio is shown in Illustration 13A-17.

Illustration 13A-17
Return on assets ratio

Ratio	Formula	Indicates:	Kellogg 2004	Kellogg 2003	General Mills 2004	Industry 2004	Page in book
Return on assets ratio	Net income / Average total assets	Overall profitability of assets	8.5%	7.7%	6%	7%	437

Kellogg had an 8.5% return on assets in 2004. This rate is higher than that of General Mills and the industry average.

Note that Kellogg's rate of return on stockholders' equity (48%) is substantially higher than its rate of return on assets (9%). The reason is that Kellogg has made effective use of **leverage**. **Leveraging** or **trading on the equity** at a gain means that the company has borrowed money at a lower rate of interest than the rate of return it earns on the assets it purchased with the borrowed funds. Leverage enables management to use money supplied by nonowners to increase the return to owners.

A comparison of the rate of return on assets with the rate of interest paid for borrowed money indicates the profitability of trading on the equity. If you borrow money at 8% and your rate of return on assets is 11%, you are trading on the equity at a gain. Note, however, that trading on the equity is a two-way street: For example, if you borrow money at 11% and earn only 8% on it, you are trading on the equity at a loss.

Kellogg earns more on its borrowed funds than it has to pay in interest. Thus, the return to stockholders exceeds the return on the assets because of the positive benefit of leverage. Recall from our earlier discussion that Kellogg's percentage of debt financing as measured by the ratio of debt to total assets (or debt to equity) was higher than General Mills's and the industry average. It appears that Kellogg's high return on stockholders' equity is due in part to its use of leverage.

13. **Profit margin ratio.** The return on assets ratio is affected by two factors, the first of which is the profit margin ratio. The **profit margin ratio**, or rate of return on sales, is a measure of the percentage of each dollar of sales that results in net income. It is computed by dividing net income by net sales for the period. Kellogg's profit margin ratio is shown in Illustration 13A-18.

Illustration 13A-18
Profit margin ratio

Ratio	Formula	Indicates:	Kellogg 2004	Kellogg 2003	General Mills 2004	Industry 2004	Page in book
Profit margin ratio	Net income / Net sales	Net income generated by each dollar of sales	9.3%	8.9%	10%	7%	235

Kellogg experienced a slight increase in its profit margin ratio from 2003 to 2004 of 8.9% to 9.3%. Its profit margin ratio was greater than the industry average of 7% but less than General Mills's 10%.

High-volume (high inventory turnover) enterprises such as grocery stores and pharmacy chains generally have low profit margins. Low-volume enterprises such as jewelry stores and airplane manufacturers have high profit margins.

14. **Asset turnover ratio.** The other factor that affects the return on assets ratio is the asset turnover ratio. The **asset turnover ratio** measures how efficiently a company uses its assets to generate sales. It is determined by dividing net sales by average total assets for the period. The resulting number shows the dollars of sales produced by each dollar invested in assets. Illustration 13A-19 shows the asset turnover ratio for Kellogg.

Illustration 13A-19
Asset turnover ratio

Ratio	Formula	Indicates:	Kellogg 2004	Kellogg 2003	General Mills 2004	Industry 2004	Page in book
Asset turnover ratio	Net sales / Average total assets	How efficiently assets are used to generate sales	.92	.87	.60	1.17	439

The asset turnover ratio shows that in 2004 Kellogg generated sales of $0.92 for each dollar it had invested in assets. The ratio rose from 2003 to 2004. Kellogg's asset turnover ratio is below the industry average of 1.17 times but well above General Mills's ratio of .60.

Asset turnover ratios vary considerably among industries. The average asset turnover for utility companies is .45, for example, while the grocery store industry has an average asset turnover of 3.49.

In summary, Kellogg's return on assets ratio increased from 7.7% in 2003 to 8.5% in 2004. Underlying this increase was an increased profitability on each dollar of sales (as measured by the profit margin ratio) and a rise in the sales-generating efficiency of its assets (as measured by the asset turnover ratio). We can analyze the combined effects of profit margin and asset turnover on return on assets for Kellogg as shown in Illustration 13A-20.

Ratios:	Profit Margin = Net Income / Net Sales	×	Asset Turnover = Net Sales / Average Total Assets	=	Return on Assets = Net Income / Average Total Assets
Kellogg					
2004	9.3%	×	.92 times	=	8.5%
2003	8.9%	×	.87 times	=	7.7%

Illustration 13A-20
Composition of return on assets ratio

15. **Gross profit rate.** Two factors strongly influence the profit margin ratio. One is the gross profit rate. The **gross profit rate** is determined by dividing gross profit (net sales less cost of goods sold) by net sales. This rate indicates a company's ability to maintain an adequate selling price above its cost of goods sold.

As an industry becomes more competitive, this ratio declines. For example, in the early years of the personal computer industry, gross profit rates were quite high. Today, because of increased competition and a belief that most brands of personal computers are similar in quality, gross profit rates have become thin. Analysts should closely monitor gross profit rates over time. Illustration 13A-21 (page 678) shows Kellogg's gross profit rate.

Ratio	Formula	Indicates:	Kellogg 2004	Kellogg 2003	General Mills 2004	Industry 2004	Page in book
Gross profit rate	Gross profit / Net sales	Margin between selling price and cost of goods sold	45%	44%	41%	32%	234

Illustration 13A-21
Gross profit rate

Kellogg's gross profit rate increased slightly from 2003 to 2004.

16. **Earnings per share (EPS).** Stockholders usually think in terms of the number of shares they own or plan to buy or sell. Expressing net income earned on a per share basis provides a useful perspective for determining profitability. **Earnings per share** is a measure of the net income earned on each share of common stock. It is computed by dividing net income by the average number of common shares outstanding during the year.

The terms "net income per share" or "earnings per share" refer to the amount of net income applicable to each share of *common stock*. Therefore, when we compute earnings per share, if there are preferred dividends declared for the period, we must deduct them from net income to arrive at income available to the common stockholders. Kellogg's earnings per share is shown in Illustration 13A-22.

Illustration 13A-22
Earnings per share

Ratio	Formula	Indicates:	Kellogg 2004	Kellogg 2003	General Mills 2004	Industry 2004	Page in book
Earnings per share (EPS)	(Net income − Preferred stock dividends) / Average common shares outstanding	Net income earned on each share of common stock	$2.16	$1.93	$2.82	na	55

Note that no industry average is presented in Illustration 13A-22. Industry data for earnings per share are not reported, and in fact the Kellogg and General Mills ratios should not be compared. Such comparisons are not meaningful because of the wide variations in the number of shares of outstanding stock among companies. Kellogg's earnings per share increased 23 cents per share in 2004. This represents an 11.9% increase from the 2003 EPS of $1.93.

17. **Price-earnings ratio.** The **price-earnings ratio** is an oft-quoted statistic that measures the ratio of the market price of each share of common stock to the earnings per share. The price-earnings (P-E) ratio reflects investors' assessments of a company's future earnings. It is computed by dividing the market price per share of the stock by earnings per share. Kellogg's price-earnings ratio is shown in Illustration 13A-23.

Illustration 13A-23
Price-earnings ratio

Ratio	Formula	Indicates:	Kellogg 2004	Kellogg 2003	General Mills 2004	Industry 2004	Page in book
Price-earnings ratio	Stock price per share / Earnings per share	Relationship between market price per share and earnings per share	20.7	20.1	16.3	19.9	662

At the end of 2004 and 2003 the market price of Kellogg's stock was $44.66 and $38.80, respectively. General Mills's stock was selling for $46.05 at the end of 2004.

In 2004 each share of Kellogg's stock sold for 20.7 times the amount that was earned on each share. Kellogg's price-earnings ratio is higher than General Mills's ratio of 16.3 and the industry average of 19.9 times. Its higher P-E ratio suggests that the market is more optimistic about Kellogg than about General Mills and the other companies in the industry. However, it might also signal that its stock is overpriced.

18. **Payout ratio.** The payout ratio measures the percentage of earnings distributed in the form of cash dividends. It is computed by dividing cash dividends declared on common stock by net income. Companies that have high growth rates are characterized by low payout ratios because they reinvest most of their net income in the business. The payout ratio for Kellogg is shown in Illustration 13A-24.

Illustration 13A-24
Payout ratio

Ratio	Formula	Indicates:	Kellogg 2004	Kellogg 2003	General Mills 2004	Industry 2004	Page in book
Payout ratio	Cash dividends declared on common stock / Net income	Percentage of earnings distributed in the form of cash dividends	47%	52%	39%	37%	556

The 2004 and 2003 payout ratios for Kellogg are comparatively high in relation to that of General Mills (39%) and the industry average (37%).

Management has some control over the amount of dividends paid each year, and companies are generally reluctant to reduce a dividend below the amount paid in a previous year. Therefore, the payout ratio will actually increase if a company's net income declines but the company keeps its total dividend payment the same. Of course, unless the company returns to its previous level of profitability, maintaining this higher dividend payout ratio is probably not possible over the long run.

Before drawing any conclusions regarding Kellogg's dividend payout ratio, we should calculate this ratio over a longer period of time to evaluate any trends, and also try to find out whether management's philosophy regarding dividends has changed recently. The "Selected Financial Data" section of Kellogg's Management Discussion and Analysis shows that over a 5-year period earnings per share rose 49%, while dividends per share grew only 1.5%.

In terms of the types of financial information available and the ratios used by various industries, what can be practically covered in this textbook gives you only the "Titanic approach": That is, you are seeing only the tip of the iceberg compared to the vast databases and types of ratio analysis that are available on computers. The availability of information is not a problem. The real trick is to be discriminating enough to perform relevant analysis and select pertinent comparative data.

Glossary

Asset turnover ratio A measure of how efficiently a company uses its assets to generate sales, computed as net sales divided by average total assets. (p. 677)

Available-for-sale securities Securities that are held with the intent of selling them sometime in the future. (p. 651)

Average collection period The average number of days that receivables are outstanding, calculated as receivables turnover divided into 365 days. (p. 671)

Cash debt coverage ratio A cash-basis measure used to evaluate solvency, computed as cash from operations divided by average total liabilities. (p. 674)

Change in accounting principle Use of an accounting principle in the current year different from the one used in the preceding year. (p. 650)

Comprehensive income A measure of income that includes all changes in stockholders' equity during a period except those resulting from investments by stockholders and distributions to stockholders. (p. 650)

Current cash debt coverage ratio A cash-basis measure of short-term debt-paying ability, computed as cash provided by operations divided by average current liabilities. (p. 670)

Current ratio A measure that expresses the relationship of current assets to current liabilities, calculated as current assets divided by current liabilities. (p. 670)

Days in inventory A measure of the average number of days it takes to sell the inventory, computed as inventory turnover divided into 365 days. (p. 672)

Debt to total assets ratio A measure of the percentage of total assets provided by creditors, computed as total debt divided by total assets. (p. 673)

Discontinued operations The disposal of a significant component of a business. (p. 647)

Earnings per share The net income earned by each share of common stock, computed as net income less dividends on preferred stock divided by the average common shares outstanding. (p. 678)

Extraordinary items Events and transactions that meet two conditions: (1) unusual in nature and (2) infrequent in occurrence. (p. 648)

Free cash flow A measure of solvency, calculated as cash from operations less capital expenditures and cash dividends. (p. 674)

Gross profit rate An indicator of a company's ability to maintain an adequate selling price above its cost of goods sold, computed as gross profit divided by net sales. (p. 677)

Horizontal analysis A technique for evaluating a series of financial statement data over a period of time to determine the increase (decrease) that has taken place, expressed as either an amount or a percentage. (p. 654)

Inventory turnover ratio A measure of the liquidity of inventory, computed as cost of goods sold divided by average inventory. (p. 671)

Leveraging Borrowing money at a lower rate of interest than can be earned by using the borrowed money; also referred to as trading on the equity. (p. 676)

Liquidity ratios Measures of the short-term ability of the enterprise to pay its maturing obligations and to meet unexpected needs for cash. (p. 659)

Payout ratio A measure of the percentage of earnings distributed in the form of cash dividends, calculated as

cash dividends declared on common stock divided by net income. (p. 679)

Price-earnings (P-E) ratio A comparison of the market price of each share of common stock to the earnings per share, computed as the market price of the stock divided by earnings per share. (pp. 662, 678)

Pro forma income A measure of income that usually excludes items that a company thinks are unusual or non-recurring. (p. 661)

Profit margin ratio A measure of the net income generated by each dollar of sales, computed as net income divided by net sales. (p. 676)

Profitability ratios Measures of the income or operating success of an enterprise for a given period of time. (p. 660)

Quality of earnings Indicates the level of full and transparent information that is provided to users of the financial statements. (p. 661)

Receivables turnover ratio A measure of the liquidity of receivables, computed as net credit sales divided by average net receivables. (p. 671)

Return on assets ratio An overall measure of profitability, calculated as net income divided by average total assets. (p. 676)

Return on common stockholders' equity ratio A measure of the dollars of net income earned for each dollar invested by the owners, computed as income available to common stockholders divided by average common stockholders' equity. (p. 675)

Solvency ratios Measures of the ability of the enterprise to survive over a long period of time. (p. 659)

Sustainable income The most likely level of income to be obtained in the future; calculated as net income adjusted for irregular items. (p. 646)

Times interest earned ratio A measure of a company's ability to meet interest payments as they come due, calculated as income before interest expense and income taxes divided by interest expense. (p. 673)

Trading on the equity Same as leveraging. (p. 676)

Trading securities Securities bought and held primarily for sale in the near term to generate income on short-term price differences. (p. 651)

Vertical analysis A technique for evaluating financial statement data that expresses each item in a financial statement as a percent of a base amount. (p. 656)

Demonstration Problem

The events and transactions of Dever Corporation for the year ending December 31, 2007, resulted in these data.

Cost of goods sold	$2,600,000
Net sales	4,400,000
Other expenses and losses	9,600
Other revenues and gains	5,600
Selling and administrative expenses	1,100,000

Gain from discontinued division	570,000	
Loss from tornado disaster (extraordinary loss)	600,000	

Analysis reveals the following.

1. All items are before the applicable income tax rate of 30%.
2. The plastics division was sold on July 1.
3. All operating data for the plastics division have been segregated.

Instructions

Prepare an income statement for the year, excluding the presentation of earnings per share.

Solution to Demonstration Problem

DEVER CORPORATION
Income Statement
For the Year Ended December 31, 2007

Net sales		$4,400,000
Cost of goods sold		2,600,000
Gross profit		1,800,000
Selling and administrative expenses		1,100,000
Income from operations		700,000
Other revenues and gains	$ 5,600	
Other expenses and losses	(9,600)	(4,000)
Income before income taxes		696,000
Income tax expense ($696,000 × 30%)		208,800
Income before irregular items		487,200
Discontinued operations: Gain from discontinued division, net of taxes of $171,000 ($570,000 × 30%)		399,000
Extraordinary item: Tornado loss, net of income tax savings $180,000 ($600,000 × 30%)		(420,000)
Net income		$ 466,200

Action Plan
* Remember that material items not typical of operations are reported in separate sections net of taxes.
* Associate income taxes with the item that affects the taxes.
* On a corporation income statement, report income tax expense when there is income before income tax.

Self-Study Questions

Answers are at the end of the chapter.

 All of the Self-Study Questions in this chapter employ decision tools.

(SO 2) **1.** In reporting discontinued operations, the income statement should show in a special section:
 (a) gains on the disposal of the discontinued component.
 (b) losses on the disposal of the discontinued component.
 (c) Neither (a) nor (b).
 (d) Both (a) and (b).

(SO 2) **2.** Cool Stools Corporation has income before taxes of $400,000 and an extraordinary loss of $100,000. If the income tax rate is 25% on all items, the income statement should show income before irregular items and an extraordinary loss, respectively, of
 (a) $325,000 and $100,000.
 (b) $325,000 and $75,000.
 (c) $300,000 and $100,000.
 (d) $300,000 and $75,000.

3. Which of the following would be considered an   (SO 3) "Other comprehensive income" item?
 (a) gain on disposal of discontinued operations.
 (b) unrealized loss on available-for-sale securities.
 (c) extraordinary loss related to flood.
 (d) net income.

(SO 4) **4.** In horizontal analysis, each item is expressed as a percentage of the:
(a) net income amount.
(b) stockholders' equity amount.
(c) total assets amount.
(d) base-year amount.

(SO 4) **5.** Adams Corporation reported net sales of $300,000, $330,000, and $360,000 in the years 2005, 2006, and 2007, respectively. If 2005 is the base year, what percentage do 2007 sales represent of the base?
(a) 77%.   (c) 120%.
(b) 108%.   (d) 130%.

(SO 5) **6.** The following schedule is a display of what type of analysis?

	Amount	Percent
Current assets	$200,000	25%
Property, plant, and equipment	600,000	75%
Total assets	$800,000	

(a) Horizontal analysis.
(b) Differential analysis.
(c) Vertical analysis.
(d) Ratio analysis.

(SO 5) **7.** In vertical analysis, the base amount for depreciation expense is generally:
(a) net sales.
(b) depreciation expense in a previous year.
(c) gross profit.
(d) fixed assets.

(SO 6) **8.** Which measure is an evaluation of a company's ability to pay current liabilities?
(a) Current cash debt coverage ratio.
(b) Current ratio.

(c) Both (a) and (b).
(d) None of the above.

(SO 6) **9.** Which measure is useful in evaluating the efficiency in managing inventories?
(a) Inventory turnover ratio.
(b) Days in inventory.
(c) Both (a) and (b).
(d) None of the above.

(SO 6) **10.** Which of these is *not* a liquidity ratio?
(a) Current ratio.
(b) Asset turnover ratio.
(c) Inventory turnover ratio.
(d) Receivables turnover ratio.

(SO 6) **11.** Plano Corporation reported net income $24,000; net sales $400,000; and average assets $600,000 for 2007. What is the 2007 profit margin ratio?
(a) 6%.
(b) 12%.
(c) 40%.
(d) 200%.

(SO 7) **12.** Which situation below might indicate a company has a low quality of earnings?
(a) The same accounting principles are used each year.
(b) Revenue is recognized when earned.
(c) Maintenance costs are capitalized and then depreciated.
(d) The company's P-E ratio is high relative to competitors.

Go to the book's website, **www.wiley.com/college/ kimmel**, to access additional Self-Study Questions.

Questions

All of the Questions in this chapter employ decision tools.

1. Explain sustainable income. What relationship does this concept have to the treatment of irregular items on the income statement?

2. Indicate which of the following items would be reported as an extraordinary item on Food Feast Corporation's income statement.
(a) Loss from damages caused by a volcano eruption.
(b) Loss from the sale of short-term investments.
(c) Loss attributable to a labor strike.
(d) Loss caused when the Food and Drug Administration prohibited the manufacture and sale of a product line.
(e) Loss of inventory from flood damage because a warehouse is located on a flood plain that floods every 5 to 10 years.

(f) Loss on the write-down of outdated inventory.
(g) Loss from a foreign government's expropriation of a production facility.
(h) Loss from damage to a warehouse in southern California from a minor earthquake.

3. Top Drawer Inc. reported 2006 earnings per share of $3.26 and had no extraordinary items. In 2007 earnings per share on income before extraordinary items was $2.99, and earnings per share on net income was $3.49. Do you consider this trend to be favorable? Why or why not?

4. Caradco Inc. has been in operation for 3 years. and uses the FIFO method of pricing inventory. During the fourth year, Caradco changes to the average cost method for all its inventory. How will Caradco report this change?

5. (a) Sharon Weber believes that the analysis of financial statements is directed at two characteristics of a company: liquidity and profitability. Is Sharon correct? Explain.
   (b) Are short-term creditors, long-term creditors, and stockholders interested in primarily the same characteristics of a company? Explain.

6. (a) Distinguish among the following bases of comparison: intracompany, industry averages, and intercompany.
   (b) Give the principal value of using each of the three bases of comparison.

7. Two popular methods of financial statement analysis are horizontal analysis and vertical analysis. Explain the difference between these two methods.

8. (a) If Simon Company had net income of $350,000 in 2006 and it experienced a 24.5% increase in net income for 2007, what is its net income for 2007?
   (b) If 6 cents of every dollar of Simon's revenue is net income in 2006, what is the dollar amount of 2006 revenue?

9. Name the major ratios useful in assessing (a) liquidity and (b) solvency.

10. James Slater is puzzled. His company had a profit margin of 10% in 2007. He feels that this is an indication that the company is doing well. Jill Farvell, his accountant, says that more information is needed to determine the company's financial well-being. Who is correct? Why?

11. What does each type of ratio measure?
    (a) Liquidity ratios.
    (b) Solvency ratios.
    (c) Profitability ratios.

12. What is the difference between the current ratio and working capital?

13. ⬅ Fast Buck, a retail store, has a receivables turnover ratio of 4.5 times. The industry average is 12.5 times. Does Fast Buck have a collection problem with its receivables?

14. ➡ Which ratios should be used to help answer each of these questions?
    (a) How efficient is a company in using its assets to produce sales?
    (b) How near to sale is the inventory on hand?
    (c) How many dollars of net income were earned for each dollar invested by the owners?
    (d) How able is a company to meet interest charges as they fall due?

15. In September 2004 the price-earnings ratio of General Motors was 11.3, and the price-earnings ratio of Microsoft was 28.14. Which company did the stock market favor? Explain.

16. What is the formula for computing the payout ratio? Do you expect this ratio to be high or low for a growth company?

17. ➡ Holding all other factors constant, indicate whether each of the following changes generally signals good or bad news about a company.
    (a) Increase in profit margin ratio.
    (b) Decrease in inventory turnover ratio.
    (c) Increase in current ratio.
    (d) Decrease in earnings per share.
    (e) Increase in price-earnings ratio.
    (f) Increase in debt to total assets ratio.
    (g) Decrease in times interest earned ratio.

18. The return on assets for Elverum Corporation is 7.6%. During the same year Elverum's return on common stockholders' equity is 12.8%. What is the explanation for the difference in the two rates?

19. Which two ratios do you think should be of greatest interest in each of the following cases?
    (a) A pension fund considering the purchase of 20-year bonds.
    (b) A bank contemplating a short-term loan.
    (c) A common stockholder.

20. Happy Daze Inc. has net income of $300,000, average shares of common stock outstanding of 50,000, and preferred dividends for the period of $20,000. What is Happy Daze earnings per share of common stock? Art Fonz, the president of Happy Daze, believes that the computed EPS of the company is high. Comment.

21. Identify and explain factors that affect quality of earnings.

22. ➡ Explain how the choice of one of the following accounting methods over the other raises or lowers a company's net income during a period of continuing inflation.
    (a) Use of FIFO instead of LIFO for inventory costing.
    (b) Use of a 6-year life for machinery instead of a 9-year life.
    (c) Use of straight-line depreciation instead of accelerated declining-balance depreciation.

Brief Exercises

🔧 All of the Brief Exercises in this chapter employ decision tools.

BE13-1 On June 30 Rojas Corporation discontinued its operations in Mexico. On September 1 Rojas disposed of the Mexico facility at a pretax loss of $480,000. The applicable tax rate is 25%. Show the discontinued operations section of Rojas's income statement.

Prepare a discontinued operations section of an income statement.
(SO 2)

Prepare a corrected income statement with an extraordinary item.
(SO 2)

BE13-2 An inexperienced accountant for Barlay Corporation showed the following in Barlay's 2007 income statement: Income before income taxes $300,000; Income tax expense $48,000; Extraordinary loss from flood (before taxes) $60,000; and Net income $192,000. The extraordinary loss and taxable income are both subject to a 20% tax rate. Prepare a corrected income statement beginning with "Income before income taxes."

Indicate how a change in accounting principles is reported.
(SO 2)

BE13-3 On January 1, 2007, Cannon Inc. changed from the LIFO method of inventory pricing to the FIFO method. Explain how this change in accounting principle should be treated in the company's financial statements.

Prepare horizontal analysis.
(SO 4)

BE13-4 Using these data from the comparative balance sheet of De Rosa Company, perform horizontal analysis.

	December 31, 2007	December 31, 2006
Accounts receivable	$ 520,000	$ 400,000
Inventory	780,000	600,000
Total assets	3,220,000	2,800,000

Prepare vertical analysis.
(SO 5)

BE13-5 Using the data presented in BE13-4 for De Rosa Company, perform vertical analysis.

Calculate percentage of change.
(SO 4)

BE13-6 Net income was $500,000 in 2005, $480,000 in 2006, and $537,600 in 2007. What is the percentage of change from (a) 2005 to 2006, and (b) from 2006 to 2007? Is the change an increase or a decrease?

Calculate net income.
(SO 4)

BE13-7 If Parthenon Company had net income of $672,300 in 2007 and it experienced a 17% increase in net income over 2006, what was its 2006 net income?

Analyze change in net income.
(SO 5)

BE13-8 Vertical analysis (common-size) percentages for Bellamy Company's sales, cost of goods sold, and expenses are listed here.

Vertical Analysis	2007	2006	2005
Sales	100.0%	100.0%	100.0%
Cost of goods sold	59.2	62.4	64.5
Expenses	26.0	26.6	28.5

Did Bellamy's net income as a percent of sales increase, decrease, or remain unchanged over the 3-year period? Provide numerical support for your answer.

Analyze change in net income.
(SO 4)

BE13-9 Horizontal analysis (trend analysis) percentages for Kirvida Company's sales, cost of goods sold, and expenses are listed here.

Horizontal Analysis	2007	2006	2005
Sales	96.2%	104.8%	100.0%
Cost of goods sold	102.0	97.0	100.0
Expenses	108.6	95.4	100.0

Explain whether Kirvida's net income increased, decreased, or remained unchanged over the 3-year period.

Calculate current ratio.
(SO 6)

BE13-10 These selected condensed data are taken from recent balance sheets of Bob Evans Farms (in thousands).

	2005	2004
Cash	$ 5,267	$ 3,986
Accounts receivable	25,330	22,282
Inventories	24,416	19,540
Other current assets	2,226	1,664
Total current assets	$57,239	$ 47,472
Total current liabilities	$188,628	$145,847

Compute the current ratio for each year and comment on your results.

BE13-11 The following data are taken from the financial statements of Tall Tail Company.

Evaluate collection of accounts receivable.
(SO 6)

	2007	2006
Accounts receivable (net), end of year	$ 560,000	$ 540,000
Net sales on account	4,700,000	4,000,000
Terms for all sales are 1/10, n/45.		

Compute for each year (a) the receivables turnover ratio and (b) the average collection period. What conclusions about the management of accounts receivable can be drawn from these data? At the end of 2005, accounts receivable was $500,000.

BE13-12 The following data were taken from the income statements of Long Haul Company.

Evaluate management of inventory.
(SO 6)

	2007	2006
Sales revenue	$6,420,000	$6,240,000
Beginning inventory	970,000	837,000
Purchases	4,640,000	4,661,000
Ending inventory	1,020,000	970,000

Compute for each year (a) the inventory turnover ratio and (b) days in inventory. What conclusions concerning the management of the inventory can be drawn from these data?

BE13-13 Staples, Inc. is one of the largest suppliers of office products in the United States. It had net income of $708.4 million and net revenue of $14,448.4 million in 2004. Its total assets were $6,503.0 million at the beginning of the year and $7,071.4 million at the end of the year. What is Staples, Inc.'s (a) asset turnover ratio and (b) profit margin ratio? (Round to two decimals.) Provide a brief interpretation of your results.

Calculate profitability ratios.
(SO 6)

BE13-14 Royal Ware Company has stockholders' equity of $400,000 and net income of $60,000. It has a payout ratio of 25% and a return on assets ratio of 16%. How much did Royal Ware pay in cash dividends, and what were its average total assets?

Calculate profitability ratios.
(SO 6)

BE13-15 Selected data taken from the 2004 financial statements of trading card company Topps Company, Inc. are as follows (in millions).

Calculate cash-basis liquidity and solvency ratios.
(SO 6)

	2004
Net sales for 2004	$295.9
Current liabilities, February 28, 2004	39.5
Current liabilities, February 26, 2005	47.5
Net cash provided by operating activities	22.9
Total liabilities, February 28, 2004	64.2
Total liabilities, February 26, 2005	71.2
Capital expenditures	2.6
Cash dividends	6.5

Compute these ratios at February 26, 2005: (a) current cash debt coverage ratio (b) cash debt coverage ratio, and (c) free cash flow. Provide a brief interpretation of your results.

Exercises

All of the Exercises in this chapter employ decision tools.

E13-1 Prentiss Company has income before irregular items of $270,000 for the year ended December 31, 2007. It also has the following items (before considering income taxes): (1) an extraordinary fire loss of $50,000 and (2) a gain of $40,000 from the disposal of a division. Assume all items are subject to income taxes at a 30% tax rate.

Prepare irregular items portion of an income statement.
(SO 2)

Instructions

Prepare Prentiss Company's income statement for 2007, beginning with "Income before irregular items."

Evaluate the effects of unusual or irregular items.
(SO 1, 2, 6)

E13-2 The *Wall Street Journal* routinely publishes summaries of corporate quarterly and annual earnings reports in a feature called the "Earnings Digest." A typical "digest" report takes the following form.

ENERGY ENTERPRISES (A)

	Quarter ending July 31	
	2007	**2006**
Revenues	$2,049,000,000	$1,754,000,000
Net income	97,000,000	(a) 68,750,000
EPS: Net income	1.31	0.93

	9 months ending July 31	
	2007	**2006**
Revenues	$5,578,500,000	$5,065,300,000
Extraordinary item	(b) 1,900,000	
Net income	102,700,000	(a) 33,250,000
EPS: Net income	1.36	0.53

(a) Includes a net charge of $26,000,000 from loss on the sale of electrical equipment
(b) Extraordinary gain on Middle East property expropriation

The letter in parentheses following the company name indicates the exchange on which Energy Enterprises' stock is traded—in this case, the American Stock Exchange.

Instructions

Answer the following questions.
(a) How was the loss on the electrical equipment reported on the income statement? Was it reported in the third quarter of 2006? How can you tell?
(b) Why did the *Wall Street Journal* list the extraordinary item separately?
(c) What is the extraordinary item? Was it included in income for the third quarter? How can you tell?
(d) Did Energy Enterprises have an operating loss in any quarter of 2006? Of 2007? How do you know?
(e) Approximately how many shares of stock were outstanding in 2007? Did the number of outstanding shares change from July 31, 2006 to July 31, 2007?
(f) As an investor, what numbers should you use to determine Energy Enterprises' profit margin ratio? Calculate the 9-month profit margin ratio for 2006 and 2007 that you consider most useful. Explain your decision.

Prepare horizontal analysis.
(SO 4)

E13-3 Here is financial information for Ride Away Inc.

	December 31, 2007	December 31, 2006
Current assets	$128,000	$ 80,000
Plant assets (net)	400,000	360,000
Current liabilities	91,000	65,000
Long-term liabilities	144,000	90,000
Common stock, $1 par	138,000	115,000
Retained earnings	155,000	170,000

Prepare vertical analysis.
(SO 5)

Instructions

Prepare a schedule showing a horizontal analysis for 2007 using 2006 as the base year.

E13-4 Operating data for Poseidon Corporation are presented on page 687.

	2007	2006
Sales	$800,000	$600,000
Cost of goods sold	500,000	408,000
Selling expenses	120,000	72,000
Administrative expenses	72,000	48,000
Income tax expense	32,000	21,600
Net income	76,000	50,400

Instructions
Prepare a schedule showing a vertical analysis for 2007 and 2006.

E13-5 The comparative balance sheets of Philip Morris Companies, Inc. are presented here.

Prepare horizontal and vertical analyses.
(SO 4, 5)

PHILIP MORRIS COMPANIES, INC.
Comparative Balance Sheets
December 31
($ in millions)

Assets	2004	2003
Current assets	$ 25,901	$21,382
Property, plant, and equipment (net)	16,305	16,067
Other assets	59,442	58,726
Total assets	$101,648	$96,175

Liabilities and Stockholders' Equity		
Current liabilities	$ 23,574	$21,393
Long-term liabilities	47,360	49,705
Stockholders' equity	30,714	25,077
Total liabilities and stockholders' equity	$101,648	$96,175

Instructions
(a) Prepare a horizontal analysis of the balance sheet data for Philip Morris using 2003 as a base. (Show the amount of increase or decrease as well.)
(b) Prepare a vertical analysis of the balance sheet data for Philip Morris for 2004.

E13-6 Here are the comparative income statements of Erik Corporation.

Prepare horizontal and vertical analyses.
(SO 4, 5)

ERIK CORPORATION
Comparative Income Statements
For the Years Ended December 31

	2007	2006
Net sales	$572,000	$520,000
Cost of goods sold	477,000	450,000
Gross profit	$ 95,000	$ 70,000
Operating expenses	60,000	45,000
Net income	$ 35,000	$ 25,000

Instructions
(a) Prepare a horizontal analysis of the income statement data for Erik Corporation using 2006 as a base. (Show the amounts of increase or decrease.)
(b) Prepare a vertical analysis of the income statement data for Erik Corporation for both years.

E13-7 Nordstrom, Inc. operates department stores in numerous states. Selected financial statement data (in millions) for 2005 are presented on page 688.

Compute liquidity ratios.
(SO 6)

	End of Year	Beginning of Year
Cash and cash equivalents	$ 360.3	$ 340.3
Receivables (net)	645.7	666.8
Merchandise inventory	917.2	901.6
Other current assets	649.2	616.1
Total current assets	$2,572.4	$2,524.8
Total current liabilities	$1,341.2	$1,122.6

For the year, net credit sales were $7,131.4 million, cost of goods sold was $4,559.4 million, and cash from operations was $660.3 million.

Instructions
Compute the current ratio, current cash debt coverage ratio, receivables turnover ratio, average collection period, inventory turnover ratio, and days in inventory at the end of the current year.

Perform current ratio analysis.
(SO 6)

E13-8 Trolls Incorporated had the following transactions involving current assets and current liabilities during February 2007.

Feb.	3	Collected accounts receivable of $15,000.
	7	Purchased equipment for $20,000 cash.
	11	Paid $3,000 for a 3-year insurance policy.
	14	Paid accounts payable of $14,000.
	18	Declared cash dividends, $6,000.

Additional information:
As of February 1, 2007, current assets were $100,000 and current liabilities were $40,000.

Instructions
Compute the current ratio as of the beginning of the month and after each transaction.

Compute selected ratios.
(SO 6)

E13-9 Maury Company has these comparative balance sheet data:

MAURY COMPANY
Balance Sheets
December 31

	2007	2006
Cash	$ 25,000	$ 30,000
Receivables (net)	65,000	60,000
Inventories	60,000	50,000
Plant assets (net)	200,000	180,000
	$350,000	$320,000
Accounts payable	$ 55,000	$ 60,000
Mortgage payable (15%)	100,000	100,000
Common stock, $10 par	135,000	120,000
Retained earnings	60,000	40,000
	$350,000	$320,000

Additional information for 2007:
1. Net income was $25,000.
2. Sales on account were $400,000. Sales returns and allowances amounted to $25,000.
3. Cost of goods sold was $198,000.
4. Net cash provided by operating activities was $48,000.
5. Capital expenditures were $25,000, and cash dividends were $18,000.

Instructions
Compute the following ratios at December 31, 2007.
(a) Current.
(b) Receivables turnover.
(c) Average collection period.
(d) Inventory turnover.
(e) Days in inventory.
(f) Cash debt coverage.
(g) Current cash debt coverage.
(h) Free cash flow.

E13-10 Selected comparative statement data for the giant bookseller Barnes & Noble are presented here. All balance sheet data are as of December 31 (in millions).

Compute selected ratios.
(SO 6)

	2004	2003
Net sales	$4,873.6	$5,951.0
Cost of goods sold	3,386.6	4,323.8
Net income	143.3	151.9
Accounts receivable	74.6	60.5
Inventory	1,274.6	1,526.1
Total assets	3,301.5	3,507.3
Total common stockholders' equity	1,165.9	1,259.7

Instructions
Compute the following ratios for 2004:
(a) Profit margin.
(b) Asset turnover.
(c) Return on assets.
(d) Return on common stockholders' equity.
(e) Gross profit rate.

E13-11 Here is the income statement for New Do, Inc.

Compute selected ratios.
(SO 6)

NEW DO, INC.
Income Statement
For the Year Ended December 31, 2007

Sales	$400,000
Cost of goods sold	230,000
Gross profit	170,000
Expenses (including $14,000 interest and $24,000 income taxes)	88,000
Net income	$ 82,000

Additional information:
1. Common stock outstanding January 1, 2007, was 30,000 shares, and 40,000 shares were outstanding at December 31, 2007.
2. The market price of New Do, Inc., stock was $17.60 in 2007.
3. Cash dividends of $21,000 were paid, $5,000 of which were to preferred stockholders.

Instructions
Compute the following measures for 2007.
(a) Earnings per share.
(b) Price-earnings ratio.
(c) Payout ratio.
(d) Times interest earned ratio.

E13-12 Zubick Corporation experienced a fire on December 31, 2007, in which its financial records were partially destroyed. It has been able to salvage some of the records and has ascertained the following balances.

Compute amounts from ratios.
(SO 6)

	December 31, 2007	December 31, 2006
Cash	$ 30,000	$ 10,000
Receivables (net)	72,500	126,000
Inventory	200,000	180,000
Accounts payable	50,000	10,000
Notes payable	30,000	20,000
Common stock, $100 par	400,000	400,000
Retained earnings	113,500	101,000

Additional information:
1. The inventory turnover is 4.0 times.
2. The return on common stockholders' equity is 20%. The company had no additional paid-in capital.
3. The receivables turnover is 11.2 times.
4. The return on assets is 16%.
5. Total assets at December 31, 2006, were $605,000.

Instructions
Compute the following for Zubick Corporation.
(a) Cost of goods sold for 2007.
(b) Net credit sales for 2007.
(c) Net income for 2007.
(d) Total assets at December 31, 2007.

Problems: Set A

Prepare vertical analysis and comment on profitability.
(SO 5, 6)

P13-1A Here are comparative statement data for East Company and West Company, two competitors. All balance sheet data are as of December 31, 2007, and December 31, 2006.

	East Company		West Company	
	2007	**2006**	**2007**	**2006**
Net sales	$1,849,035		$546,000	
Cost of goods sold	1,080,490		238,000	
Operating expenses	230,000		82,000	
Interest expense	6,800		1,600	
Income tax expense	62,030		31,000	
Current assets	325,975	$312,410	83,336	$ 79,467
Plant assets (net)	526,800	500,000	139,728	125,812
Current liabilities	66,325	75,815	35,348	30,281
Long-term liabilities	113,990	90,000	29,620	25,000
Common stock, $10 par	500,000	500,000	120,000	120,000
Retained earnings	172,460	146,595	38,096	29,998

Instructions
(a) Prepare a vertical analysis of the 2007 income statement data for East Company and West Company.
(b) Comment on the relative profitability of the companies by computing the 2007 return on assets and the return on common stockholders' equity ratios for both companies.

Compute ratios from balance sheet and income statement.
(SO 6)

P13-2A The comparative statements of Jack Frost Company are presented here.

JACK FROST COMPANY
Income Statements
For the Years Ended December 31

	2007	**2006**
Net sales	$1,890,540	$1,750,500
Cost of goods sold	1,058,540	996,000
Gross profit	832,000	754,500
Selling and administrative expenses	506,000	479,000
Income from operations	326,000	275,500
Other expenses and losses		
Interest expense	25,000	19,000
Income before income taxes	301,000	256,500
Income tax expense	86,000	77,000
Net income	$ 215,000	$ 179,500

JACK FROST COMPANY
Balance Sheets
December 31

Assets	2007	2006
Current assets		
Cash	$ 60,100	$ 64,200
Short-term investments	74,000	50,000
Accounts receivable	107,800	102,800
Inventory	133,000	115,500
Total current assets	374,900	332,500
Plant assets (net)	615,300	520,300
Total assets	$990,200	$852,800
Liabilities and Stockholders' Equity		
Current liabilities		
Accounts payable	$160,000	$145,400
Income taxes payable	43,500	42,000
Total current liabilities	203,500	187,400
Bonds payable	210,000	200,000
Total liabilities	413,500	387,400
Stockholders' equity		
Common stock ($5 par)	290,000	300,000
Retained earnings	286,700	165,400
Total stockholders' equity	576,700	465,400
Total liabilities and stockholders' equity	$990,200	$852,800

All sales were on account. Net cash provided by operating activities for 2007 was $240,000. Capital expenditures were $120,000, and cash dividends were $80,000.

Instructions
Compute the following ratios for 2007.
(a)	Earnings per share.	(h)	Days in inventory.
(b)	Return on common stockholders' equity.	(i)	Times interest earned.
(c)	Return on assets.	(j)	Asset turnover.
(d)	Current ratio.	(k)	Debt to total assets.
(e)	Receivables turnover.	(l)	Current cash debt coverage.
(f)	Average collection period.	(m)	Cash debt coverage.
(g)	Inventory turnover.	(n)	Free cash flow.

P13-3A Condensed balance sheet and income statement data for Here and There Cor- poration are presented here.

Perform ratio analysis, and discuss change in financial position and operating results.
(SO 6)

HERE AND THERE CORPORATION
Balance Sheets
December 31

	2007	2006	2005
Cash	$ 30,000	$ 20,000	$ 18,000
Receivables (net)	50,000	45,000	48,000
Other current assets	90,000	85,000	64,000
Investments	55,000	70,000	45,000
Plant and equipment (net)	500,000	370,000	258,000
	$725,000	$590,000	$433,000
Current liabilities	$ 85,000	$ 80,000	$ 30,000
Long-term debt	185,000	85,000	20,000
Common stock, $10 par	320,000	300,000	300,000
Retained earnings	135,000	125,000	83,000
	$725,000	$590,000	$433,000

HERE AND THERE CORPORATION
Income Statements
For the Years Ended December 31

	2007	2006
Sales	$640,000	$500,000
Less: Sales returns and allowances	40,000	30,000
Net sales	600,000	470,000
Cost of goods sold	425,000	300,000
Gross profit	175,000	170,000
Operating expenses (including income taxes)	117,000	94,000
Net income	$ 58,000	$ 76,000

Additional information:

1. The market price of Here and There's common stock was $6.00, $9.00, and $7.00 for 2005, 2006, and 2007, respectively.
2. You must compute dividends paid. All dividends were paid in cash.

Instructions
(a) Compute the following ratios for 2006 and 2007.
    (1) Profit margin.
    (2) Gross profit.
    (3) Asset turnover.
    (4) Earnings per share.
    (5) Price-earnings.
    (6) Payout.
    (7) Debt to total assets.

(b) Based on the ratios calculated, discuss briefly the improvement or lack thereof in the financial position and operating results from 2006 to 2007 of Here and There Corporation.

Compute ratios; comment on overall liquidity and profitability.
(SO 6)

P13-4A The following financial information is for Inca Company.

INCA COMPANY
Balance Sheets
December 31

Assets	2007	2006
Cash	$ 70,000	$ 65,000
Short-term investments	55,000	40,000
Receivables	104,000	90,000
Inventories	230,000	125,000
Prepaid expenses	25,000	23,000
Land	130,000	130,000
Building and equipment (net)	260,000	175,000
Total assets	$874,000	$648,000
Liabilities and Stockholders' Equity		
Notes payable	$170,000	$100,000
Accounts payable	65,000	42,000
Accrued liabilities	40,000	40,000
Bonds payable, due 2009	250,000	150,000
Common stock, $10 par	200,000	200,000
Retained earnings	149,000	116,000
Total liabilities and stockholders' equity	$874,000	$648,000

INCA COMPANY
Income Statements
For the Years Ended December 31

	2007	2006
Sales	$880,000	$790,000
Cost of goods sold	640,000	575,000
Gross profit	240,000	215,000
Operating expenses	192,000	170,000
Net income	$ 48,000	$ 45,000

Additional information:

1. Inventory at the beginning of 2006 was $115,000.
2. Receivables (net) at the beginning of 2006 were $88,000.
3. Total assets at the beginning of 2006 were $630,000.
4. No common stock transactions occurred during 2006 or 2007.
5. All sales were on account.

Instructions
(a) Indicate, by using ratios, the change in liquidity and profitability of Inca Company from 2006 to 2007. (*Note:* Not all profitability ratios can be computed nor can cash-basis ratios be computed.)
(b) Given below are three independent situations and a ratio that may be affected. For each situation, compute the affected ratio (1) as of December 31, 2007, and (2) as of December 31, 2008, after giving effect to the situation. Net income for 2008 was $40,000. Total assets on December 31, 2008, were $900,000.

Situation	Ratio
1. 18,000 shares of common stock were sold at par on July 1, 2008.	Return on common stockholders' equity
2. All of the notes payable were paid in 2008.	Debt to total assets
3. The market price of common stock was $9 and $12 on December 31, 2007 and 2008, respectively.	Price-earnings

P13-5A   Selected financial data of Target and Wal-Mart for 2004 are presented here (in millions).

Compute selected ratios, and compare liquidity, profitability, and solvency for two companies.
(SO 6)

	Target Corporation	Wal-Mart Stores, Inc.
	Income Statement Data for Year	
Net sales	$48,163	$258,681
Cost of goods sold	31,790	198,747
Selling and administrative expenses	10,696	44,909
Interest expense	559	996
Other income (expense)	(2,158)	143
Income tax expense	1,119	5,118
Net income	$ 1,841	$ 9,054
	Balance Sheet Data (End of Year)	
Current assets	$12,928	$ 34,421
Noncurrent assets	18,464	70,491
Total assets	$31,392	$104,912
Current liabilities	$ 8,314	$ 37,418
Long-term debt	12,013	23,871
Total stockholders' equity	11,065	43,623
Total liabilities and stockholders' equity	$31,392	$104,912

	Beginning-of-Year Balances	
Total assets	$28,603	$ 94,808
Total stockholders' equity	9,443	39,461
Current liabilities	7,523	32,519
Total liabilities	11,637	55,347

	Other Data	
Average net receivables	$ 5,670.5	$ 1,411.5
Average inventory	5,051.5	25,506.5
Net cash provided by operating activities	3,160	15,996
Capital expenditures	3,004	9,245
Dividends	237	1,328

Instructions

(a) For each company, compute the following ratios.

(1) Current.	(8) Return on assets.
(2) Receivables turnover.	(9) Return on common stockholders' equity.
(3) Average collection period.	(10) Debt to total assets.
(4) Inventory turnover.	(11) Times interest earned.
(5) Days in inventory.	(12) Current cash debt coverage.
(6) Profit margin.	(13) Cash debt coverage.
(7) Asset turnover.	(14) Free cash flow.

(b) Compare the liquidity, solvency, and profitability of the two companies.

Problems: Set B

All of the Problems in this chapter employ decision tools.

Prepare vertical analysis and comment on profitability.
(SO 5, 6)

P13-1B Here are comparative statement data for Night Company and Day Company, two competitors. All balance sheet data are as of December 31, 2007, and December 31, 2006.

	Night Company		Day Company	
	2007	**2006**	**2007**	**2006**
Net sales	$350,000		$1,200,000	
Cost of goods sold	180,000		624,000	
Operating expenses	51,000		278,000	
Interest expense	3,000		10,000	
Income tax expense	17,000		54,000	
Current assets	130,000	$100,000	700,000	$650,000
Plant assets (net)	400,000	270,000	1,000,000	750,000
Current liabilities	60,000	52,000	250,000	275,000
Long-term liabilities	50,000	68,000	200,000	150,000
Common stock	360,000	210,000	950,000	700,000
Retained earnings	60,000	40,000	300,000	275,000

Instructions

(a) Prepare a vertical analysis of the 2007 income statement data for Night Company and Day Company.

(b) Comment on the relative profitability of the companies by computing the return on assets and the return on common stockholders' equity ratios for both companies.

Compute ratios from balance sheet and income statement.
(SO 6)

P13-2B The comparative statements of Fraggle Rock Company are shown on page 695.

FRAGGLE ROCK COMPANY
Income Statements
For the Years Ended December 31

	2007	2006
Net sales	$780,000	$624,000
Cost of goods sold	440,000	405,600
Gross profit	340,000	218,400
Selling and administrative expense	146,880	149,760
Income from operations	193,120	68,640
Other expenses and losses		
Interest expense	9,920	7,200
Income before income taxes	183,200	61,440
Income tax expense	35,000	14,000
Net income	$148,200	$ 47,440

FRAGGLE ROCK COMPANY
Balance Sheets
December 31

Assets	2007	2006
Current assets		
Cash	$ 23,100	$ 21,600
Short-term investments	44,800	33,000
Accounts receivable	106,200	93,800
Inventory	116,400	64,000
Total current assets	290,500	212,400
Plant assets (net)	485,300	439,600
Total assets	$775,800	$652,000
Liabilities and Stockholders' Equity		
Current liabilities		
Accounts payable	$148,200	$132,000
Income taxes payable	25,300	24,000
Total current liabilities	173,500	156,000
Bonds payable	132,000	120,000
Total liabilities	305,500	276,000
Stockholders' equity		
Common stock ($10 par)	140,000	130,000
Retained earnings	330,300	246,000
Total stockholders' equity	470,300	376,000
Total liabilities and stockholders' equity	$775,800	$652,000

All sales were on account. Net cash provided by operating activities was $94,000. Capital expenditures were $47,000, and cash dividends were $55,000.

Instructions
Compute the following ratios for 2007.
(a) Earnings per share.
(b) Return on common stockholders' equity.
(c) Return on assets.
(d) Current.
(e) Receivables turnover.
(f) Average collection period.
(g) Inventory turnover.
(h) Days in inventory.
(i) Times interest earned.
(j) Asset turnover.
(k) Debt to total assets.
(l) Current cash debt coverage.
(m) Cash debt coverage.
(n) Free cash flow.

P13-3B The condensed balance sheet and income statement data for Whitcomb Corporation are presented on page 696.

Perform ratio analysis, and discuss change in financial position and operating results.
(SO 6)

WHITCOMB CORPORATION
Balance Sheets
December 31

	2007	2006	2005
Cash	$ 30,000	$ 24,000	$ 20,000
Receivables (net)	110,000	48,000	48,000
Other current assets	80,000	78,000	62,000
Investments	90,000	70,000	50,000
Plant and equipment (net)	603,000	400,000	360,000
	$913,000	$620,000	$540,000
Current liabilities	$ 98,000	$ 75,000	$ 70,000
Long-term debt	230,000	75,000	65,000
Common stock, $10 par	400,000	340,000	300,000
Retained earnings	185,000	130,000	105,000
	$913,000	$620,000	$540,000

WHITCOMB CORPORATION
Income Statements
For the Years Ended December 31

	2007	2006
Sales	$800,000	$750,000
Less: Sales returns and allowances	40,000	50,000
Net sales	760,000	700,000
Cost of goods sold	420,000	400,000
Gross profit	340,000	300,000
Operating expenses (including income taxes)	200,000	215,000
Net income	$140,000	$ 85,000

Additional information:
1. The market price of Whitcomb common stock was $5.00, $3.50, and $2.30 for 2005, 2006, and 2007, respectively.
2. You must compute dividends paid. All dividends were paid in cash.

Instructions
(a) Compute the following ratios for 2006 and 2007.
   (1) Profit margin.   (5) Price-earnings.
   (2) Gross profit rate.   (6) Payout.
   (3) Asset turnover.   (7) Debt to total assets.
   (4) Earnings per share.

(b) Based on the ratios calculated, discuss briefly the improvement or lack thereof in the financial position and operating results from 2006 to 2007 of Whitcomb Corporation.

Compute ratios; comment on overall liquidity and profitability.
(SO 6)

P13-4B Financial information for Yazbeck Company is presented here.

YAZBECK COMPANY
Balance Sheets
December 31

Assets	2007	2006
Cash	$ 50,000	$ 42,000
Short-term investments	80,000	50,000
Receivables	100,000	87,000
Inventories	410,000	300,000
Prepaid expenses	30,000	31,000
Land	75,000	75,000
Building and equipment (net)	570,000	400,000
Total assets	$1,315,000	$985,000

Liabilities and Stockholders' Equity

Notes payable	$ 120,000	$ 25,000
Accounts payable	160,000	90,000
Accrued liabilities	50,000	50,000
Bonds payable, due 2009	180,000	100,000
Common stock, $5 par	500,000	500,000
Retained earnings	305,000	220,000
Total liabilities and stockholders' equity	$1,315,000	$985,000

YAZBECK COMPANY
Income Statements
For the Years Ended December 31

	2007	2006
Sales	$1,000,000	$940,000
Cost of goods sold	655,000	635,000
Gross profit	345,000	305,000
Operating expenses	235,000	225,000
Net income	$ 110,000	$ 80,000

Additional information:
1. Inventory at the beginning of 2006 was $350,000.
2. Receivables at the beginning of 2006 were $80,000.
3. Total assets at the beginning of 2006 were $1,175,000.
4. No common stock transactions occurred during 2006 or 2007.
5. All sales were on account.

Instructions
(a) Indicate, by using ratios, the change in liquidity and profitability of the company from 2006 to 2007. (*Note:* Not all profitability ratios can be computed nor can cash-basis ratios be computed.)
(b) Given below are three independent situations and a ratio that may be affected. For each situation, compute the affected ratio (1) as of December 31, 2007, and (2) as of December 31, 2008, after giving effect to the situation. Net income for 2008 was $125,000. Total assets on December 31, 2008, were $1,450,000.

Situation	Ratio
1. 50,000 shares of common stock were sold at par on July 1, 2008.	Return on common stockholders' equity
2. All of the notes payable were paid in 2008.	Debt to total assets
3. The market price of common stock on December 31, 2008, was $6.25. The market price on December 31, 2007, was $5.	Price-earnings

P13-5B Selected financial data for Black & Decker and Snap-On Tools for 2004 are presented here (in millions).

Compute selected ratios, and compare liquidity, profitability, and solvency for two companies.
(SO 6)

	Black & Decker	Snap-On Tools
	Income Statement Data for Year	
Net sales	$5,398.4	$2,407.2
Cost of goods sold	3,432.9	1,319.8
Selling and administrative expenses	1,336.3	945.1
Interest expense	57.9	23.0
Other income	(33.0)	(1.1)
Income tax expense	163.2	38.7
Net income (before irregular items)	$ 441.1	$ 81.7

	Balance Sheet Data (End of Year)	
Current assets	$2,927.2	$1,192.6
Property, plant, and equipment (net)	754.6	313.6
Other assets	1,849.0	783.9
Total assets	$5,530.8	$2,290.1
Current liabilities	$1,792.6	$ 674.2
Long-term debt	2,179.5	505.2
Total stockholders' equity	1,558.7	1,110.7
Total liabilities and stockholders' equity	$5,530.8	$2,290.1

	Beginning-of-Year Balances	
Total assets	$4,222.5	$2,138.5
Total stockholders' equity	846.5	1,010.9
Current liabilities	1,312.1	567.2
Total liabilities	3,376.0	1,127.6

	Other Data	
Average receivables (net)	$ 927.6	$ 618.7
Average inventory	845.9	346.5
Net cash provided by operating activities	619.1	146.8
Capital expenditures	117.8	38.7
Cash dividends	67.5	57.7

Instructions

(a) For each company, compute the following ratios.
   (1) Current ratio.
   (2) Receivables turnover.
   (3) Average collection period.
   (4) Inventory turnover.
   (5) Days in inventory.
   (6) Profit margin.
   (7) Asset turnover.
   (8) Return on assets.
   (9) Return on common stockholders' equity.
   (10) Debt to total assets.
   (11) Times interest earned.
   (12) Current cash debt coverage.
   (13) Cash debt coverage.
   (14) Free cash flow.

(b) Compare the liquidity, solvency, and profitability of the two companies.

Problems: Set C

Visit the book's website at **www.wiley.com/college/kimmel** and choose the Student Companion site to access Problem Set C.

Continuing Cookie Chronicle

(Note: This is a continuation of the Cookie Chronicle from Chapters 1 through 12.)

CCC13 The comparative balance sheet of Cookie & Coffee Creations Inc. at October 31, 2009 for the years 2009 and 2008, and the income statements for the years ended October 31, 2008 and 2009, are presented on the following page.

COOKIE & COFFEE CREATIONS INC.
Balance Sheet
October 31

Assets	2009	2008
Cash	$ 34,324	$13,050
Accounts receivable	3,250	2,710
Inventory	7,897	7,450
Prepaid expenses	6,300	6,050
Equipment	96,500	75,500
Accumulated depreciation	(25,200)	(9,100)
Total assets	$123,071	$95,660

Liabilities and Stockholders' Equity		
Accounts payable	$ 3,650	$ 2,450
Income taxes payable	10,251	11,200
Dividends payable (on common stock)	28,000	25,000
Salaries payable	2,250	1,280
Interest payable	188	0
Note payable—current portion	3,000	0
Note payable—long-term portion	4,500	0
Preferred stock, no par, $6 cumulative— 3,000 and 2,500 shares issued, respectively	15,000	12,500
Common stock, $1 par—23,180 shares issued	23,180	23,180
Additional paid in capital—treasury stock	250	250
Retained earnings	32,802	19,800
Total liabilities and stockholders' equity	$123,071	$95,660

COOKIE & COFFEE CREATIONS INC.
Income Statement
Year Ended October 31

	2009	2008
Sales	$485,625	$462,500
Cost of goods sold	222,694	208,125
Gross profit	262,931	254,375
Operating expenses		
Depreciation expense	17,850	9,100
Salaries and wages expense	147,979	146,350
Other operating expenses	43,186	42,925
Total operating expenses	209,015	198,375
Income from operations	53,916	56,000
Other expenses		
Interest expense	413	0
Loss on sale of computer equipment	2,250	0
Total other expenses	2,663	0
Income before income tax	51,253	56,000
Income tax expense	10,251	11,200
Net income	$ 41,002	$ 44,800

Additional information:

Natalie and Curtis are thinking about borrowing an additional $20,000 to buy more kitchen equipment. The loan would be repaid over a 4-year period. The terms of the loan provide for equal semi-annual payments of $2,500 on May 1 and November 1 of each year, plus interest of 5% on the outstanding balance.

Instructions

(a) Calculate the following ratios for 2008 and 2009.
  1. Current ratio
  2. Debt to total assets
  3. Gross profit rate
  4. Profit margin
  5. Return on assets (Total assets at November 1, 2007, were $33,180.)
  6. Return on common stockholders' equity (Total common stockholders' equity at November 1, 2007, was $23,180.)
  7. Payout ratio

(b) Prepare a horizontal analysis of the income statement for Cookie & Coffee Creations Inc. using 2008 as a base year.

(c) Prepare a vertical analysis of the income statement for Cookie & Coffee Creations Inc. for 2009 and 2008.

(d) Comment on your findings from parts (a) to (c).

(e) What impact would borrowing an additional $20,000 to buy more equipment have on each of the ratios in (a) above, assuming that no changes are expected on the income statement and balance sheet? Comment on your findings.

(f) What would justify a decision by Cookie & Coffee Creations Inc. to buy the additional equipment? What alternatives are there instead of bank financing?

   BROADENING YOUR PERSPECTIVE

Financial Reporting and Analysis

FINANCIAL REPORTING PROBLEM: *Tootsie Roll Industries, Inc.*

BYP13-1 Your parents are considering investing in Tootsie Roll Industries common stock. They ask you, as an accounting expert, to make an analysis of the company for them. Fortunately, excerpts from a recent annual report of Tootsie Roll are presented in Appendix A of this textbook.

Instructions

(a) Make a 5-year trend analysis, using 2000 as the base year, of (1) net sales and (2) net earnings. Comment on the significance of the trend results.

(b) Compute for 2004 and 2003 the (1) debt to total assets ratio and (2) times interest earned ratio. (See note 6 for interest expense.) How would you evaluate Tootsie Roll's long-term solvency?

(c) Compute for 2004 and 2003 the (1) profit margin ratio, (2) asset turnover ratio, (3) return on assets ratio, and (4) return on common stockholders' equity ratio. How would you evaluate Tootsie Roll's profitability? Total assets at December 31, 2002, were $646,080,000, and total stockholders' equity at December 31, 2002, was $526,740,000.

(d) What information outside the annual report may also be useful to your parents in making a decision about Tootsie Roll?

COMPARATIVE ANALYSIS PROBLEM: *Tootsie Roll vs. Hershey Foods*

BYP13-2 The financial statements of Hershey Foods are presented in Appendix B, following the financial statements for Tootsie Roll Industries in Appendix A.

Instructions

(a) Based on the information in the financial statements, determine each of the following for each company:
  (1) The percentage increase (i) in net sales and (ii) in net income from 2003 to 2004.
  (2) The percentage increase (i) in total assets and (ii) in total stockholders' equity from 2003 to 2004.
  (3) The earnings per share for 2004.

(b) What conclusions concerning the two companies can be drawn from these data?

RESEARCH CASE

BYP13-3 The October 15, 2002, issue of the *Wall Street Journal* included an article by Jesse Drucker titled "Motorola's Profit: 'Special' Again?"

Instructions

Read the article and answer the following questions.

(a) For how many consecutive quarters, including the quarter anticipated in the article, has Motorola reported a "special" item on its income statement? What is the total amount of these special charges over this period?

(b) What justification does Motorola give for reporting these charges as special items on its income statement, rather than reporting them as ordinary expenses?

(c) In the second quarter of 2002, what was Motorola's pro forma income, and what was its net income according to generally accepted accounting principles (GAAP)?

(d) According to the article, do Wall Street analysts give more attention to GAAP income or pro forma income? Do analysts agree on how to treat special charges, such as those of Motorola?

INTERPRETING FINANCIAL STATEMENTS

BYP13-4 The Coca-Cola Company and PepsiCo, Inc. provide refreshments to every corner of the world. Selected data from the 2004 consolidated financial statements for The Coca-Cola Company and for PepsiCo, Inc., are presented here (in millions).

	Coca-Cola	**PepsiCo**
Total current assets	$ 12,094	$ 8,639
Total current liabilities	10,971	6,752
Net sales	21,962	29,261
Cost of goods sold	7,638	13,406
Net income	4,847	4,212
Average (net) receivables for the year	2,131	2,915
Average inventories for the year	1,336	1,477
Average total assets	29,335	26,657
Average common stockholders' equity	15,013	12,734
Average current liabilities	9,429	6,584
Average total liabilities	14,322	27,917
Total assets	31,327	27,987
Total liabilities	15,392	14,464
Income taxes	1,375	1,372
Interest expense	196	167
Cash provided by operating activities	5,968	5,054
Capital expenditures	755	1,387
Cash dividends	2,429	1,329

Instructions

(a) Compute the following liquidity ratios for 2004 for Coca-Cola and for PepsiCo and comment on the relative liquidity of the two competitors.

(1) Current ratio. (4) Inventory turnover.

(2) Receivables turnover. (5) Days in inventory.

(3) Average collection period. (6) Current cash debt coverage.

(b) Compute the following solvency ratios for the two companies and comment on the relative solvency of the two competitors.

(1) Debt to total assets ratio.

(2) Times interest earned.

(3) Cash debt coverage ratio.

(4) Free cash flow.

(c) Compute the following profitability ratios for the two companies and comment on the relative profitability of the two competitors.

(1) Profit margin.

(2) Asset turnover.

(3) Return on assets.

(4) Return on common stockholders' equity.

FINANCIAL ANALYSIS ON THE WEB

BYP13-5 *Purpose:* To employ comparative data and industry data to evaluate a company's performance and financial position.

Address: **http://www.investor.reuters.com** (or go to **www.wiley.com/college/kimmel**)

Steps
(1) Identify two competing companies.
(2) Go to the above address.
(3) Type in the first company's name.
(4) Choose **Ratios**.
(5) Print out the results.
(6) Repeat steps 3–5 for the competitor.

Instructions
(a) Evaluate the company's liquidity relative to the industry averages and to the competitor that you chose.
(b) Evaluate the company's solvency relative to the industry averages and to the competitor that you chose.
(c) Evaluate the company's profitability relative to the industry averages and to the competitor that you chose.

Critical Thinking

DECISION MAKING ACROSS THE ORGANIZATION

BYP13-6 You are a loan officer for Lakeland Bank of Port Washington. Edmund Jeffries, president of E. Jeffries Corporation, has just left your office. He is interested in an 8-year loan to expand the company's operations. The borrowed funds would be used to purchase new equipment. As evidence of the company's debt-worthiness, Jeffries provided you with the following facts.

	2007	2006
Current ratio	3.1	2.1
Asset turnover ratio	2.8	2.2
Cash debt coverage ratio	.1	.2
Net income	Up 32%	Down 8%
Earnings per share	$3.30	$2.50

Jeffries is a very insistent (some would say pushy) man. When you told him that you would need additional information before making your decision, he acted offended, and said, "What more could you possibly want to know?" You responded that, at a minimum, you would need complete, audited financial statements.

Instructions
With the class divided into groups, answer the following.
(a) Explain why you would want the financial statements to be audited.
(b) Discuss the implications of the ratios provided for the lending decision you are to make. That is, does the information paint a favorable picture? Are these ratios relevant to the decision?
(c) List three other ratios that you would want to calculate for this company, and explain why you would use each.

COMMUNICATION ACTIVITY

BYP13-7 R.J. Falk is the chief executive officer of Ventura Electronics. Falk is an expert engineer but a novice in accounting. Falk asks you, as an accounting major, to explain (a) the bases for comparison in analyzing Ventura financial statements and (b) the limitations, if any, in financial statement analysis.

Instructions
Write a memo to R.J. Falk that explains the basis for comparison and the factors affecting quality of earnings.

ETHICS CASE

BYP13-8   Sandra Maxwell, president of XL Industries, wishes to issue a press release to bolster her company's image and maybe even its stock price, which has been gradually falling. As controller, you have been asked to provide a list of 20 financial ratios and other operating statistics for XL Industries' first-quarter financials and operations.

Two days after you provide the data requested, Chinda Khuon, the public relations director of XL, asks you to prove the accuracy of the financial and operating data contained in the press release written by the president and edited by Chinda. In the news release, the president highlights the sales increase of 25% over last year's first quarter and the positive change in the current ratio from 1.5:1 last year to 3:1 this year. She also emphasizes that production was up 50% over the prior year's first quarter.

You note that the release contains only positive or improved ratios and none of the negative or deteriorated ratios. For instance, no mention is made that the debt to total assets ratio has increased from 35% to 55%, that inventories are up 89%, and that although the current ratio improved, the current cash debt coverage ratio fell from .15 to .05. Nor is there any mention that the reported profit for the quarter would have been a loss had not the estimated lives of XL plant and machinery been increased by 30%. Chinda emphasized, "The Pres wants this release by early this afternoon."

Instructions
(a) Who are the stakeholders in this situation?
(b) Is there anything unethical in the president's actions?
(c) Should you as controller remain silent? Does Chinda have any responsibility?

Answers to Business Insight and Accounting across the Organization Questions

p. 649
Q: If a company takes a large restructuring charge, what is the effect on the company's current income statements versus future ones?
A: The current period's net income can be greatly diminished by a large restructuring charge. The net incomes in future periods can be enhanced because they are relieved of costs (i.e., depreciation and labor expenses) that would have been charged to them.

p. 660
Q: How might management influence a company's current ratio?
A: Management can affect the current ratio by speeding up or withholding payments on accounts payable just before the balance sheet date. Management can alter the cash balance by increasing or decreasing long-term assets or long-term debt, or by issuing or purchasing common stock.

p. 663
Q: Why might adding extra pages to the annual report not be beneficial to investors and analysts? What should be management's overriding objective in financial reporting?
A: When given too much information, investors may suffer from "information overload"—they may have a hard time sorting out what is important from what is not. Management's overriding financial reporting objective should be to provide an accurate depiction of the company's financial position and operating results in a clear and concise fashion. It should provide as much detail as is necessary to accomplish that.

Answer to Tootsie Roll Review It Question 3, p. 653

Tootsie Roll reported "Other comprehensive earnings" of $778,000 in 2004. "Comprehensive earnings" exceeded "Net earnings" by 1.2% [($64,952 − $64,174) ÷ $64,174].

Answers to Self-Study Questions

1. d   2. d   3. b   4. d   5. c   6. c   7. a   8. c   9. c   10. b
11. a   12. c

REMEMBER TO GO BACK TO THE NAVIGATOR BOX ON THE CHAPTER-OPENING PAGE AND CHECK OFF YOUR COMPLETED WORK.

Specimen Financial Statements: Tootsie Roll Industries, Inc.

The Annual Report

Once each year a corporation communicates to its stockholders and other interested parties by issuing a complete set of audited financial statements. The **annual report**, as this communication is called, summarizes the financial results of the company's operations for the year and its plans for the future. Many annual reports are attractive, multicolored, glossy public relations pieces, containing pictures of corporate officers and directors as well as photos and descriptions of new products and new buildings. Yet the basic function of every annual report is to report financial information, almost all of which is a product of the corporation's accounting system.

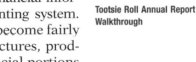

Tootsie Roll Annual Report Walkthrough

The content and organization of corporate annual reports have become fairly standardized. Excluding the public relations part of the report (pictures, products, and propaganda), the following items are the traditional financial portions of the annual report:

Financial Highlights
Letter to the Stockholders
Management's Discussion and Analysis
Financial Statements
Notes to the Financial Statements
Management's Report on Internal Control
Management Certification of Financial Statements
Auditor's Report
Supplementary Financial Information

In this appendix we illustrate current financial reporting with a comprehensive set of corporate financial statements that are prepared in accordance with generally accepted accounting principles and audited by an international independent certified public accounting firm. We are grateful for permission to use the actual financial statements and other accompanying financial information from the annual report of a large, publicly held company, Tootsie Roll Industries, Inc.

Financial Highlights

Companies usually present the financial highlights section inside the front cover of the annual report or on its first two pages. This section generally reports the total or per share amounts for five to ten financial items for the current year and one or more previous years.

Financial items from the income statement and the balance sheet that typically are presented are sales, income from continuing operations, net income, net income per share, dividends per common share, and the amount of capital expenditures. The financial highlights section from **Tootsie Roll Industries'** **Annual Report** is shown on page A-2. We have also included Tootsie Roll's discussion of its corporate principles and corporate profile.

The financial information herein is reprinted with permission from the Tootsie Roll Industries, Inc. 2004 Annual Report. The complete financial statements for Tootsie Roll Industries are also available on the book's companion website and on the Take Action! CD that is available as a supplement.

Corporate Profile

Tootsie Roll Industries, Inc. has been engaged in the manufacture and sale of confectionery products for 108 years. Our products are primarily sold under the familiar brand names, Tootsie Roll, Tootsie Roll Pops, Caramel Apple Pops, Child's Play, Charms, Blow Pop, Blue Razz, Cella's chocolate covered cherries, Mason Dots, Mason Crows, Junior Mints, Charleston Chew, Sugar Daddy, Sugar Babies, Andes, Fluffy Stuff cotton candy, Dubble Bubble, Razzles, Cry Baby, Nik-L-Nip and El Bubble.

Corporate Principles

We believe that the differences among companies are attributable to the caliber of their people, and therefore we strive to attract and retain superior people for each job.

We believe that an open family atmosphere at work combined with professional management fosters cooperation and enables each individual to maximize his or her contribution to the company and realize the corresponding rewards.

We do not jeopardize long-term growth for immediate, short-term results.

We maintain a conservative financial posture in the deployment and management of our assets.

We run a trim operation and continually strive to eliminate waste, minimize cost and implement performance improvements.

We invest in the latest and most productive equipment to deliver the best quality product to our customers at the lowest cost.

We seek to outsource functions where appropriate and to vertically integrate operations where it is financially advantageous to do so.

Melvin J. Gordon, Chairman and Chief Executive Officer and Ellen R. Gordon, President and Chief Operating Officer.

We view our well known brands as prized assets to be aggressively advertised and promoted to each new generation of consumers.

We conduct business with the highest ethical standards and integrity which are codified in the Company's "Code of Business Conduct and Ethics."

Letter to the Stockholders

Nearly every annual report contains a letter to the stockholders from the chairman of the board or the president, or both. This letter typically discusses the company's accomplishments during the past year and highlights significant events such as mergers and acquisitions, new products, operating achievements, business philosophy, changes in officers or directors, financing commitments, expansion plans, and future prospects. The letter to the stockholders signed by Melvin J. Gordon, Chairman of the Board and Chief Executive Officer, and Ellen R. Gordon, President and Chief Operating Officer, of Tootsie Roll Industries is shown on the next pages.

To Our Shareholders

Sales in 2004 increased to $420 million compared to 2003 sales of $392 million. This represents a new record level of sales for the company.

Net earnings in 2004 were $64 million as compared to $65 million in 2003. On a per share basis, earnings increased from $1.22 in 2003 to $1.23 in 2004. The increase in earnings per share results from fewer shares outstanding in 2004 due to stock repurchases.

Other highlights of 2004 include:

- We purchased Concord Confections, the largest acquisition in the company's history.

- Cash dividends were paid for the sixty-second consecutive year, earning us recognition as a "Dividend Aristocrat" by Standard & Poors and a "Dividend Achiever" by Mergent.

- Our fortieth consecutive annual 3% stock dividend was distributed in April.

- Again this year, capital expenditures were made for projects that will improve operating efficiencies and support growth.

Our conservative financial posture coupled with many years of profitable operations enabled us to make these significant outlays without incurring undue leverage or putting the company at financial risk. Of the $154 million borrowed in August in conjunction with the Concord purchase, approximately 40% or $62 million was paid back, and cash and investments, net of interest bearing debt, was $86 million by year end.

We remain prepared to capitalize on appropriate investment opportunities as they may arise. These may include initiatives to develop niche products, investment in strategically or economically prudent capital projects and pursuit of additional complementary business acquisitions. We remain active in our evaluation of opportunities in each of these areas.

Sales and Marketing

We have long recognized the competitive advantage of having strong brands which position us well against the continuing onslaught of low priced foreign imports, private label imitators and branded competition from other confectionery manufacturers.

In 2004 we again offered focused promotional programs such as bonus bags, shippers and combo packs to high volume classes of trade. These programs reinforce the attributes of quality and value that consumers expect and generate high-turn, profitable use of shelf and floor space that retailers demand.

We also successfully continued our sales initiatives in the growing dollar store class of trade. Consumers who frequent these outlets tend to be value oriented in their purchasing decisions, and find that our brands deliver excellent quality at an affordable price.

Halloween was once again our strongest sales period. Our bagged goods, in particular our popular mixed bags assortments such as Childs Play, continued to sell well through the mass merchandise, drug, supermarket and warehouse club venues.

Outside of Halloween, our line of "theater" products continued to receive good consumer acceptance in the drug, mass merchandise, supermarket and dollar store trade classes. This family of products presents many of our most popular candies to consumers in large "theater sized" reclosable boxes with attractive display panels.

Brands featured in this line include four varieties of Dots as well as Crows, Sugar Babies, Mini-Charleston Chews and Junior

Financial Highlights

	December 31,	
	2004	2003
	(in thousands except per share data)	
Net Sales	$420,110	$392,656
Net Earnings	64,174	65,014
Working Capital	110,376	180,818
Net Property, Plant and Equipment	178,750	129,163
Shareholders' Equity	570,179	536,581
Average Shares Outstanding*	52,366	53,305
Per Share Items*		
Net Earnings	$1.23	$1.22
Cash Dividends Paid	.28	.27

*Adjusted for stock dividends.

Mints. In 2004 we introduced a new item in the theater box format-Junior Caramels. These boxed candies put the company in a strong position in regard to sales to theaters and to home video sections of self-service outlets.

Junior Caramels

Junior Caramels consist of delicious, soft caramel centers enrobed in a shell of rich milk chocolate and polished to a beautiful shine. They were offered on a limited introductory basis in 2004, and met with enthusiastic consumer acceptance. National rollout is planned for 2005. Junior Caramels are an excellent example of the type of niche product extension we continually seek.

We also brought out two popular items from mixed assortments, and introduced them as stand-alone, "Limited Edition" goods. Packaged in foil bags to preserve freshness, Chocolate Tootsie Pops and Vanilla Tootsie Rolls gave consumers an opportunity to indulge in their personal favorite treats.

Limited Edition Tootsie Rolls and Tootsie Pops

Excitement about the Tootsie Pop brand was further stimulated by the addition of a sixth flavor to our traditional five-flavor mix. Consumers can now enjoy one of three tantalizing new "mystery" flavors, watermelon, strawberry or blue raspberry, in every package they buy.

Mean Green Blow Pops

In the Blow Pop line, we updated the packaging with enhanced graphics on a brighter white, opaque background. We also introduced Mean Green, an intensely lime flavored translucent candy shell surrounding a bright green, sour lime flavored bubble gum center. Its distinctive packaging cautions consumers to "Prepare to be Limed!"

Concord Confections

In keeping with our stated goal of making complimentary business acquisitions, in August we purchased Concord Confections, maker of Dubble Bubble, to our knowledge the largest maker of bubble gum in the world. This icon brand comes in two primary formats.

Dubble Bubble

"Chunk gum" is the familiar pink colored, tutti-frutti flavored bubble gum wrapped in wax paper bearing the instantly recognizable red oval Dubble Bubble trademark. "Gum balls" are brightly colored, spherically shaped and come in many sizes and flavors, primarily for sale in gumball machines and tube packs. Dubble Bubble is the market leader in both the chunk and ball gum categories.

Many other brands were included in the acquisition. Some of these are:

Razzles—the magic dextrose candy that turns into gum while you eat it.

Cry Baby—gum so sour it can bring a tear to your eye!

Nik-L-Nip—chewable wax bottles filled with tasty juice.

Along with these and other brands, the Concord acquisition included its principal manufacturing facilities located near Toronto.

Our sales and marketing departments are integrating Concord's broad product assortment and developing appropriate promotional strategies for these new items.

Advertising and Public Relations

Our products again received extensive cable television exposure through special interest features. The Food Network's *Unwrapped* program produced new segments on Fluffy Stuff Cotton Candy, Super Blow Pops and Tootsie Fruit Rolls. These are in addition to previous *Unwrapped* shows that feature nearly all of our major brands.

Tootsie Rolls and Tootsie Pops were spotlighted in "Snack Food Tech" on *Modern Marvels*, the History Channel's signature series. That show, based on engineering accomplishments, explored the snack food industry from early discoveries to the present innovative technologies employed today.

Exposure on these highly rated shows, including periodic replays, generates positive awareness of our products.

We also utilized cable television to convey our classic "How Many Licks?" Tootsie Pops advertising message. The 2004 campaign was directed toward cartoon and family programs, and generated the inevitable letters from many consumers who succumbed to the urge to convey just how many licks it does take. Alas, the precise answer remains elusive, lending credence to Mr. Owl's wise observation: "the world may never know!"

The company has had a long history of making products for military rations. We continue to receive many gratifying letters from soldiers in Iraq and elsewhere, commenting on how Tootsie Rolls in their ration kits brightened their day or brought forth a nostalgic reminder of home.

There were also numerous articles and stories in newspapers and other publications throughout the year publicizing our products. Many of these focus on holiday themes such as "popular Halloween candies" or "what's new for the Easter season." Other articles highlight certain consumer trends such as the current popularity of nostalgic 'retro' products and feature many of our brands, which have stood the test of time and remain consumer favorites.

Manufacturing and Distribution

We continue to invest in projects that support growing product lines, keep our production facilities as efficient as possible and improve product quality.

We began new capital projects of these types during the year and completed several other major initiatives, which began in prior years. As technology evolves, we have continued to realize benefits through automation.

We have long found merit in sharing ideas among facilities. As with past acquisitions, we anticipate that the addition of Concord's operations will enhance this process. Accordingly, we have eagerly begun to share ideas and best practices between our other manufacturing and distribution centers and Concord.

Our distribution centers are physically capable of handling the volume of Concord inventory, enabling us to focus on the complex process of integrating these products into our supply chain. This effort is already well underway.

Purchasing

Prices for key raw materials and packaging were generally favorable during the year. In particular, cocoa eased substantially from recent

historically high levels. However, this saving was nearly offset by increased costs in edible oils.

We are in the process of bringing the procurement activities for Concord on line with our purchasing systems. Where possible we will leverage this additional volume in our competitive bidding, hedging and forward purchase programs to ensure that the company's purchases are sourced as economically as possible, with minimum exposure to short-term market fluctuations.

Information Technology and Internal Controls

Integrating Concord into our systems was a major operational initiative during 2004. Planning was completed, certain systems have been brought over and the remaining system areas will be converted to our platform during the first half of 2005.

Projects of this scope reinforce the wisdom of past investments of time and money toward developing state-of-the-art business systems and data management protocols. We remain convinced that information technology is a prime strategic tool to support future growth.

Also during 2004 we, as well as other large public companies, undertook the substantial task of documenting and testing our system of internal controls in order to meet the requirements of the Sarbanes-Oxley Act. Completing this process in a timely fashion required commitment and cooperation throughout our organization. We are pleased to note that our controls over financial reporting, which we always believed to be good, are now documented and tested.

International

Our international sales increased during 2004. We manufacture and sell products in Mexico under the Tutsi trademark. We also sell Tootsie, Charms and Concord products to Canada and over 30 other countries in Europe, Asia and South and Central America. Our legacy product line, coupled with newly acquired Dubble Bubble products, offer a compelling and broad assortment of items that can be extended to additional foreign markets.

In Appreciation

We believe that people have been the key ingredient in our recipe for success over the years. Excellence is required at every level of the organization to meet the growing demands in today's increasingly competitive marketplace. Accordingly, we wish to thank our many loyal employees, customers, foreign distributors, suppliers and sales brokers for their efforts on behalf of the company during 2004. We also thank our shareholders for their support through the years.

We remain committed to growing the sales and profits of the company and believe that we are well positioned in this regard as we enter 2005.

Melvin J. Gordon

Melvin J. Gordon
Chairman of the Board and
Chief Executive Officer

Ellen R. Gordon

Ellen R. Gordon
President and
Chief Operating Officer

Management Discussion and Analysis

The management discussion and analysis (MD&A) section covers three financial aspects of a company: its results of operations, its ability to pay near-term obligations, and its ability to fund operations and expansion. Management must highlight favorable or unfavorable trends and identify significant events and uncertainties that affect these three factors. This discussion obviously involves a number of subjective estimates and opinions. The MD&A section of Tootsie Roll's annual report is presented below.

Management's Discussion and Analysis of Financial Condition and Results of Operations

(in thousands except per share, percentage and ratio figures)

FINANCIAL REVIEW

This financial review discusses the company's financial condition, results of operations, liquidity and capital resources, market risks and other matters. It should be read in conjunction with the Consolidated Financial Statements and related footnotes that follow this discussion.

FINANCIAL CONDITION

The strong financial condition in which the company entered 2004, coupled with profitable operations during the year, enabled us to make the largest acquisition in the company's history without incurring undue leverage or placing the company at financial risk. Working capital ended the year at $110,376, down from $180,818 at the beginning of the year. The decrease of $70,442 is due to lower cash and short-term investments and higher current debt used to finance the Concord acquisition, partially offset by the working capital acquired.

Interest bearing debt was $99,500 at year end, $62,000 lower than the peak of $161,500 on August 31, 2004 immediately following the acquisition. Debt was paid down through a combination of cash flow provided by operating activities and investment maturities.

Shareholders equity increased to $570,179 in 2004 from $536,581 primarily due to net earnings during the year, net of cash dividends and share repurchases. The company has paid cash dividends for sixty-two consecutive years and has distributed a stock dividend for forty consecutive years.

The company has a simple financial structure, and aside from an immaterial amount of operating leases, the company has no "off-balance sheet" financing arrangements. We maintain a conservative financial posture and funds generated from operations plus maturities of short term investments are expected to be adequate to meet the company's financing needs over the coming year. These funds may be augmented by prudent borrowing for significant investments such as was done for the Concord acquisition.

RESULTS OF OPERATIONS

2004 vs. 2003

Net sales in 2004 grew to a record $420,110, an increase of $27,454 from 2003 sales of $392,656. Sales benefited from successful marketing and promotional programs, including pre-Halloween sales programs that have traditionally made our third quarter the highest selling period of the year and did so again this year.

However, the sales increase in 2004 is attributable to sales resulting from the Concord acquisition as core brand sales were approximately even with the prior year.

Cost of goods sold increased from 56.7% to 58.2% of sales. This increase is due to lower margins on acquired brands, lower production volumes in several core product lines, approximately $1,800 in start-up costs associated with a new production line and a $600 inventory adjustment for a discontinued product line. These expenses were partially offset by somewhat lower raw material and packaging costs.

Due to the seasonal nature of our business and corresponding

variations in product mix, gross margins have historically been lower in the second half of the year, and this was the case in 2004. The impact of the factors discussed above was concentrated in the fourth quarter. As a result, fourth quarter gross margins were lower than in 2003.

Selling, marketing and administrative expense increased as a percent of sales to 20.4% in 2004 from 19.8% in 2003. The increase is due to expenses associated with Concord and approximately $1,500 higher freight costs related to fuel surcharges, as well as higher fees associated with Sarbanes-Oxley compliance and general cost increases.

Other income declined from $5,594 in 2003 to $4,784 in 2004 due to higher interest expense and lower investment earnings, both related to financing the Concord acquisition. The consolidated effective tax rate declined from 33.6% in 2003 to 32.2%. This decline generally reflects a reduction in foreign income taxes.

Consolidated net earnings were $64,174 and $65,014 and earnings per share were $1.23 and $1.22 in 2004 and 2003, respectively. Average shares outstanding declined from 53,305 to 52,366 due to share repurchases.

2003 vs. 2002

Net sales were $392,656 in 2003 compared to $393,185 in 2002, a decrease of $529 or 0.1%. Factors effecting sales growth were generally sluggish US economic conditions, higher promotional expense and lower sales in Mexico. Seasonal sales again peaked in the third quarter due to Halloween sales and promotions.

Cost of goods sold as a percentage of net sales was

NET SALES
Millions of dollars

$397 $392 $393 $393 $420
00   01   02   03   04

NET EARNINGS
Per Share

$1.37 $1.19 $1.22 $1.22 $1.20
00   01   02   03   04

56.7% and 56.5% for 2003 and 2002, respectively. Higher costs for our principal ingredients and increased plant overhead costs incurred during 2003 were generally offset by selective price increases. Gross margins were lower in the second half of the year due to seasonality and corresponding variations in product mix.

Selling, marketing and administrative expenses were $77,756 in 2003 as compared to $75,751 in 2002, an increase of 2.6%. These costs were 19.8% of sales in 2003 versus 19.3% in the prior year.

SHAREHOLDERS'
EQUITY
Millions of dollars

CASH DIVIDENDS
Per Share

Accordingly, earnings from operations were $92,353 in 2003, or $2,877 below the $95,230 attained in 2002. Other income was $5,594 in 2003 as compared to $5,458 in 2002. The increase of $136 is primarily attributable to a $541 property tax refund in 2003, partially offset by lower interest income due to lower interest rates.

The consolidated effective tax rate decreased from 34.1% in 2002 to 33.6% in 2003. This decline generally reflects a reduction in state income taxes.

Net earnings were $65,014 and $66,388 and earnings per share were $1.22 in both 2003 and 2002. Earnings per share remained constant on lower net earnings due to share repurchases. Average shares outstanding declined from 54,592 in 2002 to 53,305 in 2003.

LIQUIDITY AND CAPITAL RESOURCES

Cash flows from operating activities were $76,228 in 2004, $83,466 in 2003 and $75,473 in 2002. Both the decline in 2004 and the increase in 2003 were principally attributable to changes in accounts receivable due to the timing of sales and customer payments. Also, while inventories grew in each of 2004, 2003 and 2002, the 2004 increase was higher because of the addition of Concord items to our supply chain.

Cash flows from investing activities reflect the purchase of Concord Confections for $218,229 as well as capital expenditures of $17,948 and a $72,138 net decrease in marketable securities associated with financing the acquisition. In 2003, capital expenditures were $12,150 and marketable securities increased by a net of $38,233. In 2002, capital expenditures were $10,308 and marketable securities increased by $19,263.

Cash flows from financing activities reflect a borrowing of $154,000 for the acquisition and $62,000 of payments against this loan. Share repurchases were $16,407, $40,096 and $32,313 in 2004, 2003 and 2002, respectively. Cash dividends of $14,877, $14,410 and $14,614 were paid in 2004, 2003 and 2002, respectively. 2004 was the sixty-second consecutive year in which we have paid cash dividends.

MARKET RISKS

The company is exposed to market risks related to commodity prices, interest rates, equity prices and foreign exchange.

Commodity price risks relate to ingredients (primarily sugar, cocoa, corn syrup and vegetable oils). The company believes its competitors face similar risks, and the industry has historically adjusted prices to compensate for adverse fluctuations in commodity costs.

To mitigate the impact of commodity cost fluctuations, the company enters into commodity futures contracts to hedge anticipated purchases of certain ingredients (primarily sugar). These contracts are effective as hedges under Statement of Financial Accounting Standards (SFAS) 133, "Accounting for Derivative Instruments and Hedging Activities." The unrealized gains and losses on such contracts are deferred as a component of accumulated other comprehensive earnings (loss) and are recognized as a component of cost of goods sold when the related inventory is sold.

Interest rate risks relate to the company's investments in debt securities (primarily municipal bonds) with maturities of generally up to four years. The majority of these have historically been held to maturity, which limits the company's exposure to interest rate fluctuations. Interest rates on the company's debt obligations are reset weekly.

Equity price risk relates to the company's investments in mutual funds.

Foreign exchange risk relates to the company's foreign operations including Concord and purchase commitments.

The company has no outstanding guarantees of obligations to third parties.

Commodities

The potential change in fair value of commodity derivative instruments (primarily sugar futures contracts) held by the company, assuming a 10% change in the underlying commodity price, was $858. This analysis only includes commodity derivative instruments and, therefore, does not consider the offsetting effect of changes in the price of the underlying commodity. This amount is not significant compared with the net earnings and shareholders equity of the company.

Equity price

At December 31, 2004, the company has investments in mutual funds of $25,332. These investments primarily relate to hedging deferred compensation liabilities, and any potential change in their fair value would be offset by a corresponding change in such liabilities.

Interest rates

The accompanying chart summarizes the maturities of the company's investments in debt securities at December 31, 2004.

Less than 1 year	$ 28,701
1 - 2 years	53,014
2 - 3 years	18,293
Total.	$100,008

Foreign exchange

Prior to the acquisition of Concord, the company's operations outside of the United States represented less than 10% of its consolidated operations. Accordingly, the company did not use derivative financial instruments to hedge its foreign currency assets or liabilities or its overall investments in its foreign subsidiaries.

Certain of Concord's manufacturing expenses, including labor and a portion of its packaging, ingredients and supplies are sourced in Canadian dollars. From time to time the company may use forward foreign exchange contracts and derivative instruments to mitigate its exposure to these costs as well as those related to firm commitments to purchase equipment from foreign

vendors. As of December 31, 2004 the company had not entered into any forward foreign exchange contracts with respect to the Canadian dollar, and other outstanding foreign exchange contracts were not material.

CRITICAL ACCOUNTING POLICIES

Preparation of the company's financial statements involves judgments due to uncertainties affecting the application of accounting policies, and the likelihood that different amounts would be reported under different conditions or using different assumptions. In the opinion of management, the company does not have any individual accounting policy that is "critical." However, following is a summary of the more significant accounting policies and methods where estimates are used.

Revenue recognition

Revenue, net of applicable provisions for discounts, returns, allowances, and certain advertising and promotional costs, is recognized when products are delivered to customers and collectibility is reasonably assured. The accounting for such promotional programs is discussed below.

Provisions for bad debts are recorded as selling, marketing and administrative expense. Such provisions have not exceeded 0.2% of net sales for 2004, 2003 and 2002 and, accordingly, have not been significant to the company's financial position or results of operations.

Intangible assets

Effective January 1, 2002 the company adopted SFAS No. 142, whereby goodwill and other indefinite lived assets are not amortized, but are instead subjected to annual testing for impairment. The company's intangible assets consist

primarily of trademarks, the values of which the company has determined are not impaired.

This determination is made by comparing the carrying value of the asset with its estimated fair value, which is calculated on the basis of discounted projected future cash flows. These projected future cash flows are dependent on a number of factors including future business plans and projected operating results. Although the majority of the company's trademarks relate to well established brands with a long history of consumer acceptance, projected cash flows are inherently uncertain. A change in the assumptions underlying the impairment analysis, such as a reduction in projected cash flows or the use of a different discount rate, could cause an impairment in the future.

Customer incentive programs, advertising and marketing

Advertising and marketing costs are recorded in the period to which such costs relate. The company does not defer the recognition of any amounts on its consolidated balance sheet with respect to such costs. Customer incentives and other promotional costs are recorded at the time of sale based upon incentive program terms and historical utilization statistics, which are generally consistent from year to year.

The liabilities associated with these programs are reviewed quarterly and adjusted if utilization rates differ from management's original estimates. Such adjustments have not historically been material to the company's operating results.

Investments

The company invests in certain high-quality debt securities primarily Aa or better rated municipal bonds. The accounting for such investments is outlined in Note 1 and does not involve any significant estimates on the part of management. Due to their relatively short maturities, changes in interest rates have an immaterial effect on the principal value of these investments and no credit losses have been incurred.

Guarantees

The Financial Accounting Standards Board issued Interpretation No. 45 relating to the accounting for and disclosure of certain types of guarantees. The disclosure provisions are effective for financial statements with years ending after December 15, 2002. No disclosures were required for the company as a result of adoption of this standard, as it has no such guarantees outstanding.

Other matters

In the opinion of management, other than contracts for raw materials, including commodity hedges and outstanding purchase orders for packaging, ingredients and supplies, all entered into in the ordinary course of business, the company does not have any significant contractual obligations or future commitments. The company's outstanding contractual commitments as of December 31, 2004, all of which are normal and recurring in nature, are summarized in the accompanying chart.

The company provides split dollar life insurance benefits to certain executive officers and records an asset equal to the cumulative premiums paid on the related policies, as the company will fully recover these premiums under the terms of the plan.

The results of our operations and our financial condition are expressed in the following financial statements.

Open Contractual Commitments as of December 31, 2004

Payable in	Total	Less than 1 year	1 to 3 Years	3 to 5 Years	More than 5 Years
Commodity hedges	$8,588	$5,176	$3,412	$ —	$ —
Purchase obligations	68,919	68,919	—	—	—
Split dollar insurance	8,256	3,441	4,815	—	—
Interest bearing debt	99,500	6,333	85,667	—	7,500
Operating leases	1,350	851	499	—	—
Total	$186,613	$84,720	$94,393	$ —	$7,500

Note: the above amounts exclude deferred income tax liabilities of $25,995, post retirement health care and life insurance benefits of $10,075 and deferred compensation and other liabilities of $30,020 because the timing of payments relating to these items cannot be reasonably determined.

Financial Statements and Accompanying Notes

The standard set of financial statements consists of: (1) a comparative income statement for three years, (2) a comparative balance sheet for two years, (3) a comparative statement of cash flows for three years, (4) a statement of retained earnings (or stockholders' equity) for three years, and (5) a set of accompanying notes that are considered an integral part of the financial statements. The auditor's report, unless stated otherwise, covers the financial statements and the accompanying notes. The financial statements and accompanying notes plus some supplementary data and analyses for Tootsie Roll Industries follow.

CONSOLIDATED STATEMENT OF

Financial Position

TOOTSIE ROLL INDUSTRIES, INC. AND SUBSIDIARIES   (in thousands)

Assets

December 31,

	2004	2003
CURRENT ASSETS:		
Cash and cash equivalents	$ 56,989	$ 84,084
Investments	32,369	86,961
Accounts receivable trade, less allowances of $2,440 and $1,970	28,456	18,131
Other receivables	9,001	3,076
Inventories:		
Finished goods and work-in-process	37,384	28,969
Raw materials and supplies	21,393	17,117
Prepaid expenses	5,719	4,416
Deferred income taxes	1,382	951
Total current assets	192,693	243,705
PROPERTY, PLANT AND EQUIPMENT, at cost:		
Land	14,973	8,265
Buildings	61,714	44,960
Machinery and equipment	244,367	206,697
	321,054	259,922
Less—Accumulated depreciation	142,304	130,759
	178,750	129,163
OTHER ASSETS:		
Goodwill	74,002	38,151
Trademarks	193,342	79,348
Investments	96,640	112,431
Split dollar officer life insurance	66,094	62,499
Investement in joint venture	10,232	—
	440,310	292,429
	$811,753	$665,297

(The accompanying notes are an integral part of these statements.)

(in thousands except per share data)

Liabilities and Shareholders' Equity   December 31,

	2004	2003
CURRENT LIABILITIES:		
Bank loan	$ 6,333	$ —
Accounts payable	19,315	11,947
Dividends payable	3,659	3,589
Accrued liabilities	44,722	38,834
Income taxes payable	8,288	8,517
Total current liabilities	82,317	62,887
NONCURRENT LIABILITIES:		
Bank loan	85,667	—
Deferred income taxes	25,995	22,631
Postretirement health care and life insurance benefits	10,075	9,302
Industrial development bonds	7,500	7,500
Deferred compensation and other liabilities	30,020	26,396
Total noncurrent liabilities	159,257	65,829
SHAREHOLDERS' EQUITY:		
Common stock, $.69-4/9 par value—		
120,000 shares authorized—		
34,760 and 34,082, respectively, issued	24,139	23,668
Class B common stock, $.69-4/9 par value—		
40,000 shares authorized—		
17,515 and 17,145, respectively, issued	12,163	11,906
Capital in excess of par value	397,745	357,922
Retained earnings, per accompanying statement	149,055	156,786
Accumulated other comprehensive earnings (loss)	(10,931)	(11,709)
Treasury stock (at cost)—		
58 shares and 56 shares, respectively	(1,992)	(1,992)
	570,179	536,581
	$811,753	$665,297

CONSOLIDATED STATEMENT OF

Earnings, Comprehensive Earnings and Retained Earnings

TOOTSIE ROLL INDUSTRIES. INC. AND SUBSIDIARIES   (in thousands except per share data)

For the year ended December 31,

	2004	2003	2002
Net sales	$420,110	$392,656	$393,185
Cost of goods sold	244,501	222,547	222,204
Gross margin	175,609	170,109	170,981
Selling, marketing and administrative expenses	85,705	77,756	75,751
Earnings from operations	89,904	92,353	95,230
Other income, net	4,784	5,594	5,458
Earnings before income taxes	94,688	97,947	100,688
Provision for income taxes	30,514	32,933	34,300
Net earnings	$ 64,174	$ 65,014	$ 66,388
Net earnings	$ 64,174	$ 65,014	$ 66,388
Other comprehensive earnings (loss)	778	(657)	(1,139)
Comprehensive earnings	$ 64,952	$ 64,357	$ 65,249
Retained earnings at beginning of year	$156,786	$148,705	$161,345
Net earnings	64,174	65,014	66,388
Cash dividends ($.28, $.27 and $.26 per share, respectively)	(14,547)	(14,362)	(14,304)
Stock dividends	(57,358)	(42,571)	(64,724)
Retained earnings at end of year	$149,055	$156,786	$148,705
Earnings per share	$ 1.23	$ 1.22	$ 1.22
Average common and class B common shares outstanding	52,366	53,305	54,592

(The accompanying notes are an integral part of these statements.)

CONSOLIDATED STATEMENT OF

Cash Flows

TOOTSIE ROLL INDUSTRIES, INC. AND SUBSIDIARIES   (in thousands)

For the year ended December 31,

	2004	2003	2002
CASH FLOWS FROM OPERATING ACTIVITIES:			
Net earnings	$ 64,174	$ 65,014	$ 66,388
Adjustments to reconcile net earnings to net cash provided by operating activities:			
Depreciation and amortization	11,680	11,379	12,354
Amortization of marketable securities	1,885	2,534	1,407
Purchase of trading securities	(2,507)	(3,154)	(2,602)
Changes in operating assets and liabilities:			
Accounts receivable	673	4,266	(2,886)
Other receivables	1,574	490	619
Inventories	(4,567)	(2,579)	(2,734)
Prepaid expenses and other assets	(5,054)	(4,864)	(6,502)
Accounts payable and accrued liabilities	2,478	2,582	5,052
Income taxes payable and deferred	2,712	3,827	318
Postretirement health care and life insurance benefits	773	1,151	701
Deferred compensation and other liabilities	2,227	2,651	2,554
Other	180	169	804
Net cash provided by operating activities	76,228	83,466	75,473
CASH FLOWS FROM INVESTING ACTIVITIES:			
Acquisition of business, net of cash acquired	(218,229)	—	—
Capital expenditures	(17,948)	(12,150)	(10,308)
Purchase of held to maturity securities	(22,049)	(57,823)	(64,956)
Maturity of held to maturity securities	44,113	25,643	46,797
Purchase of available for sale securities	(83,987)	(57,578)	(34,795)
Sale and maturity of available for sale securities	134,061	51,525	33,691
Net cash used in investing activities	(164,039)	(50,383)	(29,571)
CASH FLOWS FROM FINANCING ACTIVITIES:			
Proceeds from bank loan	154,000	—	—
Repayment of bank loan	(62,000)	—	—
Shares repurchased and retired	(16,407)	(40,096)	(32,313)
Dividends paid in cash	(14,877)	(14,410)	(14,614)
Net cash provided by (used in) financing activities	60,716	(54,506)	(46,927)
Decrease in cash and cash equivalents	(27,095)	(21,423)	(1,025)
Cash and cash equivalents at beginning of year	84,084	105,507	106,532
Cash and cash equivalents at end of year	$ 56,989	$ 84,084	$105,507
Supplemental cash flow information:			
Income taxes paid	$ 28,966	$ 31,561	$ 34,099
Interest paid	$ 879	$ 172	$ 309
Stock dividend issued	$ 56,959	$ 42,513	$ 64,371

(The accompanying notes are an integral part of these statements.)

Notes to Consolidated Financial Statements

TOOTSIE ROLL INDUSTRIES, INC. AND SUBSIDIARIES

($ in thousands except per share data)

NOTE 1—SIGNIFICANT ACCOUNTING POLICIES:
Basis of consolidation:

The consolidated financial statements include the accounts of Tootsie Roll Industries, Inc. and its wholly-owned subsidiaries (the company), which are primarily engaged in the manufacture and sale of candy products. All significant intercompany transactions have been eliminated.

The preparation of financial statements in conformity with generally accepted accounting principles in the United States of America requires management to make estimates and assumptions that affect the reported amounts of assets and liabilities and disclosure of contingent assets and liabilities at the date of the financial statements and the reported amounts of revenues and expenses during the reporting period. Actual results could differ from those estimates.

Certain reclassifications have been made to the prior year financial statements to conform to the current year presentation.

Revenue recognition and other accounting pronouncements:

Products are sold to customers based on accepted purchase orders which include quantity, sales price and other relevant terms of sale. Revenues are recognized when products are delivered to customers and collectibility is reasonably assured. Shipping and handling costs of $31,795, $28,217 and $28,579 in 2004, 2003 and 2002, respectively, are included in selling, marketing and administrative expenses. Accounts receivable are unsecured. Revenues from a major customer aggregated approximately 20.8%, 20.6% and 19.6% of total net sales during the years ended December 31, 2004, 2003 and 2002, respectively.

In November 2004, the Financial Accounting Standards Board (FASB) issued Statement of Financial Accounting Standards (SFAS) No. 151, "Inventory Costs—an amendment to ARB No. 43, Chapter 4," which amends guidance in accounting for abnormal amounts of idle facility expense. The company believes that the pronouncement is generally not applicable to the company's operations and to the extent it may be applicable it is not expected to have a significant impact on the company's consolidated financial statements.

Cash and cash equivalents:

The company considers temporary cash investments with an original maturity of three months or less to be cash equivalents.

Investments:

Investments consist of various marketable securities with maturities of generally up to four years. The company classifies debt and equity securities as either held to maturity, available for sale or trading. Held to maturity securities represent those securities that the company has both the positive intent and ability to hold to maturity and are carried at amortized cost. Available for sale securities represent those securities that do not meet the classification of held to maturity, are not actively traded and are carried at fair value. Unrealized gains and losses on these securities are excluded from earnings and are reported as a separate component of shareholders' equity, net of applicable taxes, until realized. Trading securities relate to deferred compensation arrangements and are carried at fair value.

Hedging activities:

From time to time, the company enters into commodities futures contracts that are intended and effective as hedges of market price risks associated with the anticipated purchase of certain raw materials (primarily sugar). To qualify as a hedge, the company evaluates a variety of characteristics of these transactions, including the probability that the anticipated transaction will occur. If the anticipated transaction were not to occur, the gain or loss would then be recognized in current earnings. The company does not engage in trading or other speculative use of derivative instruments. The company does assume the risk that counter parties may not be able to meet the terms of their contracts. The company does not expect any losses as a result of counter party defaults.

The company's derivative instruments are being accounted for as cash flow hedges and are recorded on the balance sheet at fair value. Changes therein are recorded in other comprehensive earnings and are reclassified to earnings in the periods in which earnings are affected by the hedged item. Substantially all amounts reported in accumulated other comprehensive earnings (loss) are expected to be reclassified to cost of goods sold. During the years ended December 31, 2004, 2003 and 2002, ineffectiveness related to cash flow hedges was not material.

Inventories:

Inventories are stated at cost, not to exceed market. The cost of substantially all of the company's inventories ($54,794 and $42,735 at December 31, 2004 and 2003, respectively) has been determined by the last-in, first-out (LIFO) method. The excess of current cost over LIFO cost of inventories approximates $5,868 and $6,442 at December 31, 2004 and 2003, respectively. The cost of certain foreign inventories

($3,983 and $3,351 at December 31, 2004 and 2003, respectively) has been determined by the first-in, first-out (FIFO) method. Rebates, discounts and other cash consideration received from a vendor related to inventory purchases is reflected as a reduction in the cost of the related inventory item, and is therefore reflected in cost of sales when the related inventory item is sold.

Property, plant and equipment:

Depreciation is computed for financial reporting purposes by use of the straight-line method based on useful lives of 20 to 35 years for buildings and 5 to 20 years for machinery and equipment. Depreciation expense was $11,680, $11,379 and $12,354 in 2004, 2003 and 2002, respectively, including $744 relating to equipment disposals.

Carrying value of long-lived assets:

The company reviews long-lived assets to determine if there are events or circumstances indicating that the amount of the asset reflected in the company's balance sheet may not be recoverable. When such indicators are present, the company compares the carrying value of the long-lived asset, or asset group, to the future undiscounted cash flows of the underlying assets to determine if an impairment exists. If applicable, an impairment charge would be recorded to write down the carrying value to its fair value. The determination of fair value involves the use of estimates of future cash flows that involve considerable management judgment and are based upon assumptions about expected future operating performance. The actual cash flows could differ from management's estimates due to changes in business conditions, operating performance, and economic conditions. No impairment charges were recorded by the company during 2004, 2003 or 2002.

Postretirement health care and life insurance benefits:

The company provides certain postretirement health care and life insurance benefits. The cost of these postretirement benefits is accrued during employees' working careers. The company also provides split dollar life insurance benefits to certain executive officers. The company records an asset equal to the cumulative insurance premiums that will be recovered upon the death of a covered employee(s) or earlier under the terms of the plan. Split dollar premiums paid were $3,620, $4,237 and $6,890 in 2004, 2003 and 2002, respectively.

Intangible assets:

The company accounts for intangible assets in accordance with SFAS No. 142, "Goodwill and Other Intangible Assets," which was adopted by the company on January 1, 2002. In accordance with this statement, goodwill and intangible assets with indefinite lives are not amortized, but rather tested for impairment at least annually. All trademarks have been assessed by management to have indefinite lives because they are expected to generate cash flows indefinitely. The company

has completed its annual impairment testing of its goodwill and trademarks during the fourth quarter of each of the years presented, and no impairment was found.

Income taxes:

Deferred income taxes are recorded and recognized for future tax effects of temporary differences between financial and income tax reporting. Federal income taxes are provided on the portion of income of foreign subsidiaries that is expected to be remitted to the U.S. and become taxable, but not on the portion that is considered to be permanently invested in the foreign subsidiary.

Foreign currency translation:

The company has determined the functional currency for each foreign subsidiary. The U.S. dollar is used as the functional currency where a substantial portion of the subsidiary's business is indexed to the U.S. dollar or where its manufactured products are principally sold in the U.S. All other foreign subsidiaries use the local currency as their functional currency. Where the U.S. dollar is used as the functional currency, foreign currency translation adjustments are recorded as a charge or credit to other income in the statement of earnings. Where the foreign currency is used as the functional currency, translation adjustments are recorded as a separate component of comprehensive earnings (loss).

Joint venture:

The company's 50% interest in two Spanish companies is accounted for using the equity method. The company records an increase in its investment in the joint venture to the extent of its share of the joint venture's earnings, and reduces its investment to the extent of dividends received. No dividends were received during 2004.

Comprehensive earnings:

Comprehensive earnings includes net earnings, foreign currency translation adjustments and unrealized gains/losses on commodity hedging contracts and marketable securities.

Earnings per share:

A dual presentation of basic and diluted earnings per share is not required due to the lack of potentially dilutive securities under the company's simple capital structure. Therefore, all earnings per share amounts represent basic earnings per share.

The Class B Common Stock has essentially the same rights as Common Stock, except that each share of Class B Common Stock has ten votes per share (compared to one vote per share of Common Stock), is not traded on any exchange, is restricted as to transfer and is convertible on a share-for-share basis, at any time and at no cost to the holders, into shares of Common Stock which are traded on the New York Stock Exchange.

NOTE 2—ACCRUED LIABILITIES:

Accrued liabilities are comprised of the following:

	December 31,	
	2004	2003
Compensation	$13,839	$12,213
Other employee benefits	5,261	4,998
Taxes, other than income	2,248	2,531
Advertising and promotions	13,710	11,525
Other	9,664	7,567
	$44,722	$38,834

NOTE 3—BANK LOAN AND INDUSTRIAL DEVELOPMENT BONDS:

The bank loan is payable in quarterly installments through August of 2006. As a result of prepayments made in 2004, the next quarterly installment is due in December, 2005. The loan is collateralized by investments in marketable securities and is subject to other terms and conditions, none of which are significant. Interest is LIBOR based, and the average rate was 2.0% in 2004.

Industrial development bonds are due in 2027. The average floating interest rate was 1.3% and 1.2% in 2004 and 2003, respectively.

NOTE 4—INCOME TAXES:

The domestic and foreign components of pretax income are as follows:

	2004	2003	2002
Domestic	$89,164	$96,170	$ 98,978
Foreign	5,524	1,777	1,710
	$94,688	$97,947	$100,688

The provision for income taxes is comprised of the following:

	2004	2003	2002
Current:			
Federal	$26,303	$27,904	$32,303
Foreign	731	485	553
State	1,070	1,202	1,523
	28,104	29,591	34,379
Deferred:			
Federal	2,907	3,465	(286)
Foreign	(605)	(252)	176
State	108	129	31
	2,410	3,342	(79)
	$30,514	$32,933	$34,300

Significant components of the company's net deferred tax liability at year end were as follows:

	December 31,	
	2004	2003
Deferred tax assets:		
Deferred compensation	$ 9,937	$ 8,855
Post retirement benefits	3,493	3,076
Reserve for uncollectible accounts	480	480
Other accrued expenses	2,380	2,337
Foreign subsidiary tax loss carry forward	1,164	157
Foreign subsidiary tax credit carry forward	2,039	2,098
Inventory reserves	1,106	1,080
Other	1,512	1,231
	22,111	19,314
Valuation reserve	(1,183)	(1,522)
Total deferred tax assets	$20,928	$17,792
Deffered tax liabilities:		
Depreciation	$19,638	$18,333
Deductible goodwill and trademarks	15,840	12,835
Accrued export company commissions	3,087	2,825
VEBA funding	711	460
Inventory reserves	2,233	2,629
Prepaid insurance	985	—
Other	3,047	2,390
Total deferred tax liabilities	$45,541	$39,472
Net deferred tax assets	$24,613	$21,680

At December 31, 2004, the tax benefit of foreign subsidiary tax loss carry forwards expiring by year are as follows: $27 in 2005, $11 in 2009, $928 in 2011, $27 in 2012 and $171 in 2014.

Also at December 31, 2004, the amounts of the foreign subsidiary tax credit carry forwards expiring by year are as follows: $48 in 2005, $244 in 2007, $222 in 2008, $198 in 2009, $329 in 2010, $342 in 2011, $328 in 2012, $279 in 2013 and $49 in 2014. A valuation allowance has been established for these carry forward credits to reduce the future income tax benefits to amounts expected to be realized.

The effective income tax rate differs from the statutory rate as follows:

	2004	2003	2002
U.S. statutory rate	35.0%	35.0%	35.0%
State income taxes, net	0.8	0.9	1.0
Exempt municipal bond interest	(1.2)	(1.6)	(1.8)
Foreign tax rates	(1.9)	—	—
Other, net	(0.5)	(0.7)	(0.1)
Effective income tax rate	32.2%	33.6%	34.1%

The company has not provided for U.S. federal or foreign withholding taxes on $13,411 and $7,763 of foreign subsidiaries' undistributed earnings as of December 31, 2004 and December 31, 2003, respectively because such earnings are considered to be permanently reinvested. It is not practicable to determine the amount of income taxes that would be payable upon remittance of the undistributed earnings.

On October 22, 2004, the President signed the American Jobs Creation Act of 2004 (the "Act"). The Act creates a temporary incentive for U.S. corporations to repatriate accumulated income earned abroad by providing an 85% dividends received deduction for certain dividends from controlled foreign corporations. The deduction is subject to a number of limitations and, as of today uncertainty remains as to how to interpret certain provisions of the Act. As such, the Company has not yet determined whether, and to what extent, it may repatriate earnings that have not yet been remitted to the U.S. and therefore makes no estimate as to the amount of future remittances.

The Act also provides for a deduction for income from qualified domestic production activities, which will be phased in from 2005 through 2010. This provision also is subject to a number of limitations which effect the effective tax rate in 2005 and later. The company has not yet determined the extent to which its effective rate will change.

Certain Mexican tax laws were amended during 2004. These become effective primarily during 2005. The company has considered these amendments in determining the 2004 income tax provision, and will continue to monitor their impact during 2005.

NOTE 5—SHARE CAPITAL AND CAPITAL IN EXCESS OF PAR VALUE:

	Common Stock		Class B Common Stock		Treasury Stock		Capital in excess of par value
	Shares	Amount	Shares	Amount	Shares	Amount	
	(000's)		(000's)		(000's)		
Balance at January 1, 2002	34,139	$23,708	16,319	$11,332	(53)	$(1,992)	$323,981
Issuance of 3% stock dividend	1,009	700	488	339	(2)	—	63,332
Conversion of Class B common shares to common shares	48	33	(48)	(33)	—	—	—
Purchase and retirement of common shares	(948)	(658)	—	—	—	—	(31,655)
Balance at December 31, 2002	34,248	23,783	16,759	11,638	(55)	(1,992)	355,658
Issuance of 3% stock dividend	1,017	706	502	349	(1)	—	41,458
Conversion of Class B common shares to common shares	116	81	(116)	(81)	—	—	—
Purchase and retirement of common shares	(1,299)	(902)	—	—	—	—	(39,194)
Balance at December 31, 2003	34,082	23,668	17,145	11,906	(56)	(1,992)	357,922
Issuance of 3% stock dividend	1,009	701	513	356	(2)	—	55,901
Conversion of Class B common shares to common shares	143	99	(143)	(99)	—	—	—
Purchase and retirement of common shares	(474)	(329)	—	—	—	—	(16,078)
Balance at December 31, 2004	34,760	$24,139	17,515	$12,163	(58)	$(1,992)	$397,745

Average shares outstanding and all per share amounts included in the financial statements and notes thereto have been adjusted retroactively to reflect annual three percent stock dividends.

While the company does not have a formal or publicly announced stock repurchase program, the company's board of directors periodically authorizes a dollar amount for share repurchases.

Based upon this policy shares were purchased and retired as follows:

Year	Total Number Of Shares Purchased	Average Price Paid Per Share
2004	474	$34.56
2003	1,299	$30.82
2002	948	$34.03

NOTE 6—OTHER INCOME, NET:

Other income (expense) is comprised of the following:

	2004	2003	2002
Interest and dividend income	$3,784	$4,465	$5,556
Interest expense	(912)	(172)	(309)
Joint venture income	232	—	—
Foreign exchange gains (losses)	453	(78)	(206)
Royalty income	698	542	371
Capital gains (losses)	(163)	112	(35)
Rental income	413	88	2
Miscellaneous, net	279	637	79
	$4,784	$5,594	$5,458

NOTE 7—EMPLOYEE BENEFIT PLANS:

Pension plans:

The company sponsors defined contribution pension plans covering certain nonunion employees with over one year of credited service. The company's policy is to fund pension costs accrued based on compensation levels. Total pension expense for 2004, 2003 and 2002 approximated $3,135, $3,073 and $2,867, respectively. The company also maintains certain profit sharing and savings-investment plans. Company contributions in 2004, 2003 and 2002 to these plans were $806, $796 and $709, respectively.

The company also contributes to multi-employer defined benefit pension plans for its union employees. Such contributions aggregated $1,007, $1,048 and $1,055 in 2004, 2003 and 2002, respectively. The relative position of each employer associated with the multi-employer plans with respect to the actuarial present value of benefits and net plan assets is not determinable by the company.

Deferred compensation

The company sponsors three deferred compensation plans for selected executives and other employees: (i) the Excess Benefit Plan, which restores retirement benefits lost due to IRS limitations on contributions to tax-qualified plans, (ii) the Supplemental Plan, which allows eligible employees to defer the receipt of eligible compensation until designated future dates and (iii) the Career Achievement Plan, which provides a deferred annual incentive award to selected executives. Participants in these plans earn a return on amounts due them based on several investment options, which mirror returns on underlying investments (primarily mutual funds). The company hedges its obligations under the plans by investing in the actual underlying investments. These investments are classified as trading securities and are carried at fair value. At December 31, 2004 and 2003, these investments totaled $25,300 and $21,200, respectively. All gains and losses in these investments are equally offset by corresponding gains and losses in the company's deferred compensation liabilities.

Postretirement health care and life insurance benefit plans:

The company provides certain postretirement health care and life insurance benefits for corporate office and management employees. Employees become eligible for these benefits based upon their age and service and if they agree to contribute a portion of the cost. The company has the right to modify or terminate these benefits. The company does not fund postretirement health care and life insurance benefits in advance of payments for benefit claims.

The changes in the accumulated postretirement benefit obligation at December 31, 2004 and 2003 consist of the following:

	December 31,	
	2004	2003
Benefit obligation, beginning of year	$ 9,302	$8,151
Net periodic postretirement benefit cost	992	1,327
Benefits paid	(219)	(176)
Benefit obligation, end of year	$10,075	$9,302

Net periodic postretirement benefit cost included the following components:

	2004	2003	2002
Service cost—benefits attributed to service during the period	$521	$ 638	$462
Interest cost on the accumulated postretirement benefit obligation	514	604	481
Amortization of unrecognized net gain	(43)	85	(30)
Net periodic postretirement benefit cost	$992	$1,327	$913

For measurement purposes, a 9.0% annual rate of increase in the per capita cost of covered health care benefits was assumed for 2004; the rate was assumed to decrease gradually to 5.5% for 2011 and remain at that level thereafter. The health care cost trend rate assumption has a significant effect on the amounts reported. The weighted-average discount rate used in determining the accumulated postretirement benefit obligation was 5.75% and 6.0% at December 31, 2004 and 2003, respectively.

Increasing or decreasing the health care trend rates by one percentage point in each year would have the following effect on:

	1% Increase	1% Decrease
Postretirement benefit obligation	$1,315	$(1,075)
Total of service and interest cost components	$ 212	$ (170)

The company estimates future benefit payments will be $364, $355, $424, $447 and $455 in 2005 through 2009, respectively, and a total of $2,633 in 2010 through 2014. In December 2003, the FASB issued a revised SFAS No. 132, "Employers' Disclosures about Pensions and Other Post-retirement Benefits," which the company adopted in 2003. In January 2004, the FASB issued Staff Position No. 106-1, "Accounting and Disclosure Requirements Related to the Medicare Prescription Drug, Improvement and Modernization Act of 2003" (FSP 106-1) which the company adopted during 2004. The company intends to integrate its retiree prescription drug benefit with the federal benefit that will become available to Medicare eligible retirees in 2006. In accordance with FSP 106-1 the company's accumulated postretirement benefit obligation has been reduced by an unrecognized gain of $864 as of December 31, 2004 related to the federal benefit.

NOTE 8—COMMITMENTS:

Rental expense aggregated $1,012, $962 and $941 in 2004, 2003 and 2002, respectively.

Future operating lease commitments are not significant.

NOTE 9—SEGMENT AND GEOGRAPHIC INFORMATION:

The company operates as a single reportable segment encompassing the manufacture and sale of confectionery products. Its principal manufacturing operations are located in the United States and Canada, and its principal market is the United States. The company also manufactures and sells confectionery products in Mexico, and exports products to Canada as well as to over 30 countries worldwide.

The following geographic data include net sales summarized on the basis of the customer location and long-lived assets based on their physical location.

	2004	2003	2002
Net Sales:			
United States	$387,280	$362,373	$361,446
Foreign	32,830	30,283	31,739
	$420,110	$392,656	$393,185

Long-lived assets:			
United States	$293,618	$283,362	$297,894
Foreign	58,098	5,013	5,738
	$351,716	$288,375	$303,632

NOTE 10—DISCLOSURES ABOUT THE FAIR VALUE AND CARRYING AMOUNT OF FINANCIAL INSTRUMENTS:

The carrying amount approximates fair value of cash and cash equivalents because of the short maturity of those instruments. The fair values of investments are estimated based on quoted market prices. The fair value of the company's bank loan and industrial development bonds approximates their carrying value because they have a floating interest rate.

During the third quarter of 2004 approximately $36,000 of held to maturity investments were liquidated in connection with financing the acquisition of Concord Confections. As a result, the $101,000 balance of held to maturity securities was reclassified to available for sale. This change in classification was not significant to the company's 2004 net earnings or comprehensive earnings.

The carrying amount and estimated fair values of the company's financial instruments are as follows [in table below]:

	2004		2003	
	Carrying Amount	Fair Value	Carrying Amount	Fair Value
Cash and cash equivalents	$ 56,989	$ 56,989	$ 84,084	$ 84,084
Investments held to maturity	—	—	136,801	137,609
Investments available for sale	103,676	103,676	41,346	41,346
Investments in trading securities	25,332	25,332	21,243	21,243
Bank loan and industrial development bonds	99,500	99,500	7,500	7,500

A summary of the aggregate fair value, gross unrealized gains, gross unrealized losses and amortized cost basis of the company's investment portfolio by major security type is as follows:

	December 31, 2004			
			Unrealized	
Available for sale:	Cost	Fair Value	Gains	Losses
Municipal bonds	$ 100,630	$ 100,008	$ —	$ (622)
Mutual funds	2,714	3,668	954	—
	$ 103,344	$ 103,676	$ 954	$ (622)

	December 31, 2003			
	Amortized		Unrealised	
Held to Maturity:	Cost	Fair Value	Gains	Losses
Municipal bonds	$ 136,356	$ 137,170	$ 814	$ —
Unit investment trusts of municipal bonds	445	439	—	(6)
	$ 136,801	$ 137,609	$ 814	$ (6)
Available for sale:				
Municipal bonds	$ 53,061	$ 53,202	$ 141	$ —
Mutual funds	2,454	3,075	621	—
	$ 55,515	$ 56,277	$ 762	$ —

Available for sale securities of $14,931 were included in cash and cash equivalents at December 31, 2003. There were no securities with maturities greater than four years and gross realized gains and losses on the sale of available for sale securities in 2004 and 2003 were not significant.

NOTE 11—COMPREHENSIVE INCOME:

The following table sets forth information with respect to accumalated other comprehensive income (loss):

	Foreign Currency Translation Adjustment	Unrealized Gain (Loss) on Investments	Unrealized Gains (Losses) on Derivatives	Accumulated Other Comprehensive Earnings (Loss)
Balance at January 1, 2002	$ (9,977)	$ 449	$ (385)	$ (9,913)
Unrealized gains (losses)	(1,533)	(798)	(65)	(2,396)
(Gains) losses reclassified to net earnings	—	60	1,429	1,489
Tax effect	—	273	(505)	(232)
Net of tax amount	(1,533)	(465)	859	(1,139)
Balance at December 31, 2002	(11,510)	(16)	474	(11,052)
Unrealized gains (losses)	(647)	784	890	1,027
(Gains) losses reclassified to net earnings	—	2	(1,690)	(1,688)
Tax effect	—	(290)	294	4
Net of tax amount	(647)	496	(506)	(657)
Balance at December 31, 2003	(12,157)	480	(32)	(11,709)
Unrealized gains (losses)	193	(585)	2,594	2,202
(Gains) losses reclassified to net earnings	—	155	(1,237)	(1,082)
Tax effect	—	159	(501)	(342)
Net of tax amount	193	(271)	856	778
Balance at December 31, 2004	$(11,964)	$ 209	$ 824	$(10,931)

NOTE 12—ACQUISITION:

On August 30, 2004, the company purchased certain assets and assumed certain liabilities from Concord Confections, Inc. and its affiliates (collectively Concord) including its 50% equity interest in a Spanish joint venture. Cash consideration paid of $218,229 was funded by the liquidation of $64,229 of marketable securities and a bank term loan of $154,000. The results of Concord's operations have been included in the company's condensed consolidated financial statements since August 30, 2004. Concord holds a strong market position in the bubble gum category and its products are sold primarily under the Dubble Bubble brand name and trademark.

The acquisition has been accounted for under SFAS 141, "Business Combinations," and accordingly the purchase method of accounting has been used. The allocation of purchase price is based on management's determination and professional valuations of the fair value of the assets acquired and liabilities to be assumed. The final allocation to goodwill could be affected by the final determination of the required minimum working capital amount that was to be provided under the terms of the Concord purchase contract. The adjusted purchase price was allocated as follows:

Calculation of adjusted purchase price:

Cash consideration paid for net assets acquired	$218,229
Direct transactions fees and expenses	1,000
Less—Adjustment to purchase relating to minimum working capital required	(6,642)
Total adjusted purchase price	$212,587

Allocation of adjusted purchase price:	
Net working capital	$ 7,722
Step up of inventories	1,622
Investment in joint venture	10,000
Property, plant and equipment	43,399
Indefinite lived trademarks	113,994
Goodwill—deductible for income tax	35,850
Total adjusted purchase price	$212,587

The following table includes the unaudited pro forma net sales, net earnings and net earnings per share for 2004 and 2003 as if the company had acquired Concord as of January 1, 2003. Pro forma adjustments are necessary to reflect costs and expenses of financing the purchase, including additional interest expense relating to bank borrowings and the decrease in investment income reflecting the sale of marketable securities, and changes in depreciation expense resulting from fair value adjustments to net tangible assets.

The unaudited pro forma combined financial information presented does not reflect any cost savings or synergies that might be realized, including the anticipated elimination of substantially all of the Concord historical senior executive compensation and other management expenses which aggregated approximately $3,872 and $10,283 net of income taxes for the twelve months of 2004 and 2003, respectively. The pro forma results also reflect $495 and $12,007 of historical foreign exchange gains net of tax for 2004 and 2003, respectively.

UNAUDITED PRO FORMA COMBINED INCOME STATEMENT OF TOOTSIE ROLL AND CONCORD FOR THE TWELVE MONTHS ENDED DECEMBER 31, 2004 AND 2003

	2004 Combined Pro forma	2003 Combined Pro forma
Net sales	$479,278	$467,522
Net earnings	$ 64,673	$ 71,802
Earnings per share	$ 1.24	$ 1.35

The pro forma results are not necessarily indicative of what actually would have occurred if the acquisition had been completed as of the beginning of the presented periods, nor are they necessarily indicative of future consolidated results.

Management's Report on Internal Control and Management Certifications of Financial Statements

The Sarbanes-Oxley Act of 2002, requires managers of publicly traded companies to establish and maintain systems of internal control on the company's financial reporting processes. In addition, the Act requires the company's top management to provide certifications regarding the accuracy of the financial statements. The reports of Tootsie Roll are shown below.

Management's Report on Internal Control Over Financial Reporting

The management of Tootsie Roll Industries, Inc. is responsible for establishing and maintaining adequate internal control over financial reporting, as such term is defined in the Securities Exchange Act of 1934 (SEC) Rule 13a-15(f). Our management conducted an evaluation of the effectiveness of the company's internal control over financial reporting as of December 31, 2004 as required by SEC Rule 13a-15(c). In making this assessment, we used the criteria established in *Internal Control—Integrated Framework* issued by the Committee of Sponsoring Organizations of the Treadway Commission (the COSO criteria). Based on our evaluation under the COSO criteria, our management concluded that our internal control over financial reporting was effective as of December 31, 2004.

Management has excluded Concord Confections, Ltd. from its assessment of internal control over financial reporting as of December 31, 2004 because it was acquired by the company in a purchase business combination during 2004. Concord Confections, Ltd. is a wholly-owned subsidiary whose total assets and total revenues represent 29% and 6%, respectively, of the related consolidated financial statement amounts as of and for the year ended December 31, 2004.

Our management's assessment of the effectiveness of our internal control over financial reporting as of December 31, 2004 has been audited by PricewaterhouseCoopers, LLP an independent registered public accounting firm, as stated in their report which appears on page 19 [see pages A-23 and A-24 in this textbook].

Tootsie Roll Industries, Inc.

Chicago, Illinois
March 11, 2005

Required Certifications

In 2004, the Company's Chief Executive Officer submitted to the New York Stock Exchange the required Annual CEO Certification certifying that he was not aware of any violation by the Company of the exchange's corporate governance listing standards, other than that the certification itself was inadvertently filed later than within 30 days subsequent to the 2004 annual stockholders' meeting date as required.

The Company filed with the Securities and Exchange Commission the certifications required of the Company's Chief Executive Officer and Chief Financial Officer required under Section 302 of the Sarbanes–Oxley Act of 2002 as exhibits to the Form 10-K for the years ended December 31, 2003 and 2004.

Auditor's Report

All publicly held corporations, as well as many other enterprises and organizations (both profit and not-for-profit, large and small) engage the services of independent certified public accountants for the purpose of obtaining an objective, expert report on their financial statements. Based on a comprehensive examination of the company's accounting system, accounting records, and the financial statements, the outside CPA issues the auditor's report.

The standard auditor's report consists of three paragraphs: (1) an introductory paragraph, (2) a scope paragraph, and (3) the opinion paragraph. In the **introductory paragraph**, the auditor identifies who and what was audited and indicates the responsibilities of management and the auditor relative to the financial statements. In the **scope paragraph** the auditor states that the audit was conducted in accordance with generally accepted auditing standards and discusses the nature and limitations of the audit. In the **opinion paragraph**, the auditor expresses an informed opinion as to (1) the fairness of the financial statements and (2) their conformity with generally accepted accounting principles. The Report of PricewaterhouseCoopers LLP appearing in Tootsie Roll's Annual Report is shown here.

Report of Independent Registered Public Accounting Firm

To the Board of Directors and Shareholders of Tootsie Roll Industries, Inc.:

We have completed an integrated audit of Tootsie Roll Industries, Inc. 's 2004 consolidated financial statements and of its internal control over financial reporting as of December 31, 2004 and audits of its 2003 and 2002 consolidated financial statements in accordance with the standards of the Public Company Accounting Oversight Board (United States). Our opinions, based on our audits, are presented below.

Consolidated financial statements

In our opinion, the accompanying consolidated balance sheets and the related consolidated statements of earnings, comprehensive earnings, retained earnings, and cash flows present fairly, in all material respects, the financial position of Tootsie Roll Industries, Inc. and its subsidiaries at December 31, 2004 and 2003, and the results of their operations and their cash flows for each of the three years in the period ended December 31, 2004 in conformity with accounting principles generally accepted in the United States of America. These financial statements are the responsibility of the Company's management. Our responsibility is to express an opinion on these financial statements based on our audits. We conducted our audits of these statements in accordance with the standards of the Public Company Accounting Oversight Board (United States). Those standards require that we plan and perform the audit to obtain reasonable assurance about whether the financial statements are free of material misstatement. An audit of financial statements includes examining, on a test basis, evidence supporting the amounts and disclosures in the financial statements, assessing the accounting principles used and significant estimates made by management, and evaluating the overall financial statement presentation. We believe that our audits provide a reasonable basis for our opinion.

Internal control over financial reporting

Also, in our opinion, management's assessment, included in the accompanying Management's Report on Internal Control Over Financial Reporting, that the Company maintained effective internal control over financial reporting as of December 31, 2004 based on criteria established in *Internal Control—Integrated Framework* issued by the Committee of Sponsoring Organizations of the Treadway Commission (COSO), is fairly stated, in all material respects, based on those criteria. Furthermore, in our opinion, the Company maintained, in all material respects, effective internal control over financial reporting as of December 31, 2004, based on criteria established in *Internal Control—Integrated Framework* issued by the COSO. The Company's management is responsible for maintaining effective internal control over financial reporting and for its assessment of the effectiveness of internal control over financial reporting. Our responsibility is to express opinions on management's assessment and on the effectiveness of the Company's internal control over financial reporting based on our audit. We conducted our audit of internal control over financial reporting in accordance with the standards of the Public Company Accounting Oversight Board (United States). Those standards require that we plan and perform the audit to obtain reasonable assurance about whether effective internal control over financial reporting was maintained in all material respects. An audit of internal control over financial reporting includes obtaining an understanding of internal control over financial reporting, evaluating management's assessment, testing and evaluating the design and operating effectiveness of internal control, and performing such other procedures as we consider necessary in the circumstances. We believe that our audit provides a reasonable basis for our opinions.

A company's internal control over financial reporting is a process designed to provide reasonable assurance regarding the reliability of financial reporting and the preparation of financial statements for external purposes in accordance with generally accepted accounting principles. A company's internal control over financial reporting includes those policies and procedures that (i) pertain to the maintenance of records that, in reasonable detail, accurately and fairly reflect the transactions and dispositions of the assets of the company; (ii) provide reasonable assurance that transactions are recorded as necessary to permit preparation of financial statements in accordance with generally accepted accounting principles, and that receipts and expenditures of the company are being made only in accordance with authorizations of management and directors of the company; and (iii) provide reasonable assurance regarding prevention or timely detection of unauthorized acquisition, use, or disposition of the company's assets that could have a material effect on the financial statements.

Because of its inherent limitations, internal control over financial reporting may not prevent or detect misstatements. Also, projections of any evaluation of effectiveness to future periods are subject to the risk that controls may become inadequate because of changes in conditions, or that the degree of compliance with the policies or procedures may deteriorate.

As described in Management's Report on Internal Control Over Financial Reporting, management has excluded Concord Confections, Ltd. from its assessment of internal control over financial reporting as of December 31, 2004 because it was acquired by the Company in a purchase business combination during 2004. We have also excluded Concord Confections, Ltd. from our audit of internal control over financial reporting. Concord Confections, Ltd. is a wholly-owned subsidiary whose total assets and total revenues represent 29% and 6%, respectively, of the related consolidated financial statement amounts as of and for the year ended December 31, 2004.

PricewaterhouseCoopers LLP

Chicago, Illinois
March 11, 2005

Supplementary Financial Information

In addition to the financial statements and the accompanying notes, companies often present supplementary financial information. Tootsie Roll has provided quarterly financial data, stock performance information, and a five-year summary of earnings and financial highlights.

Quarterly Financial Data (Unaudited)

TOOTSIE ROLL INDUSTRIES, INC. AND SUBSIDIARIES

	(Thousands of dollars except per share data)				
2004	First	Second	Third	Fourth	Total
Net sales	$80,046	$77,157	$156,971	$105,936	$420,110
Gross margin	34,730	34,992	64,804	41,083	175,609
Net earnings	11,493	11,828	26,976	13,877	64,174
Net earnings per share	.22	.22	.52	.27	1.23
2003					
Net sales	$75,570	$77,725	$147,201	$ 92,160	$392,656
Gross margin	32,601	35,541	61,932	40,035	170,109
Net earnings	10,909	12,317	26,945	14,843	65,014
Net earnings per share	.20	.23	.51	.28	1.22
2002					
Net sales	$78,991	$77,131	$146,298	$ 90,765	$393,185
Gross margin	35,505	35,411	61,560	38,505	170,981
Net earnings	12,772	12,316	26,616	14,684	66,388
Net earnings per share	.23	.23	.49	.27	1.22

Net earnings per share is based upon average outstanding shares as adjusted for 3% stock dividends issued during the second quarter of each year. The sum of the per share amounts may not equal annual amounts due to rounding.

2004-2003 QUARTERLY SUMMARY OF TOOTSIE ROLL INDUSTRIES, INC. STOCK PRICE AND DIVIDENDS PER SHARE

STOCK PRICES*

	2004		2003	
	High	Low	High	Low
1st Qtr	$37.86	$35.00	$30.91	$27.30
2nd Qtr	$37.60	$32.41	$32.37	$28.75
3rd Qtr	$32.60	$29.08	$32.05	$29.60
4th Qtr	$34.63	$29.24	$36.94	$32.08

*NYSE—Composite Quotations

Estimated Number of shareholders at March 2005:
Common Stock	18,000
Class B Common Stock	5,000

DIVIDENDS

	2004	2003
1st Qtr	$.0681	$.0662
2nd Qtr	$.0701	$.0680
3rd Qtr	$.0700	$.0680
4th Qtr	$.0700	$.0680

NOTE: In addition to the above cash dividends, a 3% stock dividend was issued on April 14, 2004 and April 16, 2003. Cash dividends are restated to reflect 3% stock dividends.

Five Year Summary of Earnings and Financial Highlights

TOOTSIE ROLL INDUSTRIES, INC. AND SUBSIDIARIES

(Thousands of dollars except per share, percentage and ratio figures)

(See Management's Comments starting on page [A-6 of this textbook])

	2004	2003	2002	2001	2000
Sales and Earnings Data (2)					
Net sales	$420,110	$392,656	$393,185	$391,755	$396,816
Gross margin	175,609	170,109	170,981	173,858	188,585
Interest expense	912	172	309	356	866
Provision for income taxes	30,514	32,933	34,300	35,100	42,071
Net earnings	64,174	65,014	66,388	65,687	75,737
% of sales	15.3%	16.6%	16.9%	16.8%	19.1%
% of shareholders' equity	11.3%	12.1%	12.6%	12.9%	16.5%
Per Common Share Data (1)					
Net earnings	$ 1.23	$ 1.22	$ 1.22	$ 1.19	$ 1.37
Cash dividends declared	.28	.27	.26	.26	.24
Stock dividends	3%	3%	3%	3%	3%
Additional Financial Data (2)					
Working capital	$110,376	$180,818	$161,852	$188,250	$145,765
Net cash provided by operating activities	76,228	83,466	75,473	80,915	82,591
Net cash used in investing activities	164,039	50,383	29,571	19,165	64,177
Net cash provided by (used in) financing activities	60,716	(54,506)	(46,927)	(16,100)	(46,036)
Property, plant & equipment additions	17,948	12,150	10,308	14,148	16,189
Net property, plant & equipment	178,750	129,163	128,869	132,575	131,118
Total assets	811,753	665,297	646,080	618,676	562,442
Long term debt	93,167	7,500	7,500	7,500	7,500
Shareholders' equity	570,179	536,581	526,740	508,461	458,696
Average shares outstanding (1)	52,366	53,305	54,592	54,985	55,432

(1) Adjusted for annual 3% stock dividends.

(2) Certain reclassifications have been made to prior year numbers to conform to current year presentation.

Specimen Financial Statements: Hershey Foods Corporation

HERSHEY FOODS CORPORATION

CONSOLIDATED STATEMENTS OF INCOME

For the years ended December 31, In thousands of dollars except per share amounts	2004	2003	2002
Net Sales	**$4,429,248**	$4,172,551	$4,120,317
Costs and Expenses:			
Cost of sales	2,679,531	2,544,726	2,561,052
Selling, marketing and administrative	847,540	816,442	833,426
Business realignment and asset impairments, net	—	23,357	27,552
Gain on sale of business	—	(8,330)	—
Total costs and expenses	3,527,071	3,376,195	3,422,030
Income before Interest and Income Taxes	**902,177**	796,356	698,287
Interest expense, net	**66,533**	63,529	60,722
Income before Income Taxes	**835,644**	732,827	637,565
Provision for income taxes	**244,765**	267,875	233,987
Income before Cumulative Effect of Accounting Change	**590,879**	464,952	403,578
Cumulative effect of accounting change, net of $4,933 tax benefit	—	7,368	—
Net Income	**$ 590,879**	$ 457,584	$ 403,578
Earnings Per Share—Basic—Common Stock			
Income before Cumulative Effect of Accounting Change	$ 2.38	$ 1.81	$ 1.51
Cumulative Effect of Accounting Change, net of $.02 Tax Benefit	—	.03	—
Net Income	$ 2.38	$ 1.78	$ 1.51
Earnings Per Share—Basic—Class B Common Stock			
Income before Cumulative Effect of Accounting Change	$ 2.17	$ 1.64	$ 1.37
Cumulative Effect of Accounting Change, net of $.02 Tax Benefit	—	.03	—
Net Income	$ 2.17	$ 1.61	$ 1.37
Earnings Per Share—Diluted			
Income before Cumulative Effect of Accounting Change	$ 2.30	$ 1.76	$ 1.47
Cumulative Effect of Accounting Change, net of $.02 Tax Benefit	—	.03	—
Net Income	$ 2.30	$ 1.73	$ 1.47
Cash Dividends Paid Per Share:			
Common Stock	$ .8350	$ .7226	$ .6300
Class B Common Stock	.7576	.6526	.5675

The notes to consolidated financial statements are an integral part of these statements.

HERSHEY FOODS CORPORATION

CONSOLIDATED BALANCE SHEETS

December 31, In thousands of dollars	2004	2003
ASSETS		
Current Assets:		
Cash and cash equivalents	$ 54,837	$ 114,793
Accounts receivable—trade	408,930	407,612
Inventories	557,180	492,859
Deferred income taxes	46,503	13,285
Prepaid expenses and other	114,991	103,020
Total current assets	1,182,441	1,131,569
Property, Plant and Equipment, Net	1,682,698	1,661,939
Goodwill	463,947	388,960
Other Intangibles	125,233	38,511
Other Assets	343,212	361,561
Total assets	$ 3,797,531	$ 3,582,540
LIABILITIES AND STOCKHOLDERS' EQUITY		
Current Liabilities:		
Accounts payable	$ 148,686	$ 132,222
Accrued liabilities	472,096	416,181
Accrued income taxes	42,280	24,898
Short-term debt	343,277	12,032
Current portion of long-term debt	279,043	477
Total current liabilities	1,285,382	585,810
Long-term Debt	690,602	968,499
Other Long-term Liabilities	403,356	370,776
Deferred Income Taxes	328,889	377,589
Total liabilities	2,708,229	2,302,674
Stockholders' Equity:		
Preferred Stock, shares issued: none in 2004 and 2003	—	—
Common Stock, shares issued: 299,060,235 in 2004 and 149,528,776 on a pre-split basis in 2003	299,060	149,528
Class B Common Stock, shares issued: 60,841,509 in 2004 and 30,422,096 on a pre-split basis in 2003	60,841	30,422
Additional paid-in capital	28,614	4,034
Unearned ESOP compensation	(6,387)	(9,580)
Retained earnings	3,469,169	3,263,988
Treasury—Common Stock shares, at cost: 113,313,827 in 2004 and 50,421,139 on a pre-split basis in 2003	(2,762,304)	(2,147,441)
Accumulated other comprehensive income (loss)	309	(11,085)
Total stockholders' equity	1,089,302	1,279,866
Total liabilities and stockholders' equity	$ 3,797,531	$ 3,582,540

The notes to consolidated financial statements are an integral part of these balance sheets.

HERSHEY FOODS CORPORATION

CONSOLIDATED STATEMENTS OF CASH FLOWS

For the years ended December 31,	2004	2003	2002
In thousands of dollars			
Cash Flows Provided from (Used by)			
Operating Activities			
Net income	**$ 590,879**	$ 457,584	$ 403,578
Adjustments to reconcile net income to net cash provided from operations:			
Depreciation and amortization	**189,665**	180,567	177,908
Deferred income taxes	**(81,931)**	38,895	137,817
Gain on sale of business, net of tax of $2,624	—	(5,706)	—
Business realignment initiatives, net of tax of $9,988 and $12,470, respectively	—	15,488	21,509
Cumulative effect of accounting change, net of tax of $4,933	—	7,368	—
Changes in assets and liabilities, net of effects from business acquisitions and divestitures:			
Accounts receivable—trade	**17,319**	(36,636)	(9,250)
Inventories	**(40,043)**	9,095	8,843
Accounts payable	**(11,266)**	7,715	(8,542)
Other assets and liabilities	**132,827**	(81,427)	(106,520)
Net Cash Provided from Operating Activities	**797,450**	592,943	625,343
Cash Flows Provided from (Used by)			
Investing Activities			
Capital additions	**(181,728)**	(218,650)	(132,736)
Capitalized software additions	**(14,158)**	(18,404)	(11,836)
Business acquisitions	**(166,859)**	—	—
Proceeds from divestitures	**—**	20,049	12,000
Net Cash (Used by) Investing Activities	**(362,745)**	(217,005)	(132,572)
Cash Flows Provided from (Used by)			
Financing Activities			
Net change in short-term borrowings	**331,245**	897	4,130
Long-term borrowings	**—**	3,194	304
Repayment of long-term debt	**(883)**	(18,633)	(9,578)
Cash dividends paid	**(205,747)**	(184,686)	(167,821)
Exercise of stock options	**79,634**	55,120	86,491
Incentive plan transactions	**(81,933)**	(85,347)	(158,507)
Repurchase of Common Stock	**(616,977)**	(329,433)	(84,194)
Net Cash (Used by) Financing Activities	**(494,661)**	(558,888)	(329,175)
(Decrease) Increase in Cash and Cash Equivalents	**(59,956)**	(182,950)	163,596
Cash and Cash Equivalents as of January 1	**114,793**	297,743	134,147
Cash and Cash Equivalents as of December 31	**$ 54,837**	$ 114,793	$ 297,743
Interest Paid	**$ 66,151**	$ 65,347	$ 64,343
Income Taxes Paid	**289,607**	207,672	57,495

The notes to consolidated financial statements are an integral part of these statements.

HERSHEY FOODS CORPORATION

CONSOLIDATED STATEMENTS OF STOCKHOLDERS' EQUITY

In thousands of dollars	Preferred Stock	Common Stock	Class B Common Stock	Additional Paid-in Capital	Unearned ESOP Compensation	Retained Earnings	Treasury Common Stock	Accumulated Other Comprehensive Income (Loss)	Total Stockholders' Equity
Balance as of January 1, 2002	$—	$149,516	$30,434	$ 3,263	$(15,967)	$2,755,333	$(1,689,243)	$ (86,132)	$1,147,204
Net income						403,578			403,578
Other comprehensive income								107,203	107,203
Comprehensive income									510,781
Dividends:									
Common Stock, $.63 per share						(133,285)			(133,285)
Class B Common Stock, $.5675 per share						(34,536)			(34,536)
Conversion of Class B Common Stock into Common Stock		12	(12)						—
Incentive plan transactions				(298)					(298)
Exercise of stock options				(3,517)			(34,790)		(38,307)
Employee stock ownership trust/benefits transactions				1,145	3,193				4,338
Repurchase of Common Stock							(84,194)		(84,194)
Balance as of December 31, 2002	—	149,528	30,422	593	(12,774)	2,991,090	(1,808,227)	21,071	1,371,703
Net income						457,584			457,584
Other comprehensive (loss)								(32,156)	(32,156)
Comprehensive income									425,428
Dividends:									
Common Stock, $.7226 per share						(144,985)			(144,985)
Class B Common Stock, $.6526 per share						(39,701)			(39,701)
Incentive plan transactions				455					455
Exercise of stock options				1,519			(9,781)		(8,262)
Employee stock ownership trust/benefits transactions				1,467	3,194				4,661
Repurchase of Common Stock							(329,433)		(329,433)
Balance as of December 31, 2003	—	149,528	30,422	4,034	(9,580)	3,263,988	(2,147,441)	(11,085)	1,279,866
Net income						590,879			590,879
Other comprehensive income								11,394	11,394
Comprehensive income									602,273
Dividends:									
Common Stock, $.835 per share						(159,658)			(159,658)
Class B Common Stock, $.7576 per share						(46,089)			(46,089)
Two-for-one stock split		149,529	30,422			(179,951)			—
Conversion of Class B Common Stock into Common Stock		3	(3)						36
Incentive plan transactions				36					
Exercise of stock options				23,248			2,114		25,362
Employee stock ownership trust/benefits transactions				1,296	3,193				4,489
Repurchase of Common Stock							(616,977)		(616,977)
Balance as of December 31, 2004	$—	$299,060	$60,841	$28,614	$ (6,387)	$3,469,169	$(2,762,304)	$ 309	$1,089,302

The notes to consolidated financial statements are an integral part of these statements.

Time Value of Money

STUDY OBJECTIVES

After studying this appendix,
you should be able to:

1 Distinguish between simple and compound interest.

2 Solve for future value of a single amount.

3 Solve for future value of an annuity.

4 Identify the variables fundamental to solving present value problems.

5 Solve for present value of a single amount.

6 Solve for present value of an annuity.

7 Compute the present value of notes and bonds.

Would you rather receive $1,000 today or a year from now? You should prefer to receive the $1,000 today because you can invest the $1,000 and earn interest on it. As a result, you will have more than $1,000 a year from now. What this example illustrates is the concept of the **time value of money**. Everyone prefers to receive money today rather than in the future because of the interest factor.

Nature of Interest

Interest is payment for the use of another person's money. It is the difference between the amount borrowed or invested (called the **principal**) and the amount repaid or collected. The amount of interest to be paid or collected is usually stated as a rate over a specific period of time. The rate of interest is generally stated as an annual rate.

The amount of interest involved in any financing transaction is based on three elements:

1. **Principal (p):** The original amount borrowed or invested.
2. **Interest Rate (i):** An annual percentage of the principal.
3. **Time (n):** The number of years that the principal is borrowed or invested.

SIMPLE INTEREST

Simple interest is computed on the principal amount only. It is the return on the principal for one period. Simple interest is usually expressed as shown in Illustration C-1 on the next page.

STUDY OBJECTIVE

1

Distinguish between simple and compound interest.

Illustration C-1
Interest computation

Interest	=	Principal p	×	Rate i	×	Time n

For example, if you borrowed $5,000 for 2 years at a simple interest rate of 12% annually, you would pay $1,200 in total interest computed as follows:

$$\text{Interest} = p \times i \times n$$
$$= \$5,000 \times .12 \times 2$$
$$= \$1,200$$

COMPOUND INTEREST

Compound interest is computed on principal **and** on any interest earned that has not been paid or withdrawn. It is the return on (or growth of) the principal for two or more time periods. Compounding computes interest not only on the principal but also on the interest earned to date on that principal, assuming the interest is left on deposit.

To illustrate the difference between simple and compound interest, assume that you deposit $1,000 in Bank Two, where it will earn simple interest of 9% per year, and you deposit another $1,000 in Citizens Bank, where it will earn compound interest of 9% per year compounded annually. Also assume that in both cases you will not withdraw any interest until three years from the date of deposit. Illustration C-2 shows the computation of interest to be received and the accumulated year-end balances.

Illustration C-2   Simple versus compound interest

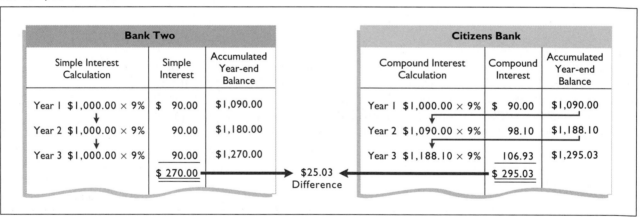

Note in Illustration C-2 that simple interest uses the initial principal of $1,000 to compute the interest in all three years. Compound interest uses the accumulated balance (principal plus interest to date) at each year-end to compute interest in the succeeding year—which explains why your compound interest account is larger.

Obviously, if you had a choice between investing your money at simple interest or at compound interest, you would choose compound interest, all other things—especially risk—being equal. In the example, compounding provides $25.03 of additional interest income. For practical purposes, compounding assumes that unpaid interest earned becomes a part of the principal, and the accumulated balance at the end of each year becomes the new principal on which interest is earned during the next year.

Illustration C-2 indicates that you should invest your money at the bank that compounds interest annually. Most business situations use compound interest. Simple interest is generally applicable only to short-term situations of one year or less.

SECTION ONE
FUTURE VALUE CONCEPTS

Future Value of a Single Amount

The **future value of a single amount** is the value at a future date of a given amount invested, assuming compound interest. For example, in Illustration C-2, $1,295.03 is the future value of the $1,000 investment earning 9% for three years. The $1,295.03 could be determined more easily by using the following formula:

STUDY OBJECTIVE

2

Solve for future value of a single amount.

$$FV = p \times (1 + i)^n$$

Illustration C-3
Formula for future value

where:

FV = future value of a single amount
p = principal (or present value)
i = interest rate for one period
n = number of periods

The $1,295.03 is computed as follows:

$$
\begin{aligned}
FV &= p \times (1 + i)^n \\
&= \$1,000 \times (1 + .09)^3 \\
&= \$1,000 \times 1.29503 \\
&= \$1,295.03
\end{aligned}
$$

The 1.29503 is computed by multiplying (1.09 × 1.09 × 1.09). The amounts in this example can be depicted in the time diagram shown in Illustration C-4.

Illustration C-4
Time diagram

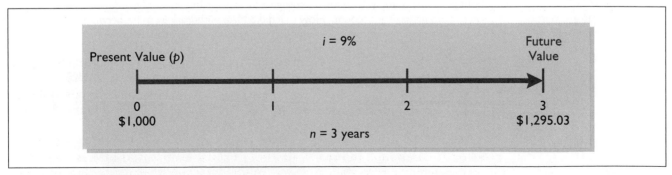

Another method used to compute the future value of a single amount involves a compound interest table. This table shows the future value of 1 for n periods. Table 1 on the next page is such a table.

TABLE 1   Future Value of 1

(n) Periods	4%	5%	6%	8%	9%	10%	11%	12%	15%
1	1.04000	1.05000	1.06000	1.08000	1.09000	1.10000	1.11000	1.12000	1.15000
2	1.08160	1.10250	1.12360	1.16640	1.18810	1.21000	1.23210	1.25440	1.32250
3	1.12486	1.15763	1.19102	1.25971	1.29503	1.33100	1.36763	1.40493	1.52088
4	1.16986	1.21551	1.26248	1.36049	1.41158	1.46410	1.51807	1.57352	1.74901
5	1.21665	1.27628	1.33823	1.46933	1.53862	1.61051	1.68506	1.76234	2.01136
6	1.26532	1.34010	1.41852	1.58687	1.67710	1.77156	1.87041	1.97382	2.31306
7	1.31593	1.40710	1.50363	1.71382	1.82804	1.94872	2.07616	2.21068	2.66002
8	1.36857	1.47746	1.59385	1.85093	1.99256	2.14359	2.30454	2.47596	3.05902
9	1.42331	1.55133	1.68948	1.99900	2.17189	2.35795	2.55803	2.77308	3.51788
10	1.48024	1.62889	1.79085	2.15892	2.36736	2.59374	2.83942	3.10585	4.04556
11	1.53945	1.71034	1.89830	2.33164	2.58043	2.85312	3.15176	3.47855	4.65239
12	1.60103	1.79586	2.01220	2.51817	2.81267	3.13843	3.49845	3.89598	5.35025
13	1.66507	1.88565	2.13293	2.71962	3.06581	3.45227	3.88328	4.36349	6.15279
14	1.73168	1.97993	2.26090	2.93719	3.34173	3.79750	4.31044	4.88711	7.07571
15	1.80094	2.07893	2.39656	3.17217	3.64248	4.17725	4.78459	5.47357	8.13706
16	1.87298	2.18287	2.54035	3.42594	3.97031	4.59497	5.31089	6.13039	9.35762
17	1.94790	2.29202	2.69277	3.70002	4.32763	5.05447	5.89509	6.86604	10.76126
18	2.02582	2.40662	2.85434	3.99602	4.71712	5.55992	6.54355	7.68997	12.37545
19	2.10685	2.52695	3.02560	4.31570	5.14166	6.11591	7.26334	8.61276	14.23177
20	2.19112	2.65330	3.20714	4.66096	5.60441	6.72750	8.06231	9.64629	16.36654

In Table 1, n is the number of compounding periods, the percentages are the periodic interest rates, and the 5-digit decimal numbers in the respective columns are the future value of 1 factors. In using Table 1, you would multiply the principal amount by the future value factor for the specified number of periods and interest rate. For example, the future value factor for two periods at 9% is 1.18810. Multiplying this factor by $1,000 equals $1,188.10—which is the accumulated balance at the end of year 2 in the Citizens Bank example in Illustration C-2. The $1,295.03 accumulated balance at the end of the third year can be calculated from Table 1 by multiplying the future value factor for three periods (1.29503) by the $1,000.

The demonstration problem in Illustration C-5 shows how to use Table 1.

Illustration C-5
Demonstration problem—
Using Table 1 for *FV* of 1

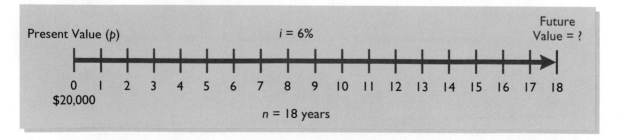

John and Mary Rich invested $20,000 in a savings account paying 6% interest at the time their son, Mike, was born. The money is to be used by Mike for his college education. On his 18th birthday, Mike withdraws the money from his savings account. How much did Mike withdraw from his account?

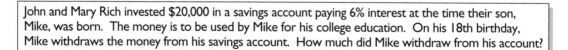

Present Value (*p*)   *i* = 6%   Future Value = ?

0 1 2 3 4 5 6 7 8 9 10 11 12 13 14 15 16 17 18
$20,000

n = 18 years

Answer: The future value factor from Table 1 is 2.85434 (18 periods at 6%). The future value of $20,000 earning 6% per year for 18 years is **$57,086.80** ($20,000 × 2.85434).

Future Value of an Annuity

The preceding discussion involved the accumulation of only a single principal sum. Individuals and businesses frequently encounter situations in which a **series** of equal dollar amounts are to be paid or received periodically, such as loans or lease (rental) contracts. Such payments or receipts of equal dollar amounts are referred to as **annuities**.

The **future value of an annuity** is the sum of all the payments (receipts) plus the accumulated compound interest on them. In computing the future value of an annuity, it is necessary to know (1) the interest rate, (2) the number of compounding periods, and (3) the amount of the periodic payments or receipts.

To illustrate the computation of the future value of an annuity, assume that you invest $2,000 at the end of each year for three years at 5% interest compounded annually. This situation is depicted in the time diagram in Illustration C-6.

Illustration C-6   Time diagram for a three-year annuity

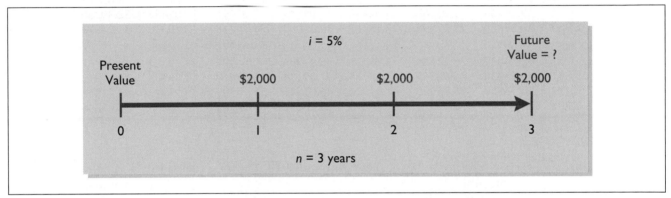

The $2,000 invested at the end of year 1 will earn interest for two years (years 2 and 3), and the $2,000 invested at the end of year 2 will earn interest for one year (year 3). However, the last $2,000 investment (made at the end of year 3) will not earn any interest. The future value of these periodic payments could be computed using the future value factors from Table 1, as shown in Illustration C-7.

Year Invested	Amount Invested	×	Future Value of 1 Factor at 5%	=	Future Value
1	$2,000	×	1.10250		$2,205
2	$2,000	×	1.05000		2,100
3	$2,000	×	1.00000		2,000
			3.15250		**$6,305**

Illustration C-7   Future value of periodic payment computation

The first $2,000 investment is multiplied by the future value factor for two periods (1.1025) because two years' interest will accumulate on it (in years 2 and 3). The second $2,000 investment will earn only one year's interest (in year 3) and therefore is multiplied by the future value factor for one year (1.0500). The final $2,000 investment is made at the end of the third year and will not earn any interest. Consequently, the future value of the last $2,000 invested is only $2,000 since it does not accumulate any interest.

Calculating the future value of each individual cash flow is required when the periodic payments or receipts are not equal in each period. However, when the periodic payments (receipts) are **the same in each period**, the future value can be computed by using a future value of an annuity of 1 table. Table 2 is such a table.

TABLE 2 Future Value of an Annuity of 1

(n) Periods	4%	5%	6%	8%	9%	10%	11%	12%	15%
1	1.00000	1.00000	1.00000	1.00000	1.00000	1.00000	1.00000	1.00000	1.00000
2	2.04000	2.05000	2.06000	2.08000	2.09000	2.10000	2.11000	2.12000	2.15000
3	3.12160	3.15250	3.18360	3.24640	3.27810	3.31000	3.34210	3.37440	3.47250
4	4.24646	4.31013	4.37462	4.50611	4.57313	4.64100	4.70973	4.77933	4.99338
5	5.41632	5.52563	5.63709	5.86660	5.98471	6.10510	6.22780	6.35285	6.74238
6	6.63298	6.80191	6.97532	7.33592	7.52334	7.71561	7.91286	8.11519	8.75374
7	7.89829	8.14201	8.39384	8.92280	9.20044	9.48717	9.78327	10.08901	11.06680
8	9.21423	9.54911	9.89747	10.63663	11.02847	11.43589	11.85943	12.29969	13.72682
9	10.58280	11.02656	11.49132	12.48756	13.02104	13.57948	14.16397	14.77566	16.78584
10	12.00611	12.57789	13.18079	14.48656	15.19293	15.93743	16.72201	17.54874	20.30372
11	13.48635	14.20679	14.97164	16.64549	17.56029	18.53117	19.56143	20.65458	24.34928
12	15.02581	15.91713	16.86994	18.97713	20.14072	21.38428	22.71319	24.13313	29.00167
13	16.62684	17.71298	18.88214	21.49530	22.95339	24.52271	26.21164	28.02911	34.35192
14	18.29191	19.59863	21.01507	24.21492	26.01919	27.97498	30.09492	32.39260	40.50471
15	20.02359	21.57856	23.27597	27.15211	29.36092	31.77248	34.40536	37.27972	47.58041
16	21.82453	23.65749	25.67253	30.32428	33.00340	35.94973	39.18995	42.75328	55.71747
17	23.69751	25.84037	28.21288	33.75023	36.97351	40.54470	44.50084	48.88367	65.07509
18	25.64541	28.13238	30.90565	37.45024	41.30134	45.59917	50.39593	55.74972	75.83636
19	27.67123	30.53900	33.75999	41.44626	46.01846	51.15909	56.93949	63.43968	88.21181
20	29.77808	33.06595	36.78559	45.76196	51.16012	57.27500	64.20283	72.05244	102.44358

Table 2 shows the future value of 1 to be received periodically for a given number of periods. We can see from Table 2 that the future value of an annuity of 1 factor for three periods at 5% is 3.15250. The future value factor is the total of the three individual future value factors as shown in Illustration C-7. Multiplying this amount by the annual investment of $2,000 produces a future value of $6,305.

The demonstration problem in Illustration C-8 shows how to use Table 2.

Illustration C-8
Demonstration problem—
Using Table 2 for *FV* of an
annuity of 1

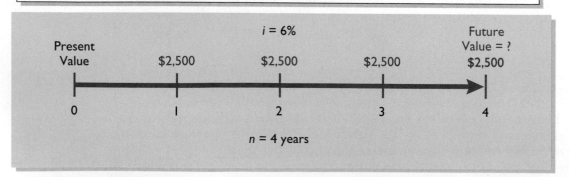

John and Char Lewis' daughter, Debra, has just started high school. They decide to start a college fund for her and will invest $2,500 in a savings account at the end of each year she is in high school (4 payments total). The account will earn 6% interest compounded annually. How much will be in the college fund at the time Debra graduates from high school?

i = 6%

Present Value
$2,500 $2,500 $2,500 $2,500
Future Value = ?

0   1   2   3   4

n = 4 years

Answer: The future value factor from Table 2 is 4.37462 (4 periods at 6%). The future value of $2,500 invested each year for 4 years at 6% interest is **$10,936.55** ($2,500 × 4.37462).

SECTION TWO
PRESENT VALUE CONCEPTS

Present Value Variables

The **present value** is the value now of a given amount to be paid or received in the future, assuming compound interest. The present value, like the future value, is based on three variables: (1) the dollar amount to be received (future amount), (2) the length of time until the amount is received (number of periods), and (3) the interest rate (the discount rate). The process of determining the present value is referred to as **discounting the future amount**.

In this textbook, we use present value computations in measuring several items. For example, Chapter 10 computed the present value of the principal and interest payments to determine the market price of a bond. In addition, determining the amount to be reported for notes payable and lease liability involves present value computations.

> **STUDY OBJECTIVE**
> **4**
> Identify the variables fundamental to solving present value problems.

Present Value of a Single Amount

To illustrate present value, assume that you want to invest a sum of money that will yield $1,000 at the end of one year. What amount would you need to invest today to have $1,000 one year from now? If you want a 10% rate of return, the investment or present value is $909.09 ($1,000 ÷ 1.10). The formula for calculating present value is shown in Illustration C-9.

> **STUDY OBJECTIVE**
> **5**
> Solve for present value of a single amount.

$$\text{Present Value} = \text{Future Value} \div (1 + i)^n$$

Illustration C-9   Formula for present value

The computation of $1,000 discounted at 10% for one year is as follows:

$$\begin{aligned} PV &= FV \div (1 + i)^n \\ &= \$1,000 \div (1 + .10)^1 \\ &= \$1,000 \div 1.10 \\ &= \$909.09 \end{aligned}$$

The future amount ($1,000), the discount rate (10%), and the number of periods (1) are known. The variables in this situation can be depicted in the time diagram in Illustration C-10.

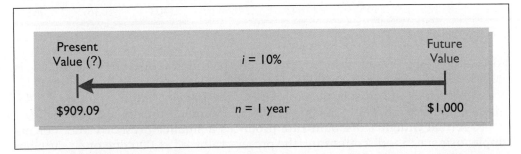

Illustration C-10
Finding present value if discounted for one period

If the single amount of $1,000 is to be received **in two years** and discounted at 10% [$PV = \$1,000 \div (1 + .10)^2$], its present value is $826.45 [($1,000 ÷ 1.21), depicted as shown in Illustration C-11 on the next page.

Illustration C-11
Finding present value if
discounted for two periods

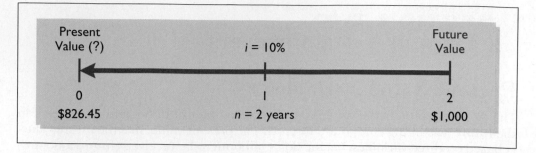

The present value of 1 may also be determined through tables that show the present value of 1 for n periods. In Table 3, n is the number of discounting periods involved. The percentages are the periodic interest rates or discount rates, and the 5-digit decimal numbers in the respective columns are the present value of 1 factors.

When using Table 3, the future value is multiplied by the present value factor specified at the intersection of the number of periods and the discount rate.

TABLE 3   Present Value of 1

(n) Periods	4%	5%	6%	8%	9%	10%	11%	12%	15%
1	.96154	.95238	.94340	.92593	.91743	.90909	.90090	.89286	.86957
2	.92456	.90703	.89000	.85734	.84168	.82645	.81162	.79719	.75614
3	.88900	.86384	.83962	.79383	.77218	.75132	.73119	.71178	.65752
4	.85480	.82270	.79209	.73503	.70843	.68301	.65873	.63552	.57175
5	.82193	.78353	.74726	.68058	.64993	.62092	.59345	.56743	.49718
6	.79031	.74622	.70496	.63017	.59627	.56447	.53464	.50663	.43233
7	.75992	.71068	.66506	.58349	.54703	.51316	.48166	.45235	.37594
8	.73069	.67684	.62741	.54027	.50187	.46651	.43393	.40388	.32690
9	.70259	.64461	.59190	.50025	.46043	.42410	.39092	.36061	.28426
10	.67556	.61391	.55839	.46319	.42241	.38554	.35218	.32197	.24719
11	.64958	.58468	.52679	.42888	.38753	.35049	.31728	.28748	.21494
12	.62460	.55684	.49697	.39711	.35554	.31863	.28584	.25668	.18691
13	.60057	.53032	.46884	.36770	.32618	.28966	.25751	.22917	.16253
14	.57748	.50507	.44230	.34046	.29925	.26333	.23199	.20462	.14133
15	.55526	.48102	.41727	.31524	.27454	.23939	.20900	.18270	.12289
16	.53391	.45811	.39365	.29189	.25187	.21763	.18829	.16312	.10687
17	.51337	.43630	.37136	.27027	.23107	.19785	.16963	.14564	.09293
18	.49363	.41552	.35034	.25025	.21199	.17986	.15282	.13004	.08081
19	.47464	.39573	.33051	.23171	.19449	.16351	.13768	.11611	.07027
20	.45639	.37689	.31180	.21455	.17843	.14864	.12403	.10367	.06110

For example, the present value factor for one period at a discount rate of 10% is .90909, which equals the $909.09 ($1,000 × .90909) computed in Illustration C-10. For two periods at a discount rate of 10%, the present value factor is .82645, which equals the $826.45 ($1,000 × .82645) computed previously.

Note that a higher discount rate produces a smaller present value. For example, using a 15% discount rate, the present value of $1,000 due one year from now is $869.57 versus $909.09 at 10%. Also note that the further removed from the present the future value is, the smaller the present value. For example, using the same discount rate of 10%, the present value of $1,000 due in **five years** is $620.92 versus the present value of $1,000 due in **one year**, which is $909.09.

The following two demonstration problems (Illustrations C-12, C-13) illustrate how to use Table 3.

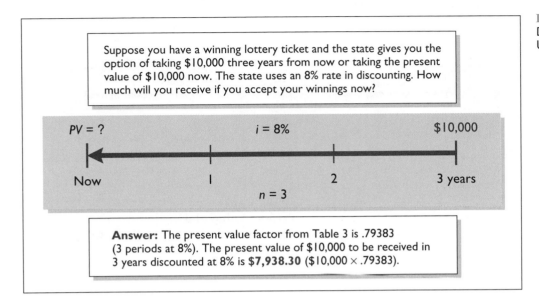

Illustration C-12
Demonstration problem—
Using Table 3 for *PV* of 1

Suppose you have a winning lottery ticket and the state gives you the option of taking $10,000 three years from now or taking the present value of $10,000 now. The state uses an 8% rate in discounting. How much will you receive if you accept your winnings now?

PV = ?   i = 8% $10,000

Now   1   2   3 years
           n = 3

Answer: The present value factor from Table 3 is .79383 (3 periods at 8%). The present value of $10,000 to be received in 3 years discounted at 8% is **$7,938.30** ($10,000 × .79383).

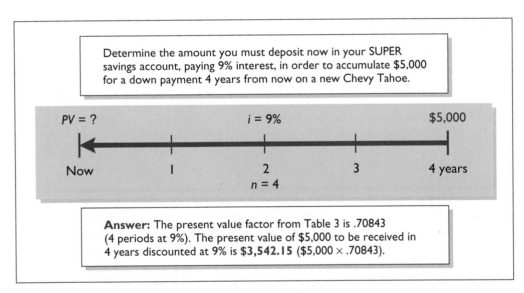

Illustration C-13
Demonstration problem—
Using Table 3 for *PV* of 1

Determine the amount you must deposit now in your SUPER savings account, paying 9% interest, in order to accumulate $5,000 for a down payment 4 years from now on a new Chevy Tahoe.

PV = ?   i = 9% $5,000

Now   1   2   3   4 years
               n = 4

Answer: The present value factor from Table 3 is .70843 (4 periods at 9%). The present value of $5,000 to be received in 4 years discounted at 9% is **$3,542.15** ($5,000 × .70843).

Present Value of an Annuity

The preceding discussion involved the discounting of only a single future amount. Businesses and individuals frequently engage in transactions in which a series of equal dollar amounts are to be received or paid periodically. Examples of a series of periodic receipts or payments are loan agreements, installment sales, mortgage notes, lease (rental) contracts, and pension obligations. As discussed earlier, these periodic receipts or payments are **annuities**.

The **present value of an annuity** is the value now of a series of future receipts or payments, discounted assuming compound interest. In computing the present value of an annuity, it is necessary to know (1) the discount rate, (2) the number of discount periods, and (3) the amount of the periodic receipts or payments. To illustrate the computation of the present value of an annuity, assume that you will receive $1,000 cash annually for three years at a time when the discount rate is 10%. This situation is depicted in the time diagram in Illustration C-14. Illustration C-15 shows computation of the present value in this situation.

Illustration C-14 Time diagram for a three-year annuity

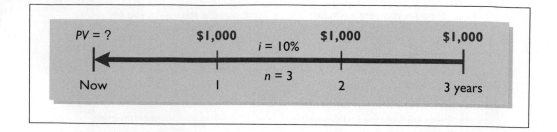

Illustration C-15 Present value of a series of future amounts computation

Future Amount	×	Present Value of 1 Factor at 10%	=	Present Value
$1,000 (one year away)		.90909		$ 909.09
1,000 (two years away)		.82645		826.45
1,000 (three years away)		.75132		751.32
		2.48686		**$2,486.86**

This method of calculation is required when the periodic cash flows are not uniform in each period. However, when the future receipts are the same in each period, there are two other ways to compute present value. First, the annual cash flow can be multiplied by the sum of the three present value factors. In the previous example, $1,000 × 2.48686 equals $2,486.86. Second, annuity tables can be used. As illustrated in Table 4 below, these tables show the present value of 1 to be received periodically for a given number of periods.

TABLE 4   **Present Value of an Annuity of 1**

(n) Periods	4%	5%	6%	8%	9%	10%	11%	12%	15%
1	.96154	.95238	.94340	.92593	.91743	.90909	.90090	.89286	.86957
2	1.88609	1.85941	1.83339	1.78326	1.75911	1.73554	1.71252	1.69005	1.62571
3	2.77509	2.72325	2.67301	2.57710	2.53130	2.48685	2.44371	2.40183	2.28323
4	3.62990	3.54595	3.46511	3.31213	3.23972	3.16986	3.10245	3.03735	2.85498
5	4.45182	4.32948	4.21236	3.99271	3.88965	3.79079	3.69590	3.60478	3.35216
6	5.24214	5.07569	4.91732	4.62288	4.48592	4.35526	4.23054	4.11141	3.78448
7	6.00205	5.78637	5.58238	5.20637	5.03295	4.86842	4.71220	4.56376	4.16042
8	6.73274	6.46321	6.20979	5.74664	5.53482	5.33493	5.14612	4.96764	4.48732
9	7.43533	7.10782	6.80169	6.24689	5.99525	5.75902	5.53705	5.32825	4.77158
10	8.11090	7.72173	7.36009	6.71008	6.41766	6.14457	5.88923	5.65022	5.01877
11	8.76048	8.30641	7.88687	7.13896	6.80519	6.49506	6.20652	5.93770	5.23371
12	9.38507	8.86325	8.38384	7.53608	7.16073	6.81369	6.49236	6.19437	5.42062
13	9.98565	9.39357	8.85268	7.90378	7.48690	7.10336	6.74987	6.42355	5.58315
14	10.56312	9.89864	9.29498	8.24424	7.78615	7.36669	6.98187	6.62817	5.72448
15	11.11839	10.37966	9.71225	8.55948	8.06069	7.60608	7.19087	6.81086	5.84737
16	11.65230	10.83777	10.10590	8.85137	8.31256	7.82371	7.37916	6.97399	5.95424
17	12.16567	11.27407	10.47726	9.12164	8.54363	8.02155	7.54879	7.11963	6.04716
18	12.65930	11.68959	10.82760	9.37189	8.75563	8.20141	7.70162	7.24967	6.12797
19	13.13394	12.08532	11.15812	9.60360	8.95012	8.36492	7.83929	7.36578	6.19823
20	13.59033	12.46221	11.46992	9.81815	9.12855	8.51356	7.96333	7.46944	6.25933

Table 4 shows that the present value of an annuity of 1 factor for three periods at 10% is 2.48685.[1] This present value factor is the total of the three individual present value factors, as shown in Illustration C-15. Applying this amount to the annual cash flow of $1,000 produces a present value of $2,486.85.

The following demonstration problem (Illustration C-16) illustrates how to use Table 4.

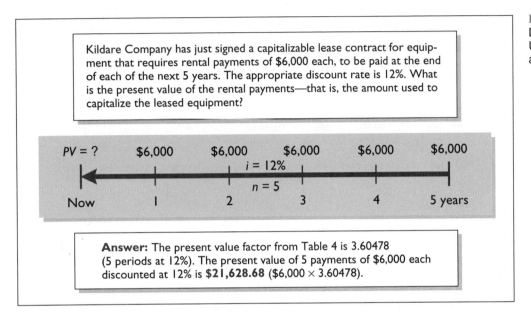

Illustration C-16
Demonstration problem—
Using Table 4 for *PV* of an
annuity of 1

Time Periods and Discounting

In the preceding calculations, the discounting was done on an annual basis using an annual interest rate. Discounting may also be done over shorter periods of time such as monthly, quarterly, or semiannually.

When the time frame is less than one year, it is necessary to convert the annual interest rate to the applicable time frame. Assume, for example, that the investor in Illustration C-14 received $500 **semiannually** for three years instead of $1,000 annually. In this case, the number of periods becomes six (3 × 2), the discount rate is 5% (10% ÷ 2), the present value factor from Table 4 is 5.07569, and the present value of the future cash flows is $2,537.85 (5.07569 × $500). This amount is slightly higher than the $2,486.86 computed in Illustration C-15 because interest is computed twice during the same year; therefore interest is earned on the first half year's interest.

Computing the Present Value of a Long-Term Note or Bond

The present value (or market price) of a long-term note or bond is a function of three variables: (1) the payment amounts, (2) the length of time until the amounts are paid, and (3) the discount rate. Our illustration uses a five-year bond issue.

STUDY OBJECTIVE
7
Compute the present value of notes and bonds.

---

[1]The difference of .00001 between 2.48686 and 2.48685 is due to rounding.

The first variable (dollars to be paid) is made up of two elements: (1) a series of interest payments (an annuity) and (2) the principal amount (a single sum). To compute the present value of the bond, both the interest payments and the principal amount must be discounted—two different computations. The time diagrams for a bond due in five years are shown in Illustration C-17.

Illustration C-17 Present value of a bond time diagram

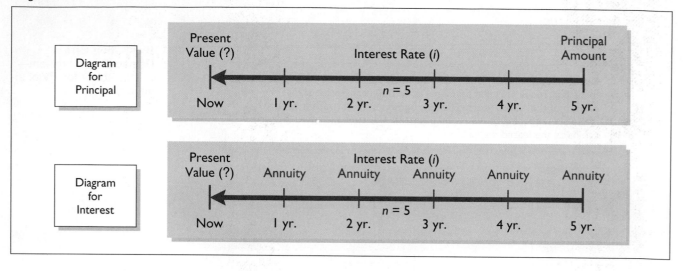

When the investor's market interest rate is equal to the bond's contractual interest rate, the present value of the bonds will equal the face value of the bonds. To illustrate, assume a bond issue of 10%, five-year bonds with a face value of $100,000 with interest payable **semiannually** on January 1 and July 1. If the discount rate is the same as the contractual rate, the bonds will sell at face value. In this case, the investor will receive (1) $100,000 at maturity and (2) a series of ten $5,000 interest payments [($100,000 × 10%) ÷ 2] over the term of the bonds. The length of time is expressed in terms of interest periods—in this case—10, and the discount rate per interest period, 5%. The following time diagram (Illustration C-18) depicts the variables involved in this discounting situation.

Illustration C-18 Time diagram for present value of a 10%, five-year bond paying interest semiannually

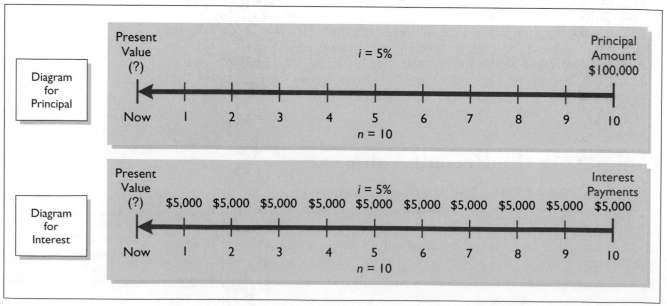

Illustration C-19 shows the computation of the present value of these bonds.

10% Contractual Rate—10% Discount Rate	
Present value of principal to be received at maturity	
$100,000 × PV of 1 due in 10 periods at 5%	
$100,000 × .61391 (Table 3)	$ 61,391
Present value of interest to be received periodically over the term of the bonds	
$5,000 × PV of 1 due periodically for 10 periods at 5%	
$5,000 × 7.72173 (Table 4)	38,609*
Present value of bonds	**$100,000**

*Rounded

Illustration C-19 Present value of principal and interest—face value

Now assume that the investor's required rate of return is 12%, not 10%. The future amounts are again $100,000 and $5,000, respectively, but now a discount rate of 6% (12% ÷ 2) must be used. The present value of the bonds is $92,639, as computed in Illustration C-20.

10% Contractual Rate—12% Discount Rate	
Present value of principal to be received at maturity	
$100,000 × .55839 (Table 3)	$55,839
Present value of interest to be received periodically over the term of the bonds	
$5,000 × 7.36009 (Table 4)	36,800
Present value of bonds	**$92,639**

Illustration C-20 Present value of principal and interest—discount

Conversely, if the discount rate is 8% and the contractual rate is 10%, the present value of the bonds is $108,111, computed as shown in Illustration C-21.

10% Contractual Rate—8% Discount Rate	
Present value of principal to be received at maturity	
$100,000 × .67556 (Table 3)	$ 67,556
Present value of interest to be received periodically over the term of the bonds	
$5,000 × 8.11090 (Table 4)	40,555
Present value of bonds	**$108,111**

Illustration C-21 Present value of principal and interest—premium

The above discussion relied on present value tables in solving present value problems. Electronic hand-held calculators may also be used to compute present values without the use of these tables. Many calculators, especially the "business" calculators, have present value (PV) functions that allow you to calculate present values by merely inputting the proper amount, discount rate, periods, and pressing the PV key.

Summary of Study Objectives

1 *Distinguish between simple and compound interest.* Simple interest is computed on the principal only, while compound interest is computed on the principal and any interest earned that has not been withdrawn.

2 *Solve for future value of a single amount.* Prepare a time diagram of the problem. Identify the principal amount, the number of compounding periods, and the interest rate. Using the future value of 1 table, multiply the principal amount by the future value factor specified at the intersection of the number of periods and the interest rate.

3 *Solve for future value of an annuity.* Prepare a time diagram of the problem. Identify the amount of the periodic payments, the number of compounding periods, and the interest rate. Using the future value of an annuity of 1 table, multiply the amount of the payments by the future value factor specified at the intersection of the number of periods and the interest rate.

4 *Identify the variables fundamental to solving present value problems.* The following three variables are fundamental to solving present value problems: (1) the future amount, (2) the number of periods, and (3) the interest rate (the discount rate).

5 *Solve for present value of a single amount.* Prepare a time diagram of the problem. Identify the future amount, the number of discounting periods, and the discount (interest) rate. Using the present value of a single amount table, multiply the future amount by the present value factor specified at the intersection of the number of periods and the discount rate.

6 *Solve for present value of an annuity.* Prepare a time diagram of the problem. Identify the future amounts (annuities), the number of discounting periods, and the discount (interest) rate. Using the present value of an annuity of 1 table, multiply the amount of the annuity by the present value factor specified at the intersection of the number of periods and the interest rate.

7 *Compute the present value of notes and bonds.* Determine the present value of the principal amount: Multiply the principal amount (a single future amount) by the present value factor (from the present value of 1 table) intersecting at the number of periods (number of interest payments) and the discount rate. Determine the present value of the series of interest payments: Multiply the amount of the interest payment by the present value factor (from the present value of an annuity of 1 table) intersecting at the number of periods (number of interest payments) and the discount rate. Add the present value of the principal amount to the present value of the interest payments to arrive at the present value of the note or bond.

Glossary

Annuity A series of equal dollar amounts to be paid or received periodically. (p. C-5)

Compound interest The interest computed on the principal and any interest earned that has not been paid or withdrawn. (p. C-2)

Discounting the future amount(s) The process of determining present value. (p. C-7)

Future value of a single amount The value at a future date of a given amount invested, assuming compound interest. (p. C-3)

Future value of an annuity The sum of all the payments or receipts plus the accumulated compound interest on them. (p. C-5)

Interest Payment for the use of another's money. (p. C-1)

Present value The value now of a given amount to be paid or received in the future assuming compound interest. (p. C-7)

Present value of an annuity The value now of a series of future receipts or payments, discounted assuming compound interest. (p. C-9)

Principal The amount borrowed or invested. (p. C-1)

Simple interest The interest computed on the principal only. (p. C-1)

Brief Exercises

(Use tables to solve exercises.)

Compute the future value of a single amount.
(SO 2)

BEC-1 Jerry Cora invested $8,000 at 5% annual interest, and left the money invested without withdrawing any of the interest for 12 years. At the end of the 12 years, Jerry withdrew the accumulated amount of money. (a) What amount did Jerry withdraw, assuming the investment earns simple interest? (b) What amount did Jerry withdraw, assuming the investment earns interest compounded annually?

BEC-2 For each of the following cases, indicate (a) to what interest rate columns and (b) to what number of periods you would refer in looking up the future value factor.

Use future value tables.
(SO 2, 3)

(1) In Table 1 (future value of 1):

	Annual Rate	Number of Years Invested	Compounded
Case A	6%	3	Annually
Case B	8%	5	Semiannually

(2) In Table 2 (future value of an annuity of 1):

	Annual Rate	Number of Years Invested	Compounded
Case A	5%	8	Annually
Case B	4%	6	Semiannually

BEC-3 Logan Company signed a lease for an office building for a period of 12 years. Under the lease agreement, a security deposit of $10,000 is made. The deposit will be returned at the expiration of the lease with interest compounded at 4% per year. What amount will Logan receive at the time the lease expires?

Compute the future value of a single amount.
(SO 2)

BEC-4 Summitt Company issued $1,000,000, 10-year bonds and agreed to make annual sinking fund deposits of $80,000. The deposits are made at the end of each year into an account paying 5% annual interest. What amount will be in the sinking fund at the end of 10 years?

Compute the future value of an annuity.
(SO 3)

BEC-5 Brad and Nancy Unruh invested $7,000 in a savings account paying 4% annual interest when their daughter, Laurel, was born. They also deposited $1,000 on each of her birthdays until she was 18 (including her 18th birthday). How much was in the savings account on her 18th birthday (after the last deposit)?

Compute the future value of a single amount and of an annuity.
(SO 2, 3)

BEC-6 Mike Snyder borrowed $25,000 on July 1, 2007. This amount plus accrued interest at 9% compounded annually is to be repaid on July 1, 2012. How much will Mike have to repay on July 1, 2012?

Compute the future value of a single amount.
(SO 2)

BEC-7 For each of the following cases, indicate (a) to what interest rate columns and (b) to what number of periods you would refer in looking up the discount rate.

Use present value tables.
(SO 5, 6)

(1) In Table 3 (present value of 1):

	Annual Rate	Number of Years Involved	Discounts per Year
Case A	12%	6	Annually
Case B	10%	11	Annually
Case C	6%	10	Semiannually

(2) In Table 4 (present value of an annuity of 1):

	Annual Rate	Number of Years Involved	Number of Payments Involved	Frequency of Payments
Case A	12%	20	20	Annually
Case B	10%	5	5	Annually
Case C	6%	4	8	Semiannually

BEC-8 **(a)** What is the present value of $20,000 due 9 periods from now, discounted at 10%?

Determine present values.
(SO 5, 6)

(b) What is the present value of $20,000 to be received at the end of each of 6 periods, discounted at 9%?

BEC-9 McCovey Company is considering an investment which will return a lump sum of $500,000 five years from now. What amount should McCovey Company pay for this investment to earn a 9% return?

Compute the present value of a single amount investment.
(SO 5)

BEC-10 Harrington Company earns 10% on an investment that will return $875,000 eight years from now. What is the amount Harrington should invest now to earn this rate of return?

Compute the present value of a single amount investment.
(SO 5)

Compute the present value of an annuity investment.
(SO 6)

BEC-11   Ritz Company is considering investing in an annuity contract that will return $30,000 annually at the end of each year for 15 years. What amount should Ritz Company pay for this investment if it earns a 5% return?

Compute the present value of an annuity investment.
(SO 6)

BEC-12   Orear Enterprises earns 8% on an investment that pays back $120,000 at the end of each of the next 6 years. What is the amount Orear Enterprises invested to earn the 8% rate of return?

Compute the present value of bonds.
(SO 5, 6, 7)

BEC-13   Santo Railroad Co. is about to issue $200,000 of 10-year bonds paying a 9% interest rate, with interest payable semiannually. The discount rate for such securities is 8%. How much can Santo expect to receive for the sale of these bonds?

Compute the present value of bonds.
(SO 5, 6, 7)

BEC-14   Assume the same information as BEC-13 except that the discount rate was 10% instead of 8%. In this case, how much can Santo expect to receive from the sale of these bonds?

Compute the present value of a note.
(SO 5, 6, 7)

BEC-15   Garcia Taco Company receives a $50,000, 6-year note bearing interest of 6% (paid annually) from a customer at a time when the discount rate is 8%. What is the present value of the note received by Garcia?

Compute the present value of bonds.
(SO 5, 6, 7)

BEC-16   Lucky Treasures Enterprises issued 9%, 8-year, $2,000,000 par value bonds that pay interest semiannually on October 1 and April 1. The bonds are dated April 1, 2007, and are issued on that date. The discount rate of interest for such bonds on April 1, 2007, is 10%. What cash proceeds did Lucky Treasures receive from issuance of the bonds?

Compute the present value of a machine for purposes of making a purchase decision.
(SO 6, 7)

BEC-17   Andrew Larson owns a garage and is contemplating purchasing a tire retreading machine for $16,100. After estimating costs and revenues, Andrew projects a net cash flow from the retreading machine of $2,690 annually for 8 years. Andrew hopes to earn a return of 10 percent on such investments. What is the present value of the retreading operation? Should Andrew purchase the retreading machine?

Compute the present value of a note.
(SO 6)

BEC-18   Harry Hart Company issues an 8%, 5-year mortgage note on January 1, 2007, to obtain financing for new equipment. Land is used as collateral for the note. The terms provide for semiannual installment payments of $112,825. What were the cash proceeds received from the issuance of the note?

Compute the maximum price to pay for a machine.
(SO 6, 7)

BEC-19   Reagan Company is considering purchasing equipment. The equipment will produce the following cash flows: Year 1, $35,000; Year 2, $45,000; Year 3, $55,000. Reagan requires a minimum rate of return of 10%. What is the maximum price Reagan should pay for this equipment?

Compute the interest rate on a single amount.
(SO 5)

BEC-20   If Shelly Remington invests $2,393.90 now and she will receive $10,000 at the end of 15 years, what annual rate of interest will Shelly earn on her investment? [*Hint:* Use Table 3.]

Compute the number of periods of a single amount.
(SO 5)

BEC-21   Elliot Dane has been offered the opportunity of investing $36,061 now. The investment will earn 12% per year and at the end of that time will return Elliot $100,000. How many years must Elliot wait to receive $100,000? [*Hint:* Use Table 3.]

Compute the interest rate on an annuity.
(SO 6)

BEC-22   Rene Barone made an investment of $9,128.55. From this investment, she will receive $1,000 annually for the next 20 years starting one year from now. What rate of interest will Rene's investment be earning for her? [*Hint:* Use Table 4.]

Compute the number of periods of an annuity.
(SO 6)

BEC-23   Cortney Eldred invests $6,710.08 now for a series of $1,000 annual returns beginning one year from now. Cortney will earn a return of 8% on the initial investment. How many annual payments of $1,000 will Cortney receive? [*Hint:* Use Table 4.]

Reporting and Analyzing Investments

STUDY OBJECTIVES

After studying this appendix,
you should be able to:

1 Identify the reasons corporations invest in stocks and debt securities.

2 Explain the accounting for debt investments.

3 Explain the accounting for stock investments.

4 Describe the purpose and usefulness of consolidated financial statements.

5 Indicate how debt and stock investments are valued and reported in the financial statements.

6 Distinguish between short-term and long-term investments.

Why Corporations Invest

Corporations purchase investments in debt or equity securities generally for one of three reasons. First, a corporation may **have excess cash** that it does not need for the immediate purchase of operating assets. For example, many companies experience seasonal fluctuations in sales. A Cape Cod marina has more sales in the spring and summer than in the fall and winter. The reverse is true for an Aspen ski shop. Thus, at the end of an operating cycle, many companies may have cash on hand that is temporarily idle until the start of another operating cycle. These companies may invest the excess funds to earn—through interest and dividends—a greater return than they would get by just holding the funds in the bank. The role that such temporary investments play in the operating cycle is depicted in Illustration D-1 on the next page.

A second reason some companies such as banks purchase investments is to generate **earnings from investment income**. Although banks make most of their earnings by lending money, they also generate earnings by investing in debt and equity securities. Banks purchase investment securities because loan demand

STUDY OBJECTIVE 1

Identify the reasons corporations invest in stocks and debt securities.

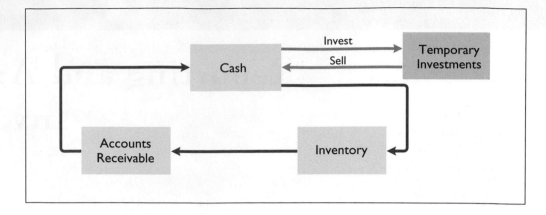

varies both seasonally and with changes in the economic climate. Thus, when loan demand is low, a bank must find other uses for its cash.

Pension funds and mutual funds are corporations that also regularly invest to generate earnings. However, they do so for *speculative reasons*. That is, they are speculating that the investment will increase in value and thus result in positive returns. Therefore, they invest primarily in the common stock of other corporations.

Third, companies also invest for **strategic reasons**. A company may purchase a noncontrolling interest in another company in a related industry in which it wishes to establish a presence. Alternatively, a company can exercise some influence over one of its customers or suppliers by purchasing a significant, but not controlling, interest in that company. Or, a corporation may choose to purchase a controlling interest in another company in order to enter a new industry without incurring the costs and risks associated with starting from scratch.

In summary, businesses invest in other companies for the reasons shown in Illustration D-2.

Illustration D-2   Why corporations invest

Reason	Typical Investment
To house excess cash until needed	Low-risk, high-liquidity, short-term securities such as government-issued securities
To generate earnings I need 1,000 Treasury bills by tonight BANK	Debt securities (banks and other financial institutions); and stock securities (mutual funds and pension funds)
To meet strategic goals	Stocks of companies in a related industry or in an unrelated industry that the company wishes to enter

Accounting for Debt Investments

Debt investments are investments in government and corporation bonds. In accounting for debt investments, companies must make entries to record (1) the acquisition, (2) the interest revenue, and (3) the sale.

RECORDING ACQUISITION OF BONDS

At acquisition, the cost principle applies. Cost includes all expenditures necessary to acquire these investments, such as the price paid plus brokerage fees (commissions), if any.

For example, assume that Kuhl Corporation acquires 50 Doan Inc. 12%, 10-year, $1,000 bonds on January 1, 2007, for $54,000, including brokerage fees of $1,000. Kuhl records the investment as:

Jan. 1	Debt Investments	54,000	
	Cash		54,000
	(To record purchase of 50 Doan Inc. bonds)		

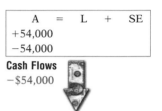

A = L + SE
+54,000
−54,000

Cash Flows
−$54,000

RECORDING BOND INTEREST

The Doan Inc. bonds pay interest of $3,000 semiannually on July 1 and January 1 ($50,000 $\times$ 12% $\times \frac{1}{2}$). The entry for the receipt of interest on July 1 is:

July 1	Cash	3,000	
	Interest Revenue		3,000
	(To record receipt of interest on Doan Inc. bonds)		

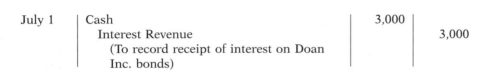

A = L + SE
+3,000
        +3,000 Rev

Cash Flows
+$3,000

If Kuhl Corporation's fiscal year ends on December 31, it accrues the interest of $3,000 earned since July 1. The adjusting entry is:

Dec. 31	Interest Receivable	3,000	
	Interest Revenue		3,000
	(To accrue interest on Doan Inc. bonds)		

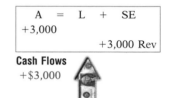

A = L + SE
+3,000
        +3,000 Rev

Cash Flows
no effect

Kuhl reports Interest Receivable as a current asset in the balance sheet. It reports Interest Revenue under "Other revenues and gains" in the income statement.

Kuhl records receipt of the interest on January 1 as follows.

Jan. 1	Cash	3,000	
	Interest Receivable		3,000
	(To record receipt of accrued interest)		

A = L + SE
+3,000
−3,000

Cash Flows
+$3,000

A credit to Interest Revenue at this time would be incorrect. Why? Because the company earned and accrued the interest revenue in the preceding accounting period.

RECORDING SALE OF BONDS

When Kuhl sells the bond investments, it credits the investment account for the cost of the bonds. The company records as a gain or loss any difference between the net proceeds from the sale (sales price less brokerage fees) and the cost of the bonds.

Helpful Hint The accounting for short-term debt investments and long-term debt investments is similar. Any exceptions are discussed in more advanced courses.

Assume, for example, that Kuhl Corporation receives net proceeds of $58,000 on the sale of the Doan Inc. bonds on January 1, 2008, after receiving the interest due. Since the securities cost $54,000, Kuhl has realized a gain of $4,000. It records the sale as follows.

A	=	L	+	SE
+58,000				
−54,000				
				+4,000 Rev

Cash Flows
+$58,000

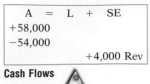

Jan. 1	Cash	58,000	
	Debt Investments		54,000
	Gain on Sale of Debt Investments		4,000
	(To record sale of Doan Inc. bonds)		

Kuhl reports the gain on the sale of debt investments under "Other revenues and gains" in the income statement and reports losses under "Other expenses and losses."

Accounting for Stock Investments

STUDY OBJECTIVE
3
Explain the accounting for stock investments.

Stock investments are investments in the capital stock of corporations. When a company holds stock (and/or debt) of several different corporations, the group of securities is an **investment portfolio**.

The accounting for investments in common stock depends on the extent of the investor's influence over the operating and financial affairs of the issuing corporation (the **investee**). Illustration D-3 shows the general guidelines.

Illustration D-3
Accounting guidelines for stock investments

Investor's Ownership Interest in Investee's Common Stock	Presumed Influence on Investee	Accounting Guidelines
Less than 20%	Insignificant	Cost method
Between 20% and 50%	Significant	Equity method
More than 50%	Controlling	Consolidated financial statements

Companies are required to use judgment instead of blindly following the guidelines.[1] We explain and illustrate the application of each guideline next.

HOLDINGS OF LESS THAN 20%

In the accounting for stock investments of less than 20%, companies use the cost method. Under the **cost method**, companies record the investment at cost, and recognize revenue only when cash dividends are received.

---

[1]Among the factors that companies should consider in determining an investor's influence are whether (1) the investor has representation on the investee's board of directors, (2) the investor participates in the investee's policy-making process, (3) there are material transactions between the investor and the investee, and (4) the common stock held by other stockholders is concentrated or dispersed.

Recording Acquisition of Stock

At acquisition, the cost principle applies. Cost includes all expenditures necessary to acquire these investments, such as the price paid plus brokerage fees (commissions), if any.

Assume, for example, that on July 1, 2007, Sanchez Corporation acquires 1,000 shares (10% ownership) of Beal Corporation common stock at $40 per share plus brokerage fees of $500. The entry for the purchase is:

July 1	Stock Investments	40,500	
	Cash		40,500
	(To record purchase of 1,000 shares of Beal common stock)		

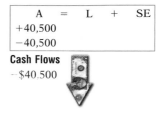

Recording Dividends

During the time the company holds the stock, it makes entries for any cash dividends received. Thus, if Sanchez Corporation receives a $2 per share dividend on December 31, the entry is:

Dec. 31	Cash (1,000 × $2)	2,000	
	Dividend Revenue		2,000
	(To record receipt of a cash dividend)		

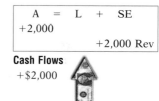

Sanchez reports Dividend Revenue under "Other revenues and gains" in the income statement.

Recording Sale of Stock

When a company sells a stock investment, it recognizes the difference between the net proceeds from the sale (sales price less brokerage fees) and the cost of the stock as a gain or a loss.

Assume, for instance, that Sanchez Corporation receives net proceeds of $39,500 on the sale of its Beal Corporation stock on February 10, 2008. Because the stock cost $40,500, Sanchez has incurred a loss of $1,000. It records the sale as:

Feb. 10	Cash	39,500	
	Loss on Sale of Stock Investments	1,000	
	Stock Investments		40,500
	(To record sale of Beal common stock)		

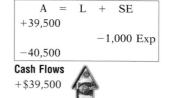

Sanchez reports the loss account under "Other expenses and losses" in the income statement, and would show a gain on sale under "Other revenues and gains."

HOLDINGS BETWEEN 20% AND 50%

When an investor company owns only a small portion of the shares of stock of another company, the investor cannot exercise control over the investee. But when an investor owns between 20% and 50% of the common stock of a corporation, it is presumed that the investor has significant influence over the financial and operating activities of the investee. The investor probably has a representative on the investee's board of directors. Through that representative, the investor begins to exercise some control over the investee—and the investee company in some sense becomes part of the investor company.

For example, even prior to purchasing all of Turner Broadcasting, Time Warner owned 20% of Turner. Because it exercised significant control over major decisions made by Turner, Time Warner used an approach called the equity method. Under the **equity method, the investor records its share of the net income of the investee in the year when it is earned**. An alternative might be to delay recognizing the investor's share of net income until a cash dividend is declared. But that approach would ignore the fact that the investor and investee are, in some sense, one company, making the investor better off by the investee's earned income.

Under the equity method, the company initially records the investment in common stock at cost. After that, it adjusts the investment account **annually** to show the investor's equity in the investee. Each year, the investor does the following: (1) It increases (debits) the investment account and increases (credits) revenue for its share of the investee's net income.[2] (2) The investor also decreases (credits) the investment account for the amount of dividends received. The investment account is reduced for dividends received because payment of a dividend decreases the net assets of the investee.

Recording Acquisition of Stock

Assume that Milar Corporation acquires 30% of the common stock of Beck Company for $120,000 on January 1, 2007. The entry to record this transaction is:

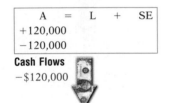

A = L + SE
+120,000
−120,000
Cash Flows
−$120,000

Jan. 1	Stock Investments	120,000	
	Cash		120,000
	(To record purchase of Beck common stock)		

Recording Revenue and Dividends

For 2007 Beck reports net income of $100,000. It declares and pays a $40,000 cash dividend. Milar must record (1) its share of Beck's income, $30,000 (30% × $100,000), and (2) the reduction in the investment account for the dividends received, $12,000 ($40,000 × 30%). The entries are:

A = L + SE
+30,000
+30,000 Rev
Cash Flows
no effect

(1)

Dec. 31	Stock Investments	30,000	
	Revenue from Investment in Beck Company		30,000
	(To record 30% equity in Beck's 2007 net income)		

A = L + SE
+12,000
−12,000
Cash Flows
+$12,000

(2)

Dec. 31	Cash	12,000	
	Stock Investments		12,000
	(To record dividends received)		

After Milar posts the transactions for the year, the investment and revenue accounts are as shown in Illustration D-4.

---

[2]Conversely, the investor increases (debits) a loss account and decreases (credits) the investment account for its share of the investee's net loss.

Illustration D-4
Investment and revenue
accounts after posting

Stock Investments				Revenue from Investment in Beck Company	
Jan. 1	120,000	Dec. 31	**12,000**		Dec. 31 **30,000**
Dec. 31	**30,000**				
Dec. 31 Bal.	138,000				

During the year, the investment account increased by $18,000. This $18,000 is Milar's 30% equity in the $60,000 increase in Beck's retained earnings ($100,000 − $40,000). In addition, Milar reports $30,000 of revenue from its investment, which is 30% of Beck's net income of $100,000.

Note that the difference between reported income under the cost method and reported revenue under the equity method can be significant. For example, Milar would report only $12,000 of dividend revenue (30% × $40,000) if it used the cost method.

HOLDINGS OF MORE THAN 50%

A company that owns more than 50% of the common stock of another entity is known as the **parent company**. The entity whose stock is owned by the parent company is called the **subsidiary (affiliated) company**. Because of its stock ownership, the parent company has a **controlling interest** in the subsidiary company.

When a company owns more than 50% of the common stock of another company, it usually prepares **consolidated financial statements**. Consolidated financial statements present the assets and liabilities controlled by the parent company. They also present the total revenues and expenses of the subsidiary companies. Companies prepare consolidated statements **in addition to** the financial statements for the individual parent and subsidiary companies.

As noted earlier, prior to acquiring all of Turner Broadcasting, Time Warner accounted for its investment in Turner using the equity method. Time Warner's net investment in Turner was reported in a single line item—Other investments. After the merger, Time Warner instead consolidated Turner's results with its own. Under this approach, Time Warner included the individual assets and liabilities of Turner with its own assets. That is, Turner's plant and equipment were added to Time Warner's plant and equipment, its receivables were added to Time Warner's receivables, and so on. A similar sort of consolidation went on when AOL merged with Time Warner.

Consolidated statements are useful to the stockholders, board of directors, and management of the parent company. Consolidated statements indicate to creditors, prospective investors, and regulatory agencies the magnitude and scope of operations of the companies under common control. For example, regulators and the courts undoubtedly used the consolidated statements of AT&T to determine whether a breakup of AT&T was in the public interest. Listed here are three companies that prepare consolidated statements and some of the companies they have owned. Note that one, Disney, is Time Warner's arch rival.

STUDY OBJECTIVE

4

Describe the purpose and usefulness of consolidated financial statements.

Helpful Hint If the parent (A) has three wholly owned subsidiaries (B, C, and D), there are four separate legal entities but only one economic entity from the viewpoint of the shareholders of the parent company.

PepsiCo	Cendant	The Walt Disney Company
Frito-Lay	Howard Johnson	Capital Cities/ABC, Inc.
Tropicana	Ramada Inn	Disneyland, Disney World
Quaker Oats	Century 21	Mighty Ducks
Pepsi-Cola	Coldwell Banker	Anaheim Angels
Gatorade	Avis	ESPN

Valuing and Reporting Investments

STUDY OBJECTIVE

5

Indicate how debt and stock investments are valued and reported in the financial statements.

The value of debt and stock investments may fluctuate greatly during the time they are held. For example, in a 12-month period, the stock of Time Warner hit a high of $58\frac{1}{2}$ and a low of 9. In light of such price fluctuations, how should companies value investments at the balance sheet date? Valuation could be at cost, at fair value (market value), or at the lower-of-cost-or-market value.

Many people argue that fair value offers the best approach because it represents the expected cash realizable value of securities. Fair value is the amount for which a security could be sold in a normal market. Others counter that, unless a security is going to be sold soon, the fair value is not relevant because the price of the security will likely change again.

CATEGORIES OF SECURITIES

For purposes of valuation and reporting at a financial statement date, the accounting profession classifies debt and stock investments into three categories of securities:

1. **Trading securities** are bought and held primarily for sale in the near term to generate income on short-term price differences.
2. **Available-for-sale securities** are held with the intent of selling them sometime in the future.
3. **Held-to-maturity securities** are debt securities that the investor has the intent and ability to hold to maturity.[3]

Illustration D-5 shows the valuation guidelines for these securities. **These guidelines apply to all debt securities and all stock investments in which the holdings are less than 20%.**

Illustration D-5
Valuation guidelines

Trading

"We'll sell within ten days."

At fair value with changes reported in net income

Available-for-sale

"We'll hold the stock for a while to see how it performs."

At fair value with changes reported in the stockholders' equity section

Held-to-maturity

"We intend to hold until maturity."

At amortized cost

Trading Securities

Trading securities are held with the intention of selling them in a short period of time (generally less than a month). *Trading* means frequent buying and selling. As indicated in Illustration D-5, companies report trading securities at fair value (an approach referred to as mark-to-market accounting); they report changes from cost **as part of net income**. The changes are reported as **unrealized gains or losses** because the securities have not been sold. The unrealized gain or loss is the difference between the **total cost** of trading securities and their **total fair value**. Companies classify trading securities as a current asset.

---

[3]This category is provided for completeness. The accounting and valuation issues related to held-to-maturity securities are discussed in more advanced accounting courses.

As an example, Illustration D-6 shows the costs and fair values for investments classified as trading securities for Pace Corporation on December 31, 2007. Pace Corporation has an unrealized gain of $7,000 because total fair value ($147,000) is $7,000 greater than total cost ($140,000).

Trading Securities, December 31, 2007			
Investments	Cost	Fair Value	Unrealized Gain (Loss)
Yorkville Company bonds	$ 50,000	$ 48,000	$(2,000)
Kodak Company stock	90,000	99,000	9,000
Total	$140,000	$147,000	**$ 7,000**

Illustration D-6
Valuation of trading securities

The fact that trading securities are a short-term investment increases the likelihood that Pace will sell them at fair value for a gain. Pace records fair value and the unrealized gain through an adjusting entry at the time it prepares financial statements. In the entry, the company uses a valuation allowance account, Market Adjustment—Trading, to record the difference between the total cost and the total fair value of the securities. The adjusting entry for Pace Corporation is:

Helpful Hint Companies report an unrealized gain or loss in the income statement because of the likelihood that the securities will be sold at fair value since they are a short-term investment.

Dec. 31	Market Adjustment—Trading	7,000	
	Unrealized Gain—Income		7,000
	(To record unrealized gain on trading securities)		

A	= L	+	SE
+7,000			
			+7,000 Rev

Cash Flows
no effect

The use of the Market Adjustment—Trading account enables the company to maintain a record of the investment cost. Actual cost is needed to determine the gain or loss realized when the securities are sold. The company adds the Market Adjustment—Trading balance to the cost of the investments to arrive at a fair value for the trading securities.

The fair value of the securities is the amount companies report on the balance sheet. They report the unrealized gain on the income statement under "Other revenues and gains." The term *income* in the account title indicates that the gain affects net income. If the total cost of the trading securities is greater than total fair value, an unrealized loss has occurred. In such a case, the adjusting entry is a debit to Unrealized Loss—Income and a credit to Market Adjustment—Trading. Companies report the unrealized loss under "Other expenses and losses" in the income statement.

The market adjustment account is carried forward into future accounting periods. No entries are made to this account during the period. At the end of each reporting period, a company adjusts the balance in the account to the difference between cost and fair value at that time. It closes the Unrealized Gain—Income account or Unrealized Loss—Income account at the end of the reporting period.

Available-for-Sale Securities

As indicated earlier, available-for-sale securities are held with the intent of selling them sometime in the future. If the intent is to sell the securities within the next year or operating cycle, a company classifies the securities as current assets in the balance sheet. Otherwise, it classifies them as long-term assets in the investments section of the balance sheet.

Companies also report available-for-sale securities at fair value. The procedure for determining fair value and unrealized gain or loss for these securities is the same as that for trading securities. To illustrate, assume that Elbert Corporation has two securities that are classified as available-for-sale. Illustration D-7 provides information on the cost, fair value, and amount of the unrealized gain or loss on December 31, 2007. There is an unrealized loss of $9,537 because total cost ($293,537) is $9,537 more than total fair value ($284,000).

Illustration D-7
Valuation of available-for-sale securities

Available-for-Sale Securities, December 31, 2007			
Investments	Cost	Fair Value	Unrealized Gain (Loss)
Campbell Soup Corporation 8% bonds	$ 93,537	$103,600	$10,063
Hershey Foods stock	200,000	180,400	(19,600)
Total	$293,537	$284,000	$(9,537)

Both the adjusting entry and the reporting of the unrealized loss from Elbert's available-for-sale securities differ from those illustrated for trading securities. The differences result because these securities are not going to be sold in the near term. Thus, prior to actual sale it is much more likely that changes in fair value may reverse the unrealized loss. Therefore, Elbert does not report an unrealized loss in the income statement. Instead, it reports it as **a separate component of stockholders' equity**. In the adjusting entry, Elbert identifies the market adjustment account with available-for-sale securities, and identifies the unrealized gain or loss account with stockholders' equity. The adjusting entry for Elbert Corporation to record the unrealized loss of $9,537 is:

Helpful Hint The entry is the same regardless of whether the securities are considered short-term or long-term.

A	= L	+	SE	
			−9,537 Eq	
−9,537				

Cash Flows
no effect

Dec. 31	Unrealized Gain or Loss—Equity	9,537	
	Market Adjustment—Available-for-Sale		9,537
	(To record unrealized loss on available-for-sale securities)		

If total fair value exceeds total cost, Elbert would record the adjusting entry as an increase (debit) to Market Adjustment—Available-for-Sale and a credit to Unrealized Gain or Loss—Equity.

For available-for-sale securities, the company carries forward the Unrealized Gain or Loss—Equity account to future periods. At each future balance sheet date, the account is adjusted with the market adjustment account to show the difference between cost and fair value at that time.

BALANCE SHEET PRESENTATION

For balance sheet presentation, companies must classify investments as either short-term or long-term.

Short-Term Investments

STUDY OBJECTIVE 6
Distinguish between short-term and long-term investments.

Short-term investments (also called **marketable securities**) are securities held by a company that are (1) **readily marketable** and (2) **intended to be converted into cash** within the next year or operating cycle, whichever is longer. Investments that do not meet **both criteria** are classified as long-term investments. In a recent survey of 600 large U.S. companies, 202 reported short-term investments.

READILY MARKETABLE. **An investment is readily marketable when it can be sold easily whenever the need for cash arises.** Short-term paper[4] meets this criterion because a company can readily sell it to other investors. Stocks and bonds traded on organized securities markets, such as the New York Stock Exchange, are readily marketable because they can be bought and sold daily. In contrast, there may be only a limited market for the securities issued by small corporations and no market for the securities of a privately held company.

Helpful Hint Trading securities are always classified as short-term. Available-for-sale securities can be either short-term or long-term.

INTENT TO CONVERT. **Intent to convert means that management intends to sell the investment within the next year or operating cycle, whichever is longer.** Generally, this criterion is satisfied when the investment is considered a resource that the company will use whenever the need for cash arises. For example, a ski resort may invest idle cash during the summer months with the intent to sell the securities to buy supplies and equipment shortly before the next winter season. This investment is considered short-term even if lack of snow cancels the next ski season and eliminates the need to convert the securities into cash as intended.

Because of their high liquidity, companies list short-term investments immediately below Cash in the current assets section of the balance sheet. Short-term investments are reported at fair value. For example, Weber Corporation would report its trading securities as shown in Illustration D-8.

WEBER CORPORATION Balance Sheet (partial)	
Current assets	
Cash	$21,000
Short-term investments, at fair value	**60,000**

Illustration D-8
Balance sheet presentation of short-term investments

Long-Term Investments

Companies generally report long-term investments in a separate section of the balance sheet immediately below "Current assets," as shown in Illustration D-9. Long-term investments in available-for-sale securities are reported at fair value. Investments in common stock accounted for under the equity method are reported at equity.

WEBER CORPORATION Balance Sheet (partial)		
Investments		
Bond sinking fund	$100,000	
Investments in stock of less than 20% owned companies, at fair value	50,000	
Investment in stock of 20%–50% owned company, at equity	150,000	
Total investments		$300,000

Illustration D-9
Balance sheet presentation of long-term investments

---

[4]Short-term paper includes (1) certificates of deposits (CDs) issued by banks, (2) money market certificates issued by banks and savings and loan associations, (3) Treasury bills issued by the U.S. government, and (4) commercial paper issued by corporations with good credit ratings.

PRESENTATION OF REALIZED AND UNREALIZED GAIN OR LOSS

Companies must present in the financial statements gains and losses on investments, whether realized or unrealized. In the income statement, companies report gains and losses, as well as interest and dividend revenue, in the nonoperating activities section under the categories listed in Illustration D-10.

Illustration D-10
Nonoperating items related to investments

Other Revenue and Gains	Other Expenses and Losses
Interest Revenue	Loss on Sale of Investments
Dividend Revenue	Unrealized Loss—Income
Gain on Sale of Investments	
Unrealized Gain—Income	

As indicated earlier, companies report an unrealized gain or loss on available-for-sale securities as a separate component of stockholders' equity. To illustrate, assume that Muzzillo Inc. has common stock of $3,000,000, retained earnings of $1,500,000, and an unrealized loss on available-for-sale securities of $100,000. Illustration D-11 shows the financial statement presentation of the unrealized loss.

Illustration D-11
Unrealized loss in stockholders' equity section

MUZZILLO INC. Balance Sheet (partial)	
Stockholders' equity	
Common stock	$3,000,000
Retained earnings	1,500,000
Total paid-in capital and retained earnings	4,500,000
Less: **Unrealized loss on available-for-sale securities**	(100,000)
Total stockholders' equity	$4,400,000

Note that the presentation of the loss is similar to the presentation of the cost of treasury stock in the stockholders' equity section. (It decreases stockholders' equity.) An unrealized gain would be added in this section. Reporting the unrealized gain or loss in the stockholders' equity section serves two important purposes: (1) It reduces the volatility of net income due to fluctuations in fair value. (2) It informs the financial statement user of the gain or loss that would occur if the company sold the securities at fair value.

Companies must report, as part of a more inclusive measure called *comprehensive income*, items such as unrealized gains and losses on available-for-sale securities, which affect stockholders' equity but are not included in the calculation of net income. For example, Tootsie Roll reported other comprehensive income in 2004 of $778,000. Note 11 to Tootsie Roll's financial statements shows that one component of this amount was unrealized gains and losses on investment securities. Comprehensive income is discussed more fully in Chapter 13.

STATEMENT OF CASH FLOWS PRESENTATION

As shown previously in Illustrations D-8, 9, and 11, the balance sheet presents a company's investment accounts at a point in time. The "Investing activities" section of the statement of cash flows reports information on the cash inflows and outflows during the period that resulted from investment transactions.

Illustration D-12 presents the cash flows from investing activities from the 2004 statement of cash flows of The Walt Disney Company. From this information we learn that during the year 2004 Disney received $14 million from the sale or redemption of investments and that it purchased $67 million of investments.

THE WALT DISNEY COMPANY Statement of Cash Flows (partial) September 30, 2004 (in millions)	
Investing Activities	
Investments in parks, resorts and other property	$(1,427)
Acquisitions (net of cash acquired)	(48)
Dispositions	—
Proceeds from sale of investments	**14**
Purchases of investments	**(67)**
Other	44
Cash used by investing activities	$(1,484)

Illustration D-12
Statement of cash flows presentation of investment activities

Summary of Study Objectives

1 *Identify the reasons corporations invest in stocks and debt securities.* Corporations invest for three common reasons: (a) They have excess cash. (b) They view investment income as a significant revenue source. (c) They have strategic goals such as gaining control of a competitor or supplier or moving into a new line of business.

2 *Explain the accounting for debt investments.* Entries for investments in debt securities are required when companies purchase bonds, receive or accrue interest, and sell bonds.

3 *Explain the accounting for stock investments.* Entries for investments in common stock are required when companies purchase stock, receive dividends, and sell stock. When ownership is less than 20%, the cost method is used—the investment is recorded at cost. When ownership is between 20% and 50%, the equity method should be used—the investor records its share of the net income of the investee in the year it is earned. When ownership is more than 50%, consolidated financial statements should be prepared.

4 *Describe the purpose and usefulness of consolidated financial statements.* When a company owns more than 50% of the common stock of another company, consolidated financial statements are usually prepared. These statements are especially useful to the stockholders, board of directors, and management of the parent company.

5 *Indicate how debt and stock investments are valued and reported in the financial statements.* Investments in debt and stock securities are classified as trading, available-for-sale, or held-to-maturity securities for valuation and reporting purposes. Trading securities are reported as current assets at fair value, with changes from cost reported in net income. Available-for-sale securities are also reported at fair value, with the changes from cost reported in stockholders' equity. Available-for-sale securities are classified as short-term or long-term depending on their expected realization.

6 *Distinguish between short-term and long-term investments.* Short-term investments are securities held by a company that are readily marketable and intended to be converted to cash within the next year or operating cycle, whichever is longer. Investments that do not meet both criteria are classified as long-term investments.

Glossary

Available-for-sale securities Securities that are held with the intent of selling them sometime in the future. (p. D-8)

Consolidated financial statements Financial statements that present the assets and liabilities controlled by the parent company and the aggregate profitability of the affiliated companies. (p. D-7)

Controlling interest Ownership of more than 50% of the common stock of another entity. (p. D-7)

Cost method An accounting method in which the investment in common stock is recorded at cost and revenue is recognized only when cash dividends are received. (p. D-4)

Debt investments Investments in government and corporation bonds. (p. D-3)

Equity method An accounting method in which the investment in common stock is initially recorded at cost, and the investment account is then adjusted annually to show the investor's equity in the investee. (p. D-6)

Fair value Amount for which a security could be sold in a normal market. (p. D-8)

Held-to-maturity securities Debt securities that the investor has the intent and ability to hold to their maturity date. (p. D-8)

Long-term investments Investments that are not readily marketable or that management does not intend to convert into cash within the next year or operating cycle, whichever is longer. (p. D-10)

Mark-to-market A method of accounting for certain investments that requires that they be adjusted to their fair value at the end of each period. (p. D-8)

Parent company A company that owns more than 50% of the common stock of another entity. (p. D-7)

Short-term investments (marketable securities) Investments that are readily marketable and intended to be converted into cash within the next year or operating cycle, whichever is longer. (p. D-10)

Stock investments Investments in the capital stock of corporations. (p. D-4)

Subsidiary (affiliated) company A company in which more than 50% of its stock is owned by another company. (p. D-7)

Trading securities Securities bought and held primarily for sale in the near term to generate income on short-term price differences. (p. D-8)

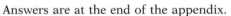

Self-Study Questions

Answers are at the end of the appendix.

(SO 2)   **1.** Debt investments are initially recorded at:
  (a) cost.
  (b) cost plus accrued interest.
  (c) fair value.
  (d) None of the above

(SO 2)   **2.** Stan Free Company sells debt investments costing $26,000 for $28,000 plus accrued interest that has been recorded. In journalizing the sale, credits are:
  (a) Debt Investments and Loss on Sale of Debt Investments.
  (b) Debt Investments, Gain on Sale of Debt Investments, and Bond Interest Receivable.
  (c) Stock Investments and Bond Interest Receivable.
  (d) The correct answer is not given.

(SO 3)   **3.** Karen Duffy Company receives net proceeds of $42,000 on the sale of stock investments that cost $39,500. This transaction will result in reporting in the income statement a:
  (a) loss of $2,500 under "Other expenses and losses."
  (b) loss of $2,500 under "Operating expenses."

  (c) gain of $2,500 under "Other revenues and gains."
  (d) gain of $2,500 under "Operating revenues."

4. The equity method of accounting for long-term   (SO 3) investments in stock should be used when the investor has significant influence over an investee and owns:
  (a) between 20% and 50% of the investee's common stock.
  (b) 20% or more of the investee's bonds.
  (c) more than 50% of the investee's common stock.
  (d) less than 20% of the investee's common stock.

5. Which of these statements is *not* true?
  Consolidated financial statements are useful to: (SO 4)
  (a) determine the profitability of specific subsidiaries.
  (b) determine the aggregate profitability of enterprises under common control.
  (c) determine the breadth of a parent company's operations.
  (d) determine the full extent of aggregate obligations of enterprises under common control.

(SO 5) 6. At the end of the first year of operations, the total cost of the trading securities portfolio is $120,000 and the total fair value is $115,000. What should the financial statements show?
   (a) A reduction of an asset of $5,000 and a realized loss of $5,000.
   (b) A reduction of an asset of $5,000 and an unrealized loss of $5,000 in the stockholders' equity section.
   (c) A reduction of an asset of $5,000 in the current assets section and an unrealized loss of $5,000 under "Other expenses and losses."
   (d) A reduction of an asset of $5,000 in the current assets section and a realized loss of $5,000 under "Other expenses and losses."

(SO 5) 7. In the balance sheet, Unrealized Loss—Equity is reported as a:
   (a) contra asset account.
   (b) contra stockholders' equity account.
   (c) loss in the income statement.
   (d) loss in the retained earnings statement.

(SO 5) 8. If a company wants to increase its reported income by manipulating its investment accounts, which should it do?
   (a) Sell its "winner" trading securities and hold its "loser" trading securities.
   (b) Hold its "winner" trading securities and sell its "loser" trading securities.
   (c) Sell its "winner" available-for-sale securities and hold its "loser" available-for-sale securities.
   (d) Hold its "winner" available-for-sale securities and sell its "loser" available-for-sale securities.

(SO 6) 9. To be classified as short-term investments, debt investments must be readily marketable and be expected to be sold within:
   (a) 3 months from the date of purchase.
   (b) the next year or operating cycle, whichever is shorter.
   (c) the next year or operating cycle, whichever is longer.
   (d) the operating cycle.

Questions

1. What are the reasons that corporations invest in securities?

2. (a) What is the cost of an investment in bonds?
   (b) When is interest on bonds recorded?

3. Mary Cunningham is confused about losses and gains on the sale of debt investments. Explain these issues to Mary:
   (a) How the gain or loss is computed.
   (b) The statement presentation of gains and losses.

4. Nickle Company sells Craig's bonds that cost $40,000 for $45,000, including $2,000 of accrued interest. In recording the sale, Nickle books a $5,000 gain. Is this correct? Explain.

5. What is the cost of an investment in stock?

6. To acquire Alyssa Corporation stock, Elena Reuter pays $75,000 in cash plus $1,500 broker's fees. What entry should be made for this investment, assuming the stock is readily marketable?

7. (a) When should a long-term investment in common stock be accounted for by the equity method?
   (b) When is revenue recognized under the equity method?

8. Mack Corporation uses the equity method to account for its ownership of 25% of the common stock of Foley Packing. During 2007 Foley reported a net income of $80,000 and declares and pays cash dividends of $10,000. What recognition should Mack Corporation give to these events?

9. What constitutes "significant influence" when an investor's financial interest is less than 50%?

10. Distinguish between the cost and equity methods of accounting for investments in stocks.

11. What are consolidated financial statements?

12. What are the valuation guidelines for trading and available-for-sale investments at a balance sheet date?

13. Debbie Gocker is the controller of G-Products, Inc. At December 31 the company's investments in trading securities cost $74,000 and have a fair value of $72,000. Indicate how Debbie would report these data in the financial statements prepared on December 31.

14. Using the data in question 13, how would Debbie report the data if the investment were long-term and the securities were classified as available-for-sale?

15. Tundra Company's investments in available-for-sale securities at December 31 show total cost of $197,000 and total fair value of $210,000. Prepare the adjusting entry.

16. Using the data in question 15, prepare the adjusting entry assuming the securities are classified as trading securities.

17. Where is Unrealized Gain or Loss—Equity reported on the balance sheet?

18. What purposes are served by reporting Unrealized Gains (Losses)—Equity in the stockholders' equity section?

19. Reuter Wholesale Supply owns stock in Yount Corporation, which it intends to hold indefinitely because of some negative tax consequences if sold. Should the investment in Yount be classified as a short-term investment? Why?

Brief Exercises

Journalize entries for debt investments.
(SO 2)

BED-1 Molina Corporation purchased debt investments for $41,500 on January 1, 2007. On July 1, 2007, Molina received cash interest of $1,660. Journalize the purchase and the receipt of interest. Assume no interest has been accrued.

Journalize entries for stock investments.
(SO 3)

BED-2 On August 1 Alshare Company buys 1,000 shares of ABC common stock for $30,000 cash plus brokerage fees of $600. On December 1 the stock investments are sold for $38,000 in cash. Journalize the purchase and sale of the common stock.

Journalize transactions under the equity method.
(SO 3)

BED-3 Morgan Company owns 40% of Holt Company. For the current year Holt reports net income of $150,000 and declares and pays a $50,000 cash dividend. Record Morgan's equity in Holt's net income and the receipt of dividends from Holt.

Prepare adjusting entry using fair value.
(SO 5)

BED-4 Cost and fair value data for the trading securities of Shellankamp Company at December 31, 2007, are $62,000 and $57,000, respectively. Prepare the adjusting entry to record the securities at fair value.

Indicate statement presentation using fair value.
(SO 6)

BED-5 For the data presented in BED-4, show the financial statement presentation of the trading securities and related accounts.

Prepare adjusting entry using fair value.
(SO 5)

BED-6 In its first year of operations Carpenter Corporation purchased available-for-sale stock securities costing $72,000 as a long-term investment. At December 31, 2007, the fair value of the securities is $68,000. Prepare the adjusting entry to record the securities at fair value.

Indicate statement presentation using fair value.
(SO 6)

BED-7 For the data presented in BED-6, show the financial statement presentation of the available-for-sale securities and related accounts. Assume the available-for-sale securities are noncurrent.

Prepare investments section of balance sheet.
(SO 6)

BED-8 Bragg Corporation has these long-term investments: common stock of Sword Co. (10% ownership) held as available-for-sale securities, cost $108,000, fair value $115,000; common stock of Epee Inc. (30% ownership), cost $210,000, equity $250,000; and a bond sinking fund of $150,000. Prepare the investments section of the balance sheet.

Exercises

Journalize debt investment transactions, and accrue interest.
(SO 2)

ED-1 Pettengill Corporation had these transactions pertaining to debt investments:

Jan. 1   Purchased 60 10%, $1,000 Gant Co. bonds for $60,000 cash plus brokerage fees of $900. Interest is payable semiannually on July 1 and January 1.
July 1   Received semiannual interest on Gant Co. bonds.
July 1   Sold 30 Gant Co. bonds for $32,000 less $400 brokerage fees.

Instructions
(a) Journalize the transactions.
(b) Prepare the adjusting entry for the accrual of interest at December 31.

Journalize stock investment transactions, and explain income statement presentation.
(SO 3)

ED-2 Gonzalez Company had these transactions pertaining to stock investments:

Feb. 1   Purchased 1,000 shares of GET common stock (2% of outstanding shares) for $8,000 cash plus brokerage fees of $200.
July 1   Received cash dividends of $1 per share on GET common stock.
Sept. 1   Sold 500 shares of GET common stock for $5,500 less brokerage fees of $100.
Dec. 1   Received cash dividends of $1 per share on GET common stock.

Instructions
(a) Journalize the transactions.
(b) Explain how dividend revenue and the gain (loss) on sale should be reported in the income statement.

ED-3 Gocker Inc. had these transactions pertaining to investments in common stock:

Jan. 1 Purchased 1,500 shares of Sealey Corporation common stock (5% of outstanding shares) for $60,000 cash plus $1,400 broker's commission.

July 1 Received a cash dividend of $7 per share.

Dec. 1 Sold 900 shares of Sealey Corporation common stock for $38,000 cash less $800 broker's commission.

   31 Received a cash dividend of $7 per share.

Instructions
Journalize the transactions.

ED-4 On January 1 Didde Glaser Corporation purchased a 25% equity investment in Mortonsen Corporation for $150,000. At December 31 Mortonsen declared and paid a $60,000 cash dividend and reported net income of $320,000.

Instructions
(a) Journalize the transactions.
(b) Determine the amount to be reported as an investment in Mortonsen stock at December 31.

ED-5 These are two independent situations:

1. Ritter Cosmetics acquired 10% of the 250,000 shares of common stock of Lye Fashion at a total cost of $14 per share on March 18, 2007. On June 30 Lye declared and paid a $75,000 dividend. On December 31 Lye reported net income of $244,000 for the year. At December 31 the market price of Lye Fashion was $16 per share. The stock is classified as available-for-sale.

2. Hollandsworth Inc. obtained significant influence over Perez Corporation by buying 30% of Perez's 30,000 outstanding shares of common stock at a total cost of $11 per share on January 1, 2007. On June 15 Perez declared and paid a cash dividend of $35,000. On December 31 Perez reported a net income of $120,000 for the year.

Instructions
Prepare all the necessary journal entries for 2007 for (a) Ritter Cosmetics and (b) Hollandsworth Inc.

ED-6 At December 31, 2007, the trading securities for Winsor, Inc., are as follows.

Security	Cost	Fair Value
A	$18,500	$16,000
B	12,500	14,000
C	23,000	20,000
Total	$54,000	$50,000

Instructions
(a) Prepare the adjusting entry at December 31, 2007, to report the securities at fair value.
(b) Show the balance sheet and income statement presentation at December 31, 2007, after adjustment to fair value.

ED-7 Data for investments in stock classified as trading securities are presented in ED-6. Assume instead that the investments are classified as available-for-sale securities with the same cost and fair value data. The securities are considered to be a long-term investment.

Instructions
(a) Prepare the adjusting entry at December 31, 2007, to report the securities at fair value.
(b) Show the statement presentation at December 31, 2007, after adjustment to fair value.
(c) Karen Eaton, a member of the board of directors, does not understand the reporting of the unrealized gains or losses on trading securities and available-for-sale securities. Write a letter to Mrs. Eaton explaining the reporting and the purposes it serves.

Prepare adjusting entries for fair value, and indicate statement presentation for two classes of securities.
(SO 5, 6)

ED-8 Markowitz Company has these data at December 31, 2007:

Securities	Cost	Fair Value
Trading	$110,000	$125,000
Available-for-sale	100,000	90,000

The available-for-sale securities are held as a long-term investment.

Instructions
(a) Prepare the adjusting entries to report each class of securities at fair value.
(b) Indicate the statement presentation of each class of securities and the related unrealized gain (loss) accounts.

Problems

Journalize debt investment transactions and show financial statement presentation.
(SO 2, 5, 6)

PD-1 Hutchinson Farms is a grower of hybrid seed corn for DeKalb Genetics Corporation. It has had two exceptionally good years and has elected to invest its excess funds in bonds. The following selected transactions relate to bonds acquired as an investment by Hutchinson Farms, whose fiscal year ends on December 31.

2007

Jan. 1 Purchased at par $500,000 of Eldridge Corporation 10-year, 8% bonds dated January 1, 2007, directly from the issuing corporation.
July 1 Received the semiannual interest on the Eldridge bonds.
Dec. 31 Accrual of interest at year-end on the Eldridge bonds.

Assume that all intervening transactions and adjustments have been properly recorded and the number of bonds owned has not changed from December 31, 2007, to December 31, 2009.

2010

Jan. 1 Received the semiannual interest on the Eldridge bonds.
Jan. 1 Sold $300,000 of Eldridge bonds at 110. The broker deducted $7,000 for commissions and fees on the sale.
July 1 Received the semiannual interest on the Eldridge bonds.
Dec. 31 Accrual of interest at year-end on the Eldridge bonds.

Instructions
(a) Journalize the listed transactions for the years 2007 and 2010.
(b) Assume that the fair value of the bonds at December 31, 2007, was $470,000. These bonds are classified as available-for-sale securities. Prepare the adjusting entry to record these bonds at fair value.
(c) Show the balance sheet presentation of the bonds and interest receivable at December 31, 2007. Assume the investments are considered long-term. Indicate where any unrealized gain or loss is reported in the financial statements.

Journalize investment transactions, prepare adjusting entry, and show financial statement presentation.
(SO 2, 3, 6)

PD-2 In January 2007 the management of Mann Company concludes that it has sufficient cash to purchase some short-term investments in debt and stock securities. During the year, the following transactions occurred.

Feb. 1 Purchased 1,000 shares of PTI common stock for $40,000 plus brokerage fees of $1,000.
Mar. 1 Purchased 500 shares of ATF common stock for $20,000 plus brokerage fees of $500.
Apr. 1 Purchased 70 $1,000, 8% CRT bonds for $70,000 plus $1,200 brokerage fees. Interest is payable semiannually on April 1 and October 1.
July 1 Received a cash dividend of $0.60 per share on the PTI common stock.
Aug. 1 Sold 200 shares of PTI common stock at $42 per share less brokerage fees of $350.
Sept. 1 Received $2 per share cash dividend on the ATF common stock.

Oct. 1 Received the semiannual interest on the CRT bonds.
Oct. 1 Sold the CRT bonds for $75,000 less $1,000 brokerage fees.

At December 31 the fair values of the PTI and ATF common stocks were $39 and $30 per share, respectively.

Instructions
(a) Journalize the transactions and post to the accounts Debt Investments and Stock In-vestments. (Use the T account form.)
(b) Prepare the adjusting entry at December 31, 2007, to report the investments at fair value. All securities are considered to be trading securities.
(c) Show the balance sheet presentation of investment securities at December 31, 2007.
(d) Identify the income statement accounts and give the statement classification of each account.

PD-3 On December 31, 2006, Lank Associates owned the following securities that are held as long-term investments.

Journalize transactions, prepare adjusting entry for stock investments, and show balance sheet presentation. (SO 3, 5, 6)

Common Stock	Shares	Cost
A Co.	1,000	$50,000
B Co.	6,000	36,000
C Co.	1,200	24,000

On this date the total fair value of the securities was equal to its cost. The securities are not held for influence or control over the investees. In 2007 the following transactions occurred.

July 1 Received $2.00 per share semiannual cash dividend on B Co. common stock.
Aug. 1 Received $0.50 per share cash dividend on A Co. common stock.
Sept. 1 Sold 500 shares of B Co. common stock for cash at $8 per share less brokerage fees of $100.
Oct. 1 Sold 400 shares of A Co. common stock for cash at $54 per share less broker-age fees of $600.
Nov. 1 Received $1 per share cash dividend on C Co. common stock.
Dec. 15 Received $0.50 per share cash dividend on A Co. common stock.
31 Received $2.00 per share semiannual cash dividend on B Co. common stock.

At December 31 the fair values per share of the common stocks were: A Co. $47, B Co. $6, and C Co. $24.

Instructions
(a) Journalize the 2007 transactions and post to the account Stock Investments. (Use the T account form.)
(b) Prepare the adjusting entry at December 31, 2007, to show the securities at fair value. The stock should be classified as available-for-sale securities.
(c) Show the balance sheet presentation of the investments and the unrealized gain (loss) at December 31, 2007. At this date Lank Associates has common stock $2,000,000 and retained earnings $1,200,000.

PD-4 Grey Company acquired 20% of the outstanding common stock of Baden Inc. on January 1, 2007, by paying $1,400,000 for 50,000 shares. Baden declared and paid a $0.50 per share cash dividend on June 30 and again on December 31, 2007. Baden reported net income of $800,000 for the year.

Prepare entries under cost and equity methods, and prepare memorandum. (SO 3)

Instructions
(a) Prepare the journal entries for Grey Company for 2007 assuming Grey cannot exer-cise significant influence over Baden. (Use the cost method.)
(b) Prepare the journal entries for Grey Company for 2007 assuming Grey can exercise significant influence over Baden. (Use the equity method.)
(c) The board of directors of Grey Company is confused about the differences between the cost and equity methods. Prepare a memorandum for the board that explains each method and shows in tabular form the account balances under each method at December 31, 2007.

Journalize stock transactions, and show balance sheet presentation.
(SO 3, 5, 6)

PD-5 Here is Railsback Company's portfolio of long-term available-for-sale securities at December 31, 2006:

	Cost
1,000 shares of Marquis Inc. common stock	$52,000
1,400 shares of B. Ogle Corporation common stock	84,000
800 shares of H. Aaron Corporation preferred stock	33,600

On December 31 the total cost of the portfolio equaled the total fair value. Railsback had the following transactions related to the securities during 2007.

Jan. 20   Sold 1,000 shares of Marquis Inc. common stock at $60 per share less brokerage fees of $600.

     28   Purchased 400 shares of $10 par value common stock of M. DeVito Corporation at $78 per share plus brokerage fees of $480.

     30   Received a cash dividend of $1.15 per share on B. Ogle Corporation common stock.

Feb. 8   Received cash dividends of $0.40 per share on H. Aaron Corporation preferred stock.

     18   Sold all 800 shares of H. Aaron preferred stock at $30 per share less brokerage fees of $360.

July 30   Received a cash dividend of $1 per share on B. Ogle Corporation common stock.

Sept. 6   Purchased an additional 600 shares of the $10 par value common stock of M. DeVito Corporation at $82 per share plus brokerage fees of $800.

Dec. 1   Received a cash dividend of $1.50 per share on M. DeVito Corporation common stock.

At December 31, 2007, the fair values of the securities were:

B. Ogle Corporation common stock	$64 per share
M. DeVito Corporation common stock	$67 per share

Railsback uses separate account titles for each investment, such as Investment in B. Ogle Corporation Common Stock.

Instructions
(a) Prepare journal entries to record the transactions.
(b) Post to the investment accounts. (Use separate T accounts for each investment.)
(c) Prepare the adjusting entry at December 31, 2007, to report the portfolio at fair value.
(d) Show the balance sheet presentation at December 31, 2007.

Prepare a balance sheet.
(SO 6)

PD-6 The following data, presented in alphabetical order, are taken from the records of Wenger Corporation.

Accounts payable	$ 250,000
Accounts receivable	90,000
Accumulated depreciation—building	180,000
Accumulated depreciation—equipment	52,000
Allowance for doubtful accounts	6,000
Bond investments	400,000
Bonds payable (10%, due 2018)	380,000
Buildings	900,000
Cash	82,000
Common stock ($5 par value; 500,000 shares authorized, 300,000 shares issued)	1,500,000
Discount on bonds payable	20,000
Dividends payable	50,000
Equipment	275,000
Goodwill	230,000
Income taxes payable	70,000
Investment in Houston Inc. stock (30% ownership), at equity	240,000
Land	460,000

Merchandise inventory	170,000
Notes payable (due 2008)	70,000
Paid-in capital in excess of par value	200,000
Prepaid insurance	16,000
Retained earnings	310,000
Short-term stock investment, at fair value	185,000

Instructions

Prepare a balance sheet at December 31, 2007.

_____

Answers to Self-Study Questions

1. a   2. b   3. c   4. a   5. a   6. c   7. b   8. c   9. c

PHOTO AND LOGO CREDITS

Chapter 1   Opener: Photo by Alex Wong/Getty Images. Page 7: Graeme Duddri/Retna. Page 8: Mike Fuentes/Getty Images News and Sport Services. Page 9: Hai Wen China Tourism Press/The Image Bank/Getty Images. Page 16: Lynn Goldsmith/Corbis Images. Page 22: Tootsie Roll Industries, Inc. Page 25: Hershey Foods Corporation.

Chapter 2   Opener: Jeanne Strongin. Page 50: Reprinted by permission of Coca-Cola. Page 50: Reprinted by permission of Yahoo! Page 51 (top): Digital Vision. Page 51 (bottom): National Magazines/Retna UK. Page 52: Reprinted by permission of The Marcus Corporation. Page 55: James Schnepf/Liaison Agency, Inc./Getty Images. Page 57: James Schnepf/Liaison Agency, Inc./Getty Images. Page 58: James Schnepf/Liaison Agency, Inc./Getty Images. Page 60: PhotoDisc, Inc./Getty Images. Page 61: Vladimir Pcholkin/FPG International/Getty Images. Page 63: James Schnepf/Liaison Agency, Inc./Getty Images. Page 66: SUPERSTOCK. Page 71: Reprinted by permission of Tweeter Home Entertainment Group. Pages 75 and 76: Reprinted by permission of Circuit City.

Chapter 3   Opener: Tom DiPace/Sports Chrome Inc. Page 106: PhotoDisc, Inc./Getty Images. Page 112: AFP/Corbis Images. Page 116: Koichi Kamoshida/AsiaPac/Getty Images.

Chapter 4   Opener: Witte Thomas E/Gamma-Presse, Inc. Page 161: Tom Mareschal/Getty Images. Page 164: Robyn Beck/AFP/Getty Images. Page 168: Elle Wagner/Copyright John Wiley & Sons, Inc. Pages 184 & 185: Reprinted by permission of Humana, Inc.

Chapter 5   Opener: Stone/Getty Images. Page 221: Courtesy Morrow Snowboards, Inc. Page 226: Robert W. Ginn/PhotoEdit. Pages 228 & 229: Reprinted by permission of Wal-Mart. Page 231: Dennis Galante/Stone/Getty Images. Page 237: Bonnie Kamin/PhotoEdit.

Chapter 6   Opener: VCG/FPG International/Getty Images. Page 269: Mario Ruiz/ZUMA/Corbis Images. Page 270: L.D. Gordon/The Image Bank/Getty Images. Page 279: PhotoDisc, Inc./Getty Images. Page 282: Courtesy Samsung Electronics America. Page 285: Reprinted by permission of The Manitowoc Company, Inc.

Chapter 7   Opener: Don Farrall/PhotoDisc, Inc./Getty Images. Page 319: Michael Newman/PhotoEdit. Page 320: Terence John/Retna. Page 322: Nick Koudis/PhotoDisc, Inc./Getty Images. Page 323: PhotoDisc, Inc./Getty Images. Page 327: "2004 Report to the Nation on Occupational Fraud and Abuse." Association of Certified Fraud Examiners. Reprinted by permission. Page 334: Reprinted by permission of Delta Airlines, Inc.

Chapter 8   Opener: William Whitehurst/Corbis Stock Market. Page 379 (top): Ken Bank/Retna UK. Page 379 (bottom): Joe Polillio/Stone/Getty Images. Page 382: Kazuhiro Nogi/Getty Images News and Sport Services. Page 385: Patrick Bennett/Stone/Getty Images. Page 386: EyeWire, Inc./Getty Images. Page 387: Ken Bank/Retna UK. Page 392: Joe Sohm/Alamy Images. Page 394: Dennis Galante/Stone/Getty Images. Page 414: Reprinted by permission of The Scotts Company LLC.

Chapter 9   Opener: Teri Hanson/AP/Wide World Photos. Page 422: Louis Lanzano/AP/Wide World Photos. Page 425: GoodShoot/Age Fotostock America, Inc. Page 432: Reprinted by permission of Southwest Airlines. Page 432: Reprinted by permission of AirTran Airways. Page 438: Justin Sullivan/Getty Images. Page 444: Andy Lions/Photonica/Getty Images.

Chapter 10   Opener: Harry Melchert/Landov LLC. Page 479: Dominique Sarraute/The Image Bank/Getty Images. Page 481: Christian Kober/Getty Images. Page 491 (top): PhotoDisc, Inc./Getty Images. Page 491 (bottom): PhotoDisc, Inc./Getty Images. Page 494: Neil Beer/PhotoDisc, Inc./Getty Images. Page 496: Scott Mills/Alamy Images. Pages 445 and 446: Reprinted by permission of Coca Cola.

Chapter 11   Opener: Nike/Getty Images News and Sport Services. Page 537: Ricky John Molloy/Stone/Getty Images. Page 542: Courtesy Nike, Inc. Page 545: Alex Fevzer/Corbis Images. Page 550: Darren Robb/Stone/Getty Images. Page 554: Reprinted by permission of Textronix, Inc. Page 555: Reprinted by permission of Columbia Sportswear Company. Page 556: Reprinted by permission of Sara Lee Corporation.

Chapter 12   Opener: Rudi Von Briel/PhotoEdit. Page 589: Darren McCollester/Getty Images News and Sport Services. Page 592: Neil Barclay/Retna. Page 594: William Whitehurst/Corbis Images. Page 600: "Why GM's Plan Won't Work" by David Welch and Dan Beucke reprinted from May 9, 2005, pp. 85–93 issue of BUSINESS WEEK by special permission, copyright © 2005 by The McGraw-Hill Companies. Page 605: PhotoDisc, Inc./Getty Images. Page 606: PhotoDisc, Inc./Getty Images. Page 609: Courtesy Intel. Page 610: Intel Corporation/OR. Page 610: Courtesy Intel.

Chapter 13   Opener: Elle Wagner/Copyright John Wiley & Sons, Inc. Page 649: Steven Bronstein/The Image Bank/Getty Images. Pages 655, 657, 664, 668 & 669: Provided by Kellogg Company. All rights reserved. Used with permission. Page 660: SUPERSTOCK. Page 663: Steve Cole/PhotoDisc, Inc./Getty Images.

Appendix D   Page D-13: Digital Vision/Getty Images.

ACCOUNTING CONCEPTS (Chapters 1–4)

Characteristics	Assumptions	Principles	Constraints
Relevance	Monetary unit	Revenue recognition	Materiality
Reliability	Time period	Full disclosure	Conservatism
Comparability	Economic entity	Matching	
Consistency	Going concern	Cost	

INVENTORY (Chapters 5 and 6)

Ownership

Freight Terms	Ownership of goods on public carrier resides with:
FOB Shipping point	Buyer
FOB Destination	Seller

BASIC ACCOUNTING EQUATION (Chapter 3)

| Basic Equation | Assets = Liabilities + Stockholders' Equity |

Expanded Basic Equation

Assets = Liabilities + Common Stock + Retained Earnings − Dividends + Revenues − Expenses

Debit / Credit Effects

	Dr.	Cr.
Assets	+	−
Liabilities	−	+
Common Stock	−	+
Retained Earnings	−	+
Dividends	+	−
Revenues	−	+
Expenses	+	−

ADJUSTING ENTRIES (Chapter 4)

	Type	Adjusting Entry	
Prepayments	1. Prepaid expenses	Dr. Expenses	Cr. Assets
	2. Unearned revenues	Dr. Liabilities	Cr. Revenues
Accruals	1. Accrued revenues	Dr. Assets	Cr. Revenues
	2. Accrued expenses	Dr. Expenses	Cr. Liabilities

Note: Each adjusting entry will affect one or more income statement accounts and one or more balance sheet accounts.

Interest Computation

Interest = Face value of note × Annual interest rate × Time in terms of one year

CLOSING ENTRIES (Chapter 4)

Purpose

1. Update the Retained Earnings account in the ledger by transferring net income (loss) and dividends to retained earnings.
2. Prepare the temporary accounts (revenue, expense, dividends) for the next period's postings by reducing their balances to zero.

ACCOUNTING CYCLE (Chapter 4)

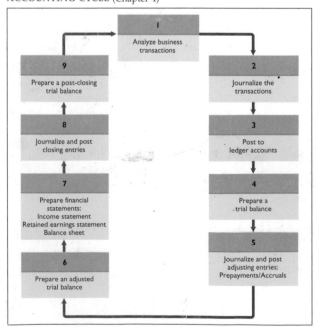

Perpetual vs. Periodic Journal Entries

Event	Perpetual	Periodic
Purchase of goods	Inventory Cash (A/P)	Purchases Cash (A/P)
Freight (shipping point)	Inventory Cash	Freight In Cash
Return of goods	Cash (or A/P) Inventory	Cash (or A/P) Purchase Returns and Allowances
Sale of goods	Cash (or A/R) Sales Cost of Goods Sold Inventory	Cash (or A/R) Sales No entry
End of period	No entry	Closing or adjusting entry required

CASH (Chapter 7)

Principles of Internal Control

Establishment of responsibility
Segregation of duties
Documentation procedures
Physical, mechanical, and electronic controls
Independent internal verification
Other controls

Bank Reconciliation

Bank	Books
Balance per bank statement	Balance per books
Add: Deposits in transit	Add: Unrecorded credit memoranda from bank statement
Deduct: Outstanding checks	Deduct: Unrecorded debit memoranda from bank statement
Adjusted cash balance	Adjusted cash balance

Note: 1. Errors should be offset (added or deducted) on the side that made the error.
2. Adjusting journal entries should only be made for items affecting books.

STOP AND CHECK: Does the adjusted cash balance in the Cash account equal the reconciled balance?